# The Chicago Architectural Club

Prelude to the Modern

Annual Christmas Banquet
Chicago Architectural Club
Auditorium Dec. 20, '06.

TCR

# The Chicago Architectural Club

Prelude to the Modern

Wilbert R. Hasbrouck

THE MONACELLI PRESS

First published in the United States of America in 2005
by the Monacelli Press, Inc.
611 Broadway
New York, NY 10012

Library of Congress Cataloging-in-Publication Data

Hasbrouck, Wilbert R.
    The Chicago Architectural Club : prelude to the modern /
Wilbert R. Hasbrouck.
       p.   cm.
    Includes bibliographical references and index.
    ISBN 1-58093-144-8
    1. Chicago Architectural Club—History.   2. Architectural draw-
ing—Illinois—Chicago—19th century. 3.  Architectural drawing—
Illinois—Chicago—20th century. 4.  Architectural drawing—Study
and teaching—Illinois—Chicago.  I. Title.
NA2706.U6H37 2004
720'.28'406077311—dc22
                                        2004018042

Printed and bound in China

**GRAHAM FOUNDATION**

This publication was supported by a grant from the Graham
Foundation for Advanced Studies in the Fine Arts.

Typeset by Michael J. Bertrand

# Contents

Preface  *7*

Prologue  *13*

1. In the Beginning  *17*

2. Organization and Establishment  *35*

3. Acceptance and Competitions  *59*

4. Robert Clark and National Recognition  *79*

5. Before the World's Columbian Exposition  *103*

6. Designing the Fair  *129*

7. The Great Fair and Beyond  *153*

8. Broadening Horizons  *177*

9. Cooperation and Continued Success  *203*

10. Philosophical Debates at the End of the Century  *227*

11. The Young Turks Take Charge  *251*

12. Steinway Hall and the Traveling Scholarship  *277*

13. The Traditionalists Return  *303*

14. A Struggle for Dominance  *327*

15. Midlife Crises and Citywide Work  *379*

16. Back to the Art Institute  *419*

17. Wartime and Decline  *443*

18. Working Together to Survive  *483*

19. New Excitement in Architecture  *509*

20. A New Home  *537*

21. Depression, Decline, and Demise  *565*

Epilogue  *595*

Appendixes:  A.  Constitution and Bylaws  *599*

                B.  Glessner and Kimball House Agreements  *601*

                C.  List of Members  *604*

Chronology  *612*

Bibliographic Note and Acknowledgments  *628*

Index  *631*

*For Marilyn,*
*to whom I owe everything*

# Preface

During the past century, dozens of books and hundreds of articles have been written about the myth and reality of Chicago's architecture and its far-reaching influence. From 1885 until 1940, the world looked to Chicago for some of the most innovative buildings ever conceived. Where, when, and how did the men who produced this work learn to be architects? How were they able to convert the sometimes rudimentary sketches their superiors handed them into drawings that could be used for construction? What inspired them to refine designs and produce the drawings for buildings now considered icons of the early modern movement? This book is about how these young men became architects in the late nineteenth and early twentieth centuries. The buildings they crafted for their employers and later designed for their own clients are incidental to the story.

There are a dozen or so names usually associated with the Chicago School of architecture, a term used here in its broadest sense to include the incredible domestic architecture that paralleled the movement toward ever taller, bigger, more complex and impressive urban office structures. John Wellborn Root and his partner, Daniel Hudson Burnham, have to be at the head of any list of architects of the Chicago School. The list should also include, in no particular order: Dankmar Adler, Louis Sullivan, William Holabird, Martin Roche, William Le Baron Jenney, William Mundie, Joseph Lyman Silsbee, Richard E. Schmidt, Hugh M. G. Garden, and ultimately Ludwig Mies van der Rohe, all of whom were instrumental in the development of Chicago's tall buildings. Walter Burley Griffin, Marion Lucy Griffin (née Mahony), George Grant Elmslie, William Drummond, Howard Van Doren Shaw, Robert C. Spencer Jr., Dwight Heald Perkins, and, of course, Frank Lloyd Wright should be remembered as well. Virtually all of this second group trained in the offices of those named above, where the great steel-framed urban structures were designed. Following their apprenticeships, many of them chose to emulate their mentors' innovative spirit and went on to make their own contributions to the domestic architecture first called the Chicago School and later referred to as the Prairie School.

All these names are known to any historian of the modern movement in architecture. But who remembers delineator Paul Lautrup, who served as Burnham & Root's chief draftsman? Or H. R. Wilson, who helped found the Western Association of Architects, or Peter B. Wight, who fought side by side with Montgomery

Ward to keep Chicago's lakefront "open, clear and free" (as it was described on a now-famous 1836 map of Chicago on the shore of Lake Michigan), despite Daniel Burnham's efforts to install the Field Museum in the center of Grant Park? On the same list of forgotten, mostly young movers and shakers on the Chicago scene is Francis W. Kirkpatrick, who became president of the Chicago Architectural Club in 1898 and went on to spearhead its reorganization, which led to the now-fabled 1901 and 1902 exhibitions at the Art Institute of Chicago. J. C. Llewellyn and N. Max Dunning are hardly household names, but they were key figures in founding the Architectural League of America, spreading the ideas of the Chicago Architectural Club far beyond the shores of Lake Michigan. And there were others, such as W. G. Wuehrmann, Fred M. Hodgdon, Bernard C. Greengard, Otto A. Silha, Elmer J. Fox, and Rudolph J. Nedved, who all dedicated their intellectual abilities to the betterment and advancement of the profession of architecture, along with hundreds of aspiring architects who worked toward the same end between the Chicago Fire of 1871 and the Second World War.

In the late nineteenth century, Chicago was a frontier city growing by hundreds of people every day. Accommodations for living and business were in desperate demand. Architecture was an unproved profession—perhaps not even a profession at all. There were no real requirements of someone claiming the title of architect, no licensing, no laws regulating what he could or should do or what his responsibilities were to his clients and the public. There were a few men who had an education beyond secondary school, some of whom had training at the college level, but they were the exception to the rule at a time when "architects" with the most rudimentary training, almost no understanding of basic engineering, and only the slightest knowledge of aesthetics were the norm. Even those who did have an education and experience had an almost insurmountable problem. It was extremely difficult to employ draftsmen who could execute their work with competence and skill. The average office of a dozen or so men was fortunate to have a staff with more than one member who was able to take the principal's sketches and turn them into working drawings. This predicament was not due to lack of intelligence or disinterest; other than architectural periodicals and the few books that were available, the average aspiring architect had nowhere to learn his trade.

No one was more aware of this than the young "draughtsmen" themselves.[1] Much of what they learned was from older, more experienced draftsmen in established offices who had been trained in Europe or elsewhere and had a reasonable understanding of styles, classical proportions, and the mechanics of assembling a set of drawings. These men were not, however, in leadership positions. They were generally subordinate to experienced architects, self-trained men with a talent for conceiving basic schemes for anxious moneyed clients who needed buildings quickly. It was the senior draftsmen, however, who directed the production of drawings for the buildings the great names brought into the office, and who were responsible for refining and detailing the basic schemes. The junior staff members who assisted them faced an extraordinarily difficult learning curve.

This book is an attempt to understand the methods by which these young men learned the techniques and skills needed to become accomplished draftsmen and architects at a time when formal training as such was essentially nonexistent, beginning around 1885 and continuing well into the twentieth century. The need for competent, if not highly skilled, draftsmen following the Chicago Fire was critical. Well-executed buildings depended on such a workforce, both mechanically

1. The term "draughtsman" was already becoming archaic in 1885. By the turn of the century it was rarely used, and "draftsman" had become the preferred term.

and aesthetically. For the most part, design was either limited to whatever pattern book the architect-builder had available, or buildings lacked appropriate proportion and classic ornament almost entirely. Many historians have argued that this very lack of knowledge of classical architecture was a key element in the development of the Chicago School. In too many cases, however, the results were less than desirable.

Buildings were being built by the hundreds in the early 1880s when James H. Carpenter, a forty-two-year-old, English-born itinerant draftsman in Chicago, realized that the need for trained men to finalize designs and produce working drawings had reached a critical stage. Just what Carpenter's motives were has never been determined, but it was he who brought eighteen colleagues together to form the Chicago Architectural Sketch Club in the spring of 1885. It was through the efforts of this club that young draftsmen learned the history, styles, and functions of architecture to a degree that they were able to translate first their employers' and later their own clients' needs into buildings. This organization, more than any other individual, firm, or professional society, was responsible for the evolution and development of the Chicago School of architecture.

The Chicago Architectural Club, as it was later renamed, existed for just over half a century. During that time more than sixteen hundred people passed through its roster of members. From the beginning, the club maintained a level of activity that would be unheard of today. It met as a group at least once a fortnight and sometimes twice that often. Committees also held regular meetings and sponsored competitions both simple and complex. They had brief sketching evenings where small prizes were awarded and invited established colleagues to speak on a wide range of topics. Several of the most famous essays on the development of modern architecture were first delivered at the club. For thirty years, the Annual Traveling Scholarship Competition provided funds for the winner to spend a year in Europe.

The Chicago Architectural Club thus became an instrument of learning for several generations of architects, first in the absence of formal education at the college level and later as an alternative. It began as a system of lectures, social interchange, competitions, and entertainment designed to cultivate an understanding of architecture. Its leadership always came from within, although the advice of established architects was regularly sought out and followed. The membership assembled an excellent library, and members were, in general, well read if not formally educated. The club's affairs were managed by men who followed architectural trends and educational efforts throughout the United States with some diligence. They worked closely with other clubs and organizations, including the Architectural League of America and the Society of Beaux-Arts Architects, whose educational techniques were for the most part eventually adopted by the club.

The education of members was all-consuming, to the point that it sometimes encouraged an irrational suspicion of formal training and established organizations such as the American Institute of Architects and the Illinois Society of Architects. It wasn't until the last few years of the club's existence, in fact, that cooperation with these groups that served their senior colleagues became the norm. Eventually the club joined forces with the Chicago Chapter of the American Institute of Architects and the Illinois Society of Architects to form an umbrella group called the Architects Club of Chicago. That group acquired the W. W. Kimball House on Prairie Avenue and made arrangements to turn the John J. Glessner House into a permanent home for all of Chicago's architects. Unfortunately, those plans were torpedoed by the Great Depression. By 1936, the Glessner House had become an impossible dream and the Kimball House was lost.

By the time Ludwig Mies van der Rohe arrived in Chicago in 1938, the Chicago Architectural Club had essentially lost its purpose. Most architects were now being formally educated, often at institutions the club had had a hand in establishing, and the techniques the club had used so successfully for half a century were no longer needed. With the onset of the Second World War, the Chicago Architectural Club effectively ceased to exist. Its ideas, however, lived on—particularly that of the architect as a respected professional.

After World War II, Chicago reaffirmed its reputation as the leading city of architecture in the world. There was, unfortunately, no place for young designers to call their own. (Both the American Institute of Architects and the Illinois Society of Architects still catered only to licensed practicing architects.) Thirty-three years after the end of the Second World War that would change. In the fall of 1979 a notice was circulated among a number of younger architects and designers suggesting that the Chicago Architectural Club be reconstituted. Architect Stanley Tigerman was the originator of the notice. He and several colleagues decided that the new club would be less concerned with basic education, since virtually all its members were college graduates and most were accomplished designers or academicians. Instead, it would be an outlet for their dreams and a place to debate issues. In keeping with the mission of the original club, however, lectures, competitions, exhibitions, and social interchange were among its goals. It was decided that membership would be a privilege limited to eighty men and women. Architect Carter H. Manny, the director of the Graham Foundation for Advanced Studies in the Fine Arts, generously offered the use of the landmark Madlener House for club meetings.

On November 19, 1979, Stanley Tigerman opened the first meeting of thirty-nine people. It took only minutes to agree to the nuts and bolts of the organization. The founding members then heard an opening lecture on the history of the original Chicago Architectural Club.[2] Twenty-five years later, the Chicago Architectural Club continues to serve the young men and women in the Chicago architectural community in much the same way it did a century earlier.

Wilbert R. Hasbrouck
October 2004

2. My lecture, "The Early Years of the Chicago Architectural Club," was recorded and published in *Chicago Architectural Journal* 1, no. 1 (1981).

THE
CHICAGO
ARCHIT
ECTURAL
CLUB

PRELUDE
TO
THE
MODERN

DEARBORN AVENUE NEAR DIVISION ST.

STATE ST NEAR DIVISION ST.

LAKE SHORE DRIVE NORTH SIDE

FRAGMENTS FROM CHICAGO ARCHITECTURE
SKETCHED BY CICERO HINE

MICHIGAN AV. AND ELDRIDGE CT.

HOTEL CHARLEVOIX RUSH ST.

*Cicero Hine regularly contributed sketches of this nature to* Inland Architect
*(IA)*

# Prologue

In January of 1895 a notice was sent to members of the Chicago Architectural Sketch Club advising that a special meeting would be held the following month. At that meeting, John Robert Dillon, secretary of the club, noted the following:

> *RESOLUTION:* The Chicago Architectural Sketch Club, on the evening of February 11, 1895, by a vote of the whole membership decided to have its name changed to The Chicago Architectural Club and to incorporate under that name.

With this action, which was not officially recorded until more than three years later, the Chicago Architectural Club became the premier organization of its kind in the United States. It was no longer strictly a "sketch" club, with membership restricted to apprentice architects. It now represented the broader architectural community of Chicago. The club was one month short of ten years old.

The official reasons for the name change remain somewhat obscure. The club's records during the first half of 1895 are among the least complete of an otherwise well-documented organization. There are, however, some later published accounts that comment on the change. Peter B. Wight, in his 1896 review of the Ninth Annual Exhibition of the Chicago Architectural Club, wrote, "the word 'sketch' was, two [sic] years ago, obliterated from its name when it made its regular membership open to all practicing architects."[1] He went on to comment on the exhibition in general, concluding, "The club is on the right track and doing excellent work."

More than a year later, the December 1897 issue of the *Inland Architect and Building News* carried an article titled "The Work of the Chicago Architectural Club," under the byline of Robert Craik McLean.[2] He wrote, "The work of the Chicago Architectural Club . . . is surprising in its scope and influence upon the student-architect when examined in detail . . . Carried on, as it is, by young men whose daily employment is over the drafting boards of the architects of Chicago, with little or no guidance except their own bright conception of the needs of their fellows, aided by the traditions of the club, which stretch back twelve years to the time of its organization, in the office of the *Inland Architect*, by a few draftsmen who have since become prominent among the best designers in the country, they teach and are taught and work together for the common purpose of advancement in

CASC membership card (courtesy John Bushnell)

1. *Inland Architect* 27, no. 3 (April 1896): 22–23.

2. Robert Craik McLean (1854–1933) was born in Waukegan, Illinois, where he received his early education. He began his career in journalism in Chicago around 1878, and became the editor of the *Inland Architect and Building News* in 1883. In 1905 he became the editor of the *Western Architect*, and remained in that job until he retired in 1930. He died at his retirement home in Bradford Woods, Pennsylvania.

*Robert Craik McLean in his* Inland Architect *office, ca. 1886
(courtesy Jessie McFarland McLean and Robert Prestiano)*

their chosen art." The article went on to discuss the activities of the club in some detail, particularly its educational aspects.

McLean was certainly qualified to comment on the Chicago Architectural Club, for it was he, more than anyone else, who was responsible for its existence. As the founding editor of the *Inland Architect*, which began publication in 1883,[3] he regularly reported on the activities of professional societies involved with architecture and the building trades in mid-America, including the American Institute of Architects and the Western Association of Architects, as well as groups such as the Plumbers' Association and the Chicago Master Masons. Often his articles would note that he had been present at the meetings, and many times he would be listed as an officer of some sort. (One cannot help but wonder whether he actively promoted the activities of the builders' associations primarily to fill the pages of his magazine—although, of course, he couldn't have done so without their enthusiastic cooperation.) Every issue of the *Inland Architect* had a column of "Association Notes," listing forthcoming meetings, and several of the various groups claimed the *Inland Architect* as their official journal. The most prominent coverage, however, was given to the many architectural clubs throughout the United States, particularly in the Midwest. McLean maintained both a professional and a personal interest in the club in Chicago, where the *Inland Architect* was published, until his death more than forty years after the club was founded.

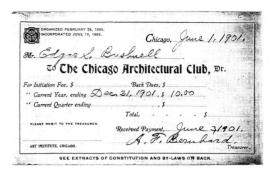

*CAC membership card (courtesy John Bushnell)*

3. The *Inland Architect and Builder* debuted in February 1883. (Its six-month volumes were always published in February and August. Occasionally extra issues were released in numerical sequence; consequently the issues do not always correspond with the months.) The name was changed to the *Inland Architect and News Record* in 1887, although the journal is referred to throughout this book as the *Inland Architect*.

*Cover of the banquet program for the first meeting of the Western Association of Architects (IA)*

# In the Beginning

## CHAPTER ONE

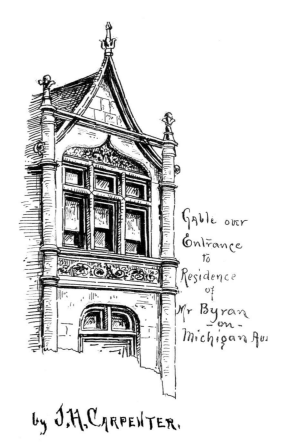

*J. H. Carpenter drawing (IA)*

Ten years before the name change was announced in 1895, the originators of what was to become the Chicago Architectural Club used the pages of the *Inland Architect* to announce their intention to organize. In February of 1885, under the headline "Draughtsmen's Sketching Clubs," editor Robert Craik McLean published the following notice:

> The leading draughtsmen in Chicago offices are contemplating the organization of a club for the purpose of increasing their knowledge of design and construction, their power of delineation, and for general sociability. The movement takes tangible form in a brief note received, which says:
>
> > *Editors Inland Architect and Builder,*—Will you please consider the proposition to invite the draughtsmen who desire to form a sketching club, to send their names directed, if you please, to yourselves, or to "T. Square," in care of your office? The intention is to commence at once. By giving this movement your consideration, you will oblige,
> >
> > THE DRAUGHTSMEN.

McLean added an editorial comment: "The idea is a good one, and if properly organized and conducted by the right parties, cannot but result in a permanent and increasing good."[1]

The note had been sent by "T. Square," a pseudonym of J. H. Carpenter,[2] a leading draftsman in Chicago who had contributed an article titled "Architects' Draughtsmen" to the *Inland Architect* a few months earlier.[3] Written in the somewhat flowery rhetoric of the time, the article was essentially an admonition to employers of aspiring architects—i.e., junior draftsmen—to find a way to train young people in the skills of architecture.

In 1885, "draughtsman" was a title used to describe a wide range of jobs, from those of the most junior assistants in an architectural firm to longtime senior employees. It was a title that commanded respect. Generally speaking, the draftsmen did the day-to-day work of preparing the drawings for the buildings designed by the principals or senior men in the firm. There was rarely any training available for aspiring draftsmen before they entered an architect's office. They learned from being told what to do by older men, from the many journals of architecture that published methods of preparing drawings, and from numerous books covering all

1. *Inland Architect* 5, no. 1 (February 1885): 9.

2. James H. Carpenter (1842-1897) was born in England. He was listed in the 1890 census as a "contractor." He wrote regularly for the *Inland Architect* and by 1885 was listing himself as an "architect and construction engineer." He probably had some formal education but was largely self-taught. A skilled "perspectivist" whose drawings often appeared in the pages of the *Inland Architect*, he apparently worked independently, since his name, as delineator, appeared on the drawings of a number of different architects. After editor Robert McLean revealed that "T. Square" was Carpenter's nom de plume, Carpenter wrote under his own name.

3. "Architects' Draughtsmen, 'By T. Square,'" *Inland Architect* 4, no. 4 (November 1884): 55–56. J. H. Carpenter was no stranger to the published word. He had also written a small book, *Hints on Building* (Hartford, CT: Press of the Case, Lockwood & Brainard Company, 1883). Following the organization of the Chicago Architectural Sketch Club, that book was serialized with only minor revisions in the *Inland Architect*. Later, he published *The Complete House Builder* (Chicago: Donohue, Henneberry & Co., 1889), a volume "containing fifty plans and specifications of dwellings, barns, churches, public buildings." Carpenter's books are extremely rare today but can be found on microfilm in Henry-Russell Hitchcock's *American Architectural Books: A List of Books, Portfolios, and Pamphlets on Architecture and Related Subjects Published in America Before 1895* (Minneapolis: University of Minnesota, 1962).

aspects of the work required of draftsmen in architects' offices. There were also trade schools where the basic techniques of draftsmanship and preparation of construction drawings were taught, but formal educational opportunities for aspiring architects were few and far between. In the Midwest, only Michigan and Illinois had universities where architecture was taught.

Young men, and a very few women, usually entered architects' offices as apprentices. Some did so as young as twelve to fourteen years of age. Few remained long in what was a rigorous apprenticeship, but those who did learned construction drawing techniques and preparation of perspectives, as well as the basic mathematics and engineering needed to produce the plans required to construct the increasingly complex buildings of the late nineteenth century. Some of these apprentices became very proficient and were proud to be called draftsmen. Nevertheless, they realized that as buildings became more complicated, some method of learning outside the architect's office was becoming essential.

As one of the few draftsmen with some formal education, J. H. Carpenter was most concerned about those who had little or no training beyond high school, if that. He began his article, "Hardly any profession excites the imagination of young men with the state of feeling that the architectural [profession] does. The possibility of creating structures which shall be monuments of fame, lures each one to believe he may be the favored one, and if the candidate for the honor starts out to accomplish this purpose it is usually with the idea of reaching his ambition's desire with the least amount of trouble and by the shortest road possible . . . haste seems to be the only rule." He went on to point out that a draftsman soon arrived at a point where "he cannot reach a higher place because he is unfitted." Not only did draftsmen lack the knowledge needed to advance, but they had no way of getting that knowledge.

Somewhat undiplomatically, Carpenter suggested that this was the fault of the employer, who too often took the position that he was wise to let his draftsmen remain ignorant—that he was not a teacher and if he were, his employees would move on to jobs with better salaries as soon as they had acquired the knowledge they needed to advance. Carpenter argued that knowledgeable draftsmen were worth more to an employer and should be paid accordingly. In his words, "if the student is worth more to another he is certainly worth quite as much where he is." In closing, his article took a somewhat paternalistic tone, suggesting that young men "must help themselves to gain the requisite knowledge." His final paragraphs were specific and to the point: "We would suggest the forming of sketching clubs, such as now exist in some cities . . . This union, by united effort, could first learn of each other and then seek information from various sources . . . Discussion among us all of plans to prosper our cause should follow our thought on this subject, and no one will rejoice more than we at any step made toward improvement and progress in our profession—the grandest and noblest of all studies and practice."

J. H. Carpenter and his fellow draftsmen in Chicago would have been aware of sketching clubs from published accounts in architectural journals and other magazines of the period. For example, they might have seen the article that appeared in the *Century Magazine* in March 1883, titled "The Architectural League of New York,"[4] a rather lengthy essay outlining the organization and activities of the league. The author, Roger Riordan, wrote that "the League began some two or three years ago in haphazard meetings in the room of one of the members . . . Here all the young architects in the city became acquainted with one another, and found that they had a common cause and a mission which they were called on to perform as a body. From chance gatherings in this room a step was made toward corporate existence by the institution of monthly meetings at the rooms of the several members,

4. Roger Riordan, "The Architectural League of New York," *Century Magazine* 25, no. 15 (March 1883): 698–708.

*The only known surviving example of architect J. H. Carpenter's work are these row houses built in 1887 on Chicago's South Side (WRH)*

*Carpenter published this example of his work in 1883 and again in 1889 (CHB)*

and so many were anxious to attend them that a regular club organization with fortnightly meetings and a home of its own, soon became possible. The new society met for a few times in the halls of its friends, the Salmagundians, but found permanent quarters before long in the top-story-back in Fourteenth street." Riordan's article included several sketches of members' work and noted that "the League has already had its first annual dinner . . . [but it] was not organized for merely convivial purposes. In its great object of enabling its members to advance themselves by comparing notes on all subjects that interest them, and bring into plan, by means of the fortnightly competitions, faculties and talents that would remain undeveloped by ordinary practice the League has been successful to an unexpected degree. A good many of the older architects in the city have shown an active interest in it. Its list of lecturers comprises nearly every name of note in the profession." The description of the league's activities could easily have applied to those of the Chicago Architectural Sketch Club five years later. It was certainly an exemplary model for the Chicago draftsmen to emulate.[5]

Carpenter's thought-provoking article must have had a profound effect on young draftsmen in Chicago, causing them to reflect on the difficulties of advancing in their field. They were not the only ones preoccupied with the issue of advancement. At about the same time—during 1884 and early 1885—there was a burst of organizational activity on the part of architects in Chicago. Although architects were becoming an intrinsic part of Chicago's economy and its professional circles, due to the building boom in the early 1880s that followed the Great Fire of 1871[6] and the brief recession in the late 1870s, the Illinois Chapter of the American Institute of Architects had been moribund for years, often holding only a single annual meeting attended by less than twenty architects. Many architects felt the need of a more active association that would present a united front to society.

In March of 1884, the *Inland Architect* had published a letter from H. R. Wilson,[7] then an obscure Chicago architect, suggesting that an association of Midwestern architects be formed.[8] Robert McLean had encouraged further suggestions, and by May a number of architects had responded. In June, he had asked more architects to endorse the plan. Over the summer, he had continued to encourage the

5. The Architectural League of New York was organized in January of 1881. A group of five young men met in rooms occupied by Cass Gilbert and C. H. Johnston at 40 Irving Place in New York. The league is well documented: nearly all of its records—including meeting minutes, membership applications, financial records, and data concerning competitions and exhibitions—have been saved. This material is now on deposit at the Archives of American Art in Washington, D.C., in eighty-nine loosely organized file boxes of records. I am indebted to Rosalie Genevro, executive director of the Architectural League of New York, for bringing this resource to my attention.

6. *Industrial Chicago, The Building Trades,* vol. 1 (Chicago: Goodspeed Publishing Company, 1891), 121. The Chicago fire of October 8–9, 1871, destroyed more than twenty thousand buildings over an area of twenty-one hundred acres. The total loss exceeded $190 million.

7. Horatio Reed Wilson (1857–1917) was born in Jamestown, New York. He studied architecture abroad and in 1878 apprenticed with architect C. J. Hull. He entered a partnership with Oliver W. Marble in 1889. After Marble's death, he practiced alone until 1893, when Benjamin Marshall joined him to form Wilson & Marshall. From 1902 until his death in 1917, he practiced without a partner, as head of H. R. Wilson & Co.

8. *Inland Architect* 3, no.2 (March 1884): 24.

*The* Century Magazine *published this drawing of a meeting of the Architectural League of New York in 1883 (CM)*

9. *Inland Architect* 4, no. 2 (September 1884): 19.

10. A verbatim transcript of the proceedings was published in *Inland Architect* 4, extra no. (November 1884): 2 et seq.

11. Paul C. Lautrup (1848–1913) was born and educated in Denmark. He came to the United States in 1869 and began his career in Washington, D.C., ca. 1876, working for the supervising architect of the Treasury, where he was eventually named chief designer. His first signed drawing for a Chicago architect was done for William Le Baron Jenney in 1882. Thereafter he signed numerous drawings for Chicago firms. In 1882 he was named chief draftsman for Burnham & Root but continued to do freelance work. In 1883, he opened his own office as a designer and perspectivist. He was listed as an associate member of the Chicago Architectural Sketch Club in 1893. His work is briefly reviewed by Eileen Michels in "A Developmental Study of the Drawings Published in *American Architect* and in *Inland Architect* through 1895" (PhD diss., University of Minnesota, 1971).

idea, and in September, he wrote that "more than two hundred architects have responded to our circular calling for a convention of members of the profession . . . to meet in Chicago November 12." He went on to conclude, "the need of a movement of this kind in the west, and coming, as they do, from our farthest northern, southern, and western boundaries, the widespread extent of the movement is indicated."[9] While not specifically stated, the primary intention of such a movement was to form an association of architects that would be broadly representative, enhancing the image of the architect professionally, politically, and socially—objectives that were commonly associated with the American Institute of Architects but had never been realized in the west, as the AIA was essentially an East Coast organization.

On November 12–14, 1884, 140 architects from throughout the Midwest, and as far away as the West Coast and the Gulf of Mexico, had met in Chicago, and the Western Association of Architects was born.[10] The WAA was to become a major force in the architectural world during the next five years; nevertheless, it did not have any provision for draftsmen, except to recognize that their services were important. At the closing banquet of the organizational convention, chairman D. H. Burnham acknowledged as much when he proposed a toast to "the draughtsmen" and called on Paul C. Lautrup to respond.[11] Lautrup, who was then Burnham's chief draftsman, delivered "a witty speech, which was heartily enjoyed and applauded throughout. He closed with the following: 'I have been a draughtsman all my life, and I have often thought I would feel very happy to be an architect. I see many heads around me now that have taken me into real fellowship. You have given me the honor to say a few words for the draughtsman, and I feel that though I am simply a draughtsman, I have been generously received this evening among architects. So much honor has been paid tonight to the draughtsmen that in the name of all other draughtsmen, I thank you deeply.'"[12]

Despite Lautrup's response to the toast, his fellow draftsman J. H. Carpenter was not happy with the conspicuous absence of any specific role for the draftsman, or young architect, in what was to become the primary professional association of architects in the west. Although Carpenter would have been fully aware of the convention, he probably did not attend, since he was not an architect. (He was proud to be a draftsman and was never listed as an architect in any Chicago directory.) Nearly every architect's office in Chicago was represented, usually by principals or partners. The fact that the new association, like the AIA, made no proviso for the education and training of young men must have been rankling, to say the least. Exactly when Carpenter's article was written and submitted to McLean is not known, but logic suggests that it was written with the author's full knowledge of the events at the WAA convention, as it appeared in the same issue of the *Inland Architect* as the verbatim record of the entire convention. It is also reasonable to conclude that Carpenter's byline, "T. Square," was used to protect himself from repercussions by current or future employers.

*Horatio R. Wilson can be rightly credited as the father of the Western Association of Architects (MofI)*

During the early days of the Western Association of Architects, the young draftsmen who would found the Chicago Architectural Sketch Club were very much aware of the organization and its responsibility for the steady enhancement of the reputation of architects and architecture. Once organized, in fact, the WAA became a national organization, expanding rapidly throughout the Midwest and as far afield as California, Minnesota, and Louisiana. Within weeks of the WAA's November 1884 meeting, McLean reported that several state architectural associations had been formed. The Architectural Association of Minnesota, which had already been in place for four years, reported in February of 1885 that it was continuing its work but was offering its members the privilege of membership in the WAA and would henceforth operate under the WAA's rules.

The previous month, McLean had announced, "Architects of the State of Illinois are requested by the secretary and board of directors of the W.A.A. to meet in Chicago on the 16th inst. for the purpose of forming a state association under the laws of the national association. Although the proposed state association will be largely composed of Chicago architects, those at other points should not fail to be present, that their interests may be fully represented, and they may take a broader form than if composed purely of those whose interests lie in one direction. It is the desire of the directors in this, as well as in the formation of all state bodies, that the interests, not only of the majority, but of each individual member of the profession, may be fully served, and the harmony that marked the formation of the national association may be perpetuated in each of its branches."[13] Thus the WAA was clearly meant to be inclusive rather than exclusive, as the national and local AIA had been since its inception in 1857.

In February 1885, the *Inland Architect* noted that Missouri was planning a similar state association under the rules of the WAA.[14] The next month it was reported that the Illinois State Association of Architects had met on Saturday, March 13, 1885. John W. Root had been elected chairman of the Executive Committee, and Louis Sullivan had been appointed a committee of one to procure articles of incorporation. The secretary had reported forty-nine charter members.[15]

The activities of the Western Association of Architects and the Illinois state association seem to have had little effect on the Illinois Chapter of the AIA. During the months when the organization of architects was paramount in the minds of

*Seal of the Western Association of Architects (IA)*

12. *Inland Architect* 4, extra no. (November 1884): 15.

13. *Inland Architect* 4, no. 6 (January 1885): 1.

14. *Inland Architect* 5, no. 1 (February 1885): 9.

15. *Building Budget* 1, no. 1 (March 1885): 6.

*A panoramic view of Chicago's Loop, looking north from Harrison and Dearborn streets, after the Great Fire of 1871 (WRH)*

16. While McLean and others often referred to the "Chicago" Chapter of the AIA, it was actually the Illinois Chapter until the mid-1920s.

17. *Inland Architect* 5, no. 4 (May 1885): 67.

practitioners in Illinois and neighboring states, there was no mention of the Illinois Chapter of the AIA in any of the various architectural journals, until May of 1885, when the *Inland Architect* reported, under the heading "Chicago Chapter, AIA,"[16] that "the Chicago Chapter of the American Institute of Architects held their first meeting in several years at the Grand Pacific Hotel last month. It was in the form of a banquet, about a dozen architects being present, L. D. Cleveland presiding. The officers elected at the last meeting of [the] chapter; August Bauer, president; L. D. Cleveland, vice-president; Jas. R. Willett, treasurer, Samuel A. Treat, secretary; were reelected for the coming year."[17] The chapter continued to meet from time to time for the next five years, but it had ceased to be much of a force in the architectural

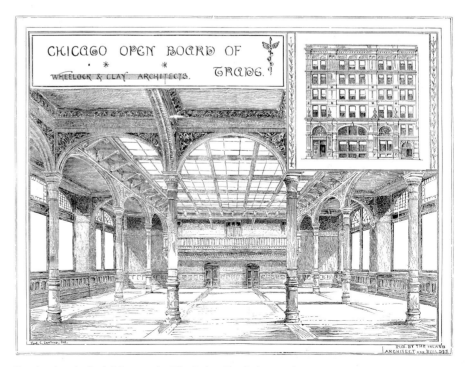

*Drawing done by Paul C. Lautrup for Wheelock & Clay (IA)*

community in Illinois. It was not until 1889, when the WAA and the national AIA merged into a single body, followed shortly thereafter by the merging of the Illinois Association of Architects and the Illinois Chapter of the AIA, that the Illinois AIA became the respected organization it is now.[18]

While Chicago's architects continued their frenzy of organizational activities, two unrelated events transformed the city's landscape and fired the imaginations of architects and draftsmen alike. First, William Le Baron Jenney, an engineer and architect,[19] designed and built the Home Insurance Building. His site superintendent was William Bryce Mundie.[20] Jenney had received the commission in 1883, and construction had begun in 1884. The building was completed in 1885, at about the time the Chicago Architectural Sketch Club was organized. Tall, aesthetically pleasing, and structurally innovative, it stood in a prominent location in the heart of Chicago's business district. The urgent demand for taller buildings that could provide more office space on a finite amount of land had already taxed the architectural community to its limits, reinforcing the importance of engineering, but by the mid-1880s, with the construction of the Home Insurance Building, it was clear that design had become an increasingly important factor.[21]

The other significant event in 1885 was the arrival—for the second time—of Henry Hobson Richardson, one of America's premier architects. Richardson had been responsible for the American Merchants Union Express Company Building, built in Chicago just after the fire in 1873. A five-story building with somewhat eclectic detailing, it was not considered a major effort by the East Coast master. Its foundations failed almost immediately and it had to be repaired and essentially rebuilt between 1874 and 1880, under the supervision of Chicago architect Peter B. Wight. Richardson did not return to Chicago for more than a decade, but when he did it was with a vengeance.

Just as the Chicago Architectural Club was being organized in April of 1885, Richardson received the commission to design the Marshall Field Warehouse. In May of the same year he was commissioned to design a residence for John J. Glessner, and two months later he was asked to design a house for Franklin McVeagh.[22] Richardson's Chicago clients moved in the same social cir-

18. In 2004 there are several chapters of the AIA in Illinois, of which Chicago is the largest. For statewide matters, the AIA operates under an umbrella organization called the Illinois Council of the AIA.

19. William Le Baron Jenney (1832–1907) was born in Fairhaven, Massachusetts. He received a public school education and after a course in engineering at the Lawrence Scientific School in Cambridge, Massachusetts, he eventually entered the École Centrale des Arts et Manufacturers in Paris, where he earned his diploma in 1856. He served as an engineer during the Civil War, rising to the rank of brevet major. He began working in Chicago in 1868, took William B. Mundie as his partner in 1891, and remained in active practice until 1903. He became an honorary member of the Chicago Architectural Sketch Club in 1892.

20. William Bryce Mundie (1863– 1939) came to Chicago from Toronto in 1884. He was the son of a Canadian architect and the grandson of a Scottish architect. Mundie went to public school and was a graduate of the Hamilton Institute. Upon his arrival in Chicago, he immediately began work for William Le Baron Jenney, an association that lasted until Jenney's death. He became a member of the Chicago Architectural Sketch Club in 1886 and was elected an honorary member in 1916.

21. The best contemporary discussion of architecture and construction from 1871 to 1891 can be found in *Industrial Chicago,*

*William Bryce Mundie around the time he began to work with W. L. B. Jenney (MofI)*

*Henry Hobson Richardson, ca. 1885 (VanR)*

*Paul Lautrup's drawing of William Le Baron Jenney's Home Insurance Building, under construction at the time the Chicago Architectural Sketch Club was organized (IA)*

cles and knew each other well. Construction began on the Field Building in November of 1885 and on the Glessner and McVeagh houses around March of 1886. None of the buildings was finished before Richardson's sudden death on April 27, 1886, and the work was completed by his successor firm, Shepley, Rutan & Coolidge. Edward Cameron, who had come to Chicago in 1885 to act as site superintendent for all three buildings, never joined the Chicago Architectural Sketch Club, but two other draftsmen then in Richardson's Brookline, Massachusetts, office, Alfred H. Granger and Dwight Heald Perkins, became prominent members.

While it is unlikely that the CASC members were aware of the Richardson commissions at the time the club was founded, during the next few years they would be greatly influenced by them, as would the rest of Chicago's architectural

22. The best concise description of these three buildings can be found in Jeffrey Karl Ochsner, *H. H. Richardson, Complete Architectural Works* (Cambridge and London: MIT Press, 1982), 380–93.

community.[23] What came to be known as Richardson Romanesque became de rigueur during the next decade or so, particularly in competition entries produced by members of the various architectural clubs in the Midwest, including the Chicago Architectural Sketch Club.

On the other hand, the club's founders would have been fully aware of the Home Insurance Building. It was the most prominent building under construction in the city in early 1885, and its structural system and overall aesthetic served as the model for a number of new structures over the next few years, laying the groundwork for what became known as the Chicago School of architecture. In 1885, Chicago may still have been a frontier city, but its architects were open to new ideas. Jenney's and Richardson's avant-garde work was exactly what Chicago's young practitioners needed to move into a new era of architecture.

Thus it appears that when J. H. Carpenter asked the editors of the *Inland Architect* in February of 1885 to "invite the draughtsmen who desire to form a sketching club to send their names," he was very much in tune with the prevailing spirit of the time. A new architecture was being born in Chicago and it was the draftsmen who would produce the drawings from which it would be built. Carpenter's plan was to fill the void that existed between practicing architects and draftsmen, many of whom expected to one day become architects. He knew similar clubs had been organized in New York, Boston, and elsewhere, and he expected Chicago to follow suit. His timing was perfect.

Following Carpenter's letter of February 1885, Robert Craik McLean published the complete bylaws of the Des Moines Sketch Club, "a similar club organized in that city . . . that the Chicago draughtsmen may see what has already been done in this line." Those bylaws were brief and not aimed primarily at architects. The Chicago group found little there other than a challenge to do better. They would succeed beyond anyone's expectations.

In March of 1885, McLean reported that the organizational meeting of the Chicago Architectural Sketch Club had been held.[24] He gave no date for the meeting, but there is a date of February 26, 1885, recorded in a brief history of the club published in 1891 as part of *Industrial Chicago, The Building Trades*.[25] Following McLean's comments on the organizational meeting, the *Inland Architect* published an article under the headline "A Draughtsmen's Association Formed."[26] It began: "In accordance with the suggestion made last month the draughtsmen of Chicago are organizing themselves into a club for mutual improvement. A preliminary meeting for consultation was called and took place at the office of the *Inland Architect and Builder*. As the design of T. Square—Mr. J. H. Carpenter—who called the meeting, was to secure a limited number of the leading draughtsmen, the work proposed for the initial meeting being preliminary, a general invitation was not issued, and the call was responded to by all addressed, with the exception of two who live out of town."

Clearly, since only a "limited number of the leading draughtsmen" were asked to attend that initial organizational meeting, it was the intent of the organizers to maintain control over what they proposed. Interest was obviously high. Twenty invitations were sent out, and eighteen men attended the meeting. McLean reported that the charter members included Harry Lawrie, W. A. Otis, J. H. Carpenter, Ed-

THE AMERICAN EXPRESS CO<sup>S</sup> BUILDING
Nos 72, 74, 76, 78 & 80 Monroe St. Chicago, Ill.

*H. H. Richardson's American Express Building, demolished in 1919 (WRH)*

23. An excellent discussion of Richardson's influence on Chicago and the Midwest is in Paul Clifford Larson, *The Spirit of H. H. Richardson on the Midland Prairies*, ed. Susan M. Brown (Minneapolis: University of Minnesota and Ames, Iowa, State University Press, 1988).

24. *Inland Architect* 5, no. 2 (March 1885): 18.

25. *Industrial Chicago*, 306–8.

26. *Inland Architect* 5, no. 2 (March 1885): 24.

*The Marshall Field Warehouse Building, completed in 1886 and demolished in 1936 (IA)*

ward Dewson, W. J. B. McCullough, C. A. Kessell, George Beaumont, Harry Wheelock, Irving K. Pond, Myron H. Church, William Zimmerman, Cicero Hine, L. B. Dutton, W. G. Williamson, G. A. Hawkins, J. T. Warine, J. T. Hetherington, and T. D. Hetherington. Conspicuous in their absence were William Bryce Mundie and Paul Lautrup ("the dean of Chicago's draftsmen, the best pen and ink perspective artist in the west and a model to be emulated"),[27] both of whom soon became involved. Most of the men had already made a name for themselves as the delineators of important buildings by prominent architects in the Midwest. Although not yet architects, they were not amateurs, and nearly all had published work to their credit. Their average age was about twenty-seven years, and most had some education beyond high school and several years of experience. At forty-two, Carpenter was apparently the oldest.[28]

Robert Craik McLean was not listed as a charter member, probably by his own choice, since he was not a draftsman. The club's organizational meeting was held in his office, but he obviously did more than merely provide a place for the initial meetings. The article in the March 1885 issue of the *Inland Architect* noted, "R. C. McLean was called to the chair, and Harry Wheelock asked to act as secretary." (Wheelock's duties ended when officers were elected, but McLean's work continued when he was elected to be the first treasurer of the club.)

McLean's article went on to say, "After a unanimous vote being made to proceed to organize an association of draughtsmen, the entire meeting was taken up with the discussion of the best plan to adopt." He continued, "The general idea and the most popular expression that was incorporated in the remarks of those present was to the effect that the association should be simply a club for improvement and enjoyment, and that the work done should be in thorough harmony with the architect, and that it should not in any manner approach trades-unionism." Apparently, Carpenter's choice of words in his article "Architects' Draughtsmen" was a concern to those present at the February meeting. Carpenter had used the phrase "this union, by united effort," which sounded uncomfortably close to trade unionism. The draftsmen considered themselves professionals, not tradesmen, and they wanted to make that clear.

Several of those present made speeches, all of which supported the idea of forming a club. "The arguments in favor of such an organization were many, one of the strongest being that because of the general inexperience among draughts-

27. Michels, "A Developmental Study," 108.

28. Thirteen of the eighteen charter members were between the ages of twenty-two and thirty-two when the club was formed. Myron Church was thirty-two and Harry Wheelock and W. B. Williamson, at twenty-two, were the youngest.

*The Franklin McVeagh House by H. H. Richardson (VanR)*

*The Glessner House by Henry Hobson Richardson (WRH)*

men . . . it should be the work of the association to improve each member in . . . design. The tenor of each speech seemed to be that the draughtsmen were anxious for improvement . . . It was thought best to have a junior class, in which all draughtsmen of one year's experience should be eligible . . . and that all should accompany their application for membership with a sketch." It was apparent that they wanted to attract younger men who needed the education and experience they expected the club to provide.

Lawrie, Beaumont, Zimmerman, Carpenter, and Pond were appointed to prepare a constitution and bylaws. It was suggested that they obtain copies of similar documents from the "British association," the "junior association of Glasgow," and the clubs of Boston, New York, and Des Moines. Williamson, Kessell, and Dewson were appointed to find permanent quarters for the club. They agreed to meet two

*Chicago's Royal Insurance Building was designed by William W. Boyington in 1884; this Jackson Street facade was drawn by Myron H. Church (IA)*

*Quincy Street facade of the Royal Insurance Building, drawn by W. G. Williamson (IA)*

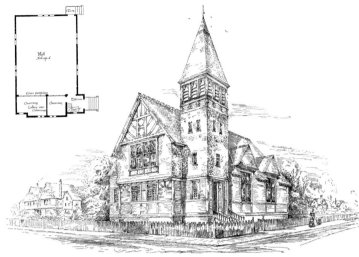

*House for J. K. Barry in Chicago, designed by J. J. Flanders and drawn by William Zimmerman (IA)*    *Woodlawn Presbyterian Church, designed and drawn by Harry Lawrie (IA)*

weeks later to "perfect" the organization. McLean concluded his report on that initial meeting, "The movement should receive the support of every draughtsman who wishes for advancement in his profession, and it is being heartily indorsed by the architects."

The eighteen men who met that Saturday afternoon, February 26, 1885, in McLean's office at the *Inland Architect* took the organization of the Chicago Architectural Sketch Club seriously. The Constitution and By-Laws Committee clearly spent some time on its assignment during the two weeks between the initial meeting and the second organizational meeting on March 12. The committee had been advised to review the constitutions and bylaws of other clubs. While the bylaws of the Des Moines Sketch Club had not been helpful, the charters prepared by the Architectural League of New York in 1881 and the Boston Society of Architects in 1867[29] were more useful.

McLean reported in the April issue of the *Inland Architect* that "the organization which was inaugurated by the leading draughtsmen last month was perfected on the 12th ult. The Committee on Constitution and By-laws made its report, and after earnest discussion, section by section, it was adopted."[30] In the same issue, he published a complete copy of the bylaws and the constitution,[31] a concise statement of the club's purpose and the rules of organization, including seven articles that defined the members' qualifications, officers, the official name, and provisions for amendments. Perhaps the most significant section was Article III—Methods. It read as follows:

> The methods of this association shall be:
> By regular meetings of its members.
> By increasing the facilities for study.
> By readings or lectures on professional subjects.
> By the friendly discussion of practical matters.
> By competition in design and drawing for exhibition.
> By visiting selected buildings.
> And by any other means determined upon by the Association.

29. The Boston Society of Architects was formed in 1867. It was followed by the Architectural Association of Boston in 1883, from which the Boston Architectural Club, which still survives, evolved in 1889. There is an excellent, albeit brief, history of the Boston Architectural Club titled "BAC: The First Hundred Years," by Susan Lewis, in *Practice: A Publication by the Boston Architectural Center* (Fall/Winter 1999/2000): 14–15.

30. *Inland Architect* 5, no. 3 (April 1885): 37.

31. A copy of that document is included hereinafter, in Appendix I.

Other sections were equally succinct. Article IV—Membership read, "This Association shall consist of Senior, Junior and Honorary members." Article VI provided for qualifications of each class of membership. Senior members were to have had at least three years' experience in an architect's office or in kindred arts. Junior members were required to have had at least one year of similar experience. Honorary members were to be elected by the membership on the basis of demonstrated interest in the association. Junior members and honorary members had all the privileges of full membership except that of voting, and they were not eligible for office.

While no written record of how the Constitution and By-laws Committee approached its task has survived, a review of the early constitution and bylaws of the Architectural League of New York and the Boston Society of Architects reveals that the club drew heavily from both in assembling its charter. In several instances, the language was nearly verbatim. An examination of the constitution of the Architectural League of New York[32] reveals its methods were to be accomplished through "the reading of Essays, Lectures upon topics of general interest, Competitions in Architectural design, Exhibitions of members' work, Formation of a Library, Formation of a collection of drawings, photographs and casts, Establishment of a traveling scholarship, and any other means calculated to promote the object of the Association," all of which was echoed in the language of the Chicago charter. The Boston Society of Architects had a corresponding section in its constitution that was even closer to what the Chicagoans proposed.[33] Its Article III read, "The means of accomplishing this end may be: Regular meetings of the members for the discussion of subjects of general importance; the reading of essays; lectures upon topics of general interest; a school for the education of architects; exhibitions of architectural drawings; a library; a collection of designs and models; and any other means calculated to promote the objects of the Society."

The CASC's bylaws were somewhat lengthier than the constitution and essentially expanded on the major points of that document. Much of its language also recalled that of the New York and Boston groups, but it was not identical. The nine articles covered membership application procedures, elections, conduct of meetings, officers' duties, and committee functions. Certain articles, in particular, were key to the future success of the club, expanding on the "methods" outlined in the constitution. Article II of the bylaws concerning "Election of Members," for instance, was quite straightforward, but some of its items made the club unique among similar groups. Section 8 stated, "Each member shall be required to deliver a paper or submit at least two drawings during the year, which shall remain the property of the club." To this section was added, "NOTE—It is desired that, when possible, sketches shall conform to the uniform sizes, 8 x 12, or 14 x 17, and made with pen and ink, that they may be photo-engraved." Both the Boston Architectural Club and the Architectural League of New York had already established a record of publication of members' work, and the leaders of the Chicago club were obviously thinking about the ever-growing importance of getting their members' work in print. It was the only real way for draftsmen to improve their status in the stratified world of the architectural community in late-nineteenth-century Chicago. More than a dozen national and regional architectural journals were being published in the United States in 1885, and many more—all eager to fill their pages—were about to be launched. If ever there was a time to gain notoriety through architectural publications, 1885 was it.

In the late nineteenth century, well-illustrated architectural literature was just beginning to be readily available. While books on building and architecture had been

32. It was impossible to locate a complete copy of the original constitution of the Architectural League of New York. There is, however, a copy of the *Architectural League of New York, Officers, Constitution, Members,* dated 1888. It is likely that few, if any, changes in the constitution had been made between the time of the group's organization (1881) and the publication of that document.

33. The *Constitution and By-Laws of the Boston Society of Architects,* published in March 1887, probably includes the same language used by the Chicago Architectural Sketch Club in 1885.

published in the United States during the previous century, the illustrations were usually engravings and print runs generally weren't very large. The use of photographs of any kind was still in its infancy. There was, however, a burst of publication of serial journals devoted to architecture between 1855 and 1885, and they had become quite common, almost to the point of saturating the market, by the time the Chicago Architectural Sketch Club was formed.

There had been several abortive attempts at starting periodical journals of architecture after the mid-nineteenth century.[34] The *Crayon*, founded in 1855, was the first journal to publish the activities of the American Institute of Architects, but since it was devoted to all the visual arts, not just architecture, the AIA designated the *Architects' and Mechanics' Journal* as its official organ in 1859. Within two years, that relationship soured, and in 1861 the *Architects' and Mechanics' Journal* ceased publication, although in its brief life it had established a policy of printing plans, elevations, and perspectives of architects' work.

During the years following the Civil War several other journals were launched, but most of them were short-lived. The *Architectural Review and American Builder's Journal* began publishing in 1868, and the *American Builder and Journal of Art* was established in the same year; the former lasted only two and a half years, while the latter survived until 1895, when it merged with the *National Builder*. Both of these journals published a wide variety of plans, drawings, and details. Convincing architects to submit material, however, was a major problem for publishers. Most architects were extremely proprietary of their work and feared plagiarism. Nevertheless, the number and quality of journals publishing architects' work continued to increase, among them the *Manufacturer and Builder* (1869–97), the *Technologist* (1870–77), and the *American Architect and Builders Monthly* (1870–71). The latter, while it only lasted for a year, did publish elaborate illustrations.

About this time, shortly after the Chicago Fire, a major figure emerged in architectural publishing. James Ripley Osgood (1836–1892) had been working with publishers Tichnor & Fields since 1855, and in 1872, he acquired the rights to a photomechanical process called "heliotype." Invented in England, it used a sensitized gelatin "plate" to print paper photographs and line drawings at a reasonable cost. In 1873, Osgood established his own firm and began publishing his first journal, the *Architectural Sketchbook,* in cooperation with the Boston Portfolio Club, which was affiliated with the Boston Society of Architects. (Virtually all the material in the journal was supplied by members of the Boston Society of Architects.) Following the journal's apparent success, Osgood started the *New York Sketchbook* six months later, in January of 1874. Like its predecessor, it was issued monthly[35] and was probably modeled after European publications like the German *Architektonische Skizzenbuch,* the French *Croquis d'Architecture*, or the English *Architectural Association Sketchbook*.[36] The European journals, however, used much larger plate sizes than Osgood's publications, and focused on the work of established practitioners instead of younger men, unless they had won competitions.

The *New York Sketchbook* was an independent serial publication, not affiliated with any architectural organization, and it eventually became the more impressive of Osgood's sketchbooks. Both, however, were reasonably successful, which prompted Osgood to launch the *American Architect and Building News* in 1876. During its early years, most of its subscribers were on the East Coast, but it had a substantial number of readers in Chicago, including most of the practicing architects. Eventually it became a major national journal of architecture, and today it survives as the *Architectural Record*.[37]

*J. R. Osgood in 1892 (AA)*

34. M. N. Wood, "The 'American Architect and Building News' 1876–1907" (PhD diss., Columbia University, 1983), is the best source of data on American architectural journals of the nineteenth century.

35. Copies of both the *Architectural Sketchbook* and the *New York Sketchbook* are quite rare and seldom found complete; they were monthly serials, and today most of the few copies still extant are in bound volumes.

36. These European serial publications can be found in most large architectural library collections. They were certainly available to the founders of the Chicago Architectural Sketch Club.

37. The *American Architect and Building News* may be the longest continuously published architectural journal in the United States. It first appeared on January 1, 1876. Never a great financial success, it survived after thirty years through mergers with other journals: it merged with the *Inland Architect* in 1909, the *Architectural Review* in 1921, and *Architecture* in 1936. It retained its name through all these mergers. In 1938, however, it merged with the *Architectural Record*, the name that survives today.

Osgood's two *Sketchbooks* stopped publication at the end of 1876. They had served his purpose by demonstrating that there was a demand for an architectural journal with well-executed illustrations. Osgood anticipated that his new, more ambitious journal would satisfy a broad, receptive audience. What he didn't realize was that a national magazine did not necessarily address regional or local concerns, and during the decade after the *American Architect and Building News* began publishing, several regional journals were established, among them the *California Architect and Building Review* in San Francisco (1879), the *Western Architect and Builder* in St. Louis (1879), and the *Northwestern Architect* in Minneapolis (1884). Chicago alone saw the launch of three journals: the *Sanitary News,* the *Building Budget*, and the *Inland Architect and Builder.*

Osgood's *Sketchbooks* had shown that regional architects' work could find an audience, and sketch clubs throughout the country began to publish their members' work in a similar manner. It is therefore easy to understand the motivation of the founders of the Chicago Architectural Sketch Club when they specified in their charter that members must submit drawings that could be easily reproduced. They knew that publication of members' work would enhance the desirability of membership in the club and, more important, encourage members to do superior work.

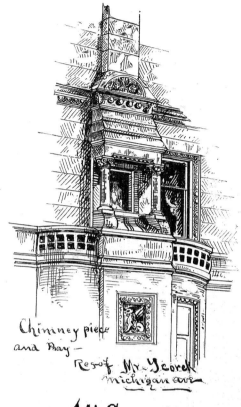

*J. H. Carpenter sketch (IA)*

Another critical element of the original charter was the provision for an Executive Committee to manage the affairs of the club. It included the club's five officers and two other members who would appoint committees and control the club's funds, as well as acting on membership applications and settling disputes among the members. The committee was also responsible for managing competitions and choosing judges, an important function during the first few years when competitions were held several times a year.

The constitution and bylaws put in place at the second organizational meeting on March 12, 1885, served the club well until June of 1889, when it incorporated. The most important revision made then was to admit practicing architects as associate members in order to encourage them to do more than attend meetings sporadically as guests. It was not until 1895, when the membership elected to admit architects as members, that it became necessary to make major revisions to the original charter. Still, the basic tenets remained intact.

Upon approval of the constitution and bylaws in March of 1885 at the club's second organizational meeting, temporary chairman Robert McLean called for nominations from the floor for officers. J. H. Carpenter was elected president, Irving K. Pond and Harry Lawrie, first and second vice presidents, and W. G. Williamson was chosen as secretary. By virtue of his position, Williamson was exempt from paying dues, "in consideration of the onerous duties of the Secretary."

The secretary's job was extremely important, since the club was meticulous about seeing that each meeting was reported in detail to the architectural journals published in Chicago and elsewhere. In addition to the *Inland Architect*, minutes of the club's meetings were sent to the *Building Budget* and the *Sanitary News,* both of which were published in Chicago and were strong supporters of the club in its early days. Later, the club's activities were regularly reported in the *American Architect and News Record* and regional publications such as the *Northwestern Architect* and *Architecture and Building.*[38]

Robert Craik McLean was elected treasurer and was responsible for collecting dues of twenty-five cents a month plus a three-dollar initiation fee. He served until a second slate of officers was elected on November 23, 1885.[39] Shortly after his

38. In the late nineteenth century, the *Brickbuilder* and the *Brochure Series* covered the club's activities. During the twentieth century, several other periodicals also reported on the club's affairs; all are cited hereinafter.

39. *Sanitary News* 7, no. 100 (January 2, 1886): 80.

# The Sanitary News.
## An Illustrated Weekly Journal.

*The* Inland Architect, *the* Building Budget, *and the* Sanitary News *were all critical to the success of the Chicago Architectural Sketch Club, as they published news of club activities in almost every issue during the first decade of the club's existence (WRH)*

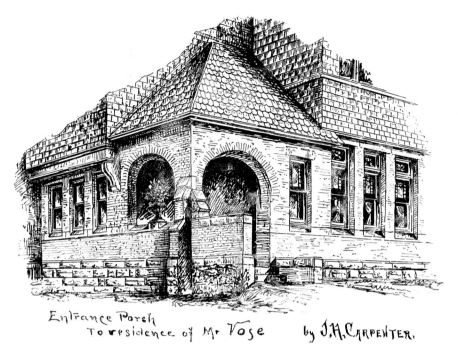

Entrance Porch
To residence of Mr Vose    by J.H.CARPENTER.

*Sketch by J. H. Carpenter (IA)*

tour of office was up, he was elected an honorary member and remained so until his death. Charter members Edward Dewson and George Beaumont were asked to serve on the seven-man Executive Committee during that first, abbreviated year of the club's existence. The Committee on Rooms, appointed at the initial meeting in McLean's office, "reported that there was a possibility of the [Illinois] Architects' Association combining with them in renting quarters, and that it would be wise, in their opinion, to wait until permanent action could be taken with this in view."[40] The sketch club chose to go its own way. It had received a communication "from the directors of the Builders and Traders' Exchange, offering the club the use of their committee room, for holding meetings until the club had secured permanent quarters, which was accepted with thanks."[41] The founders' decision to accept that offer was probably prudent, as it separated them from their senior colleagues in the Illinois Architects' Association and gave them freedom to control their own destiny.

At the end of the second organizational meeting, it was reported that the charter members had "decided to make the first [regular] meeting [of the club] one of general interest and as informal as possible, and members were directed to invite as large a number of draughtsmen as possible, that they might hear the Constitution and By-Laws read, and apply for membership, after which the meeting adjourned." Thus began a journey that was to last more than half a century.

40. *Inland Architect* 5, no. 3 (April 1885): 38.

41. The Builders and Traders' Exchange was organized in January of 1884. It was a professional society for contractors, builders, tradesmen, and craftsmen from all parts of the construction industry. Architects were not admitted to membership but could have the "privileges of the floor" upon application, and several other trade associations used the group's facilities for their meetings. It published an annual handbook, which included a list of members and other information of use to people in the building trades. The organization survived well into the twentieth century.

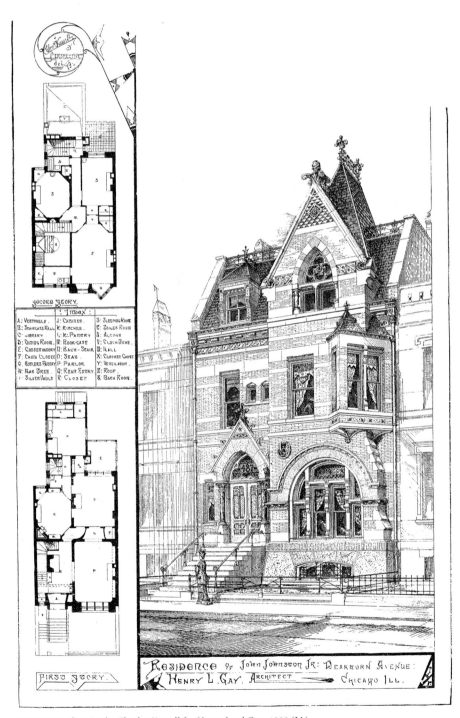

*Presentation drawing by Charles Kessell for Henry Lord Gay, 1883 (IA)*

# Organization and Establishment

CHAPTER TWO

The first regular meeting of the Chicago Architectural Sketch Club was held at the Builders and Traders' Exchange in the National Life Insurance Building[1] in Chicago's business district on a Monday evening, March 27, 1885. The club's eighteen founders had spread the word among their colleagues, and some fifty draftsmen showed up to hear what the club had to offer. President J. H. Carpenter, who delivered the opening address, outlined the proposed course of action discussed at the two organizational meetings: the prime objective of the club would be to educate potential architects, and the methods were to be those outlined in the constitution and bylaws ("by lectures and papers on professional subjects, by friendly discussion of matters of interest which lie nearest the desires of the members, by the contribution of sketches, by competition on special subjects, and by exhibitions of works completed. Visits to buildings in course of construction will be made in bodies.").[2] Carpenter also announced the motto of the club: "Design in beauty and build in truth."

It was noted that some of those present were "members of Le Ecole Des Beaux Arts of Paris and the academies of arts in London and Berlin, and it is expected that some of the features of these bodies will be introduced." Harry Lawrie and George Beaumont related their experiences with similar organizations in Scotland and England. It was suggested that some of the features of the European groups be incorporated in the Chicago Architectural Sketch Club, and there was also discussion of plans for future activities.

It was agreed that regular meetings would be held on alternate Monday evenings beginning three weeks later, on April 13, 1885.[3] The fifty or so draftsmen who attended that first regular meeting were apparently impressed, since a number of them applied for membership.[4] As a general rule, the meetings were alternately educational and recreational. The subject for discussion and illustration at the following meeting was announced as "Entrances."

Two events occurred at the meeting on April 13 that were to help establish the protocol of the sketch club for the next decade. First, architect Henry Lord Gay, owner of the Permanent Exhibit and Exchange and editor of the *Building Budget,* had sent a note that club president Carpenter read aloud. In it, Gay stated that he was fitting up an assembly room for the Illinois Architects' Association, where he desired to build a mantel. He offered prizes for designs to be submitted in compe-

*Henry Lord Gay (MofI)*

1. Originally called the Major Block, this building was one of the few to survive the Chicago Fire of 1871, although it needed significant repairs. Before it was demolished in 1914, it stood on the southeast corner of Madison and La Salle streets, at what was then 161 La Salle Street; today its address would be 1–17 South La Salle Street. (Chicago street addresses were changed in 1909.)

2. *Sanitary News* 5, no. 61 (April 4, 1885): 136. Essentially the same information was reported in the *Inland Architect* and the *Building Budget.*

3. The *Inland Architect,* the *Sanitary News,* and the *Building Budget* began a policy of announcing that the club met "every alternate Monday, temporary quarters, Builders and Traders [sic] Exchange."

4. According to *Inland Architect* 5, no. 3 (April 1885): 38, forty applications were received, while the *Sanitary News* reported that twenty-six men tendered applications. Apparently, twenty-six applications were received from a total of forty guests. It can probably be assumed that the new applicants were accepted subject to the payment of dues. No list of attendees at this meeting has survived.

*Before moving into its own quarters in January of 1888, the Chicago Architectural Sketch Club met in the Builders and Traders' Exchange in the National Life Insurance Building, on the southeast corner of La Salle and West Madison streets; originally called the "Major Block," it was nearly destroyed in the fire of 1871 (LO)*

tition by members of the club: first prize, a year's subscription to any English architectural publication; second prize, a year's subscription to any American periodical costing four dollars; and third prize, a year's subscription to the *Building Budget*. The mantel was to be of brick, any style, with an opening of five feet. The designs, signed with noms de plume, were due April 23. Thus, the first of many competitions was inaugurated.

The second event was the attendance of a distinguished visiting speaker, W. H. Junge, the first in a long list of important members of the construction and architectural communities who would speak before the club. Junge was the Chicago representative of the Boston Terra Cotta Company, which had its offices at 15 East Washington Street in one of the spaces provided by Gay's Permanent Exhibit and Exchange. Junge's company had just published an elaborate 130-page catalog, which he made available to club members,[5] and his lecture covered the manufacture and use of terra-cotta. An extensive question, answer, and discussion period followed, and the next month a full transcript of his presentation was published in the *Inland Architect* with a synopsis of the discussion.[6] Thus, a precedent was established whereby the club would sponsor knowledgeable professionals and their remarks would later be published.

Because Junge's presentation had prevented the scheduled discussion of entrances, it was agreed that members would prepare and submit drawings of entrances for the next meeting. The club had not yet established a syllabus for the year, but plans were under way for additional speakers, competitions, and club nights, where members would address issues of common interest. The remainder of the second regular meeting was devoted to a discussion of the duties of members. Officers' and directors' responsibilities were quite clear, but individual members were admonished to be prepared to perform short-term committee tasks, participate in in-house competitions, and occasionally give brief presentations of various kinds. Serious participation was expected, but humor and entertainment

5. Catalogs of this nature were an important tool used by manufacturers to promote their products. They were usually distributed annually, and unfortunately, as recipients often discarded older editions, they are extremely rare today.

6. *Inland Architect* 5, no. 4 (May 1885): 64–65.

were also encouraged. A review of the club's minutes indicates that the rank and file were very much involved. Within a few weeks, regular meetings were formalized to the point that members knew exactly what to expect.

At the next meeting on April 27, the names of twelve new members were announced, and President Carpenter stated that "the competition to be worked out during the coming month would be the design for a hall mantel." The similarity of the club's first competition to the one offered by Henry Lord Gay can probably be explained by the fact that the submission deadline for Gay's competition was too soon to allow for the degree of participation many members would have liked. In any case, Carpenter advised the membership that the club's own mantel competition would proceed and that entries would be due on May 24. He also noted that the Executive Committee had been working with Gay to refine the rules of his competition and that the deadline for submission of designs had been extended to May 18. It was agreed that the subscriptions to architectural journals that Gay had offered as prizes would be used to form the nucleus of a club library. Prizes were rarely awarded in the club's own competitions. The members themselves usually reviewed and discussed the submissions and voted to determine winners, and all competition drawings remained the property of the club.

Several members had submitted sketches of entrances, which were examined and discussed at some length. President Carpenter and George Beaumont both gave

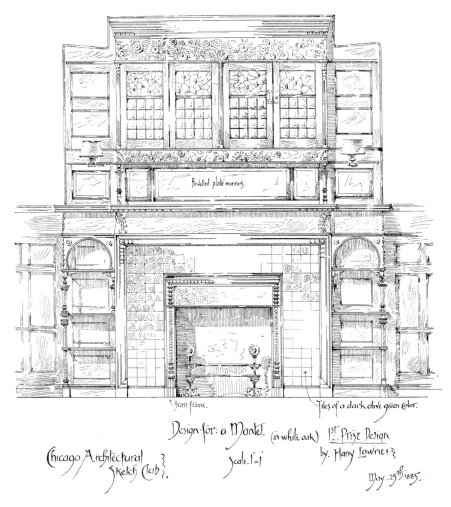

*Drawing published by the* Inland Architect *(IA)*

brief but thoughtful speeches on what an entrance should be and its importance to the overall design of the building it served. Beaumont concluded his remarks with the assertion that "architectural draughtsmen were far in advance of the position occupied by them in years past,"[7] perhaps recalling a lack of training in his own youth.

At the end of the evening, the entrance designs were put to a vote, and the one by W. G. Williamson was deemed the best. A humorous design by Carpenter titled "An Entrance in German Renaissance" received second place. (Carpenter was a gregarious person and an excellent caricaturist who often brought a bit of levity to the proceedings.) Before adjourning for the evening, Carpenter advised the membership that the next meeting would feature a discussion of the use of stained glass. Edward Dewson, one of the founders of the club, was the featured speaker.[8]

In the May issue of the *Inland Architect*, Robert McLean noted that Dewson's "interesting paper" would be printed in the next issue. The *Sanitary News* made the same promise. It never appeared, however, possibly because of copyright restrictions, as it was a revision of an article Dewson had published in another journal two years earlier.[9] McLean closed his May news item with a brief promotional note for the CASC. He wrote that "it should be understood by [prospective] members that the sketch club is thoroughly cosmopolitan and its membership is open to anyone who can fill the requirements of the constitution and by-laws, and that each drawing presented in competitions must be under a nom de plume." Competitions were to become an important aspect of the club's activities during the next decade, and the nom de plume served two purposes: it hid the names of competitors from the jurors and it allowed those whose proficiency with pen or pencil left much to be desired to avoid embarrassment.

✳

As the club's membership grew, Henry Lord Gay continued to take an interest, promoting it to the larger architectural community. In June 1885, he published an item in the *Building Budget* titled "An Invitation," in which he praised an exhibition

7. *Sanitary News* 6, no. 65 (May 2, 1885): 6.

8. Edward Dewson (ca. 1848–1915) was an excellent draftsman whose work appeared in various journals between 1880 and 1895, illustrating the designs of a number of architects. He practiced in Boston from 1877 to 1882, when he left for Chicago, where he remained until 1887. He then returned to Boston, where he lived until 1891, after which he was listed as an architect in New York City. His drawings and advertisements appeared regularly in the *Decorator and Furnisher*, a New York journal, starting in 1888, usually under the name Boston Designing and Draughting Company, or a variation thereof. In 1896 he was named editor of that journal.

9. Edward Dewson, "America's Stained Glass," *Catalog of the Art Department* (1883). The article was illustrated with a title drawing incorporating an initial letter, as well as a tailpiece, both apparently illustrating stained-glass designs and signed by Dewson.

*One of the first published images of the club's work, this drawing was done on April 1, 1885 (IA)*

The Permanent Exhibit and Exchange at the northwest corner of Wabash and Washington in downtown Chicago (BBU)

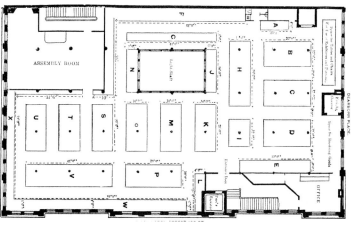

Floor plan of the Permanent Exhibit and Exchange, 1885 (BBU)

held in conjunction with the inaugural meeting of the Western Society of Architects in November 1884, suggesting that a similar one should be held in the fall of 1885 and that members of the sketch club should participate.[10] Gay offered to make all the arrangements, provide space at the Permanent Exhibit and Exchange, and assume all the expenses, except for the cartage of exhibition materials. He also stated that he was considering "providing some valuable prizes for the members of the Architectural Sketch Club, and will next month announce the theme and state the prizes . . . [and] it is desired that all architects and members of architectural sketch clubs, in this and other cities, will personally respond to this invitation at an early day."[11]

Immediately following that article, Gay reported that the Competition for a Mantel he had proposed in April had been adjudicated.[12] Five entries had been received, and the jury consisted of the Executive Committee of the Illinois State Association of Architects, along with Louis Sullivan, Samuel Treat, Charles Palmer, and William Holabird. It was the first of several groups of distinguished architects who were to evaluate the club's competitions. First, second, and third prizes were awarded to "Hurry" (W. G. Williamson), "Gas-Lite" (whose identity was not made

10. *Inland Architect* 4, no. 2 (September 1884): 1. There had been an exhibition of architectural drawings at the Permanent Exhibit and Exchange during the organizational convention of the Western Association of Architects. Gay had "issued a circular offering to furnish . . . space . . . advertise the exhibit, and throw it open free to the public." The exhibit opened a week before the convention and remained in place for two weeks.

11. *Building Budget* 1, no. 4 (June 1985): 33. There is no record that such an exhibition ever took place. There was, however, a similar exhibition at the second convention of the Western Association of Architects held in St. Louis in November of 1885, to which the CASC contributed drawings.

12. Ibid., 33–34.

Edward Dewson drew this tailpiece illustration to complement his article "America's Stained Glass" (NEMMI)

*Sketch of the interior of the Permanent Exhibit and Exchange by Edward Dewson (BBU)*

known), and "Circle and Triumph" (Eugene L. Caukin). The jury members discussed the merits of the entries that were not awarded prizes, and for the most part they were complimentary. They did express concern that one person had uncharitably stated "that it was asking a great deal for the small amount offered." The jury responded, "We regret that such a feeling and spirit should exist at all, and we feel assured that it does not exist in the minds of any enthusiastic student of architecture, and we should all be enthusiastic—or nothing." They also noted that they had heard from several members who regretted not being able to participate due to time constraints. The jury was effusive in its praise of the club and closed its remarks by stating, "We will not be slow to offer any aid to the club that is within our power to give, and we are happy to record the decision of the Committee of the Sketch Club, who have accepted our offer to use the assembly room for the meetings of their Society." This last statement was apparently a misunderstanding on the part of both the Illinois Association of Architects and Henry Lord Gay, since there is no record of such an acceptance and the fiercely independent club continued to meet at the Builders and Traders' Exchange for the remainder of 1885. The location had a good deal to offer: there was no rent, it was centrally located, and it was large enough to accommodate upward of a hundred people. Furthermore, between meetings club members were granted use of the rooms, which had a substantial library of books on architecture and building,[13] as well as most of the current journals of architecture.

The club's in-house mantel competition was reviewed by the membership at the regular meeting on May 25, one of the few early meetings that was not reported in any detail in the architectural press. It was noted that the first meeting in June would focus on a competition for a "gate lodge." That meeting, held on June 8, was another that was not reported in the local journals. On June 22, however, the entries for the "gate lodge" were the feature of the evening. A large number of entries were exhibited, and the membership voted to award first place to I. K. Pond, sec-

13. The Builders and Traders' Exchange's annual handbook included a list of books in its library. In 1887, it listed 233 titles, many of which were multivolumes.

ond to W. G. Williamson, and third to R. B. Williamson. As usual, there were no prizes per se, but interest was obviously high. The secretary reported that "quite a number of sketches were on exhibition giving evidence of great interest in the club by its members."[14]

The idea of architectural competitions had begun to catch on throughout the Midwest, and at the same meeting it was announced that a communication had been received from the Anderson Pressed Brick Company, offering the club prizes totaling twenty-five dollars for the best four sketches of a window and doorway featuring its product: first prize would receive ten dollars (about a week's pay for a junior draftsman); second prize would receive seven dollars; third would receive five; and fourth, three. The offer was accepted by the club, and all agreed that the prize money would be added to the treasury.

Mantel design competitions were popular, especially among suppliers of materials used in their construction. In early August, as part of a long article on the forthcoming convention of the Western Association of Architects, the *Sanitary News* reported that the Pickel Marble and Granite Company of St. Louis was offering several prizes for the design of a wood mantel. (Why it was wood instead of marble or granite remains a mystery.) In the same article, it was noted that the St. Louis Hydraulic Pressed Brick Company was inviting designs for mantels made out of plain and/or molded brick from the firm's most recent catalog. While the two companies soliciting the designs were not related, they had apparently combined efforts to encourage competitive designs; the rules for submission were identical and all designs were to be sent to St. Louis, labeled "Convention of Western Association of Architects at St. Louis, Nov. 11, 1885." The designs were to carry a nom de plume and were required to include a statement that they were original and had not been used or previously published.[15] The article carried the byline of C. E. Illsley, president of the WAA, who also served as associate editor of the *Inland Architect.* Illsley had seen to it that both competitions were published in the *Inland Architect* as well, along with the rules. They were clearly being offered to generate interest in the coming WAA convention, while promoting the sponsors. These two competitions, along with the one sponsored by the Anderson Pressed Brick Com-

14. *Sanitary News* 6, no. 72 (June 27, 1885): 75.

15. *Sanitary News* 6, no. 79 (August 8, 1885): 124.

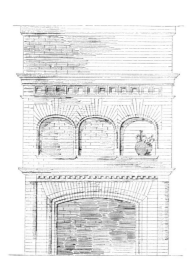  

*First-, second-, and third-prize drawings in mantel competition sponsored by Henry Lord Gay*

*Irving K. Pond's competition drawing for a gate lodge, the only known surviving work of the club's activity from this period, is in the Pond archive at the Bentley Library of the University of Michigan (IA)*

pany and the club's own competition for a gate lodge, presented CASC members with a variety of problems to solve during the summer of 1885.

On July 6, the club formally accepted the journal subscriptions that had been offered by Henry Lord Gay for his mantel competition a few weeks earlier. The focus of the evening, however, was "a talk on perspective drawing by Irving K. Pond."[16] Pond described in great detail the various techniques used in sketching architectural subjects. He covered topics such as perspective, line work, and shading in a very professional manner, supplementing his prepared text with illustrations on a blackboard and inviting comments and questions. Many of the younger members found the lecture especially valuable in view of the competitions then under way, all of which required perspective drawings. While several of the founders were superb draftsmen, a number of the new, younger members had little, if any, training in architectural presentation.

Pond was an excellent choice to discuss the subject. At the time, he was twenty-eight years old, and his sketching technique was loose, expressive, and easily recognizable. His lecture and demonstration of sketching was reported in depth by the *Inland Architect* and in a brief note in the *Sanitary News*. In keeping with

16. Irving K. Pond (1857–1939), a club founder, was born in Michigan and educated at the University of Michigan, where he received a civil engineering degree in 1879. He came to Chicago and, after a year in the office of W. L. B. Jenney, joined S. S. Beman for three years. He then took a two-year tour of Europe and, upon his return in 1885, established his own office, where he was joined by his younger brother, Allen, in 1886. I. K. Pond maintained a lifelong interest in the Chicago Architectural Sketch Club and was elected an honorary member in 1909.

the club's philosophy of mixing business with pleasure, President Carpenter responded to Pond's lecture with a short speech on caricature, which was followed by remarks from Beaumont, Williamson, and others. The most important comments, however, came from Robert Craik McLean.

McLean, who was always on the lookout for material he could use in the pages of the *Inland Architect*, took advantage of Pond's lecture to outline the requirements for drawings intended for publication, stressing the need for absolutely black ink, white paper, and proper scale. During the next few months, drawings by members of the club were featured in almost every issue of the *Inland Architect*. They were often competition drawings or work from the offices where the members toiled during the day. Sometimes other drawings appeared as well—vignettes of initial letters at the beginnings of articles or small sketches within the text added to enhance the journal's appearance. In his long article on Pond's sketching techniques, McLean closed with one of his classic statements about the CASC: "The meeting was attended by the more enthusiastic members, and the interest taken in the discussion was indicated by the lateness of the hour when the meeting adjourned."[17] The Chicago Architectural Sketch Club had become an important part of the lives of its members, and McLean had every intention of keeping it that way.

During the next several weeks, the club continued its regular fortnightly meetings. Many subjects were addressed, but education and professionalism were always the major concerns of the club's senior members. In August, President Carpenter made some very pointed remarks to the assembled members regarding the "proneness of draughtsmen generally to regard their work as 'simply a day's work, and the sooner done the better'; not looking upon their work with any degree of professional pride."

Two weeks later the speaker of the evening presented a paper on "the professional standing of draughtsmen." The subject was received with enthusiasm, and a spirited discussion followed. At that same meeting, there was considerable concern expressed about the need for planning the coming year's activities. It was

17. *Inland Architect* 6, no. 1 (July 1885): 91–92.

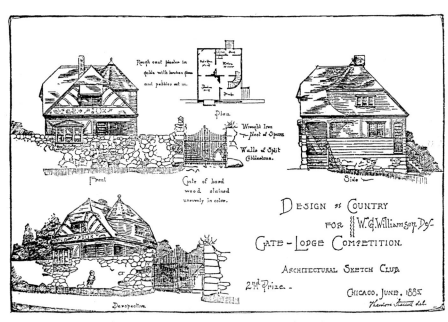

*The second prize for the Gate Lodge Competition went to W. G. Williamson, although there are two names on this drawing; apparently Williamson had some help (IA)*

*The six buildings illustrated above, left to right—Burnham & Root's Montauk Building (1882), John J. Flanders's Mallers Building (1884), S. S. Beman's Pullman Building (1884), W. W. Boyington's Royal Insurance Building (1884), Cobb & Frost's Chicago Opera House Block (1885), and William Le Baron Jenney's Union League Club (1885)—were all either recently completed or under construction when the Chicago Architectural Sketch Club was formed (ATA)*

agreed that the Executive Committee should begin "at once laying out lines of studies for the coming winter . . . and it was suggested that the club form a sketching class and engage an instructor."[18] McLean began his reporting in the September *Inland Architect* by announcing, "The meetings of this club are becoming more and more interesting, and it is to be hoped that the draughtsmen who have heretofore stayed away with the fear that the club would not be a success, will now lose no time in making application for membership. There are many benefits to be derived, and a hearty welcome will be extended to those who have not yet become interested."

As the summer of 1885 drew to a close, the *Sanitary News* reported that "the pleasant weather and a slight 'let up' in the studios resulted in an unusually large attendance [at the club meeting on September 14]."[19] Members of the club had been heavily committed to the work being done in the Chicago's various architectural offices, and club affairs had suffered during the summer months, but at the September 14 meeting it appeared that club work was about to start up again. The Anderson Pressed Brick Company had offered yet another competition, this time for the best sketch of a gable-end of a building.

At the same early fall meeting, President Carpenter advised the membership that the club had been offered the use of a room at the Art Institute of Chicago for its meetings. The only stipulation was that the club would pay for the use of any gas and janitorial services. Furthermore, club members were offered the opportunity to take classes at the institute at a reduced rate. (Eighteen dollars was the normal yearly fee, but CASC members would be able to attend for only eight dollars.) The members considered the offer, but at a special meeting a week later they decided to remain at the Builders and Traders' Exchange and declined the offer with thanks. There is no record of why that decision was made, but the members' desire

18. *Inland Architect* 6, no. 2 (September 1885): 30.

19. *Sanitary News* 6, no. 85 (September 1885): 173.

for independence was undoubtedly a major part of the reason. If they couldn't accept potential domination by the Illinois Association of Architects, the possibility of being overwhelmed by the Art Institute of Chicago would have seemed even more daunting. Furthermore, an extension to the Art Institute—a new structure designed by Burnham & Root—was being built at the time and the new space would not have been ready for more than a year.

While the members of the Chicago Architectural Sketch Club were defining their organization and its goals in the fall of 1885, the new structure at the Art Institute was just one of the many new buildings under construction in Chicago's business district. The period from 1881 to 1900 has been referred to as the golden age of building in Chicago.[20] Just before and during the organization of the Chicago Architectural Sketch Club, several seminal buildings of the early modern movement were designed and built: the Montauk (Burnham & Root, 1882), the Home Insurance (William Le Baron Jenney, 1885), the Pullman (S. S. Beman, 1884), the Calumet (Burnham & Root, 1884), the Chicago Opera House (Cobb & Frost, 1885), the Mallers (John J. Flanders, 1884), and a number of others were either under construction or in the planning stages. It is difficult to establish exactly how much each club member was involved in any specific building, but it is certain that they were involved. Thus, the drafting tables of their day jobs were as much a learning experience as their evenings at the club, although not always as pleasant. The hard work in the offices was also felt by the architects, and all were welcome to enjoy a respite in the rooms of the club.

During the next decade and beyond, virtually every major architect in the city participated in the affairs of the CASC. The men who would become the icons of the Chicago School of architecture were pleased to participate and club members wanted their counsel. The Chicago Architectural Sketch Club provided

20. Frank A. Randall, *History of the Development of Building Construction in Chicago* (Urbana, Illinois: University of Illinois Press, 1949), 93. This work is absolutely indispensable to any serious study of the Chicago School of architecture.

Design for a Brick Mantel
by Harry Lawrie.

*Perspective Sketch.*

*Brick mantel by Harry Lawrie (IA)*

a forum and an eager, intelligent audience for John Root, Louis Sullivan, Daniel Burnham, W. L. B. Jenney, and others with similar talents. Fortunately, much of what they had to say was recorded and published by Robert Craik McLean and his competitors. These architects, later revered by historians, would almost certainly have appeared before the CASC at the request of their employees who were active in the club. Many major figures in Chicago architecture used the club as a platform to present some of their most important critical and theoretical thoughts.

In October, the club entertained a Mr. Fehleisen of the Des Moines Sketch Club, who "offered some interesting remarks relative to the club in his city."[21] The Des Moines group included a broad spectrum of those working in the arts, but architects were only a peripheral part of the organization. Chicago club members were courteously unimpressed, as their interest was in what was happening in Chicago. On the same evening, members who were planning to enter the two mantel competitions were warned that their submissions were expected to be in the club secretary's hands by November 3, so they could be sent en masse to the WAA convention in St. Louis, where they were to be exhibited. (Later, in December, there was considerable concern when, without explanation, the drawings were not permitted to be shown at the convention. The prizes were, however, still awarded.) The evening also featured a talk by President Carpenter on the construction of theaters. While Carpenter didn't claim to be an architect, his experience as a draftsman on projects of this nature certainly qualified him to speak. Following his presentation, some time was spent in sketching, the subject being the design of a chimney. These sketches, done at a small scale and using the techniques and materials recommended by McLean, were published in the *Inland Architect,* the *Building Budget,* and the *Sanitary News.*

Election of officers for 1886 was postponed until November 23, 1885, due to a small turnout two weeks earlier. Nevertheless, both President Carpenter and Harry Lawrie spoke at some length to the members who did attend. Carpenter "reviewed the history of the club and spoke of its remarkable success, and of its brilliant future." Lawrie then "spoke for some time on 'Mouldings in their Different Phases' . . . He illustrated his remarks on the blackboard."[22] The meeting and election two weeks later was reported to have been "one of the most interesting and enjoyable that has been held for some time."[23] It was not recorded as an "annual meeting," but it served the same purpose. (The first Annual Meeting, Banquet, and Exhibition would come in 1886.) Harry Lawrie[24] was elected president for 1886, and George Beaumont and former president J. H. Carpenter were elected vice presidents. W. G. Williamson became secretary, and C. A. Kessell took over from Robert McLean as treasurer. Those officers, together with I. K. Pond, M. H. Church, and McLean, constituted the Executive Committee. All were founders of the club who maintained tight control over the group and would continue to do so for some time. The *Building Budget* reported that the membership now numbered forty-four.[25]

Following the election and some brief remarks by the new president and officers, the results of the mantel competition sponsored by the St. Louis Hydraulic Pressed Brick Company were announced. Most of the prizes went to Chicagoans, led by Harry Lawrie who was awarded the first prize of thirty dollars. Other prizes went to draftsmen from Kansas City, Des Moines, and St. Louis.

*Thumbnail sketch by Harry Lawrie (IA)*

21. *Sanitary News* 6, no. 91 (October 1885): 220.

22. *Sanitary News* 7, no. 93 (November 14, 1885): 14.

23. The November 23 meeting and election was reported in *Sanitary News* 7, no. 96 (December 5, 1885): 43, the *Building Budget,* and the *Inland Architect.*

24. Harry Lawrie (1858–1935) was born and educated in Glasgow, Scotland. He had nine years of experience working in Glasgow and Edinburgh before coming to Chicago in 1883. He worked with Burnham & Root until 1886, when he joined W. W. Clay. In early 1887 he moved to Omaha, Nebraska, where he became a partner in Mendelssohn and Lawrie, later Mendelssohn, Fisher & Lawrie. He remained in Nebraska until his death around 1935.

25. *Building Budget* 1, no. 9 (November 1885): 83. The December *Inland Architect* reported forty-three members. McLean probably did not consider himself a real member since he was not a draftsman. The *Sanitary News* reported forty-one members in its December 12 issue.

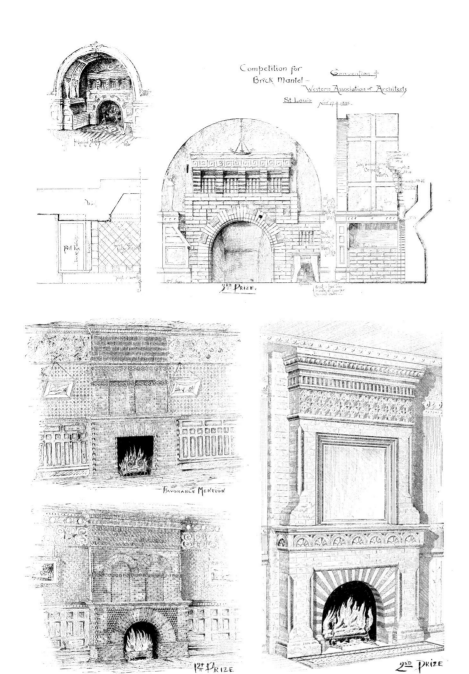

Competition for
Brick Mantel.

Convention of
Western Association of Architects
St Louis Nov 17 1885

2ND PRIZE.

FAVORABLE MENTION

1ST PRIZE

2ND PRIZE

Mantel competition drawing for St. Louis exhibition (IA)

Sketches -
- in Chicago.
By Schaefer

Drawing by sketch club member (IA)

By the end of 1885, the club had met twenty times (including the two organizational meetings and the special meeting to consider the Art Institute's offer of space). The club's success was recognized by the *Building Budget* in a short unsigned statement, probably by editor Henry Lord Gay: "The result of some of the work done by this club indicates that . . . no small power of originality and artistic skill is possessed by some of its members. The development of the society is an encouraging indication that the draftsmen are seeking improvement, not only by a skillful handling of the pencil, but by interchange of thought and social contact.

Harry Lawrie (MofN)

The architects should not delay in giving some substantial expression of their encouragement and good wishes for the welfare of this club."[26]

These sentiments were echoed in an editorial by Robert Craik McLean: "Draughtsmen's Associations are fast becoming a recognized and important element in the architectural economy of the West. Stimulated by . . . Des Moines, Chicago, . . . and an association . . . [recently] started at Milwaukee . . . The aims of each are similar, the sociability of comradeship and the better and more thorough advance in the technique of the architectural profession, both as regards general design and that calling for a more distinctive artistic talent in the designing of furniture, stained glass, etc., all of which comes within the legitimate province of the sketch clubs. The State Association of Illinois, at a recent meeting, took steps toward the formal recognition of that at Chicago, and this example should be followed by all state associations, and architects, as individuals, should do all in their power to encourage their growth. Until proper schools are established throughout the country for the teaching of architecture, a day we hope not far distant, upon the draughtsmen's clubs will rest the important work of education in a large degree."[27]

Draftsmen's clubs were beginning to proliferate throughout the Midwest, and many took the Chicago club as a model. For example, on November 14, 1885, the Milwaukee Architectural Club had been organized with Alfred Claus as president and Charles Barkhausen as secretary (both pro tem). Two committees had been immediately appointed to look into general arrangements and bylaws, and Dwight E. Green had been asked to communicate with the *Inland Architect* for information about the Chicago Architectural Sketch Club. Two weeks later, Claus and Barkhausen had visited Chicago "in the interests of the club."[28] By March, the club had secured rooms in the Follensbee Block in Milwaukee.

The first meeting of the next Chicago Architectural Sketch Club year was held on December 7, 1885, with president Harry Lawrie in the chair.[29] The most important event of the evening was the report of the Executive Committee regarding "a programme for the year, which included papers to be read upon six practical subjects, six papers on art subjects, and eight competitions." The *Inland Architect* reported that the syllabus was incomplete and would be ready shortly. The *Sanitary News*, however, reported five days later that the "programme for the coming year's work" was as follows:[30]

PRACTICAL ESSAYS.
1. Foundations, by Harry Lawrie
2. Brick Work, by George Beaumont
3. Stone Work, by Mr. Church
4. Terra Cotta
5. Iron Work, by C. W. Trowbridge
6. Hard Wood Finish

ART ESSAYS.
1. Polychromatic Architecture, by I. K. Pond
2. Greek and Roman Architecture, by C. A. Kessell
3. Architecture of the Middle Ages, by M. G. Holmes
4. Interior Decoration
5. Applied Ornament, by W. G. Williamson

26. *Building Budget* 1, no. 9 (November 1885): 83.

27. *Inland Architect* 6, no. 6 (December 1885): 95. This was the lead editorial and, while unsigned, it was certainly by McLean.

28. *Inland Architect* 6, no. 6 (December 1885): 103–4.

29. Ibid.

30. *Sanitary News* 7, no. 97 (December 12, 1885): 51.

SUBJECTS FOR COMPETITIONS.

1. Entrance Gate
2. Clock Tower
3. Drinking Fountain
4. Tombstone
5. Eight-room Dwelling
6. Library to contain fifty thousand volumes with Reading Room, etc.
7. Country Shop-Front
8. Village Chapel to seat two hundred and fifty persons

The club planned twenty-six meetings for 1886, one every two weeks. Its mission as an educational vehicle was now established, with the founders still in charge. (Of the scheduled speakers, only C. W. Trowbridge and M. G. Holmes were not founding members.) The draftsmen were teaching themselves, as the founders had envisioned; regular presentations by distinguished guests would come later.

During the 1886 year, virtually all the scheduled items were addressed. Lawrie's paper on foundations was delivered on December 21, 1885, and published in the January 1886 issue of the *Inland Architect*. The second scheduled paper, George Beaumont's on brickwork, was delivered later than expected, on April 12, 1886, and published in the May issue. The only major deviation from the syllabus was the scheduled lecture on stonework by Myron Church. He actually presented a paper titled "A Course of Study for Jr. Members" on January 18, 1886, which was published in the February issue of the *Inland Architect*. Church had researched the curricula of various institutions, and his paper was enthusiastically received, generating considerable conversation about the training of architects at universities. He spent a good deal of time discussing the two-year program at MIT, even though the three schools he had researched—MIT, Cornell, and Illinois—all offered four-year

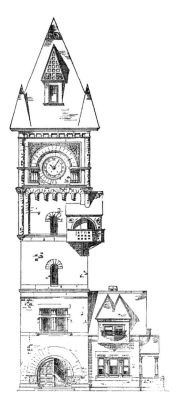

*Clock Tower Competition drawings (IA)*

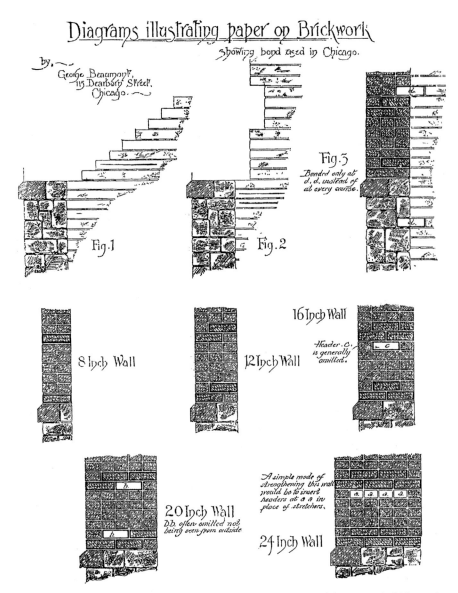

George Beaumont illustrated his lecture on brickwork with stereopticon slides, some of which are shown here (IA)

programs. He noted that while he was acting in concert with the bylaws of the club in addressing the junior members, his remarks would also benefit the younger senior members.

Church was not alone in his concerns regarding education. It was an issue that was regularly discussed within the club and other similar groups. The problem was not only the cost and difficulty of finding a way to stop working and go to school for several years, but the dearth of institutions offering study in architecture. Groups like the Chicago Architectural Sketch Club did their best to fill the gap, and interest in education during this period was the primary concern of the club's officers. They were highly successful in getting important architects, builders, and businessmen from Chicago to speak to the membership. Between 1885 and 1889, nearly a hundred major addresses were delivered at the club. Speakers included John Root, Dankmar Adler, D. H. Perkins, Louis Sullivan, and George Maher. It was not only the great or near-great figures who spoke. Few remember A. W. Hampe, W.

E. Kleinpell, or J. G. McCarthy, but they all lectured as well. William Le Baron Jenney was followed by his partner of later years, William Mundie, and Paul Mueller, then with Adler & Sullivan, spoke several times. Their remarks were usually published in one of the various journals of architecture. In many cases, these presentations are the only evidence we have of the philosophy of the major architects of the period. Their subjects ranged from the practical to the theoretical. Critical comments on recent architecture were made regularly and the history of architecture was often the subject of lectures. Sometimes the members themselves addressed their colleagues, usually on practical subjects such as the use of masonry design, terra-cotta, iron and steel, and interior decoration. Experienced draftsmen were often more knowledgeable in these fields than their employers.

Nevertheless, there remained a dire need for formally trained architects at the end of the nineteenth century, and only MIT, Cornell, Columbia, Syracuse, and Illinois offered architecture programs. Fewer than a hundred degrees were granted in the United States in the spring of 1886, producing but a fraction of the number of trained people needed in architectural offices throughout the country. The situation would change only marginally during the next decade, despite the best efforts of groups like the Chicago Architectural Club.

The University of Illinois, then called Illinois Industrial University, was the only nearby school that trained architects. Planning for its architectural program had begun in 1868 at the Champaign campus, and the first class was enrolled in the fall of 1870. Nathan Ricker, a member of that class, became its first graduate in architecture in 1873, and consequently the first person granted a degree in architecture in the United States. Not surprisingly, perhaps, Ricker's work at the University of Illinois became legendary.

Nathan Clifford Ricker was born in Maine in 1843.[31] After graduating from high school, he was employed as a teacher, worked in government service, and did factory work until the mid-1860s when, on a visit to Illinois, he purchased a wagon and blacksmith's shop. Three years later, he decided to enroll in the university to further his education and, because of his past education and experience, was granted standing as a second-year student. He was scheduled to graduate in June of 1872, but the Chicago Fire in October of 1871 prompted him, and his primary instructor, Harold M. Hansen, to leave the university to work in Chicago, where he remained until the fall of 1872. Hansen did not return to the university, and Ricker was asked to assume a temporary appointment and take charge of instruction in architecture, including his own. It was a task that would last until his death in 1924.

When Ricker completed his degree in March of 1873, he accepted a permanent appointment in charge of the department of architecture, with the understanding that he would have a six-month period to review similar programs in Europe. He returned to begin his teaching duties in September of 1873, and for the next twelve years taught all the architecture courses at the university. In 1877, he was given an assistant, a recent graduate named Joseph C. Llewellyn.[32] During the next decade, Ricker worked tirelessly to develop a sophisticated architectural program. He translated numerous French and German texts for use by his students and began to assemble a library.[33] Often the only means of reproducing his translations was to make blueprints of his typescripts, a process he used for several years.

By the time the Chicago Architectural Sketch Club was formed in 1885, Ricker had been appointed dean of engineering, in addition to being head of the Depart-

*Nathan Clifford Ricker (RL)*

31. The best information on Ricker is in Alan K. Laing, *Nathan Clifford Ricker (1843–1924), Pioneer in American Architectural Education* (Urbana: University of Illinois, 1973).

32. Joseph C. Llewellyn was to become a major figure in the activities of the Chicago Architectural Club in the late nineteenth century. See chapters 10 and 11.

33. Today the Ricker Library at the University of Illinois is one of the world's great architectural libraries.

*Nathan Ricker designed this building for the University of Illinois in 1872 (RL)*

34. One of Ricker's in-depth discussions of architectural education was published in the *Sanitary News* on November 20, 1886, in the same issue that covered the third annual meeting of the Western Association of Architects and the second annual meeting of the Chicago Architectural Sketch Club.

35. Between 1885 and 1890, nearly forty new buildings of eight stories or more were designed and built in Chicago's central business district. If one includes buildings of lesser height, the number reaches into the hundreds. Many more were executed in other areas of the city and its environs, and Chicago architects' services were in demand throughout the Midwest.

36. Blueprinting and other duplicating techniques were in their infancy, and most beginners—as well as some more experienced men—spent a good deal of time "tracing." That is, after original construction details were worked out, "tracers" would copy the details for contractors and workmen to use in the field. It was not efficient, but it did afford junior personnel a way to learn how to prepare construction drawings. As experienced draftsmen prepared original drawings, they often invented their own details and kept their own personal files of such details for use in the future.

ment of Architecture. He also carried on a small private practice and acted as architect for a number of university buildings. More important, he wrote and spoke widely on architectural education to organizations such as the Chicago Architectural Sketch Club, the Western Association of Architects, and the American Institute of Architects.[34] From time to time, he also served as a juror for competitions sponsored by the club.

In 1885, when the Chicago Architectural Sketch Club was organized, the University of Illinois, under Ricker, was granting about twenty degrees in architecture each year. At that time, there were approximately 125 architectural firms in Chicago, most of which had more than one draftsman on staff. The need for experienced draftsmen to direct and supervise production of drawings and to address the technical problems of tall building design far exceeded the number of available graduates.[35] Some of the slack was taken up by the city's trade schools, such as the Athenaeum and the Chicago Manual Training School, but neither was able to supply the manpower needed during this period. Chicago architects worked in a constant manpower crisis.

The basic problem was that, with a few exceptions, draftsmen's knowledge of classic details and the techniques of assembling sets of construction documents was rudimentary at best. The exceptions were those men who took it upon themselves to study and learn these basics for use in their day-to-day work. Most young men in architects' offices, however, even recent graduates, were rarely well versed in such matters.[36] The Chicago Architectural Sketch Club, under the leadership of its founding members and with the support of a large segment of the architectural profession in the city, sought to educate these novice practitioners. An

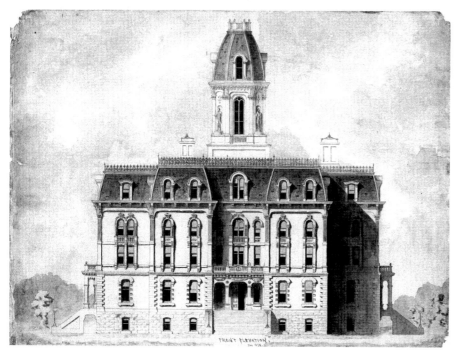

*This design was prepared by J. C. Llewellyn while he was a student at the University of Illinois, ca. 1876; its similarity to Ricker's drawings of the same period is striking (WRH)*

examination of the twenty-six biweekly meetings in 1886 clearly demonstrates their efforts.

The club's activities covered three areas: first, members prepared and delivered papers, both of a practical nature and an artistic bent; second, they sponsored competitions that honed design and presentation skills; and finally, they provided social interchange among the younger draftsmen of Chicago, who could learn through conversation, demonstration, argument, and sometimes partying. In short, they learned to network. Occasionally they combined serious efforts with recreation. For example, in midsummer of 1886, the club decided to take a sketching trip to Janesville, Wisconsin.[37] They left by rail on Saturday, July 10. They had been invited to spend the weekend at the home of Mr. William Butts. About ten members took part and more than forty sketches and watercolors were produced over the weekend. The following Monday evening, those drawings were exhibited at the club rooms for comment by those who stayed behind. The idea of exhibitions was germinating.

Most of the club's eighteen founders had been appearing in the architectural journals of Chicago, as well as in national publications, for several years, and they had the foresight to include in the bylaws the provision that drawings by members, including competition drawings, would remain the property of the club. Clearly their plan was to find a means to put this work before their senior colleagues in offices throughout Chicago and, eventually, before a wider audience. Publication was the reward for increasing one's skill, and in order to gain that skill, knowledge of architecture gained through education and practice was necessary. That was the goal of the founders of the Chicago Architectural Sketch Club, and opportunities to realize this goal came rather quickly.

37. *Sanitary News* 8, no. 126 (July 3, 1886): 128, and *Sanitary News* 8, no. 128 (July 17, 1886): 147.

Within a year of the founding of the club, the *Northwestern Architect*, a Minneapolis journal, suggested that there be an architectural exhibit at the Minneapolis Industrial Exposition in August of 1886 and an invitation to participate was published widely. Every architectural association and club was invited to submit the work of its members.[38] The CASC members discussed the matter and eventually elected to send a consignment of drawings in one lot. The exhibition opened on August 23, and the drawings were on view until October 2. It was the first time the club's work was exhibited outside of Chicago.

Encouraged by Minneapolis exhibition, the members began plans in October for an exhibition of their own. They decided to hold it in the rooms of the Builders and Traders' Exchange during the national convention of the Western Association of Architects scheduled for November 18. The 1886 syllabus had not called for an annual meeting or banquet, but the members had met and elected officers in November of 1885 and it was logical to do so again in November of 1886. It was relatively easy to expand the annual meeting into an exhibition. The Executive Committee put forth some straightforward rules on what could be exhibited in a circular, noting that the following types of drawings would be permitted:[39]

1. Club drawings exhibited at the Industrial Exposition in Minneapolis.
2. Pen and ink drawings of buildings in perspective.
3. Water-color drawings of buildings in perspective.
4. Miscellaneous sketches in pen and ink.
5. Miscellaneous sketches in water color.
6. Sketches from nature (Buildings, landscapes, etc.) in pen and ink and water color.
7. Sketches from photographs of foreign buildings.
8. Sketches from photographs of domestic buildings.
9. Club competition drawings.
10. Sketches in pencil made at the club, and others.
11. Sketches in oil.
12. Initiation sketches.

Only drawings by members of the club were to be accepted and framing would be at the option of the contributor. Copies or prints of any kind were not acceptable. Since the drawings sent to Minnesota were still in Minneapolis at the time the rules were distributed, the committee agreed to provide a separate space for them when they were returned. Charter members were reminded that some had not submitted initiation sketches and were asked to so designate some of the drawings they submitted. The last sentence of the rules stated, "In order that this exhibit may be properly catalogued, a complete list of drawings must be presented with them when they are handed in, and each drawing marked *on the back* with name and address of the owner. No drawings received after the 12th inst can be catalogued."[40]

The Executive Committee soon realized that having both an exhibition and an annual meeting in November of 1886, with election of officers and all the other housekeeping matters such an occasion required, would be very difficult. Therefore, they moved the annual meeting up to November 8 and called a special meeting a week later, on November 15, to open what was to become the first annual exhibition of drawings sponsored by the club, an event that would continue for the next half century.

The *Inland Architect* for December 1886 reported that the "inauguration of an annual exhibit of club drawings and annual banquet" had been held on November 15, and "the exhibit of drawings, about 200 in number, was a surprise to all but those

38. *Sanitary News* 8, no. 123 (June 12, 1886): 83. The data regarding the proposed exhibition were widely distributed.

39. The circular has not survived but the information it contained, excerpted here, was published in *Inland Architect* 8, no. 7 (November 1886): 53.

40. The reference to cataloguing is interesting in that no catalog of this first exhibition has been found. The earliest catalog of an exhibition located is that for 1894. There are, however, references to other early catalogs in addition to this one for 1886. It and later catalogs may have simply been printed lists of entries, which did not survive.

who have watched the advancement of the club for the past two years."[41] The *Building Budget* noted that "the display consisted of initiation sketches, twenty-two in number; club competition drawings, sketches in oil, sketches in pen and ink, embracing miscellaneous designs of buildings, of decorations, of interior and exterior architectural detail; perspectives of buildings and drawings from nature, including some fine water color sketches and pencil drawings . . . There has never been displayed in the West so creditable an exhibit of architectural and artistic sketches of a general character, as has been gathered from one year's work by this club. The original designs and able handling of some of the work presented is indicative of a skill, which will surely . . . find employment in the actual construction of Chicago architecture at no distant day."[42]

41. *Inland Architect* 8, no. 8 (December 1886): 75.

42. *Building Budget* 2, no. 9 (November 1886): 138.

*Drawing from the* Inland Architect

The opening of the exhibition was followed immediately by an elaborate banquet. Only members of the club, directors of the Builders and Traders' Exchange, and the three architects who served on the Adjudicating Committee (Root, Jenney, and Sullivan) were invited to the banquet. Upward of forty members and guests attended, and letters of regret were received from several prominent men who were unable to be there. Following the dinner, a series of toasts were offered, including one to "The Architect," to which John Wellborn Root, the only member of the Adjudicating Committee to attend, responded.[43] His "response was an unusually fine address to the draughtsmen. It . . . merited the enthusiastic manner in which it was received." It was at this meeting that John Wellborn Root became the first nonmember to be proposed for honorary membership. He accepted the honor in an "appropriate manner."[44]

The remainder of the evening was spent with various members entertaining the group with songs, recitations, and general good fellowship. The camaraderie generated was evident in the published reports of the affair, and the evening set the tone for future exhibitions and annual meetings. Every published syllabus thereafter—beginning two weeks later with the one for 1887—would provide for an annual banquet and exhibition.

The exhibition at the Builders and Traders' Exchange remained in place for only a short time, probably less than two weeks. It was seen by the members of the exchange, of course, but the public was also welcomed, as were the attendees of the Second Annual Convention of the Western Association of Architects, which was taking place in Chicago at the time. Published reports of the exhibition were universally positive, and the club members, particularly the junior members, were elated about the response.

The CASC was not, however, the only group sponsoring exhibitions. The WAA had a small show at the same time in the rooms of the Permanent Exhibit and Exchange, where the convention was located. The drawings displayed were primarily done by local architects, and many had been delineated by club members. More important, in January 1887, the Second Annual Exhibition of the Architectural League of New York was held at the Salmagundi Club in New York City. The Chicago club had agreed to participate. That exhibition opened on January 10, on the heels of the Chicago exhibition, and ran for a month. The catalog of the league exhibition contained 189 entries, mostly work from New York offices, but material from Boston, Philadelphia, and Europe was also shown. Chicago was the only club specifically mentioned in a comprehensive review of the show published in the *Sanitary News*.[45] The reviewer, Martha Howe-Davidson, noted that Harry Lawrie exhibited a drawing, T. O. Fraenkel had several sketches and a drawing of a country house, and R. M. Turner had sent a sketch of a doorway. The Chicago work was described in some detail in a favorable tone. Members of the CASC would continue to be represented in the Architectural League's annual show for many years.

❖

Membership in the Chicago Architectural Sketch Club reached about fifty members in 1886. The roster fluctuated as members married, moved away, or established their own offices. There was a continual supply of new members, usually from architectural offices of men who were already in the club or from those who had seen the annual exhibitions and wanted to take part. Larger offices in particular, such as Holabird & Roche, Burnham & Root, and Adler & Sullivan, were constantly in need

43. John Wellborn Root (1850–1891) was born in Georgia. He was sent to England in 1864 to avoid the Civil War. He received his early architectural education there, including some study at Oxford. He returned to the United States before graduation and entered City College in New York. While a student, he worked for James Renwick and James Snook. Root came to Chicago after the Great Fire of 1871 and worked in the office of Carter, Drake & Wight, where he met Daniel H. Burnham. In 1873, they established a partnership that lasted until Root's untimely death in 1891. Burnham & Root pioneered the early modern movement in Chicago. Root was a great supporter of the CASC and spoke many times before the club.

44. *Inland Architect* 8, no. 8 (December 1886): 75.

45. *Sanitary News* 9, no. 157 (February 1887): 167.

of knowledgeable draftsmen who understood enough about architecture and construction to be able to work somewhat independently after receiving basic guidance from senior colleagues. Those architects recognized the value of what the club was doing, and established firms encouraged young men to participate. Much of the architectural education of the younger members of the profession in Chicago was in the hands of the club. It performed admirably.

At the end of 1886, the club once again prepared a syllabus for the coming year. It was announced that twenty-one lectures and competitions had been scheduled for 1887, and when no special event was on the agenda, there would be "club evenings" that would "be devoted to designing and to sketching from still life."[46] The first lecture of the year was to be delivered by honorary member John Wellborn Root. For the next five years, Root would use the club as a platform to deliver his most reasoned thoughts on architecture to the architectural community.

46. *Sanitary News* 9, no. 153 (January 1887): 118.

*William Bryce Mundie's drawing of a clock and bell tower, awarded second prize by the Architectural League of New York in 1887 (IA)*

# Acceptance and Competitions

CHAPTER THREE

The first meeting of the Chicago Architectural Sketch Club in 1887, at the Builders and Traders' Exchange as usual, was called to order by president George Beaumont,[1] who had assumed the office upon the resignation of Harry Lawrie. Lawrie, who had been unanimously reelected to the presidency on December 6, 1886, had immediately resigned to accept a position in Omaha, Nebraska. Oscar Enders had also tendered his resignation,[2] in order to join Lawrie in Omaha. (Reporting on their farewell dinner, the *Inland Architect* observed that "Mr. Enders, while one of the youngest, is looked upon as one of the most promising members of the club"; the journal also praised Lawrie for his efforts over the previous two years and reminded him to maintain a relationship with the club.)[3]

That evening, Lawrie was elected to honorary membership, the first member to be so honored. President Beaumont then had the pleasure of introducing architect John Wellborn Root as the speaker for the first meeting of 1887. Root gave his now-famous paper, "Style," which was published the following month in the *Inland Architect*.[4] More than sixty members were present, and the paper, which is still regarded as one of the important philosophic contributions to the early modern movement in architecture, was extremely well received; the *Inland Architect* described it as "the best ever written on the subject." To those young men who heard Root speak that evening, it must have been an epiphany.

After a sincere vote of appreciation by the members, Root responded "in a manner which will always be remembered by the club," discussing the relationship between the architect and his draftsmen in a way that made it clear he understood their value. He closed by observing that the Chicago Architectural Sketch Club held a leading position among the draftsmen's clubs of the country and that the work they were doing was not only important, but would help them advance to the front of the profession when they went into practice for themselves.[5]

Following Root's speech, Beaumont announced that the 1887 syllabus was complete. While similar to the previous year's, it was even more ambitious. Ten formal evenings and eleven in-house club competitions were planned, with only December having none. (December was reserved for parties.) Speakers had already been contacted and their names were published with the syllabus, which included a date for an annual banquet and exhibition in November. The syllabus was followed during the year with only minor modifications, those being addi-

1. George Beaumont (1854–1922) was born and educated in Leeds, England. He was a member of the Royal Institute of British Architects and in 1879 won the medal of the Leeds and Yorkshire Architectural Association. He came to Chicago in 1885 and was active in the CASC, the WAA, the AIA, and the Chicago Architects' Business Association. He established his own office in 1886 and practiced until his death in 1922.

2. Oscar Enders (1865–1926) was born in Milwaukee, where he received his education. He came to Chicago in 1886 and became a member of the CASC the same year. In 1887, he moved to Omaha, Nebraska, where he remained for a few months, returning to Chicago in early 1888. By 1895 he was in St. Louis, where he was instrumental in organizing the St. Louis Architectural Club. He remained a designer throughout his life, spending most of his career working with architect Isaac Taylor. During the last years of his life he returned to Chicago, where he was employed by Graham, Anderson, Probst & White until his death in 1926.

3. *Inland Architect* 8, no. 9 (December 1886): 95.

4. Root's paper was published as "revised by the author" in *Inland Architect* 8, no. 10 (January 1887): 99 et seq. It has been published several times since, most notably in Donald Hoffmann, ed., *The Meanings of Architecture, Buildings and Writings by John Wellborn Root* (New York: Horizon Press, 1967).

5. *Inland Architect* 8, no. 10 (January 1887): 107.

*George Beaumont (MofI)*

*Oscar Enders (MCAA)*

tional activities that often occurred more or less spontaneously between regular meetings.

During the first five years of the club's existence, there was a meeting of some sort nearly every week, and records indicate that while turnout was occasionally low, usually due to bad weather, not a single meeting was ever canceled. Speakers were generally chosen at the beginning of the year and, for the most part, they were quite dependable. During the six-year period from 1886 through 1892, more than a hundred lectures were presented to the club, and major presentations by well-known figures were usually attended by standing-room-only audiences. Many of these papers were later published in the *Inland Architect*.

Unlike the formal lectures, regular club evenings could be boisterous, noisy, and even raucous. They were usually spent sketching details or designs that were assigned without advance notice. At the end of the evening, members would vote on the best drawing, and occasionally these drawings would appear interspersed throughout the text of the *Inland Architect*. It was not uncommon for members to produce irreverent sketches, including caricatures of fellow draftsmen. While these evenings weren't planned in the usual sense, they were certainly expected. (The final sentence of the 1891 syllabus stated that "through the year it is proposed to entertain the members with frequent informal meetings and socials, and in general the year promises to be a notable one with the club"; a year earlier the last sentence read, "Every alternate Monday evening will be devoted to drawing, sketching, brushwork and designing.")

Work on the scheduled monthly competitions was usually begun during these evenings, but members were permitted to complete their drawings between meetings. Unlike the club-evening sketches, however, scheduled competitions were not judged by the membership. To avoid favoritism, and to obtain the advice and counsel of practitioners, the club had invited a committee of three architects to "adjudicate upon the drawings." In March of 1886, R. C. McLean had made the following motion, seconded by F. L. Lively:

> RESOLVED: That a committee of three architects, consisting of Architects John W. Root, Louis H. Sullivan and W. L. B. Jenney, be asked to act as judges upon the mantel competition, and all future competitions of the club during the current year.[6]

Thus the club bound itself to three of the most prominent architects in Chicago and the world. Jenney, Sullivan, and especially Root were to serve the club for most of their professional lives, and although none was ever an ordinary member of the

6. *Inland Architect* 7, no. 4 (March 1886): 35.

*John Wellborn Root, ca. 1886 (courtesy Don Hoffmann)*

*Louis H. Sullivan, ca. 1886 (AIC/SC)*

*William Le Baron Jenney, ca. 1886 (AIC/FR)*

club, they were all accorded honorary membership. While the resolution had appointed them for "the current year," they continued to meet and act as the competition jury for several years.

In addition to their work on the Adjudicating Committee, all three jury members were regular speakers at club meetings, and they and their partners also took part in local and national architectural organizations. Root was particularly active, serving on the Executive Committee of the Illinois State Association of Architects and later as secretary to the national organization of the American Institute of Architects. His partner, Daniel H. Burnham, was active in the AIA and other architectural groups, and served as president of the AIA in 1894–95. Jenney was an officer in the Illinois AIA, as well as being heavily involved in national affairs. Sullivan, who was secretary of the Illinois State Association of Architects in the late 1880s, was often quoted in published records of that group's activities, and his longtime partner, Dankmar Adler, was involved in city, state, and national architectural organizations until his death in 1900.

Sullivan was the first to give up his duties on the Adjudicating Committee. He last appeared as a member in early 1890. Apparently his professional responsibilities were overwhelming. He was in the midst of getting Chicago's Auditorium Building built, as well as serving a number of other important clients. His position on the jury was taken by J. L. Silsbee.[7] John Root remained an active member until he died in January of 1891. During the months following his death, reports of the committee's activities appeared in journals from time to time, but the members were not named. One can assume that Jenney remained an active participant, since his name continues to appear in reports of various club affairs. At the Sixth Annual Banquet on November 16, 1891, Jenney was the respondent to one of the toasts, as reported in a long article in the *Northwestern Architect*.[8] The article, probably written by the recently elected club secretary, John E. Youngburg, stated, "There is no event of note in the history of the club which Mr. Jenney is not humorously or instructively identified with. Time makes no change established by precedent except as the stock of famous vintages, he improves, and becomes merrier by age. A C.A.S.C. banquet without Mr. Jenney's genial presence would be like a banquet without wine." While Youngburg's language is a bit obtuse, its spirit is clear.

Over the years, the Adjudicating Committee's letters of comment on the competitions were often printed in the *Inland Architect,* the *Building Budget,* and the *Sanitary News*. These letters demonstrate the jury's serious approach to its assignments. Usually short and to the point, they were sometimes also humorous and occasionally critical. In September of 1886, John Root wrote, "The committee . . . desires to report . . . that drawings submitted in this last competition are by no means up to the level which has been attained by the sketch club." At the end of the article, McLean added his own comment: "This criticism of the adjudicating committee is not undeserved . . . The Club . . . has needed . . . this timely hint, and . . . will, with the next competition, show the adjudicating committee that their deficiencies have been largely owing to the exceedingly busy season, which has prevented much club work which would have otherwise been accomplished.—ED."[9] His agreement with the committee's criticism was apparently short-lived, as his editorial in the following issue stated, "In reviewing the year's work we feel that the club deserves words of congratulation. No kindred association in the country has shown a like amount of work performed . . . The adjudicating committee upon the club competition drawings has, by suggestion and criticism, influenced the members to use their best efforts, and while the competitions have not been all they

*Joseph Lyman Silsbee, ca. 1870 (HUA)*

7. Joseph Lyman Silsbee (1845–1913) was born in Salem, Massachusetts. He earned a BA from Harvard in 1866 and then studied at MIT for three years. He moved to Chicago around 1883, where he worked primarily as a residential architect. He is often remembered for employing several men who became key figures in the Prairie School: Frank Lloyd Wright, John Edelman, George Maher, and George Elmslie all served in his office.

8. *Northwestern Architect* 9, no. 11 (November 1891): 102–4. This article described the banquet and activities of the evening in great detail. The banquet was also reported in abbreviated form in *Inland Architect* 18, no. 5 (December 1891): 65–66.

9. *Inland Architect* 8, no. 4 (September 1886): 32.

*The entries for the Buffalo Architectural Sketch Club's Competition for a City Front were remarkably similar to work done by the Chicago club (IA)*

could be . . . there is a strong feeling that the work of the coming year will make up for any deficiency in the past."[10]

The club rose to the challenge. For several years, competitions were a major staple of its activities. During Harry Lawrie's tenure in 1886, there were eight competitions.[11] Eleven were scheduled for 1887,[12] twelve for 1888,[13] and twelve again in 1889.[14] The 1890 syllabus had only six on the agenda, including a "Rendering from a Photograph" and an essay contest on "Expression in Form."[15] A similar program was announced for 1891, with six competitions that included a "water color from a photograph" and a "Design and artistic rendering from the following quotation (to be selected)."[16] For 1892, the syllabus listed ten competitions.[17]

The competitions ranged from simple (a menu card for the annual meeting) to complex (an "Artist's House by the Sea, with an interior sketch of the studio arrangement. To be rendered in Sepia. The interior sketch may be in brown ink with pen rendering").[18] Winners' drawings were often published in the *Inland Architect*, and from time to time in the *Building Budget* and the *Sanitary News* as well, where they were sometimes juxtaposed with examples of work from other sketch clubs.

The club's own competitions were not, of course, the only ones available to CASC members, and while the prizes offered were modest by today's standards—generally about a week's salary for first place—the real reward was getting the work published. It gave the draftsmen status in the architectural community, and that was what the younger members of the Chicago Architectural Sketch Club wanted more than anything else.

❊

The club continued its rigorous schedule of in-house competitions and sketch nights throughout 1887, and in October, members had another opportunity to put

10. *Inland Architect* 8, no. 6 (October 1886): 35.

11. *Sanitary News* 7, no. 97 (December 12, 1885): 51.

12. *Sanitary News* 9, no. 153 (January 7, 1887): 118.

13. *Inland Architect* 10, no. 9 (January 1888): 101.

14. *Inland Architect* 12, no. 6 (January 1889): 98.

15. *Inland Architect* 14, no. 7 (December 1889): 83.

16. *Inland Architect* 16, no. 7 (December 1890): 81.

17. *Northwestern Architect* 10, no. 21 (February 1892): 16.

18. *Inland Architect* 14, no. 7 (December 1889): 83.

their work before a distinguished group of architects. The national organization of the American Institute of Architects had accepted an invitation to hold its annual convention in Chicago, at the Permanent Exhibit and Exchange rooms at 15 East Washington Street. Henry Lord Gay, who ran the Exchange, was always willing to offer his exhibition room to any group who might be interested in what his building-supplier tenants were showing. On this occasion, he asked practicing architects to display their work as well, and one evening of the convention was set aside to view the drawings and material exhibitions before regular business took place.[19] Nearly all the Chicago drawings shown were delineated by members of the sketch club for their employers. For the most part, they had been prepared for actual projects, and while they prominently displayed the architects' names, they credited the delineators as well. A few drawings from other parts of the country—Dayton, Ohio; Washington, D.C.; Green Bay, Wisconsin; Cleveland; and Philadelphia—were also shown.

A month later, the 1887 annual meeting of the Chicago Architectural Sketch Club was held on November 6, with sixty-five members present. After the usual housekeeping tasks, George Beaumont was reelected president, and it was "recommended that some . . . action be taken" to seek permanent quarters for the club. There was growing concern that the club needed a home of its own. No decisions were made, but the idea had been planted. The remainder of the evening was devoted to finalizing plans for the annual banquet and exhibition.[20]

The club's Second Annual Banquet and Exhibition took place on November 14, 1887, as scheduled in the syllabus published almost a year earlier. The club had been preparing for some time. The exhibition rules were similar to those of the previous year and a Hanging Committee consisting of C. A. Kessell and E. J. Wagner, with president George Beaumont as chairman, had made the arrangements with help from various volunteers. Invitations suggested that members and guests allow an hour to view the exhibition before sitting down to dinner at nine.

By this time, the Chicago Architectural Sketch Club had aroused enough public interest for the show to merit coverage in the popular press. The most extensive

19. *Sanitary News* 10, no. 26 (October 29, 1887): 309.

20. *Inland Architect* 8, no. 7 (November 1886): 3.

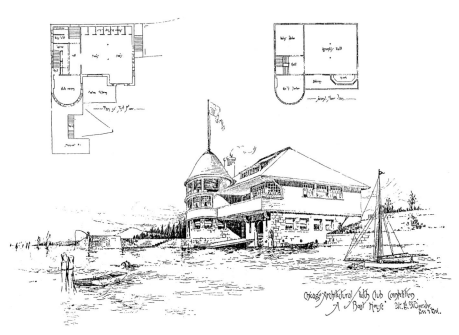

*Drawing from the* Inland Architect

*Sketches from the 1887 exhibition at the Builders and Traders' Exchange (CH)*

21. "Many Pretty Designs," *Chicago Herald*, Tuesday, November 15, 1887. I am indebted to Harold T. Wolff for bringing this reference to my attention.

22. *Sanitary News* 11, no. 198 (November 19, 1887): 34–35.

23. Ibid. The reference to a catalog confirms its existence for this exhibition, as well as for the previous year.

newspaper review was in the *Chicago Herald*.[21] The unsigned review was positive and included five line drawings from the exhibition in addition to an exhaustive description of many of the nearly two hundred drawings in the show. The reviewer went to great lengths to name a number of the exhibitors and to describe their work. It appears that he was also present at the banquet, since he described the evening in some detail.

The event was reported extensively in the architectural press, most vividly perhaps in the *Sanitary News*, where the author wrote, "While the Clover club of the Quaker city crosses its legs under the mahogany and discusses the unique cuisine of the Bellevue, the New England society is content with an annual dinner at Delmonico's and listens to profound dissertations by learned and cultured gentlemen, the Architectural Sketch Club satisfies its yearnings in this direction by an annual banquet at the Builders and Traders' Exchange."[22] The places of each of the nearly fifty members and guests "were designated by a card, about five by eight inches, bearing a beautiful design emblematic of their profession, and in the centre of which was the guest's name." The card was a design by F. L. Linden.

The reviewer continued, "President Beaumont, after bidding those present a hearty welcome, gave a brief resume of the club's labors and aims. 'From a small beginning,' he said, 'it has developed into a well organized, useful and artistic club. The aims of the club are mutual improvement and the advancement of the members to a higher standard of mutual attainments. The club is conducted on broad cosmopolitan principles, and any architectural draughtsman or worker in the allied arts, of integrity, honor and sobriety can become a member on the presentation of an initiation sketch of sufficient merit to pass an examination by the executive committee. We have among our honorary members, architects of high standing, who have practiced their profession in this city for years. Our club nights are devoted to sketching, and other evenings to the reading and discussion of papers on various subjects relating to architecture.' In concluding his remarks he told the junior members that the leisure hours were better and more ennoblingly spent in the pursuit of art than over the billiard table, and admonished them to strive after a higher education." Following Beaumont's remarks, the members and guests enjoyed the elaborate menu and heard a number of laudatory toasts and short speeches. There was a great deal of musical talent present, both vocal and instrumental, and the festivities continued until a late hour.

The item immediately following the report of the annual meeting in the *Sanitary News* was a lengthy, nearly full-page review of the exhibition. The unnamed reviewer, like his colleague from the *Chicago Herald*, was generous in his praise, noting that there were 166 drawings hung on the four walls of the room. He listed twenty-six members whose work was shown and described many of the drawings in great detail. He observed that there "was a somewhat larger number of drawings presented at the exhibition last year, but there is a notable improvement in the quality . . . undoubtedly due to the sketching expeditions inaugurated by the club the past year . . . which resulted in much pleasure as well as profit to the participants." He was not, however, pleased with the room where the show was held and found it "not at all suitable for the purpose. The dark and gloomy weather which prevailed for the first day or two of the week made it all the worse." The reviewer noted that "the Club drawings which occupy the first place in the catalogue, are composed of initatation [*sic*] and competition drawings, of which those of W. R. [*sic*] Mundie and H. T. Hazelton are specially worthy of mention." He identified the various drawings by number, which suggests that a catalog was published, and concluded that "those who have not visited it will find it worth while to go around and take a peep at the productions of the 'future greats.'"[23]

The *Inland Architect* had similar, if somewhat briefer, praise for the show, although the article did comment that "the exhibit has been visited by a large number of citizens, and received universal praise," which was exactly what both the founders and the general membership had hoped would happen.[24] In the future, much of their efforts throughout the year would be directed toward producing a successful annual exhibition.

After the show, the club's first priority was to find larger, more appropriate quarters where it could have more control over its activities. Within a week of the opening of the 1887 exhibition, at the next regular meeting, a number of members subscribed to a fund of about five hundred dollars, to be used for finding, leasing, and refitting new rooms for the club.[25] Since only about a third of the members were present at this initial fund-raising, all concerned felt it would be relatively easy to proceed. They were right. The membership responded positively, and a committee was formed to find a new space.[26] Some thought was given to increasing the initiation fees and dues, but the idea was tabled, as it was considered more important to expand the membership first, and members were asked to spread the word that all architectural draftsmen in the city were invited to join.

The Executive Committee noted that the club wanted to have rooms that were centrally located, well lighted and heated, and could be used by the members both days and evenings. They specified that they wanted a large meeting room as well as a library and reading room. These programmatic requirements were filled within a few weeks, when the Art Institute of Chicago offered space in its recently completed building on Michigan Avenue at Van Buren Street. The new building had ample space on the top floor that was not yet needed for museum functions.

Before the club could move to its new quarters, the Architectural League of New York once again held its annual exhibition.[27] This time it opened in mid-December at the Fifth Avenue Art Galleries in New York City. The league had outgrown the Salmagundi Club. Over three hundred pieces were exhibited, including forty-four designs that had been submitted for the league's National Draughtsmen's Competition for Gold and Silver Medals. (The gold medal had been awarded to James A. McLeod of Minneapolis for his design of "a low-arched tower of rough boulders and . . . a roof of Spanish red tile . . . The silver medal was given to 'Tuxedo,' a sketch by 24 year old W. B. Mundie of Chicago, showing a high tower with a rounded turret, a red tile roof crowning a structure of rough stones and brick." It was the first national recognition of a member of the Chicago Architectural Sketch Club.)

Since the club's own exhibition drawings remained in place for three weeks, from November 14 through December 5, the first meeting of the new year was a club evening on December 5, 1887, when the drawings were taken down. Two weeks later, on December 19, the membership was treated to an evening with John K. Allen, editor of the *Sanitary News*, who gave a paper on "Architecture in the South of Ireland."[28] Allen was an excellent speaker who illustrated his lecture with lantern slides. It was the first reported time that members had invited ladies to attend; from that day forward, women were often participants in the club's social events. It would be some time, however, before the first female member would be listed on the rolls of the club.

24. *Inland Architect* 10, no. 5 (December 1887): 85.

25. *Sanitary News* 11, no. 199 (November 26, 1887): 45.

26. *Sanitary News* 11, no. 203 (December 24, 1887): 95.

27. Ibid.

28. *Inland Architect* 10, no. 9 (January 1888): 101.

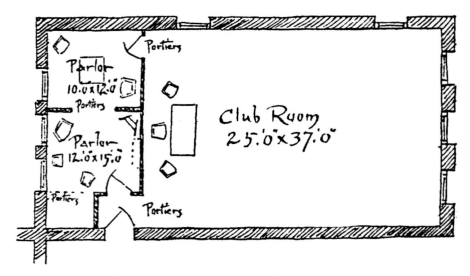

*Sketches of the CASC club rooms and furnishings by W. G. Williamson, published in the March 1888 issue of the* Inland Architect

Two important events were announced at the end of Allen's presentation: the 1888 syllabus was ready and new quarters had been found. The syllabus was published in part in the *Sanitary News* on December 24, 1887, and the full program was published in the *Inland Architect* in January 1888.[29] It called for twenty-six meetings, starting on December 5, 1887, and ending with what was now known as the annual exhibition and banquet, on November 19, 1888. Informal club evenings were again scheduled between meetings where prominent architects and others spoke to the membership. In addition to John Allen, who had opened the year on December 19, scheduled speakers included Root, Jenney, and Sullivan, as well as W. B. Mundie and Richard E. Schmidt. Lesser names included Martin Moylan, who spoke on "Practical Plumbing," and members F. L. Lively, J. H. Carpenter, and C. A. Kessell. Only two formal evenings were unassigned when the syllabus was published, and they were quickly filled by W. B. Lord and Fritz Wagner of the Northwestern Terra Cotta Company, who agreed to speak on February 13 and August 27, respectively. Remarkably, every scheduled meeting was held, although some were delayed for various reasons, and at least one additional evening meeting, an informal reception, was held on May 4. The members also participated in a number of unscheduled activities outside the club rooms, such as sketching trips, visits to building sites, and even athletic events.

The 1888 syllabus called for twelve competitions—one every four weeks—with drawings to be turned in at the beginning of each formal meeting. Root, Sullivan, and Jenney continued to serve on the Adjudicating Committee. All the competitions were executed and most were published, and brief, informal competitions continued to be popular at club evenings.

The search for a new permanent home had been concluded rather quickly, and in January of 1888, the *Inland Architect* reported on "an important move . . . which will place the club in surroundings, and it is hoped in membership, first among artistic bodies in the country. This was the passage of a resolution directing the executive committee to engage quarters for the club at the newly completed Art Institute . . . and a room 50 by 25 feet was secured."[30]

Immediately after finalizing the lease arrangements, the Executive Committee circulated a subscription paper among the membership to raise additional money for the improvements that would be necessary before the club could move into the

29. Ibid.
30. Ibid.

new space. It was also suggested that there would be "no better time than the present . . . for honorary members and other friends of the club to show their appreciation of the work the club is doing for the advancement of architectural knowledge by contributing to this fund."[31] Several friends of the club responded, and the members themselves contributed several hundred dollars. These funds, combined with the money raised a few weeks earlier, proved sufficient to furnish quarters that would serve the club for several years. (It also helped that F. L. Linden, who had decorated the new Art Institute Building, had his workers finish the club's space at no extra charge.) Funds were also needed to subdivide the space and purchase furniture. A striking element in the scheme was a magnificent entry door with an art glass panel incorporating the letters *CASC* in its design.

The club room was published in the *Inland Architect* after the first meeting was held there on January 16, 1888.[32] The article observed that when the club was first organized "the Builders and Traders' Exchange immediately offered the club the free use of its assembly hall, and to this generosity the club owes much of its success, and now that a permanent home for the club has been secured this disinterested friendship of the builders of Chicago is not forgotten." The last meeting in the old space provided for nearly three years by the Builders and Traders' Exchange had been held on January 2, 1888, and it was adjourned early so members could lend a hand on the work being done on the new space.

The reporter for the *Inland Architect* (probably Robert Craik McLean) not only published the plan of the new space, but included sketches of the interior and the furniture drawn by charter member W. G. Williamson. He also made a point of describing, in somewhat humorous terms, various members who had contributed substantially to the club. He added, with obvious praise for all the members, that "to describe the notable members would be to describe them all, for each has to a greater or lesser extent become known through their drawings in the architectural publications, and each has much architectural honor in store for him in the future."

John Root was the scheduled speaker at the first meeting in the new space, and the article reported that "the event of the evening is a paper by Architect John W. Root, and, for the time being, he, the greatest architectural genius in the West, if not in the country, is a draftsman among draftsmen . . . he seems to enjoy the bright questions, practical ideas, and ingenious theories that are so freely expressed by the members, drawn out, and encouraged as they are by the feeling of thorough fellowship existing between every member and their guest."[33] Root's paper, "Broad Art Criticism," had been published in the previous issue of the *Inland Architect*,[34] when these comments appeared in print. He was clearly a role model for the club members, although, at thirty-eight years old, he was essentially a member of their generation.

As he often did, McLean couldn't resist commenting on the success of the club and its roots, in which he still took a strong proprietary interest. He noted in his article that "the causes which have lead [*sic*] to the establishment and success of this as well as other similar clubs in the United States, are peculiar. Sketching . . . has never been . . . so important a part of a draftsman's training as at present." He went on to discuss the need to educate draftsmen who would become architects, lamenting that the average draftsman could not afford the time or the expense of attending one of the "several leading colleges" and "must work by day and study by night, if he would rise in his profession," and, therefore, "the draftsmen are seeking among themselves to institute clubs like this for their mutual improvement . . . While the study of architecture is the main object, and the papers read and the club competitions all have some bearing on that profession, the club is essentially a sketch club," and furthermore, "until the time comes when Chicago has an architectural school properly organized, the sketch club will fill its niche and fill it well."

31. Ibid.

32. *Inland Architect* 11, no. 3 (March 1888): 33–34.

33. For the first time, the modern "draftsman" is used in lieu of the archaic "draughtsman."

34. *Inland Architect* 11, no. 1 (February 1888): 3–5. It has since been republished in Hoffmann, *The Meanings of Architecture.*

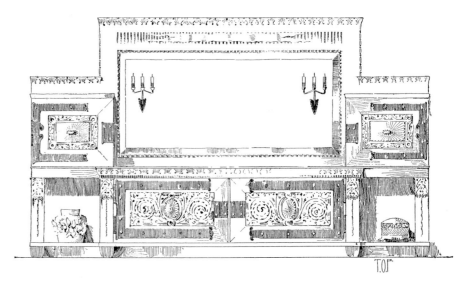

*Theodore O. Fraenkel's first-place drawing of a sideboard (IA)*

35. *Sanitary News* 11, no. 210
(February 14, 1888): 178.

All in all, the first meeting in the new space was a decided success. Two weeks later, at the first club evening in the new rooms, it was suggested that the entry fee be raised from three to ten dollars.[35] There was now rent to be paid and other incidental expenses related to the new quarters. Nevertheless, the proposition was tabled. The Executive Committee hoped that the recent publicity the club received because of the move would increase membership. Perhaps they were also encouraged when three new members—the first new faces in several weeks—were admitted at that same meeting.

*The Auditorium Building, under construction above in the fall of 1887, would have progressed only a modest amount by the time the club visited en masse in the spring of 1888 (IA)*

Attendance at club activities was excellent in the new space. Not only was it conveniently located on Michigan Avenue, but it was open during the day and most evenings, so it was a convenient place to meet, talk, and draw. The club subscribed to most of the current architectural periodicals, and now that members no longer had immediate access to the library at the Builders and Traders' Exchange, they began assembling a library of their own, an activity they continued for the next forty-five years. While the club rooms were not large, there was adequate space for fifty or sixty members and their guests to hear speakers, and on club evenings, when members brought out their sketch pads, it was a comfortable place to draw. There was also an abundance of wall space where competition entries and other work could be shown.

The members' pride in their new space prompted them, for the first time, to hold a purely social evening—an informal reception—in the club rooms to which they invited their ladies as well as honorary members and other friends of the club. They set the date for Friday, May 4, not a regular meeting night. It was a great success. The *Sanitary News* reported that "the hall was tastefully draped and decorated for the occasion."[36] Food and drink was served, and a casual program that included songs, instrumental music, and recitations by both members and guests was presented. The evening ended with "a series of legerdemain sketches by Oscar Enders, which were exceptionally well executed." (Enders's short-lived residence in Omaha was over, and he had returned to both Chicago and the club.)

*M. G. Holmes's perspective of a sideboard took second place in the competition (IA)*

❖

The 1888 schedule had opened with John Root's presentation on January 16 and been followed a fortnight later by a practical lecture on slate by W. B. Lord. William Le Baron Jenney had presented a paper titled the "Evolution of Style," followed two weeks later on April 9 by Louis Sullivan's paper "Style."[37] Each of these men commanded the respect of the club's members, but Sullivan's lyrical presentations always brought out the membership in full. His paper was well received and he was immediately nominated and elected to honorary membership, something he treasured until the end of his life. That same evening the competitions for a sideboard and a park fountain were declared closed and the drawings were submitted to the Adjudicating Committee for review. The committee also advised the membership that it had examined the drawings submitted on January 16 and February 13 for a "staircase and hall" and a "French residence front." W. G. Williamson and O. C. Christian were awarded first and second place in the first competition, and O. C. Smith and T. O. Fraenkel took similar honors in the second. Smith and Fraenkel had the pleasure of seeing their winning entries command a full page in the April 1888 issue of the *Inland Architect*. The results of the competition for a sideboard were announced on May 7; T. O. Fraenkel, M. G. Holmes, and W. B. Mundie took the first three places.

❖

One of the basic objectives outlined in the club's constitution was "visiting selected buildings." It seems to have been pretty much ignored by all concerned until the April 28, 1888, meeting, when it was announced that "next Saturday afternoon the members will meet at the club rooms at 2 P.M., and in a body visit the Auditorium Building for the purpose of examining its construction and gaining information."[38]

36. *Sanitary News* 12, no. 223 (May 12, 1888): 20.

37. Sullivan's paper was published in full in *Inland Architect* 11, no. 6 (May 1888): 59–60.

38. *Sanitary News* 12, no. 221 (April 28, 1888): 305.

A good number of members took advantage of the plan and were privileged to have fellow member Paul Mueller as their guide.[39]

The May 7 meeting was poorly attended due to inclement weather.[40] The scheduled talk, "Practical Plumbing" by Martin Moylan, was therefore postponed until May 21, normally a club evening. The members also agreed to extend the deadline for the "Eight-room frame dwelling" competition until the same date. These postponements forced the club to cancel its usual evenings of sketching and, while it was difficult to deny an invited speaker such a privilege, it was annoying to some members that scheduled lectures by members and competition deadlines were postponed. The matter more or less came to a head on June 4, when secretary W. G. Williamson read a communication to the assembled members from R. E. Schmidt giving his reasons for "omitting to read a paper entitled 'Student Days.'"[41] Schmidt's reasons were not recorded, but his note prompted some spirited discussion as to how to deal with delayed presentations and the occasional extension of competition deadlines, which some felt was unfair to those who had made a point of coming to hear a specific lecture or those who completed their submissions in

39. *Sanitary News* 12, no. 223 (May 12, 1888): 20. A brief item notes that "a vote of thanks was extended to Mr. Paul Mueller."

40. Ibid.

41. *Sanitary News* 12, no. 227 (June 9, 1888): 70.

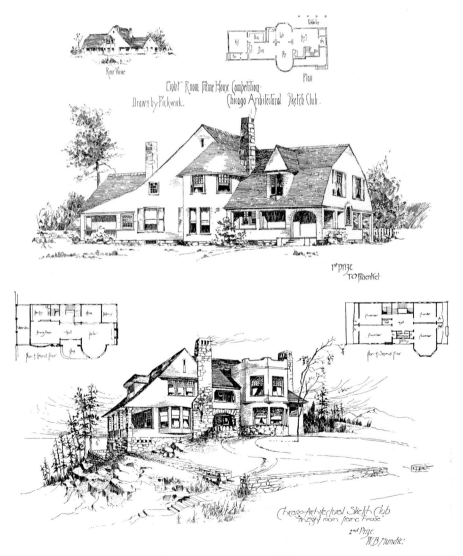

*T. O. Fraenkel won the Eight-Room Frame Dwelling Competition of 1888 and W. B. Mundie took second place (IA)*

the time allotted. Later that same evening, O. C. Christian, who only occasionally participated in competitions, offered a motion "not to allow the date of competitions to be postponed." The motion was not passed, but its spirit was followed; future competition drawings were usually delivered on or before their scheduled deadlines, and cancellation of a scheduled lecture became a rare event.

The June 4 meeting also featured the reading of a communication from the Buffalo Architectural Club[42] asking "Chicago draughtsmen to co-operate . . . in forming a national league of such clubs, of which there are about ten throughout the United States. The object of the league would be the arranging of competitions. It would also be beneficial to the many draughtsmen and would greatly help to increase the memberships of the clubs now existing, as only club members would be eligible to membership, and be the means of organizing many more clubs." The CASC elected to leave the request in the hands of its secretary, who was asked to communicate with the Buffalo group for more details.

The Buffalo club's letter was never published in full, but it was circulated among most of the sketch clubs then in existence. Robert Craik McLean was quick to realize the possibilities of such a league of clubs, and in June of 1888 he spoke out strongly in favor of such an organization.[43] During the next decade, there would be a number of attempts to form a league of architectural clubs, but it was not until 1899 that such an organization was actually realized.

The first meeting in July of 1888 featured a paper by Frank Lively on Greek architecture. The *Inland Architect* reported[44] that it was "received with applause" and "showed close study in not only the forms of Greek architecture, but in its history as well," and that while it was "too long for publication in an architectural journal . . . it is exceedingly valuable." The *Inland Architect* had often published lengthy papers before, but apparently McLean felt that Lively's paper was too esoteric for many of his readers. It was one of the few times such a decision was made. It was, however, extensively reviewed in the *Sanitary News*.[45] Both the *Inland Architect* and the *Sanitary News* also carried a brief note that the competition for "Furniture design on one sheet" was "indefinitely postponed," perhaps because the members of the club considered themselves architects and had little interest in the design of freestanding furniture. The club's competition for the design of a two-foot-square carved wood panel, however, was not canceled; the drawings were to be full-size and were due on July 30.

During the summer of 1888, club members began to work—and play—outside the club rooms. On July 2, William Gibb invited the other members on a sketching trip to Riverside, Illinois. Shortly thereafter, it was noted in the *Sanitary News* that the "members of the Architectural Sketch Club have purchased light, mouse colored jackets to wear while on sketching excursions. If the weather is favorable, they will take the 8 or 11 o'clock C.B.&Q. R.R. train for Riverside Park Sunday. The place selected is known as Shantytown, near the limestone quarry in the town of Lyons. The Des Plaines river runs through the town and affords them ample facilities for bathing and fishing."[46] The outing proved to be a success and resulted in a number of sketches that were later displayed in the club rooms.

The following week, the *Sanitary News* reported that "one of the most interesting amateur baseball games of the season was witnessed Saturday week, at Jackson park between the employees, mostly draughtsmen, of Architects Burnham & Root and Cobb & Frost."[47] The two lineups published indicate that nearly all the players were members of the Chicago Architectural Sketch Club. (The final score was 17–5 in favor of Burnham & Root.) Following the baseball item, the *Sanitary News* reported that the Adjudicating Committee had awarded first place in the eight-room frame house competition to T. O. Fraenkel and second place to W. B.

*The competition for a "carved wood panel, full size" resulted in several drawings such as this Renaissance design (IA)*

42. Ibid.

43. *Inland Architect* 11, no. 7 (June 1888): 70.

44. *Inland Architect* 11, no. 8 (July 1888): 87.

45. *Sanitary News* 12, no. 10 (July 14, 1888): 125–26.

46. *Sanitary News* 12, no. 231 (July 7, 1888): 120.

47. *Sanitary News* 12, no. 233 (July 21, 1888): 139.

Mundie[48] (both entries were published in the September issue of the *Inland Architect*). Third prize went to nom de plume "No. 12," who was not identified. The committee also reported that Charles Whittlesey had won first place in the park fountain competition, with second and third places going to C. A. Kessell and O. C. Christian. At that same meeting, held on July 16, Kessell read a letter to the club from a former member, W. R. Rae, then in Los Angeles. In his letter, Rae deplored the fact that the public spirit seen in the erection of magnificent buildings in Chicago was not possessed by Los Angeles capitalists, and said he missed Chicago and his colleagues at the Chicago Architectural Sketch Club.

On July 30, Fritz Wagner was scheduled to give a paper on terra-cotta, but he was out of town, so the Executive Committee rescheduled his presentation for August 27. The entries for the carved panel competition were also due, and a number of the members' drawings were handed in to the secretary. While the subject was somewhat unusual, several of these designs were published during the next few months.

The baseball game and the outing to Riverside were still very much in the minds of the members at the July 30 meeting, and they were extremely pleased to hear that contractor Oliver Sollitt had invited the entire membership to visit his home in northern Illinois for a long weekend of sketching and general camaraderie.[49] Sollitt owned a farm he called "Sunset," near Fox Lake, which was supposedly easy to reach. It was agreed that all who wished to attend would take a three o'clock train after work on Saturday afternoon, August 25, and return to Chicago early the following Monday morning. Thirty members accepted the invitation.

The *Inland Architect* reported the outing in great detail, which suggests that editor Robert Craik McLean was probably part of the group.[50] The members engaged a special parlor car that took them to the village of McHenry, fourteen miles from the farm. Sollitt had arranged to have carriages at the station to take the group to a steamer that would transport them up Fox River to their destination, and all aboard had brought sketching materials that were put to good use as they traveled up the river. They were delayed somewhat when one of the pumps on the boat broke down, but they eventually arrived just before dark. From a distance, the lights of the Chinese lanterns Sollitt had hung for the occasion shimmered across the lake. McLean was in good form when he described their arrival, noting that a "greeting of a 'jolly lot of ladies' and a splendid supper awaited the arrival of the excursionists. After supper . . . sleeping assignments were made, by which some were to be snugly housed in the cottage, others in a tasty little boat-house on the edge of the lake, and the remainder in tents nearby." He noted that "Friedberg's band"—musicians who had accompanied them from the city—"furnished the music for guests and other invited friends to the number of two hundred to dance by until the 'wee sma' hours' came on, then the cottagers turned in to rest, and the boat-house contingent turned in, to turn out as soon as the 'tenters were sandwiched' for the night, and razed the textile walls upon their unsuspicious heads, the result of which may be inferred if not described." Obviously, the group was prepared to enjoy themselves, even if it meant the loss of a night's sleep. The night was short in any case: McLean reported that the "next day roll was called at 4 A.M., and the visitors deployed as sketchers up to breakfast-time. After breakfast . . . boat-riding was done up to dinner-time, and then an adjournment to the steamer, in company with lady companions . . . and the day spent at the 'lotus beds' and Wilmot until 10 P.M., including the run home." Just what the "lotus beds" and "Wilmot" signified is left to our imagination. McLean ended his description by noting that "to catch the 5:30 A.M. train at McHenry the next day necessitated an early retiring. Four A.M. found the delegation 'leaving with regret, sitting on two straws for a seat in a hay wagon, for a ride over one of those delightful country roads.'"

48. Ibid., 139–40.

49. Oliver Sollitt (1860–ca. 1925) established his contracting firm in 1890. The name later became Sollitt Construction Co. He retired around 1920 and moved to Florida.

50. *Inland Architect* 7, no. 2 (September 1888): 17.

The group returned to Chicago on Monday morning just in time to reach their respective offices by the usual eight o'clock starting time. Work at the drafting boards undoubtedly suffered, as the weary workers struggled to stay alert until quitting time. There was a resurgence of energy after work, however, when most of them made their way to the club rooms at the Art Institute for the regular Monday meeting. Several matters had to be addressed. Two weeks earlier the club had received an invitation to submit drawings to the Kansas City Exposition,[51] and a small committee had been appointed to collect and forward the drawings. After due consideration it was decided to decline the invitation, since "the time was too short to collect strictly architectural drawings, so much of the club-work has been sketching from nature."[52] In the meantime, secretary W. G. Williamson had received "a communication from the secretary of the Milwaukee exposition inviting the members to send an exhibit of drawings to the coming exposition, which was accepted." President Beaumont directed the committee appointed to collect the Kansas City drawings to transfer its efforts to the Milwaukee Exposition.

Beaumont then appointed a committee consisting of C. A. Kessell, treasurer E. J. Wagner, and himself to select a suitable gift to thank Oliver Sollitt for his courtesy over the past weekend. They chose to present Sollitt with a large photograph of the ruins of the Coliseum in Rome, framed in antique English oak with a suitable inscription handsomely carved in the right-hand corner.[53]

With the evening's business concluded, the speaker—Fritz Wagner, then assistant superintendent of the Northwestern Terra Cotta Company—was introduced. Despite some nodding heads in his audience, Wagner delivered his lecture in a manner appreciated by all, but the discussion that followed was understandably brief, and a tired group of draftsmen went home to a much needed night's rest.

Two weeks later the club received its first formal resignation. It was from George W. Maher, who had recently organized his own practice after several years of working with Joseph Lyman Silsbee. Apparently he felt opening his own office as an architect precluded his continued membership in the club. While his resignation was accepted, Maher continued to take part in club activities, and he subsequently rejoined. His name appears as a member in exhibition catalogs a few years later.

The September issue of the *Inland Architect* published several drawings by club members, including one of a Milwaukee building by Oscar Enders. Enders was still a member of the club but was now working in Milwaukee, where his brother, Frank, an artist, also lived and worked. His presence in Milwaukee may have been part of the reason that much of the September 10 meeting was devoted to making arrangements to accept an invitation to the Milwaukee Exposition. With a fellow club member already in Milwaukee, a trip to the exposition was almost certain to be a success. After a good deal of discussion, it was agreed that all who wished to make the trip should meet after their offices closed at noon on Saturday, September 22, to set off.[54] Oscar Enders agreed to make arrangements for accommodations.

The trip was a decided success. The Chicago, Milwaukee & St. Paul passenger train took the club members directly to downtown Milwaukee, where Frank Enders met them. They were treated to an afternoon tour of the city and were then dropped off at the Republican House Hotel, where they had dinner before visiting the Exposition Building. They found the one hundred drawings they had sent from Chicago hung in a separate, well-lighted room, each one neatly framed. Frank Enders, the head of the Exposition Art Department and a well-regarded artist in his own right, had directed the installation. After seeing the exhibition, the members returned to their hotel and, unlike their experience at Sollitt's farm, had a good night's rest. They rose early on Sunday and took carriages and boats to Jones Island, where they devoted the day to sketching until it was time to take the train back to Chicago.

51. *Sanitary News* 12, no. 237 (August 11, 1888): 184.

52. *Inland Architect* 12, no. 2 (September 1888): 17.

53. *Sanitary News* 12, no. 241 (September 15, 1888): 231.

54. *Sanitary News* 12, no. 244 (October 6, 1888): 244.

*The club's drawings were hung at the Milwaukee Exposition Building, an extraordinary structure (MCHS)*

*Drawing by Oscar Enders (IA)*

The following evening was a regular club meeting where C. A. Kessell presented an essay titled "Vacation Notes Abroad." While his paper was received with courtesy, much of the evening was devoted to recalling the events in Milwaukee. Oscar Enders was thanked for his efforts, and his brother, Frank, was elected an honorary member in thanks for his work on the installation.[55] Two weeks later the members heard from the Enders brothers, thanking them for participating and advising that the drawings would be returned the following week.[56]

*Menu card for the club's third annual banquet (IA)*

The timing was excellent in view of the approaching annual meeting and exhibition. It was agreed that all drawings for the exhibition must be in the hands of the Exhibition Committee by November 10 to give the committee time to properly hang the work. The elegant installation in Milwaukee prompted all concerned to be especially mindful of how the drawings would be seen for the first time by the public in the club's own rooms at the Art Institute. Following the discussion of how and when they were to be handled, President Beaumont introduced club member William Bryce Mundie, who gave a major address titled "Originality in Design."[57]

At the Fourth Annual Meeting of the Chicago Architectural Sketch Club on November 5, three matters were addressed: the annual election was held, the Adjudicating Committee reported on the two most recent competitions, and final arrangements were made for the annual banquet and exhibition only two weeks away.[58] Retiring president George Beaumont opened the meeting by calling on secretary W. G. Williamson, who "gave a brief history of the activity of the club in the past year. He referred to the sketching trips and competitions, which had not been as freely entered into by the members as they should have been. The club, he said, had gained four seniors, three juniors, and five honorary members, and was sailing along on the crest of the billows." Treasurer E. J. Wagner then reported that the club had paid all its bills and that "$400 remained in the coffers."

Nearly every member was present when nominations of officers for the coming year were put forth. After W. G. Williamson was elected president, he immediately took the chair and read a communication from the Adjudicating Committee advising that "in the competition for the best design for a church tower and gable, Oscar Enders was awarded first place; A. Heim [*sic*], second place; and W. G. Williamson, third place." In the entrance doorway competition, A. Heun was given first place; A. W. Hompe, second; and C. B. Schaefer, third. All present agreed that these were indeed winning entries, but at the same time, the officers in particular were critical of their colleagues for not entering competitions more often, as prizes were repeatedly awarded to a small group of regulars. (This concern was one that would be resolved during the next few months, when the Executive Committee announced new incentives for entering club competitions.) It was announced that the syllabus for the coming year was not quite finished but would be ready before the end of the year.[59] The remainder of the evening was spent discussing and assigning duties for the annual banquet and exhibition.

The Third Annual Banquet and Exhibition was held on November 19, 1888, in the club's rooms at the Art Institute.[60] More than two hundred drawings in various media were exhibited, and the members assembled early to enjoy drinks and review the year's work.[61] There was an excellent turnout. Of the fifty-five active and honorary members on the roll, forty-three were present, along with thirteen guests.

Retiring president George Beaumont served as toastmaster at the banquet, and he "rapped for order, which he received in a degree which was complimentary under the circumstances, and called upon" various guests and honorary members to respond to toasts following the elaborate dinner. W. L. B. Jenney, Louis H. Sullivan, and Henry Lord Gay all spoke, as did others. Jenney congratulated the members on the quality of their work and admonished them to enjoy themselves, noting that

55. *Sanitary News* 12, no. 243 (September 29, 1888): 259.

56. *Sanitary News* 12, no. 247 (October 27, 1888): 312.

57. Mundie's address was reprinted in full in *Inland Architect* 12, no. 5 (November 1888): 53–55. It was one of the longest papers delivered to the club, and Mundie always considered it to be one of the most important statements of his design philosophy.

58. Ibid., 58; *Sanitary News* 13, no. 249 (November 10, 1888): 18.

59. The *Sanitary News* published a partial syllabus on December 8, 1888, and the final version was printed on page 98 of the January 1889 *Inland Architect*.

60. The annual banquet was treated extensively in both *Inland Architect* 7, no. 7 (December 1888): 70–71, and the opening article in the *Sanitary News* for November 19, 1888. The quotations and comments hereinafter regarding that event are taken from these two accounts.

61. *Inland Architect* 7, no. 7 (December 1888): 70.

"when later they engaged in active professional work . . . the routine and detail of office work" would reduce "opportunities for sketching and watercolor work."

Sullivan responded to a toast to the Adjudicating Committee with the suggestion that "the draftsman's work should grow, and each design have a definite purpose. A certain conception should be formulated before the design was commenced." Sullivan was obviously harking back to his days at the École des Beaux-Arts, when it was customary for students to quickly prepare an *esquisse*, a rapid but thoughtful response to a written problem. That initial response, once approved by the faculty, was expected to be developed in detail, without major revisions, in the weeks that followed, before a specified deadline. He suggested that in the club's competitions there should be some well-defined program, as they were, in his opinion, far too general. As an example, Sullivan noted that "hitherto it had been a competition for a tower in a park. The rule did not say whether it was to be 50 or 100 feet high, or whether the park was level or hilly." He went on to suggest that the work should "invite a critical spirit but from two standpoints, that of recreation and of serious work. It would not be amiss for the club to pay more attention to systematic and serious work . . . Without . . . serious study there can be no architects. Serious study compels the study and appreciation of values." Clearly, Sullivan was concerned with the direction the club was taking. He and a number of others felt that while watercolor work and outings for sketching were valuable, members should address themselves to matters of a more architectural nature.

William B. Mundie, who had become increasingly active in club affairs during the previous year, responded to a toast to the Chicago Architectural Sketch Club, commenting that "it had been said that the club was organized for the purpose of infringing upon the rights of the architects in general. This was not true. The club was organized for the development of the artistic talent of the members. It had also been said that it was sort of a trades' union, but no greater insult could have been offered to the members than that. The club was not organized for anything but solid work."

The evening was not all seriousness. Recitations and songs composed for the occasion were performed by both members and guests. One of the songs written by club poet R. B. Williamson and sung to "Vive la Compagnie" was printed in its entirety by the *Inland Architect* in its article on the annual banquet and exhibition opening. (It was noted that publication would show "how some things that seem immensely funny when spoken or sung under certain conditions look in cold type.")

In Chicago's fair city
There's buildings so pretty,
Designed by the boys of the C. A. S. C.
The boys are so jolly,
They're artists, by golly,
And on every street corner their buildings you see.
*Chorus.*—Then here's to the artists,
For they are the smartest;
Then hurrah for the boys of the C. A. S. C.

There is Fraenkel and Enders,
They go on great benders
When out with the boys of the C. A. S. C.;
They go home at night,
Hang their hats on the light,
And hate in the morning the sunlight to see.—*Chorus.*

There is W. B. Mundie,
Who gets up on Sunday,
And sketches the sun coming over the lake:
(The day-breaking sinner)
Then goes home to dinner,
And fills up his basket on pud, pie and cake.—*Chorus.*

There's Williamson's brother—
He's just such another—
He stays out at night and paints red the West Side;
This night-prowling divil
Is ever quite civil,
And a downright good heart is cased in his hide.—*Chorus.*

Our treasurer's a lalla;
He collects every dollar
That belongs to the club called the C. A. S. C
And those in arrears
Will get boxed on the ears;
If they do not pay up they will get the G. B.—

Now at every club meeting,
When Beaumont is speaking,
And arguing a question with Gibb, don't you :
Parliamentary rules
Were made but for fools,
And not for the boys of the C. A. S. C. ?—*Chc*

Now while you are here
Partake of good cheer,
And make the night merry as long's you can s
So drink and be jolly,
This night of our folly,
And remember this banquet of C. A. S. C.—*C*

One guest, D. G. Phimister, who would later have a major influence on club activities, recited a selection from *Macbeth* and the "Charge of the Light Brigade." He was called back for an encore recitation of "Spartacus." Several speakers noted that prizes had been awarded to various members during the year but the only award of the evening was given to Oscar Enders—a baseball bat "bearing the quotation from Shakespeare: 'Fairy-like, I fanned the air three time,' in commemoration of his 'slugging' at the ball game last summer."[62] The banquet closed with the singing of "Auld Lang Syne" in chorus.

The reviews of the exhibition were almost unanimously positive. The *Sanitary News* reported that "the walls are this week covered with the handiwork of the members in water-colors, pen, and pencil, the first-named predominating. The exhibition is much superior in design and execution to the work of last year; and while the talent of the club is fully appreciated by all, it is at the same time an agreeable surprise to note the general standard of excellence to which their work has attained."

The *Inland Architect*'s comments were in a similar vein: "In regard to the exhibit of watercolor work, which represented not the year's work of the club, but its recreation, too much cannot be said in praise. From a purely artistic standpoint it is probably the finest exhibit of amateur watercolor sketching ever exhibited in Chicago, and whatever the draftsmen may be in the designing and constructing of buildings, as artists, with a conception for color and a skill in interpreting and expressing it, the members of the Chicago Architectural Sketch Club certainly stand well in the line of watercolor artists." Clearly, the sketching outings had produced nonarchitectural works that were a major part of the Third Annual Exhibition.

Perhaps the most enigmatic article on the club's 1888 exhibition was published by the *American Architect and Building News* in its "Chicago" column.[63] Although no catalog has ever been found for any club exhibition prior to 1894, the correspondent wrote that "there were more than two hundred numbers in the neatly printed catalogue, and a very great majority of the subjects were landscape in water-color—a class of work to which the club seems to have especially devoted itself in the last twelve months." He went on to praise the work highly. (This article certainly constitutes evidence that the club published catalogs of its early exhibitions.)

Two weeks later, the club held its first meeting under the newly elected officers.[64] The coming year's syllabus was not quite ready,[65] but the first competition was announced. It was to be a design for a stone mantel, and would close on December 31, four weeks later. The chair also announced that New York architect F. A. Wright, who had been a guest at the club's annual banquet two weeks earlier, had handed the president an invitation for the members to submit designs to the New York Architectural League's exhibition opening on December 22.[66]

The December 17, 1888, meeting was to have been a regular club evening, but instead it was the occasion of an extremely important announcement. After several weeks of quiet discussion, it was announced that "Robert Clark, of Clark, Raffen & Co., has given $1,000 to the Chicago Architectural Sketch Club."[67] The money was to be put into the hands of three trustees, who would invest it. The income would be "devoted to the purchase of two medals, gold and silver, which are to be competed for annually, under the management of a jury of the club, the first competition taking place next October. The judges are to be five architects, and the medals are to be awarded at the annual banquet in December. Any draughtsman under thirty can compete. Robert Clark also gave the dies and medals for the first year. Henry Lord Gay, of the Institute of Building Arts, has been active in arranging the details."

The Robert Clark Testimonial Competition, as it was called, catapulted the Chicago Architectural Sketch Club onto the national scene. It was to become a major element of the club's activities for the next decade.

62. *Sanitary News* 13, no. 251 (November 24, 1888): n.p.

63. *American Architect and Building News* 24, no. 678 (December 22, 1888): 289. Articles such as the "Chicago" column were published without bylines, although it has been suggested that Peter B. Wight was the journal's Chicago correspondent, which can be supported stylistically by comparing the "Chicago" columns of this period with Wight's other writings.

64. This event was reported in the same issue of the *Inland Architect* as the annual meeting, but in a separate article on page 82.

65. While the syllabus was "not quite complete," a partial listing of forthcoming events was published in *Sanitary News* 13, no. 253 (December 8, 1888): 63. The full syllabus was printed in *Inland Architect* 12, no. 9 (January 1889): 98.

66. *Inland Architect* 7, no. 7 (December 1888): 82. This article reported that the Architectural League of New York would hold a special reception on the evening of the exhibition opening. Immediately following was an item reporting that "the draftsmen of Detroit organized a sketch club about seven months ago," clearly modeled on the Chicago club.

67. This announcement was also made by means of a press release, first published in *Sanitary News* 13, no. 256 (December 29, 1888): 98.

National Exhibition
Architectural Drawings
and
Sketches

Pikes Opera House
Nov. 20 – 26. 1889
Held under the auspices of the
Cincinnati Architectural
Club

*The cover of the catalog issued by the Cincinnati Architectural Club during the joint convention of the American Institute of Architects and Western Association of Architects (IA)*

# Robert Clark
# and National Recognition

CHAPTER FOUR

The last day of 1888 was the occasion of a New Year's Eve affair at the rooms of the Chicago Architectural Club. The recently completed syllabus for 1889[1] called for a "Reception to Mr. Robert Clark, donor of gold and silver medals."[2] The evening began with the members and their guests "participating in the bounties of the buffet, prolonged by social intercourse,"[3] and in due time the meeting was called to order by president W. G. Williamson.

Williamson opened with the following: "Members of the Sketch Club, the object of our meeting tonight is simply to receive Mr. Robert Clark, the liberal donor to our club of $1,000, for the purpose of establishing a fund to supply a gold and silver medal to be awarded in competitions of the club, to members who are under thirty years of age. The idea is, as I understand it, to invest this $1,000 at six or seven per cent, and the interest thus derived is to be expended in these medals."

The Robert Clark Testimonial Competition was a result of the efforts of Henry Lord Gay, the editor of the *Building Budget*, who had worked with architects Boyington, Adler, Jenney, and Burnham to encourage Clark's donation. He also had the advice and council of the immediate past president of the club, George Beaumont, and the current president, W. G. Williamson. These men, probably with substantial input from Robert Clark's old friend Dankmar Adler, met several times with Clark. The final terms of the gift provided for an annual competition that would not be confined to members of the Chicago Architectural Sketch Club, but would be national in scope.

A resolution had been prepared by a committee of five architects who had defined the rules of the competition as follows:

Chicago, December 14, 1888

*Resolved:* That the donation of Mr. Robert Clark will best serve the interests of the architectural profession if its income be applied for the award of a medal or medals, to be annually awarded to the victor or victors in an architectural competition by draftsmen (not practicing architects, and under thirty years of age), these competitions to be instituted under the auspices of the Chicago Architectural Sketch Club. In case of the disbandment of the C.A.S.C., the fund to revert for the same purpose to the Western Association

*Robert Clark (CN)*

1. *Inland Architect* 7, no. 9 (January 1889): 98. The syllabus for 1889 started on December 3, 1888, and concluded on November 18, 1889.

2. Robert Clark (1829–1909) was born in Scotland and moved to Chicago with his parents in 1849. In 1854, he and his father formed John Clark & Son to supply iron of all kinds to builders. In 1867, the firm became Clark, Raffen & Co. Clark's father was lost in the Chicago Fire, but the firm continued to operate under the name of Aetna Iron Works, providing iron to various Chicago buildings including the Central Music Hall Building designed by Dankmar Adler in 1879. Adler and Clark became lifelong friends. Clark had a strong sense of civic duty and was elected alderman of the Sixteenth Ward of Chicago in 1864. He held the office of supervisor of North Town, Chicago, in 1869–70 and from 1870 to 1874 was a member of the Chicago Board of Education. He later served in the same capacity for Cook County. He was also deeply involved in the Fullerton Avenue Presbyterian Church. Clark had a broad interest in the arts and wrote at least one book, *Our Twelve Months' Tour*, published in 1885, an account of a yearlong vacation he had taken two years earlier with his wife and daughter. He died in 1909 at the age of eighty.

3. This quotation and those that follow regarding the New Year's Eve meeting, unless otherwise noted, are from *Inland Architect* 12, no. 9 (January 1889): 96–97.

of Architects, or to such architectural association with which it may become merged, unless the trustees, when appointed, shall deem it wise at any time to transfer the said income over, for the same purpose as above mentioned, to a school devoted to architectural education which may be hereafter established in Cook county, in which case at the option of the said trustees, they may cease to apply said income to the sketch club competitions, and instead thereof, use it for providing medals for competitions of a similar character in the school proposed, and under rules found by its faculty; it being understood that the medals presented at these annual competitions shall be known as the "Robert Clark Testimonial." It is decided (by this committee appointed to suggest the disposition of the fund contributed by Mr. Clark), that he shall appoint his own trustees to carry out the resolutions as above provided.

It is the sense of this committee, and we believe will be the unanimous voice of the architectural profession, when informed of this testimonial, that Mr. Robert Clark has, in his voluntary offering, created a precedent which we hope and believe will extend to a reality, the possibilities of which are outlined in this resolution, namely, a school of architecture established in Cook county.

And we hereby tender to him the warmest expression of our appreciation of his kindness.

> William W. Boyington,
> Dankmar Adler,
> W. L. B. Jenney,
> Daniel H. Burnham,
> Henry Lord Gay.[4]

The five-man committee that prepared the resolution was made up of the individuals involved in negotiating the award. This resolution would be their final act as a group. It is clear that they took their task seriously, and the basic rules laid down in the resolution were followed by the club. (Just why the reference to "a school devoted to architectural education" was included was not immediately apparent, but that issue would be addressed by the club in the future.) Robert Clark did appoint trustees for the fund. W. G. Williamson and Alexander Kirkland were named as the first two and, in view of his work in arranging for the gift, Henry Lord Gay was probably the third.[5] After the donation was announced, the club assumed rather broad powers in the implementation of the competition, including the decision that five architects would serve on the jury, three from Chicago and two from out of town.[6] They agreed that the medals would be awarded at the annual banquet and that the first competition would take place starting in October of 1889. (Later, when sufficient funds had accumulated, the club elected to offer a third-prize bronze medal in addition to the gold and silver medals Clark had offered, as well as bronze medals for honorable mention and CASC complimentary.) These decisions had all been made by the time the reception for Robert Clark was held.[7]

After President Williamson's brief description of Clark's offer, he added, "Mr. Clark is present, and we would be pleased to hear from him." Clark spoke to the assembled members, and his remarks were recorded and printed verbatim in the *Inland Architect*. "Mr. Chairman," he said, "I am somewhat at a loss . . . I am an old man of sixty years of age, but I'm somewhat of a young man too. I believe in the progress of art . . . in the scintillations of genius. I believe you young gentlemen . . . have a grand future before you . . . I am simply an old blacksmith . . . nothing more . . . who has a slight appreciation of art and wants to do what he can toward its development in his adopted country."

4. *Inland Architect* 12, no. 9 (January 1889): 98.

5. *Sanitary News* 13, no. 256 (December 29, 1888): 98.

6. *Sanitary News* 13, no. 263 (February 16, 1889).

7. *Inland Architect* 12, no. 9 (January 1889): 96.

Following Clark's initial comments, secretary C. A. Kessell stood and suggested, "I do not think we can do a better thing, or honor ourselves more than by adding a blacksmith to our preferred list. I think we need a blacksmith in our organization and I would like to nominate Mr. Robert Clark as an honorary member of the Chicago Architectural Sketch Club, and make a motion to that effect." The motion received several seconds from the floor and was then carried by acclamation. Clark was to remain an honorary member until his death two decades later.

Robert Clark's generous act had come as a surprise to most of the club members on that New Year's Eve. Medals for the efforts of young draftsmen were not, however, unknown to them. Oscar Enders, who had just learned that the New York Architectural League had awarded him a silver medal, then rose to speak on his own good fortune. "My joy knows no bounds," he said. "You can all imagine how a young man would feel being the possessor of a medal won in a competition. You are all well aware that I, one of your fellow-workers, have been successful in the New York League competition, and right here I will say I owe all to the Chicago Architectural Sketch Club. If I had staid where I was four years ago, I would have been nothing more than a vampire draftsman. An institution of this kind can do a vast amount of good. It incites one to progress in design and construction, and affords the glorious opportunity to argue the intricate points of the profession."[8]

Enders's remarks set the tone for a second, surprise announcement. After Robert Clark's initial comments, Robert Craik McLean noted that "Mr. D. G. Phimister has also provided funds for a medal to be competed for."[9] Phimister was present as well, and his remarks indicate that he was a bit perturbed at being overshadowed by Clark's gift. He announced that he had "a word or two . . . to say . . . in regard to this medal question," and went on to observe that he had been "sitting at dinner with Mr. Williamson. It was, I believe, previous to Mr. Clark's donation, and we were talking casually of the club, when it came into my head that your young men would be benefited by having a medal to be contested for, and under the impulse of the moment, I said I would give a $50 gold medal to be competed

8. Little is known of D. G. Phimister (1846–1911). He was listed, in 1893, as a carpenter member of the Builders and Traders' Exchange. After 1892, he was also listed as an honorary member of the Chicago Architectural Sketch Club.

*Oscar Enders received a silver medal from the New York Architectural League for this 1888 design (IA)*

*Alfred P. Evans's 1892 design won a New York Architectural League gold medal (IA)*

for." He continued in the same vein for a few minutes, but the question of his donation was not mentioned again that evening.

The Clark and Phimster medals were not the first such prizes offered to draftsmen. The practice of awarding medals by architectural clubs had been inaugurated by the Architectural League of New York two years earlier. Members of The Chicago Architectural Sketch Club had already been successful in the New York competitions. In the first annual competition sponsored by the Architectural League of New York, Chicago's William Bryce Mundie had been awarded the silver medal for second place. The following year, as noted above, Oscar Enders won the silver medal and Robert C. Spencer, who was still working in Boston but was to become a prominent member of the Chicago Club in a few years, was given an honorable mention in the same competition. Oddly, both Mundie's and Ender's drawings were not published by the League until the 1889–90 catalog of the New York Exhibition was published. The fifth (1889–90) and sixth (1890–91) Architectural League competitions had no Chicagoans on the list of honorees, but in the seventh (1891–92) there were several entries from Chicago, including all three Garden brothers, Hugh, Frank, and Edward. More important were the winners, with Alfred P. Evans of Chicago taking the gold, and Hobart A. Walker of Oak Park, Illinois, awarded the silver medal.[9] These awards undoubtedly spurred both Clark and Phimister to come forward with their offers.

Ex-president George Beaumont was also asked to speak, and he brought up the subject, often discussed in the past, of the need for a school of architecture in Chicago. He suggested that "Mr. Clark's donation . . . [could be] the nucleus of a great architectural school in this city . . . There is no reason in the world why we should not have a school . . . that shall be second to none anywhere." R. C. McLean then recounted at length his own long-standing efforts to start an architectural school in Chicago. He had done all he could to convince his colleagues in the architectural community that such a school was urgently needed and had gone so far as to visit the president of Northwestern University in suburban Evanston to try to induce him to support the idea. Although he had not succeeded, he was still unwilling to give up. He ended his comments by asserting, "We will overcome all difficulties. We will have a school of architecture in Chicago."

Robert Clark immediately responded, "We will not only have an architectural school in Chicago, but we will raise an endowment fund for it. I stand ready today

9. Evans became a member of the Club in 1893, but Walker never did.

*Hobart A. Walker's 1892 design received a silver medal from the New York Architectural League (IA)*

to place $5,000 on that basis—I mean toward a permanent fund for a permanent school for the education of Architects." The evening continued with a vigorous discussion about starting a school of architecture and, just after the New Year arrived, the members adjourned.

The generosity of Clark and Phimister immediately brought the Chicago Architectural Sketch Club members to the attention of their colleagues throughout the United States. The January 1889 issue of the *Inland Architect* devoted nearly half its editorial page to the forthcoming competitions resulting from the two gifts, as well as to the already established Architectural League of New York competition.[10]

The club's Executive Committee immediately began planning for both the Clark and Phimister competitions. It also had the simultaneous task of managing the activities of the club, no small responsibility since the syllabus called for a meeting every two weeks and in-house competitions every month. A total of sixteen speakers were scheduled for the 1889 year. (A major change, however, was that the scheduled lectures were all by regular or honorary members of the club, most of whom were prominent members of Chicago's architectural community. Outsiders did not appear.) Furthermore, alternate meeting nights were devoted to sketching in the club rooms, continuing a precedent now firmly established.

The first meeting of the new year, on January 14, featured a stereopticon presentation of views from Egyptian ruins with an accompanying lecture by John K. Allen.[11] Two weeks later, W. L. B. Jenney read his paper, "A Few Practical Hints."[12] That same evening, the club's Adjudicating Committee reported on its split decision on the results of the competition for a stone fireplace. T. O. Fraenkel, Oscar Enders, and W. E. Kleinpell took the first three places. R. A. Dennell, A. Heun, and C. D. Schaefer received favorable comments as well. It was also announced that the club competition for a "wrought-iron gate for a residence with stone posts" was closed.[13] During the discussion of the competition results, the chair advised that the club had received an invitation from the publishers of *Railway Review* maga-

10. *Inland Architect* 12, no. 9 (January 1889): 90.

11. *Inland Architect* 13, no. 1 (January 1889): 12. John K. Allen was the editor of the *Building Budget*. He eventually became an honorary member of the CASC. He had a great interest in architecture and as long as he was at the helm of the *Building Budget*, the activities of the club were regularly reported there.

12. Ibid.

13. Ibid.

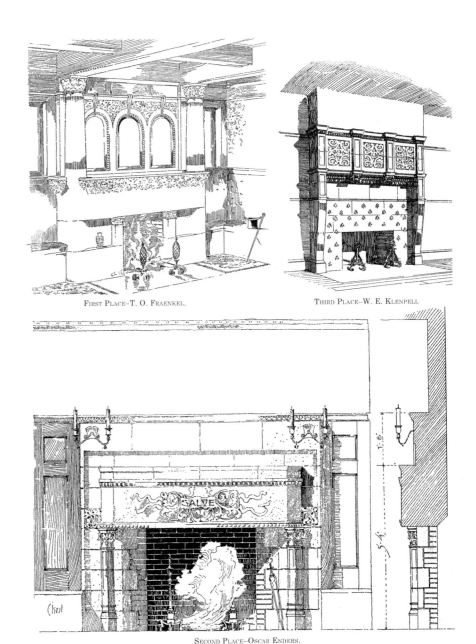

FIRST PLACE–T. O. FRAENKEL.

THIRD PLACE–W. E. KLENPELL.

SECOND PLACE–OSCAR ENDERS.

*The top three prizewinners in the stone fireplace design competition were published in the* Inland Architect

zine, offering a prize of twenty-five dollars for the best railway depot that could be constructed for five thousand dollars. The proposal was referred to the Executive Committee for consideration.

The evening ended with a lengthy, rather spirited discussion of the possibility of revising the bylaws to admit members from other cities. Similar clubs throughout the country, specifically those in New York and Boston, had such bylaws and there was some interest in following those cities' lead. The matter was tabled for the time being, but two weeks later, on February 11, a resolution was drafted and presented to the members. It proposed that "non-resident" members be allowed all the privileges of membership except those of voting and holding office. An addendum to the resolution provided for Chicago members who left the city for a year or more to have their dues reduced. The resolution was discussed at length and it was agreed that it would be put to a vote in four weeks.[14]

14. *Sanitary News* 13, no. 263 (February 16, 1889): 184.

A month later, the resolution was passed unanimously, and the bylaws were revised to admit out-of-town members.[15] The bylaw amendments were not specified, but apparently covered the admission of both nonresidents and "worthy men of artistic talent as associate members to be known as sustaining members," which was noted later that year at the annual meeting held in December of 1889.[16] It had been the original intent of the club to invite only draftsmen to be members, but as time passed and the club's activities became more and more interesting, practicing architects were becoming anxious to participate. Many of the original members had become "architects," simply because they had opened their own offices. These men continued as members of the club, but until the last half of 1889, new memberships were restricted to draftsmen.

It was now becoming apparent that the club had reached a point where the organization should be formalized by incorporation, a task that took several weeks but was done in June of 1889. The incorporators were William G. Williamson, William B. Mundie, Oswin C. Christian, Charles A. Kessell, Ernest J. Wagner, Theodore O. Fraenkel, and Frank C. Linden. The corporate documents stated that the "object for which it is formed is the mutual improvement of members and the advancement of knowledge of art and architecture."[17]

*The first Robert Clark jury: Dankmar Adler, Lorado Taft, Samuel Treat, Henry Ives Cobb, and Nathan Ricker*

The major issue before the club at the February 11 meeting, however, concerned the selection of a jury for the first Robert Clark Testimonial Competition. Some members were in favor of having the regular Adjudicating Committee of Jenney, Root, and Sullivan handle this duty, but others felt it was too great a burden to impose on them and, since they were all honorary members of the club, there might be an appearance of favoritism to club members. It had already been decided that the jury should consist of five members, three from Chicago and two from elsewhere. The club, meeting as a committee of the whole, chose the jury. Numerous names were suggested and by consensus the members agreed on the following: Dankmar Adler, Henry Ives Cobb, Lorado Taft, N. Clifford Ricker, and Richard M. Hunt.[18] (Adler was the only one who had been involved in the original donation and the drafting of the resolution establishing the ground rules.) All were contacted and all but Hunt accepted. His place was assumed by architect Samuel A. Treat. The selection of the Phimister competition jury had been accomplished in the first week of June by simply asking the regular Adjudicating Committee to add that task to their list of duties.[19] They accepted without comment.

Before adjourning the February 11 meeting, the club was pleased to accept an invitation from fellow member Paul Mueller, then with Adler & Sullivan, for another visit to the construction site of the Auditorium Building on Saturday, February 23, 1889. The building, which was dominating the architectural scene in Chicago, was the city's largest and had been for some time its tallest. (Mueller, Adler & Sullivan's site superintendent, would remain with the firm for several more years before he es-

15. *Inland Architect* 13, no. 4 (April 1889): 59.

16. *Inland Architect* 14, no. 7 (December 1889): 80–81.

17. The original corporate documents, dated June 19, 1889, are still extant in the Illinois secretary of state's office. Copies are in the author's collection.

18. *Sanitary News* 13, no. 263 (February 16, 1889): 184.

19. *Sanitary News* 14, no. 279 (June 8, 1889): 69.

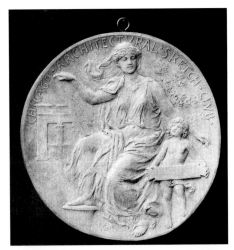

*Plaster model of the Clark medal by sculptor Johannes Gelert (IA)*

*The Auditorium Building under construction on October 1, 1888: although it had progressed a great deal since the club's first visit a year before, it would have been only minimally further along when the club returned to visit the site again in early 1889 (AIC/SC)*

20. *Sanitary News* 14, no. 274 (May 4, 1889): 6.

21. *Inland Architect* 13, no. 4 (April 1889): 59–60.

22. Johannes Sophus Gelert (1852–1923) was a logical choice for the job. A tenant at the Art Institute of Chicago, where the sketch club had their club rooms, Gelert had modeled several sculptural elements for John Wellborn Root's buildings, as Root was a close friend of his, and had also produced the memorial sculpture commemorating the Haymarket Riots.

23. *Inland Architect* 16, no. 2 (March 1890).

24. The only known example of one of the medals is in the collection of the author. It is silver, measures an inch and a half in diameter, and was awarded to W. L. Pinkham of San Francisco in 1891. It was discovered in 1999 in New York City at a shop dealing with medallic art.

tablished himself as an independent contractor.) There was a large turnout for the tour, and the members enjoyed the visit very much. (One wonders if Frank Lloyd Wright, a recent employee of Adler & Sullivan, participated as well.) Several weeks later, in May of 1889, Adler & Sullivan would move into a temporary space on the tenth floor of the Wabash Avenue side of the building, where the office would remain until the sixteenth-floor space was finished in July.[20]

The pressure of other matters seems to have delayed entries for the February competition for a country house in the colonial style, and entrants were given a two-week extension. The members also agreed to have a competition for the design of the Phimister medal. At the March 11 meeting, it was reported that fifteen designs had been received (although it had been hoped that each member would submit a design). The plan seems to have been to incorporate the various ideas into a single composite design.[21] The Phimister medal design was never published, but the competition itself did proceed.

The Clark medal was not a club design. It was modeled by Chicago sculptor Johannes Gelert,[22] who maintained a studio in the Art Institute Building at 200 Michigan Avenue in Chicago, the same building where the club had its rooms. A plaster model of the medal was published in the *Inland Architect* in March of 1890, several months after the medals were struck.[23] In his design of the medal, Gelert provided for a small, raised "ribbon" on the reverse side, where the date could be added. The recipient's name was engraved on the edge.[24] The first medals were to be awarded in 1889 at the Chicago Architectural Sketch Club's annual banquet.

*William B. Mundie's winning entry for the competition for a wrought-iron gate is on the far right. Others from left were submitted by H.C. Trost (Second Place), Oscar Enders (Honorable Mention), and below Mundies drawing is Richard Schmidt's (Honorable Mention), and finally Arthur Harris (Third Place) drawing at lower right.*

The club was now devoting an extraordinary amount of effort to competitions, in addition to its regularly scheduled activities. The Adjudicating Committee reported in February that the entries for the wrought-iron gate competition had been reviewed, and W. B. Mundie, H. C. Trost, and A. Heun had been awarded first, second, and third place, respectively. Three other club members received honorable mentions.[25]

The membership accepted the invitation from *Railway Review* to participate in a competition to design a suburban railway station. Submissions were due by March 28. A number of entries were received and promptly adjudicated, and there was a twenty-five-dollar prize for the best design. The Executive Committee chose to divide the prize money into first, second, and third prizes of twelve, eight, and five dollars.[26] The prize money was distributed on April 8 to T. O. Fraenkel, Harry Braun, and W. G. Williamson. Awards for an in-house competition for a club bookcase were announced on the same evening, with Arthur Heun, W. H. Henderson, and R. A. Dennell taking the honors.

The Chicago club's heavy involvement in competitions was not overlooked by clubs from other cities, largely because winning entries were usually published in the architectural journals. The club often received requests from other groups asking for advice on conducting competitions. For example, at the February 25 meeting, president W. G. Williamson noted that he had received a letter from the Columbus, Ohio, sketch club on the subject of competitions, as well as a communication from New York inquiring as to the best means of organizing a sketch club.[27] The Architectural League of New York was not, apparently, serving the needs of its younger members in regard to sketch, design, and competitions.

Competitions took up much of the members' free time. That work was generally done outside the club rooms. During the 1888–89 year, those competitions varied widely. Some were extremely complex, such as the colonial-style country house or the design for a city residence on a twenty-five-foot lot. Others were smaller but perhaps no less demanding, such as the March effort to design a bookcase for a draftsman and the last project of the year, in December, a menu card for the annual banquet and exhibition. The most demanding, however, were the Clark Testimonial Competition and the Phimister Medal Competition.

The Phimister medal was offered on a onetime basis, and entries were restricted to members of sketch clubs throughout the United States, with no age limitations. The Clark medal, on the other hand, was open to any draftsman

25. *Sanitary News* 13, no. 265 (March 2, 1889): 208.

26. Ibid.

27. Ibid.

*Theodore Fraenkel's first-place design for the Railway Station Competition (RR)*

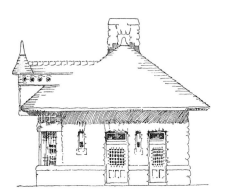

*W. G. Williamson's Railway Station Competition entry (RR)*

*Henry Braun's second-place design (RR)*

under the age of thirty. The programs for the two competitions were announced and published in early July of 1889.[28] The *Inland Architect* offered only brief editorial comment when the programs were published, noting that a circular of information was available regarding either competition from the secretary of the club in care of the *Inland Architect.* The announcement for the Clark competition read as follows:

> *To the Architectural Draftsmen of the United States:*
>
> Mr. Robert Clark, of Chicago, being desirous of actively aiding the development of architectural design and draftsmanship in this country, has placed at the disposal of the Chicago Architectural Sketch Club, a sum of money, the interest of which is intended to provide the award of a gold and a silver medal to be given annually to the victors in a competition, free to architectural draftsmen under thirty years of age and not practicing architects.
>
> To the undersigned committee has been intrusted the working out of a programme for this year's competition, which is as follows: Designs, illustrated by drawings drawn to a scale of 1/8 inch to the foot, are required for an apartment house for tenants of moderate means, say with an annual income of from $1,200 to $1,800. This building is to be four stories in height, and is to have basement and attic. No elevator will be required. The site is at the intersection of a boulevard and a side street, its dimensions as shown on the accompanying diagram.
>
> The first story is not to be used for stores. The drawings are to be India ink line drawings, and to consist of plans of basement, first and second stories, of one geometrical elevation, and one perspective. The point of sight of the perspective is to be on a line bisecting the obtuse angle of the site and two hundred feet distant from the same, and fifteen feet above the street grade.

28. Identical, full-text announcements for both competitions appeared in *Inland Architect* 13, no. 8 (July 1889): 102–3; *Building* 11, no. 1 (July 1889): 8; and *Sanitary News* 14, no. 284 (July 6, 1889): 117.

The drawings are to be marked with a symbol or *nom de plume* and accompanied by a sealed envelope marked in the same manner, containing the name and address of the author of the corresponding drawing. All drawings are to be delivered to the secretary of the Chicago Architectural Sketch Club at the Art Institute Building, in Chicago, on or before noon, October 1, 1889.

In awarding the prizes the committee will take into account not only the degree of merit of the draftsmanship but also that of plan and design

> Dankmar Adler, architect,
>
> Henry Ives Cobb, architect,
>
> Lorado Taft, sculptor,
>
> N. Clifford Ricker, architect,
>
> Samuel A. Treat, architect

The Phimister announcement was presented in a similar manner under the heading "The Phimister Medal Competition":

An invitation is extended to all members of sketch clubs in the United States to enter this competition, secretaries of clubs to collect drawings from their members. Drawings to be sent, express paid, to Charles A. Kessell, secretary of Chicago Architectural Sketch Club, Art Institute, Chicago, Illinois, on or before September 23, 1889, and marked Phimister Competition.

The following is the competition in detail as arranged by Architects John W. Root, W. L. B. Jenney and L. H. Sullivan, who will act as judges:

Drawings to be marked with a motto or device, a corresponding motto or device on a sealed envelope containing name and address of competitor.

The problem is a public library for a rich suburb. The library to contain 50,000 volumes; to have a large entrance hall as a gallery for American works of art, and also a summer reading room in the shape of an arcade or colonnade or terrace.

Material and cost not given.

To be two (2) plans, one perspective; two (2) elevations, not shown in the perspective; one sheet of sections. Wash drawings in India ink or sepia. Drawings to be 1'8 inch scale on sheets 22 by 28. Drawings to be sent flat.

Charles A. Kessell, Secretary C.A.S.C.

In early 1889, the club began working closely with allied groups elsewhere in the United States, especially neophyte organizations that needed advice on getting started. William Bryce Mundie took it upon himself to prepare a lengthy paper titled "Sketch Clubs," which he presented to his colleagues at the Chicago Architectural Sketch Club on March 11. It was published the following month in the *Inland Architect*.[29] The same issue included George Beaumont's paper, "History and Development of the Chicago Architectural Sketch Club."[30] These two articles became a blueprint for other groups to follow in forming clubs throughout the country. The club also began responding to requests for exhibition material from other clubs and in May of 1889 the members agreed to send a selection of drawings to the Columbus Sketch Club for exhibition.[31] That club had been formed in 1887 and was modeled after the Chicago club. The drawings it requested were for its first exhibition, held in the rooms of the Orpheus Club in Columbus. St. Louis and Cincinnati also sent material for the exhibition, which opened on July 9; a report in the national architectural press suggests that they operated in a manner very similar to the Chicago Architectural Sketch Club.[32]

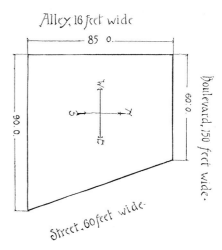

*Site drawing for the first Clark competition, provided to every competitor (IA)*

29. *Inland Architect* 13, no. 4 (April 1889): 55–57.

30. Beaumont had delivered this paper to a meeting of the Illinois State Association of Architects on March 18, 1889, a week after Mundie's paper was delivered to the club.

31. *Sanitary News* 14, no. 278 (June 8, 1889): 69.

32. *Sanitary News* 14, no. 285 (July 14, 1889): 142.

*These drawings for a "25-foot city front" were all well executed but showed little of what was to come in Chicago during the next decade: from left, this page, drawings by W. B. Mundie, first place W. R. Rae, second, R. M. Turner, third, and Richard Wood: Facing page, drawings by T. O. Fraenkel, W. B. Mundie, and T. O. Fraenkel (note that Mundie and Fraenkel each had two entries) (IA)*

This increased fraternization with other clubs, however, did not distract Chicagoans from what they considered a more urgent matter—the need for an architectural school in Chicago. Most local arts' groups were in favor of such a school and, apparently, they looked to the sketch club for leadership. In April 1889, the club's secretary read a communication from the Chicago Woman's Club, which requested that "in the formation of the contemplated architectural school, there should be no distinction between sexes, and that students of either sex should be admitted."[33]

George Beaumont's paper on the history of the sketch club had prompted a vigorous discussion among members of the Illinois State Association of Architects regarding the possibility of establishing an architectural school in Chicago. While not the primary point of his presentation, it had again raised the need for more formal training of young men as architects. Following Beaumont's presentation several members of the Illinois State Association, led by Dankmar Adler and Normand Patton, suggested that their group was ideally suited for "the establishment of such an institution," although one major concern was cost. Adler speculated that "at least $25,000 a year would be required."

Perhaps the most compelling statement was made by Patton, who remarked that Chicago and Western architects were "getting beyond the period in which they could go east for ideas. The Easterners are now coming west for ideas. Chicago architects are originating designs, and there is no reason why Chicago should not be a centre for the West and Northwest." He went on to suggest that a committee be formed to consider the subject. The chair appointed Patton, Henry W. Hill, and George Beaumont, and they were asked to report back at an early date.[34] One of the points to be investigated was the possibility that an existing institution could add an architectural school to its present program. The Newberry

33. *Inland Architect* 13, no. 4 (April 1889): 60.

34. *Sanitary News* 13, no. 268 (March 23, 1889): 243; *Inland Architect* 13, no. 4 (April 1889): 58.

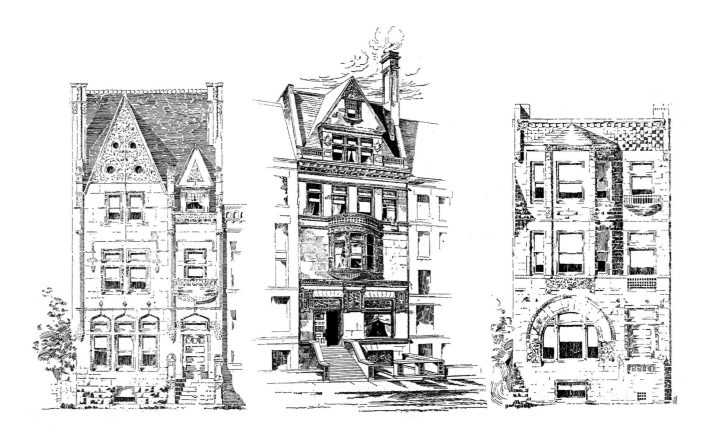

Library, which was then planning a large architectural library, was considered a definite candidate.

Several of the sketch club's late spring and summer lectures focused on keeping interest in this issue alive. An important element in the club's campaign to establish a school was a paper presented by R. A. Dennell on July 1, 1889. Titled "Architectural Students," it outlined a course of study for an aspiring architect that, Dennell suggested, might take "four to eight years." His paper was a carefully crafted statement that essentially said that becoming an architect required both formal study and actual practice. Formal study would address technical issues as well as instruction in the art of drawing, which was, in Dennell's opinion, the essence of architecture. He noted that young men should "draw continually, mostly freehand, from photographs, sculpture, life, nature, casts; in fact, everything. For training in design, entering the C.A.S.C. competitions is fine practice." Dennell supported what the sketch club was doing, but he felt that the technical aspects of architecture needed more attention. The lecture was published in the *Inland Architect* the following September.[35]

Dennell's paper, combined with the efforts of the Illinois State Association of Architects and pressure from other groups, proved to be extremely influential. In September, the Art Institute of Chicago announced that "with the beginning of the new school year, Monday, September 23, classes in architecture will be opened as a part of the regular course of the art school."[36]

While the activities of various organizations clearly had an effect on the decision makers at the Art Institute, one must, in fairness, note that plans for providing instruction in architecture at the institute had been under consideration for some time. In its *Tenth Annual Report,* published in June of 1885, the Art Institute noted

35. *Inland Architect* 14, no. 2 (September 1889): 22.

36. Ibid., 23. This article immediately followed R. A. Dennell's published paper.

*Louis J. Millet (PC)*

*William A. Otis (WHS)*

37. *Tenth Annual Report of the Board of Trustees* (June 1889), 19–20.

38. Louis J. Millet (1856–1923) was born and educated in New York City, and trained at the École des Beaux-Arts and in the architectural section of the École des Arts Decoratifs in Paris. He returned to Chicago around 1880 with his friend George L. Healy, possibly at the suggestion of Louis Sullivan, whom they had met in Paris. In 1881, they formed Healy & Millet, a prominent and successful decorating firm that collaborated on a number of important projects with Adler & Sullivan. Millet taught at the Art Institute of Chicago from 1889 until 1918. He died in Chicago in 1923.

39. William A. Otis (1855–1929) was born in New York. He was educated at the University of Michigan and the École des Beaux-Arts, where he met Louis Sullivan. He moved to Chicago in 1882 and worked in the office of William Le Baron Jenney, where he became a partner in 1886. He left in 1889 to enter private practice and to teach at the new School of Architecture at the Art Institute of Chicago. Otis, who designed a number of notable buildings in and around Chicago, began a ten-year partnership with Edwin H. Clark in 1914; subsequently his firm was known as Otis & Fuller.

40. *Inland Architect* 12, no. 9 (January 1889): 96.

41. *Sanitary News* 14, no. 279 (June 8, 1889): 69.

42. *Sanitary News* 14, no. 278 (June 1, 1889): 58.

43. Fraenkel's essay was published in full in *Inland Architect* 13, no. 8 (July 1889): 100–101. He provided several excellent line drawings as illustrations.

that "the departments of modeling and decorative designing, which were introduced four years ago, are now fully established and doing excellent work. A department of architecture will next urge itself upon our attention, and there are encouraging elements in the interest of the architectural societies and private architects. While it would be impossible to open a comprehensive school of architecture without a considerable endowment, it may be possible to establish certain classes for architectural students at the Art Institute this fall."[37]

The published announcement of the new curriculum advised that classes would be held three evenings a week and that a drafting room would be accessible at all times. The plan was to make the classes "available to draftsmen and other persons engaged in actual practice." Louis J. Millet[38] and William A. Otis[39] were named as regular teachers in the program. It was also noted that "among the well-known architects who have promised to lecture are John W. Root, W. L. B. Jenney, D. H. Burnham, I. K. Pond, John M. Ewen, and it is confidently expected that others equally competent will be added to the list." The announcement also acknowledged the influence of the Chicago Architectural Sketch Club by stating that "the friendly attitude of the architectural societies and of the sketch club toward such a serious effort to found an art school is assured." The article closed with an expression of concern about financing, as no endowment was yet in place. One wonders if this concern was shared by Robert Clark, who had declared only a few months earlier that he stood "ready today to place $5,000 . . . towards a permanent fund for a permanent school for the education of architects."[40] There is no evidence that he ever made good on that promise.

Clark had, of course, been preoccupied with starting the competition for which he had provided funds for gold and silver medals. Perhaps he wanted to see the results of the competition before committing himself further. The Phimister medal drawings were being prepared simultaneously.

The summer season of 1889 included a number of activities that were more recreational than academic. It opened with an exhibition at the club rooms of watercolors executed by the members on sketching trips.[41] It was the first show of strictly nonarchitectural work by the members. Similar events would occur in the future, but seldom with the fanfare that accompanied the annual exhibition of architectural drawings. The baseball game held the year before between Burnham & Root and Cobb & Frost had aroused interest among a number of club members, and this year the club challenged Burnham & Root to a game, calling themselves the Sketch Club Team. The game was played in Washington Park on Decoration Day (i.e., Memorial Day).[42] Sketching trips were still very much in vogue as well. The first one during the summer of 1889 was in late June on a Saturday afternoon.

On July 1, the club secretary received a number of excellent entries for the in-house competition for the design of a "25-foot City Residence, three stories high, French Chateau style." In August, the competition for a hall seat had a similar response, and designs for a "Carved Wood Panel (12 by 16 inches), Indian style, full size" were turned in later that month. That competition may have been inspired by T. O. Fraenkel's essay, "Wood Carving," which he delivered to the club on May 6, 1889.[43] Although the twenty-five-foot city residence designs were excellent, and six of the entries were published, the carved wood panels were severely criticized. Jury member L. H. Sullivan noted that he "found the 'designs very poor and lean and lacking that delicacy of significance characteristic of Indian work.' He did not make a choice." Root and Jenney gave the honors to Joseph Wexelberger for both first and

*Example of a carving by T. O. Fraenkel (IA)*

third prize, to Arthur Heun for second, and to A. C. Berry for fourth. In the hall-seat competition, Sullivan and Root gave the first three places to Fernand Parmentier, O. C. Christian, and T. O. Fraenkel. Jenney added Alexander Robertson's name in lieu of Fraenkel's.[44] Most of these competitions were published, with the winners identified.

The competitions for a house doorway and a rendering in pen and ink from a photograph were both postponed at the August 26 meeting to allow the members to devote time to "the Clark, Phimister, and other monetary competitions."[45] Only the pen-and-ink competition was ever rescheduled. It was put on the agenda the following year for the month of September. The house doorway design was apparently forgotten.

Despite the widespread publicity and the encouragement offered to competitors in the form of valuable and prestigious medals, the response to the Clark and Phimister competitions was disappointing. The Phimister Medal Competition drawings were due on September 23 and the Clark Testimonial Competition drawings a week later. There is no evidence of how many submissions were received for the Phimister competition, but only five entries were submitted in the Clark competition, none of them from Chicago. Not only were very few entries received, but they were, in the eyes of the editor of the *Building Budget,* unacceptable. He wrote that in "both, the results are unsatisfactory, either in consequence or a scarcity of competitors, or in an almost complete lack of originality in design or appreciation of correct rules of architectural composition."[46] Notwithstanding this severe criticism, the *Building Budget* was the only journal to publish the winners. The first- and second-place designs for the Clark competition, by Claude Fayette Bragdon of Rochester, New York, and A. Beatty Orth of Pittsburgh, Pennsylvania, both appeared in the October issue. The drawing by the winner of the Phimister Gold Medal, T. G. Holyoke, was published in the same issue. (A variation of that drawing was printed in the club's first publication, *Sketches,* issued in December of 1892, along with a second drawing that appears to be another Phimister entry, although it was not identified as such.) No Phimister jury report was ever published.

Some hint of what may have gone wrong can be inferred from the information published on the Clark competition drawings in the "Report of Committee on Awards" delivered to the club on October 15, 1889:[47]

> *To the Chicago Architectural sketch club:*
> GENTLEMEN—The undersigned Committee on Competition of the Clark Medals beg leave to report as follows:
> It was their endeavor in making the "programme" for the competition, to impart to the same an element of responsibility and character approximating as nearly as possible to the competitions for work actually to be done by the "draughtsman" in his future career. They regret to have found by the

44. *Building Budget* 11, no. 11 (September 14, 1889): 90.

45. *Inland Architect* 14, no. 2 (September 1889): 24.

46. *Building Budget* 5, no. 8 (October 1889): 122.

47. *Building Budget* 11, no. 19 (November 9, 1889): 157.

*These drawings for a twenty-five-foot French Chateau–style facade are little different from the earlier drawings for a twenty-five-foot street front. Frrom left, R. A. Dennell (mention), Oswin C. Christian, Charley A. Kessell, and C. Bryant Schaefer. On the facing page are the first-place entry by Addison C. Berry, second place by Arthur Heun, third place by Arthur Niemz, and mention by Fernand Parmentier (IA)*

limited number (five) of designs submitted, that the draughtsmen of the United States are not disposed to attempt the solution of problems of a practical nature.

After careful examination of the designs submitted, the Committee awards first prize to the plans marked "Jan-I-Tor," the work of A. Beatty Orth, of Pittsburgh, Pa., and the second prize to the plans marked with an "Ace of Spades," the work of Claude Fayette Bragdon, of Rochester, N.Y. In making this award, your committee endeavored to place itself as nearly as possible in the mental attitude of a capitalist about to make an investment in a building of the kind called for in its "programme," and has based its decision first, upon the qualities of the plan as that of an income producing property under the conditions of the programme, and secondarily, upon the general design of exterior and draughtsmanship.

Respectfully submitted,

> Lorado Taft,
> Henry Ives Cobb,
> N. Clifford Ricker,
> D. Adler,
> *Committee.*[48]

A careful reading of this report reveals that the jury was disappointed that the entrants were not sophisticated or experienced enough to solve the problem in the manner of an architect serving a real client. In preparing the program, the jury had misjudged the abilities of the young draftsmen who, for the most part, were not formally educated.

The five entries in the first Clark Testimonial Competition were not described by the jury, but the gold and silver medal winners were published without comment. Robert Craik McLean did comment on the matter in one of his most critical

48. The fifth member of the committee, Samuel A. Treat, was on a trip to Europe at the time and did not participate in judging the drawings.

statements regarding the work of draftsmen in the United States.[49] His editorial was headlined "Unsatisfactory Result of the Clark Medal Competition." He stated:

> We have not met Mr. Robert Clark since the committee appointed to award the prizes founded by his munificence has had its meeting, but we doubt not that the thought uppermost in his mind after hearing the result of the competition must have been one of regret that there is, among the draftsmen of the United States, so little desire to grapple with the solution of the more burdensome and difficult problems which are daily placed before the architect; that there were but five participants in the first competition for the Clark medal, and that these few participants failed, almost to a man, to comprehend that the problem was not the designing of some vague, indefinite kind of an apartment house, but the designing of an apartment house of certain fixed dimensions, and adapted to the wants of families with a certain stated fixed income. We understand that the committee in fixing this income had in mind the fact that it comprehended within its range the salaries paid the average draftsman; that in propounding this problem it endeavored to come as near home to his actual wants as possible; and that it believed that there would be many among the draftsmen of the United States who had given this matter grave consideration, and were eager to give expression to their thoughts and studies as to how people of their means could be advantageously and satisfactorily housed. This competition seems to demonstrate that the draftsmen of the United States have little desire to fit themselves for the responsibilities and duties which will devolve upon them when they emerge from their present condition into that of full-fledged architects, and that they are only willing to make mere drawings in competition for "a clock tower on a village green," "a monumental bridge," "a country inn," or to solve any problem of the class which calls upon their skill in draftsmanship, but imposes upon them no restraint and no responsibilities. Would it not be time for these young men to begin to

49. *Inland Architect* 14, no. 5 (November 1889): 46–47.

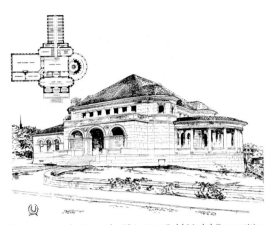

*Prizewinning design in the Phimister Gold Medal Competition by T. G. Holyoke; a watercolor of the same view was published in* Sketches *(BBU)*

50. One Clark entry was sent but never received. The March 1890 issue of the *Inland Architect* published a letter dated February 2, 1890, from one James P. Jamieson of Philadelphia, who described his frustration that his drawings had not been judged because of a mix-up in the delivery.

51. *Building Budget* 5, no. 8 (October 1889): 122. Because the *Building Budget* was issued at the end of the month and the *Inland Architect* at the beginning, the two journals would have been in the hands of subscribers at about the same time.

feel that if ever they wish to rise in the world, if ever they wish to become architects with large practice they must be ready at all times to face problems involving limitations and conditions of every conceivable character, desirable and undesirable, and that, very often, the more distasteful, the more harassing, the more embarrassing the limitations and conditions of a given problem intrusted to them, the greater must be their effort to secure a satisfactory result, and that their usefulness, and, therefore, their success in future life will be measured by the ability displayed by them in handling these difficult and disagreeable tasks.

The dearth of entries received in the Clark competition can also probably be attributed to the program, which was beyond the abilities of most draftsmen under thirty.[50] It was complex, requiring skills beyond the ability to draw well. A workable solution had to be found before the drawings could be executed and many potential participants simply weren't up to it. This problem may also explain why the results of the Phimister competition were equally disappointing.

In the October 1889 issue of the *Building Budget*, which appeared at about the same time as the November issue of the *Inland Architect*, the editorial addressed the same problem discussed by McLean.[51] After a few comments concerning the two competitions and what amounted to a failure, the writer, probably Henry Lord Gay, asked a rhetorical question, "How can competitions be more ably arranged to enlist the true spirit of architectural ambitions?" He went on to say that "to successfully solve such problems, or even to attempt their elucidation, is of greater importance to the *architectural* draughtsmen than any other class of designing, if he aspires to become a practicing architect. But the inclinations of club members seem to lead them to ignore these important practical lessons. They prefer to cover the walls of their club rooms with hastily sketched water colors—clever drawings from nature made during holiday rambles. Some of the members

*Julius Harder's design for the Phimister competition was not identified as such, or as a winner, when it was published in* Sketches

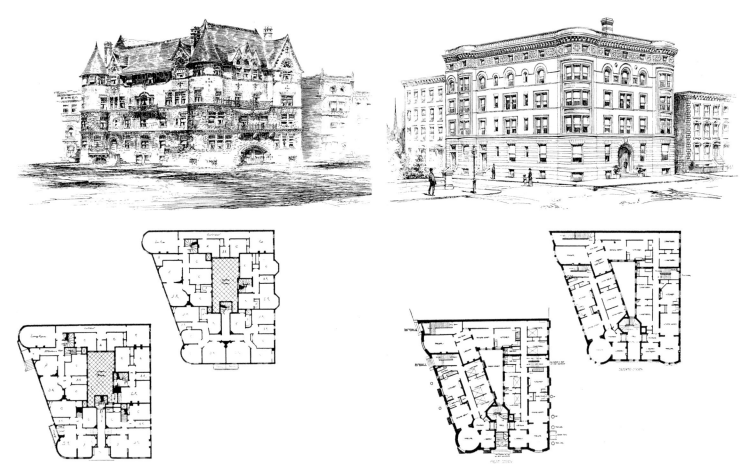

*Only five entries were received in the first Clark Testimonial Competition, none of which were exceptional; Claude Bragdon's design, at right above, took the gold medal, while the drawing on the left by A. Beatty Orth, was awarded the silver medal (BBU)*

of the C.A.S.C. are superior water color artists, but when they indulge in the pastime of sketching to the entire exclusion of practical studies, their performances parallel the acrobatic evolutions of a show company of Zouaves; these flights of clever colorings of sunlight and shade effects on objects, on land and water, these pretty pictures, have no closer relation to the fixed rules of architectural composition, to the laws of construction, than do the lightening like evolutions, somersaults and one leg balances of the Zouaves, to the strict regulations and thorough discipline of the real soldier." The column concluded with the statement that "the disappointment in the results of these two competitions should prove salutary to the outgrowth of a praiseworthy success in the future of the Architectural Sketch Clubs. Particularly the C.A.S.C. can ill afford to have a repetition of this year's competitions. They must live worthy of their name. An architectural sketch club is not a water color society, it implies something more important; it is a preparatory school, and such problems as have recently been laid before it, which it has so prominently neglected, must be taken up as its all important work. Its friends and patrons expect it of them." In spite of these comments, the club members did not become discouraged. The Phimister competition was a onetime event, but the Clark Testimonial Competition was to continue into the foreseeable future. It went on to become what it was intended to be, a national event of considerable merit.

Despite their disappointment with the number of entries in their two national competitions, the club members continued their active program of events. Shortly after the Phimister competition closed, Louis Sullivan, who had served as one of the jurors, delivered another memorable paper to the Chicago Architectural Sketch Club: "The Artistic Use of the Imagination." Sullivan's lecture and the discussion that followed clearly demonstrated the importance of imagination to any student who wished to become an architect. The *Inland Architect* reported that the event made a deep impression.[52] Sullivan always commanded the attention of the membership and that October 7, 1889, meeting had the largest attendance of the year. It was literally standing room only.

With men like Louis Sullivan regularly participating in the affairs of the Chicago Architectural Sketch Club, it is not surprising that the club continued to be looked to for leadership beyond Chicago. Support began to form for some sort of formal amalgamation of architectural clubs throughout the United States. The subject had been suggested by the Buffalo Architectural Club the previous year, and in 1889 the Cincinnati Architectural Club once again raised the idea of a national league. The Chicago group discussed that possibility at some length but took no action. It would be a decade before such an organization would be formed.

In the fall of 1889, two events captured the interest of CASC members. The Cincinnati Architectural Club announced that it was sponsoring an exhibition of architectural drawings and sketches that would take place during the joint convention planned by the American Institute of Architects and the Western Society of Architects in Cincinnati later that year.[53] Invitations were sent to all sketch clubs in the United States and Canada. Several medals were promised, including the Hinkle Gold Medal for the best exhibition of club work. The best individual work was to receive the Anderson Silver Medal, and the Builders' Exchange offered a medal for the best watercolor perspective. Shortly after the announcement, the Wayne Hardware Company promised a silver medal for "best design and drawings, complete, of the hardware necessary to complete a door, namely, hinges, 5 by 5, mortise lock, knobs and combined escutcheons. Also, a window . . . The design to be Romanesque."[54]

There was a positive response to the Cincinnati club's invitation from many clubs throughout the United States. Chicago, Boston, New York (both the sketch club and the league), St. Louis, Detroit, Philadelphia, Columbus, St. Paul, Minneapolis, and others all agreed to be represented. Prior to the opening of the exhibition, the names of several prominent draftsmen were published as being included in the exhibition.[55] Following those names was a note from the Cincinnati club that still another medal was being offered. It was to be a "Subscription gold medal . . . for the best free-had [*sic*] drawing of original architectural detail, and will be open to all draughtsmen *under twenty-one years of age,* who are in the employ of an architect in good standing."

The second event of interest to members of the Chicago club was the announcement of the Fifth Annual Exhibition (1889–90) of the Architectural League of New York.[56] The Third Annual Competition for the Gold and Silver Medals of the Architectural League was being held in conjunction with the exhibition.[57] A number of Chicagoans entered the competition, but none was rewarded with a medal. The club was honored, however, by the publication of two previous winners in the 1889 catalog: William B. Mundie's silver-medal entry of 1887 was the frontispiece and Oscar Enders's 1888 entry, also a silver-medal winner, was included as

52. The lecture was published in *Inland Architect* 14, no. 4 (October 1889): 38. Comments concerning the paper were on page 42 of that issue.

53. The complete rules for exhibitors can be found in *Building Budget* 11, no. 11 (September 14, 1889): 90, as well as the *Sanitary News* from the same month.

54. *Inland Architect* 14, no. 4 (November 1889): 42.

55. *Building Budget* 11, no. 16 (October 19, 1889): 131–32.

56. Ibid.

57. Ibid.

well. The gold and silver medals, all struck from the same die, were from a design by Edwin Howland Blashfield, which the Architectural League would continue to use for the next century.[58]

The annual business meeting of the Chicago Architectural Sketch Club was held on November 4, 1889.[59] After reports on the status of the club and other matters, nominations of officers for the coming year were accepted from the floor. There was near unanimous agreement that president W. G. Williamson be reelected for another term, and he was so chosen on the first ballot. He then rose to say that due to circumstances beyond his control he was forced to decline the honor. On the second ballot, William Bryce Mundie was elected president, the first non-charter member to be so named. Charles A. Kessell and O. C. Christian were elected vice presidents, and William Gibb was chosen as secretary, with E. J. Wagner continuing another year as treasurer. Wagner had been very successful as treasurer, not only in the collection of dues, but also in regularly renting the club rooms to outside groups, which greatly enhanced the club's financial position. The Executive Committee was filled out with F. L. Linden and T. O. Fraenkel. Only Kessell was a founding member of the club. A new generation was assuming control.

Two weeks after the election of officers for 1890, the Fourth Annual Banquet and Exhibition of the Chicago Architectural Sketch Club was held at the club rooms in the Art Institute of Chicago. By now the affair had attained bacchanalian proportions. R. C. McLean reported in the *Inland Architect* that "the club rooms were decked in gala array. The newly frescoed walls, the work of Mr. Linden, with the blending of gray and lavender tints, formed a fitting background for the club sketches in watercolor and sepia that were hung on every side. In the assembly hall the effect was superb. Above the president's rostrum a wash drawing of the national capitol was draped with the stars and stripes, and in front of this was placed the piano, festooned with flowers. The tables were arranged along either side of the hall, and at the lower end seats were reserved for the president and guests. These were decorated with vases of red and yellow roses. The entire arrangement was creditable to the taste of the club members."[60] McLean's colorful description of the event continued: "The usual happy flow of spirits characterized this, the club's fourth annual gathering. The club members and guests assembled around what was in this case truly a festive board."

President W. G. Williamson spoke briefly before dinner, thanking his colleagues for their help in the past year and taking "pleasure in handing over the reins." He pointed out that "we may well be called the best sketch club in the country, and deserving of the honors that have been bestowed upon us individually and collectively." He thanked both Robert Clark and D. G. Phimister for their support during the year and alluded briefly to his concern that more members had not participated in the two competitions. He closed by noting that many of the club's drawings had been lent to the Cincinnati club exhibition and were not available to be shown on this important evening. (That situation was rectified a month later, when the club had an informal reception for members and friends to show those drawings, which had been returned and hung in the club rooms.)[61]

The opening of the Fourth Annual Exhibition proceeded, followed by the usual elaborate dinner. Glasses were raised in toasts to various participants in the profession, and prominent members and guests responded. Among the speakers

*Edwin Howland Blashfield's design for the medals awarded by the New York Architectural League (IA)*

58. Edwin Howland Blashfield (1848–1936) was born in New York City and studied with Bonnat in Paris. In addition to designing the medal for the Architectural League of New York, he is noted for his work as a muralist.

59. *Inland Architect* 14, no. 5 (November 1889): 54.

60. *Inland Architect* 14, no. 7 (December 1889): 80–81.

61. Ibid., 83. The 1890 syllabus was published along with a brief report of this informal showing held on December 16, 1889.

*Menu card*

were John W. Root, W. L. B. Jenney, and Lorado Taft, as well as D. V. Purington, president of the Builders and Traders' Exchange. One of the few serious notes of the evening was president-elect Mundie's comment that "paying dues and attending meetings did not constitute the full duty of members." He reminded the members present that the next year's syllabus would be ready soon and "each competition arranged for must be entered into by every member."

J. G. McCarthy, a member of the Builders and Traders' Exchange, responded to a toast to "A Contractor's Knowledge of Architecture." His comments came in the form of a quotation from Longfellow:

> In the elder days of Art,
> Builders wrought with greatest care
> Each minute and unseen part;
> For the gods see everywhere.

He ended his remarks by suggesting that "a well organized god might be a valuable adjunct to every architect's office." Songs were sung (most of the lyrics were original compositions by the members) and recitations of all sorts were delivered. The meeting was a decided success. Forty-one members had attended, along with fifteen guests, including several honorary members.

Two days later, the long-anticipated National Exhibition of Architectural Drawings and Sketches opened in Cincinnati at Pike's Opera House.[62] It was timed to coincide with the consolidation convention of the Western Association of Architects and the American Institute of Architects being held at Burnet House in Cincinnati. Several hundred citizens of Cincinnati and visiting architects attended a special reception the night before the official opening. After guests had had the opportunity to inspect the exhibition, Cincinnati architect George W. Rapp called the group to order and introduced national AIA president Richard Morris Hunt, who welcomed them to the city. He, in turn, introduced John Wellborn Root, who expressed his pleasure at the drawings and gave a brief description of some of what the joint AIA and WAA convention hoped to accomplish in the next few days.

The work exhibited was not confined to that of sketch clubs. Much space was devoted to drawings produced by nationally recognized firms such as Shepley, Rutan & Coolidge, Cram and Wentworth, Plympton and Trowbridge, and William Le Baron Jenney. While some participants did not acknowledge affiliation with either a firm or a club, a third of the thousand drawings shown were contributed by nine sketch clubs from throughout the United States. Of the 333 sketch-club entries, 140 were from Chicago. "A Residence in Milwaukee" by Oscar Enders was singled out for special praise. New York was conspicuous in its absence, no doubt because the Architectural League's annual exhibition was about to open. There were, however, a number of drawings and watercolors from individual New York draftsmen. Albert R. Ross of New York won the "Subscription Gold Medal for the best free-hand drawing of original architectural detail by a draughtsman under the age of twenty one." The Philadelphia T-Square Club was awarded the Hinkle Gold Medal for the best club exhibit. The Anderson Silver Medal for individual work went to C. Blackall of Boston, and his colleague, C. Howard Walker, took home the Builders' Exchange Silver Medal for his watercolor drawing by a draftsman under the age of twenty-one. Chicago's only medal was an honorable mention awarded to Julius Beeckman.

There was a handsomely printed catalog, although only forty-seven plates illustrating items from the exhibition were included. Chicago was represented by just two illustrations of club members' work. The catalog was, however, a superb

62. The exhibition was reported and reviewed in several architectural journals, the most comprehensive of which were *Building Budget* 11, no. 23 (December 7, 1889): 201, and *Inland Architect* 14, no. 7 (December 1889): 82. The *Building Budget* article devoted more space to the actual exhibit, while the *Inland Architect* covered the proposed activities of the joint AIA and WAA convention that was to begin the next day.

63. The Cincinnati catalog of 1889 is extremely rare. In his *American Architectural Books*, Henry-Russell Hitchcock lists only three libraries that have copies, although it is available at many libraries on microfilm.

example of what would be done by sketch clubs in the future. Somewhat larger than most of the catalogs previously published (nine inches by twelve inches), it included a supplementary catalog, or checklist, that was apparently given to visitors for reference while they viewed the exhibition.[63]

The *Inland Architect* called the show "the greatest exhibit of architectural work this country has ever seen." It was to have enormous impact on future exhibitions of architectural sketch clubs in the United States, particularly on those of the Chicago Architectural Sketch Club. Exhibitions and their accompanying catalogs were to become one of the most important records of work done by architects, experienced as well as young, during the next fifty years; today they are an unparalleled treasure of information.

*The Hinkle medal, awarded to the Philadelphia T. Square Club at the Cincinnati Exhibition (BS)*

Pen & Ink Sketch
of existing Building

Cin Archtl. Club Competition

SECOND PLACE–ARTHUR STEDMAN

BUFFALO    FIRST PLACE–R. A. GREENFIELD.

TORONTO    FIRST PLACE–ERNEST WILBY.

*The* Inland Architect *printed work from architectural clubs throughout the country—including, from top to bottom, the Cincinnati club, the Buffalo Architectural Club, and the Toronto club, all of which was remarkably similar during this period (IA)*

# Before the World's Columbian Exposition

CHAPTER FIVE

The year 1890 was the beginning of an exceptionally active period for American architectural organizations in general and those in Chicago in particular. The consolidation convention held by the American Institute of Architects and the Western Association of Architects in Cincinnati had been successfully concluded in late November of 1889. The name that survived was the American Institute of Architects. Now it was time for architects throughout the United States to join in a mutual effort to promote their profession. The first step was to reorganize the various state and city groups into chapters of the new AIA. The Chicago Architectural Sketch Club, like most architectural clubs, was not considered a candidate. State associations previously connected with the WAA, on the other hand, were expected to merge with local or state AIA chapters, and Illinois was one of the first states to take that step.

The Western Association of Architects and its key members had almost always been Chicago architects. The Illinois State Association of Architects was organized within a few weeks of the establishment of the WAA, and had been incorporated in March of 1885, shortly before the organization of the Chicago Architectural Sketch Club. The Illinois association was organized in accordance with the rather loose rules of the WAA, which stipulated that such groups should be affiliated with the parent association, just as the AIA chapters were organized under the umbrella of the national AIA. The Illinois Chapter of the AIA had never been particularly active, and there was a great deal of crossover membership with the Illinois Association of Architects.

When it became apparent in 1889 that the consolidation of the AIA and the WAA was virtually certain, the architects of the two groups in Illinois began discussions concerning a merger. On January 20, 1890, they joined together to become the Illinois Chapter of the American Institute of Architects, with John Addison as president.[1] The newly formed chapter immediately began to take an active part in the professional affairs of architecture in Chicago and the state of Illinois. One of its first steps was to negotiate with Henry Lord Gay to transfer control of the Institute of Building Arts. This organization was the successor to the Permanent Exhibit and Exchange, which Gay had started in 1883. Its primary purpose had been to provide an exhibition space for building material suppliers and meeting facilities for architects' and builders' associations. Gay collected rents from the exhibitors and

1. Arthur Woltersdorf, "The First Forty-Eight Years of the Chicago Chapter, A.I.A," *Chicago Chapter AIA Leaflet*, no. 52 (April 1929), is one of the best sources of information on the early days of the organization.

*Design by Edward Dewson (his monogram is at the bottom right) for awards presented by the Institute of Building Arts to exhibitors, drawn while Dewson was editor of the* Decorator and Furnisher *(DF)*

published the *Building Budget* to help promote the endeavor. The Institute of Building Arts was located at 25 East Washington Street, where a number of architectural events had taken place over the past several years. It was an ideal location and operation for the Illinois Chapter of the AIA.

The Institute of Building Arts was quite successful under the mantle of the AIA, and income from rentals of the space was sufficient to permit membership dinners without charge. The chapter continued to operate the Institute of Building Arts until the lease on its space expired in 1898. It then moved to rooms in the Art Institute of Chicago, where it was to remain for many years.[2]

The consolidation of the AIA and the WAA engendered a certain feeling of stability among architects in Illinois for the next decade. The Illinois Chapter of the AIA, however, did not involve itself to any great degree in matters other than design. Its efforts in the field of education were relatively modest, and it remained for others—primarily the Chicago Architectural Sketch Club—to address this issue. The business of architecture was also given short shrift, and it was not until 1897, when the Chicago Architects' Business Association was formed, that the architects of Illinois were to have a voice in the legal ramifications of architecture.[3] More important to the architectural community as a whole in 1890 was the planning then under way for the World's Columbian Exposition. It had been under discussion for many years in the United States Congress and the state legislature, and by early 1890, a national commission appointed by President Benjamin Harrison was about to designate Chicago as the city that would host the event.

An exposition commemorating the discovery of America had been under consideration for more than twenty years, with a number of metropolitan areas in the

2. Ibid.

3. The Chicago Architects' Business Association was made up of a core group from the Illinois Chapter of the AIA, but included others as well. It achieved its first goal, the licensing of architects, in 1897.

*Library and meeting room of the Illinois Chapter of the American Institute of Architects at the Institute of Building Arts, Chicago, designed by Peter B. Wight (IA)*

*The original consultants for the design of the World's Columbian Exposition: from left, John Wellborn Root, Frederick Law Olmsted, Daniel H. Burnham, and Henry Codman (IA)*

United States actively campaigning for the privilege of being the host. Chicago put together a team of civic leaders that included 250 members of the business community who were relentless in their pursuit of the fair. The city was so confident that it would win the right to hold the fair that a corporation made up of prominent citizens was formed several weeks before Congress authorized an act providing for an "international exhibition of arts, industries, manufactures, and the products of the soil, mine, and sea" to be held in Chicago. President Harrison signed the bill on April 25, 1890. (The Chicago corporation had already chosen a prestigious board of directors to manage the fair, on April 4, 1890.)[4] Burnham & Root was asked to consult on the preliminary plans. Frederick Law Olmsted and his partner, Henry Codman, were brought in to assist in the selection of a location. By the fall of 1890, the four consultants had agreed on Jackson Park, then essentially a swamp on the south side of Chicago. Planning then began in earnest, with Burnham acting as chief of construction and Root serving as consulting architect.

The process went relatively smoothly until, after a meeting of most of the architects who were to design the major fair buildings, John Wellborn Root suddenly

4. The best concise description of the events leading up to the fair and its overall planning and execution can be found in Thomas S. Hines, *Burnham of Chicago* (Chicago: University of Chicago Press, 1974), chap. 4.

*Jackson Park was essentially a swamp before it was designated the site of the World's Columbian Exposition (AIC/CDA)*

became ill and died on January 15, 1891. His death had a profound effect on Chicago's architectural community. At the time, Root was a member and secretary of the national board of directors of the American Institute of Architects. He was also an active member of the Illinois Chapter of the AIA and had served as president of the Illinois Association of Architects prior to the merger of the AIA and WAA. More important, at least to the members of the Chicago Architectural Sketch Club, was his longtime interest and support of their organization as a regular lecturer and member of the Adjudicating Committee. He was held in extraordinarily high regard by the draftsmen and younger architects of Chicago. Many of his most important papers on architecture were first delivered to the Chicago Architectural Sketch Club and later published in the *Inland Architect*.[5] The 1891 syllabus, the following year, was the first not to include his name.

The 1890 syllabus was filled with the names of major speakers, including Root's.[6] He spoke in the spring on "Architectural Design and Fireproof Construction," and his partner, Daniel Burnham, who had always supported the club as well (although not to the same degree as Root), was scheduled to speak on "The Practice of Architecture" in August. Burnham's personal schedule was such that his paper was delivered earlier, on June 2, 1890.[7] It was on that evening that he first publicly stated that if

> a man or a firm is ambitious to carry on a great general practice, there must be
> in the organization:
>> A very great designer.
>> An exceptionally strong chief engineer.
>> A mechanical engineer.
>> A business man.
>> Each of these will have his hands full if he is faithful, and only with such
> an organization, I say again, can a large general practice live and keep going.

One cannot help but wonder if this was when the young Frank Lloyd Wright first heard these words. If Wright was not present, certainly Louis Sullivan was, and the two of them eventually developed a philosophy very different from Burnham's. Both Sullivan and Wright spent the rest of their lives devoting their attention to their clients' needs and delegating only those elements that others could attend to after the basic decisions had been made.

In addition to Root and Burnham, the popular E. J. Wagner was scheduled twice in 1890, and other speakers included Arthur Heun, H. C. Trost, Lorado Taft, W. G. Williamson, Dankmar Adler, Paul Mueller, and W. L. B. Jenney, as well as some lesser-known figures. The club planned only six competitions in addition to the annual Robert Clark Testimonial Competition, to be certain that members had sufficient time to compete. The Executive Committee was seeking quality and hoping that a larger number of members would participate. For the first time, the club decided to offer a prize to the member who stood highest in competitions for the year ending on October 20. It was to be one of the monographs of American architecture by the late H. H. Richardson. One serious concern was that most of the competitions were entered by only a few of the most active members. Membership had increased and by February of 1890 there were "fifty-six active members, with good prospects of a large increase within the next two or three months," according to the *Inland Architect*.[8] The anticipated increase in membership did, in fact, come to pass. At the annual meeting in November of 1890, it was reported that "the year commenced with fifty seven names on the roll, of which four senior members resigned and one, Mr. William Henderson, died. There has been admitted during the

5. The best source of Root's published lectures is Hoffmann, *The Meanings of Architecture*, which identifies the original source of each lecture.

6. The 1890 syllabus was published in *Inland Architect* 14, no. 7 (December 1889): 83.

7. *Inland Architect* 15, no. 5 (June 1890): 75.

8. *Inland Architect* 15, no. 2 (March 1890): 38.

year seven senior, twelve junior and one honorary member, making a present total membership of seventy-seven."[9] Business was good for architects in 1890, which undoubtedly helped in maintaining and adding to the club's roll.

The Chicago Architectural Sketch Club was not the only club looking at success as the last decade of the nineteenth century opened. *Architecture and Building* magazine editorialized in January 1890, "In looking over our files of the past year we find that there has been more activity among the sketch clubs of the country than for any other year in our history. Among the new clubs established in 1889 may be mentioned that of St. Louis organized in January, that of Columbus, O., in February, and that of New York organized in May."[10] The writer continued, "Eleven sketch clubs are now in operation, among which that of Chicago seems to be the most active, its meetings are held semi-monthly, its membership is unusually large, and considerable interest has been created in its work by funds which have been donated to it to stimulate competitive work." The editorial went on to describe in some detail the basic purposes of sketch clubs and ended with: "It is to the sketching clubs that we look for the greatest progress in future work; it is to them we shall one day look to see promises fulfilled and possibly new phases of art developed and carried to the highest point of human attainment."

*Architecture and Building* continued to publish material on architectural clubs in general and the Chicago Architectural Sketch Club in particular. In March of 1890, for example, it published a list of fourteen clubs throughout the United States, with addresses and the names of club secretaries. For reasons unclear, immediately following the list were two articles concerning clubs not on the list. The Sketch Club of San Francisco was noted with a list of forthcoming competitions, and the Cornell Architectural Sketch Club rated a brief item regarding its latest competition for "an entrance to a city house."[11] While most of the prominent clubs were included in the list, some were conspicuously absent. Neither Minneapolis nor St. Paul was listed, although both had thriving clubs that had been published in the *Inland Architect*, and their work was comparable to that of Chicago and other established clubs. The second annual meeting of the St. Paul club was reported in the March 1890 issue of the *Inland Architect*.[12] Among other things, the club president's comments, printed verbatim, acknowledged a debt to Chicago: "We all need an incentive for each and every member to go into every problem without reserve," he said. "This I think may be accomplished by following the admirable example of the sketch club that stands alone in the history of clubs. I need scarcely add that I refer to the Chicago Architectural Sketch Club. Let us give to the member who stands best at the end of the year, both in the number of competitions entered and the number of mentions received, some good and instructive book or photograph that he may keep as an evidence of his industry and faithfulness to the club work. I think that when we are better known in the city and the work we are doing is appreciated, that some art lover like Mr. Clark, of Chicago, or Mr. Phimister will appear and be proud to have his name upon a medal for the club to strive for." Clearly, the members of the St. Paul club had been following the work of their Chicago colleagues in the architectural journals that regularly published their activities.

The same month, the *Inland Architect* also published the winners of the first six places in the "Competition for a Village Smithy," the first competition of the year. First place went to William B. Mundie, who submitted a spectacular drawing; the other winners included Arthur Heun, O. C. Christian, Oscar Enders, C. Bryant Schaefer, and T. O. Frankel. The skill exhibited in these entries was clear when they were published, a month after they had been adjudicated. For reasons never noted, the February competition for a "Novelty for the World's Fair" was never published or even mentioned in the press. The third competition of the year, however, got a

9. *Inland Architect* 16, no. 5 (November 1890): 62.

10. *Architecture and Building* 12, no. 1 (January 4, 1890): 9.

11. *Architecture and Building* 12, no. 10 (March 8, 1890): 117–18.

12. *Inland Architect* 15, no. 2 (March 1890): 37–38.

*The "Village Smithy" drawings showed extraordinary talent; William B. Mundie's took first place (IA)*

great deal of attention. It was a design for an "Artist's House by the Sea." When the drawings were received, the secretary of the club noted that "fourteen designs were received. The committee awarded first place to W. B. Mundie, second place to T. O. Fraenkel, and third place to C. Bryant Schaefer. The competition as a whole is the best of the year, both in execution and in number of drawings." The competition ended in May and the winners were published in the July issue of the *Inland Architect.*

The next competition, in June of 1890, was for a "Litch Gate for a Country Cemetery." Thirteen drawings were submitted and, once again, they proved to be of very high quality. The first- and second-place drawings, both by Oscar Enders, who also won third prize, were published in the September issue of the *Inland Architect.*[13] No comment was made about Enders winning all three prizes. In the same issue, a drawing from the Cincinnati Architectural Club was published. A few weeks earlier, the *Inland Architect* had published winning competition drawings

13. *Inland Architect* 16, no. 2 (September 1890).

*The "Artist's House by the Sea" drawings, these by C. Bryant Schaefer, were also excellent, although they were still Victorian (IA)*

THE·CHICAGO·SKETCH·CLVB
COMPETITION·FOR·A
LICH·GATE

EACH IN HIS NARROW CELL FOREVER LAID
THE RVDE FORE FATHERS OF THE HAMLET SLEEP
THOMAS GRAY

*Oscar Enders showed his virtuosity with a pen by winning all three places in the competition for "A Litch Gate for a Country Cemetery"; the first two designs are shown here (IA)*

from the Buffalo Architectural Sketch Club and the Toronto Architectural Sketch Club.[14] These drawings had a certain generic similarity. All of them were small perspectives with minuscule floor plans as insets, executed in pen and ink. The influence of the Chicago Architectural Sketch Club was clear.

Other than a competition announced on September 1 for the design of the menu card for the forthcoming annual banquet in November, the litch gate was the last scheduled competition in 1890. The club continued its fortnightly meetings, however, and on alternate evenings had brief in-house competitions as much for recreation as anything else. Beginning in July, evenings were devoted to "sketching and social" activity, "drawing from a cast," "brush drawing," and "designing in pencil." The more formal evenings continued to have a variety of speakers, most of whom presented papers. The emphasis of the club's activities continued to be educational, primarily efforts to improve the members' chances of entering into private practice. An exception to this policy, or at least an announced exception, was a paper delivered by I. K. Pond on May 19, 1890, titled "A Sketch of Travel."[15] The paper was a detailed memoir of his grand tour of Europe, taken in 1883–84. He opened his comments, "In other papers before the club, if I remember rightly, I have sought, more or less, to instruct. In this I shall not try to be instructive. I am willing to 'let the dead past bury its dead,' so far as instructive papers are concerned, but I do wish to go to the past and rake up a few embers which have been smoldering for some time now." What Pond did was impress upon his colleagues, particu-

14. *Inland Architect* 15, no. 3 (April 1890), and *Inland Architect* 15, no. 4 (May 1890).

15. *Inland Architect* 15, no. 5 (June 1890): 71–74. The entire paper was printed but without any sketches. Before the Chicago Architectural Sketch Club was formed, Pond had provided the *Inland Architect* with several articles on his travels in Europe, which had been extensively illustrated with his sketches.

The Gate of Justice
Alhambra

*I. K. Pond's 1885 sketch of the Alhambra (IA)*

larly the younger members of the club, the importance of travel to an architect's education. He did not "instruct" in the usual sense, but he did make it clear that others would do well to follow his example.

Travel for aspiring architects, as far as Pond and his contemporaries were concerned, meant Europe. Travel suggestions were often published in the various journals. For example, in September of 1888, the *Engineering and Building Record* published a long letter from T. M. Clark of Boston titled "Cost and Route for an Architectural Draughtsman's Trip in Europe." It was in response to a brief inquiry from a "Draughtsman" published the previous month.

Clark's letter went into considerable detail, specifying costs, useful guidebooks, traveling methods, and the best and least expensive accommodations. He also urged the traveler to keep a "memorandum book" to record what he saw during his trip, and suggested that the best way to get photographs was to buy them "on the spot."

A week later a second letter on the subject appeared over the signature of architect J. A. Schweinfurth. He went into even more detail, describing routes, costs, and the best cities to visit. He ended his letter with the statement that a "draughtsman" can "safely work on a basis of $125 per month including the purchase of about 1,000 photographs." Immediately following his letter was one from C. H. Blackall that, while shorter, gave essentially the same information.[16]

Most, but not all, of the members who opened offices for private practice curtailed their activities in the club. I. K. Pond, for example, had been a founder of the club and was very active in the early days. He won one of the early competitions, was elected first vice president in 1885, and was a member of the Executive Committee in 1886. In July of 1885, he presented a paper on perspective drawing, and the syllabus for 1886 noted that he would present an "art essay" on "Polychromatic Architecture" on March 16.

Three months later, I. K. Pond's younger brother, Allen B. Pond, came to Chicago to join him. Although Allen Pond was not educated in architecture or engineering, the two brothers had been planning for some time to open an office to practice architecture.[17] They did so shortly after Allen arrived in Chicago. I. K. Pond then decided that, as a practicing architect, he should no longer take part in the day-to-day affairs of the club. He did not, however, give up his membership. In fact, he remained a member of the club until its demise, and his death, in 1939, more than fifty years later.

There were two in-house competitions in 1890 that did not involve design and one that did. The first, a "Rendering from Photo in Pen and Ink," which had been postponed the previous year, was rescheduled for September. At the same time, the syllabus called for a "Menu Card Design" for the annual banquet. Only three drawings for the menu card were received. Arthur Heun was awarded first place. In the rendering competition, fourteen entries were received. All were identified in the *Inland Architect*. Oscar Enders took first place. W. R. Gibb and E. C. Jensen were both given second prize, and Emery Roth and A. Y. Robinson took third and fourth place, respectively. The work of Enders, Gibb, and Jensen was published in the *Inland Architect* along with a copy of the photograph used in the competition.[18]

The other competition that didn't involve design was an essay, "Expression in Form," limited to nine hundred words. Six papers were submitted, and all were

16. T. M. Clark's letter was in the September 22, 1888, issue of the *Engineering and Building Record,* and the J. A. Schweinfurth and C. H. Blackall letters followed a week later in the same journal.

17. There is a great deal of information regarding the activities of Irving Kane Pond (usually referred to as "I. K.") and Allen Bartlett Pond (referred to as "A. B.") in the Pond Family Papers deposited at the Bentley Library at the University of Michigan. The brothers wrote to each other at least once a week, and their parents and sister were also regular correspondents. Much of this correspondence has survived. I am grateful to the Bentley Library for permitting access to this material.

18. *Inland Architect* 16, no. 5 (November 1890).

*The subject of the club's competition for a rendering from a photograph, which received an enthusiastic response (IA)*

19. *Inland Architect* 16, no. 3 (October 1890): 29–31.

20. Ibid., 30–32.

published in the *Inland Architect* along with the Adjudicating Committee's report.[19] Only Silsbee and Jenney signed the report giving first place to Peter C. Stewart, second to C. B. Schaefer, and third to J. C. Youngberg. A. Beatty Orth of Pittsburgh, who had won the gold medal in the previous year's Clark Testimonial Competition, came in fourth, with J. A. Miller and H. J. Ross taking the last two places. Root was out of town when the report was issued, but he still felt the need to review the papers, and he submitted his own comments in an essay that is now more memorable than the competition papers themselves.[20] It was reprinted in *The Meanings of Architecture*, edited by Donald Hoffmann, in 1967. In his introduction, Hoffmann states that Root's essay "is pregnant with the principles of organic func-

*The winners of the competition for a rendering from a photograph: from left, first-place design by Oscar Enders, and second-place entries by Elmer C. Jensen, and William R. Gibb*

tionalism. Significantly, he advises young architects to read Viollet-le-Duc's *Discourses* and Edward Lacy Garbett's *Rudimentary Treatise on the Principles of Design in Architecture* (1850), both important sources of organic theory."

The most important competition in 1890 was, once again, the Robert Clark Testimonial Competition, which was announced on August 1 and closed on October 31.[21] After the disappointment of the previous year, when only five designs had been received and none was given high marks by the jury, the Clark committee elected to simplify the competition. They wrote the program as follows:

> It is required to design for the equestrian statue of General Robert E. Lee, recently erected at Richmond, Virginia, a pedestal which shall be unlike the one upon which the statue is now set. The design shall comprise the pedestal and the approaches and surroundings of the monument, and no limitation as to the cost or material or dimensions of the pedestal, and its accessories are imposed by the committee.
>
> The site of the monument for the purpose of the competition shall be immediately outside the entrance to a public park and at the end of a broad boulevard, on each side of which are tall and elegant buildings, apartment houses, hotels, etc.
>
> Drawings shall be rendered on two sheets, one containing such ground plans, elevators and sections as may be required to illustrate fully the intention of the designer, and the other a perspective drawn to any scale and rendered in any manner desired by the individual competitors. The size of the sheets shall be 16 x 28 inches, and they are not to be rolled for purposes of shipment.
>
> Drawings will be received until, and not later, than noon to the first day of November at the office of the Chairman of the Committee, room 1600, Auditorium Tower, Chicago . . . An excellent illustration of the statue for which the pedestal is to be designed can be found in the Supplement to *Harper's Weekly* of March 29, 1890.
>
> D. Alder [*sic*], Chairman
> Henry Ives Cobb
> N. Clifford Picker [*sic]*
> Lorado Taft
> Samuel A. Treat

21. The Clark competition program was published in *Northwestern Architect* 10, no. 9 (September 1890): 68. It also appeared in various other journals at about the same time.

There were no more competitions scheduled following the Clark Testimonial Competition, although the members did continue to sketch and judge their own work at regular sketching evenings. Several important lectures were delivered in the fall of 1890. Paul Mueller, from the office of Adler & Sullivan, spoke on "Practical Ironwork" on September 8, and J. Beeckman gave a paper on the "History of Perspective" two weeks later. The last lecture of the year was by W. L. B. Jenney, who spoke on "Steel in Building Construction" on October 6. His paper was published two months later in the *Inland Architect.*[22]

A number of competition drawings were published during the year in the *Inland Architect,* although editorial coverage of the club in 1890 was far less extensive than it had been in previous years. McLean more or less made up for lost time, however, by publishing lengthy accounts of the club in both the November and December issues. In November he opened his comments by stating, "The two closing meetings of the club year were important,"[23] and went on to report on several of the competitions and the sixth annual meeting on November 3. He included a note that the "secretary spoke with much feeling, which was shared by every member present, of the affliction of one of the club's most active members and second vice president, Mr. O. C. Christian, who became insane through overwork some months ago. One of the charter members, he was always first to lend his assistance in any club work, always kind and warm hearted and ready to encourage and help members in their work. The walls of the club rooms bear many evidences of his skill as a draftsman, and his artistic feeling for nature." Christian had been included in the 1890 syllabus as the featured speaker on October 20. He was to have spoken on "Interior vs. Exterior."

McLean also reported on the election of officers for the coming year, an event

22. *Inland Architect* 16, no. 7 (December 1890): 7–77. The title was changed to "An Age of Steel & Clay."

23. *Inland Architect* 16, no. 5 (November 1890): 62.

*This statue of Robert E. Lee was the subject of the Clark competition in the fall of 1890 (IA)*

that always took place at the annual meeting. W. G. Williamson was elected president, T. O. Fraenkel and W. B. Mundie were named first and second vice presidents, and W. R. Gibb and E. J. Wagner were reelected secretary and treasurer, respectively. Arthur Heun and F. L. Linden were asked to serve on the Executive Committee. After the election, committees were appointed to prepare for the Annual Exhibit and Banquet on November 17, 1890.

Before the exhibition and banquet were held, the Clark Testimonial Competition Committee, headed by Dankmar Adler, met and adjudicated the entries. They were delighted with the number of submissions, twenty-five in all, and commented at some length on each.[24] Even the first- and second-place winners came under serious criticism, and some of the unplaced drawings were reviewed in a devastating manner. Comments in the report included "'Columbia,' which is an exceptionally attractive drawing, is nothing more than an adaptation of [another] monument." "Columbia" was, in fact, the first-place entry. As to the third-place design, "Spearhead," the committee reported that "the top is too bald and out of proportion with the frieze." One entrant had "not grasped the technique of watercolor sketching," and another unplaced designer was admonished to "study of the problem he is at work on, instead of endeavoring to design a whole city."

Oddly enough, comments on the unplaced drawings were sometimes more favorable than those on the winning designs. The principal problem seemed to be that the committee felt that most of the competitors were not familiar with the classic forms of architecture. They closed their report: "In making these criticisms of the different drawings, it is hoped that the one great deficiency noticed will be appreciated, and that is, the absolute necessity of careful study of good existing work to educate one's ideas of design." The members of the Clark jury—Adler, Cobb, Treat, Ricker, and Taft—were essentially establishment architects who were not ready for any sort of radical innovation. Young men were expected to build on what had been accomplished in the past. In the next decade, this attitude would be challenged by a number of key members of the Chicago Architectural Sketch Club.

With the adjudication of the Clark Testimonial Competition completed but not yet announced, the annual banquet and exhibition of members' work on November 17 could proceed as planned. Robert Craik McLean reported the occasion in considerable detail in the *Inland Architect*:[25]

> The club rooms were profusely decorated with plants, flowers, festoons of evergreen and smilax. The best watercolors of the best artists in the club adorned three walls of the assembly room, while on the fourth wall were arranged the twenty-five drawings of the Clark medal competition, the prize drawings being framed in evergreen.
>
> Covers were laid for seventy; the tables taxed the capacity of the hall to the utmost and every seat was filled. There were gathered about the board draftsmen who are winning national reputations, and many friends who have already achieved world-wide distinction in their art, and are still willing to lend their presence and counsel wherever it will give pleasure to those who emulate their successes, while they share the good fellowship that comes from the association with genius that knows no age.
>
> William Bryce Mundie, President of the Club and winner of the Clark gold medal, occupied a central position at the head of the table. On his right those veteran architects and engineers, William Le Baron Jenney and James R. Willett, were young fellows again for the evening, the swamp bridge building and fort planning during the war as chiefs of engineers on Sherman's staff or the vicissitudes of architectural practice since having only touched their hair

24. *Building Budget* 6, no. 12 (November 1890): 143–44.

25. *Inland Architect* 16, no. 7 (December 1890): 78–79.

*William B. Mundie's winning design for the gold medal for his Clark design (BBU)*

with gray, their hearts being as green as in their student days, of which these gatherings remind them. Lorado Taft, the sculptor, was there, and Dankmar Adler, the architect of the Auditorium, another architect with a war experience as captain of artillery. Other guests there were to lend dignity and pleasure to the occasion, while the absent Mr. Root was represented by a glorious bowl of punch, sent with his compliments, and regrets that important business prevented attendance.

Neither McLean nor any of those present at the banquet could have known that Root's thoughtful gift was to be the last gesture of this great friend of the Chicago Architectural Sketch Club. A month later, John Wellborn Root was dead.

Encouraged by generous quaffs of Root's punch and a supply of wine at the tables, all of which were complemented by an extraordinary spread of food, the festivities proceeded. Dankmar Adler announced the winners of the Clark medals, including several bronze medals made possible by a surplus of funds in the Clark

*Arthur Heun won second place and received a silver medal (BBU)*

*James C. Green from Denver took the bronze medal (BBU)*

Testimonial account. Upon completing the presentations, Adler spoke of his long friendship with Robert Clark. The medal recipients gave brief acceptance speeches, and then William Le Baron Jenney rose to respond to a toast to "The Draftsman." His rather lengthy comments were humorous to a fault. He concluded: "Then there are the draftsmen collectively. A jolly set of mighty good fellows they are, who well know how to give a banquet and to entertain their guests and each other right royally. Long life to them. Will the guests join me? Here is to their health, every one of them." As usual, the banquet lasted well past midnight; in fact, McLean reported that "at four o'clock the lights were turned out, and the fifth annual banquet of the C.A.S.C. closed a complete success."

A month after the annual meeting, the first draft of the syllabus for 1891 was published.[26] The general plan was similar to that of previous years except that July was designated vacation month. There were again only six scheduled competitions plus the Clark Testimonial, which was to be announced later. Only twenty-one dates were noted, but the Executive Committee commented that "it is proposed to entertain the members with frequent informal meetings and socials, and in general the year promises to be a notable one with the club."

The death of John W. Root understandably put a damper on activities in early 1891. The first two scheduled presentations, William Kleinpell's paper on "Dormers" and W. Schlessinger's lantern show on "the castles of King Louis of Bavaria," were not reported in the architectural press and may have been canceled due to Root's demise. On February 9, however, D. H. Perkins read his paper, originally scheduled for February 23, on "System in Architects' Offices."[27]

Perkins, then only twenty-three years old, had already acquired a wealth of experience and was certainly qualified to speak. Born in 1867 in Tennessee, he had come to Chicago with his parents at age twelve, and shortly thereafter his father died. Without completing high school, he began work in the office of architect F. R. Schock, where he remained until late summer in 1885. After some private tutoring by a family friend, he left Chicago for Boston.[28] He enrolled in the two-year curriculum of architecture under William R. Ware at the Massachusetts Institute of Technology. He remained in Boston for three years, serving as an instructor at MIT and working part-time for Henry Hobson Richardson[29] before returning to Chicago in 1888. He was employed briefly in the office of Wheelock & Clay before he joined Burnham & Root as John Wellborn Root's principal assistant. After Root's death and with Burnham's total commitment as chief of construction for the World's Columbian Exposition, Perkins became the de facto head of the firm's downtown office in the Rookery Building. As such, he had complete responsibility for all aspects of the affairs of the office. Burnham rarely came into the office. When Perkins needed Burnham's advice and counsel, he went to Jackson Park, where the work on the fair was handled in a "shack" Burnham had had built for that purpose.[30]

When Root died, there were more than a dozen major buildings on the drawing boards or in the late stages of design in the Burnham & Root office. The Women's Temple, the Masonic Temple, the First Regiment Armory, Ashland Block, and the Monadnock Block were just a few of these projects, all of which were in Chicago. Several new buildings were also under way in other parts of the United States. Perkins was faced with an enormous workload, but fortunately he had assistance. Engineer John Meigs Ewen was listed as "Engr. And Gen. Mgr, Burnham & Root, Architects" during 1890–94 in *The Book of Chicagoans, 1905*. Thus, Perkins

*Menu card for the club's fifth annual banquet (IA)*

26. Ibid., 81.

27. The entire paper, along with the discussion that followed, was published in *Northwestern Architect* 11, no. 2 (February 1891): 26–28.

28. *Sanitary News* 6, no. 85 (September 19, 1885): 173.

29. In the author's collection is a check for ten dollars signed by Richardson and dated April 20, 1886, just a few days before Richardson's death on April 27, 1886. According to Dwight Perkins's son Lawrence, the check represented a week's salary.

30. Charles Moore, *Daniel H. Burnham: Architect, Planner of Cities*, 2 vols. (Boston and New York: Houghton Mifflin Company, 1921), 53–54.

*Henry Hobson Richardson's office staff in 1886; the figure circled is Dwight Perkins (SBRA)*

would have had the benefit of his experience. Ewen was not, however, an architect, and during the same period he was listed as "Vice-Pres. And Gen. Mgr." for general contractor George A. Fuller & Co. Just how much "managing" Ewen did at Burnham & Root is left to conjecture, but he certainly would have been a great help to Perkins, particularly in the area of contracting. Perkins was listed as the "mngr." at 1142 the Rookery, Burnham & Root's office, in the local telephone directory. He also had a staff of experienced men to assist in field superintendence. Most of the build-

*Buildings under construction while Dwight Heald Perkins was manager of Burnham & Root's office: from left, the Women's Temple, the Masonic Temple, the First Regiment Armory, the Ashland Block, the Monadnock Building (north end) (PC)*

ings under construction were built without a "general" contractor in the sense that the term was to become used as standard practice within the next decade. Instead, the architect was charged with handling numerous contracts for various elements of the work, and a "superintendent" was assigned to handle coordination in the field. Perkins was able to delegate much of the work after drawings had been completed and construction had either started or was to begin shortly. He did not, however, delegate the design of any new buildings.

One structure that came into the office around the time Root died was a refectory building for the Chicago Park District to be built in Washington Park just west of the site of the World's Columbian Exposition.[31] Washington Park was connected to the Jackson Park location of the great fair by means of the "Midway" between Fifty-eighth and Sixty-first streets.

Today the Washington Park Refectory is the oldest surviving original park building in the South Park System of Chicago.[32] It was completed in late 1891 with finishing touches added in early 1892 and has been in continuous service since then. While it is possible that Root was involved in the early stages of planning the building, its size and scale, as well as its design and documentary evidence, suggest that Dwight Perkins was solely responsible for it. The only other similar building designed by the office of Burnham & Root was the Jackson Park Pavilion (1888), now demolished, which was very different in form and design, although the program and function of the two buildings were essentially identical. Furthermore, the Washington Park Refectory was an unprecedented design for the period. It was, in fact, a precursor of the Prairie designs of ten years later. The low-pitched hipped roofs, the horizontal emphasis created by the long, thin roman brick, the two-story-high central core balanced by a one-story porch, and the loggia all became strong elements of the Prairie style. Five years later, Perkins was to become, along with

31. Chicago Park District records indicate that the office of Burnham & Root began work on the design early in 1891. The plans were "resubmitted to the Architects with a view of rearrangements" on May 27, 1891, under the title "Annual Estimate, 1891." By this time, Root had been dead for several months and Burnham was fully occupied by the fair. Any changes would have been made by Perkins.

32. The Washington Park Refectory was restored in its centennial year (1991) by the author's architectural firm, Hasbrouck Peterson Associates. It was during the early stages of this restoration that much of the information concerning the early history of the building was discovered, largely through research in the archives of the Chicago Park District.

Frank Lloyd Wright and various other Young Turks, a leader of the Prairie movement in early modern architecture.

Dwight Perkins was a great admirer of Louis H. Sullivan and the Refectory's similarity to Sullivan's Transportation Building then being designed and built at the World's Columbian Exposition is obvious. The Transportation Building was published in the *Inland Architect* at the very time Perkins would have been designing the Refectory. Perkins would certainly have made a point of seeing it under construction during his weekly visits to Burnham at his headquarters in Jackson Park. The form of the Refectory is more than casually similar to that of the Transportation Building, and stylistically it owes much more to Sullivan than to Root. It is, in fact, a seminal building of the Prairie School of architecture.

In February of 1891, when Perkins spoke to the Chicago Architectural Sketch Club, he had been in the Burnham & Root office for about two and a half years. His responsibilities had been magnified by both Root's death and Burnham's absence. He had undoubtedly given the subject of his paper, "System in Architects' Offices," a great deal of thought and may have committed much of it to paper for his own benefit. He began with a comment that clearly indicates his intellectual curiosity and knowledge of architectural history: "The type of monasteries built in the ninth century in St. Gall, Switzerland, is best studied from an ideal plan which happens to have been preserved in a monastic library."[33] He continued, "The plan (says Ferguson in his history) does not pretend to represent any particular establishment but is a project of what was then considered a perfect monastery." His point was that his paper would deal with ideal conditions in an architect's office, large or small. His thoughts were obviously an extrapolation of the remarks Burnham had made to the club during his presentation the previous June regarding the organization of an architect's office. Perkins expanded on Burnham's philosophy of the business of architecture, going into considerable de-

33. The plan Perkins referred to was published as Walter Horn and Ernest Born, *The Plan of St. Gall, A Study of the Architecture & Economy of & Life in a Paradigmatic Carolingian Monastery,* 3 vols. (Berkeley: University of California Press, 1979). A shorter version (Lorna Price, *The Plan of St. Gall in Brief*) was published in 1982 by the same press.

*The Jackson Park Refectory Building as it appeared when completed; it was restored in 1991 (IA)*

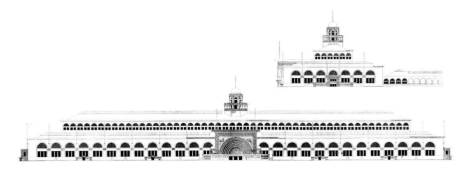

*It is highly likely that Perkins was influenced by the Transportation Building at the World's Columbian Exposition when he designed the Jackson Park Refectory (IA)*

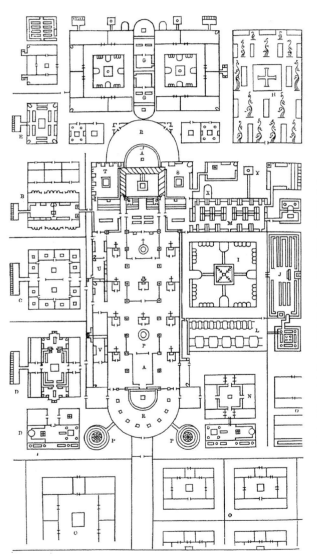

*Plan of St. Gall*

On the north side of the church (AA) was situated the abbot's lodging (B), with a covered way into the church, and an arcade on each face; his kitchen and offices were detached, and situated to the eastward. To the westward of this was the public school (C); and still farther in that direction the hospitium or guest-house (D), with accommodation for the horses and servants of strangers attached to it.

Beyond the abbot's house to the eastward was the dispensary (E), and beyond that again the residence of the doctor (F), with his garden for medical herbs and simples at the extreme corner of the monastery.

To the eastward of the great church was situated another small double apse church (GG), divided into two by a wall across the centre.

On either side of this church was a cloister, surrounded by apartments: that on the north was the infirmary, next to the doctor's residence, and to it the western portion of the chapel was attached. The other was the school and residence of the novices. Beyond these was the orchard (H), which was also the cemetery of the monks; and still farther to the southward were situated the kitchen-garden, the poultry-yard, the granaries, mills, bakehouses, and other offices. These last are not shown in the woodcut for want of space.

On the south side of the church was situated the great cloister (I). On the south side of this was the refectory (J), with a detached kitchen (K), which also opened into the great wine-cellar (L); opposite to this was the dormitory (M), with various dependent buildings.

The westward of this was another hospitium (N), apparently for an inferior class of guests; and to the southward and westward (OO) were placed the stable for horses, cattle, sheep, and all the animals required for so large an establishment, and all arranged with as much skill and care as could be found in the best modern farms.

*Photograph of Burnham & Root's drafting room on the top floor of the Rookery, taken during Dwight Perkins's tenure around 1890looking north toward the light well (AIC/DHB)*

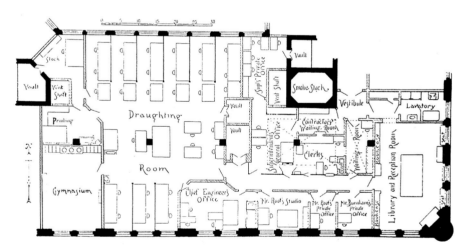

*Plan of Burnham & Root's office at the time the photo was taken (ER)*

34. "The Organization of an Architect's Office, No. 1," *Engineering and Building Record* 21 (January 1890): 84.

35. The Rookery was restored in the late twentieth century, and the library space is still extant. Unfortunately, the private offices of both Burnham and Root, which had survived, were destroyed.

tail on the activities in an architect's office, from the first meeting with the client to the last payments to the contractor and architect. It was an excellent description of how the organization and operation of architectural offices had evolved over the previous decade. With Burnham & Root in the forefront, Chicago architects had literally reinvented the procedure used to provide their services quickly and efficiently.

Burnham & Root's office was, of course, very large. Located on the top floor of the Rookery, it had been published in the January 1890 issue of the *Engineering and Building Record*.[34] There was room for at least forty employees plus ancillary features such as two vaults, a gymnasium, a printing room, space for contractors, and a magnificent library.[35] There was also room in the attic for addi-

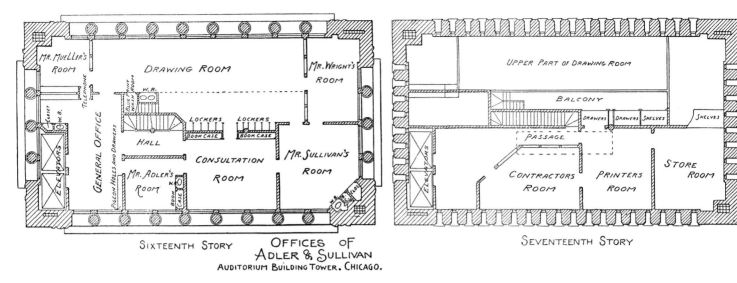

SIXTEENTH STORY    OFFICES OF
ADLER & SULLIVAN
AUDITORIUM BUILDING TOWER. CHICAGO.

SEVENTEENTH STORY

*Adler & Sullivan's office on the top two tower floors of the Auditorium Building (ER)*

tional drafting stations. It was the physical embodiment of Burnham's idea of the ideal office. During the year before Perkins delivered his paper, other offices had also been described in the architectural press. Adler & Sullivan's new space, on two floors in the tower of the recently completed Auditorium Building, was published with a brief description in the June 1890 issue of the *Engineering and Building Record*.[36] A month later the offices of Patton & Fisher, located on the top floor of the Montauk Block in Chicago, were published in the *Inland Architect*.[37] The lengthy article, a full page, included a floor plan and a sketch of "Alcoves in Draughting Room." While smaller than the two previous examples, it could accommodate about ten employees and had facilities for clients and contractors to meet with the principals and review plans. Other offices in other cities were also published during this same period. The profession of architecture and the system of delivery of services was becoming sophisticated. The members of the Chicago

36. "New Offices of Adler & Sullivan, Architects, Chicago," *Engineering and Building Record* 22, no. 1 (June 7, 1890): 5.

37. "A City Architect's Office," *Inland Architect* 15, no. 6 (July 1890): 85.

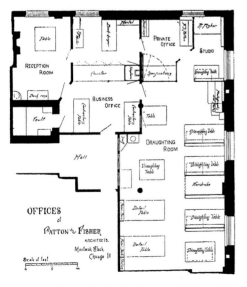

OFFICES
of
PATTON & FISHER
ARCHITECTS.
Montauk Block
Chicago Ill

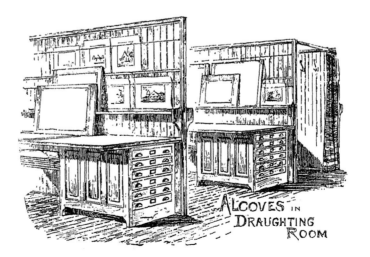

ALCOVES IN
DRAUGHTING
ROOM

*Patton & Fisher's office in the Montauk Building (IA)*

Architectural Sketch Club, most of whom were aspiring architects, had been following the progress of the profession with great interest, and Dwight Perkins's paper concerning the operation of Burnham & Root's office was received with considerable enthusiasm.

The architectural community was consumed with planning for the World's Columbian Exposition during the early months of 1891. The architecture of the exposition was clearly expected to be magnificent, but there was concern among architects that there should be some method of exhibiting both building materials and architectural work in the form of drawings, models, and similar material. This had been discussed by various journals during the previous year or so, but no actual plans for an architectural exhibition had been made. The Illinois Chapter of the American Institute of Architects had taken the lead when it met in December of 1890. Dankmar Adler was the leading proponent of such a plan. He made a plea to his colleagues in the Illinois chapter, saying that there should "be instituted a department in the Columbian Exposition which will illustrate the progress of architecture in the different countries, from barbarism to the present day."[38] He went on to describe in some detail what he expected to be accomplished by such an endeavor. He also noted that the American Institute of Architects would meet in Chicago during the fair and, that efforts were under way to arrange for a "congress of the architects of the world" during the same period. Adler hoped that "if this special exhibit could be made particularly interesting to the participants in this congress, the result would be of incalculable benefit to our country, to our city and to our profession." Following Adler's comments, the Illinois Chapter of the AIA asked him to chair a committee to plan the event. The committee consisted of "Messrs. D. Adler, S. A. Treat, F. Baumann, H. L. Gay and S. V. Shipman." Shipman was the president of the chapter and the only one named who had no connection with the Chicago Architectural Sketch Club.

There is no record that suggests that members of the club were asked to help plan the proposed exhibition of architects' work. In January the committee reported to the chapter that it had met with representatives of the fair, and progress was being made. Eventually, the plans for the fair did include an exhibition of architects' work from throughout the United States and elsewhere, but it was never considered a major element by the planners of the World's Columbian Exposition. The idea, however, did give rise to the idea that the Illinois Chapter of the AIA should hold its own exhibition, which came about in 1892.[39]

Despite the preoccupation with other matters in early 1891—Root's death being foremost in the members' minds—the activities of the club continued. The first two competitions of the year, a design for an upright piano in January and a watercolor from a photograph in March, proceeded on schedule. Drawings for both were exhibited at the club rooms on March 23. Despite the colorful exhibition of the entries, the evening was cast in gloom when it was announced that "notice was received from the Art Institute directors that the rooms occupied by the club must be vacated during the coming spring or summer, as they were wanted for school purposes." The club rose to the challenge and members Williamson, Wagner, and Youngburg were immediately delegated as a committee to find new quarters.[40] That accomplished, the conversation turned to the competition designs on the walls of

38. *Inland Architect* 17, no. 1 (February 1891): 6–7.

39. The Illinois Chapter of the AIA held its first annual exhibition at the Art Institute of Chicago from March 1, 1892, through March 15, 1892. A catalog of the exhibition is in the author's collection.

40. *Inland Architect* 17, no. 2 (March 1891): 25.

the club room. The piano design had attracted eighteen entries. Emery Roth and P. C. Stewart tied for first place, with H. C. Trost and E. C. Jensen taking second and third. The watercolors from a photograph had not yet been adjudicated and the report on that competition was deferred. The committee reported nearly two months later that Arthur Heun's watercolor took first place, with F. L. Linden, O. G. Brown, and R. E. Schmidt receiving the next three commendations.[41] None of these entries was published.

At the meeting on May 4, when the winners of the watercolor from a photograph awards were revealed, it was also announced that "new quarters had been secured in the Athenaeum building, which adjoins the Art Institute building, where an entertainment by club members will be given May 18, open to members only."[42] The change in quarters didn't cause the club to miss a beat in its activities.

The Athenaeum Building was a natural location for the Chicago Architectural Sketch Club. Built in 1886 and extensively remodeled in 1891, it was located next door to the original Art Institute Building on the south side of Van Buren Street. The mission of the Athenaeum, while broad, was heavily oriented toward architecture. Organized just after the Chicago Fire of 1871, it was a training school for young men and women who wished to enter business or the trades. It was sometimes referred to as the People's College. Its advertisements noted that its curriculum provided "Best advantages for students of Architecture, Carpentry, Mechanics, etc. with classes in Architectural and Mechanical Drawing, Mathematics, Physics and Wood Carving. Standard Business and Shorthand School; also a fine Library and Gymnasium."[43] Several members of the Chicago Architectural Sketch Club had attended or were attending classes there. The move to the new quarters was accomplished with a minimum of difficulty. Not a single meeting was delayed and only one presentation was canceled: Robert McLean's paper, "What I Know About Draftsmen," which had been scheduled for May 18, the evening the club reopened in its new space with a reception for members only.

While the club did not find it necessary to cancel any of its regular meetings, the schedule of speakers in the 1891 syllabus was altered substantially. Root's demise had forced some adjustments in the early part of the year, and the club never really did get back on schedule. W. B. Mundie, George Beaumont, Fritz Wagner, and Arthur Dawson had all been on the agenda for March through May, but there is no evidence that any of them made their planned presentations. However, on May 4,

41. The upright piano case adjudication was published in *Northwestern Architect* 11, no. 3 (March 1891): 40. The jury for the watercolor from a photograph published its findings in *Inland Architect* 17, no. 4 (May 1891): 51.

42. *Inland Architect* 17, no. 4 (May 1891): 51.

43. This quotation is included in an advertisement in *Architects, Contractors, and Material Dealers' Directory of the City of Chicago* (Chicago: J. D. Wirt Publishing Co., 1893), 170.

44. Ernest Albert (1857–1946) was a practicing artist who, early in his career, sometimes produced architectural drawings for architects.

*Sketches from the club's upright piano competition (NWA)*

*The Athenaeum Building on the south side of Van Buren Street, just east of Wabash Avenue (PC)*

45. *Inland Architect* 17, no. 4 (May 1991): 51. Albert's paper was published in full on pages 44–47. A similar citation appeared in the *Northwestern Architect* in June 1891.

46. The Clark medal competition was announced in several architectural journals in virtually identical language, indicating that the same material was sent to each journal. In most cases, it appeared as a straight news item, but it was featured, with comments, on the editorial page of *Inland Architect* 17, no. 6 (July 1891): 66.

47. *Inland Architect* 18, no. 3 (October 1891): 26. Once again, the information the Clark competition merited inclusion by McLean on the editorial page.

before the move, the club was privileged to hear scenic artist Ernest Albert[44] discuss his work in painting, stage construction and settings, and tricks of the stage "in a masterly manner."[45] Albert's paper, "Scenic Art," had been scheduled for June 15 but was moved up to fill in for other cancellations. At that same meeting it was announced that the report of the committee for the bridge and tollgate competition was postponed. If it was ever adjudicated, or even took place, it was never recorded. The club secretary also announced that the next "competition for June 1 is a design to a given line." This competition also seems to have been either canceled or otherwise lost. It was never published and does not appear in any of the records of the club. Finally, before adjourning for the summer, J. E. Youngburg's paper "Architect's Up to Date," scheduled for June of 1891, was canceled as well.

During the summer months the club had no scheduled events other than an "excursion and picnic" in August. There was one important activity left to address: the third Clark medal competition, announced in early July.[46] The same men continued to serve on the Clark committee: Dankmar Adler as chairman, with Henry Ives Cobb, Samuel A. Treat, N. Clifford Ricker, and Lorado Taft as regular members. After the disappointing results of the first competition and only slightly better entries in the second, the committee elected to go back to basics in 1891. The program noted that "competitors are supposed, in pursuance of their studies, to have visited Athens, either in person or in the study of books, cuts and photographs. It is assumed that they have made a special study of the Acropolis." In an editorial announcing the program in full, McLean commented that the committee "have, in selecting the subject, shown that, in their opinion, the student should first learn his alphabet and demand of him evidence thereof." The subject was to be "drawings or sketches, geometrical or perspective, of the Acropolis as a whole, or any part of its structures, or of any detail or details of either of these in their present condition or of restorations according to standard authorities."

After describing the rules for submission, the Clark committee noted that "the Award will be based upon the degree of actual and critical knowledge displayed in the choice of the subject selected for illustration and in the mastery of the same shown in the drawings, as well as upon skill, taste and judgment in rendering." They also stated that they expected this competition to be the first of a series of kindred subjects. Obviously, the committee felt that knowledge of historic subjects was critical to the education of young architects. McLean, in his July editorial, clearly agreed and stated that he expected that "a large number of drawings should result." Finally, he suggested that draftsmen should refer to the comments published in the *Inland Architect* regarding the previous competition and thus "avoid many errors." McLean's expectations of "at least fifty draftsmen . . . who are willing to study the Acropolis" were not met. When the competition closed on October 1, nine competitors had submitted drawings,[47] and only one entry came from a member of the club. Winners would not be named until the annual meeting in November.

It seems likely that in the fall of 1891 the members of the Chicago Architectural Sketch Club were preoccupied with work on the World's Columbian Exposition. There may have been little incentive to devote time to a project rooted in history more than two thousand years past when history was being made in Chicago. The excitement of having an opportunity to work on the planning of what was expected to be the largest and most impressive example of classical architecture ever assembled must have been overwhelming. More than half the membership was working directly or indirectly on the great fair. For the next eighteen months, preparations would preoccupy the architects of Chicago at the same time they were creating what was to become known as the Chicago School of architecture. It was an exciting time to be a young architect in Chicago.

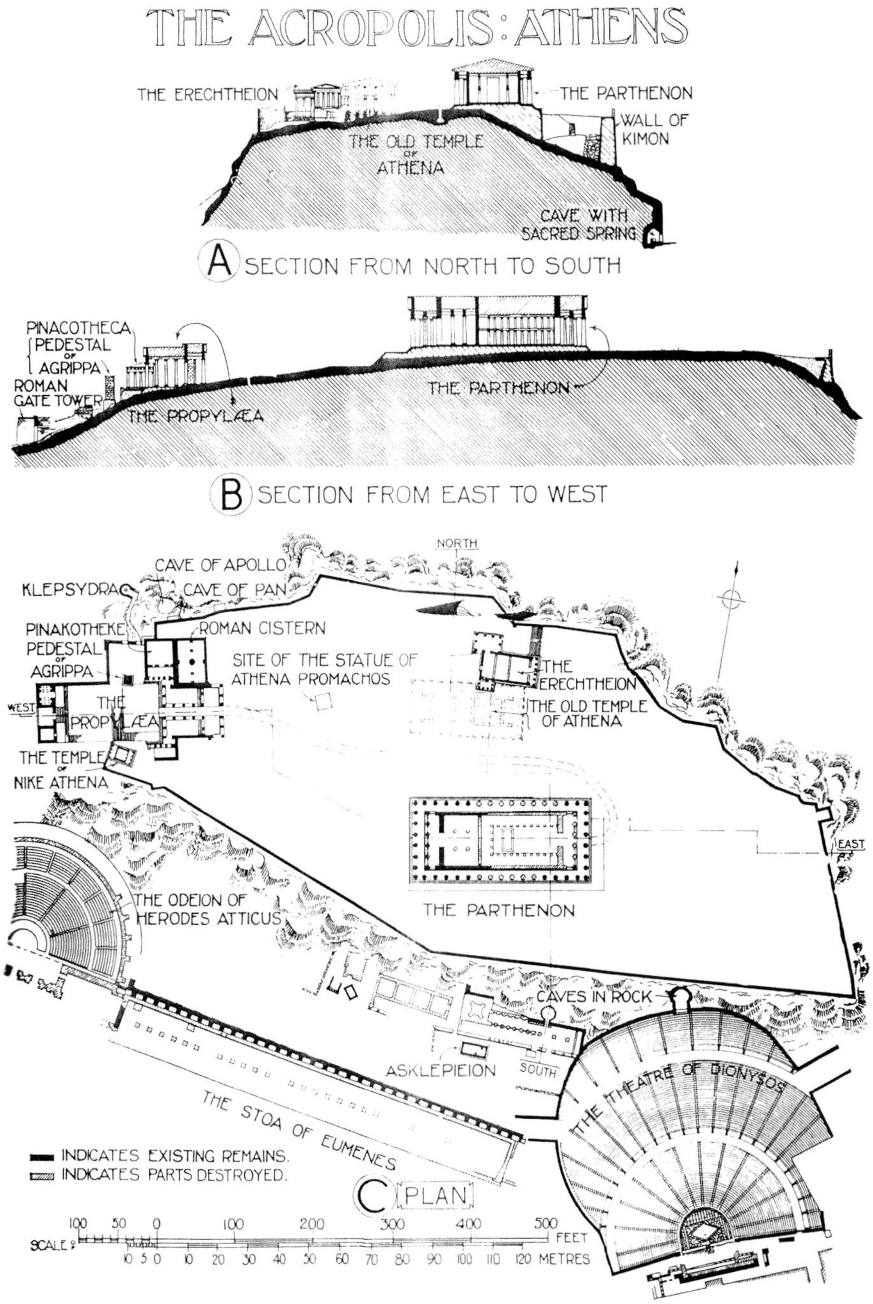

# THE ACROPOLIS: ATHENS

THE ERECHTHEION

THE PARTHENON

WALL OF KIMON

THE OLD TEMPLE OF ATHENA

CAVE WITH SACRED SPRING

(A) SECTION FROM NORTH TO SOUTH

PINACOTHECA
PEDESTAL OF AGRIPPA
ROMAN GATE TOWER

THE PROPYLÆA

THE PARTHENON

(B) SECTION FROM EAST TO WEST

NORTH

CAVE OF APOLLO
CAVE OF PAN
KLEPSYDRA
ROMAN CISTERN
PINAKOTHEKE
PEDESTAL OF AGRIPPA

SITE OF THE STATUE OF ATHENA PROMACHOS

THE ERECHTHEION
THE OLD TEMPLE OF ATHENA

WEST
THE PROPYLÆA

THE TEMPLE OF NIKE ATHENA

EAST

THE ODEION OF HERODES ATTICUS

THE PARTHENON

CAVES IN ROCK

ASKLEPIEION

SOUTH

THE STOA OF EUMENES

THE THEATRE OF DIONYSOS

■ INDICATES EXISTING REMAINS.
▨ INDICATES PARTS DESTROYED.

(C) PLAN

SCALE 9
100  50  0        100       200       300       400       500
FEET
10 5 0   10   20   30   40   50   60   70   80   90  100  110  120 METRES

*Drawing from the first edition (1896) of Sir Bannister Fletcher's* History of Architecture; *similar material was provided to the entrants in the 1891 Robert Clark Testimonial Competition*

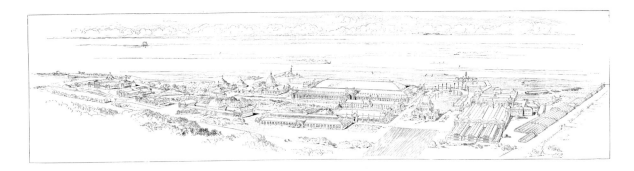

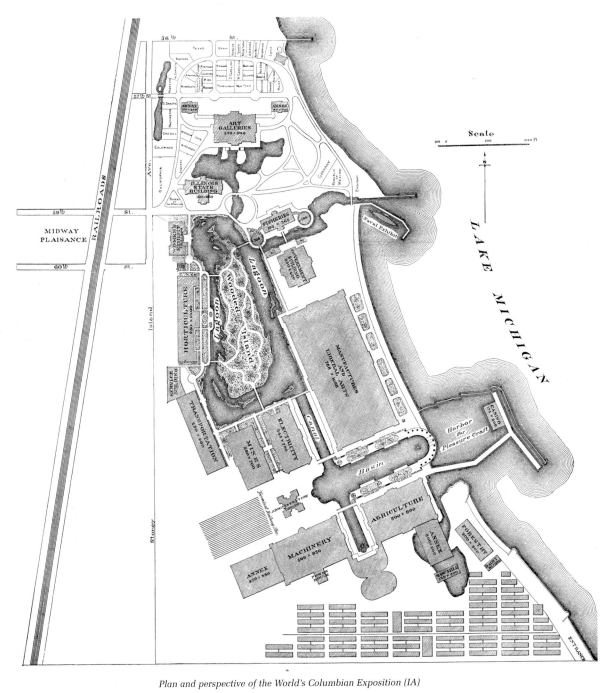

*Plan and perspective of the World's Columbian Exposition (IA)*

# Designing the Fair
## CHAPTER SIX

During the summer of 1891, Chicago's architects and the Chicago Architectural Sketch Club members in particular were extremely busy. Seventeen major buildings for Chicago's Loop were in the late planning stages or under construction in 1891 and 1892, and nine more would be finished in 1893. This was in addition to the literally hundreds of smaller commercial buildings and residential commissions under way. At the same time, most large firms, and some small ones, were designing buildings to be built elsewhere in the United States. All this was going on while the buildings for the World's Columbian Exposition were being designed and built.

Daniel Burnham and John Wellborn Root had been appointed consultants for the World's Columbian Exposition in 1890, and by the fall of that year, they had prepared a preliminary plan. Burnham carried the title of chief of construction, although later he would have the additional title of director of works. (He used the titles interchangeably depending on what he was dealing with at the time.) Root's title was consulting architect. When they accepted these tasks, it was agreed that Burnham & Root would continue to handle private clients. In order to facilitate the work of the fair while attending to their practice, they stipulated that the offices of the World's Columbian Exposition must be near their office in the Rookery. They set up the exposition offices in the east wing of the top floor of the building. One door of the library of Burnham & Root led to the firm's private space on the south wing of the building and a second door opened directly into the office of the World's Columbian Exposition. They also took space in the attic for drafting rooms and had a small "shed" built on the roof for printing. These rooms would be used for less than a year, and early in 1891 plans were prepared for a "service building" to be built in Jackson Park. Burnham moved there when it was finished on May 1, 1891, and spent the better part of the next two years at the site. The service building, the first of many to be designed by Charles Atwood,[1] was built to permit around-the-clock use. It was torn down a year later to make way for a permanent service building, since more space was needed until the fair opened. The first service building, which Burnham often referred to as the "shack," included offices for him and several of his principal assistants, a drafting room, and sleeping quarters. The permanent service building included those facilities as well as a medical clinic, a telegraphic center, a small gymnasium, and sleeping space and bathrooms for Burnham and others who needed to be at the

*Burnham & Root's library was accessible to both the architectural office and the World's Columbian Exposition office (IA)*

1. Charles B. Atwood (1848–1895) was recruited by Burnham to take John Root's place after Root's death. Born in Massachusetts and educated at Harvard, Atwood worked in Boston and New York City for more than twenty years before moving to Chicago. When he arrived, Burnham asked him to work at Jackson Park as the principal on-site designer for the World's Columbian Exposition buildings that hadn't already been assigned to others. When the fair was over, Atwood became a partner at D. H. Burnham and Company, where he remained until his death in 1895.

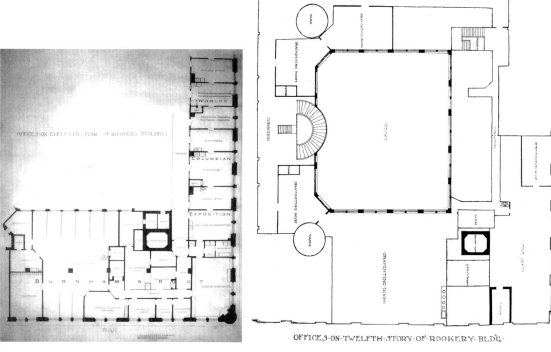

OFFICES·ON·TWELFTH·STORY·OF·ROOKERY·BLDG·

*Plans from the* Final Report of the Chief of Construction *(AIC)*

*Charles Atwood (PC)*

site virtually all the time. It was in the service buildings that most of the drawings for the fair buildings were produced.

Burnham & Root had set about selecting designers for the various fair buildings in the fall of 1890, and by January of 1891 most of the architects had been identified. After they finished conferring with the invited designers, the final list of architects assigned to the primary buildings was established as follows: Peabody & Stearns, Machinery Hall; George B. Post, Manufacturers and Liberal Arts; Richard M. Hunt, Administration Building; Henry Ives Cobb, Fisheries Building; Jenney & Mundie, Horticulture Building; S. S. Beman, Mines and Mining Building; McKim, Mead & White, Agriculture Building; Van Brunt & Howe,

*This photograph of the Service Building for the World's Columbian Exposition was the first taken by C. D. Arnold, the fair's official photographer; Burnham called the building "the shack" (AIC/CDA)*

Electricity Building; Adler & Sullivan, Transportation Building; Burling & White-house, the Venetian Village.

The remaining buildings, except for state and government structures, were assigned to others by Burnham. About half the buildings at the fair were designed by Chicago firms. Every state was given a site for a state-sponsored building, some of which were designed by Chicago firms. Burnham's *Final Report* included the names of nearly a hundred architects who designed buildings for the fair. Some of these men, or firms, designed several. Charles Atwood, for example, designed more than seventy-five, including the Fine Arts Building, the only one to become a permanent structure. The preparation or final review of the drawings and construction of all these buildings had to be supervised by Daniel Burnham and his staff.

That staff was made up largely of Chicago draftsmen whose work involved much more than mere on-site supervision. Even the principal "design" architects for the large primary structures provided relatively small, and in some cases almost rudimentary, design drawings, and Burnham's drafting corps prepared the construction documents. Many of the smaller buildings were designed and executed entirely under the auspices of the chief of construction. It was the only way to maintain control over a massive project that had to be completed in an extraordinarily short time.

During the 1891–92 period, more than half the members of the Chicago Architectural Sketch Club were involved in the design and construction of the World's Columbian Exposition buildings. In the fall of 1892, the club's secretary, John E. Youngburg, sent a long letter to the editor of the *Northwestern Architect* wherein he stated that "forty of the sketch club members are directly or indirectly connected with the designing and construction of the World's Columbian Exposition buildings."[2] Among those was the club president at the time, Charles A. Kessell, who was the foreman of a team of draftsmen in the office of the chief of construction.[3] There were others involved who were not members of the club, of course, including representatives of various out-of-town firms as well as independent draftsmen.

The publication of the designs for the fair buildings was a major concern of the managers and architects, who wanted to publicize the fair and ensure that their work was widely recognized. The means employed to accomplish these goals was to prepare high-quality perspective renderings and elevations, and publish and exhibit them as widely as possible. Plans were sometimes included, but usually at a small scale. Most of the buildings, particularly the larger ones, were essentially huge sheds with interiors designed to exhibit materials at the fair. The impressive exteriors were molded of a plaster-like material called "staff." It was not designed for long service and, had the buildings not been demolished after the fair, they would have deteriorated within two or three years.

The first building published by the *Inland Architect* was W. W. Boyington's State of Illinois Building, which appeared in the March 1891 issue.[4] The elevation drawings were not signed, but the style is one that was to be replicated on almost every drawing of fair buildings published during the next year. Clearly, they were prepared by the World's Columbian Exposition's Department of Construction. The very small plan and perspective, on the other hand, were prepared by a delineator who signed his name "von H." The same issue of the *Inland Architect* published two alternate designs for the U. S. Government Building, both with the same plan. The perspectives were credited to the supervising architect of the Treasury Department, Jas. H. Windrim, and bore the initials R. H. A. as the delineator. The tiny published plan was in the same style as that of the State of Illinois Building. Elevation drawings of the first-, second-, and third-prize winners of the competition for the Women's Building (the only structure at the fair to be awarded by competition)

*The Rookery (WRH)*

2. *Northwestern Architect* 10, no. 11 (November 1892): 70–71. The letter was dated September 13, 1892.

3. Charles A. Kessell (1853–1896) was born in Norway and moved to Chicago when he just was a year old. A founder of the Chicago Architectural Sketch Club, he served as treasurer for two years and was elected president in 1892. While working with Burnham's staff at the World's Columbian Exposition, he was responsible for the construction drawings for the Administration and Fisheries buildings, the Choral Hall, and several minor works. His work as a draftsman and watercolorist was held in high regard by his colleagues. His obituary can be found in *Inland Architect* 27, no. 2 (March 1896): 10.

4. *Inland Architect* 17, no. 1 (February 1891): 1, noted that the sketches had been delivered. The following month, they appeared in the *Inland Architect,* executed by the Department of Construction.

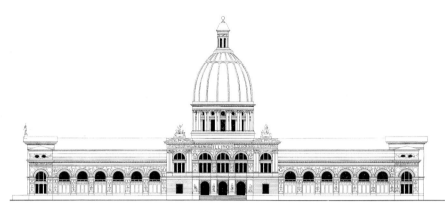

*The State of Illinois Building by William W. Boyington was the first World's Fair building published in the* Inland Architect

5. Sophia G. Hayden (1868–1953) was the first woman to receive a degree in architecture from MIT. She was born in Chile and at the age of six was sent to live with her grandparents in Boston. She was admitted to MIT in 1886 and graduated with honors in 1890. In 1891, she entered a "women's only" competition to design the Women's Building for the World's Columbian Exposition. Hayden won the competition but never practiced architecture during her long life. Her original drawings for the Women's Building are now at the Chicago Historical Society.

6. Frederick O. Cloyes (1862–1926) was born and educated in Illinois. Little is known of his work after the fair. He apparently continued to work as a senior draftsman until he was licensed as an architect in 1906. He partnered with John H. Murphy in Chicago for a few years, eventually moving to Maywood, Illinois. He died in the Elgin State Hospital in 1926.

7. The best reference to E. Eldon Deane (ca. 1859–ca. 1915) and his work is in Michels, "A Developmental Study." Deane's drawings can be found in a number of architectural journals published in the last quarter of the nineteenth century.

were also published. Sophia G. Hayden was the architect.[5]

The March *Inland Architect* also featured two large, preliminary foldout drawings of bird's-eye views of the fairgrounds. Neither was signed, but the style suggests that they were prepared in the office of the chief of construction. During the next several months the *Inland Architect* would continue to publish fair buildings in each issue. When they appeared, they would nearly always be credited to the Department of Construction. This would continue through November of 1891, when the last drawings of the primary buildings were published. During 1892 most of the drawings concerning the fair published by the *Inland Architect* were of state and other minor buildings. From time to time, until the opening of the fair on May 1, 1893, construction photographs of various buildings would also appear. Virtually all issues of the journal included editorial comments on the progress of the design and construction of the fair buildings.

The style of the World's Columbian Exposition drawings was such that it is clear that they were prepared, if not by the same hand, at least under the direction of a single supervisor. That person was F. O. Cloyes, chief draftsman for the Department of Construction.[6] Cloyes's name first appeared as an associate member of the Chicago Architectural Sketch Club in December of 1892.

Another key figure who assisted in the preparation of presentation drawings was E. Eldon Deane. Deane was considered by some to be the "dean" of architectural draftsmen on the East Coast.[7] He had studied at the London Architectural Association and began publishing drawings in the *American Architect and Building News* in 1883. He was actually on the staff of that journal for several years begin-

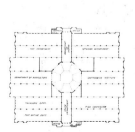

*Plan of U.S. Government Building (IA)*

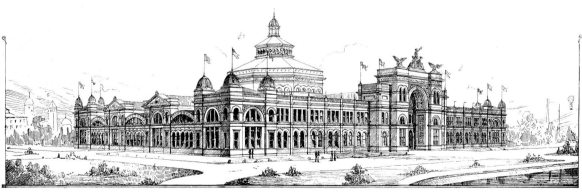

*Two designs for the U.S. Government Building—both with the same floor plan—were submitted for consideration; this one was built (IA)*

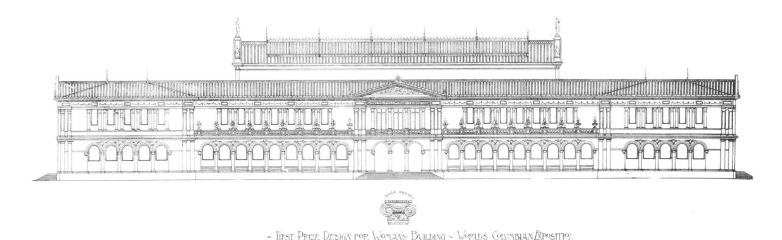

~ First Prize Design for Woman's Building ~ World's Columbian Exposition

*Drawing from the* Inland Architect

ning in 1886, but apparently was permitted to do freelance work at the same time. Drawings carrying his signature as delineator were often included in architectural exhibitions on the East Coast. In 1891, he appeared in Chicago, probably as a freelancer, and his drawings of the fair buildings began appearing in the *Inland Architect* in August of 1891. His perspectives of the Mines and Mining Building, the Women's Building, and the Manufacturers and Liberal Arts Building were all published that month. His drawing of the Agriculture Building was published in September. His "Official Plat" and bird's-eye perspective of the entire fairgrounds, published in October, were the last of his drawings for the World's Columbian Exposition to appear in the *Inland Architect*.[8] Deane's drawings of fair buildings did, however, continue to appear elsewhere, including a number of promotional items for the fair.

Meanwhile, on September 7, 1891, the Chicago Architectural Sketch Club began planning for a new year of activity. The meeting was "devoted to sociability and the inspection of an exhibit of water-colors by E. Eldon Deane."[9] In reporting on that meeting, the *Inland Architect* noted that "a number of new members were admitted, among whom was Julius Harder, well-known for his success in competitions of the New York Architectural League, etc." Deane's name does not reappear

8. The drawings prepared by Deane, as well as several other drawings of the major World's Fair buildings, were published before the fair opened in *The Buildings of the World's Columbian Exposition* (New York: New York Photogravure Co., 1892). Eleven of the major buildings were included, and six were signed by Deane. They were all elaborations of line drawings published in the *Inland Architect*. Deane did do other work during his stay in Chicago. For example, he was responsible for nearly all the perspective line drawings in an elaborate promotional book titled *Masonic Temple,* which, although undated, must have been prepared early in 1892 as a rental aid.

9. *Inland Architect* 18, no. 2 (September 1891): 22.

*Sophia G. Hayden (PC)*

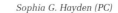

*Agricultural Building* from North-east

*Drawing of the Agriculture Building by E. Eldon Deane (IA)*

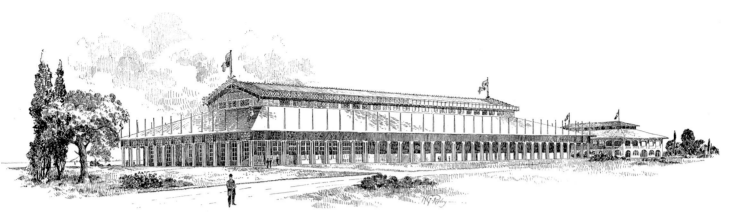

*W. M. Kenyon drawing of the Electricity Building by Van Brunt & Howe (IA)*

in the records of the World's Columbian Exposition, but he seems to have remained in Chicago for a time after executing the drawings noted above. He did drawings for various other Chicago firms and was published from time to time in the *Inland Architect* for the next few years. After his Chicago experience, he returned to Boston, where he remained until 1894, when he moved to New York. He continued to do renderings for architectural firms throughout the United States until his death around 1905.

E. Eldon Deane was not the only perspectivist who prepared drawings of the World's Columbian Exposition for publication. Perspectives by Theo. Pietsch, N. Tharp, J. W. Johnson, and W. M. Kenyon were also published as drawings from the Department of Construction. Other than Deane, the largest number of published drawings was credited to H. G. Ripley.[10] All these men had, or would have in the future, some connection to the Chicago Architectural Sketch Club. Most were members or associate members, and some served as delineators for exhibitors at the club's annual exhibitions during the next decade or so. The World's Columbian Exposition drawings were exhibited in a number of places, the most prominent being the Seventh Annual New York Architectural League Exhibition, from late December 1891 through early January 1892.

The activities in preparation for the World's Columbian Exposition in Jackson Park, as well as in architects' offices throughout Chicago, apparently curtailed some of the activities of the club in the fall of 1891, but certain events still took place. Scheduled presentations at the new club rooms in the Athenaeum Building were delivered by Charles Kessell, W. A. Morse, and A. B. Pond. The club held its annual business meeting on November 2. Officers elected for the 1892 year included Charles A. Kessell, president; W. E. Kleinpell, first vice president; Arthur Heun, second vice president; John E. Youngburg, secretary; and Ernest J. Wagner, treasurer. Frank L. Linden and T. O. Fraenkel were chosen to serve with the officers on the Executive Committee.[11] Only one of the founders, president C. A. Kessell, was now part of the management of the club. The seeds of the early modern movement were being sown, and younger members were assuming control.

Nearly a year later, in a letter to the editor of *Northwestern Architect* dated September 13, 1892, the club's secretary, John E. Youngburg, made some revealing comments about the status of the club at the time of the 1891 election.[12] He wrote, "The present club year was inaugurated on the days of grace, when the gloomy ab-

10. Hubert G. Ripley (1869–1942) was born in Massachusetts, and at the age of nineteen entered MIT to study architecture. He graduated in 1890 and immediately moved to Chicago, where he worked with Burnham and Atwood on the World's Columbian Exposition. He returned to Boston after the fair and, after many years in various offices, entered into partnership with Addison B. Le Boutillier in 1928, where he remained until his death in 1942.

11. *Inland Architect* 18, no. 4 (December 1891): 65–66.

*H. G. Ripley drawing of the Forestry and Dairy Building by C. B. Atwood (IA)*

sence of interest, and exchequer contaminated by an all too frequent absence of the presiding functionaries had reduced the club to penury and imminent dissolution." Apparently, the previous year's officers and many members had simply grown tired or had moved into active architectural practice and were not addressing the issues of interest to the membership. The intense pressures that many of them faced with the incredible amount of work necessary to prepare for the World's Columbian Exposition were robbing them of time they would have normally spent on club affairs. This was exacerbated by the amount of work in most of the private offices in Chicago. The Youngburg letter's reference to a "penury" problem also suggests that the club was in dire straits financially. For reasons not recorded, the 1891 treasurer, E. J. Wagner, was the only officer reelected for the 1892 year.

Youngburg went on to say, "The sketch club began to lose its prestige at home, and the famous C.A.S.C. was about to conduct its own obsequies, when as coming to the surface for the third time, at the annual meeting, three names on the executive committee were exchanged. The success or failure of a legitimate enterprise depend on the management and the present club standing indicates with few exceptions that success was courted in an ardent and persistent manner. The president Mr. C. A. Kessell, has brought about results in the club which must make his predecessors blush with silent envy." Youngburg's language is a bit tortured, but his description of the club's woes is clear. Certain past officers were simply not doing their duty. His letter went on to describe in some detail the work of Arthur Heun, Frank Linden, T. O. Fraenkel, and several other club members, which he reviewed with great frankness. He praised some past officers for their work and excused some current members for their lack of attention to club affairs. He noted that "every minute of draughtsman time this year is needed at his place of business for we are living in the greatest architectural period in the history of the country." Nevertheless, he had harsh words for members who were not, in his opinion, participating in club events at the same level they had in the past. Youngburg ended his letter with comments about the various programs already completed in the club year and what was yet to come. His letter apparently roused a number of members to greater participation, since the next few months were among the most impressive of the early years of the Chicago Architectural Sketch Club.

12. This letter, which appeared in *Northwestern Architect* 10, no. 11 (November 1892): 70–71, is referred to hereafter as the "Youngburg letter."

Designing and building for the fair and the club's activities were only some of the concerns of the architectural community during the fall of 1891 and early 1892. The Art Institute of Chicago announced that its classes in architecture had been very successful and that it was continuing to refine the program. It published a circular outlining the entire two-year curriculum of three terms each year, but concluded that "not much in the way of a scientific architectural school could be conducted in the evening, because the attendance was chiefly of draughtsmen from the offices of practicing architects, who were too hard worked to keep up their studies successfully. At the end of the second year it is decided that the methods of the French schools of architecture are not applicable to our conditions, and that textbooks, stated recitations, and the presence of teachers nearly or all the time are necessary."[13] The idea of "ateliers" in architects' offices was not working, and the Art Institute elected to conduct classes in a traditional manner. Accordingly, it put together a comprehensive class schedule that effectively eliminated the possibility of students working full-time in architectural offices. Louis J. Millet continued to serve as the primary architecture instructor, with William R. French in charge of overseeing the school. Architects W. A. Otis, W. L. B. Jenney, and Irving K. Pond continued as instructors and engineer W. MacHarg taught a course on sewerage and ventilation. A permanent studio was provided at the school for use by the students during and between classes. They also had access to all the other facilities of the School of the Art Institute of Chicago.

The appointment of Walter Francis Shattuck (1871–ca. 1949) as an instructor in mathematics was an important step in the development of the program. He had been asked to join the faculty during the summer of 1891 after graduating from the School of Architecture at the University of Illinois. Shortly thereafter, he wrote to Nathan C. Ricker, his former professor at the University of Illinois, saying that he was "very much please[d] with the prospect before me, and I think that I have been in very good luck to obtain such a place."[14] He went on to say that the school would need new desks for the studio and asked Ricker if he "would ask one of the boys to make a sketch for me and put the dimensions on." Shattuck was given a great deal of responsibility at the school. He was in charge of "recitations, geometry, trigonometry and perspective, spending three hours every day in the class rooms and drafting rooms." He would remain at the school for most of his professional life. After the turn of the century, many members of the Chicago Architectural Club would owe him a great deal for the education they received. He became a member of the club in 1904.

*Walter Francis Shattuck (IIT)*

13. "Instruction in Architecture: Art Institute, Chicago," *Inland Architect* 18, no. 2 (September 1891): 20.

14. His undated letter was written on the letterhead of D. M. Osborne & Co., a manufacturer of harvesting machines. Shattuck graduated from the University of Illinois in 1891.

15. *Inland Architect* 18, no. 4 (November 1891): 35–36. The comments following this first quotation are all from the editorial cited here.

While the School of the Art Institute embarked on the 1891 fall term, Chicago's full-time architects were presented with a major competition. The City of Chicago announced that a public library was to be built "on one of the most prominent lake shore sites in the city."[15] In an unsigned editorial, R. C. McLean made no effort to hide his disdain for the technique used by the library board in requesting competitors for the new building. He noted that "the astute building committee has apparently determined to hold a close rein on the architects, it has invited and limited their capacity for mischief to the more unimportant and chiefly ornamental parts of the building. The architects are not to make the plans nor meddle with them unnecessarily." He went on to describe in somewhat humorous but obviously contemptuous terms how the Building Committee had set down rules that effectively prevented a building of any merit whatsoever from being designed. He ended his remarks, "It should not be forgotten that, so far as known, the building committee, which has worked out these instructive plans, has never accomplished nor attempted the planning of a library before, nor, indeed, of any other public building. In view of their success the query naturally arises, 'Why did they not take another six months and design the exterior also, instead of paying five thousand dollars to architects and giving them til January 2, 1892, to do it in?'"

The rules of the library competition, apparently available to McLean in November 1891, were published in full in the March 1892 issue of the *Inland Architect*.[16] McLean's fears about the results of the competition were well founded. Architects Shepley, Rutan & Coolidge of Boston won the competition and the building was built. They were able to plan the exterior but their hands were tied when it came to the interior layout. Eventually, they were able to revise the plans provided by the Building Committee slightly to permit certain amenities such as restrooms, but few other changes were allowed. Unfortunately, the basic scheme originally put forth by the Building Committee was essentially realized. The difficulties with that scheme haunted the library for nearly a century. The internal circulation problems were never solved and it was not until the late twentieth century, when the building was converted to the Chicago Cultural Center by Holabird & Root, that it was able to be used as a public building should be used. In fairness to Shepley, Rutan & Coolidge, the exterior of the building and some of the interior public spaces were extraordinary in the classic sense.

Two other results of the competition did have an effect on the architectural profession in Chicago and the Chicago Architectural Sketch Club. Shepley, Rutan & Coolidge established a permanent office in Chicago and shortly thereafter designed the new Art Institute of Chicago Building, which still stands in Grant Park at the foot of Adams Street on Michigan Avenue. More immediately important to the club was the arrival of Robert C. Spencer, who had been employed in the firm's Boston office and was sent to Chicago in 1892 to assist on the library project. Spencer began attending club functions shortly after arriving in Chicago. In September of 1893 the club sponsored an exhibition of his watercolor sketches, most of which had been executed during his Rotch Traveling Fellowship tour of Europe in 1891 and 1892. During the next several years Spencer was to become a key member of the club.

Two weeks after the 1891 annual meeting and election of officers for the coming year, the club held its annual banquet and exhibition of members' work.[17] On November 16, 1891, "the walls [of the club rooms at the Athenaeum] were covered with drawings showing the representative merit of active members, interspersed with casts, art loans, etc." The Clark medal competition drawings were also exhibited. The nine entries for the third annual Clark competition, which closed on October 1, had been received and adjudicated, and awards were presented at the annual banquet.[18] Winners were announced as follows: the gold medal went to George G. Will of Omaha, Nebraska, and the silver medal went to Walter E. Pinkham of San Francisco, California.[19] Although no other medals were awarded, third through eighth places went to F. R. Hirsh of New York, M. G. [*sic*] Garden of Chicago, F. H. Briggs of New York, F. C. Baldwin of Detroit, Adolph Thule of Omaha, and C. M. Olsen of Omaha. The ninth entrant was not named. The *Inland Architect* also reported that at the annual banquet "all active members of the club were present; also the majority of Honorary and associate members were in atten-

16. *Inland Architect* 19, no. 2 (March 1892): 24–25. The rules were a classic example of how not to run a competition.

17. *Inland Architect* 18, no. 4 (December 1891): 65–66. The annual meeting was also reported in great detail in *Northwestern Architect* 9, no. 11 (November 1891): 102–4.

18. *Inland Architect* 18, no. 3 (October 1891): 26.

19. Walter E. Pinkham's silver medal is now in the collection of the author. Pinkham, who also won a silver medal in the 1892 competition, was the only man to win two Clark Testimonial medals.

Menu card for club's sixth annual meeting (NWA)

dance." It was noted that "dinner was served in the assembly hall of the club rooms, which, although commodious in the past for entertainments, is now hardly adequate for this use owing to the rapidly increasing membership." The evening's festivities proceeded along lines similar to previous years, with dinner at nine followed by numerous toasts responded to by various distinguished guests, including Charles Atwood, Lorado Taft, W. L. B. Jenney, and Dankmar Adler. I. K. Pond "responded to 'The Draughtsman off Duty.' The pith of his clever, impromptu remarks was that the draughtsman, on and off duty, is a draughtsman still, and whether still or quiet, he is still a draughtsman. The draughtsman is always off duty." The meeting continued until the wee hours with music, club songs, recitations, and a new song composed for the club by Fritz Wagner. All present agreed that the evening was "the most brilliant banquet in the history of the club."

On November 30, the club devoted its entire meeting to the formulation of the coming year's syllabus.[20] Reports of the meeting noted that "as an indication of the prominence the sketch club has attained among the senior profession, the members of the executive committee were much encouraged by the hearty manner in which those gentlemen who were chosen to address the club consented, and solicited suggestions which could make the papers especially interesting." The new officers were making a great, and successful, effort to revitalize the club.

The Executive Committee was very concerned that the 1892 year be of interest to all members. The selection of competitions was extremely important, and the subjects were chosen from a collection of suggestions offered by members. The syllabus called for ten competitions, more than in any previous year. The goal was to encourage the participation of a large segment of the members. For the first time it was proposed that the club publish a "catalog of sketches" of work by the members. The second competition for 1892 was, in fact, directly related to promoting a club catalog, with the subject being a "Frontispiece for [the] C.A.S.C. Catalogue." The first competition in January was a competition for a club seal. The third competition of the year was to be a design for a public drinking fountain.

The *Northwestern Architect* hinted at the contents of the club syllabus in early 1892 but did not publish it until March.[21] By that time it had already appeared in the *Inland Architect,* where it was cited as "perhaps the very best syllabus ever

20. *Northwestern Architect* 9, no. 12 (December 1891): 112.

Robert Clossen Spencer produced this watercolor sketch in Europe after winning the Rotch Traveling Scholarship (AIC)

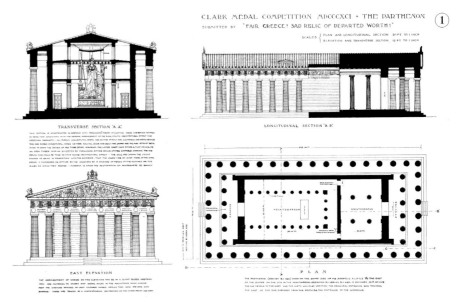

Winning entry by George G. Will for the 1891 Clark Testimonial Competition (IA)

*Walter E. Pinkham of San Francisco took the silver medal in the 1891 Clark competition with this drawing* (Sketches)

*Hugh M. G. Garden won third place in the 1891 Clark competition, but no medal was awarded for his drawing, shown here* (Sketches)

arranged by the club, both in the practical work outlined and in the importance of those who will present the several papers in their particular field of work."[22] That article also listed, for the first time, "the present membership of the club." Included were sixty active members, eleven associate members, and fourteen honorary members, for a total of eighty-five men. Following the syllabus and member list, the *Inland Architect* reported that the first meeting held in 1892 was on January 14 (although, in fact, it took place on January 11), when Lorado Taft spoke on "Classic Sculpture and its Relations to Architecture." That meeting had been announced to the membership by secretary John E. Youngburg's hand-drawn postcard, which suggested that members "Bring Club Seal Drawings."

In the same column, the *Inland Architect* writer noted that "the impetus which has been given to classic sculpture and architecture since the location of the Exposition in Chicago, to building in general, is indicative of much diligent study and review among the Chicago Architectural Sketch Club members who constitute a large majority of those directly interested in its execution, and Mr. Taft, who is at work on several groups that will embellish the Fair buildings was importuned to appear before the club with his rare collection of slides. He was greeted with a large and enthusiastic audience that was completely captured." There is no question that the fair had generated an intense interest in classical architecture. Perhaps Louis Sullivan's lament thirty years later concerning the effect of the fair's architecture was well founded.

The club seal drawings were provided to the Adjudicating Committee shortly after Lorado Taft's lecture. The design of a club seal, the year's first competition, had attracted a number of entries that were printed without comment in various journals over the next few weeks, usually introducing articles related to the activities of the club, although no winners' names were ever published.[23]

In March Paul Lautrup, who was by then an associate member, presented a "dissertation . . . upon 'Vanishing Points.'"[24] Lautrup was held in high regard by the younger members of the architectural community, who envied and emulated his technique of draftsmanship. The *Inland Architect* noted that "at the conclusion of his remarks Mr. Lautrup was enthusiastically applauded, and a hearty vote of thanks was accorded him for his enjoyable and instructive discourse."

That same evening it was announced that the fourth competition of the year would be based on a verse from Samuel Rogers: "Mine be a cot beside the hill; / A beehive's hum shall soothe my ear; / A willowy brook that turns a mill, / With

*This postcard invitation was typical of those used to alert members to meetings* (AIC/DHB)

21. *Northwestern Architect* 10, no. 3 (March 1892): 16.

22. *Inland Architect* 19, no. 1 (February 1892): 12.

23. Discussion of the need for a seal comes up from time to time in the published minutes of club activities. Apparently no winner was chosen from the January 1892 competition. There is, however, an original invitation to the CASC annual banquet dated November 1890 that survives in the Nathan Ricker Archive at the University of Illinois. It is sealed with red wax with an impression of the obverse of the Robert Clark Testimonial Medal. The impression is a positive one, therefore a medal was not used to make it. The sealer either used the actual Clark medal die or had a seal prepared for this purpose.

24. *Inland Architect* 19, no. 2 (March 1892): 26.

C·A·S·C· COMPETITION
DESIGN FOR CLVB SEAL

*Designs for a club seal (NWA)*

many a fall shall linger near." The third competition, for a public drinking fountain, had not been adjudicated in time for the March meeting but the first two design competitions of the year (for the club seal and the catalog cover) had been turned in. In the year's second competition, eight designs had been submitted for the cover of the forthcoming club catalog. The idea of a catalog had first been put forth in late 1891, and during 1892 much effort was devoted to making the club's first official publication a successful vehicle to demonstrate the skills of the membership.

Architectural club catalogs were not a new idea. New York and Boston had both been publishing annual catalogs for some time. They were usually, but not always, done in conjunction with an exhibition. In late December of 1891, the New York Architectural League had published an extensive catalog of its annual exhibition that included a number of drawings for the buildings of the World's Columbian Exposition. That catalog listed a total of 539 entries in the exhibition, many of which were illustrated. In addition to drawings of the fair, the entries for the league's Annual Medal Competition were listed and many of the drawings were published. Several Chicagoans were included, notably all three Garden brothers, Hugh, Frank, and Edward, none of whom were winners, although the gold medal was awarded to Chicagoan Alfred P. Evans and the silver medal went to Hobart A. Walker of Oak Park, Illinois, both noted earlier. Neither was a member of the Chicago Architectural Sketch Club at the time, but Evans joined in 1893. The 1891 New York catalog was much admired by the members of the Chicago club, as were the Cleveland and Boston catalogs in 1889 and 1890. Furthermore, in March of 1892 the Illinois Chapter of the American Institute of Architects had arranged for its first annual exhibition of drawings by practicing architects at the Art Institute of Chicago, and a catalog was issued.[25] Its thirty-two pages, plus covers, listed 242 exhibits, but only thirty-nine, some of them multiple examples of the same projects, were by eight Chicago architectural firms. Several of the entries for the annual

MINE BE A COT
BESIDE THE HILL;

A BEEHIVE'S HVM
SHALL SOOTHE MY EAR;

A WILLOWY BROOK
THAT TVRNS A MILL,

WITH MANY A FALL
SHALL LINGER NEAR.

SAMVEL ROGERS

*Watercolor by Theodore Fraenkel for his competition entry, illustrating the poem at left (Sketches)*

medal competition of the New York Architectural League were included, with the Garden brothers noted as having been in the exhibition, but neither of the two Chicago medalists, Alfred Evans or Hobart Walker, was represented. There were a number of St. Louis firms included in the exhibition, all of which had been in the St. Louis show prior to coming to Chicago. The club had not been invited to participate as a group, but many of the drawings from Chicago architects' offices had been delineated by club members. The exhibition received only lukewarm reviews in the press.[26] Ultimately, the most important influence on the Chicago Architectural Sketch Club was the publication of the catalog. The club members now realized that publication of their work, particularly in conjunction with an exhibition, would be relatively easy and extremely beneficial. The rudimentary catalogs that had been prepared for the annual exhibitions since they were first inaugurated in 1886 did not include illustrations and were apparently simply printed lists of the exhibits. It became clear that a well-produced catalog would outlive an exhibition, particularly if it was illustrated and made available to the public.

In the competition for the "Frontispiece for C.A.S.C. Catalogue," as it was listed in the syllabus, many "meritorious drawings were submitted." No list of entrants was published, but it was noted that W. J. Beauley ranked first and R. E. Smith second.[27] Both of their designs were published, along with that of E. G. Garden. None of them, however, was used in the catalog, which was finally produced in late 1892. The problem was that each of the published designs suggested that the work illustrated was either a single year's work, or in the case of Beauley's design, did not fit the horizontal format eventually agreed upon. The cover design used, while not attributed to a particular member, was signed with the initials "FLL," indicating that it was prepared by Frank L. Linden. But it was only a small part of the work that had to be addressed during the summer and fall of 1892 before the catalog could go to press. It was under the general direction of chairman W. E. Klein-

25. This is the first known catalog of an architectural exhibition in Chicago. It was titled *Catalogue of the First Annual Exhibition* and was published under the joint auspices of the Art Institute of Chicago and the Illinois Chapter of the American Institute of Architects.

26. The exhibit was "not as successful as we might have wished, as only a few Chicago architects took advantage of the opportunity to display their work." *Northwestern Architect* 10, no. 4 (April 1892): 24.

27. Ibid., 20–21.

*Prizewinning entries for a catalog cover, which were never used*

*Emery Roth took third place in the Drinking Fountain Competition (NWA)*

Sketches *cover; note Frank L. Linden's initials worked into the design at the bottom right (Sketches)*

pell and committee members Julius Harder, Henry C. Trost, and Stephen M. Wirts. Fellow member E. S. Bushnell made the final arrangements for production.

Work on the catalog went on largely outside the club rooms, while the regular activities of the club continued. The competition designs for a public drinking fountain were received and adjudicated. E. G. Garden took both first and second honors and E. Roth was third. These three entries were published in the March 1892 issue of *Northwestern Architect,* but there was no further publicity of this competition.

There was a full schedule of lectures, competitions, and entertainment during 1892, as well as at least two sketching trips. One unscheduled lecture took place on May 9, when Charles Francis Browne spoke on "Practical Hints on Outdoor Sketching by an Artist."[28] In keeping with the social aspects of the club, an evening of entertainment had been planned early in the year on Washington's Birthday, under the leadership of Messrs. Heun, Hoeppner, Gibb, Lund, and Schaefer. The evening was described at length in the April 1892 issue of the *Northwestern Architect* in an unsigned article, probably by secretary John Youngburg.[29] It was noted that a "recapitulation of previous entertainments revealed the fact that the drama, one of the most essential functions of entertainment for large audiences, had not been attempted." The enter-

28. This lecture was reproduced verbatim in *Northwestern Architect* 10, no. 6 (June 1892): 35–36. It was followed by a verbatim transcript of an unattributed lecture titled "The Decorative Features of Sculpture," which appears to be the one Lorado Taft delivered at the club on January 14.

29. *Northwestern Architect* 10, no. 4 (April 1892): 23–24.

*Edward G. Garden won both first (left) and second place (right) in the Drinking Fountain Competition (NWA)*

tainment leaders began the evening with what must have been a hilarious version of the second act of *The School for Scandal,* with Youngburg appearing as Lady Teazle, even though the part required him to sacrifice "the crowning glory of manhood's balmy days—a well fed mustache." Without the mustache, he was also able to fill the role of a "well fed boy" in another skit later in the evening. Other members presented their own version of a scene from *Julius Caesar* as well as a number of other "dramatic" presentations adapted to fit their own special talents. The evening ended when "club songs, old and new, were sung exhilarated by a judicious sampling of carefully selected refreshments, a shadow dance by Messrs. Youngburg & Hoeppner, piano solos by C. B. Schaefer and Arthur Heun, and numerous selections by the guitar and mandolin club . . . concluded the most brilliant entertainment the club has given." The club members knew how to relax even if it required hard work.

Many of the key architectural and engineering figures from Burnham's Department of Construction at the World's Columbian Exposition spoke to the club during the summer and fall. And in October of 1892, for the first time, a woman was the invited speaker.[30] Lucy Fitch Perkins, Dwight Perkins's wife, spoke "to a large audience of members of the club and ladies" on Egyptian hieroglyphics with accompanying illustrations in watercolor copied from papyrus. Her subject was certainly appropriate since, concurrently, the Robert Clark Testimonial Competition drawings were being prepared with an Egyptian theme. Lucy Perkins was an accomplished artist, author, and teacher. The membership, particularly those who were entering the Clark competition, welcomed her program. Her voice continued to be heard in the architectural, artistic, and literary communities of Chicago for the next half century.

The last speaker of the season, on October 30, was Fritz Wagner of the Northwestern Terra Cotta Company.[31] Wagner "in his inimitable style caricatured the draftsmen, depicting the different types of draftsmen in a good-natured way that awoke much applause." He continued in a more serious note with advice as to what a draftsman should provide to a contractor to ensure that a building under consideration was properly built. It was noted that "his lectures are always well attended and deemed of greatest value by the club."

At the conclusion of Wagner's talk, the results of the Robert Clark Testimonial Competition were revealed. Originally, the 1892 program for the competition was to have been announced in February and was expected to close on October 1, 1892, but it did not appear in the architectural press until May of 1892, and the results were delayed until the end of October.[32] The program required a design for the entrance to a large cemetery combining a waiting room, a crematory, and a chapel. The competition officially closed on September 15, having been shortened considerably from the syllabus dates.[33] As usual, it was open to all architectural draftsmen under thirty years of age, but not to practicing architects. For the first time the announcement noted that in addition to the gold and silver medals, there would be three bronze medals. Dankmar Adler, N. Clifford Ricker, Henry Ives Cobb, S. A. Treat, and Lorado Taft continued to serve as jurors. Thirteen sets of drawings were received, with a wide geographical area represented. The jury picked Axel Sandbloom's drawing of a "Cemetery Entrance and Crematory (Egyptian)" to win the gold medal. His was the only submission by a member of the club to receive an award. (Nearly a year later, the club "announced that the gold medal design . . . should also bear the name of Mr. John Johnson, it being the joint production of these two gentlemen.")[34] For the second year in a row, Walter E. Pinkham from San Francisco took the silver. The third-prize bronze medal went to John Zettel of Cincinnati. An honorable mention bronze medal was awarded to Henry H. Braun of New York City and a "complimentary" bronze medal was presented to John Rich-

*Lucy Fitch Perkins (WRH)*

30. *Northwestern Architect* 10, no. 10 (October 1892): 80.

31. *Inland Architect* 20, no. 4 (November 1892): 44.

32. *Inland Architect* 19, no. 4 (May 1892): 44. A similar announcement was published the same month in the *Northwestern Architect.*

33. The dates may have changed because other clubs throughout the country were postponing the announcement of dates for their own competitions until the deadline of the Clark competition had been set. Apparently, they did not want interest in their own competitions to be diminished.

34. *Inland Architect* 21, no. 1 (February 1893): 15.

*Axel Sandbloom, who won first place in the 1992 Clark competition with this design, later acknowledged that he had had help from John Johnson (Sketches)*

mond of St. Joseph, Missouri.

The CASC Catalogue Committee had been waiting for the results of the Clark competition before settling on the final work to be included in their 1892 publication. That was not, however, the committee's only concern. Chairman W. E. Kleinpell had, a few weeks earlier, spoken out by "roundly scoring many members for entirely ignoring the repeated appeals of the committee for the subject matter of the catalogue, and in many instances the absolute refusal of some members to render the 'ads' assigned to them. These were given another week to finish their work after which time they will be reported to the executive committee, when the question will arise and be voted on, why should they be members of the C.A.S.C."[35] The "ads" that Kleinpell spoke of were drawings prepared by club members for suppli-

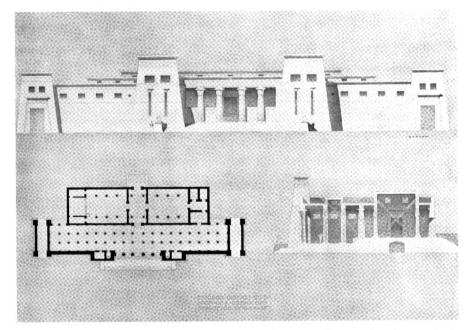

*Walter E. Pinkham's second-place Clark competition drawing for 1992; Pinkham was the only person to win two Clark medals, both for second place (Sketches)*

ers who paid a fee to appear in the publication, thereby covering the cost of production. The drawings for ads are, in many ways, as interesting as some of the members' work in the body of the portfolio. Most are pen-and-ink line drawings, and the delineators can be identified either by full signatures or initials.[36] Ultimately, the committee somewhat arbitrarily chose the members' drawings to be included in the catalog. The only certainty in the early days of planning the publication was that several of the Clark Testimonial Competition drawings would be included. When final selections were made, it was agreed that instead of a catalog, it would be a "portfolio of work" of the club spanning several years.[37]

In July of 1892, while the Clark competition was under way, the club officers announced that there would be a special prize "Competition for Memorial to the late J. W. Root," limited to members of the club.[38] It was to be a permanent memorial located in Jackson Park with a construction budget of fifteen thousand dollars. In McLean's editorial comments, he stated that the competition "gives to draftsmen a rare opportunity for not only displaying their designing ability, but, by the number of drawings presented in the competition, making a slight tribute to the memory of an architect who was the friend of all draftsmen, and particularly of the C.A.S.C." Three prizes were offered, contributed by Daniel Burnham and John Ewen, of seventy-five, fifty, and twenty-five dollars in gold. Daniel Burnham, Lorado Taft, Charles B. Hutchinson, and Charles Follen McKim were to be the jurors. McLean concluded his remarks, "In the absence of club meetings during the summer months, each member should keep this competition in mind and . . . present a drawing . . . worthy of the great object for which it is designed." The competition was to close on October 17, only two weeks after the Clark drawings were due. Secretary Youngburg had anticipated having the winning entries exhibited at the annual banquet, but the jury was not able to meet that deadline.[39] The drawings were not adjudicated until January of 1893 and were not part of the annual exhibition held on November 28, 1892.

On November 14, T. O. Fraenkel was elected president despite the enthusiasm expressed earlier for the reelection of Charles Kessell, who many members felt had literally saved the club from extinction. Two weeks later at the annual banquet, Kessell, who had declined to serve another year, graciously commented that "from the commencement of the club to this, its seventh annual banquet, the history of the club was architectural liberty and freedom exemplified by the work of the club. Ever progressive, its present success was not the result of any one year but of the faithful work of officers and members each year since its inception."[40] He was pleased to turn over the reins to Mr. Fraenkel.

The rest of the newly elected slate of officers included William R. Gibb and Frank L. Linden as first and second vice presidents, respectively. John Youngburg and E. J. Wagner were reelected secretary and treasurer. Both would resign two months later, to be replaced by Hugh M. G. Garden and E. A. Hoeppner. Julius Harder and Stephen M. Wirts were asked to serve as directors.

At the annual meeting, it was announced that the classes in charcoal, black-and-white, and watercolor would be conducted in the winter months, as well as still life and drawing from a model. Instruction would be under the direction of Charles E. Boutwood and held in the club rooms at the Athenaeum. Since the normal workweek of draftsmen included at least a half day on Saturday, the classes were to be held on Sunday mornings beginning at ten o'clock. Club member C. Bryant Schaefer was responsible for organizing them.

The annual exhibition and banquet was always held two weeks after the annual meeting and election of officers. On November 28, the club's Seventh Annual Banquet took place in the club rooms at the Athenaeum where the Sixth Annual

35. *Northwestern Architect* 10, no. 11 (November 1892): 70–71.

36. The portfolio released was *Sketches* (Chicago: Press of the Henry O. Shepard Company, 1892).

37. The book was produced in an oblong format, bound in heavy terra-cotta colored boards with a printed ornamental device on the cover, and tied with heavy cord instead of being bound in the usual manner. It was thirteen and a half inches wide by eleven inches high, with 138 unnumbered pages (sixty-nine leaves). The first two leaves included a prologue and a list of members. Forty leaves, printed one side only, of drawings followed, all identified by author and some dated. The last club drawing had an advertisement on its verso and was followed by twenty-five leaves of advertisements printed on both sides, some with several per page. Most of the advertisements were obviously drawn by club members, and some were signed.

38. The competition was recorded in the 1892 syllabus as beginning on April 18, 1892. The announcement did not appear in the architectural press until July; it was included as an editorial comment in *Inland Architect* 19, no. 6 (July 1892): 68.

39. *Inland Architect* 20, no. 6 (January 1893): 66.

40. *Inland Architect* 20, no. 5 (December 1892): 55.

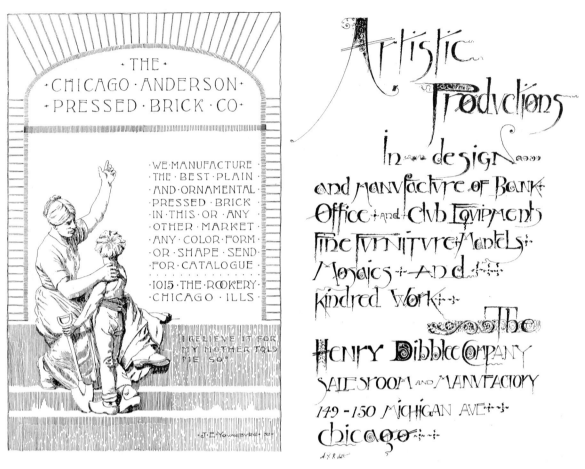

*Two ads in* Sketches *drawn by John E. Youngburg and A. S. Robertson (*Sketches*)*

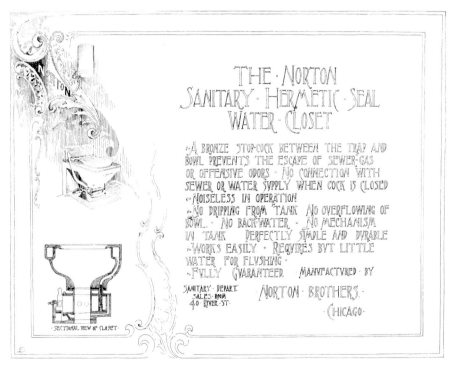

*Full-page ad prepared by C. Bryant Schaefer; all the* Sketches *ads were done by club members (*Sketches*)*

Exhibition of members' work was hung. There had been other exhibitions during the year from time to time, the most prominent an "Art Loan Exhibit" of watercolor and pen drawings rendered from famous architectural triumphs and historical ruins by Mr. J. M. Goodwin, during a trip to Greece and Italy.[41] Goodwin, who was temporarily working with Charles Atwood at the World's Fair drafting office, was from Richard M. Hunt's office in New York. His exhibition, although up only a few days in September, was much admired by the club members and set the tone for a much larger than usual annual exhibition.

The *Inland Architect* reported after the Sixth Annual Exhibition that "the walls were hung with the latest productions of the club, and the rooms were decorated in green and yellow and festooned with flowers."[42] More than a hundred members and guests were assembled for the evening. Among other things, the club's newly published portfolio, *Sketches,* was on display, and the club's treasurer did a land office business in sales at a dollar a copy. After the usual elaborate dinner washed down with a variety of wines, the evening's program got under way. Messrs. Wagner, Wirts, and Hoeppner, who had arranged the menu, were enthusiastically thanked and their effort was pronounced "a work of art." An Entertainment Committee consisting of Messrs. Williamson, Fraenkel, Youngburg, Gibb, and Garden provided an excellent program, which had to be revised on the spot due to the absence of several proposed participants. Printed on the menu card, it read as follows:

AFTER DINNER.
    President's Address.

| | |
|---|---|
| D. H. Burnham | Visitors of '93 |
| W. G. Williamson | Friends of the C.A.S.C. |
| Dankmar Adler | The Clients |
| Lorado Taft | Staff |
| W. A. Morse | The Camera |
| I. K. Pond | Color in architecture |
| Charles Atwood | Development of the Architectural Draftsman |
| Fritz Wagner | Architectural Hobbies |

INCIDENTALS.

| | |
|---|---|
| Club Song | "Rub, rub, rub—The Boss is Watching" |
| Club Song | "My Sketch Club, 'Tis of Thee" |
| Club Song | "We'll Drown the Bogie Man" |
| Joseph Ohlheuser | Violin Solo |
| E. C. Jensen | Song |
| Richard Place | Piano Solo |
| W. R. Gibb | Recitation |

Daniel Burnham had sent his regrets, as had his World's Fair colleague Charles Atwood. Henry Bacon, also on the World's Fair staff, was not on the program but nevertheless remarked on what was being done at Jackson Park and spoke of "the work at the World's Fair as marking a period in the architectural history of this country." He also commented on the quality of the sculpture at the fair, noting that the "fine friezes and figures will educate the public as they never have been before, and give them a better appreciation of the architect's work." Sculptor Lorado Taft was not able to attend but he would certainly have appreciated and applauded Bacon's comments. W. G. Williamson was absent, although his (unrelated) colleague R. B. Williamson filled in for him with his usual array of songs written for the occasion.

41. Youngburg letter, *Northwestern Architect* 10, no. 11 (November 1892): 70–71.

42. *Inland Architect* 20, no. 5 (December 1892): 55.

*Monument marking the grave of John Wellborn Root, Graceland Cemetery, Chicago: the central carving depicts the entrance to Root's unbuilt design for the Art Institute of Chicago (IA)*

Irving K. Pond gave a speech on a serious note, ending with "a plea for the study of color, not waiting for its forms and suggestions to come to us, but to go to nature for inspiration and direction." The evening was pronounced a success no matter who spoke, since genial Fritz Wagner was there to enliven the proceedings with his wit. He was the last speaker. When he spoke, "chairs were generally drawn toward the end of the board where a circle of rhine wine bottles marked the entrenchments of that gentleman, who always begins with a preliminary volley of chaff and ends by giving his auditors hard, practical truth. His speech was one of the best the club has ever listened to."

All these comments were recorded and later printed in the December issue of the *Inland Architect*.[43] The author, probably R. C. McLean, ended his article, "The banquet was in every way a success and closed in the usual way, which is by forming a circle around the tables with joined hands and singing 'Auld Lang Syne.'" It was to be the last annual banquet where members' work of the previous year would be formally exhibited. There would be no Chicago Architectural Club exhibition in 1893. Instead, several small exhibitions would be held in the club rooms and plans would be made for a new method of exhibiting members' work starting in 1894.

Contrary to what had taken place in the past, the club did not begin its 1893 year in December of 1892. Apparently other activities were making too great a demand on the membership. The construction of the buildings of the World's Columbian Exposition was in full force, hampered by a severe winter, and a large number of major and minor buildings were under construction in the business district of Chicago, as well as in outlying areas. Architects were all consumed with the need to finish their work before the great fair opened on May 1, 1893. Club members were the among primary production and superintending personnel who executed the work.

The first club meeting of 1893 took place on January 9. The 1893 syllabus had not yet been published and would not appear in the architectural press until March.[44] Some of the activities of the January 9 meeting were published in the *Inland Architect* under the caption "Root Memorial Competition of the C.A.S.C." Daniel Burnham and John Meigs Ewen had contributed a total of $150 as prize money for the first three places. The results had been scheduled to be announced at the annual banquet the previous November, but the adjudication had not been completed. In January three members of the jury, Lorado Taft, Charles B. Hutchinson, and Charles Atwood, forwarded their comments on the competition.[45] Burnham was noted as being "unable to be present," and Stanford White had previously sent in his opinion in the absence of his partner, Charles Follen McKim, who was in Europe. It was also noted that William Ware had offered his services in lieu of the absent Mr. Burnham.

After apologizing for not having completed their work in time for the annual banquet, the committee commented that "this competition expresses the scholastic and artistic talent of the club." They went on to advise that first prize (seventy-five dollars) be awarded to Mr. P. J. Weber ("Caridad"), second (fifty dollars) to F. M. Garden ("Sisyphus"), and third (twenty-five dollars) to Ernest F. Guilbert ("Wellborn"). Mr. A. C. Berry ("Oneida") was awarded honorable mention. The jury noted that "the competition was very spirited, and each of the eighteen competitors expended his best talent in an effort to perpetuate the memory of the Sketch Club's most illustrious member." The winning design was, unfortunately, not built. Instead, a Celtic cross stands over John Wellborn Root's grave at Graceland Cemetery in Chicago, as the result of a suggestion by Charles Atwood, who recalled that "Root admired the Celtic Crosses." Atwood "took for a model those crosses left by the Druids in Argyleshire, in Scotland, notably that called the St. Martin's cross, and

43. *Inland Architect* 20, no. 4 (December 1892): 55.

44. *Inland Architect* 21, no. 2 (March 1893): 27.

45. *Inland Architect* 20, no. 6 (January 1893): 66.

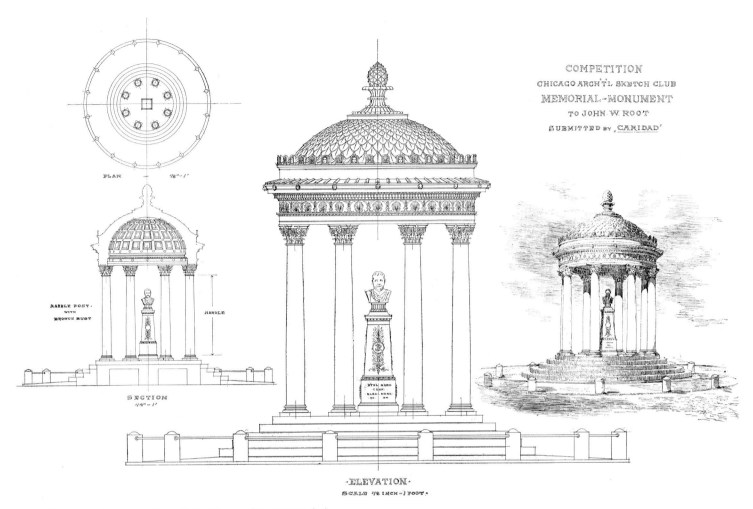

COMPETITION
CHICAGO ARCH'T'L SKETCH CLUB
MEMORIAL·MONUMENT
TO JOHN·W·ROOT
SUBMITTED BY 'CARIDAD'

PLAN ⅛"–1'

MARBLE POST
WITH
BRONZE BUST

MARBLE

SECTION
⅛"–1'

ELEVATION
SCALE ½ INCH–1 FOOT

*Peter J. Weber's winning entry for the J. W. Root Memorial Competition (IA)*

John Wegman completed the work of designing one of the most graceful monuments this country has seen."[46]

The January meeting of the club focused on other matters in addition to the results of the Root Memorial Competition. No speaker was scheduled, but the club was pleased to hear a report from George R. Davis, director general of the World's Columbian Exposition. There was also a problem to be resolved in that several men were claiming authorship of one of the anonymous prize-winning drawings from the Robert Clark Testimonial Competition (if resolved, it was never reported). Finally, it was necessary to appoint committees for the coming year, including a new Adjudicating Committee for the regular club competitions. Messrs. Charles Coolidge, C. S. Frost, and William Zimmerman agreed to assume this task, which had been so admirably handled since 1885 by John Root, Louis Sullivan, and William Le Baron Jenney.

Less than a week after the first meeting of 1893, on January 13, secretary John Youngburg and treasurer E. J. Wagner both resigned. Their positions were filled by Hugh M. G. Garden and E. A. Hoeppner, respectively. No reason for the resignations was recorded, but shortly thereafter the new treasurer was asked to provide a $3,500 bond to the club, and the secretary was directed to secure a safety deposit box for the storage of valuable papers.[47]

In February of 1893, the *Inland Architect*, as part of its regular practice of not-

46. *Inland Architect* 25, no. 3 (April 1895): 27.

47. *Treads and Risers* 3, no. 1 (January 1930): 21. The published records of the club are quite scant during the early months of 1893. Unfortunately, no original records have ever come to light. Research for this book turned up three issues of *Treads and Risers*, published by the Chicago Architectural Sketch Club between 1928 and 1931. In the above cited issue, there is an article titled "Our History," in which several items not noted elsewhere give a fair indication of what transpired during the period in question. The article covers only late 1892 through the annual meeting of 1893, but probably does not include all the events of that period. A diligent search did not locate any other issues of the journal. It is highly likely that "Our History" was prepared using original records, and its style suggests that it is one of a series. Finding the remaining issues of the journal would be helpful in reconstructing the activities that took place before 1892 and after 1893.

*Frank M. Garden took second place in the Root Memorial Competition (IA)*

ing club activities, published a brief review of the "catalog of architectural drawings lately compiled and published by the members of the Chicago Architectural Sketch Club."[48] The article went on to say, "The members of this Club are all young men of great promise and in not a few cases of acknowledged ability, and their influence on the architecture of the future cannot fail to be a wholesome one . . . Considered as a whole, however, this book is a most artistic publication, reflecting great credit on its projectors." He was referring, of course, to *Sketches*. Copies were still available at a dollar each from Mr. A. R. Dukkee, who worked in the Unity Building.

The *Inland Architect* article also reported that on January 23, Mr. A. L. Schlesinger had read a paper "lavishly illustrated with lantern-slides" on the subject "Castles of King Louis II, of Bavaria." Club members entertained themselves on February 6 with one of their "characteristic evenings which have become a feature of the Club, where good fellowship prevails and where the members mingle among each other with that true spirit of fraternal intercourse which is the first binding tie that holds such societies together." That "bohemian" evening was also reported in *Treads and Risers* nearly thirty years later.[49]

A sad note at the February 20 meeting was the announcement of the death of "one of the oldest and most active members of the club," Mr. O. C. Christian. The club made a donation of a hundred dollars to his widow. On the same evening, members were entertained by an informal talk by Harry Bacon regarding "the draftsman abroad." This meeting and those noted earlier were all included in the 1893 syllabus, which was finally published in the March issue of the *Inland Architect*.[50] It was one of the least definitive to date. A "club competition,—subject to be given" was noted for March 6, and C. B. Atwood was scheduled to speak on "A Few

48. *Inland Architect* 21, no. 1 (February 1893): 15.

49. *Treads and Risers* 3, no. 1 (January 1930): 21.

50. *Inland Architect* 21, no. 2 (March 1893): 27.

*Charles Coolidge (SBR&A)*

*Charles S. Frost (MofI)*

*William Zimmerman (CD)*

Reflections on Design" on March 20. The other plans for the year included several evenings where it was noted that the "subject to be announced" was not yet formalized, although the speakers were named. The only firm meeting was that of October 16, when A. G. Brown was to speak on "The California Mission Buildings." Four competitions were listed in the syllabus: February 20, a "Monumental Mantel"; April 7, "A Little Church"; June 12, a "Design for the Main Entrance to an Office Building"; and October 2, a "Water Approach or boat landing." The Robert Clark Testimonial Competition was also "to be announced later." Near the end of the syllabus it was suggested that "for particulars regarding water-color and drawing classes, see secretary." The last sentence noted that "alternate Monday evenings are informal club nights."

There was no indication in the 1893 syllabus that the club rooms at the Athenaeum were about to be lost or that a new space was needed, although club records indicate that on February 27, the membership had been advised that new space would be necessary.[51] The Executive Committee was empowered to act, and they secured the northeast corner rooms on the ninth floor of the Masonic Temple Building. The lease took effect on May 1, 1893, the same day the World's Columbian Exposition opened. Most of the members had already seen much of the architecture, and the exhibits for that matter, at the fair since many of them either worked at the site or on buildings to be built on the grounds. Much of their leisure time in March and April was spent planning for and executing the work needed to move into their new quarters. The meeting scheduled for May 8 was to be a "business meeting" according to the syllabus. It was actually the first meeting in the new space and very little "business" took place.

51. *Treads and Risers* 3, no. 1 (January 1930): 21.

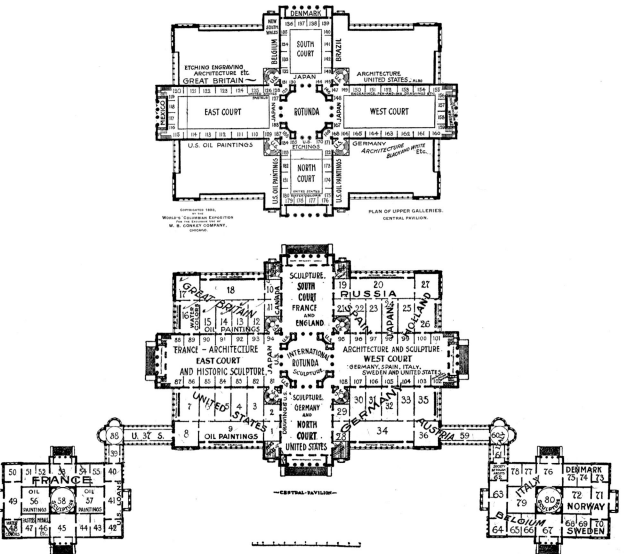

*Perspective from the southwest and floor plans of the Fine Arts Building (WCEC, BWCE)*

# The Great Fair and Beyond

CHAPTER SEVEN

The opening of the World's Columbian Exposition, on May 1, 1893, was the beginning of a period in Chicago's still youthful life that would be remembered for decades. Whether or not one approved of the classical designs on the more than six-hundred-acre site, and most did, the fair was impressive to Chicagoans and visitors alike.[1] May 1 was not only the beginning of the fair, but also the end of one of the most productive periods of construction in the history of cities.

With its more than a hundred buildings, the fair had been conceived, designed, and built in just over three years. The decade before the opening of the fair, beginning in 1883, is generally considered to have been a golden era, when the birth of modern commercial architecture took place. While other cities were building during the same period, nowhere was architecture so avant-garde as in Chicago. Records were broken time and again as new buildings displaced old. Many buildings that were ten years old in 1883 were already obsolete, having been built in haste after the 1871 fire, and they were replaced with little concern. The ever bigger, taller, and more impressive structures built in their place were crowned by Adler & Sullivan's Auditorium Building and Burnham & Root's Masonic Temple.

It was on the ninth floor of the Masonic Temple that the Chicago Architectural Sketch Club found a home when it left the Athenaeum in late April 1893. The club took a two-thousand-square-foot space in the northeast corner at an annual rental of two thousand dollars, with an option for four more years at the same rate.[2] The members moved in on May 8, after decorating and furnishing the new space.[3]

It was perfect for the club. It was near the elevators and had several large windows, including three bay windows looking north and east with a clear view of the lake. The rent was high, but in early 1893 the club was financially stable and new members were being welcomed regularly. As soon as the move to the Masonic Temple was known to be imminent, an entertainment committee began plans for a gala opening.[4] Printed invitations went out to the membership well in advance and all were urged to bring ladies, friends, and especially prospective members. The evening went off as planned, with about two hundred members and guests present. The newly decorated rooms were enhanced with flowers and palms, and the walls were covered with the work of members. The sole business of the evening was a decision to admit nonresident members for a period of six months during the World's Columbian Exposition. (The only restriction was that these

*Detail of the Masonic Temple drawn by E. Eldon Deane (MTB)*

1. An excellent treatise on the impression made by the World's Fair—and, more important, Chicago's new commercial architecture—on European visitors is covered in Arnold Lewis, *An Early Encounter with Tomorrow, Europeans, Chicago's Loop, and the World's Columbian Exposition* (Urbana: University of Illinois Press, 1997).

2. *Treads and Risers* 3, no. 1 (January 1930): 21. It is interesting to note that the rent was one dollar per square foot, which gives a good indication of office rents of the period.

3. Ibid.

4. *Inland Architect* 21, no. 3 (April 1893): 40.

*The Chicago Architectural Sketch Club moved into the new Masonic Temple at the northwest corner of State and Randolph streets in May of 1893; note the Central Music Hall at the lower right, designed by Dankmar Adler (photo by Graybar, courtesy WRH)*

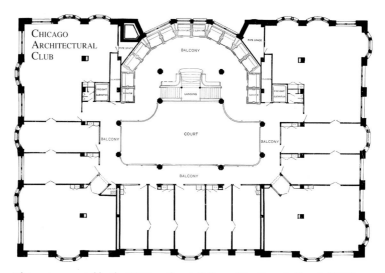

*The space occupied by the CASC on the ninth floor of the Masonic Temple (MTB)*

guests should be connected with the architectural profession and would be required to pay an initiation fee of two dollars.) After that bit of business was completed, charter member W. G. Williamson spoke briefly on the history and progress of the club. The remainder of the evening was devoted to good fellowship, music, and at least one dramatic reading. The announced goal of the evening had been that "strangers will enjoy the evening as generally as the oldest member." All concerned felt that this goal was met.

The new space and completion of work on the fair apparently inspired the members to fill in the empty dates on the syllabus and return to the kind of fortnightly activity that had been the hallmark of the club for the past decade. The May 8 meeting was followed with a club night on May 15, and two weeks later, artist John H. Vanderpoel presented a paper on sketching and art in general, followed by the presentation of a bronze bust of the late John W. Root, which sculptor Johannes Gelert had modeled and donated to the club.[5] (Gelert had, of course, also modeled the Robert Clark Testimonial Medal.) Julius Harder read his paper on "Design in Connection with the Building of the World's Fair" at the June 12 meeting as scheduled. Harder had been part of Burnham's team at the fair, working closely with Charles Atwood, and he was "thoroughly conversant with all the details of his subject."[6] It was the last scheduled meeting before the club adjourned for the summer.

Prior to the summer hiatus, the club had one important task to complete. The program for the Fifth Annual Robert Clark Testimonial Competition had to be prepared and distributed. For reasons unrecorded, the Adjudicating Committee was almost entirely replaced. Only Lorado Taft continued to serve from the previous year. New members included D. H. Burnham, Charles A. Coolidge, and Samuel A. Treat, with W. L. B. Jenney as chairman. They prepared the program calling for "a design for an elevated railroad terminal station for Suburban traffic, in the business centre of a large city." It was a complex problem. Apparently the jury felt that the problems put before competitors in the past had been too simple. The building was to be located on a site 225 feet wide by 125 feet deep between two 80-foot-wide streets, set back from a major thoroughfare a distance of 150 feet. The building could be smaller than the lot size but the space between the building and the major street was to be an "approach or park." The building was to have three floors, the first with a lobby, stairways, offices, and all necessary conveniences. The second floor was to be on a level with the platform and include a general waiting room as well as women's and men's waiting rooms, toilet rooms, a ticket office, a depot master's office, and a stairway to the company's headquarters on the third floor. The program specified sheet sizes and drawings required, and indicated that a site plan was to be included as well. As usual, the competition was open to draftsmen under thirty years of age who were residents of the United States and were not practicing architects. The program was printed for distribution to the membership and was also sent to several national journals with a cover letter from secretary Hugh M. G. Garden dated June 26, 1893.[7] The drawings were due at the club rooms on or before Monday, October 2, 1893.

In addition to publishing the program for the Clark competition, Robert Craik McLean followed up with an editorial in the August issue of the *Inland Architect* in which he commented that the program "presents an interesting problem, its attractiveness largely lying in the difficulty of solution . . . The problem for this year should receive a strong indorsement through a large number of draftsmen being represented . . . [it] closes October 2 and work should commence now."[8]

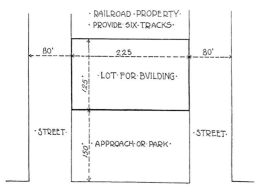

*Site plan for the fifth annual Clark competition, published along with the program in several journals (BB)*

5. That sculpture is now in the permanent collection of the Chicago Historical Society.

6. *Treads and Risers* 3, no. 1 (January 1930): 21.

7. The program was printed in the May issue of the *Brickbuilder* and the July issues of *Architecture and Building*, the *Inland Architect*, and the *American Architect and Building News*. It was the first time that the *Brickbuilder* had included the affairs of the club in its pages. Apparently, the program had been printed with Robert Clark's name spelled "Clarke," since it appears in each journal with that error.

8. *Inland Architect* 22, no. 1 (August 1893): 2.

✤

During the summer months of 1893, the members of the club had an opportunity to see some of their own work, as well as the work of their colleagues from elsewhere in the United States and the rest of the world, exhibited in the form of presentation drawings and models at the World's Columbian Exposition. The idea of an architectural exhibition at the fair had been put forth in the late 1880s, with Dankmar Adler as the foremost proponent of the plan. It was a struggle, but eventually the fair managers agreed. Work from New York, Boston, and Philadelphia constituted the great majority of the drawings, with a smattering from elsewhere, Chicago being represented by a modest number of architects.

Several official catalogs of the exhibits at the fair were published, including one for "Fine Arts" in which the architectural exhibits were listed.[9] The catalog had several sections devoted to subjects such as sculpture, oil paintings, and watercolors. Architecture had its own section, but it was noted that work in this category was also drawn from other sections. There was a Jury of Acceptance for each category. The architecture jury had representatives from New York, Pennsylvania, and Massachusetts, plus a national jury in Chicago chaired by Dankmar Adler. The official catalog listed nearly three hundred exhibits, each one briefly identified. It did not, however, list all the material shown. The various reviews of the exhibited material sometimes referred to exhibit numbers that were not in the catalog.[10] Firms and individuals from Chicago included Adler & Sullivan, Fraenkel & Schmidt, O. C. Rixson, Shepley, Rutan & Coolidge, and Alfred Evans, who had recently been awarded a gold medal by the New York Architectural League. The space allotted to the architectural drawings was in the Fine Arts Building, primarily in the major spaces around the rotunda on the first and second floors. The United States was assigned to the west court of the upper galleries of the central pavilion. Little was made of this aspect of the fair, but we are indebted to the official photographer, C. D. Arnold, for a splendid image showing both levels of the west court and the architectural material exhibited therein.[11]

There was actually more interest in the drawings exhibited at the fair than the managers had expected. Architects from throughout the world attended the fair and were eager to see what their colleagues were doing. Furthermore, a World Congress of Architects was scheduled to meet in Chicago at the same time. This attention, combined with the interest evidenced in the drawings shown at the Art Institute of Chicago the previous year, encouraged the Chicago Architectural Club to find ways to exhibit its members' work in a manner that would be more accessible to the public. The first meeting in the fall of 1893 was also encouraging. It was an exhibition of the work of Robert C. Spencer.[12]

✤

Spencer had come to Chicago in 1892 to work with Boston architects Shepley, Rutan & Coolidge on the construction of the Chicago Public Library. The firm had won a competition for the building and shortly thereafter also won the commission to design the new Art Institute of Chicago. Spencer was involved in both projects. He had been at MIT and upon completing the two-year program in 1888, he worked for a short time with Boston architects Wheelwright & Haven. He did some work for the Boston office of Hartwell & Richardson in the early part of 1890, followed by work in the office of Shepley, Rutan & Coolidge. Spencer won the Rotch Traveling Scholarship for 1891–92, which gave him the opportunity to spend two years in Europe. When he returned, he rejoined Shepley, Rutan & Coolidge in the Chicago

9. *Official Catalogue of Exhibits, Department K, World's Columbian Exposition* (Chicago: W. B. Conkey Co., 1893). The catalog listed drawings, oil paintings, etchings, and pastels from the United States and other countries. The Department of Fine Arts was under the direction of chief Halsey C. Ives, and Louis J. Millet served as superintendent of architectural and decorative exhibits.

10. Reviews appeared in *American Architect and Building News* 41, no. 918 (July 29, 1893), and the British journal, the *Builder*. The review in the latter was reprinted in *American Architect and Building News* 41, no. 927 (September 30, 1893).

11. C. D. Arnold and H. N. Higinbotham, *Official Views of the World's Columbian Exposition* (Chicago: World's Columbian Exposition Company, Department of Photography, ca. 1893). Most of these photographs are now in the collection of the Art Institute of Chicago in large format.

12. Robert C. Spencer Jr. (1865–1953) was at the University of Wisconsin when Frank Lloyd Wright attended in 1886–87. There is no evidence that they knew each other during that period, but their later friendship suggests that they may have been acquainted while they were in Madison, Wisconsin. Spencer was also at MIT while Dwight Perkins was there, and it is likely that they were acquainted. Not only was the architectural department relatively small, but Perkins was working with H. H. Richardson when he died and, shortly thereafter, Spencer worked in the Boston office of Shepley, Rutan & Coolidge, Richardson's successor firm.

*Robert Clossen Spencer (PC)*

*Robert Spencer worked in the office of Hartwell & Richardson in Boston after graduating from MIT; his skill as a draftsman is evident in the drawing above*

*Interior photo of the Fine Arts Building showing some of the architectural drawings in place (AIC)*

office and began, almost immediately after his arrival, to participate in the affairs of the Chicago Architectural Sketch Club.

On September 4, 1893, the club held an informal reception for Spencer's exhibit.[13] There were "about sixty of Mr. Spencer's superb collection of watercolor sketches . . . hung on the walls of the club reception room, and [they] were studied with a marked degree of interest by about fifty of the club members who were present. The sketches were made by Mr. Spencer in Europe during 1891 and 1892, as the winner of the Rotch Traveling Scholarship." The evening ended with a presentation by Spencer concerning the "pleasures and difficulties" of a draftsman traveling abroad. His traveling partner in Europe, George Dean, was also present for the evening.[14] The *Inland Architect*'s item concerning the evening's reception and exhibit stated that "several other new faces were observed, which shows that the membership of the club is already being added to and with a high class of draftsmen, which gives an encouraging outlook for the year's work."

Clearly the Spencer exhibit was a success, and two weeks later it was reported that "Mr. T. O. Fraenkel exhibited a superb collection of watercolors, done during the summer."[15] Fraenkel had been on the schedule for a "subject to be announced" for October 2, but his presentation was moved up two weeks to September 18. At the same time, the club had visitors from the Denver Architectural Sketch Club, who offered honorary membership to the president and secretary of the Chicago Architectural Sketch Club. Both accepted with thanks. (The Denver club had been organized in 1889 and was modeled after the Chicago club.)

The Spencer and Fraenkel shows demonstrated that it was relatively easy to mount exhibitions, but many felt that not enough of the members' work was being shown and they were concerned that what was being shown was not being seen by the right people. Ideally, they wanted their work to be exhibited in a public venue. The nearly completed new Art Institute of Chicago presented a challenge and an opportunity for exhibitions, but before they could use the space, they had to wait for its completion and wind up other club affairs by year's end.

The syllabus for 1893 called for three meetings between Fraenkel's exhibition on September 18 and the annual meeting on November 13, but none of those meetings was recorded. Perhaps the membership was simply exhausted from other activities and the meetings were "club evenings" with no speakers or special events. It was also, of course, the time when the World's Columbian Exposition was winding down. The official closing date was October 31, 1893. There were grand plans for closing the fair, but on October 28 Carter Harrison, Chicago's mayor, was assassinated and the closing ceremonies were subdued. The fair's end came at a time when architects and developers were just beginning to realize that the long building boom in Chicago was over. The following months were extremely difficult for architects and even more so for many of the members of the sketch club, who were laid off in droves.

The annual meeting did take place as scheduled on November 13, 1893.[16] Hugh M. G. Garden was elected president, and Stephen M. Wirts and Alfred R. Schlesinger were named first and second vice presidents, respectively. The position of secretary went to Edward G. Garden, and E. J. Wagner was reelected treasurer. Edgar S. Belden and F. L. Linden filled out the Executive Committee. The other business for the evening, selection of subjects for the annual syllabus, was placed in the hands of the Executive Committee.[17]

Two weeks later, on November 27, 1893, the Chicago Architectural Sketch Club's Eighth Annual Banquet was held in the quarters on the ninth floor of the Masonic Temple. About eighty members attended, along with a number of guests, in-

13. *Inland Architect* 22, no. 3 (October 1893): 30.

14. George Robinson Dean (1864–1919) met Spencer while he was employed by Shepley, Rutan & Coolidge in Boston (1889–91). Although he didn't win a scholarship, he did travel in Europe with Spencer. In 1892–93, Dean was in the atelier of Henri Duray in Paris. When he returned to the United States, he, like Spencer, rejoined Shepley, Rutan & Coolidge in the firm's Chicago office, and he remained there until he entered private practice in 1895. An active member of the Chicago Architectural Sketch Club, he was elected president on November 26, 1894, and again on October 7, 1895.

15. *Inland Architect* 22, no. 3 (October 1893): 30.

16. *Inland Architect* 22, no. 5 (December 1893): 46.

17. No published syllabus for 1894 has been found. The records for late 1893 and 1894 are scant. It was the responsibility of the secretary to distribute information to the press after each meeting. A change of secretaries in early 1894 may account for the dearth of published data. An exception was the reporting on the Sixth Annual Clark Testimonial Competition and announcements and reviews of the Seventh Annual Exhibition of members' work.

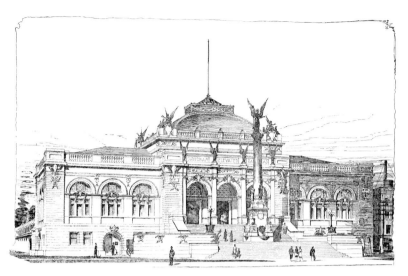

*W. Pell Pulis's first-place design for an elevated terminal station for the 1893 Clark competition, reminiscent of the recently completed Art Institute of Chicago, but more elaborate (CASC/94)*

*One of the two honorable-mention designs in the 1893 Robert Clark Testimonial Competition, by Edward G. Garden (CASC/94)*

*Francis L. Norton's second-place design was not published; Ben W. Trunk took the third-place bronze medal for this design (CASC/94_*

cluding the president and several others from the Chicago Society of Artists, thus initiating an association that was to last for several years. It was the first time that there had not been an exhibition of the members' work opening on the evening of the annual banquet, but plans were already under way for the Seventh Annual Exhibition in the spring of 1894. In the meantime, in lieu of showing members' work, the club mounted an exhibition of the Clark Testimonial Competition drawings, which opened to the public on November 28, the day after the annual dinner.

The Fifth Annual Robert Clark Testimonial Medal Competition was a far greater success than previous years' Clark competitions. Despite the complexity of the problem—a design for an elevated railway terminal—thirty competitors, the largest number ever, submitted drawings. Furthermore, many of the entries were quite sophisticated. It is difficult to ascertain just why there were more and better entries, but it may have been because the competition program was more widely published than in the past. In any case, the result was a total of 154 sheets of drawings, each measuring twenty-two by twenty-eight inches. The rules had called for a ground-floor plan, second-floor plan, front and side elevations, a transverse or longitudinal section, and a perspective and block plan. There was more than enough material to hang an excellent exhibition.

The jury—Jenney, Treat, Coolidge, Burnham, and Taft—had received the drawings nearly two months before the annual banquet. Their report, dated November 9, 1893, advised that they had met several times before taking the first ballot on November 7.[18] It took three ballots before a consensus was reached. On the first ballot, each juror noted his choices for the first three places. They opened their comments with the statement that "there is no design which is markedly superior to others in both plan and elevations, all having some serious defect in either the one or the other. The essential features of the plan should be an abundance of light and the greatest facilities for passing from the street, by a convenient ticket office and gate-keeper, to the trains, and a careful separation of the people descending from the trains, from those coming up; if these conditions are not fulfilled, the station can never be a success. Many of the designs which otherwise have merit were thrown out for want of attention to this one fundamental principle, or for lack of adequate arrangements to insure its working with large numbers of people."

The jury had obviously given a good deal of thought to what they expected in a design for an elevated railway terminal. Apparently, they had decided among themselves what was to be addressed before reviewing the entries and governed themselves accordingly. Most of the jury's comments were somewhat critical, but favorable criticism was also included in most cases. Phrases such as "shows intelligent study," "the plan is well laid out," and "well drawn and rendered" are intermixed with an obvious effort to point out shortcomings and how they might have been addressed. Several comments were made concerning the rendering techniques. One rendering, that of John Richmond from St. Joseph, Missouri, was not selected as a medal winner, but was singled out as "a drawing of great merit that we will be pleased to see in possession of the Sketch Club, framed and hung upon their walls." The gold medal went to W. Pell Pulis ("Fraternity") of St. Louis, the silver to Francis L. Norton ("Greek") of Staten Island, New York, and the bronze to Ben W. Trunk ("L") of St. Joseph, Missouri. Honorable-mention bronze medals were awarded to E. G. Garden ("Ace of Spades") of Chicago and M. P. McArdle ("One of the House of the Craft") of St. Louis. In addition to the special note concerning John Richmond's rendering, the jury also commended the perspective by H. W. Jackson of Saginaw, Michigan.[19] At the end of the committee's report, it was noted that "the principal drawings in the competition have been sent to New York for exhibition, and will on their return be published."

18. *Inland Architect* 22, no. 5 (December 1893): 46–47. The report was printed in full with a list of all the entrants and their pseudonyms, as well as a recapitulation of the Adjudicating Committee's comments. For some reason, the names of the jurors were not noted; the report was simply signed "The Committee."

19. Five of the seven drawings were reproduced in the *Catalogue [of the] Seventh Annual Exhibition* issued as part of the exhibition at the Art Institute of Chicago that took place in May of 1894. All were listed in the catalog, except H. W. Jackson's drawing, which, while commended, was not illustrated, and Norton's drawing, which "could not be reproduced."

*W. F. McArdle won an honorable mention in the competition (CASC/94)*

*John Richmond's design for the 1892 Clark competition did not win an award but was recognized for excellence in rendering (CASC/94)*

✳

With the closing of the World's Columbian Exposition came two events of great interest to Chicago's cultural community and to the Chicago Architectural Sketch Club. First, the new building for the Art Institute of Chicago was completed and opened to the public, and second, immediately after the opening, the School of the Art Institute made space available to the Chicago School of Architecture, the name given to the combined enterprise of the Art Institute and the Armour Institute. The architecture school had been in existence for four years, first as a two-year program and then, after the new space was made available, as a four-year curriculum. The sketch club, with the full endorsement of the Illinois Chapter of the AIA, had been one of the strongest advocates of a full four-year program in Chicago for the training of architects. It had finally happened.

The new building for the Art Institute was one of the permanent fruits of the World's Columbian Exposition. When the fair was first proposed for Chicago, there was a strong movement in favor of locating it on the lakefront in what is now Grant Park. The site of the present Art Institute Building was occupied by the old Interstate Exposition Building constructed in 1873 from plans by W. W. Boyington. It had been used for "fairs and exhibitions, and had housed the Republican Conventions in 1880 and 1884."[20] In 1885 it was standing empty, and two leading Chicagoans, N. K. Fairbank and F. W. Peck, had proposed remodeling it into a theater for an opera festival. They called on Dankmar Adler and his partner, Louis Sullivan, who agreed to handle the project. Together they conceived the idea of retaining the shell of the huge building and constructing a new auditorium inside. The result was a 6,200-seat space built almost entirely of wood. It was an acoustical masterpiece, and became, in effect, a prototype for Adler & Sullivan's Auditorium Building of 1889. The opera festival for which it was designed lasted only two weeks, and for nearly five years the space was used for a variety of purposes. When the World's Columbian Exposition was planned, its site was considered the ideal place for boarding Illinois Central trains to Jackson Park, and more important, the perfect place for a permanent Art Institute of Chicago.

Funds for the new Art Institute Building were not in place when plans were first put forth. There were really two sources of money. First, the officers of the Art Institute elected to sell their relatively new building at Van Buren and Michigan to the Chicago club for their new clubhouse. Other funds were solicited from individ-

20. Hugh Morrison, *Louis Sullivan, Prophet of Modern Architecture* (New York: W. W. Norton, 1935): 67 et seq.

*The Art Institute of Chicago as proposed by Shepley, Rutan & Coolidge: the lions were not installed immediately and the other sculptures shown were never installed (IA)*

uals and businesses, but there was a two hundred thousand dollar shortfall. So, as a second source of funds, the institute officers prevailed upon the managers of the World's Columbian Exposition. In return for the financing needed, they agreed that the new Art Institute Building would be made available for the many World Congresses that were to be held concurrently with the great fair.

The Chicago office of Shepley, Rutan & Coolidge was engaged as the architect for the new building. The classic exterior was completed in a remarkably short time, but in the interior only the two large lecture halls in the north and south wings, called Columbus and Washington, were completed in order to accommodate the various congresses scheduled to take place during the fair. Some of the small galleries were finished as well, and exhibits were mounted during the six months of the fair. When the fair was over, the lecture halls were demolished and gallery spaces were constructed in the interior to put "the building in order, and the structure as far as completed was thrown open to the public on the 8th of this month." It was completed in December of 1893, less than three months after the fair was over, a remarkable achievement.[21]

The new Art Institute consisted of only the westernmost element of the building with arms extending on the north and south. There was a shorter element in the center that provided for the staircase hall. It would be several years before the entire structure west of the Illinois Central tracks would be finished. Nevertheless, the new space was admirably fitted for the collections of the Art Institute, and there was ample room for the institute schools, which had been housed for a few months in temporary quarters on Wabash Avenue. The only department to occupy the new building immediately was the Chicago School of Architecture.

The school's four-year curriculum was made up of a combination of the offerings of the Armour Institute and the Art Institute of Chicago, with Armour teach-

21. *Inland Architect* 12, no. 5 (December 1893): 47.

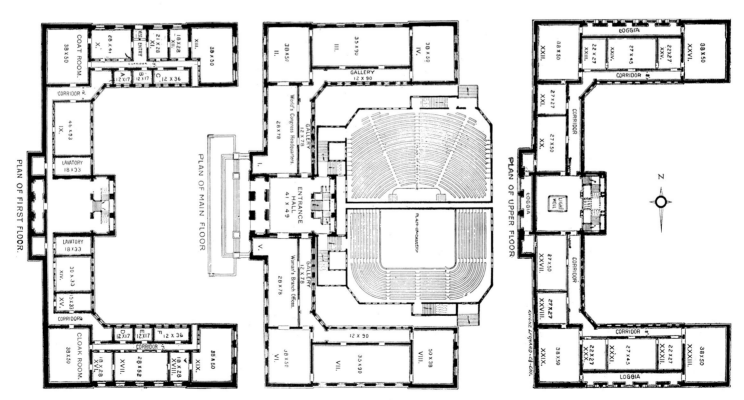

*Plans showing the configuration of the Art Institute of Chicago during the World's Columbian Exposition (WCPR)*

ing the technical classes and the Art Institute handling the aesthetics.[22] The evening classes and the two-year program were phased out. It was the culmination of several years of lobbying by both the Chicago Architectural Sketch Club and the Chicago Chapter of the American Institute of Architects.

The Art Institute was under the overall direction of William M. R. French. Louis J. Millet served as a professor of architecture and Walter Shattuck as an assistant professor, both full-time faculty members. Lecturers, all of whom maintained full-time practices, included architects William A. Otis, I. K. Pond, W. L. B. Jenney,

*The Art Institute was originally essentially two large meeting halls, one of which is shown here; during the World's Columbian Exposition these halls were the site of numerous congresses (WRH)*

and engineers W. S. MacHarg and Wiber M. Stine. All were either members of the Chicago Architectural Sketch Club or participants in club activities. Within a short time, a Thumb Tack Club of student architects was organized under the direction of professor Shattuck, with the support of the Chicago Architectural Sketch Club.

There were no meetings of the club scheduled after November 27 in the 1893 syl-

22. There is an excellent, albeit brief, description of the Chicago School of Architecture in *Inland Architect* 12, no. 5 (December 1893): 47–48.

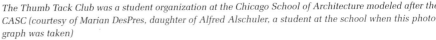

*The Thumb Tack Club was a student organization at the Chicago School of Architecture modeled after the CASC (courtesy of Marian DesPres, daughter of Alfred Alschuler, a student at the school when this photograph was taken)*

labus. The 1894 syllabus had been "left in the hands of the Executive Committee," and the next meeting of the club would be postponed until after the holidays.[23] In a sharp departure from previous years, the 1894 syllabus was never published. In fact, very little was published regarding the club's activities for the first half of 1894. It had always been the secretary's responsibility to record the minutes of the meetings and to distribute them to the various architectural journals for publication. (For performing this task, the secretary's dues were waived.) There was some confusion in early 1894 when Edward G. Garden, who had been elected secretary in November of 1893, resigned and moved to St. Louis. His place was filled by second vice president A. Schlesinger, who served until July 14, when John Robert Dillon was appointed to serve out the rest of the year. Schlesinger's term as second vice president was taken by Arthur Heun, who had already served in that position and on the Executive Committee in 1890–91. The change of secretaries caused a lapse in the information provided to the press, and the first six months of 1894 are difficult to document. Only one regular meeting was reported, that of February 26, and it was published only in the *Inland Architect*, which noted that the meeting was an "exceedingly busy one, it being the first important regular business meeting of the year. Arthur Heun presided."[24] Classes in watercolor, pen and ink, and clay modeling under the direction of W. B. Mundie, E. C. Jensen, and Annibale Guerini, respectively, were announced as being free to members. The classes would take place evenings and Sunday mornings and were likely a response to the University of Illinois at Champaign's new policy of offering similar classes as part of its architecture curriculum.[25]

There had also been a suggestion that the Illinois Chapter of the AIA and the Chicago Society of Artists consider a "consolidation of interests" with the sketch club. The idea was discussed, and while the club and the AIA continued to have a good relationship, it was with the Chicago Society of Artists that a more permanent affiliation was established. The club had invited the Chicago Society of Artists to the 1893 annual banquet and all concerned agreed that there were a good deal of common interests among the members of the two groups. The society had been formed in 1888, and incorporated on April 17, 1889. Its object was "the advancement of art in Chicago, the cultivation of social relations among its members and the general building up of such an art home as will be a credit to art and Chicago, where the works of its members as well as others can be properly placed before the public."[26]

A review of the membership lists of the two groups reveals a rather substantial amount of cross membership. In 1894, all but two of the officers and directors of the society were also members of the sketch club, as they had been in 1891–92 and 1892–93. In fact, in February of 1892, when the Chicago Society of Artists held its Fourth Annual Black and White Exhibition of drawings and sketches, many had been executed by members of the sketch club. A few weeks later in the society's Fourth Annual Exhibition of members' work, sketch club members were again represented, this time with oil paintings, watercolors, and similar items. There was a strong mutual interest in exhibiting to as wide an audience as possible. Until early in 1894, the Society of Artists had used various members' studios as its headquarters, but it then elected to find a permanent home. The Chicago Architectural Sketch Club faced a similar problem. The need for appropriate space for classes and a more club-like atmosphere than that provided by the space on the ninth floor of the Masonic Temple prompted the club to give up its lease and join the Society of Artists at the former Lyman Blair House located at 274 South Michigan Avenue.[27] It was the southernmost building in a block of expensive private houses, all of which would disappear in the twentieth century as property on Michigan Avenue

23. *Inland Architect* 12, no. 5 (December 1893): 46.

24. *Inland Architect* 23, no. 2 (March 1894): 21.

25. The University of Illinois classes were described in an article titled "Artistic Architecture at the University of Illinois," in the May 12, 1894, issue of *Architecture and Building*.

26. This description is taken from the *Catalogue [of the] Seventh Annual Exhibition, Chicago Architectural Sketch Club*. The organization's work was documented in that catalog.

was developed commercially. In 1894, commercial buildings were already being built in the area on the southern fringe of the business district. Just across the street from the new clubhouse was the Bucklen Building, a six-story structure designed by the office of Oscar Cobb in 1884.

The new clubhouse was a two-story Italianate structure with a number of rooms ideally suited for classes and other activities, plus a large coach house where lectures could be held.[28] The first published reference to the new quarters was in the catalog of the Seventh Annual Exhibition, issued in May of 1894. No other notice of the move was published, but in December of 1894, an item in the *Inland Architect* recapping the year's activities noted that "for the first time in its history the C.A.S.C. occupies its own home, at 274 Michigan avenue, whose latch-string always hangs outside for its friends."[29] The first notice to include the new address was in the September 1894 issue of the *Inland Architect,* when the program for the Sixth Annual Robert Clark Testimonial Competition was published.[30]

Between March and December, the only published notices of club activity pertained to the Robert Clark Testimonial Competition or the Seventh Annual Exhibition, with one exception. A two-paragraph item in the July 1894 issue of the *Inland Architect* noted that the club members had "been on their usual summer sketching trip, spending several days at Burlington, Wisconsin."[31] They camped on a river and spent most of their time sketching in the field. Several side trips were taken, including a boat trip upstream. The article noted that "in the evening barges conveyed them and the Boutwood and Vanderpoel painting classes to Brown Lake, when five boat loads were launched upon the water. A German sangerbund [*sic*], upon floats, filled the air with music and colored fire, while the moon and lantern-lit shores formed the background of an evening worth long remembrance. Trips were made in all directions for sketches. Old houses, poplar trees, water, meadow and sunset furnished a sufficient variety of subjects for the pleasure of all." The article went on to say that among "the most enthusiastic present were Messrs. H. M.

27. The Lyman Blair House was situated on the northwest corner of Michigan Avenue at Peck Court, now Eighth Street. The Conrad Hilton Hotel now occupies this location.

28. Over the next few years, some club members gave the clubhouse as their address. Whether they actually worked or lived there is difficult to ascertain.

29. *Inland Architect* 24, no. 5 (December 1894): 48.

30. *Inland Architect* 24, no. 2 (September 1894): 17.

31. *Inland Architect* 23, no. 6 (July 1894): 64–65.

*The Lyman Blair House on Michigan Avenue served as the CASC's club house for several years (CHS)*

*Sketches from the club's "Picturesque Chicago" competition (IA)*

G. Garden, Schaefer, Johnson and Buck; also Messrs. Dean and Chaffee, who made the outward trip on their wheels. Probably another excursion will occur in the fall. The C.A.S.C. has always been commendably forward in encouraging outdoor sketching. The weekly classes at the club rooms will continue through the summer for the benefit of those who attend."

After forgoing the usual exhibition of members' work in 1893, the club began making plans for the Seventh Annual Exhibition early in 1894. With the opening of the new Art Institute Building, including the four-year program for students of architecture, the club took advantage of its good relationship with the institute and worked out an agreement to show work in the new galleries. The club published a circular, dated March 28, 1894, outlining the rules for exhibitors.[32] It noted that "there is to be held a joint exhibition of works of architecture and the allied arts of the City of Chicago in the galleries of the Art Institute, opening Thursday, May 10. It will remain open for two weeks. Works will be received until Tuesday, May 1." The circular included an application blank and a shipping label. Drawings were to be sent to Alfred R. Schlesinger, secretary, CASC, at the Masonic Temple club rooms. Applications were due on or before April 7. The rules stated that the following types of material could be exhibited:

1. Architectural perspectives and elevations in all renderings.
2. Architectural sketches in all renderings.
3. Landscape architecture.
4. Interior architecture.
5. Interior decoration.
6. Interior furnishings (samples and sketches).
7. Architectural and decorative metal work (wrought iron, bronze and brass).
8. Sculpture (ornamental, figurative, architectural) in all renderings.

The rules banned any material previously exhibited in Chicago. They also prohibited photographs of buildings or photographic reproductions of drawings or renderings, with the exception of photographs used for reproduction in the catalog. Exhibitors were encouraged to furnish cuts or photos of their work for use in the catalog (maximum full-page size, four and a half by six inches).

After the rules had been published, the *Inland Architect* commented on the new venue. McLean wrote that the Chicago Architectural Sketch Club exhibition "shows in a remarkable degree what persistent effort will accomplish . . . This year, with the encouragement of the Illinois Chapter of the American Institute and the

32. The circular was published in several journals, sometimes in edited form, including *Inland Architect* 23, no. 3 (April 1894): 34, and *Architecture and Building* 20, no. 15 (April 14, 1894).

cooperation of the Society of Artists, the club secured the Art Institute in which to hold the exhibition and put themselves into closer touch with the art appreciative public. As a sketch club it has for years occupied the first place among draftsmen's organizations, and its influence has done much to promote those in other cities . . . Its benefit to individual members who have gone to other cities has been great, and through the publication of its competition drawings they have become known to architects everywhere. The officers who have thus advanced the local prominence of the club into something of a broader character by the planning and execution of this seventh exhibition of the club's work cannot be too highly commended."[33] This editorial was written before the show opened, but McLean would have been completely familiar with the club's plans. He never faltered in his admiration and promotion of its activities.

The planned exhibition was also noted by the local press. In a lengthy column ten days before the show opened, the *Chicago Tribune* noted that "some months ago the Executive committee of the Chicago Architectural Sketch club sent out invitations to all architects and workers in kindred arts to participate in an exhibition to be held at the Art Institute in May . . . At this moment there are stored in the Art Institute many of the best productions from the pen and brush of architects and decorative artists of this city awaiting to be placed in the galleries for public inspection."[34] The author went on to discuss what was to be shown in some detail, but clearly he had not seen the actual material. He discussed the rules for entry and named the jurors for the various categories. He also noted that none of the work shown had been published previously, and all of it would be in the catalog prepared under the direction of Alfred R. Schlesinger.[35] He ended his comments by stating, "The general character, the high standard of selection, and the wide cooperation which have marked this venture are indicative of the enthusiasm in matter of art which pervades the professional life of the city. Public sanction will encourage that spirit and make Chicago the center of artistic life in America."

The Seventh Annual Exhibition went off as planned, opening on May 10, 1894. It was a great success insofar as it was attended by many people and was favorably reviewed. It was to be open only two weeks. As one would expect, Robert Craik McLean published a thoughtful review in the *Inland Architect*. It did not appear, however, until an even longer review had been published in the *American Architect and Building News* as part of a regular column called "Chicago," by an anonymous author (probably P. B. Wight).[36] The reviewer had clearly seen the exhibition and opened his comments by saying, "The great interest of this month to architects is the exhibition now being held at the Art Institute under the auspices of the Architectural Sketch Club." He was apparently as interested in the exhibition of decorative elements of various kinds as he was in the architectural drawings. He commented at length on plaster friezes, models, stained glass, metalwork, tapestry, and furniture. He felt that the surrounding materials, particularly the rugs, furniture, and tapestry, made an attractive setting for the drawings. The need for several juries to select the items to be exhibited received favorable comment, as did the recent offer by the Illinois Chapter of the AIA to provide an annual gold medal to the club member who had shown the most promise over the previous year. The reviewer gave a good deal of space to comments on the activities of the club and quoted from the catalog that the club was organized "by a few architects' assistants and designers in the allied arts, the object being then, as it is now, the mutual improvement of its members, and the advancement of art and architecture, accomplished by friendly competitions and a series of lectures and essays, relating to all matters pertaining to architecture or the arts." For some unexplained reason, no acknowledgment of the Chicago Society of Artists' participation was made in this or

33. *Inland Architect* 23, no. 4 (May 1894): 38.

34. "Art for Builders," *Chicago Tribune*, Sunday, April 29, 1894. I am indebted to Harold Wolf for bringing this item to my attention.

35. The 1894 *Catalogue [of the] Seventh Annual Exhibition, Chicago Architectural Sketch Club* is the earliest known catalog of the club's annual exhibitions.

36. "Chicago," *American Architect and Building News* 44, no. 962 (June 2, 1894): 101–2.

the *Inland Architect* review.

The *American Architect and Building News* reviewer was especially impressed by the stained-glass exhibit of the Linden Glass Company, as well as "some very artistic displays in furniture, giving the designers their full share of credit." Winslow Brothers also got high praise for its ironwork, but he was disappointed that the designer was not named. Comments on the architectural sketches were included near the end of his article, with high praise for Robert C. Spencer's watercolors and for a large drawing of "the design of the main staircase of the Art Building, exhibited by Shepley, Rutan & Coolidge." Lawrence Buck and Ernest Albert were also singled out for praise, but no mention was made that six of Albert's ten watercolors were done for a young architect named Frank Lloyd Wright. Wright's line drawing for the Milwaukee Public Library Competition was also illustrated but no delineator was identified. The reviewer concluded by noting that "taken as a whole, the exhibition is most interesting and far exceeds any previous display of the kind made in the city before." In the following paragraph, he stated that "the unveiling of Mr. Edward Kemeys's lions . . . was made a feature of the opening night of the Club exhibition . . . [and] we are devoutly thankful and proud of them." More than a century later, they still flank the entrance to the Art Institute of Chicago.

The review published in the *Inland Architect* appeared just a few days after the review in the *American Architect and Building News*.[37] It, too, was critical of the show for devoting so much space to furniture and other manufactured items shown by "leading merchants and manufacturers of Chicago." The reviewer did note that the exhibition remained in place three weeks, one week longer than originally announced.

The *Inland Architect's* reviewer found great merit in the decorative artwork, sculpture, stained glass, and architectural modeling. He was concerned that the material needed more room for hanging, although some pieces benefited from being "hung in close proximity to casts of some of the most superb examples of sculptural ornament that the world has ever seen from Chartres and Notre Dame of Paris." Those casts were one of the residual benefits of the Columbian Exposition, contributed to the Art Institute of Chicago by various foreign exhibitors who did not want to ship them back to Europe. He also commented that the "furniture was accorded a privilege that no architect received, by each exhibitor being allowed to exhibit his works in a group. The large Lecture Room of the Institute, in which the exhibition was held, therefore somewhat resembled a furniture sample and show room . . . It was good free advertising for certain dealers and they made the most of

*Robert Spencer's drawing of the central staircase at the Art Institute of Chicago (PC)*

37. *Inland Architect* 23, no. 5 (June 1894): 53.

*This watercolor rendering of the Frederick Bagley House in Hinsdale, Illinois is one of several drawings executed by Ernest Albert for Frank Lloyd Wright and shown in the 1894 exhibition (CASC/94)*

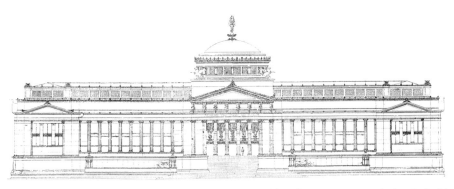

*Frank Lloyd Wright's competition design for the Milwaukee Public Library owes a great deal to the buildings at the World's Columbian Exposition, particularly the Fine Arts Palace by Charles Atwood; it was shown in the 1894 CASC exhibition (CASC/94)*

it. But in justice to the individual designers of these pieces, the names of those who were known appeared in the catalogue."[38] The article also stated that the exhibition was made up "largely of the works of practicing architects who are not members [of the club]." Some unnamed "authority" had advised the reviewer that more than half the drawings submitted had been rejected by the jury of selection. In any case, very few drawings were executed by club members, except those done for their employers, which listed the members only as delineators.

Finally, the anonymous reviewer had mixed praise for the catalog. He noted that it was "profusely illustrated, is a work of art in itself . . . But it was notable for many inaccuracies, and showed inefficient proofreading."[39] He also faulted the committee for relying on outsiders to mount the exhibition. His final comment was "Even if they do not make a scientific classification of exhibits, they should hang their own productions by themselves." In future exhibitions, they took his advice.

❖

38. The exhibition was held before the interior of the Art Institute was completed. There were two lecture rooms, on the north and south, one of which became Fullerton Hall; the other was in the space now dedicated to the Ryerson and Burnham Libraries. It is likely that the latter space was used for the exhibition, since it never had sloped seating.

39. A careful examination of the catalog reveals that several names are misspelled and captions for the Clark Testimonial Competition drawings are inaccurate, as previously noted.

40. There are two primary sources of information concerning the founding of the Permanent Exhibit and Exchange. The first is in a "precursory issue" of the *Building Budget* published in February of 1885. The second is a rather lengthy article in *Industrial Chicago*, 309 et seq. The latter article borrows heavily from the former, but also includes a description of the many exhibitions in what was by then known as the Institute of Building Arts.

The Seventh Annual Exhibition of the Chicago Architectural Sketch Club was not the only show in town during May of 1894. The Illinois Chapter of the AIA held a special exhibition of building materials at the Institute of Building Arts at the same time. The display was prompted by the enlargement of the space to two full floors.

Henry Lord Gay, who had organized the Permanent Exhibit and Exchange in 1883 as a profit-making venture, had envisioned an institution that would "concentrate everything worth knowing and seeing in Architectural construction in one general display."[40] The exhibit space, which was located in the heart of downtown Chicago on Washington Street at the corner of Wabash Avenue, was a success, and numerous manufacturers took advantage of the reasonable rents to display their goods. A major attraction was Gay's practice of making space available for all sorts of architectural meetings. The Western Association of Architects met there many times, as did several other groups, including the Illinois Association of Architects, the predecessor of the Illinois Chapter of the AIA. A critical part of promoting the space was the *Building Budget*, the journal Gay edited and published.

After ownership and operation of the Permanent Exhibit and Exchange was assumed by the Illinois Chapter of the AIA in 1890, the name was changed to the Institute of Building Arts. Few changes other than increasing the number of exhibitors were made until 1894, when the AIA expanded operations and took over a new floor in the building. The correspondent for the *American Architect and Building News* reported that "interest has so increased in the Institute of Building Arts that it now appears to stand on a firm and substantial basis . . . last week a reception has been held . . . the principal occasion being the opening of new rooms, which it was found necessary to add to the old ones. The chief room is the library, where those books that are owned by the Chapter are kept, as well as numerous photographs received from various World's Fair sources. This room is naturally used as a sort of club room by members of the Institute [the AIA] when such a room is needed by them. The building-material exhibit has been much enlarged and formed an interesting feature of this spring reception."[41]

The First Annual Chicago Building Trades and Material Exhibition was reviewed in the same journals as the Seventh Annual Exhibition of the Chicago Architectural Sketch Club. In fact, the review of the Building Trades and Material Exhibition was included in the same "Chicago" column of the *American Architect and Building News* as the sketch club review cited earlier. The *Inland Architect* also gave the Building Trades and Material Exhibition full coverage.[42] Its article noted that the institute had "held a special exhibition of building materials" and that it had added "a floor about 40 by 70 feet . . . so that it now has about 8000 feet, all on the second floor in one of the best business streets of Chicago." The article described the library facilities and other amenities and reported that four hundred guests had assembled on May 14 for a formal dedication of the new space. On that occasion, the "first award was made of the gold medal of the [Illinois] Chapter [of the AIA] for the best design from an architectural standpoint, contributed by a member of the Chicago Architectural Club to the current exhibition of that society."[43] The jurors, P. B. Wight, S. A. Treat, and Frederick W. Perkins, had found only ten eligible drawings by club members. The members presented a petition to the jury suggesting that due to the dearth of drawings, they might consider not awarding the medal. Nevertheless, the jury had little problem choosing a winner. A watercolor perspective titled "Study for an Office Building," by Hugh M. G. Garden, was judged "preeminently above all others." The *Inland Architect* reviewer wrote that the design was "not only the best sent in by the club, but was one of the very best in the whole exhibition." Unfortunately it was not illustrated and has not been found.

All of Chicago's architects and the officers of the art societies, with their wives, had been invited to the May 14 gala, and the evening was a great success. It served to unite the architectural, arts, and building trade organizations in the city to a degree never before experienced. There were no more formal events that evening, but

41. *American Architect and Building News* 44, no. 962 (June 2, 1894): 101–2.

42. *Inland Architect* 23, no. 5 (June 1894): 53.

43. The medal was not actually presented until the following January, probably because it had not yet been struck.

*Two views of the installations at the First Annual Chicago Building Trades and Material Exhibition held at the Institute of Building Arts in 1894, which coincided with the Chicago Architectural Sketch Club's Seventh Annual Exhibition (BBU)*

on the two following Mondays there were special inspection days at the institute, first for architects and then for members of the Builders and Traders' Exchange and the Real Estate Board. Finally, on June 1, the day before the club's exhibition at the Art Institute closed, there was a special reception for both architects and exhibitors.

The exhibition at the Institute of Building Arts was an ideal complement to the Chicago Architectural Sketch Club's exhibition at the Art Institute. Only a few drawings were shown, but there were hundreds of examples of the very latest in building materials, photographs, and other items of interest to architects and draftsmen, including a number of valuable books from the Central Society of Architects of France, which had been exhibited at the World's Fair and subsequently donated to the Chicago Chapter of the AIA. There was a large collection of photographs from the Photogrammetric Society of Berlin, as well as images published by the French National Commission for Ancient Monuments, also residual benefits from the World's Columbian Exposition. It was during the exhibition that the widow of the late W. Henri Adams presented the chapter with most of his library and collection of pictures and photographs.[44] This material was all available for study by the architectural community.

Following the club's intense activities in the late spring of 1894, the summer months were very quiet. Three competitions took place, but other than being published in the *Inland Architect*, they were scarcely noticed by the press. The first, a design for a "Road House for Cyclists," was won by John Johnson, who also took first place in the fall competition for a sketch of a "City Park Bridge" and second place for his series of sketches in the competition for "Picturesque Chicago." First place in the "Picturesque Chicago" competition was awarded to Elmer C. Jensen. The drawings were published in the October and December 1894 issues of the *Inland Architect* without comment. The only other club events reported in the press were the usual summer sketching trips.

44. An intensive search of several Chicago library collections did not reveal any of these items. Some may now be in the Ryerson and Burnham Libraries at the Art Institute of Chicago, but if so, they are not identified as such.

C·A·S·C· COMPETITION
"A ROAD HOUSE FOR CYCLISTS"
SUBMITTED BY "CYCLE"

*John Johnson took first place in the club's competition for "A Road House for Cyclists" (IA)*

John Johnson's first-place drawing in the competition for a "City Park Bridge" (IA)

Sketch from the "Picturesque Chicago" competition (IA)

The fall of 1894 was a period of modest activity as well, except for work on the annual Clark competition. Excitement returned only when the annual meeting was held on November 26, 1894. That meeting, in the new space the club shared with the Chicago Society of Artists, was, according to the *Inland Architect,* "large and enthusiastic, the 'old boys' were out in force, and, as of old, 'Heppy' assumed his 'unanimous' role."[45] George R. Dean was elected president, and Elmer C. Jensen and Frank M. Garden were chosen as first and second vice presidents. John Robert Dillon was elected secretary, a position to which he had been appointed the previous July. Edgar S. Belden, from the previous year's Executive Committee, was asked to be treasurer. The Executive Committee was filled out by Arthur Woltersdorf and John W. Johnson. The entire slate of the Executive Committee was made up of young men who had, during the previous year or so, become extremely active in the affairs of the club.

There was no banquet at the annual meeting, as had been customary in the past, and business was held to a minimum. The organizers of the annual exhibition were lauded, as were the instructors and participants in the various classes in watercolor, pen and ink, and clay modeling. The new clubhouse was admirably suited for these events. The point was made that the "classes are of a character which are a benefit to draftsmen in their everyday work, and are progressive and for every man according to his needs. The classes are free to members of the C.A.S.C." The most important event of the evening, other than the election of officers, was the announcement of the winners of the Robert Clark Testimonial Competition.

When the Clark competition began in 1889, there were five jurors—Lorado Taft, Henry Ives Cobb, C. Nathan Ricker, S. A. Treat, and chairman Dankmar Adler—all of whom served four years. In 1893, Ricker and Cobb were replaced by W. L. B. Jenney and Charles Coolidge. There was a complete change in 1894, with a new three-man jury consisting of Irving K. Pond, Frank Lloyd Wright, and chairman W. B. Mundie. No reason for the change was recorded, but in view of the problems experienced in the early days of the competition, it may have been agreed that a younger group might prepare a program more attractive to the young designers expected to enter the competition. The change was made although the 1893 competition had been the most successful in terms of number of entries. In any case, there was a new jury and the 1894 competition proved quite successful.

Irving K. Pond (BHL)

Frank Lloyd Wright (Tal)

William Bryce Mundie (MofIL)

45. *Inland Architect* 24, no. 5 (December 1894): 48.

46. The program was published in at least two architectural journals with only minor variations: *Inland Architect* 24, no. 2 (September 1894): 17, and *Architecture and Building* 21, no. 11 (September 15, 1894).

47. The results were published in *Architecture and Building* 21, no. 24 (December 15, 1894): 290, and *Brickbuilder* 3, no. 12 (December 1894): 247. *Inland Architect* 24, no. 5 (December 1894): 48, carried the results as part of its reporting on the annual meeting of the CASC.

48. According to the catalog published in early January 1895 covering the competition and its results, there was a fifth medal, an honorable mention, awarded to someone whose name was not given. There were actually two entries for which competitors were not identified. Only one copy of the catalog seems to have survived; it is at the Ryerson and Burnham Libraries of the Art Institute of Chicago. Printed in red and black, it is approximately six by ten inches and consists of eight pages bound with a gold cord tied in a bow on the vertical (long) side. The title, printed on the cover, is *Chicago Architectural Sketch Club Exhibition of the Sixth Annual Clark Testimonial Drawings*. There is an ornamental wreath in the center of the cover surrounding the letters *CASC*. At the bottom of the cover is "Chicago, January vii, mdcccxcv." The text includes a brief history of the competition, the conditions, and the program, followed by a list of entrants' names, with the winners heading the list. The newly elected officers of the club are listed on the last page, along with the address, 274 Michigan Avenue, where the exhibition was held.

49. Leyden's and Rice's entries were published in *Architecture and Building*, Leyden's in volume 22, no. 24 (June 15, 1895), and Rice's in volume 23, no. 17 (October 26, 1895). In each case, the designs were given two full pages, one for the facade and one for the perspective. Gillespie's entry was published only in the catalog of the Eleventh Annual Exhibition of the Architectural League of New York.

As usual, the program for the competition was published in circular form and distributed to the architectural press and any potential entrant who requested a copy.[46] Entrants were admonished to do all their own work or face rejection. Prizes were to be gold, silver, and bronze medals for the first three places and special bronze medals for those receiving honorable mention. Winning drawings would become the property of the club.

The 1894 competition called for the design of the facade for an "Art Club" situated on a residential boulevard. Dimensions were given and it was noted that the "lot is not situated on a corner, and little or no attention is to be paid to the sides of the building, beyond indicating the proper return of the cornice, etc., in the perspective." It was to be a three-story building in "Classic or Renaissance" style. The size of the drawings was specified along with the usual instructions as to noms de plume and data for identification. The drawings were to be delivered to the secretary, John Robert Dillon, at the clubhouse on or before Thursday, November 15, 1894.

There were a total of sixty-five entries and 130 drawings. The Adjudicating Committee had submitted the results to Dillon, who made the formal announcement. The committee wrote that "the competition as a whole was a decided success. The draftsmanship [was] excellent, with but few exceptions. Considering the age limit of thirty years, the same cannot be said of the main feature in a competition, that is, that a building shall look like and suggest what it is intended for." This comment seems to be straight out of the philosophy of Louis Sullivan, who was held in extraordinarily high regard by the club members and, of course, by jury member Frank Lloyd Wright. The jury went on to state that "the great majority of contestants submitted designs too suggestive of art galleries, institutes, etc., too monumental in their arrangement of parts, and the disposition of detail too lavish," noting that the drawings had "an unusual high order of merit." Ultimately, four designs were selected by written vote of each judge. The gold medal went to Willard Hirsh of Cleveland, Ohio; the silver to Edwin R. Clark of Lowell, Massachusetts; the bronze to Ernest F. Guilbert of Chicago; and Albert Kahn of Detroit received a special bronze medal and an honorable mention. The names of the winners were published in at least three journals.[47]

The Clark drawings were hung in the clubhouse shortly after New Year's in 1895. All sixty-four entries were displayed and "an artistically printed catalogue gave the names of the competitors."[48] For some inexplicable reason, the winning designs were never published in any of the journals that usually gave the Chicago Architectural Sketch Club a great deal of space. A careful search revealed only three designs from the competition that found their way into print, and none was a prizewinner. The first was the work of Thomas F. H. Leyden of Chicago, who had become a member of the Chicago Architectural Sketch Club in May of 1894, just a few weeks before the competition was announced. The second was by Florence Chauncey Rice from New York City, who became the first woman to be published as part of the Chicago Architectural Sketch Club's programs. Finally, the design of Charles H. Gillespie of New York City was exhibited and published in the Eleventh Annual Exhibition of the Architectural League of New York in 1896.[49]

Thus, the year following the World's Columbian Exposition ended on a positive note with the first really successful Robert Clark Testimonial Competition following the first of what was to become an annual exhibition of the members' work at the Art Institute of Chicago for the next three decades. Flush with success, the club was ready to expand its horizons.

*Entries of Thomas F. H. Leyden of Chicago (left) and Charles H. Gillespie of New York City (right) in the 1894 Clark competition: neither received an award, although they were both exhibited in the 1895 New York Architectural League Exhibition (A&B and ALNY)*

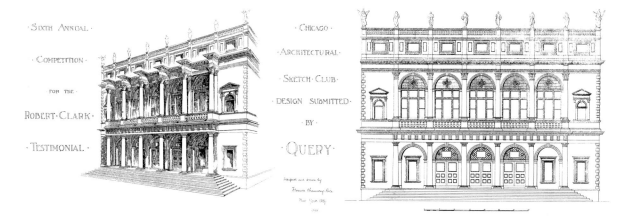

*Florence Chauncey Rice's entry in the 1894 Clark competition; Rice was the first woman published as a participant in any CASC event (A&B)*

+ CHATEAU DE JOSSELIN +

+ FRANCE +

+ INITIATION SKETCH +

FOR THE

+ CHICAGO ARCHITECTURAL SKETCH CLUB +

# Broadening Horizons

CHAPTER EIGHT

Early in 1895, the *Inland Architect* reported, "The first meeting of the eleventh year of the Chicago Architectural Sketch Club, which occurred on January 7, was an auspicious event and one of the most distinguished in its history."[1] It was the formal opening of the new clubhouse, although the CASC had been in residence for several months while the building was being redecorated to accommodate the members and their colleagues from the Chicago Society of Artists. Not only were the Clark Testimonial Competition drawings on exhibit, but Daniel H. Burnham was the featured speaker. The paper he read, "The Organization, Design and Construction of the Columbian Exposition," had been evolving since the end of the great fair in the fall of 1893.

Burnham had resigned as chief of construction of the World's Columbian Exposition when the fair closed at the end of October in 1893. (Ernest Graham, his assistant at the fair, was appointed manager to tie up loose ends.) His one major remaining responsibility was to prepare an elaborate final report of the work he and his colleagues had done.[2] Burnham's last few months as chief of construction had been extremely demanding, although the actual design, contracting, and supervision of construction was essentially finished. His activities then became a combination of completing the work of his staff at Jackson Park, preparing to return to his private practice, and probably most demanding, serving as chairman of the World Congress of Architects and president of the American Institute of Architects.

The Twenty-Seventh Annual National AIA Convention had opened on July 31, 1893, coinciding with the World's Congress of Architects, in the new Art Institute of Chicago Building in Grant Park. Burnham had already agreed to serve as chairman of the World's Congress of Architects and, on the day the convention opened, he was elected president of the AIA. During the week of July 31, Burnham, E. C. Shankland, and Frederick Law Olmsted each read major papers regarding the Columbian Exposition, all of which were later published in the *Inland Architect*.[3] It was these papers, plus his own vast knowledge, on which Burnham based his paper delivered to the Chicago Architectural Sketch Club on January 7, 1895. No copy of that paper has been found, but McLean described it in his report on the club meeting: "Mr. Burnham's paper was a remarkable condensation of facts and was illustrated by the large number of original plats, drawings, etc., which were used in

1. *Inland Architect* 24, no. 6 (January 1895): 59.

2. Burnham's *Final Official Report of the Director of Works of the World's Columbian Exposition* was completed in June 1894. It was produced in holograph form with tipped-in photographs and maps on heavy twenty-by-twenty-six-inch sheets bound in eight scrapbook volumes, with three accompanying volumes of photographs. The original has been in the archives of the Art Institute of Chicago for many years. (It was finally published, in an abridged format, by Garland Publishing, Inc., in 1989, but the reproduction was not well done and the copy is difficult to read; its most valuable asset is the introduction by Joan E. Draper.) The *Final Official Report* has been used as a source for relatively few books about the World's Fair, although it contains important facts that are not available elsewhere and have been ignored by previous authors. Several of the chapters are actually revisions of papers prepared earlier by Burnham and his colleagues; citations for those papers are included hereinafter.

3. D. H. Burnham, "The Organization of the World's Columbian Exposition," *Inland Architect* 22, no. 4 (August 1893): 5–8; Edward C. Shankland, "The Construction of the Buildings, Docks, Piers, Bridges, etc., at the World's Columbian Exposition," *Inland Architect* 22, no. 4 (August 1893): 8–9; and Frederick Law Olmsted, "The General Scheme and Plans of the World's Columbian Exposition," *Inland Architect* 22, no. 5 (September 1893): 18–21. Numerous other papers were delivered during the week, including "Polychromatic Treatment of Architecture" by Louis H. Sullivan, which was not published.

*Daniel H. Burnham, elected president of the American Institute of Architects in the summer of 1893 (IA)*

*Burnham was presented with this elaborate loving cup by his colleagues in New York City in appreciation for his work on the World's Columbian Exposition*

*Johannes Gelert modeled this bust of John Wellborn Root, presented to the club in 1893 (CHS)*

the frequent consultations of the architectural commission. These with the bits of inside history connected with those conferences made the paper of exceeding interest to Mr. Burnham's auditors. It is, probably, also the most accurate condensation of the history of the Fair that could be written."[4]

The very fact that Burnham chose to deliver this important paper to the Chicago Architectural Sketch Club indicates his respect and admiration for the club and its activities. The club returned the favor by turning out in full force to hear what he had to say. McLean reported that "there were present, besides almost the full membership of the club and many visiting draftsmen, distinguished architects, members of the directory of the American Institute of Architects, which was in session in Chicago . . . It was probably the first time that a sketch club of draftsmen ever entertained so distinguished a body of architects, and the fact was appreciated by the club members." The club further honored Burnham and his deceased partner, John Wellborn Root, by prominently displaying the bust of Root modeled by sculptor Johannes Gelert and the loving cup presented to Burnham at a dinner held in his honor in New York City by his "fellow-architects and the citizens of New York" in appreciation of what he had accomplished at the World's Columbian Exposition.[5]

Following Burnham's paper, the first annual gold medal of the Illinois Chapter of the AIA was presented to Hugh M. G. Garden for the best architectural drawing by a member of the club. (Garden had been selected for this award several months earlier for his submission to the Seventh Annual Exhibition at the Art Institute of Chicago.) After some brief housekeeping matters, the remainder of the evening was spent in pleasant conversation between club members and their guests. Near the end of the evening it was announced that the syllabus for the remainder of the year was still being put together, but an important event in the near future would be a plan for reorganization, whereby the club would "enlarge its membership into the general character of an art society, while still retaining as its main feature that of an architectural sketch club." The real meaning of the proposed change was that in the future practicing architects would be admitted as regular members. The activities of the evening "so impressed a number of the visiting architects, that several requested to be placed on the associate list of the club, among them being the treasurer of the Institute." Daniel Burnham, who had been only

4. *Inland Architect* 24, no. 6 (January 1895): 59.

5. Moore, *Daniel H. Burnham,* 69 et seq.

mildly active as an associate member in the past, chose to become a full member as soon as the constitution of the club was revised a few weeks later.

A week after the very successful opening meeting, the club had its first in a series of "Bohemian" nights at the clubhouse—evenings of entertainment only. The following week, the club heard a paper prepared by New York architect Thomas Hastings titled "Planning." The author was not present, but he had forwarded his paper and a group of slides to illustrate it. The subject, certainly prompted by the work done at the World's Columbian Exposition, was to be a matter of great concern to the club members during the next several years. Despite a furious blizzard, more than forty members turned out. After the formal program, classes for the coming year were announced. Elmer Jensen and J. W. Johnson would hold a class in pen-and-ink drawing every Thursday. A major fringe benefit of that class was publication: pen-and-ink sketches and pencil drawings from the previous year had been published in the December 1894 issue of the *Inland Architect* and again in February of 1895. Sculptor Richard Bock agreed to teach modeling on Friday nights,[6] and the class in watercolor was offered on Sunday morning under the tutelage of W. Bryce Mundie, Arthur Heun, and George R. Dean. Louis Millet would teach "Architecture" on Tuesday evenings, and he would also critique the work of the candidates for the next Illinois AIA gold medal.

All the class information was included in the 1895 syllabus, which was formally announced on January 21.[7] It was somewhat different from those of the previous decade. Instead of announcing specific speakers, it merely stated that "on each alternate Monday night, beginning January 7, there will be a lecture or illustrated paper on an architectural subject by men prominent in their profession. Every other Monday night will be devoted to entertainment, at which refreshments will be served." The club established a policy of designating three or four members as "hosts" for each meeting. It was their responsibility to arrange the entertainment on bohemian nights and to provide refreshments.[8]

The syllabus also called for an in-house competition every two months. Prizes would be given to the three members who made the best averages in these competitions during the year. The annual exhibition was to be held again at the Art Institute in May, with detailed information to be provided later. The syllabus also announced the programs for the Illinois Chapter AIA gold medal and the Clark medal competitions. Both were complex problems, the subject of the Illinois chapter competition being "A Building for the Study of Botany" and the Clark Testimonial Competition, "An Art School." The syllabus indicated that 1895 would be a year of intense activity with something scheduled nearly every day or evening, except during July and August, which were to be "vacation months." The new clubhouse, shared with the Chicago Society of Artists, provided the space and ambience to make all this possible.

Following Daniel Burnham's presentation and the formal opening of the new clubhouse on January 7, the club took the steps necessary to revise the constitution and broaden the base of the membership. The Executive Committee and a few senior members had been at work on this for some time. The law required a thirty-day notice to make such a change, and therefore a notice was sent to the membership during the week of January 7, advising that a special meeting would be held on February 11 to vote on the new constitution. February 11 was a regular bohemian night at the club, and the card sent to advise of the vote served two purposes.[9] It bid the membership "to attend a 'Rip Snorter at the Club House,' stating that 'provisions and proviso would be provided and Frou Frous be on tap.'" The reporter

*A typical example of the class work done at the Chicago Architectural Sketch Club between 1893 and 1895 (IA)*

6. Richard W. Bock (1865–1949) was born in Prussia and came to Chicago with his family in 1869. He planned at an early age to be a sculptor and studied with several artists in Chicago, New York, Berlin, and Paris, after which he returned to Chicago, by way of New York, in 1891 and shortly thereafter was employed as a modeler-sculptor at the World's Columbian Exposition. Eventually, he worked with Louis Sullivan, Dwight Perkins, Frank Lloyd Wright, and others of similar talent. He also executed numerous commissions in his own right. He worked in California from time to time and moved there in 1944. Bock taught at several institutions and retired in California, where he died in 1949.

7. *Inland Architect* 25, no. 1 (February 1895): 8.

8. This policy was soon emulated by other clubs. In *Brochure Series* 1, no. 3 (March 1895): 45, it was reported that "the Sketch Club of New York is following the lead of the Chicago Architectural Club in delegating to one or two of its members the office of Entertainment Committee for one evening, when these members act as hosts and provide for the entertainment of the club. This plan has resulted in an increased attendance at the meetings, and is giving general satisfaction."

9. The card has not survived but it was quoted in *Brochure Series* 1, no. 1 (January 1895): 15. This was the first of many notes published by the *Brochure Series* concerning the Chicago Architectural Club, and other clubs' activities, under the heading "Club Notes."

for the *Brochure Series* didn't quite know what the "exact significance of the cabalistic description" was, but he assumed that the membership understood. The second half of the card "announced that the new Constitution and By-Laws would be finally voted upon at the same meeting." The vote was taken, it passed, and the club moved on with a new name.

Starting in March of 1895, published reports of the club's activities began appearing under the heading "The Chicago Architectural Club."[10] It was still the duty of the club's secretary to provide information to the various journals, so it was John Robert Dillon who recorded the change of name in the club's minutes. For reasons unclear, the recording of that change with the Illinois secretary of state, as required by law, was not done until May of 1898,[11] when the papers were filed by secretary N. Max Dunning.

An immediate result of the change in rules to admit practicing architects was a substantial increase in the number of members. In early 1893 there were sixty-five active members on the rolls, and the total of 110 included eight nonresidents, twenty-four associates, and thirteen honorary members. In 1894 the club added six nonresidents and ten associates, while the number of active and honorary members remained the same. However, after the rules were changed in 1895, the club added twenty-seven active members, ten of whom had been nonresidents, a category no longer used. The following year, 1896, saw 115 names on the active list for a total of 162 members in all categories. Associates and honorary members remained stable in 1895 and 1896. Apparently those in the associate category were given the option of becoming full members or remaining associates. Honorary members were elected by the active members, but there weren't any named during this period. The larger membership provided the funds needed to broaden the club's programs and its influence in the architectural community. More important, many of the new members were practicing architects who brought a mature point of view to the club. Their presence also served to entice young members who wished to become part of the larger architectural community.

The 1895 syllabus had included both the annual Robert Clark Testimonial Competition, which would not close until late in the year, and the Illinois Chapter AIA Gold Medal Competition. The latter was to close on April 29; the winner would be announced at the annual exhibition and his work would be published in the exhibition catalog along with all the other prizewinning drawings. The subject of the competition, "A Building for the Study of Botany," was expanded in the printed "programme" to include the study of "Botany, Zoology and Mineralogy." It was to be situated in a botanical garden and was to include: a broad vestibule or portico; a lecture hall arranged in the form of an amphitheater with a seating capacity of seven hundred to eight hundred; three specimen rooms with access to the main hall, and specimens to be used for the illustration of lectures; and three smaller rooms connected with the above for use by instructors and for lectures.

The program also specified the size and scale of the drawings. All were to be marked with a nom de plume and delivered to the club secretary no later than Monday, April 29, 1895. The Adjudicating Committee was appointed by the Chicago Chapter of the AIA and included Charles S. Frost, T. O. Fraenkel, and August Fiedler. Work on the Illinois Chapter AIA Gold Medal Competition began immediately after the rules were published. Much of the work was done at the clubhouse,

10. Prior to the name change, the activities of the Chicago Architectural Sketch Club had been reported primarily in the *Inland Architect*, the *Sanitary News*, and the *Building Budget*, which later merged with the *Northwestern Architect*. After the name change, the club got wider coverage in the *Brochure Series*, the *Brickbuilder*, *Architecture and Building*, and occasionally the *American Architect and Building News*.

11. The document attesting to the name change survives in the files of the Illinois secretary of state. Dated May 4, 1898, it was filed in Springfield, Illinois, on May 17, 1898, and is in box 487, no. 17725. The entire text of the document is printed in a small bound book titled *Charter, Constitution, By-Laws, House Rules, Officers and Members of the Chicago Architectural Club*.

where Louis J. Millet acted as principal critic and adviser for the work in progress. Elmer C. Jensen, then employed in the office of Jenney & Mundie, took first place in the competition.[12] His design, along with those of Hugh M. G. Garden,[13] John Johnson,[14] Charles E. Birge,[15] and Fred Pischel,[16] were all exhibited at the Eighth Annual Exhibition at the Art Institute of Chicago.

The mounting of the Eighth Annual Exhibition was a major effort. A small coterie of members understood that long after the exhibition had closed, the accompanying catalog would remain as a permanent record of the architecture of the period.

12. Elmer C. Jensen (1870–1955) was born in Chicago and was educated in public school followed by two years at the Art Institute of Chicago. He entered the office of William Le Baron Jenney in 1885, where he remained for the rest of his career. The firm became Jenney & Mundie in 1891 and was renamed Jenney, Mundie & Jensen in 1907. In 1936, it became Jenney, Mundie, Bourke & Havens. It survives today as Jensen & Halsted and is believed to be the oldest architectural firm in continuous practice in Chicago. Jensen became a member of the CASC in 1890.

13. Hugh Mackie Gordon Garden (1873–1961) was born in Toronto, where he received his basic education followed by a degree from Bishops College School in Lennoxville, Canada. He moved to Chicago in 1891 after a brief stay in Minneapolis. A skilled draftsman, he worked in several offices before establishing himself as an independent designer.

14. Little is known of John Johnson except that he worked for Jenney & Mundie for many years and his name often appeared as a delineator for the firm's projects. His participation in the 1892 Clark competition as a partner of the winner, Axel Sandbloom, was belatedly acknowledged in *Inland Architect* 21, no. 1 (February 1893): 15.

15. Charles E. Birge (1871–1942) was born in Iowa and educated at the University of Wisconsin, followed by MIT and the École des Beaux-Arts. An accomplished perspectivist, he began his career in Chicago, where he worked with D. H. Burnham and was responsible for some of the drawings in the *Plan of Chicago*.

16. This seems to be the only time Pischel was recorded in print. Nothing else is known of him.

*Elmer C. Jensen's gold medal–winning entry in the AIA's 1895 competition (CASC/95)*

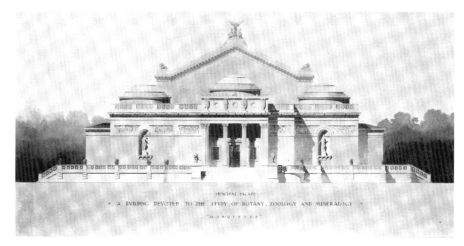

*Hugh M. G. Garden's 1895 AIA competition entry (CASC/95)*

*Charles E. Birge's AIA competition design, shown in the 1895 CASC exhibition (CASC/95)*

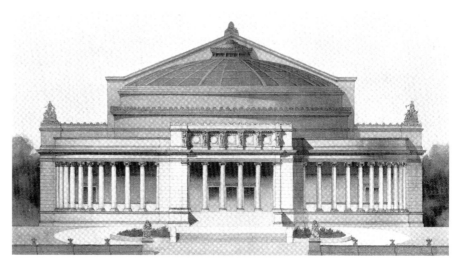

*John Johnson's AIA competition design, as published in the 1895 CASC catalog (CASC/95)*

This point was not lost on other clubs in the nation, nor on the architectural press. The *Brochure Series* editorial in March of 1895 stated that "an illustrated catalogue has come to be one of the important features of exhibitions of architectural drawings, and these catalogues are now exceedingly valuable records of recent progress in architecture."[17] It went on to comment on recent catalogs from club exhibitions in Philadelphia, New York, St. Louis, and Boston. It also editorialized on the many competitions held by various architectural organizations and the steady increase in the number of architectural clubs throughout the United States. The editorial continued, "When in our January [1895] issue it was announced that we should devote a certain amount of space and attention to the architectural clubs of the country, we had no idea of the extent to which these organizations had developed within the last year or two. The work of a few of the older clubs was familiar to us, but it is a surprise to find that nearly every city of importance in the United States has an active and flourishing society of draughtsmen and young architects."[18]

The dates for the club's annual exhibition at the Art Institute were not fixed until April, when it was announced that an "exhibition of works of architecture and the allied arts will be held in the galleries of the Art Institute, opening Thursday, May 23, 1895."[19] The circular inviting participation advised that the following material would be accepted: Architectural perspectives and elevations, architectural sketches, landscape designs, interior architecture, decoration, and furnishings, as well as decorative metalwork and sculpture of an architectural nature. No material that had been previously exhibited in Chicago would be accepted. It was noted that "the jury of admission will be selected from prominent members of the professions." This last stipulation was not really followed, since the jury was actually three members of the club, I. K. Pond, R. C. Spencer, and T. O. Fraenkel, all of them just on the cusp of prominence.

The Eighth Annual Exhibition opening was "largely attended, and proved of much interest, not only to the members but to the many visitors who took the opportunity to view the drawings on the walls."[20] In contrast to the previous year's show, more than half the exhibits were by Chicagoans. There were a total of 321 numbered exhibits, 278 of which were in the architectural category. The remainder were under a special listing for the "Chicago Ceramic Club and Others," most of them exhibits from the Chicago Society of Artists, the club's cotenant at 274 Michigan Avenue.[21] The catalog recognized the relationship between the two groups by giving both a full page at the front listing officers, directors, and committees. At that time the Society of Artists claimed 150 members, and the architectural club had a total membership of 138. A review of the membership lists of both groups indicates that the fairly substantial overlap continued, particularly in the officer and director categories. The announcement and invitation to exhibitors had stated that the 1895 exhibition was to be of "works of architecture and the allied arts,"[22] but this was not noted in the exhibition catalog, and the work of members of both groups, and nonmembers as well, was intermixed.

The architectural exhibits were listed under individual names or firm names. There were nearly fifty members represented, including several with multiple exhibits. D. H. Burnham and Company exhibited fifteen panels of three large buildings in Chicago, Detroit, and Buffalo. Myron Hunt had sixteen numbered exhibits of large-scale drawings, samples of tiles, and various sketches of architectural subjects from his recent tour of Europe. There were twenty exhibitors from outside Chicago, including five from the École des Beaux-Arts in Paris. In addition, the recently organized Cleveland Architectural Club had eight subjects exhibited by five men.[23] The Chicago Architectural Club's annual exhibition was becoming de rigueur for architects everywhere.

*Cover of the 1895 CASC catalog featuring a photograph of a bas-relief by Richard W. Bock; casts of the original were sold for a dollar (CASC/95)*

17. *Brochure Series* 1, no. 3 (March 1895): 41.

18. Ibid., 45.

19. *Inland Architect* 25, no. 3 (April 1895): 32.

20. *Architecture and Building* 22, no. 21 (May 25, 1895): 256.

21. The best reference on Chicago ceramics is generally thought to be Sharon S. Darling, *Chicago Ceramics & Glass* (Chicago: Chicago Historical Society, 1979). It doesn't include any references to the Chicago Ceramic Club, although several groups with similar names are cited therein. The catalog of the Eighth Annual Exhibition of the Chicago Architectural Club lists seventeen exhibitors from the "Chicago Ceramic Club and Others." Several of those names are included in Darling's book as members of various ceramics clubs in Chicago.

22. *Inland Architect* 25, no. 3 (April 1895): 32.

23. *Brochure Series* 1, no. 3 (March 1895): 43. The organization of the Cleveland Architectural Club merited a full page after it was formed on November 22, 1894.

GUARANTY BUILDING
BUFFALO N.Y.

ADLER AND SULLIVAN·
·ARCHITECTS· CHICAGO

*Last work by Adler & Sullivan; perspective by Hugh M. G. Garden*

Notices of the exhibition appeared in several local newspapers, all brief. There was, however, a major review in the *Inland Architect* written by architect Peter B. Wight.[24] Wight's thoughtful and lengthy four-page article demonstrates what a senior member of the architectural establishment felt about exhibitions of this nature. He was in his fifty-eighth year in 1895, having been in practice in Chicago since 1871. While never in the top echelon of Chicago architects, he was successful, was a fellow of the AIA, a member of the Municipal Art League and related organizations, and had been writing articles for various journals for many years. He was certainly familiar with the architectural scene in Chicago.

His review opened with a brief comment about the exhibition space, which he felt was an improvement over the previous year. He noted that the "few manufactured articles exhibited are pieces of genuine artistic value, and the enterprising shopkeepers who got much gratuitous advertising last year by having their wares exhibited under the auspices of an Architectural Sketch Club have been unable to

24. *Inland Architect* 25, no. 5 (June 1895): 47–50.

do the same thing this year with a club of architects." Clearly he felt that the club was in better hands now that it admitted "architects" as members. In fact, had he checked the list of officers and directors, he would have discovered that it was still very much in control of the younger men, all of whom had been active before the senior men were admitted. He commented favorably on the catalog, particularly the cover, which was a photograph of a low-relief sculpture by Richard Bock. (Bock, one of the club's instructors in its regular program of classes, was not listed as a member of the club until two years later.) Wight pointed out that the exhibits were not only by architects, but also by students, draftsmen, and amateurs, as well as a "special exhibit of Ceramic decoration by members of the Chicago Ceramic Club and others . . . [that had been] carefully selected by some person of critical judgment, for there is not one piece of 'amateurish' work in it." He was sufficiently impressed to name all the exhibitors from the Ceramic Club.

Wight was concerned that no real attempt had been made to classify the exhibits, especially in the catalog. He even made some suggestions as to how such classification might have been done. He covered the AIA Gold Medal Competition drawings to some degree, but gave the highest praise to Hugh Garden's entry rather than that of Elmer C. Jensen, who took top honors. He gave even higher praise to the work of established architects such as Adler & Sullivan, D. H. Burnham and Company, Holabird & Roche, W. A. Otis, Patton & Fisher, D. H. Perkins, Pond & Pond, Shepley, Rutan & Coolidge, Clinton J. Warren, and Willett & Pashley, and to Richard Morris Hunt of New York City. He couldn't resist editorializing a bit, adding that "Adler & Sullivan, D. H. Burnham & Co., and Mr. Hunt are the only ones that show what the real work of an architect is."

Wight commended Adler & Sullivan's exhibit, which included "perspective study . . . drawings, models, and terra cotta work." He also commented favorably on the "perspective of the whole building [the Guaranty of Buffalo], drawn and shaded in ink, and side by side are Mr. Sullivan's pencil drawings of ornament which he furnishes to well trained modelers who understand his motive." He was equally impressed that D. H. Burnham and Company showed "working drawings for three buildings about to be commenced," but was not entirely pleased with the buildings those drawings represented. He noted that "all are what are generally called skyscrapers . . . from one of the most prominent offices in America . . . [illustrating] the want of purpose in design which has characterized the works of our leading architects for the past five years or more. Here are three buildings, all for nearly the same purpose and all distinguishable mainly for their great height, designed in three different styles of architecture." They were the Ellicott Square Building in Buffalo, the Winnebago in Chicago, and the Mobley Building in Detroit. He noted that in none "of these designs can we trace the influence of the works of the late John W. Root. Considered as drawings, they approach perfection, and show the methods used in the best regulated architects' offices both in drawing and duplication of copies." Clearly, Wight saw the need for a more original architecture in the development of the tall office building, which, he implied, was a truly American style. It doesn't take a great deal of imagination to realize that his comments on these designs for skyscrapers held a veiled reference to the architecture of the Columbian Exposition.

Wight was laudatory in his comments regarding most of the perspective drawings, calling special attention to the work of Holabird & Roche, Shepley, Rutan & Coolidge, and Patton & Fisher. He was a bit disturbed that Trinity Church of Boston was exhibited under the name of Shepley, Rutan & Coolidge, with no acknowledgment that its design was actually by Henry Hobson Richardson. Other practicing architects received recognition, if not praise. Wight bestowed his most careful and generally favorable criticism on the contributions of "students and draftsmen, [for] we here have contribu-

*Louis Sullivan's sketches for the ornament on the Guaranty Building,(IA)*

*Watercolor of the main entrance to the Yerkes Observatory by Ernest F. Guilbert (CASC/95)*

tions which fairly show the present condition of the several architectural schools and their influence upon the younger practitioners, from John Comes, Cudel & Herz [*sic*], T. O. Fraenkel, J. Friedlander, Paris, H. Hornbostel, Fred M. Mann, Gold Medalist of the *Beaux Arts* Society Competition, L. Henry Morgan, Paris, O. C. Rixson, Schmid & Schieden, R. E. Schmidt, John Van Pelt, Paris, and Frank L. Wright." He also looked with favor on a number of renderings by "architect's [*sic*] artists exhibited in their own name," giving high marks to the watercolor work of Ernest F. Guilbert.

Wight saved his highest praise for the sketches and studies of ancient buildings done by younger members of the club as the result of traveling scholarships and independent study. Charles E. Birge, Elmer Grey, Myron Hunt, W. B. Mundie, and Robert C. Spencer were singled out along with a number of names that have otherwise been lost in the annals of architectural history. He also wrote about the work of nonarchitects—Oliver D. Grover's mural paintings, Fred Hahn's wood carving, Christina Reade's designs in stained glass and wall decoration, and strictly decorative material submitted by others. He did not ignore the items shown by building material suppliers. He was especially kind to the hardware exhibit assembled by the Yale & Towne Manufacturing Company, which he noted was "the most prominent among the exhibits of artistic design applied to manufactures." Yale & Towne actually got more space in Wight's review than any other exhibitor, because of a "large collection of illustrations of the new art called 'Yale Stylo-Chiselry,' which is an improved process of etching on metallic plates." The technique, essentially an etching process, used wax over metal; when partially removed, it allowed an acid to etch into the metal, creating a delicate image.[25] Wight was so taken with the results of the process that he included one of the images as an illustration in his review.

He closed his classic review with praise for the exhibition, noting that "it is a pleasure to record words of encouragement for the enthusiastic young club which may well be proud to assume the responsibility for it. It has dropped the work 'sketch' from its title during the past year, and many of the older architects have joined it. Still its Bohemianism is the ruling element. May it ever be young in spirit if not in years."

Wight's was not the only thoughtful review of the Eighth Annual Exhibition. The *American Architect and Building News* also commented on the event, but the

25. No other reference to the process was located in other literature of the period; apparently it never became popular, despite the fact that it produced an elegant image.

Yale & Towne Manufacturing Company's hardware exhibit, praised by Peter B. Wight: note the first escutcheon plate on the left, designed by Louis Sullivan, and the interesting drinking fountain, two items to the right of the Sullivan piece (IA)

anonymous reviewer found little to praise.[26] He wrote that "the general opinion seems to be that the display was equal to that of last year, although there certainly has been a larger amount of inferior work admitted than previously." He was particularly critical of the school drawings. He thought some were "extremely good, and of especial interest to all draughtsmen and students . . . well worthy of study." On the other hand, he was disappointed that others, in particular those from the École des Beaux-Arts, were "badly rendered and generally soiled and dirty." He felt that drawings that "were not deemed by the French school as worthy even of a 'mention'" should not have been included and that "a little more pruning . . . by the jury would be well received."

As far as the catalog was concerned, the writer had praise only for Richard Bock's cover. He was annoyed that the engraved plates for illustrations were not prepared by the club but by the exhibitors themselves. Therefore, "any exhibitor who desires more advertising has plates made of his own works and they are inserted in the catalogue. As a result, frequently the poorest things . . . are the most prominent . . . while many of the really best things are those never impressed on the attention of the casual observer." The obvious solution, according to the reviewer, was to sell a few more pages of advertising and use the funds to have plates made of drawings selected by the club. He had no objection to advertising; in fact, he noted that the ads "were not overpowering, but kept well in a secondary place, although some of them were certainly artistic in arrangement and design." He concluded by stating that "a few more pages of well paid for advertisements might be tolerated, if the actual engraving of exhibits could be more intelligently and reasonably selected." His point had merit.

When the Eighth Annual Exhibition closed on June 10, the Chicago Architectural Club still had a few matters to attend to before taking July and August off. The syllabus had announced that there would be "a regular club competition due every two months; programmes for these competitions will be announced two months before each competition is closed." Those competitions and their closing dates were: February 25, "A Park Shelter"; April 29, "A Pen-and-Ink Rendering from a Photograph"; June 24, "A City Front"; August 26, "Picturesque Chicago"; October 28, "a Mosaic Floor"; December 30, "a Full Size Detail of an Archaeological Subject." The first two competitions, the park shelter and the pen-and-ink rendering from a photograph, were never published. Three members of the club, however, were listed as showing

26. *American Architect and Building News* 49, no. 1022 (July 27, 1895): 38–39. The comments on the exhibition were included in the "Chicago" column, which was penned by an anonymous correspondent.

their work on these projects at the Eighth Annual Exhibition at the Art Institute of Chicago. Charles E. Birge exhibited his entry for a park shelter and a sketch from a photo. Charles F. Eppinghausen entered two sketches from photographs, and Harry Dodge Jenkins entered a single example of similar work. The other competitions were due after the exhibition. No example of the city front competition has surfaced, but the "Picturesque Chicago" drawings were noted several times in various journals.

With an original deadline of August 26, the latter competition was eventually scheduled to close during the club's vacation period. The closing date was changed to September 2, to coincide with what was becoming the traditional opening of the new year.[27] The club was gradually adjusting its schedule to conform more or less to the schedules of other cultural institutions, the most prominent being the Chicago School of Architecture at the Art Institute.

Following the closing of the exhibition, the Chicago Architectural Club's immediate concern was the Seventh Annual Competition for the Robert Clark Testimonial Medal. The Adjudicating Committee was completely new, and only three members had been appointed. In a break from past practice, they were all members of the Chicago Architectural Club. Louis J. Millet was chairman, and R. C. Spencer Jr. and Irving K. Pond served with him. The program was published in pamphlet form and circulated to the club's membership, other clubs throughout the United States, and several architectural journals.[28] The usual rules for competitors applied (under thirty years of age, residents of the United States, and not practicing architects).

The 1895 Clark Testimonial Competition program called for the design of "An Art School" that would house a large collection of paintings, statuary, and architectural fragments. It was the wish of the gentleman owner of this material to share his collection with his townsmen and to provide facilities for the study of architecture, painting, and sculpture. The building was to be one story with a high basement, facing a town square, and its greatest dimension was not to exceed 150 feet. The interior room requirements were described in some detail and were to include an entrance gallery lighted from above, a large glass-covered court for architectural fragments, an amphitheater to seat two hundred, a library, four classrooms, and the usual subsidiary rooms. The required drawings were a plan and a section, as well as one front elevation, all to be presented in rendered form, without frames, on sheets of twenty-eight by forty inches. The closing date was Friday, November 15, when the drawings were to be delivered to the club secretary at the clubhouse at 274 Michigan Avenue. Thirty-two entries were received and adjudicated.

❋

The months of July and August were intended to be vacation months, but classes continued to be held at the clubhouse. The summer classes started in June, with Charles

27. *Architecture and Building* 23, no. 8 (August 24, 1895): 96, and *Brochure Series* 1, no. 8 (August 1895).

28. The program for the 1895 Clark competition appeared in *Architecture and Building* 23, no. 2 (July 13, 1895): 23; *American Architect and Building News* 49, no. 1022 (July 27, 1895): 41–42; and *Brochure Series* 1, no. 7 (July 1895): 107–98. It had already appeared in abbreviated form in *Inland Architect* 25, no. 1 (February 1895): 8.

*The Adjudicating Committee for the Seventh Annual Clark Testimonial Medal was completely new; it included chairman Louis J. Millet (WRH), Robert C. Spencer (WRH), and Irving K. Pond (BHL)*

E. Birge directing the pen-and-ink work and Arthur Heun as the instructor for the watercolor class.[29] These and other activities of the club were apparently popular and well attended. In June 1895, an editorial in the *Brochure Series* stated that "the Chicago Architectural Club has given evidence this year of very great activity, and its work has been directed in many channels and with good effect. Its lectures, classes, competitions, smokers, Bohemian nights, receptions, ladies' nights, expeditions to places of interest, and finally its exhibition of last month have all been excellently chosen to instruct, interest, and amuse its members, and incidentally promote the general cause of architectural education. The long list of attractions has held the interest of its members without flagging. In the classwork it has had the services and advice of the best and most competent men connected with the profession; and in all directions it is to be congratulated upon the good work done."[30] The club was attracting national attention. The *Brochure Series* was, of course, an East Coast publication. It regularly published a column of "Club Notes," and while Chicago got its share of coverage, clubs on the East Coast and elsewhere in the United States were also covered. *Architecture and Building* was also regularly covering the work of the Chicago Architectural Club. Apparently the club secretary, John Robert Dillon, was performing his task of keeping the media informed with some diligence most of the time. Occasionally, however, major events occurred with little or no attention.

The September 2 meeting came and went with only brief notices in the architectural press. It may have been just due to a lack of space for publication, but the only references to the work of the club during this period were somewhat vague. For example, in September of 1895, the *Brochure Series* report on the recent organization of the Detroit Architectural Club and its activities ended with the statement that "a number of the other clubs have begun early in the systematic work of the year. The Philadelphia, Baltimore, Cleveland and Chicago clubs in particular are starting with unusual vigor and promise."[31] The following month the journal reported that "the Chicago Architectural Club is keeping its members guessing to know what scheme of work or entertainment will come next on its programme." The writer apparently was concerned that no syllabus had been prepared for the fall of 1895. He didn't realize that the club officers were still adhering to the rather loose outline for the entire year published the previous January.

Reports of club activities did appear on a fairly regular basis later in the fall of 1895. The September 2 meeting included an informal exhibition of summer work as well as a showing of the "Picturesque Chicago" drawings, which had been judged and published several months earlier.[32] Members John Johnson and Elmer C. Jensen, both of whom submitted several sketches, were singled out for highest honors in the in-house competition. Two weeks later, the clubhouse was the site of an exhibition of competitive drawings submitted for a city house of moderate cost, loaned to the club by the Brickbuilder Publishing Company of Boston. It was described as "most interesting because of the splendid showing made by the competitors on this practical subject."[33] At the same meeting, the in-house competition for a mosaic floor was announced. Details were presented in a printed flyer, but the results of that competition were never published, nor was there ever any mention of the results of the "Full Size Archeological Subject" competition listed in the syllabus.

The remaining meetings in September included a good deal of "politicking [about] the manufacture of slates for the annual election of officers."[34] The election was held on October 7, and George R. Dean was chosen as president, and Richard

29. *Architecture and Building* 22, no. 25 (June 22, 1895): 303.

30. *Brochure Series* 1, no. 6 (June 1895): 89.

31. *Brochure Series* 1, no. 9 (September 1895): 141.

32. *Inland Architect* 24, no. 5 (December 1894).

33. *Architecture and Building* 23, no. 14 (October 5, 1895): 168. No Chicagoans were named as competitors.

34. *Architecture and Building* 23, no. 13 (September 28, 1895): 156.

E. Schmidt and Myron Hunt became first and second vice presidents. Frank M. Garden was elected secretary and E. T. Wilder, treasurer. The Executive Committee was filled out with John Robert Dillon and Arthur George Brown. All were experienced members who had been active in club affairs. It was the earliest election ever, and it established a precedent for the next six years whereby the club year began in the fall instead of late in the year as it had in the past. No syllabus was published for the 1895–96 year, although a brief outline of activities was included in the January 1896 issue of the *Inland Architect*, in an item concerning club activities.[35]

Following the election and a bohemian night on October 14, the first formal meeting of the 1895–96 year was held on October 21, and vice president Myron H. Hunt delivered the paper "An Impecunious Draughtsman Abroad."[36] Hunt, who was then employed in the office of Shepley, Rutan & Coolidge, had just returned from an extended trip in April of 1895.[37] His lecture was illustrated by "a number of sketches made by Chicago men abroad, showing their methods of working in the field." On that same evening, the club's classes for the coming season were announced. Hugh Garden was to teach watercolor, George Dean was to head the class on architecture, and Charles E. Birge was to continue his class on pen and ink, as would Richard W. Bock on modeling.

The club continued to meet regularly every week, alternating bohemian evenings and formal meetings, usually with a speaker. President George Dean gave one of the formal presentations on November 4, a lantern slide exhibition illustrating the Chateau de Blois. From time to time the club would have joint meetings with colleagues from the Chicago Society of Artists, who shared the clubhouse. On November 25, a scheduled bohemian night, the two clubs collaborated on a program featuring architect Normand S. Patton, then president of the Municipal Improvement League, who spoke on "Architectural and Artistic Possibilities of the Lake Front." The announcement noted that it was "a subject of special interest to architects, artists and sculptors."[38] It would be of more long-term interest than most of those present that evening realized. During the next decade, the Chicago Architectural Club and various other civic groups would regularly address the problems of the lakefront. Ultimately, that interest would result in the 1909 *Plan of Chicago,* sponsored by the Commercial Club of Chicago and executed by Daniel H. Burnham and Edward H. Bennett.

On December 2, 1895, a lantern slide presentation of historic buildings of Rome was followed by an informal discussion of the subject. At the end of the evening, the results of the Robert Clark Testimonial Competition were announced, and the drawings were unveiled for display at the clubhouse.[39]

There had been thirty-two entries (plus two that arrived too late for consideration), eleven from Chicagoans. Five medals were awarded by the Adjudicating Committee—chairman Louis J. Millet, R. C. Spencer Jr., and Howard Van Doren Shaw taking the place of Irving K. Pond, who for reasons not explained had resigned from the committee. The first three prizes went to Addison B. Le Boutillier from Boston, Massachusetts, William L. Welton from Lynn, Massachusetts, and John F. Jackson from Buffalo, New York. The only members of the Chicago Architectural Club to be honored were Harry C. Starr and Edward T. Wilder, who received first and second honorable mention bronze medals, respectively. The committee's report was submitted in great detail with extensive critical comments outlining the rationale for the awards. It included, as it had the previous year, a complete list of the competitors.

The committee noted that the "main criticism that can be made of the designs in general is, that while the subject was one which manifestly called for great simplicity in planning, a large proportion of the designs exhibited far too elaborate and complex plans; as a consequence, many of the designers, in order to introduce added and un-

35. *Inland Architect* 6, no. 6 (January 1896): 63.

36. *Architecture and Building* 23, no. 17 (October 26, 1895): 206.

37. *Brochure Series* 1, no. 5 (May 1895): 78.

38. *Architecture and Building* 23, no. 22 (November 30, 1895): 265.

39. The first brief notices of the Clark competition results appeared in *Architecture and Building* 23, no. 23 (December 7, 1895), and *Brochure Series* 1, no. 12 (December 1895): 191. The full text of the Adjudicating Committee's report was published in *Inland Architect* 26, no. 6 (January 1896): 62–63. This is the source of the quotes that follow. All these notices appeared after the winners' drawings were unveiled at the club.

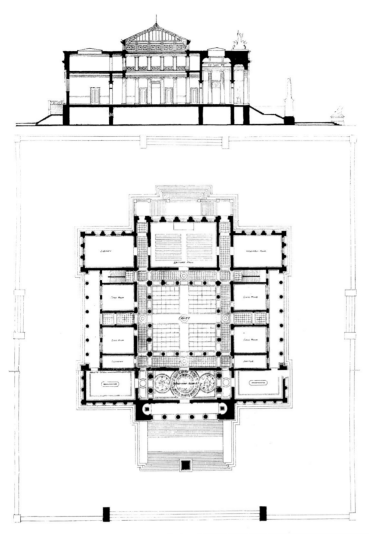

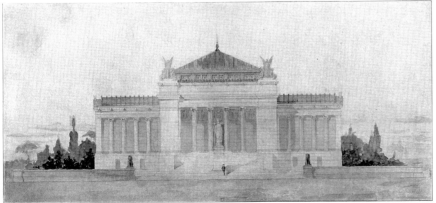

*Gold medal–winning entry by Addison B. Le Boutillier of Boston, from the 1895 Clark Testimonial Competition (IA)*

necessary features, and still keep to the given dimensions, had reduced the actual sizes of intercolumniations, passageways, etc., in a manner which would, in execution, render them impracticable. Some of the plans were entirely unsymmetrical, and these were generally so devised as to allow of [*sic*] a symmetrical elevation, a result which evidently taxed the designer's ingenuity to the extent of necessitating certain expedients, the use of which was hardly in conformity with the dignity of the subject."

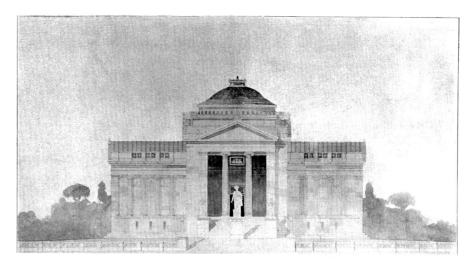

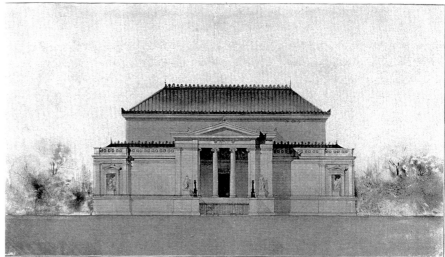

*Drawings by William Leslie Welton, top, and John F. Jackson, bottom, winners of the silver and bronze medals in the 1895 Clark competition (IA)*

The entire report was in the same vein; that is, almost excessively critical of not only the non-winners but the medalists themselves. One unusual statement in the report was that "it was evidently not the intention of those who wrote out the subject," which seems to imply that the jury did not prepare the program. Later the jury stated that they had "inquired very carefully into the possibilities of the side and rear elevations . . . [but since] no drawings of these elevations were required, the matter was more or less one of conjecture." This, again, seems to imply that the jury had not written the program. It is likely that I. K. Pond alone was the author of the program. He had been on the original jury but had resigned before the competition was adjudicated.

However the competition was drafted, Millet, Spencer, and Shaw took great pains to review all the entries and to report their findings in detail. Each of the medal winners merited a detailed explanation of why his work was considered meritorious. Perhaps the most telling statement was the jury's comment regarding the gold-medal winner: "Design No. 30 seemed to solve the various difficulties in the most acceptable manner, and in consequence was awarded the gold medal." Design No. 30 was the work of first-prize winner Addison B. Le Boutillier of Boston, Massachusetts. More than a century later, the influence of the World's Columbian Exposition was obvious; the modern movement was still to come.

The last meeting of the year was a Christmas party on December 23. (The published announcement noted that "presents for the Christmas tree for club friends are requested on or before Monday noon, addressed to the committee.")[40] The Clark drawings were still in situ, but would be taken down shortly thereafter to enable the *Inland Architect* to prepare plates for publication of the winners in its January issue.[41]

Since the club no longer had its annual members' exhibit in December, the Clark drawings were all that hung on the walls during the annual Christmas party.[42] With more than sixty sheets, it made for a festive background. R. C. McLean reported that in the spirit of the season, the walls were also "hung with green, and against this background were set posters of gorgeous hue and fantastic design. The authorship of these was mixed, for those by club members—proclaiming in all the colors in or out of the spectrum, that a Christmas 'Bohemian night' would be held on December 23."[43] Rather than the kind of sit-down banquet that had been held in the past, those present were provided with "red hots, sandwiches, stone mugs for beer, and a container of wine which . . . did not remain full long."

The guest list included P. B. Wight and George Beaumont, the recently elected president of the Illinois Chapter of the AIA, who was, of course, a founder of the club. He was there to present the gold medal the chapter awarded for the most meritorious work of the year. He took advantage of being given the floor: "In a few words Mr. Beaumont sketched the history of the club . . . referring to the important work done . . . and incidentally regretting to find that the word 'Sketch' had been dropped from the club title, and then called for Mr. Elmer C. Jensen, who had won the medal, to receive it from his hands."[44] Jensen's award was no surprise since it had been published in the *Catalogue [of the] Eighth Annual Exhibition* in May of 1895. After a "neat speech of acceptance" from Jensen, the remainder of the evening was "spent in general enthusiasm." Songs were sung and poems recited and, according to McLean, it was the kind of evening that "establishes that spirit of comradeship which the French call *esprit du corps,* and which is the indescribable something which binds men together and keeps the spirit of emulation in its proper and most helpful channel." McLean closed his article with a brief overview of club's 1895–96 activities, which had "opened with the annual meeting, on October 7, 1895," and mentioned that the Ninth Annual Exhibition had already been arranged to be held at the Art Institute of Chicago and would open March 27, 1896.

Before the Christmas party ended, AIA president Beaumont apparently had informal conversations with some of the club officers to review what had been done during the previous few months in regard to a plan for a new "Lake Front Park" (which would later be renamed Grant Park). This became the genesis of an extremely important activity of the club in early 1896.

George Beaumont had been elected president of the Illinois Chapter of the American Institute of Architects at the chapter's annual meeting on September 16, 1895.[45] The rest of the slate of officers elected that evening included vice presidents Peter B. Wight and Normand S. Patton. Dwight Perkins was named secretary and L. G. Hallberg, treasurer. All except Hallberg were members of the Chicago Architectural Club. Following their election, Patton reported that the chapter's Committee on Buildings and Grounds under his chairmanship "had prepared during the year a complete plan for the improvement of the Lake Front Park, on land to be recovered from Lake Michigan." The work had been undertaken as a joint venture with the

40. *Architecture and Building* 23, no. 25 (December 21, 1895): 301.

41. *Inland Architect* 26, no. 6 (January 1896). The gold, silver, and bronze medalists were all published.

42. The announcement of the Christmas party was included in *Architecture and Building* 23, no. 25 (December 21, 1895). Invitations were probably sent on printed postcards to members and friends of the club.

43. *Inland Architect* 26, no. 6 (January 1896): 63. The usual description of the annual end-of-the-year party included all the events reported here.

44. There is some confusion as to when the presentation actually occurred. The *Inland Architect* article previously cited suggests that the presentation was done on December 23, 1895. A brief item in *Architecture and Building* 24, no. 2 (January 11, 1896): 28, states that "the presentation of the gold medal of the Illinois Chapter of the American Institute of Architects, awarded to Elmer C. Jensen in the second annual 'Chapter Medal' Competition, took place on Monday evening, January 6, at the club house."

45. *Inland Architect* 26, no. 3 (October 1895): 27.

Municipal Improvement League, one of several reform groups active in Chicago in the late nineteenth century. The plan had been referred to various other committees "for consideration, and to Frederick Law Olmsted for criticism." Two similar but not identical versions of that plan were prepared, one dated July 1895 and the other dated August 1895. The major difference was the design and location of the Field Columbian Museum. In both cases, it was sited at the south end of the park, not in the center as Daniel Burnham advocated. The *Inland Architect* reported further that "it was not expected that the plan would be adopted as a whole, but it would put on record a comprehensive scheme that may be the foundation of what may be done when the work is taken up in earnest." The committee was asked to continue its work and the following month Normand S. Patton, who also served as president of the Municipal Improvement League, spoke to a joint meeting of the Chicago Society of Artists and the Chicago Architectural Club.[46]

Patton's subject was "Architectural and Artistic Possibilities of the Lake Front," one he had been considering for some time. His interest was an outgrowth of the general admiration of the public and architects alike for what had been accomplished in Jackson Park, where landfill was used to recover parkland that was incorporated into the design of the Court of Honor at the World's Columbian Exposition. There were strong feelings in the art and architectural communities of Chicago that something similar could and should be done in Lake Front Park. Key personnel in addition to Patton were Peter B. Wight and Samuel A. Treat, senior members of the Illinois Chapter of the AIA. In 1894 they had formed a committee that spearheaded the organization of the Municipal Improvement League—an organization of organizations—which took up the cause. (The Builders and Traders' Exchange, the Chicago Real Estate Board, the Chicago Society of Artists, and the Western Society of Engineers all formed three-man committees whose charge was to "confer upon public buildings and grounds and arrange for a permanent organization." Together with Patton's AIA group, these committees became the Municipal Improvement League.)[47]

The league's constitution stated that "the purpose of this League shall be to secure for our city such an arrangement, design, and adornment of our public buildings and grounds, streets, boulevards, and other public works as shall most contribute to the convenience and enjoyment of the public; shall stimulate an appreciation of art and give to the city a fit expression of its greatness." S. A. Treat, the 1894 president of the local AIA, immediately offered the chapter's space at the Institute for Building Arts as a permanent meeting place.

Within a few weeks of the organization of the Municipal Improvement League, Chicago businessman Washington Porter announced his own plan for major improvements to the lakefront. His plan, which was described but not published in the local press, included beautification of the shoreline of Lake Michigan from the mouth of the Chicago River to Jackson Park.[48] It was essentially the same as Daniel H. Burnham's first plan for lakefront improvements prepared in 1896. Burnham's plan, however, included the construction of what would become the Field Museum of Natural History in the heart of Lake Front Park on axis with Congress Street. This was, of course, prohibited by a law that was codified as a result of the efforts of Montgomery Ward.[49] After this initial plan, Burnham did little with regard to the improvement of Lake Front Park for the next several years. Patton and Wight, on the other hand, continued their efforts.

Two weeks after Washington Porter's plan was publicized, the Municipal Improvement League announced that it would take up the question of creating a park on the lakefront.[50] While league members did not specifically mention Porter's proposal, they did advise that they would review a somewhat less ambitious plan that had been put forth by alderman Martin B. Madden, who had been advocating var-

*Normand S. Patton (PC)*

46. *Architecture and Building* 23, no. 22 (November 30, 1895): 265.

47. The Municipal Improvement League was launched on October 26, 1894, by representatives of each of the named organizations. It was reported in the *Chicago Tribune* on Saturday, October 27, 1894.

48. "His Lake-Front Plan, Washington Porter Outlines a Scheme for Improvement," *Chicago Tribune*, November 30, 1894.

49. Montgomery Ward spent many years and a substantial sum of money in his fight to keep the lakefront "forever open, clear and free" (in words of Gurdon Saltonstall Hubbard, William F. Thornton, and William B. Archer, who wrote the now-famous phrase across the bottom of a map of the shores of Lake Michigan in 1836). He even designated funds in his estate to continue the battle after his death. Chicagoans today owe him a great debt for his efforts, epitomized by the magnificence of Grant Park (known as Lake Front Park in the late nineteenth century).

50. *Chicago Tribune*, December 16, 1894.

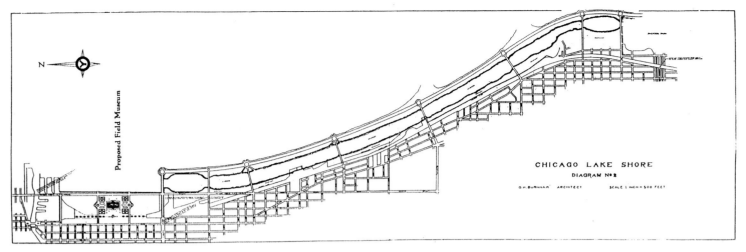

*D. H. Burnham's 1896 plan to improve Chicago's lakefront (IA)*

ious schemes for improving Lake Front Park since the end of the Columbian Exposition.[51] In the same announcement, the members of the league were listed, with Patton, Treat, and Wight continuing to represent the AIA. Prominent members of the other organizations were named, including L. J. Millet, Lorado Taft, and John Vanderpoel, who represented the Chicago Society of Artists. There was no official representation from the Chicago Architectural Club, but all three members of the Chicago Society of Artists were also members of the Chicago Architectural Club. The two organizations were still sharing quarters and activities in the clubhouse on Michigan Avenue overlooking Lake Front Park. Patton, Treat, and Wight agreed to prepare preliminary plans for the proposed improvements.

Twenty years later Peter B. Wight prepared a speech that he delivered several times in Chicago and elsewhere, wherein he recapped what took place during the first half of 1895 when he was responsible for preparing the promised preliminary plans.[52] He wrote that his "attention was first drawn to the matter during the lean years immediately after the World's Columbian Exposition. In 1894, the architects, builders and real estate men being without much to do . . . organized . . . The Municipal Improvement League." He "acted as a sort of factotum under [Patton]" since he was one of the "unemployed" and proceeded "to lay out a plan of the proposed park . . . mostly the work of Mr. Patton, and was very beautiful." Both Wight and the league as a whole

51. Martin B. Madden (1855–1928) was born in England. In 1860, he moved to Chicago, where he attended public school. Madden graduated from Bryant and Stratton Business College in 1873 and then from an engineering trade school. He owned a quarry near Chicago and was vice president and director of the Builders and Traders' Exchange in 1886–87. He was elected Fourth Ward alderman in 1889 and served until 1897. In 1905, he was elected to Congress and served until his death in 1928.

52. The speech was titled "The Lake Front of Chicago with Special Reference to the Improvement of Grant Park." A typescript copy is on deposit in the special collections of the Ryerson and Burnham Libraries at the Art Institute of Chicago. While it is not dated, its content suggests it was produced around 1915.

*Charles Atwood's design for an art museum for the lakefront, prepared shortly before his death in 1895 and shown in the New York Architectural League's 1896 exhibition (NYAL/96)*

*Martin B. Madden (CPL)*

seem to have been disappointed by the response to this first plan, which was not published. In retrospect, he wrote that the "League lost interest in the work, for . . . they received no public encouragement." The principal problem seemed to be that there were too many suggestions for what should be included in the plan. Therefore, in 1895, Wight decided that since "I was still one of the 'unemployed,' that I [would] reconcile all those divergent ideas as to how the park should be." Purely as an exercise, he put together a plan incorporating all available lakefront data between Division Street (1200 North) and Fourteenth Street (South), hoping "that it would attract the attention of other interested parties. A few blue prints were made and distributed and a reproduction of part of it was published by *The Chicago Tribune*."[53] It was this plan that was the basis of Normand Patton's work in July and August of 1895, which became the subject of his report to the Illinois Chapter of the AIA on September 16, 1895, a few weeks short of a year after the work had begun, and which he had used as the basis of his speech to the Chicago Architectural Club on November 25, 1895. It was this subject that George Beaumont discussed with the Chicago Architectural Club officers at their Christmas party a month later. It was a fortuitous conversation.

❖

The Chicago Architectural Club took up the challenge of further development of the lakefront plan, and as the planning began, it received another challenge from the Illinois Chapter of the AIA. In February of 1896, the club was presented with a "programme" for the "third annual competition for the gold medal" of the Illinois Chapter of the AIA.[54] The competition "proposed to place in the new Lake Front Park a pavilion, which shall be devoted principally to band music." It was to be very large, with seats for three thousand and room for seventy-five pieces in the band. Various ancillary facilities were also specified. The program suggested that the "competitor should keep in mind the work of the club on the Lake Front Park, and suit his design to the place assigned for the pavilion." The usual requirements for scale, size of sheets, and the use of a nom de plume were included in the invitation to participate. Concurrently, the club was working on its own plan for the lakefront, with several members participating. Members were also encouraged to prepare designs for individual elements of the proposed Lake Front Park, such as a fountain, shelters, and monuments.

When the AIA's gold medal competition was announced in early February of 1896, there was some urgency to complete the work in time for the annual exhibition scheduled to open at the Art Institute on March 27, 1896.[55] The club also released a syllabus in early February, although it was in narrative form and did not specify individual program dates. Even though the club year had begun in the fall of 1895, the syllabus was issued "for the year 1896." It reported that having been "encouraged by the growth and activity of the club in the past year, it is proposed to broaden more than ever our range of action . . . the club proposes to take up the study of serious problems, which will be studied by the members organized as a class, having a regular time of meeting. The first of these, which will be entered upon immediately, will be the central portion of the new Lake Front Park, which has been delegated to this club by the Municipal Improvement League."[56] The syllabus reiterated that regular meetings would be held every Monday, alternating between bohemian and formal nights. Summer months were again to be devoted to outdoor work, such as sketching trips and bicycle tours, during which time regular meetings would be discontinued. Classes would, however, continue in architecture, sketching, modeling, and watercolor, and the club rooms would be kept open for use by the membership. The syllabus included a "Music Pavilion Competition" for the AIA gold medal and noted that the Robert Clark Competition program

53. "Lake Front Plans: Report Received by Municipal Improvement League," *Chicago Tribune*, August 10, 1895.

54. *Inland Architect* 27, no. 1 (February 1896): 8.

55. Just when the exhibition opened is a matter of some confusion. It was announced for March 27, 1896, in several journals, but the catalog notes an opening of March 31, 1896. This date was published in *Architecture and Building* on April 11, 1896, along with a note that an informal reception was held on that date. A few days later, in its April 1896 issue, the *Brickbuilder* noted that the exhibition had opened on April 7. The various reviews of the exhibition all use the date March 31, 1896.

56. *Architecture and Building* 24, no. 7 (February 15, 1896): 83–98.

would be announced before summer vacation. The last meeting of the club before the opening of the annual exhibition was on March 24 in the club rooms. The speaker was George Twose, on "An Architectural Conjecture," a subject never elaborated on but probably covering some aspect of the arts and crafts, since that was his major interest.[57] A week later, on bohemian night, the final touches were completed on the hanging of the Ninth Annual Exhibition of the Chicago Architectural Club at the Art Institute of Chicago. The exhibition opened on Tuesday, March 31, with an informal reception hosted by the club's officers, along with Director French and Secretary Carpenter of the Art Institute. The chairman of the exhibition committee, John Robert Dillon, was also in the receiving line. He had moved to Detroit earlier in the year to take a new position, but had returned for the opening.[58]

The exhibition was a resounding success, which might be partially explained by an editorial in the *Inland Architect* written by Robert Craik McLean. Nearly three months before the exhibition, he wrote that "the ninth annual exhibition of the Chicago Architectural Club promises to be the most noted of all of those held by this progressive organization. It may [be] that the friendly rivalry of the Cleveland Club has something to do with this, for the latter now seems to be a strong second to the Chicago club in the matter of exhibitions."[59] Cleveland was not alone in activities outside of Chicago. A month later the *Brochure Series* noted that a new Providence Architectural Club had been formed and that the Detroit Architectural Club had been especially active.[60] The article went on to say that "the interest in the work of architectural clubs as organizations is unquestionably growing. The latest evidence of this is the highly commendable plan for a series of competitions which have lately been initiated by the *American Architect* . . . The plan is . . . announced . . . to be competed for by any non-practicing member of an established association. The designs are to be submitted to the members of the various associations and the three from each association which are considered best are to be sent to the *American Architect*. They are then to be published without comment and each association is to choose, from the whole number submitted, the three designs which it considers best. Prizes will then be awarded . . . the first being $50." It went on to say, "As bearing on club work, anything which will lead to a greater activity in matters in which the whole club is interested will certainly have a beneficial result."

Clearly the "whole club" in Chicago was interested in the designs and competitions for improvements to the lakefront. In addition to the club's large plan for the proposed Lake Front Park, which was obviously based on Wight's plan, and a similarly large perspective of that plan, there were several other designs submitted to the exhibition for various elements to be sited in the proposed park. Two of the AIA's annual gold medal competitive designs for a music pavilion were exhibited. Finally, the *American Architect* competitions elicited a number of entries from the Sketch Club of New York, the Cleveland Architectural Club, the Detroit Architectural Club, the St. Louis Architectural Club, and the T-Square Club of Philadelphia. Several schools were also represented, including the University of Pennsylvania and Columbia College. The usual contingent of Chicagoans, members, and other individuals also exhibited in the show, with a total of 432 listings in the catalog.

The exhibition was reviewed widely, both locally and in the national architectural press. Literally every newspaper in Chicago announced the opening, and no less than six reviews of varying length were published.[61] The most comprehensive reviews, however, appeared in the architectural journals. *Architecture and Building*, the *Brickbuilder*, and the *Inland Architect* all covered the exhibition.[62] Peter B. Wight's review in the *Inland Architect* was by far the most interesting.

Wight was a prolific writer, and he had always had an interest in the activities of the club. As a senior architect in Chicago, his comments were generally held in

57. George M. R. Twose was born in England and trained as an architect. He was a resident of Hull-House and served as secretary to the Chicago Arts and Crafts Society. He taught furniture making and was deeply involved in the exhibitions of the Arts and Crafts Society.

58. *Architecture and Building* 24, no. 15 (April 11, 1896): 179, and *Brochure Series* 2, no. 2 (February 1896): 23.

59. *Inland Architect* 26, no. 6 (January 1896): 55.

60. *Brochure Series* 2, no. 2 (February 96): 21–23.

61. The notices of the pending opening and the reviews in Chicago newspapers can be found in the microfilm files at the Art Institute of Chicago.

62. *Architecture and Building* 24, no. 15 (April 11, 1896): 179; *Brickbuilder* 5, no. 4 (April 1896): 69; and *Inland Architect* 27, no. 3 (April 1896): 22–23.

*Peter B. Wight's 1895 master drawing of the lakefront from Division to Fourteenth streets (ONHS)*

*These drawings prepared by Peter B. Wight, Normand Patton, and the Chicago Architectural Club in 1895 and 1896 show the evolution of thought regarding the development of Lake Front Park, later known as Grant Park. Below are the two plans Normand Patton prepared in 1895, while president of the Municipal Improvement League. He was serving as the representative of the Illinois Chapter of the AIA, where he was vice president. Patton's goal was to stimulate interest in the development of the park. He never claimed that these plans were definitive. Following Patton's work, Wight assembled all the data available regarding the lakefront from Division Street on the north to Fourteenth Street on the south and prepared the large plan shown at right. It incorporated much of what Patton had proposed but went further. Wight, who had long been opposed to building the Field Columbian Museum in the park, showed a site for it at the south end of the park just above Twelfth Street. The drawing at right just below Wight's, is the Chicago Tribune's sketch, the first plan made public. Finally, at bottom right is the only surviving example of the Lake Front Park design work done by the Chicago Architectural Club in the spring of 1896. This plan, which was eight feet long, was exhibited in the Ninth Annual Exhibition in April of 1896.*

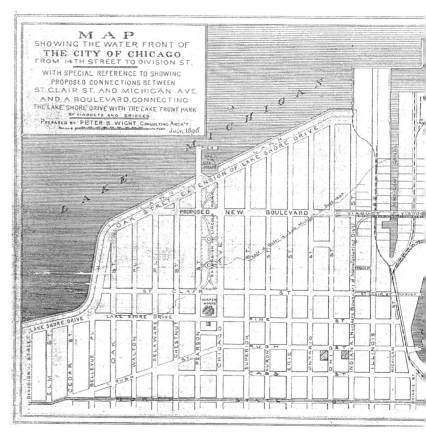

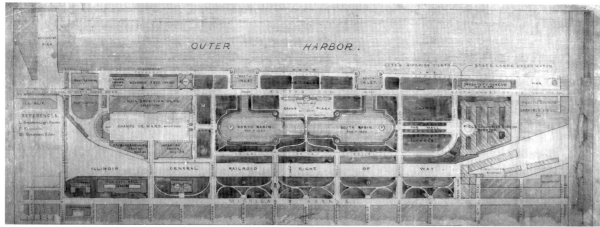

*Normand Patton's first drawing of Lake Front Park, July 1896 (ONHS)*

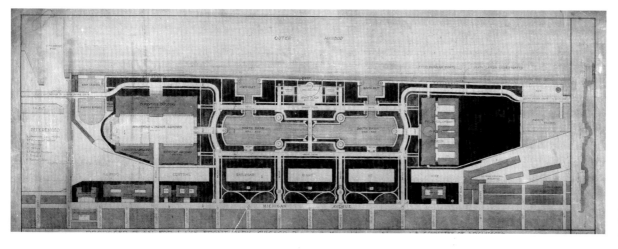

*Normand Patton's second drawing of Lake Front Park, August 1896 (ONHS)*

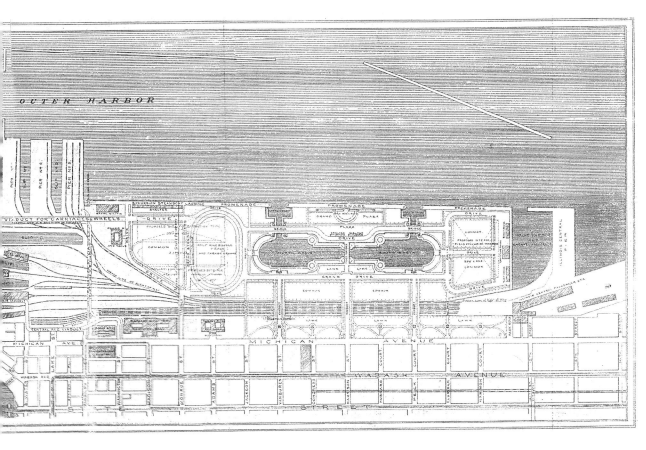

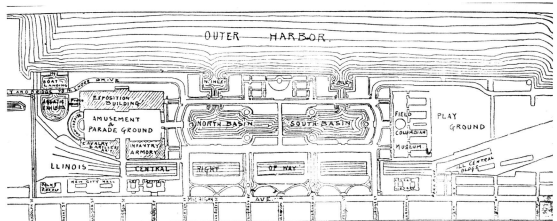

*The* Chicago Tribune *published this crude tracing of Normand Patton's master plan for the lakefront (CT)*

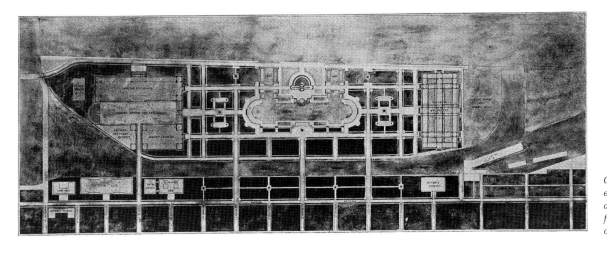

*CASC plan for Lake Front Park, exhibited in the club's 1896 catalog (shown upside down to conform to the orientation of the others)*

high regard. He had reviewed the club's exhibition the previous year, and his lack of work in 1896 gave him the time to look carefully at what the club had to offer and compare thoughts on the two exhibitions. Wight was, of course, particularly interested in what the club had done in regard to planning improvements to Lake Front Park. (He had made the material he had assembled for his grand drawing of the lakefront available to the club in the months prior to the exhibition.)

Wight's review was published in the April 1896 issue of the *Inland Architect*.[63] After commenting favorably on Robert C. Spencer Jr.'s design for the cover of the catalog (the only illustration used in the review), he went on to state that "this is the best exhibition the club has held . . . its distinctive characteristic is found in its illustration of the present condition of architectural education in America, as exemplified by the professional schools and the voluntary associations of students and draftsmen." He lauded the efforts of the younger practitioners, particularly those who were still learning. He wanted to see their work, not the work of mature architects. He went so far as to suggest that "it would be most wise in the future to omit all executed work and the designs of professional architects of more than two years practice." His early remarks were directed at the exhibitions of the schools and other architectural clubs, without naming individuals. He reserved his most positive comments for the work the Chicago Architectural Club had done as a group to prepare plans for the proposed Lake Front Park. He noted that the club exhibited "nine drawings specially prepared and fathered by the club as a body, being designs for the improvement of the new Lake Front park . . . [while] individual contributions of the members of the Chicago Architectural Club are all hung in the east room, grouped around the official club drawings."

Wight devoted more than half his review to the Lake Front Park drawings, of which a total of twelve were shown, some by individuals rather than by the club as a whole. He had been instrumental in the club's work in this effort. After he provided the club with all the material he and his colleagues from the Municipal Improvement League had assembled, the club decided "to adhere to their main features, and appointed a committee consisting of George R. Dean, president of the club, and Hugh M. G. Garden to embody their suggestions and modifications in a new set of drawings." As noted earlier, the members prepared a huge ground plan of Lake Front Park and a colored perspective showing how the park would appear from "an elevated point over Lake Michigan." Several other drawings by individuals were shown supplementing these master plans. There was a park shelter by Hugh Garden and a facade drawing of the proposed Field Museum by George Dean. Howard Van Doren Shaw showed a design for a bridge over the Illinois Central Railroad tracks to connect with South Shore Drive, and two of the designs for a music pavilion located in Lake Front Park submitted in competition for the Illinois Chapter of the AIA's gold medal were also shown. These drawings, with first mention going to Henry J. Ross and second to E. C. Jensen, were displayed only at the exhibition.[64] No record of them appears elsewhere. While Wight and others were deeply impressed by the work the club had done toward the development of Chicago's lakefront, the 1896 exhibition had a wide variety of other material as well. For example, Dwight Perkins and Robert Spencer showed a small but exquisite design for a church that was clearly a precursor of the early modern movement work soon to make itself known.

The final portion of Wight's review was addressed to the "possible rivalry between long-established and well-endowed professional schools of architecture." He was somewhat concerned about the influence of "French methods," and noted that it would be appropriate if "our able professors of architecture [would] exert a little American independence." He was, however, impressed with the work of the Chicago Architectural Club.

*Robert Spencer designed the cover for the 1896 catalog (WRH)*

63. *Inland Architect* 27, no. 3 (April 1896): 22–23.

64. Henry J. Ross exhibited two drawings, numbers 79 and 80, and E. C. Jensen also showed two drawings, numbers 66 and 67. One sheet of each entry was a plan and elevation and the other was a perspective. While they are listed in the catalog, neither was illustrated.

*Dwight Perkins and Robert Spencer's design for a church, a bright spot in the 1896 catalog (CAC/96)*

Despite the glowing reviews and obvious success of the exhibition, the 1896 catalog was a disappointment. Only thirty-two of the more than four hundred exhibits made it into the catalog's pages, and most of them, with the exception of Shaw's bridge over the Illinois Central tracks and the church by Perkins and Spencer, were mundane at best. The important work concerning the designs for the lakefront in particular was omitted. Only a tiny drawing of the club's plan for Grant Park was published.

With the closing of the Ninth Annual Exhibition, the Chicago Architectural Club apparently took a breather and followed the recommendation in the syllabus that the "months of June, July and August will be devoted entirely to outdoor work, sketching trips, bicycle tours, etc."[65] P. B. Wight, however, continued his work on a plan for Lake Front Park. The last activities for the 1895–96 year came in the fall, when Lucy Fitch Perkins discussed the "Artistic Possibilities of Chicago" at a meeting on September 28, followed a week later by the election of the 1896–97 officers on October 5.[66] Richard E. Schmidt was elected president, Dwight Perkins and Adolph Bernhard were elected first and second vice presidents, and Arthur G. Brown and Dan Everett Waid were made secretary and treasurer, respectively. Hermann von Holst and Harry D. Jenkins filled out the Executive Committee. All these men would continue to be active in the club and would distinguish themselves in the future. A week after the election, several of the retiring officers, Messrs. Dean, Garden, Lilleskau, and Hunt, held a retirement reception at the clubhouse. The first regular meeting of 1896–97 was held on October 12, 1896. Classes in architecture, pen and ink, and watercolor were to begin immediately, as was the Eighth Annual Robert Clark Testimonial Competition. It was to be an exciting year.

65. No published material concerning the club's activities has been located for the months of May through August 1896.

66. *Brickbuilder* 5, no. 10 (October 1896): 180.

*Hugh M. G. Garden's drawing of a "Sketch of Proposed Shore Drive Over Depressed Tracks," designed by Howard Van Doren Shaw (CAC/96)*

*Steinway Hall, nearing completion in late 1896; its loft became the drafting room of choice for key participants in the Chicago Architectural Club in 1897 (CHS)*

# Cooperation and Continued Success

CHAPTER NINE

The first order of business for the Chicago Architectural Club during the 1896–97 year was the announcement of the Eighth Annual Robert Clark Testimonial Competition in late September 1896. The program, "A Bath House for a Small City," was heavily influenced by the work of the club and others in developing plans for Chicago's Lake Front Park.[1] The word "small" was a rather obvious attempt to indicate a community other than Chicago, but the remainder of the program was clearly aimed at Lake Front Park.

The bathhouse was to be a one-story-and-basement structure with a "large hall for conversation and the promenade; it may be lighted from above." Two "lounging" rooms were required, one for men and another for women. Fifty dressing rooms were called for, as well as ten bathrooms, but only one toilet room. No specifics were given as to what would be in the basement or on the first floor. Only two drawings were required, one a plan including the site and the other a front elevation. Sheet sizes were designated as thirty-three by forty-six inches.

The drawings were to be delivered to the club secretary on or before January 15, 1897. The program was issued by the Adjudicating Committee, which consisted of Louis J. Millet, chairman, Charles A. Coolidge, and Jeremiah Kiersted Cady. Millet was the only juror who had served the previous year.

No syllabus for the 1896–97 year has surfaced, but it is possible to reconstruct the club's activities during the next few months by the regularly published notices of what occurred at the meetings. After the first "regular" meeting on October 12, the club continued its normal once-a-week meetings, alternating between formal lectures and bohemian nights. By November of 1896, the officers had arranged for the Tenth Annual Exhibition to be held at the Art Institute of Chicago, opening on March 2, 1897.[2] At the same time, they announced that "the question of taking up architectural history in connection with the club class in architecture, by having lectures once or twice a month . . . was considered." On November 30, Dankmar Adler spoke on "The Influence of Steel Construction and Plate Glass upon Style."[3] His presentation was a well-prepared essay elaborating on the dictum "form follows function" set forth by his former partner, Louis H. Sullivan. He suggested that architects should "welcome the prosaic output of the furnace and mill, and even the unpromising and garish sheet of plate glass." Near the end, he stated that while he had quoted "form follows function," he had "modified it into the words 'func-

*Sketch by Charles F. Eppinghausen, 1895 (IA)*

1. The Robert Clark Testimonial program was printed and distributed to the membership and anyone else who requested a copy. It was published in several journals, including *Brickbuilder* 5, no. 10 (October 1896): 180; *Inland Architect* 28, no. 3 (October 1896): 29; and *Architecture and Building* 25, no. 15 (October 10, 1896): 174.

2. *Brickbuilder* 5, no. 11 (November 1896): 207.

3. Adler had delivered this speech at the Thirtieth National Convention of the AIA held in Nashville, Tennessee, October 20–22, 1896. Much later, Frank Lloyd Wright remembered the presentation at the Chicago Architectural Club and suggested to AIA convention program chairman Arthur C. Holden that it be reprinted for distribution to AIA conventioneers in New York City in 1952. It was reproduced in pamphlet form along with three other essays on the same subject presented in Nashville in 1896. A copy is in the collection of the author.

tion and environment determine form.'" His lecture indicated the club's increased interest in the technical aspects of architecture, something the large, complex buildings of the late nineteenth century were forcing young architects to understand.

Three weeks later, on December 21, the last meeting of 1896 was devoted to architectural history with a lantern slide show and a general discussion on Tuscany.[4] The *Inland Architect* reported in its December issue that "the fall season of the club has demonstrated that its members are active and enterprising. The meetings every Monday evening are well attended, and as each meeting has a special committee to look after its welfare and provide an interesting programme, either in the way of a feast of wisdom or a flow of—other things with 'red hots,' as a decorative feature, the attendance is large and enthusiastic."[5]

*The Clark adjudicating committee, 1897, Louis J. Millet (WRH), Charles A. Coolidge (SBRA), and Jeremiah K. Cady (WRH).*

The club was not the only architectural group in Chicago active in late 1896. The local chapter of the AIA had continued its interest in the development of plans for the lakefront and was now pressing for the licensing of architects. More important perhaps was the organization of a new group to be known as the Chicago Architects' Business Association at the Sherman House on December 19, 1896.[6] There had been at least one preliminary meeting before then, when a committee had been appointed to draft a constitution and bylaws that were approved at the organizational meeting. The society was to be "a protective one, to work for needed reforms in the method, manner, and by whom plans are drawn and building operations conducted in Chicago." While it was not specifically stated in the first news release, initially the primary purpose of the group was to pass legislation in Illinois to require the licensing of architects. CABA quickly became a statewide organization.

The Chicago Architects' Business Association grew out of the longtime interest the Illinois Chapter of the AIA had in getting a licensing law passed. The chapter had first introduced a licensing bill to the Illinois legislature in 1886. It did not pass, nor did several later attempts succeed. The chapter had met on December 14, five days before the new group formally organized, and devoted the entire meeting to the current bill before the state legislature. (The bill discussed that evening did not pass, but it was essentially the same as the one that was passed later in 1897.) The AIA was not for the most part a business-oriented group, however, and many members felt that another group would be more effective in getting legislation passed.

There were twenty-five architects present at the December 14 meeting, including L. G. Hallberg, J. M. Van Osdel, P. B. Wight, D. H. Perkins, H. B. Wheelock, and George Beaumont, all of whom had been or still were active in the affairs of the Chicago Architectural Club. The December 19 organizational meeting of the Chicago Architects' Business Association included Van Osdel, who was elected president, Wheelock, Hallberg, and S. A. Treat, as well as several others prominent in the architectural community. The membership and interests of the three groups,

4. *Brickbuilder* 5, no. 12 (December 1896): 223.

5. *Inland Architect* 28, no. 5 (December 1896): 53.

6. This group survived for over a century. It changed its name to the Illinois Society of Architects in 1914 and merged with the Association of Licensed Architects in 1999.

the CAC, the AIA, and the CABA, overlapped to a great degree. The CABA was the largest in terms of membership, the CAC had fewer and younger members, and the Illinois Chapter of the AIA was the smallest, mostly made up of older, established practitioners, nearly all Chicagoans.

CABA's first effort was to get the Illinois Licensing Act passed by the state legislature, and it reviewed the efforts of a number of other states over the previous decade, all of which ended in failure. The Executive Committee decided to take a unique approach to passing the law by asking Charles W. Nothnagel, one of their own, to stand for election to the state legislature.[7] Nothnagel won the seat and devoted most of his legislative efforts during the next year to convincing his colleagues in the legislature to support the Illinois Licensing Act. He succeeded, and on June 3, 1897, "An Act to provide for the Licensing of Architects, and Regulating the Practice of Architecture as a Profession" was passed.[8] Nothnagel was rewarded by being issued the first license and thus became the first person in the world to become a licensed architect. He was not immediately named to the State Board of Architectural Examiners, probably because he was an elected representative, but he was appointed the following year and he then served for about two and a half years. After that he continued to work from time to time as a paid lobbyist for the Chicago Architects' Business Association when the group had concerns regarding matters before the legislature.

*Charles W. Nothnagel, the first man to hold an architect's license (CABA)*

While their older colleagues were addressing the business side of the architectural profession during the first half of 1897, the members of the Chicago Architectural Club continued their extraordinary schedule of weekly meetings, classes, and competitions. The Eighth Annual Clark Testimonial Competition drawings for a bathhouse were submitted on January 15, 1897, by thirty-seven competitors. The results were announced in February by the Adjudicating Committee, which found it appropriate to "comment very favorably on the drawings submitted, no other contest under the auspices of the club having brought out, on the whole, such excellent results."[9] For reasons never made clear, these drawings were the last to be submitted in a Robert Clark Testimonial Competition. The competition was never held again. The last Robert Clark gold medal was awarded to David G. Meyers of Boston for a "combination of excellences in plan, exterior, design and rendering." The committee found itself in a quandary about awarding second place. Two of the entries, those of John F. Jackson of Buffalo, New York, and Oscar M. Hekanson of Philadelphia were considered to be of "such nearly equal merit that they chose to make a new precedent and award two Silver medals, one of which was their own contribution." A bronze medal was awarded to Arthur Shrigley of Lansdowne, Pennsylvania, and honorable mentions went to John F. Sheblessy and Thomas Livingston, both from Chicago. The submissions by Pierre Liesch of Boston and William L. Welton of Everett, Massachusetts, were "commended" without being awarded prizes. After adjudication, the Clark drawings were exhibited at the clubhouse on Michigan Avenue and later, in March, thirteen of the entries, including all those named above, were exhibited in the Tenth Annual Exhibition. That show, originally scheduled to open at the Art Institute of Chicago on March 2, did not open until March 23.

The three-week delay was caused by a conflict with the opening of the first annual exhibition at the American Academy in Rome on March 2, which was lauded by one local newspaper as "one of the most intellectual and suggestive exhibitions of the season."[10] It was not, however, even close to the size of the Chicago Architectural Club exhibition that followed, in terms of numbers of exhibitors or ex-

7. Charles W. Nothnagel (ca. 1860–ca. 1920) was a practicing architect in Chicago for at least twenty-five years. His name appears with various partners between 1885 and 1910. He was listed as a member of the AIA, 1897–99, and a member of the CABA, 1898–1906, although he was never a member of the Chicago Architectural Club. Nothnagel served two and a half years, from 1899 to 1901, on the State Board of Architectural Examiners. He was last listed as a licensed architect with a Chicago address in 1909. Little else is known of him or his practice.

8. An excellent article titled "A New Look at the Beginnings of the Illinois Architect's Licensing Law," by Paul Kruty, can be found in *Illinois Historical Journal* 90, no. 3 (Autumn 1997): 154–72.

9. The *Brickbuilder* published a brief item noting the medal winners in volume 6, no. 2 (February 1897): 24, and *Architecture and Building* published the complete "Judges' Report" in volume 26, no. 8 (February 20, 1897): 94. The "Judges' Report" was then published two months later in *Inland Architect* 29, no. 3 (April 1897): 29.

*The last Robert Clark competition gold medal went to David G. Meyers of Boston, whose design is shown here in plan and elevation (CAC/97)*

10. This quotation was taken from the *Chicago Times Herald* of March 3, 1897. Nearly all the Chicago newspapers reviewed or commented on the American Academy's first annual exhibition.

11. *Catalogue of the First Annual Exhibition of the American Academy in Rome, Open March 2 to March 14 Inclusive* (Chicago: Art Institute, 1897). The first twenty pages of the catalog describe the academy and its activities, with illustrations, and conclude with a list of the twelve "Past and Present Beneficiaries of the American Academy in Rome." A listing of the exhibits appears on pages 21–46.

12. William K. Fellows (1870–1948) was born in Winona, Minnesota, where he received his early education. He studied architecture at Columbia University while working in various New York offices, then joined D. H. Burnham and Company in Chicago around 1895. His traveling scholarship enabled him to spend eighteen months in Europe. Upon his return around 1897, he entered into partnership with George C. Nimmons in Chicago. Later (ca. 1911) he joined Dwight Perkins and John Hamilton to create Perkins, Fellows & Hamilton. That firm survived until 1925, after which Fellows practiced alone until he retired in 1936.

Fellows's traveling scholarship award was reported by several Chicago newspapers. Clippings are in the microfilm files at the Art Institute of Chicago, but the names of the newspapers are not noted. One of the articles stated that "Mr. Burnham made no effort to conceal his delight over the fact that a man in his office had won the scholarship."

hibits. Only twelve "beneficiaries" were listed in the catalog—nine architects, two sculptors, and one painter.[11] The sole Chicagoan was William K. Fellows, who had been awarded the Columbia Traveling Scholarship the year before while employed as a draftsman by D. H. Burnham and Company.[12] Fellows had also taught at the School of the Art Institute of Chicago while in the Burnham office. He was not, however, one of the exhibitors in that first annual exhibition of the American Academy in Rome. Of the twelve beneficiaries, nine were participants in the exhibition. Apparently students at the academy spent a good deal of their time traveling, observing, and sketching historic structures, and nearly all the exhibits were the results of such endeavors. The few illustrations in the catalog suggest that most of the

*Two 1897 silver medals went to John F. Jackson of Buffalo, New York (top) and Oscar M. Hekanson of Philadelphia (above) (CAC/97)*

work done was executed in the manner then in vogue at the École des Beaux-Arts in Paris.

It seems highly likely that D. H. Burnham had used his influence to supplant the opening of the Chicago Architectural Club's exhibition with that of the American Academy in Rome. Burnham had been instrumental in organizing the academy in 1894. He had by then completed his work as chief of construction for the World's Columbian Exposition and was serving as the president of the American Institute of Architects. His friend Charles F. McKim of New York City prevailed upon him to help raise funds to establish the American Academy in Rome. Burnham responded by sending letters to several of his Chicago colleagues, noting that "Mr. McKim hopes to make this not a local New York movement, but a national one, and has asked me to help him by interesting a few of the leading men here. I have undertaken to raise $2,000.00, and have already sent forward over a dozen checks for

*Victor Traxler's silver-medal design for the annual Chicago AIA competition (CAC/97)*

$100.00 each, including my own."[13] Burnham continued his interest in the academy until his death in 1912. He would have certainly been happy to intervene with the director of the Art Institute to see to it that the exhibition took place.

The delay may have actually been an advantage for the club, giving them additional time to assemble material and plan the show. The Exhibition Committee elected to hang literally every item submitted, including many competition drawings, and it became the largest exhibition mounted by the club to date.

At the same time the last Clark Testimonial Competition was under way, the Illinois Chapter of the AIA had sponsored its Fourth Annual Gold Medal Competition, which was open to members of the Chicago Architectural Club "who had not been in independent practice more than two years."[14] As in the previous year, there was very little publicity. The program was not included in any of the usual publications and the only references to it were somewhat oblique notes in items concerning other club events. The Adjudicating Committee was never named. The program apparently called for the design of the facade of a city residence. The most revealing information was in the April issue of the *Inland Architect,* where it was noted under "Our Illustrations" that "there were twelve designs submitted in the competition . . . [and it] . . . was recommended by the judges that no gold medal be awarded, but that three silver medals of merit be presented."[15] The only medal winner identified was Victor Traxler, whose drawing was illustrated in the *Inland Architect* and in the Tenth Annual Exhibition catalog. None of the other entrants or other medal winners has been identified. It is likely, however, that other entries were exhibited since some of the titles listed in the catalog seem to match the titles in the competition.

The delayed Tenth Annual Exhibition opened on March 23 after a gala reception for members and their guests the previous evening. More than eight hundred drawings, plans, elevations, projects for decorative paintings, and sculptures were shown. The catalog, while the basic size and format of the previous year, was a sophisticated publication that set a high standard for future exhibitions in Chicago and elsewhere. All 170 members of the club were listed with addresses. One hundred nineteen advertisers were included, many of whom showed "cuts" of buildings designed by club members and other exhibitors. In contrast to the year before, when few Chicagoans exhibited, about half the exhibits were from local professionals. There were also fairly large contingents from New York City, Boston, and Philadelphia. A number of clubs from other cities were well represented, including St. Louis, Philadelphia, and New York, as well as several universities. In a departure from previous years, there were a substantial number of exhibits in the field of decorative arts. Artist Joseph Pennell showed more than 120 drawings and lithographs, which were available for purchase.

The exhibition was reviewed widely, both in architectural journals and in the popular press, and the response was almost universally positive.[16] The *American Architect and Building News* began its review, "The Tenth Annual Exhibition . . . was one of exceptional merit, and the three galleries which held it were so filled with strong and charming things as to prove attractive to all kinds of visitors, whether professional or otherwise."[17] The following month, the *Brickbuilder* wrote that "the exhibition at the Chicago Art Institute, under the auspices of the Chicago Architectural Club . . . eclipsed all former exhibits."[18] At the end of the review, the reporter noted that "the Art Institute has provided club rooms for the use of the Chicago Architectural Club in the Institute Building." The journal had first re-

13. This quotation is taken from an original letter in the author's collection dated June 11, 1894, with D. H. Burnham's signature. It is addressed to Mr. Henry J. Willing, 115 Monroe Street, Chicago.

14. *Brickbuilder* 6, no. 5 (May 1897): 83.

15. *Inland Architect* 29, no. 3 (April 1897): 29.

16. The *Brickbuilder* and the *American Architect and Building News* both had notes advising of the forthcoming exhibition, and both later reviewed it. No less than eight Chicago daily newspapers reported on the exhibition, from brief notices to full-fledged reviews by the *Chicago Tribune* and the *Chicago Post.*

17. *American Architect and Building News* 56, no. 1112 (April 24, 1897): 29.

ported that move in its April issue.[19] With no explanation, the club had quietly moved out of its joint-tenancy club rooms further south on Michigan Avenue, and a new era of activity had begun. The club would remain in its new quarters at the Art Institute until 1904. The club's association with the Chicago Society of Artists at the clubhouse on Michigan Avenue had been a very positive experience. It enabled the club to broaden its interests, particularly in the cultural affairs of Chicago. Classes had become more viable, with the space available in the clubhouse, and several members had actually rented office space in the building. Most important, perhaps, they had a highly visible headquarters where not only members but important visitors could present their views to the cultural community of Chicago. The space they were to occupy at the Art Institute for the next several years gave them similar opportunities, with the added advantage of being identified with what was then, and remains today, the city's premier cultural institution. In the *Brickbuilder*'s remarks concerning the move, it was noted that "New York architects can appreciate the enthusiasm of the Chicago club over the new departure by imagining the Metropolitan Museum located near their business center, and offering them not only the use of private club rooms, but access to all the gallery, lecture, and school room privileges." The move proved to be entirely satisfactory for many reasons, not the least of which was that the club had its own private entrance on the north side of the principal wing of the Art Institute, thus permitting the members to come and go without walking through the museum itself.

The club moved into its new quarters on May 1, 1897.[20] The formal opening was held on May 24, when Daniel Burnham gave a short address.[21] (Perhaps he was making amends, if he had, in fact, usurped the club's opening date a few weeks earlier.) Burnham's remarks were printed in the *Inland Architect* with a preface by R. C. McLean, who wrote that the "admission of this architectural club to membership in the Art Institute is part of a wise plan lately adopted by the directors . . . and the quarters assigned them in the north end of the building are in every way attractive."

Burnham began his somewhat flowery comments, "The house in which we have met tonight was built and dedicated to those activities which, more than others, have led men away from ignorance and brutality toward the source of those eternal laws that express themselves upon the earth in forms of never changing beauty." He continued, "You now desire to make your home in this temple of fine arts. Fortune has been kind to you and has opened the door, and I deem it the great-

18. *Brickbuilder* 6, no. 5 (May 1897): 83.

19. *Brickbuilder* 6, no. 4 (April 1897): 70.

20 *Brickbuilder* 7, no. 5 (May 1898): 106. The following year, in early May of 1898, the Illinois Chapter of the AIA followed the lead of its younger colleagues in the Chicago Architectural Club and took permanent rooms at the Art Institute of Chicago. It was a good move with a number of advantages, not the least of which was the closer proximity to the club.

21. Burnham's address has survived in its original form and in two variations. There are two copies deposited at the Art Institute of Chicago. One is probably a first carbon copy that is most likely the speech Burnham actually delivered to the club members. The other is also a carbon copy, but it has been extensively marked up for a typesetter. Certain phrases have been altered, and some sentences have been heavily edited or deleted. The editing appears to be in Burnham's hand. A second hand is evident in the headings. This copy was clearly used as the basis for the printed version that appeared in *Inland Architect* 29, no. 5 (June 1897): 46–47.

*The Chicago Architectural Club occupied room 107 in the basement of the Art Institute of Chicago (AIC)*

*Published design for the Stevens Point Normal School by Perkins & Selby (IA)*

est honor of my life that I am allowed to stand on the threshold and bid you welcome." He went on to comment on the hopes he had for the members of the club as architects and his expectations of greatness from them. He could not help relating the work of the future to the work of past masters when he noted that it was important that "before beginning the design of an important building, [one must] submit himself to the influence of one of [the] nobler works of art." Little did he know that only two blocks away, in Steinway Hall, an event was taking place that would forever change the grammar of the architecture of Chicago and the world.

On May 1, 1897, while the Chicago Architectural Club was moving into its new rooms at the Art Institute of Chicago, Myron Hunt, Robert C. Spencer, and Frank Lloyd Wright were moving into Steinway Hall to share space with Dwight Heald Perkins. Perkins had designed Steinway Hall as his first major Chicago office building after leaving D. H. Burnham and Company in 1893. In his design, Perkins provided a small office for himself on the eleventh floor with access to the loft under the roof in the attic above. It was not his first commission.

Exactly when Perkins left D. H. Burnham and Company is uncertain. He probably phased himself out starting in mid-1893, when Burnham resigned as chief of construction for the World's Columbian Exposition and returned to his offices on the top floor of the Rookery. It was a critical time in Chicago, as a major depression was under way. Architects were particularly hard hit and work was scarce largely because of the massive overbuilding prior to the World's Columbian Exposition. The downturn lasted for some time. The *Brickbuilder* reported in May of 1897 that "the business depression and the large number of new office buildings in Chicago have combined to make offices a drug in the market. Good offices can be rented at a very low price."[22]

Seventy years later, Dwight Perkins's daughter, Eleanor, wrote that "in June, when the Fair was in full swing, Mr. Burnham's duty to it ceased, and he came back to his own office. As agreed four years before, Dwight was to leave the office in December and begin private practice."[23] Burnham had asked Ernest Graham, Charles Atwood, and E. C. Shankland to be his partners and he simply could not keep

22. *Brickbuilder* 6, no. 5 (May 1897): 84.

Perkins in a position of authority over them, since they were all senior to him. Burnham apparently offered Perkins some assistance in establishing his own office, but just what that assistance was has never been made clear. Eleanor Perkins also wrote that in 1893 Burnham "began urging the members of his office force to do private work on their own time, and keep themselves as busy as possible." She further noted that her father had been "so fortunate as to get a normal school at Stevens Point, Wisconsin to do." Her memory was correct. A sketch of the building Perkins designed was published, first in the Stevens Point *Gazette* on October 25, 1893, and then in the November 1893 issue of the *Inland Architect*.[24] That drawing was also exhibited in the 1894 club exhibition at the Art Institute of Chicago. The *Gazette* wrote in August of 1893 that local officials had "left for Milwaukee . . . yesterday for the purpose of submitting several competitive plans to supervising Architect Koch and deciding upon the one that shall be adopted for Stevens Point."[25] Apparently some preliminary plans were in hand, but two weeks later the Stevens Point regents published a circular advising that "plans and specifications for the new building . . . will be received until Sept. 8th." The circular gave "full instructions to architects, as to location, elevations, cost, material, heating, ventilating, etc.," and concluded by saying that "the building should be of a pure style of architecture, befitting its uses, and impressive to the eye by harmony of line and beauty of proportions, rather than by showy ornamentation or eccentric features."[26] Then, on September 12, the same paper wrote, "the fortunate architects will be Messrs. Starbuck & Rose, of Milwaukee." Two weeks later, the *Gazette* reported that the first set of plans "were found defective . . . and rejected accordingly. Other plans were looked over, and on Monday those presented by Perkins & Selby, Chicago architects, [were] adopted by the committee. Capt. Burnham, the great World's Fair architect, is the head of the above firm, and while his name does not appear in this connection, the plans for the Normal were drawn under his immediate supervision. Three sets will be ready for contractors to figure on by Oct. 12th . . . [and] bids will be opened on the 20th."[27] After some delays in finding the right contractor, the job was given to E. Bonnett & Son of Whitewater in the amount of $51,900.[28] Perkins & Selby immediately announced that they had employed a local man, M. T. Olin, to supervise the work on site. The building was completed in September of 1894. The *Stevens Point Journal* reported that members of the State Board of Regents were in town "Tuesday last for the purpose of inspecting the new Normal Building. Messrs. D. H. Perkins and George W. Selby of Chicago, the architects who prepared the plans and specifications for the building, were also here."[29] Two weeks later there was a formal dedication of the building.[30]

It is clear that Dwight Perkins left the office of D. H. Burnham and Company only after getting a major commission for a large building, apparently with the knowledge and probably the help of Daniel H. Burnham. When Perkins left Burnham's office, a colleague from the staff, George W. Selby, joined him. The two opened an office in the Marshall Field Annex Building at the corner of Wabash and Washington, a building designed by D. H. Burnham and Company on Perkins's watch. The building, still standing and in use, was clearly influenced by Richardson's Marshall Field Warehouse, which Perkins would have been aware of; in fact, he may have had some small part in the preparation of its construction drawings while serving in Richardson's office.[31] Since Perkins & Selby's listing appears in the 1894 *Chicago Business Directory*, it is apparent that the office was open in late 1893. Despite the severe depression in Chicago, the firm did have work. The Normal School in Wisconsin was under con-

23. Eleanor Ellis Perkins, "Perkins of Chicago," unpublished manuscript from the author's collection, 1966.

24. The Stevens Point Normal School has never been included in any published work of architectural history of which I am aware. I am indebted to W. R. Nelson of Amherst, Wisconsin, who kindly shared information concerning the history of the Normal School Building.

25. "The Site Selected," *Gazette*, August 16, 1893.

26. *Gazette*, August 30, 1893.

27. "Plans Adopted," *Gazette*, September 27, 1893. The article's language suggests that Perkins & Selby took the commission with Burnham's knowledge.

28. "The New Normal," *Gazette*, November 8, 1893.

29. "The Building Accepted," *Stevens Point Journal*, September 29, 1894.

30. Justus F. Paul, *The World Is Ours* (Stevens Point: University of Wisconsin-Stevens Point Foundation Press, 1994). This history of Stevens Point Normal School, now the University of Wisconsin-Stevens Point, covers the construction of the Perkins & Selby building in some detail, albeit abbreviated. The book is not footnoted, but there is a bibliographic note. The content makes it clear that Paul made use of many of the same references used herein.

*Perkins & Selby's office in the Marshall Field Annex Building, completed in 1893 and still standing (WRH)*

STEINWAY HALL

VAN BUREN STREET

Between Michigan and Wabash Avenues

F. HOIT DEL

LYON, POTTER & CO.
(STEINWAY PIANOS)
Will remove to this new building named Steinway Hall on or before May 1st, '95.

*Rendering of Steinway Hall, signed by Henry F. Hoit (CHS)*

31. An excellent essay, "The Marshall Field Annex and the New Urban Order of Daniel Burnham's Chicago," by Ann Lorenz Van Zanten, is in *Chicago History* (Fall-Winter 1982): 130–41. Van Zanten credits the design to Charles Atwood and cites several possible sources. She notes that the building was completed in August 1893.

32. *Inland Architect* 23, no. 5 (June 1894): 56.

33. *Inland Architect* 24, no. 1 (August 1894): 10.

struction and in June of 1894, the *Inland Architect* announced that Perkins & Selby was designing a two-story residence in Evanston.[32] In the same issue, Frank Lloyd Wright announced the design of the W. H. Winslow House in River Forest, Illinois, and the four Roloson town houses on the South Side of Chicago. Two months later, in August 1894, the same journal noted that Perkins & Selby had "completed drawings for the ten-story [*sic*] 'Temple of Music,' to be erected on Van Buren Street between Wabash Avenue and Michigan Avenue."[33] After a lengthy description of the building's program, the item ended with the statement that the "building will be commenced as soon as the ground is clear." This was what was to become known as Steinway Hall. Its developer and owner was William H. Winslow. Thus Frank Lloyd Wright and Dwight Perkins shared a client before they shared an office.

Construction of the Winslow House and Steinway Hall proceeded rapidly. Both were essentially completed in early 1895. In May of 1895 it was reported that "Mr. Dwight H. Perkins, of the firm of Perkins & Selby, Marshall Field Building,

Chicago, opened a new office on May 1 at 1107 Steinway Hall Building, Chicago."[34] Selby did not join Perkins in the new space, since the partnership was apparently not successful.[35] The office at 1107 Steinway Hall was a small room on the east side of the eleventh floor with its own winding staircase to the loft above. (It was also possible to get to the loft from a public staircase on the west side of the main corridor.) It seems that Perkins had intended to move into Steinway Hall from the beginning. The stair from room 1107 was probably built during construction of the building. He was one of the first tenants to move in.

Steinway Hall was published widely in the professional press. The first notice, in *Architecture and Building*, reported that Steinway & Sons had "opened a hall in the Western metropolis (Chicago) which is described as the most beautiful and perfect one in the United States."[36] It was also included in other journals, always with detailed descriptions.[37] The building was described as being in the Renaissance style. The first six of the eleven stories were occupied by Lyon, Potter & Co., the western agents for Steinway pianos. The five remaining floors were devoted to offices and studios for musicians with a small lecture and recital hall on the seventh floor. Later on, the top floor was devoted almost entirely to architects' offices and still later, a number of other architects took space in the building. It was the eleventh floor, however, where the Young Turks in architecture found a home in which they could talk, argue, and develop a new style that was not reliant on traditional forms. Dwight Perkins was the catalyst for this extraordinary prelude to the early modern movement in architecture.

Perkins occupied room 1107 in Steinway Hall for two years before he was joined by Hunt, Spencer, and Wright. He was not, however, alone. Francis W. Kirkpatrick was already sharing Perkins's space by late 1896, probably as an employee, although he soon began to work on his own. Perkins also had at least one other draftsman during that period, Henry F. Hoit, who had joined him after graduating from MIT in 1896. It was Hoit who prepared the drawings of Steinway Hall that were published in the *Brickbuilder* in 1896[38] and the superb perspective used by Lyon, Potter & Co. (i.e., Steinway Pianos) in its promotional material. He would remain with Perkins until 1901, when he joined Van Brunt & Howe in Kansas City, Missouri. Perkins's cousin, Marion Mahony, who had also attended MIT, graduated in 1894. She worked with Perkins from time to time before and after he moved into the building. There were probably others in Perkins's office as well.

During Perkins's first two years at Steinway Hall, he had a good deal of work.[39] While his address was room 1107, his drafting room was in the loft above. During construction, the original plans had been revised to add skylights to the loft space. (Some time later, windows were added on the east, north, and west walls of the eastern half of the loft to provide even more light.) Perkins had far more space than he needed, and in the spring of 1897, when he invited several colleagues to join him, the union of friends was announced in the "Chicago Real Estate" column of the *Sunday Inter Ocean*.[40] The paper reported that "an interesting experiment in architectural practice has recently been inaugurated in Steinway Hall by four young men, R. C. Spencer, who took the Rotch traveling scholarship in 1888; Frank Wright, who was formerly with Adler & Sullivan; Myron Hunt, who came from the office of Shepley, Rutan & Coolidge, and Dwight Heald Perkins, from the office of D. H. Burnham. These young men, believing in the principles of cooperation rather than in the idea of competition, have united in a general office, the expenses of which are prorated according to the amount of use each one makes of the telephone, typewriter, etc. Uniting in this way upon impersonal expenses, they keep their private offices and their practice absolutely individual. It is essentially a cooperative scheme and they are in no sense partners. At the same time they have the

*Henry F. Hoit (MWHM)*

34. *Brochure Series* 1, no. 5 (May 1895): 77.

35. "As a partner, Selby failed him and did no work of any kind, and Dwight was obliged to carry out the letter of the partnership agreement and pay him three thousand dollars to get rid of him." Perkins, "Perkins of Chicago," 89.

36. "The Steinway Hall," *Architecture and Building* 22, no. 21 (May 25, 1895): 248.

37. *Brickbuilder* 5, no. 10 (October 1896): 198, and *Engineering News* 34, no. 16 (October 17, 1895): 251. Both articles were illustrated.

38. *Brickbuilder* 5, no. 10 (October 1896): plates 55–58.

39. In those first two years of Perkins's occupancy of room 1107 in Steinway Hall, there were at least twelve announcements of buildings he was designing, divided almost evenly between private homes and commercial projects. There is no question that Perkins had a successful practice at a time when architects in general were suffering due to a severe depression.

40 "Chicago Real Estate," *Sunday Inter Ocean*, May 2, 1897.

advantage of great reductions in rent and running expenses. This, however, is not the greatest advantage which they feel that they gain by the arrangement. Convinced that the time has come when Chicago is ready to demand more artistic work as well as building which will meet every demand of utility, they have set themselves high standards, which by mutual criticism and encouragement they strive to maintain. The pecuniary advantage derived from co-operation they feel to be insignificant beside the benefit of the inspiration coming from association with each other and contact with each other's ideas. This experiment is certainly worth a trial and there seems every reason for prophesying for it a brilliant success. It is evidence of a progressive spirit and is along general lines of social evolution." Thus, four of Chicago's brightest young designers were united in one office in a single large drafting room. All but Frank Lloyd Wright were members of the Chicago Architectural Club, and one could argue that he was a de facto member since he had served on the Clark competition jury and had spoken before the club a number of times. His work had been shown in a number of the club's exhibitions and would continue to be shown in the future.

Perkins and his new colleagues were certainly kindred spirits. All four were about the same age, Perkins being thirty, Spencer thirty-two, Hunt twenty-nine, and Wright thirty. Their social backgrounds were somewhat diverse, but their educations all had points of similarity, as did their architectural experience. Spencer, Hunt, and Perkins had all attended MIT, in the two-year program. Perkins studied there from the fall of 1885 through the spring of 1887, after which he spent another

*Dwight Heald Perkins, Myron Hunt, Robert Clossen Spencer, and Frank Lloyd Wright (PC)*

year as an instructor while working part-time for Henry Hobson Richardson. Hunt spent two years at Northwestern University before attending MIT from 1890 to 1892. He then was employed by Richardson's successors, Shepley, Rutan & Coolidge, first in Boston and later in Chicago. Spencer had already received a degree in mechanical engineering from the University of Wisconsin at Madison when he began his studies at MIT in the fall of 1886. He was at the University of Wisconsin in 1886 when Wright was there, but being older, may not have known him well, if at all. In addition to what was then an excellent education, both Spencer and Hunt had taken an extensive European tour. Wright's formal education was the most sparse in that he had spent less than a year at the University of Wisconsin, as a special student. All four of these young men were experienced in architecture with time in the offices of Burnham & Root (Perkins), Shepley, Rutan & Coolidge (Hunt and Spencer), and Adler & Sullivan (Wright). They were all well prepared to provide services to clients. As an adjunct to their practice, all remained heavily involved in the affairs of the Chicago Architectural Club for the next several years.

Room 1107 or, more accurately, the loft above it, became for all practical purposes an extension of the Chicago Architectural Club. It was where what eventually came to be called the Prairie School of architecture coalesced and became the epitome of the modern movement in architecture in Chicago. During the decade after Perkins brought in Wright, Spencer, and Hunt, Steinway Hall became the office building of choice for numerous other architects, many of whom were sympathetic to the same philosophy. Marion Mahony had already worked with Perkins, and was then working with Wright at least part of the time. Henry Hoit was still in Perkins's office as well. Just how Francis W. Kirkpatrick fit into the picture is unclear, but he probably worked with Perkins while beginning his own independent practice. He would shortly become a key figure in the affairs of the Chicago Architectural Club. Adamo Boari, Birch Burdette Long, and Webster Tomlinson soon were sharing room 1107 and the loft above. Walter Burley Griffin went directly from the University of Illinois to Perkins's office in 1899. According to Eleanor Perkins, Jules Guerin was also part of the original group. The Pond brothers, Irving K. and Allen B., were listed as being in room 1109 in 1897, which suggests that they moved there in 1896. Both were active in the Chicago Architectural Club. Irving K.

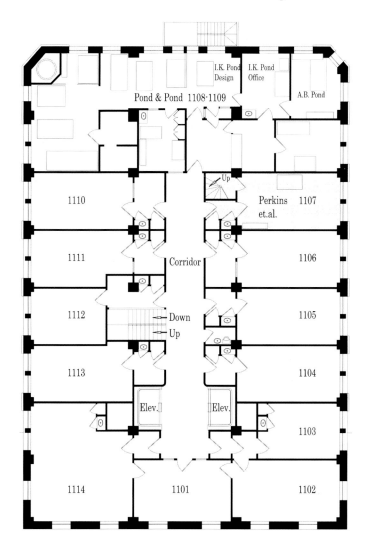

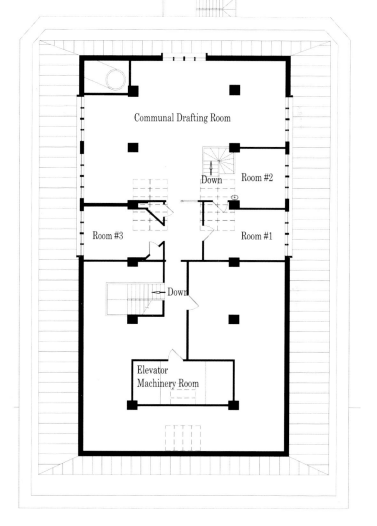

*Plan of eleventh floor at Steinway Hall (Drawn by David Waldo)*

*Plan of twelfth-floor loft at Steinway Hall; note the windows added on the north side (Drawn by David Waldo)*

*Irving K. and Allen B. Pond in their office on the eleventh floor of Steinway Hall (Bentley)*

had been a founder and his brother, Allen, became a member in 1890. Pond & Pond occupied a suite originally intended to be four rooms, each the same size as room 1107, at the north end of the eleventh floor. When the brothers moved into Steinway Hall they were well established as a firm. Plans they prepared for their space designated it as room 1108/09.[41] Later they expanded into room 1107, when Perkins left the building in 1906 to become the architect for the Chicago Board of Education. Pond & Pond had the longest tenure in building, staying until 1923. They were somewhat of an anchor in Steinway Hall and saw numerous other architects come and go during their more than twenty-five year tenure in the building.

Other tenants in Steinway Hall during the late nineteenth century included Theodore Pietsch, W. Carbys Zimmerman, and Arthur Niemz, who had been with Dankmar Adler until his death in 1899. As time passed, more architects came to Steinway Hall, although not all to the eleventh floor. Arthur Heun, Lawrence Buck, and H. G. Hodgkins were there. Nearly all were dues-paying members of the Chicago Architectural Club. They came to be called what H. Allen Brooks has referred to as the "Steinway Hall Group."[42] The most active period of the Steinway Hall Group was from 1897 through 1907, when they not only produced an enormous volume of architecture, but dominated the activities of the Chicago Architectural Club.

In 1897, while Perkins, Spencer, Hunt, and Wright were establishing themselves in Steinway Hall, another activity was taking place, which would affect them and others during the next several months. The American Luxfer Prism Company hired Frank Lloyd Wright as a consultant to assist in developing and promoting the company's product.[43]

Luxfer prisms were small four-by-four-inch blocks or tiles of glass about one-quarter-inch thick, with horizontal, V-shaped ribs on the inside set in rows in a metal frame, which was installed in exterior window walls. The ribs, or prisms, bent the sunlight that fell on the tiles and reflected it into the building, enhancing the quality of light in the interior. In the days before modern electric lighting, this was a boon to building owners, since it provided a far better level of interior light than had previously been available, permitting much larger floors.

✳

The American Luxfer Prism Company was organized in 1896 and adopted its name in April of 1897.[44] It was well financed by some of the most important figures from Chicago's development community. The board of directors included Cyrus H. McCormick, Charles H. Wacker, Levi Z. Leiter, George A. Fuller, and John M. Ewen, who was the company's first president, as well as Edward C. Waller and William H. Winslow. Ewen had served many years as chief engineer for Burnham & Root and was, when he became president of the American Luxfer Prism Company, also pres-

41. There are two sources of plans for Steinway Hall. George A. Fuller Company, the builder, published a book of the firm's work in 1899 that included a photograph and a typical plan of the building. More important are several surviving plans of the space occupied by Pond & Pond that are now in the Pond Archive at the Bentley Historical Library at the University of Michigan. These drawings show several variations (revisions) of the Pond & Pond offices during the first decade of the twentieth century.

42. The first serious study of the architects who occupied Steinway Hall was an article by H. Allen Brooks titled "Steinway Hall, Architects and Dreams" in *Journal of the*

*Society of Architectural Historians* 19, no. 1 (March 1960): 171–75.

43. The best concise study of Luxfer prisms is Dietrich Neumann, "'The Century's Triumph in Lighting': The Luxfer Prism Companies and their Contribution to Early Modern Architecture," *Journal of the Society of Architectural Historians* 54, no. 1 (March 1995): 24–53. When facts from that article are used here, they are cited in footnotes. While Neumann's excellent work is an important starting point, most of the references here came from research into this period of the Chicago Architectural Club's activities.

44. Neumann, "Luxfer Prism Companies," 25.

*Luxfer Iridian Plates & Patent Numbers*

*Frank Lloyd Wright's designs for Luxfer prisms were used to illustrate the handbook prepared by the American Luxfer Prism Company (UofMINN)*

ident of the George A. Fuller Company, one of Chicago's major construction firms. Both Waller and Winslow were clients of Frank Lloyd Wright, who had designed Winslow's home in River Forest and was working with Waller on several projects. Waller was a principal in the development of the Rookery Building, where the American Luxfer Prism Company and Winslow had their offices.

A key element in the success of the American Luxfer Prism Company was Winslow's invention of a system of electro-glazing, whereby thin copper ribbons were placed between the four-inch prism tiles and then electroplated in a bath of copper sulfate. The process built up a rim of copper on the edges of the ribbon and made the glass tiles more or less rigid and easy to handle. The process was not unlike that used by Tiffany in assembling his remarkable multicolored glass shades. Winslow's idea was patented in January 1897, one of the company's 162 design and mechanical patents for various aspects of the prisms and their installation. Frank Lloyd Wright, acting as a design consultant, prepared forty-one different designs for the glass prism tiles.[45] At least one of them was mass produced and can still be found in installations throughout the United States.

Wright's work as a consultant to the American Luxfer Prism Company apparently started at about the time he moved into 1107 Steinway Hall. During the latter half of 1897 he produced the various designs for the glass-block tiles for his clients. Much of this work was done at Steinway Hall, but in late 1897 Wright evidently found it more convenient to work at the company's offices on the north side of the eleventh floor of the Rookery. The 1898 *Chicago Business Directory* lists Wright in room 1123 of the Rookery. Later that year Wright produced a small printed announcement noting that thereafter his studio would be in Oak Park, except between the hours of twelve o'clock and two, when he would be at his downtown office in room 1119 of the Rookery. The brochure noted that the Rookery office was strictly "for business purposes, consultation and matters in connection with superintendence." Plans of both the Oak Park Studio and the Rookery office were included, but it is highly unlikely that Wright ever built the office proposed for room 1119 at the Rookery. In 1899 he was listed in room 1104 of the Rookery, and in 1900 he was once more listed in Steinway Hall in room 1106, a space he shared with H. Webster Tomlinson in a short-lived partnership. By 1899 the Luxfer Prism Company had left the Rookery, and Wright would no longer have had the use of their offices. In any case, he continued to list his downtown address as 1106 Steinway Hall until 1907, when he left the building for good. It is doubtful that he continued to use the loft above, although he remained friends with his colleagues in room 1107. Wright has written that his fee for the work he did for the American Luxfer Prism Company was used to build his Oak Park Studio. That fee must have been substantial. During the same period, he continued work for E. C. Waller, who had offices in the Rookery. Waller would be Wright's client, friend, and supporter for many years to come.

The most important work Wright did for the American Luxfer Prism Company was producing designs for prototypical business buildings using Luxfer prisms. Two designs have survived, both for the facade of an eleven-story building. They were published in the January 1898 issue of the *Inland Architect* and in the supplement to the February 12, 1898, issue of the *American Architect and Building News,* to announce a competition sponsored by the company to promote its product by getting architects to suggest uses for the prisms.[46] The drawings were done in a similar style, probably by one of Wright's colleagues in the loft above room 1107 of Steinway Hall. (Wright rarely did his own presentation drawings.) The second design was strangely reminiscent of Louis Sullivan's work, although it was somewhat conventional, and has seldom been discussed. Wright never referred to it in later years, and its derivative style suggests that it was an afterthought, perhaps cre-

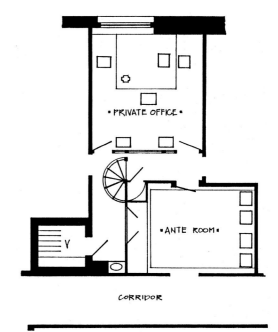

Unbuilt office Frank Lloyd Wright planned on the north side of the top floor of the Rookery (WRH)

Henry Webster Tomlinson (PC)

45. Ibid., 26–28. Neumann states that Wright submitted forty-one designs, most of which were "simple ornamental line drawings, somewhat reminiscent of the system of geometrical and organic ornament developed by his former employer, Louis Sullivan."

46. *Inland Architect* 30, no. 6 (January 1898): 63–64 and two unnumbered plates, and *American Architect and Building News* 59, no. 189 (February 12, 1898): 1–3. Both journals published full-page illustrations of Wright's two designs.

*First design suggested by Frank Lloyd Wright as an example of how Luxfer prisms might be used in an office building (IA)*

*Second Luxfer prism design by Frank Lloyd Wright (IA)*

ated to comply with the requirements of the forthcoming competition. The first design, on the other hand, was pure Wright. The most interesting surviving drawing is now in the archives at Taliesin. It is a hard line drawing clearly showing how Wright intended to use the assembled prisms to define the architecture. This drawing may have been, at least partially, in Wright's own hand. (Unfortunately, Wright revised the drawing in later years to show how he would have done it then. One half of the building is, however, still in its original form.)

Wright's suggested designs for Luxfer prisms were included in a *Hand-Book* prepared by the American Luxfer Prism Company released in January 1898.[47] It was included as part of the program for the competition, and stated that the company wished to set "forth in a definite and comprehensive manner new possibilities in the use of Luxfer prisms as a building material."[48] The prizes offered were substantial, with two thousand dollars going to "the design of greatest merit" and the fifth prize set at two hundred dollars. There were also to be prizes of a hundred dollars each for the "ten designs next in point of merit." Guidelines were minimal, suggesting only that the competitors might review the Luxfer Prism handbook, which would provide "a thorough understanding of the subject." The competitors' drawings were to be delivered to the company at its offices in the Rookery no later than March 15, 1898, and awards were to be announced on March 21.[49] Apparently two months was not enough time to get sufficient response, and the due date was extended to June 15, 1898. The winners' names and designs were published in the September issues of the *Inland Architect* and the *American Architect and Building News*.[50] All the five thousand dollars in prize money was awarded, with Robert C. Spencer taking the first place of two thousand dollars, Adamo Boari taking second with a thousand, and S. S. Beman taking third with five hundred. The three principal winners were all Chicagoans connected to the Chicago Architectural Club. Boari was not listed as a member but was a regular participant in the affairs of the Steinway Hall group.[51] Beman had become an associate member in 1894 and was a supporter and an occasional speaker at club functions. The remaining prizes went to Curtis Hoffman (fourth prize of three hundred dollars) and Frederick S. Sewell (fifth prize of two hundred dollars), both from Chicago. There were ten prizes of a hundred dollars each that went to J. E. Fisher of Bloomington, Illinois, Hugo F. Liedberg of Chicago, Frederick S. Sewell of Chicago, Field & Medary of Philadelphia, J. L. Wees (two awards) of St. Louis,

47. *Pocket Hand-Book of Useful Information and Tables Relating to the Use of Electro-glazed Luxfer Prisms* (Chicago, 1898).

48. The rules of the competition were published along with Wright's designs in an edited version in the *Inland Architect*, and in their entirety in the *American Architect and Building News (Trade Supplement)*.

49. The March 21 deadline would have been just in time for the drawings to be shown at the Chicago Architectural Club's 1898 exhibition, although the extension, published in *Inland Architect* 31, no. 4 (May 1898): 38–39, made that impossible, so some of the drawings were exhibited in the 1899 exhibition.

50. *Inland Architect* 32, no. 2 (September 1898): 15–16, and *American Architect and Building News* 61, no. 1187 (September 24, 1898): 103.

51. Adamo Boari (1863–1928) was first noted as being in room 1107 of Steinway Hall when Perkins et al. combined forces there. Boari was born in Italy and studied civil engineering before emigrating to Brazil in 1889. He moved to Chicago around 1892 and apparently did some technical work with D. H. Burnham at the World's Columbian Exposition. While he was never a serious part of the Eighteen, he did work for Wright from time to time. (Rendering number 441 in Bruce Brooks Pfeiffer, ed., *Frank Lloyd Wright, 1887–1901* [Tokyo: A.D.A. Edita, 1986], has Boari's name written across the bottom.) In 1904 Boari moved to Mexico after winning a competition to design the Mexico City Opera House. He never returned to Chicago, but moved to Rome, where he died in 1928 after a distinguished career.

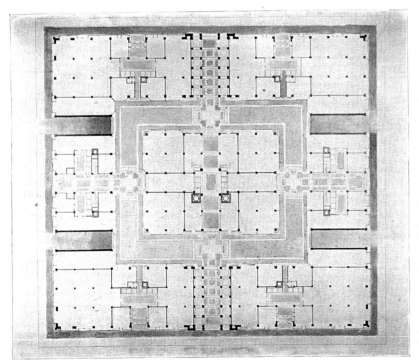 

*Plan and interior perspective of Robert Spencer's winning design for the use of Luxfer prisms (IA)*

*Adamo Boari (PC)*

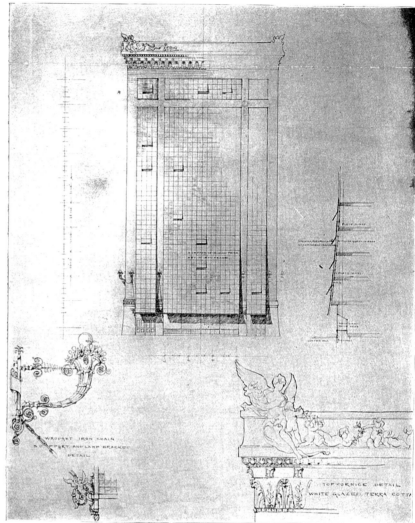

*Adamo Boari's second-place design, published in the* Inland Architect *(IA)*

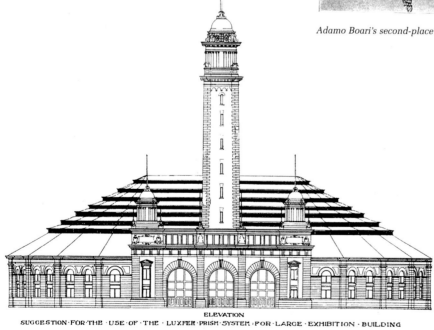

ELEVATION
SUGGESTION·FOR·THE·USE·OF·THE·LUXFER·PRISM·SYSTEM·FOR·LARGE·EXHIBITION·BUILDING

*S. S. Beman's third-place design for the Luxfer Prism Competition (IA)*

Alfred Fellheimer of Chicago, David S. Williams of Fort Snelling, Mississippi, and Howard Bowen of St. Louis. (It is interesting to note that two competitors, Sewell and Wees, each received two awards. Second-place winner Adamo Boari also did two designs but apparently submitted only one, or perhaps his second design was not considered of sufficient merit to win an award. It did, however, have enough merit to be shown in the club's 1899 exhibition and illustrated in the catalog.) It was the first and last showing of the Luxfer Prism Competition. The competition had occupied a good deal of the time of Wright and his colleagues in Steinway Hall during the fall of 1897 and the early months of 1898. It was not, of course, the only activity that was important to the Steinway Hall group during that period. They all had clients to serve, and most of them remained active in the affairs of the Chicago Architectural Club.

✤

The last days of spring and the early summer of 1897 after the Tenth Annual Exhibition were, as usual, a quiet time for the club. The move to new quarters in the Art Institute of Chicago on May 1, 1897, had effectively ended the club's activities before summer vacation. The last formal meeting in the old quarters at 274 Michigan Avenue had been on April 19, when Peter B. Wight delivered an address titled "Fundamentals of the Development of Style."[52]

Wight, who had always taken an interest in the club's activities, particularly during its work on Lake Front Park, spoke eloquently. He was concerned with two questions that had recently been raised: Is architecture a living art? and Can architecture again become a living art? Both questions had been discussed in recent meetings of the Illinois Chapter of the AIA, but Wight was quick to point out that the "spirit of inquiry is not local; it may be seen in the writings of older architects all over the civilized world." In his presentation, Wight briefly reviewed how the evolution of styles had been dealt with in the past elsewhere in the world, but he soon returned to events that directly affected the Chicago Architectural Club. First, he referred to the work of John Root, commenting on "the admirable life of John Wellborn Root, whom most of you knew . . . The best of his essays were written for this club, and the best of them all on 'Style' which was read by him just ten years ago, has been re-read before you by one of your own members very recently." He was referring to the club's meeting on February 26, 1897, when Hugh M. G. Garden had read Root's paper before the assembled membership. Wight went on to touch on lectures and papers by Louis Sullivan, Ralph Adams Cram, and Leopold Eidlitz. He was primarily concerned with architects who slavishly followed either historic styles or whatever style was currently in vogue. He urged his audience not to merely follow their seniors like sheep. He told them that he "would not advise anyone to turn his back on all the historical styles any more than I would tell him to close and forget the book of history, which I know he cannot do. The fundamentals of the development of style are found first in the materials that we have to use to build our house with, as they always have been throughout all time. Let the architect design for his materials, and not fit materials to his design . . . If any of his materials had no counterpart in history he is free to use them without regard to it. Here he at once begins to feel his emancipation from precedents . . . As time goes on and successive works come to his hand, every liberal departure from the models he originally followed will be one step more in the development of style." Wight, by advocating originality in architecture while respecting the past, was proselytizing in the spirit of Louis Sullivan. He was also in concert with the ideas of Frank Lloyd Wright, Robert Spencer, Myron Hunt, and Dwight Perkins, who

52. Wight's address was printed in *Inland Architect* 29, no. 4 (May 1897): 32–34. His critical comments on architecture were often published, especially during the late nineteenth century when he was not otherwise employed. The best study of Wight is that of the architectural historian Sarah Bradford Landau, who wrote a long essay titled "P. B. Wight: Architect, Contractor, and Critic, 1838–1925," issued on the occasion of a 1981 exhibition of Wight's work at the Art Institute of Chicago. Landau notes that Wight's "words seem to predict twentieth-century modernism."

were all about to produce a new architecture in shared facilities at Steinway Hall. Peter B. Wight was clearly far more an advocate of a new architecture than was Daniel Burnham.

Following the club's move to the new rooms at the Art Institute, the opening night festivities, and a last bohemian night of the year on June 7, the members essentially took the summer off from club affairs. The new rooms remained open, but there were no scheduled events. During that summer the young practitioners who had joined Dwight Perkins in Steinway Hall began a relationship that would affect architecture in Chicago and the world to an extent that could not have been anticipated. The work they did for the American Luxfer Prism Company helped bind them into a cohesive group of avant-garde designers, and other events helped to weld them together as well. The Chicago Architectural Club was a major vehicle for their public activities during the next several years, but it was not the only organization of interest to them.

During the summer and early fall of 1897, while the Steinway Hall group were becoming established in their new quarters, they were introduced to another society that would influence their theories on design and the architecture they produced. It was probably their next-door neighbor on the eleventh floor of Steinway Hall, Allen B. Pond, who introduced them to the activities at Jane Addams's Hull-House on the near West Side of Chicago. Pond had been secretary of the organization since its inception in 1888.[53] He and his brother, I. K. Pond, occupied room 1109 of Steinway Hall, a space four times the size of room 1107. A. B. Pond made it a practice to attend numerous meetings of various clubs formed under the umbrella of Hull-House, mostly for social purposes.[54] In December of 1897 the *Hull-House Bulletin* noted that "an informal meeting was held at Hull-House in October, to discuss the advisability of forming a local arts and crafts society. At subsequent meetings, attended by an increasing number of sympathizers, the idea was farther [*sic*] discussed, and a society was formed."[55] The article published an extract from the constitution of the society and stated that meetings were being "held in the Hull-House Lecture Hall on the first and third Fridays of each month, and a paper dealing with some special craft is read and discussed at each meeting. It is intended to

*Allen B. Pond, ca. 1888 (BHL)*

53. While not educated as an architect, A. B. Pond became a distinguished practitioner along with his brother, Irving K. Pond, who had been a founder of the Chicago Architectural Club. Pond & Pond was formed in 1886, and the firm designed all the buildings in the Hull-House complex. A. B. Pond maintained his interest in Hull-House throughout his life and served on its board of trustees until his death in 1929.

54. Under the direction of social reformer Jane Addams, Hull-House provided activities for the benefit of disadvantaged citizens of the near West Side of Chicago. While they were not restricted to the poor, they were generally intended to give people something to do while teaching them social and personal skills to enhance their lives. There were more than a dozen clubs for women, children, boys, and girls for which Hull-House provided rooms and direction on a daily basis. There were also a number of "general societies," primarily for adults. Almost anyone or any group could form such an organization merely by demonstrating that it would benefit the community. The Arts and Crafts Society was one such group; formed at Hull-House on October 22, 1897, it was an immediate success.

55. *Hull-House Bulletin* (December 1, 1897): 9. The same column was repeated in the January–February 1898 issue with the addition of a list of the next three meetings of the society.

*Hull-House complex on Chicago's West Side, designed by Pond & Pond (PC)*

hold an exhibition about the end of February." The following month a schedule of lecturers was published, including "Mr. Androvette" on "Modern Stained Glass," "Messrs. Winslow Bros." on "Wrought Iron Work," and "Fritz Wagner" on "Terra Cotta." Those subjects and lecturers were, of course, very much in the spirit of what was happening at the Chicago Architectural Club. The arts and crafts exhibition held a few weeks later was done in conjunction with the Chicago Architectural Club's Eleventh Annual Exhibition. The exhibition catalog included the complete constitution of the new society, which had been adopted on October 31, 1897, and a list of all the founding members.[56] Included were Mr. and Mrs. Myron Hunt, Marion Mahony, A. B. and I. K. Pond, R. C. Spencer, Frank Wright, Mr. and Mrs. Herman Winslow, and Mr. and Mrs. Dwight Perkins, all of whom were involved in some manner with the Chicago Architectural Club. Several other prominent members of the club and the architectural and design community were also listed as members. The Chicago Arts and Crafts Society was to become a major force in the cultural affairs of the city due in no small part to the participation by members of the Chicago Architectural Club.

While the organization of the Chicago Arts and Crafts Society was under consideration, the Chicago Architectural Club began its 1897–98 year's activities with a meeting on Monday evening, September 13. It was a formal meeting without a speaker. Instead, the floor was opened to a general discussion, "How to Make the Most of the Club's Privileges this Coming Season." Those privileges were the advantages that had accrued to the members since the club had been admitted to the Art Institute of Chicago with rooms on the premises. Without naming names or defining the events of the evening, the *Brickbuilder* reported that "many of the leading members offer valuable suggestions which will no doubt materialize as the season advances."[57]

The following month, on October 11, 1897, the club held its annual meeting and election of officers. Edward G. Garden was elected president,[58] Frank Kirkpatrick and William C. Eggebrecht were chosen as first and second vice presidents, N. Max Dunning assumed the secretary's position, and his employer, Joseph C. Llewellyn, was asked to be treasurer. August C. Wilmanns and Frank Upman filled out the Executive Committee. For the second consecutive year, no syllabus was published, and the club's activities must be derived from a careful study of brief items that appeared regularly in the architectural press.

The last of the annual Robert Clark Testimonial competitions had taken place in 1896. Nevertheless, a competition very similar to the Clark event was announced early in the 1897–98 club year. The October 1897 issue of the *Inland Architect* reported that a "club member" had made a donation of a gold medal for a competition for "A Clubhouse for Architects."[59] Only one medal was to be awarded, although mention was made of the next two drawings in order of merit. The club member was later identified as associate member Henry R. Dillon. The rules of the competition were similar but not identical to those of the Clark competition.

The announcement of the competition began, "The programme for this competition was inspired by the desire to bring architecture into closer relation to its sister arts, sculpture and painting, thus broadening the architect's artistic horizon. The architect will feel more and more the stimulus created by having constantly before him the best examples of the three arts. He will unconsciously strive to give art its proper place in his work appreciating that it will be judged by future genera-

56. *Catalogue of the Eleventh Annual Exhibition of the Chicago Architectural Club*, 118–43.

57. *Brickbuilder* 6, no. 9 (September 1897): 189.

58. This was the second time that Edward G. Garden had held office in the Chicago Architectural Club. He had been elected secretary on November 13, 1893, only to resign on February 6, after which he moved to St. Louis and was instrumental in forming the St. Louis Architectural Club. He served as president of that club in 1895. Why he returned to Chicago is unknown, but he went back to St. Louis in February 1898 after having served only four months as president.

59. *Inland Architect* 30, no. 3 (October 1897): 33.

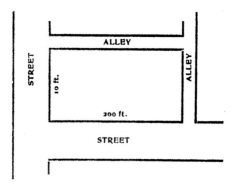

*Published site plan for the Dillon Competition for "A Clubhouse for Architects" (IA)*

tions, and that an architect can do much toward uplifting the taste and artistic feeling of the people. It is evident from this introduction that the building is to be monumental, bearing witness to its high function as a shrine of true art." The program then described in some detail the rooms and spaces required. Sculpture and painting were to be prominently featured, especially on the first floor, and the second floor was to be entirely devoted to the needs of the club. A plan of the site was published with the program. Clearly, it was to be a clubhouse for a group like the Chicago Architectural Club, although that was not specifically stated. The drawings were to be delivered on or before January 15, 1898. That deadline was later extended to March 14, 1898.

Without a published syllabus it is impossible to recreate all the club's activities in the fall of 1897. Some events were reported, the earliest being an address by W. A. Otis on November 1 on the development of architectural styles. Shortly thereafter, president E. G. Garden arranged to exhibit the working drawings of the new Chicago Public Library, which were discussed by his brother F. M. Garden, who had been the superintendent of construction at the building for Shepley, Rutan & Coolidge. At the end of the month, on November 29, Frank Lloyd Wright led a discussion on "Arts and Crafts," obviously prompted by his newfound interest in the Chicago Arts and Crafts Society. General William Sooy-Smith, P. B. Wight, and W. B. Mundie were also noted as speakers during this period, but neither subjects nor dates were recorded.

Formal lectures and bohemian nights continued to be an important part of the club's activities. The club also continued the now well-established practice of providing classroom instruction to members in pen-and-ink drawing and watercolor work, with Birch Burdette Long and Harry D. Jenkins as tutors. In a departure from the past, the club took a new direction in its effort to teach design. Taking a cue from the recently organized Society of Beaux-Arts Architects, the club established several "projets" under the direction of prominent members of the club. Dwight Perkins, R. C. Spencer, George Dean, E. G. Garden, Elmer Jensen, Frank Upman (later succeeded by N. Max Dunning), W. B. Mundie, and Myron Hunt agreed to act as "patrons" and to lead a team of younger members during the coming year. The plan was for each group to select a project, develop it together, and present it to the full club for criticism. The initial presentation was held at the first meeting of 1898, on January 10. Ultimately, it was expected that each team's projet results would be exhibited at the club's annual exhibition. It did not work out as well as planned, however, because only the Spencer and Dunning groups were able to produce work of sufficient merit to be exhibited, but the others were presented at club meetings.

In another departure from past efforts, the club joined forces with the Chicago Chapter of the AIA to sponsor a series of five lectures by professor William Henry Goodyear of the Brooklyn Academy. The series began on November 18 when he spoke on "Horizontal Curves and other optical refinements in Greek Architecture." Two weeks later his subject was "Surveys showing structural optical refinements in Italian Churches." The next three weeks were devoted to "Pisa Cathedral," "The Egyptian Lotus in Greek decorative art," and "The Roman Ruins of Eastern Syria."[60] While all this was under way, the club also managed to have a "Ladies Night" on December 6. The evening was sponsored by Mr. and Mrs. Dwight Perkins, Mr. and Mrs. R. C. Spencer, Mr. and Mrs. Myron Hunt, and several others, all of whom had some connection with the Steinway Hall group.

In the December issue of the *Inland Architect*, Robert Craik McLean penned another of his perennial essays, "The Work of the Chicago Architectural Club."[61] After commending the club for having established itself at the Art Institute, he ob-

60. Brochure Series 3, no. 12 (December 1897): 197.

61. *Inland Architect* 30, no. 5 (December 1897): 47–48.

served that the work was being carried on "by young men whose daily employment is over the drafting boards of the architects of Chicago, with little or no guidance except their own bright conception of the needs of their fellows, aided by the traditions of the club, which stretch back twelve years to the time of its organization, in the offices of *The Inland Architect*, by a few draftsmen who have since become prominent among the best designers in the country, they teach and are taught and work together for the common purpose of advancement in their chosen art." McLean's admiration for what the club had accomplished never wavered. His editorial was a fitting end to the year 1897.

## The Modern Phase of Architecture.

BY LOUIS H. SULLIVAN.

THE Cleveland meeting of the Architectural Clubs of the country will mark, I believe, the auspicious opening of a new era in the growth of architectural thought.

It should, in the nature of things, be of serious import to us of the present and active generation, to know what the generation to follow thinks and feels.

Its thoughts may be immature, its feelings vague and formless; yet, nevertheless, in them the future life of our art is surely working out its destiny; and the sincerity of them is not to be denied.

Youth is the most ambitious, the most beautiful, but the most helpful stage of life. It has that immediate and charming idealism which leads in the end toward greatness; but it can know little of the sorrow and bitterness of the struggle for greatness. Youth is ineffable. I have said good-bye to mine; with solicitude I welcome yours.

Perceiving, as I do, the momentous sway and drift of modern life; knowing, as I do, that the curtain has risen on a drama, the most intense and passionate in all history, I urge that you cast away as worthless the shopworn and empirical notion that an architect is an artist—whatever that funny word may mean—and accept my assurance that he is and imperatively shall be a poet, and an interpreter of the national life of his time.

Do you fully realize how despicable is a man who betrays a trust?

Do you know, or can you foresee, or instinctively judge how acutely delicate will become, in your time, the element of confidence and dependence between man and man and between society and the individual?

If you realize this, you will realize at once and forever, that you, by birth, and through the beneficence of the form of government under which you live—that you are called upon, not to betray, but to express the life of your own day and generation. That society will have just cause to hold you to account for your use of the liberty that it has given to you, and the confidence it has reposed in you.

You will realize, in due time, as your lives develop and expand, and you become richer in experience, that a fraudulent and surreptitious use of historical documents, however suavely presented, however cleverly plagiarized, however neatly repacked, however shrewdly intrigued, will constitute and will be held to be a betrayal of trust.

You know well what I mean. You know in your own hearts that you are to be fakers or that you are to be honest men.

It is futile to quibble or to protest, or to plead ignorance or innocence, or to asseverate and urge the force of circumstances.     *     *     *     *     *

If you take the pains truly to understand your country, your people, your day, your generation; the time; the place in which you live; if you seek to understand, absorb, and sympathize with the life around you, you will be understood and sympathetically received in return. Have no fear as to this.

Society soon will have no use for people who have no use for it. The clairvoyance of the age is steadily unfolding; and it will result therefrom, that the greatest poet will be he who shall grasp and deify the commonplaces of our life—those simple, normal feelings which the people of his day will be helpless, otherwise, to express—and here you have the key with which, individually, you may unlock, in time, the portal of your art.

I truly believe that your coming together will result in serious things. You have my sympathy. I am with you in spirit; for in you resides the only hope, the only sign of dawn that I can see, making for a day that shall regenerate an art that should be, may be and must be, the noblest, the most intimate, the most expressive, the most eloquent of all.

Your youth is your most precious heritage from the past: I am with you.

*Essay and decorative border by Louis Sullivan, published in the* Inland Architect

# Philosophical Debates at the End of the Century

CHAPTER TEN

The Chicago Architectural Club held its 1897 Christmas party on December 29 in its rooms at the Art Institute of Chicago. An elaborate, heavily ornamented tree was the feature of the evening, which was hosted by president Edward G. Garden and his brother Frank along with other officers of the club. Gifts were exchanged, songs were sung, and the food and conversation was enjoyed by all. With that bohemian evening behind them, the club members settled down to more serious efforts at their regular fortnightly meetings with bohemian evenings sandwiched in between. Those serious evenings began with the first exhibition of projet drawings on January 10, 1898, followed by the second and third presentations on January 31 and February 14.[1] The eight patrons and their teams had put together projets that their colleagues were delighted and eager to criticize on these supposedly formal evenings, which were sometimes very bohemian in character. The January 31 showing was by Robert C. Spencer and his team; the other groups were not identified.[2]

All the members, of course, continued to participate in other, more serious events between these showings. For example, P. B. Wight, the secretary of the newly appointed Illinois Board of Architectural Examiners, delivered a lecture at the club rooms on January 24 regarding the recently passed law governing the practice of architecture in the state of Illinois.[3] The members also spent a good deal of time honing their drawing skills and quite often were requested to "come to the club rooms prepared with pencils, sketch blocks, and bright ideas, to participate in a competition for the design of a building," the governing conditions of which were announced on that evening. A time limit of a half hour was allotted for the preparation of sketches, with general criticism and discussion of the problem following.[4] The spirit and camaraderie of the early days of the "sketch" club had been revived.

The activities of the club and its individual members were sometimes reported in the local press and often in the architectural press. In February, the *Brochure Series* noted that "Theodore W. Pietsch of Chicago" had been awarded a diploma by the École des Beaux-Arts in Paris.[5] This was a rare event, since most American students at the École did not stay long enough to receive a diploma. Upon his return to Chicago, Pietsch became an active member of the Chicago Architectural Club.

On February 1, 1898, an event occurred that would influence the club's governance and activities for the next several years. The recently elected president,

1. *Brickbuilder* 7, no. 1 (January 1898): 2, and *Brochure Series* 4, no. 1 (January 1898): 9.

2. *Brochure Series* 4, no. 2 (February 1898): 32.

3. *Brickbuilder* 7, no. 2 (February 1898): 26.

4. Ibid. These events were reported to the media by the secretary as the bylaws specified. Unfortunately, the sketches made on such evenings were usually discarded and none have surfaced.

5. *Brochure Series* 4, no. 2 (February 1898): 31.

6. There is also information concerning Kirkpatrick in the 1900 U.S. Census, vol. 76, E. D. 1155, sheet 17, line 80. He was listed as Francis W. Kirkpatrick, architect, 1227 Chicago Avenue, Evanston, Illinois. His birthplace was Kansas and he was noted as being twenty-seven years old, having been born in October 1872. (Census records do not list the day of birth.) His wife, "Amy L. O.," was born in November 1875 in Minnesota and twenty-four years old. McDonough's *Architects' and Contractors' Directory* for 1902–03 lists him as an architect working in room 1142 of the Rookery, in the office of D. H. Burnham and Company. Kirkpatrick left Chicago in 1902 and in 1903–4 he was listed as an Illinois licensed architect with J. H. Felt & Company, living in St. Joseph, Missouri. In 1905, the St. Joseph directory notes that he had "moved to Kansas City, Mo." That same year he was listed as an architect for the Board of Public Works in Kansas City, Missouri.

Edward G. Garden, resigned to return to St. Louis, where he would practice for the remainder of his career. His position was filled by first vice president F. W. Kirkpatrick.

Francis (Frank) W. Kirkpatrick is somewhat of an enigma. Little is known about him, except that he worked in room 1107 at Steinway Hall at the time of his election to the board of directors of the Chicago Architectural Club on October 11, 1897. He was first listed as a member of the club in the 1896 exhibition catalog, where his address was shown to be on the near West Side of Chicago. During the next two years he continued to be listed at various (apparently home) addresses in that area. In 1897 he was listed in the *Chicago Business Directory* as an architect occupying room 1107 at Steinway Hall, and he continued to be listed there for several years. Whether he was employed by one of his more prominent colleagues in Steinway Hall or was an independent practitioner is not clear. The fact that he was listed as an architect in the *Chicago Business Directory* suggests that he was independent. Furthermore, his listing in the 1897 directory indicates that he was in Steinway Hall at the end of 1896, before Wright, Hunt, and Spencer joined Perkins in room 1107.[6]

Whatever Kirkpatrick's background and practice may have been, when he became president of the Chicago Architectural Club, there was a major change in the philosophy behind the club's activities. Except for secretary N. Max Dunning, the other members of the club's board of directors in 1898 were, for the most part, only modest contributors to the affairs of the club. Following Kirkpatrick's assumption of the office of president, the committee structure of the club, which controlled the annual exhibition, became heavily dominated by the men who were to become known

*Semi-detached houses, F. W. Kirkpatrick's only published work in Chicago (IA; photo by Fuermann & Williams)*

first as the Chicago School, and later as the Prairie School of practitioners. That situation would continue for the next five years. Not only would the annual exhibitions now be devoted to the modern movement taking place in Chicago, but the club would take a much more active interest in social changes that could be brought about by architecture. The club's committee structure was formalized and meetings were scheduled far in advance. A syllabus was once again published, and members knew what to expect and what was expected of them as the year progressed.

The first task facing Kirkpatrick when he assumed the presidency was the Eleventh Annual Exhibition scheduled for March 23 through April 15, 1898. Kirkpatrick had less than two months to prepare, and he did so by appointing himself chairman of the Exhibition Committee, along with six other members—Birch Burdette Long, Clarence Hatzfeld, Victor A. Matteson, Harry Starr, Hugo Arnold, and a single club officer, secretary N. Max Dunning. He set up a Jury of Admission consisting of Louis J. Millett, J. K. Cady, and Robert C. Spencer Jr., and appointed a three-man group consisting of Hugh Garden, Elmer Jensen, and George Dean to serve as the Hanging Committee. Finally, he asked the club treasurer, J. C. Llewellyn, to chair the Catalogue and Finance Committee, which included H. V. von Holst and Kirkpatrick. All these men were among the avant-garde of the Chicago architectural community.

The Eleventh Annual Exhibition of the Chicago Architectural Club opened as scheduled on March 23, 1898. The date had been established in late 1897, and the rules for the exhibitors had been published in the February issue of the *Inland Architect*.[7] Those rules were essentially identical to what had been established in the past, but they were accompanied by an interesting letter to the club from the committee in charge of AIA chapter medals, which were awarded annually to members of the club for the best overall performance during the year. Signed by the chapter's president, Dankmar Adler, and secretary, Dwight Perkins, the letter suggested, without actually saying so, that the chapter was rather disappointed that the membership was not taking a greater interest in vying for the gold, silver, and bronze medals. They had expected that those medals would go to the members who participated in and won places in the weekly sketch classes and other events during the year, which were held on regular sketch nights. Points were also given for members who took major competition prizes. (Apparently no records of those events were kept, and thus no winners of the medals can be named.) The AIA letter noted that since the club already had several competitions, the AIA did not wish to merely add another. What it had wanted was to "encourage each to put forth an extra effort, not for the purpose of securing a medal, but to assist in maintaining a high standard for the club's share of the [annual] exhibit." It went on to say that "the Chapter wishes, therefore, to acknowledge the purely architectural abilities of the club as represented by individual work presented . . . [and] does not reserve the right to withhold its award." It chose to find another method of awarding medals and brief, somewhat generic rules were noted along with the names of the judges, Peter B. Wight, W. W. Clay, and Harry B. Wheelock.

The members of the Chicago Chapter of the AIA were clearly discouraged by the club's response to what they had been trying to do. Their plan had been to recognize the most active and talented club members. They didn't feel that the membership appreciated their efforts. Since they had already committed to awarding a gold, silver, and bronze medal in 1898, they simply awarded those medals to the first-, second-, and third-place winners of the Clubhouse for Architects Competition sponsored by Henry F. Dillon.[8] Those awards had been selected by the CAC Jury of Admission appointed by Kirkpatrick.

Despite the confusion about the AIA awards, the Eleventh Annual Exhibition

7. *Inland Architect* 31, no. 1 (February 1898): 7–8.

8. The awards were publicized in two ways. First, a caption for the *Inland Architect*'s illustrations of the Dillon competition winner noted that the first prize was a "Design by Victor Traxler, Chicago; Awarded the Henry R. Dillon Gold Medal and also Gold Medal by the Illinois Chapter, The American Institute of Architects." Second, a brief essay in the 1898 exhibition catalog stated that Traxler had won the gold medal and that John Robert Dillon was given second place. In the catalog listing, Dillon was named as "First Mention" and John F. Sheblessy as "Second Mention." Ten names were listed in the catalog as competitors. It is assumed that the silver and bronze medals of the AIA were awarded to the first and second mention designs.

*Victor Traxler's winning design for "A Club House for Architects," awarded the Dillon medal and the AIA gold medal (IA)*

*The Boulder, modeled by Richard W. Bock, still flanking the entrance to Frank Lloyd Wright's studio in Oak Park, Illinois (DH)*

9. The format of the catalog suggests that combining the two groups into a single book may have been an afterthought.

10. It was reviewed by the *Chicago Tribune,* the *Chicago Evening Post,* the *Chicago Times Herald,* and other local papers as well. Clippings of these reviews are available on microfilm at the Art Institute of Chicago. Unfortunately, those clippings are not always fully identified bibliographically. It was also reviewed in the architectural journals and various art journals, some of which are noted hereinafter.

11. *Chicago Tribune,* April 3, 1898, and *Chicago Times Herald,* March 15, 1898.

went on as scheduled, in conjunction with an exhibition sponsored by the Arts and Crafts Society. The joint exhibition occupied several rooms on the second floor of the Art Institute of Chicago. The Chicago Architectural Club dominated the exhibition, especially the catalog, with nearly 150 pages and more than a hundred advertisers, many of whom took out full pages. No mention is made of the editor or designer of the catalog, but the cover carries the monogram of Birch Burdette Long, who often did graphics of this nature. After a title page, a complete roster of club members and officers was included, as well as a preface and a brief description of the results of the Dillon prize. This was followed by a listing of the 559 entries in the exhibition, with illustrations interspersed between advertisements. No mention is made of the Arts and Crafts Society until page 117, where there is a second title page for that group alone. Following that title page is a copy of the society's constitution and a list of its 123 members. These names are particularly interesting. Several members of the Chicago Architectural Club are listed, often both husband and wife. Of the core group from Steinway Hall, Perkins, Spencer, Hunt, and Wright are all there, but Spencer's and Wright's wives are conspicuously absent. On the other hand, Marion Mahony and Blanche Ostertag, both of whom worked with the Steinway Hall architects on a regular basis, were listed. The membership was about evenly divided between men and women. The members list was followed by a listing of 540 exhibits from the Arts and Crafts Society. There were no illustrations of these exhibits.[9]

The joint exhibition was well received, and according to the popular press, it attracted hundreds of visitors every day.[10] Two critics commented at length on sculptor Richard Bock's work for the building Dwight Perkins had designed for the Trans-Mississippi International Exposition in Omaha, Nebraska, then in the planning stages.[11] Both remarked extensively on the quality of the architecture and the sculpture, and commented favorably on *The Boulder* by Richard Bock, which was not listed in the catalog but was obviously in the show. This was an important piece Bock designed to be installed on the exterior of Frank Lloyd Wright's studio in Oak Park. Two versions of it are still in place. The two critics also praised the Illinois building designed for the Trans-Mississippi Exposition by Hugh M. G. Garden. In all the local reviews, the Arts and Crafts Society's contribution took second place, usually at the end of each critic's article.

*Richard Bock's sculpture adorns the Machinery and Electricity Building designed by Dwight Heald Perkins for the Trans-Mississippi International Exposition at Omaha (IA)*

The most favorable review of the exhibition was published by the Chicago art journal *Brush and Pencil*.[12] This is not surprising since the article was written by N. Max Dunning,[13] secretary of the club and the patron of several of the club's projets. Dunning's review began by noting that "the event of greatest importance during the last month in art circles in Chicago has been the exhibition of the Chicago Architectural Club at the Art Institute." He called it "the largest and most excellent collection of architectural drawings ever hung in the west," and made only a passing comment that the Arts and Crafts Society was exhibiting with "us" this year. He wrote that the "strictly architectural exhibition consists of designs of buildings for all purposes" and that "principal architects of this and other countries . . . have responded admirably . . . by sending examples of their projected and completed work." Dunning noted that drawings from New York, Philadelphia, and Boston were exhibited, but that "Chicago has held up her end in the exhibition, as she usually does" and that the "most notable exhibits in the Chicago group are those sent over by Messrs. Shepley, Rutan & Coolidge, Pond & Pond, H. M. G. Garden, Handy & Cady, Robert C. Spencer, Jr., D. H. Perkins, Frank Wright, Arthur Heun, Richard E. Schmidt, Waid & Cranford, Joseph C. Llewellyn, George R. Dean, Howard Shaw and Henry L. Ottenheimer." With a few obvious exceptions these were the Young Turks of Chicago most of whom were in some manner associated with the Steinway Hall group.

Dunning also commented briefly on the history of the Chicago Architectural Club and noted that despite the "severe depression in business of the past few years . . . the club seems to be on the top of the tidal wave . . . membership has been rapidly increasing and now numbers over one hundred and fifty names." He noted that the lectures and classes sponsored by the club had been very successful, as had the "idea of dividing the club into squads of members, each to work out some practical problem . . . under the guidance of some architect . . . who volunteered his services that the younger members might profit by his instruction." Dunning's own group of nine men chose to design a "Residence for a retired Florist," which was shown in the exhibition. Robert C. Spencer led another group that designed an "Elevated Station for the Union Loop," and D. H. Perkins headed a group that designed a cold

12. *Brush and Pencil* 2, no. 4 (April 1898): 20–29.

13. N. Max Dunning (1874–1946) was born in Wisconsin and studied at the University of Wisconsin for four years. He moved to Chicago in 1894 and joined the office of J. C. Llewellyn, where he remained until 1900, when he won the Chicago Architectural Club Traveling Scholarship. After a year in Europe he opened his own office in Chicago. He lived in Chicago for the remainder of his life, except for intermittent government service in Washington, D.C.

*Robert Clossen Spencer's design for H. N. Kelsey on Sheridan Road in Wilmette, Illinois (IA)*

storage warehouse. Both of these designs were also exhibited. Similar comments regarding these projets were included in other reviews. One even commented on a projet that never made it to the exhibition. That reviewer noted that "George R. Dean's recruits worked on a plan for a palace for winter sports, but unfortunately the drawing is not exhibited, as it was buried under the walls that fell in the studio of Healy & Millet."[14] None of these designs was ever published. The reviews that appeared in the public press were all quite favorable to both the club and the Arts and Crafts Society. The professional press was not always so kind.

The *Brickbuilder* commented that the "annual architectural exhibition is the event at the Art Institute at the present writing."[15] The reviewer was concerned that "the most prominent architects of Chicago do not take as active part as they might." Like the mainstream press, the journal was favorably impressed by the work of the projet groups and Perkins's work for the Trans-Mississippi Exhibition. It also noted that the simultaneous exhibit by the Arts and Crafts Society "was surprisingly good both in quantity and quality." The reviewer from the *American Architect and Building News* had essentially the same opinion. He opened by stating that "to say that the present architectural exhibit exceeded in interest those of preceding years would be a remark very wide of the truth." He spoke highly of work sent by the various schools of architecture but was disappointed that the works of "the Chicago Architectural Club were weak and amateurish." His most favorable comment was that "the real interest of the architectural exhibit this year to the public has not been the architectural exhibit all, however, but that of the Society of Arts and Crafts." Several of the arts and crafts exhibitors were singled out for praise, including "T. S. [*sic*] Ashbee of Essex House, London." It was the first of several times that Ashbee would exhibit in Chicago.

The most comprehensive review of the Arts and Crafts Society exhibition was published by *Brush and Pencil* in the same issue that N. Max Dunning's review of the Architectural Club's work had appeared. It was written by one of the primary figures from the exhibiting group, the Arts and Crafts Society's secretary, George M. R. Twose.[16] Twose was an excellent writer and he covered the exhibition in a very professional manner, discussing a number of the items in the exhibition as well as

14. Unidentified newspaper clipping from the microfilm file of scrapbook items at the Art Institute of Chicago (ca. March 1898).

15. *Brickbuilder* 7, no. 4 (April 1898): 87.

*Robert Spencer's rendering of the first Quadrangle Club at the University of Chicago designed by Howard Van Doren Shaw; it has been moved, but still stands on the campus (IA)*

the exhibitors. Several illustrations were included. He ended his review by stating that "the exhibition as a whole, good as it was, gave greater promise for the future. And that is an achievement."

The exhibition closed on April 15, 1898. It was the only time that the Arts and Crafts Society and the Chicago Architectural Club would exhibit together, but it was not the end of cooperative efforts of the overlapping memberships.

Following the exhibition, President Kirkpatrick and his fellow officers applied their efforts elsewhere while scheduled events continued during late April, May, and June. There were classes, lectures, bohemian nights, and other programs at least once a week and sometimes several times a week. Theodore Pietsch, who had recently finished the course at the École des Beaux-Arts, spoke to the membership on "Student Life in Paris" on May 2.[17] Two days later, at the Fourth Annual Congress of the Central Art Association, the club provided five speakers—Dean, Handy, Spencer, Perkins, and Millet—all of whom spoke on the general subject of architecture.[18] Their presentations were done under the chairmanship of W. L. B. Jenney. George R. Dean spoke on "Some Modern Ideas in Architecture," and the other four followed him with "Ten-Minute Discussions." Handy spoke on "A Plea for More Honest Living," Spencer covered "Is There an American Style of Domestic Architecture?," and Perkins talked about "Criticism of Architecture by the Public." The session ended with Louis Millet giving an informal talk with questions and answers by the entire group. On May 5, Frank Lloyd Wright delivered a lecture on "Art in the Home" at the same venue, followed by W. O. Partridge, who spoke on "The Relation of Art to Practical Life."[19] Wright had disappointed an audience a week earlier when his lecture had been scheduled at the Art Institute and he did not show up.[20] The earlier talk was apparently to be a warm-up for his speech before the Central Art Association. Wright, a notorious nonjoiner, was actually a member of the Central Art Association and served on its Special Committee for Industrial Art.[21]

16. *Brush and Pencil* 2, no. 4 (April 1898): 74–79.

17. *Brickbuilder* 7, no. 5 (May 1898): 93. This talk was published in *Inland Architect* 31, no. 5 (June 1898): 44–46.

18. *Brickbuilder* 7, no. 5 (May 1898): 93, and *Inland Architect* 31, no. 5 (June 1898): 44–46.

19. The program of the Fourth Annual Congress of the Central Art Association held in Chicago May 3–5, 1898, lists all these activities. (A copy is in the collection of the Art Institute of Chicago.) While they were not official events of the Chicago Architectural Club, they were organized by some of the most active members of the club. It is clear that the club was heavily involved in the artistic community of Chicago.

20. *Chicago Evening Post*, April 2, 1898.

21. See the program of the Fourth Annual Congress of the Central Art Association referenced above.

Wright and his friends in the club were especially busy in their private practices during this period. Wright was heavily involved in his work for the Luxfer Prism Company, and his colleague Robert C. Spencer not only had a great deal of private work but was also busy preparing his design for the Luxfer Prism Competition. Among other things, Chicago's Central Art Association also took measures on "behalf of the trans-Mississippi Exposition, 'to erect, furnish, and decorate a modern $10,000 house containing ten rooms, wherein will be used the most approved building material of the present time. The following committee of architects, Geo. R. Dean, Frank L. Wright, and R. C. Spencer, Jr., has been selected by the Central Art Association to design a home which may be considered typical of American architecture.'"[22] Since Wright chaired the Special Committee for Industrial Art, he was almost certainly the instigator of this project for a "typical" house. Apparently the plans were never completed and no house was built. There probably just wasn't enough time to do all of what was expected of him and his colleagues at Steinway Hall. Or perhaps it was simply a problem of getting Dean, Wright, and Spencer to agree on a design.

With the Eleventh Annual Exhibition and the Congress of the Central Art Association over, most of the club members had reached a point of exhaustion from club affairs, but there were two final events before the summer recess. The last bohemian night of the 1898 season was held on June 6. Much was in the news about the possibility of the Spanish-American War, and the membership committee sent out a special "red, white and blue postal card which was inscribed: 'War! War! War!!! Grand trooping of the colors at the rooms of the Chicago Architectural Club on Monday evening, June 6.'"

The evening's hosts were all given military titles and admonished the members to "volunteer in an attack upon the Commissary Department." The only business was the presentation of medals for the Henry R. Dillon Club House Competition. The card also noted that "a 'gang' excursion by water to Milwaukee to inspect the new Public Library will be planned."

That excursion took place on June 18, when some twenty members of the club sailed to Milwaukee to spend two days seeing not only the new library designed by Ferry & Clas but other architectural marvels as well. After too much of Milwaukee's "amber fluid" and a pleasant night spent at the Hotel Davidson, the members returned to Chicago the following day. It was the last event of the club year.

The end of formal club activities for the year did not signal an end to the work of its young president, Frances W. Kirkpatrick, who was not particularly happy with the activities of the club. With the help of secretary N. Max Dunning and his colleagues at Steinway Hall, he set about reorganizing the club's structure. Much of the assistance he got came from conversations he had outside the club rooms. Those conversations included a number of Kirkpatrick's fellow club members, but were centered on four close acquaintances: Robert C. Spencer, Dwight H. Perkins, I. K. Pond, and Frank Lloyd Wright.

It was almost certainly during the interregnum of club activities in the summer of 1898 when the luncheon group that Frank Lloyd Wright referred to as the "Eighteen" began meeting. Wright claimed to be its leader. Robert C. Spencer, Dwight H. Perkins, and I. K. Pond were all part of the group, but each remembered it somewhat

22. *Brickbuilder* 7, no. 5 (May 1898): 107.

differently and by other names. None of them acknowledged Wright as the leader. Whatever name was used by the young architects who gathered for lunch from time to time during this period, they were undoubtedly inspired by, if not actually a subgroup of, the "Committee on the Universe," which had been meeting for some time at the Tip Top Inn on the ninth floor of the Pullman Building. I. K. Pond recalled forty years later that the room where they met had been "decorated by Louis Tiffany . . . in his best styles: and here, for a number of years including the building and duration of the World's Colombian Exposition, met in weekly enclave the Deipnosophists, or the Wise Diners . . . known also as 'The Committee on the Universe!' The conversation was choice,—learned and witty. The names of [some of] the 'Diners' may be of interest: Halsey Ives, of St. Louis, Chief of the Fine Arts at the Exposition, and Charles Kurtz his assistant; Lorado Taft sculptor, Henry Fuller, novelist and writer on art; Alexander McCormick newspaper man and . . . Frederick Gookin . . . Arthur Wheeler and I tagged along . . . The Deipnosophists gave . . . burlesque Art Exhibits which furnished the inspiration for similar and extremely popular entertainments 'put on' later by the Chicago Literary Club . . . Two of the very brilliant and poignant meetings of the Deipnosophists were fun, the farewell dinner to my brother [Allen Pond], when he sought change of scene in England . . . and then, the welcoming dinner when . . . he returned revived in body and spirit."[23]

That dinner inspired the publication of a booklet titled *Exhibition of Sketches and Studies by Allen B. Pond.*[24] It had no drawings but instead thirty-two paragraphs of humorous comment on the work of A. B. Pond, who was not known for his ability as a sketch artist. It is useful since all the comments are signed. It was from this source that I. K. Pond probably identified the members of the group forty years later. Architects Edgar D. Martin and Dwight Perkins were both included, as was Avery Coonley, later a client of both Wright and Perkins, plus several other prominent figures from Chicago's intellectual and artistic communities, all of whom had established relationships. Young architects would have been somewhat intimidated by such a group and would have been more comfortable with men at their own level of accomplishment.

Dwight Perkins seems to have been referring to the same group when he spoke of the "Committee of the Universe," as recorded in the oral history of his son, Lawrence B. Perkins, now deposited at the Art Institute of Chicago. Thus, what Frank Lloyd Wright remembered as the Eighteen, Dwight Perkins recalled as the Committee of the Universe. In 1939, Robert C. Spencer wrote about the same group when the Illinois Society of Architects asked him to prepare a paper on the Chicago School of architecture. He noted that "by some we were [known as] the 'Ten Percent Club' because we believed in adequate fees."

Frank Lloyd Wright had his own version of events. In 1957, he wrote that "before long a little luncheon club formed, comprised of myself, Bob Spencer, Gamble Rogers, Handy and Cady, Dick Schmidt, Hugh Garden, Dean, Perkins, and Shaw, several others; eighteen in all. We called the group the 'Eighteen.'"[25] Perkins recalled that the group met at the City Club of Chicago, but Spencer remembered that they met "once a month at the old Bismarck Restaurant for a steak dinner in one of the private dining rooms . . . At these little informal dinners we could discuss (and 'cuss') our architectural problems and theories more freely and intimately than at A.I.A. Chapter meetings." The truth is probably that they met in various places and that the discussions covered a broad range of subjects including the workings of the Chicago Architectural Club, in which all of them were involved.

Just who the Eighteen were has been the subject of debate for many years. H. Allen Brooks has written that in addition to the "ten participants mentioned by Wright can be added six others, the second Dean brother (George or Arthur), Alfred

23. This quotation is from Irving K. Pond's handwritten biography, "The Sons of Mary and Elihu Pond," now deposited in the library of the American Academy of Arts in New York City. A copy is in the author's collection.

24. The only copy of this booklet that seems to have survived is at the Newberry Library in Chicago. The interior title varies from the one on the cover. It reads: "Catalogue of Sketches and Studies by Allen Bartlit Pond made during his recent tour in Europe." Below a printer's device is added, "With Critical notes by members of the Society of the Deipnosophists sometimes reverently dubbed The Committee on the Universe," followed by "Chicago, February 4, 1897."

25. Frank Lloyd Wright first alluded to the group without naming it in his article "In the Cause of Architecture," published in *Architectural Record* 23, no. 3 (March 1908): 156. He coined the term the "Eighteen" in *A Testament* (New York: Horizon Press, 1957), 34. A copy of Lawrence Perkins's oral history (1986) is in the author's collection. The date referenced is on page 7. A copy of Spencer's paper is also in the author's collection.

Granger, Arthur Heun, Myron Hunt, and Irving and Allen Pond . . . It is also possible that Webster Tomlinson should be included too."[26] Spencer did not name the luncheon group per se, but he did speak of several of the men on Wright's list as colleagues in the early modern movement. Likewise, Perkins did not provide a list, but he did suggest the names of two men who may have been involved, Hermann V. von Holst and Charles Zeublin. Von Holst was at that time heavily involved in the Chicago Architectural Club. Zeublin was a professor of sociology at the University of Chicago and a close friend of Perkins's. He was also a founding member of the Chicago Arts and Crafts Society. Zeublin's interest in housing for the poor and in the arts and crafts, as well as his educated opinion as to how architecture could be instrumental in curing some of the ills of Chicago's tenement housing problems, would have had a major impact on the young group's thinking. That influence would be seen in the activities of architects individually and collectively during the next several years, particularly in work carried out at the Chicago Architectural Club, initiated under the leadership of president Francis W. Kirkpatrick, who *must* have been one of the Eighteen. He was sharing office space with Perkins at Steinway Hall and would have been fully cognizant of both private and club work being talked about and done by his colleagues.

After Kirkpatrick's first few hectic months, he was relieved to have an opportunity to rethink the organization of the club. His first weeks in office were difficult, particularly the overseeing of the fifteen other men on the Exhibition Committee. Not only was Kirkpatrick chairman of that committee, he also served on the subcommittee for catalog and finance. The exhibition, while large, had been criticized for its content, probably because there were few rejections. The added problem of having a dual exhibition with the Arts and Crafts Society made it even more difficult. After the exhibition, when Kirkpatrick and his most active officer, secretary N. Max Dunning, vowed to reorganize the club, they did not have to go far to find direction.

*N. Max Dunning (PC)*

In 1895, after the club had rewritten its constitution and changed its name to permit practicing architects to become full members, many did so, making the club much more representative of the architectural community as a whole. For reasons never explained, the new name and constitution were not immediately recorded with the Illinois secretary of state as required by law. Kirkpatrick and Dunning discovered this oversight and quickly set out to remedy the situation. On May 4, 1898, they executed the necessary documents legalizing the changes made in January 1895. The amendment added to the constitution provided for an Executive Committee in addition to the officers, consisting of six "at large" members serving staggered three-year terms, thus ensuring that experienced men would always be at the helm. This innovation was finally implemented with the election in the fall of 1898.

The changes established under Kirkpatrick's leadership provided for four standing committees in addition to the Executive Committee—namely, the Exhibition, the Lecture, the Bohemian, and the Smoker committees. Other than the Executive Committee, it was the Exhibition Committee that was considered the most important. It included six members of the Executive Committee at large and the treasurer of the club. Funds for the annual exhibition were kept separate. Thus, the Exhibition Committee was small and, in theory, there would always be "holdover" members, since the at-large members served three-year staggered terms.

When Kirkpatrick assumed the presidency, it was too late to reorganize the club's committee structure that year, and the new system was put in place after the

26. H. Allen Brooks, *The Prairie School: Frank Lloyd Wright and His Midwest Contemporaries* (Toronto and Buffalo: University of Toronto Press, 1972), 31.

elections for the 1898–99 year. The Exhibition Committee for 1898 was chaired by Kirkpatrick. Of the six members of the committee, N. Max Dunning was the only other officer to serve. There had been three subcommittees that year, a Jury of Admission, a Hanging Committee, and a Catalogue and Finance Committee, for a total of sixteen members involved in the organization and delivery of the annual exhibition, which was far too cumbersome. The membership welcomed the new seven-man system, a structure that would serve for the next several years. Kirkpatrick arranged all this, undoubtedly with the advice and council of his friends at 1107 Steinway Hall, probably over lunch with the Eighteen. Although he did not originally plan for a Hanging Committee, he ultimately realized that such a group was essential to the successful mounting of the exhibition. The Hanging Committee chose the material to be shown and supervised the actual hanging of the exhibits. They controlled the exhibition.

The club's programs after the fall 1898 elections were tightly scheduled: The first and third Monday of each month was a lecture, the second a smoker, and the fourth a bohemian night. Dunning later noted that the "functions of the club work may be said to be three in number—the educational, the social and the semi-social. The educational interests are advanced through the medium of lectures, classes, *Projets* and competitions." The projet system was becoming an important aspect of the club's work. An outgrowth of the system that had been used for years at the École des Beaux-Arts, it had migrated to the United States through men who had spent time in Paris or who had been instructed by graduates of the École (examples of the latter group include Spencer, Hunt, and Perkins).

When Kirkpatrick was thrust into the presidency, the projet system of competitions had already been used by the club in the fall of 1897, when eight teams were set up to compete with one another and to present their work to the club as a whole. Apparently he felt that the system was working well, and under his leadership it was formalized. Its success can probably be attributed to its methods and techniques, which generated a great deal of cooperative effort and were of substantial value to the younger members, particularly those who had not had the benefit of a formal education. On the other hand, the casual competitions that early members of the club had enjoyed and learned from became less and less a part of the club's activities, a great loss of individual creativity.

The first meeting of the Chicago Architectural Club's 1898–99 year was a bohemian meeting on September 19. The major topic of discussion was the results of the Luxfer Prism Competition, which had just been published in the September issue of the *Inland Architect*.[27] The other topic of the evening was the forthcoming election of officers at the annual meeting scheduled for October 3. Before that meeting, the members were entertained at a smoker held by the Chicago Builders' Club on September 28. They did not participate in the program for the evening, being strictly guests. The meeting did, however, demonstrate the continued importance of the club to its colleagues in the building trades. A few days later, at the annual meeting and election of officers,[28] president Francis W. Kirkpatrick handed over his gavel to Joseph C. Llewellyn and quietly faded away.[29] He was never listed again as a member of the Chicago Architectural Club.

The club's new president, Joseph C. Llewellyn, was joined by A. G. Zimmer-

27. *Inland Architect* 32, no. 2 (September 1898): 15–16

28. The Chicago Architectural Club's annual meeting was no longer a time of celebration. Without an exhibition of work on the club room walls or a banquet, it was simply another evening, although the election of officers was a special event.

29. Kirkpatrick's name did not appear in the 1899 catalog of the Chicago Architectural Club, although he continued to be listed in Chicago business directories at 1107 Steinway Hall through 1902. The March 28, 1903, issue of *Construction News* notes that he "has resigned his position with D. H. Burnham & Co., and will establish himself in the practice of architecture in St. Joseph, Mo." In 1903, he still maintained his Illinois architect's license but he was listed as living in St. Joseph, Missouri. After 1904, he was no longer listed as a licensed architect in Illinois.30. *Brickbuilder* 7, no. 10 (October 1898): 202.

Joseph C. Llewellyn (PC)

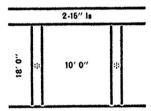

Sketch published with the program for a competition for "Terra Cotta as a Building Material" (IA)

30. *Brickbuilder* 7, no. 10 (October 1898: 202.

31. The date for this event was recorded in the "Calendar, 1898–99" as being October 17, and in *Brickbuilder* 7, no. 11 (November 1898): 240, as being October 24. The *Brickbuilder* is probably correct, since it goes on to note several other events held during October and November of 1898.

32. *Inland Architect* 32, no. 3 (October 1898): 28.

33. *Inland Architect* 32, no. 5 (December 1898): 49–50, plus unnumbered plates.

man and Henry K. Holsman as vice presidents. N. Max Dunning continued as secretary, with August C. Wilmanns as treasurer. Under the new rules, Birch Burdette Long and Charles A. Carr were elected to three-year terms on the Executive Committee, Henry W. Tomlinson and Clarence Hatzfeld to two-year terms, and H. V. von Holst and W. H. Eggebrecht completed the committee with one-year terms. These six men, plus treasurer Wilmanns, also served as the Exhibition Committee. Under the new rules, they appointed a Jury of Admission and a Hanging Committee of seven: Dwight Perkins, Frank Handy, Alfred Granger, George Dean, Robert Spencer, I. K. Pond, and Howard V. D. Shaw. The avant-garde of Chicago architecture would have virtual dictatorial control over the club's annual exhibitions for the next four years.

After the election on October 3, Fritz Wagner of the Northwestern Terra Cotta Company announced that his firm would sponsor a competition for the club. He "offered three prizes: first, of $50; second, of $30; third, of $20, for the three best designs for a terra-cotta column and lintel with wall surface above."[30] Two weeks later Wagner and his colleague William D. Gates spoke to the club on the subject of "Terra Cotta as a Building Material."[31] The rules for the competition were published in the October 1898 issue of the *Inland Architect*.[32] They included a small sketch with size limits and a brief description of terra-cotta and its uses. Drawings required were "an elevation . . . and such details and sections as may be necessary." They were to be delivered to the club secretary on or before noon on November 14. At the end of the printed rules was an addendum: "NOTE.—Mr. Wagner has kindly loaned for the use of the members a series of photographs of the Guarantee [*sic*] building, Buffalo, which will be hung on the walls of the club rooms during the progress of this competition." The just completed Guaranty Building was, of course, from the hand of Louis Sullivan, a longtime friend and honorary member of the club.

The terra-cotta competition drawings were delivered on time and promptly adjudicated, probably by Wagner and Gates. The results were illustrated with a long comment in the *Inland Architect* in December of 1898.[33] George Dean's design for "A Zoological Entrance" took first honors, and Axel Sandblom and Birch B. Long were awarded second and third place, respectively. An anonymous comment, probably by Wagner or Gates, noted that "this problem was one of the most instructive that has come before the club for solution. Its value in demonstrating how intimately facility of construction is connected with architectural design was recognized and that a designer should treat every material according to its specific qualities and emphasize its character. Thus the terra cotta column competition was a step in the right direction." After praising the qualities of terra-cotta, the author stated that "of the designs submitted that of Mr. George R. Dean was by far the most satisfactory. It is original, thoroughly practical, and exquisite in coloring." The second-prize design was "very credible architecturally and well adapted for the material." The third-place design "shows good color treatment and is more feasible, but will offer more difficulties for practical execution than the others."

The 1898–99 club year was the first in several years for which a syllabus was published. It was not printed, however, until March and then only as part of the Twelfth Annual Exhibition catalog. The "Calendar, 1898–99" indicated that the club was following the newly established rules that specified four meetings a month. The subjects of those meetings, and sometimes the results of them, were usually published in one or more of the professional journals. Speakers included both prominent practitioners and tradesmen, among them I. K. Pond, Louis Sullivan, Lorado Taft, and Frank Lloyd Wright. Since the calendar was published in March, it was able to list the actual names of those who had already spoken to the club. The meetings scheduled after the annual exhibition closed on April 16, 1899,

*Second and third place entries in the terra-cotta competition by Axel Sandbloom and Birch Burdette Long (IA)*

*George R. Dean's winning design in the terra-cotta competition (IA)*

were identified only as "Lecture," "Smoker," "Bohemian," without naming names.

The calendar also listed the competitions in which the members had participated. The Terra-Cotta Column Competition was noted as having closed on November 14, 1898, followed by "A Church Window," which closed on January 16, 1899, and was won by Samuel H. Levy, then "A Schoolhouse Entrance," which closed on February 10, with first prize going to Carleton Monroe Winslow. All these competition winners were listed in the exhibition catalog, but without illustrations. The last competition mentioned was for a "Catalogue Cover for Twelfth Annual exhibition," closing on March 18, 1899, with barely enough time to get it to the printer. First prize for the cover, which was used, went to William H. Eggebrecht. George R. Dean was given second prize, and his design was published in the catalog. It was clearly an adaptation of his design for the terra-cotta competition.

George R. Dean's second-place design for the exhibition catalog was his only design to appear in the catalog. He did, however, command eight full pages of text in the front of the book. His essay "Modern Architecture" had already been read before the Chicago Architectural Club, but here it was presented in a slightly revised form. It was the primary, but not the first, essay in the catalog. Hermann V. von Holst, secretary of the Exhibition Committee, opened the catalog with a two-page offering titled "To Our Friends," proselytizing about the work of the Chicago Architectural Club and similar clubs throughout the United States. He was pleased with the results of canvasing other clubs to join in Chicago's effort and commented that a step "in the right direction are the yearly exhibitions of the architectural clubs in the large cities." He went on to say he hoped that "all the principal clubs of the country will cooperate in a satisfactory arrangement of dates and interchange of exhibits." The long-range plan was that "an 'unaffected school of modern architecture in America' will change more and more from a mere vision to a reality." He was suggesting that a new modern architecture was being developed.

*Hermann V. von Holst, active in the Chicago Architectural Club for more than a decade (PC)*

*George Dean, a loyal member of the club, established an extensive practice with his brother (CD)*

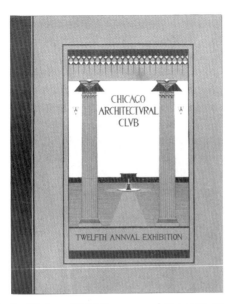

*William Eggebrecht's cover design for the catalog of the Twelfth Annual Exhibition was used; George Dean's runner-up design was printed inside the catalog (CAC/12)*

His comments were a precursor to the plan that would be put in place the following year when the Architectural League of America was organized. That plan would establish an exhibition circuit of drawings from each club that would be shown throughout the nation.

George Dean's essay was more philosophical.[34] He was laying the groundwork for a "new architecture," a subject he had written and talked about for some time. Dean was concerned with just what "modern architecture" was. Early in his essay he stated, "For the purpose of this paper I wish to limit it to its strictest meaning." He then reviewed the architecture of the ancients, suggesting that in every era, work was modern largely because it drew its forms from the daily life of the citizens who used the buildings. He noted that "simple growth went on—the art following the development of the people, logical in the use of its materials, and conforming to the wants of man, growing in strength and beauty as the race gained power—as different in one race as its climate or needs differed from another's. This law controlled until the fifteenth century."

Dean's comments were generally directed toward the ornament of architecture and the way local plants and climate affected buildings in the past. He often referred to "nature" and its effect on architecture. He also commented on the enormous influence the invention of the printing press had on literature, but observed that when architecture was put into books, it essentially killed original thought. The literature of architecture, he said, "furnished a set of measurements for architects—not in general, but to the width of a line for every portion of every building." He went on to say that "for three hundred years all progress in the arts was stopped . . . Architects, most deluded of all, reared buildings from descriptions and covered them with decoration . . . which in nature they had never seen." Dean then wrote that "within this century, the other arts have one by one returned to the great mother, nature, for inspiration." He strongly believed that these other arts—painting and sculpture—were ahead of architecture in throwing off the yoke of the past. After reviewing the work of several masters, he stated that it "remained for Manet to discover the subduing and harmonizing effect of atmospheric color . . . [and thus opening up] the process of evolution."

Dean's language was often convoluted and one must read carefully to under-

34. Dean's essay, "Modern Architecture," was published in the *Catalogue of the Twelfth Annual Exhibition of the Chicago Architectural Club,* 13–20. It is noted that it had been "read before the Chicago Architectural Club," but it hasn't been established when this happened.

stand his insights. He saved his most critical comments for the schools of architecture. He was convinced that they were relying too heavily on rote memorization of historic styles and not enough on teaching young architects to think. Near the end of his essay he commented that "for four hundred years we have choked in our efforts to suck blood from dry bones. How long shall we continue . . . ?" In his opinion:

> The evil, especially in America, is the architectural school. The instructors are not architects. The pupils have too much instruction and too little guiding. Their minds are crammed with a knowledge which will prevent the natural growth of any problem which may confront them . . . When an American builds as an American sees America, then and not until then will we have an American style . . . There are, at present, technical difficulties to overcome. It is necessary, in order to produce the numerous complicated drawings which constitute the plans of a building in the time allotted by our rapid age, not to mention the economy required to prevent financial failure, to observe a system. This condition is not, however, prohibitory to the forming of a new style, for it has been successfully overcome in many large and notable buildings.

Dean also stated that "here and there, in domestic architecture, [we find] character without the use of precedent, and with nature as the model." Throughout his essay, Dean referred to nature as a guiding element in the development of architectural style, clearly demonstrating that he believed that nature had been in the forefront in virtually all the work of the past, and that young men of the late nineteenth century should look to nature in the future.

This essay reveals much of Dean's basic thought on the development of an "American" architecture. It is obvious that he had been influenced by both John Root and Louis Sullivan. It seems certain that he was a regular at the meetings of what Frank Lloyd Wright called the "Eighteen." Wright's later writings were filled with references to his debt to "nature," although they were much more developed than those in George Dean's essay of 1899.

The 1899 catalog was somewhat more orderly than the 1898 catalog, but it had even fewer of the Young Turks than the year before. There were 113 exhibitors, thirty-six from Chicago, and five institutions. A number of members from the Chicago Architectural Club were represented, largely through the projet drawings, which were exhibited as a group. Other exhibitors included Dean, Fellows, Hugh Garden, Birch Long, Dwight Perkins, and Robert Spencer. Frank Lloyd Wright had been represented in the 1898 catalog by a single item, "No. 542, Examples of Electro glazing, Luxifer [sic] Prism Co." The remaining exhibits were overwhelmingly

*Robert Clossen Spencer's design for the Spencer Memorial Library in Geneva, Ohio, suggests a family connection, although none has been found; the name is simply a coincidence (CAC/12)*

*Adamo Boari's second-prize design for the Luxfer Prism Competition was illustrated in the 1899 CAC catalog; another version is shown in the background, on the left (CAC/12)*

from the East Coast and did not, for the most part, represent anything like the avant-garde in architecture. The 1899 catalog, under the new rules put in place the year before under Kirkpatrick's leadership, would have been expected to be more daring. It was not. There were 151 exhibitors, plus eight more from institutions in 1899. Thirty-nine were from Chicago, several being individuals or organizations other than architects. The American Luxfer Prism Company was again represented, this time with three examples of "Luxfer Electro-Glazed Art Glass," plus the first- and second-place winners of the company's competition from the previous year. Robert Spencer's first-place design was listed in the catalog without an illustration,

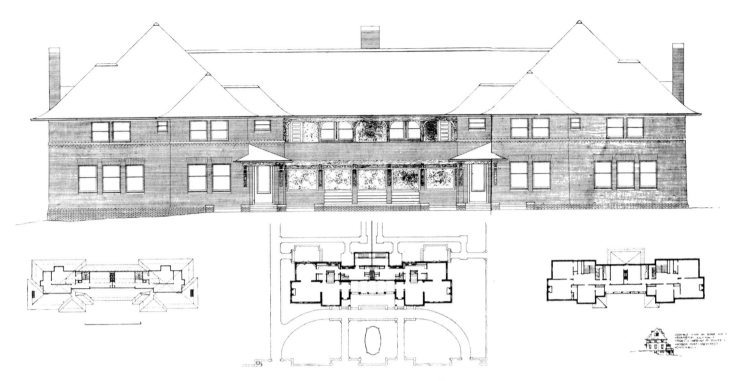

*Several of the occupants of 1107 Steinway Hall claimed credit for the design of the Catherine M. White Double House in Evanston, Illinois, but it was exhibited by Myron Hunt (CAC/12)*

but Adamo Boari's second-place design merited a full page. The published Boari design was not the same one printed the previous year in the *Inland Architect*.[35] That Boari design had been similar to the example prepared by Frank Lloyd Wright and included with the competition rules. The second-place design by Boari published in the catalog was entirely different. It consisted of what appeared to be a bundle of four cylinders over a flared base and an ornamented crown. The design published by the *Inland Architect* is in the background of the illustration.

In addition to the Luxfer Prism entries, Birch Burdette Long and club president J. C. Llewellyn were both represented, as were Pond & Pond and Richard Schmidt. Myron Hunt had twelve items in the catalog including one drawing, a "Residence for J. E. Nolan, Evanston, Ill. Rendered by F. W. Kirkpatrick." This was the only time Kirkpatrick's name ever appeared as an exhibitor of any kind in one of the club's catalogs.[36] Hunt also exhibited the Catherine M. White double house in Evanston, Illinois, which has been cited from time to time as one of the buildings benefiting from the cooperative efforts in Steinway Hall's loft drafting room. Oddly enough, Dwight Perkins was not in the catalog but his wife, Lucy Fitch Perkins, was, with four examples of a "Decoration for Child's Room," one of which was illustrated. With the exception of Hunt's offerings and perhaps the work of Pond & Pond, the only illustration in the 1899 catalog that seemed to evoke the early modern movement was Robert C. Spencer's design for "A Spencer Memorial Library at Geneva, Ohio." This clean-lined design is clearly a precursor of the Prairie School that would be so prominent in the next decade. One other illustration in the catalog, which may not have been exhibited, is a rendering of the facade of the Ayer's Building by Holabird & Roche. Its full-page drawing, probably a paid advertisement, carried the name of the architect and the contractors, W. A. & A. E. Wells, who had a half-page advertisement on the facing page. It was not listed in the index of architectural exhibits.

*Lucy Fitch Perkins showed this "Decoration for Child's Room" in the 1899 exhibition (CAC/12)*

35. *Inland Architect* 32, no. 2 (September 1898): 15–16.

36. Kirkpatrick's name does appear in the *T-Square Club, Catalogue of the Architectural Exhibition, Philadelphia, January 14 to February 2, 1899*. He is listed under a section called "Drawings Entered by the Chicago Architectural Club" for two entries for a "Design for a Church . . . by H. M. G. Garden and F. W. Kirkpatrick, Associated," one an exterior and the other an interior.

The rules for the Twelfth Annual Exhibition of the Chicago Architectural Club had been published in February of 1899.[37] They were similar to those of the previous year, except that it was noted that work from New York, Philadelphia, Boston, Cleveland, and St. Louis would be included. Furthermore, the announcement stated that "works as are selected from this exhibition by the juries of the St. Louis and Boston Architectural Clubs (who will hold exhibitions in the order named, following the close of this one), will be delivered direct to such exhibitions when the consent of the exhibitor is expressed on the entry and identification blanks." A month later the *Inland Architect* reported that "special representatives of the club were sent to the Eastern cities and secured a large number of important exhibits, and the efforts to make this display of architectural work perfect in quality and large in quantity has been most successful."[38] The idea of more widespread exhibition of young architects' work was spreading. It would be formalized a few months later with the formation of the Architectural League of America.

The Twelfth Annual Exhibition of the Chicago Architectural Club opened with a flood of publicity. Every local newspaper announced that the exhibition was either forthcoming or had already opened, and several did lengthy reviews.[39] Generally speaking, the popular press was kind, particularly to exhibits by persons other than architects. Newspaper reviewers were much more enamored of the work of East Coast architects and the local arts and crafts exhibits than they were of the architectural work of Chicagoans. The most lengthy review ran in the *Chicago Chronicle*, whose reviewer noted that the "present collection . . . is the largest and most important exhibit gathered together by [the Chicago Architectural Club]."[40] The reviewer also commented favorably on the contributions by "Miss Ida Burgess, Charles H. Barr and the Grueby Faience Company," none of whom were architects, suggesting that he found the "objects" in the exhibition to be of at least as much interest as the architecture. He, like other local reviewers, thought the drawings of "Navel Architecture" were fascinating, although just why this material was included in the exhibition was never explained. He did find the work of Spencer, Pond & Pond, Perkins, Dean, and a few others to be of merit. While it had little to do with the exhibition, this same critic noted at the end of his review that the club has access to the "assembly room in the basement of the Art Institute [where it] is occupied by enthusiastic members of the association every Monday evening from October to June."

The professional press also publicized the exhibition, and in several cases published full reviews. The *Brickbuilder* noted only that the "younger members of the profession are at present interested in the Twelfth Annual Exhibition of the Chicago Architectural Club, which opened on the 30th inst. at the Art Institute. An unusually large number of drawings has been received from other cities, and the average quality of the work is exceptionally high."[41] The longest and most favorable review was the one published in the *Inland Architect*.[42] It stated that the exhibition was "the largest, best arranged and most comprehensive exhibition yet held by this club, and, as a whole, is immensely creditable to the club, and particularly to the committees that had the work of collecting, classifying and selecting." It also quoted at some length from an article by sculptor Lorado Taft, although his comments were not aimed at the work of Chicagoans.[43] He spoke favorably only of the work of Pond & Pond for Hull House, but he did like the colored drawings for a "frieze for a child's room" submitted by Lucy Fitch Perkins. He also spoke well of the "Terra Cotta Column" design submitted by Birch Burdette Long, even though it won only third-place honors in the competition.

After quoting Taft, the editors of the *Inland Architect* ended with comments of their own. They thought that "the medal drawings of a crematory, by Theodore

37. *Inland Architect* 33, no. 1 (February 1899): 7.

38. *Inland Architect* 33, no. 2 (March 1899): 20.

39. There are a number of newspaper clippings, now on microfilm, included in the Art Institute of Chicago scrapbooks. Not all are identified, but they appear to include at least eight Chicago newspapers, as well as others from Boston, Detroit, and Philadelphia. The articles range from one or two sentences to full-page reviews illustrated with line drawings of the exhibition entries.

40. "Display Architectural Designs: Interesting Exhibition Now to Be Seen at the Art Institute," *Chicago Chronicle*, April 2, 1899.

41. *Brickbuilder* 8, no. 4 (April 1899): 81.

42. *Inland Architect* 33, no. 3 (April 1899): 27–28.

43. There is evidence that this was published in the *Chicago Record*; Taft's original article cannot be located.

Wells Pietsch, are a decided addition to the collection of drawings" and that "the dreamy effect of light and shade in R. C. Spencer, Jr.'s, drawing for a memorial library was most beautiful and held the attention of many." They also liked the exhibition of naval architecture, but concluded, "A large amount of space is given to academic work, and possibly, as the exhibition is by draftsmen, it is not out of place, but one could wish that the line could be drawn at competition drawings, if the exhibit must go beyond those of executed work, for in one way they mar the general effect."

The most critical review was an anonymous column in the *American Architect and Building News*.[44] The reviewer began, "The Chicago Architectural Club is . . . holding its twelfth annual exhibition at the Art Institute . . . A few rather bored-looking people walk through the rooms and a still smaller number make the rounds with any apparent interest." His review had minimal praise for a selected few exhibits while being highly critical of others. For example, he noted, "There is the usual work from the schools, of the least possible interest to the ordinary visitor, but full of worth and benefit for the student. Columbia's showing is not as strong as in some previous years, while Illinois comes out better than heretofore . . . [Their] work is so well mounted that it looks at its very best on the walls, though in itself having often less merit than that from some of the other schools." He also commented favorably on the work of Wilson Eyre and Frost & Granger, and like others, on R. C. Spencer's design for a "memorial library." He saved his most vitriolic criticism for the Montgomery Ward Building, although he did not identify the architect, Richard Schmidt:

> Aside from the matter of rendering, but as a question of design, if one wants a good rousing monstrosity, one need not hunt far or long for it when one is in the room with the elevation for the Montgomery Ward Building. The structure is ostensibly a ten or eleven storied one, coming in nicely within the limit of the ordinance for high buildings, but in the centre of the facade rises a tower about forty feet square, with six or seven stories more above the cornice. These seven stories have their height almost doubled by the addition of an extinguisher-shaped composition surmounted with an apparently Classic arch or kiosk, bearing aloft a draped female figure, sacred perhaps to the millinery interests.

This reviewer did look with favor on the submissions from the supervising architect of the Treasury and that "of our local school-architect, Mr. Mundie . . . [and] his design for the North Division High School, a pleasing brick structure with high Colonial entrance or portico." He also liked the "very attractive group of little perspectives . . . of the art colony at Oregon, Illinois, by Pond & Pond." Finally, he commented favorably on the designs submitted in the Luxfer Prism Competition.

The most positive review of the exhibition was published in *Brush and Pencil,* by Robert C. Spencer Jr.[45] Spencer's review was quite professional and generally favorable, but he was disappointed by the apparent lack of interest by the general public. In the first paragraph of his review he noted that "the regular throng of visitors was there—everywhere except in the south wing. My dear young brother architects who may chance to read this page, don't imagine for a day that your 'hot' water colors, and cold ink washes are being admired by throngs of prospective clients in search of architectural talent which has hitherto remained unknown to public fame because denied the right to express itself in materials more substantial than graphite and soluble pigments applied to what F. Hopkinson Smith has styled: 'Bald, beastly, God-forsaken white paper.'"

He continued, "A considerable number of the visitors to the Art Institute stroll

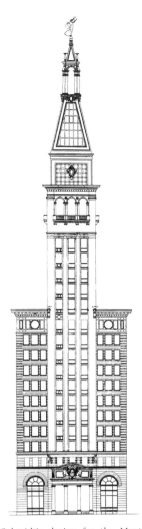

*Richard E. Schmidt's design for the Montgomery Ward Building on Michigan Avenue, submitted to the 1899 exhibition (PSR)*

44. *American Architect and Building News* 64, no. 1218 (April 29, 1899): 36–37.

45. Robert C. Spencer Jr., "The Architectural Club's Annual Exhibition at the Art Institute of Chicago," *Brush and Pencil* 4, no. 2 (May 1899): 88–96.

aimlessly through these rooms—apparently because they have come to see the contents of the building and wish to make sure of seeing everything that is to be seen while there." Spencer was not disappointed in the show itself, however. He wrote that "it seems strange that such a really good thing should receive so little public patronage and appreciation. It is true that the architects of Chicago—particularly those whose names are identified with large and important work—make a very limited and weak showing; but the collection as a whole is one of the best ever exhibited by the Architectural Club, and it is more systematically and effectively hung than ever before." He commented favorably on the work of several of his fellow Chicagoans, as well as those from out of town. Midway through his review he stated that "to undertake any serious comprehensive architectural criticism . . . would be a very tedious, thankless and presumably useless task. There are better ways of reforming our recreant and misguided colleagues whose work is important enough and sufficiently respectable and well-dressed to pass the jury, than to find fault in a personal or individual way with the counterfeit presentations of the buildings they have built, or think they would like to build . . . it may not be amiss to add a word to the widespread protest now being aroused among us by the wholesale importation via New York City, at the hands, chiefly, of the individuals composing the Beaux Art Society—of what Ralph Adams Cram, of Boston, has aptly styled, 'Boulevard Architecture.' It would take more space than remains to clearly present the glaring faults and weaknesses of this exaggerated style, and call attention to the sad results which would attend the spread of the disease inland."

He wrote that "our only safety in Chicago lies in the comparative indifference of the public to architecture of any sort, and the weakness in numbers of the local disciples of the *fin de siecle* French ideas of architecture, which seem to render worse than null the splendid training still given by the Paris School in monumental planning massing, and construction, unless the student has a tremendous amount of originality and American spirit." Clearly, Spencer was espousing the philosophy that he and his colleagues in Steinway Hall and environs had been developing. He was not condemning the Beaux-Arts training per se; he was condemning the idea that only drawing on historicism would produce a proper architecture. The stage was set for an American architecture to emerge, and in 1899 Spencer was one of its chief spokesmen. The Chicago Architectural Club would be the vehicle to carry the message to the general public.

46. The complete text of this letter, along with editorial comment supporting the idea, was published in *Inland Architect* 33, no. 4 (May 1899): 30.

47. *Inland Architect* 33, no. 5 (May 1899): 41–43, and *Brickbuilder* 8, no. 6 (June 1899): 109–15. Both journals printed extensive reviews of the events at the convention. There were other less comprehensive reports published elsewhere as well.

Within two weeks of the closing of the exhibition, the club's secretary, N. Max Dunning, issued a circular letter to other clubs in the United States inviting them to join in a "convention of delegates, from all architectural clubs of the United States, to be held at Cleveland, Ohio, Friday and Saturday, June 2 and 3, 1899."[46] There were three primary aims outlined in the letter. First, each club would review its organization and suggest what worked well for the success of its group. Second, an exhibition schedule would be set up to permit each club to show the work of the others in its own city. Third, they hoped to establish a "Code Governing Competitions." The tentative schedule was left open for other subjects to be brought before the assembled delegates. Each club was permitted only one voting delegate, but as many members as wished to attend were invited.

The convention was a resounding success and was reported in depth in both the *Inland Architect* and the *Brickbuilder*.[47] The *Brickbuilder* reported that "ninety-seven registered delegates represented thirteen societies: the Architectural League and the Society of Beaux Arts Architects of New York, the architectural clubs of St. Louis,

*Assembly Room of the Associated Technical Club in Cleveland, where the Architectural League of America was born (Cleveland AC)*

Chicago, Cleveland, Boston, Philadelphia, Pittsburgh, Detroit, and Toronto (Canada), and the Illinois, Pittsburgh, and Cleveland Chapters of the American Institute of Architects." At the end of the convention, the T-Square Club of Philadelphia, the Architectural League of New York, and the clubs from Chicago, St. Louis, Detroit, Cleveland, and Pittsburgh were named as charter members of the new league. Within a year the Boston Architectural Club, the Society of Beaux-Arts Architects, the Pittsburgh Chapter of the AIA, the Architectural Eighteen from Toronto, the Cincinnati Chapter of the AIA, and the Washington Architectural Club had also joined.

The *Brickbuilder* reported that the "majority of the delegates were the younger element of the profession, averaging about thirty-two years of age, and being about evenly divided between practicing architects and prominent draftsmen, and they brought the greatest enthusiasm to the work." The *Inland Architect* actually named the delegates. Fourteen men from Chicago attended, not all of whom were members of the club. Frank Lloyd Wright was listed as a delegate, as was Robert Craik McLean. J. C. Llewellyn was elected chairman of the convention, and N. Max Dunning was named secretary. A year later they would be elected president and secretary of the Architectural League of America.

A key goal of the convention was to organize a system, or "circuit," whereby each club would schedule its annual exhibition in a manner that would not conflict with other clubs' exhibitions. The great advantage of this, of course, was the ability of each club to send examples of its members' work to other cities for exhibition. This innovation had considerable success; for the next decade or so it was the policy of each club to show the work of others. Often the same drawings from various clubs would show up in several other cities in the same year. The discussion of this "exchange" was kicked off by a paper by Henry W. Tomlinson of Chicago titled "The Annual Exhibition." Another major concern was how to produce a catalog at a reasonable cost. Dwight H. Perkins felt that "the whole idea of the catalogue advertising was a 'hold up' of the contractors and characterized as a most undignified proceeding."[48]

48. The Chicago club originated the idea of asking for patrons to sponsor the catalog rather than simply advertising. Patrons' names were listed but the amounts of their individual contributions were not included, nor were examples of their work. This was the club's policy for several years thereafter.

*"Progress before Precedent," the motto of Albert Kelsey, the first president of the Architectural League of America, was resented by a number of founders of the league; it can be seen in the circular motif of his design at right (PC)*

A number of papers were read before the assembled delegates, all recorded verbatim by a stenographer. Excerpts from that record were used in various journals, but the entire transcript was published under the direction and editorship of N. Max Dunning.[49] The transcript included all the papers read at the convention, both formal and extemporaneous. It included, for example, Louis Sullivan's paper, "The Modern Phase of Architecture," which Dunning read for him.[50]

The most ambitious use of the convention transcript was in the preparation of the *Architectural Annual.* This beautifully produced volume was edited by architect Albert Kelsey, who was the first president of the Architectural League of America. (J. C. Llewellyn served only as president of the convention.) The red-cloth cover was embossed in black and gold with a circular emblem inscribed with the words "Progress before Precedent," a motto that Kelsey felt expressed the sentiments of the league. Later, there was considerable controversy about this motto, and it was used only for a short time. One could argue, however, that it did succinctly express the sentiments of the delegates, particularly those from the Chicago club, who believed that in order to have a truly American architecture, the precedents of the past had to be put aside.

The *Architectural Annual* was very popular. So popular, in fact, that a second printing was announced, without change, before the first edition was completely sold out. It was instrumental in spreading the word about architectural clubs and was as near to a national yearbook of architecture as could be presented at the end of the nineteenth century. Each of the member clubs was described in some detail in the appendix. Also included were brief descriptions of the national AIA and each of its chapters throughout the United States. Two pages were devoted to the Royal Institute of British Architects, its officers, and related societies. Other data included descriptions of the various universities offering an architectural curriculum and brief resumes of each of the most popular architectural journals then in print. Finally, there was a listing of all the American graduates of the École des Beaux-Arts and the winners of the various traveling scholarships offered by clubs and universities. Kelsey prepared an opening essay for the book, covering a broad spectrum of the profession, its strong points, and its shortcomings. He ended his statement by saying that "most necessary to-day are clearly-conceived ideals, self assurance, based upon rigorous training, a healthier point of view, realization of the needs of the age, and a judicious application of standards that are in accordance with Amer-

49. N. Max Dunning, ed., *Report of the First National Convention of Architectural Societies* (Cleveland, Ohio, June 2 and 3, 1899). This obscure booklet recorded the proceedings of the convention verbatim. Excerpts appeared elsewhere, but the entire text is available only from this source.

50. This paper was published in *Inland Architect* 33, no. 5 (June 1899): 40. It was also published the following year in the *Architectural Annual.*

of activity greater than any they had experienced in the past. Indeed, the 1899–1900 year was the beginning of an extraordinary period for the Chicago Architectural Club, and for the modern movement in architecture. As the twentieth century approached, the club was clearly the dominant force in architecture in the city of Chicago.[51]

about half of what it had in 1893. Times were difficult, and Wight was concerned that many members would not be able to pay their annual license fees, much less their AIA dues. On the other hand, he noted that "the Club, composed half or more of draughtsmen, and some practicing architects and amateurs has about 150 members, and seems to be flourishing . . . while the Chapter is languishing." I am grateful to Chicago architect Kathy Nagle for bringing this letter to my attention. She found it in the files of the AIA library in Washington while doing research on the history of the Chicago Chapter of the AIA.

CHICAGO ARCHITECTURAL CLUB EXHIBIT OPENS TO-NIGHT.

David Swing Settlement Buildings.

Typical Farm Home.

HANGING DRAWINGS IN THE ART INSTITUTE.

*Sketch published in the* Chicago Record-Herald *before the Thirteenth Annual Exhibition opened in 1900; the two inset drawings are actual exhibition items (PC)*

# The Young Turks Take Charge

CHAPTER ELEVEN

In order to clearly understand the activities of the Chicago Architectural Club at the beginning of the twentieth century, one must look at what it was doing in 1900, 1901, and 1902 as a whole. The club's work during this period is well documented and the exhibition catalogs were among the best ever produced, but it was a time when Chicago architecture was at its lowest point in many years. In mid-1900 the *Brickbuilder* reported that "Chicago building operations for March are the worst for any month in twelve years, and show how completely building operations have been paralyzed by labor troubles. Permits were issued for only three buildings exceeding three stories in height, and only sixty-six permits were granted for two-story buildings."[1]

The club's activities were heavily influenced by other organizations and individuals, many of whom were only peripherally involved in architecture. Evidence of this influence can be found in the catalog for the exhibition of 1900.[2] Not only was the book lengthy, it was the most carefully edited of any of the exhibition catalogs published up until that time. It was divided into sections, including several pages devoted to "Societies engaged in Public Improvement in Chicago." These groups were listed with their officers and brief resumes of their missions. Included were the Art Commission, the Art Association of Chicago, the Municipal Art League of Chicago, the Chicago Woman's Club, the Illinois Chapter of the American Institute of Architects, the Chicago Architects' Business Association, the Arts and Crafts Society, and the Chicago Improved Housing Association. The Architectural League of America got its own full page describing the new organization. Not specifically mentioned, but still very much involved, was the Municipal Improvement League, which was still promoting improvements to Lake Front Park. There was a great deal of overlapping membership between these organizations, and the Chicago Architectural Club had relationships with all of them.

In the opening "Greetings" page, the club's Exhibition Committee acknowledged that all these organizations were making major contributions to Chicago. They wrote that "the Architectural Club has noticed the great interest that has been taken in civic beauty by citizens, by our municipal officers, and by clubs and societies . . . Recognizing the increasing interest in municipal art, and believing in its ultimate accomplishment, the Architectural Club gladly lends itself to the combining and correlating of these activities. To that end, it has invited the Improved

1. *Brickbuilder* 9, no. 6 (June 1900): 106.

2. The full title, on the interior title page, was *Annual of the Chicago Architectural Club, Being the Book of the Thirteenth Annual Exhibition 1900*. It was edited by Dwight H. Perkins.

Housing Association to share in this exhibition, and has availed itself of the cordial assistance of the Arts and Crafts Society." The involvement of these two groups was actually the result of activities that started around the time of the election of club officers the previous fall.

✤

The election of the 1899–1900 officers of the Chicago Architectural Club took place on October 2, 1899. Three current officers, president J. C. Llewellyn, second vice president Henry K. Holsman, and treasurer August C. Wilmanns, were reelected. Along with them, Robert C. Spencer was elected first vice president and Birch Burdette Long became secretary. These last two were both working at 1107 Steinway Hall. The six-man Executive Committee now included Henry W. Tomlinson, Charles A. Carr, and Clarence Hatzfeld as carryovers. Since Birch B. Long had been elected secretary, there were three open slots, which were filled by Walter H. Kleinpell, Max Mauch, and Edgar S. Belden. Belden resigned shortly thereafter and his place was taken by Carleton M. Winslow. All these men were deeply involved in the day-to-day affairs of the Chicago Architectural Club and most, if not all, were probably participants in the "Eighteen" luncheon meetings.

Prior to the 1899–1900 elections, two important events occurred that would affect the club during the next year, one more than the other. The Illinois Chapter of the AIA had announced a new program for its annual medal competition, and the Charity Organization Society of the City of New York had begun planning the Tenement House Exhibition of 1900, which included a Model Tenement Competition. Both of these events would attract members of the Chicago Architectural Club, and the Tenement House Exhibition would travel to Chicago, after its initial showing in New York in February 1900, to become part of the Thirteenth Annual Exhibition of the Chicago Architectural Club.

The Illinois Chapter of the AIA had never been pleased with club members' response to its annual offer of gold, silver, and bronze medals for those who demonstrated the greatest proficiency in design. The chapter did not, however, want to stop awarding these medals. In July of 1899, it had announced that the medals to be awarded in 1900 would be done so under a new set of rules. It had proposed "a competition which will at once test the designing ability and rendering of club members and stimulate the sentiment in the direction of 'municipal improvement' in the proper grouping of buildings."[3] The competition was for a major civic improvement on the east side of Michigan Avenue between Monroe and Randolph streets. The first notice, published in the *Inland Architect* and signed by Peter B. Wight, included a plan of the area and a preliminary program. The plan was actually a refinement of one Wight had prepared in 1896 when he and his colleagues in the Municipal Improvement League had first begun advocating major improvements to Lake Front Park. Details were minimal, but two months later, in the October issue of the *Inland Architect*, the "conditions of the competition" were published.[4] The program called for two buildings, a city hall fronting on Michigan Avenue on the centerline of Madison Street and an educational building between Washington and Randolph streets, also on Michigan Avenue facing the Chicago Public Library. The rules did not specify a detailed program for either building. Contestants were encouraged to interview city officials to learn the requirements of such buildings. Three floor plans, two elevations, and a cross section of the city hall were required. Only exterior drawings of the educational building were necessary. Contestants were, however, required to furnish a watercolor perspective of the entire site, and they were encouraged, but not required, to include the future ex-

3. *Inland Architect* 33, no. 6 (July 1899): 49–50.

4. *Inland Architect* 34, no. 3 (October 1899): 21.

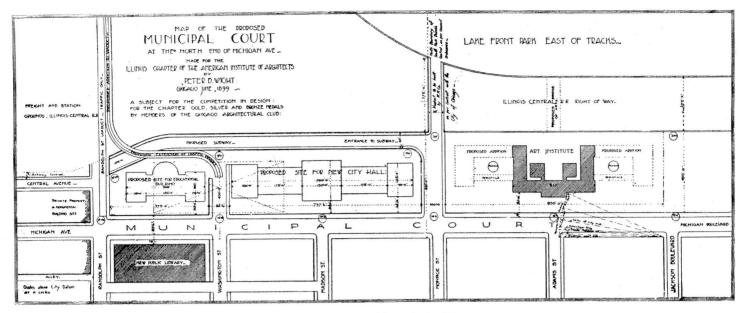

*Plan of the area north of the Art Institute and east of Michigan Avenue given to participants in the AIA competition for "municipal improvement" of Lake Front Park; note the indication of the camera location, where a photograph was to be taken (IA)*

pansion on the north side of the Art Institute in their perspective. A photograph taken from the point of view of the required perspective was supplied to each competitor along with a plan of the entire area showing the point of origin of the photograph. The obvious aim of the competition was to encourage the young members of the club to address the design of a large project that would enhance the city of Chicago. The drawings were to be delivered to the secretary of the Art Institute four weeks before the opening of the annual exhibition of 1900.

It soon became evident that the project was simply beyond the abilities of most individuals. In the same issue of the *Inland Architect* where the final program was published, it was noted that "on October 16, the president [of the club] announced that the program for the competition for the Illinois Chapter medal was much too elaborate for individuals to accomplish in the time given, and that the chairman of the committee had decided that the competition should be by the *projet* system, with teams of men working together, and the groups working on the competition should take the place of the regular classwork of the year."[5] In January of 1900 the *Brickbuilder* noted that the jury for the AIA competition was to be Charles A. Coolidge, S. S. Beman, and W. Carbys Zimmerman.[6] No announcement of the winners, if any, of the competition was ever published. Ultimately, only one projet team showed its work in the exhibition of 1900. Headed by N. Max Dunning, the team included Clarence Hatzfeld, Burton F. Morse, Walter H. Kleinpell, Francis M. Bartolomae, Charles A. Carr, and Carlton Monroe Winslow. The catalog listing indicated that they exhibited only the principal facade and the first- and fourth-story plans of their design for a city hall, but those drawings were not published.

New York City's Tenement House Exhibition, under the auspices of the Charity Organization Society, had a much greater impact on the club.[7] As part of its work, the Tenement House Committee had sponsored a competition for tenement designs for lot sizes varying from twenty-five by a hundred feet to a hundred feet square. The prospectus for both the exhibition and the competition was published in the January 1900 issue of the *Inland Architect*.[8] It described in some detail just what would be included in the exhibition. There were to be models, drawings, and

5. Ibid., 23.

6. *Brickbuilder* 9, no. 1 (January 1900): 18.

7. The Tenement House Committee was the vehicle used by Lawrence Veiller to promote housing reform in New York City. Veiller was a tireless reformer who worked for decades, starting in the late nineteenth century. The Tenement House Exhibition of 1900 was an idea he first proposed in early 1898. The plan was to demonstrate that "the working-man is housed worse [in New York City] than in any other city in the civilized world." This quotation is taken from Roy Lubove's *The Progressives and the Slums: Tenement House Reform in New York City, 1890–1917* (University of Pittsburgh Press, 1962). The best concise review of the Tenement House Exhibition can be found in Kevin P. Murphy, "'Bringing the So-Called Slums to the People Uptown': The Tenement House Exhibition of 1900 and Housing Policy in New York City" (PhD diss., New York University, 1993). I am grateful to Stephen Long, director of the Resource and Study Center of the Lower East Side Tenement Museum in New York City for bringing this to my attention.

8. *Inland Architect* 34, no. 4 (January 1900): 47.

*No photograph taken in 1900 has surfaced, but this is a shot of the same site taken in 1919 (WRH)*

photographs, all demonstrating the deplorable conditions of tenements in New York City and various means of ameliorating these problems. In that respect, the Tenement House Committee proposed to hold "a special competition, open to all architects, for an average city block (200 x 400 feet) of model tenements made up of independent units; the object of such competition being to obtain plans of model units which, while embodying in themselves the advantages of economy of construction, convenience of plan, good light and ventilation, cheerful outlook, and as great as possible a concentration of light and air space, shall, when repeated or combined in block form, secure these advantages in a still higher degree." The Tenement House Committee also proposed to hold a series of conferences on the subject of tenement housing during the period the exhibition was in place in New York. Finally, it planned to have the exhibition travel to Chicago, Boston, and other cities, as well as the Paris Exposition of 1900.

The *Inland Architect* article was the first to give details of the planned exhibition and competition, but it was not the first notice to appear in the architectural press. The *American Architect and Building News* had reported in August 1899 that the exhibition and the competition were forthcoming.[9] The writer commented, "Our readers will at once think of the Shattuck competition, in Boston, for designs for a very similar group of buildings, [and] the Shattuck plans . . . [will be] interesting to refer to." The Shattuck Competition, which had taken place in 1898, called for a design for approximately fifty artisans' houses on a single block of land. There were two categories, a limited competition for fifteen invited competitors, only one of whom was from Chicago, and an open competition that drew twenty-nine entries. The results were published in November of 1898.[10] During the next several weeks most of the entries were published individually. The houses were to have been designed for a family with a single breadwinner who had an income of between twelve and twenty dollars a week. The "houses" generally varied from three to five rooms, and rents were between six and twelve dollars a month. None of the schemes was built, so those figures may not have been realistic. The tenement house plans in New York, on the other hand, were expected to be model units that would eventually be built. Rents were intended to be in the same range. The only Chicagoan identified as a competitor in the Shattuck Competition was S. S. Beman, who was invited to participate in the limited part of the competition. His was the only entry to be exhibited at the Chicago Architectural Club's exhibition of 1900, where it was displayed next to examples from the Tenement House Competition.

The response to the Tenement House Competition was overwhelming.[11] The time allowed for entries was short, but nearly two hundred were received. First and second prizes were awarded, three entries were given third prize, and twenty-six were "commended" or "highly commended" for excellence. All the major prizes went to New York firms. Elmer C. Jensen of Chicago was one of those commended for his submission, and Adamo Boari, a peripheral member of the Steinway Hall group, was one of those highly commended. A number of the winning designs were included in the Tenement House Exhibition. Unfortunately, only a few of the prize designs were shown in Chicago and in the 1900 exhibition catalog. The New York Tenement House Exhibition closed on February 24, and the Chicago Architectural Club exhibition opened on March 20. Despite the efforts of Chicago's Improved Housing Association, there was simply not enough time to get all the material to Chicago before the catalog went to press. The Chicago club's Exhibition Committee, in a brief foreword to the section of the catalog where the available entries were illustrated, expressed regret "that the exhibit of the Improved Housing Association could not reach Chicago in time for listing and illustration in this book. It has been

9. *American Architect and Building News* 65, no. 1232 (August 5, 1899): 41.

10. *American Architect and Building News* 62, no. 1196 (November 26, 1898): 73–76.

11. The winners were not published until April 1900, when a list appeared in *Inland Architect* 35, no. 3 (April 1900): 23.

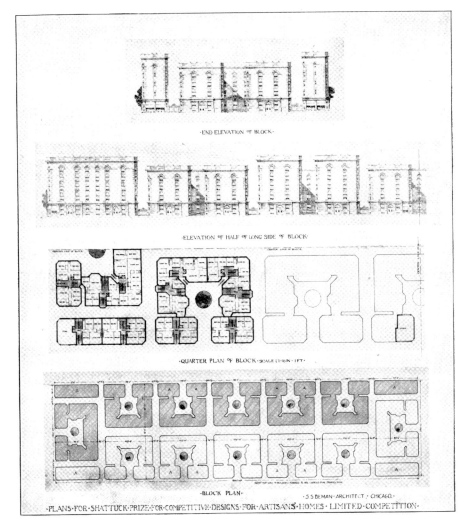

·END·ELEVATION·OF·BLOCK·

·ELEVATION·OF·HALF·OF·LONG·SIDE·OF·BLOCK·

·QUARTER·PLAN·OF·BLOCK·SCALE·1-16·IN·=1·FT·

·BLOCK·PLAN·

·S·S·BEMAN·ARCHITECT·CHICAGO·

·PLANS·FOR·SHATTUCK·PRIZE·FOR·COMPETITIVE·DESIGNS·FOR·ARTISANS·HOMES·LIMITED·COMPETITION·

*Solon Spencer Beman design for the "Shattuck" competition (CAC/1900)*

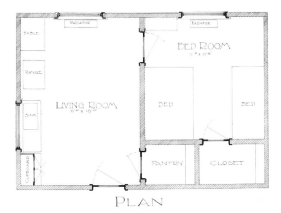

PLAN

*The plan of the two-room tenement constructed full size for the 1900 exhibition (CAC/1900)*

*Photograph of the interior of the two-room tenement, published in* House Beautiful *(HB)*

possible to procure the prize designs in the tenement house competition, and they are published here by the cooperation of the *Construction News.* We add to their publication a design for a similar problem by Mr. Beman [his Shattuck design], made some time ago, and sketches of the Langdon Apartments [by D. H. Perkins], one portion of which is now built on the West Side." Thus, while the New York material was not, for the most part, illustrated or listed in the Chicago catalog, it was part of the exhibition.

An important addition to the material from New York illustrated in the catalog was the construction of a "two-room tenement erected full size in the galleries of the Art Institute by the Architectural Club, and furnished and decorated by the Arts and Crafts Society." The model apartment was furnished with inexpensive items that, it was felt, could be afforded by a family with a primary wage earner who had an income of two dollars a day. The price of each item was noted on the object itself in the apartment. The plan of that living unit commanded a full page in the catalog, followed by a "Statement Concerning the Arts and Crafts Exhibit" by George M. R. Twose, secretary and prime mover of the Chicago Arts and Crafts Society.[12] Twose noted that his group was motivated to participate in the exhibition because the New York Tenement House Committee had opened the discussion of appropriate housing and he felt that the Arts and Crafts Society had a great deal to

12. *Book of the Thirteenth Annual Exhibition,* 104–8.

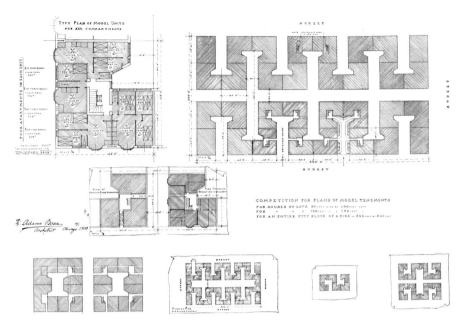

*Adamo Boari's highly commended plans for the Tenement House Competition (CAC/1900)*

contribute by building and furnishing a model of what could be, as opposed to the huge, square-block model provided as an example of the deplorable conditions then existing in New York. Twose noted in his essay that "just as the Tenement House Exhibition shows the conditions of light, air and sanitation that every one ought to possess, so the Arts and Crafts society aims to show the same status of household articles." The model apartment, exhibited along with the material from New York and a number of similar designs by Chicagoans, was an important part of the club's exhibition of 1900. The club was now directing much of its energy toward civic activities that, combined with the key members' interest in the development of new forms, set the tone for club affairs and laid the foundation for a new architecture.

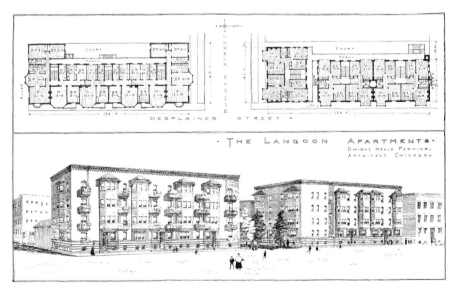

*Dwight Heald Perkins's Langdon Apartments, shown in the 1900 exhibition (CAC/1900)*

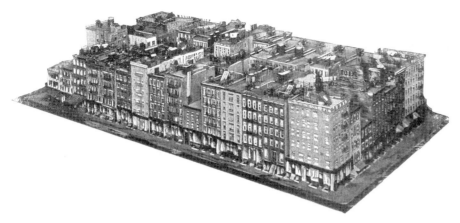

*Model of a square block of existing tenements, shipped to Chicago from New York City for the 1900 exhibition (PC)*

The 1900 exhibition and its catalog occupied a great deal of the club's time in early 1900. In addition to the exhibition, the club continued its weekly programs of sketch nights, lectures, competitions, and bohemian, or entertainment, nights. On January 15, Joseph Twyman[13] gave a presentation on tapestries, with exhibits.[14] A week later, Frank M. Garden recounted his recent experiences in the Klondike, complete with lantern slides. The bohemian night of January 29 was an evening of *Faust* presented by eight members with music, costumes, and food.[15]

After the club's reorganization under the presidency of Francis W. Kirkpatrick in 1898, the new structure provided for tighter control of club affairs by the Executive Committee, which had a great deal of continuity, as its members were now elected for staggered multiyear terms. By now the officers and the Executive Committee were drawn primarily from the young men who made up what Frank Lloyd Wright called the Eighteen. (The group varied in number between 1896 and 1900 and may have included as many as twenty or more participants.) Several of these people worked in Steinway Hall, and those who didn't shared a similar philosophy. What they were seeking was an American architecture. Wright claimed in later years to have been the leader of the group, but it is highly likely that there was no leader per se. Participation seems to have been broad and vocal. Of the group, George R. Dean, Robert C. Spencer Jr., Dwight Perkins, and Frank Lloyd Wright were all outspoken and highly literate. Literate enough, in fact, to have recorded many of the seminal ideas propagated by the group. Each of these men found time to record his thoughts and, in many cases, to get his words into print.

Another important figure in the group was a nonarchitect, Charles Zueblin, a professor of sociology, then at the University of Chicago.[16] He was part of a subgroup of the Eighteen whose interests went beyond architecture to exploring the means of improving life, particularly for the working class, through architecture. The Pond brothers, I. K. and Allen, Dwight Perkins, and Frank Lloyd Wright were all interested in this aspect of architecture. By the turn of the century, Pond & Pond had been involved for more than a decade with the design of social service buildings for the Hull-House complex founded by Jane Addams. The firm had also designed the David Swing Settlement Building and the Chicago Commons project. Dwight Perkins had designed the University of Chicago Settlement House, as well as a similar project for Northwestern University. His Langdon Apartments for low- to middle-income residents on the near West Side of Chicago were also done during the last

*Charles Zueblin (WRH)*

13. Joseph Twyman (1842–1904) was born and educated in England, where he developed a great interest in the work of William Morris. In 1870, he came to the United States, where he worked with J. J. McGrath. By 1890 he had his own decorating firm in the McVickers Theater Building (coincidentally, he and Adler & Sullivan had worked together on the interior). Later he joined the Tobey Furniture Company as chief of the Department of Decoration, where his longtime interest in William Morris was reflected in the Morris Room he set up in the company's warerooms. During the same period he was also instrumental in developing the South Park Workshop Association as an arm of the William Morris Society. He became an associate member of the Chicago Architectural Club in 1900.

14. Twyman spoke again on February 18, when his subject was "Furniture." That talk was published in *Inland Architect* 35, no. 3 (April 1900): 19–20.

15. *Brickbuilder* 9, no. 2 (February 1900): 39–40.

16. Charles Zueblin (1866–1924) was born in Indiana and moved to Philadelphia as a child, where he received his early education in the public schools. He studied at Northwestern University and Yale, with further study in Leipzig, Germany. He founded the Northwestern University Settlement House in 1891. Zueblin was made an instructor in sociology at the University of Chicago when it was founded in 1892. Around 1903, he moved to the East Coast, where he remained until his death. Zueblin was brought to my attention by the late Lawrence B. Perkins, Dwight's son, who insisted that Zueblin was a key figure in the Eighteen and influenced his father's thinking. Zueblin wrote extensively; his most relevant work covering the period under review is *A Decade of Civic Development* (Chicago: University of Chicago Press, 1905).

*David Swing Settlement Building, designed by Pond & Pond (CAC/1900)*

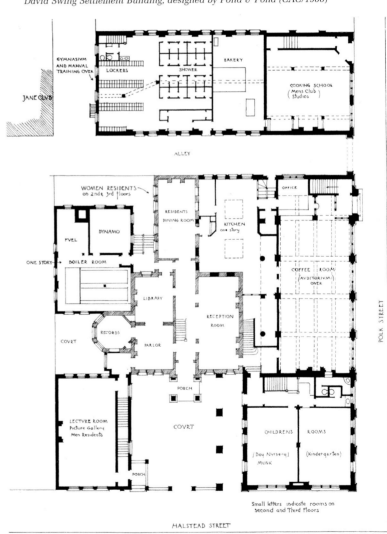

"HVLL HOVSE"　　　　　　　POND & POND ARCHITECTS

*The Hull-House complex expanded after 1900 to cover almost an entire block; the original Hull-House is indicated by the lightly shaded walls in this plan (CAC/1900)*

*Northwestern University's Settlement House by Dwight Heald Perkins is still standing (CAC/1900)*

years of the nineteenth century. All these designs were included in the club's exhibition of 1900. Wright had been interested in low-cost housing for several years but, although he showed a number of his other projects in the 1900 exhibition, he showed only one example of his work of this nature. That was the Abraham Lincoln Center, a project for his uncle, Jenkin Lloyd Jones, who caused Wright and his associate on the project, Dwight Perkins, a great deal of consternation.

The Abraham Lincoln Center, also called All Souls or Lincoln Center, was essentially a community center. Wright had begun work on it in early 1897. Perkins had joined him shortly thereafter. Both Wright and Perkins were members of All Souls Church, the sponsoring entity. Perkins was probably brought on board because of his experience in designing similar social service projects. Wright, on the other hand, had had experience in the design of low-cost housing, such as the Francisco Apartments and Francisco Terrace. Neither of these projects, however, involved providing services other than housing. Although the Abraham Lincoln Center was shown at the club's exhibition of 1900, that particular design was not built. In fact, the design went through a number of configurations before Wright and Perkins finally gave up trying to satisfy Jenkin Lloyd Jones. The structure finally built was disowned by Wright and Perkins, although it still had hints of both men's contributions to the design.[17]

The Chicago Architectural Club exhibition of 1900 opened on March 20. The accompanying catalog was released at the same time. It had a total of 160 pages without advertising. Instead of ads, the Exhibition Committee had asked "patrons" to contribute to the funding of the catalog, and there were 129 responses from architects, contractors, sculptors, and a number of ordinary citizens. The Exhibition Committee consisted of eight members of the club, including Dwight Perkins, who was the editor of the catalog, and two outsiders, David Knickerbacker Boyd from Philadelphia and Julius F. Harder from New York City. There was also a Hanging Committee of five members plus representatives from New York and Philadelphia. Perkins also served on this committee. The catalog was the club's most ambitious to date. The cover, with a new logo designed by Robert C. Spencer, was printed in green, gold, and black. That cover was "to be used annually" for future exhibi-

17. The Abraham Lincoln Center Building has been strangely absent from most documentation of Wright's work during this period, which is odd considering that it occupied an extraordinary amount of Wright's time. There have been two studies of the project that shed light on what actually happened. The first, completed in September 1970 by the author's office, was done as a consulting service for Andrew Heard, the restoration architect when the building was converted and adapted for use by Northwesern University. The second study, by Joseph Siry, was titled "The Abraham Lincoln Center in Chicago" and published in the *Society of Architectural Historians Journal* in September 1991.

*Frank Lloyd Wright and Dwight Perkins were engaged by Wright's uncle, Jenkin Lloyd Jones, to design the Abraham Lincoln Center in mid-1895. They prepared a number of designs, five of which are illustrated at right. The first was published in the January 1900 issue of* Architectural Review *with an article by Robert Spencer and was then shown in the 1900 Chicago Architectural Club Exhibition. Shortly thereafter, a slightly smaller second version was published, followed by a third version, and a fourth in concrete. Other designs are hinted at in the literature surrounding this project but no other unbuilt designs were published. Ultimately, Wright and Perkins quit in frustration. Jenkin Lloyd Jones then proceeded without their help, and the final building, the fifth scheme at the far right, was built without the architects' supervision (PC)*

tions.[18] The catalog was divided into sections starting with a "Greeting" from the Exhibition Committee, followed by a list of the patrons and an essay by Art Institute of Chicago curator James F. Gookins, who wrote eight pages of what could only be described as Chicago boosterism. He began with an outline of the benefits and detriments of living in Chicago and concluded with a call for a massive public effort to improve literally everything about the city. One could argue that Gookins's essay was the first published demand for a comprehensive plan for Chicago. Such a plan would be realized within the next decade.

The essay was followed by a report of a competition sponsored by the Art and Literature Department of the Chicago Woman's Club for a small triangular space called Oak Park, bounded by North State and Rush streets. The published design was by Birch Burdette Long. It did not win a prize because its cost was expected to exceed a thousand dollars. It was, nevertheless, chosen for construction since it was acknowledged to be "not only the best, but a very original and appropriate scheme."[19] When it was completed it was described in the *Brickbuilder* as a "most beautiful and unique example of terra-cotta work." The journal went on to note that it was "the first time in local architectural history, glazed terra-cotta has been used, in which rich polychromatic effects have been obtained . . . The design is as refined and original as the craftsmanship, and should prove a valuable object-lesson to the community in the possibilities of a modern architecture suited to modern and local materials."[20]

Robert C. Spencer then had a long illustrated essay titled "The Farmhouse Problem," and there was a full page of text from the Exhibition Committee regretting that the Improved Housing Association had been unable to get the Tenement House Exhibition material in time for it to be illustrated and listed in the catalog. This was followed by a brief discussion of the material that was exhibited. There was a single-page unsigned essay on the items exhibited by social service organizations such as Hull-House.

18. *Brickbuilder* 9, no. 3 (March 1900): 62. The entire cover was never used again, but the logo designed by Spencer appeared on virtually every piece of printed material distributed by the club for many years.

19. Ibid.

20. *Brickbuilder* 9, no. 12 (December 1900): 256–57.

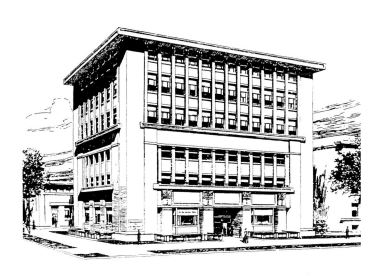

A major part of the catalog was a ten-page section illustrating Frank Lloyd Wright's work, all of which was published a few weeks later in the June issue of the *Architectural Review* as part of an article by Robert C. Spencer Jr.[21] It was unusual, indeed stunning, for a single individual to be granted so much space in the exhibition and catalog. This and similar intrusions into the club's affairs by Wright over the next two years would eventually cause a schism in the club that would bring about almost total exclusion of the work of the early modernists from exhibitions for several years.

The Architectural League of America was given a page to briefly describe its current efforts and announce its forthcoming convention in Chicago during the month of June. (One cannot help but wonder if Spencer's article on Wright was not deliberately timed to coincide with the convention of the Architectural League.) The back of the book included the club's second syllabus in two years, called "Calendar 1899–1900," a roster of club officers, and a complete list of members. The

21. Robert C. Spencer, "The Work of Frank Lloyd Wright," *Architectural Review* 7, no. 6 (June 1900): 61–72, plates 35–39. This was reprinted by the Prairie School Press as a booklet in facsimile in 1976.

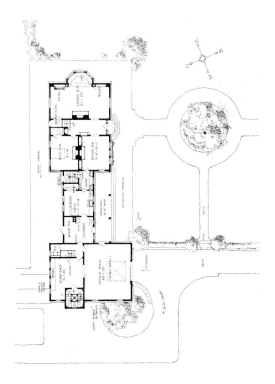

*Robert C. Spencer's drawing of his solution for the "Farmhouse Problem," shown in the 1900 exhibition (CAC/1900)*

final part of the catalog was an incomplete listing of exhibitors. Interspersed between these articles and essays were illustrations of the exhibits, both drawings and photographs. It was an impressive document then and remains so to this day. Very little, other than the work of Frank Lloyd Wright, represented the avant-garde work of the Eighteen who got together on a regular basis to talk architecture. That would come later, but it would be short-lived.

A press preview of the exhibition was held from ten o'clock in the morning until four o'clock in the afternoon on March 19, the day before the show opened to the public. There had already been a good deal of advance publicity. Every newspaper in Chicago had items of varying length concerning the exhibition, usually emphasizing the participation of the Improved Housing Association and the participation of the Tenement House Committee from New York. The first reviews of the exhibition appeared in Chicago newspapers the day it opened and others within the next few days.[22] The *Chicago Inter Ocean* noted that "the thirteenth annual exhibition of architecture and the allied arts of the Chicago Architectural club at the Art Institute opened last night with a grand reception, which filled the south wing of the building with people who love beautiful and comfortable homes . . . Room after room is filled with fine elevations and perspectives of all that is old and all that is new, all that is domestic and all that is foreign, all that is good and all that is cozy and beautiful to human abodes . . . the first two rooms are for the humanitarian and the practical reformer. They are given up to the exhibit of the Chicago Improved Housing association, which includes exhibits from the Tenement Housing Committee of the New York Charity Association, and exhibits from London, Berlin, Paris and every great city in Europe."[23] Nearly every review had similar comments regarding the Improved Housing Association's part of the exhibition. They did not, however, neglect the work of Chicago draftsmen and architects. The *Chicago Record* reviewer noted that "in entering the first room of the exhibit proper, the eye is greeted by a large fireplace in golden mosaic."[24] A number of the reviewers were

22. The *Chicago Tribune*, the *Chicago Record*, the *Chicago Inter Ocean*, and the *Chicago Reporter*, as well as several other papers, had reviews immediately. A week later the *Chicago Record*, the *Chicago Post*, and the *Times Herald* printed much longer reviews, some with illustrations.

23. "Work of Architects," *Chicago Inter Ocean*, March 21, 1900.

24. *Chicago Record*, March 27, 1900.

*Frank Lloyd Wright's design for the Husser House fireplace, probably done with the help of Blanche Ostertag (AREV/AV)*

fascinated by this fireplace. The reviewer for the *Chicago Inter Ocean* noted that there were "certain exhibits that attracted particular attention. One of these is a facing for a fireplace—a glass mosaic with gold effects, which is something entirely new. The gold is burned on the glass and by the use of new methods, color effects have been produced which, it is said, are unusual. The design is a wisteria vine and blossoms, and the effect is remarkable. Frank L. Wright is the architect, Miss B. Ostertag, the designer, and Grannim [*sic*] & Hilgart, the makers."[25] Thus we are treated to contemporary descriptions of the fireplace that was ultimately installed in the house for Mr. and Mrs. Joseph Husser. It was not, however, listed or illustrated in the catalog.

The exhibition was apparently very successful. All the local papers commented on the number of visitors and how they enjoyed the architecture. The portion of the exhibition devoted to tenements got at least equal coverage. (It occupied two of the five rooms on the south end of the Art Institute where the exhibition was featured.) Nearly every newspaper article was positive. Typical was the item published by the *Chicago Record* on March 20. The paper noted that the "thirteenth annual exhibit of the Chicago Architectural Club will be on view in the South Gallery of the Art Institute to-night and until next Monday. Nearly 700 specimens of the work of the architects of the world and their fellow-craftsmen will be shown, many of the displays being practical models of homes, hotels and tenement houses. One new feature is the attention paid to farmhouses and country dwellings." It went on to say, "Associated with the Architectural Club in the exhibition are the Improved Housing Association and the Arts and Crafts Society. They have constructed a two-room unit for a tenement house. The object of the model is to show how well-planned tenements may be comfortable and healthful at a small cost. In this same line is an exhibit of a lodging house to accommodate over 1,000 men on the plan of the Mills hotels. Plans for the beautifying of public parks at small cost are shown. The design submitted by Birch Burdette Long for the improvement of the Bellevue place triangle is among these. The Hull house, Chicago Commons and structures of similar nature are shown by photographs and drawings. James Gamble Rogers shows designs for the Chicago institute."[26]

Several architectural journals published more lengthy reviews, the best of which was Robert Craik McLean's for the *Inland Architect,* which was, as usual, highly laudatory: "This year the Chicago Architectural Club has combined its most complete exhibition of illustrated architecture with a sociological exhibit . . . which shows how the other half ought to live, as well as by photographic illustrations of how they do live."[27] McLean was impressed by the quality of the exhibits, particular the use of color in the drawings. He noted that "the most attractive residence design was that of the Farson House, by George W. Maher, of Chicago; the most unique the model of the Chicago Bank, carved in wood, from Jenney & Mundie's design, and the most extensive of the designs submitted in the Phoebe Hurst Competition . . . There was breadth and economic value in Robert C. Spencer's farm houses."[28] He commented that "the cursory visitor saw beauty in line and color everywhere and was deeply impressed with the fact that the draftsman of fifteen years ago was more or less a mechanic, while today he is no less mechanical in his knowledge, but his appreciation of the beauty of a line has led him to seeing the relation of color and of form, and that the higher the art instinct was developed the better the design was apt to be." McLean described a number of other exhibits and near the end of his review noted that "the whole picture is full of the thought of the enthusiasm of the Chicago Architectural Club and the grinding perseverance of those individual members who have from year to year worked for the perfection and success of the annual exhibition of which this is easily the best."

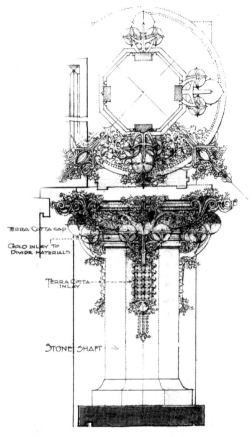

*Model of the Husser House column capital illustrated in the* Brickbuilder *without identification (above); the same column drawing from Wright's studio (below) (Arev)*

25. *Chicago Inter Ocean*, March 21, 1900.

26. "Chicago Architectural Club Exhibit Opens To-Night," *Chicago Record*, March 20, 1900.

27. *Inland Architect* 35, no. 3 (April 1900): 18–19.

28. Neither the Farson House nor the wood model of the bank was included in the catalog's list of exhibits; apparently a number of entries were not included.

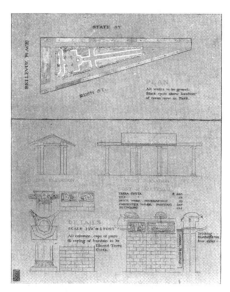

*Plan of Birch Burdette Long's "Design for a Park Improvement," published with the perspective (CAC/1900)*

While most newspaper and journal reports of the 1900 exhibition were favorable, there were adverse reactions as well. There were several dissidents, largely from the Eighteen, who were disturbed by what they saw at the exhibition. Their sentiments were put in print by George R. Dean, who had already expressed his concerns about modern architecture the previous year.[29] Shortly after the close of the exhibition, Dean wrote an essay titled "Progress before Precedent," which was published in the *Brickbuilder*.[30] The text was less than two pages, but appended to it were several pages of comments regarding Dean's thoughts that he had solicited from prominent architects throughout the United States. (Copies had been sent to a number of architects for comment before publication and twenty-five of the responses were published along with the article.)

Dean was concerned that the Architectural League of America was using the expression "Progress before Precedent" in a number of its publications, and that the motto was subject to misinterpretation. He pointed out that the expression "was not used at the Cleveland Convention which resulted in the Architectural League of America, and to my mind does not express the character of the movement, if, indeed, by analysis it can be made to express anything." He was correct that the term was not used at the convention but only later, when Albert Kelsey, the first president of the Architectural League of America and editor of the *Architectural Annual,* used it in an essay in the first volume of that publication.[31]

George Dean's article in the May 1900 issue of the *Brickbuilder* was clearly written before the *Architectural Annual* of 1900 was issued. Internal evidence suggests that the *Annual* was published in late May of 1900. Dean had obviously seen a draft or a preliminary copy of it before writing his article. In his essay, Dean noted that "precedent in architecture has two very distinct and entirely different meanings. If that of slavishly copying the forms of ancient architecture is meant, let us say 'Progress without Precedent.' If, however, the meaning is the following of principles which led the great architects to produce monuments of art which we revere and fondly worship, let the maxim be 'Precedence and Progress'; for Progress will follow, and we may hope . . . to develop monuments as much greater than theirs as our civilization is broader, richer, and more powerful." He discussed the use of materials and ornament in the context of current building. He then stated that "what the young men of the League desire is an architecture free from vulgar importations." He expressed a certain amount of disgust with the European forms being used in the United States, but he also said that "the young men of the League do not wish to banish from their lives all early architecture." His argument was essentially that what the young architects of America really wanted was an architecture that reflected current conditions and society. They wanted an "American Architecture."

Unlike most reviewers, Dean was extremely critical of the club's exhibition and its catalog. He wrote that his colleagues could see improvement in their own work, but they were discouraged to "see such exhibitions as the one at Chicago this year, and the book of the exhibition which is worse. But they realize that club politics and individual incapacity are always rampant, and take new heart. The fact that the club was able to produce a book at all without the aid of advertisements speaks volumes for those who had the work in charge, and shows the interest the people take in architecture."

Dean continued, "Not that the exhibition is worse than those which preceded it, but the opportunities were greater. The Chicago Architectural Club was a prime mover in the League, formed, as its constitution says, 'To encourage an indigenous and inventive architecture, and to lead architectural thought to modern sources of inspiration.'" Toward the end of his essay Dean wrote, "the club's action in crowding the exhibition and book with the trite architecture of the past to the exclusion

29. George Dean had published an essay on the subject in the June 1898 exhibition catalog and a revised version in *Arts for America* the same month. Dean was one of the Eighteen and during the late nineteenth century wrote several times on the subject of modern architecture.

30. *Brickbuilder* 9, no. 5 (May 1900): 91–97.

31. Albert Kelsey, ed., *The Architectural Annual, An Illustrated Review of Contemporaneous Architecture*, vol. 1 (Philadelphia, 1900).

of the many good things done throughout the West during the last year is inexcusable . . . [but] Whatever disappointment we feel, we must not attach too much importance to a slight defeat. The architecture has come to stay . . . It is safe to say that the number of young men in the Middle West who are working on these lines has more than doubled in the last year." While Dean expected that some of his colleagues would simply copy the work of the innovators, he noted that this "will correct itself when the people discriminate between the original and the copy as well as they do at present in painting."

A careful review of the book of the exhibition for 1900 seems to support George Dean's concerns. Although close to seven hundred exhibits were listed, only a handful were in the spirit of the emerging modern movement. Furthermore, much of the publicity—and there was a great deal—had been devoted to the work assembled by Chicago's Improved Housing Association. Related to that was some of the better work of Pond & Pond and Dwight Perkins in the field of settlement house design, most notably for Hull-House, Northwestern University, and the University of Chicago. The Abraham Lincoln Center by Wright and Perkins fell in this same category, but most of the rest of the show was devoted to traditional designs from throughout the United States and Europe. Unfortunately, the only exhibit from the AIA competition for the design of a municipal improvement in Lake Front Park, listed in the catalog as "Projet: A City Hall on the Lake Front, Chicago," was not illustrated, and none of those drawings has survived. Another exhibit not illustrated was Adamo Boari's Mexican National Capitol Competition entry. Genuinely avant-garde work such as that emerging in Chicago was scant.

On the other hand, Birch Burdette Long's "Design for Park Improvement" was superb. The designs for farmhouses by Robert C. Spencer Jr. gave a strong preview of what Spencer was capable of and what he would do in the future. Myron Hunt and Howard Shaw both had some highly credible designs in the exhibition and, of course, there were Frank Lloyd Wright's eleven examples of work (six photographs, four sketches, and the aforementioned All Souls buildings for which he and Dwight Perkins shared credit). It is almost certain that Wright's contribution to the exhibition was a last-minute endeavor, probably engineered by Spencer, who was first vice president of the club and on both the Hanging and Publicity committees. The first major national article on Wright, "The Work of Frank Lloyd Wright," by Spencer, was already in the works and would be published in the *Architectural Review* a few weeks later.[32] All Wright's exhibits in the 1900 show, plus a number of his other designs, were published in that article.

The controversy over the content of the exhibition and the motto "Progress before Precedent" was exacerbated by Dean's article in the *Brickbuilder*, particularly by the comments from architects throughout the United States that were published with it, many of them major figures in the architectural world of the turn of the century. Opinions were diverse, but several qualified their comments in a manner that left them squarely on the fence. C. H. Blackall of Boston, for example, said, "The maxim sounds good, but like all epigrammatic expressions is right or wrong, depending upon its interpretation and application." Glenn Brown, secretary of the AIA at the time, noted that "progress has always been founded on precedent. No great art movement has grown from nothing." Walter Cook of New York City thought that "formulating of maxims . . . is usually an entirely harmless recreation, and exercises no great influence upon any individual." Most agreed with Dean that the present education of architects was deficient, and virtually all felt that his brief essay was good, if only to stimulate debate.

Of the Chicagoans who commented, W. L. B. Jenney remarked that "undoubtedly the maxim is a good one. We should not be blind copyists." Irving K. Pond was less clear, although one statement of his seemed to put him on the side of the tra-

*"Park Improvement" shelter, still standing in Oak Park on Chicago's near north side (WRH)*

*Birch Burdette Long's "Design for a Park Improvement," as published in the 1900 CAC catalog*

32. Spencer, "The Work of Frank Lloyd Wright."

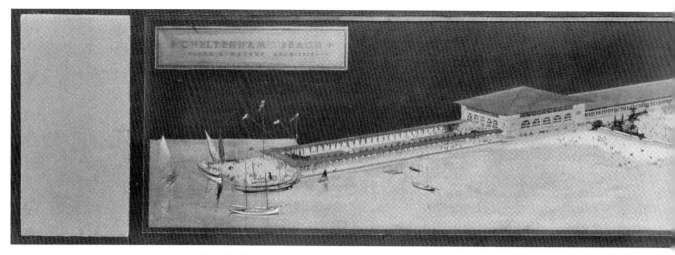

*Frank Lloyd Wright's design for Cheltenham Beach, published as a full-page spread in the* Architectural Review, *the signatures of the delineators, Charles A. Corwin and Hugh M. G. Garden, can be seen in the lower right. (ARev)*

ditionalists. He noted, "I am in the dark, and I am equally blind as to just how nature study is to inspire a new architecture any more than it did an old (which it never did)." If Pond did participate in the discussions with the Eighteen, this kind of contribution would have put him very much in opposition to the majority of the group, and to Louis Sullivan and Frank Lloyd Wright in particular.

In his published response, Sullivan wrote, "In my judgement a maxim or shibboleth, such as 'Progress before Precedent,' is in itself neither valuable nor objectionable." He went on to say, "Talk and good intentions we have, but talk and good intentions do not build beautifully rational buildings. Talk may be had for the asking . . . but delicate clarity of insight, sturdy singleness of purpose, and adequate mental training are notably so rare in our profession as almost to be freakish." A careful reading of his words suggests that he knew of the conversations and debates of the Eighteen, but like Mies van der Rohe fifty years later, he was saying "build, don't talk."

Frank Lloyd Wright's articulate letter was near the end of the twenty-five published. He opened by saying, "George Dean is right. An alliterative slogan is trite at best. His feeling against the present hidebound condition of architecture as a fine art, and his hope for its future, are characteristic of a growing group of young men in the Middle West." He ended his remarks with a personal note: "And Dean,—Are you not just a little harsh and unreasonable in calling for fruit from seed planted the day before yesterday?"

George Dean's thought-provoking article, and the responses thereto, fomented activity in the early modern movement that would change architecture forever. An audience had been found and the ideas that resulted in new forms and new uses of materials were being discussed throughout architectural communities everywhere. The Chicago architects, largely those in the Eighteen, were the Midwest leaders of new theory and thought. They were not alone, as their colleagues in Vienna, England, Germany, Scotland, and elsewhere were embarking on similar endeavors. It would be a few years before the modern movement became a worldwide phenomenon, but as the twentieth century dawned, the key elements of a new architecture were in place.

The Chicago Architectural exhibition of 1900 closed on April 2. A great many of the individual exhibits were packed and sent to St. Louis for the Second Annual

Exhibition of the St. Louis Architectural Club in accordance with the plans set out at the organizational meeting of the Architectural League of America the year before in Cleveland. Prior to being shown in Chicago, most of the foreign exhibits and a great many of the domestic ones had already been shown in Philadelphia and New York City. From St. Louis, the drawings went on to other exhibitions sponsored by the members of the Architectural League of America, including Detroit, Cleveland, and Pittsburgh.[33] Conspicuous in their absence on the circuit were the items shown in Chicago by Frank Lloyd Wright, who was not a member of the Chicago Architectural Club.

In May of 1900, the club's immediate concern was preparing for the Second Annual Convention of the Architectural League of America scheduled for June 7–9.[34] Chicago was the host club. Just as the exhibition was closing, the club announced a competition for "the immediate improvement of its club rooms in the most artistic manner possible."[35] The competition was open to all members. Whether a winner was named or the work done was never recorded. There may simply have been too much to do beyond cleaning up the club's rooms and Fullerton Hall at the Art Institute of Chicago where the convention was to be held. The location had been agreed to the year before, but a great deal of work was needed before the meeting. A large contingent of draftsmen and architects from all the clubs that made up the original members of the league were expected, plus other individuals and representatives of various architectural organizations. About thirty-five delegates, representing twelve architectural clubs and societies, and a hundred visitors attended.[36]

By all reports the convention was a resounding success.[37] Most of the meetings were held in Fullerton Hall at the Art Institute. The Chicago Architectural Club's rooms in the same building were open for use by small groups and for refreshments after the formalities were over. J. C. Llewellyn, president of the club, opened the meeting and introduced Albert Kelsey, president of the league. Kelsey delivered an opening address, noting that the league had been a great success during its first year and had received invitations from architectural organizations in England, France, and, not least, the American Institute of Architects, to participate jointly in the future. He reopened the debate as to whether or not the motto "Progress before Precedent" was appropriate, but did not belabor the point. Several committees reported their efforts during the year, including work on competition codes, scholarships, and the like.

33. This "circuit" of exhibitions was described in *Brush and Pencil* 5, no. 2 (November 1899): 93–94.

34. The meeting dates were published in Chicago's *Book of the Thirteenth Annual Exhibition* in March. The same information was published in *Brickbuilder* 9, no. 5 (May 1900): 108, and *Inland Architect* 35, no. 4 (May 1900): 1.

35. *Brickbuilder* 9, no. 4 (April 1900): 83.

36. *Inland Architect* 35, no. 5 (July 1900): 40 et seq., listed the delegates and visitors. Chicago, understandably, had the largest contingent.

37. *Inland Architect* 35, no. 5 (June 1900): 40–44, and *Brickbuilder* 9, no. 6 (June 1900): 111–18. The convention was reported in depth by all the major architectural journals. It was also reported by other journals, but the most extensive coverage was in a booklet published after the convention titled *Report of the First National Convention of Architectural Societies, Chicago, Illinois, June 7, 8 and 9, 1900.*

The second day's work was directed toward the business and philosophy of architecture and the reading of papers by various delegates. Elmer Grey[38] gave what was considered "one of the most noteworthy addresses,"[39] calling for his fellow architects to follow the league's constitution, which expressed the need to "encourage an indigenous and inventive architecture, and to lead architectural thought to modern sources of inspiration."[40] He went on to suggest that those "qualities in our architecture will, when obtained, appear in its style." He proposed to define "style," to discuss the terms "indigenous" and "inventive," and to "attempt to show how . . . we can best go about to attain to an 'indigenous and inventive architecture' in America." Grey noted that "style is not the external adornment of a building; it is the vital quality of it which has resulted from conditions inherent in its making and which include situation, cost, material requirements, the constructional means available for meeting those requirements and the ornament with which it was thought fitting to clothe it." Later he stated:

The poets never tire of calling our attention toward the unity of life, toward the intimate relation all living things bear to one another, and toward the fact that this relation is a far more intimate one than we almost always feel it to be. Scientific research . . . insists upon the oneness of all nature and of all life; upon the fact that each plant in nature is not a self-dependent organism, but that its health and its life is governed by a force which controls and sustains all living things; . . . a man is not an independent organism . . . his fortunes are governed by a higher ambition than his own, and that, though he is given free will to choose between the good and the bad, his final destiny will rest upon obedience or disobedience to physical, moral and spiritual laws over which he has no control . . . And so it is in art. For the artist is not an independent worker having supreme control over the quality and number of his creations. He is a part of a divine order of life from which all his efficiency springs, and the originality and sustained excellence of his work depend upon the degree to which he becomes conscious of his relation to that order, and upon his recognition of and obedience to its laws in their application to his life.

*Elmer Grey (AR)*

38. Elmer Grey (1871–1963) was not educated as an architect. A self-taught designer and a skilled delineator, Grey was a draftsman in Milwaukee who often participated in the affairs of the Chicago Architectural Club. He moved to California in 1903, and in 1904 joined former Chicagoan Myron Hunt in a partnership that lasted six years. He then practiced alone until his death in 1963.

39. *Brickbuilder* 9, no. 6 (June 1900): 113.

40. *Inland Architect* 35, no. 5 (June 1900): 36–37. Grey's entire speech is reproduced here verbatim, along with several other presentations from the convention. The quotations that follow are from this source. The speech was also published in *Brickbuilder* 9, no. 6 (June 1900): 121–24.

*Chicago participants at the Second Annual Convention of the Architectural League of America in Chicago; only nine were voting delegates (IA)*

*Robert Craik McLean's photograph of a group attending the Architectural League Convention (IA)*

He continued in the same general vein for several paragraphs, eventually returning to the subject of architecture as it grows out of such thoughts. Near the end of his presentation he stated that "beautiful things of lasting quality in architecture . . . are the result of an assimilation of many kinds of order, and of beauty, and of truth, into the soul of the artist, where they undergo an unconscious process of transmutation into the reactions which his imagination brings forth and which his knowledge, his skill and his character shape into new material form. He may obtain this nourishment from all sources which he finds will enrich him; from nature, from human experience, from religion, from literature, from painting, from the architecture of the past. But whatever sources he selects should be capable of refreshing him continuously." Grey told his audience that "the architecture of a country which will be truly representative in style, and which will endure with a lasting beauty, will voice the highest ideals of its people and will spring from the hearts of conscientious men who have accomplished the architectural expression of its noblest national life." He ended by saying, "To further the growth of such an architecture in every possible manner should be our ambition."

Grey's presentation "struck the keynote that aroused an enthusiastic spirit early in the convention, an interest, moreover, which was sustained to the hour of adjournment . . . At the conclusion of the reading of Mr. Grey's paper, the chairman asked Mr. Louis H. Sullivan to express his views upon the subject."[41] Sullivan was in the audience and had listened to Grey's presentation with great interest. He had no notes and had not planned to speak but, as reported in the *Brickbuilder*, "for half an hour he held the audience to a man, in rapt attention. He never raised his voice, used no superlatives, and indulged in no clever clap-trap phrases to compel attention. Slowly, quietly, and surely he gained the attention and eager interest of every one in the room."[42] Sullivan could make his points without "unpleasant references to the servile copyists, but, in alluding to their work, merely said 'Francis I. is dead; all the people of that period are dead,—and they will stay dead!' . . . the analogy was pat and convincing. So he talked on without hitch and without losing the continuity of his remarks, and always following along the lines of his own philosophy."[43] Clearly, Elmer Grey's remarks had been well received by the master.

Immediately after Sullivan's impromptu talk, Frank Lloyd Wright presented his own paper, "The Architect." He prefaced his comments with the statement that

41. *Brickbuilder* 9, no. 6 (June 1900): 113.

42. Ibid.

43. Sullivan's remarks were recorded by a stenographer at the convention. They were reproduced verbatim in *Inland Architect* 35, no. 5 (June 1900): 42–43.

"after listening to the master it hardly seemed proper to listen to the disciple."[44] Nevertheless, he spoke at length; his paper was the longest of any to be presented at the convention.[45] Wright began with what seems today to have been a condemnation of his colleagues, stating that "a vital point of difference between [the] professional man and [the] man of business is that money-making to the professional man should, by virtue of his assumption, be incidental; to the business man it is primary. Money has its limitations; while it may buy quantity, there is something beyond it, and that is 'quality.'" He "blasted" the "plan factory," the "shyster," and the "charlatan."[46] He was outspoken in his distaste for the state of architecture and the architects of the time. He felt that the architect had "been submerged, overwhelmed by the commercialism of his time." He pointedly declared that his colleagues were selling "ready made imported architecture . . . as a poultice or porous plaster would be applied . . . and is accepted with a clamor for 'more' through lack of acquaintance with the real thing, lack of an ideal and of educational force in the profession itself." He lectured his audience about the apparent lack of integrity in the profession and urged them to "help his lame, halt, and blind profession again to its place by respecting his art and respecting himself . . . that will make a man of business see that a Greek temple made over to trade is an unhallowed joke, and that he is the butt when genuine dignity and beauty might be his for less money; that will make the householder realize that if he would live in a Louis XV environment, he is but a step removed from the savage, with a ring in his nose; and make it felt that architecture is not a matter of the scene painting of periods, nor a mere matter of scene painting in any sense whatever." This was seminal Wright philosophy, which would, over the years, be refined and restated. He suggested a positive role for the profession when he stated that "the architect should help the people to feel that architecture is a destroyer of vulgarity, sham, and pretense, a benefactor of tired nerves and jaded souls, an educator in the higher ideals and better purposes of yesterday, to-day, and to-morrow."

Wright then spoke at length on "education," noting that the "education of the architect should commence when he is two days old—'three days is too much'—and continue until he passes beyond, leaving his experiments by the wayside to serve his profession as warning signs or guide-posts." (Was this a reflection of his own mother's decision, while he was still in the womb, that he was to be an architect?) He was concerned that his colleagues were depending too much on the past and he suggested that "the architect primarily should have something of his own to say, or keep silence. If he has that something to say in noble form, gracious line, and living color, each expression will have a 'grammar' of its own, using the term in its best sense, and will speak the universal language of Beauty in no circumscribed series of set architectural phrase as used by people in other times, although a language in harmony with elemental laws to be deduced from the beautiful of all peoples in all time."

As he approached the end of his paper, Wright grew more philosophical, more poetic, and his years with Sullivan became evident. He could not resist stating that "in the arts every problem carries within, its own solution, and the only way yet discovered to reach it is a very painstaking way—to sympathetically look within the thing itself, to proceed to analyze and sift it, to extract its own consistent and essential beauty, which means its common sense truthfully idealized. That is the heart of the poetry that lives in architecture." This was Sullivan slightly revised, but clearly etched in Wright's memory from those long nights in the Auditorium Tower when Sullivan poured out his soul to his young apprentice.

Wright's paper was well received, particularly after Elmer Grey and Louis Sullivan had set the stage. The editor of the *Brickbuilder* commented, "His paper was

44. Ibid.

45. The full text was published in *Brickbuilder* 9, no. 6 (June 1900): 124–28. The speech was delivered on June 8, 1900, Frank Lloyd Wright's forty-third birthday.

46. Ibid. The best brief description of Wright's speech is on page 124.

a fearless and outspoken utterance on a subject of moment to every person interested in architecture."

The remaining two days of the convention were somewhat anticlimactic. On Friday evening the delegates met in the rooms of the Chicago Architectural Club at the Art Institute of Chicago to handle various housekeeping duties. Reports were heard on the activities of member clubs and league committees, and assignments were handed out to individuals. On Saturday, the convention continued with presentations on "the licensing of Architects" and a paper from New York architect Ernest Flagg titled "American Architecture as Opposed to Architecture in America," read by Dwight Perkins in Flagg's absence. Despite missing the convention, Flagg would become a major figure in the debate on "pure design" during the next year. The last session was devoted to planning for the next year, choosing a site for the 1901 convention (Philadelphia), and electing officers. Chicago Architectural Club president Joseph C. Llewellyn was chosen as president of the league for 1900–1901, and N. Max Dunning was chosen as secretary.

On the evening of Saturday, June 9, with the affairs of the convention behind them, the voting delegates, visiting delegates, local members, and their guests, over two hundred in all, met in the dining room of the Auditorium Hotel for a reception and banquet in honor of the visitors to Chicago.[47] Daniel H. Burnham acted as toastmaster and introduced incoming president Llewellyn, who outlined his plans for the coming year. After brief presentations by representatives from Boston and Philadelphia, Louis Sullivan took the podium and read his now famous paper, "The Young Man in Architecture." The editor of the *Brickbuilder* noted that he "was listened to with the closest attention, and many present must have returned to their homes strengthened and stimulated by his earnest words." Oscar Enders then entertained the group with one of his humorous songs, after which Dwight Perkins gave the concluding address whereby he "summed up the sentiment of the convention."

Shortly after the convention was over, President Llewellyn exercised his prerogative, provided for in the new constitution of the Architectural League of America, by appointing the league's Executive Board at the first of their monthly meetings. He asked the Executive Committee of the Chicago Architectural Club to assist him and together they chose Richard E. Schmidt of Chicago as vice president, Emil G. Lorch of Detroit as corresponding secretary, Hugh M. G. Garden of Chicago as recording secretary, August Wilmanns of Chicago as treasurer, and Robert C. Spencer Jr. of Chicago and Newton A. Wells from the University of Illinois as the other members of the board.[48] Control of the league's affairs was firmly in the hands of Chicagoans, most of whom were proponents of the emerging modern movement. It was expected that the board would meet regularly to conduct the affairs of the league between conventions. The first full meeting was in August of 1900, when they assigned various duties to each of the clubs. Chicago had responsibility for publicity and promotion.[49] That group was chaired by Henry K. Holsman, who served with William K. Fellows and Walter Burley Griffin. There was a special committee on "Municipal Improvement" chaired by H. K. Bush-Brown of New York, on which Dwight Perkins served.

With the club's president heavily involved in the affairs of the Architectural League of America, the Chicago Architectural Club essentially took the summer off, in accordance with its usual practice. By fall, however, it was time to return to club activities. The first meeting of the 1900–1901 year was held in the club rooms

47. Ibid. The closing events of the convention are described in some detail on pages 114–15.

48. *Brickbuilder* 9, no. 7 (July 1900): 152.

49. *Brickbuilder* 9, no. 9 (September 1900): 195.

*The Auditorium Building dining room, where the Architectural League held its closing banquet, set up for dinner (CT)*

on September 16.[50] There was a large turnout and "the work of the coming year" was thoroughly discussed. The proposal that a traveling scholarship be established and supported by the club was heartily endorsed and the Executive Committee was given power for its establishment. Reports from "the secretary and treasurer, showed that after an unusually active year the club had not only increased in membership, but that the finances showed a large increase upon the previous year. This, the secretary thought, was largely due to the abolition of the advertising feature in the exhibition catalogue." The income from patrons had been greater than from advertisers in the past, and there was no expense for printing advertisements.

The club held its annual meeting on October 1 and elected Henry K. Holsman[51] as president.[52] Other officers included Robert C. Spencer Jr. as first vice president, Peter J. Weber as second vice president, Birch Burdette Long as secretary, and Adolph Bernhard as treasurer. The full slate included an Executive Committee made up of Walter H. Kleinpell, chairman, Charles A. Carr, Max Mauch, Burton E. Morse, J. Nelson Watson, and E. Charles Hemmings.[53]

The fall of 1900 also saw a turnaround in architectural activity in Chicago. After nearly eight years of a severe depression that coincided with extreme unrest in the labor community, work for architects began to reappear. In the same issue of the *Brickbuilder* that the new Chicago Architectural Club officers were announced, it was noted that Dwight Perkins had been appointed architect of Hitchcock Hall at the University of Chicago. Pond & Pond was recorded as designing a new Northwestern University Settlement Building, Shepley, Rutan & Coolidge was working on several new buildings for the University of Chicago, and D. H. Burnham was preparing plans for a new building for Marshall Field & Company that would occupy the entire front between Randolph to Washington streets on State Street in Chicago. Similar activity was being reported throughout the United States. The architectural drought was over.

50. *Inland Architect* 36, no. 3 (October 1900): 23–24.

51. Henry K. Holsman (1867–1963) was born in Iowa and educated at Grinnell College. He came to Chicago in 1891 and, after ten years as an architect, he designed an automobile and established Holsman Automobile Works. That enterprise survived until 1910, when he returned to architecture. He practiced for the rest of his life, often working as both architect and developer. He was active in many organizations including the AIA, where he was a fellow.

52. *Brickbuilder* 9, no. 10 (October 1900): 214.

53. These names are taken from a copy of *Charter, Constitution, By-Laws, House Rules, Officers and Members of the Chicago Architectural Club.* Officers since 1885 are listed, as are all 1904 members.

Chicago had a distinguished, if somewhat controversial, visitor in the fall of 1900. Charles Robert Ashbee was an Englishman who was deeply involved in the cultural and artistic affairs of Great Britain.[54] An architect and designer, he is most often remembered today for his exquisite designs for decorative objects, often in hand-wrought silver. He was a key figure in the arts and crafts movement in London, where he had organized a workshop called the Guild of the Handicraft. He had been in the United States once before, in 1896, but had not ventured as far west as Chicago. His three-month 1900 journey started on the East Coast and progressed through several New England states and then westward to Illinois and Missouri, after which he traveled east again, delivering lectures along the way.

The primary purpose of his journey was to arouse interest in and raise funds for the National Trust of Great Britain. His lectures generally addressed the issues of the arts and crafts movement and related subjects such as city planning and architecture.[55] Ashbee reported that he "addressed altogether ten meetings in Chicago."[56] An early lecture was at Hull-House, where he met Frank Lloyd Wright during dinner. They became friends and Wright served as host and guide during his visit. Most of what they saw, of course, was Wright's own work. Ashbee was particularly impressed with the Joseph W. Husser House in Buena Park on the North Side of Chicago.[57]

Ashbee spoke to the Illinois Chapter of the AIA on November 26. Later that evening he was a guest of the Chicago Architectural Club at the annual Thanksgiving dinner.[58] The evening, a regular bohemian night, was a resounding success that ended with the entire assemblage rising to sing "God Save the Queen," accompanied by a string band. Ashbee's next meeting with the club, a week later on December 5, was not as successful.

The Chicago Architectural Club was host to what became Ashbee's most talked-about lecture in Chicago. He was to speak on "The Work and Object of the National Trust for Places of Historic Interest or Beauty" at Fullerton Hall at the Art Institute of Chicago.[59] He addressed what began as a packed house, starting with some rather innocuous comments about Chicago and its cultural assets, or lack of same, but soon digressing into a diatribe concerning a "nameless" city. He stated that "this city, typifies all that a city should not be. Her citizens are all that true citizens should not be. Her two rivers are covered with the slime of factory refuse. Soft coal is burned and chimneys tall and unsightly belch forth a pall of filth. The citizens care not for improving the conditions of the metropolis, which has more than a million souls, but tell you, on the contrary, that they intend to stay only long enough to make their fortunes and then move to a pleasanter place—New York or some other City."[60] He continued in this vein for some time. His audience assumed that the nameless city was Chicago. He had, of course, been visiting for several weeks. When the lights were turned down to show the stereopticon views, more than half the audience got up and left in anger. Only a handful were still present when the lights came back on and Ashbee told them that he had been referring to Pittsburgh, not Chicago. Later, during another lecture, "he discussed the misunderstanding, but gave no quarter—it was the Chicagoans who had thought he meant them."[61] It was their error, he felt, not his!

In the end, Ashbee's trip to Chicago was not a total failure. Eleven civic groups formed a loose association to "apply the principles of the National Trust to the conditions of Chicago, and affiliate with or send representatives to the Central American Council in Washington whenever that should be formed . . . Several ladies and gentlemen also joined the informal committee, and Mr. Frank Lloyd Wright, one of the

*Charles Robert Ashbee (PC)*

54. The best and most reliable study of Ashbee (1863–1942) is Alan Crawford, *C. R. Ashbee: Architect, Designer & Romantic Socialist* (New Haven: Yale University Press, 1985).

55. Ashbee's trip is described in detail in *A Report by Mr. C. R. Ashbee to the Council of the National Trust for Places of Historic Interest and Natural Beauty, on his visit to the United States in the Council's Behalf, October, MDCCCC, to February, MDCCCCI* (Essex House, March 1901).

56. Ibid., 10.

57. This was recorded in Ashbee's journal on December 8, 1900.

58. *Inland Architect* 36, no. 5 (December 1900): 39.

59. His lecture was announced in both the *Chicago Chronicle* and the *Chicago Times Herald* on December 2, 1900.

60. *Chicago Tribune*, December 6, 1900. The lecture was reported in several other Chicago newspapers as well.

61. Crawford, *C. R. Ashbee*, 97.

leading spirits among the younger architects, and of whose work the city may well be proud, was appointed secretary."[62] Ashbee left Chicago shortly after his unfortunate experience at the Chicago Architectural Club. He would continue to correspond with and meet Frank Lloyd Wright from time to time for more than thirty years.[63]

✳

After the election of officers on October 1, the Chicago Architectural Club focused on preparing the syllabus for the coming year. (No copy of that document has surfaced, but it is possible to reconstruct the activities of the club through published notices of its events.) By the end of October, the syllabus was set. It was to follow, generally, the pattern of the previous year with four meetings each month. The first Monday would be a lecture, the second a smoker, usually with sketching and criticism of competition work, the third a second lecture, and the fourth a bohemian night. Classes continued to be offered in sketching and watercolor, and competitions were a regular feature. The club also offered its services to the City of Chicago for the design of shelters and enclosures for five public playgrounds, an initiative undoubtedly prompted by the completion of the shelter designed by Birch Burdette Long the year before. The work was delegated to Messrs. Perkins, Llewellyn, Spencer, Holsman, F. M. Garden, Fellows, Long, Watson, and Lilleskau.

The meetings at which competitions were critiqued or announced were the most heavily attended. Early in 1901 it was announced that the Thomas Moulding Company had "offered $50 for prizes in a competition for design of a city clubhouse. The competition will be conducted under the general code governing competitions in design of the club."[64] The design was to incorporate "litholite," a cast material made up of crushed stone and portland cement. The drawings were due before six o'clock on March 8, and the awards were made on March 18. The first prize of twenty-five dollars went to Alfred S. Alschuler, the second (fifteen dollars) to Birch B. Long, and the third (ten dollars) to Paul V. Hyland.[65] None was ever identified in any publication as the winner of the competition.[66] Those prizewinners were somewhat overshadowed by the results of the Annual Traveling Scholarship Competition Awards, which were announced the same evening. The latter was, by far, the most prestigious and important competition for 1900–1901.

During the fall of 1900, there had been a major effort to establish a Scholarship Committee and an Annual Traveling Scholarship prize of $250.[67] This fund started a tradition that would last for nearly forty years, providing money for a member to travel in Europe. The recipient was to be selected through competition. The first year it involved a five-stage program for "the residence of an American Minister in an important foreign city."[68] The program was distributed to the members in October of 1900, but it was first published in the catalog of the Fourteenth Annual Exhibition in 1901, in a section at the end titled "Announcement."[69] Here, the final title of the competition was "A United States Embassy in a European Capital." The intent was to defray the expenses of the winner on a European tour devoted to architectural study. The club appropriated $250 in prize money. This amount was to be appropriated annually, although in later years it grew larger. For the first year, George R. Dean subscribed an additional fifty dollars, and William Bryce Mundie added another twenty-five, for a total award of $325.

The first Annual Traveling Scholarship Competition involved an elaborate series of design problems extending over five months, with a separate sub-competition each month, the subject in each case being a part of the larger problem. There were separate critics each month. The subjects included a block plan of buildings and grounds (critic, Dwight H. Perkins); entrance gates (critic, George R. Dean); plans

62. *A Report by Mr. C. R. Ashbee,* 10. This was also reported in a number of Chicago newspapers, but with the name of the secretary listed either as "Frank D. Wright" or "Frank D. White." It seems certain that Frank Lloyd Wright was the correct name and that the other names were simply errors.

63. There are several pieces of correspondence in the Taliesin archives between the two men.

64. *Inland Architect* 37, no. 2 (March 1901): 16.

65. *Construction News* (March 23, 1901): 184.

66. There is an illustration in the *Chicago Architectural Annual* for 1902 of a "Suggestion for Treatment of the Garden, Standard Club," which appears to meet the Thomas Moulding Company Competition specifications. The caption reads: "Scheme for the treatment of the interior court of a city club house, to be executed in cement and enamelled tiles with a tiled floor and the columns in grey limestone." The author of the drawing is not named.

67. *Brickbuilder* 9, no. 11 (November 1900): 237.

68. *Carpentry and Building* (December 1900): 322–23.

69. The only copy of that program to survive was printed in the *Catalogue of the Fourteenth Annual Exhibition.*

and elevations of buildings (critics, James Gamble Rogers and Frank Lloyd Wright); interiors of a ballroom and a grand hall (critics, Louis J. Millet, Edward G. Garden and Louis H. Sullivan); and a bird's-eye view of buildings and grounds (critics, Robert C. Spencer Jr., professor Seth Temple, and Louis H. Sullivan). Once a month, the most recent competition drawings were hung for judgment. The critics, who had already had an opportunity to study the designs, reviewed the drawings before the assembled membership. The subject was then open for discussion, and a ballot was taken.

Five members of the club survived the five-month Traveling Scholarship Competition. From the first, the interest was intense. The jurying and balloting were held at every mid-month meeting starting in November. There were more than a dozen serious competitors and the voting was close. Several dropped out as the competition progressed. On the last evening of judgment, in mid-March, five members were still in the running. The winners were chosen by an elaborate point system. N. Max Dunning (who received twenty-one points) took first honors with John H. Phillips (seventeen points) coming in second. William E. Drummond (sixteen points) took a close third place. Thomas E. Tallmadge (seven points) and Birch Burdette Long (six points) were fourth and fifth.[70] The final vote was reported in the *Inland Architect* as follows: "Nelson Max Dunning was the successful competitor in the traveling scholarship competition of the Chicago Architectural Club, having received the largest average of votes in the four [*sic*] competitions . . . The competition was ably contested and was the subject of intense interest and discussion during the winter months, and called forth all the abilities of the contestants. Mr. Dunning's brilliant victory was closely contested by John H. Phillips, William E. Drummond, Burch Burdette Long and T. E. Tallmadge, who completed the series, the pace having left by the wayside half a dozen others who appeared in the first of the series."[71]

The scholarship competition occupied a good deal of the club's time during the fall of 1900 and the early months of 1901, but it was not the members' only activity. Other events that took place in the 1900–1901 year included several informal evenings, or smokers, at which various questions were raised in preparation for the debates that were expected to be held at the Third Annual Convention of the Architectural League of America in Philadelphia later in the year. The principal concern of the members was the value of an architectural education as it was then conceived. The members were still involved in practical matters, but as a group they were beginning to realize that the architecture of the future would evolve from sophisticated discussions and debates of theory and philosophy. There was no lack of interest.

At the turn of the century, the Chicago Architectural Club was prepared to address problems of the profession far beyond local issues.

70. The most comprehensive announcement of the competition and its winners was in *Construction News* (March 23, 1901): 184.

71. *Inland Architect* 37, no. 3 (April 1901): 24.

*This extraordinary drawing by Louis H. Sullivan was used as the frontispiece of the 1902* Chicago Architectural Annual, *published by the Chicago Architectural Club. Sullivan's monogram is centered near the base of the drawing (CAC/02)*

# Steinway Hall and the Traveling Scholarship

CHAPTER TWELVE

The beginning of the twentieth century found the Chicago Architectural Club alive, well, and flourishing. There were 152 members, including ninety active residents, sixteen nonresidents, thirty-three associate members, and thirteen honorary members. They had excellent quarters at the Art Institute of Chicago and their weekly programs, classes, competitions, and planning for the annual exhibition were more than enough to keep them busy. The officers and committee members were now drawn largely from the young men who had offices at Steinway Hall, or from the Eighteen who met from time to time at informal luncheons to discuss and argue about architecture. Those debates were to have a profound effect on the emerging modern movement in architecture, the activities of the Chicago Architectural Club in general, and Frank Lloyd Wright's contribution to the club in particular.

This group of architects had come together in 1897 after Dwight Perkins asked his friends Myron Hunt, Robert Spencer, and Frank Lloyd Wright to join him and others in his office and loft space at the top of Steinway Hall. Shortly thereafter, the Chicago Arts and Crafts Society was formed at Hull-House, and several of these young men, their wives, and others were instrumental in founding it. Others gravitated to the core group and together they, through the Chicago Architectural Club, created a platform for discussion that, combined with the presentations and rebuttals at the 1899 and 1900 conventions of the Architectural League of America, brought the search for an American architecture into focus.

Louis Sullivan had been the acknowledged leader in innovative architecture in Chicago for more than a decade. He had written and spoken widely on his theories and had become highly respected, particularly among younger practitioners. Virtually every public speech concerning the infant modern movement then developing in Chicago cited Sullivan's leadership. He was always present, in spirit if not in person, at the luncheon debates of the Eighteen. He spoke, by proxy, at the first convention of the Architectural League of America in Cleveland. (H. Webster Tomlinson read his speech in his absence.) Sullivan spoke twice again at the second league convention in Chicago in 1900.

The question had been raised after the 1899 league convention as to whether or not there was an American architecture, and if so, what exactly it was and where it was headed. Between conventions, the debate was kicked off by George R. Dean, who wrote several articles culminating in "Progress before Precedent," published

*Logo designed by Robert C. Spencer Jr. used by the Chicago Architectural Club for over a decade in the early twentieth century*

1. *Brickbuilder* 9, no. 5 (May 1900): 91–97.

2. Elmer Grey did not represent a club at the convention, as Milwaukee didn't yet have such a group. Grey often participated in the affairs of the Chicago Architectural Club.

3. *Brickbuilder* 9, no. 6 (June 1900): 113.

4. *Inland Architect* 35, no. 5 (June 1900): 42–43.

5. *Hull-House Bulletin* 2, no. 7 (November 1897): 1. Notice of it appeared under the heading "Public Entertainments."

6. The first notice of that constitution was published in *Hull-House Bulletin* (January–February 1898): 11–12. Excerpts were included under the heading "General Societies." The full document was published in the *Catalogue of the Eleventh Annual Exhibition of the Chicago Architectural Club* on page 118. It was noted that it was adopted on October 31, 1897.

7. This lecture, which Wright had delivered previously in slightly different forms, was a major effort on his part. He continued to use it in various forms for the rest of his life. There have been several analyses of "The Art and Craft of the Machine"; the two most useful are Martha Pollak, ed., *The Education of the Architect* (Cambridge, MA: MIT Press, 1997), 3–36, and Margaret G. Klinkow, "Frank Lloyd Wright's Art and Craft of the Machine, 1897–1902" (master's thesis, University of Illinois, 1997).

8. *The Catalogue of the Fourteenth Annual Exhibition* gives the delivery date as March 6. Other data, including Jane Addams's diary, indicate that it was actually given on March 1.

in May of 1900,[1] which had set the stage for further debate at the 1900 convention in Chicago. Most of the presentations in Chicago were directed at the current state of architecture in America. Two themes, practice and education, were at the forefront. A speech by Elmer Grey of Milwaukee[2] had "struck the keynote that aroused an enthusiastic spirit early in the convention, an interest, moreover, which was sustained to the hour of adjournment."[3] It was this talk that had prompted Louis Sullivan to comment extemporaneously on the state of architecture. Fortunately, his remarks were recorded.[4] Sullivan had spoken again at the closing of the convention. Immediately following his first speech, Frank Lloyd Wright had given a presentation he called "The Architect." He believed that it was time for architects to become thoroughly professional, and his remarks were part of a philosophy that had been developing during the previous seven years.

After Wright had left the office of Adler & Sullivan in late 1893, he had begun formulating a personal approach to architecture. He did not do this in a vacuum. He, of course, had the advantage of countless late-night discussions with Louis Sullivan in the Auditorium Tower. Much of his philosophy was refined over lunch with his colleagues who made up the Eighteen. Dwight Perkins, George Dean, Robert Spencer, Myron Hunt, and Charles Zueblin all participated in these discussions, which were not always amicable. Zueblin in particular often disagreed with Wright and Dean, but his approach helped to move the discussion along. It was Dean and Spencer who generally sided with Wright and, through their writings, spread the word of the early modern movement. Wright's proselytism had begun a short time before the formation of the Arts and Crafts Society of Chicago. His first public lecture outlining his basic philosophy, "Use of Machinery," had been delivered at Hull-House on October 31, 1897.[5] The constitution of the Arts and Crafts Society was adopted the same evening.[6] Its language had clearly been influenced by Wright's speech and, in fact, it is likely that he had had a hand in its preparation. In effect, it supported the idea of handicrafts but recognized the need for machines.

Wright's 1897 speech and the Arts and Crafts Society's constitution had laid the groundwork for his major address at Hull-House, "The Art and Craft of the Machine."[7] That speech was delivered on March 1, 1901.[8] He gave it again with minor variations to the Western Society of Engineers on March 20, a week before the opening of the Chicago Architectural Club's Fourteenth Annual Exhibition. The entire text of the speech at Hull-House was printed in the catalog of the exhibition.

The most elegant of any of the club's catalogs to date, it was oblong and bound in brown paper over boards with a decorative tan wraparound paper with the title, the club logo in white highlights, and the outline stamped in gold. The previous year's cover, designed by Robert C. Spencer Jr., was to have been used on future catalogs, but only the logo—a circle enclosed in a square incorporating the letters *CAC*—was used from the previous year. The body of the book was printed on coated beige paper with red highlights on the title page and the initial letter of the opening paragraph of Wright's essay, which began on the twelfth unnumbered page.

The 1901 catalog was very different from the 1900 catalog, which had been well received by most media critics, but severely criticized by architect George Dean, primarily because of its illustrations. Much of the work shown in the 1900 exhibition was traditional, and the avant-garde work (except for that of Frank Lloyd Wright) was ignored both by the press and in the catalog. The 1901 catalog was assembled by a board of editors chaired by Hugh M. G. Garden, with Dwight Perkins and Robert Spencer assisting. There was a six-man Exhibition Committee chaired by Walter H. Kleinpell and a Jury of Admission made up of the Exhibition Committee and the board of editors. The Hanging Committee was the same, with the addition of Birch Burdette Long and N. Max Dunning. Nearly all these men

*"Proposed Peristyle and Arch at the Foot of Market Street, San Francisco," the first full-page illustration in the 1901 catalog (CAC/01)*

*Birch Burdette Long's title page drawing for the 1901 exhibition catalog, clearly influenced by Japanese prints (CAC/01)*

were drawn from the officers and directors of the Chicago Architectural Club who, in turn, were primary participants in the Eighteen luncheon group and/or had offices in Steinway Hall. George Dean had suggested a year earlier that "the club should appoint each year men of discernment and innate artistic worth, men capable of forming a heart judgment, men who know a good thing, whose duty it shall be to search out those things which have merit, and on the walls and in the book give them such place that the public may feel the importance of the movement and know for what the club stands." From the point of view of those who practiced in the "new movement," Dean got his wish. Both the catalog and the exhibition, for the first time, reflected the thinking and the architecture of the Young Turks of Chicago.

The 1901 catalog opened with a tiny pencil-sketch frontispiece by Harvey Ellis, followed by a poster designed by Claude Fayette Bragdon. Their appearance reflected the broadening influence of the Chicago Architectural Club. Neither was a Chicagoan, but their work was very much in the spirit of the men in control of the exhibition. The title page, in two colors, was designed by Birch Burdette Long. It incorporated a drawing titled "The Garden—A Decoration," which was shown at the exhibition. It was clearly done in the style of a Japanese print and was probably influenced by Frank Lloyd Wright. (Long was, at that time, one of those sharing office space with Perkins, Wright, and others at Steinway Hall.) The next four pages of the catalog listed the various committees, club officers, and two pages of "Patrons of the Exhibition." San Francisco architect Willis Polk got the following two pages, showing his drawings of a "Proposed Peristyle and Arch at the Foot of Market Street, San Francisco."[9] The following twenty-two pages were devoted to Wright's "The Art and Craft of the Machine." The next fifty-four pages were illustrations from the exhibition. Two of the last six pages were devoted to an "Announcement" that described the terms of the five-month-long competition for "A United States Embassy in a European Capital." The final pages of the catalog listed all the members of the Chicago Architectural Club. With each copy came a smaller booklet titled *Catalog of Exhibits and Supplementary List of Patrons.*[10] It had no illustrations but contained a complete list of all the exhibitors and their entries, 393 in all, plus a supplementary list of patrons not included in the main catalog.

9. William Jefferson Polk (1867–1924) was born in Jacksonville, Illinois. He soon moved to St. Louis, where he was apprenticed to architect J. B. Legg while he was still a child. He began designing buildings as a teenager and, between 1885 and 1900, was essentially an itinerant architect. Although he had little formal education, he was an excellent designer and a superb delineator. During the 1890s, he did a great deal of work in San Francisco, and in 1901 he joined D. H. Burnham and Company in Chicago, where he remained for two years. He became a member of the CAC in 1901. He left Chicago in 1903 and spent two years studying in Paris. Upon his return, he became manager of Burnham's San Francisco office. He left around 1910 and ran his own practice until his death in 1924.

10. This small catalog (sixteen unnumbered pages) was probably given away to visitors at the exhibition. The official catalog had to be purchased and its price, fifty cents, was apparently more than most people wished to spend.

The content of both the catalog and the exhibition was very different from that of the year before. Of the sixty-six illustrations in the catalog, nearly half were done by Chicagoans, mostly members of the club. Only about a third were traditional. The exhibition itself had a similar proportion of work from young Chicago practitioners. Richard Bock, Lawrence Buck, Frost & Granger, Myron Hunt, Nimmons & Fellows, and Dwight Perkins all had several exhibits. Louis Sullivan, Hugh Garden, Robert Spencer, George Maher, and Pond & Pond were all represented, in some cases by multiple examples in a special room devoted to Chicago architects. Examples of "circuit drawings" from other clubs affiliated with the Architectural League of America were also included.

The exhibition opened on March 28, 1901 and, generally speaking, the reviews were positive. Typical of those reviews was one that appeared in the *Brickbuilder*.[11] The author wrote that: While the number of exhibits is less than in recent years, the standard of quality is high and presents unusual interest and variety. There are comparatively few *projets* from the schools which usually take up much space and do not greatly interest the average visitor. Chicago has a room of selected drawings, the well-known contributors being Mr. Sullivan, with photographs of the Guaranty and Condict Buildings, his cottage at Ocean Springs, Miss., and a very fiercely polychromatic Russian Church in blue, purple, scarlet, and gold; Birch Long's imaginary garden, embassy gates, and Jackson Park sketches show a charming originality and artistic feeling; Hugh Garden's little theater and country house are particularly nice, both in design and drawing. They are in marked contrast to the design he exhibited in 1900 of a house for Charles H. Hodges; Richard Schmidt's hospital, drawn by Mr. Garden, is a very dignified and restrained piece of design, somewhat suggestive of 'the new movement'; and Mr. Spencer and Pond & Pond have some characteristic country houses.[12] He went on to say "The feature of the exhibition is undoubtedly the collection of drawings from San Francisco, chiefly contributed by Willis K. Polk. There are also a number of interesting things from Bliss & Faville and Coxhead & Coxhead. The star drawing is Mr. Polk's line rendering, a very large bird's-eye of the proposed peristyle at the foot of Market Street . . . The

11. *Brickbuilder* 10, no. 4 (April 1901) 85–86.

12. Sullivan's "fiercely polychromatic" drawing, no longer extant, was of the Holy Trinity Russian Orthodox Cathedral still standing at 1121 North Leavitt in Chicago. There is a second, much more muted, drawing of the cathedral still hanging in the rectory at the site. For a detailed discussion of the cathedral, see Theodore Turak, "A Celt Among Slavs: Louis Sullivan's Holy Trinity Cathedral," *Prairie School Review* 9, no. 4 (1972): 5–22.

*Drawing of Louis Sullivan's Holy Trinity Russian Orthodox Church from the 1901 CAC exhibition; the building is still standing in Chicago, although its exterior surfaces have a simpler finish (AIC/SC)*

*Hugh Garden's rendering for his design of a theater in Marion, Illinois (CAC/01)*

*Hugh Garden's design for Charles H. Hodges, exhibited in 1900 (Michael Levitin and Meredith Wise/Mendes)*

*Hugh Garden's design for a house in Highland Park, Illinois (note his monogram at lower right); this and his theater design both show the influence of Japanese prints (CAC/01)*

city and hills beyond are managed with unusual artistic skill and a remarkably clever technique. Altogether the club is very grateful to Mr. Polk."[13] (It is likely that Polk was also responsible for getting California architects Bliss & Faville and Coxhead & Coxhead to show their work.) Just why Polk's work was so attractive to Chicagoans is difficult to understand since it was essentially traditional in form and spirit. Nevertheless, Robert C. Spencer was prompted to comment in his review in *Brush and Pencil* that "from a pictorial standpoint, the collection of drawings contributed by Willis Polk, of San Francisco, attracted more attention . . . [by Chicagoans] than anything from the hands of their colleagues. For boldness, freedom, and beauty of technique, without hard contrast or forced effects, they have not been surpassed by any American architect."[14] Several other reviews in the local press and the national architectural journals had similar comments. In retrospect, the most surprising thing about the reviews was the almost complete lack of critical comment on the drawings for the club's first Traveling Scholarship Competition. It was an incredible oversight.

13. Polk had come to Chicago in March to meet D. H. Burnham and discuss job opportunities. The twenty-one drawings he exhibited were representative of the work he had done during the previous decade on the West Coast, which he had undoubtedly brought to Chicago to show Burnham. It seems likely that they were last-minute additions to the exhibition and the catalog.

14. *Brush and Pencil* 8, no. 2 (May 1901): 114.

*The entrance to Birch Burdette Long's fourth-place design for the 1901 Traveling Scholarship Competition, shown in the 1902 catalog (CAC/02)*

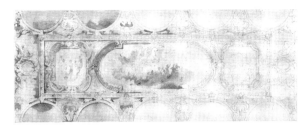

*Four designs for the ballroom of "A United States Embassy for a European Capital," all submitted for the first Traveling Scholarship Competition: from the left, first-place drawing by Nelson Max Dunning; second place by John H. Phillip; third place by William Drummond; and fifth place by Thomas Eddy Tallmadge (CAC/01)*

Four of the five finalists in the First Annual Traveling Scholarship Competition—Dunning, Phillips, Drummond, and Tallmadge—each showed three of their drawings in the exhibition, and they all rated a prominent place in the catalog. The renderings of the "Ball Room" done by each commanded a full page. The drawing of the first-place winner, N. Max Dunning, was perhaps the least impressive. Like the drawings of Phillips and Drummond, it was Sullivanesque in character. Tallmadge's fifth-place drawing was much more traditional. All were clearly influenced by the Auditorium dining room. Perhaps they had heard that Sullivan would be jurying that portion of the competition.

The perspectives and site plans of the finalists were exhibited in the 1901 exhibition, but were not published in the catalog. For reasons never made clear, the only work of the competition winner, N. Max Dunning, that was illustrated was the ballroom perspective. Birch Burdette Long's fourth-place design was recognized in 1902 with an illustration of his drawing of "An American Embassy, The Entrance," but none of his other drawings was published. The plans prepared by second- and third-place competitors Phillips and Drummond were published in the catalog for 1902, titled the *Chicago Architectural Annual*.[15]

The published work of Phillips and Drummond deserves some attention. The plans of these two entries were very different. Phillips provided an H-shaped configuration on a site that fronted a large body of water. The site was rectangular with what appears to be the ambassador's residence at the rear, facing an expansive garden at the side of the embassy. A smaller garden was located at the back of the embassy. The formal entrance to the embassy was on the water side of the site with a minor entry on the short side of the property and a driveway with a porte cochere entrance on the opposite side in the center of the site. The raised central portion of the embassy was intended to be extremely formal with access to the garden in the rear. The rooms were essentially symmetrical except for the ballroom, which occupied one wing of the H-shaped plan. The surviving drawing of the ballroom is, perhaps, the most Sullivanesque of the published interior drawings of this space. There are two other large rooms and a number of smaller rooms on this level.

15. The 1902 catalog was one of the club's most elaborate publications. It included several items shown in the 1901 exhibition, in addition to drawings from the First Annual Traveling Scholarship Competition.

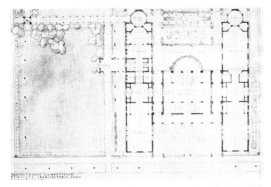

*John H. Phillips's plan for his 1901 Traveling Scholarship Competition entry*

Apparently the offices and working spaces were on the lower level. No plan of that level has survived.

William Drummond's plan took a different approach. The site appears to front on a river or canal, with the primary entrance on the other side. The plan is much less formal, with the ambassador's residence sited in the same manner as in the Phillips plan. Drummond provided for two areas of lawn, the smaller highly formalized and the larger with a grove opposite the ambassador's residence. The primary entrance appears to have had a rather tight carriageway for visitors. There were two other carriage entries, one that led to a porte cochere and the ambassador's residence, and another that permitted guests to enter the embassy under cover at what really was the rear of the property on the ground level. Drummond's published plan was only the ground level. There were at least two other levels, including the central ballroom wing, an octagon lighted all around with clerestory windows. All in all, the Drummond plan is an exercise in geometry, with various volumetric shapes that seem to be placed to complete both a two- and three-dimensional design as much as to satisfy the needs of the building's occupants. Nevertheless, it would have been a handsome structure very much in the spirit, if not the sophistication, of the Chicago's early modern movement and the work of Louis Sullivan.

Louis Sullivan, his philosophy, and his architecture were all very much on the minds of Chicago's architects during late 1900 and early 1901, while the Traveling Scholarship Competition was under way. Sullivan had instigated a debate on the teaching and development of an American architecture at the organizational meet-

*John H. Phillips's perspective of his second-place entry in the 1901 Traveling Scholarship Competition for a United States embassy (CAC/02)*

*William Drummond's design took third place in the 1901 Traveling Scholarship Competition (CAC/02)*

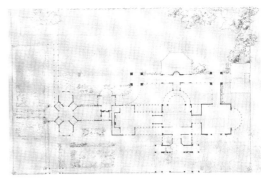

*William Drummond's plan for his 1901 Traveling Scholarship Competition entry*

ing of the Architectural League of America in Cleveland in 1899. His short but eloquent essay, "The Modern Phase of Architecture," had been received with great enthusiasm by nearly all those present. Basically, he had been telling his younger colleagues that they needed to take a new approach to architecture. During the following two years, a number of young men, including George Dean, Robert Spencer, Elmer Grey, and Frank Lloyd Wright, had taken up the challenge of defining just what the proper course of education for an architect should be. During the 1900–01 year, the Chicago Architectural Club devoted an inordinate amount of time to preparing to debate two important questions at the 1901 convention of the Architectural League of America. Those questions, noted in the "Announcement" section of the 1901 exhibition catalog, were:

1.  Is it advisable that the architectural student devote the time necessary to obtain a so-called classical education as a foundation for refined culture and taste, or can the same refinement be gained by studies more closely allied to architecture?
2.  a. Should architectural design and the study of historic styles follow and be based upon a knowledge of pure design?
    b. How can pure design be best studied?

The "Announcement" went on to say, "And as these touch what is fast becoming the 'sore spot' of architectural education in America, it has not been difficult to arouse interest. It is proposed to publish the debates on this and the other questions proposed by the Educational Committee of the League, in the hope that these much-mooted problems may be either solved or answered."

By the end of the nineteenth century, Louis Sullivan had become obsessed with the idea that in order have a "modern" architecture, the teaching of architecture must be changed. Even before his thought-provoking essay had been presented to the Cleveland assembly, he had been communicating his ideas to the young architects of Chicago. For example, on January 23, 1899, he had addressed the Chicago Architectural Club on "The Principles of Architectural Design."[16] It was a subject he felt he understood and he had wanted very much to convey his thoughts to his younger colleagues. The following year he had spoken twice at the Chicago convention of the Architectural League of America, delivering his now-famous

16. *Brickbuilder* 8, no. 2 (February 1899): 22.

lecture "To the Young Man in Architecture." During the remaining months of 1900, Sullivan had essentially divorced himself from the American Institute of Architects. He had refused, not too politely, a request to speak at the next AIA convention. The AIA had made a second overture and Sullivan had replied, "Until the AIA puts itself squarely on record as an advocate of advanced thinking . . . until it indicates clearly that it is alive and stands for realities, not figments, symbols or simulacre, that it desires to stand not as a lethargic and repressive but as a liberating and upbuilding force, I choose to take no part in its councils."[17] Sullivan had continued his letter-writing battle with various members of the AIA for several months. His attention had been diverted in late 1900 when he had been "discovered" by a new Chicago journal called the *Interstate Architect & Builder*.[18] The journal had published a number of Sullivan's letters and illustrated several of his works during the last few months of 1900. In December of that year it had agreed to publish fifty-two of his articles on American architecture. These "Kindergarten Chats" became Sullivan's magnum opus. The first chapter had appeared in the February 16, 1901, issue a few weeks before the Chicago Architectural Club's Fourteenth Annual Exhibition opened. (It is tempting to suggest that Sullivan had tried out some of his thoughts on members of the Steinway Hall group or the Eighteen.) The "Chats" appeared weekly in the *Interstate Architect & Builder* until February 8, 1902, but they received little attention from the architectural press, a disappointment to Sullivan, who had expected them to become the basis for a new educational system for young architects who would develop a modern American architecture. It is, however, virtually certain that the "Chats" were read by the leaders of the Chicago Architectural Club. When they first appeared, the club was already preparing for the debate on education at the next convention of the Architectural League of America.

❖

While the Fourteenth Annual Exhibition was still under way, the club leaders proceeded to make two major changes to their constitution: they moved the annual meeting and election of officers to the first Monday in May and reduced the number of members on the Executive Committee to five officers and two others. (The number of regular meetings was also reduced to two each month.) The new constitution was approved on April 8, 1901.[19] Accordingly, on the first Monday in May 1901, the club elected Robert C. Spencer Jr. president, and Emil Lorch and E. C. Hemmings first and second vice presidents, respectively. John H. Phillips was chosen as secretary and Adolph F. Bernhard as treasurer. Robert E. Bourke and Thomas E. Tallmadge filled out the Executive Committee. The committee immediately began to outline "a program for next year's work [to be] undertaken at once . . . that the members may take it up in earnest early in the fall."[20]

Following the annual meeting and election of officers, retiring president Henry K. Holsman presented an "annual report" to the membership.[21] He spoke at some length regarding the work of the club during the previous year. He was pleased with the increase in membership and the participation of the members in the affairs of the club, but he was upset that Charles Ashbee, in his report to the British National Trust, had not "remembered the cordiality of the Architectural Club." Holsman ended his remarks on a more positive note. The same article noted that he was "about to address a communication to Andrew Carnegie with a view to obtaining an endowment for a permanent traveling scholarship large enough to enable a student to spend a year or two in architectural study abroad. The fund is to be administered and competed for under the rules of the Architectural Club. Mr. Holsman believes such a prize is within the lines of Mr. Carnegie's benefactions,

17. This quotation is from a letter to AIA secretary Glenn Brown, from Louis Sullivan, dated July 25, 1900, now in the archives of the American Institute of Architects in Washington, D.C.

18. The *Interstate Architect & Builder* was published in Chicago in between 1898 and 1903.

19. The change in the constitution was not published in any of the usual journals. It is noted in the *Charter, Constitution, By-Laws, House Rules, Officers and Members of the Chicago Architectural Club*.

20. Construction News (May 11, 1901): 303.

21. *Construction News* (June 1, 1901).

and for this reason he thinks that it is possible that it will be granted." No such grant was ever forthcoming. Nevertheless, the membership of the club and a number of local benefactors took it upon themselves to support the Annual Traveling Scholarship Competition for the next three decades. In the meantime, the officers and several key members of the club were devoting more and more time to the question of how architecture should be taught.

The debate regarding how to teach architecture, particularly "pure design," which was expected at the forthcoming meeting of the Architectural League of America in Philadelphia, had not been taken up by the Chicago club by mere chance. The club had been assigned the subject by the Committee on Education of the league after the 1900 convention in Chicago, probably at the suggestion of the league's Executive Committee, which was made up of Chicagoans, all active members of the club. Joseph C. Llewellyn was president, and he was assisted by Hugh M. G. Garden, Richard G. Schmidt, Emil Lorch, and Robert C. Spencer Jr. The league's Committee on Education did not include any Chicagoans. It was a three-man group consisting of Albert Kelsey of Philadelphia, professor James M. White from the University of Illinois, and John Watrous Case of Detroit, who served as chairman. In an article published in May before the convention, Robert C. Spencer Jr. noted that the Committee on Education had assigned special topics to various clubs for discussion.[22] He went on to say, "To New York, Philadelphia, and Chicago were assigned the questions, 'Should the study of architectural design and of the historic styles follow and be based upon a knowledge of pure design?' and 'How can pure design best be studied?' An interesting evening was spent at the club not long ago in discussing these questions, which are awakening a powerful interest among the younger men in the profession, and . . . at Philadelphia . . . Chicago will advocate the affirmative, as opposed to the present methods of the leading architectural schools here and abroad."

Emil Lorch, who identified himself as being from both Detroit and Chicago, was a prime mover of the discussions in Chicago prior to the convention. This was probably due, in part, to an interest in education fostered by his work with some of the faculty of the Chicago School of Architecture.[23] Lorch spoke to the Chicago Architectural Club on March 4, 1901, on "A New Departure in Study of Architectural Design."[24] He revised that paper and delivered it to the assembled convention of the Architectural League of America in Philadelphia on May 24, 1901. The *Inland Architect* recognized the importance of Lorch's leadership in the campaign to improve architectural education. In June of 1901, it reported, "under the leadership of Mr. Emil Lorch, for the past two years, the League has devoted much attention to the discussion of the necessity for the study of pure design in architectural education in place of the time-honored practice of training the student along classical and historical lines . . . the questions formulated by the Committee on Education [essentially an expanded version of those published in the Chicago exhibition catalog] were sent to a number of the best-known exponents in the field of architectural education." Several responses were received, the most pertinent being those from C. Howard Walker, Arthur W. Dow, and Denman W. Ross, all respected practitioners in the field of design. Dow and Ross responded jointly, and their comments were published by the *Inland Architect* along with several papers on the subject presented at the convention. Following Lorch's paper were others by Robert C. Spencer Jr. for Chicago, Julius F. Harder for the New York Architectural League, William Rae for Toronto's Architectural Eighteen Club, and J. W. Case for the Detroit Architectural Club.

22. Robert C. Spencer Jr., "The Work of the Younger Architects," *Brush and Pencil* 7, no. 2 (May 1900): 113–20.

23. Emil Lorch joined the staff of the Art Institute of Chicago in 1899 as secretary to director W. M. R. French. He was not directly involved with the institute's School of Architecture, but he made several efforts to influence the way design was taught. He was close friends with Louis J. Millet, dean of the school, and Louis Sullivan. Lorch and Sullivan shared an interest in "modernizing" architectural education. In the spring of 1901, the school's advisory group of architects (Burnham, Shaw, Rogers, Frost, and Coolidge) led a campaign to replace Lorch and some time later he left Chicago.

24. *Brush and Pencil* 8, no. 5 (August 1901): 253–62. The paper was published earlier, in somewhat different form, as delivered to the convention in Philadelphia, in *Inland Architect* 37, no. 5 (June 1901): 34. It was what led to the "interesting evening" Spencer referred to in his article. The March 4 meeting was reported in advance in *Construction News* (March 2, 1901): 133.

*Emil G. Lorch*

Despite the anticipation and preparation for a debate on the subject by the Chicago representatives, it did not happen. All the papers presented were, to some degree at least, in agreement that architectural education needed to be refined, but none of the papers gave concrete ideas of how this was to be done. The recorded minutes of the convention do not mention any debate whatsoever. Incredibly, the subject disappeared from the journals and Louis Sullivan was left to continue a lonely campaign for educating "the young man in architecture" by means of his "Kindergarten Chats," which were published in the *Interstate Architect & Builder* until early 1902.[25]

Just why the issue was not pursued by the Architectural League of America, or for that matter the Chicago Architectural Club, has never been explained. Emil Lorch lost his position at the Art Institute of Chicago, and none of the other protagonists was directly involved with an educational institution. A review of the yearbooks of the Chicago School of Architecture indicates that many of the students there during Lorch's tenure and for a while after were influenced by Sullivan's work and the work of the younger architects who were to make up what is today called the Prairie School. The principal techniques used in virtually all the schools at the beginning of the twentieth century were adaptations of the system that had been used so successfully for decades by the École des Beaux-Arts in France. Furthermore, the Society of Beaux-Arts Architects had been organized in New York City in 1894 by former students of the French school. They advocated the Beaux-Arts teaching system, built on a network of ateliers that essentially provided private training, usually under the supervision of a senior practitioner, or patron, in his own office using "programmes" published by the Society of Beaux-Arts Architects.[26] The "students" in ateliers of this kind paid for the privilege of attending.

There was already at least one atelier in Chicago. An announcement in the *Brickbuilder* in early 1900,[27] reported that "Mr. F. J. Fitzwilliam, a former pupil of D'Espouy & De Monclos in Paris, and of Masqueray in New York, has opened in the Auditorium Building, a school for instruction in architectural composition and presentation to be known as the Atelier Fitzwilliam."[28] Four months later it was announced that there was to be a "Special Sketch Competition" at the Fitzwilliam atelier.[29] That announcement stated that the atelier would, "beginning with the month of September, 1900, inaugurate a special nine months' series of sketch problems, which are intended to be worked up spontaneously without criticism." Participants were asked to send their sketches plus a one-dollar entrance fee for the first competition or eight dollars to enter them all. There were to be twenty-five cash prizes, totaling $145, in September. Fitzwilliam obviously expected that enough students would participate to cover the cash prizes and make the atelier profitable. The first sketch problem was "A Fountain Niche." Programs for each month's problem appeared in the next three issues of the *Brickbuilder,* after which no more notices appeared. Apparently, the atelier was not successful. It disappeared in 1901, after several of its students' designs had been shown in the CAC exhibition of 1901. It would be some time before the Chicago Architectural Club established its own atelier.

❋

When the Architectural League of America had completed its work in Philadelphia, its last official act was to reelect Chicago's Joseph C. Llewellyn as president. N. Max Dunning continued as the league's secretary. In accordance with the league's by-laws, Llewellyn then appointed his officers, once more naming Richard E. Schmidt as vice president, Emil Lorch as corresponding secretary, Hugh M. G. Garden as

25. Sullivan tried for years to get his "Kindergarten Chats" published in book form but never succeeded. The book was finally issued in 1934 through the efforts of his literary executor, George Grant Elmslie. Louis H. Sullivan, *Kindergarten Chats, On Architecture, Education, and Democracy,* ed. Claude F. Bragdon (Scarab Fraternity Press, 1934). It was reissued by Wittenborn in 1949 in paperback, and is available today in an edition published by Dover.

26. It is interesting to note that the principal advocates for change—Sullivan, Lorch, Spencer, et al.—had all studied under the Beaux-Arts system either in France or America.

27. *Brickbuilder* 9, no. 4 (April 1900): 82.

28. Little is known of F. J. Fitzwilliam other than the information in the *Brickbuilder* announcement. He was not licensed to practice architecture in Illinois at the time.

29. *Brickbuilder* 9, no. 8 (August 1900): 176.

recording secretary, and August C. Wilmanns as treasurer. Robert C. Spencer Jr. and Newton A. Wells from the University of Illinois were asked to continue serving on the Executive Committee. The league also selected Toronto as the place for the 1902 convention.[30] The 1901 convention was over.

With the Architectural League of America convention behind them and the 1901 exhibition over, the newly elected officers of the Chicago Architectural Club began planning the 1901–2 club year. *Construction News* reported that the principal work of the club after the election was "the arrangement of a program for next year's work, and it is understood that this will be undertaken at once by the executive committee, that the members may take it up in earnest early in the fall. One of the interesting problems which they have under contemplation is a plan for the improvement of the lake front."[31]

The summer of 1901 was one of great activity in the building professions and trades in Chicago. *Construction News* reported that "draughtsmen are in demand in Chicago. The majority of architects are busier than they have been for many years. Young men who were getting $5 a week six months ago are now drawing a salary of $25 . . . Some architects find it necessary to employ at night the forces of other firms who are not so busy . . . There is no indication of a let up soon."[32] In November of the same year, *Carpentry and Building* reported, "With the exception of the year 1892, it is probable that the twelve months of this year will witness a larger volume of business in the building line in the city of Chicago than any corresponding period in the past decade."[33]

This level of work in Chicago was probably the reason that the records of activity by the Chicago Architectural Club for the last half of 1901 are so sketchy. After June of 1901 when the new officers were announced, there were no notices in any of the usual architectural journals concerning the affairs of the club until December, when a brief item in *Construction News* reported that R. M. Combs of the Thomas Moulding Company, James Van Inwegen of the Tiffany Enameled Brick Company, and H. L. Matz of the Chicago Hydraulic Pressed Brick Company had spoken at a regular meeting in early December. It is, however, possible to reconstruct one important activity the club undertook in late 1901.

Following the success of the five-part competition for the club's Annual Traveling Scholarship awarded in 1901, the members elected to have a similar competition in 1901–02. The *Chicago Chronicle* announced in early January of 1902 that the Chicago Automobile Club was planning to build a "country clubhouse several miles from the city."[34] The idea of such a clubhouse had been under consideration for several months, but it was only when the Chicago Architectural Club "offered as a prize for the best specifications for an automobile clubhouse or inn, a trip to Europe" that the plan gained momentum. The rules of the competition stipulated, according to the *Chicago Chronicle,* "that the porches and terraces shall be excellent viewpoints from which to witness the arrival and departure of machines in the club runs and races." The *Chronicle's* article was clearly quoting from the rules of the competition that had been provided to the club's membership. The article described the program for the competition in some detail, noting that "in front of the building the road is to be widened into a plaza to permit the congregation of a large number of vehicles without obstruction of traffic. The building is to face the road, with the main floor porch and terraces located about fifteen feet above the level of the road. A large interior court is to be provided on the level of the road, and if desired there may be passageways under the main floor for the automobiles to reach

30. *Inland Architect* 37, no. 5 (June 1901): 39.

31. *Construction News* (May 11, 1901): 303.

32. *Construction News* (May 25, 1901).

33. *Carpentry and Building* (November 1901): 271.

34. "Auto Club to Build," *Chicago Chronicle,* January 7, 1902.

the court. On the ground floor there is to be a large room or vestibule extending up through the main floor. This room is to be under cover, but open to the air and is to be located on the interior court, about which is to be grouped the stabling accommodations and workshop." The article went on to say that both men and women were to be accommodated in the clubhouse, and that there were to be "storerooms, laundry and boiler room, kitchens, pantries, bedrooms, stalls for the automobiles and places where the machines may be supplied with fresh power, gasoline, steam or electricity." The newspaper did not specify how the competition was being managed, but when the winners were announced in March, it was noted in the *Chicago Tribune* that "four competitions were held, the first being determined on sketches showing the general architectural scheme; second, the plans and elevations of building; third, the sections or interior perspectives of lounging-room and dining-room, showing color scheme; fourth, a perspective of the whole."[35] There was another article on the same day in the *Chicago American*, where it was reported that "following a spirited contest, John H. Phillips was awarded the annual scholarship of the Chicago Architectural club at its meeting at the Art Institute last night. Several ballots were taken before the matter was finally decided. The votes for the three highest were John H. Phillips, nineteen; Jarvis Harbeck, thirteen; and Jules B. Benedict, eleven."[36] Thus it is clear that the 1901–2 Traveling Scholarship Competition was handled in very much the same way as the first competition a year earlier. Unfortunately, no record of the jury members has survived and, as noted in the 1902 *Architectural Annual,* the competition "closed too late for publication." The editor of the *Annual* went on to say that "the competition this year was very successful from the standpoint of the number of competitors and general excellence of work produced." While the winners were not included in the *Annual,* the drawings of Phillips, Harbeck, and Benedict were in the exhibition along with another competitor, Harry C. Starr. (It is interesting to note that Jarvis R. Harbeck is listed as being at 1107 Steinway Hall.) No drawings of any of the competitors for the 1902 award have been located.

✤

The Fifteenth Annual Exhibition of the Chicago Architectural Club opened on March 28, 1902, at the Art Institute of Chicago. It was open to the public for three weeks and generated a great deal of interest, both in the architectural press and in the local newspapers. The *Chicago Chronicle* had a major article as well as a minor story following the opening of the exhibition.[37] The shorter of the two was illustrated with one of Robert Spencer's designs "for 'A Northern Farmhouse.' . . . a good example of the drawings on exhibition." That brief article also noted that "drawings representing the highest art in architecture will be on exhibition at the Art Institute tonight," and the author wrote that "space will be given to arts allied to architecture." The longer article in the *Chronicle* devoted most of its space to a description of the huge drawings exhibited by MIT professor Desire Despradelle for his Beacon of Progress.

Desire Despradelle had been educated at the École des Beaux-Arts, and in 1893 became head of the Department of Architecture at MIT.[38] He exhibited ten drawings, the largest of which was fifteen feet high by ten feet wide. Designed to be built at the site of the Columbian Exposition of 1893, the Beacon was totally beyond the realm of reality. The *Chronicle*'s article concluded, "Whether or not the dreams of M. Depradelle [*sic*] will ever be realized, the drawings for the wonderful monument are marvelous conceptions, worth seeing from the viewpoint of the artistic, the elaborateness of design and the possibilities of the future." Other crit-

35. "Local Draftsman Wins Trip Abroad by Auto Tavern Plans," *Chicago Tribune,* March 18, 1902.

36. "Wins 6 Months Trip Abroad," *Chicago American,* March 18, 1902.

37. *Chicago Chronicle,* March 28, 1902. Both articles are on microfilm at the Art Institute of Chicago. The brief item is titled "Exhibition of Architecture and Art" and the major article is "Plans a Great Monument."

38. The best biography of Despradelle (1862–1912) is in *Pencil Points* (May 1925): 59 et seq.

*Northern farmhouse by Robert C. Spencer Jr.; note his monogram at lower left (CAC/02)*

ics devoted less time to Despradelle's fantasy and more to the remainder of the exhibition.

The *Inland Architect*, for example, noted in its review, "Our old friend—the Despradelle dream—that has appeared from time to time in exhibitions during the last decade . . . Without asserting that it is original in its design, it is nevertheless original in its conception."[39] The same critic wrote, "This year there is a larger variety of work than usual, and this is divided so that each room presents some special feature in which some phase of building predominates." He noted that "the first room . . . is given to architecture in larger conceptions . . . The second presents decorative effects, interior design, stained glass, etc. . . . The third . . . that which is especially domestic in design . . . The fourth is very general in its display, but there, too, domestic architecture is most in evidence." The reviewer was impressed by the work of Ralph Adams Cram, Lawrence Buck's renderings for D. H. Burnham, and Wilson Eyre's "original conceptions."

39. *Inland Architect* 39, no. 3 (April 1902): 25–26.

*Desire Despradelle's widely published and much discussed "Beacon of Progress" (CAC/02)*

*Detail of Desire Despradelle's "Beacon of Progress" (CAC/02)*

*First-floor plan (left), and perspective (above), Dwight Perkins's design for Hitchcock Hall at the University of Chicago, exhibited in 1902 (CAC/02)*

FIRST FLOOR PLAN

The unsigned review, probably by Robert Craik McLean, did not mention the work of Frank Lloyd Wright or that of any of the other young avant-garde architects of Chicago who, in fact, dominated the exhibition. He did note, however, that the "catalogue, which was compiled and edited by George R. Dean, deserves mention and special praise for the manner in which that gentleman has recognized its purpose, and brought into skillful use, and in a practical way, all that an artist in types or harmonious arrangement could admire." In short, the catalog was beautiful, but he couldn't bring himself to comment favorably on its content.

That content was truly extraordinary. The drawings by the previous year's Traveling Scholarship winner, discussed earlier, were in the catalog but not in the exhibition itself. Despradelle's Beacon of Progress must have been an impressive introduction to exhibition visitors, and to readers of the catalog, but the work they saw as they entered the galleries would have been far more important and impressive. Not only were several examples of Robert C. Spencer's avant-garde designs for farmhouses included, but his colleagues from Steinway Hall were also represented with excellent examples of the emerging modern movement in architecture. Dwight Perkins's design for Hitchcock Hall at the University of Chicago was shown along with his work for the university at its Morgan Park Academy on Chicago's South Side, as was the recently completed Settlement House and two of Perkins's private

*Dwight Perkins's gymnasium for the Morgan Park Academy in southwest Chicago (CAC/02)*

*Louis Sullivan's drawing of a house designed for Mrs. Nettie F. McCormick, exhibited in 1902 (CAC/02)*

residences. Myron Hunt's two-family house in Evanston was exhibited along with Elmer Grey's contribution to the *Ladies' Home Journal* series of house designs. Architect George Dean had three full pages of designs, as did Arthur Heun. Pond & Pond had six designs in the catalog. Hugh Garden, Richard E. Schmidt, and S. S. Beman were also represented. Louis Sullivan was not only represented with a splendid frontispiece in the catalog, but two of his house designs and several of his distinctive ornamental pieces were exhibited. All this material, along with an extensive display of Frank Lloyd Wright's work, made the 1902 catalog one of the most memorable in the history of the club. The modern movement in architecture had made itself known, and Chicago was its birthplace.

The *Inland Architect* was not the only journal to review the exhibition. The *Chicago Post* included its comments on the exhibition as part of a larger article on the arts in Chicago.[40] It noted that "success in the guise of public interest has been the portion of the exhibition of the Architectural club in the south galleries of the Art Institute. Even the pay days have been notable for the crowd of visitors and the throng before the drawings of lovely homes and picturesque country houses on free days proves that an art which comes near to personal comfort touches a chord of sincere appreciation." The reporter went on to say, "Frank Lloyd Wright's room is

40. "Success Greets Architectural Club," *Chicago Post*, April 5, 1902.

*Robert C. Spencer's "Gardener's Cottage at Lake Delavan" reflected his interest in farm buildings (CAC/02)*

especially attractive. It is a cozy place and teems with original ideas." He was impressed with the chairs, tables, and other items shown by Wright, all of which he found to be "object lessons in good taste." He had little to say about the rest of the exhibition, mentioning only "Jessie M. Preston['s] examples in bronze for electric candelabras and lamps." Neither Wright nor the other exhibitors were so favored in the review published by the *American Architect.*

The review in that journal's "Chicago" column was in some ways thoughtful, but the reviewer was certainly not in the same camp as the members of the Chicago Architectural Club.[41] In fact, his attitude might be described as caustic or even hostile. His opening paragraph noted that "the Exhibition . . . is in many ways creditable, though there are some features which are questionable for a general exhibition."

He briefly discussed Despradelle's Beacon of Progress, but felt it was impractical, although interesting to the average man, since "such grandeur and size cannot help but appeal." He was concerned that "while the list of exhibitors shows nearly as many outside of Chicago as in, the impression of the Exhibition is that it is given over, not only to Chicago, but to the less-important class of work of the younger men, who chiefly compose the club membership. In fact, in many ways the exhibits brought most into prominence are of the arts-and-crafts type, rather than the strictly architectural class of designs. Moreover, the few examples of large and serious work that are exhibited seem to have been relegated into the background as much as possible. Nor is there illustrated a single example of the larger work that must of necessity endure long after that of a smaller nature has been forgotten." He could not accept that the descendants of the great Chicago School buildings that had made their mark ten years earlier had been "relegated into the background" simply because few were being built due to the recent seven-year depression or that the smaller buildings exhibited were, in fact, the precursors of the architecture of the future. In 1902, the early modern movement was typified by small to medium-size buildings produced primarily by small to medium-size offices.

The *American Architect* reviewer continued his remarks:

> Collected under the banner of Mr. Frank L. Wright, doubtless most of the designs bearing his hall-mark, one of the smaller galleries is given up entirely to his exhibit. From the standpoint of professional ethics it seems questionable whether such a pronounced personal exhibit should have its place in a general architectural exhibition, as it certainly smacks of advertising more than anything else. Having selected one of the small rooms, with a door for entrance and one for exit directly opposite each other, a low partition is run across from one door to the other, forming a distinct room. The color-scheme of this small division is very charming. Warm light browns and grays are com-

41. *American Architect* 76 (April 26, 1902): 29–30.

*George Dean's work had a decidedly modern tone, as evidenced in this dining hall for Strawberry Island, exhibited in 1902 (CAC/02)*

bined, the walls being some brownish burlap banded with strips of some soft-finished wood. The exhibited designs on the walls are all framed to harmonize with the general color-scheme. Brown-leather covers stretch across desks and tables, on which dull copper vases hold effective bunches of gray milkweed pods, brown grasses, teazles, etc. Tall copper and bronze vases in the style of "L'Art Nouveau" hold slender brown seed-cups of some of last year's plants; bits of colored and leaded glass, a marble font of good design, a bronze figure, chairs and tables from Mr. Wright's own house, all have a place in this room. This is all very well as far as it goes, and it certainly is *pretty*, almost "too pretty," as Mr. Raffaelli has put it, for such a place as this. Why in an architectural exhibit, the chief one in Chicago for the year, why should Mr. Wright's tables and chairs, and his teazles and milkweeds and pine-branches cover so much space? When one sees the seriously beautiful work, even in domestic architecture, that is being done in other parts of our country, notably in the East, one is ashamed of the trivial spirit that is abroad here among us. There is a set of younger men here in Chicago who foster all this sort of thing. They have among them men with the artistic spirit and feeling, but their aim seems to be always to strive for the semi-grotesque, the catchy. Their compositions lack the best principles of honest design. Their aim seems to be to impress upon the beholder the belief that they are so filled with artistic inspirations and ideas that the flood cannot be held back for a minute, but must be dashed down onto paper as fast as ink or lead can carry it. There *is* a certain dash about it. These men treat the world like one huge studio, but how will these things look, say, even twenty years from now? Like a dusty studio from which the life has gone. There certainly will be no acquired dignity born of time. The designs hardly amount to designs and the execution is usually so extremely cheap that one questions the honesty of the whole thing. Not only in the profession but out of it do people here constantly take this short cut, which they think leads to perfection in art. It is a dangerous thing and one which will hurt the best interests of art and architecture in the section of the country where it most flourishes. Originality, tempered with honest endeavor and careful thought and work, gives a fine flavor, one that the more it prevails in a community just so much better is it for that community; but careless self-sufficiency, that is a different thing.

The reviewer wrote only briefly on the rest of the exhibition, confining his remarks to the observation that there had been "two notably fine houses finished on the North Side in Chicago this year, one a beautiful Colonial on Wellington Avenue, the other an equally good French Renaissance on North State Street. Only one of

*Frank Lloyd Wright's classic high-backed chairs first appeared in the January 1900 issue of the* Architecture Review; *Wright exhibited the same photograph in the 1902 CAC show (CAC/02)*

*George Dean's Alpha Delta Phi Chapter House for Cornell University, one of his most elaborate designs (CAC/02)*

*Arthur Heun exhibited this design for a residence in Winnetka in 1902 (CAC/02)*

these houses appears at the Exhibition and that only in one form, somewhat over-shadowed in spirit by teazles and pine-branches, and this is the only showing, though they both are unquestionably the strongest examples of domestic architecture here for several years." A review of the catalog does not reveal which houses these were.

The reviewer also commented on the catalog, noting that it was "quite an imposing affair . . . While supposedly free from advertisement, and for this purpose published by contributions solicited from architects and others interested in the club, it must be recognized by nearly every one that this catalog is nothing but a huge advertisement for a few exhibitors. Aside from all questions of professional ethics on advertising, which the club committee would have been wise to have considered, it seems decidedly impolitic for the architects themselves to have permitted it. The works of different men are placed in the catalog in groups in the reproductions of drawings and photographs . . . generally done quite unostentatiously, but when Mr. Frank Wright's portion is reached, we are introduced to his fourteen pages with a title-page effect in which is the inscription, "The Work of Frank Lloyd

*Pond & Pond's design for a country house was built in Oregon, Illinois, as part of an artists' colony (CAC/02)*

Frank Lloyd Wright's section of the 1902 Chicago Architectural Exhibition catalog had its own internal title page; the terra-cotta capital modeled by Richard W. Bock includes two storks on either side of an inscribed plan of Wright's studio; the sculpture of Wright's son, also by Bock, stands on a Wright-designed chair (CAC/02)

Wright." A Wright chair, vases and the bronze figure, before alluded to, and the usual architectural jetsam compose the material of the title-page composition. The reviewer was obviously not a fan of Frank Lloyd Wright. "To glance at the [*Architectural Annual*] one would think that this 'L'Art Nouveau' of ours was the only manner of existence in architecture here, and it is a positive relief to turn to some of Mr. Sullivan's charming designs, a cast-iron grille arc-lamp for one thing, and some beautiful details of his in the large building for Gage Brothers on Michigan Avenue." With this conclusion, it is clear that the reviewer totally missed the point that Sullivan's work was the inspiration for the designs he found so distasteful. He also missed the fact that much of the material in the catalog was either from previous years' exhibits or had never been shown at all. The current year's Traveling Scholarship drawings were omitted, and several of the Sullivan items, most notably the Gage Building photographs, the cast-iron grill, and the arc lamp, were not in the exhibition, although they were in the *Annual*. One wonders if the reviewer actually looked carefully at the exhibition and the *Annual*, or if his goal was merely to criticize the young men whose work was gaining popularity in Chicago. The review was unsigned, and the reviewer, who was apparently a Chicagoan, has never been identified. The editor of the *Architectural Annual* is, however, known. It was George Dean, as noted by another reviewer, one of the stalwarts of the Eighteen and an outspoken advocate of the need for an American architecture. In addition to his editorial duties, Dean had also served on the Jury of Admission to the exhibition, with Richard E. Schmidt and Robert C. Spencer Jr. Clearly the goal was to present

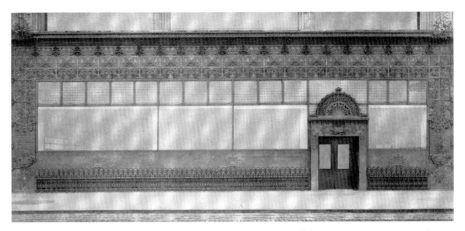

*Street-level facade of the Gage Building on Michigan Avenue; Louis Sullivan's cast-iron ornament has all been removed, but the building still stands (CAC/02)*

the work of the young disciples of Sullivan who were developing a new architecture. As time went by, they became the core of the Prairie school of architecture.[42] For the time being, they formed the leadership of the Chicago Architectural Club. One other professional journal commented on both the 1902 exhibition and the *Annual.* The *Architectural Review* noted in its May 1902 issue under "Current Periodicals" that "the dullness of the magazines for the month is unapproachable, yet we have only to turn to the *Architectural Annual* and the catalogue of the exhibition of the Chicago Architectural Club to see that work is being done, which is, at all events, interesting: whether it is significant or not must remain to be proved."[43] Later in the same column the reviewer wrote that the exhibition "was strident with the clamoring of the Sullivan School of Architecture. It was novel, it was interesting and it was thoroughly sincere; much of it was entirely good, some of it was too fantastic for really serious consideration, but it was all vital and characteristic, far more representative of the present epoch than the common run of trade architecture that flows through the columns of so many of the architectural periodicals." That reviewer understood what was happening in Chicago.

Some members of the club, however, were not completely happy with the decidedly biased selection process for the 1902 exhibition. A few went so far as to publish an "official announcement" of a "Gallery de Grotesque" to be held at the rooms of the club in the basement of the Art Institute at the same time the exhibition was being held in the galleries upstairs.[44] The *Chicago Journal* article stated:

42. The best discussion of the 1902 exhibition and its catalog is in Brooks, *The Prairie School,* 45–47.

43. *Architectural Review* 9, no. 5 (May 1902): 105.

44. "Art in Its Humorous Phases," *Chicago Journal,* April 9, 1902

*George W. Maher's building for James A. Patten in Evanston, with Maher's distinctive ornament on either side (CAC/02)*

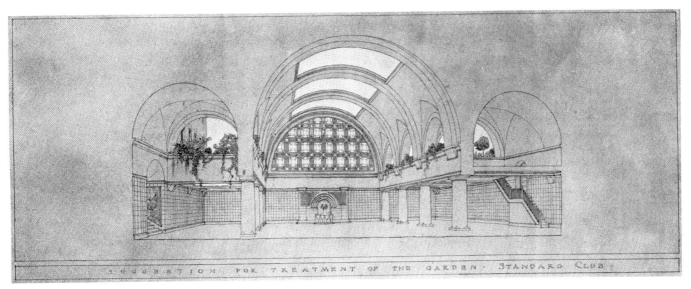

*Drawing of the Standard Club garden, exhibited by Richard E. Schmidt (CAC/02)*

There will be doings at the Chicago Architectural Club, Art Institute, during the week of April 21 to 28. The "Gallery de Grotesque" will be held . . . Just what this will be may be judged from the following extracts from the official announcement: "The exhibition is held to mark the auspicious opening of a new era of architectural thought, and will illustrate the latest fashions and designs for the year 1902. You are invited to submit plain, ornamental, and free-hand drawings, hektograph renderings, hand-painted perspectives, wash-drawings in domestic finish or polish, articles of bric-a-brac comprising vawses, glass—either cut, blown, or double-thick—carvings, in compo or jig-saw, and all articles which make up the artistic inconveniences of buildings.

"Exhibition held under the marquis of Queensbury code.
"Hanging committee from county jail, kindness of Sheriff Shitman. Nails furnished free. Exhibitors will supply their own hammers.
"Booths by Booth Packing company.
"State if you wish exhibits forwarded on circuit, which includes St. Louis, Toronto, Ash Heap, Scrap Pile, and City Dump."

Whether or not such a "Salon des Refuse" was actually held cannot be determined, but it does demonstrate that not all the members were happy with the exhibition. The language of the announcement seems to suggest that the reviewer at the *American Architect* may have had some involvement.

Shortly after the closing of the exhibition, the club held its annual meeting at its rooms in the Art Institute of Chicago and elected new officers. It was an entirely new slate: Arthur G. Brown was elected president, with H. W. J. Edbrooke and William J. Beauley as first and second vice presidents. J. B. Benedict and Harry C. Starr were elected secretary and treasurer, respectively. N. Max Dunning and Thomas E. Talmadge were named to fill out the Executive Committee. None was part of the Steinway Hall group, with the possible exception of Dunning, who was on the periphery, although all had been active in the club for several years.[45] Only Tallmadge was a relative newcomer, having joined the club in early 1901.

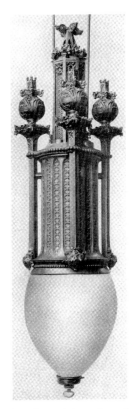

*Cast-iron "Arc Lamp" designed by Louis Sullivan, shown in the 1902 exhibition*

Ghetto Fish Market *by W. J. Beauley was shown at the Chicago Architectural Club's First Annual Water Color Exhibit in 1902 (CT)*

*Walter Francis Shattuck (PC)*

45. *Inland Architect* 39, no. 4 (May 1902): 36.

46. This paper was printed in full in *Inland Architect* 39, no. 5 (June 1902): 41. It was an adaptation of one of his "Kindergarten Chats."

47. The exhibition was reported in several Chicago newspapers between September 22 and 24, including the *Chicago Tribune,* the *Chicago Inter Ocean,* the *Chicago American,* and the *Chicago Record-Herald.*

48. *"Architects' Club Gives a Fine Exhibit,"* Chicago American, September 23, 1902.

With new officers in place it was again time to choose members to attend the forthcoming annual meeting of the Architectural League of America. In addition to the league president, J. C. Llewellyn, the club sent Dwight Perkins and A. C. Wilmanns as its representatives. W. E. Kleinpell also attended as chairman of the Exhibition Circuit Committee. Louis Sullivan did not attend, but was represented by a paper read by E. J. Russell of St. Louis, titled "The Formation of Knowledge."[46] The convention again devoted a good deal of time to the issue of education, but the presentations were shorter and received far less attention from the architectural press than in past years. After the formal presentations were over, the convention chairman, E. J. Russell, appointed committees for the following year including Llewellyn on Publicity and Promotion, Perkins on Auxiliary Promotion, W. E. Kleinpell on Exhibition Circuit, and J. H. Phillips (who was not present) on the Foreign Exhibits Committee. Before adjourning, Frederick S. Lamb of New York was elected president, and the league chose St. Louis for its next annual meeting in October of 1903. Chicago's influence had faded to nearly nothing, insofar as the Architectural League of America was concerned. The east was now in charge.

While there were no regular meetings of the Chicago Architectural Club in the summer of 1902, the members continued to be active in the various classes offered to those who wished to enhance their skills. The watercolor classes were well attended and, in a new approach, the members chose to paint city scenes rather than country views, which involved long treks out of town. It was also a way to draw and paint buildings instead of landscapes. The senior members of the club decided that a good way to kick off the 1902–3 season in September would be to have an exhibition of the summer's work. Thus, on September 22, 1902, the club opened an "annual" exhibition of summer sketches.[47]

The *Chicago Tribune* reported that it was the "fifth annual water color exhibit of the Chicago Architectural Club," but no other similar exhibition had ever been recorded. ("Fifth" was probably a typographical error, and should have read "first.") The article went to say that the exhibit would include "over 200 paintings, representing mainly the work of the younger members of the Club . . . [and] many of the pictures show scenes in Chicago with which the public is unfamiliar . . . [including] paintings of buildings, scenes along the river and lake front, and unfrequented streets." W. J. Beauley, J. B. Benedict, and H. D. Jenkins were singled out by the *Tribune,* which reported that forty-five of the club's members had contributed to the exhibition.

The *Chicago American* was also laudatory and in addition to those members named above, added Tallmadge, Behr, Starr, and Hugo Zimmerman to the list of exhibitors who had excellent work on display.[48] The opening was, according to the same source, "the first regular meeting of the year after the Summer vacation. It was a real old-fashioned Bohemian night." The article noted that the "hosts for the evening were: T. E. Tallmadge, R. C. Spencer, Jr., A. F. Bernhard, R. E. Bourke, E. Charles Hemmings, J. H. Phillips and J. B. Benedict." The club year appeared to be off to a good start.

In its article regarding the exhibition of watercolors, the paper also noted that through an "agreement with the Art Institute [the club] has entered a number of its young men in the classes of the regular school. It is now ambitious to found endowed scholarships, and is looking up gifts and subscriptions. So far $1,000 for the purpose has found its way into the coffers of the society." It went on to report that "a glimpse at the exhibition of students' work in place this week is enough to convince the most critical that the Chicago Architectural Club is inspiring the younger members to do original work. There is evidence of a desire to see the pictorial everywhere and to proceed to draw it in the most honest way. The idea has taken root among the members of the sketch classes that it is all nonsense to spend half a day going out of town to hunt a picturesque place for drawing. They believe that pictorial effects may be found in every alley, in the streets and parkways, and interesting bits nearly everywhere. So they spend their time in working rather than hunting for a place and not finding it. This explanation accounts for the street scenes, roof views, corner lots and attractive studies in color."

The club's interest in establishing scholarships at the Art Institute—which, with the technically oriented Armour Institute, constituted the Chicago School of Architecture—was not surprising. It had always been supportive of the school, and senior members of the club often lectured there. The principal faculty members, including Walter Shattuck, William K. Fellows, and Louis Millet, had always participated in club affairs. Finally, the club had been instrumental in establishing the students' Thumb Tack Club. It was a sort of mini-version of the Chicago Architectural Club, not unlike similar groups that provide social life in architecture schools today.

In the Ghetto *by H. D. Jenkins was shown in the first CAC Water Color Exhibit in 1902 (CP)*

In the fall of 1902 club members took a great interest in civic affairs, particularly in two areas. A number of members testified before the Chicago City Council on the revision of the city's building ordinances,[49] and virtually all the members took part in the debate concerning the development and beautification of Grant Park, a prelude to Daniel H. Burnham's *Plan of Chicago*.[50] Both subjects would continue to be of interest to the club, growing in importance as the members became more involved in civic affairs.

The members were also occupied by other matters in the fall. Not the least of their concerns was the formulation of a program for the 1903 Traveling Scholarship Competition, which was released in late November.[51] Similar to the previous two years' programs, it was a four-part affair with the first drawings due on December 20, 1902. Before club members could get totally immersed in the 1903 competition, however, they had one last task to perform regarding the 1902 competition. The winner of that prize, John H. Phillips, had been announced in March of 1902, but there had never been a formal presentation of his award. That was done at the club's annual New Year's party at the rooms in the Art Institute. Seventy members gathered in the basement quarters around a banquet table to celebrate the New Year and to honor John Phillips on January 5, 1903.[52] W. J. Beauley acted as toastmaster. President A. G. Brown spoke of the plans for the next year and then made the presentation to Phillips, who responded that he would "return with a fund of information." Former presidents Robert C. Spencer Jr. and Joseph Llewellyn each spoke, followed by J. W. Hoover of the University of Pennsylvania, the guest for the evening. The remainder of the evening was spent in good fellowship and discussing the forthcoming year. Chicago's avant-garde was still very much in evidence, but a new generation of officers was now in charge.

49. *Brickbuilder* 11, no. 12 (December 1902): 263.

50. In the spring of 1902, it had been announced in several Chicago newspapers that the land between Michigan Avenue and the Illinois Central tracks immediately north of the Art Institute would be developed as a park. Shortly thereafter, Marshall Field announced that he would donate $10 million toward the construction of a major museum to be built south of the Art Institute and east of the ICRR tracks. Both plans, particularly the second, were subjected to intense public scrutiny.

51. *Inland Architect* 40, no. 5 (December 1902): 40–41.

52. *Chicago Inter Ocean* and *Chicago Record-Herald*, January 6, 1902.

*Lobby of the club rooms in the Dexter Building (PC)*

# The Traditionalists Return

CHAPTER THIRTEEN

When 1903 began, the 1902 exhibition and catalog were only memories. Nevertheless, some club members were still smarting from the adverse publicity and, more important, were upset that a small group of members had taken over the show. Those angry members vowed it would not happen again. In late 1902, the club chose March 26 through April 17, just over three weeks, for the dates of the 1903 exhibition. Those dates were published in early February, and preparations began immediately.[1]

One major event carried over from 1902 was the Traveling Scholarship Competition, now firmly established as an annual activity. The program for the third annual competition had been announced in November of 1902,[2] but most of the work and the actual competition took place in 1903. The subject was "A Monumental Crossing for the Illinois Central Railway at the Midway Plaisance." Even with the Columbian Exposition now a decade behind them, club members were still concerned about what was happening at the Jackson Park site of the great fair. The Illinois Central Station at Fifty-ninth Street, which had been a major entrée to the fair, was now the primary station serving the University of Chicago and its environs. The competition program assumed that the South Park commissioners had converted the "sunken garden in the center of the midway into a watercourse or canal connecting the lagoons of Jackson and Washington Parks, and that bridges will be erected at each crossing." The program also assumed that the Illinois Central Railroad was "desirous that its crossing be in keeping with the plans of the South Park Commissioners." The program called for the crossing to be "treated in a monumental way and, together with the street crossing at Stony Island and Madison avenues, it forms the subject of this competition." It was a monumental problem in all respects.

Competitors were limited to those under the age of twenty-eight, but there was no stipulation that they had to be members of the club. The Scholarship Committee was made up of Willis Polk, chairman, along with Dwight H. Perkins and Pierce Anderson. Polk, who was still relatively new in Chicago, was now taking an active part in club affairs, although he would soon leave for Europe and, upon his return, go back to San Francisco.[3] Pierce Anderson had also only recently become a member of the club, in 1902. Perkins, of course, had been a longtime active member. The committee was not the jury of the competition. That task was left to "all active members of the club, excepting the competitors, [who] will constitute a committee

1. *Brickbuilder* 12, no. 2 (February 1903): 43.

2. The program was printed in pamphlet form for the membership, but it was also published twice in the architectural press, in *Inland Architect* 40, no. 5 (December 1902): 40, and *Construction News* (January 31, 1903): 68.

3. *Inland Architect* 43, no. 2 (March 1904): 16. Willis Polk (1867–1924) lived and worked in San Francisco until 1901, when he joined D. H. Burnham and Company in Chicago for nearly two years.

of the whole to decide by ballot the merits of the designs submitted." The program noted that at "the regular meeting following the receipt of the drawings, a critic will be appointed and a discussion of the drawings by the jury will be had. At the next meeting the vote is to be taken, but the ballot at each meeting will be sealed and the result will not be announced until the final competition is closed."

Those who entered the competition were given a detailed site plan and instructions to provide all the amenities needed for a railway station with both express and suburban service. Driveways were to extend to station level, which required long ramps for horse-drawn carriages. Comfort facilities for the public were mandated, and it was specified that a "promenade at a level no lower than the station platform must be provided to permit crowds to view the plaisance and canal." The competitors were required to submit their solutions in four parts as follows: The first drawings—a general plan including the adjacent street crossings, an elevation of the west side of the railway crossing, and an east-west section—were due on December 20, 1902. Those drawings were reviewed and voted on by the members a week later. The votes were counted and the totals accrued as the competition progressed. The next set of drawings, due no later than January 17, 1903, were to be a plan of the crossing and station with elevations and two sections. These too were juried and voted on promptly. The third set of drawings was due on or before February 7, and was to include three sheets of details of any parts of the scheme the designer considered of special interest. These were the only sheets where the size (twenty-four by forty inches) was specified. Again, they were voted on the following week. The final drawings, a perspective view of the railway crossing taken from the intersection of Madison Avenue and Sixtieth Street, the horizon line at grade 25, were due not later

*Birch Burdette Long's winning design in the 1903 Traveling Scholarship Competition (CAC/03)*

than March 14, 1903. Since the first- and second-place drawings were published in the exhibition catalog, the drawings were probably delivered early. The exhibition opened on March 26. The rules specified that "rendering" would not count in the first three submissions, but in the fourth submission, the perspective, rendering would count for 50 percent. No competitor was allowed to skip any of the four parts of the competition, and each was asked to keep tracings of his work since the drawings would not be returned.

The 1902–3 Traveling Scholarship Competition was not popular with the membership. The program was complex and probably beyond the abilities of many of the younger members. It was also a time when literally all the members were working full-time during a continuing building boom in Chicago.[4] (Many were working full-time for their employers and for others at night.) There was simply little time left for a complex competition. Consequently, very few members submitted drawings in the initial round in December of 1902. When Birch Burdette Long was announced as the winner of the scholarship, *Construction News* reported that there "were five entries in the first [competition] held in December, but gradually the number decreased until only Mr. Long and Ralph W. Weirick, [ a young architect in the employ of Frost & Granger, remained . . . The competition was close, the difference being only three points. Mr. Long . . . came to Chicago in 1894 and three years ago established himself independently."[5]

Birch Burdette Long had been an active participant in the affairs of the Chicago Architectural Club since becoming a member in April of 1896. His entry in the Woman's Club Competition of 1900 for a park shelter had actually been built. (It had not, however, been chosen as the winner, having been deemed too expensive to meet the competition's criteria.) He had also been a finalist in the first Traveling Scholarship Competition in 1901. Long was closely associated with the Steinway Hall group and had worked with and for several of them, primarily as a renderer.

Less is known about Ralph W. Weirick, whose design received an honorable mention. At the time of the competition, he was employed in the office of Frost & Granger, where the president of the club, Arthur G. Brown, was chief designer.[6] Weirick first appeared as a member of the Chicago Architectural Club in March of 1901. He was listed as a licensed architect for the first time in 1902. By then, he

4. *Construction News* for March 28, 1903, reported that "D. H. Burnham & Co. now have a force of ninety men on the pay roll, probably a larger number than at any time in the history of Mr. Burnham's private practice." Burnham was able to maintain such a staff as he had a national practice and was not subject to local changes in demand for architectural services. The building boom continued into 1903, but would end within a few months. All in all, however, the first decade of the twentieth century was a strong period for construction.

5. Ibid., 198.

*Ralph W. Weirick's design, not nearly as sophisticated as that of B. B. Long (CAC/03)*

would have had to have obtained his license by examination. He is listed again in 1903, after which he no longer appears in the annual listings issued by the Chicago Architects' Business Association.

Both Long and Weirick exhibited their entries in the 1903 exhibition, and both projects were illustrated in the catalog. Weirick showed his perspective, a detail of an end pavilion, and an elevation. Long showed his block plan and his bird's-eye perspective. The latter was a splendid drawing and commanded the premier space in the catalog. His design was monumental and clearly met the requirements of the competition. It included the entire area between Stony Island Avenue on the east and Madison Avenue (an extension of what is now Blackstone) on the west. The assumed canal connecting the Jackson and Washington park lagoons was a central feature and became the setting for the classical colonnades that enclosed the railroad station and the promenade for pedestrians. Gentle ramps on either side provided carriage and pedestrian access to track level. Long had solved the problem posed by the competition. Since cost was not a factor, his design was easily chosen as the winner.

Weirick's design paled in comparison. He, too, commanded a full page in the catalog, but his drawing was not as well executed as Long's, nor was his design as sophisticated. It was Romanesque almost to a fault, with nine pairs of huge arches on either side of the tracks. Rather steep ramps led up from street level to track level. The published perspective does not indicate how pedestrians got to track level, but stairs were probably provided between the pairs of arches with access at either end. Weirick's design does not focus on or take advantage of the proposed canal, nor does it suggest any treatment between the railroad right-of-way and the two streets, Stony Island and Madison, which were specifically named as part of the program.

The Sixteenth Annual Exhibition catalog for 1903 was, like the 1901 and 1902 catalogs, issued in two parts. The forty-eight-page (plus covers) illustrated catalog was for sale at the exhibition. An eight-page, self-covered *List of Exhibits* either came with the catalog or was given free to visitors who did not buy the full catalog. The catalog was somewhat larger than it had been in previous years (ten by twelve inches), and it was printed in red and black on two kinds of paper, enameled for the illustration pages and rough paper for most of the text. The usual lists of patrons and members were included, as well as a two-page, unsigned essay with some innocuous remarks on the club and its activities. No hint of controversy appears anywhere in the book. The illustrations, with a very few exceptions, were traditional to a fault. Only two seem to be avant-garde. Atchison & Edbrooke showed a drawing of an apartment building for Evanston, Illinois, which clearly was heavily influenced by Louis Sullivan (but not a copy), and a bit of ornament by Nimmons

6. Arthur G. Brown (1869–1934) was born in California and arrived in Chicago in 1889. He worked for a number of firms before becoming chief designer for Frost & Granger in 1901. He became a member of the Chicago Architectural Club in 1892.

*Atchison & Edbrooke's excellent design for an apartment building in Evanston, Illinois (CAC/03)*

*Stable design for "Mr. Sollitt" by Holabird & Roche, with a hint of modernism (CAC/03)*

& Fellows showed the same influence. There was a rather nice design by Holabird & Roche for a "Stable for Mr. Sollitt," and Howard Van Doren Shaw exhibited a "Country House" of some merit. Peabody & Beauly exhibited a tiny rendering of a house to be built in Wilmington, Illinois, which still stands. Here and there throughout the catalog are sketches of historic buildings in Europe by N. Max Dunning, the previous year's Traveling Scholarship winner. For some reason, several small sketches of San Francisco by Willis Polk that had been in the 1901 exhibition were shown again, as was a design for a "City Residence" by Victor Traxler that had appeared before. In short, the 1903 catalog was very different from that of 1902 or, for that matter, from any of those issued previously. It illustrated what was generally happening in the Midwest and elsewhere, but did not emphasize the cutting-edge work of the young architects of Chicago. That work, however, was still being done, although it would be essentially ignored by the club's exhibitions for the next several years.

The 1903 exhibition opened to the press on the afternoon of March 25. The following day it opened to the public for just over three weeks. There were 490 exhibits listed in the catalog, although there were more actually shown if one takes into account the exhibits that had several items included under a single number. The response from the local popular press was fairly extensive, although not always laudatory. The first review, in the *Chicago Tribune,* noted that "hundreds of architects and many guests and their wives attended the reception."[7] The rest of the

*Nimmons & Fellows's Sullivanesque entry in the 1903 exhibition (CAC/03)*

*Rendering of a house for Wilmington, Illinois, by Peabody & Beauley (CAC/03)*

*House in Wilmington, Illinois, still standing; the resemblance to the rendering at left is too close to be coincidental (WRH)*

*Sketch by N. Max Dunning*

article was devoted largely to out-of-town exhibits, although the two Traveling Scholarship winners were mentioned but not analyzed or critiqued. The *Chicago Post* devoted much more space to the exhibition.[8] It too mentioned Long and Weirick as the scholarship winners, but it also commented on many other entries. The reviewer was disappointed that more space was not devoted to "model Lodging houses" or "plans for ideal flat buildings." He stated that he joined "in regrets with the man who is searching for a little home which may come up to his notions of house planning. Such things as these belong to the commonplace bread and butter side of life, and the men of the architectural club have carefully kept them in the background in this their one great exhibition of the year." Clearly the critic was writing for the newspaper's subscribers rather than for architects. The reviewer noted that there were "many pretentious buildings for residences of the wealthy, churches and public establishments and ideal structures which will never materialize in stone, brick and mortar." He went on to comment on the many exhibits from other cities and particularly from various universities. A number of Chicagoans were briefly noted with special attention given to a few such as "Blanche Ostertag, [who exhibited] two panels and an over mantle made for the dining rooms of J. J. Husser in Venetian coloring, with decorative design and text." That design, of course, was to be installed in the house done by Frank Lloyd Wright for Husser three years earlier. It was as close as Wright was to get to being included in the 1903 exhibition. After his overt domination of the 1902 exhibition, he would be persona non grata in the Chicago Architectural Club exhibitions until 1907.

The *Chicago Record-Herald* also published a short review of the exhibition.[9] Its comments were confined to a brief statement regarding the Traveling Scholarship Competition that didn't name the winners and the observation that "Chicago architects are not only in eager demand at home but in favor all over the United States." It concluded with a paragraph noting that "citizens who love beauty in intimate association with the practical will find more than one visit to this exhibition delightful and inspiring." It included two illustrations from the exhibition, a watercolor, *Schwabs Station, Germany,* by William Jean Beauley and a rendering by Richard E. Schmidt, *Restaurant Building, Chicago.* The latter was, like many of the illustrations in the 1903 catalog, a building of no real significance except for the novelty of being a German restaurant in Chicago.

The *Chicago Tribune* published a second, more comprehensive, review of the 1903 exhibition after it had been open for a few days.[10] In preparation, the reviewer had obviously spent some time at the show. He was impressed by the more monumental work, such as that of D. H. Burnham and Company. The firm exhibited both its recently designed First National Bank and a preliminary sketch for a new railroad station that was eventually erected in Washington, D.C. The *Tribune* was also one of the few newspapers to comment in any detail on Birch Burdette Long's winning design for the Traveling Scholarship.

A careful reading of all the local reviews of the 1903 exhibition reveals that none of the reviewers was willing or prepared to take a genuinely critical stand. One last review, which appeared in the *American Architect and Building News,* deserves attention not so much for what it said, but for what it did not say. In the previous year it was this journal's review that had been so devastating in its commentary on the extensive representation of avant-garde work and, in particular, that of Frank Lloyd Wright. In 1903 the reviewer had only this to say: "The annual exhibition of the Architectural Club held in the Institute this spring was carried along legitimate lines more strictly than it was last year, and the result was a more dignified whole, though doubtless it took the fancy of the general public less than did the cat-tails and ceramics of last years. It was an exhibit of serious work and

7. "Work of Architects Shown," *Chicago Tribune*, March 27, 1903.

8. *Chicago Post*, March 28, 1903.

9. *Chicago Record-Herald,* March 29, 1903.

10. "Architectural Beauty," *Chicago Tribune*, April 5, 1903.

contained much of merit and worth."[11] The reviewer was, to say the least, conservative in his views.

Before the exhibition closed, there was one last item in the *Chicago Post,* in which a reporter asked "why local architects of note have not made a representative showing, and the reply given by the men interrogated is that they have so much actual work to do that there is no leisure left in which to make ornamental drawings or build castles in the air."[12] He also noted that the exhibition did include "a number of instructive drawings by the older men, though it was undoubtedly a glorious opportunity for the younger set, who made so excellent an exhibition last year in the club rooms, to come forward and show what they could do." He went on to say that with "this in mind, it is none too early for them to begin thinking of what may be accomplished by home architects in the next year's exhibition."

The club moved on toward the next year by electing the new officers on May 4, 1903, barely two weeks after the exhibition had closed. The new officers included William K. Fellows as president, with J. L. Hamilton and T. E. Tallmadge as first and second vice presidents. Paul V. Hyland and Harry C. Starr were elected secretary and treasurer, respectively.[13] (Starr resigned in September before his duties really began and was replaced by Edward O. Nelson.) Hugo H. Zimmerman and Horace S. Powers filled out the Executive Committee. The 1903–4 officers were decidedly more attuned to the new movement in modern architecture than their predecessors. Only Tallmadge and Starr (for a few weeks) were holdovers from the previous year.

For several years it had been customary for the officers of the club, assisted by committee chairs, to prepare and offer several competitions during the club year. These varied from one-night problems juried by the membership at the end of the evening to the annual Traveling Scholarship Competition, which took from four to five months to complete. There is no record of the club participating regularly in competitions sponsored by other organizations before 1903. In May 1903, however, an opportunity was presented to the members to participate in competitions offered by a companion organization, the Society of Beaux-Arts Architects.[14]

The society had been organized in 1894 by a group of men in New York City who had studied architecture at the École des Beaux-Arts in Paris. The original object of the society was to perpetuate the principles of the École and maintain the associations the members had made while studying in Paris. In addition to the obvious social aspects of the organization, the members were very much interested in architectural education. A primary goal was to establish ateliers and other means of training young men (and women) in architecture. By 1903, the group had become large enough to offer "a course of study for architectural draughtsmen, modeled on the system adopted by the Ecole des Beaux-Arts, with the intention of cultivating among them the principles of their art which the members of the society have learned in Paris."[15] The classes were offered in two forms: Class B, in which all were welcome, and Class A, in which a student would be welcome only after receiving certain awards in Class B. Upon completion, the students were awarded certificates of proficiency.

At first the atelier competitions were held only in New York City under rules similar to those in Paris. Later the programs were revised so that students from throughout the United States could participate. The society advertised in architectural journals that it had "established a free course of study, open to draughtsmen and students of any city, modelled on the general plan pursued at the *Ecole de*

11. "Letter from Chicago," *American Architect and Building News* 81, no. 1457 (July 11, 1903): 11–12.

12. *Chicago Post,* April 11, 1903.

13. A detailed search of periodicals of the period revealed no information concerning the election. The officers noted were published in the *Charter, Constitution, By-Laws, House Rules, Officers and Members of the Chicago Architectural Club.* It is interesting to note that the bylaws printed in this small book do not provide, as the original bylaws did, that the secretary would be excused from paying dues in view of the tasks he was required to perform. It is probably for this reason that very few references to the club and its activities are found in newspapers or periodicals after 1903. Much of the data about the club for the next five years (1904–10) must be derived from the published catalogs and various peripheral references.

14. The actual name of the organization was the Beaux-Arts Society of Architects, and it was under that name that it was incorporated in 1894. The name was apparently cumbersome, as it was almost always referred to in print and by its members as the Society of Beaux-Arts Architects, a change that was made official in 1912.

15. The offer was published in pamphlet form, but the terms and conditions were published in *Brickbuilder* 12, no. 5 (May 1903): 110, and in somewhat abbreviated form in *Architectural Review* 10, no. 5 (May 1903): 56.

*Beaux-Arts* in Paris, and comprising frequent problems in orders, designs, archaeology, etc."[16] The result was the establishment of ateliers in larger American cities, including Chicago. The "problems" were published in professional magazines, and later in a monthly journal called the *Bulletin of the Beaux-Arts Society of Architects*. It became a simple matter for local architectural clubs to use these problems as part of their own programs. The Chicago Architectural Club, to a limited degree, did this. It did not, however, ignore its regular programming efforts.

The greatest impact the Society of Beaux-Arts Architects had in the United States was the almost universal adoption at the university level of at least some of the techniques used at the École des Beaux-Arts. While ateliers did spring up, including one sponsored by the Chicago Architectural Club a few years later, it was the formal college-level schools of architecture that were most affected. There were already, of course, a great many teachers of architecture with École des Beaux-Arts experience before the society had been formed, and their philosophy was now reinforced. A number of the key members of the Chicago Architectural Club had been trained by former École students. MIT had been following the basic principles of the École for many years and several schools—Columbia, Michigan, and others—also taught in that manner, albeit generally in a classroom setting rather than in ateliers.

In addition to the competitions offered by the Society of Beaux-Arts Architects, there were other competitions available to young practitioners. The *Brickbuilder* regularly sponsored competitions that attracted large numbers of participants. In June 1903 it announced a "Competition for a Public Library" with prizes totaling eight hundred dollars.[17] (The prize money was provided by terracotta manufacturers who advertised in the magazine.) The announcement filled a full page and was reprinted in July and August. The jury, published in the November issue, included Robert S. Peabody of Peabody & Stearns, D. Despradelle, then a professor of architecture at MIT, C. A. Coolidge of Shepley, Rutan & Coolidge, the only Chicago juror, Clarence H. Blackall, who was both an architect and a critic, and W. C. Hall, president of the Perth Amboy Terra-Cotta Company. It was a distinguished and able jury. Nearly three hundred designs were submitted, and the magazine devoted a special issue in January 1904 to the competition. Twenty-five designs were published, including several from Chicago. The three prizewinners plus a first-mention design were shown in the 1904 Chicago Architectural Club exhibition as a group. Chicagoan William Gray Purcell, who did not win a prize, also exhibited his design.

✳

16. This advertisement first appeared in *Brickbuilder* 12, no. 5 (May 1903): 110.

17. "Competition for a Public Library," *Brickbuilder* 12, no. 6 (June 1903): 132.

18. Field's offer was widely covered by several Chicago newspapers. The most comprehensive articles were published on February 19, 1903, in the *Chicago Inter Ocean* and the *Chicago Tribune*. The $10 million figure varied from time to time over the next few years while the location of the museum was being debated. When Marshall Field died in 1906, his will provided $8 million for the museum with the proviso that the city furnish a site, without cost, within six years.

Before any of these competitions was under way, there was another matter that took a good deal of the club's time and attention. Chicago's Grant Park (the South Park commissioners had voted to change the name from Lake Front Park in 1901) was very much in the news in the summer of 1903. A few months earlier, in February, Chicago's merchant prince, Marshall Field, had offered the City of Chicago the sum of $10 million to erect a museum on the lakefront to take the place of the Field Columbian Museum in Jackson Park.[18] That museum, originally the Fine Arts Building, was the only major surviving structure from the World's Columbian Exposition and, while it was more or less a permanent structure, it was not really of sufficient stability to serve much longer as a public museum. The decade since the fair had not been kind to it. Furthermore, it had never been the intent of Chicago's South Park commissioners to maintain it as the permanent Field Museum. The plans prepared in 1895 and 1896 by the Municipal Improvement League and the Chicago Architectural Club had both shown the "Field Columbian Museum" sited

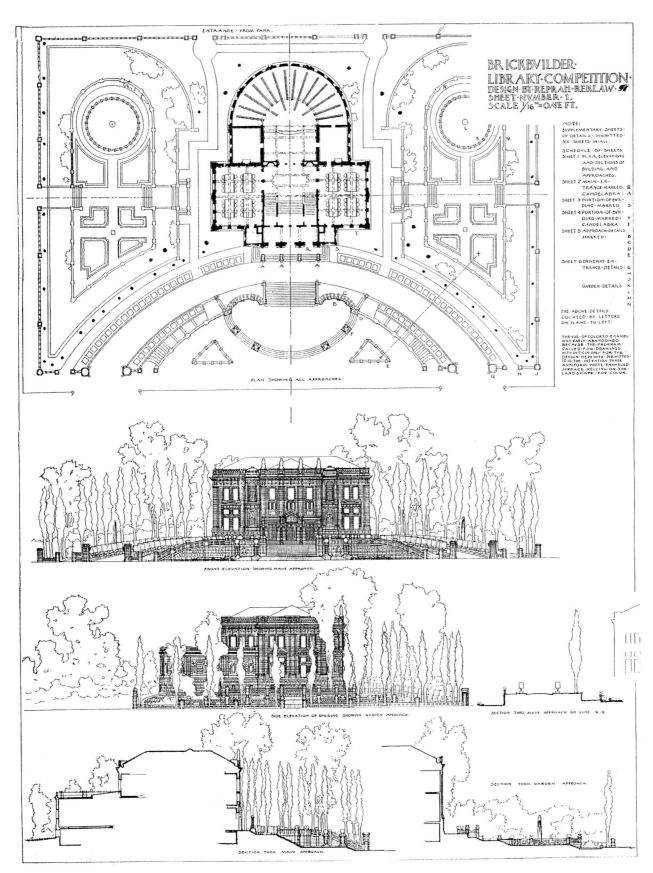

*Brickbuilder* competition design by Chicagoans W. W. Harper and Frank C. Walker (BB)

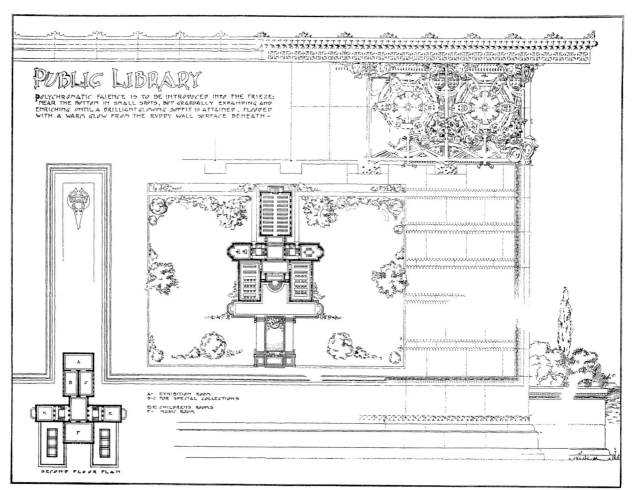

PUBLIC LIBRARY

POLYCHROMATIC FAIENCE IS TO BE INTRODUCED INTO THE FRIEZE:
NEAR THE BOTTOM IN SMALL SPOTS, BUT GRADUALLY EXPANDING AND
ENRICHING UNTIL A BRILLIANT GLOWING SOFFIT IS ATTAINED . FLOODED
WITH A WARM GLOW FROM THE RUDDY WALL SURFACE BENEATH —

A— EXHIBITION ROOM
B-C FOR SPECIAL COLLECTIONS

D-E CHILDRENS ROOMS
F— MUSIC ROOM

SECOND FLOOR PLAN

*William Gray Purcell's Sullivanesque design for the 1903* Brickbuilder *competition did not win a prize (BB)*

at the south end of what was then called Lake Front Park.

Field's offer to fund the new building came at a time when the debate over how to treat the lakefront of Chicago was very much in the minds of civic leaders. The key architectural figures in this discussion were Daniel H. Burnham and Peter B. Wight. Burnham had long been an advocate of lakefront improvements, including the development of Grant Park, where he felt the new museum should be the centerpiece of Chicago's civic pride. Wight, on the other hand, believed that the lakefront should remain essentially free of structures. He had a powerful ally in A. Montgomery Ward, who had fought for years to prevent any buildings other than the Art Institute from being built in Grant Park.

Members of the Chicago Architectural Club had been interested in the development of the park since 1894, when the Municipal Improvement League, under the leadership of Normand Patton, had spent a good deal of time and effort to develop plans for the underused property. Wight was then, and continued to be for several years, a major proponent of the development of the park. Burnham had taken a similar interest but with a different and broader point of view. He was interested in the lakefront both near the downtown and south as far as Jackson Park, while Wight had confined himself to the area between Division Street on the north and Fourteenth Street on the south. It was he who had encouraged the Chicago Architectural Club to develop a plan for the park in 1896 based primarily on his own ideas, including a scheme to install city hall in the park west of the Illinois Central tracks between Randolph and Monroe streets. He was, however, adamant that no other structures should be built in the park between Randolph and Roosevelt Road. Burnham's plans would have made the proposed Field Museum the centerpiece of the park, located on axis with Congress Street. It was the latter idea that Burnham and his colleagues proposed after Marshall Field offered his $10 million for a museum in early 1903.

Daniel Burnham was heavily committed to a number of clients throughout the United States in 1903. His architectural practice was generally devoted to very large projects. He had also just finished work on a "Plan for Washington, D.C.," under the auspices of the McMillan Commission, and he was an invited participant in a competition for a plan for several new buildings at the Military Academy at West Point. At the same time, he was a serving as a consultant to the City of Cleveland for the improvement of that city's downtown lakefront property.[19] Nevertheless, he found time to contact the office of his old friend and colleague Frederick Law Olmsted to get what he considered the best advice available for the planning of Grant Park as a site for the proposed Field Museum.[20] He worked with John C. Olmsted, son of Frederick Olmsted, who had passed away in 1903. John and his brother Frederick Law Olmsted Jr. had continued the firm as Olmsted Brothers after their father's illness had become acute. Burnham provided Olmsted Brothers with the basic data available, probably including the work done by the Municipal Improvement League, Peter B. Wight, and Normand Patton, as well as the schemes he and Charles Atwood had prepared shortly after the World's Columbian Exposition. They would also have had access to the plan prepared by the Chicago Architectural Club, which was exhibited at the club's 1896 annual exhibition. The fact remained that Burnham's early work had always shown a major civic structure as the centerpiece of Lake Front Park, while none of the other plans did so. Since Burnham was the Olmsted brothers' primary Chicago contact, it is understandable that they followed his basic plan.

The Olmsted brothers' preliminary plan for Grant Park was ready in July 1903.

19. Daniel Burnham's efforts in the field of city planning are well documented; the most complete study is Cynthia R. Field, "The City Planning of Daniel Hudson Burnham" (PhD diss., Columbia University, 1974). Field expands on the work of Thomas Hines, whose *Burnham of Chicago* is an important source for anyone interested in Burnham's life and work.

20. Frederick Law Olmsted (1822–1903) was one of Burnham's primary advisers during the Columbian Exposition, and the two remained friends. In 1895, Olmsted suffered a severe mental breakdown from which he never recovered. The work in his office was carried on by his staff, and in 1897, after the death of Charles Eliot, the firm became Olmsted Brothers. John Charles and Frederick Jr. guided it well into the twentieth century.

John C. Olmsted, along with Burnham, presented it to H. N. Higinbotham (Marshall Field's representative) and several members of the South Park Commission, which would eventually have governing authority over the property.[21] Their preliminary plan called for the museum to be exactly where Burnham had proposed, in the center of the park. It also called for "municipal buildings" to be located between Randolph and Monroe streets west of the Illinois Central tracks, but did not suggest any other buildings in the park. It did suggest that several recreation fields be included in the park, largely at the north end. A yacht basin was proposed on axis with Roosevelt Road, east of the Illinois Central tracks.

The plan was widely published in the Chicago newspapers with generally favorable comments. It was not, however, received with favor by Peter B. Wight and A. Montgomery Ward. Most of the members of the Chicago Architectural Club favored the plans the club itself and the Municipal Improvement League had put forth in 1896. John C. Olmsted returned to Brookline, Massachusetts, and prepared a slightly variant but more finished plan dated September 22, 1903.[22] The suggested location for municipal buildings had been eliminated, as had the athletic facilities at the north end of the park. It was this plan that was discussed at length and in great detail by public and professional planners during the next five years. A major obstacle to its implementation was that when the state legislature had authorized the South Park Commission to control the land that made up Grant Park, it had included a proviso that the owners of the property on Michigan Avenue fronting on the park would have a veto on any structure to be built in the park. This covenant was written in such a way that any single property owner could exercise the right to refuse permission for the Park District or the City of Chicago to build in the park. This provision of the law was not completely settled until nearly a decade later when the courts held that it was enforceable, and, as A. Montgomery Ward had argued for years, that the land that made up Grant Park should remain "Forever Open, Clear and Free."[23]

❧

While the Grant Park plans were being considered in Chicago, the work Daniel Burnham was doing in Cleveland was also appearing in the mainstream press. What was really happening was that architects and civic planners were beginning to understand that they didn't need a world's fair to realize a well-planned city. What they needed was the determination to build the "city beautiful." The members of the Chicago Architectural Club were young enough and idealistic enough to believe it could and should be done. While the plans for Chicago, Cleveland, and other great cities were never realized down to the last minute detail, those plans did prompt architects, developers, civic leaders, and politicians to insist on more livable cities. The Chicago Architectural Club took up the challenge.

During the months between September 1903 and April 1904, Dwight H. Perkins led a group of ten members of the Chicago Architectural Club in preparing plans for the arrangement of public and private buildings in a manner that would enhance the lives of all city dwellers. While they did not specifically state that their work was to be executed in Chicago, it was their own city they had in mind as they prepared their drawings and reviewed those being done elsewhere. When the Seventeenth Annual Exhibition of the Chicago Architectural Club opened on March 31, 1904, this work was the focus of attention in literally all the Chicago news reports. The Chicago Inter Ocean noted that "especial attention is being paid to the 'group system' for arranging public buildings, which the club is advocating as applicable to Chicago. Extensive drawings and designs are being exhibited, showing

21. There were certain legal requirements that needed to be met before the South Park commissioners could have decision-making authority over the lakefront property between Randolph Street and Park Row (Eleventh Place). The authority passed to the commissioners on January 20, 1904, by means of legislation passed by the Illinois state legislature. See "Lake Front Park," Chicago Economist, January 2, 1904.

22. The July 1903 plan was published in the Chicago Chronicle on July 31, 1903. There is, in the Olmsted archive in Brookline, Massachusetts, a plan dated July 27, 1903, that is almost identical to the published July plan (which was probably traced for publication). The September 22, 1903, plan is also still extant in the Olmsted archive.

23. This phrase comes from a map of Chicago prepared in 1836 by G. S. Hubbard, W. F. Thornton, and W. B. Archer, whereon they noted that the land designated as Grant Park would be a "Public Ground—A Common to Remain Forever Open, Clear and Free of any Buildings, or Other Obstruction Whatever." A. Montgomery Ward based his argument on this map.

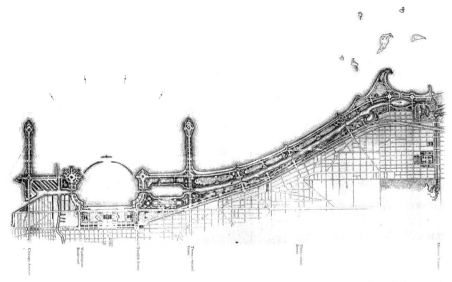

*Plan for the Chicago lakefront from Grant Park to Jackson Park; published in* The Plan of Chicago; *the scheme was an elaboration of Atwood's plan of 1896 (PofC)*

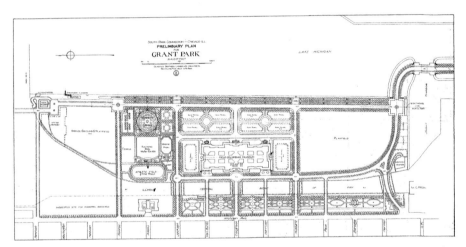

*Preliminary plan for Grant Park prepared for D. H. Burnham by Olmsted Brothers in July 1903 (ONHS)*

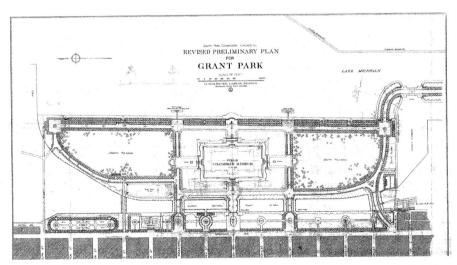

*Olmsted Brothers' revised plan of September 1903 for Grant Park, which stimulated a great deal of debate (ONHS)*

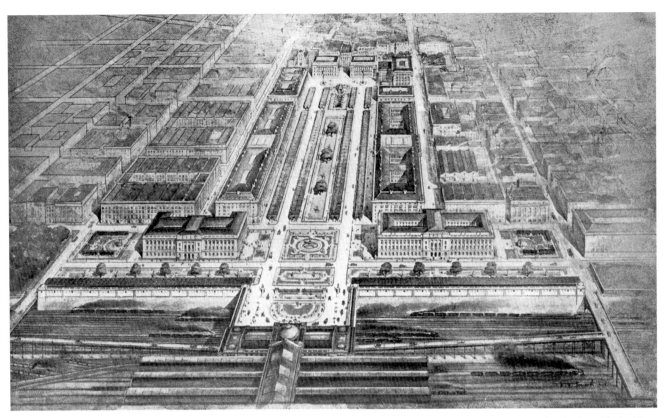

*D. H. Burnham, John Carrere, and A. W. Brunner's 1904 design for downtown Cleveland's public buildings (ALNY/04)*

the work now under construction at Cleveland, Ohio, which provides for the arrangement of all public buildings around a square, in the same manner as the structures were disposed around the Court of Honor at the World's Columbian exposition." The critic went on to say, "The plan is not only for the arrangement of public buildings, but for commercial structures and will be carried out to a certain extent in the reconstruction of City Hall park in New York City. In Cleveland, there is a public square four blocks in length by one in width and culminating in an ornamental pier on the lake front. This square will be lined with public buildings, constructed on the 'uniform cornice line.'" The item concluded with a quote from Dwight H. Perkins: "It is the purpose of the Club to arouse public sentiment in favor of such a reconstruction in Chicago."

When the 1904 exhibition opened, Dwight H. Perkins was cited as being the chairman of a "committee of ten" that was preparing a report suggesting that Chicago should adopt a plan similar to that of Cleveland, which would, in Perkins's words, "relieve the congestion of downtown Chicago."[24] He went on to say, "The backbone of our project is to relieve at one blow the congestion of our present business district, and enlarge it so it will be great enough for all time. The plan is extremely simple and captures everyone. Our work also will include the development of the lake front. Dockage facilities will be greatly enlarged. A plan for the lake front park, with proper distribution of its buildings will be included. When our committee prepares the plans the club will see how great a political influence it can wield to put the project into operation. It devolves upon the architects to wake up Chicago. Eventually we shall reach all of Chicago's Business men. We depend upon them to carry out our plan." The article closed with an editorial note that "several receptions will be given by the club to acquaint its friends with the Cleveland and Washington plans. No details of the Chicago project will be divulged until the plans are prepared by the committee." If the report by Perkins and his committee of ten

24. "Ideal Chicago Seen in Plans, Architectural Club Devises a Project for Harmony in Future Buildings," *Chicago Tribune*, April 17, 1904.

was ever delivered, or even prepared for that matter, there is no record of it. It may simply have been an idea that some of the club members had after reviewing the Cleveland and Washington plans, which Perkins felt could be accomplished, based on his own experience.

During the previous few months Perkins had begun preparing his now little-known but extremely important report concerning a metropolitan park system, which ultimately resulted in the establishment of the Forest Preserve District of Metropolitan Chicago.[25] That *Metropolitan Park System* report had been commissioned by the City of Chicago on September 28, 1903, just as Olmsted Brothers was completing the "Revised Preliminary Plan" for Grant Park.[26] From September 1903 through December 1904, Perkins devoted a good deal of time and energy to his work on the *Metropolitan Park System* report. It was, to some degree, a labor of love since his fee was only fifteen hundred dollars. He was assisted by several prominent members of the business community and his colleague and fellow member of the Architectural Club Jens Jensen.[27] One of the members of the Cook County Board's Outer Belt Park Commission was Daniel Burnham who, in 1907–8, incorporated Perkins's recommendations virtually verbatim into the *Plan of Chicago*.

While the Chicago Architectural Club was following the events outlined above during the summer and fall of 1903, the regular affairs of the club continued. Classes in sketching and watercolor were conducted and lectures continued to be offered at alternate club meetings, now held twice a month. The club continued its Traveling Scholarship Competition, but for some reason, the program for the 1903–4 competition was never published. The terms and conditions of the competition can, however, be surmised from items in newspaper accounts and critics' comments concerning the 1904 exhibition at the Art Institute of Chicago.

The program called for the design of a "creche," or day care center, to be erected in a manufacturing district of a large city. The rules called for an initial "sketch plan" and a "sketch elevation" to be submitted, followed by a final plan, an elevation and section, details, and finally, a perspective of the completed design. As

25. The *Report of the Special Park Commission to the City Council of Chicago on the Subject of a Metropolitan Park System* (Chicago, 1905) became the basis of the Forest Preserve District that now surrounds Chicago. The title page noted that it was a "report compiled by Dwight Heald Perkins, 1904," although was actually printed in 1905.

26. The plan was dated September 22, 1903.

27. Jens Jensen (1859–1951) came to Chicago from Denmark in 1884. He was employed in Chicago's West Park System, eventually becoming superintendent of Humboldt Park. He left that position in 1900 to enter private practice. During this period he worked with Perkins on the plans that resulted in the formation of the Cook County Forest Preserve System. He continued to work sporadically on Chicago's park system, but most of his work was in the private sector.

*Thomas Tallmadge's winning design was the only published entry from the 1904 Traveling Scholarship Competition; no plan was included with this newspaper illustration (CTR)*

usual, the various elements were submitted separately over a period of several months, at which time they were critiqued and club members voted on the best work of the evening. The voting was cumulative, and as the competition progressed, some of the competitors dropped out. The final evening found ten contestants still in the running. Thomas Tallmadge was declared the winner, with Roy Eliel taking second place.[28] Both were exhibited in the 1904 show at the Art Institute of Chicago.

The Seventeenth Annual Exhibition of the Chicago Architectural Club was shown at the Art Institute of Chicago from March 31 to April 20, 1904. It was similar in size and character to previous years' exhibitions, with a total of 469 exhibits. The 1904 catalog, however, was a far cry from earlier catalogs. It was small, in paper wraps, and the only illustrations were a frontispiece of the Art Institute Building and a photograph titled "Interior of New Club Room—Chicago Architectural Club," which was then located in the Dexter Building at 84 Adams Street above a restaurant that provided food for the members.[29] The club had been evicted, for the second time, from the Art Institute of Chicago.[30] It is likely that the club was simply unable to afford a catalog, since it was now obligated to both pay rent and furnish and decorate its new club rooms. In any case, the catalog was not published by the club. It was noted on the title page that it was "Printed for the Art Institute, Chicago, 1904." Whatever the reason, the catalog was a modest undertaking. Eighty firms and individuals, mostly building suppliers and architects, were listed in the catalog as "patrons" of the exhibition. Following that list was a page of "Standing Officers, 1903–04," with no additional editorial content. The other thirty-four pages were simply a list of exhibitors with their addresses and their contributions to the exhibition. There were no illustrations of exhibits. Few of the exhibits were from the young progressives of previous years. Only Pond & Pond and Dwight Perkins from Steinway Hall had entries, and both showed work of only modest interest. Probably the most interesting thing about the 1904 catalog was the illustration of the "Dexter Building Club Rooms," a variation of which appeared in another, more important publication in 1904. That was the small, hardbound book referenced earlier, the *Charter, Constitution, By-Laws, House Rules, Officers and Members of the Chicago Architectural Club,* which was published in 1904 shortly after the election of the 1904–5 officers. Not only did it include the items listed in its long title, but it included four illustrations of the new club rooms.[31] They were views of the "Entrance Lobby," the "Club Room Looking North," the "Dining Room," and "Club Room Looking South," the latter being similar to the image that appeared in the 1904 catalog and was included in one of the reviews of the exhibition. These are the only photographs of any of the spaces used by the Chicago Architectural Club until it moved to the Kimball House many years later.

From these photographs it is easy to conclude that the club was now in its heyday insofar as facilities were concerned. The new quarters included both a lounge area and a dining room, as well as an entrance lobby. Food was provided by the restaurant on the ground floor and there was a permanent staff at the club, probably two persons. The rooms were finished in the style of the emerging Prairie School, with furnishings virtually all in the arts and crafts style, as were the hanging light fixtures and wall sconces. The lounge room was accessorized with Teco pottery donated by William Gates, a few pieces of sculpture, and small framed pictures. The Gates pieces included heavy terra-cotta cups with the letters *CAC* impressed on the handles and a huge ceremonial stein that was used only occasionally.[32] There was an upright piano, two large tables, two desks, a large drawing case, and numerous chairs, many of which were rockers. The walls appear to have been fabric in two colors below a classic plaster cornice. The fabric would have permitted drawings to be hung without visible damage to the walls during competitions or other events. It was a club where the members could be comfortable for lunch or dinner but, more im-

28. Thomas Eddy Tallmadge was born in Washington, D.C., on April 24, 1876. Seven years later he moved to Evanston, a suburb of Chicago, with his family. After a public school education, he studied architecture at MIT, graduating in 1898. He spent the following summer in Europe and then began his career in the office of Daniel H. Burnham. Tallmadge became a member of the Chicago Architectural Club in 1901. He was still in Burnham's office when he won the Chicago Architectural Club Traveling Scholarship. Tallmadge used his scholarship money to pay for a trip to Europe. Upon his return in 1905, he persuaded a coworker at Burnham's office, Vernon Watson, to form a partnership, which lasted nearly thirty years. Today he is remembered as much for his writing and teaching as for his architecture, although much of his firm's work is held in high regard. Less is known of the second-place winner. Roy Eliel joined the Chicago Architectural Club in 1897. His first and only exhibition with the club was his entry in the 1904 Traveling Scholarship Competition. He continued to be listed as a member through 1910, and thereafter is not included. There is no record that he was ever licensed.

29. The Dexter Building was designed by Burnham & Root and built in 1883. The street number was changed to 39 West Adams in 1909. It was torn down in 1961 to make room for the Dirk-

sen Federal Center Building, part of the new Federal Center complex designed by Mies van der Rohe.

30. Notice of the club's eviction is published in the Report of the Director, Art Institute of Chicago, 1903–4. It covered the period June 1, 1903, to June 1, 1904, but does not say when the club was asked to vacate room 107, which it had occupied for several years. (The previous eviction, noted in chapter 5, was in March 1891.)

31. Three of these photographs also appeared in the club's 1905 catalog, and the slightly different view in the catalog was published in an unnamed newspaper; a copy survives in the Art Institute clipping file for April of 1904.

32. The stein was illustrated and described in *Clay Worker* 37 (January 1902). Obviously, it was made before the club moved out of the Art Institute of Chicago.

*Club room in the Dexter Building, looking south (PC)*

*Club room in the Dexter Building, looking north (PC)*

*Club mug with CAC impressed on the handle (WRH)*

*William D. Gates of the American Terra Cotta and Ceramic Company donated this giant stein to the club: over 20 inches high and finished in Gates's classic matte green surface, it reads, "If you can't keep it down, throw it up" (CW)*

*Club dining room in the Dexter Building (PC)*

portant, a place to call their own. It was here they met for their regular meetings, entertained guests, and held many of their classes.

The new Chicago Architectural Club rooms were dedicated on the afternoon of March 12, less than three weeks before the Seventeenth Annual Exhibition opened at the Art Institute of Chicago.[33] Clearly a great deal of attention, as well as time and money, had been devoted to the new club rooms, and this may explain why the 1904 catalog was so modest. The long list of "patrons" in the 1904 catalog also suggests that some of those who made contributions may have actually been helping out with the expenses of finishing and furnishing the new space. The design of the club rooms was clearly done by the members who had been for several years the leaders of the club. The influence of Spencer, Perkins, Garden, Wright, and their colleagues was clearly evident. They had not, however, been prominent or even visible in the 1903 exhibition, nor did they have a major part in the 1904 exhibition.

Some of the members who were persona non grata at the exhibition again mounted a show of their own a few days before the official club exhibition opened. On the same day the new club rooms were dedicated, the *Chicago Post* wrote that on March 17, an "exhibition of water colors, sketches, drawings and practical plans relating to 'House and Garden Architecture' will be opened in the town hall of Riverside. This is, in certain features, a departure from the usual architectural exhibitions . . . [and] a number of well-known architects have interested themselves to make it a success and among the exhibitors are eminent men from the East. Among those standing sponsor for the collection which will be presented are Olmsted Brothers of Brookline Mass., Coolidge & Carlson of Boston, Lord & Hewlett and Wilson Eyre of New York, J. Wilkenson Elliott of Chewick, Pa., and from Chicago come Arthur Heun, Alfred H. Granger, Howard Shaw, Robert C. Spencer, Jr., Dwight Heald Perkins, Hugh M. G. Garden, Richard E. Schmidt, James Gamble Rogers, Pond & Pond, George Maher, H. R. Wilson, Joseph C. Llewellyn, H. L. Ottenheimer, J. L. Silsbee, John N. Tilton, H. H. Waterman, William W. Clay, William A. Otis and

33. *Brickbuilder* 13, no. 3 (March 1904): 66.

Frank Lloyd Wright." About half these names also appeared as exhibitors in the Seventeenth Annual Exhibition. Unfortunately, no catalog or other listing of the exhibits shown in Riverside has surfaced, and what was shown is not known. An examination of the exhibits of the thirteen men who were in both shows indicates that the material in the club's 1904 exhibition was generally of a traditional nature or simply sketches rather than designs. It seems likely that the club's Exhibition Committee, headed by J. L. Hamilton, was not prepared to have the exhibition dominated by avant-garde work in 1904 and took the easy way out by omitting it. On the other hand, two members of the Jury of Admission, a subcommittee of the Exhibition Committee, showed their work in both venues. Those men, James Gamble Rogers and George W. Maher, had not been heavily involved in the exhibitions of 1900, 1901, and 1902, and probably maintained at least a casual relationship with members of both camps. It is also possible that other material shown in Riverside was hung in the regular 1904 exhibition that opened two weeks later as well. Whatever the case, the Riverside exhibition got only minimal attention from the press, while the Seventeenth Annual Exhibition of the Chicago Architectural Club was enthusiastically reviewed by both local newspapers and professional journals.

The first article concerning the 1904 exhibition was an illustrated notice in the *Chicago Tribune* announcing that Thomas E. Tallmadge's design for a creche had won the annual Traveling Scholarship prize for 1904.[34] Tallmadge's perspective of the winning design was illustrated, the only time any of the 1904 exhibits was illustrated. The article referred to the award as the "Falkenau prize," which was not entirely correct. Victor Falkenau had provided the five hundred dollars in prize money, but the award was still called the CAC Annual Traveling Scholarship.[35] During the next few days similar items announcing the prize appeared in several other Chicago newspapers, and on March 30 most of those papers noted that the exhibition would open with a reception at the Art Institute on March 31 between eight and eleven o'clock.

The reviews of the exhibition often led with a paragraph regarding the report Dwight Perkins was putting together on a "group system" of public buildings.[36] The reviewers commented extensively on Burnham's designs for downtown Cleveland, as well as his competition designs for the United States Military Academy at West Point (which did not win). Cram, Goodhue & Ferguson's winning design for that project actually got less attention in these brief reviews.

The longest, although not necessarily the most thoughtful, review in the Chicago newspapers was the one published by the *Chicago Post*.[37] It began with what had become an almost mandatory comment that the club's annual exhibition was better than ever. The reviewer stated that every "succeeding year the exhibitions of the Chicago Architectural Club increase the sphere of their interests and draw more largely upon the attention of the general public." He was probably correct in his assumption that the club was aiming at the general public rather than demonstrating what was being done by the most advanced thinkers in the architectural world. He noted that there were "469 numbers of drawings, water colors, photographs, vases and panels in terra cotta" and pointed out that the "arrangement of the exhibits has been made with skill and in such a way that the untutored layman may find something to delight his eyes on every wall. The enthusiast dreaming of a city beautiful may linger before Burnham, Carrere and Brunner's scheme of public buildings for the City of Cleveland; the millionaire['s] . . . country home . . . and . . . the seeker for a suburban retreat must find something to his liking." These opening statements were almost condescending, suggesting that the layman might not be up to understanding the more avant-garde work then rising in the suburbs of Chicago. The reviewer pointed out that the "residences of any suburb are eloquent examples of lack of intelligence and common sense from an exterior point of view

34. "Prize Design in Competition for Day Nursery in a Manufacturing District," *Chicago Tribune,* March 18, 1904.

35. Victor Falkenau (1859–1922) was born in New Jersey and educated at City College in New York. In 1882, he moved to Chicago, where he did some development work and was a client of Adler & Sullivan in the late 1880s. By 1897, he was president of Falkenau Construction Co., Inc. He maintained a lifelong interest in architecture and became a member of the CAC in 1904.

36. See the *Chicago Examiner,* the *Chicago Inter Ocean,* and the *Chicago Post* for April 1, 1904.

37. *Chicago Post,* April 3, 1904.

and interior convenience, both of which are the corner stones of good architecture. Only by repeating examples of simple, honest art in household construction may the public be taught to lay aside foolish ornament and unwholesome planning. The exhibitions of the Architectural Club should have an educative side which would help the good work along." It is a bit difficult to follow the reviewer's logic, but it seems that he was advocating traditional architecture. Later in his review he appeared to reverse himself, suggesting that the architect should be allowed "to build without interference. Too much meddling has spoiled the plan of many an architect, too much figuring has lowered him to the tune of commercial spirit, and art and harmony are in the background." His final comment in this vein seems to be in support of the residential avant-garde; he wrote that until "the average man is converted to the needs of a city beautiful and willing to begin on his own street, it is folly to think of great plans of regeneration. Better begin the work on a small scale."

After his opening and somewhat confusing remarks, the *Chicago Post* reviewer devoted a few paragraphs to Thomas Tallmadge's winning design for the Traveling Scholarship Competition and to the second-place winner, Roy Eliel. He followed with some positive comments on the exhibited work of previous scholarship winners and mentioned a number of other works in the show. W. B. Mundie's designs for the Chicago Board of Education and similar work by W. B. Ittner in St. Louis were noted without any comment on the part of the reporter. Most of the remainder of the long article was essentially a list of the exhibits, with only minimal comment on the quality of the work. He ended with some favorable words on the Teco vases and terra-cotta panels exhibited by the Northwestern Terra Cotta Company, which he felt had "an artistic value."

A day later the *Chicago Tribune* had its turn.[38] It was more objective in its comments, which were generally favorable but with little reference to the cutting-edge architecture gaining a foothold in the Midwest. Early in the article the writer noted that "the architect may not be quite a painter or a sculptor yet it will go hard to deny the solid, honest, esthetic, artistic work here set forth in his creations in brick, stone, and iron; his bridges, towers, mansions, warehouses, churches. There is in them both beauty and strength." The contributions by past Traveling Scholarship winners Birch Burdette Long, John H. Phillips, and John Molitor were singled out for praise. Their exhibits were, of course, virtually all sketches of historic scenes in Europe. The *Tribune* also noted that "the two most ambitious projects occupy a large portion of the wall space in the largest room of the Institute." They were the designs for the improvement of New York City, primarily bridges, by Palmer & Hornbostel, and the Cram, Goodhue & Ferguson winning competition design for the improvement of West Point. The designs of D. H. Burnham and Company and Frost & Granger for the same project were not mentioned, nor was the work done by Burnham, Carrere & Brunner in Cleveland. Frost & Granger's design for the Chicago Northwestern Railway Station in Chicago did get a favorable note. The *Chicago Tribune* ended its review with a statement that "the exhibition is impressive for the vast amount of architectural talent in the country, its wide distribution, and the luxury and immense resources of a land that can command such elegance in its public and private structures." Obviously the writer was impressed that many of the exhibits came from outside Chicago.

Several other newspapers had briefer comments during the next few days; none covered the exhibition in any depth. It was left to the *Inland Architect* to cover it for the professional journals.[39] Its unsigned article was not particularly critical, but was essentially a description of the exhibition. The writer noted that the "larger part of space was given to public works" and described each briefly. He noted that the work of Palmer & Hornbostel in New York consisted largely of bridges, and that several models were exhibited. He also commented at some length

38. "Artistic Architects," *Chicago Tribune*, April 3, 1904.

39. "The Chicago Architectural Club Exhibition," *Inland Architect* 43, no. 4 (May 1904): 29–30.

*Louis Sullivan's design for a facade for a theater without a specific site (AR)*

on the inclusion of displays from various colleges and universities. He was impressed that in "New York the committee there, Messrs. Long and Phillips, who recently removed to that city from Chicago, secured through their personal efforts most of the Eastern exhibits." Not only was work from universities and New York cited, but it was noted that there was a "large variety of designs for structures all over the United States." The writer then listed most of the exhibits without any particular comments and ended with praise for the terra-cotta of the Northwestern Terra Cotta Company. Like the other reviewers, he did not find it necessary to report that the work of the young modernists of two to four years earlier was conspicuous in its absence. Not only were many of the younger avant-garde designers once again absent from the annual exhibition, but without an illustrated catalog, the work that was shown was not preserved for analysis by future critics. The sleek modernism that would make itself known in the work of Eliel Saarinen, Holabird & Root, and others in the 1920s was apparent only in scattered and, for the most part, ignored entries. The unlikely and seldom-heralded team of Frost & Granger followed its 1903 exhibition of work, precursive of art deco, on the Hall Bartlett House with an elaborate design for West Point buildings and the Chicago Northwestern Railway Station, which were largely ignored. William B. Mundie exhibited several of his designs for the Chicago public school system, as did William B. Ittner, who did a similar service for the Saint Louis public school system. Both deserved attention. While some reviewers did comment on the Northwestern Terra Cotta Company's exhibit, they did not note that William Gates, president of the company, which showed Teco designs by William Mundie, had his own exhibit that included an elaborate mosaic panel executed by Orlando Giannini, one of the craftsmen of choice of the young modernists working out of Steinway Hall. The reaction of the

*Both S. S. Beman's Third Church of Christ Scientist (top), shown in the 1902 exhibition, and Frost & Granger's Hall Bartlett House (above), shown in 1903, revealed an extraordinary affinity to the art deco work that appeared twenty years later (CAC/02/03)*

*Ernest Flagg's traditional design for the United States Naval Academy, shown in the 1903 exhibition (CAC/03)*

press and many practitioners to the excesses of the 1902 exhibition lingered. Some time was still needed to heal those wounds.

Even Louis Sullivan, the mentor of the modernists, was mentioned only once, in an unidentified sidebar clipping, now in the files of the Art Institute of Chicago, in which the reviewer wrote, "Lovers of fine draughtsmanship should not fail to see Louis H. Sullivan's beautiful design for the facade of the front of a theater executed in pencil." That critic could not deny Sullivan his due, but he and the rest of the writers in Chicago did not yet understand the importance of the work of the Steinway Hall group and their colleagues in the Chicago Architectural Club, who were, while the 1904 exhibition was being shown, changing the architecture of the world.

# PROGRAM OF EVENTS

# GRAND ATHLETIC TOURNAMENT

## At Terra Cotta, Illinois
## July 4th, 1905

Hon. W. D. Gates, Mayor of Terra Cotta, Illinois, has extended an invitation to the members and ladies of the Chicago Architectural Club, to be his guests, July 4th, 1905.

July 4th is hereby declared a holiday and all members are enjoined from pushing graphite on that day. Anyone so attached to their plans can bring them along.

By order of the High Moguls, all you have to do is to be present at the C. & N.-W. Depot, Wells and Kinzie Streets, at 8:30 A. M., everything else being arranged for.

Train Leaves Chicago       8:45 A. M.
Train Leaves Terra Cotta   5:30 P. M.

Address of Welcome by Mayor Gateski.

Response by Admiral Nelsoninski.

Grand Tramp down de track led by Mayor Gateski and Admiral Nelsoninski to de Orange Grove.

Upon the ringing of Cow-Bells, guests will assemble for lunch.

Hot Tomales, Fried Possum, Baked Elephant, Duck Eggs, Omega Oil, Carrots—will constitute the menu.

*Smokables* — Fire-Crackers will be distributed for those wishing to smoke up.

Highland Fling, by W. B. (day before Tuesday).

Fritz Wagner will play the Bagpipes.

Exhibition of Fancy Fly-Casting by Mr. O. Gianninni.

Base-Ball Game between the T-square and Triangle Clubs.

Mr. Horse-Power, Umpire.
Mr. Cabin Slot, Scorekeeper.
Mr. Slide-Kelly-Kelly-Slide, Referee.

*Athletic Competition* —A series of games and races will be arranged for. All present are invited to compete for the prizes which will be offered.

Solo, by Mr. Holmes going home.

Come one! Come all!! and spend a delightful day in the woods with us. Send in postal immediately so that proper arrangements can be made.

### ARTHUR J. T. BENNETT
Chairman House Committee

*Poster invitation to the outing at Gates Potteries, "printed in gorgeous colors on yellow paper" (WA)*

# A Struggle for Dominance

CHAPTER FOURTEEN

The Seventeenth Annual Exhibition of the Chicago Architectural Club closed on April 20, 1904. About two weeks later, on the first Monday in May, the club elected a new slate of officers. J. L. Hamilton moved up to president,[1] with Harry L. Marsh and Edward B. Pattison as first and second vice presidents. M. M. Levings became secretary, and Edward O. Nelson was reelected treasurer. Hugo H. Zimmerman remained on the Executive Committee, and Alfred S. Alschuler took the place of Horace S. Powers. As in the previous year, the club appointed a large Exhibition Committee, twelve in all, headed by the second vice president, Edward B. Pattison. Pattison also served on the Finance Committee with Otto Silha. These men were responsible for a period of stability in the club that was to last for the rest of the decade.

Now ensconced in their new quarters on the second floor of the Dexter Building, the members set about using the space to its best advantage. They held most of their regular meetings there but, more important, they used the club rooms as a club. There was a lounge area with comfortable chairs and an expanding library that eventually grew to several hundred books. The club also subscribed to all the current professional publications, often taking several subscriptions to each of the most popular periodicals. With its central location between State and Dearborn streets on Adams, it was an ideal place to spend one's lunch hour. The facilities were open in the evening for dinner or club affairs that often included wives and other guests. The fabric-covered walls permitted the most recent competition drawings and other similar material to be mounted for viewing. The CAC had become a club in the truest and broadest sense.

By late summer of 1904 plans were under way for the coming year. While the club continued to have regular guest lecturers and bohemian nights, the major efforts of the officers and the Executive Committee were the organization of competitions and planning of the annual exhibition.

They also regularly monitored and criticized plans for Grant Park on Chicago's lakefront. Daniel Burnham continued to advocate the development of the park with the Field Columbian Museum as its centerpiece. He had a number of allies in this effort, headed by N. H. Carpenter of the Art Institute of Chicago and H. N. Higinbotham, who represented Marshall Field in the discussions. It was Field, of course, who had offered to provide the funds to build the museum, but only if the Park District provided a site. From September of 1903 through Septem-

*The Dexter Building, where the club had quarters on the second floor (CCB)*

1. John L. Hamilton (1878–ca. 1968) was born in Bloomington, Illinois, and shortly thereafter moved to Chicago, where he was educated at the Chicago Manual Training School. He began private practice in 1905, when he formed Perkins & Hamilton, later to become Perkins, Fellows & Hamilton.

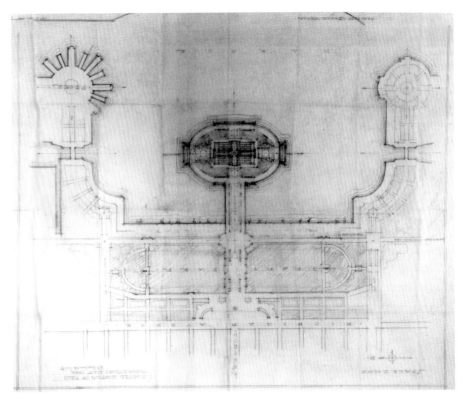

*Burnham's plan to put the Field Museum on an island in the lake got little support (F. M. Weinstein)*

ber of 1904, the Olmsted brothers tinkered with their plan for Grant Park, but little was changed.[2] They continued to show the Field Museum in the center of the park on axis with Congress Street. It was, however, too soon to proceed because the proposed site was still under the water of Lake Michigan. Burnham went so far as to suggest an alternate plan for building an island for the museum off the shore in Lake Michigan. Apparently he thought such a plan might defeat his opponents and solve some legal problems of building in the park. It did not fly. A number of legal hurdles had to be faced before filling in the lake, and this gave the opponents of the Grant Park museum site time to promote alternatives. Ultimately, the opponents won out.

With Peter B. Wight making the architectural arguments and A. Montgomery Ward leading the legal battle, Burnham's museum-in-the-park plan did not go forward, even after his *Plan of Chicago* was published in 1909. In that seminal document the museum was sited in the center of the park. Ultimately, it was built, following Burnham's death, at the south end of the park on land recovered from Lake Michigan after the Illinois Central Railroad gave up its riparian rights east of the 12th Street Chicago Passenger Station. The final plan of Grant Park was essentially the same as the one the Chicago Architectural Club had proposed and exhibited in 1896, insofar as the location of the Field Museum was concerned. In fact, the entire park resembled the club's 1896 plan, except that no boat basin was installed in the center of the park and no municipal buildings were proposed for the area between Randolph and Monroe streets.

Many of the proposals for Grant Park, including plans prepared for inclusion in the *Plan of Chicago,* were exhibited in the club's rooms. Burnham also exhibited parts of his plan from time to time in the club's annual exhibitions. For example, in 1905 he showed his current plan for Grant Park, as well as several other drawings, including one of Sherman Park (named for his father-in-law, John B. Sher-

2. Olmsted Brothers provided the South Park commissioners with a new plan dated 1904, which varied only slightly from the plan dated September 1903.

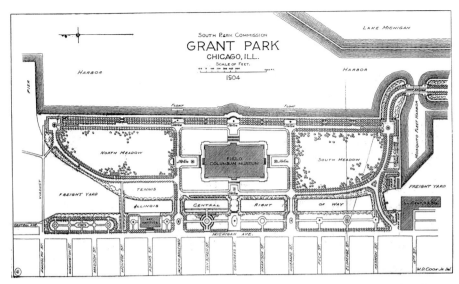

Burnham expected the Field Museum to be the centerpiece of Grant Park, as indicated on this plan prepared by Olmsted Brothers for the South Park Commission in 1904 (OHS)

man). In 1907 he exhibited his plan for a waterway centered in the Midway Plaisance at the University of Chicago. Eventually, of course, all Burnham's drawings for the *Plan of Chicago* were exhibited widely in other venues.

The Chicago Architectural Club's primary civic activities between 1903 and 1906 were directed at reviewing plans for the improvement and development of Chicago's lakefront. The members were, however, heavily involved in other activities as well. Meetings were held as in the past, but were not reported regularly in the architectural press for two reasons. First, the recently revised constitution did not relieve the secretary from paying dues, as it had earlier in recognition of the time-consuming task of reporting the club's activities to the press. Second, the

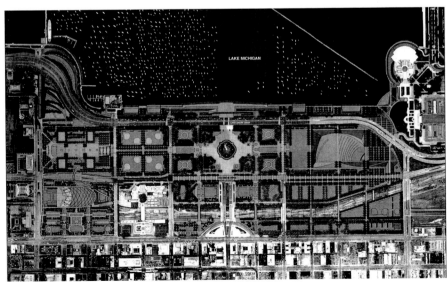

The Field Museum was ultimately located southeast of Grant Park, as shown in this recent plan of the park (CPD)

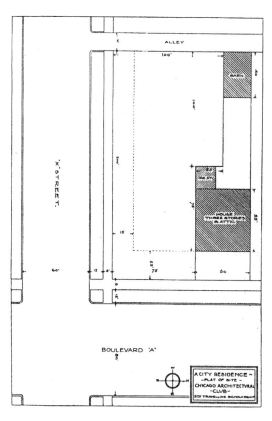

*Site plan for the Fifth Annual Traveling Scholarship Competition (IA)*

club's champion at the *Inland Architect*, Robert Craik McLean, left the magazine after the October 1904 issue to join the *Western Architect* as editor. Thereafter, the *Inland Architect* published news of the Chicago Architectural Club only sporadically. The first notice of the club's work in the fall of 1904 appeared in the *Inland Architect's* December issue, when the competition for the club's Fifth Annual Traveling Scholarship was announced.[3] The club held other competitions, but the Traveling Scholarship Competition was second in importance only to the annual exhibition. It was held every year until 1938, except during the World War I years of 1916–18, when virtually all club activity ceased.

The program for the Fifth Annual Traveling Scholarship Competition was issued "in neat pamphlet form."[4] The subject was a city residence to be built for a public-spirited citizen of ample means interested in the collection of art, and was to include, in addition to the residence proper, a gallery, collection rooms, and servants' quarters. The program went into considerable detail, describing the family that would live there and all the rooms required. The pamphlet provided a site plan and even suggested the materials to be used on the exterior of the house. Like previous Traveling Scholarship competitions, it was held in multiple stages, although in this case only two. The first stage, due on January 23, 1905, called for plans and a perspective, all at a relatively small scale. These were to be exhibited in the club rooms after being juried in secret by a three-man jury made up of Irving K. Pond, Howard Van Doren Shaw, and P. J. Weber. The second-stage drawings were due on February 27 and were to be "detail drawings showing more completely the work of previous sketches." The program noted that the competitors were "allowed to vary from their original design, but the motives of the original conception must be well recognized in the final drawings." C. Herrick Hammond won first honors. The prize money, $650 as in the previous year, was donated by Victor Falkenau. The *Chicago Evening Post* wrote that in addition to Hammond, "second place honor was assigned to Alfred Alschuler and Christian Morgensterne; and others of the fourteen architects

3. That announcement appeared twice in the December 1904 issue of *Inland Architect* 44, no. 5, on the editorial page and pages 36–37, with a complete description of the rules of the competition.

4. *Inland Architect* 44, no. 5 (December 1904): 36–37. No copy of the pamphlet referred to has been located.

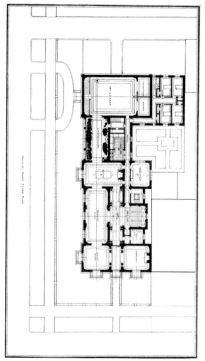

*C. Herrick Hammond's winning design for the Fifth Annual Traveling Scholarship Competition (CAC/05)*

entering the contest whose drawings are in the exhibition are Charles H. Kable, acknowledged third, and Vernon W. Behel, Walter B. Griffin, Mark M. Levings and Frank C. Walker."[5]

During the next five years the Traveling Scholarship Competition continued to be held in essentially the same manner, that is, in stages that were each juried separately. The final tally of accumulated votes determined the winner. There were, however, very few notices of the competition in the professional press, and in no case was the entire program published during this period. There was a notice that Fritz Wagner "subscribed" the funds for the Sixth Annual Traveling Scholarship in 1906.[6] In the 1906 exhibition catalog, credit was given to the Northwestern Terra Cotta Company for the gift. (Wagner was, of course, an officer of that company.) Like the earlier competitions, the sixth competition was juried in stages, but each stage called for a different design. The first stage was "An Episcopal Church," the second was "A yacht Club-house for Grant Park," and the third was "A recreation pier for a public park." Herbert Green was the winner of the prize, and Walter Parker took second place, with third going to Joseph W. Wilson. All three entries were shown in the 1906 exhibition. Eleven drawings were illustrated on seven pages.

The Seventh Annual Traveling Scholarship Competition in 1907 was the first to be announced in the *Western Architect,* where the club's old friend and honorary member Robert Craik McLean was now serving as editor. The brief notice stated that the competition would be "divided in two parts, the program for the first part being given, the second part to follow at a later date."[7] The subject was a branch municipal court. It had the odd condition that the same building was to be built in three sections of the city, each on an ordinary city block. The second part of the program was never published. The prize of five hundred dollars was donated by Mr. E. G. Elcock of the Hansel-Elcock Company, and the winner was, as usual, to use the funds for European travel.[8] The winner was Will Reichert. His winning designs were never published. Reichert had joined the Chicago Architectural Club in 1905 and lived in Palos Park, Illinois. He is listed as a member of the club in 1907, but in an apparent oversight his name is not on the membership list in 1908, even though he was second vice president of the club and chairman of the Exhibition Committee. In October 1908 he was listed as a newly licensed architect in the state of Illinois.[9] His name reappears as a member in 1910. That year and the year before,

5. *Chicago Evening Post*, April 1, 1905.

6. *Inland Architect* 47, no. 1 (February 1906): 18.

7. *Western Architect* 10, no. 2 (February 1907): 22.

8. Edward G. Elcock was born in Belfast, Ireland, on May 22, 1859, and came to the United States in 1867 with his family. He helped organize the Hansel-Elcock Company, steel manufacturers, in 1888 and became president of the firm in 1904. He was elected an honorary member of the Chicago Architectural Club in 1909.

*Herbert Green's design for an Episcopal church was submitted in part one of the Sixth Annual Traveling Scholarship Competition (CAC/06)*

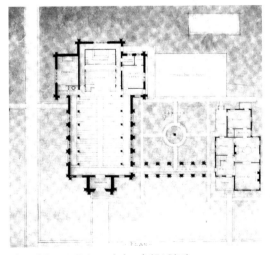

*Plan of Green's Episcopal church (CAC/06)*

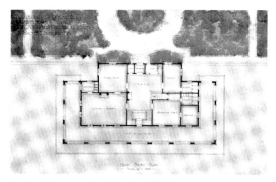

*Herbert Green's yacht club plan (CAC/06)*

*Herbert Green's part-two competition submission for a yacht club was quite simple but impressed the jury (CAC/06)*

the firm of Ottenheimer, Stern & Reichert took part in the annual exhibition. During the next several years, it became a prominent Chicago firm and was published widely.

The only published notice of the Eighth Annual Traveling Scholarship Competition was in the February 1908 issue of the *Inland Architect*.[10] It was included as part of a paragraph concerning the club's activities and said only that "the subject for the Traveling Scholarship competition, now under way is, 'Public Gymnasium and Baths.'" No other published data appeared until the *Inland Architect* published a review of the annual exhibition in April of 1908.[11] The journal noted that "attention is drawn to the prize and mention drawings submitted in the Traveling Scholarship competition . . . It was one of the most successful competitions yet held by the Chicago Architectural Club. The prize design by George Ausumb [*sic*] is illustrated in this number. It shows much breadth in conception and treatment of the problem, and unusual skill in rendering. The First Mention design by

9. *Inland Architect* 52, no. 5 (November 1908): 65.

10. *Inland Architect* 51, no. 2 (February 1908): 10.

11. "Chicago Architectural Club Exhibition, 1908," *Inland Architect* 51, no. 4 (April 1908): 30–31.

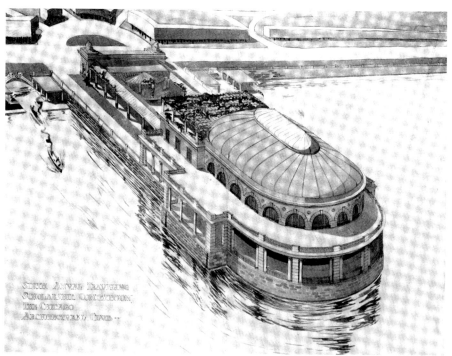

*"Recreation Pier for a Public Park," Herbert Green's final, prizewinning design in the Sixth Annual Traveling Scholarship Competition (CAC/06)*

Walter Parker's final design for the Sixth Annual Traveling Scholarship Competition (CAC/06)

Episcopal church design by Walter Parker, which won him second place in the Sixth Annual Traveling Scholarship Competition (CAC/06)

"Recreation Pier" by Joseph Wilson, who won third place in the Sixth Annual Traveling Scholarship Competition (CAC/06)

Arthur H. Knox's design for an Episcopal church for the Sixth Annual Traveling Scholarship Competition (CAC/06)

Vernon S. Watson and the Second Mention by Paul T. Haagen are well conceived and rendered." All three entries were shown in the exhibition and illustrated in the 1908 catalog. For the first time the exhibition included both the preliminary drawings, or *esquisse,* and the final drawings for each of the three winners. The prize money for the 1908 traveling fellowship was again donated by E. G. Elcock, who would do so the next year as well.

The program for the Ninth Annual Traveling Scholarship Competition was announced in December of 1908.[12] Complete details were not given, but the subject was "An Athenaeum for Teachers." The item in the *Inland Architect* noted that it was "to be designed to accommodate the 7,000 teachers in the Chicago public schools and is to have suitable provision for educational conventions and lectures." It was the first program to include a requirement for landscape work. The jury was made up of W. K. Fellows, Dwight H. Perkins, Pierce Anderson, and S. S. Beman.

12. *Inland Architect* 52, no. 6 (December 1908): 78.

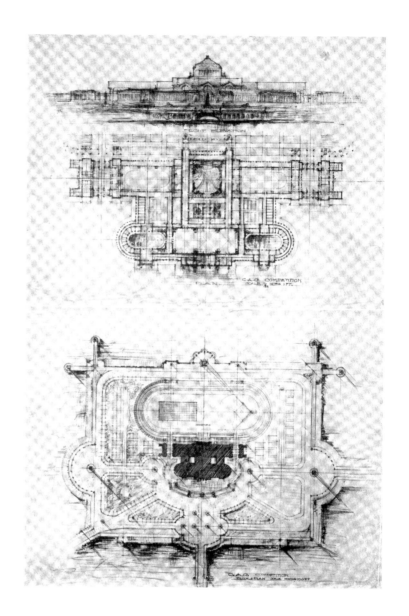

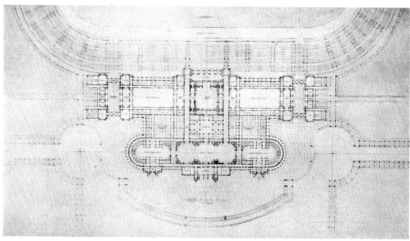

*George Awsumb's* esquisse *was done in the classic style of the École des Beaux-Arts (top); his final plan (above) followed his original sketch with great fidelity, as expected at the École (CAC/08)*

*George Awsumb's final, winning design for the Eighth Annual Traveling Scholarship Competition showed little sign of the emerging modernism in the Midwest (IA)*

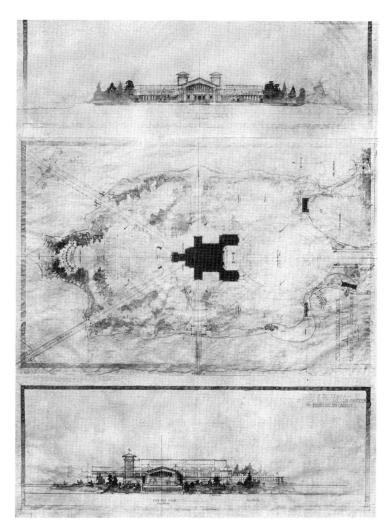

*Vernon Watson's esquisse for the Eighth Annual Traveling Scholarship followed the form of the Beaux-Arts, but the influence of Midwestern modernism is apparent (CAC/08)*

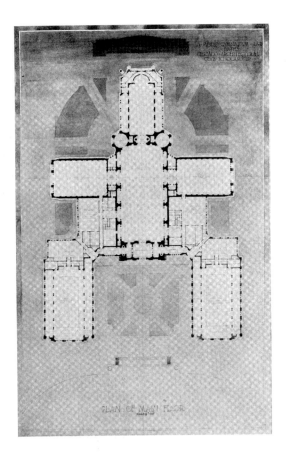

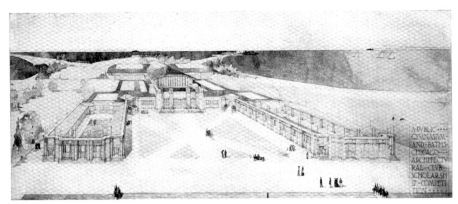

*Vernon Watson's final Eighth Annual Traveling Scholarship design seems to have reverted to classic forms in both plan (left) and perspective (above) (CAC/08)*

The winner was announced at the annual exhibition. Taking first honors was Hugh Dunning, brother of N. Max Dunning, who had won the first Traveling Scholarship nine years earlier. Robert Teal Hyett was awarded first mention, but no other prizes were listed. Both Hugh Dunning's and Robert Hyett's drawings were shown in the exhibition and illustrated in the annual catalog but, oddly, neither was listed as an exhibitor.[13]

The tenth anniversary of the Traveling Scholarship Competition was not announced in the professional press, but it was noted in the 1910 *Book of the Twenty-Third Annual Exhibition*. The subject was "A Building in the Interests of Navigation and Sanitation." Just what that meant was not recorded, although the designs published in the catalog suggest that it was a building providing both docking facilities and, perhaps, some sort of structure to house sanitary equipment to prevent the pollution of the lake it abutted. First prize went to Clarence G. Brown, a gold medal was awarded to E. R. James for second place, and L. E. Wilkinson was mentioned. All were published in the annual catalog.

The Traveling Scholarship competitions held between 1905 and 1910 were an important aspect of the Chicago Architectural Club's activities. They were not, however, the only competitions in which the members of the club participated. They continued to have one- or two-hour sketch competitions at their biweekly meetings at the club rooms, although these were rarely published or otherwise acknowledged. A number of members were also regular participants in the biannual competitions sponsored by the *Brickbuilder*. That journal, owned by Rogers & Manson of Boston, would publish elaborate programs from time to time, always specifying that the design be done using brick or terra-cotta as the primary material. The winners would then be published in the journal. Occasionally as many as twenty designs would be published, and Chicagoans would often be included. Rogers & Manson would sometimes submit the winning designs for inclusion in the club's annual exhibition and catalog. The company began this in 1904 and continued in 1905, 1906, 1907, 1908, and 1910. Occasionally a member would submit his design to the exhibition even if it was not a prizewinner. William Gray Purcell did this in 1904, 1905, and 1906.[14] In 1905, Rogers & Manson exhibited the three top entries in its Village Church Competition, none by a Chicagoan. One member of the Chicago Architectural Club, Paul V. Hyland, exhibited his entry in the same competition. J. W. Wilson, who took third place in the Sixth Annual Traveling Scholarship Competition, also took third place in the *Brickbuilder's*

13. Hugh Dunning's drawings were also shown in the First Annual Exhibition of the Minneapolis Architectural Club, held between April 17 and May 3 of the same year. A number of other Chicagoans, including Frank Lloyd Wright, Richard E. Schmidt, Lawrence Buck, Dean and Dean, and N. Max Dunning, were also shown in that exhibition. See *Western Architect* 12, no. 5 (May 1908): 51–55.

14. William Gray Purcell (1880–1965) was born in Oak Park, Illinois. He was educated there and at Cornell University. After graduation he worked a short time for Louis Sullivan, but then took an extended trip to the West Coast to see the work of Myron Hunt, Elmer Grey, and John Galen Howard. He returned to Chicago in 1906. After another extended trip, this time to Europe, he joined George Feick Jr. (1881–1945) in partnership in Minnesota. In 1909, George Grant Elmslie joined the firm, which became Purcell, Feick & Elmslie and later Purcell & Elmslie.

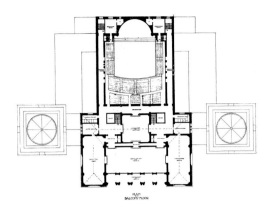

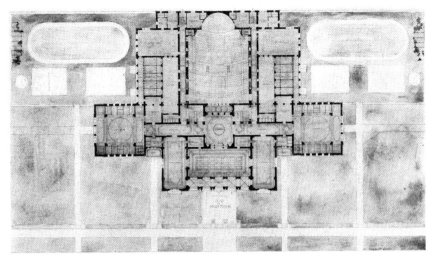

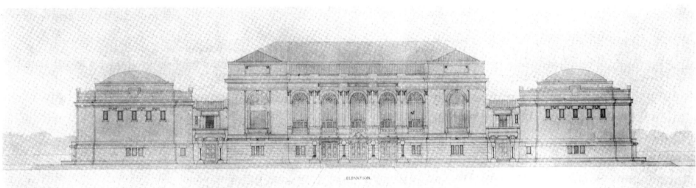

*Plans and rendered elevation of Hugh Dunning's gold-medal-winning scheme for the Ninth Annual Traveling Scholarship Competition (CAC/09)*

*Robert Hyett's second-place design for the Ninth Annual Traveling Scholarship Competition (CAC/09)*

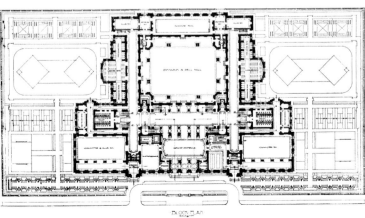

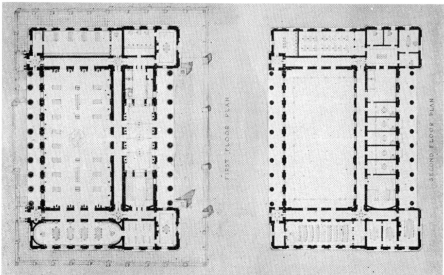

*E. R. James won a gold medal for his second-place design in the Tenth Annual Traveling Scholarship Competition (CAC/10)*

*L. E. Wilkinson received a "first mention" in the Tenth Annual Traveling Scholarship Competition (CAC/10)*

earlier Competition for a Fireproof House.[15] That drawing was published in the journal in 1905.

Other Chicago Architectural Club members who participated in the various competitions sponsored by the *Brickbuilder* included John H. Phillips, whose two entries were published in 1906. The first was for a competition for "An Office

15. This design and a photograph of Wilson were published in *Brickbuilder* 14, no. 7 (July 1905): 133, 146–47. The design was a collaboration with Nimmons & Fellows.

*William Gray Purcell's bank, designed for the* Brickbuilder's *1904 competition (CAC/05)*

*J. W. Wilson took third place in* The Brickbuilder's *1905 competition for a fireproof house (BB)*

16. Phillips's design for an office building appeared in *Brickbuilder* 15, no. 2 (February 1906): 21. His design and that of Arthur Knox for the Architectural Faience Competition were in the same issue on pages 37–38. Phillips's design for the railroad station competition was in the same volume as well, on page 213, and N. Max Dunning's design was on pages 226–27.

Building" in which he did not place, and the second was for "An Architectural Faiance [*sic*]" for which he won second place. Chicagoan Arthur Knox also got a mention in that competition. Phillips appears to have been a regular in the *Brickbuilder* competitions, because he also entered the "Village Railroad Station" competition in 1906. He did not win, but his design was published. In the same year, N. Max Dunning's *Brickbuilder* competition drawing for a village railroad station was published although, like Phillips, he did not receive a prize.[16] No Chicagoans appeared in any of the *Brickbuilder* competitions in 1907, but George Awsumb's entries for a Terra Cotta Theater in 1908 and a Public Bath and Gymnasium Building in 1910 were both published in the *Brickbuilder*. Virtually all these competition

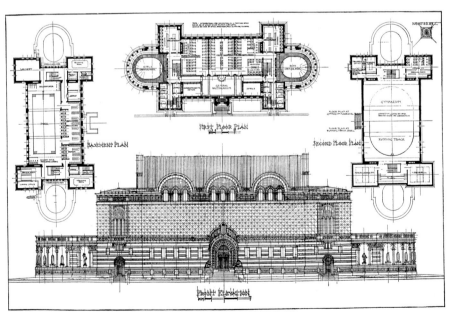

*George Awsumb's "Public Bath and Gymnasium Building," designed for the* Brickbuilder's *1910 competitions (BB)*

drawings were shown in the club's annual exhibition at the Art Institute of Chicago and most, if not all, were also shown in the club rooms on Adams Street. There were many smaller sketch competitions as well that would be shown on the walls of the club for a few days after their completion.

In early 1906 the Municipal Art League of Chicago offered three prizes—one hundred, seventy-five, and fifty dollars—for the design of practical electric lampposts for the City of Chicago and the Chicago Park District. The announcement of the competition also stated that the "designs will be exhibited at the Art Institute. The park and city authorities will give them careful attention with a view to their adoption . . . Several of the daily newspapers have promised to publish pictures of the leading designs." Ten of the designs were published in the *Inland Architect*,[17] and the *Chicago Daily News* published three of the winning designs.[18]

Two of the prizes went to students at the Art Institute of Chicago: Arthur Gunther won first prize and Enoch Bognild took third. Second place went to a member of the Chicago Architectural Club, John Lilleskau. This was apparently not the only time the Municipal Art League worked with the Chicago Architectural Club on a competition of this nature. Shortly after the announcement of these prizes in March 1906, the league issued an undated circular titled "Undertakings of the Municipal Art League of Chicago," in which it was noted under the subtitle "Competitions in Designs for Lamp Posts" that "in conjunction with the Chicago Architectural club, the Municipal Art League has inspired architects to create artistic designs for reinforced concrete lamp posts. The last competition was for electroliers for the Lincoln Park board. The Art League gives publicity to these movements and honors to the best designers." It went on to say that "an important officer in the United States postal service having invented a remarkable combination of lamp post and various utility boxes, the League has undertaken to secure from designers and artistic treatment for it. The Architectural Club will unite with us in this effort, and it is expected that this will bring about a decided improvement in such street fixtures,

17. *Inland Architect* 47, no. 4 (May 1906).

18. "Prize Winning Designs for Lamp Posts," *Chicago Daily News*, March 10, 1906.

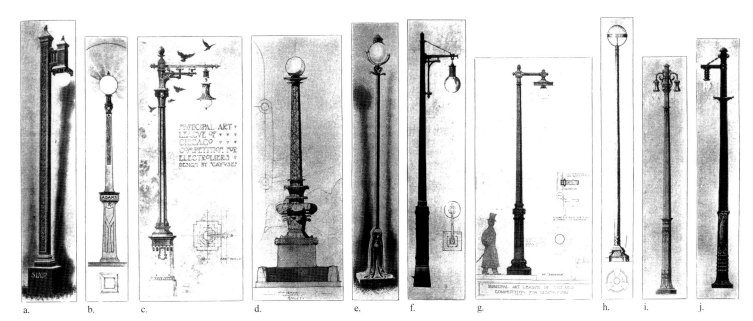

a.  b.  c.  d.  e.  f.  g.  h.  i.  j.

*Designs entered in the Municipal Art League's 1906 lamppost competition, left to right, by* a. Hugh A. Price, b. J. M. Anderson, c. W. W. Harper, d. William L. Welton, e. Hugh A. Price, f. Arthur Gunther (first-prize winner), g. John Lilleskau (second-prize winner), h. Enoch Vognied (third-prize winner), and i., j. E. Pierron (last two entries) (IA)

now so generally confused and lacking in beauty." The league also had plans "to secure an artistic form of street news stands to replace the present ugly make-shifts which have disgraced Chicago these many years." Two years later, it was noted in the *Inland Architect* that the "activities of the club for a month or two have been largely enlisted in two competitions for municipal improvements. The competition for a public comfort station was judged January 6; that for Cast Iron Lamp Posts is in progress."[19] A month later the *Inland Architect* reported that judgment "has been rendered and prizes awarded in the Street Lamp competition. C. H. Hammond secured the first prize, H. H. Green, second prize and A. J. Knox, third prize."[20] No record of the winners has come to light for the prizes awarded for the public comfort stations. In any case, the joint effort demonstrates the interest in civic improvements that the Chicago Architectural Club shared with its sister organization, the Municipal Art League.

These competitions, which the Chicago Architectural Club regularly participated in, were important but were not the only civic responsibility the club members assumed. They continued to monitor and exhibit the work of Daniel Burnham and his evolving plan of Chicago. Although they did not always agree with him, particularly in regard to his placement of the Field Museum in the heart of Grant Park, they did not speak out forcefully on the matter. They were criticized for this by Robert Craik McLean, who wrote in the February 1908 issue of the *Western Architect* that "the Chicago Architectural Club is one of the strongest forces for the guidance and advancement of civic art that the city can boast, yet the representative speakers at the banquet of the club failed to present the real argument in their criticism of the city's commercialism." Whatever was said at that meeting has not been recorded, but apparently the speakers primarily discussed minor things rather than the big picture. McLean went on to say that they "expended their force in expressing undoubted truths in regard to the city's lack of artistic beauty in small things, and forgot the large ones that will be a permanent blot upon the city of the future unless they are planned now with care and foresight . . . They forgot that no art can succeed that is not hand in hand with commerce, any more than a successful commercial growth can be sustained without art as a basis . . . There is fortunately a force at work whose domination is at least hopeful. The vision . . . is being carefully and firmly continued by Burnham." McLean noted that Burnham had the moneyed men of Chicago with him, but that it "is only by educating the present generation in its feasibility and importance, that there is any certainty of its successful completion a generation hence. And this work the Architectural Club can aid in. It can still call attention to the small things, but it should lend all its support to the movement which is in the direction of those permanent structural works which form the basis for future beauty and commercial prosperity."[21] McLean clearly felt that what the club was doing was fine, but he wanted it to broaden its horizons.

The Chicago Architectural Club was broadening its view by again participating heavily in the Architectural League of America, which it had helped to organize in 1899. J. C. Llewellyn had been president of the league in the 1900–1901 year and was reelected the following year. The club was always represented at the league's annual conventions and usually held several key committee appointments. Officers of the league continued to be drawn from a single city, thus facilitating communication between conventions. After the convention was held in Chicago in 1900, it was in Philadelphia (1901), Toronto (1902), and St. Louis (1903). There was no con-

19. *Inland Architect* 51, no. 2 (February 1908): 10.

20. *Inland Architect* 51, no. 3 (March 1908): 23.

21. *Western Architect* 2, no. 2 (February 1908): 13.

vention in 1904 during the tenure of president William B. Ittner of St. Louis. The Sixth Annual Convention was finally held in Pittsburgh in April 1905. After this rather lackluster, and long, period between national meetings, the league once again turned to Chicago for leadership. N. Max Dunning was chosen as the speaker for the convention and then elected president of the Architectural League of America on April 18, 1905. It was the third time that Chicago had held the top office of the league.[22]

The affairs of the Sixth Annual Convention of the Architectural League of America were reported verbatim in a supplement to the *Inland Architect and News Record* distributed with its April 1905 issue. There was a good deal of minutia included in that document, but several items of importance were also covered. The delegates were disappointed in the results of the "circuit," whereby drawings from each club were shown at the annual exhibitions of other clubs. The problem seems to have been that most architects were reluctant to have their work away from the office for long periods of time when it might have been used for promoting work at home. It was suggested that perhaps the league should have its own annual that would show representative work from each club.[23] It was also concluded that the league should sponsor a traveling scholarship competition much like the ones run by the CAC and several other clubs throughout the country. Eventually, the delegates agreed that both a traveling scholarship competition and an annual would be desirable. During the next three years, from 1906 to 1908, annuals were published. They were generally uniform in size but varied substantially in content. The 1906 annual was very much like the exhibition catalogs of Chicago, Boston, and New York. It included an essay titled "The Functions of a Traveling Scholarship" by the 1906 winner Chaster Boyce Price of St. Louis. His winning design for a railroad station was the lead illustration. The first-mention design by Norman T. Vorse of Washington, D.C., was also illustrated. The annual included brief essays by Bertram Grosvenor Goodhue, George B. Ferry, and John Lawrence Mauran. The illustrations were quite evenly distributed among the various clubs, with the East Coast getting a slight edge in number. Chicago was well represented with drawings and photographs by Howard Shaw, Allen Weary (for D. H. Burnham), Lawrence Buck, R. C. Spencer Jr., Thomas Tallmadge, Pond & Pond, Frank Lloyd Wright, and others. Sullivan's Wainwright Building was illustrated, as were two office buildings by Kees & Colburn of Minneapolis, which were obviously influenced by Sullivan's building. Many, but not all, of the illustrations had been published earlier in local club exhibitions. Unfortunately, there was no listing of exhibitors nor was there any in-

*N. Max Dunning, 1905*

22. J. C. Llewellyn was elected president in 1901 and then reelected in 1902. N. Max Dunning worked in J. C. Llewellyn's office during 1901–2 and beyond, so he was fully aware of the responsibilities of the office.

23. There was a book called the *Architectural Annual* published in 1899 and 1900, but publication ceased after that, and information concerning the league was disseminated through various architectural journals. The *Architectural Annual* was revived from 1906 to 1908 in a smaller format.

*Chester B. Price of St. Louis won the Architectural League of America's first Traveling Scholarship Competition with this design for a railroad station (ALA/06)*

dication of whether or not there was an actual exhibition of the work illustrated. The 1906 annual, which got national distribution, was instrumental in publicizing the avant-garde work being done in the Midwest.

The 1907 Architectural League annual was similar in size to the 1906 edition, but editorially it was quite different. Fourteen of the sixteen clubs that made up the Architectural League of America each had a chapter wherein they provided a list of officers, at least one brief essay, and representative examples of work from their members. Only the National Sculpture Society and the Boston Architectural Club were not represented. It was well produced and, in some cases, provides information regarding individual clubs that is unavailable elsewhere. Nowhere in the 1907 annual is there any mention of a traveling scholarship competition. The Publishing and Editing Committee did take it upon itself to hold a competition for the cover of the 1907 annual. The winning design by Chester H. Walcott of Chicago, which was used, was one of thirty-three submitted. First and second mentions went to J. N. Watson of St. Louis and Frank L. Molby of Washington, D.C., whose drawings were published in the annual.

The 1908 Architectural League annual was the same basic format, but the content was different from that of its predecessors. There were several essays in the early pages followed by "illustrations . . . intended to show the work of the students in some of the principal architectural schools of the country." Ten institutions, including two active ateliers, were represented. Boston, which had not been included the previous year, got the lion's share of illustrations by showing work from Harvard, MIT, the Boston Architectural Club, and the Boston Architectural Club Atelier. They and the other eastern schools all had several exhibits. For some unexplained reason, the only western group represented was the Architects Club of the University of Illinois, which got its own section at the end of the book.

There were no more annuals published by the Architectural League of America. The recorded proceedings of the conventions in 1908 and 1909 have numerous references to the problems of publication.[24] The death knell of the annuals came on December 14, 1909, when the chairman of the Annual Committee, Louis C. Newhall, "respectfully recommended that the publication of the *Annual* be discontinued."[25] The annual had never been high on the league's list of priorities, but the early issues in 1899 and 1900 and the later ones in 1906, 1907, and 1908 are among the best visual evidence of its activities.

The Architectural League of America had been founded as a loose confederation of architectural clubs. It was, essentially, a young men's group. As time passed, it became more and more devoted to the education of young men as architects. By 1905, during the sixth convention, more than half the published information concerning the proceedings was devoted in one way or another to education. This issue had been raised five years earlier but had not aroused much interest. The Chicago delegates who had been prepared to debate the issue found no one with whom to debate. By 1905, with licensing of architects becoming more of an issue and the need for trained and qualified senior draftsmen increasing, formal education became the primary focus of the league. Much discussion ensued regarding the best course of study for aspiring architects. Work in an established office under the apprentice system was still much in vogue, but it took years to produce skilled men. Universities were rapidly developing sophisticated courses of study but with little practical work as part of that study. The most prominent organization of professional architects other than the American Institute of Architects, which did not offer educational courses, was the Society of Beaux-Arts Architects. Organized in 1894 by Americans who had studied at the École des Beaux-Arts in Paris, the society had founded the Beaux-Arts Institute of Design, headquartered in New York

24. Those proceedings were published verbatim in two small booklets: *Proceedings of the Ninth Annual Convention of the Architectural League of America, 1908* and *Proceedings of the Tenth Annual Convention of the Architectural League of America, 1909*. Extensive excerpts were also published in several professional journals of the period.

25. *Proceedings of the Tenth Annual Convention* (December 14, 1909).

City, in 1895 to promote educational activities based on the principles taught in Paris. The primary function of the institute was to provide a framework of competition programs and other material for use in ateliers throughout the United States. These ateliers were semi-classroom situations that took place after normal working hours in the offices of senior architects referred to as patrons. The students, who either paid a small fee or worked for the patron during the day, spent several hours each evening solving design problems prepared by the Beaux-Arts Institute of Design. The drawings were then juried at the institute headquarters in New York, and the students progressed through a series of levels until they were considered accomplished enough to be certified by the institute.

After much debate, the Architectural League of America chose to adopt, or at least highly recommend, the system of education by atelier established by the Beaux-Arts Institute of Design. At the 1905 convention in Pittsburgh, the following recommendation was made: "Each club in this League is requested to organize, where a Beaux Arts atelier is not already in operation, to elect the best designer, and one acceptable to the Beaux Arts Society, in the club or community as patron, and then to make application to the Beaux Arts Society for the problems in design issued by them."[26] Just before this recommendation, the "Proceedings" had recorded those cities that already had established ateliers. Among them was Chicago, where it was noted that an atelier was in place under the direction of architect B. E. Holden at 175 Dearborn Street, Chicago, Illinois.[27] (The atelier active in Chicago in 1900 under the direction of Mr. F. J. Fitzwilliam, which disappeared in 1901, was not part of the Chicago Architectural Club, nor is there evidence that Fitzwilliam's students exhibited at the club, although they may have shown work under their own names.)

Prior to the league's call for ateliers, a new slate of directors for the Chicago Architectural Club had been elected on the first Monday of May in 1904. It was headed by president J. L. Hamilton and included five officers and two others rounding out a governing board of seven. This arrangement was in keeping with the revised constitution of 1901. The number of directors remained the same until the 1909–10 election, when a "Patron of the Atelier," Theodore A. Lescher,[28] and a "Massier of the Atelier," Samuel Marx,[29] were added to the list of officers. (This was the first acknowledgment of an atelier with a direct connection to the Chicago Architectural Club.) In following years, these positions were not listed as being officers of the club. Those listings, however, do offer documentary evidence that the club's atelier was in place by May of 1909, and possibly earlier. The following year, 1910–11, the traditional seven directors were listed in the exhibition catalog.

Following Hamilton's presidency, which ended in May of 1905, the club was led successively by Edward O. Nelson (1905–6), Alfred S. Alschuler (1906–7), H. V. Von Holst (1907–8), C. H. Hammond (1908–9), and Elmo C. Lowe (1909–10). In virtually every case, these men had served in a lesser capacity on the Executive Committee prior to their presidency. In most years, the major committees were headed by members of the Executive Committee, with the exception of the president, who served ex officio on all committees. Generally, it was the second vice president who served as chairman of the Exhibition Committee. He had a particularly demanding task, with several subcommittees serving under him, including a Jury of Admission, a Hanging Committee, and a Finance Committee. The finances of the exhibition were always kept separate from the funds of the club as a whole.

The activities of the club during this period of stability can be deduced from

26. "Supplement to the Inland Architect and News Record, Proceedings of the Sixth Annual Convention of the Architectural League of America," *Inland Architect* 45, no. 3 (April 1905): 5.

27. Little is known of Ben Edwin Holden. He was first listed as a licensed architect in 1902, at 175 Dearborn Street, where he remained for several years. In 1909 he was listed as being in the Railway Exchange Building. No further references to his atelier have been found. There is no evidence that he was ever a member of the Chicago Architectural Club; he did not exhibit there, nor did any member of his atelier.

28. Oddly enough, Theodore A. Lescher was never listed as a member of the Chicago Architectural Club, nor was he included in any of the Chicago Architects' Business Association handbooks in the lists of architects licensed in Illinois.

29. Samuel Marx (1885–1964) graduated from MIT in 1907, then spent a year in Paris, where he was in Atelier Umdenstock & Duquesne. Throughout his life, he was active in a number of architecture-related groups. He was particularly noted for his elegant interiors, often furnished with pieces of his own design.

the occasional notes in various periodicals regarding the regular meetings and from the reviews of the annual exhibitions at the Art Institute of Chicago. For example, in February of 1905, the *Inland Architect* wrote that "the activities of the Chicago Architectural Club for the coming year are suggested by the February program which comprises various papers to be read before the club. After a social evening on February 6, a lecture by Louis H. Sullivan is announced for February 13. This will be followed by an illustrated talk on Fireproofing by E. V. Johnson on February 20 and a lecture by Alfred H. Granger on February 27. The club has commenced classes in water-color and also pen and ink work which promises to be largely attended. The pen and ink class has been organized by Max Dunning and the revival of that art, which fifteen years ago reached a perfection that was remarkable at the time but lost since, is most valuable at this time when the delicacy of line and proportion is so frequently lost in brush work and bad drawing."[30] The journal followed up a month later by reporting that "a large and representative gathering of members of the Chicago Architectural Club on February 13 listened to a paper by Louis H. Sullivan on 'Natural Thinking, a Study in Democracy.'" The reporter noted that it was part of a much longer paper Sullivan was at work on, and he likened the paper to "a combination of Rosseau and Ruskin."[31] He went on to say that the presentations of both E. V. Johnson and Alfred H. Granger had also been well received. He ended his article with the announcement that the "eighteenth annual exhibition of the Chicago Architectural Club will be held in the fireproof galleries of the Art Institute, Chicago, from March 30 to April 19." A month later the *Inland Architect* reviewed the annual exhibition in an unsigned article.[32] It was only one of many reviews of that show to be published.

In a break from the past, invitations to the annual exhibition of the club in 1905 were issued by the Art Institute of Chicago. Previously, invitations had either been issued by the club itself or jointly by the club and the Art Institute. The invitations were sent early enough so that nearly every daily newspaper in Chicago announced that the "opening reception of the annual exhibition of the Chicago Architectural Club [would be on] March Thirtieth, Nineteen Hundred and Five, from Eight to Eleven o'clock." It would be on view until April 10. These notices were published between March 27 and March 31, 1905.

The first newspaper review appeared in the *Chicago American* on April 1. Generally positive, it admonished its readers to "pay more heed to architectural work, watch its progress, be jealous of every experiment." Later the reviewer would comment that the "exhibition as a whole reflects a little too strongly the beaux-arts' training of Paris, endorses too emphatically the present fashion for the classic." He went on to say that it "may be architectural to design a modern palatial residence in 'the high Roman fashion' . . . But to apply scraps and rags of classic design to a modern skyscraper seems to me most inexpressive and futile." He was particularly critical of various designs from New York City, but he was not wholly in agreement with the work of local architects either. He noted that "the strong design of Nimmons & Fellows for a large group of buildings on the West Side for Sears, Roebuck & Company is sadly weakened by its bits of classic detail. Here we have a solid brick construction, frankly expressive in the main of a modern commercial purpose, but the architects must needs [*sic*] their sturdy tower upon a weak-kneed, white marble Roman portico, with Corinthian columns and top it with a story of arches and pilasters supporting their red tiled roof. And their low building for the offices has a classic entrance topped by a pediment, which one longs to slice off and cast away, leaving the honest brick opening bare." The reviewer was clearly in sympathy with the work of Louis Sullivan and his followers in the Steinway Hall

30. *Inland Architect* 45, no. 1 (February 1905): 8.

31. *Inland Architect* 45, no. 2 (March 1905): 20.

32. *Inland Architect* 45, no. 3 (April 1905): 29.

*Invitation issued by the Art Institute of Chicago for the Chicago Architectural Club's 1905 exhibition (AIC)*

group. Oddly enough, this same reviewer commented favorably on the room in the exhibition "devoted to the memory of the late Joseph Twyman, being filled with his designs for mural decorations, furniture, brasses, screens, etc. The room contains beautiful objects and expresses the personality of a sincere artist and clever designer."

The work of Joseph Twyman was heavily oriented toward the English arts and crafts movement. While he did not design in the style being developed by the younger men of Chicago, they admired his work and took it as a starting point. He was also personally well liked by members of the architectural community.

*Nimmons & Fellows's design for the Sears, Roebuck & Company complex on Chicago's West Side was praised by critics who reviewed the 1905 exhibition (AIC)*

Twyman was enamored of the work of William Morris and often lectured about it. He spoke at least twice to the Chicago Architectural Club.[33] His work was also published twice in the *House Beautiful*.[34] After his untimely death in 1904, the club elected to show his work in a setting designed specifically for that purpose. The Twyman room was furnished with pieces from the "William Morris Room," which Twyman had assembled for the Toby Furniture Company. Many of the pieces were from Twyman's personal collection. Nearly every reviewer of the Eighteenth Annual Exhibition commented favorably on this memorial to Joseph Twyman. The *Inland Architect* noted that "it is with considerable approbation that one finds a room given up to a memorial exhibit of the works of Joseph Twyman, who was foremost in this country in interpreting the art of William Morris." The *American Art News* noted that the "memorial room [had] many exquisite examples of furniture craft and designs by this Morrisite. The exhibit is made, in fact, under the auspices of the William Morris Society."[35]

Only the review included as part of the "Letter from Chicago" column in the *American Architect* was less than enthusiastic about the 1905 exhibition.[36] The reviewer noted that "taken as a whole, the exhibit is not as interesting as it has been in some previous years. It fills three galleries and with the Twyman Memorial Room and the exhibition of the Alumni Association of Decorative Designers occupies a dignified space."[37] His entire review was somewhat condescending. He briefly described several exhibits, including "the usual perennial display of huge water-colors from the office of D. H. Burnham & Co. of possible improvements on the Lake Front. The sketches are too much in the nature of bird's eye views, devoid of details to afford much satisfaction to the beholder." Discussing the same work, a colleague who wrote an otherwise undistinguished review for the *Inland Architect* observed that a "notable example is Jules Guerin's sketch in color of D. H. Burnham's suggestion for the lake front of Chicago. This is a drawing, possibly thirty feet long, showing about seven miles of water front."[38] Clearly the reviewer for the *American Architect* had little understanding of the importance of the work D. H. Burnham was showing. Burnham also exhibited plans for several other parks, all of

33. His papers were "Furniture," *Inland Architect* 35, no. 3 (April 1900): 19–20, and "The Art and Influence of William Morris," *Inland Architect* 42, no. 6 (January 1904): 43–45.

34. See *House Beautiful* 2, no. 3 (August 1897), and *House Beautiful* 13, no. 3 (February 1903): 169–77.

35. *American Art News* 3, no. 74 (April 8, 1905).

36. *American Architect* 87, no. 1533 (May 13, 1905): 152–53.

37. The exhibition of the Alumni Association of Decorative Designers was held at the same time as the club exhibition, but was not part of it. The Twyman Room, on the other hand, was part of the club's Eighteenth Annual Exhibition and was included in its catalog.

38. *Inland Architect* 45, no. 3 (April 1903): 29.

*Twyman room, built as part of the Chicago Architectural Club's 1904 exhibition (CAC/05)*

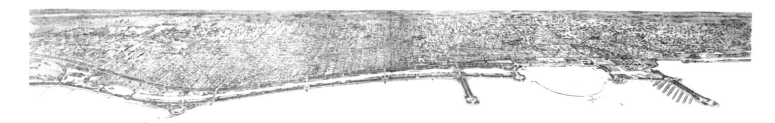

*Detail of Grant Park from the thirty-foot-long drawing Jules Guerin prepared of the lakefront for* The Plan of Chicago *(PofC)*

which would ultimately be included in his *Plan of Chicago.* Toward the end of his review, the *American Architect* reporter did manage a sort of faint praise for the Twyman Room, stating that it "is interesting historically, one might almost say. Many of the objects are now such matters of everyday use, that they hardly excite a comment, but when they were designed by Mr. Twyman, he brought them as a pioneer brings his first implements to a country where such things were not known. There is much to-day to excel these examples, but they only show not that Mr. Twyman did his work less well, but that we have all profited by his and other men's efforts to rise to a higher standard."

The only signed review of the Eighteenth Annual Exhibition was in the form of a letter to the editor dated April 17, 1905, that appeared in the *Chicago Record-Herald* on April 19. A Mr. Frederic E. Dewhurst wrote that the Twyman exhibit "merits the attention of the general public, not only because it affords an illustration of the versatility of one of our own citizens, who worked modestly and quietly among the things he loved, but especially because it affords a tangible expression of the outreaching of art into a wider realm of life."[39] Twyman's work clearly had the respect of both architects and the cultured general public.

With the 1905 annual exhibition behind them, the Chicago Architectural Club members took their usual steps toward another year's work. They were undoubtedly pleased when, shortly after electing a new slate of officers headed by Edward O. Nelson, they read an excellent editorial in the *Western Architect* by Robert Craik McLean. McLean wrote that "the rise and fall of pen and ink perspective drawing might make an interesting chapter in the history of architectural delineation of the past twenty years."[40] He noted that Paul C. Lautrup had been instrumental in developing such work, but that about ten years earlier the art had begun to decline. He was pleased to note, however, that "the renewal of the pen and ink art is urged by the Chicago Architectural Club and Max Dunning, who is perhaps its best exponent now in the club, gave his time during the past winter to a class in pen and ink . . . [and such] work will be illustrated from time to time in these pages."

During the club's 1905 exhibition, one of the major multiple exhibits was sponsored by the American Terra Cotta Company. Its display received favorable comments from nearly all reviewers, such as the one from the *Chicago American,* who wrote that it was appropriate that "the club does not confine us to purely architectural designs, but shows projects for decorative painting and sculpture, furniture,

39. Albert Nelson Marquis, ed., *The Book of Chicagoans, 1905* (Chicago, 1911). Frederic Eli Dewhurst (1855–1906) was a clergyman who had a great interest in architecture and the other arts and often expressed his opinions in this manner.

40. *Western Architect* 4, no. 6 (June 1905): 1.

*Pen-and-ink drawing by N. Max Dunning (CAC/05)*

*Frank Lloyd Wright pottery designs, executed by Gates Potteries*

41. *Chicago American*, April 1, 1905.

42. The best discussion of Wright's designs for Gates is included in Sharon S. Darling, *Teco: Art Pottery of the Prairie School* (Erie, PA: Erie Art Museum, 1989). Darling is the acknowledged expert on William Gates and his work.

pottery, etc. Some of the terra cotta exhibits are interesting, especially that beautiful panel by the American Terra Cotta company showing green and purple fishes in a green sea, the color admirably handled under the soft glaze, and the curving waves lightly modelling the surface. The Teco vases from Gates Potteries also have great beauty of color and surface, and if Mr. Wright's geometrical designs do not always convince me, still they are interesting experiments."[41]

The reference to "Mr. Wright's geometrical designs" suggests that Frank Lloyd Wright had been represented in the exhibition by proxy. That is, his pottery designs were shown by Gates, an associate member of the club, who regularly exhibited work from his company, the American Terra Cotta and Ceramic Company, as well as Gates Potteries, a division of his firm devoted to the manufacture of beautiful pottery. In 1903, his larger firm had exhibited several "Vases designed by members of Chicago Architectural Club," which may well have included items designed by Wright. In 1904, the firm had exhibited "Teco Vases designed by W. B. Mundie." The 1905 exhibition included items from both the parent firm and Gates Potteries. It is only through the newspaper item referenced above that we know that at least some of the pieces were designed by Frank Lloyd Wright. The following year, 1906, the American Terra Cotta and Ceramic Company exhibited several terra-cotta objects, including a "Terra cotta statue for residence of Mrs. Dana, Springfield, Illinois." Mrs. Dana's house was one of Wright's most ambitious designs. The statue was modeled by Richard Bock. Gates Potteries also exhibited several unidentified pieces of Teco pottery. Although Frank Lloyd Wright was not represented as an individual exhibitor in any of these years, Gates would have had no problem exhibiting Wright's designs, as he clearly thought highly of them.[42]

Gates thought highly of all his colleagues at the Chicago Architectural Club. He had provided a number of his pottery pieces for the club's rooms and was a regular speaker as well as an exhibitor. In 1905, Gates's business was going particularly well, and he took it upon himself to entertain the club on the Fourth of July at his home in Terra Cotta, Illinois. The officers of the club heartily endorsed the idea of a day away from Chicago to celebrate the holiday.[43] The chairman of the House Committee arranged to have a poster printed and distributed as an invitation. Plans called for the members and wives, girlfriends, sisters, and children to meet at a special train at 8:45 a.m., which took the group, numbering 150, to Terra Cotta for a full day of food, sports, and entertainment, all of which was reported in both the *Western Architect* and the *Clay Worker* in July of 1905. Gates, of course, realized the value of the positive public relations created by the event, but there is little doubt that he genuinely enjoyed the day, probably as much or more than any of his guests.

During the fall of 1905, the principal talk in architectural circles was the just-completed competition for the new Cook County Courthouse and the submissions to the Architectural League of America competition for its first annual scholarships. Drawings for both competitions were exhibited on the walls of the club rooms in the Dexter Building on Adams Street. Holabird & Roche took first place with its courthouse design, and the two Architectural League scholarships to Harvard were awarded to Eugene L. Pietsch and Frank G. Dillard, both from the St. Louis Architectural Club.[44]

The club was in good financial condition in the fall of 1905, and with its new centrally located rooms and a series of excellent programs with prominent speakers, it continued to be the dominant architectural organization in Chicago. Louis Sullivan spoke to the club in mid-October, presenting a chapter from his still-evolving "Kindergarten Chats." Those who were in attendance "were greatly interested both in the reader's matter and manner." The same article noted that a week later "Henry G. Foreman spoke of 'The Outer Belt Park System for Chicago.'" Foreman was one of the members of the Special Park Commission of Chicago, which had engaged Dwight Perkins to develop what soon became the Forest Preserve District of Cook County.[45]

There was good reason that the club was becoming affluent during this period. The *Inland Architect* reported in December of 1905 that "the great improvement in building operations in the West in the past few years has reached its climax in the record for 1905 in Chicago. With no unusual event as a stimulus, in the face of high prices for material and labor, and the retarding influence of one of the most bitter labor struggles in recent years, there was built this year the equivalent of forty-seven miles of single frontage at a cost of $62,500,000. This is only about $1,000,000 less than the total for 1892 when preparation for the World's Fair caused unbounded activity."[46] Chicago was booming during a period when inflation had been essentially nonexistent for nearly a quarter of a century.

The year 1906 began with the seventh annual meeting of the Architectural League of America in late January in New York City. Chicagoan N. Max Dunning was president and had the pleasure of noting that the league had arranged for a total of three scholarships to be awarded each year to Harvard University. The league continued to be primarily interested in education and to encourage the establishment of ateliers by its member clubs throughout the United States. The Chicago group, however, after having held the presidency of the league three of the first seven years,

*Richard Bock modeled this terra-cotta sculpture for the entryway of Frank Lloyd Wright's Susan Lawrence Dana House (PC)*

43. The first published notice of the event appeared in *Western Architect* 4, no. 7 (July 1905): 6–8; a few days later a second article was published in *Clay Worker* 44, no. 1 (July 1905).

44. *Inland Architect* 46, no. 3 (October 1905): 36.

45. *Inland Architect* 46, no. 4 (November 1905): 48.

46. *Inland Architect* 46, no. 5 (November 1905): 50.

began to reduce its commitment to the league's affairs. They were far more interested in their own activities in Chicago.

The club again chose to have its annual exhibition at the Art Institute of Chicago, this year between March 29 and April 18. The members agreed that the "allied arts" would be welcome in 1906. The Exhibition Committee that year was headed by chairman Otto A. Silha, second vice president of the club, and John D. York, secretary for the exhibition.

No less that twenty-four men were assigned to work on the exhibition in 1906. For reasons unclear, several men included as part of the exhibition group were not members of the club. Painter Albert Fleury was on the Hanging Committee, and two former members, John H. Phillips and Birch B. Long, both now in New York, were named to the Jury of Admission. That same jury had Clarence H. Blackall from Boston and John Molitor of Philadelphia serving as out-of-town members. The apparent goal was to have an exhibition that would show the best architecture of the United States. This was alluded to in an introductory essay in the catalog by Elmer C. Jensen, who wrote that "the character of both the exhibitions and the catalogues should be raised to and maintained on a high professional basis, so that the best men in the profession would make serious efforts to prepare special material for exhibition." The 1906 exhibition reflected this attitude. Nearly half the exhibitors were from places other than Chicago. Chicagoans did, however, get the lion's share of illustrations in the catalog. It was similar to the previous year's effort, albeit somewhat thinner. As it had been for the past several years, it was financed by "patrons" whose names were published in the front of the hardbound book.

Frank Lloyd Wright appeared in the 1906 catalog only because his work was shown by the American Terra Cotta and Ceramic Company. He did, however, have another presence at the 1906 exhibition. Wright had made his first visit to Japan a year earlier, returning in April 1905. While in Japan, he had indulged his interest in Japanese prints, bringing several hundred home with him when he returned to Chicago. During the next year both he and his wife gave a number of lectures to various groups in the Chicago area on Japan and, in particular, Japanese prints. Wright recognized that he needed to know more about his collection and enlisted the aid of Frederick Gookin, an acknowledged expert on Japanese prints at the Art Institute of Chicago. With Gookin's help, he planned a small exhibition of prints at the Art Institute timed to coincide with the Nineteenth Annual Exhibition of the Chicago Architectural Club. Wright designed the space where the prints were shown. The room was immediately adjacent to the galleries of the Architectural Club's exhibition and, in fact, passing by that space was the most convenient way to reach the club's exhibition.

About three weeks before the opening of both exhibits, Wright delivered a lecture at the Art Institute on "Art Education in Japanese Schools."[47] Then, while both exhibitions were in place, he spoke to the Chicago Architectural Club at one of the regular Monday evening meetings on "'A Lesson From the Japanese,' illustrated by drawings and art made by the pupils of the Takamatzu Industrial Art School of Takamatzu, Japan."[48] All this could hardly have been a coincidence. Frank Lloyd Wright was ending his estrangement from the Chicago Architectural Club.

Further on in the news item that reported Wright's appearance before the club, it was noted that "in gallery 31, leading to the exhibition of the Architectural Club, is a collection of 213 color prints by Hiroshige from the private collection of Japanese prints belonging to Frank Lloyd Wright." After a rather complete description of the exhibition catalog and its contents, the reviewer proceeded to discuss the annual exhibition of the Chicago Architectural Club. His generally positive comments took up less than half the space devoted to the Japanese print exhibit. He did note that one

47. *Chicago Post*, March 10, 1906.

48. *Chicago Evening Post*, April 7, 1906.

*Frank Lloyd Wright's 1906 exhibition of Hiroshige prints, immediately adjacent to the Chicago Architectural Club's exhibition at the Art Institute of Chicago (Tal)*

exhibit was "particularly novel, and of local interest." He was referring to the model of the new Cook County Courthouse designed by Holabird & Roche. For reasons never explained, this model was not included in the catalog of exhibits for 1906.

The published reviews of the 1906 exhibition were far less detailed than in the past. Most local newspapers confined themselves to a few sentences at most, often mentioning only the winners of the current Traveling Scholarship. The *Chicago Evening Post* did note that the exhibition "presents an interesting review of the conditions that are prevailing among those who plan buildings and those who construct them. If the mind could recall the exhibition of a decade ago, the contrast between past and present would be striking. The architect of the past, as a rule, confined his activities to drawings, plans and making estimates; the architect of the present not only has the early rulings of his profession as a basis of technical exploits, but beholds confronting him more than one aesthetic demand which must have its bearings upon his plans and must be allowed harmonious play in his finished work." He went on to discuss the importance of "mural decoration, sculpture, and landscape gardening or architecture" to the architect's work. His review did not really discuss the exhibition so much as the broadening of the profession of architecture. This was, of course, exactly what the club's Exhibition Committee had hoped to convey in the 1906 exhibition. The *Post* reviewer ended his article with the statement that "few organizations, among professional men, are as thoroughly educational in purpose as the Chicago Architectural Club. The club has a membership of about 300, including an active body of nearly 200 young architects who benefit from association with the older and experienced men."[49] The tone of the article suggests that it was almost certainly the result of an interview with key members of the club rather than a review of the exhibition itself.

On the heels of the exhibition, the club resumed its high level of activity, concluding its 1905–06 year with another great Fourth of July celebration.[50] This time

49. "Exhibitions Next Week," *Chicago Evening Post*, March 31, 1906.

*Invitation to the extravaganza on July 4, 1906, typical of the kind of graphics being done by the club at the time (AIC)*

the members, their families, and friends were guests of the Brownell Improvement Company of Thornton, Illinois.[51] The newly elected officers of the club, led by president Alfred S. Alschuler, were all in attendance.[52] Members were again taken to the site by special train and spent the day enjoying themselves with sports events and food, all at the expense of their hosts.

The 1906–7 year opened with an offer from the Colonial Fireplace Company of prizes totaling fifty dollars for the three best designs of mantels in brick, tile, terracotta, or metal. Drawings were to be delivered by November 10, 1906. The jury consisted of Thomas Tallmadge, Elmer Jensen, and Harry Jenkins. It was announced that "this being the first of the series of competitions arranged for this winter, it is hoped that it will be well patronized by all the club members."[53] The "culmination of the social events of the year was the annual Christmas banquet (see frontispiece) which was held December 20 at the Auditorium Hotel."[54] The subject of the evening was the "Beautifying of Chicago," and the main speaker was Daniel H. Burnham. He gave the members a hint of what was to come in the *Plan of Chicago.* The club continued its regular series of lectures, bohemian nights, and sketching evenings, but once again, its primary preoccupation was with the Traveling Scholarship Competition and the exhibition. It was to be the Twentieth Annual Exhibition, and the members took the anniversary seriously. The Exhibition Committee was headed by second vice president C. H. Hammond, who had eighteen men on various subcommittees to assist him. The largest subcommittee was the Jury of Admission, with I. K. Pond, Alfred Granger, and Howard Van Doren Shaw representing Chicago. Five men from Boston served, as well as two from New York City, Birch B. Long and John H.

50. A humorous invitation was sent to the membership on June 20, 1906, with the signature of Edward J. Poulsen, chairman of the House Committee. Among other things, the invitation noted: "ALL MEMBERS ARE ENJOINED FROM PURSUING MENTAL, PHYSICAL, OPTICAL, EMOTIONAL AND SPIRITUAL WORK ON THAT DAY. *LET COLONIAL PATRIOTISM REIGN."*

51. The Brownell Improvement Company was a contractor for public improvements and a supplier of building materials. It had an office in downtown Chicago and a plant in Thornton, Illinois.

52. *Western Architect* 5, no. 7 (July 1906): 67.

53. *Western Architect* 5, no. 10 (October 1906): 120.

54. *Inland Architect* 49, no. 1 (January 1907): 22.

Phillips, both former Chicagoans now listed as nonresident members.

The 1907 catalog, hardbound with an ornamental gold stamping on its red cover, was very much in the style of the Prairie school. It was a handsome publication similar in format to the catalogs published in 1905 and 1906. There was no advertising, but more than a hundred sponsors were listed, many of whom were members of the club. The introductory essay was by H. V. von Holst, who was an active member but did not hold office in 1907–8. He wrote, "In visiting an exhibition it is natural to compare and criticize. But of what nature should this criticism be? A celebrated French painter said the best way to study a work of art was to look for its meaning, for the underlying idea, and for its good points first of all; the bad points would reveal themselves without being searched for. If this spirit guides us, our enjoyment will be keen, and the profit to ourselves great; it will give us new ideas and new courage for our daily tasks."

The 1907 exhibition was the first to last a full month. The invitation was issued jointly by the Art Institute of Chicago and the Chicago Architectural Club. Opening night was Monday evening, April 1, 1907. Several local newspapers announced the opening, but only a few printed reviews. Perhaps they were put off because the Traveling Scholarship entries were "still in the hands of the judges." Some papers did publish brief reviews, but only two treated the show as the major event it was. The *Chicago Record-Herald* published a review by Isabel McDougall.[55] She seemed a bit confused by what she had seen, observing, "At the first view of an architectural exhibition with its rather puzzling array of ground plans, everyone takes refuge in the perspectives and renderings that they can readily understand." She found the most interesting elements to be the work of D. H. Burnham and Company, particularly the plans for Washington, D.C. She also found the firm's work on Chicago's Midway Plaisance of interest, largely because of the splendid rendering by Lawrence Buck. Most of the rest of her comments were reserved for out-of-town exhibitors. The same paper also published an illustration of a relief casting titled *Labor,* which it identified as having been modeled by Carl Bell and Leon Herinant for installation at the Clark Street entrance of the new county building. As in the previous year, this element of the Cook County Courthouse was neither listed nor illustrated in the catalog. The *Chicago Evening Post* had a brief review wherein the reporter noted that the Hanging Committee had "filled the five galleries of the south wing of the Art Institute with drawings and water colors and have displayed considerable art in arrangement."[56] The reviewer was particularly impressed with the work of D. H. Burnham, but saved his highest praise for Frank Lloyd Wright. For the first time since he dominated the 1902 exhibition, Wright was back and once again had his own space in the exhibition.[57] The reviewer wrote that in a "smaller gallery the works of Frank Lloyd Wright are disposed in excellent taste that has reached a fine art. The quiet color of the walls, the restfulness of the small molding decoration, the framing of prints unite with objects of decoration and furniture to stimulate more than passing interest." The *Chicago Record-Herald* followed its early initial review with a longer essay in which the writer covered the entire exhibit in some detail, but he also reserved his most favorable comments for the work of Frank Lloyd Wright. He noted that "Frank Lloyd Wright's work is installed by itself in the small gallery adjoining. Here is a man who follows no precedents, but boldly devises a style of his own and his audacities create the same commotion that an original genius creates in any profession. They have also created for him a considerable following, so that he is actually of those rare architects who have the honor of founding a school."[58] Thus the founding of what was to be first called the Chicago school and later the Prairie school was recognized in print. The *Chicago Record-Herald* was not the only paper to have two reviews of the 1907 exhibition.

Labor *sculpture, shown at the 1907 exhibition, still stands near the entrance to Chicago's County Building (WRH)*

55. Isabel McDougall, "Architects' Annual Exhibition," *Chicago Record-Herald*, March 31, 1907.

56. *Chicago Evening Post*, April 6, 1907.

57. The 1907 exhibition is the only exhibition until this time to have been photographed in situ. Only Wright's work was photographed, and we can assume that he arranged for the pictures to be taken.

58. *Chicago Record-Herald*, April 8, 1907.

*Photographs showing the installation of Frank Lloyd Wright's work in the 1907 exhibition; Wright was able to show a great deal of his work in a relatively small space. (The photo on this page is from* Ausgefurte Bauten *and that on the following page is from the Taliesin Archive)*

The *Chicago Examiner* printed one review on April 6 and a second on April 13, both under the byline of Harriet Monroe.[59] In her first review, Monroe was quite critical, and early on she noted that the exhibition was "a haphazard kind of show, interesting for the variety of its exhibits, but not fairly representative of recent architecture . . . Some of our best men send important designs, but a greater number send nothing at all. Among Chicago architects, for example, Louis Sullivan, Schmidt, Garden and Martin, Arthur Heun, Nimmons and Fellows, and others are conspicuous for their absence: and from other cities the list would be much longer. Of architects showing original designs, thirty-four have offices in Chicago and twenty-four in other cities; and there are thirty-three exhibitors of decorative sculpture and painting, glass, furniture, students' projects, and sketches of foreign buildings." Miss Monroe was pleased with the "increasing respect which our architects feel for the surroundings of buildings." She was also impressed with the planning work of D. H. Burnham and Company, "who are now studying this problem for Chicago, but do not yet present their Chicago scheme." She gave Burnham's work more attention than that of any other exhibitor. She was appalled by what she thought was "the most important building shown, the most depraved example of renaissance design tortured and misapplied, is the enormous Christian Science Church of Boston, shown by Brigham, Coveney & Bisbee of that city." The review continued pretty much in this vein, with praise for some and condemnation for others. Clearly, she had taken care to look at the exhibition. She did not, however, touch upon the work exhibited by Frank Lloyd Wright in her first review.

Harriet Monroe's column on April 13, however, focused on the work shown by Frank Lloyd Wright. Wright and Monroe knew each other and had, from time to time, traded correspondence, not always in a completely amicable fashion. She began her column by stating, "one of the smaller galleries . . . is given over to the work of Frank Lloyd Wright of Oak Park. There are many exhibits in this comprehensive group—beautiful drawings of dwellings, a church or two, an outdoor resort, and models for large buildings, specimens of glass, furniture, lamps, etc." She continued, "Mr. Wright has cut loose from the schools and has elaborated his own

59. Harriet Monroe, "Architects' Twentieth Annual Exhibition," *Chicago Examiner*, April 6, 1907; Harriet Monroe, "An Interesting Experiment," *Chicago Examiner*, April 13, 1907.

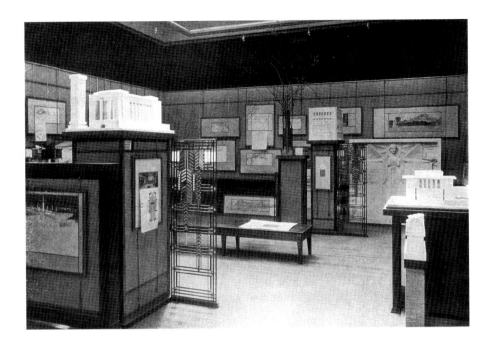

system of design, like the art-nouveau enthusiasts abroad. He believes that the three Greek orders have done their utmost in the service of man, until in modern hands their true meaning is distorted and lost. Therefore he thinks it is time to discard them and all their renaissance derivatives, and begin fresh from the beginning. At least he believes such a rebirth to be the only course for him." From this it seems clear that Miss Monroe had not only seen and studied Wright's work, but undoubtedly discussed his theories and philosophy with him.

She continued, "His work is thus a most interesting experiment, dependent for its success wholly upon the designer's creative force and inborn sense of architectural proportions and harmonies. The experiment has been worked out chiefly in the suburbs of Chicago, and is thus of special importance to us. Therefore this roomful of Mr. Wright's designs—so unusual, at times even bizarre—demands more than a questioning glance and a passing word."

Her review was not entirely positive. She went on to ask, "What is his measure of success? His limitations are obvious enough. We pass by his more ambitious buildings—the plaster models for Unity Church at Oak Park, for the Larkin Company administration building at Buffalo, and for a huge, square nameless structure [apparently Lincoln Center], all of which look too much like fantastic blockhouses, full of corners and angles and squat, square columns, massive and weighty, without grace or ease or monumental beauty. Manifestly his imagination halts here; it labors and does not yet achieve beautiful and expressive buildings for public worship and business. Again, his decorative designs—his glass screens, lamp shades, vases, furniture—seem to me too square and squat, without unity, of structure or grace of line." Such language could only have antagonized Wright.

Her final paragraph struck a more positive note: "But if at these two ends of the scale, Mr. Wright's system of design seems inadequate to the strain imposed upon it, his dwellings, on the contrary, show its charm. Some of these low-browed, slant roofed, unobtrusive houses, with groups of little windows and broad verandas nestling under the eaves, with gardens and walls and pergolas framing them in—some of these seem to grow out of the ground as naturally as the trees, and to express our hospitable suburban American life, a life of indoors and outdoors, as spontaneously as certain Italian villas express the more pompous and splendid life of those old gorgeous centuries. Especially graceful in the grouping of lines and masses are the dwellings of Avery Coonley at Riverside, of Elizabeth Stone at Glencoe, of T. P. Hardy at Racine, and of V. H. Metzger away up on a rocky hill at Sault Ste. Marie." Wright did not take kindly to Monroe's comments. Apparently he expected her, as a longtime friend, to be more adulatory. She, on the other hand, obviously felt the need to do an honest evaluation of his work. Wright sent off a lengthy response wherein he demonstrated that he didn't understand honest criticism at all. That letter, reproduced here in full, is now in the Harriet Monroe archive at the University of Chicago.

Monroe devoted the remainder of the column to a few generally positive remarks regarding other architects and their work in the exhibition and other matters of current interest in the world of art in Chicago. Her comments on the work of Frank Lloyd Wright were very much in the spirit of the young practitioners of Chicago who had begun work in the lofts of Steinway Hall ten years earlier. Even if he did not agree with her criticism, Wright was now indeed the leader of a "school" of architecture—first among a number of not quite near equals, perhaps, since a school cannot be the work of only one man. He and his colleagues would continue to work in their distinctive style for the next decade, and they would always pay homage to the man who began it all, Louis H. Sullivan.

❧

When the Twentieth Annual Exhibition of the Chicago Architectural Club was over, the members met on May 6 in their club rooms[60] and elected Herman V. von Holst as president for the 1907–8 year.[61] He had not previously served as an officer, but he had been a member since 1897, had served on the club's Executive Committee in 1898 and on the Jury of Admission in 1906, and had written the opening essay in the 1907 exhibition catalog. He was, and would remain, an active member of the Chicago Architectural Club for many years.

The club continued its busy schedule of classes, lectures, and competitions through the end of 1907 and into 1908. Late in 1907 the members chose March 31 through April 19 as the dates for their Twenty-first Annual Exhibition at the Art Institute of Chicago. They decided to make the exhibition "more local in character than those held heretofore, and it is planned to include more exhibits of the auxiliary arts of sculpture and painting than usual."[62] This had, of course, been their de facto policy for the past two years. Thought had been given to including more work of all kinds from other cities, but ultimately this was rejected largely because of the desire of the membership to show their own work rather than the work of others. Furthermore, more and more architectural clubs were being formed throughout the United States, most of which had their own exhibitions. Cooperative efforts other than those promoted by the Architectural League of America were becoming very difficult. New York, Boston, Philadelphia, and other cities had the same problem.[63] A major effort by the Architectural League of America to encourage the exchange of material from various clubs to be shown on a "circuit" of exhibitions was coming to an end. The league had worked with all concerned on the various club exhibitions to ensure that there would be no conflicts in scheduling. It worked, but not very well. Several clubs did send material on the circuit, but the best material did not always make the rounds. It was time-consuming and expensive, and many members needed their exhibition drawings as promotional material. Furthermore, there was some feeling that the exhibitions were seen primarily by architects and not by potential clients, which was really the point.

*Hermann V. von Holst, 1907 (PC)*

60. *Inland Architect* 50, no. 1 (July 1907): 11; *Western Architect* 10, no. 7 (July 1907): 53.

61. Hermann Valentin von Holst was born in Freiburg, Baden, Germany, on June 17, 1874. He moved to Chicago as a youth when his father joined the faculty of the University of Chicago, where he eventually became chairman of the Department of History. Von Holst received a BA from the University of Chicago in 1893 and a BS in architecture from MIT in 1896. He returned to work in Chicago for Shepley, Rutan & Coolidge and immediately became active in the Chicago Architectural Club. In 1901, he traveled in Europe, where he had several watercolors exhibited at the Paris Salon. Upon his return to Chicago, he opened a small practice and taught at the School of Architecture from 1904 through 1906. He was elected president of the Chicago Architectural Club in 1907, after writing the introductory catalog essay for that year's show. (Wright was one of the major exhibitors that year, which seems to belie Wright's claim that they barely knew each other when von Holst took over Wright's practice when he left for Europe in late 1909.) Von Holst later became an expert in prison design and had a successful if not distinguished practice. He died in 1955.

62. *Inland Architect* 51, no. 2 (February 1908): 10.

63. There is evidence that more than fifty architectural clubs existed in the United States between 1885 and 1910. Some lasted only a short time, others for many years; groups such as the Boston Architectural Club and the Architectural League of New York are still active.

My dear Miss Monroe - and at the beginning let
me say that to me "My dear Miss Monroe" for
the moment is a TYPE and this rude but not ill-
natured resentment is inscribed to the "type".

Architects have learned, long since, that
the professional critic's commodity, ~~remarks
otherwise of the "type"~~, when related to architecture at least either has to be "steered"
from the inside or intelligently so prejudiced
or deliberately manufactured so or it is quite
apt to be of the "I-may-not-know-what -Art-is-
but-I-know-what-I-like" variety, -bromidic and
utterly useless.

Personally, I am hungry for the honest,
genuine criticism that searches the soul of the
thing and sifts its form. Praise isn't needed
especially. There is enough of that, such as it
is, but we all need intelligent painstaking inquiry
leading into the nature of the proposition to be
characterized before with airy grace the subject
is lightly touched up with House Beautiful English
for the mob.

The struggle behind vital work of any kind is
naturally difficult enough but it is precisely the
Harriet Monroe in this sense in society that makes
the struggle unnecessarily grim and temporarily
thankless. Her commodity has no power to harm the
inherent virtue of good work but it does serve to
hamper the man and to confuse and hinder a practical issue that deserves all the help and strength
that, grudgingly enough in any case, may come to
it from a public in these matters diffident or in-
different. Fashion and Sham rule the day. When an
independent effort to be true to a worthy ideal
has the courage to lift its head it deserves something more than the capricious slap-stick of "the
type", even if the slap appeals to the gallery,
in other words to "our very best people".

Personally, again, I have met little more
than the superficial snap-judgment insult of the
"artistically informed". I am quite used to it,
glad to owe it nothing in any final outcome. But,
meanwhile the Cause suffers delay! That is the
price the public pays for "the type" and it is the
serious side of the matter.

I cannot believe you altogether insensible
to fundamental qualities but what a flimsy charac-
terization of the Ideal behind the work to which
I have given my life, you have on record!— "The
old orders all worked out", (starting on a new
stunt to bring down "the gallery" too I suppose).
"Progress before precedent" perhaps? Believe me,
dear Miss Monroe, it is all not one half so silly.
Need I say that it is the very spirit that gave
life to the old forms that this work courts?
That it is the true inspiration that made of the
time honored precedent in its own time a living
thing that it craves? Venerable traditional forms
are held by this work still too sacred to be parad-
ed as a meretricious mask for the indecencies and
iniquities of the market place!

Long ago, yes ages ago, from Nature came
inspiration to the Architect and back to Nature
with the principles deduced from these dead forms
or formulas we will go again for inspiration.
I know we shall find it for the Gods still live.

In the average of this work you saw merely a
curious experiment with certain boxes, withal a
"square" and a "squat" that offended your dainty
love of fleshly curves and sensuous graces, a love
that after all is in the last analysis rather cheap
and not merely because it is common. But, is it
impossible that the exquisite delicacy of the living
nature that we all love may bloom more vividly
where the "Architectural", which is primarily the
background for this life, itself becomes a more
quiet and restrained convention than has yet been
practiced? Why usurp what by nature belongs to
the other members of the family - Sculpture, Painting, Literature and Music? For one I decline to
be obsessed as are most artists and almost all

arts by the literal or by literature. My conception of the architectural art is somewhat
higher than that.

Need I remind you that the pyramid is
just a pyramid - that's all?—the obelisk a huge
billet of stone up-ended?- a Greek temple a
rectangle with angular excrescences? -the Parnasi
a box with a lid?

Perhaps it might be well to mention in this
connection that one of the "huge", formless, nameless structures of your story was a small scale
plaster model for a cast concrete column for
Unity Church. In the edifice the column itself
stands two feet six inches by thirteen feet high.
This is one of the buildings wherein imagination
halts!

Concerning our perennial friend the "squat"—
we happen to be living on the prairie, the prairie
has a beauty of its own. A building on the prairie
should recognize the features of its quiet level
and accentuate them harmoniously. It should be
quiet, broad, inclusive, a welcome associate of
trees and flowers not a nervous, fussy interloper,
and should be "married" to the ground. Hence,
broad, sheltering eaves over determined masses,
gentle roofs, spreading base and outreaching walls.

What is publicly set forth in this little
collection could hardly be American Architecture.
No- not yet- but I say that if a given type, (like
the type or like it not, be handled with the organic consistency and such individuality as is manifest in this aggregation here, then, an American
Architecture is a possibility and will be a definite
probability when conscientious efforts of this
nature wherever they may be found, receive the
encouragement on their native heath that they
already have received in conservative old England
or in France where these square, squat experiments
with boxes have been accorded the rare virtue of
originality without eccentricity. Buildings, like
people, must be honest, must be sincere and withal
as lovable and gracious as may be. But, unfortunately for the man who dares, we, as a people, artistically,
have a deadly and painfully provincial horror of
doing the "incorrect thing" which the self-conscious
dangerous small-knowledge of the provincial art
critic only serves to intensify, making it just so
much more difficult for us as a people to come into
our own.

Some day, as Mc Andrews prayed in his "Hymn",
even the "first class passenger" will understand
that the classic is no matter of the dead letter of
former glory and will know that the old spirit which
was so vital then is vital now and living in forms
the news papers pronounce eccentric. They may even
proclaim that after all these forms are truly classic
in the best sense of that much abused term.

But why be serious? Are not the limitations
already obvious and fixed? The progress made already marked in the public prints by such shoddy
fustian from the architectural rag-bag, -as "Ottenheimer's clock", such cheneille as "Wilson's graceful residences"?

sincerely Frank Lloyd Wright.

Wright's letter to Harriet Monroe, now at the University of Chicago in her archive.
The originals are on different sizes of paper as shown (UofCLib)

*Louis Sullivan's incredible design for the Owatonna Bank teller's screen; several have survived, but they are no longer in service at the bank (PC)*

Early in 1908, the *Western Architect* editorialized that "the Chicago Architectural Club is one of the strongest forces for the guidance and advancement of civic art that city can boast, yet the representative speakers at the annual banquet [in December of 1907] of the Club failed to present the real argument in the criticism of the city's commercialism."[64] The writer, R. C. McLean, went on the criticize the club for neglecting the big picture.

The club took McLean's words seriously. The members were extremely interested not only in Burnham's work but in other aspects of the development of the city, as reflected in their competitions and the material they exhibited. Perhaps the best evidence of the club's devotion to the beautification of Chicago was demonstrated in N. Max Dunning's introductory essay for the 1908 annual exhibition. He was writing about the value of architectural clubs in general, but was directing his remarks in particular at the Chicago Architectural Club. He ended his four-page comment, "the Chicago Architectural Club must put its shoulder to the wheel and work with others to the end that the Chicago of the future will stand supreme, not alone in Commerce and Industry, but in Art as well." The 1908 catalog bore out this commitment.

The Twenty-first Annual Exhibition catalog followed the same basic format used since 1905 (a format that would continue to be used through 1909). It opened with a dedication page to William Le Baron Jenney, a longtime supporter of the club who had died in 1907. The early pages of the catalog were devoted to a list of the "Committee on Annual Exhibition," followed by an acknowledgments page and a page of "Patrons." N. Max Dunning's essay was titled "The Function of Architectural Clubs in General, and the Chicago Architectural Club in Particular." A list of current officers and members was included, as well as a page devoted to the club's Traveling Scholarship, with a list of all past winners and the 1908 winner, George Awsumb. There were twenty-one pages of illustrations and a list of exhibitors. The catalog was edited by John Lilleskau.

The exhibition for 1908 was similar to previous exhibitions but had more material of a purely decorative nature. Sculpture, decorative objects, glass, and murals were much in evidence. There was also a much higher percentage of photographs as opposed to drawings. The exhibition, which opened to the public on April 1, was reviewed by most local newspapers and received attention from the professional press as well. The *Chicago Evening Post* opened its review, "To enjoy the twenty-first annual exhibition of the Chicago Architectural Club with any degree of appreciation, the layman viewer must invite an architect, a mural painter, a sculptor or an interior decorator to go with him through the galleries. Each of these will point out the advancement in his chosen profession and denote the place that he occupies in planning and building houses for public or for private uses. Only under conditions such as these can the private citizen see the worth of the collections of drawings and various objects."[65] (The review generally supported what N. Max Dunning had written in his foreword: "Through the medium of these exhibitions, there can be little doubt the public has been and is being brought to a better appreciation of good work, and its taste is being cultivated.") The reviewer went on to describe the exhibition in some detail in a positive manner. He wrote at some length about the various pieces of sculpture, including work by Richard Bock and Leonard Crunelle. He also found *The Maiden at the Fountain* exhibited by Beil & Hermant to be of interest. Apparently that work was purchased during the show by the Woman's Outdoor Art League for installation in Chicago. The reviewer praised a number of the younger architects' work, including that of George Maher, D. H.

64. *Western Architect* 2, no. 2 (February 1908): 13.

65. *Chicago Evening Post*, April 4, 1908.

*Dwight Perkins's Carl Schurz High School, still in service (CAC/08)*

*This sculpture by Richard Bock was the frontispiece of the 1908 catalog (credit?)*

Perkins, Lawrence Buck, and P. J. Weber. He reserved his most laudatory words, however, for the decorative arts. He found that a "gorgeous piece of color is Miss Blanche Ostertag's figure of Michael, from the group of 'The Everlasting Covenant,' for the hall of Mrs. J. J. Husser of this city." The Husser House had, of course, been designed by Frank Lloyd Wright nearly a decade earlier. Wright was not mentioned in the catalog or in any of the reviews. He was, however, almost certainly represented, once again, in a rather unusual way at the exhibition.

During the month prior to the club's 1908 exhibition at the Art Institute, galleries 25, 26, 27, 28, 30, and 31 were occupied by a Loan Exhibition of Japanese Colour Prints. The original dates were March 5 to March 25, 1908, but the show was extended a few days due to its popularity.[66] The prints were from the collections of Clarence Buckingham, F. W. Gookin, J. C. Webster, John H. Wrenn, and Frank Lloyd Wright. Six hundred and fifty-five prints were shown in a setting designed by

*William B. Ittner exhibited this St. Louis school building in 1907; its debt to Perkins is apparent (CAC/08)*

66. An unidentified newspaper article, hand-dated March 22, 1908, suggests that the Japanese print exhibition was held over until March 28.

Wright, in a manner similar to what he had done two years earlier, although in a much larger space. That space was the same, except for gallery 31, as that used by the Chicago Architectural Club's exhibition. A number of photographs of the Japanese print exhibition have survived showing the space as designed. In view of the very short time between the two exhibitions, and the fact that 655 Japanese prints had to be taken down and more than 450 architectural exhibits installed, it is highly likely that the club simply used much of the material already in place, including wall coverings, for its exhibition. Aesthetically, it would have been entirely appropriate.

Whether or not the Japanese print installation design was used in part for the 1908 club exhibition, there is reason to believe that Wright was deeply involved in two other similar designs at the same time. He was working on the design of Browne's Bookstore and the Thurber Galleries during this period. Furthermore, while he did not show any work at the 1908 annual exhibition, he did have several items included in the First Annual Exhibition of the Minneapolis Architectural Club. He had been showing his work at other clubs' exhibitions from time to time since his first *Ladies' Home Journal* design had appeared in the 1900–1 exhibition of Philadelphia's T-Square Club.

An unsigned article in the *Chicago Examiner* reported during the Japanese print exhibition that "memories of other exhibitions of the year must fade into insignificance in the presence of the loan collections of Japanese prints which grace the galleries of the Art Institute . . . The walls of the six lofty galleries of the south wing of the institute have been covered with a soft gray butcher's paper which gives out rosy reflections in contrast to the color harmonies of the pictures. These have been arranged with artistic regard for tonal values, and framed in natural wood, gray toned, are hung against a becoming background by long, white vertical cords. Filling the middle floors of the larger galleries are designs of screens completed by square pillars constructed of the wood and grayish paper and containing more prints. And as a final touch to complete the most artistic work of installation that has ever been exhibited in this, and in perhaps in any city of the country or the

*Frank Lloyd Wright's exhibition of Japanese prints, held at the Art Institute just prior to the club's 1908 exhibition (AIC)*

world, are pots of blooming pink and white azaleas, topping every pillar and diffusing their ethereal fragrance . . . Entering the galleries from the corridor, the imagination is held spellbound by the loveliness . . . in a setting evolved by Mr. Frank Lloyd Wright and his associates."[67]

There was also an overlap with other exhibitions in 1908. The Municipal Art League of Chicago had "an exhibition of drawings, photographs, mural paintings and sculptural models brought from New York . . . in galleries 48 and 25."[68] Gallery 25 was part of the Chicago Architectural Club exhibition and gallery 48 was adjacent to it. Some reviewers actually confused the two and reported as if they were a single show. The *Chicago Evening Post,* however, gave the Municipal Art League material its just due. James W. Pattison, secretary of the Municipal Art League, wrote that "after becoming accustomed to interiors of buildings which have been decorated with mural paintings, the bareness and forlorn lonesomeness of one lacking in this interesting and attractive finish are painful. Four large decorative panels have been brought from New York City by . . . the Municipal Art League . . . in order to make plain . . . the beauty of our edifices by introducing paintings to keep company with the architecture."[69] He went on to identify the murals as being by Francis Newton, Albert Herter, Van Ingen, and Luis F. Mora, all prominent New York muralists. There were several other smaller murals, sculptures, and preliminary sketches, all of which were exhibited in "the far east room in company with the exhibit of the Architectural Club." Pattison also mentioned that several "smaller objects with the nine works of painting and sculpture purchased for the Municipal Art Gallery by the Art League, are in the new east corridor. The Municipal Art League is most appreciative of the courtesy of the management of the Art Institute in that they secured space for this showing in the galleries which were already well filled."

The 1908 Chicago Architectural Club exhibition and the simultaneous showing by the Municipal Art League were well received by the public and press alike. The *Inland Architect* ended a favorable review by saying that "the Chicago Exhibition as a whole was one of the best in arrangement, character and number of exhibits, and their rendering, yet held the work of local architects."[70] The *Chicago Record-Herald* wrote that such a display would be of interest to "many who are not especially fond of paintings. In this connection the exhibition which closes to-day ought to be very profitably spent. One might easily call it an architectural exhibit, an art craft show, an exhibition of pictures and of sculptures, all combined. Particularly praiseworthy has been the matter of housing, with bits of ornamental pottery about, textiles of different kinds here and there and the happy effect of stained glass hanging in the windows of the corridor."[71] There is no question of the success of the 1908 exhibition.

With the exhibition behind them, the members met at their club rooms on May 4 for the annual meeting.[72] C. Herrick Hammond was chosen as president. Floyd A. Naramore and Will Reichert were elected first and second vice presidents, respectively. Elmo C. Lowe became the secretary, with Paul T. Haagen as treasurer. Elmer Nettenstrom and E. L. Downs were asked to fill out the Executive Committee. June, July, and August were essentially vacation months, although the club rooms did stay open and planning for the coming year took place.

The club continued a policy of working closely with other architecturally oriented groups. On June 8, the Illinois Chapter of the AIA announced that it, along

67. "Loan Exhibition Merits High Praise," *Chicago Examiner,* March 7, 1908.

68. Art Institute of Chicago, Twenty-ninth Annual Report, 42.

69. James W. Pattison, "Municipal Art in Chicago," *Chicago Evening Post,* April 7, 1908.

70. *Inland Architect* 51, no. 4 (April 1908): 30–31.

71. Maude I. G. Oliver, *Chicago Record-Herald,* April 18, 1908.

72. *Western Architect* 2, no. 2 (June 1908): 74.

with the Chicago Architects' Business Association and the Chicago Architectural Club, would sponsor two lectures by C. R. Ashbee of London on "Arts and Crafts."[73] Ashbee's unfortunate experience with the architectural community a decade earlier had apparently been forgotten. The arrangements were made by Peter J. Weber, chairman of the AIA's Committee on Entertainment, who was also a longtime member of both the Chicago Architectural Club and the Chicago Architects' Business Association. At the same meeting, the AIA considered, but rejected, the idea of establishing an atelier of its own. The AIA members felt that "this might react unfavorably upon the atelier now in operation by the School of Architecture of the Art Institute." Finally, the AIA recognized the importance of the Municipal Art League movement by authorizing a standing committee on municipal art to confer with the league. This relationship was to prove fruitful over the next several years, as the two groups worked toward creating a "Chicago Beautiful."

September of 1908 saw the inauguration of the tenth convention of the Architectural League of America in Detroit.[74] The Chicago Architectural Club was represented by H. V. von Holst, E. C. Lowe, P. C. Heayden, H. K. Holsman, I. K. Pond, N. Max Dunning, and J. C. Llewellyn. Two downstaters from the University of Illinois were present, Newton A. Wells and L. E. Wilkinson. Wells was serving as chairman of the league's Education Committee, on which H. V. von Holst also served. (The third member of the committee, F. M. Mann, was not at the convention.) Wells and Von Holst were elected chairman and secretary, respectively, of the convention. Chicago had taken only a minor role in the league after N. Max Dunning's tour as president starting in 1905, and this new activity demonstrated the club's continued concern with education. It had now been three years since the 1905 convention when the league began focusing on the education of young architects. Now education was again thrust into the forefront of the convention. The Education Committee's report was the most comprehensive of any presented, and the subject was part of virtually every other presentation at the convention. Also important was the strong feeling by a number of the delegates, including the league's president-elect Frank C. Baldwin, that the league should consider a closer relationship with the American Institute of Architects. In his remarks accepting the presidency, Baldwin stated that if "you want a man, who will hold . . . that . . . the [league] is the preparatory school for that greater college, the American Institute . . . that is my pretty strong conviction." He worked tirelessly to carry out that conviction, while promoting the league's dedication to education, but it was too late. By 1911 the Architectural League of America had ceased to exist, except on paper.[75] The rank-and-file members had lost their enthusiasm, and individual clubs went their own way. In the meantime, the Chicago Architectural Club had taken the advice of its colleagues in the league and established its own atelier.

❉

The exact date of the formation of the Chicago Architectural Club atelier is difficult to determine. The first atelier to exhibit at the Chicago Architectural Club was Atelier Masqueray from New York City in 1898. It showed fourteen items, none of which were illustrated in the catalog. By the fall of 1908 there had been at least three ateliers in Chicago. The Fitzwilliam atelier, organized in 1900, had lasted only about a year. B. E. Holden had an atelier in 1905, about which little is known. The origin of the Chicago Architectural Club atelier was most likely the Atelier Bennett, which first appeared at the annual club exhibition in 1909, suggesting that it was founded in 1908.[76] Eight items were exhibited; the designers weren't named, but they were noted as being in "Class B," which was the nomenclature used by the

73. *Inland Architect* 51, no. 6 (June 1908): 60. This issue included a report of a meeting on June 8. In July, the *Western Architect* reported that on June 21, the chapter had held a "summing up of the year's work," where the forthcoming Ashbee visit was confirmed.

74. The entire transcript of the convention, including most of the reports, was printed in *Inland Architect* 52, no. 3 (September 1908).

75. The records of the Architectural League of America are now housed at the Bentley Library at the University of Michigan. Its final days are outlined in chapter 15.

76. Edward H. Bennett was D. H. Burnham's colleague in the preparation of the *Plan of Chicago* during 1907–9. He became a member of the Society of Beaux-Arts Architects in 1908 after having studied at the École de Beaux-Arts in Paris, at Atelier Paulin, in 1895. After Burnham's death, he became a prominent city planner in his own right.

Society of Beaux-Arts Architects. The Bennett atelier continued to exhibit every year thereafter until 1914 (except 1913). In 1914 the name was changed to Atelier Bennett-Rebori, and in 1916, the last year it appeared in the catalog, it became the Atelier Rebori.[77] In 1915 the first exhibits from Atelier Puckey appeared in the annual exhibition catalog with the notation that it represented "Chicago Architectural Club, Art Institute." It would continue in this manner through 1917. The descriptions of the exhibits indicate that all were problems developed from the "programmes" regularly issued by the Beaux-Arts Institute of Design. These ateliers were all apparently loosely connected to the Chicago Architectural Club after 1909. While different names were used, depending on the patron or patrons, the sponsor was always the club, even when two groups were acting at the same time. What scant evidence is available concerning the early days of the club atelier suggests that it followed the programs of the Beaux-Arts Institute of Design from the beginning, a practice that became more common as the atelier matured. The club atelier operated continuously until the demise of the club just before the Second World War. Atelier facilities were in the club rooms, which were open to the membership virtually around the clock. The atelier—along with the Traveling Scholarship Competition and the annual exhibition—became a primary focus of the Chicago Architectural Club.

In the fall of 1908, just as it was moving toward establishing its own atelier, an important competition was offered to the club. The Universal Portland Cement Company proposed a "Prize Competition for a Suburban House."[78] The announcement noted that the "chief interest at present in the club concerns the prize competition for designs of concrete houses open to all architects and architectural draftsmen residing within a radius of fifty miles from Chicago . . . F. A. Naramore is chairman of [the] competition committee and will furnish full information upon request."[79] The prizes were substantial for the time. First prize was to be two hundred dollars, second was seventy-five, and third was twenty-five. Furthermore, the announcement noted that the sponsoring firm reserved the right to publish the entries, and that "many or all of the designs will be exhibited at the Chicago Cement Show in February." The time allotted for the competition was relatively short. It was announced on October 31, drawings were due on December 17, and the jury's awards were made on December 21.

The Universal Portland Cement Company Competition was a success. There were a substantial number of entries, nineteen of which were published in a booklet entitled *Plans for Concrete Residences*.[80] Of those nineteen entries, one of which was anonymous, eight were members of the Chicago Architectural Club. (Several became members later.) R. C. Ostergren took first honors, followed by Paul Topping Haagen. Both were club members. A joint entry by Frank W. and Walter S. Church took third place. There were two honorable mentions, William G. Wuehrmann and Hugh Dunning. N. Max Dunning's design was published but was not a winner. Another interesting non-winner was the entry by "M. L. Mahoney [sic]." It showed the influence of Frank Lloyd Wright to an extraordinary degree. The entrant was, of course, Marion Mahony, who had left Wright's office to join Walter Burley Griffin in his practice in the loft of Steinway Hall.

A week before the Universal Portland Cement Competition drawings were due, English architect Charles R. Ashbee returned to Chicago to give the lecture that had been arranged the previous June.[81] He had been invited by the Illinois Chapter of the AIA with the cooperation of the Chicago Architects' Business Association and the Chicago Architectural Club, who were guests of the AIA, with their ladies, on this occasion. At a reception and dinner in the Art Institute's club room before his formal speech, Ashbee "gave an informal talk on some phases of the [arts and

77. Andrew Rebori (1886–1966) was an important early modern architect whose work has often been overlooked. He graduated from Armour Institute in 1907. He then worked in the offices of Cass Gilbert and Jarvis Hunt somewhat sporadically between 1909 and 1918, and was in private practice after that, until his death in 1966. He taught at the Chicago School of Architecture from 1909 to 1914.

78. The first notice of this competition was in *Inland Architect* 52, no. 5 (November 1908): 64. It did not identify the sponsor. The entire program was printed in a booklet published by the Universal Portland Cement Company in early 1909, along with the winners and a number of the other designs.

79. F. A. Naramore was first listed as a member of the Chicago Architectural Club in 1908. He was not listed as a licensed architect in Illinois. He was probably an employee of the Universal Portland Cement Company.

80. *Plans for Concrete Residences, Being a Selected Number of Designs with Descriptions and Estimates of Cost, Submitted in a Competition of the Chicago Architectural Club* (Chicago and Pittsburgh: Universal Portland Cement Company, 1909).

81. "Illinois Chapter, AIA," *Inland Architect* 52, no. 6 (December 1908): 78.

*Robert C. Ostergren's design for a concrete house took first prize in the 1909 Portland Cement Competition (PCA)*

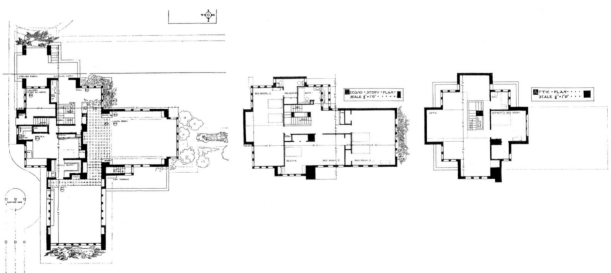

*Marion L. Mahony's design for the Portland Cement Competition; Frank Lloyd Wright's influence is clear (PCA)*

crafts] movement in England. He stated that he was delighted to be again in Chicago after an absence of eight years. He complimented this city upon having the fire and snap for accomplishment, not found elsewhere—the spiritual fire that leads to great things." After these brief remarks and following dinner, the group "adjourned to Fullerton Hall . . . and heard Mr. Ashbee's lecture on the 'Arts and Crafts Movement in England.'" There is no evidence that he lectured again during his visit, but he did stay on until after Christmas, renewing his friendships with Louis Sullivan, Jane Addams, and Frank Lloyd Wright, with whom he stayed in Oak Park. He was far less taken by Chicago than he had been on his first visit. He recorded in his journal that "the soul of the city is sick." From Chicago, he went to the West Coast and then back east and on home to England. He would next meet his friend Wright nearly two years later, in 1910, when Wright asked him to write the introduction to the German publication *Frank Lloyd Wright, Ausgefuhrte Bauten.* This was apparently the only lasting impact of Ashbee's second visit to Chicago.[82]

While Ashbee was in Chicago during December of 1908, the Art Institute of Chicago mounted an extensive show called the Annual Exhibition of Art Crafts.[83] It was a major exhibition with 840 items. Concurrently, the institute had an exhibition of mural decorations and windows designed by Frederic C. Bartlett for the new University Club Building, as well as a number of other related items all shown in the spaces usually used by the Chicago Architectural Club. A number of members of the club were exhibitors and, of course, all this was of interest to Ashbee.

82. The best source of information concerning Ashbee and Chicago is Crawford, *C. R. Ashbee.*

83. Bulletin of the Art Institute of Chicago 2, no. 3 (January 1909): 35, 37, 43.

*Frederic C. Bartlett's cartoons for the new University Club windows, exhibited at the Art Institute; when completed, they were installed at the club and are still there (AIC)*

*

Early in 1909, the *American Architect* published "Judgements" and "Criticisms" of the problems submitted by various ateliers in response to programs put forth by the Society of Beaux-Arts Architects.[84] In January the results of two Class B problems were published, with Chicago's Atelier Bennett receiving two mentions. The first went to club member F. C. Walker for his solution to "An Aqueduct," and the other went to Earl H. Reed for the design of "A Villa." A month later, F. C. Walker was named again, along with A. S. Ingeman. Shortly thereafter, Walker also won a "special competition" for a "monumental fireplace." The atelier was obviously active by the end of 1908, if not earlier.

Late 1908 and the first weeks of 1909 were busy times for the Chicago Architectural Club, with Ashbee's visit, the Exhibition of Art Crafts , and the preparations for the Ninth Annual Traveling Scholarship Competition that were completed during December of 1908. The dates of the Twenty-second Annual Exhibition were established during the same period. The catalog noted that it was set to open on March 9 and run through March 23, 1909. This was the first of a number of errors in the catalog. It actually opened with a private viewing and reception for the press on March 2 and did not close until March 28. For reasons never discussed, the public opening was not until March 9. The invitations were issued jointly by the Art Institute of Chicago and the Chicago Architectural Club. The opening reception was on a Tuesday evening. At the same time, the Art Institute issued a second invitation to a "private view of paintings of Frank C. Peyraud," and noted on that card that "the Annual Exhibition of the Architectural Club opens at the same time."

The catalog of the 1909 annual exhibition followed the same general format that had been used since 1905. It was edited by Arthur B. Tuttle. In contrast to recent exhibitions, the 1909 show and catalog emphasized drawings, although photographs were still accepted. The Exhibition Committee was chaired by second vice president William G. Reichert, who had become very active after winning the Seventh Annual Traveling Scholarship in 1907. The Jury of Admission was chaired by H. V. von Holst with John B. Fisher, Paul F. Mann, Thomas E. Tallmadge, and Hugo Zimmerman. W. L. Kalter was the treasurer of the exhibition fund. For the most part, these men were part of the avant-garde contingent of the club. The Young Turks were returning. Dwight Perkins, now an officer with the Illinois AIA, wrote the opening essay for the catalog, titled "Drawing and Drawings in Connection with the Architectural World." He wrote that drawing "is the great universal language not only of the fine arts but of all the industrial arts as well. No process involving physical things can exist without it." Perkins would maintain his relationship with the club for many years to come. The catalog listed 236 members, in all categories, the largest number to date. The data concerning the Traveling Scholarship followed the membership list, after which there were thirty-seven pages of illustrations. The end of the catalog had a "complete" list of exhibitors and exhibits, 329 in all, heavily oriented to Chicago work. Walter Burley Griffin had three photographs of the Orth House, and Spencer & Powers had a total of twenty-eight photographs, three of which were illustrated. One of the more interesting exhibits was H. D. Jenkins's large drawing of a "Proposed New Harbor for Chicago," illustrated but not listed. A careful reading of the catalog confirms that it was rather sloppily edited. Many exhibits discussed in reviews of the exhibition were not in the catalog, and some illustrations were not included in the list of exhibits.

Because the press was admitted to the exhibition early, reviews were published before the public saw the show. The first was in the *Chicago Evening Post* three days before the opening night.[85] The reviewer noted than an "interesting fea-

84. *American Architect* (January 13, 1909): 15; *American Architect* (March 3, 1909): 79.

85. *Chicago Evening Post*, March 6, 1909.

*Walter Burley Griffin exhibited several photographs of his work in 1909; this is the W. S. Orth House in Chicago (CAC/09)*

*One of the photographs exhibited by Spencer & Powers in 1909 (CAC/09)*

ture of the twenty-second annual exhibition . . . will be the large number of foreign exhibitors." This statement apparently refers to out-of-town, rather than European, exhibitors, since according to the catalog there were no exhibitors from outside the United States. The catalog listed, along with the fifty-eight Chicago exhibitors, seventeen from Philadelphia, twelve from New York, four from Boston, and one from Detroit—about 40 percent from outside of Chicago. The catalog also failed to list the winning Traveling Scholarship design by Hugh B. Dunning, although it was given two full pages in the front of the book. George B. Herlin, H. C. Skigly, and Wm. R. Bajor, who won the first, second, and third prizes for the students' Home Traveling Scholarship offered by the Art Institute of Chicago, were erroneously included under the listing for Cram, Goodhue & Ferguson of New York. Other similar errors and omissions suggest that the catalog was hastily assembled.

*Harry Dodge Jenkins's huge drawing for a "Proposed New Harbor for Chicago" provoked discussion during the 1909 exhibition (CAC/09)*

There were several short notices of the exhibition in local newspapers, but only one of substance. Maude I. G. Oliver's review in the *Chicago Record-Herald* was comprehensive and made a point of correcting some of the errors in the catalog.[86] Her review was accompanied by illustrations of Charles J. Mulligan's sculpture and the Hutchinson Medal, which was awarded to Matthew Neu of the Chicago School of Architecture (the name that by then was regularly used to refer to the combined effort of the Armour Institute and the Art Institute of Chicago). The most interesting review was by Robert Craik McLean, editor of the *Western Architect*, who made a point of reminding his readers that he had been one of the founders of the club in 1885.[87] He didn't really review the exhibition so much as he simply spoke in a highly favorable manner about the club and its history, although one paragraph of his comments may explain the problems found in the catalog. He wrote that "changing of the date of the [Philadelphia] T Square Club's exhibit prevented the showing of many drawings that had been promised for the Chicago exhibition . . . [and one must] . . . realize the extra work which this entailed upon the exhibition committee." McLean also alluded to earlier exhibitions, writing, "There is criticism, too, to meet. Time was when special exhibits of club members were permitted, and because this was abolished it is said that some of the most talented members refuse to exhibit their work. One year almost the entire exhibit was monopolized by a member for his private showing; and whose work has undoubted merit and interest, but who took an unfair and unwarranted advantage of this to the general obscuring of the other exhibitors. It was probably for this reason that the special exhibit, otherwise a most attractive and logical method, was abolished. But the members who take exception are wrong, for it is the club, and the advancement of their art that counts, and not the individual." He was clearly referring to 1902, when Frank Lloyd Wright dominated the exhibition. McLean had never been a proponent of Wright's work during his tenure as editor of the *Inland Architect*, and it is odd that he now seemed, in sort of a left-handed manner, to be supporting Wright. Whatever the case, after 1909, under McLean's editorship, the *Western Architect* began to publish Wright more or less regularly along with other members of the Prairie school.

The following month, McLean reported that the "first annual exhibition of the Minneapolis Architectural Club was held . . . from April Seventeenth to May third."[88]

He did not mention that he was on the Catalog Committee for the exhibition.[89] His lengthy article went into great detail about the content of the exhibition and the work put forth by the members of that club to realize such success. He commented on the many exhibits from other cities, as well as those from Chicago, a number of which were apparently sent directly to Minneapolis when the show closed. Frank Lloyd Wright was represented by nine entries, and several others of the Prairie school were prominent. During the first decade of the twentieth century, Wright was officially represented only twice in Chicago club exhibitions, but he and his Prairie school colleagues often appeared in club shows of other cities, including Cleveland, Pittsburgh, Detroit, Boston, and Philadelphia. Wright's famous "Home for a Prairie Town," designed for and published in the *Ladies' Home Journal*, was actually displayed at several other club exhibitions, including Toronto, New York, and Philadelphia, before it was shown in Chicago.

❋

With the Twenty-second Annual Exhibition over, the Chicago Architectural Club met in early May to elect Elmo C. Lowe as president for the 1909–10 year, with T.

86. Maude I. G. Oliver, *Chicago Record-Herald*, March 28, 1909.

87. "Exhibition, Chicago Architectural Club," *Western Architect* (April 1909): 43

88. "Minneapolis Architectural Club Exhibition," *Western Architect* (May 1909): 51–55.

89. *Catalogue of the First Annual Exhibition of the Minneapolis Architectural Club, 1909* (Minneapolis, n.d., ca. 1909). The catalog is extremely rare; the Minnesota Historical Society's librarian very kindly furnished me with a photocopy for reference.

E. Tallmadge, Paul Haagen, George Awsumb, Elmer Nettenstrom, T. A. Lescher, Samuel Marx, John Fisher, and Redmond Corse filling out the rest of the Executive Committee. Plans for the coming year began immediately, but not before the club and most of Chicago's architectural intelligentsia were treated to the results of Daniel H. Burnham's long struggle with his *Plan of Chicago.*

The *Plan of Chicago* was a direct outgrowth of Burnham's work on the World's Columbian Exposition of 1893. He had become intensely interested in planning large projects—both buildings and their surroundings. Several cities, some already discussed, engaged Burnham to help plan their long-term growth. From 1894 forward he worked on large-scale plans for Washington, D.C., Cleveland, San Francisco, and Manilla, as well as other sites in the Philippines. During this period, he continued to talk and present plans for various aspects of the city of Chicago, primarily along the lakeshore. In 1906, after years of conversation, he had finally agreed to head a group that would prepare a plan for Chicago. He enlisted the help of Edward H. Bennett, who had already assisted him on several earlier plans, and began work. The results were shown piecemeal from time to time, sometimes at the annual exhibitions of the Chicago Architectural Club. Burnham's colleagues, the Olmsted brothers, who had been working with him on a plan for Grant Park, showed an elaborate model of the park at the Art Institute of Chicago a year before Burnham's final plan was published.

Finally, in 1909 it was announced that the final product was to be issued in the form of a magnificent "volume of more than 150 pages, profusely illustrated by colored reproductions of the paintings of Jules Guerin, Fernand Janin, and other artists who have been so long at work."[90] A few days after the release of the book, the "drawings, plans, and perspectives showing the scheme for the development of Chicago, prepared under the direction of Daniel H. Burnham . . . [were] . . . on exhibition, after July 8, in Room 16" at the Art Institute of Chicago.[91] The preparation of the *Plan of Chicago* had long been known to Chicagoans, but when the entire collection of drawings, as well as the beautiful volume describing it, were finally issued, it had an immense and enduring influence on the people of Chicago. Virtually every newspaper in Chicago and many in other cities wrote extensively on the plan with almost universal praise. Civic groups hastened to endorse it, and Burnham was in great demand as a speaker and proponent of the plan. The Chicago Architectural Club was but one of many groups to look with favor on the plan. It had, of course, been advocating such a movement for years. The local AIA chapter endorsed the plan in early October 1909 and promised help in implementing it. Burnham was present at the meeting where the Illinois AIA voted unanimously to support the plan, and after hearing the group's comments rose and responded as follows: "'It is quite likely,' said Mr. Burnham, 'that in 1950 or thereabouts some Chicagoan, browsing about some old bookstand, may run across a copy of our plan book. "Well," he may say, "those fellows did pretty well back in 1909, according to

90. *Chicago Tribune,* July 4, 1909; Daniel H. Burnham and Edward H. Bennett, *The Plan of Chicago* (Chicago: The Commercial Club, 1909). The plan has been reprinted twice, first by Da Capo Press, in 1970, and then by Princeton Architectural Press, in 1993.

91. *Bulletin of the Art Institute of Chicago* (July 1909): 3–4.

*In 1908, Olmsted Brothers showed this elaborate model of Grant Park, done with Daniel Burnham (PC)*

their modest ideas of Chicago's greatness, but they certainly didn't go half far enough." However, we have gone a good way. We believe we have a plan in a general way which shows Chicago as it should be.'"[92] Burnham knew he had done a great job, but he was wise enough to leave room for others to improve upon it. The *Plan of Chicago* has had an enormous impact on the city of Chicago and American city planning into the twenty-first century.

Burnham spoke with many groups in Chicago about his plan, including the Chicago Architectural Club. The club members, however, did not completely approve of his plan. They could not endorse the idea of the Field Museum being built in the center of Grant Park. It was a gross violation of what they had been advocating for more than a decade. On the other hand, they did approve of the overall master plan and continued to suggest ideas for years to come, particularly for the improvement of the lakefront and Grant Park.

In the meantime, the club continued its mission to entertain and educate the young architects of Chicago. A major figure in this effort was Burnham's colleague Edward H. Bennett, who served as patron of what was essentially the club's atelier. Following the release of the *Plan of Chicago*, it was Bennett more than Burnham who continued to work in the area of city planning, but he also maintained his interest in training younger members of the architectural community.

During the fall of 1909, the club members returned to their usual agenda of meetings that alternated between bohemian nights and more formal evenings with senior speakers from the architectural and construction community. The club had regular sketch nights and began to encourage members who participated in the club's atelier to do their work in the club rooms at the Dexter Building. Every year, as Christmas approached, the club had a number of purely social affairs, where wives and other guests were invited to participate, but in 1909, the members did something entirely new: they staged a musical comedy. The play was performed twice at the Bush Temple Theater, on December 10 and 11.[93] Titled *A Modern Miracle,* it was written by Robert H. Moulton, who was totally deaf, and the music was composed by Edward G. Oldefest, both members of the club. According to the *Tribune,* the play dealt "with the adventures of a wealthy American in a Paris architectural school in search of ideas for a palatial residence." (It was also noted that the principal performance was preceded by a "minstrel show.") All of the parts were performed by "architects and draftsmen of Chicago. The parts will be taken by members of the club, and in addition to a strong cast of principals there will be a chorus of thirty men and girls." In view of the dearth of women members, most of the female parts were taken by men, and the description suggests that the result was hilarious. The *Tribune* also noted that this would be "the first of a series of theatrical entertainments planned by the club, which numbers 250 members, including practically all of the architects and draftsmen of Chicago." There is no documentation of later performances, but this one was significant enough for the *Chicago Tribune* to include a wonderful cartoon of "Architects in Roles of Actresses as Seen by Artist."[94]

By the end of 1909, with its theatrical escapade behind it, the club had already established dates for the 1910 exhibition at the Art Institute of Chicago. It was scheduled for April 5 through May 1 and would commemorate the twenty-fifth anniversary of the founding of the club. For unknown reasons there was very little published about other activities of the club in the early months of 1910. In sharp contrast, the activities of the Illinois Chapter of the AIA and the Chicago Architects'

92. "Illinois Chapter Formally Indorses Burnham Idea and Promises to Assist Commercial Club in Its Efforts," *Chicago Record-Herald*, October 12, 1909.

93. The performance was featured in the *Chicago Tribune* three times. Before the performance, articles appeared on December 5 and December 9, and a review was published on December 11, 1909. All were written in a humorous vein. The Bush Temple Building still stands at the northwest corner of Clark Street and Chicago Avenue.

94. The cartoon was signed "Ross." An H. J. Ross became a member of the club in 1890, and it is possible that he drew the cartoon.

Business Association were published regularly. Virtually every meeting of the two groups was recorded in Chicago's *Construction News*. I. K. Pond got a lengthy article with a portrait when he was elected president of the national AIA.[95] It is likely that Pond was responsible for an exhibition at the Art Institute of the work of the late Charles F. McKim of New York, who had been an active member of the national organization and was instrumental in the formation of the American Academy in Rome. Before the exhibition came to Chicago, it had hung in the AIA's recently acquired home in Washington, the Octagon House.[96] It was popular with the members of all three architectural societies in Chicago.

During this time, one issue that served to unite the CAC, the AIA, and the CABA was the totally unsubstantiated charge by members of the Chicago Board of Education against Chicago School Board architect Dwight H. Perkins, who was accused of "Incompetency . . . Extravagance . . . and Insubordination."[97] The three groups called a special joint meeting on February 5, 1910, to "protest against the prosecution of Dwight Heald Perkins by the Board of Education."[98] They were unanimous in their support of Perkins, but to no avail. He was forced out of his position as School Board architect. He went on to form one of the most successful private architecture firms in Chicago, specializing in the design of schools throughout the Midwest.

Not until the Twenty-third Annual Exhibition did the club's activities again get publicity either locally or nationally, and then it was confined largely to local newspaper items. We can, however, tell a good deal about the members' activities by looking closely at their annual catalog. They continued the policy of assigning the club's second vice president, in this case Paul T. Haagen, to be the chairman of the Exhibition Committee. The Twenty-third Annual Exhibition catalog was to be the last of the series begun in 1906 to follow a basic format. The 1910 catalog was the same size as in recent past years, bound in printed paper over boards. (There was also a paper-bound edition.) The cover design was done by longtime member Hugh M. G. Garden and carried his distinctive monogram. After the frontispiece and title page, there was a small photograph of a painting by G. A. Bauman titled *The Builders,* one of two by Bauman in the exhibition. It was followed by a list of the club's officers and the members directly involved with the exhibition. For the first time, the club listed a "Manager of the Exhibition," one L. C. Vinson. He was not a member of the club, and his name does not appear in any of the publicity about the exhibition. Apparently, he was a paid adviser responsible for all the organizational aspects of the show, probably including getting contributions from "Patrons of the Exhibition." The last time advertising had been included in the club's catalog was in 1900. Members prided themselves on not taking advertising, and a number of other clubs throughout the United States emulated them. That is, they simply asked contractors, building suppliers, and some architects to contribute funds to offset the cost of the exhibition. Since 1901, those contributors had been listed in the catalog by name only. In 1910 they were listed by profession, and their complete addresses were included in the front of the catalog immediately following an acknowledgments page. There were 164 patrons listed, more than ever before.

There was a two-page foreword to the catalog written by founding member Irving K. Pond. In 1910 Pond was beginning a tour of duty as president of the American Institute of Architects. He had previously served in the same capacity for the Illinois Chapter of the AIA. Pond was highly regarded by his colleagues and there is no doubt of his pride and sincerity when he wrote in his introduction that "the ideals for

Drawing published in the Chicago Tribune, *lampooning the club's theatrical efforts (courtesy of Harold T. Wolff)*

95. *Construction News* 29, no. 1 (January 29, 1910). Pond had been elected at the AIA National Convention held in Washington, D.C., December 14–16, 1909.

96. *Construction News* 29, no. 4 (January 22, 1910): 50.

97. *Construction News* 29, no. 8 (February 19, 1910): 140. These charges and the trial that followed were widely publicized in both the popular and the professional press during the early months of 1910; the complete story of this unfortunate event has never been fully covered.

98. *Construction News* 29, no. 23 (June 11, 1910): 396.

*G. A. Bauman's painting* The Builders *(CAC/10)*

which the club first stood have not changed . . . the inspiring ideals were fellowship and development, the underlying motives were social and educational . . . The altruistic spirit which impels the individual to extend unselfish aid to the community, to the municipality animates the architectural brotherhood as it seems to animate no other body of professional men . . . not only in its Club activities but in the activities of the individual members . . . The Chicago Architectural Club animated by these lofty ideals and noble purposes deserves the highest respect and support of the community it seeks to serve."

As usual, the catalog included a list of all the past winners of the club's Traveling Scholarship, as well as the name of the current winner, Clarence G. Brown. The American Radiator Company was acknowledged as the donor of the six hundred dollars in prize money for the scholarship. The gold medal for the runner-up design was the gift of Charles W. Gindele.[99] That was followed by a listing of the membership of the club, which by now included 266 names in all categories. Fifty-six pages of illustrations, about equally divided between photographs and drawings, were followed by a list of exhibitors who showed 685 items, of which 143 were in an addendum. There were 130 exhibitors, of which forty-nine were from out of town, the largest contingent being twenty-five from New York.

The 1910 club catalog noted that the Illinois Chapter of the AIA had, in 1909, "re-established a gold medal of honor for award to designers of buildings represented in the Annual Exhibition of the Chicago Architectural Club." That medal had been awarded in 1909 to Pond & Pond for its Women's Baptist Missionary Home Training School in Chicago. The medal could not have been announced in the 1909 catalog, since it was not chosen by the AIA jury until the exhibition was in place. In 1910, the jury included George C. Nimmons, president of the AIA, along with Samuel A. Treat, J. C. Llewellyn, Thomas E. Tallmadge, Dwight H. Perkins, William K. Fellows, and E. C. Lowe, who was president of the CAC. They met at the exhibition on April 19 before it opened and chose the Blackstone Hotel designed by Marshall & Fox to receive the medal. It was presented on May 9, 1910.[100] A month later, at the AIA's annual meeting on June 14, the gold medal was awarded to Benjamin H. Marshall, who announced that he was presenting the chapter with a check for a thousand dollars to establish the Caleb H. Marshall Scholarship in memory of his recently deceased father.

The invitation to the opening of the 1910 exhibition at the Art Institute of Chicago was appended to an invitation to a concurrent exhibit of paintings by Gardner Symons. The first notice of the club's showing was one sentence in the *Chicago Evening Post* on April 2, 1910. A day later the *Chicago Tribune* noted that "a reception at the Art Institute on Tuesday evening will inaugurate two important exhibitions. The Chicago Architectural Club will give its annual show, and about twenty-five paintings by Gardner Symons will be exhibited." The *Chicago Record-Herald* published a similar notice on the same day, and several other newspapers announced the opening on its first day, April 5. Only the *Chicago Evening Post* provided a preview of the exhibition.[101] Its comments reflect some of the architectural activities in Chicago at the time. The reviewer wrote that "the plans of buildings for civic and business enterprise show something of the stress of the times which is filling the draughting rooms with work and keeping the busy architects from making show drawings for an exhibition." He went on to mention several of the architects who were in the exhibition, as well as some of the other material in the show. Eventually nearly every Chicago paper published brief reviews, some with photographs.[102] Two longer reviews appeared, both on April 10. The *Chicago Tribune* reported, after an introductory item about Gardner

99. The driving force behind the American Radiator Company's first-prize gift of six hundred dollars was the company's president, Clarence M. Woolley. Along with Charles W. Gindele, he was also responsible for the gold medal awarded for second place. After 1915, however, the donors were no longer listed. Gindele was elected an honorary member of the club in 1910.

100. This event was reported twice in *Construction News*, on May 7, 1910, and on May 14, 1910, in a longer version.

101. *Chicago Evening Post*, April 5, 1910.

Symons, that "it is an off year with the Architectural club, which has fewer important projects to show than usual." The writer went on to discuss a number of easily forgettable projects. He did acknowledge that there were several important polychrome panels exhibited by the Northwestern Terra Cotta Company, which were designed by Louis Sullivan. He did not, however, comment on the numerous projects by the younger, more avant-garde members, who had returned to the exhibition almost en masse. Walter Burley Griffin, Spencer & Powers, Jens Jensen, George Maher, Charles E. White, Tallmadge & Watson, Lawrence Buck, Chatten & Hammond, Nimmons & Fellows, Patton & Miller, and Pond & Pond were all well represented. Several younger men, including Alfred Alschuler and T. Ralph Ridley, also showed work of considerable merit in the spirit of the early modern movement. The long review in the *Chicago Record-Herald* was similar in tone. The reviewer seemed to be more interested in the mounting of the show than he was in the exhibits themselves.

The *Bulletin of the Art Institute of Chicago* published a brief after-the-fact item in its July 1910 issue.[103] It was simply a news item, not a review. The only article on the 1910 exhibition to appear in the professional press was in the *Inland Architect*.[104] It was a straight reported piece, totally uncritical. It too, ignored the fact that the Young Turks of architecture had returned to the annual exhibition with a vengeance. The men listed above, who were generally considered part of the avant-garde movement, had a total of 105 exhibits, and there were twelve more by the two younger men. There were also a number of older architects with serious entries that the reviewers overlooked. The local press was simply not ready to acknowledge the developing American architecture.

The Perkins affair, the reestablishment of the AIA gold medal as part of the annual exhibition, and the Chicago Architectural Club's move to the Art Institute of Chicago all served to bring the club and its sister organizations together in 1910 and thereafter. One indication of this was that the AIA, at its annual meeting, noted that a step had been "taken which it is thought will be a great convenience to those who are also members of the Architectural Club, as that body meets every Monday evening and the Chapter one Monday of each month. The time of holding the meeting was changed by the Chapter from Monday to Tuesday evening."[105] Thus the chapter deliberately found a way to avoid any conflict of meeting times.

*Spencer & Powers's design of the T. B. Smith House in Terre Haute, Indiana, the frontispiece for the 1910 exhibition catalog (CAC/10)*

*The Blackstone Hotel by Marshall & Fox, winner of the local AIA gold medal (PC)*

*Benjamin H. Marshall (MofC)*

102. In addition to those already noted, items appeared in the *Record-Herald*, the *Examiner*, and the *Chicago Daily News* on April 6, 1910. Other reviews are noted below.

103. *Bulletin of the Art Institute of Chicago* 4, no. 1 (July 1910): 7.

104. *Inland Architect* 15, no. 5 (May 1910): 56.

105. *Construction News* 30, no. 6 (August 6, 1910): 96.

*Charles E. White's design for F. F. Badger (CAC/10)*

Late in 1910, on November 12, the Illinois AIA held another of its "special" meetings, this time to discuss the issue of education. A number of distinguished guests were present, including Clifford Ricker and several colleagues from the University of Illinois, as well as Emil Lorch, then head of the Department of Architecture at Michigan. Horace Ingram, Samuel Marx, T. Ralph Ridley, and Edward G. Oldefest represented the Chicago Architectural Club. All of them were then serving on the club's Executive Committee. The purpose of the meeting was to focus on architectural education and the work then being done in the Midwest. In his opening remarks, Illinois AIA president George C. Nimmons noted that "in the East they are classicists or confine themselves to a great extent to a historical style. In Chicago we adopt something entirely different. The first break away from an historical style was Mr. Sullivan and he did it beautifully; we can trace the gradual growth in grace of his style until we reach his transportation building, where we get a newness of design and a beauty that has never been equaled that has been a constant source of inspiration to younger men."[106] Professor Lorch followed, saying that "American

106. *Construction News* 30, no. 19 (November 19, 1910): 16.

*Cottage in Evanston, Illinois, by Tallmadge & Watson (CAC/10)*

*"An English Suburban Residence," exhibited in 1910 by T. Ralph Ridley (CAC/10)*

*S. M. Speigel's house in Winnetka, designed by Lebenbaum & Marx (CAC/10)*

schools are better . . . than the foreign schools . . . and recommended the atelier system." The Chicago Architectural Club, which had established its own atelier two years earlier, thereafter began to devote even more time to the education of its younger members. Club members, in fact, devoted so much time to the atelier that the Art Institute of Chicago would eventually ask them to find other quarters for the atelier work, since the School of the Art Institute could simply no longer spare its classrooms for that purpose.

It was the end of the first decade of the twentieth century, and the club was now firmly established as one of the most important forces in architecture in Chicago. It was not alone, of course, since the local chapter of the American Institute of Architects was very much in evidence, and the Chicago Architects' Business Association was also a strong voice. A review of the officers and directors of these organizations reveals that virtually all had been or still were members of the Chicago Architectural Club. The impact of the club on the architects of Chicago was impressive, to say the least.

*Louis Sullivan's exquisite, multilayered screen for the Schlesinger & Meyer Building (CAC/13)*

# Midlife Crises and Citywide Work

CHAPTER FIFTEEN

Nineteen eleven was the midpoint in the life of the Chicago Architectural Club, which would continue to influence the architects of Chicago and the United States for another quarter century. During much of that period, it would be the premier professional group of architects in Chicago, certainly among the younger men and women of the city. The second decade of the twentieth century was the beginning of a time when virtually all the major architects of Chicago either were, or had been, members of the club.[1] It now became normal practice for the three primary architectural groups in Chicago to cooperate on a regular basis. In June of 1910 the *Western Architect* commented, "It is probable that the most systematic organization of architectural interests in the country exists at Chicago . . . there is also a joint meeting of representatives from the several bodies once a month. The Illinois Chapter of the American Institute of Architects gives its attention wholly to ethical subjects, the Chicago Architects' Business Association, made up largely of chapter members, considers the business side of the profession, the Chicago Architectural Club, its educational work."[2] The club began to devote even more of its time to educational activities and, in doing so, continued to evolve. It became more and more dedicated to the education of young hopefuls in the field and found ways to cooperate with both the Illinois Chapter of the American Institute of Architects and the Chicago Architects' Business Association. It was, in fact, a training ground for full-fledged practitioners of the art of architecture. Its constituency covered the gamut from the youngest apprentice with, at most, a high school education to graduates of any of the now numerous college- and university-level schools of architecture. The Chicago Architectural Club had a good deal to offer to all.

The club still maintained its rooms in the Dexter Building, but social events were given less emphasis and major competitions and the annual exhibition at the Art Institute of Chicago took up more time and energy than in the past. The regular meetings with the two groups of senior architects gave members the opportunity to convey their thoughts to older colleagues without the need for as many public relations activities as they had performed in the past. Unfortunately, the secretary no longer distributed the minutes of regular meetings to the press and, consequently, far less information on the club's week-to-week activities was published. Only the annual exhibition and a few minor events were regularly reported in the press.

1. This trend was confirmed with the 1909 AIA national convention, when all the Chicago delegates were current or former members of the Chicago Architectural Club, as reported in *Inland Architect* 52, no. 5 (November 1908): 65.

2. *Western Architect* 15, no. 6 (June 1910): 58.

The Twenty-fourth Annual Exhibition was announced in January 1911.[3] It was to be held at the Art Institute from March 7 to March 26, 1911. Entry forms were to be returned to the club not later than February 6. For the first time the announcement noted that the Illinois Chapter of the AIA had reestablished its gold medal of honor for a design to be chosen from the exhibits at the show. Any building completed within the previous five years was eligible. The following month, the chapter announced that it had put together a program for the selection, by competitive examination, of the recipient of the Caleb H. Marshall Scholarship.[4] The elaborate rules called for nominations from members of the AIA and involved several days of examinations in artistic abilities, design, freehand drawing, and reading in two languages followed by a thesis based on that reading. It was a onetime competition with an award of a thousand dollars to be used by the winner to attend a university of his choice, subject to approval by the jury. The jury was to be selected by a committee made up of R. C. Spencer Jr., chairman, Peter B. Wight, C. H. Hammond, Thomas E. Tallmadge, and Walter B. Griffin. All were, or had been, members of the Chicago Architectural Club. Nominations were to be in the hands of the AIA chapter's secretary by April 15, and the examinations were scheduled to begin on May 15. They were actually held from May 29 through June 5. Only four candidates presented themselves, and the jury, which consisted of Hugh Garden, Peter Weber, and Horace Powers, gave the award to F. W. Morse.[5] Just how Mr. Morse used his thousand dollars was never recorded, and no more Caleb H. Marshall scholarships were awarded.

In mid-February of 1911 a group of the founders of the Chicago Architectural Sketch Club announced a reunion of the early members of the club. Apparently they asked anyone who was present in the first year or so, since most of those who reportedly attended were not actually those who had been recorded as founders in the March 1885 issue of the *Inland Architect*.[6] On February 21, 1911, the reunion was held at the Sherman House.[7] Those in attendance were W. G. Williamson, Thomas H. Mullay, Arthur G. Brown, Frank L. Lively, C. Bryant Schaefer, and E. J. Wagner. Only Williamson was actually a founder, although the others were all members of the original Chicago Architectural Sketch Club. Plans were made to interview other early members and suggestions for other activities were made. A number of members suggested that perhaps a reunion of "all those who at any time joined the club, including its many friends" should take place. One long-absent founder was heard from, namely Robert Craik McLean, then residing in Minneapolis, and his letter was quoted in full in the news article. He noted that he was stating "from memory, to be corrected by the club's history, several meetings were held. That at the first meeting there were seven or eight draftsmen present, among them being I. K. Pond, W. G. Williamson, Harry Laurie [*sic*], Teddy Fraenkel, George Beaumont, Charley Kessell and Billy Gibb." Of these, only Fraenkel and Gibb did not appear as founders in that long-ago article concerning the formation of the club, although they were early members. McLean ended his letter with statement that "the club's secretary can give you accurate data regarding the founding of the club that was compiled by a committee of charter members some years ago." Unfortunately, such a document has never surfaced.

❖

The Annual Traveling Scholarship Competition continued to be the club's major competition. It was held every year until 1915, after which it was suspended due to the onset of the First World War. Rarely, if ever, were the terms of the competition published after 1909. Most, but not all, of the winning designs were repro-

3. *Construction News* 31, no. 3 (January 21, 1911): 10.

4. *Construction News* 31, no. 7 (February 18, 1911): 10.

5. *Construction News* (June 17, 1911): 8.

6. *Inland Architect* 5, no. 2 (March 1885): 24.

7. *Construction News* 31, no. 9 (March 4, 1911): 10.

*William B. Betts's design for "A Monument to a Great American General," winner of the Eleventh Annual Traveling Scholarship Competition in 1911 (CAC/11)*

duced in the annual exhibition catalogs. Generally they were included in the many reviews of the exhibition that appeared in the public and professional press.

There is a good deal of confusion concerning the announced winners of the Annual Traveling Scholarship and other competitors between 1909 and 1913. For example, Hugh Dunning's design for "An Athenaeum for Teachers" was the announced winner of the 1909 scholarship competition, and his name continued to be listed as such in every catalog until 1917, when it was noted that "two Scholarships were awarded this year." Frank C. Walker's design for "A Monumental Fireplace" was listed as the second winner. Neither he nor his work had been listed or illustrated in the 1909 catalog or any subsequent catalog. Only the work of Hugh Dunning and the runner-up, Robert Teal Hyett, was illustrated in 1909. Clarence Brown won the competition in 1910. In 1911 W. B. Betts was the announced winner for his design of "A Monument to a Great American General." His design was illustrated in the 1911 catalog, along with that of Christian U. Bagge, who was a runner-up. That year, the page where all past winners except Walker were listed noted that "this year the Club holds two competitions for prizes of $600 and gold medals." The 1912 catalog, however, listed John Calvin Leavell as the 1911 Traveling Scholarship winner and Betts and Walker as winners of "Special Competitions." Leavell's design for "A Monumental Stairway" was never listed or published in the 1911 catalog. Not until 1917 was it noted that there had been two scholarships awarded in 1911, and both Betts and Leavell were then acknowledged as winners.

There is little record of the competition programs sponsored by the club in 1912–13. Arthur C. Hanifin[8] was recorded as having won the 1912 Annual Traveling Scholarship prize of six hundred dollars, donated by Clarence M. Woolley of the American Radiator Company, for his design for "A Theater in a Large City Park," and E. Dean Parmelee was awarded the second prize, a gold medal donated by Charles W. Gindele. Neither the program nor the designs were ever published, but Hanifin and Parmelee were both acknowledged in the 1912 exhibition catalog, although not in the list of exhibitors. Obviously the Thirteenth Annual Traveling Scholarship Competition was part of the schedule in 1913, but like the year before the only published record of the program for that competition was the name of the

*Christian Bagge won a gold medal for his runner-up design in 1911 (CAC/11)*

8 Arthur C. Hanifin is something of an enigma. His was the only winning entry in the Traveling Scholarship Competition that was never published. He was listed as a CAC member beginning in 1907, when he was recorded as "inactive" and his address was given as D. H. Burnham and Company in San Francisco. In 1910 he was listed with two addresses, the first at 1417 Railway Exchange Building in Chicago (D. H. Burnham's office) and the second at 1405 Monadnock, where he remained until 1914. In 1914, he was listed as a nonresident member living in New York City, which suggests that he stopped there after his Traveling Scholarship-funded trip to Europe. In 1915 he was back in Chicago at 449 Woodland Park, probably a home address. He continued to live in Chicago for the next few years, and in 1920 his address was given as the office of Holabird & Roche at 104 S. Michigan. In 1921, he was listed as an Illinois licensed architect living in Oakland, California. His name never appeared in the list of licensed architects living in Illinois, but in 1912 and 1915 he was listed as a member of the Chicago Architects' Business Association, an organization that required a license as a prerequisite for membership. Census records from 1910 indicate that he was born in Pennsylvania around 1884 and was the son of Myra C. and John C. Huey in Chicago, which suggests that his father was dead and his mother had remarried. The date of his death is unknown, although there is a death certificate for an "Arthur Hannifin" on record in Chicago for 1927.

*Rudolph G. Wolff's design for "A Municipal Tribune," winner of the 1913 Traveling Scholarship Competition (CAC/13)*

project, "A Municipal Tribune," noted along with the winners in the 1913 catalog issued when the annual exhibition opened on May 6. That year, however, the winner's design was published, along with the work of several others. Rudolph G. Wolff took first prize and W. J. Schaefer was the winner of the gold medal for second place. B. C. Greengard, William G. Wuehrmann, and A. A. Schwartz were cited as first-, second-, and third-mention entries. The first prize of six hundred dollars was again donated by the American Radiator Company, and Schaefer's gold medal was contributed by Charles W. Gindele, a tradition he had started in 1910, which would continue through 1915.

There had been one other "Special Competition" in 1913, sponsored by the Chicago Face Brick Association. It was for "A Four Thousand Dollar Brick

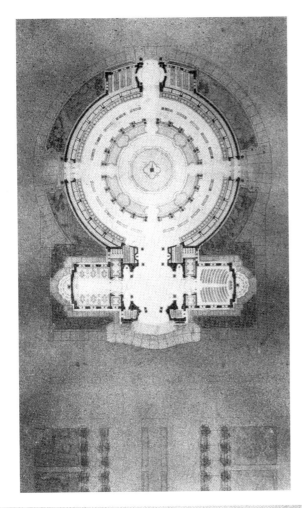

*W. J. Schaefer won the 1914 Annual Traveling Scholarship Competition with his design for an aquarium (CAC/14)*

House." William Wuehrmann, who won the competition, was listed in the 1913 catalog as the winner of a "Special Competition" for that year and continued to be so listed in every catalog through 1916, after which this category of winners was dropped. Wuehrmann's winning design was not illustrated in the 1913 catalog, but it did appear along with another design, assumed to be the second-place winner but not identified as such, in an obscure journal called *Construction Details*.[9] Both designs also appeared in a small pamphlet issued by the Hydraulic-Press Brick Company, in which twenty-six designs were illustrated and identified

9. *Construction Details* 3, no. 4 (April 1913): 4–5.

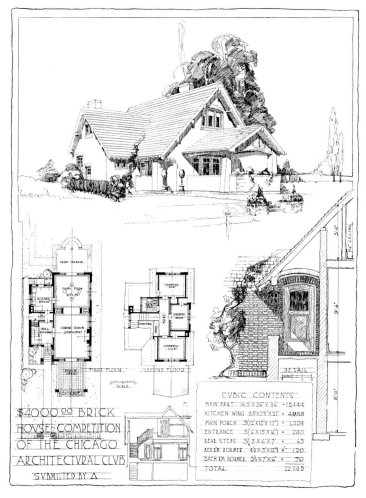

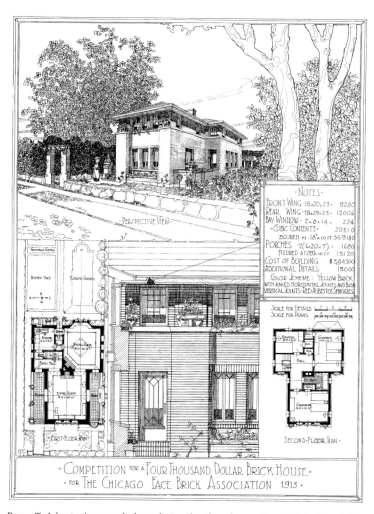

William G. Wuehrmann's design for a four-thousand-dollar house won first place in the Chicago Face Brick Association's competition of 1913, done under the auspices of the Chicago Architectural Club (CD)

Percy T. Johnston's second-place design for the Chicago Face Brick Association Competition (CD)

with designers' names, but there was no information about how they ranked in the competition. (The apparent second-place winner was identified in the pamphlet as Percy T. Johnston.[10] Stylistically, it was highly reminiscent of the work of Walter Burley Griffin and Marion Mahony, but there is no evidence that Johnston was ever in their office.)[11]

As the second decade of the twentieth century began, two very different approaches to architecture were being carried on simultaneously in Chicago. The Steinway Hall group, who looked to Louis Sullivan for inspiration and to Frank Lloyd Wright for new forms, was decidedly the smaller but more vocal of the two groups. The second group had a more formal attitude toward architecture and found inspiration in the traditional teaching methods used at the École des Beaux-Arts in Paris. The two camps seldom quarreled but they did debate, often in the rooms of the Chicago Architectural Club.

There were two rallying points for these divergent points of view. Both were essentially Chicago ateliers. What might be considered the first, and for a time the most influential, atelier was the Oak Park Studio of Frank Lloyd Wright, where a

10. Percy Thorwald Johnston (1890–1934) was born in Chicago to Swedish parents. He took the Illinois architects' licensing exam three times before passing in 1914, after which he practiced at various addresses in Chicago.

11. *Suggestions for Small Hytex Homes* (St. Louis, MO: Hydraulic-Press Brick Company, n.d., ca. 1914).

small but intensely loyal and dedicated group of young men, and a few women, worked with Sullivan's acknowledged disciple to invent what amounted to an entirely new architecture. No French patron could have been more demanding or respected than Frank Lloyd Wright in the heyday of his studio between 1900 and 1908. Walter Burley Griffin, Marion Mahony, William Drummond, Barry Byrne, John Van Bergen, and several others learned architecture from Wright through an apprentice system whereby they designed and saw built dozens of buildings in the style of what was then called "the new school of the middle west," which we know today as the Prairie School of architecture.

The second group congregated around men who had studied in Paris and returned to Chicago to make their mark on the architecture of the early twentieth century. A number of ateliers, most notably the one headed by Edward H. Bennett and several successors, were established in Chicago, usually with a strong relationship with the Chicago Architectural Club. Students at these quasi-schools, who regularly met and participated in architectural competitions sponsored by the New York–based Beaux-Arts Institute of Design, rarely worked on actual building projects but did labor prodigiously over their drafting tables in quest of medals and other prizes. There is no question that they were learning scale, proportion, and traditional forms, and the integration of these elements into elegant designs, albeit designs based on historic architecture. It was this second group, by far the largest, that was most accepted by society as a whole in the second decade of the twentieth century. It was, after all, reflecting the architecture that had been de rigueur in the eastern United States for a half century or more and had been legitimized by the World's Columbian Exposition only twenty years earlier.

It has always been a puzzle why the Prairie School never established itself as a long-lasting influential movement. Part of the answer is that Wright's Oak Park Studio closed in 1909 when he left Chicago to spend nearly two years, during two separate trips, in Europe. His staff members, for the most part, then opened their own offices. While some had some success over the next decade, without Wright's charisma or client base few were able to match his quality of work or level of success. As a group, the most positive effect they had on the public would come in 1911, when the work they mounted at the club's annual exhibition received critical acclaim.

In the meantime, the Chicago Architectural Club continued to sponsor its annual traveling scholarships, regular lectures, and other events, which attracted young hopefuls as they had in the past. These were the same people who continued to work, for the most part, over the drafting tables of the great and near-great firms that had emerged in Chicago since the World's Columbian Exposition. The club's own atelier sponsored many, if not most, of the competitions, and provided an environment in which the Annual Traveling Scholarship drawings could be executed in a manner very much like designs done in Paris. After 1910, the entries became more and more like the work produced in Paris for the École des Beaux-Arts. The huge, beautifully rendered, symmetrical drawings no longer included the innovative details so much admired by Sullivan, Wright, and their colleagues of ten years earlier. The purely American approach to architecture propagated in Wright's studio had simply vanished. A new generation had assumed leadership of the club, and not until after the First World War would the kind of fresh work seen at the turn of the century be present again in Chicago. This time it would be in the sleek forms that had first appeared in the work of architects on the fringe of the early modern movement, such as Frost & Granger's Hall Bartlett House (1903) and S. S. Beman's Christian Science Church interiors. Ultimately, the modern movement would resurface again in the art deco buildings of the twenties with Finnish architect Eliel Saarinen as the leader and Frank Lloyd Wright a reluctant follower who eventually embraced the new aesthetic.

When the Chicago Architectural Club changed its general direction between 1909 and 1912, it did not curtail its activities. Work continued as it had in the past; it was only the architecture that was somewhat different. After Rudolph G. Wolff, a member of the Bennett atelier, won the Thirteenth Annual Traveling Scholarship Competition, W. J. Schaeffer won for his design for "An Aquarium" in 1914, and Fred M. Hodgdon's design for "A Summer and Winter Garden" was chosen as the winner in 1915. The 1916 catalog stated that there was to be a competition that year, but it was never officially announced or carried out. Instead, the 1917 catalog noted that "the European Traveling Scholarship was temporarily discontinued in 1916, and will not be resumed until after the close of the war. This year an American Traveling Scholarship will be awarded; the winner will spend two months traveling in the East, primarily for the study of Colonial Architecture." The competition for the Annual Traveling Scholarship, referred to in the 1917 catalog as the "European Traveling Scholarship," was resumed in 1920.

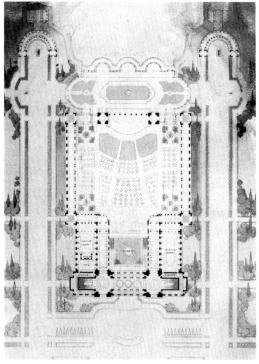

*Fred M. Hodgdon's 1915 design for "A Summer and Winter Garden" (CAC/15)*

In addition to the scholarship winner's designs, the exhibition catalog regularly illustrated winning designs from the Chicago School of Architecture. With technical classes held at the Armour Institute and design taught at the Art Institute of Chicago, the school had a close relationship with the Chicago Architectural Club. Its Home Traveling Scholarship, for a design of a home for the Chicago Chapter of the AIA, was won in 1911 by Bernard C. Greengard. (The Home Traveling Scholarship was awarded for travel in the United States.) Second prize went to Homer S. Sailor, who would join Louis Sullivan upon graduation. In 1912, C. D. Faulkner won this competition for "A Fine Arts Building" and in 1913 C. Halperin was the winner. There is no evidence that the scholarship was awarded after 1913, although the Chicago School of Architecture continued to exhibit student work in the annual exhibition of the Chicago Architectural Club.

A number of other organizations also maintained a close relationship with the Art Institute of Chicago. In October of 1910, the *Bulletin of the Art Institute of Chicago* had published an article that noted "it has been the constant policy of the Art Institute to assist . . . by furnishing rooms for meetings . . . [to] many societies and clubs."[12] It went on to list twenty-three arts-oriented groups that used the institute's facilities. The article noted that "a club-room for the meetings of such societies has been maintained for many years past. A much larger and more commodious room (No. 160 of the ground floor) will hereafter be appropriated to this use and will be handsomely fitted up. The entrance to the new room will be

12. *Bulletin of the Art Institute of Chicago* 4, no. 2 (October 1910): 22.

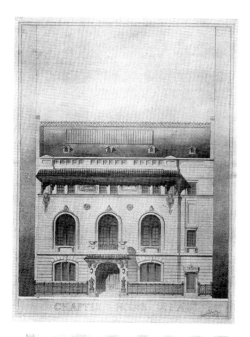

*Bernard C. Greengard won the Home Traveling Scholarship in 1911, while he was a student at the Art Institute of Chicago, with his design for a building to house the Chicago Chapter of the AIA, above; Homer S. Sailor's scheme, top right, took second prize in the competition (CSAC)*

*C. D. Faulkner's 1912 Fine Arts Building (left) won the Home Traveling Fellowship for that year; J. H. Bischof's design (right) took second place (CSAC)*

from the hall under the main entrance to the building." Since the Chicago Architectural Club was still maintaining its own quarters on the second floor of the Dexter Building, it rarely used the Art Institute room for regular meetings, but the Illinois Chapter of the AIA and the Chicago Architects' Business Association did meet there.

   The AIA moved into the new space at the Art Institute and held its first regular meeting there on November 8, 1910[13] The Chicago Architectural Club and the Chicago Architects' Business Association were special guests for the evening. The AIA made the room its regular headquarters and meeting space for the next fourteen years.[14] From time to time the three groups would meet together at the Art Institute when mutual interests made it convenient. The Chicago Architectural Club's

13. *Construction News* 31, no. 24 (June 17, 1911): 9.

14. I am indebted to Kathleen Nagle for her essay "Building the Profession: 125 Years of AIA in Chicago" in *Special History Edition of Architecture Chicago* 12 (1994): 7–21.

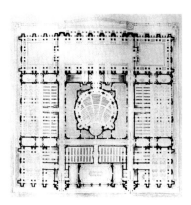

*C. Halperin's winning entry in the 1913 Home Traveling Competition (CSAC)*

primary use of the facilities of the Art Institute of Chicago continued to be for the mounting of its annual exhibition.

The club's Twenty-fourth Annual Exhibition in March of 1911 was handled in a new manner. In a major departure from the past, the club asked second vice president Horace C. Ingram to act as manager of the exhibition and catalog instead of merely appointing him chairman of the exhibition. It did not hire an outside, non-member manager as it had done in 1910. Ingram relieved other members of many of the day-to-day activities required to mount the exhibition, and it seems that he received payment for his duties, even though he was otherwise employed. He was apparently able to take time off from his full-time position when it was required. Ingram was chief designer for Postle & Mahler, which had eighteen exhibits in the show, some of which carried his name as designer. He also had one exhibit under his own name.

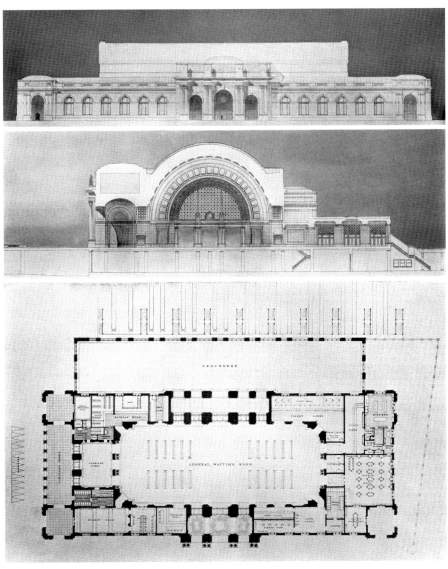

*Postle & Mahler's entry in the 1911 exhibition; the designer was Horace C. Ingram, who served as manager of the exhibition that year (CAC/11)*

Most young architects were extremely busy in 1911 and had little time for club affairs. It was reported that "building operations of Chicago for 1911 broke all previous records."[15] Therefore the club, and Ingram, named two advertising representatives, Edward G. Oldefest and Robert H. Moulton. Ingram and Oldefest were both architects and members of the Executive Committee. Moulton, on the other hand, was a freelance writer, not an architect.[16] There is no evidence of which duties each of the three was assigned, but Oldefest and Ingram most likely solicited patrons to support the exhibition, while Moulton solicited advertising. He may have assisted in editing and assembling the catalog for printing as well.

For the first time in more than ten years, the catalog had paid advertising. There were still patrons, but the list was far shorter than in previous years, probably because only their names and addresses were printed in the book, while advertisers got anywhere from a quarter to a full page of space. Thirty-three patrons were listed, but the index included well over a hundred paid advertisers.

The rest of the catalog was laid out in very much the same manner as in the previous six years, except that the overall size was slightly larger. There were a total of 544 exhibits. Chicago architects made up the majority of exhibitors, with a sprinkling of East and West Coast firms and several exhibits from schools. The American Academy in Rome had seventy-six exhibits, none from Chicagoans.

The exhibition opened in the east wing of the Art Institute on Tuesday evening, March 7, to members and friends by invitation only. The actual opening was preceded by a banquet for club members and invited guests.[17] Nearly a hundred guests attended and "brought the younger men into the social atmosphere of those farther along in the profession." The *Chicago Post* noted two days after the formal opening that "the Municipal Art League gallery tour, conducted by Horace C. Ingram, vice president, with the presence of Edwin F. Gillette, president of the Architectural Club, was an innovation which tended to popularize the show by bringing the delegates of the women's clubs in touch with professional work in house planning and the allied arts intimately associated with building." There was clearly a conscious effort to interest a broad spectrum of the public in the exhibition. Similar reports were published by a number of Chicago newspapers, but the professional press was conspicuously absent.

There were several "skyscrapers" on view that were singled out for comment by reviewers. Holabird & Roche's Monroe Building was admired, as was Cass Gilbert's proposed forty-five-story Woolworth Building in New York City. The *Inter Ocean* reported that there was "on exhibition a model of the memorial to be erected on the battle field of Gettysburg which was designed by J. Devereaux York of Chicago."[18] It also noted that "the sketch, which won the $600 prize offered by the club, which depicts a memorial to a great general, done by William Betts, has also been hung." No mention of the design of "A Monumental Stairway" by John C. Leavell, who was later named the second-place winner of the same prize, appeared in any of the newspaper accounts.

One of the more interesting reviews was written by Maude I. G. Oliver and appeared in the *Chicago Record-Herald*.[19] After commenting in general terms about the show, she wrote:

There are two schools of architecture in this country to-day. One is based upon the theory that the present is entitled to build upon the legacy of the past, adapting but not copying historic periods. This school, of course will allow all manner of digression from original sources, as wide variance, in fact, as individual imagination will allow.

The other school believes in discarding all foundations and building from

15. "The number of buildings erected [in Chicago] was 11,106, having a frontage of 299,032 feet, costing $105,269,700." *Brickbuilder* 21, no. 3 (March 1912): 88.

16. Robert H. Moulton was born in Nashville, Tennessee, on June 8, 1880. He had a BS from the Missouri School of Mines in Columbia, Missouri. He worked as a reporter in Chicago from 1908 to 1909, and as a freelance writer after 1909. Most of his published work was illustrated with his own photographs.

17. "New Style in Skyscrapers," *Chicago Post*, March 7, 1911. The *Post* followed up with two more articles concerning the exhibition, on March 10 and 11, 1911.

18. "Remarkable Achievements in Building Construction," *Chicago Inter Ocean*, March 8, 1911.

19. Maude I. G. Oliver, *Chicago Record-Herald*, March 19, 1911.

*Holabird & Roche's Monroe Building, Chicago (CAC/11)*

the ground up . . . [and] once a certain level of development has been reached
by such a procedure, the finishing process is capable of a very high degree of
excellence. A really beautiful stage of this sort, it is safe to say, is rapidly crys-
tallizing in what is known as 'The Chicago School.' This is quite a concerted
movement . . . virtually local and already evinces a healthy, consistent growth,
that bespeaks a vigorous future.

It was the first time that the early modern movement in Chicago, which had
been christened the Chicago School some years earlier by Hugh M. G. Garden,
had been recognized by a critic in the popular press for what it was, a new architecture.

The new architecture of the Midwest was strongly oriented toward residential
work, but many of the commercial buildings in Chicago, Milwaukee, St. Louis, and
the twin cities of Minneapolis and St. Paul were also adopting the new aesthetic.[20]
The style of the residential work and some of the smaller commercial buildings,

20. The best discussion of the
development of residential
work in the Midwest is Brooks,
*The Prairie School.* The commercial work of the period ca.
1900–1920 hasn't been covered
as extensively, although Carl
Condit's *Chicago School of
Architecture* is admirable as far
as it goes.

*George W. Maher's Northwestern University Gymnasium (CAC/11)*

21. By far the best chronology of Wright's European ventures and his later return to practice is Anthony Alofsin, *Frank Lloyd Wright, The Lost Years, 1910–1922, A Study of Influence* (Chicago: University of Chicago Press, 1993). Alofsin's work is an excellent example of scholarship covering a period in Wright's life that had been largely ignored.

22. There are extensive records, although not complete, of the Dwight Bank at the Art Institute of Chicago.

23. Oskar Gross (1871–1963) was born in Vienna, Austria, on November 29, 1870. He studied in Vienna, Munich, and Paris and came to the United States in 1902. He won numerous awards for his work and collaborated with several American architects as a muralist.

which ultimately came to be called the Prairie school, was being promoted vigorously in the early years of the second decade of the twentieth century. Frank Lloyd Wright, who is often cited as the prime advocate of the movement, had left Chicago in late September of 1909 and did not return to full-time practice until midyear of 1911 after two trips to Europe.[21] Thus he was not involved in the 1911 exhibition. His former colleagues from Steinway Hall, a number of former employees, and others took on the challenge of promoting the new architecture. Lawrence Buck, William Drummond, Elmer Hunt, George Maher, Dwight Perkins, and several of their colleagues who were prominent members of the architectural community were actively working in the new movement and took advantage of the 1911 exhibition to show their work. Wright, whose last official showing at a Chicago Architectural Club exhibition had been in 1907, was once again represented in a somewhat peripheral manner. In 1906 he had designed the First National Bank in Dwight, Illinois. In the 1911 exhibition Oskar Gross exhibited "Panels for Bank of Dwight" along with several other sketches for decorative panels that appear to have been murals. An examination of the plans of the bank suggests where they may have been installed.[22] They are not illustrated in the catalog. Because Gross is known to have stopped doing murals in 1912, it is highly likely that these panels were among the last he did and that they were sketches of panels that had either already been installed in the bank or were never realized.[23]

The 1911 exhibition was extremely successful. The club was at a high point in many ways. The public had turned out to see the work exhibited and membership,

*John Devereaux York's "Memorial for the Battle Field of Gettysburg" (CAC/11)*

*Hunt & Grey's Throop Institute, Pasadena, California (CAC/11)*

*Woolworth Building, New York, by Cass Gilbert (CAC/11)*

at 254 in all categories, was as high as it ever would be. Despite this success, however, there are hints that the 1911 exhibition was not financially successful. Perhaps the delegation of duties to a paid manager-member and an outsider (Horace Ingram and Robert Moulton), plus the printing of the advertising was more expensive than anticipated. In any case, for the next three years the catalogs were once again produced like the ones between 1905 and 1910, and the number of pages, particularly of illustrations, was substantially reduced.

One element of the 1911 exhibition was not noted in the reviews, although it was covered in an editorial that appeared in *Construction News*.[24] The article began, "Nothing has taken place in the architectural profession in the west in recent years that is so deserving of commendation as the action of the committee in declining to award the gold medal of the Illinois chapter to the work exhibited at the Art Institute in Chicago this year." It went on to state that this was not the fault of those who exhibited but of the buildings that qualified for the award. There was "nothing out of the ordinary." The journal praised certain works that for various

24. *Construction News* 31, no. 16 (April 22, 1911): 9.

*W. D. Douglas Residence by Howard Van Doren Shaw (CAC/11)*

reasons did not qualify, but also somewhat gently chastised the more senior architects who did not exhibit work that deserved the "only medal, the only reward of merit that has ever been established by a professional organization in this country." The editors were clearly disappointed. The editorial concluded by asking, "Isn't it worth working for? The consensus of opinion among men qualified to judge is that it is."

When the exhibition closed, the members of the Chicago Architectural Club gathered on the first Monday in May to elect officers for the coming year. Prior to the meeting they had made revisions to the club's constitution. The previous bylaws had required that the elected officers and two other directors would make up both the Executive Committee and the board of directors. The new rules called for the elimination of the two vice presidents and for the election of six directors, three for one year and three for two years. The plan was that three new directors, including one from the associate member list, would be elected each year and thus a certain continuity would be established. Edwin F. Gillette was reelected president for 1911–12, with Roy A. Lippincott and Otto A. Silha serving as secretary and treasurer, respectively. Members Mark M. Levings and Elmer T. Nettenstrom were elected for one-year terms, and Elliot R. Andrews filled the associate slot. Edward O. Nelson and Clarence G. Brown were elected for two years, along with Roger M. Combs as the associate. Committees were no longer automatically chaired by members of the Executive Committee, although several were so designated. The plan quickly proved unworkable, and the club decided a vice president was needed. Lippincott was moved up to that position. Silha stepped aside as treasurer and William G. Wuehrmann and George Awsumb were asked to serve as secretary and treasurer. The elected directors remained in place.[25]

Almost immediately after the 1911 exhibition closed, the club was once again faced with a competition, although not one that it was sponsoring. The Cement Products Exhibition Company, which had been having competitions of various sorts since 1909,[26] offered three hundred dollars in prizes for the design of a

25. There is some confusion as to who actually served in the various positions during this period and the next year or so. The information in this book is based on two sources, the annual catalog of the exhibition and the list in the *Handbook for Architects and Builders* published by the Chicago Architects' Business Association; the latter appears to be more accurate.

26. The company first exhibited the competition drawings for a suburban house in 1909. In 1910 it had a competition to guess the breaking point of a concrete cylinder; it was won by Miss Lillian M. Williamson of Chicago, whose prize was a concrete house that was actually built in Walden, Illinois (now a part of Chicago).

*Residence for C. H. Wills, Detroit, by Hermann V. von Holst (CAC/11)*

*Chicago apartment building by William Drummond (CAC/11)*

concrete bungalow to be built for Miss Lucile Bishop, who had won a contest held at the February 1911 Cement Products Exhibition in Chicago.[27] The competition was open to all architects and was for a bungalow to be built almost entirely of concrete. The jury included Sam A. Marx, Hugh M. G. Garden, and Walter Burley Griffin, all members of the Chicago Architectural Club. The jury elected to divide the three hundred dollars in prize money "equally among Frederick J. Meseke, New York City, F. W. Kerric [*sic*], South Bend, Ind., and Harry F. Robinson, Chicago, Ill." The three winning designs were all published in *Concrete*

27. The competition was announced in *Concrete* 11, no. 6 (June 1911): 31–32; the results appeared in *Concrete* 11, no. 7 (July 1911): 76.

*Lincoln Park Refectory by Perkins & Hamilton (CAC/11)*

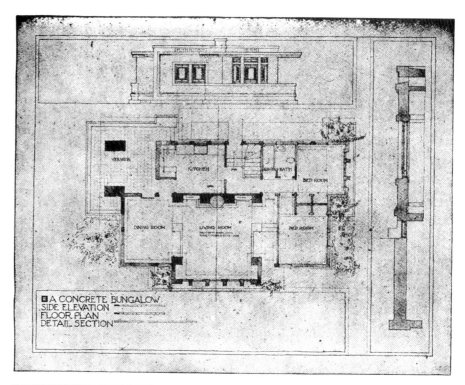

*Harry F. Robinson's design for a house built of concrete won a prize in the 1911 Cement Products Exhibition Competition (CN)*

28. Meseke's design was published in *Concrete* 11, no. 9 (September 1911); Robinson's and Kervic's designs were published in *Concrete* 11, no. 11 (November 1911): 41–42.

29. *Concrete-Cement Age* 2, no. 6 (June 1913): 262–64.

30. *Construction News* 32, no. 14 (October 7, 1911): 9. The results of the competition appeared in the same journal on December 30, 1911, on page 10.

magazine with illustrations, descriptions, and estimates of cost.[28] William Drummond and E. S. Sommers of Chicago were both given favorable mention but did not share in the prize money. Only Drummond had ever been a member of the Chicago Architectural Club. His design was shown at the club's 1912 exhibition. At the time of the competition, Robinson was employed by Walter Burley Griffin in his Steinway Hall loft. Griffin was then experimenting with concrete as a building material and, two years later, would publish his "Solid Rock House," which was built in 1911 and reproduced in the 1912 Chicago Architectural Club exhibition catalog.[29]

Just as the concrete house designs appeared in the professional press, another competition was announced by *Brick and Clay Record* magazine, headquartered in Chicago. The rules were published in several other journals, including *Construction News*.[30] The plan was to have a design for a house built of brick that

SOLID
ROCK
HOUSE

*Walter Burley Griffin's "Solid Rock House" (CAC/1912)*

could be erected on the floor of the Chicago Coliseum during the forthcoming Clay Products Exposition scheduled for March 7–12, 1912. The space allotted was only twenty feet square. The jury was made up of Hermann L. Matz, Dwight Heald Perkins, and Arthur F. Woltersdorf, all members of the Chicago Architectural Club. Of the three winners, only one was from Chicago—Alexander S. Robertson, then working with D. H. Burnham and Company. The others were from New York City and Indianapolis.[31]

Work by members of the Chicago Architectural Club received a great deal of publicity during the last half of 1911, largely through articles in professional journals and popular magazines. Robert C. Spencer Jr., for example, had two long articles in the *Brickbuilder* in October and November, both titled "The Small House of Brick in Suburbs & Country."[32] The initial page of each featured a drawing incorporating the title. Spencer included his own work, but Griffin, Tallmadge & Watson, W. G. Purcell, and Spencer & Powers, as well as Claude Bragdon and a few others from out of town, were also represented. In the November issue, several of Dwight Perkins's designs for Chicago school buildings were illustrated. Spencer had, of course, been writing about the avant-garde movement in the Midwest for several years. His articles had appeared in the *Ladies' Home Journal,* the *House Beautiful,* and several other magazines.[33] A number of the buildings featured can be identified as those that had been in the club's exhibitions at the Art Institute of Chicago.

Club members continued to be active participants in the *Brickbuilder*'s annual terra-cotta competitions, the results of which were often published. Chicagoans were rarely in the top echelon of winners but were usually represented, particularly if one or more of the jury were from the Midwest. In early 1912, the *Brickbuilder* sponsored two competitions for the design of a three-thousand-dollar bungalow built of clay products. The first was announced in January and was to be ready in time for the Clay Products Exposition in Chicago opening in March. Prizes ranged from $500 for first place to $250 for second, $150 for third, and $100 for fourth. Three months later, the *Brickbuilder* announced a second competition with very similar requirements, except that the budget was four thousand dollars. The prizes were actually smaller, starting at $300 for first, $200 for second, $150 for third, and

31. *Construction News* 32, no. 52 (December 30, 1911): 10.

32. *Brickbuilder* 20, no. 10 (October 1911): 209–17; *Brickbuilder* 20, no. 11 (November 1911): 229–241.

33. Earl H. Reed Jr., who worked for Spencer at the time, told the author that "Bob" Spencer depended heavily on these articles for a portion of his income. He also stated that he depended on his colleagues at the Chicago Architectural Club to provide him with photographs and drawings for the articles.

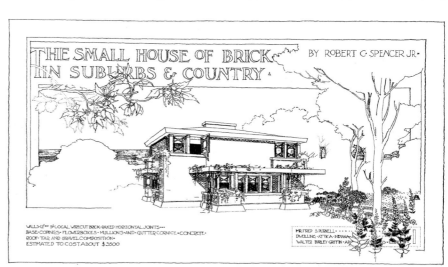

*This drawing of a design by Walter Burley Griffin, executed by Marion Mahony Griffin, accompanied an article by Robert C. Spencer in the* Brickbuilder *(BB)*

$100 for fourth. Several Chicagoans entered both competitions, but they weren't among the top prizewinners.

The Twenty-fifth Annual Exhibition was announced by a circular sent to the membership and the press. It was not, however, widely published—only *Construction News* appears to have found room for it.[34] Much of the language in the circular was identical to that of the previous year, including the notice of the proposed gold medal to be awarded by the Illinois Chapter of the AIA for the most meritorious design in the exhibition. At virtually the same time, the University of Illinois announced its competition for the award of the Francis J. Plym Fellowship in Architecture. That award, valued at a thousand dollars, had been established the previous year by a graduate of the university's School of Architecture. The selection committee for the Plym Fellowship included Irving K. Pond, Peter B. Wight, Joseph C. Llewellyn, N. Clifford Ricker, and Frederick M. Mann. All were members of the Chicago Architectural Club except Mann, who was on the faculty at the University of Illinois.

The catalog of the Twenty-fifth Annual Exhibition was similar to those published between 1905 and 1910. The cover was in brown paper with a subdued symbol of the club in the background. It was printed on dark ivory paper in dark brown ink. There were fifteen pages of text with the usual data in the front of the book followed by eighteen pages of illustrations, the fewest in many years. The index of exhibits listed only 333 items, also the fewest in several years. Nearly all the exhibitors were from Chicago, with only a scattering of East Coast firms represented. The local exhibitors were largely drawn from the avant-garde men of Steinway Hall and their colleagues. The policy of having no paid advertisers was resumed. There were, however, sixty "patrons" listed in the front of the book, nearly half of whom were architects. The amounts each contributed were not noted. Even with their help and the smaller size catalog, the exhibition put a great strain on the finances of the club.

The 1912 exhibition was covered by several of the local newspapers but hardly any of the professional journals.[35] The first review, in the *Chicago Record-Herald,* began, "This year the architectural exhibition is perceptibly diminished in extent. The standard set, however, is about on a level with that of previous seasons . . . One feature which, however, indicates rather an evolution of the allied arts than any departure in architecture itself, is the gradual adjustment of the various sister crafts to architectural needs. Especially is the current show noticeable for the co-operative spirit of the graphic arts in relation to building." The reviewer went on to praise the relationship of painting to sculpture and the exhibits of various craftsmen in those fields. He was especially impressed with sculptor Charles J. Mulligan, who showed two pieces modeled for the City Club of Chicago, a building designed by Pond & Pond. That work was never executed, although it was shown in a retouched photograph of the City Club Building published in the May 1912 issue of the *Brickbuilder.* Also shown was Mulligan's Memorial to Progress of a Century, done with architect W. Carbys Zimmerman for installation at Edwardsville, Illinois. Zimmerman exhibited a model of his design for the Illinois State Penitentiary as well. Glass mosaics from the shops of the Linden Glass Company also got high praise. Nowhere, however, did this reviewer discuss the work of the avant-garde architects who were so heavily represented. That was left to the critics at the *Chicago Evening Post* and the *Chicago Examiner.* Both commented on the decorative work in the show, but devoted most of their space to the work of

*City Club of Chicago Building, designed by Pond & Pond; the two sculptural figures flanking the entrance were never completed, but this photograph was retouched to show how it was expected to look (BB)*

34. *Construction News* 33, no. 12 (March 23, 1912): 6.

35. Local coverage included reviews in the *Chicago Record-Herald* on April 4, 1912; the *Chicago Evening Post* on April 4 and 11, 1912; the *Chicago Tribune* on April 9, 1912; and the *Chicago Examiner* on April 12, 1912. A second, related review appeared in the *Chicago Tribune* on April 21, 1912.

*Charles Mulligan's "Memorial to Progress of a Century," designed for installation at Edwardsville, Illinois (EPL)*

*William Carbys Zimmerman's model of the Illinois State Penitentiary, shown at the 1912 annual exhibition (AC)*

Walter Burley Griffin, N. Max Dunning, William Drummond, George W. Maher, and others of the emerging modern movement. The more traditional work was not ignored, and most of the reviewers devoted a special place to the "Winning Design for the Lincoln Memorial in Washington" by Henry Bacon of New York City. The rendering was by William J. Beauley, formerly a member of the Chicago Architectural Club.

The last popular press review of the 1912 exhibition appeared in the *Chicago Tribune* on April 21, 1912, under the byline of Harriet Monroe. Her comments pertained to a part of the exhibition that was neither illustrated in the catalog nor included in the list of exhibits. She wrote, "In the large south gallery of the architectural exhibition at the Institute is a frame containing three photographs. The largest is a perspective of the present Field museum from the southeast, and the other two are front and side elevations of the proposed new structure taken from a plaster model next to the painting." The museum was, of course, the Fine Arts Building at Jackson Park, the only structure to survive the 1893 World's Columbian Exposition. The plaster model had been prepared in 1911 and published in the September 12, 1911, issue of *Construction News.* Miss Monroe went on to say, "One is forced to compare the two designs to the extreme disadvantage of the latter." She discussed the various reasons for her dissatisfaction with the new design and ended her review by noting that the original was "a building which for twenty years was acknowledged by all competent judges to be one of the most beautiful of modern times." What she did not know, of course, was that it would be the last new design for a building from Burnham's office to be shown during his lifetime. He would die on June 1, 1912, while on a trip to Europe.[36]

The only professional press review of the 1912 exhibition was in *Construction News,* following a full column article under the heading "No Chapter Medal This Year."[37]

The review was somewhat neutral, noting that the exhibition was "an exceedingly interesting collection of drawings showing the work of the architects of the middle west, as well as that of several architects of New York and other eastern cities." It went on to say, "It is to be regretted that several of the leading architects of Chicago have not seen fit to exhibit." It concluded that "the most interesting de-

36. When Burnham's will was made public six weeks later, it was learned that he had left a bequest of fifty thousand dollars for the establishment of a library of architecture at the Art Institute of Chicago. That library survives to this day as part of the Ryerson and Burnham Libraries of the Art Institute of Chicago.

37. *Construction News* 33, no. 16 (April 20, 1912): 8–9.

*George Maher exhibited the Watkins Administration Building for Winona, Minnesota, in 1912 (WA)*

*Henry Bacon's design for the Lincoln Memorial in Washington, D.C. (CAC/12)*

*William Drummond's design for a lakeshore residence, from the 1912 exhibition (PSR)*

*Fine Arts Building rendering shown at the 1912 architectural exhibition (PC)*

signs exhibited are those of smaller buildings, such as residences and less important business buildings." The preceding article regarding the jury's report, however, pulled no punches in its concern about the lack of work of sufficient merit to receive the AIA's gold medal.

After a description of the jury's efforts, *Construction News* printed an excerpt of its report that stated, "The main reason for the failure to make an award is the apparent indifference of the architects of Illinois to the efforts of the Chicago Architectural Club to procure a representative exhibition of the best work recently carried out in the state . . . they feel discouraged at the failure of their efforts." The club simply could not get major firms to exhibit their best work. The report by the jury made up of Wight, Gillette, Woltersdorf, Pond, and Griffin went on to say that "the present state of affairs may result in the abandonment of these annual exhibitions, which would result in putting the architects of Chicago in contempt of their confreres throughout the country. The annual exhibitions of the club are not only expensive and unremunerative notwithstanding the great assistance given by the Art Institute, but entail the use of a great deal of time by members of the club, which they can ill afford, most of the members being employed as draftsmen and sacrificing their own time for the service." The report was signed by all the jurors except Griffin, who stated that "he had no fault to find with the conclusions of the jury. He felt that the majority of the jury demanded too great cost in the work to which the medal is to be awarded. He thought that as great competition and as much talent could be found in a small building." Probably the most important, succinct statement about the jury's report was made by I. K. Pond, who said, "The chapter must affiliate more closely with the club." Over the next few years, it did just that, and both organizations benefited from the cooperation.

*Plaster model of the new Field Museum, exhibited in 1912 (CN)*

The Chicago Architectural Club continued its efforts in the area of education, largely by sponsoring regular lectures by professionals, participating in the atelier headed by Edward H. Bennett, and sponsoring its own atelier, which had been working more or less without a patron in the club rooms at the Dexter Building. The first move toward formalizing the club's atelier came in 1912, when Francis W. Puckey was invited to chair the Jury of Admission for the 1912 exhibition. Puckey was not a member of the club, but would soon become patron of the atelier. On the jury, he was assisted by four club members, Walter Burley Griffin, George C. Nimmons, Thomas E. Tallmadge, and Roy A. Lippincott. All four were alumni or still part of the Steinway Hall group. At the time Puckey assumed responsibility for the club's atelier, he was a licensed architect, a member of the Illinois Chapter of the American Institute of Architects, and an employee of Shepley, Rutan & Coolidge.[38] Under Puckey's leadership, the Bennett atelier and its successors would ultimately become part of the club's atelier. The atelier was becoming an increasingly important part of the club's educational efforts.

The club also helped promote education by participating in the Architectural League of America. It had been instrumental in organizing the league in 1899, but after 1910, the members took a much smaller part in its activities and formed a stronger relationship with the AIA both locally and nationally.[39] There had been some support for "a closer relationship . . . between the Institute and the membership of the architectural clubs."[40] That support came primarily from the American Institute of Architects. Robert Craik McLean, who wrote of this, did not like the idea of uniting architectural clubs with the AIA. McLean advocated cooperation between the AIA and the various clubs through the Architectural League of America, which was more of a loose confederation of clubs than a national organization. He commented, "In no other way does the Architectural League of America so impress itself upon the student-draftsman as in its competitions . . . Where there is a live active Architectural Club, competitions flourish and draw out the best talent . . . it has invariably been those who were most often in evidence when a competition problem was on, who are still in evidence." The league followed McLean's advice and set up a program of architectural competitions with scholarships for the winners, although few were ever awarded.[41] By 1910, the league was declining rapidly, and the last convention was held in 1911.[42]

✤

The 1912–13 club year began in May of 1912 with the election of Otto A. Silha as president and John F. Surmann, William G. Wuehrmann, and George Awsumb as vice president, secretary, and treasurer. The plan to have three of the previous year's directors serve another year didn't work as well as expected. Only Elmer T. Nettenstrom returned for a second term. Leon Burghoffer took the place of Mark Levings, and W. W. Koch took over as associate director from Elliot R. Andrews, who agreed to serve for two more years in the class of 1914. Fritz Wagner Jr. and Jens A. Johnson were chosen as member directors through 1914.[43] Committee chairmanships were all filled by the officers and directors, some of whom served as members of several other committees. A review of the list of these members indicates that the club was being managed by seasoned men. There was clearly a need to make certain that activities, particularly the competitions and the annual exhibition, were maintained at a high level. The article in *Construction News* that announced the new officers and committee chairmanships also noted that "the

38. Francis Willard Puckey (1874–1954) was born at Wilkes Barre, Pennsylvania. His early education was at Wyoming Seminary, and in 1901 he graduated from MIT. After postgraduate work and some experience, he spent a year studying in Paris. He then worked for a year in New York before forming Old & Puckey in Chicago (1906–10). Puckey later worked for Shepley, Rutan & Coolidge (1910–15), until he organized Puckey & Jenkins in 1916, which he continued to run until his retirement in 1952. He was elected an honorary member of the CAC in 1913.

39. One of the club's founding members, Irving K. Pond, became president of the national AIA in 1910. He would, of course, have encouraged club members to maintain a strong relationship with the AIA, perhaps to the detriment of the Architectural League of America.

40. *Western Architect* 15, no. 5 (May 1910).

41. The most comprehensive description of the league's scholarship program is in the *Proceedings of the Ninth Annual Convention of the Architectural League of America, 1908*. This booklet was published in 1909 and contained a verbatim transcript of the convention held in Detroit in September 1908 ("Report of the Committee on University Fellowship," 41–43).

42. The Architectural League of America had become more and more difficult to manage, as it had only volunteer workers after 1906. In May 1907, a special committee was formed to select a permanent headquarters and a permanent secretary. It chose Washington, D.C., and H. S. McAllister.

A document titled "The Architectural League of America, A Sketch of an Association of Architectural Clubs and related Organizations, 1899–1912" is included in the papers of Emil Lorch, now deposited in the Bentley Historical Library at the University of Michigan. There are five typewritten pages of text plus four pages of what appear to be data Professor Lorch intended to insert into the body of the text. There are numerous handwritten corrections and additions indicated on the manuscript. It is not dated but is in the same file as a copy of a letter dated March 5, 1945, to "President Raymond J. Ashton, President of the National AIA." In his letter, Lorch noted that he was working on the history, but it was not yet completed. He also sent a check for $196.81, which represented the remaining funds in the league's treasury. Lorch noted that he and others from the league "hope this fund can be used in connection with the educational work of the Institute." There are several other documents in the file, some of which are referenced hereinafter.

43. *Construction News* 33, no. 19 (May 11, 1912): 12.

headquarters of the club have been transferred from the Dexter Building to club rooms in the Art Institute."

The club continued to conduct its regularly scheduled affairs in the latter half of 1912, but a number of members also competed in events sponsored by others. Late in the year, two such competitions were announced. One of them, the *Brickbuilder*'s Annual Terra Cotta Competition for a public garage, automobile sales, and service building was judged in January of 1913, with three Chicago men taking awards. Chicago architect Valere de Mari took second prize of $250, while Frederick Scholer and H. P. Beers of Chicago were given mentions. The most ambitious and important competition of 1913, however, was not one sponsored by the Chicago Architectural Club, although a number of members participated. It was the City Club of Chicago's competition for a "Scheme of Development for a Quarter-Section of Land within the Limits of the City of Chicago, Illinois."

The City Club, organized in 1903, was one of the largest and most influential civic organizations in Chicago in 1913. Its mission statement specified that "the purpose of the Club is to bring together those men who are genuinely interested in the improvement of the political, social and economic conditions of the community in which we live."[44] The 1913 competition program was prepared by the Illinois Chapter of the AIA and published in a circular signed by the club's civic secretary, George E. Hooker, on December 21, 1912.[45] The City Club was planning to hold a housing exhibition at its new building beginning on March 7, 1913, although the date was later changed to April 15 so that the Exhibition of the Public Properties of Chicago and Neighborhood Center Competition Plans could be held at the clubhouse prior to the housing show. Competitors were required to have their plans in the hands of the jury on or before noon on March 3, so that the winners (and other entries) could be shown at the preliminary exhibition. There were three prizes: the first, three hundred dollars; the second, two hundred dollars; and the third, one hundred dollars. The jury was made up of housing expert J. C. Kennedy, engineer John W. Alvord, landscape architect Jens Jensen, and architects George W. Maher and A. F. Woltersdorf.[46]

The City Club competition was very popular. Thirty-nine sets of drawings were submitted, twenty-one from Chicago. (Frank Lloyd Wright submitted a set of noncompetitive drawings that were later published along with twenty-five others.) First prize was awarded to Wilhelm Bernard of Chicago, second went to Arthur C. Comey from Cambridge, Massachusetts, and third was given to Albert and Ingrid Lilienberg from Gothenburg, Sweden.[47] After the awards were announced, the winner, Wilhelm Bernhard, was permitted to supplement his original submission with additional drawings, as were the other contributors. (This may have taken place after the major housing exhibition was opened on April 15 and the competition drawings were moved to the fourth floor.) Bernhard was, either at the time of his participation in the competition or shortly before, employed in the office of Frank Lloyd Wright.[48] The supplemental drawings he submitted, seven of which were published, had a distinctly European flavor with overtones of Wright's work. The windows in his drawings appeared to have been influenced by Wright, as did the foliage. The forms and colors are reminiscent of the work of the Nabis group popular in France in the last decade of the nineteenth century. Bernhard was not an amateur. One of his supplemental drawings was a plan for "The Shawnee Garden City" of Lima, Ohio, and the text accompanying it noted that it was "now being carried out." While it was by no means a copy of the competitive drawing he had submitted, it had a number of similarities too obvious to overlook. A careful inspection of both his competitive entry and the Lima, Ohio, plan suggests that Bernhard was an accomplished planner.[49]

44. This mission statement is quoted from the cover of the *Membership Role* published in 1916. At that time there were more than two thousand members of the City Club of Chicago. There were a substantial number of Chicago Architectural Club members, particularly the older men, who also belonged to the City Club.

45. A copy of that eight-page circular is deposited with the records of the City Club at the Chicago Historical Society. The complete program appeared in *Architecture* 27, no. 1 (January 15, 1913): 18–19. It was also published in Alfred B. Yeomans, ed., *City Residential Land Development, Studies in Planning, Competitive Plans for Subdividing a Typical Quarter Section of Land in the Outskirts of Chicago* (Chicago: University of Chicago Press, n.d., ca. 1916).

46. Walter Burley Griffin was noted in the club's housing exhibition directory as an adviser to the competition. He was also listed as one of the competitors. Jensen, Maher, and Woltersdorf were, of course, members of the Chicago Architectural Club, as was Griffin.

47. The winners were not published in the local press until after the housing show opened on Monday, March 17. The best article was "'Garden City' Plans Are Shown by Club," *Chicago Inter Ocean*, March 23, 1913. In that article, it was noted that Bernard had "his architectural training in Dresden." The winners were also published in "City Club Competition," *Western Architect* 21, no. 4 (April 1913): 39–41, XV–XVI.

48. Wilhelm Bernhard is briefly discussed in Anthony Alofsin's excellent book, *Frank Lloyd Wright, The Lost Years*, on page 72, where he is identified as a draftsman who worked at Taliesin in Wisconsin in the summer of 1912. Taylor

Woolley was also helping Wright at Taliesin but left to return home to Utah in early 1912. An architect named Edward Sanderson was managing Wright's Chicago office at the time and may have had an agreement to share in the profits, if any, of the office. Bernhard probably left Wright after winning the City Club Competition. He and Sanderson were not the only employees in Wright's Chicago office. In a handwritten letter reproduced in James A. Robinson's book *The Life and Work of Harry Franklin Robinson, 1883–1959* (Hong Kong: Hilross Development, 1989), Wright asks Robinson to work in the Chicago office and suggests that he would be managing the office. Robinson remained with the office until late 1916, when he left to join Dean and Dean. Another key person working with Wright during this period was Russell Barr Williamson, who joined the office shortly after the tragic fire at Taliesin in 1914. See Shirley DuFresne McArthur, *Frank Lloyd Wright, American System-Built Homes in Milwaukee* (Hot Springs, Virginia: The Barr Brand, 2000).

49. Bernhard, whose name suggests German origin, is first listed as a licensed architect in the 1914 *Handbook for Architects and Builders*. For the next fifteen years he continued to be listed at various addresses. There was an exhibition of architectural sketches held at the Boston Architectural Club February 21–27, 1911, by one "William [*sic*] Bernhard of Dresden," according to the official list of exhibitors. The two illustrations in the Boston Architectural Club catalog for that year have a vague resemblance to the supplemental drawings submitted by Bernhard after he won the City Club Competition. He later formed a partnership with Arthur Woltersdorf.

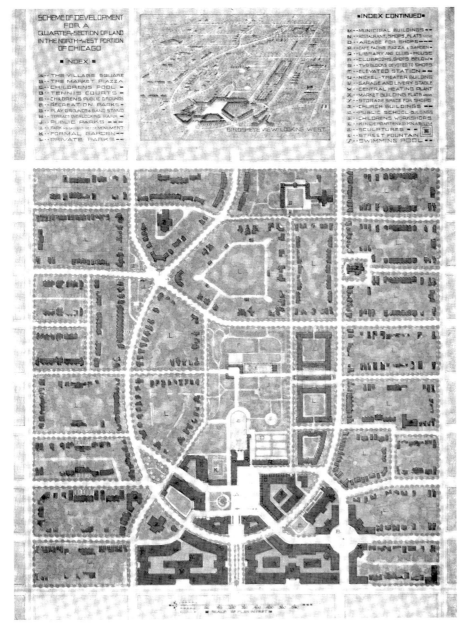

Wilhelm Bernhard's winning design for the City Club's Neighborhood Center Competition (CRLD)

One of the small, supplemental drawings Wilhelm Bernhard submitted for the City Club's competition (CRLD)

Second-prize winner Arthur C. Comey was a landscape designer who gave his address as Harvard Square in Cambridge, Massachusetts. He had, according to an *Inter Ocean* article, "formerly been associated with Olmstead [*sic*] Bros." Albert and Ingrid Lilienberg, the third-prize winners, were a husband-and-wife town-planning team. Mr. Lilienberg was, at the time, head of the city planning department in Gothenburg, Sweden. Of the thirty-nine sets of plans submitted, twenty-one were published in a book with illustrations describing the competition.[50] All but two were noted as "Competitive Plans." One of those was a "Plan by William Drummond, Developed from a Sketch submitted in Competition." The jury felt it was interesting enough to include in the exhibition, and they gave Drummond time to develop it further. It was allotted eight pages of well-illustrated text, more than any other submission, including the "Non-competitive Plan" by Frank Lloyd Wright. Wright's submission was not particularly original. It was

50. Yeomans, *City Residential Land Development*. Yeomans was also one of the competitors.

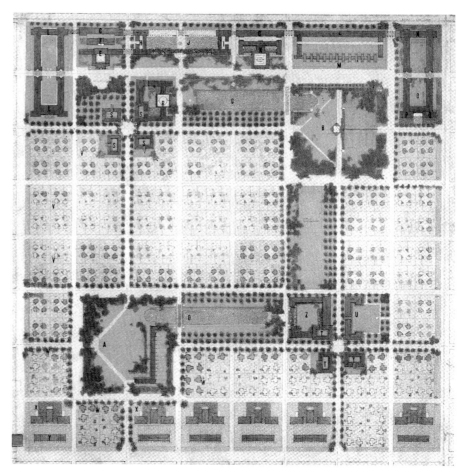

*Frank Lloyd Wright's (noncompetitive) plan for the Neighborhood Center Competition (CRLD)*

essentially a minor variation on his "quadruple block plan," which he had been working on from time to time since late in the nineteenth century. Albert Kelsey produced an "Aesthetic Review of the Plans," which was published with them. He pointed out good elements in most of the plans, with his most favorable comments directed at the winners. He was also impressed with a plan by Edgar H. Lawrence, who submitted an extraordinary octagon-in-a-square design. At the time of the competition, Lawrence was sharing an office with Walter Burley Griffin, possibly as a draftsman. Lawrence credited "W. B. Griffin, Advisory" on his plan and included a splendid perspective that must have been influenced, if not drawn, by Marion Mahony.

After the winners of the City Residential Land Development Competition were named, the City Club proceeded with its City Club Housing Exhibition. It ran from April 15 through June 1, 1913.[51] There were exhibits on every floor plus the mezzanine, including corridors and stair halls. Illustrations consisted of maps, charts, photographs, and drawings covering every possible aspect of housing in Chicago, with an emphasis on housing for the poor.

With the closing of the exhibition, the City Club immediately launched another program concerning Chicago's railway terminal problem. During June, it held six meetings at which the proponents of various plans for a new consolidated railway terminal presented their schemes. Architects who submitted plans included E. R. Graham of D. H. Burnham and Company, Jarvis Hunt, Pond & Pond, and William Drummond. Walter Moody and Charles Wacker submitted a plan developed by the

51. There was a handsome fifty-five-page exhibition catalog published. The cover was designed and signed by Wilhelm Bernard. The catalog lists 1,374 exhibits, although many numbers were "reserved" but not used; there were actually about a thousand exhibits.

*D. H. Burnham and Company's plan for the Chicago Union Station submitted as part of the City Club program; much of it was actually built and still exists today (RTPC)*

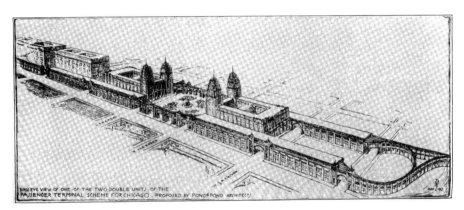

*Pond & Pond's elaborate plan for Union Station included some rather impractical raised tracks at the north end of the long station (RTPC)*

*Guenzel & Drummond's Union Station plan included freight facilities on both sides of the Chicago River and graceful new bridges (RTPC)*

staff of the Chicago Plan Commission. Several railway executives spoke to the City Club during this period. The intent was to generate interest in resolving the problem of too much downtown property devoted to railroad use. The material submitted was collected and published as a book with plans, sketches, and several perspectives.[52] All the plans were sophisticated and highly detailed. Jarvis Hunt's submission was included in the 1913 Chicago Architectural Club exhibition but was not illustrated in the catalog. Hunt had previously spoken to the City Club regarding his plan in January of 1913. His perspective of the proposed terminal was illustrated in the *City Club Bulletin* of January 23, 1913.

While the City Club exhibitions were under way, the Chicago Architectural Club announced the rules for its Twenty-sixth Annual Exhibition to be held at the Art Institute from May 6 to June 11, 1913.[53] The rules were unchanged from previous years and, once again, it was announced that the Illinois AIA gold medal had been reestablished. It was emphasized that "no award shall be made if in the opinion of the jury no work presented is sufficiently meritorious." Entry blanks were to be returned to the club by April 10, 1913.

The exhibition opened as scheduled on May 6, overlapping with the City Club Housing Exhibition for about three weeks.[54] The paperbound catalog was patterned after the one published the previous year, with essentially the same layout. It was dedicated to the memory of Daniel H. Burnham, a longtime member and supporter, who had died in 1912. The opening essay was penned by George C. Nimmons, who noted that "the Annual Exhibit provides a good opportunity for observing the progress made in Architecture, as evidenced by the many buildings and structures erected during the year. In Chicago alone, there were 11,298 buildings costing $88,000,000.00. There has probably not been any time in the world's history when Architects had more opportunity to practice their art than right now in this country." He discussed the wealth of new materials and other facilities available to his colleagues, but noted that even with all this "at hand, Architects in the opinion of many have failed to develop a style of Architecture that is at all expressive of the character of the American people." He went on to severely criticize his fellow practitioners for working primarily in historic styles. He credited this practice to a lack of interest in architecture by the public. He did, however, purport to believe that a certain sophistication was developing, that "our people are now going to begin to take an interest in Architecture, to criticize it, to study and to find real appreciation and pleasure in it, then will our Architecture grow and develop into a real national style that will do full credit to our country."

Nimmons was somewhat hard on his colleagues, and the catalog seems to bear him out. It was sparsely illustrated. The list of exhibitors reveals that it was a mixed bag of designs reflecting both the influence of the Beaux-Arts and the new school of the Midwest led by Louis Sullivan and Frank Lloyd Wright. Sullivan had a special room devoted to his work, but there was no listing of what he exhibited. His contribution was noted in the catalog only as a "Collection of Exhibits. Room 28." Two of his designs were illustrated. The second frontispiece in the catalog was a panel from Sullivan's incredible multilayered screen from the Schlesinger & Mayer Building (later known as the Carson, Pirie, Scott Building).[55] Also illustrated was Sullivan's design for a theater facade that was never built.[56] Several other Sullivan designs dating back to the World's Columbian Exposition were also shown. The awards for the Annual Traveling Scholarship, which went to Rudolph G. Wolff and W. J. Schaefer, were very much in the spirit of the Beaux-Arts, as were the mention entries by B. C. Greengard, W. G. Wuehrmann, and A. A. Schwartz. Architect and sculptor Emil R. Zettler had a particularly fine exhibit presaging the art deco style that would become so popular a decade later. There were several exhibits that

52. *The Railway Terminal Problem of Chicago* (Chicago: City Club of Chicago, September 1913) was published with transcripts of the various speeches on the subject. A second book was announced but apparently never published.

53. *Construction News* 25, no. 14 (April 5, 1913): 9.

54. *Brickbuilder* 22, no. 4 (April 1913): 98.

55. This screen, now destroyed, was on the northwest corner of the third floor in the Carson Pirie Scott Building.

56. This drawing had originally been exhibited in the 1904 CAC exhibition but was not illustrated.

*Photograph of Louis Sullivan's design for the Transportation Building at the World's Columbian Exposition, one of several shown at the 1913 annual exhibition (PC)*

exemplified the work of the new Chicago School. Richard Bock, Spencer & Powers, Lawrence Buck, Walter Burley Griffin, George Maher, George Nimmons, Dwight Perkins, Tallmadge & Watson, and Purcell, Feick & Elmslie were all well represented. Wright was given space for seven exhibits, some of which were also shown the following year, when he had a much larger display. Only a few of these architects' work was illustrated; for the most part they were included only in the list of exhibitors.

*Frank Lloyd Wright's unbuilt Madison, Wisconsin, Hotel (PACC/13)*

*Interior of Wright's Madison Hotel (PACC/13)*

57. *Annual Exhibition, 1912, Carnegie Institute, Pittsburgh Architectural Club* (Pittsburgh: Dick Press, March 1912).

58. See the *Pittsburgh Architectural Club Eighth Annual Exhibition, Carnegie Institute* (Pittsburgh: Dick Press, 1913) with a supplement, "Index of Exhibits, Eighth Annual Exhibition, March 1 to March 17 Inclusive, 1913."

A number of the avant-garde designers, including Sullivan, had also shown their work in the 1912 exhibition of the Pittsburgh Architectural Club.[57] Several of the drawings were illustrated. H. V. von Holst showed five drawings in the 1912 CAC exhibition, two of which were illustrated. He then showed at least six drawings at Pittsburgh, not all of which were identical to those he exhibited in Chicago. Wright did not show in the 1912 Pittsburgh exhibition, but he did show there in 1913, a few weeks before the Chicago exhibition.[58] The same material was shown in both venues.

The 1913 CAC exhibition was, as a whole, well received by the press. The formal opening reception was postponed for unrecorded reasons until May 15, but

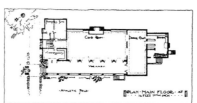

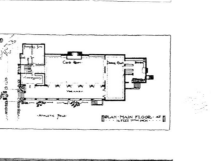

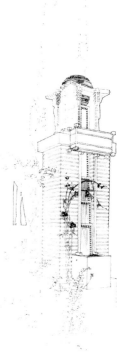

*Marion Mahony's superbly executed drawing of a light standard for Decatur (CAC/13). Marion Mahony's drawings of Hermann V. von Holst's designs for the 1912 exhibition at Pittsburgh (PACC/12)*

*Walter Burley Griffin's scheme for Canberra received attention as much for Marion Mahony's renderings as for Griffin's designs (PACC/13)*

this did not delay the mainstream press reviews. First to appear was Harriet Monroe's critique in the *Chicago Tribune.*[59] She wrote that the "retrospective exhibition of the work of Louis H. Sullivan of Chicago, which nearly fills one of the smaller galleries, is the most important part of the show. The selection is inadequate, since certain important buildings are represented merely by small photographs, but it includes such great works of modern architecture as the Wainwright memorial in St. Louis, the Getty tomb in Graceland cemetery, the Transportation building of the Columbian Exposition, the Seattle Opera house, and the Farmers' Bank of Owatonna, Minn., besides commercial buildings and residences. With these are original drawings of great beauty, iron grilles, and other decorative works." She went on to praise the work of George Nimmons for "a number of well balanced, frankly expressed designs," as well as the work of Jarvis Hunt, George W. Maher, Purcell, Feick & Elmslie, and Howard Van Doren Shaw. She briefly mentioned Frank Lloyd Wright's work and praised "Walter Burley Griffin's admirable accepted project for the planning of the federal capital of Australia . . . illustrated by a series of drawings." These drawings, for some reason, were neither listed nor illustrated in the catalog.[60] Other reviews were equally or even more laudatory. The *Chicago Evening Post* reported that the opening reception had been delayed to coincide with another exhibition.[61] It also noted that after the opening "additional exhibits from the eastern cities will be added to the collection." Its review mentioned many names not included by Harriet Monroe, but the critic once again praised the work of Louis Sullivan and his followers and noted that Griffin had submitted a "small model for the Trier Center Neighborhood, Winnetka."

The next day, the *Chicago Evening Post* followed up with a review by Thomas E. Tallmadge.[62] It was the most thoughtful of the critiques. Early on, he noted that "this year is exceptionally interesting [and] . . . more to the point, a certain spirit of freshness, a certain spirit of independence, a certain spirit of Americanism." He went on to say, "To those of us who have been pursuing the will-o-the wisp of an American style for so many years, this Americanism here evidenced is tremendously encouraging. Even the big offices which have been burying architectural hopes in twenty-storied Roman sarcophagi for so long a time seem to be waking up to a possibility of a great art born of new conditions in a new land." Tallmadge was a bit disappointed in the layout of the exhibition, but it did not prevent his praise of the master. He wrote, "The principal cause of distinction for this exhibition is the collection of drawings and photographs of the work of Louis H. Sullivan. The public should appreciate him, for Mr. Sullivan has proved the most vital force in American architecture since H. H. Richardson. To each of them it has been vouch-

59. Harriet Monroe, "Architectural Club Exhibit at Institute," *Chicago Tribune,* Wednesday, May 7, 1913.

60. They were, however, both listed and illustrated in the 1913 catalog of the Pittsburgh architectural exhibition.

61. "Architectural Club Opens Its Exhibition," *Chicago Evening Post,* Wednesday, May 7, 1913.

62. Thomas E. Tallmadge, "Spirit of Americanism Is Seen in Exhibition," *Chicago Evening Post,* May 8, 1913.

*Walter Burley Griffin*
*(PC/NLA)*

*Walter Burley Griffin's model of the New Trier neighborhood, shown in the 1913 annual architectural exhibition; only one of the buildings was built (WA)*

safed to found a school—an accomplishment achieved only by men of heroic mold." Tallmadge discussed many of the individual displays and noted that "the men who have believed in Sullivan's principles and shared his faith in an American art are well represented." He named them without specifying what they exhibited. He ended his review with lukewarm praise for the first- and second-prize winners of the annual Traveling Scholarship, which were not, of course, in the spirit of Sullivan.

The *Bulletin of the Art Institute of Chicago* had a short review of the exhibition in its July issue.[63] It suggested that the success of the exhibition was due "largely because of the cooperation of the Illinois Chapter of the American Institute of Architects." Its brief article was the only one that announced that "the annual gold medal given by the Illinois Chapter of the American Institute of Architects for the most meritorious work on exhibition by a member of the chapter was awarded to Perkins, Fellows, and Hamilton for drawings of the Lion House at Lincoln Park." The Lion House was listed, but not illustrated, in the exhibition catalog and its winning the AIA gold medal was not mentioned.[64] That award was apparently made during the exhibition, after the catalog had been printed. The best illustrated, and probably the most widely read, review of the 1913 exhibition was one by Roy A. Lippincott[65] in the *Architectural Record*.[66] Lippincott's review was generally favorable. He disagreed with Tallmadge about the layout. He commented that "as a whole, the exhibition is well hung, is good in arrangement and color and a decided credit to the jury and hanging committee."

In addition to the articles on the City Club and the Chicago Architectural Club, there were numerous news reports on the Armory Show of Modern Art, which had opened in New York in February and traveled to Chicago, where it was shown from the end of March until the middle of April.[67] There were also regular articles extolling the work of Midwestern architects. Typical of these was an article by Henry M. Hyde,[68] which appeared in the *Chicago Tribune* in September of 1913.[69] After beginning with brief quotations from the *Architectural Record* and the *Western Architect*, Hyde went on to tout the coming of the "new American School of Architecture." He wrote that "for the first time an art indigenous to the American soil is being developed. For the first time a new form, a new style, free from the traditions of the historic schools, has begun to win recognition." He commented that eastern architects were in "a contemptuous rage. The insurgents answer by calling their opponents fossils and mere copyists . . . The great American Institute of Architects is divided into bitter factions, with the majority clinging fast to the traditions of the

63. *Bulletin of the Art Institute of Chicago* 7, no. 1 (July 1913): 5.

64. Perkins, Fellows & Hamilton's Lion House had been shown at the exhibition of the St. Louis Architectural Club and illustrated in its catalog. See the *Catalogue of the Fourth Exhibition of the Saint Louis Architectural Club and Saint Louis Chapter, AIA, XIII.* Walter Burley Griffin was listed as a member of the National Advisory Committee for this exhibition, which took place from January 13 through January 19, 1903.

65. Roy Alston Lippincott (1885–1969) was married to Walter Burley Griffin's sister, Genevieve, and was therefore Griffin's brother-in-law. Lippincott worked in Griffin's Chicago office on the Canberra drawings and later in his Australian office. In 1920, he established his own practice with Edward Billson, and after 1925 he practiced alone. When the Second World War began, he moved to California, where he died in 1969.

66. *Architectural Record* 33 (June 1913): 567–73.

67. The Armory Show, officially known as the International Exhibition of Modern Art, was organized by the very small group that called itself the Association of American Painters and Sculptors. It has been memorialized in an excellent book, Milton W. Brown, *The Story of the Armory Show* (New York: Abbeville Press, 1988). In it, the author discusses the trials of putting together an exhibition of more than a thousand items in a period of a few months. (The reader cannot help but compare that effort with the work the Chicago Architectural Club did annually for more than forty years.) The Armory Show had been in New York City from February 17 through March 15, 1913. It opened in Chicago on March 24 and closed on April 16 with most, but not all, of the same works that had been exhibited in New York.

68. Henry Morrow Hyde (1866–ca. 1935) was born in Freeport, Illinois, and educated at Beloit College in Wisconsin. He wrote a number of books and articles prior to becoming the editor of *Technical World Magazine* in 1907. In 1913, he became a full-time staff writer for the *Chicago Tribune*. Hyde was a member of the Little Room, predecessor of the Cliff Dwellers, both of which had many architects as members.

69. Henry M. Hyde, "'Rebels' of West Shatter Styles of Architecture." Chicago Tribune, Friday, September 12, 1913.

*Interior of the Lion House at Lincoln Park, an exercise in elegance (P,F&H)*

[past] . . . Only Chicago remains calm and apparently uninterested. And it is exactly in Chicago that the insurgent school of American architects had its birth . . . And it is in Chicago . . . that the buildings which have aroused the scorn and indignation of eastern critics and the admiration of almost everybody else have been built and are now standing." Oddly enough, Hyde continued by commenting about the Armory Show, "Possibly the people of Chicago, some of whom went into intellectual and artistic convulsions when the insane pictures of the Cubist painters were shown at the Art Institute, might find something worth their attention in an exhibit of the native art of their own men. One even ventures the gratuitous suggestion that an exhibit at the institute of the drawings and models of buildings designed by the Chicago school of insurgent architects would be well worth while . . . Such an

*Farmer's National Bank of Owatonna, Minnesota, by Louis H. Sullivan (Stout)*

exhibit need not carry with it the indorsement of the institute, but it would be, at least, a recognition of the bold and interesting attempt of Chicago architects to add a new note to their ancient art. If the institute finds itself unable to give to such an exhibition there would seem to be nothing to prevent the Secessionists from giving a show on their own account." Hyde was particularly taken with the work of Louis Sullivan and commented on two of his recent works, the National Farmers' Bank of Owatonna, Minnesota, and the People's Bank of Cedar Rapids.[70] He quoted critic Montgomery Schuyler, who wrote in the *Architectural Record* that "there is no denying that a new work by Louis Sullivan is the most interesting event which can happen in the American architectural world today."[71] Hyde felt that Sullivan was "rather the despair of even his followers for the ease and success with which he 'puts over' original and almost bizarre forms and designs." The article was illustrated with Sullivan's Owatonna bank and the Sears School of Kenilworth, Illinois, by George W. Maher.

Hyde's article went on to name others of the early modern movement, leading off with Frank Lloyd Wright, who he claimed was "the most extreme member of the school." He also named George W. Maher, Walter Burley Griffin, Perkins, Fellows & Hamilton, George Nimmons, and Tallmadge & Watson. He stated that "they pay no attention to the conventions and rules of the classic types of architecture. They would express a new and democratic spirit." After some remarks concerning the forms the "new school" was using, Hyde ended his article by saying that "whether really the beginning of a new and greater school, whether an artistic revolution or merely a fanciful and passing fad, there is no doubt that just now the Chicago insurgents and their work is attracting more attention and causing more comment than any other architectural development in America." What Hyde did not recognize was that it was the Chicago Architectural Club that had been and was continuing to bring this avant-garde work to the attention of the public, largely through its annual exhibitions.

While Henry Hyde's article probably was little noticed outside of Chicago, the architectural press began to take much greater notice of the early modern movement between 1913 and 1916. Frank Lloyd Wright's trips to Germany in 1909–10 and 1911 had taken him away from Chicago, and his practice had suffered to such

70. The People's Bank of Cedar Rapids was completed in 1911. It continued to serve its clientele in Cedar Rapids until 1989, but was insensitively remodeled several times. In 1988 it was purchased by Norwest Bank Corporation, a holding company that also owned the Owatonna Bank designed by Louis Sullivan. Norwest Bank Corporation engaged the author to prepare a master plan for the restoration of the bank. The work was completed in 1991 in association with OPN Architects of Cedar Rapids, which was responsible for renovating the large additions done to the bank in 1951, 1966, and 1978.

71. Montgomery Schuyler, "The People's Savings Bank," *Architectural Record* 31, no. 1 (January 1912): 45–56.

*Interior of the People's Bank of Cedar Rapids in 1911 (WRH)*

*Exterior of the People's Bank of Cedar Rapids by Louis Sullivan as it appeared shortly after completion (WRH)*

a degree that he felt it necessary to do all he could to reestablish himself upon his return in April of 1911.[72] He was always ready to speak with the press and his ability to get the press to speak for him was legendary. In December of 1911, a major article on Wright's City National Bank of Mason City, Iowa, appeared in the *Western Architect*. It was followed in the next four years by no less than eleven issues of the *Western Architect* devoted to members of the early modern movement.[73] The *Brickbuilder* also carried a number of articles and illustrations of the movement, sometimes publishing the work of men who have otherwise been lost to most historians. For example, it had an excellent illustrated article in December of 1913 on the Orpheus movie theater in Chicago, designed by architects Aroner & Somers, with clear influences from Louis H. Sullivan in its ornament and massing.[74] This building, along with several other examples by this somewhat obscure firm, was published in the 1914 Chicago Architectural Club catalog.

✳

While the Twenty-sixth Annual Exhibition of the Chicago Architectural Club and the City Club Housing Exhibition were both still in place, the Chicago Architectural Club elected its officers for the 1913–14 year. George Awsumb was elected

72. Wright's two trips to Germany are described in some detail in Alofsin, *The Lost Years*.

73. These issues have been assembled in H. Allen Brooks, ed., *Prairie School Architecture, Studies from "The Western Architect"* (Toronto: University of Toronto Press, 1975). Most of these articles were essentially monographs covering the work of Purcell, Feick & Elmslie, Purcell & Elmslie, Walter Burley Griffin, William L. Steele, George W. Maher, Spencer & Powers, Guenzel & Drummond, John S. Van Bergen, Tallmadge & Watson, and Louis H. Sullivan. Other architects were covered during the same period, but not to the same degree. The work of Barry Byrne was included in 1924, 1925, and 1929 in the same magazine and in Brooks's book.

74. "A Moving Picture Theater: The Orpheus, Chicago, Ill.," *Brickbuilder* 22, no. 10 (October 1913): 233–36.

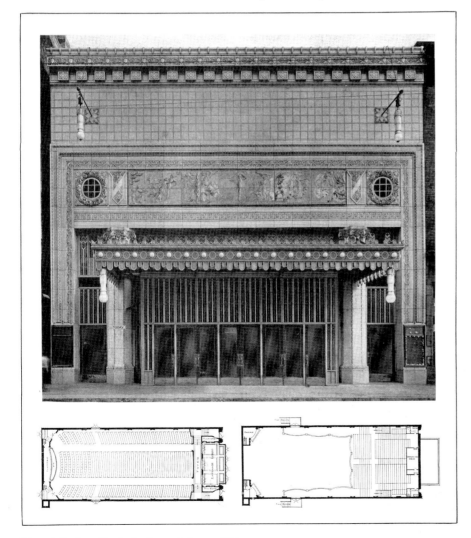

*Chicago's Orpheus Theater by Aroner & Somers (BB)*

*Walter Burley Griffin's design for a brick house, constructed on the floor of the City Products Exposition in Chicago (CN)*

president and W. G. Wuehrmann vice president. Both had won major club competitions in the past and had been regular contributors to club affairs. Harry H. Bentley and Fritz Wagner Jr. were chosen as secretary and treasurer, respectively. The club continued its policy of electing directors for two years, although of the three directors elected the year before to serve through 1914, only Jens A. Johnson continued in that office. Fritz Wagner Jr. had moved up to secretary, and the previous year's vice president, John Surmann, agreed to serve out his term as a director along with L. C. Vogel, who was new to the board. The class of 1915 was made up of Robert J. Love, J. Bernard Mullen, and R. C. Llewellyn. Both Wagner and Llewellyn were second-generation members of the board (sons of earlier members). All the committees were made up entirely of members of the board.

As usual, there was very little club activity during the summer months. Some members, however, were extremely active. Walter Burley Griffin, for example, had won the competition to design the new capitol for the City of Canberra, Australia, in 1912. After winning, Griffin entered into a partnership with architect Barry Byrne, who was to handle his work in the United States while Griffin was in Australia.[75] Griffin had rented space in the Monroe Building and moved there from Steinway Hall on May 1, 1912. Byrne would join him there in late 1913. In June 1912, Griffin was a guest speaker at the Illinois Chapter of the AIA, where he "explained in detail his design and plans for the new city."[76] The chapter then passed a resolution to "tender" its "congratulations" to Griffin.

Griffin continued practicing in Chicago while awaiting word from Australia regarding the execution of his capital city plans. He designed a small brick house for the annual Clay Products exposition held in Chicago in February of 1913. It was actually built at the exposition and was the prize in a "guessing" contest held during the show.[77] He also completed a preliminary design for the New Trier Neighborhood Center, a planned development for the village of Winnetka, Illinois. In July 1913 he was invited to Australia to discuss implementing his plan for Canberra.[78] He arrived in August. After a three-month stay, he returned to the United States for several months to wind up his affairs, after which he returned to Australia, where he was based for most of the rest of his life. Before he left, the Illinois Chapter of the AIA held a special meeting in early February 1914 in honor of Walter and his wife, Marion Mahony Griffin.[79] The club room walls at the Art Institute were covered with the work of "Mr. Griffin, and also of Mrs. Griffin . . . the first woman licensed to practice architecture in Illinois. The guests . . . were unanimous in lauding the works . . . there being a number of sketches and drawings on satin." After dinner, the president "called upon Mrs. Griffin for a few words. She told of her future plans in a most delightful way and declared that working together with her husband . . . she has more than realized her ambitions in an architectural way . . . Mr. Griffin followed and expressed his most heartfelt thanks to the members of the Institute for their kindness and good wishes." It marked the end of Griffin's participation in the affairs of the Chicago AIA and the CAC. The year 1913 would see a number of other changes that would affect the club's future.

The most wrenching event was the loss of the club's space at the Dexter Building, which it had occupied since early 1904.[80] For the next four years, until 1916, the club's address would be the Art Institute of Chicago. Members used the club room at the Art Institute as their headquarters and held most of their formal meetings there. The space was shared with a number of other arts and cultural organizations, among them the Illinois Chapter of the American Institute of Architects

75. Francis Barry Byrne (1883–1967) was born in Chicago. He attended parochial school in Chicago but left at the age of fourteen. After various other jobs, he entered Frank Lloyd Wright's studio in 1902 at the age of nineteen. In 1908, he joined Andrew Willatzen in Seattle, Washington, where he remained for four years. He then went to California and worked with Irving Gill for about a year. In 1913, he returned to Chicago and entered a partnership with Walter Burley Griffin. He remained in Chicago until 1923, when he took an extended tour of Europe. Upon his return, he opened a private practice in New York and Chicago. He died in 1967.

76. *Construction News* 33, no. 24 (June 15, 1912): 11.

77. *Construction News* 35, no. 5 (March 8, 1913): 6–7.

78. The best brief discussion of Griffin's work on Canberra is Donald Leslie Johnson, *The Architecture of Walter Burley Griffin* (South Melbourne: Macmillan of Australia, 1977): 20–23.

79. *Construction News* 37, no. 6 (February 14, 1914): 8.

80. No evidence of the actual date of the club's move has been found, but since it took possession of the space in early 1904, probably on March 1, it is likely that the lease was up in early 1912, again probably March 1, since that was a common date for lease renewals. As noted earlier, the only printed information on the move out of the Dexter Building was published in *Construction News* 33, no. 19 (May 11, 1912): 12. The 1913 exhibition catalog gives the address as the Art Institute of Chicago.

and the Chicago Architects' Business Association, which in 1913 became the Illinois Society of Architects. The Chicago Architectural Club had always had a good relationship with these groups and, in 1913, had had the help of the Illinois Chapter of the AIA in mounting the annual exhibition. By the end of 1913, the club had arranged to work with both the AIA and the ISA to sponsor the 1914 exhibition. It was an association that would last until the demise of the annual exhibitions in the 1930s.

Despite the turmoil caused by loss of the club rooms in the Dexter Building and the move to the Art Institute, the 1913 exhibition had come off well and had made a considerable impact on the public and the architectural community. Nineteen-thirteen was an important year for the early modern movement in architecture, particularly for those who were part of what was later known as the Prairie School.[81] Many of them would move beyond what the Chicago Architectural Club had to offer. Some would regress and become part of the establishment. They had little time to devote to the club's activities, and the club suffered as a result. The catalog of the annual exhibition of 1913 was simply not up to the standards set by earlier publications. Some of the best work was not illustrated and sometimes not even listed. It was also the first catalog to acknowledge the aid and assistance of the Illinois Chapter of the AIA. The club was beginning to lose its position as the most influential architectural organization in Chicago. The next few years would see changes that would, arguably, eventually lead to its demise.

81. The accomplishments of these architects have been admirably treated in Brooks, *The Prairie School*. This book is indispensable to any serious scholar of the early modern movement in architecture in the Midwest. It does not, however, cover the minor participants, nor does it cover the activities of the Chicago Architectural Club beyond their relationship to the members of the Prairie school.

BOOK OF THE 27TH
ANNVAL EXHIBITION

CHICAGO ARCHITECTVRAL
CLVB · · · 1914

*The 1914 exhibition catalog cover was the first without the Chicago Architectural Club's symbol; this was R. C. Llewellyn's copy and his signature is still visible (PC)*

# Back to the Art Institute

CHAPTER SIXTEEN

When the Chicago Architectural Club lost its space at the Dexter Building on Adams Street in 1912, it faced a problem that had not plagued it for several years. The club had become accustomed to having its own space with dining facilities, a small staff, and most important, something to call its own. It was offered, and accepted, the use of the "club room" at the Art Institute of Chicago. It was, in some ways, well suited to the CAC's needs. On the other hand, the club had to share the space with numerous other groups, including the Illinois Chapter of the AIA and the Chicago Architects' Business Association. Several other organizations also met there, and it was far more difficult for club members to meet casually and plan events specific to their interests and needs. It did, however, encourage interaction with their colleagues in other organizations.

It was the City Club of Chicago with which the Chicago Architectural Club had the strongest relationship. Not only did the members of the Architectural Club participate in the Competition for the Development of a Quarter Section of Property in Chicago, but a number of them were active in other aspects of the two exhibitions sponsored by the City Club, where the competitive plans were exhibited. The larger of the two, the Housing Exhibition, was so successful that the City Club immediately launched a similar program addressing the problem of railroad terminals in downtown Chicago shortly after that exhibition was over. Incredibly, an examination of Chicago's Loop and its immediate surroundings shows that in 1913 roughly half the property downtown was owned and used by railroads, most of which had their own passenger and freight terminals. The problem had been addressed, but not solved, in the *Plan of Chicago* completed in 1909 by Burnham and Bennett. The City Club recognized the need to provide for more efficient railroad facilities, and in June 1913 it sponsored a series of seminars in which various plans for the reorganization and consolidation of the existing terminals were considered.

The Chicago Architectural Club continued to collaborate with the City Club on efforts to enhance the quality of life in Chicago. Among their more significant activities was attending the Third National Conference of Housing held in Cincinnati on December 3–5, 1913. The City Club's delegates were Robert C. Spencer and William Drummond, both active, longtime members of the Chicago Architectural Club. When they returned, the two men gave reports that were published in the *City Club Bulletin*.[1] During the next few years, cross-membership was fairly high,

1. *City Club Bulletin* 7, no. 1 (January 12, 1914): 1–6. Both reports to the City Club were reproduced verbatim.

partially because the club rooms at the Art Institute of Chicago had no private dining space and the shared space was not always available to Architectural Club members. The Chicago Architectural Club also had a substantial overlap with the Cliff Dwellers Club, located on the top floor of Orchestra Hall immediately across the street from the Art Institute. Those facilities were available to the Architectural Club as well for lunch, dinner, and conversation.

Generally speaking, the activities of the Chicago Architectural Club were limited during the fall of 1913. It continued to operate an atelier informally under the leadership of Francis W. Puckey and, just before the end of the year, set up the program for the Fourteenth Annual Traveling Scholarship Competition. The subject was "An Aquarium." It entailed a good deal of work for the entrants but was relatively easy for the club to administer. The 1913–14 Competition Committee was chaired by Robert J. Love with the help of Jens A. Johnson and J. Bernard Mullen. Once again, the first prize of six hundred dollars was offered by Clarence M. Woolley of the American Radiator Company and the gold medal for second place was the gift of Charles W. Gindele, following the tradition begun in 1910.

By early 1914, the Chicago Architectural Club was struggling. Membership, which had hovered around two hundred for the past few years, had dropped in 1913 after a brief peak in 1912. After a drive for new members, the 1914 catalog listed 205 members in all categories, thirty-six who had not been listed before. There had been an increase in the honorary category starting in 1910, when William E. Clow, E. G. Elcock, and Charles W. Gindele were added to the list. In 1912, William D. Gates was added, and in late 1913, well before the next annual exhibition, Francis W. Puckey was made an honorary member. All had made significant contributions to the club. Associates, who were essentially nonarchitect members, seemed to remain quite stable. It was the younger men who came and went more or less arbitrarily, often joining to take advantage of the two ateliers and leaving when they felt they had learned what they needed to work in an office at a higher level or to enter practice on their own. There remained, however, a core of members who continued to work hard to maintain the activities and reputation of the club year after year.

Part of the problem may have been the establishment of what seemed to be a rival organization. The Chicago Architectural Club had originated in 1885 as a "sketch" club for draftsmen. Architects were welcomed as guests but not as full members until a decade later. Many of the original members had by that time become practicing architects. After 1895, the affairs of the club were dominated by practicing architects, albeit the younger ones, and many of the draftsmen felt somewhat left out. In the fall of 1912 the Architectural Draftsmen of North America was organized in Chicago.[2] The key organizer was B. J. Winkel, a draftsman with A. S. Coffin, which had offices in the Schiller Building. The *Construction News* article in which it was announced stated that "the object of the organization is the betterment of the condition of architectural draftsmen materially, educationally, and socially." The organization planned to help draftsmen find employment and drafting rooms where they might "do private work in the evenings, lounging and smoking rooms . . . It is the intention to make the permanent quarters so attractive and interesting that every member may feel perfectly at home there." B. J. Winkel was named the first president, with E. G. Albricht and C. Hale serving as vice president and secretary, respectively. They planned to hold an inaugural membership meeting shortly after the initial organization, "to which all draftsmen are cordially invited . . . to be held in the offices of above mentioned architect [A. S. Coffin]." The article

2. *Construction News* 34, no. 42 (October 26, 1912): 8.

went on to say, "Though practically nothing has been done to advertise the organization, it has already thirty members, and others have signified their intention to join." Little more was heard from the group until August 1913, when a second article appeared in *Construction News*.[3] It referred to "the American Technical Association (formerly the Architectural Draftsmen and Superintendents' Association)," which was almost certainly the same group under a different name. The article further noted that the group had "clubrooms in the Republic building . . . [and] has made arrangements for a stag vaudeville show to be given in the Whitney Opera House, 64 East Van Buren Street, Thursday, August 28. The entertainment is for the benefit of the treasury of the association to provide equipment and a library for the new quarters." (The Whitney Opera House was located in Steinway Hall, the building of choice for a number of architects.) No further information concerning the draftsmen's group has come to light. It may have been a thinly disguised attempt at unionization. In the March 28, 1914, issue of *Construction News,* it was reported in an article concerning the Chicago Architects' Business Association that a recent important discovery was "that architectural draftsmen have formed a union and have a charter from the American Federation of Labor." The subject was referred to the board of directors for further discussion. The group, if it was the same organization, apparently died out rather quickly.

The fact that a "draftsmen's association" was formed and apparently had some support does lend credibility to the assumption that the Chicago Architectural Club was no longer meeting the needs of those men who chose to continue as draftsmen rather than take the steps necessary to become architects. The club needed to take a long look at its activities and find a way to satisfy those who were unable to become members of either of the senior organizations, the AIA or the CABA. It took some time, but the club did eventually return to its roots insofar as serving the draftsmen of Chicago was concerned.

Apparently the 1913 exhibition had been a financial strain on the club. It had received assistance from the Illinois Chapter of the AIA, but whether that included financial aid is unknown. In the fall of 1913 the club members realized that they needed more help if they were to continue to mount their annual exhibitions at the level of quality they and the public had come to expect. Without any written agreement, they turned to the Illinois Chapter of the AIA and the Chicago Architects' Business Association for help. Together they set up a ten-man Committee on Exhibition, chaired by J. F. Surmann, who had held a similar position the previous year. William G. Wuehrmann, R. C. Llewellyn, and Fritz Wagner Jr. served with him as CAC representatives. The AIA named Arthur G. Brown, H. V. von Holst, and Thomas E. Tallmadge to the committee, and the CABA asked George Maher, J. D. York, and Arthur Woltersdorf to represent it. The Jury of Admission included Francis W. Puckey from the CAC, Martin Roche from the AIA, and George Maher from the CABA, along with Fritz Wagner Jr. as treasurer of the exhibition. All these men, although representing their respective organizations, had been or still were active members of the Chicago Architectural Club. Clearly, the club needed help, but it was not about to give away control.

In the early days of 1914, there was little published regarding the Chicago Architectural Club, but Robert Craik McLean occasionally wrote about clubs and certain members in the *Western Architect*. McLean's lead editorial in April 1914 was a humorous essay comparing Venus and Kohinoor drafting pencils.[4] Venus had been the mainstay of draftsmen for some time and Kohinoor was new to the profession. He

3. *Construction News* 36, no. 5 (August 2, 1913): 12.

4. *Western Architect* 20, no. 4 (April 1914): 33–34.

noted that "they both looked pretty good and worked well. They seemed a good deal alike and we have been trying . . . to find out the difference between them." He implied that the two pencils were very much like architects, with Venus being the older, which can be "depended not to roll off the table. Venus is not so long as Kohinoor and seems to show a different point, sort of a machine made engineering kind of pointedness." Clearly, he was suggesting that Venus represented the old school of architecture. He wrote, "Venus is guaranteed not to break a point with the roughest handling, and to make a true and even line at all times." On the other hand, he believed that "Kohinoor is firm and works well on any kind of paper. He seems . . . to be especially suitable for persons of taste and culture."

After this unusual opening, McLean identified Robert C. Spencer as Kohinoor, and the suggestion was that he typified the best of the new architecture then developing in the Midwest. He remembered that Spencer was "one of the little colony of thoughtful men who made common cause for the good of American Architecture up in the 'attic' of Steinway Hall. We who are familiar with this homelike little architectural nest believe that the surroundings must have had a wholesome effect on those who were working there." The editorial was in the same issue of the magazine devoted almost entirely to the work of Robert C. Spencer Jr. and his partner, Horace S. Powers.

The following month, McLean again wrote in a humorous vein with a serious goal, this time under the heading "Off Nights in the Architectural Club."[5] He didn't name the club he was writing about, but considering his long relationship with the Chicago Architectural Club, he was obviously talking about Chicago. His comments began, "When the pulse of the Architectural Club beats low; when members forget(?) to pay their dues and competitions lose their erstwhile attractiveness, there is always a saving few who, like the exception that proves the rule, save the situation and preserve momentum. Draftsmen are alike, gregarious, and clubs are alike, in the ebb and flow of their enthusiasms. It was in the ebb phase of its progress that a certain club was threatened with something, that was diagnosed Indiferentitis, and the doctors sought a remedy. They found it. Then the faithful got busy." He went on to describe how twelve members of this fictitious club worked together to revitalize it. He concluded, "Thus off evenings in any Architectural Club can be made interesting, enjoyable and profitable by the work of a few members using their gray matter and adding a little enthusiasm to the brew." He was apparently right, since the Chicago Architectural Club with its newfound friends in the AIA and the CABA put together an exhibition in 1914 that rivaled many of those great shows of a decade earlier. It was not, however, without controversy.

Once again, the only professional journal to announce the terms and rules of the annual exhibition was *Construction News*.[6] The language of the invitation was virtually identical to that of the previous two years, including the rules for the award of a gold medal by the Illinois Chapter of the AIA. In a departure from the past, the announcement listed all the members of the committees from the AIA, the CABA, and the CAC working on the exhibition. It was careful to note that it was still the club's exhibition, and all the officers of the club were named. Entry forms from exhibitors were to be returned by March 4 and the dates of the exhibition were set from April 9 to May 3, 1914.

The first announcement of the opening of the Twenty-seventh Annual Exhibition of the Chicago Architectural Club appeared in *Chicago Commerce* on April 3, 1914. It noted that the opening reception was to be on April 9 from eight to

5. *Western Architect* 20, no. 5 (May 1914): 41.

6. *Construction News* 37, no. 10 (March 7, 1914): 8.

eleven o'clock. The show opened as scheduled, but only after a scathing article titled "Architects Quit Big Exhibit" appeared in literally every one of the ten editions of the *Chicago American* on the same day.[7] The column was by Florence Patton,[8] who wrote, "If what purports to be a city-wide case of 'architects' peeve' develops its symptoms, there will be a dearth of Chicago architects this evening when the twenty-seventh annual exhibition of the Chicago Architectural Club opens at the Art Institute. Alleged unfairness in the handling of the exhibits and partiality shown to Eastern architects . . . threatens to disrupt the good will in the business here. The storm-center is supposed to be Frank Lloyd Wright, whose 'spirited hegira' with the former Mrs. Edwin H. Cheney of Oak Park served for so much publicity a short time ago. It is charged that Mr. Wright's display has been especially privileged and that he has an entire room for his drawings."[9] This was, of course, true. It was verified in the article by J. F. Surmann, who was chairman of the Exhibition Committee. He stated that "Mr. Wright has been especially granted three walls in a room of the exhibit, not only on account of the merit of his work, but on account of the interest attached to his private life . . . he's just as interesting to the public one way as another . . . and will draw a big crowd." His comments made it obvious that the club was eager for public support regardless of what it took to get it.

Wright was, as usual, not reticent about replying. Ms. Patton wrote that he was "calmly disparaging of the alleged attacks from the architects of the city." She quoted him as saying, "Let them talk. Let them say what they will. Let them resurrect all the old scandal of the past three years. What do I care. I have three walls for my work. I'm erecting the Imperial Hotel at Tokio [*sic*] and I'm doing other big work in the world—both the scandal and what I am doing artistically, will bring us greater crowds. Let them talk, let them talk, he said." Wright was on the same page as the chairman of the exhibition.

Further down in her column, Florence Patton wrote that "the exhibit is two thirds of the work of Eastern architects . . . another reason for the row." E. S. Hall, secretary of the Chicago Architects' Business Association, was quoted as saying, "For the past few years Chicago architects have been dropping out of the exhibition on account of a favoritism too plainly shown for work done by painters rather than architects. In the displays have been artistic showings of buildings . . . as no real architect can countenance. A painter is one thing, an architect is another." He went on to say, "For instance, Mr. Wright's work. He paints upon satin and so forth." Hall, who was an architect, obviously was confusing Wright's work with other renderings done by the young avant-garde men who had essentially dominated the previous year's somewhat truncated exhibition. The column ended with a comment from William G. Wuehrmann, vice president of the club, who noted that it had been unfortunate that Wright had been given so much space but that "Chicago men have failed to submit exhibits."

The *Chicago American* was not the only local paper to report on the controversy over the amount of Wright's work included in the exhibition. The *Chicago Examiner* printed an even more vitriolic article the following day.[10] In an item headlined "Architects in Dispute Over Wright Room," the reporter began, "A family fight among the three societies interested in the twenty-seventh annual exhibition of the Chicago Architectural Club preceded the opening view last evening in the Art Institute. The trouble is pending still. It arose because Frank Lloyd Wright, who is not a member of any of the participating organizations, has an entire room for his exhibit, which he was allowed to place himself, and because he was released from submitting the exhibit to the jury which passed upon the work of all other applicants." There had been an allegation that Wright had paid five hundred dollars

7. *Chicago American* 14, no. 240 (April 9, 1914): 1. The column appeared on the front page of every edition of the day, ten in all. More or less the same text was reprinted in each edition with minor typographic corrections.

8. Florence Patton was a regular critic for the *Chicago American*.

9. Wright's visit to Europe with Mrs. Cheney in 1909–10 and their cohabitation at Taliesin had been the subject of numerous headlines in Chicago newspapers during the years immediately prior to this article. The terrible tragedy of the murder of Cheney and others at Taliesin did not occur until later in the summer of 1914.

10. "Architects in Dispute Over Wright Room," *Chicago Examiner*, April 10, 1914.

for the privilege of having his own private show. Whether he paid anything or not simply to be permitted to show his work was never established. He was a patron of the exhibition, along with sixty-eight other architects, building suppliers, and friends of the club, and thus did make some sort of monetary contribution. He had done so previously. There is evidence that Wright had planned for some time to be represented in the 1914 exhibition. On March 30, 1914, shortly after the announcement of the exhibition, Wright wired his former employee, Taylor Woolley, who was then in Salt Lake City, to come to Chicago to assist in preparing for the exhibition.[11] Thus, he clearly intended to exhibit and he would not have made elaborate preparations, including paying Woolley for assistance, unless he was certain that his work would be shown. He was undoubtedly also trying very hard to capitalize on the recent publicity for his two "Wasmuth" publications, which he was offering for sale in the United States.[12] He expected to generate a good deal of cash from the sale of these publications, and the exhibition was an opportunity to promote interest in his work and himself.[13]

The Jury of Admission—Francis W. Puckey from the CAC, Martin Roche from the AIA, and George Maher from the CABA—was apparently not asked to pass on Wright's submissions. Puckey was quoted in the *Chicago Examiner* article as saying, "I didn't even know Mr. Wright was going to exhibit until I read about the trouble in the morning papers . . . I understand Mr. Wright is exhibiting at his own expense. It might easily put him $500 out of pocket to arrange an exhibit." W. R. French, director of the Art Institute, confirmed, "Mr. Wright paid no money to the Art Institute." George W. Maher observed, "We were very short of exhibits this year." He went on to note that "last year was a very dull year for architects. Louis Sullivan has had a room in previous years, and so has D. H. Burnham. Mr. Wright was invited to participate, as he has been before. We were very glad to get him to take a room. No exhibits were excluded on his account. He wouldn't need to submit his work to a jury. Everybody knows it is type work."

The club's vice president, W. G. Wuehrmann, stated that "it costs us more to stage an exhibit than we get out of it . . . but we wouldn't have made Mr. Wright buy his way in." The matter was later reviewed by the Illinois Chapter of the AIA, and it was concluded that the charges against Wright were false. Wright was probably delighted to show his work and agreed to do so subject to not having it juried and with the understanding that he would pay all costs incurred by him in mounting the exhibit. Whether that was a five-hundred-dollar patron's contribution or not is long lost to any records. Whatever the case, Wright's display in the 1914 exhibition was an important part of the show and the only part that was photographed.[14] No illustrations of his work appeared in the catalog of the exhibition. The photographs of his space and exhibits are among the few we have of Chicago Architectural Club exhibitions.

The *Book of the Twenty-seventh Annual Exhibition* was the first in fifteen years not to include the symbol of the club on its cover. This was probably in deference to the two other architectural organizations that had joined the club in sponsorship. The cover was a pen drawing of the Michigan Avenue facade of the Art Institute of Chicago, which had been adapted from a watercolor duplicated in a very small format on the inside cover page. The artist was not identified. The catalog was dedicated "To the Memory of Otto A. Silha, 1881–1913," the previous year's president who had died in November 1913.[15] The basic format was similar to that of recent years, with a page devoted to the Committee on Exhibition and below that, the Jury of Admission. Both were made up of members from the three sponsoring organizations. An acknowledgments page followed, thanking all concerned for their help. The patrons who supported the club with financial contributions got

11. Alofsin, *The Lost Years*, 309.

12. The Wasmuth publications were a huge two-volume monograph, *Ausgefuhrte Bauten und Entwurfe von Frank Lloyd Wright* (Berlin: Ernst Wasmuth, 1910), that was reviewed in the April 1912 issue of the *Architectural Record* by critic Montgomery Schuyler. More important, the *Architectural Review* led off its "Book Notes" in March of 1914 with a favorable review of the smaller Wasmuth publication, *Frank Lloyd Wright, Ausgefuhrte Bauten* (Berlin: Ernst Wasmuth, 1911).

13. The entire story of Wright's efforts to sell these publications is told in Alofsin, *The Lost Years*.

14. Those photographs were apparently arranged for by Wright. Most are now in the collection of the Chicago Architectural Photography Company in Chicago, although prints of several are in the archives at Taliesin and in the collection of the Art Institute of Chicago.

15. "Deaths," *Chicago Inter Ocean*, November 27, 1913, 11. Silha's death notice states that he died at Wesley Hospital on November 24 at the age of thirty-two. No cause of death is given. He left a wife, Apolena, and two brothers, Edward F. and John A., but no children.

*Frank Lloyd Wright had a separate room in the 1914 annual architectural exhibition; it was one of the few exhibition spaces ever to be photographed, and much of what he showed had not be seen before (Taliesin)*

nearly two full pages, with addresses, but no indication of what their individual donations were. There was a two-page "Welcome" from Alfred S. Alschuler, wherein he raised an old issue: "We trust that each succeeding year shall find us closer to the goal toward which we all are striving. Whether the slogan be 'Progress before precedent' or 'Precedent before progress,' we trust this annual assemblage will in

*Wright's "puppet theater," with two of his Japanese print stands in the background (Taliesin)*

*Another view of Frank Lloyd Wright's room at the 1914 exhibition (Taliesin)*

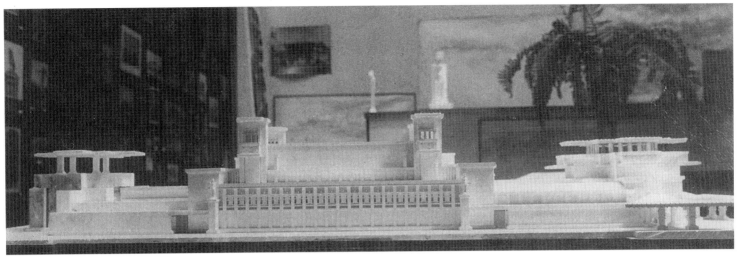

*Model of the Midway Gardens, exhibited in 1914 (Taliesen)*

any event indicate PROGRESS." He was pleased with the results of the exhibition and noted that "this opportunity for interchange of ideas . . . shall result in higher standards both for the profession and for the laity, and that the city beautiful shall no longer be a vision unfulfilled, is the wish of the Chicago Architectural Club." His welcome was followed by a page of the club's officers and committees for 1913–14, after which all the current members were listed. As in the past, the club's Annual Traveling Scholarship got its own page, with a list of all past winners including the 1914 winner, W. J. Schaeffer, for his design of "An Aquarium." R. N. Heer took home the gold medal for second place. There were only nine pages of illustrations other than the frontispieces. The "List of Exhibitors," on the other hand, included 279 regular exhibits plus a "Special Exhibit" of twenty-five buildings intended to be "a collection of exhibits that could be used in connection with the designing of buildings for a small American City of a uniform style of Architecture." Remarkably, none of those exhibits was provided by a Chicago architect or illustrated. Finally, there were thirty-one numbered exhibits under the subtitle "Work of Frank Lloyd Wright." Some of these consisted of several items under the same number, making up a total of more than fifty items shown by Wright.

The local press reviewed the exhibition extensively; sometimes the same critic wrote about it more than once. Harriet Monroe first critiqued the show on April 9, along with an art exhibit that opened the same evening.[16] She wrote that "the most important exhibit . . . is Henry Bacon's model of a monument which it is proposed to erect in Logan Square to commemorate the one hundredth anniversary of the admission of Illinois to the union." She then qualified her praise by stating that the "design is a disappointing compromise between classic prepossessions and an effort to be original." Her review noted that "Frank Lloyd Wright is to have a room at the exhibition which, save for one interesting model of a skyscraper project for San Francisco, was empty at the press view." Monroe went on to briefly discuss some of the other exhibits, but said little more of real interest.

Several days later, she went back to the show and wrote a second column.[17] This time she had more to say. She opened by noting that the exhibition was "smaller and less representative than usual, partly because the last year has been inactive." She stated that "for the third time the club has offered to Frank Lloyd Wright a gallery for a special exhibition. There is reason enough for giving Mr. Wright a special room, for, after Louis Sullivan, he is the most important of American secessionists in architecture, and is so recognized by the leading secessionists

16. Harriet Monroe, "Two Exhibitions Open at Art Institute Tonight," *Chicago Tribune*, April 9, 1914.

17. Harriet Monroe, "The Orient an Influence on the Architecture of Wright," *Chicago Tribune*, April 14, 1914.

*Shepley, Rutan & Coolidge exhibited work done for the University of Chicago (CAC/14)*

abroad. Chicago, through their little group, headed by Messrs. Sullivan and Wright, is the center of American rebellion against the historic styles in architecture, a rebellion which is now traveling to the new capital of Australia in the person of Walter Burley Griffin, formerly a draftsman in the Wright office."[18] One wonders how Wright would have responded to this paragraph. Certainly he would not have objected to being named along with Sullivan, but the reference to Griffin's success must have galled him. Monroe, who had had a somewhat bitter exchange with Wright when she wrote about his work in the 1907 exhibition, obviously could not resist the temptation to tell the world that Wright was not alone in the avant-garde of Chicago. She went on to say, "As the first hint for all occidental art comes from Greece, so Mr. Wright's first hint comes from the orient, or, more specifically, Japan. In feeling this influence he is at one with all modern thought in the arts." She noted that in his "long level lines he seems to express our need of shelter against climatic extremes more violent than the Greeks knew."

Harriet Monroe had done something few other reviewers had done. She had looked at Wright's work with the eye of a critic, perhaps because of the exchange she had had with him seven years earlier. She went on to praise the design for Midway Gardens, where, she noted, "the general public will have its first opportunity at a fair judgment of this artist, who is devoting his professional career to an effort to give us an authentic and indigenous architecture. Hitherto the public has known too little about his work. He has built an imperial hotel in Tokio [sic] for the Japanese government, a postoffice [sic] and library at Ottawa, and other buildings for the Canadian government, but most of his Chicago work is scattered in suburbs."

Another thoughtful and lengthy review of the exhibition was written by Lena May McCauley in the *Chicago Evening Post*.[19] She felt that the exhibition presented "a most hopeful sign of the times in its sphere of the arts." She further noted that the club "has escaped the restrictions of a governing clique of fossilized dictators, or members of the profession given to fads." She thought the "arrangement of the drawings is a tactful undertaking, since the exhibition is intended to inform the public as well as to serve the architect. Few matter-of-fact plans take up space, and popular interest is attracted by the handsome renderings." She was particularly impressed by the "special exhibit of twenty-six architects which could be used in connection with the designing of buildings for a small American city of a uniform style of architecture." She seemed to have no concern that those architects were literally all from the east and that Chicago was not represented at all. She did, however, grant that the "dignified installation accorded the work of Frank Lloyd Wright in a

18. It is interesting that Monroe used the word "secessionists," since it was, of course, the term used to describe the young European avant-garde architects and designers whose explorations of new forms and a new architecture paralleled those of Sullivan and Wright and their colleagues in Chicago. It is also interesting that the research for this book did not turn up any direct references to the secessionist movement in any published material regarding the Chicago Architectural Club.

19. Lena May McCauley was born in 1859 in Hagerstown, Maryland. After an excellent education at the Dearborn Seminary in Chicago, followed by graduate work in literature and science at the universities of Chicago, Wisconsin, and Illinois, she became a teacher, and eventually a principal, in the Chicago public school system. After 1900, she began writing professionally; she was named art editor of the *Chicago Evening Post* in 1902, a position she held when she wrote the article cited.

gallery aside affords the privilege of enjoyment of the individual ideas of the architect. Mr. Wright's accomplishments are unusual, in that he has original convictions and the strength of purpose to carry them out to conclusions. In a few years he has evolved a style, and so established it that it exercises a wide influence."

The *Chicago Record-Herald's* art critic, Maude I. G. Oliver, wrote a brief item on April 12 and followed up a week later with a longer, more thoughtful column.[20] About all the first column tells us is where the exhibition was held. It occupied the entire south tier of the second floor of the Art Institute, except for room 25. Her second column went into considerable detail. She was concerned about the rather haphazard organization of the exhibit and felt that like buildings should be shown together. She followed the lead of her colleagues in Chicago by devoting a good deal of space to the work of Frank Lloyd Wright. She thought that in some cases he was "carrying aestheticism too far." She also felt that this "exotic element in Mr. Wright's style is brilliant though . . . there is a sense in a Wright house, that the occupants cannot fit in. It always remains a Wright house and it always will remain a Wright house." She, more than any other critic, devoted a good deal of her space to a general discussion of the entire exhibition. She wrote of George Maher's "theories," the work of John Russell Pope, and about several banks designed by various architects. Few of these were discussed critically; she seemed to be more interested in describing everything than she was in criticizing what she saw.

There was other press coverage as well. H. Effa Webster wrote a brief comment on April 11, and the *Boston Transcript* had a short item the day before. Neither was critical. The Boston item was undoubtedly printed because of the showing of the drawings of the Lincoln Memorial designed by Henry Bacon, which was about to begin construction in Washington, D.C. Bacon was then based in New York City but had worked in Boston earlier. His design for the Lincoln Memorial had been vehemently opposed by the Illinois Chapter of the AIA, which expressed its opinion in a resolution passed in December of 1912.[21] The AIA's principal problem with the design was its Greek antecedents. It noted that there was "no connection historically, nor from the standpoint of democracy, with the work of Abraham Lincoln, nor with his life, his country or his time; but suggests rather the age of Pericles of ancient Greek history . . . [and] the Illinois Chapter of the American Institute of Architects, emphatically protests against the adoption of such a memorial." It did not, of course, succeed in its efforts to delay or force a revision of the design, today one of the most revered monuments in Washington. At the time, however, Henry Bacon was not held in high regard in Chicago because of his selection as designer of the building, and this was probably why his plans for both the memorial and his design to commemorate the one hundredth anniversary of the admission of Illinois to the Union were both omitted from the exhibition catalog.

The chapter felt strongly that the Lincoln Memorial should reflect American architecture. A major problem was that no one had yet defined just what an American architecture was. George Maher and Arthur Woltersdorf were particularly outspoken in their insistence on the promotion of such an architecture. Following the reading of the AIA's resolution, Woltersdorf, who strongly favored it, spoke to the assembled members of the Illinois AIA and said, "We have now waited 50 years and why not wait a little longer for an American expression or a truthful representation of Mr. Lincoln and what he stood for." It was not, of course, the first time this subject had been brought before the assembled members of the Chicago Chapter of the AIA. They had debated it for several months before the issue of the Lincoln Memorial was discussed.

After considerable discussion and sometimes rancorous debate, it had been decided that the chapter had an obligation to define American architecture. In Jan-

20. Maude I. G. Oliver, *Chicago Record-Herald*, April 12, and Maude I. G. Oliver, *Chicago Record-Herald*, April 19, 1914.

21. The position of the Illinois Chapter of the AIA was outlined in detail in *Construction News* 35, no. 3 (January 18, 1912): 14.

uary 1913, the Illinois Chapter of the AIA had appointed Dwight H. Perkins, George W. Maher, and Arthur Woltersdorf to a committee "whose duty it shall be to formulate a statement relating to American architecture, or modern design as distinct from classic or renaissance models. Examples of modern work in this spirit already exist in various localities in the United States, particularly in the Middle West, in numbers sufficient to entitle this tendency to recognition." The committee was instructed to recommend that the national AIA recognize and illustrate examples of such architecture in the official journal of the AIA.[22] No report from the appointed committee has come to light, but each of the men assigned to the task wrote passionately on the subject from time to time during the next few years.

None of the critics who wrote about the 1914 exhibition noted that the Illinois AIA gold medal, which had been mentioned in the request for exhibition entries, was not awarded in 1914. On May 7, after the exhibition was over, the chapter members were informed that the seven-man jury had been unable to identify an "exhibit . . . of sufficient merit or high character to warrant its being awarded the chapter's annual gold medal." One wonders if this decision might have been made before the exhibition, since there is no mention of it in the 1914 catalog as there had been in previous years. It is interesting to note, however, that a photograph of Lockby Court, an apartment building by Richard E. Schmidt of Schmidt, Garden & Martin, was the second frontispiece in the catalog. It would win the AIA gold medal the next year.

Following the success of the City Club Housing Show, the Armory Show, and the Chicago Architectural Club exhibition of 1913, the City Club announced still another competition of great interest to the members of the Chicago Architectural Club. The first notice was published in March of 1914, just before the annual exhibition.[23] It was to be for the development of a neighborhood center (not to be confused with the competition for the "Scheme of Development of a Quarter Section of Land" of a year earlier). I. K. Pond, R. C. Spencer, and Elmo C. Lowe were appointed to prepare the details of the competition, and by midyear the program for the two-stage competition was ready. The first stage would close on November 9, 1914. Eight to sixteen preliminary plans would be selected by a jury of architects and would then be entered in a final competition. These selected drawings could be refined by their designers and were to be in the hands of the City Club by January 25, 1915. The entrants were allowed a great deal of latitude. The plans could be for a fictitious site, not necessarily Chicago. Six hundred dollars in prize money was to be divided equally among the eight entrants selected by the jury. The key requirement was that the plans were to enhance neighborhood life in cities by providing better and more specifically grouped buildings and grounds for social activities.[24]

Twenty plans were submitted in the first stage of the competition.[25] Ten were selected to compete for the final prizes. The rules had changed in that there were now to be first, second, and third prizes instead of merely dividing the money equally among the finalists. The winners of the competition were to be chosen in time to be shown at the City Club's Exhibition of Public Properties of Chicago, which was scheduled to open on March 2, 1915.[26] It was another huge exhibition, with more than seven hundred items. Seventeen committees with more than fifty

22. *Construction News* 35, no. 4 (January 25, 1913): 13.

23. *Construction News* 37, no. 11 (March 14, 1914): 6.

24. *Construction News* 38, no. 1 (July 3, 1914): 5.

25. *City Club Bulletin* 7, no. 19 (November 25, 1914): 260. During this period, the City Club also had a number of other activities under way, most of which held little interest for the members of the Chicago Architectural Club. An exception was the Health Exhibition, which took place from mid-December through mid-January. One of the posters promoting the show was designed by Wilhelm Bernhard, who had won the previous year's competition for the development of a quarter section of land on the outskirts of Chicago. Bernhard's name often crops up in City Club notices recording some small task he had done for the club.

26. *City Club Bulletin* 8, no. 3 (February 24, 1915).

*Joseph Hudnut's design for a neighborhood center took third place in the City Club competition (CCB)*

men, many of whom were members of the Chicago Architectural Club, assisted in the preparation and mounting of the show, which occupied most of the City Club Building.[27] A comprehensive description was published in the *City Club Bulletin,* followed by an article describing the winners of the Neighborhood Center Competition, which was a centerpiece of the exhibition.[28]

The winners of the Neighborhood Center Competition, which was national in scope, were two women architects from New York, Anna Pendleton Schenck and Marcia Mead. Second place went to Chicago architects Guenzel & Drummond, and third place was divided between professor Joseph Hudnut of Auburn, Alabama, and civil engineer Carl Berg of Chicago. The jury for the final awards was made up of professor George H. Mead, chairman, Mary McKowell, Robert C. Spencer, Irving

27. Ibid., 71.

28. *City Club Bulletin* 8, no. 4 (March 23, 1915): 75–78, 81, 111.

*Anna P. Schenck and Marcia Mead won the City Club's competition for a neighborhood center (CCB)*

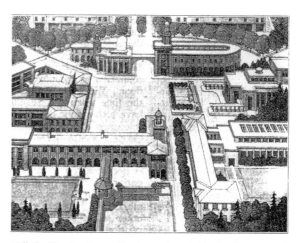

*Wilhelm Bernhard's contribution to the neighborhood center problem was part of his earlier submission for another competition for the design of a quarter section of land; these drawings appeared in the* City Club Bulletin *in 1915 (CCB)*

K. Pond, and Howard Van Doren Shaw. Charles Mulford Robinson was a consulting member. Four other plans were commended but not named as winners. Jens Jensen, Dwight H. Perkins, and Wilhelm Bernhard submitted noncompetitive plans. (Bernhard's plan was actually an elaboration of his winning entry for the development of a quarter-section of land in the City Club competition of a year earlier.) On March 5, shortly after the opening of the exhibition, the finalists discussed their entries at a meeting of the City Club. On March 9, the Illinois Chapter of the AIA held its regular monthly meeting at the City Club, where the finalists once again were present to explain their work.[29]

The City Club exhibition was open to the public from March 2 through April 15 of 1915. When it closed, parts of it traveled to various communities throughout Chicago. It was shown at the Women's Club of River Forest, a superb building designed by Guenzel & Drummond, and from there it went to the Rogers Park area of Chicago. It was well received at these and several other locations.

The Chicago Architectural Club's Twenty-eight Annual Exhibition in 1915 was held at the Art Institute April 8–28, overlapping the City Club exhibition. It was announced first in *Construction News* in mid-February,[30] where it was acknowledged that the exhibition would be a joint effort of the Chicago Architectural Club, the Illinois Chapter of the AIA, and the Illinois Society of Architects.[31] The announcement also mentioned that the AIA intended to offer a gold medal for the best design in the exhibition. It was also announced in the *Bulletin of the Art Institute of Chicago* on March 1 and again on April 1.[32] The second notice stated that "this year the Illinois Chapter of the American Institute of Architects, the Illinois Society of Architects, and the Art Institute have joined forces with the Chicago Architectural Club in managing and installing this exhibition." It also noted that "the Illinois Chapter has established a gold medal of honor as an award to designers of buildings represented in the annual exhibition." These were the first public notices of the exhibition and the combined efforts of the three architectural groups with the institute. There was, however, evidence that this cooperation had been planned for some time. In the minutes of a special meeting of the board of directors of the Illinois Society of Architects held on January 21, 1915, it was recorded that a "Report of the Exhibition Committee was given in reference to the coming Architectural Exhibition at the Art Institute wherein the expense of the exhibition was estimated not to exceed $2,000, of which amount the Art Institute would donate $1,000 and the remaining $1,000 expense would be divided equally between the Illinois Society of Architects, the Illinois Chapter A.I.A. and the Chicago Architectural Club . . . After some discussion on motion of Davidson, seconded by Barnes, the report was received and the offer accepted and the Committee notified of this fact."[33] Thus began a formal relationship between the Art Institute, the Illinois Society of Architects, the Illinois Chapter of the AIA, and the Chicago Architectural Club that would last for nearly twenty-five years.

Serious consideration had been given to forgoing an exhibition in 1915. The effort had simply become more than the club could deal with alone. Edwin F. Gillette, who had been president in 1912 during the beginning of a period of crisis for the club, wrote the foreword for the 1915 catalog. He observed that in the past, "these exhibitions had been undertaken, single-handed, by the Chicago Architectural Club . . . [but the] scope and magnitude of the affair have grown, through the years, without a corresponding increase in the club membership, until it had finally become a serious problem as to its proper handling without working an unnecessary hardship on the club." He went on to say that the "discontinuance of the Exhibition was seriously considered this year, unless outside assistance could be secured; and the question was taken up with the Art Institute, the Illinois Society

29. *Construction News* 38, no. 11 (March 13, 1915): 6.

30. *Construction News* 38, no. 9 (February 20, 1915): 7.

31. The Chicago Architects' Business Association changed its name to the Illinois Society of Architects on June 23, 1914.

32. *Bulletin of the Art Institute of Chicago* 9, no. 3 (March 1, 1915): 50, and *Bulletin of the Art Institute of Chicago* 9, no. 4 (April 1, 1915): 38.

33. Minutes, Illinois Society of Architects, Chicago Historical Society Special Collections, box 2, folder 2.

*The Lockby Court apartments by Schmidt, Garden & Martin won the AIA gold medal in 1915 (CAC/16)*

of Architects, and the Illinois Chapter American Institute of Architects, all of whom agreed to use their best efforts to carry forward the Architectural Exhibition, it being considered one of the principal features of the year." He described the efforts of each group and was pleased to conclude that the "Twenty-Eighth Annual Chicago Architectural Exhibition is opened to the public." He didn't point out that it was no longer the Chicago Architectural Club Exhibition, but was now the Chicago Architectural Exhibition.

The name was not the only change in the exhibition catalog. Each of the four sponsoring groups was given equal billing on the title page, and the officers, directors, committees, and membership lists of each of the three architectural organizations were included. Patrons continued to get their names and addresses listed. The Chicago Architectural Club Traveling Scholarship winners since 1901 were listed on their own page, as was the list of past winners of the AIA gold medal. The American Academy in Rome got two pages of descriptive material. There were 505 exhibits listed, some of which included more than one item. The greatest change was in the number of illustrations. After a dearth in the recent past, the 1915 catalog had sixty-eight illustrations about equally divided between drawings and photographs. There was a reasonable mix of local, state, and out-of-state architects, with a substantial number of student projects. These student projects had been on display at the University of Illinois for ten days starting on March 27, after having been shown at the annual national AIA convention in Washington, D.C., in December of 1914. The drawings actually arrived after the Chicago exhibition had opened and were not, therefore, on view the entire time.

Frank Lloyd Wright, whose presence had caused such a stir the year before, was not represented, but a mural for his Midway Gardens designed by John Norton was included. The catalog did not indicate the winner of the AIA gold medal, since it was awarded after the show opened. It went to Richard E. Schmidt, of Schmidt

*"An Oriental Fountain" by A. C. Webb, the Atelier Bennett-Rebori's only contribution to the 1915 exhibition (CAC/15)*

*"A Study in Superimposed Orders" by A. G. Mayger, one of ten installations in the 1915 exhibition from the Atelier Puckey (CAC/15)*

*John Norton's Midway Gardens mural design, from the 1915 exhibition (CAC/15)*

*Hewitt & Emerson's Mohammed Temple for Peoria, Illinois, is a strong statement of the early modern movement and foreshadows the art deco work of a decade later (WA)*

*Guenzel & Drummond's "Study for a Studio Building" from the 1915 exhibition (WA)*

34. Charles J. Mulligan (1866–1916) was a highly regarded sculptor who had studied with Lorado Taft. He died on March 25, 1916, a few days before the 1916 exhibit opened. It may have been because of his death that the sculpture for the City Club was never completed.

Garden & Martin for the design of Lockby Court, the Chase Apartments in Chicago, which had been exhibited in the 1914 show. The winner of the 1915 CAC Traveling Scholarship was Fred M. Hodgdon, for his design of "A Summer and Winter Garden." It was illustrated in the catalog, but the gold-medal, second-prize design, which went to Robert R. Cenek, was not. The Atelier Bennett-Rebori, which had a loose association with the Chicago Architectural Club, had only one exhibit illustrated, although six of Andrew Rebori's splendid drawings were included. The Atelier Puckey, which was sponsored by the club, had ten exhibits, two of which were shown in the catalog. Sculptor C. J. Mulligan's models for two decorative figures for the City Club Building by Pond & Pond were shown but not illustrated.[34] Oddly

*Charles Frost's design for the structure that later became the Navy Pier was first seen in the 1915 exhibition (CAC/15)*

*Schmidt, Garden & Martin's First National Bank in Pueblo, Colorado, clearly influenced by Louis Sullivan's work of twenty-five years earlier (CAC/15)*

enough, when the City Club Building was published in the *Brickbuilder* in 1912, these figures were shown in place.[35] The photograph had been retouched; the sculptures had never been carved. All concerned probably expected that the work would be executed in the near future. It never was.

The 1915 architectural exhibition was widely covered by both the popular and the professional press. No less than twenty articles appeared in various Chicago newspapers, a few before the opening and many after, but there were only a few critical comments. The *Bulletin of the Art Institute of Chicago* carried a review by Thomas E. Tallmadge, who covered the show carefully, with a number of references to "eclecticism." He wrote, "To illustrate the present tendency toward eclecticism, it might be of interest to enumerate the different architectural styles under which could be classed the principal exhibits: Classic 10, Gothic 16, Romanesque 4, Italian Renaissance 8, Spanish 1, Colonial and Georgian 8, Chinese 1, and the 'Western Style,' or as we sometimes call it, the 'Chicago School,' 28." He ended his review, "The increased attendance over previous years not only speaks well for the excellence of the exhibition but is indicative of an increased interest in architecture, which will surely be reflected in the better buildings of the future."

The first review in the professional press appeared in *Construction News* in early April shortly after the exhibition opened.[36] It was essentially a reported article with little critical comment except for a note about the very large number of attendees. The most widely distributed review was published by the *American*

35. *Brickbuilder* 21, no. 5 (May 1912): plate 57.

36. *Construction News* 37, no. 10 (April 10): 7.

37. *American Architect* 107, no. 2056 (May 19, 1915): 309–13.

*Architect*.[37] The well-illustrated article by an anonymous author noted that "no better means of measuring the architectural advance of this country can be had than that afforded by a study of this year's architectural exhibitions. Beginning with Pittsburgh and following the circuit to Boston, New York, Philadelphia, and thence to Chicago, one would recently have found himself viewing the twenty-eighth annual Chicago exhibition in the galleries of the Art Institute of that City." The reviewer acknowledged the recent problems of mounting the exhibition and described the cooperative efforts of the Art Institute and the three architectural societies of Chicago. He felt that the "result has been gratifying in the extreme . . . and it is felt that the influence and effect of this exhibition will be more far-reaching and beneficial than ever before." He was particularly impressed with the presentation of "city plans in the Middle West," of which there were several, but he was also pleased to find that in "almost every phase of modern architectural practice there was to be found examples among more than five hundred exhibits that indicated in general the temperamental qualities of the Western population and the ability of Western architects." He did not single out any specific buildings or designers, and the accompanying illustrations showed a broad representation of the exhibition. He ended his review with a listing of architects that was, as might be expected, heavily oriented toward Chicagoans.

At about the same time, the *Western Architect* covered the exhibition.[38] The article was certainly written by the magazine's editor, Robert Craik McLean. McLean opened with a brief history of the club and somewhat nostalgically recalled that the first exhibition of the club in 1886 was held primarily "to attract the attention of prospective members rather than for the edification of the laity . . . [and was] carried out with success . . . [and] the first exhibition of the first architectural club, is also the first architectural exhibition we have record of in this country."[39] McLean wrote of the club's concern about the "increasing demand for extension in its exhibition program . . . [and] that it had even contemplated the abandonment of the exhibition feature unless outside assistance could be secured." He, like other reviewers, went on to describe the cooperation between the Art Institute and the three Chicago architectural organizations, as well as the success of the 1915 exhi-

38. *Western Architect* 21, no. 5 (May 1915): 35.

39. McLean is not quite correct in stating that the Chicago club was the first club of its kind in the country, nor that its was the first exhibition. Both Boston and New York had clubs and exhibitions a few years earlier.

Peter B. Wight's portrait by Allen E. Philbrick (CHS)

Solon Spencer Beman, by Oliver D. Grover (CHS)

Dankmar Adler's portrait by Oskar Gross, now at Roosevelt University (CHS)

bition. He also wrote that "Chicago is an architecturally progressive city mainly because the architects and the contractors are progressive, one of the strongest indications being a uniform willingness to lend countenance to its architectural club enterprises, of which this annual exhibition is the most visible expression . . . The 1915 exhibition of the Chicago Architectural Club was one of the most successful and comprehensive ever given in that city." McLean's comments were widely read and his support was critical to the continued success of the club over the next two decades.

The cooperative effort of the Chicago Architectural Club, the Illinois Chapter of the AIA, and the Illinois Society of Architects to continue the annual exhibition at the Art Institute of Chicago was not the only way the three groups worked together. Shortly after the close of the exhibition, the *Chicago Tribune* published a brief item noting that the Illinois Chapter of the AIA was planning a "Hall of Fame" for Chicago architects.[40] The subhead of the article read "Foundation Laid at Annual Meeting of Illinois Chapter of American Institute of Architects." It went on to report that portraits of Daniel Hudson Burnham and Solon Spencer Beman had been presented to the chapter by their families. The "annual meeting" referred to had taken place on June 8 and was reported at some length in *Construction News*.[41] The AIA met at the Cliff Dwellers Club and one of the agenda items was the presentation of the portraits of Burnham and Beman. Following the unveiling, Louis Sullivan gave a moving oration on his longtime colleague and friend Solon Spencer Beman. He remarked, "I esteem it a high privilege to have known Mr. Beman as a friend as well as an architect." In what some might think as uncharacteristic of Sullivan, he also said that he felt that "in a large measure Mr. Beman was responsible for the creation of the true American type of architecture." Following the unveiling of the Burnham portrait, Charles L. Hutchinson, president of the Cliff Dwellers, called on Daniel Burnham's youngest son, Hubert, for a few words, after which Burnham was "eulogized in glowing terms by Charles H. Wacker, pres-

40. "Plan 'Hall of Fame' for Chicago Architects," *Chicago Tribune*, June 9, 1915.

41. *Construction News* 38, no. 24 (June 12, 1915): 6.

*Portrait of Daniel Hudson Burnham by Oliver D. Grover (CHS)*

*Frederick Baumann's portrait, by Oskar Gross (CHS)*

*William Le Baron Jenney's portrait, by Walter Ufer (CHS)*

ident of the Chicago Plan Commission." The final speaker of the evening was R. Clipston Sturgis, president of the national AIA, who had been invited to Chicago for the occasion.[42]

The Burnham and Beman portraits were presented in 1915, but the establishment of an architects' hall of fame had had its origin two years earlier at the annual meeting of the Illinois Chapter of the AIA.[43] The June 10, 1913, meeting, also held at the Cliff Dwellers Club, had been the occasion for the presentation of the first of several portraits of eminent Chicago architects, that of Peter B. Wight. The minutes of the meeting recorded that the chapter had "adopted a very unique and happy idea by which the fame of the men distinguished for their ability, attainments or devotion to the profession of architecture shall be carried down to posterity. It is proposed to collect the portraits of men thus distinguished . . . who placed their mark upon the architecture of this country. The first subject to be selected . . . is that of Peter B. Wight." The portrait by Allen E. Philbrick had been painted earlier and had been unveiled at the annual meeting of the chapter. An address by William W. Clay followed. Mr. Wight had been present and had "accepted the portrait [graciously]." Lawton Parker, Charles Francis Brown, and N. H. Carpenter, the secretary of the Art Institute, had also made brief remarks. Arthur Woltersdorf had been present and had recounted "how the idea of a collection of portraits of distinguished men had originated. The subject was one of the chance topics of discussion among a group of friends one afternoon last winter at the rooms of the Cliff Dwellers. Among those present, including himself, was Mr. Philbrick, the artist, Messrs. Beman and Weber—maybe there were others; and the more they talked about it the more they felt that it was a great opportunity to pay a tribute to the men who were so worthy of it. Mr. Philbrick had very generously offered to paint the first portrait. He said, however, that if he did so, he must be allowed to select his own subject. 'There is one man among you who has marked characteristics, and to who I think I can do justice. That man is Peter B. Wight.' We grew enthusiastic about the matter and Mr. Philbrick was encouraged to go about his work. Mr. Wight was approached and after some hesitancy he accepted the honor."

As the afternoon had progressed other names had been suggested for future portraits, including Dankmar Adler, William Le Baron Jenney, Daniel H. Burnham, and John W. Root. The group had thought it might add one or two each year, and did so for many years. As the portraits were prepared, they were hung in the club room at the Art Institute of Chicago. Eventually the collection included those already mentioned, plus Louis H. Sullivan, Frederick Baumann, and others. A bronze bust of Root, done by Johannes Gelert several years earlier, was added to the collection, and a portrait of Root done in lithographic chalk by P. B. Wight was presented to the chapter as well.[44] While the project was an AIA effort, every portrait was of a man who either was a member of or had a close relationship with the Chicago Architectural Club.

❀

During the first week of May 1915, following the close of the annual exhibition on April 28, the Chicago Architectural Club met in the club room of the Art Institute and elected officers for the coming year. The election of the 1914–15 officers had been overshadowed by the conflicts surrounding the 1914 exhibition and the results hadn't made it into print until the release of the 1915 exhibition catalog. George Awsumb had been elected president in 1914, and Ralph C. Llewellyn had served with him as vice president along with Gifford Brabant and Fritz Wagner Jr.

42. The remarks of Sullivan, Wacker, and Sturgis were all published in later editions of *Construction News*.

43. *Construction News* 35, no. 24 (June 14, 1913): 15.

44. The AIA portrait gallery eventually grew to have at least eighteen paintings plus three bronzes. They were hung in the club room of the Art Institute until 1924, when the AIA was asked to remove them. They then stayed, for about a year, at the University Club, until the Kimball House was ready for occupancy in early 1925. They remained there until the AIA left around 1938. The portraits were then put in storage until 1943, when they were given to the Chicago Historical Society. Most are still there, but only the portrait of Louis H. Sullivan and the bronze of John W. Root are permanently displayed.

as secretary and treasurer, respectively. Ralph C. Llewellyn was moved up to president for 1915–16, the first second-generation member of the club to so serve. Harry H. Bentley, a 1914–15 director, was elected vice president. Gifford Brabant and Fritz Wagner Jr. were reelected secretary and treasurer, respectively. The club continued the policy of choosing directors for two-year terms. Herbert E. Downton and J. Bernard Mullen had been elected for two-year terms the year before, and they moved up to the class of 1917. George Awsumb, the previous year's president, was asked to serve with them in lieu of Robert J. Love, who remained for another two-year term. John C. Leavell and Louis C. Vogel filled out the directors' positions. Thus, the entire slate for the previous year was reelected, albeit in different positions. Apparently the membership felt that the work done under these men should be continued. Standing committees were handled in a similar fashion. Customarily, the president served ex officio on all committees, so Llewellyn was not named to any club committee. The previous year's president, George Awsumb, essentially took his place. No new names appeared.

Plans began almost immediately for the 1916 exhibition, and it was hoped that the momentum of 1915 would continue. The cooperative efforts of the three architectural organizations had been so successful that the decision to continue in that vein was made early in the fall of 1915. The Exhibition Committee, which included members from the AIA, the ISA, and the CAC, did change somewhat but by no means completely. Once again, nearly all the participants were current or past members of the Chicago Architectural Club, and there was overlap in several other cases. Ralph C. Llewellyn was president of the CAC but also served on the Exhibition Committee representing the Illinois Chapter of the AIA. The only real change in the organization of the committee was in the Jury of Admission. In 1915 there had been only three members, I. K. Pond, H. M. G. Garden, and Andrew N. Rebori. In 1916 Pond was the only holdover and the committee was enlarged to ten mostly older men. Martin Roche, F. W. Perkins, E. C. Jensen, F. C. Bartlett, Oliver D. Grover, Charles J. Mulligan, John Holabird, Allen Philbrick, and Charles H. Prindeville made up the jury. They were not all architects. The group had decided that future exhibitions would show the work of related arts, and Philbrick, Grover, and Mulligan (two painters and a sculptor) were considered appropriate jurors from related fields. Unfortunately, Mulligan's untimely death in March of 1916 prevented him from serving a full term.

The club also reinstituted something that had been missing for some time. While it did not publish a syllabus, it did begin to report regularly on its activities again. Nearly every month the meetings were reported in the professional press, sometimes several meetings at one time. The November 27 issue of *Construction News* noted that the club "plans a most active season for the entertainment of its members." It went on to describe what was expected and concluded by noting that the club was "also doing a great deal to encourage its members to participate in architectural competitions and the results attained are most gratifying to the educational committee."[45] Both the Illinois Chapter of the AIA and the Illinois Society of Architects also made a point of reporting their activities to the press. These two groups were now extremely active, and their regularly published reports indicate that they nearly always invited the Chicago Architectural Club members to their meetings. The club reciprocated, but its most ambitious work was once again having regular speakers and sketch nights on alternate Monday evenings at the Art Institute club rooms. It also continued its atelier classes in the drafting rooms used during the day by the students of the School of the Art Institute. This double-duty use soon became a problem, and I. K. Pond reported to his colleagues at the Illinois Chapter of the AIA that the "matter has been arranged by the renting of a suitable

45. *Construction News* 40, no. 22 (November 27, 1915): 4.

*Pond & Pond's design for the University of Michigan Union Building, exhibited in 1915 (CAC/15)*

*Perkins, Fellows & Hamilton's final design for the Pontiac, Michigan, High School, also exhibited in 1915 (CAC/15)*

room in Plymouth Court, where special night work is continued, while the meetings of the club will continue to be held in the Art Institute, which will also house the library, as heretofore."[46] Apparently this proved only partially successful, since the address of the club was given in the 1916 exhibition catalog as the Art Institute, but by 1917, and again in 1918, it was given as 332 Plymouth Court, directly across the street from the City Club.

Nineteen fifteen ended three years of uncertainty for the Chicago Architectural Club. It counted 168 members in all categories—102 were regular members and the rest were associates, nonresidents, allied, and honorary members. Of the regular members, there had been about a dozen who had carried the load of the organization and done the work. Except for the atelier, which was fairly well established under the direction of patron Francis W. Puckey, meetings had been sparsely attended, especially in 1913 and 1914. When the club had seen fit to ask for help from the Illinois Chapter of the AIA and the Illinois Society of Architects, it had been somewhat revitalized. The forced move out of the drafting rooms of the Art Institute into a space of its own had had an additional positive effect.

There had been a brief glimpse of things to come when the possibility of war with Mexico was raised in April 1914. The skirmish had ended when the insurgents in Mexico backed down, but a month later World War I had begun, following the assassination of Archduke Francis Ferdinand, heir to Austria-Hungary's throne, on June 28, 1914, in Sarajevo. Although the United States did not enter the war until the spring of 1917, many of the younger members of the Chicago Architectural Club had been called to military duty, which had had a considerable impact on the activities of the club. It had been forced to cancel the Traveling Scholarship Competition, which had already been announced in early 1916. On the other hand, the problems of the previous three years had brought about a coalition of architectural organizations that would last for many years, during which time the Chicago Architectural Club would once again flourish.

46. *Construction News* 40, no. 20 (November 13, 1915): 5.

*Mural design by Alfonso Iannelli, shown in the 1916 exhibition (courtesy David Jameson)*

# Wartime and Decline

CHAPTER SEVENTEEN

Nineteen fifteen marked the end of the reign of the Chicago Architectural Club as the premier organization of architects in Chicago. It was now, for all intents and purposes, one of three equally influential organizations. The Illinois Chapter of the American Institute of Architects had steadily increased its membership and activities during the previous fifteen years, and the Illinois Society of Architects was by far the largest professional organization of architects in the state. Its 1916 *Handbook for Architects and Builders*, which listed the membership of each organization at the end of 1915, named 150 members of the statewide Illinois Chapter of the AIA in all categories (most from the Chicago metropolitan area), 375 members of the ISA, and only 114 members of the Chicago Architectural Club. Five years earlier, it had listed only 91 members of the AIA, 149 members of the ISA, and 155 members of the Chicago Architectural Club. The club had gone from being the largest of the three groups to the smallest, perhaps because the active members had grown older and moved on while fewer young men participated. There was a great deal of cross-membership. Nearly all the members of the AIA had been or still were members of the club, as were many members of the ISA. The ISA was genuinely statewide, which accounted for its much larger membership. The AIA and the ISA, of course, required their members to be architects, which the Chicago Architectural Club did not. In any case, by 1915 there was a great deal of cooperation between the three groups, each with its own mission.

The AIA addressed primarily aesthetic and ethical problems, and was part of the national organization of architects. The ISA was focused largely on city and state legislative activities and the business of architecture statewide. The Chicago Architectural Club had always been oriented toward the education of aspiring practitioners and younger men in particular. It had also set aside time for (sometimes raucous) entertainment for its members. Lectures and other presentations by prominent members of the profession continued to be an important aspect of its activities.

The club was faced with two major problems at the end of 1915. The war in Europe had reached a point where it was impossible for the club to offer its annual Traveling Scholarship. The competition was announced in 1916, but apparently never completed. The catalog that year stated, "The sixteenth annual traveling scholarship will be held in May of this year. Announcement of the subject of the

*Charles Morgan's design for the cover of the 1916 architectural exhibition (CAC/16)*

competition and of the successful competitors will be made in due course."[1] No evidence of any further action on the competition has come to light. The 1917 catalog stated that "the European Traveling Scholarship was temporarily discontinued in 1916, and will not be resumed until after the close of the war. This year an American Traveling Scholarship will be awarded; the winner will spend two months traveling in the East, primarily for the study of Colonial Architecture. Prizes aggregating $325 have been generously donated by the Chicago Face Brick Association." That scholarship was awarded in 1917, but not in 1918 or 1919. In 1920, the Traveling Scholarship Competition was reinstituted.

The second problem the club faced in late 1915 and 1916 was the draft. Club members were generally young and eligible for service in the armed forces. Many volunteered and others were conscripted. The AIA and the ISA had the same problem to a lesser degree. By 1917, the Illinois Society of Architects was listing an "Honor Roll" of architects in the military, and in 1918 the exhibition catalog noted those members in each group who were "in the service of their country." The club, although the smallest group, had by far the largest number in the military, obviously because of their relative youth. In 1919, the club's annual catalog listed several members who had died in the service. The roll of members of the Chicago Architectural Club was diminishing. The leadership made a valiant effort to stem the flow.

In the fall of 1915, the club had begun to publish its forthcoming meetings for the first time in several years. Proposed activities were announced in the local and professional press, along with the names of speakers and other scheduled events. The club's meetings during this period were held in the club room of the Art Institute of Chicago. The AIA and the ISA also held most of their meetings there. It was a congenial place, and the walls were beginning to be hung with portraits of Chicago's "hall of fame" architects.[2] The great shortcoming of the club room was that it had to be shared with numerous other arts-oriented groups, so it was not always available. When the club had been forced to move its atelier to another space on Plymouth Court, it had started using that space for its regular meetings. There was room for its atelier, and when needed, the room could be cleared for seating of members at lectures or other events. During club competitions or sketching evenings, the members took over the drafting tables used by the students of the atelier. It was not an ideal situation, but it did give members a place to relax after hours, read the latest professional journals, and socialize with their colleagues.

Nineteen sixteen began with an announcement that the "twenty-ninth annual architectural exhibition given by the Chicago Architectural Club of Illinois, Society of Architects of Illinois, League of American Institute of Architects, and the Art Institute of Chicago will be held in the galleries of the institute April 6 to April 23."[3] Although all three organizations' names were wrong, the basic information, including the dates, was correct. The same article announced that "an open competition for a design for a cover of an exhibit catalogue which may also be otherwise used in advertising. Prizes will be awarded in sums of $25, $15, and $10, and two honorable mentions will also be made." The winner was Charles L. Morgan, whose renderings would become legendary during the next two decades. Robert L. Wachter took second place. Third prize and two honorable mentions were awarded to three women, Ruth Wilson, Kathryn Holmes, and Hazel Traxler. Morgan's design was used on the cover of the catalog. The "advertising" referred to was the use of the cover design as a poster distributed around the city and in news items concerning the exhibition.[4] The competition was also announced twice in *Construction News*, along with information on the forthcoming exhibition. The practice of holding an annual competition for the catalog cover was continued every year through 1920.

1. *Twenty-Ninth Annual Chicago Architectural Exhibition* (Chicago Architectural Club, Illinois Society of Architects, Illinois Chapter of the AIA, Art Institute of Chicago, 1916).

2. Ultimately, more than twenty portraits, drawings, and busts of architects were exhibited in the club room. Eventually, most of the portraits were transferred to the Chicago Historical Society, where all but two are in storage: the bust of John W. Root is on display in the lobby and Sullivan's portrait is on permanent exhibit. The portrait of Dankmar Adler is on display in the lobby of the Auditorium Building, Daniel Burnham's portrait is in the Burnham Library, and the Perkins portrait is in the hands of his family.

3. "Decorative Design Competition," *Chicago Commerce*, January 21, 1916.

4. A copy of one of the posters is in the author's collection. It is the same as the cover of the catalog, but with wide margins.

During this period, the catalogs all had a similar look. The covers became classical in design, and the format of the content was always essentially the same. Equal credit was given to the three sponsoring groups, with the Art Institute always named as a cooperating organization. The exhibitions were always held in April, occasionally extending a few days into May. A careful review of the contents of the catalogs suggests that the Beaux-Arts was becoming more and more of a force in mid-America.

The annual Illinois Chapter AIA gold medal, awarded in 1915 after a year's hiatus, was offered again in 1916 and subsequent years, but no announcement of a winner was ever published. An unusual aspect of the announcement for the 1916 exhibition was the statement that any exhibits "which are to be sent to the T-Square Exhibition in Philadelphia, opening on May 6, should be clearly designated . . . and by mutual agreement . . . the shipment of such exhibits will be expedited so as to insure their arrival in Philadelphia in time for admission."[5]

While preparations for the exhibition were under way, another exhibition, this one of student work, was also being shown. The national AIA convention had been held in Washington, D.C., the previous December, and ten of the leading schools of architecture had been invited by the American Federation of Arts to submit work for exhibition at the Corcoran Gallery during the convention. Nine of the ten schools responded. After the convention, the exhibition traveled to each of the schools for further showing, arriving at the University of Illinois in March 1916. It opened on March 27 for ten days, after which it was sent to Chicago for the Twenty-ninth Annual Exhibition.[6] Over two hundred examples of student work were exhibited, although they were not assigned numbers in the catalog.

When the 1916 exhibition opened, the catalog listed 452 items. With the student work, it added up to more than 650 exhibits. Six galleries were required to mount the exhibition. For the first time, the catalog featured a color frontispiece, a perspective of Goodhue's proposed, but never built, Grace Church in Chicago. There were a number of drawings included in the exhibition and in the catalog that had more than casual interest. Several were from Chicago, but others were from downstate and elsewhere. For reasons now lost, the Twenty-ninth Annual

H. Wallebrecht, a student at the Chicago School of Architecture, exhibited this design for " A Municipal Campanile" (CAC/16)

5. *Construction News* 50, no. 4 (January 22, 1916): 5, and *Construction News* 50, no. 6 (February 5, 1916): 5.

6. "Many Drawings to Be Shown," *Champaign Illinois Gazette*, March 14, 1916.

James B. Dibelka's "Sketch for an Armory," clearly a modern building (CAC/16)

*John Holabird and John W. Root Jr. designed this studio as much as a party place as for business (CAC/16)*

7. Louise James Bargelt, "Art" *Chicago Tribune,* April 6, 1916; Louise James Bargelt, "In the Field of Art," *Chicago Tribune,* April 7, 1916; and Louise James Bargelt, "Art," *Chicago Tribune,* April 9, 1916.

8. Lena M. McCauley, "Art & Artists," *Chicago Post,* April 15, 1916.

9. Albrecht Montgelas, "Bragdon Star of Exhibition," *Chicago Examiner,* April 7, 1916.

Exhibition was one of the few photographed in situ. Those photographs illustrate how the exhibition was hung, and many of the illustrations in the catalog can be clearly seen.

A cursory examination of the catalog suggests that it was reasonably well edited, but published reviews often commented on exhibits that were not illustrated. Some reviewers wrote of the exhibition more than once. Louise James Bargelt penned three items, the first a fairly straightforward column covering a number of the exhibits, with special attention to Alfonso Iannelli's entry for "mural decorations for the Academy theater."[7] She called it a "weird conglomeration of colorful figures and designs . . . strikingly attractive." The next day, in another column, she used Iannelli's mural as an illustration. It was clearly an outgrowth of Iannelli's California poster designs, which had brought him to the attention of Frank Lloyd Wright, who asked him to help out with similar designs for the Midway Gardens. In her third article, Bargelt used the catalog cover as an illustration but then wrote primarily about other exhibits in place at the Art Institute at the same time.

Local newspaper reviews were generally favorable, with a few exhibits getting the lion's share of attention. One of the more unusual was a model of the proposed Madison Street bridge designed to cross the Chicago River on the west side of Chicago's Loop. It was a direct result of efforts by the AIA to influence the design of public works. Virtually every local press review lauded the work of Claude Bragdon, who exhibited a number of black-and-white drawings he had prepared for his recently published book, *Projective Ornament.* Those drawings, of course, were not really architectural. They were but one of the displays of nonarchitectural items in the exhibition. Lena M. McCauley wrote in the *Chicago Post* that the exhibition "received additional interest in water-color drawings by the talented young Frenchman, Ferdinand [*sic*] Janin, who was associated with Mr. Burnham and Mr. Bennett in the preparation of the Chicago Plan drawings."[8] Apparently these drawings were not officially part of the exhibition, but were hung nevertheless, since Ms. McCauley went on to say, "They are a delightful addition to gallery 52, in which are the English water colors loaned by Mr. Roche and others and the travel sketches by Edmund Campbell. Mr. Janin died several years ago, and his paintings are loaned by S. A. Marx." The Campbell drawings were listed in the catalog, and three watercolors under S. A. Marx's name were listed but not identified as being by Fernand Janin. The items loaned by Martin Roche included two pencil sketches by J. A. Haig and twelve originals by Joseph Nash.

One reviewer stated that Bragdon's was "the most interesting exhibit . . . [and] . . . strikes almost the only original note in what is to the greatest part a display of skill in imitating the work of the geniuses of former centuries."[9] The same writer ended his review with a note on the student drawings: "I should imagine that an institution like the Carnegie Institute of Technology has more important problems for its students to solve than the 'treatment of the banks of a river' in the fashion here presented." Similar comments regarding the exhibition as a whole were published by most of the Chicago papers. They provide a glimpse of what was happening to the vitality of the Chicago Architectural Club and to the education of architects in America. The club was no longer seeking a new architecture, but was looking to the past for inspiration.

In 1916 the Chicago Architectural Club was struggling to maintain its place in the world of architecture. Much of its original educational work had been taken up by the emerging architectural schools in America. Only three such schools had existed

*G. L. Barnum, a student at the Atelier Puckey, showed this Sullivanesque design for "A Safety Deposit Vault Building" (CAC/16)*

when the club was formed in 1885, and by 1916 nearly twenty schools were offering formal training in architecture. Virtually all these institutions followed the system developed by the École des Beaux-Arts in Paris. Furthermore, the Beaux-Arts Society of Architects, formed in 1894 by men who had attended the École, now had ateliers—offices where training was offered following the École system—in virtually every major city of the United States. The Chicago Architectural Club was significantly influenced by all this. The creative innovators who directed the club's activities during its heyday just before and after the turn of the century had grown older, attained professional status, and were now generally active in the AIA or the ISA instead of working long hours to energize the members of the Chicago Architectural Club. It was easier and less demanding to follow the lead of the Beaux-Arts Society of Architects.

At the state-sponsored École des Beaux-Arts in Paris, virtually all the design problems assigned to students were worked out in ateliers, while other subjects were covered in classrooms on the quai Malaquais and the rue Bonaparte.[10] The École required prospective students to pass rather stringent exams in mathematics, languages, and history, but there was no requirement that students actually attend classes. Architecture students in Paris were required to either join or be assigned to an atelier, where most of their work was done under the supervision of a patron. Their assignments in design, which lasted from a few days to several weeks, were judged by the faculty with the help of senior practicing architects. Deadlines for completion were absolute and late projects were not accepted.[11] Students could attend as many, or as few, classes as they wished. Examinations were offered from time to time, and passing grades earned *valeurs*. After a certain number of these were credited, the student would earn either a Certificat d'Etudes de l'École, which usually took about two to three years, or for a greater number of *valeurs* and related experience, a Diplome d'Architecte, the highest honor granted by the École. Few foreign students remained at the École long enough to receive the Certificat, much less the Diplome d'Architecte. The first Chicagoan to be so honored was Theodore W. Pietsch in January of 1898. He spoke to the Chicago Architectural Club at various times after his return to the United States but never became a member. Louis Sullivan was an example of a short-term student. He was in Paris less than a year.[12] Nevertheless, even attendance without completing the work was considered a mark of distinction. Sullivan never repudiated the somewhat limited training he received in Paris. To the end of his life he felt that the discipline imposed by the Beaux-Arts system was of great benefit to him and would have been the same to his younger colleagues.

10. The École des Beaux-Arts was closed in 1968, but the buildings still survive. An excellent explanation of how the school operated in the late nineteenth and early twentieth centuries is in Russell Sturgis, ed., *A Dictionary of Architecture and Building*, vol. 3 (New York: Macmillan, 1904), 434 et seq.

11. The word *charrette*, still used to describe working long hours to meet a deadline, comes from the French word for "cart." Supposedly, students would transport their huge drawings to the school in a cart, where they would continue to put on the final touches while en route.

12. Probably the best account of Sullivan's stay in Paris during his time at the school is Robert Twombly, *Louis Sullivan, His Life and Work* (New York: Viking, 1986), 56–76.

*Claude Bragdon's multi-plate exhibit at the 1916 architectural exhibition (AIC)*

The ateliers in the United States established by the Society of Beaux-Arts Architects quickly became one of the primary methods of architectural education in the late nineteenth and early twentieth centuries. These ateliers rarely required work other than design problems. The Atelier Bennett—which later became the Atelier Bennett-Rebori, and was finally headed by Rebori alone—had a loose association with the Chicago Architectural Club and was led by École-trained men. The club's own atelier, under the direction of Francis W. Puckey, who had also attended the École, allowed the club to remain active on a different level. It was still the young architects' group, and as such, provided entertainment and lectures by older members of the profession. Most important, it continued to be the driving force behind the annual architectural exhibition at the Art Institute of Chicago. One indication of its continuing influence on the professional community was a signed editorial in the *Western Architect* by Robert Craik McLean in December 1916.[13] Commenting on the recent AIA convention in Minneapolis, McLean expressed his disappointment that in the "prolonged discussion" of education, one aspect was neglected: "that of the Architectural clubs of the country in their development of the employed draftsmen, was not mentioned . . . [and that] . . . Of Chicago's representation at the convention, fourteen in number, all were of that spiritually connected guild which is actively engaged in giving a vitality and a new meaning to architecture in the Middle West. Thirteen of the fourteen are 'graduates' from the Chicago Architectural Club." McLean was not about to concede that the architectural clubs in America had outlived their time. Enough young Chicagoans agreed, allowing the Chicago Architectural Club to continue as a major, albeit smaller, force in the early modern movement in architecture.

McLean had already demonstrated his continuing support of the club earlier when he wrote a lengthy and largely positive review of the 1916 exhibition in the

13. *Western Architect* 24, no. 6 (December 1916): 148–52.

*Three views of the 1916 Chicago architectural exhibition in situ at the Art Institute of Chicago (AIC)*

April issue of the *Western Architect*.[14] He began his comments by acknowledging the cooperation between the AIA, the ISA, the club, and the Art Institute. The article was heavily illustrated, but it was more a discussion of the importance of the club and its contribution to the profession than any real criticism of the exhibition. He was particularly pleased with the cooperative efforts. He stated that the "new arrangement by which the entire profession in Illinois contributes to its success is most indicative of what should have been done years ago in recognition and co-operation by the architects of the city and state." It was that cooperation that secured the future of the Chicago Architectural Club for the next twenty years.

McLean's attitude toward Chicago had always been positive, even after he moved to Minneapolis to serve as editor of the *Western Architect*. Early on, however, he had not been enamored of the work of the young rebel architects of the Midwest, at first called the Chicago School and later known as the Prairie School. His attitude changed after the first decade of the twentieth century. In 1911, he published a comprehensive article on Frank Lloyd Wright, covering his City National Bank in Mason City, Iowa,[15] and in 1912 and 1913 he published two major articles on the work of Walter Burley Griffin. From 1913 through 1916 there was an absolute plethora of articles concerning the work of the avant-garde practitioners of the Midwest. During this period, there were nearly a dozen special issues of the *Western Architect* devoted entirely, or nearly so, to individual avant-garde Midwestern architects. In addition to Wright, there were issues on Purcell & Elmslie, Walter Burley Griffin, George W. Maher, Spencer & Powers, and Guenzel & Drummond, as well as John S. Van Bergen and Tallmadge & Watson. There were also a number of articles, usually by McLean, concerning work by lesser-known proponents of the new movement, such as Elmer Grey, Ottenheimer, Stern & Reichert, Wolfe & Lenzen, Cannon & Fetzer, and George Nimmons, who were producing work that was obviously influenced by Midwesterners, most of whom claimed allegiance to Louis Sullivan or, to a lesser degree, Frank Lloyd Wright. It was not at all unusual for the *Western Architect* to publish illustrations of work without accompanying text. McLean also continued to publish articles regarding the value of architectural clubs and, invariably, he used the Chicago Architectural Club as an example. Unfortunately, most other magazines, particularly those published for laymen, were concentrating on classical revival architecture.

It has been suggested that the demise of avant-garde movement was due, primarily, to the publication of architecture based on the revival of historic styles in architectural and homemakers' journals.[16] There is no question that these publications had a great impact on architecture, particularly domestic architecture. Domestic architecture was not, however, the only work that changed during this period. Public and commercial architecture also began to reflect the classical revival styles, although not to as great a degree or as quickly as has sometimes been suggested. It seems more likely that there was a broad acceptance of the teachings of men who had been trained at the École des Beaux-Arts during this time. Nevertheless, the work and theories of Louis Sullivan and his adherents were flourishing simultaneously.

By 1916, the Society of Beaux-Arts Architects had existed for some twenty years and its educational arm, the Beaux-Arts Institute of Design, had been advocating the society's system of education for more than a decade through its ateliers and members' influence as teachers in the various schools of architecture. While this system was modeled on the one developed over many years in France, it was not the same. The École in Paris did not provide students with a well-grounded background in the liberal arts, and design problems were almost always on a monumental scale. When architectural education began in America, it was deemed important that it be part of a much broader education, and instead of working in

14. Robert Craik McLean, "The Chicago Architectural Exhibition of 1916," *Western Architect* 23, no. 4 (April 1916): 32–35.

15. *Western Architect* 17, no. 12 (December 1911).

16. H. Allen Brooks discusses this phenomenon at some length in *The Prairie School* in his final chapter, "The Demise of the Prairie School." I am in general agreement with Brooks in his attribution of the change in domestic architecture to the advent of homemakers' journals and various other influences, but I believe that they were not the only factors that contributed to the change in clients' tastes, particularly in business and commercial buildings during this period. The automobile, radio, and a wide range of other emerging modern amenities would all have affected the taste of clients in the period after the First World War.

outside offices, most design work was expected to be done at classroom drafting tables, with practicing architects looking on.

Of the first three schools to offer architectural degrees in the United States—Massachusetts Institute of Technology beginning in 1868, Cornell in 1871, and the University of Illinois in 1873—only MIT was headed by a man (William R. Ware) whose background included a year at the École des Beaux-Arts. The head of Cornell, Charles Babcock, had earned a B.A. before entering the early office atelier of Richard Upjohn, where he received the bulk of his architectural education. The University of Illinois was headed by Nathan Ricker, who was the first graduate to be awarded a degree in architecture in the United States, and was then immediately appointed head of the school's new Department of Architecture. These men all felt strongly that the education of architects required something more than work in an office, and they set up programs that emphasized a broad education in architecture. Nevertheless, much of the École system still survived in those schools, particularly MIT. As time passed and other schools were established, most programs had several faculty members who believed strongly in the teachings of the École. Although students worked in classroom drafting rooms instead of the offices of architects, and attendance at other classes was mandatory, they were encouraged to get office experience during vacation periods or after hours.

When the Society of Beaux-Arts Architects set up its programs for ateliers throughout the United States in 1903, the intent was to teach young men essentially as they had been taught in Paris. It was seen as a way for young men to learn architecture while earning a living. Many American ateliers operated in locations other than private offices, and in most cases the patron charged a small fee. Often the ateliers were sponsored by architectural clubs or members of such clubs. So it was in Chicago. The Society of Beaux-Arts Architects had a policy of promoting its system to as wide an audience as possible. In fact, the bylaws of the society specifically stated that "a local Committee may be appointed to carry on the work of the Society in any town or district where three or more members or associate members of the Society in good standing, reside." Those members were encouraged to establish ateliers.

A basic policy of the society's system was to emphasize the classic historic styles and, for the most part, to adapt those styles to modern needs. It was difficult, if not impossible, for École-trained men to understand, much less endorse, the avant-garde work that had begun with Louis Sullivan and his young disciples in Chicago. Nevertheless, many were interested in developing an architecture that was truly American. The core group of young men who were most active in the Chicago Architectural Club never forgot this goal. As members matured and moved on to the AIA and the ISA, the subject of an American architecture was often brought to the fore. For example, as noted earlier, in 1912 it was reported that the Illinois Chapter of the AIA had "requested George W. Maher and Dwight H. Perkins to put into words accurately defining in so far as it is possible what is called by some progressive architecture, or the progressive spirit in architecture, which is now making itself felt, particularly in the Middle West with indications of it cropping out at other points, in order that those who are working to that end, and others who want to know what they are doing, may know just what it means. A definition is wanted of the work of just such men as Louis H. Sullivan, who has been looked upon as the founder of the school, along with whom may be associated Irving K. Pond, George W. Maher, and a number of others whose names do not readily come to mind. It is proposed to crystallize it, to give it a name and to make a place for it in the world's history."[17] There had been a lengthy discussion concerning the suggestion, after which George W. Maher, Dwight H. Perkins, and Arthur

17. *Construction News* 34, no. 25 (December 21, 1912): 12–13.

*"A Free Standing Tablet," an Atelier Puckey entry in the 1916 exhibition by F. C. Mueller (CAC/16)*

18. *Construction News* 35, no. 4 (January 25, 1913): 13.

19. The motion passed but there is no evidence that the proposed definition was ever accepted or published by the national organization of the AIA.

20. These names are from the yearbook of the Society of Beaux-Arts Architects, published in 1929.

21. These publications began around 1909 and continued for several years. Typically, they included a brief statement by the jury regarding the competition as a whole, followed by a list of the individuals who received at least a mention from the jury.

22. The grading system of the Society of Beaux-Arts Architects followed the one used in Paris: "x" was an unacceptable entry, "pass" was the lowest passing grade, and above "pass," in ascending order, were "half mention," "mention," "first mention," and "first mention place," the highest grade. This system, sometimes with minor variations, was used by most schools of architecture in the United States from around 1910 through the mid-twentieth century.

Woltersdorf had agreed to consider the preparation of such a definition. At the next meeting of the chapter, Perkins had presented the following motion:[18]

> That a committee be appointed whose duty it shall be to formulate a statement relating to American architecture, or modern design as distinct from classic or renaissance models. Examples of modern work in this spirit already exist in various localities in the United States, particularly in the Middle West, in numbers sufficient to entitle this tendency to recognition.
>
> It is the most clearly defined product of democratic ideals which has yet found expression in the art of architecture, in this country. It aims to adapt the principles which produced the great work of the past to modern conditions, and to create in accordance with them an architecture which shall be to our civilization what the Doric was to that of Greece.
>
> I also move that this committee be instructed to include in its statement an earnest recommendation to the American Institute of Architects that this tendency be recognized and illustrated by its official journal.[19]

A careful reading of the above resolution suggests that the architects of Chicago were not rejecting the teachings of the École or those members of the society who advocated the teachings in America. What they were advocating was that the society use the system developed at the École to define and develop an understanding of American architecture.

A review of the membership records of the Society of Beaux-Arts Architects indicates that by 1908 there were three members in Chicago, William E. Parsons, E. H. Bennett, and Francis W. Puckey.[20] Of these men, only Parsons became a member of the Chicago Architectural Club, but each of them eventually became the patron of an atelier with some connection to the club. Bennett was the first to do so. Work from his atelier was shown at the 1909 Chicago Architectural Club exhibition, and again in 1911, 1912, and 1914. The 1914 material was from the Bennett-Rebori atelier. Andrew Rebori, who became a club member in 1914, was never a member of the Society of Beaux-Arts Architects, but he did attend the École des Beaux-Arts and would have been eligible to be a member. Bennett's atelier was absorbed by the club in 1916, when Francis W. Puckey was named patron.

It was the practice of the Society of Beaux-Arts Architects to publish a "Criticism by the Jury" and an "Award of the Jury" for local competitions by various ateliers.[21] The great majority of those receiving "mentions" or better, often a hundred or more, were from eastern ateliers or universities.[22] Of the western submissions, Washington University in St. Louis was often noted, and the Armour Institute of Chicago (part of a joint effort with the Art Institute of Chicago) appeared on the list from time to time. The first listing from Chicago was in March of 1909, when F. C. Walker and A. S. Ingeman, both from Atelier Bennett, received mentions. Walker was a member of the Chicago Architectural Club; Ingeman was not. In April of 1909, R. Wolff received a first mention, and H. E. Davis and F. G. Kartowicm also got mentions. All were in the Bennett atelier, but only Wolff was a member of the club. In this same competition, the Chicago Architectural Club atelier was noted for the first time, although no patron was named. C. E. K. Rabig was listed as receiving a mention. As might be expected, he was a member of the club. In June of the same year, H. S. Marquand and P. T. Johnston of the Bennett atelier received mentions, and R. P. Corse of the club's atelier was also named. Only Corse was a member of the club. During the next few years, Chicago would be listed from time to time, but the great majority of winners continued to be from the eastern ateliers and schools. In January 1911, however, the Armour Institute of Technology had four students listed: R. H. Peters, C. M. Brown, A. D. Gibbs, and J. H. Bischof. They weren't members of the club, although George Vrooman, who was in the club atelier and was a member, also received a mention at the same time. Three members of the Bennett atelier—A. C. Gustafson, F. W. Morse, and C. H. Sierkes—all got mentions in January. Of these, only Sierkes was a member of the club. Two months later, the Armour Institute had twenty members (almost its entire class, and more than any other institution) listed as receiving mentions. At the same time, the Bennett atelier and the Chicago Architectural Club atelier each received only one mention. When one reviews the lists of those winners of mentions or better during this period, it is clear that the ateliers and schools where the Beaux-Arts system was most rigorously adhered to were the most often cited.

A review of the winners of the traveling scholarships awarded by the Chicago Architectural Club between 1901 and 1916 makes it clear that starting in 1908 the winners were those men who, if not trained in Beaux-Arts ateliers or schools, followed the basic rules set down by the Society of Beaux-Arts Architects. The system called for huge presentation drawings, usually done in ink wash with generally symmetrical plans and elevations inspired by classical forms. The first winner who used such a distinctly Beaux-Arts style in his presentation was George Awsumb, who won in 1908. Awsumb had been trained first, for a year, as an engineer at the University of Wisconsin. After some practical experience in construction, he returned to architectural school at the University of Illinois for three more years of study. At that time, the University of Illinois was not committed to the Beaux-Arts system, but several faculty members were familiar with it and undoubtedly conveyed their knowledge to the students. Awsumb worked with various Chicago firms for two years before winning the Eighth Annual Traveling Scholarship. He was active in the Chicago Architectural Club for many years and held several offices, including two terms as president in 1913–14 and 1914–15. His 1908 entry was the first of many to be done in the manner advocated by the Society of Beaux-Arts Architects. A review of later entries suggests that they were all executed in the Beaux-Arts style (with the possible exception of Arthur C. Hanifin's unpublished 1912 entry), which became virtually standard in most schools of architecture from around 1910 through 1950.

When the Beaux-Arts system of education became more or less ubiquitous in local ateliers as well as in schools, most of the architectural clubs throughout the United States, adopted the same presentation standards. The freedom of expression through sketching and watercolor work that had been so in vogue in the late nineteenth and early twentieth centuries began to disappear. The Beaux-Arts system stressed study of the classic styles, almost to the point of immersion. No longer were the majority of young men learning architecture at club meetings and in their

*George Awsumb's winning design for the Traveling Scholarship Competition was done in a distinctly Beaux-Arts style (CAC/16)*

respective offices as they had in earlier years. No longer was there room for the experimentation and innovation that had been so prominent in Chicago between 1885 and 1910, particularly in domestic architecture. It is a phenomenon that is a bit difficult to understand, since many of the leaders of the earlier avant-garde group had been trained by men who had studied at the École des Beaux-Arts in Paris. Sullivan, of course, was a prime example, but Perkins, Granger, Spencer, and several others who were so active around the turn of the century had also had such training. Perhaps it was because these men were surrounded by many talented but untrained "amateurs" that they realized that adherence to the strict rules of the Beaux-Arts system simply wasn't appropriate in Chicago and the Midwest. When success in architecture became predicated on attendance at accredited architectural schools, the freewheeling techniques used by the early modern movement architects were overshadowed by those of their younger counterparts.

These changes in architectural education occurred at a time when the Chicago Architectural Club was struggling for survival on more than one front. By 1917 membership had slipped to 107 active members, and by 1918 it was only 94, 31 of whom were in military service. It was, of course, the young men who were called to serve in the First World War. Many went to Europe and in 1919, as noted earlier, the exhibition catalog listed several who had died there. After the war, a number stayed in France to study European buildings or attend the École, which helped to further perpetuate the use of the Beaux-Arts system in the United States. In retrospect, all this turmoil in the years just before, during, and after the First World War undoubtedly was largely responsible for the revitalization of classical architecture, which had never really been forgotten after the 1893 World's Columbian Exposition. Ultimately, it led to the development of the great art deco buildings of the 1920s, the scale of which was consistent with the Beaux-Arts system of design. These buildings were also a logical extension of the great buildings designed in the early days of the Chicago Architectural Club.

The Chicago Architectural Club not only survived during this period, but it began to recover and prosper, largely because it and its sister groups, the AIA and the ISA, as well as most American schools of architecture, responded to the Beaux-Arts system with modern design, new materials, and an understanding of the needs of clients. Club members used the Beaux-Arts system to develop new forms that did not rely on historic antecedents. The world of architecture was changing, and the club changed with it. The change was not overnight, but in retrospect 1916 was a point from which there was no turning back.

The 1916 exhibition was a success in many ways. It was broader in scope than in previous years and it included related arts and the work of architects practicing in both contemporary and historic styles. It was well received by the public, and the Art Institute of Chicago thought well enough of it to include photographs and editorial matter on the exhibition in three of its bulletins.[23]

Ten days after the close of the Twenty-ninth Annual Chicago Architectural Exhibition, the club met to elect officers and directors for the coming year. Harry H. Bentley moved up to president, and Fritz Wagner Jr. gave up the treasurer's chair to become vice president. John C. Leavell and Frederick C. H. Stanton became secretary and treasurer, respectively. Only Herbert E. Downton remained as a director from the previous year. Franklin Marling Jr. and Robert L. Franklin were elected to fill out the 1917 term, and Archibald S. Morphett, George L. Barnum, and Arthur Kimbell were chosen for the 1918 class of directors. Not long after the election, the club elected to

23. *Bulletin of the Art Institute of Chicago* 10, no. 4 (April 1916): 170–71; *Bulletin of the Art Institute of Chicago* 10, no. 5 (May 1916): 116; *Bulletin of the Art Institute of Chicago* 10, no. 6 (October 1916): 1.

*The 1916 exhibition was beautifully mounted and included a number of nonarchitectural items such as the model of a Chicago bridge seen in the center above (AIC)*

use its quarters at 332 South Plymouth Court as its permanent address. By 1919, the club had moved again, this time to the old Athenaeum Building at 59 East Van Buren Street, where it had had space from 1891 through 1897.[24] It still used the Art Institute club room from time to time for special meetings.

Little information is available on the activities of the Chicago Architectural Club in the fall of 1916. It continued to cooperate with both the AIA and the ISA, an easy course of action since all three were then using the Art Institute club room as their headquarters. The club solidified these relationships primarily in order to continue its annual exhibitions. The three groups agreed to continue having a Joint Exhibition Committee made up of members of each organization. In late 1916, the committee was organized with five men from each group. Chairman Fritz Wagner Jr., treasurer George A. Knapp, and secretary A. J. Lawrence were chosen from the CAC, the ISA, and the AIA, respectively. Only Knapp had never been a member of the club. In fact, of the fifteen members of the committee, all but three had been members of the Chicago Architectural Club at some time. These men were then as-

24. The Chicago Architectural Club's address was always published in the annual exhibition catalog, along with a list of members. The Illinois Society of Architects also published a list of members in its annual *Handbook for Architects and Builders*. When the club left the Art Institute, its address continued to be listed as being in the building until 1922, when it moved to 40 South Clark Street.

*Chicago bridge (ISA)*

signed to various subcommittees to manage the exhibition. There was a separate group of nine men who served as the Jury of Admission, only five of whom were club members. They were drawn primarily from senior members of the profession. Dates for the Thirtieth Annual Exhibition were established in late 1916. The first documentary evidence of planning for the 1917 exhibition is in the minutes of the ISA for January 9, 1917.[25] The board of directors authorized the chairman of the ISA Exhibits Committee to work with the AIA and the Chicago Architectural Club with a total budget of two thousand dollars, half to be borne by the Art Institute and the remainder to be shared three ways between the cooperating organizations. Two months later, the Illinois Society of Architects' *Monthly Bulletin*[26] announced that the exhibition would be held "in the New Galleries of the Art Institute, between the dates of April 5th and April 29th."[27] It confirmed that Frank L. Venning had done the cover "selected in a competition" for the catalog of the forthcoming exhibition. It further advised that the ISA had arranged to exhibit "some rare antiquities of furniture, draperies and hardware loaned through the courtesy of Martin Ryerson and R. T. Crane, Jr. A special feature of design has been created as an entrance to the exhibition, which takes the form of an Italian garden. There will also be some special exhibits selected from the current exhibition being held by the Architectural League of New York."

The 1917 exhibition opened to the press on April 2, two days before the public was admitted. In the first notice the following day, the reporter, apparently quoting from a press release, noted that the "exhibition of the Chicago architects is many-sided in its attractions. The display will include exhibits illustrative of architecture," briefly describing what was to be included.[28] Most of the local papers reported on the exhibition, but in less detail than in the past. Part of the interest was in the recently completed annex to the Art Institute. The galleries were on the east side of the building and were reached directly from the top of the monumental stair just inside the main entrance. Writer Louise James Bargelt reported that at the top of the stair a "vast entrance hall is amassed in green foliage in imitation of an Italian garden." She went on to describe "Graham and Burnham's sketches of the new Union station for Chicago . . . [and] . . a sketch of the Field museum."[29] She neglected to note that a sketch of the Union Station, probably the same one, had been shown in the previous year's exhibit. Another critic, Albrecht Montgelas, wrote that "a hurried survey of the eight galleries of the new wing . . . gives the impression that more attention has been given this year to the problem of smaller residences. This is a good sign, because here is a real American problem which needs solving on original American and artistic lines as much as the problem of business structures and factory buildings, to which American architects have in the past successfully

25. Virtually all the minutes of the now-defunct Illinois Society of Architects have survived, as have a substantial number of other records. They are deposited at the Chicago Historical Society and are available to scholars. The item referenced here is in box 1, folder 1-4, page 169.

26. The Illinois Society of Architects began publishing the *ISA Monthly Bulletin* in July of 1916.

27. *ISA Monthly Bulletin* 1, no. 9 (March 1917).

28. "Architects to Come," *Chicago Evening Post*, April 3, 1917.

29. Louise James Bargelt, "Appeal to Laymen Found in Exhibit by Architects," *Chicago Tribune*, April 4, 1917.

*Sketch of Union Station by D. H. Burnham and Company, exhibited in 1916 (CAC/17)*

applied themselves. Unfortunately, the imitation of the un-American 'classic archi-tecture' in official and representative buildings is still indulged in by most of the exhibitors. This un-American spirit denying the legitimacy and beauty of our own time and life and its possibility of artistic expression, is given full sway in the arrangement of the corridor leading to the first gallery and that gallery itself. The wall decoration and the furniture standing around prepare the visitor rather for a historical exhibition than for an exhibition of work created by twentieth century American architects and decorators."[30] George Maher, Dwight Perkins, Arthur Woltersdorf, and many of their colleagues must have been delighted with Montge-las's column. Columnist Lena M. McCauley, however, did not agree. She wrote that "the Italian garden entrance . . . is an attractive introduction to the galleries . . .

30. Albrecht Montgelas, "Architects Open Exhibition at Art Institute," *Chicago Examiner,* April 6, 1917.

*George Maher's Winona Savings Bank, first shown in the 1917 Chicago architectural exhibition (CAC/17)*

*Sketch of the colonnade at the north end of Grant Park, by Chester H. Walcott (PC)*

[and] . . Beyond the corridor the large gallery is hung with three magnificent tapestries and is furnished with an ancient chest and Gothic chair."[31] She did find space to comment on the private office building recently designed and occupied by Perkins, Fellows & Hamilton, and she was interested in several other exhibits as well. She ended her comments with praise for the catalog, which she found to be "a handsomely made book, with illustrations of a value that give the publication a permanent place in every working library of an architect." Apparently she didn't compare it to the previous year's catalog. The 1917 catalog was literally identical, except for the illustrations and lists of entries. Many of the sections were actually taken verbatim from the 1916 catalog. It made for an easy editing task, but the policy of using a unique design each year had been abandoned. As a matter of fact, the same basic scheme was used again in 1918.

One especially interesting exhibit at the 1917 show was a large model of the Ravinia Park entrance to Highland Park. The design by Carl Hoerman was not illustrated, but at least two newspapers commented on it.[32] The *Chicago Examiner* noted that it was "about eight feet by three feet and shows across from the railroad station a small park fronted by a solid row of two-story buildings containing stores, offices, theatres and garages. Two covered gates form entrances through the buildings to the town behind." It survived the twentieth century and is still standing in 2004, although the surrounding buildings have changed a great deal. Another important exhibit, barely touched upon, was E. H. Bennett's plan for Grant Park, between Randolph and Jackson streets. Some portions of Bennett's plan had already been executed, most notably the colonnade and fountain at the intersection of Randolph Street and Michigan Avenue. (This delightful amenity, destroyed in the mid-twentieth century, was rebuilt as part of the Millennium Park project in 2003 using the original design but more lasting materials.)[33]

The professional press also had somewhat varied opinions about the 1917 exhibition. An anonymous review in the *American Architect* appears to have been written by someone who had not actually visited the exhibition.[34] He noted that he had "before us many clippings, some two columns in length, giving with much detail an account of this exhibition." He also wrote that the "presentation of architecture and the allied arts brings to a most successful conclusion the 1916–1917 season of architectural exhibits." It was not a comprehensive review, merely a repetition of what had been printed elsewhere. On the other hand, Robert Craik McLean had obviously seen the show, and his editorial in the *Western Architect* concerned the Chicago Architectural Club's influence on the profession. McLean, as usual, praised the club rather than the exhibition itself. He wrote that "especial significance attaches to the Chicago Architectural Club exhibition this year, the thirtieth to be presented annually by the club . . . What the Chicago Architectural Club has become it has achieved alone, though a sympathetic attitude was indicated by the local chapter . . . In fact, the present list of officers and committees of the Illinois Society of Architects reads like a section of the club's roster in 1895–96, except that Myron Hunt occupies a prominent position among Los Angeles architects."[35] He ended his remarks by noting that the cooperation between the AIA, the ISA, and the club was "the best possible evidence that the club has attained a high place in architectural achievement." He didn't mention that the club had shrunk in size or that some felt that it was no longer on the cutting edge of modern architecture.

Architect Thomas Tallmadge had no such reservations. In the same issue of the *Western Architect*, he wrote a review expressing his mixed feelings about the exhibition. He liked the new galleries at the Art Institute and commented that "the smaller and more intimate new galleries make the drawings immensely more interesting, and as the galleries virtually end in an impasse, the exhibition is no longer

31. Lena M. McCauley, "Architects Are Showing Civic Pride," *Chicago Evening Post*, April 14, 1917.

32. "Town Entrance Model Shown by Architect," *Chicago Examiner*, April 12, 1917, and "Ravinia Town Entrance," *Chicago Post*, April 17, 1917.

33. OWP&P Architects was responsible for this reconstruction.

34 "The Chicago Architectural Exhibition," *American Architect* 111, no. 2158 (May 2, 1917): 277–78, 283.

35. *Western Architect* 25, no. 4 (April 1917): 23.

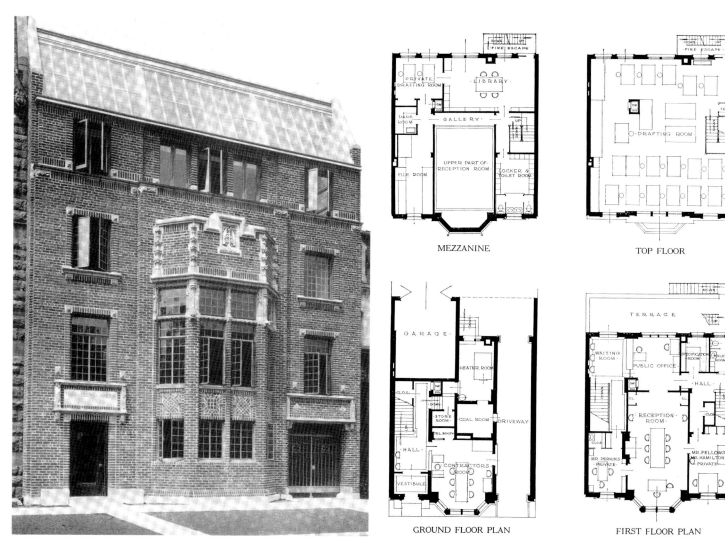

*Perkins, Fellows & Hamilton's office building, exhibited in the 1917 show; only the facade has survived (PC)*

*Plans for the Perkins, Fellows & Hamilton office building (PC)*

merely the decoration of a passage way leading to the more poignant delights of a Cubist or Futurist show." He felt that the Hanging Committee had done "wonders with unimpressive material." He was disappointed that the exhibition was essentially one of "Little Masters" and that the great skyscrapers and cathedrals were missing. Furthermore, he stated that "what is even more to be regretted is the absence of any evidence that the 'Chicago School,' as a potent style of architecture, any longer exists . . . Where are Sullivan, Wright, Griffin and the others? The absence of these men has removed from the show the last vestige of local color." He went on in this vein for several paragraphs, but eventually turned to what he liked about the exhibition. He had praise for Howard Shaw, Frederick Perkins, Pond & Pond, and George Awsumb's auditorium in "Eau Claire, Wisconsin, [which] shows a commendable originality in the treatment of the Doric order." Was this his way of endorsing the teachings of the Beaux-Arts system? He went on to commend other exhibits and concluded, "To the young men of the Architectural Club a sincere tribute should be given for the excellent exhibition splendidly presented and illustrated by a catalogue as good as the best." Tallmadge was the only reviewer to comment on the club's truncated Traveling Scholarship for 1917. He wrote that the "annual foreign Traveling Scholarship of the Chicago Architectural Club, on account of the war has been replaced by a home scholarship consisting of $325.00 donated by the Chicago Face Brick Association. The subject, a memorial library in the colonial style, gives certainly no great scope for the aspiring wings of youthful imagination and the drawings reflect the depressing program." This was the only published reference to the program for 1917. No mention was made by Tallmadge or any other reviewer of the winner of the scholarship, Roy Larson, whose design had commanded two full pages in the 1917 exhibition catalog. His name was not published until 1918, and the second- and third-place designs by Archie Morphett and George Lloyd Barnum were not listed in the catalog until 1919. There were no competitions in 1918 and 1919. Following Tallmadge's review were thirteen pages of illustrations from the catalog, including Larson's winning design. Tallmadge had too long a relationship with the club to condemn it, even if he did not care for much of what of what he saw in the 1917 exhibition. He would spend a good deal of time and effort during the next three years trying to bring his Chicago colleagues in the architectural avant-garde back to the forefront.

When the 1917 exhibition was over, the club held its annual meeting to elect officers for the coming year. The plan to have directors elected in "classes" of three to serve two years and thus provide continuity had not worked, and an entirely new slate was put in place. The 1917–18 officers included president Fritz Wagner Jr., vice president John C. Leavell, secretary Frederick C. H. Stanton, and treasurer Robert L. Franklin. The directors were A. S. Morphett, George Barnum, H. E. Downton, and Frank Venning, all active members. In a departure from past practice, two associate members, Arthur Kimbell and George Saunders, were also elected to the board.

With the United States now fully committed to the war in Europe and over a third of the club's members in the service, it was difficult to maintain an active schedule of events. The club did take advantage of invitations from the AIA and the ISA to attend their events. The longtime traditions of sketching evenings and in-house competitions were, however, essentially abandoned for the duration of the war.

There was one exhibition in the fall of 1917 that was of considerable interest to club members, although it was not one of theirs. In late October it was announced that architect Frank Lloyd Wright would once again show his collection of Japanese prints.[36] This time it was not at the Art Institute or at an Architectural Club show. It was at the Arts Club in the Wrigley Building on North Michigan Avenue. The prints were all from Wright's personal collection, most of them obtained in Japan while he was completing the design for and starting construction of the Imperial Hotel. The exhibition opened on November 12 in a setting designed by Wright, who had "transformed the club into a fitting background for the colored bits of Japanese art" and who spoke on "The General Principles of the Print" on November 22.[37] Wright's on-again-off-again relationship with the Chicago Architectural Club was not quite over. He would never again be involved as a participant in any of the club's events, but some of his work would be shown in the 1918 exhibition when the club included work of Illinois architects for the centennial year of the state as part of its annual exhibition.

By late 1917, the club and its allies in the AIA and the ISA had mutually agreed with the Art Institute of Chicago to hold the Thirty-first Annual Chicago Architectural Exhibit between March 23 and May 1 in 1918.[38] It would have been the most extensive of any exhibition to date, but it was later trimmed to April 4 through May 1. The United States had officially entered the war in Europe a year earlier, on

36. Louise James Bargelt, "Japanese Prints to Be Exhibited by the Arts Club," *Chicago Tribune*, October 28, 1917.

37. "Frank Lloyd Wright to Lecture Today on His Japanese Prints," *Chicago Tribune*, November 22, 1917.

38. *Western Architect* 26, no. 2 (February 1918): 13.

*Roy Larson's winning design for the 1917 CAC Traveling Scholarship Competition, a departure from the accepted Beaux-Arts style (CAC/17). Plans of Larson's design (CAC/17)*

April 6, 1917. Nearly one third of the active members of the Chicago Architectural Club were in military service by the end of 1917, and a number of others were involved in various government or public works projects as part of the war effort. Consequently, there was far less manpower or time to devote to the annual exhibition. Furthermore, private clients were scarce and less work was available for exhibition. Nevertheless, plans were made to hold the show in 1918 and to broaden the scope of material exhibited.

Francis W. Puckey, representing the AIA, was appointed chairman of the exhibition, while George A. Knapp and A. J. Lawrence from the CAC and the ISA were appointed treasurer and secretary, respectively. All told, there were again fifteen members on the Joint Exhibition Committee. They filled all but one of the subcommittee positions. The one exception was Thomas E. Tallmadge, who served on the Committee on Special Features. A separate nine-man Jury of Admissions, headed by William K. Fellows, was asked to review submissions prior to acceptance. That jury included several non-architects, including decorator Louis J. Millet, sculptor Emil R. Zettler, and artist Albert H. Krehbeil, who represented the allied arts. This was considered important, since the Exhibition Committee, largely due to the efforts of Puckey, in addition "to the usual showing of architectural work . . . intended to include a display of craftsmanship in as many other lines as possible." This may have been because of a lack of new buildings available for exhibition, but it was also an effort "to exert in unusual ways an educational influence upon the public and to acquaint people of Chicago with the wide scope of the architects' activities."[39] It was in this area that the Committee on Special Features came into play. Thomas Tallmadge was the moving force of this small group.[40]

After the 1917 exhibition, where he was disappointed by the absence of the

39. Ibid., 27–28.

40. Tallmadge started his private practice, Tallmadge & Watson, in 1905 and shortly thereafter began teaching architectural history at the Armour Institute (the Chicago School of Architecture). While he was a champion of the avant-garde movement in Chicago, his firm generally produced conservative designs. His partner, Vernon S. Watson, was the primary designer. Tallmadge became more and more interested in teaching and writing as his career progressed. He was a regular contributor to various journals, often as a critic.

Chicago School of avant-garde architects, Tallmadge took it upon himself to see to it that the work of Midwestern architects would be well represented in the 1918 exhibition, suggesting and promoting a showing of Illinois architecture in a celebration of the state's centennial year. He wrote an essay that was published separately from the 1918 catalog, outlining the history of architecture in Illinois.[41] In it, he described the architecture of Illinois built in the previous century. (Actually he started with a church built in 1765.) He admired the early work, particularly the Greek revival buildings of the mid-nineteenth century, but was appalled by the "war years" architecture between 1850 and 1880, and he felt that the arrival of H. H. Richardson in Chicago in the early 1880s signaled a new architecture in Illinois. The 1893 World's Columbian Exposition brought still another revelation in design, albeit rooted in the architecture of the past. In Tallmadge's opinion, it was the work of Louis Sullivan that brought about a truly new architecture in the Midwest. He wrote:

> We should be proud of the fact that the only conscious effort to break away from European precedent and to create a new style which would be distinctly American occurred in Chicago . . . [The new architecture] has been fostered by a small number of brilliant and courageous men, who in the face of opposition and indifference have carried on a losing fight, sacrificing often popularity for principle . . . The characteristics of the style are the strict avoidance of European precedent, an unusual emphasis on the horizontal line, a frank acknowledgement of the construction and materials and the use of indigenous natural forms in the ornament. The style, sometimes called the Chicago school, has been unfortunately discredited by the excesses of some of its practitioners and has often been made ridiculous by the atrocities perpetrated by ignorant contractor-architects, who have travestied some of its forms and motives in cheap flats and stores. Its best expression we see today in the small houses whose owners have not been educated up to the 'styles' and in the warehouses and commercial buildings where the logic of its forms makes a happy union with modern engineering. Peculiarly adapted to the clothing of the skeleton of the skyscraper, there are unfortunately only two examples of such use in Chicago, and both have been preeminently successful, the Garrick Theatre Building and the Gage Building, both by Mr. Sullivan.

The last half of this essay was the nearest thing to a definition of an American architecture, as argued for by Midwestern architects for several years, that ever appeared in print. Tallmadge was dedicated to the new architecture described in his booklet, and his own firm had been instrumental in promoting it during its early years. Oddly enough, it was Watson, not Tallmadge, who was the firm's designer when it was producing its most advanced designs. Tallmadge's designs were primarily ecclesiastical and rarely demonstrated the characteristics he seemingly admired so much.

The exhibition of the historic architecture of Illinois took up an entire gallery of the Thirty-first Annual Chicago Architectural Exhibit, but was not illustrated in the catalog. The only acknowledgment was a brief paragraph at the end of other listings crediting the State Historical Society, the Chicago Historical Society, the Art Institute, and Orson Smith for their help in assembling the material.[42] It did, however, get the attention of the popular and professional press.

The *Chicago Daily News* published an illustrated article in its "Home" section with the byline of Marguerite B. Williams.[43] She opened her article, "To view in a nutshell 100 years of house building from the log cabin to the creations of Frank

41. That essay was published in a six-by-eight-inch, eight-page booklet, now very rare, Thomas E. Tallmadge, *A History of Architecture in Illinois, 1818–1918.*

42. Orson Smith (1841–1923) was a banker. Born and educated in Chicago, he had a great interest in the city's history, particularly its architecture.

43. Marguerite B. Williams, *"Styles in House Planning, 1818–1918,"* Chicago Daily News, April 10, 1918.

Lloyd Wright is made possible by the historical exhibition arranged by the Chicago Architectural club at the Art Institute." While no listing of the buildings was published, Ms. Williams did mention several buildings and architects. She included three illustrations, none of which was identified in captions. They were the Charnley House, a Victorian mansion, and one of the Keith houses on Prairie Avenue. In her article, which was essentially straight reporting rather than a critique, she named the Widow Clark House, Lincoln's Springfield home, and the Kinzie House in Chicago as examples of early work. The Auditorium Building and the Glessner House were both mentioned, as was Louis Sullivan's Transportation Building at the Columbian Exposition. She used the Charnley House as an example of a current style that "ought to delight the hearts of all housewives, for it is planned so that she may care for it herself if necessary." She implied that other similar designs were included and closed by stating that the "exhibition brings home the progress of good taste in building, and it is a satisfaction to feel that the standards set by the architects in the homes of the wealthy are in a measure being sifted about among all home builders."

The *Chicago Daily News* was not the only local paper to comment on the exhibition and its emphasis on the Chicago School. In an article headlined "Architects Favor Chicago School," Lena M. McCauley noted that due "to the depression in building . . . it has been difficult to gather drawings and designs of any kind to make a novel exhibition. But the architects could not let the hour go by, and . . . have assembled what will be a creditable show and one that is enjoyable."[44] She did not cover the current work offered by architects but noted that there had been an "attempt to recall the associations of a Chicago School of architecture" and "among the architects instrumental in its success are Messrs. Sullivan, Wright, Tallmadge, Puckey, Maher, Pond and others . . . the Chicago school of architecture gallery is certain to unveil surprises."

The professional press also covered the exhibition and it too concentrated on the historical aspects of the show, emphasizing the work of the Chicago School. The unsigned review in the *Western Architect* stated that the exhibition "may be counted a success. Less may be said from the architectural standpoint, though the exhibits, almost wholly local in nature, contained some really interesting features gathered together by the Herculean efforts of the promoters, to whom all credit is due."[45] It continued, "Two features were overshadowing in their importance. One, of the most interest professionally, was the gallery given over completely to the picturing of the Morgan Park improvement for the United States Steel Corporation, by Dean and Dean, architects, an example of industrial housing of peculiar value at the present time. The other was the display of photographs and prints picturing the development of Chicago architecturally, a feature which aroused genuine interest on the part of public as well as profession." Much of the rest of the review was devoted to the historical aspects of the exhibition, but a number of the Chicago School designs, not always those in the historical gallery, were also covered favorably. Two items appeared in the *American Contractor,* both of which emphasized the historic aspects of the exhibition.[46] The same sort of article was published by the *American Architect.*[47] Nearly every article on the exhibition focused on the history of Illinois architecture. There was never a listing of the historic work exhibited, although one can piece together a partial list by reading the various articles. It was apparently devoted mostly to work produced after the World's Columbian Exposition, with Louis Sullivan's Transportation Building cited as the germ of the development of the Chicago School of architecture.

Within days of the closing of the 1918 exhibition, the Illinois Chapter of the AIA reported that "an organized effort will be made to bring together photographs and other reproductions of the work of the 'Chicago School' of architecture and al-

44. Lena M. McCauley, "Architects Favor Chicago School," *Chicago Evening Post,* April 2, 1918.

45. *Western Architect* 27, no. 4 (April 1918): 29–31, 34.

46. *American Contractor* 39, no. 1699 (April 20, 1918): 31, and *American Contractor* 39, no. 1700 (April 27, 1918): 27.

47. *American Architect* 113, no. 2210 (May 1, 1918): 521–24.

*Interior and exterior views of the Glen Ellyn Public Library by George Awsumb (CAC/18)*

*Charnley House (WRH)*

*Elbridge Keith House on Prairie Avenue (WRH)*

*Widow Clark House, as it appeared after restoration in 1978. (PC)*

*An entire gallery in the 1918 show was devoted to Dean and Dean's design for an "Industrial Village" for the United States Steel Corporation (PC)*

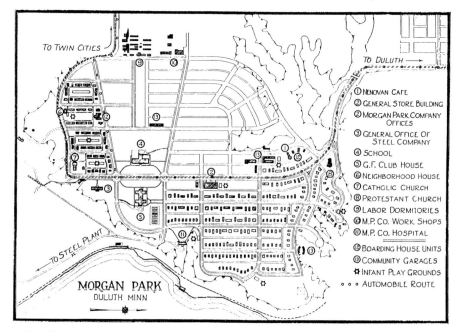

*A plan of Morgan Park, Minnesota, by Dean and Dean, from the 1918 exhibition (PC)*

lied arts. This resolution was recommended by the Executive Committee as a result of a report made by the Historical Committee under the chairmanship of Mr. Thomas E. Tallmadge."[48] The resolution read, "Resolved, That the historical committee be instructed to co-operate with the exhibition committee and the affiliate committee to prepare for a convocation of the arts to take place during the time of exhibition." The AIA planned to bring together material "as far back as the early work of John W. Root and Louis Sullivan." The overall plan was to exhibit the material at the next architectural exhibition and to include "criticisms and discussions relating to this school and to put the entire material in convenient form for publication later." The AIA credited the idea to Tallmadge's "display of the work of Chicago architecture during the last architectural exhibition." It also noted that Louis Sullivan had promised to assist in the preparation of the material. The resolution ended with the statement that the plan was to bring "to view the merits and underlying principles of [the Chicago School] and the worthy common factors of it, in such a manner that the art world may see it and a permanent record of it may be kept."[49] This is very much in keeping with a resolution passed by the Illinois Chapter of the AIA in late 1917, to "'make the profession of ever-increasing service to society,' and that the Chapter may affiliate with itself, for purposes of co-operation, other organizations." It went on to suggest that the AIA would be working with "twenty or twenty-five art and cultural societies of Chicago" and that "great good to the architect and the community may result." By the time this resolution was published, ten or twelve of the more than twenty-five other arts-oriented groups in Chicago had indicated an interest in cooperating with the chapter.[50] The 1919 catalog of the Chicago Architectural Exhibition began listing "Affiliated Societies" and "Affiliated Journals" along with the lists of members. In 1919, and again in 1920, there were eleven affiliated societies listed. Sixteen affiliated journals were listed both years. The club's first effort continued, however, to be the promotion of the development of modern architecture in Chicago, as represented by the Chicago school.

There is little doubt that the historical material gathered by Tallmadge for the 1918 annual exhibition was kept. It almost certainly formed the core of the collection planned by the AIA to promote Midwestern architecture. There was, in 1919 and again in 1920, a substantial showing of this material at the annual exhibitions. There is not, however, any hard evidence of what eventually became of the material.[51]

Of course, the idea of formally recognizing a Chicago School of architecture was not new when Tallmadge lamented its absence from the 1917 exhibition. (Although the Illinois Chapter had asked George Maher, Dwight Perkins, and Arthur Woltersdorf to prepare such a definition in late 1912, it is doubtful the definition was ever widely distributed, as they had recommended.)[52] Tallmadge and his colleagues did all they could during the next several years to perpetuate the work of the avant-garde architects who generally scorned the work of historicists following European precedents. They were only partially successful. One can argue that they failed on the domestic level but succeeded beyond their wildest dreams with the commercial architecture of Chicago.

During the 1920s, Holabird & Roche, Graham, Anderson, Probst & White, Walter W. Ahlschlager, Marshall & Fox, Burnham Brothers, Perkins, Fellows & Hamilton, Schmidt, Garden & Erikson, and others of similar merit produced work of a quality that certainly compared favorably with that of the first wave of the great Chicago School commercial buildings of the late nineteenth and early twentieth centuries. Smaller offices, such as those of Howard Van Doren Shaw, David Adler, and Andrew Rebori, were also producing excellent work. While high quality do-

*Drawing by Charles Walcott, illustrating an article by Julie Walcott in the* Chicago Daily News

48. *Western Architect* 27, no. 6 (June 1918): 51 et seq.

49. This plan was first reported in the *Western Architect,* as cited above. The actual resolution was not published until October 8, 1918, in the *Chicago Evening Post.*

50. *American Contractor* 39, no. 1688 (January 5, 1918): 39.

51. The Ryerson and Burnham Libraries at the Art Institute of Chicago and the reference center at the Chicago Historical Society both have substantial collections of photographs of Chicago's architecture. The January 1919 *Bulletin of the Art Institute of Chicago* states that the library had received "a gift of nearly one hundred photographs from Thomas E. Tallmadge, illustrating architecture in the eighties." The acquisition records at the Art Institute indicate that several hundred professionally prepared large-format photographs of Chicago buildings were acquired between 1916 and 1930. It is likely that many of them are from the collection assembled in 1918–19, although they are not identified as such.

52. *Construction News* 34, no. 25 (December 21, 1912): 12–13.

mestic work was being done, much of it was influenced to at least some degree by historicism, and it was the larger structures that gained the most notoriety as modern buildings. All the offices of the architects named above were staffed by members of the Chicago Architectural Club. Often done by men who had been trained at the École des Beaux-Arts or in ateliers or schools led by members of the Society of Beaux-Arts Architects, that work—now usually identified as art deco or moderne—was a new architecture developed by emulating the discipline of the Beaux-Arts without the dependence on historicism that dominated such training prior to the First World War. It was a golden age for Chicago architecture, which lasted until the Great Depression began in 1929. But before it could take part in the flowering of the 1920s, the club needed to regroup after the First World War, which ended in November of 1918.

The new officers of the Chicago Architectural Club elected at the annual meeting in May of 1918 included Robert L. Franklin as president, A. S. Morphett as vice president, and Sigurd A. Rognstad as treasurer, with R. J. Ashton as secretary. H. E. Downton, E. G. Oldefest, E. S. Nelson, F. M. Hodgdon, C. H. Sierkes, and Fred Crofoot were chosen as directors.[53] Their first concern was finding a new home for the club. The lease at 332 South Plymouth Court had not been renewed, and that space had never really been satisfactory in any case. It had been used as a drafting room for the atelier and occasionally some of the members socialized there, but it was not a club room in the sense they wanted. Many of their regular meetings and lectures were held in the club room at the Art Institute of Chicago. They elected to return to the Athenaeum Building on Van Buren Street, where they had headquartered from 1891 to 1893. By the end of 1918, they were established in the new space directly across the street from Steinway Hall. They would stay there less

53. These names are all taken from the catalog of the Chicago Architectural Club exhibition catalog of 1919. They were not published in any other venue that could be located.

*The proposed Union Station and Federal Building by Graham, Anderson, Probst & White (the Northwestern Station is at the far right): the station was built, the Federal Building was not (CAC/18)*

Walter W. Ahlschlager's Beatrice Creamery exhibited in 1918 had a strong modern aesthetic; today it is used as housing (CAC/18)

than two years.

The last reference to the activities of the architectural societies of Chicago in 1918 was published in the *Chicago Evening Post* in October 1918, in an article that documented the concerted effort to collect historical data and photographs of Illinois architecture.[54] The three societies—the CAC, AIA, and ISA—scheduled dates with the Art Institute of Chicago to hold the Thirty-second Annual Chicago Architectural Exhibition at the institute between April 15 and May 8, 1919. Prior to that, another smaller exhibition of interest to all three societies and the public was shown at the Art Institute. In January 1919, gallery 250 was filled with sketches of the proposed improvements to Michigan Avenue from the river to Tower Place, near Chicago's Water Tower. The idea for improving North Michigan Avenue had originated in 1908, when the Commercial Club of Chicago published its "Plan for a Boulevard to Connect the North and South Sides of the River on Michigan Avenue and Pine Street." It predated Burnham and Bennett's *Plan of Chicago* and was, to a large degree, incorporated therein.

By 1919, the decision to build a bridge over the Chicago River connecting Pine Street on the north with Michigan Avenue on the south had already been made. In 1918, Andrew Rebori had been invited to work with the Architects Committee for the North Michigan Avenue Development, a group that had as its goal the improvement of Pine Street (later North Michigan Avenue). The committee included a number of prominent architects: E. H. Bennett, Howard Van Doren Shaw, Graham, Anderson, Probst & White, Schmidt, Garden & Martin, and Jarvis Hunt, in whose office Rebori was working. Rebori was asked to assume the position of managing architect for the committee, and it was he who prepared most of the drawings for the proposed improvements of the avenue north of the river.[55] It was these drawings that were exhibited at the Art Institute of Chicago in January of 1919.[56] This work was a direct result of the basic plans laid out in 1909 in the *Plan of Chicago.*

54. "Illinois Chapter A.I.A.," *Chicago Evening Post,* October 8, 1918.

55. The best information regarding this effort and other work by Rebori is in Wim De Witt, "Andrew Rebori: Buildings and Business," *Chicago Architectural Journal* 4 (1984): 4–13.

56. A number of these drawings have survived and are now in the collection of the Chicago Historical Society.

With the war behind them and the hope of prosperity beckoning, the business and architectural communities of Chicago were ready to move forward with the development of the city as suggested a decade earlier by Burnham and Bennett. Their efforts advanced on several fronts. In January of 1919, the *Chicago Daily News* began a series of articles titled "Chicago Sketches" written by Julie C. Walcott and illustrated by architect Chester H. Walcott, a longtime member of the Chicago Architectural Club.[57] The articles were all highly positive essays on downtown Chicago that focused on subjects such as the Grant Park Colonnade, the Art Institute, and Monroe Street. During the next decade there was a major effort by businessmen and architects alike to promote the implementation of the *Plan of Chicago*. Charles H. Wacker was the moving force behind this endeavor.[58] The architects of Chicago were encouraged to always consider the *Plan of Chicago* when designing buildings for the businessmen of Chicago, and the great majority of those plans were prepared, if not designed, by members of the Chicago Architectural Club. It was the beginning of a remarkable decade.

The 1919 exhibition was directed by a sixteen-man committee made up of five members each from the ISA and the CAC, and six from the AIA. Seven of these men had served the previous year. Frank A. Childs was the chairman, A. S. Morphett was secretary, and George Knapp was treasurer. Committee members were drawn from these sixteen men, except for the Committee on Special Features, which Thomas Tallmadge served on again, along with chairman F. W. Puckey and Earl H. Reed Jr., both from the main group. Puckey also served as chairman of the Committee on Decorations and Hanging. The Jury of Admissions was again a separate group of six architects, none from the previous year, chaired by George Nimmons.

Assembling the Thirty-second Annual Chicago Architectural Exhibition was not an easy task. Wartime had stifled work during 1916–17, and 1918 was a year of regrouping. Many of the young men who had gone off to Europe either remained overseas to study or returned with ideas gleaned from their observations while there. Work of the Chicago School architects was scant, and the 1919 exhibition was the worse for its lack. In early April, the Joint Exhibition Committee issued a press release announcing that the show would open with a reception on Tuesday, April 15.[59] It set the tone for the exhibition, stating, "On account of the war and the embargo on all nonessential building, the architects have less work to show than usual; but the committee hopes to secure drawings and plans of all the best work executed by representative American architects within the last five years, whether it has been exhibited before or not." The release also noted that the exhibition would include "a number of unusual features which will be of special interest to art amateurs as well as to those interested in the latest developments of our city and community life."[60] The writer went on to say that "those who wish to see the future of the boulevard link scheme will find here the drawings of the North Michigan avenue development . . . the drawings of the Evanston Beautiful plan, the Winnetka plan . . . [and] the Lake Forest plan . . . fashioned after the original L'Enfant plan of the city of Washington." In addition to these and other city plans, the 1919 show included a number of planned communities by Dean and Dean, J. C. Llewellyn & Company, Howard Van Doren Shaw, and others. The Exhibition Committee also expected to show items of furniture, murals, and decorative arts. There were only 272 exhibits, compared to more than 360 the previous year, including in excess of a hundred items from the 1918 historical exhibit and the AIA's exhibit of twenty-seven drawings from its Farmhouse Competition.

The 1919 catalog, edited by a four-man committee chaired by Robert L.

57. Several of these drawings were shown by Walcott in the Thirty-third Annual Chicago Architectural Exhibition of 1920.

58. Charles H. Wacker (1856–1929) was chairman of the Chicago Plan Commission. He began his career in real estate and first became involved in public service when he served as a director of the World's Columbian Exposition. He served in numerous other capacities on public service committees but will always be remembered for his tireless efforts to promote the *Plan of Chicago*. Perhaps his most memorable contribution was Wacker's Manual of the Plan of Chicago, on the value of public improvements, published in 1911 and used as a textbook in Chicago schools for more than twenty years. (It has been suggested that bond issues for public improvements in Chicago were always passed so long as the voters had been in school while Wacker's manual was used as a textbook.)

59. "Architects to Exhibit," *Chicago Evening Post*, April 8, 1919.

60. "Architectural Exhibit Will Be Held in Chicago," *Evanston News Index*, April 14, 1919.

*Andrew Rebori's spectacular drawing of his idea for improving Michigan Avenue north of the river was shown at the Art Institute in a separate exhibition in early 1919 (CAC/15)*

Franklin, was nearly identical in format to the 1918 catalog. The cover design was a sketch by Allen B. Weary, a longtime member of the club. There was a page listing the Joint Exhibition Committee members, an acknowledgments page, a list of patrons (sixty-three in all), and a brief foreword by Emery B. Jackson. Jackson's essay seems to have been suggesting, without actually saying so, that it was time to think long and hard about the fact that "the spirit of revolt against the conventional and accepted is spreading around the world into every field of activity. Architecture will not escape it. Is this spirit to be one producing chaos, sweeping out from

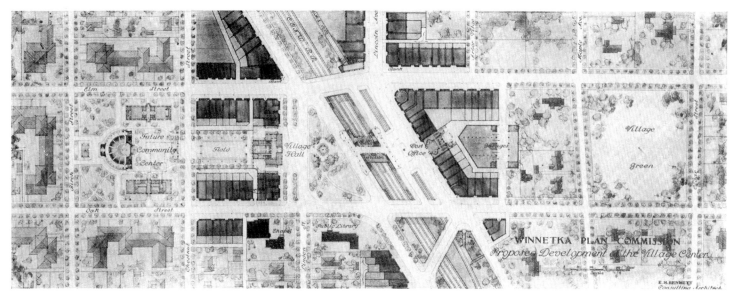

*One of the drawings produced by E. H. Bennett for his "Plan of Winnetka," shown in the 1919 exhibition (CAC/19)*

*A typical double housing unit designed by J. C. Llewellyn for the United States Housing Corporation (CAC/18)*

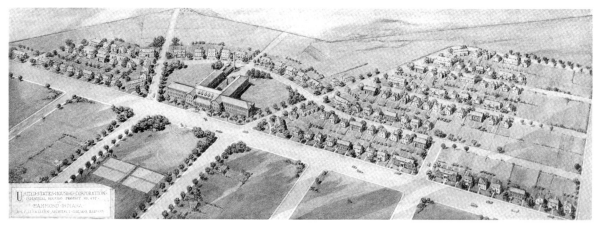

*J. C. Llewellyn's design for a United States Housing Corporation development in Hammond, Indiana (CAC/18)*

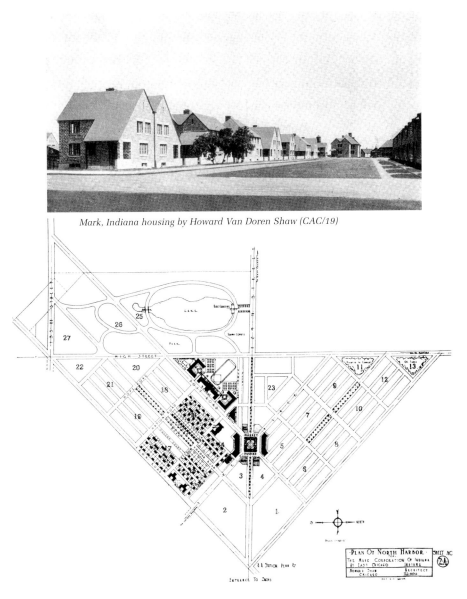

*Mark, Indiana housing by Howard Van Doren Shaw (CAC/19)*

*Plan of Howard Van Doren Shaw's industrial housing development in Mark, Indiana, exhibited in 1919 (CAC/19)*

under us the established standards of all sorts, or will this confused ferment awaken impulses which will enrich our ideals? Is a discriminating public to be our stimulus or the craving for the new and sensation to be our master?" He went on to observe that "the charm of novelty is transitory at best . . . and nothing has less charm than last year's fashions . . . Centuries of consecutive effort have built up a considerable stock of knowledge which, fitted together in an orderly way, has become our one safe, sure guide." He was, it seems clear, repudiating the work of the Chicago School and suggesting that the architects of Chicago and elsewhere should look to the past for inspiration. The 1919 exhibition reflected this attitude. After Jackson's disappointing essay came a page regarding the Traveling Scholarship, which had not been awarded since 1915. A page followed concerning the Illinois Chapter of the AIA's medal of honor for the best work shown at the exhibition, which, likewise, had not been awarded since 1915 and would not be given in 1919. There were two pages devoted to the American Academy in Rome and a complete listing of all the members of each of the three groups sponsoring of the exhibition. Several pages of illustrations were included, followed by a listing of all the exhibitors. A careful review of the illustrations and the listing of exhibits reveals almost no work of the avant-garde architects of Chicago, who, until recently, had made up the Chicago school as defined by Thomas Tallmadge.

Tallmadge did write a review of the exhibition for the *Western Architect*.[61] He began by saying that "after a careful examination of the thirty-second annual architectural exhibition, on display at the Art Institute, one begins to realize how lean, for the architects, have been the last two years. Yet the committee has put its best foot forward, displayed its boldest front and deserves much credit for skillful hanging and for making a little go a long way. The usual colored perspectives, rendered drawings, cartoons, furniture, etc., greet the eye, as in former years, but on closer inspection I find that most of these are old friends, and for the most part the rest are projects still to be consummated." Tallmadge felt that architecture in Chicago had reached "the end of an era in 1914," and was "now at the birth of a new one." He also felt that it would take a decade or more to understand the new work.

Tallmadge was impressed by the room devoted to city planning and called it the "most significant feature of the exhibition." He briefly covered the Winnetka Plan, the Evanston Plan, and the brilliant drawings by Andrew Rebori and Vernon Howe Bailey for the Michigan Avenue extension. He also noted that there was a "scheme by a lawyer, Mr. George B. Jones, for moving the capital of the United States to the environs of Chicago." That plan, which had been presented earlier to the Illinois Chapter of the AIA with a site plan by Tallmadge, was neither listed nor illustrated in the 1919 catalog.[62] Tallmadge admired the work of Myron Hunt, who had the largest number of exhibits, and Bertram Goodhue, both non-Chicagoans, as well as the Quigley Seminary by architect Zachary Davis. He was also pleased with a factory by Schmidt, Garden & Martin, and in a vague reference to the work of the Chicago School asked the reader if "it is possible that the prodigal is returning from the flesh pots of Georgian England, and 18th Century France, to his own home town? Yet here is a splendid building in the same virile American fashion that we used to admire and emulated in the addition to the Chicago Athletic Club, and in

61. *Western Architect* 28, no. 4 (April 1919): 29–30.

62. "Chicago Capital of U.S., Plan of Illinois Architects," *Chicago Tribune*, March 12, 1919. The article credits George B. Jones of the Chicago Association of Commerce as presenting the plan to the Illinois chapter of the AIA. Tallmadge is credited with preparing the map for a probable site of the capital, "in the vicinity of Fort Sheridan, stretching north as far as Lake Forest and south to Glencoe and west to the Des Plaines River."

*Schmidt, Garden & Martin's factory design, an example of the modern movement in the 1919 exhibition (CAC/19)*

the Madelener House." His last paragraph was reserved for admiration of "some clever pen renderings of Louis Sullivan's bank at Sidney, and some beautiful photographs illustrating some of its details." He also said that the "mission building by Purcell & Elmslie is brilliantly conceived and makes a flashing spot of color on a drab wall, but it is somewhat of a relief to find that it is to be built in China." It was not, in his opinion, a Chicago school building.

A careful reading of Tallmadge's reviews for 1918 and 1919 reveals a certain cynicism. He was disappointed in what he wrote about, but he overlooked some of the best work that was, in fact, representative of the maturing Chicago School, the passing of which he so lamented. The works by Schmidt, Garden & Martin and Andrew Rebori were prime examples. Tallmadge's own work, shown in 1918 and 1919, certainly was not in the spirit of the Chicago School. The two sketches by Tallmadge & Watson shown in 1918 were hardly distinctive, and his Roycemore School, done with Lawrence Buck and illustrated in 1919, was in the same vein. In fact, Tallmadge & Watson's work after 1919 regressed to the very European roots Tallmadge had previously condemned.

Most of the Chicago newspapers reviewed the 1919 exhibition and had essentially the same reaction as Tallmadge.[63] All were interested in the city plans and large-scale multiunit housing schemes, but the smaller buildings generally got short shrift. The most positive review was in the *American Architect*.[64] The unnamed author was highly impressed by the work shown, and wrote that others were similarly taken by what they saw. He stated that at the exhibition he had sat in a place where he could observe visitors and had noted that there was "a decided

63. The 1919 exhibition was reviewed or at least noted in the *Chicago Evening Post*, the *Evanston News Index*, the *Chicago Examiner*, and the *Chicago Tribune*, sometimes more than once. It was also briefly noted twice in the *Bulletin of the Art Institute of Chicago*.

64. *American Architect* 115, no. 2264 (May 14, 1919): 671–76.

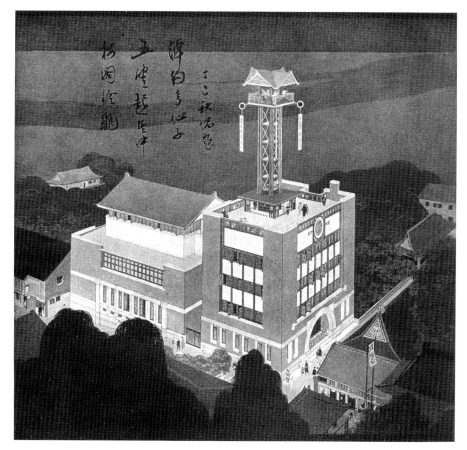

*The Sieng Tan Institutional Church by Purcell & Elmslie, for a site at Sieng Tan, Hkunan, China (PC)*

loitering in the three architectural galleries, and a keen appreciation of all that was hung on the walls . . . there were throngs of young people." He continued for several well-illustrated pages and ended his comments by saying, "When the general public come to a closer knowledge as to what an architect really is . . . they will have a better knowledge and a deeper respect for him and his work." He acknowledged that he was writing from New York City, and it is not surprising that he did not understand that the lack of critical comments concerning the avant-garde work of the Chicago School practitioners was disappointing to past and present members alike of the Chicago Architectural Club.

Thus the Thirty-second Annual Chicago Architectural Exhibition was over. One of the smallest in many years, it had nevertheless maintained the tradition begun in the late nineteenth century. One old friend of the club from the East, Wilson Eyre, had not seen fit to exhibit in the 1919 show. Perhaps it was because he had already arranged for a one-man show at the Art Institute of Chicago in October of 1919. Eyre had never practiced in the Midwest, and while he didn't exhibit in Chicago every year, he had been a regular in the annual exhibitions since 1895. He had always been active in the Philadelphia T-Square Club as well as the Architectural League of America. He was acquainted with a number of prominent members of the Chicago Architectural Club, and it was through them that he was able to mount a show at the Art Institute.[65]

When the annual meeting of the Chicago Architectural Club was held in May of 1919, the officers for the 1919–20 year were chosen. Archibald S. Morphett was moved up to president from vice president, and F. M. Hodgdon became vice president after a year as director. Sigurd A. Rognstad agreed to another year as treasurer, and Elmer J. Fox was elected secretary. C. H. Sierkes, H. E. Downton, and E. S. Nelson stayed on as directors, and P. F. Esser, F. O. Rippel, and A. J. Lawrence filled the vacant directorships. The officers immediately began to plan ways to expand the club's activities after the interruption of the war years and to get the Thirty-third Annual Architectural Exhibition under way. After meeting with their colleagues at the AIA and the ISA, as well as with the Art Institute of Chicago, they scheduled the annual exhibition for April 6 through May 5, 1920, one of the longest exhibitions yet. From the beginning, the 1920 exhibition was planned to highlight

65. Wilson Eyre (1858–1944) was an active architect for more than fifty years. He was born in Italy to American parents and came to the United States at the age of eleven. He studied in both the U.S. and Canada and had one year at MIT. He worked with various colleagues until 1911, when he joined Gilbert McIlvaine in Eyre & McIlvaine. Most of his work was carried out in Philadelphia.

*House for William McJunkin by Tallmadge & Watson, shown in 1918 (CAC/18)*

*Roycemore School in Evanston, a joint project by Tallmadge & Watson and Lawrence Buck shown in 1919 (CAC/19)*

the work of the Chicago school designers and particularly Louis Sullivan. Sullivan eagerly agreed to participate. The club also announced, early in 1920, that it was once more offering the Traveling Scholarship, for the first time since 1915. The drawings, however, were not due until April 12, several days after the exhibition opened. The subject of the competition was "A Hotel Lobby" to be designed in terra-cotta. The thousand-dollar first prize was donated by the Northwestern Terra Cotta Company, the Midland Terra Cotta Co., and the American Terra Cotta and Ceramic Company.

There had apparently been great concern among some architects that the 1920 exhibition would not actually take place. The Chicago Architectural Club was struggling to survive, and its only chance of continuing to sponsor the exhibition was to work closely with the AIA and the ISA. Both groups answered the call. The 1920 exhibition not only was held, it was one of the best presentations for some time. Robert Craik McLean wrote in the *Western Architect* in March of 1920 that "President Hammond, of the Illinois Society of Architects expresses an earnest desire that the architects of the city co-operate in a practical, active manner with the Chicago Architectural Club in its preparation for the annual exhibit of 1920."[66] After a few words of concern about architects who were complacent about the exhibition and the club, he continued, "The Club has earned its right to every ounce of aid and recognition that the practicing architects of Chicago can give it." In the same editorial he remarked that it was "especially important this year because of the disaster that has come to the League exhibition in New York through its destruction by fire on the eve of its opening, and which leaves to Chicago the duty as well as the privilege of presenting the premier exhibition of the year to the public." He ended by suggesting that "each architect will consider that it is of the highest importance that he make special preparation for their adequate presentation to an inspecting, intelligent public through the medium of the joint exhibition of the Chicago Architectural Club, the Illinois Society of Architects and the Art Institute." (Not including the AIA was probably simply an oversight.)

McLean's editorial may well have been what prompted the Joint Exhibition Committee to issue a press release outlining its plans for the 1920 exhibition nearly a month before it opened. The idea of working together and emphasizing the Chicago school of architecture was described as part of the overall plan for the exhibition. Information in that release was used by a writer at the *Chicago Daily News,* who noted that the exhibit would "have special significance as it will represent the earnest effort of a group of men to give definite expression to what has

66. *Western Architect* 29, no. 3 (March 1920): 22.

become know as the 'Chicago School' of architecture."[67] The article credited Louis Sullivan as the father of the movement and quoted him as saying, "The purpose of this movement is to arrive at a plastic architecture, in contradistinction to a purely intellectual architecture, as represented by the Greeks, and the emotionalism of the medieval period, as expressed in the Gothic cathedrals of northern France . . . The need of today is for an architecture based strictly upon utilitarian conditions, and developed in such wise [sic] that these utilitarian conditions may find full expression." He went on to say that such a philosophy would allow a building "to grow out of its conditions, and these conditions, as we face them are modern. We have been trying to solve these modern problems by application of ancient forms. An architecture of this sort, because it is the work of a free spirit, must naturally be democratic, because the essence of democracy is the expression of the free spirit of man."

The writer observed that in "recent years Mr. Sullivan has designed numerous bank buildings . . . [including one in] . . . Owatonna, Minn., . . . [and] in Sidney, Ohio." No other buildings by Chicago School architects were mentioned in the article, but he did note that "many other architects are now enrolled in this movement." Nineteen architectural firms and several sculptors and other craftsmen sympathetic to the movement were named, all of whom were expected to be in the exhibition. He also noted that the exhibition would include a number of photographs of the "decorations on the Lake Front during the Victory loan drive," which had furnished an "interesting example of the work of the Chicago School which is familiar to all." That event had been prepared under the direction of a group of architects chaired by T. E. Tallmadge. These photographs appeared in the exhibition, which opened a few weeks later. The spirit of the exhibition was not, unfortunately, reflected in the catalog's illustrations. No editor of the catalog was named, but whoever it was certainly was not sympathetic to the Chicago school.

The Joint Exhibition Committee was organized as it had been in the previous five years, although it was somewhat larger than in the past. There were nineteen members, and it was chaired by Frederick M. Hodgdon from the Chicago Architectural Club. The various subcommittees were made up primarily, but not entirely, from its members. The separate five-man Jury of Admission served as a committee of the whole without a chairman. Prior to the exhibition, the committee sponsored a competition for the catalog cover. The winner, Herbert Anderson, received the one-hundred-dollar first-prize donated by Herbert Green. Both Green and Anderson were members of the Exhibition Committee. Second prize of twenty-five dollars went to Herbert A. Smith, and Bernard C. Greengard was given a "mention." Anderson's simple design was used on the cover. The catalog was organized very much as it had been in the past. The front matter included basic information about the three sponsoring organizations, a list of patrons, a brief essay by Irving K. Pond, a page concerning the Traveling Scholarship, and information on the American Academy in Rome, followed by illustrations of the exhibits and an index of all the entries. The catalog illustrations were about equally divided between sketches and photographs. None was indicative of the work of the Chicago school.

The index of exhibits in the catalog was the longest list to appear in many years, with a total of 785 items. (There was also a separate "Index of Exhibits" printed on rough paper that was given away to visitors who did not buy the catalog.) There were 135 exhibitors, most of whom had multiple entries. New York had forty-two exhibitors, largely because of the recent fire that had prevented the Architectural League of New York from mounting its 1920 exhibition. Chicago had seventy-six exhibitors, but since Chicagoans tended to show many more items than out-of-town firms, their work dominated the show. Although few of the illustrations

67. "To Show Chicago School of Architecture," *Chicago Daily News*, March 13, 1920.

*Barry Byrne's Clarke House in Fairfield, Iowa (WRH)*

*Spencer & Powers's Hauberg House in Rock Island, Illinois (PC)*

*The Lincoln Park Refectory by Perkins, Fellows & Hamilton, shown in 1920 (PC)*

*During the Victory Loan Drive in the summer of 1918, Thomas Tallmadge headed a group of architects who designed elaborate decorations to create a carnival atmosphere in Grant Park along Michigan Avenue from the Chicago River to Roosevelt Road (CHS)*

were from Chicago school proponents, their work was very much in evidence in the list of exhibits and in the exhibition rooms. Lawrence Buck, Barry Byrne, Dean and Dean, William Drummond, Alfred Granger, George Maher, Perkins, Fellows & Hamilton, Pond & Pond, Purcell & Elmslie, A. N. Rebori, Spencer & Powers, and Tallmadge & Watson were all represented, often with multiple items. Schmidt, Garden & Martin and Holabird & Roche exhibited a number of large buildings in the spirit of the Chicago school. Holabird & Roche also exhibited several large drawings of the proposed Soldier Field.[68] Finally, Louis H. Sullivan had twenty-eight items of his own work and that of Adler & Sullivan, dating back to before the World's Columbian Exposition, as well as some of his most recent work. His work and that of his colleagues from the Chicago school was important enough to merit a room of its own, one wall of which was devoted to Sullivan's contributions since the World's Columbian Exposition.

When the Thirty-third Annual Chicago Architectural Exhibition opened with a reception on Tuesday evening, April 6, 1920, the invited guests were entertained by the Van Vlissingen Dancers, who performed a program entitled "Dancing the World Back to Nature." Eight galleries were open for viewing. The press was included in the invitation list, and a number of newspaper reviews appeared within the next few days. Most were highly favorable, and all commented on the exhibition of the work of the Chicago school. Louise James Bargelt wrote that "the group of architects known abroad as the Chicago school is splendidly represented. Louis H. Sullivan, whose Transportation building at the Columbian exposition attracted worldwide comment and praise, shows a detail of the building's famous 'golden doorway' and the Wainwright tomb in St. Louis, Mo."[69] She also commented on Holabird & Roche's design for Lakefront Stadium, later renamed Soldier Field. Several models were shown, including one of the Centennial Memorial Building by Schmidt, Garden & Martin, and a model of the work proposed by Childs & Smith for enlarging Clarendon Beach on Lake Michigan. Bargelt also commented on a number of more or less forgettable exhibits, but ended her review by saying, "It is an interesting as well as a worthwhile exhibit and should be seen in its many details in order to be appreciated."

The *Chicago Economist* reviewer felt that the exhibition "promises to surpass all former exhibitions of this character . . . Every prominent Chicago architect is participating. Each is represented by his best work, executed in and around Chicago, during the year."[70] The *Bulletin of the Art Institute of Chicago* commented that there were "an unusually large number of models . . . and an effective selection of furni-

68 *Western Architect* 29, no. 1 (January 1920): 7. The structure that was to be called Soldier Field was announced in 1919 as "A Stadium for the South Park Commissioners." It was formally named Soldier Field in 1926.

69. Louise James Bargelt, "Architectural Exhibit at the Art Institute," *Chicago Tribune,* April 11, 1920.

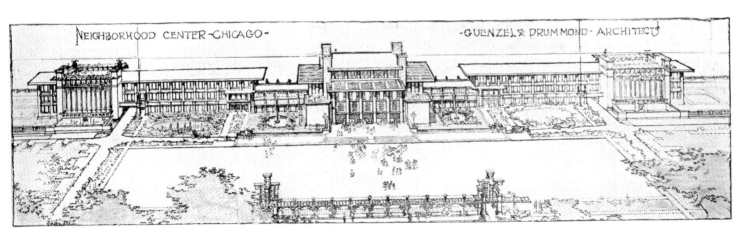

*William Drummond's design for "A Neighborhood Center," shown in 1920 although the design was done several years earlier (WA)*

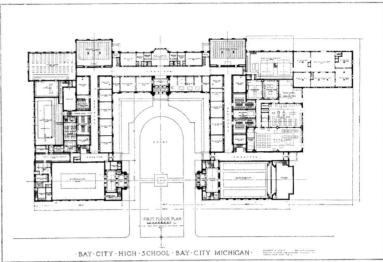

*Perspective and plan of an early version of the design for Bay City High School in Bay City, Michigan (PC)*

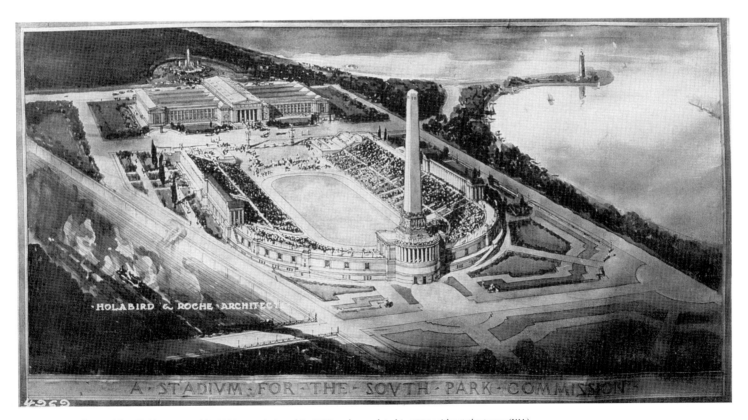

*Holabird & Roche's Soldier Field, so named in 1926, was designed in 1920 and completed in 1924 without the tower (WA)*

*Louis Sullivan's work, much of it done long before the exhibition, was nevertheless given an entire wall in the 1920 exhibition (AIC)*

ture and tapestries."[71] It also quoted extensively from Sullivan's remarks. A number of other local publications reviewed the exhibition, generally in the same vein, always with high praise for Sullivan and the Chicago School.

The professional press also reviewed the 1920 exhibition. The *Western Architect*'s unnamed reviewer apparently did not actually see the exhibition.[72] He stated that "it was not so large as we have been accustomed to witness, though comparing favorably with that of 1919." In fact, the 1920 exhibition was more than twice the size of the one held in 1919. Nevertheless, he did make some valid points. He named all the men of the Chicago School who exhibited and commended "the room given over to the 'Chicago School' in what is the most serious attempt that has been made to present the activities of that school." He also remarked that Frank Lloyd Wright's absence was notable. Finally, he gave credit where credit was due, writing that "not in years has so considerable a representation of the work of Mr. Sullivan been brought together. This is due to the labors of a special committee of which Mr. Robert C. Spencer, Jr., was chairman, and which brought to light matter with which the younger men in the profession are not familiar."[73] The *American Architect* published similar sentiments, but ended its long review by stating that "in all matters pertaining to organized architecture, the State of Illinois appears to stand as a brilliant example. On the floor of the convention in Washington during the debate on State Societies, the fact that Illinois had accomplished great and lasting results through the harmonious cooperation of the chapter and State Society was used as a strong point in argument. In this joint Chicago Architectural exhibition probably one of the most successful local exhibitions yet held, we have further evidence of the good results to be obtained by this happy combination. Some will claim that the Chapter alone would have secured equally satisfactory results, but they would have to prove it."[74] While he was right, it is unfortunate that he did not see fit to mention the Chicago Architectural Club, without which the exhibitions in Chicago would never have started, much less reached a thirty-third anniversary. The cooperation between the club, the AIA, and the ISA was now firmly established and would continue until the demise of the club nearly twenty years later.

70. "Architectural Exhibit," *Chicago Economist (Austin)*, April 16, 1920.

71. *Bulletin of the Art Institute of Chicago* 14, no. 5 (April 1920): 67–69.

72. *Western Architect* 29, no. 4 (April 1920): 33–34.

73. This is the only time Spencer was named. It's likely that the writer had confused him with Tallmadge.

74. "Thirty-third Annual Chicago Architectural Exhibition," *American Architect* 117, no. 2319 (June 2, 1920): 719–26.

Andrew N. Rebori's innovative Field House for the Lincoln Park Commission, shown in the 1920 exhibition (WA)

Andrew Rebori, sketched by fellow Cliff Dweller Theodore J. Keane in 1924 (CDC)

Andrew Rebori's design for a golf shelter for Lincoln Park, shown in 1920 (WA)

*Sketch by Charles Morgan (CAC/22)*

# Working Together to Survive

CHAPTER EIGHTEEN

At the end of 1920, two decades into the twentieth century, the Chicago Architectural Club was forced to look back on seven years of decline. There had been a brief spurt of new members following the end of the World War, but the old spark of the group was not there. It was no longer the vibrant, active organization it had been twenty years earlier. The last year when the club had mounted its annual exhibition on its own had been 1913. That year had been successful but not outstanding compared to the influence the club had had earlier. The 1914 exhibition had been better, partially due to the presence of Frank Lloyd Wright, albeit over the objections of some. It was also the first year that the Illinois Chapter of the AIA and the Chicago Architects' Business Association (later renamed the Illinois Society of Architects) had helped out with the exhibition. Nineteen fourteen was the last year that the exhibition would be identified as a Chicago Architectural Club event. Thereafter, it would be the Chicago Architectural Exhibition, and the club, the AIA, and the ISA would share credit and responsibility for mounting the show.

A greater concern than needing help with the annual exhibition was that the Illinois Chapter of the AIA and the Illinois Society of Architects were becoming more and more active in representing the architects of Chicago and Illinois, and the Chicago Architectural Club could no longer claim to be the preeminent architectural organization in Chicago. The AIA, a national organization, had relaxed its rules somewhat, and more practitioners were becoming members. In states where licensing was now a legal requirement, that alone was usually enough to qualify for AIA membership, although a certain level of ethical conduct and professionalism was also expected. The ISA, whose only requirement for membership was that one must be a licensed architect, was becoming increasingly powerful, particularly in representing architects in legislative matters. By 1915, it was the largest architectural organization in the state and was envied and emulated by state organizations throughout the United States. The membership of both the Illinois Chapter of the AIA and the ISA—particularly the leadership—was made up largely of former, or in some cases current, members of the Chicago Architectural Club. There was little competition among the three groups, and they often worked together on matters of mutual interest such as the annual exhibition.

There were several reasons for the decline of the Chicago Architectural Club. One major justification for its existence had always been the education of young men who had no means of learning the intricacies of the profession other than apprenticeship, and the club had helped to fill that void in its early years. This task became less and less important as college- and university-level two- and four-year curricula were established throughout the United States. For those who could not attend such institutions, the Society of Beaux-Arts Architects and its Beaux-Arts Institute of Design had ateliers in most major cities. It became increasingly difficult for the Chicago Architectural Club to maintain its own educational programs when they competed directly with the society for the time of its members. The club essentially embraced the Beaux-Arts system and established its own atelier. With the establishment of the club atelier, fewer members were willing to spend the time needed to organize and promote the activities of the club. At the same time, the First World War had decimated the club's numbers. By 1918, a third of the active members were in military service and others were working in some capacity for the government as part of the war effort. Furthermore, the war forced the club to cancel its very popular annual Traveling Scholarship Competition, which was not held after 1915.[1] An American Traveling Scholarship was awarded in 1917 for two months' travel in the eastern states for the study of colonial architecture, but it was hardly the same. Only a few members competed for it.

On the aesthetic front, many of the young members who had served in Europe during World War I had developed a new interest in historic architecture, and the modern movement in Chicago had suffered. It was only through the efforts of a few stalwarts, led by Thomas Tallmadge and George Maher, that the dream of creating a truly American architecture in Chicago and the Midwest had been kept alive. This small but determined group of architects had remained dedicated to the idea of the Chicago School of architecture. The Illinois Chapter of the AIA had asked George Maher, Dwight Perkins, and Arthur Woltersdorf to define the Chicago School in 1912, but the chapter had done little to promote it. Perkins, Woltersdorf, and particularly Maher were not about to abandon the idea. They were joined by architect and historian Thomas Tallmadge, who, in 1918, had used the occasion of the hundredth anniversary of the state of Illinois to present a photographic exhibit of architecture from the previous century as part of the Thirty-first Annual Architectural Exhibition. The bulk of the exhibit had shown work done after the World's Columbian Exposition.

The 1918 exhibition had received a good deal of press coverage, largely due to the historic architecture, which had prompted the Illinois Chapter of the AIA to begin a permanent collection of photographs of the work of Illinois architects. The AIA had been particularly interested in the work of the Chicago School architects led by Louis Sullivan, who had offered his support for the idea. The collected material, especially that of Sullivan, formed a major part of the 1920 exhibition, but the 1919 exhibition had been dominated by the work of various architects who were deeply involved in city planning and multiunit housing schemes. The 1919 exhibition had not been a venue for the work of the Chicago School of architecture. In 1920, Tallmadge, Maher, and several of their colleagues had made an effort to change this situation, which had resulted in one of the largest assemblages of Chicago School work ever exhibited.[2] The leaders of the club, however, had not been particularly pleased with the results. They had lost control of the exhibition and had exhausted their treasury in mounting the show.

The realization that the 1920 exhibition would not have been held except for the efforts of the AIA and the ISA had a demoralizing effect on Chicago Architectural Club members. Virtually all of the men who had done the work and served on the various committees in 1920 were former or current members of the Chicago Architectural Club. Most were older now, and they were concerned about this ven-

1. The Traveling Scholarship was announced in the 1916 annual exhibition catalog, but there is no evidence that it was ever awarded.

2. The 1920 exhibition required eight galleries to show the 785 entries. It was one of the few exhibitions that was documented by Art Institute photographers.

## ILLINOIS SOCIETY OF ARCHITECTS' MONTHLY BVLLETIN

ISA Monthly Bulletin *caption design by Hugo H. Zimmerman (ISA)*

erable institution of their youth. They set out to do what they could to remedy the problem.

❋

The Illinois Society of Architects had begun publishing its *Monthly Bulletin* in July of 1916. While it was produced primarily for members of the business-oriented ISA, it was ecumenical in nature, often publicizing the activities of the Illinois Chapter of the AIA and the events of the Chicago Architectural Club. It always, for example, published the dates and other information about the annual exhibition. In March 1917, the ISA had sponsored a competition for a new "Caption" for the *Bulletin*.[3] It had been open to ISA, AIA, and CAC members. The ISA had been disappointed with the response and had announced in June that it could not yet award any prizes due to the dearth of entries.[4] Not until February 1918 did it make a selection.[5] George W. Maher was chairman of the jury. Club member Hugo H. Zimmerman was given the first prize of fifty dollars, with the proviso that his design would be altered somewhat to make it more appropriate for the masthead. George Lloyd Barnum was named second-prize winner. No other awards were made. Henceforth, the slightly revised caption was used in the *ISA Monthly Bulletin*.

In the January 1920 issue of the *ISA Monthly Bulletin,* published before the 1920 exhibition was mounted, an unsigned article noted that the "manifest destiny of the United States is to be the leader of modern civilization. In the new Americanism now being formed in the crucible of Time will be developed an American Art, an American Music and an American Architecture." The author went to state his position in a few paragraphs, asking, "Will a true American Architecture be developed? The editor thinks so. Will the American Institute of Architects perform its full duty to the Nation and to civilization by encouraging and fostering the development of a real American Architecture? Time will tell." The editor of the *ISA Monthly Bulletin* and probable author of the article was F. E. Davidson. Davidson had been a member of the ISA since its founding and had held a number of positions including that of president in the 1916–17 year. He was almost certainly prompted to write the item by George W. Maher, who was active in both the AIA and the ISA. Maher had been an early member of the Chicago Architectural Club and was now one of the foremost proponents of the recognition of the Chicago School as an "American" architecture.

The month following Davidson's editorial, Maher wrote the first of three articles, each of which was titled "An Indigenous Architecture."[6] In his first installment, Maher stated that he was concerned that while there seemed to be a belated recognition of the creative abilities of Americans, people seemed to have forgotten the great strides made before World War I and were content to make "a fetish of precedent—content to add replica upon replica, indicating a sterility in creative or imaginative ability." He went on to assert that a "country like America demands a vital art created from its own environment, its own people, an art that will suggest a democracy and reflect the aspirations and character of the nation." He ended by acknowledging that the ISA had asked him "to write a series of short articles . . .

*Frank E. Davidson (WRH)*

3. George W. Maher, "An Interesting Competition," *Illinois Society of Architects Monthly Bulletin* (hereinafter referred to as the *ISA Monthly Bulletin*) 1, no. 9 (March 1917): 1.

4. "The May Meeting," *ISA Monthly Bulletin* 1, no. 12 (June 1917): 1.

5. "The Competition for Our New Caption," *ISA Monthly Bulletin* 2, no. 8 (February 1918): 8.

6. *ISA Monthly Bulletin* 4, no. 8 (February 1920): 1–2; *ISA Monthly Bulletin* 4, no. 9 (March 1920): 1–2; and *ISA Monthly Bulletin* 4, no. 10 (April 1920): 1–2. All three articles carried George W. Maher's byline.

suggesting certain ideas and impressions touching upon this subject. I shall aim to do this from the viewpoint of the Middle West. I hope I have a purpose to perform, perhaps in inaugurating a school of architecture in the midst of this country where the enthusiasm of the young men shall not be quenched and where full opportunity be given to encourage them to express in their work the ideals of America and the spirit of a democracy."

In his second article, Maher began by commenting on the values found in the indigenous architecture of America and noted that those works had been, for the most part, neglected "in present educational methods, especially pertaining to architecture, in failing to pay close attention and study to that which springs from the soil, from the people, since it is from such inspiration that all great national achievements originate, whether in the realm of art, poetry, literature or music . . . As a contrast in procedure, the methods now in vogue in designing, for instance important government or public work, is seemingly to ignore all native inspiration . . . the conventional methods in designing important buildings is to hark straight back to the days of Pericles, the Caesars or from precedents of a foreign clime, aiming to produce the exact architectural achievement of a people far removed in aspirations and forms of government and life from our own." He continued:

> Such an architecture is not indigenous, is not American, and does not in any sense reflect the spirit of a democracy, for which an Abraham Lincoln strove by precept and example to enable and perpetuate . . . While I have referred to many evidences in our country of an indigenous type of building reflecting American life and people, it may be stated with truth that the middle west can claim the distinction of succeeding in crystallizing into being a type of architecture that possesses certain creative and original characteristics inclusive of general plan and design which has received recognition both in this country and abroad.
>
> This type of architecture is generally known as 'The Chicago School' and is the result of a conscientious effort on the part of a group of men who reside in and near the metropolis of the west. They express in their work 'The Western Spirit' as I interpret it free from exacting precedent and yet free to adhere closely to the principles of good construction and the true spirit of design.

Oddly enough, Maher did not credit the origination of this architecture to Louis Sullivan, as he and others had so often done in the recent past. Instead, he attributed it to "the first pioneer who penetrated the virgin wilds of a new country and located near what is now known as the Chicago River, and the broad waters of Lake Michigan." In Maher's opinion, it was here that "the Chicago spirit was born in the hearts and minds of these first settlers. There is no mistake in the assertion. Here an indigenous art was fathered which in time will be a contribution to a national art reflecting an American civilization."

In the same issue of the *ISA Monthly Bulletin,* there was an item headlined "The Chicago School of Architecture," which noted that the "coming architectural exhibit at the Art Institute, Chicago, will display work of designers who aspired to establish a distinctive style."[7] It went on to list those men whose work was expected to be shown, twenty in all, beginning with Louis H. Sullivan and ending with George W. Maher. The item concluded, "Mr. George W. Maher, F.A.I.A., is a special committee of one having charge of the proposed exhibit."

In George Maher's third and final article, he became less philosophical and more specific. Early on, he wrote that "no movement of any permanent importance can evolve and properly mature unless founded upon certain fundamental princi-

7. *ISA Monthly Bulletin* 4, no. 10 (March 1920): 6.

ples related to environment surrounding life and progress . . . The 'Chicago School' or 'Movement' as well as other distinct Chicago achievements received their original impetus from the adventurous spirit of the early pioneer. The 'I will' spirit of this great metropolis of the west is indigenous, it is a Chicago product of energy inherited from the early struggle for existence, a power that is generally known and given full recognition." After a few sentences acknowledging the Chicago Fire and its aftermath, Maher went on to suggest that the Chicago School dated its birth to the World's Columbian Exposition. He flatly asserted that "'the Chicago School' of building was first expressed in a noteworthy way at the World's Columbian Exposition. This effort was the creation of the Transportation Building by Louis H. Sullivan, the architect. Here was an expression in art and architecture entirely new." He continued:

> This building . . . expressed in plan, design and ornament the purpose for which it was constructed, but also brought . . . a new vision of the possibilities of the use of materials, construction, art and architecture blended together into an original creation.
>
> "The Chicago School" in design was, therefore, as auspicious in its beginning as that of any art movement in any country and no doubt was the inspiration that encouraged other minds to seek a new expression in their work . . . "The Chicago School" dates its outward expression of note in the year 1893. It has progressed consistently from this time, ever growing in importance as recruits of independent minds have added their interest and influence to the movement.

Without naming any names other than Sullivan's, Maher credited a "widening group" of men who had responded to the new architecture of the Middle West. He noted that the practitioners of the style were mindful of the engineering needed to realize their structures and that they made no effort to hide the structural aspects of their work. It was language that would have fit nicely into architectural criticism a half century later. In this last article in his series, which coincided with the Thirty-third Annual Chicago Architectural Exhibition, Maher made a point of telling his readers that the work he was so enamored of could currently be seen at the Art Institute of Chicago. "The special room . . . at the Art Institute . . . displays the work of this school and the extent of its wide and varied influence . . . This exhibit perhaps displays a broader range of effort in plan and design than any exhibit held in Chicago or elsewhere . . . No greater educational propaganda could be suggested than that this entire exhibit be forwarded to various parts of the country where it may be viewed and explained to the general public."

The concluding words of Maher's series read: "The principles underlying this work are akin to the ideals of America and represent in a tangible way the spirit of a democracy, working through the minds of the men who have expressed it. These examples are indigenous since they spring from the soil and the people." Louis Sullivan and his many admirers must have read Maher's words with great appreciation. For the time being, at least, they were not forgotten.

When the 1920 exhibition was over, the club held its annual meeting to elect officers for the coming year. Elmer J. Fox was elected president, Paul F. Esser, vice president, Fred O. Rippel, treasurer, and Curt A. Esser, secretary. Four active members were chosen as directors: A. J. Lawrence, S. A. Rognstad, C. W. Farrier, and A. S. Morphett. Continuing the policy established the year before, two associate members, C. H. Sierkes and W. L. Pringle, were made directors. Six of these men had served on the board during the past year. The club had added more than fifty members to its roster in the previous twelve months, primarily because of the war's end and the club's atelier, now under patron William E. Parsons. The club was not, however, out of the woods. There was a great deal of work to do if it was to continue to be a force in Chicago architecture. The CAC members looked to the Illinois Chapter of the AIA and even more to the Illinois Society of Architects for help.

The first problem club members faced following the annual meeting was finding a new home. They had occupied space in the Athenaeum Building on East Van Buren Street for nearly two years, but it had been less than satisfactory. They found new quarters at 40 South Clark Street in a building where the Adventurers Club already had space.[8] The Chicago Architectural Club members were therefore able to use their sister club's dining facilities and, on occasion, its space for a large group meeting for dinner. The major disadvantage was that their floor, the fourth, was divided into numerous small rooms on different levels, and they didn't have sufficient furniture to outfit the space. They did, however, have drafting tables, which they brought in immediately to serve the students in their atelier.

When the board of directors of the Illinois Society of Architects met on July 13 just after the Chicago Architectural Club had moved to its new space, they "authorized the special Committee on Co-operation with the architectural club to solicit subscriptions from our members to make up the quota of $1,000 needed by the club to fit up its new quarters." The society also appropriated a hundred dollars toward this fund to help in furnishing the club's rooms. At the same meeting, the ISA board authorized the mailing of the *ISA Monthly Bulletin* to each member of the club and "placed at the disposal of the Chicago Architectural Club one page of each issue of the Bulletin. Members of the board of directors also pledged themselves to attend the meetings of the Architectural Club and to assist all possible in bringing about the closest relationship between the Architectural Club and the Illinois Society of Architects."[9] The only stipulation the ISA made was that the copy for the page devoted to the club was to be supplied and edited by club members, and the ISA would have no responsibility for its content.[10]

The August 1920 issue of the *ISA Monthly Bulletin* was the first with a page dedicated to the Chicago Architectural Club. (This practice would continue every month until April of 1927.) It carried a CAC heading with a list of officers, directors, standing committees, and four articles. The first article thanked the ISA for its generosity in assisting the club; the second described the new club rooms; the third was an item concerning the club's atelier; and the last was a brief note about the social features of the club. There was also an article, sans title, that voiced concern about the "dropping off of attendance at the Club Rooms at noon." It ended with several notes about various members' activities. The most interesting of the articles was the one describing the new club rooms. It noted that "the new Club Rooms at 40 South Clark Street are larger than those we have just left, and are approaching the amount of space necessary to take care of the various branches of activity of the club. The quarters consist of the entire fourth floor of the building, with only a few partitions in the rear. A small portion will be set aside for a Club Room and Reception room, and the remainder left open for the Atelier, which will also be used for the Lecture Room. The many little flights of stairs and narrow corridors up to the Club Rooms remind one of the old Paris Ateliers, and with a few decorations on the walls for directions, will lend the proper spirit. The Adventurers Club, occupying the Third Floor, are very congenial, and lend a hand at making things interesting. A little time will be required to get things in good running order, but this winter will see us going fine."

The club did not wait until winter to get going. The article regarding its atel-

8. The Adventurers Club's records indicate that the CAC moved to 40 South Clark Street in May 1920. Since the July minutes of the ISA note an offer to help the CAC "fit up" its new quarters, it is likely that the two clubs agreed to take space at the same address at the same time. In any case, there are several later references to the CAC using the Adventurers Club space occasionally, especially for dinner meetings; apparently they had an arrangement to share the kitchen and dining room.

9. *ISA Monthly Bulletin* 5, no. 1 (July 1920): 12. These matters were also noted in the ISA's minutes for the July 13, 1920, meeting.

10. *ISA Monthly Bulletin* 5, no. 2 (August 1920): 2.

*Forty South Clark Street, the Chicago Architectural Club's headquarters from mid-1920 on; the club occu-
pied the fourth floor, the Adventurers Club was on the third floor, and the first and second floors were the
home of the Economy Book Store for many years (PC)*

ier noted that it was now the only atelier in the city and acknowledged that it
would be following the Beaux-Arts Institute of Design programs. The club planned
to send out a "detailed announcement" regarding the atelier "soon for the winter
season." It had already started holding outdoor Saturday afternoon sketch classes,
which were to continue "as long as weather permits." Those classes were taught by
members C. L. Morgan and B. C. Greengard, under the overall direction of G. L. Barnum.[11] The members were also holding sketch nights, usually of two hours' duration, in the club rooms as they had done during the club's early days. They planned
that their first in-house exhibition would be one of sketches from these efforts. The
first suggested competition was for a heading for the CAC page in the *ISA Monthly
Bulletin*.[12] Apparently the members decided against such a small effort, since nothing came of it. This renewal of interest in competitions focused the club's activities
during the next few months. It was almost like old times.

The first Evening Sketch Competition was held on November 19, 1920. The
subject was "An entrance doorway to a small downtown Club." Criticism and
prizes were to be followed by refreshments. The results were disappointing, largely
because "most of the atelier men were working industriously on their Beaux Arts
projects, nearly due, and refused the opportunity to win cash prizes." The club reported that judge Earl H. Reed Jr. found little to commend, but it was suggested that
"all come out the next time with real stuff."[13] There were a great many other competitions in which the members had the opportunity to participate. The Le Brun
Traveling Scholarship was announced in October,[14] and artist Joseph Birren offered
a prize of fifty dollars to be awarded at the 1921 Chicago Architectural Exhibition
for "the best design in color showing an interior of two walls with at least one window, one door, a mantel and appropriate spaces for the distribution of . . . paintings."[15] The Chicago Own Your Own Home Exposition, to be held from March 26
through April 2, during the 1921 architectural exhibition, had also announced a

11. Ibid.

12. *ISA Monthly Bulletin* 5, no.
4 (October 1920): 7.

13. The competition was
announced in *ISA Monthly
Bulletin* 5, no. 5 (November
1920): 7, and the results were
published in *ISA Monthly
Bulletin* 5, no. 6 (December
1920): 7.

14. The Le Brun Traveling
Scholarship was a national
competition and Chicagoans
rarely entered. In 1921, however, the club recorded in the *ISA
Monthly Bulletin* that member
Paul J. McGrath had "submitted
a very creditable solution of the
problem, a Railroad Depot."

15. *ISA Monthly Bulletin* 4, no.
12 (June 1920): 6.

competition for the design of a small house, with a prize of five thousand dollars. Henry K. Holsman, president of the Illinois Chapter of the AIA, was the architectural adviser for the competition, and there was a great deal of interest in it, especially among the younger men of Chicago.[16] The ISA offered a first prize of a hundred dollars for the design of a certificate of membership in the ISA.[17] The *ISA Monthly Bulletin* mentioned it twice, in December and again in January. There was also an announcement, in January 1921, of a Farm and Garden Competition sponsored by the Woman's National Farm and Garden Association, which felt it was important enough to send the program to the club quarters by messenger. The results of each of these competitions were to be shown at the 1921 exhibition. All the competitions were under way while the club was in the process of getting its new rooms in suitable condition for use as both a headquarters and an atelier.

The Annual Traveling Scholarship Competition was still the club's most important event of its kind. The problem, a "Club House for Chicago Architectural Club," was announced in early January, and on Saturday afternoon, January 29, 1921, there was a preliminary *esquisse en loge* held in the club rooms. Nineteen members entered. It was the first time that the Beaux-Arts system of rules was officially used in the annual competition. The problem was more than a building for the club. It was a structure to house the ISA and the AIA as well, a telling indication of the relationship of the three groups. The 250-by-500-foot full-block site was just north of the Chicago River, bounded by four streets of equal importance, which were not identified. The program included a rather elaborate system of rooms for each of the three societies and noted that "the Club will have a park setting with possibilities of formal gardens and use of sculpture . . . an open air amphitheater seating a thousand people is required . . . and must not be pretentious, *but simplicity must be its keynote.*"[18]

The problem of outfitting the new space on Clark Street was partially solved by generous contributions of time and materials by suppliers, some of whom were associate members of the club. The CAC column in the December 1920 issue of the *ISA Monthly Bulletin* noted that the club was grateful for "the donation of plastering in the Club rooms from Mr. William Williams." The same issue credited Messrs. G. L. Barnum and C. W. Farrier as being "in charge of the decoration of our club rooms."[19] A month later, the club thanked "J. B. Mullen and the Sherwin-Williams Co. for the donations, respectively, of the labor and material required in the painting of our club room." The article went on to say that the "room is now finished, the furniture is moved in; and it makes a comfortable place for reading, lounging and general sociability."[20] In fact, a little more remained to be done. The April 1921 *ISA Monthly Bulletin* noted that the Architectural Decorating Company had donated a lighting fixture similar in design to those in the Burnham Library of Architecture.[21]

Under the leadership of president Elmer J. Fox, the Chicago Architectural Club was functioning well in the last half of 1920 and in early 1921. The new space at 40 South Clark Street was successful, and the need for refurbishing brought the members together for working evenings. They began a regular schedule of programs, competitions, and other events, many done in cooperation with the AIA and the ISA. Of all the affairs of the club, now the most organized and arguably the most important was the club atelier under the leadership of William E. Parsons. Parsons had graduated from Columbia University in 1898 and then studied for three years at the École des Beaux-Arts in Paris. After serving in various positions in the United States and abroad, he joined Edward H. Bennett in 1914. He became a member of the firm in 1922, when it became Bennett, Parsons & Frost. He was an experienced architect and city planner. It is not surprising that he assumed the

16. *ISA Monthly Bulletin* 5, no. 4 (October 1920): 5.

17. *ISA Monthly Bulletin* 5, no. 6 (December 1920): 8.

18. *ISA Monthly Bulletin* 5, no. 8 (February 1921): 7.

19. *ISA Monthly Bulletin* 5, no. 6 (December 1920): 7.

20. *ISA Monthly Bulletin* 5, no. 7 (January 1921): 7.

21. *ISA Monthly Bulletin* 5, no. 10 (April 1921): 9.

responsibility for the Chicago Architectural Club atelier in the fall of 1919. His employer, E. H. Bennett, had been in that position for several years, the last two of which he shared responsibility with Andrew Rebori. Parsons had never been a member of the Chicago Architectural Club, probably because he felt that his education and experience did not mesh with the activities of the club. He was, however, a good teacher and critic, and he remained the patron of the atelier for more than a decade.

Parsons had taken over as patron of the Chicago Architectural Club atelier in 1919–20. When the *ISA Monthly Bulletin* began its publication of club affairs in the fall of 1920, one of the first items noted that "the Atelier at the close of last season was large and growing." There was, however, room for expansion in the new quarters. In the second issue of the *ISA Monthly Bulletin,* on the page devoted to club affairs, the entire space was devoted to a discussion of the club atelier.[22] It began, "When a man becomes the employer of other men he assumes . . . a debt to his profession." It went on to describe the work of the club atelier and how it operated under the rules of the Beaux-Arts Society. Also included was a list of men who had won honors in the club's atelier work in the past season. No less than twenty-two honors were on that list, and some men were listed more than once. This was an extraordinary achievement, since virtually all the jurying was done in New York City by eastern architects. The long article ended by announcing that "a Business Meeting of the Atelier Parsons will be held in the Club rooms Friday evening, October 1, 1920. Everyone planning to join the Atelier should be present."

The well-organized atelier season started on October 2. Twenty-seven *esquisses* were turned in, including a "7B projet" and "20B analytique."[23] The projet competition was a private chapel on a country estate, and the analytique competition was a side entrance to a church in the Renaissance style.[24] On November 23, 1920, the atelier participants elected Herbert Anderson as *massier* and Gordon Beach as *sous massier*.[25] They also reported the various deadlines established for the work in the atelier to be turned in, which occurred approximately once a week. By the end of 1920, it was reported that twenty-five men were actively working at the atelier. The awards, chosen by juries in New York, were generally announced about two months after the final drawings were submitted. The first to be published in the *ISA Monthly Bulletin* appeared in February 1921, when ten of the eighteen drawings submitted in November received mentions and one was granted a first mention. In April another first mention and ten more mentions were announced. In June the club published the results of the year's work in its section of the *ISA Monthly Bulletin.* Twenty-four men had received at least one award in the 1920–21 year, and some as many as four, the total number of problems submitted. It was an incredible showing for what was really a very small atelier. At the end of the club year in May, the atelier patron, William E. Parsons, was elected to honorary membership in the Chicago Architectural Club. He had earned it.

The atelier occupied a good deal of the club's time during the 1920–21 year, but it was by no means the primary activity in the club rooms, as it had been in the two previous years.[26] The new space was more centrally located and larger, with room for a library and a lounging area, and members had the privilege of using the Adventurers Club dining room on the floor below. They made a valiant effort to revitalize the club and reinstitute the various social, educational, and other events that had been so popular in earlier years. It seemed to be working. After the 1920 exhibition, the Entertainment Committee arranged for a picnic and field day in July at

22. *ISA Monthly Bulletin* 5, no. 3 (September 1920): 5.

23. Most American ateliers used French terminology when discussing design work. An *esquisse* was the first quick sketch done immediately after a problem was assigned. A copy was left with the patron at the end of the day and it was compared with the final design. In theory, the final design was expected to be very close to the esquisse in form and solution. *Projet* was the name for the project as a whole.

24. *ISA Monthly Bulletin* 5, no. 4 (October 1920): 7.

25. These terms were used to describe the men who were experienced in atelier work and were in charge of the activities at the atelier in the absence of the patron. The best source of terms used in ateliers is *Pencil Points* magazine. Starting in April of 1922, Raymond M. Hood presented a series of one-page articles titled "A Vocabulary of Atelier French," which ran for several months and presented, in alphabetical order, a list of French words used in ateliers.

26. The following information concerning club activities was taken from various issues of the *ISA Monthly Bulletin* published between August 1920 and September 1921.

*Illinois Society of Architects' membership certificate, designed in a Chicago Architectural Club competition (WRH)*

the Cook County Forest Preserve, an event that was reminiscent of earlier days. Members were encouraged to use the club during noon hours and in the evenings. A pool table was acquired and a piano was available for music, extemporaneous or otherwise. The club began a serious effort to build its library, taking out subscriptions to all the current professional journals. It had a six-copy subscription to *Pencil Points*, a journal published specifically for draftsmen. Sketch nights were started again, with at least one two-hour problem each month. Generally the club devoted one evening a month to a visiting lecturer, usually with stereopticon slides. Subjects included the *Plan of Chicago,* hospital design, and school design, and late in the season the club started a class in French for would-be travelers. Some evenings were still devoted to work on the club room, which needed some finishing touches before it was completely ready for use. Members instituted a "study class" once a week for candidates for the Illinois architects' examination. While all this was going on, the Thirty-fourth Annual Chicago Architectural Exhibition was scheduled for early March of the following year. That decision was made in September of 1920, giving all concerned adequate time to prepare. Plans called for working with the AIA and the ISA once again to mount the exhibition.

As 1920 moved to a close, the competition for the design of a certificate of membership for the Illinois Society of Architects was adjudicated. Two prizes were awarded: first prize of a hundred dollars went to G. L. Barnum, and H. W. Anderson took the twenty-five-dollar second prize. Those certificates remained in use until the demise of the ISA nearly eighty years later.[27]

Cooperation between the club and its sister organizations, the AIA and ISA, was now an established fact, probably the most important factor in the revitalization of the Chicago Architectural Club following the First World War. The new club rooms on Clark Street were also important. The club had never really been pleased with the space it shared with others at the Art Institute of Chicago, and the space it had used on Plymouth Court from mid-1916 through mid-1918 was not suitable for anything other than the atelier. The move to the Athenaeum Building in 1918 had been similarly unsatisfactory. That situation can be best summed up by a passage from an article by an anonymous writer in the *ISA Monthly Bulletin* in September of 1921, when the club atelier was about to start its new year: "The first of October . . . brings back to the writer reminiscences of . . . that black Saturday afternoon a few years ago, and it certainly was black for us 'neuveaux' . . . The club was then only an atelier. That was enough too, but I mean there was no social calendar. There was a club room in the Art Institute basement, but seldom used. The Atelier was 'at home' on the top floor of an old building south of Van Buren on Dearborn Street."[28] The writer had confused the club's location and must have had mixed emotions, because a few sentences later he wrote, "There were those in the atelier that winter or two who saw some real work and who will never forget the all-night 'charettes' . . . It was that clean, honest, brotherly friendship, which existed then that Mr. Puckey as patron did so much to create . . . that made the atelier a success and the night work a pleasure." Clearly, he was remembering the difficult times with some pleasure, but he was also pleased that those days were over and that the Chicago Architectural Club had a real home for the first time since it had left the Dexter Building on Adams Street.

When the Chicago Architectural Club took space at 40 South Clark Street in mid-1920, the Illinois Society of Architects made a concerted effort to help it get back on its feet. The ISA helped out financially and "pledged themselves to attend

27. The competition was announced in *ISA Monthly Bulletin* 5, no. 7 (January 1921): 7. The results were reported to the ISA board by the Committee for Co-operation with the Chicago Architectural Club on June 13, 1921.

28. *ISA Monthly Bulletin* 6, no. 3 (September 1921): 11.

the meetings of the Architectural Club" and to assist in other ways to bring about a closer relationship between the two groups.[29] The Illinois Chapter of the AIA made a similar commitment. In October of 1920 the AIA issued a blanket invitation to members of the Chicago Architectural Club to attend all meetings of the AIA.[30] It was a period of great cooperation between Illinois's three architectural organizations. The *ISA Monthly Bulletin* regularly published information on the activities of the AIA, and the ISA was usually asked to attend state and national AIA conventions as guests. The Chicago Architectural Club chose to respond in a manner that was beneficial to all.

At a special meeting of the club on November 1, 1920, the Chicago Architectural Club made a major change to its constitution.[31] It provided for a new category of allied members, open to "any person . . . who is a member in good standing, in either the Illinois Chapter of the American Institute of Architects or the Illinois Society of Architects, or both." Annual dues were to be five dollars, with that money committed to funding the Annual Traveling Scholarship. The idea was an immediate success. A few days later, at the ISA monthly meeting, club president Elmer Fox explained the new rules to the members of the ISA. By the end of the evening, twenty-five members of the ISA had signed applications to become allied members of the Chicago Architectural Club.[32] The trend continued, and by 1921 the ISA *Handbook for Architects and Builders* listed 144 allied members of the Chicago Architectural Club. The extra dues were nearly enough to fund the Traveling Scholarship, which at the time awarded $750 to the winner. More important, it gave members of the ISA and the AIA a reason to participate in the activities of the club. It was not at all uncommon for allied members to turn up unannounced at a regular meeting of the club or at a session of the atelier to offer advice and help. Furthermore, with these senior architects on board, there was a new interest from draftsmen and other younger men in becoming part of what many referred to as the "junior" association of architects in Chicago.

The myriad activities of the club, both on its own and with the AIA and the ISA, promoted a camaraderie among Chicago architects that had not been seen for a decade. The educational and professional meetings were of great importance to the young men, as were the social events. The club's tradition of celebrating the end of the year provided an opportunity to bring all three organizations together. On the CAC page in the *ISA Monthly Bulletin* it was noted that the "most important social event of the club year is the annual party held at the Christmas season. The date this year is December 28th, and it will be held at the Art Institute. Our success last year has led us to follow a similar program. Wm. Ziegler Nourse and the Studio Players will present short plays and dances, between which there will be musical numbers. Refreshments will be served in the refectory, following the program, and there will be dancing in the club room."[33] The Art Institute was chosen largely because it offered the use of Fullerton Hall, where the entertainment could be presented. A month later, the *Bulletin* reported that "notwithstanding the sudden extreme cold weather there was a good crowd on hand to enjoy our party on the 28th." It did lament that "more of the Chapter and Society members were not there to see the club in its social aspect and to get better acquainted with us. These evenings are expected to serve the double purpose of giving pleasure and promoting club prestige and understanding."[34]

As 1921 got under way, the club began to concentrate much of its efforts on the forthcoming annual exhibition. It had begun offering the Traveling Scholarship again in 1920, but it had been announced too late for the drawings to have been exhibited or the winner announced in the 1920 exhibition. The program, "A Hotel Lobby" in terra-cotta, was never published, nor were any of the entries. The winner's

29. *ISA Monthly Bulletin* 5, no. 2 (July 1920): 12.

30. *ISA Monthly Bulletin* 5, no. 4 (October 1920): 7.

31. *ISA Monthly Bulletin* 5, no. 5 (November 1920): 7.

32. *ISA Monthly Bulletin* 5, no. 6 (December 1920): 1, 7. Those members named were listed on the club page. Additional names were published in January 1921, bringing the total to eighty-two ISA allied members. More names were added nearly every month for the following year.

33. Ibid., 7.

34. *ISA Monthly Bulletin* 5, no. 7 (January 1921): 7.

*Fine Arts Building in 1893, from the southeast (AIC/CDA)*

name, Pierre Blouke, first came to light in an article titled "The Winner of the 1920 Traveling Scholarship," published in the October issue of the *ISA Monthly Bulletin*. It was in the form of a letter from Blouke outlining his plan for his trip to Europe. During the next several months, the *ISA Monthly Bulletin* published excerpts from letters Blouke sent back from Europe. He was not the only club member traveling in Europe; Fred Hodgdon, the 1915 scholarship winner, was finally able to take advantage of his winning entry now that the war was over,[35] and the club had agreed to increase his stipend to $750 from the original $600, so that his prize money would equal that of Pierre Blouke. Another popular member of the club, Paul McGrath, was also in Europe and spent part of his trip traveling with Hodgdon.[36]

The 1921 Traveling Scholarship Competition was planned well in advance of the 1921 exhibition. The announcement appeared in January and was published in the February *ISA Monthly Bulletin*. Final drawings were due at the club rooms at noon on Monday, March 7, 1921, which allowed ample time for the winner's drawings to be hung at the annual architectural exhibition. The subject, a "Club House for Chicago Architectural Club," was one with which members were very familiar, having just finished fitting out their own new club rooms. The difference, of course, was that the competition program required a separate building that would house not only the club, but the AIA and the ISA as well. An unexpected consequence of the competition was planting the idea of such a clubhouse in Chicago. Within a few short years, it would come to pass.

The Traveling Scholarship jury, C. H. Hammond, W. J. Smith, and I. K. Pond, met on March 7, 1921. They were pleased with the overall submissions, eventually narrowing them down to four finalists. A. S. Morphett was named the winner. The remaining three, J. B. Lindquist, G. L. Barnum, and H. W. Anderson, were so near to equal in quality that the jurors elected to give each a mention. They also agreed that "because of the merit of all of the drawings submitted, the jury was quite pleased and willing to devote a full evening for a criticism at the club."[37] No record of such an evening has been found, but members of the AIA and ISA began appearing regularly at the club rooms. The 1921 scholarship winner reported to the membership that he planned to leave Chicago in the fall of 1921, traveling first to England and then on to various cities on the continent. He promised a monthly letter to keep his fellow members up to date on his travels. He also promised, upon his return, to "deliver a 'lecture' descriptive of my ramblings."[38]

Even more demanding than the annual scholarship competition was the planning and mounting of the Thirty-fourth Annual Chicago Architectural Exhibit. Early in the planning, two events occurred that altered the tone of the exhibition. First, it was decided that other groups should be admitted to the exhibition, and second, Chicago was asked to participate in an exhibition at the Paris Salon. The

35. *ISA Monthly Bulletin* 5, no. 11 (May 1921): 8.

36. *ISA Monthly Bulletin* 6, no. 1 (July 1921): 7; *ISA Monthly Bulletin* 6, no. 2 (August 1921): 11.

37. *ISA Monthly Bulletin* 5, no. 9 (March 1921): 7.

38. *ISA Monthly Bulletin* 6, no. 1 (July 1921): 7.

*Fine Arts Building in ruins in 1921 (CAP)*

major group to be added to the exhibition was the Woman's National Farm and Garden Association, which also sponsored a "course of eight lectures" at Fullerton Hall during the exhibition, dealing with issues of gardening and landscape design of the home.[39] In a prepared statement to the press a week before the exhibition opened, the chairman of the Exhibition Committee, John A. Holabird, spoke of the exhibition as being "the first concerted effort of architects . . . to reach the painters, sculptors, and workers in applied arts whose product might enlarge the scope of building plans. There are a great many young painters and sculptors in Chicago—some of them students of arts schools—who can do murals, decorative figures, and other work that has a definite place in architectural plans."[40] Holabird, who represented the AIA, was joined by three colleagues from that organization. The ISA contingent was chaired by George Maher and three other members of the society. The Chicago Architectural Club group of five members was chaired by Paul F. Esser. The Jury of Admissions was chaired by E. H. Bennett with Howard Shaw, Hugh Garden, Emery Jackson, and Arthur Aldis. Neither Jackson nor Aldis was an architect.

Before the jury had an opportunity to act, they were asked by the Illinois Chapter of the AIA to respond to a request from the Paris Salon to provide "a representative selection of drawings from American architects for their spring exhibition."[41] Chicago was included. The Chicago jury selected thirty-nine buildings by twenty-one architects. There were two each by Sullivan and Wright, five by D. H. Burnham and Company, and four by Holabird & Roche. Several other architects had one or two each. The jury sent photographs to New York, where the work of twelve Chicago architects was selected and sent on to Paris.

During this same period there was a concerted effort to find a means of restoring the former Fine Arts Building, the only major surviving structure from the World's Columbian Exposition.[42] It had been pressed into service after the fair to house museum items remaining from the fair and collected since then, and had been renamed the Columbian Field Museum. With the new Field Museum now planned for the south end of Grant Park, there was no further need for it in Jackson Park. Nevertheless, there was great public interest in restoring and reusing it. Starting in 1920, George Maher led the battle to save it. It would be nearly two decades, long after Maher's death, before the restoration was completed. In the meantime, Maher and several sympathetic colleagues on the AIA's Municipal Art and Town Planning Committee arranged to have large-scale photographs of the building shown at the 1921 exhibition. They were prints of the building as it appeared in 1893 and 1921. It was not the first or the last time the building would be shown at

39. Eleanor Jewett, "Miniature Garden Will Be Feature at Art Institute," *Chicago Tribune*, March 1, 1921.

40. "Architects to Have Exhibit at Art Institute," *Chicago Tribune*, February 27, 1921.

41. *ISA Monthly Bulletin* 5, no. 7 (January 1921): 5.

42. The idea of restoring the Fine Arts Building was not new. It had been discussed numerous times by both the AIA and the ISA over the previous five or so years. The building had survived largely because it had been built to resist fire, as it was the repository of hundreds of important works of art during the fair.

the annual exhibition. It had been shown in the 1911 exhibition and compared to a model of the proposed new Field Museum. The 1893 photograph was later used as the frontispiece for the 1923 exhibition catalog when the building's restoration was imminent. The value of Chicago's architectural history was not lost on the 1921 Joint Exhibition Committee, and they welcomed the photographs as part of the campaign to restore the building. As it turned out, they had their work cut out for them. The 1921 exhibition was to be different from any previously held.

The Exhibition Committee was forced to combine efforts with colleagues in landscape and the applied arts, largely because the Art Institute of Chicago had already committed much of the space the committee wished to use to the Woman's National Farm and Garden Association, as well as to the annual exhibition of arts and crafts and an exhibition of British arts and crafts. A report from the ISA Exhibits Committee after the show closed stated that a "departure was undertaken in this Exhibition, made necessary by the fact that the Art Institute could not give the entire space exclusively to the Architectural Exhibition, therefore, this annual Exhibition was held in collaboration with the Arts & Crafts and Landscape Societies."[43] The showing of the British arts and crafts material was actually a "division of the nineteenth annual exhibition of applied arts." One reviewer, Eleanor Jewett of the *Chicago Tribune*, wrote that the "idea this year which is worked out in the union of the architectural with the applied arts exhibit is, I suppose, a good one, in principle. In practice, I am not so sure. There are certain things like paintings, hangings, furniture, and house decorations generally, which have a definite correlation to architecture proper. There are other things . . . which belong not to architecture." Nevertheless she, like most local reviewers, felt that the two exhibits had a good deal in common and together formed a fine exhibition.

The professional press was not so kind. The *Western Architect* made no comment on the exhibition at all. The *American Architect* published an extremely neg-

43. ISA Minutes, Chicago Historical Society, box 12, folder 12–10.

*Woman's National Farm and Garden Association room at the 1921 architectural exhibition at the Art Institute of Chicago (AIC)*

ative review that began, "It is with a distinct sense of disappointment that one concludes an inspection of the 34th annual Chicago Architectural Exhibit."[44] The reviewer was disgusted with the "artistic pots, jugs and what-nots; fabrics, furniture and miniature works of sculpture." He went on to say that "an architectural exhibit should be overwhelmingly architectural." He remembered that "last year's exhibit had a room devoted to the works of a period when Chicago architects gave promise of great influence in the development of American architecture . . . Those in charge of the current exhibit have seen fit to ignore much that is distinctive of Chicago and worthy of a world's attention." The only displays he found worthy of comment were a "great plaster model of the Bahai Temple" and a few of the submissions by architectural schools. He also noted that the catalog was "scarcely worthy . . . of Chicago."

In fact, there was no real catalog for the Thirty-fourth Annual Architectural Exhibition. Instead, a small pamphlet listing the exhibitors and the patrons of the show was distributed to visitors, but no other information was included.[45] There were 298 exhibits listed, some of which appear to have been landscape designs or arts and crafts items. One hundred and forty-four patrons were listed. There was no listing of the British arts and crafts items shown at the same time, nor were any of the Woman's National Farm and Garden Association exhibits identified as such.

On May 2, 1921, nearly a month after the exhibition was over, the Chicago Architectural Club held its annual meeting to elect officers and plan for the coming year. The members did not let the adverse comments about the 1921 exhibition discourage them; the meeting was a great success. It was reported that "perhaps the outstanding feature of the occasion was the attendance . . . the fact that approximately three times as many attended as were at the preceding annual meeting was cause for considerable satisfaction. We do not like to think that the free meal, served to the members in the rooms of the Adventurers Club, before the meeting, had any in-

44. *American Architect* 119, no. 2364 (April 13, 1921).

45. This is among the rarest of the exhibition publications. It was about four and a half by seven inches, with fourteen pages plus covers. There is a copy at the Art Institute of Chicago library.

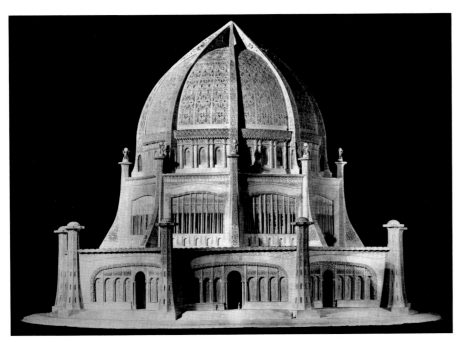

*The great plaster model of the Baha'i Temple, a crowd-pleaser at the 1921 exhibition (Baha'i photo)*

*Adventurers Club dining room, the site of many a boisterous evening hosted by the Chicago Architectural Club (courtesy Adventurers Club)*

fluence on the meeting; still it might! Four past presidents were present, but they were reticent to talk on club life during their own administrations."[46] The club treasurer reported that there was more than a thousand dollars in the bank and about the same was owed in back dues.

More important was the report of the Membership Committee, which noted that the club had gone from 182 members the previous year to 337 members, the largest number ever. Fifty of the new members were active members, one was an associate, and 122 were in the new allied category. The club had lost only twenty-one members during the year. The club librarian reported a substantial increase in the number of books in the library due to gifts and purchases. Finally, Elmer J. Fox was reelected president and treasurer Curt A. Esser moved up to vice president. J. B. Lindquist and Charles H. Markle were chosen as secretary and treasurer. Four of the previous year's directors remained in place and two new men were added, D. R. Lundberg and Fred O. Rippel. Both Lundberg and Rippel would resign their directorships in September. The positions were filled by Gerald Barry and James A. Kane. The annual meeting closed with the presentation of prizes to the winners of the seven-hour "Alford Sketch" problem, which had been held on Saturday, April 23, 1921. It was the second year that William H. Alford had offered a twenty-five-dollar prize for this event.[47]

With the summer months upon them, the club members reduced their activities to a minimum, even though the club rooms remained open and they had the privilege of using the Adventurers Club dining facilities. The library was regularly used, particularly by members reading the various architectural journals, of which there were multiple subscriptions so that all could be served as needed. The *ISA Monthly Bulletin* reported few club activities other than sporting events, visitors, and letters from travelers. It did note that the club was holding a class in French during the summer months, led by Mr. E. Le Vieque.[48] His students were drawn largely from the club's atelier. He expected to have "the Atelier boys speaking

46. *ISA Monthly Bulletin* 5, no. 10 (May 1921): 7.

47. William Hedley Alford was born in England in 1860. He studied architecture there before coming to the United States in 1884. He first worked for an architect in Omaha, Nebraska, and later moved to Ohio. He became a dealer in bank furniture in 1887 and vice president and general manager of Weary & Alford Co., designers of bank buildings and equipment. He arrived in Chicago around 1900.

48. *ISA Monthly Bulletin* 6, no. 2 (August 1921): 11.

French this winter and Atelier Parsons will be transformed into a real Paris Atelier." It was predicted that the atelier would "be as large if not larger than last year." The attitude of the members was "let's all get the real Atelier spirit and make ours the 'Atelier de Beaux Arts.'" The club was now completely in tune with the French system of teaching. The raw, almost amateurish, but nevertheless enthusiastic, approach of earlier years was gone. With it went much of the creative spark that was responsible for the Chicago School of architecture. The Beaux-Arts Institute of Design had succeeded in bringing the French system of architectural education to Chicago.

In August of 1921 the *ISA Monthly Bulletin* announced that the Atelier Parsons's "calendar for the 1921–22 season has been received . . . A Smoker will be arranged . . . at which plans will be settled . . . above all, let's get settled." The following month it was noted that the first *esquisse* of the new atelier year would be held on the first of October. The same month, a brief article suggested that "it is hoped that our next move, which will probably be next May, will be into our own Club House, capable of covering every branch of the club's activities."[49] There had been hints in both the ISA and Illinois AIA minutes that a headquarters building for the architectural community was very much on the minds of all. Ultimately, it would come to pass in a manner that no one expected.

The fall season started with an "Open House Meet" outlining the work of the atelier and encouraging members to participate. A few days later, the first sketch meeting was held, and longtime associate member G. Broes Van Dort offered a gift of fifty dollars for the best design submitted in a nine-hour sketch. The Van Dort Sketch Competition was becoming a regular feature each fall. In November, the *ISA Monthly Bulletin* announced that it "was probably the most successful competition held in the club for some time."[50] Seventeen sketches were submitted, all well done. George L. Barnum and George N. Nedved shared the fifty-dollar prize money equally, and Gerald Barry was given a mention. One of the jurors, William J. Smith, spent the following Thursday evening at the club reviewing the drawings, "giving each a very interesting and instructive criticism."

By January 1922 it was reported that "the club is constantly increasing its activities and has already outgrown its quarters . . . every Tuesday, Wednesday, Thursday and Friday evening is taken up with some special class, aside from the already large atelier, which is open and busy every day and evening . . . Monday and Friday evenings have been set aside for the study class; Tuesday and Thursday evening for the French class, and Wednesday evening for a new French class being organized. Then, once a month, an educational night program, and a social evening, with wives and girl friends, sandwiched in occasionally. Saturday afternoons are generally busy with new Beaux Arts problems, Esquisse-Esquisses, etc."[51] The report went on to encourage members to participate in as many activities as possible.

In addition to the regular activities, the club still had to plan its two major annual events, the architectural exhibition and the Traveling Scholarship Competition. The club president named a Scholarship Committee chaired by N. Max Dunning in November of 1921. He was aided by George C. Nimmons, Howard Shaw, Francis W. Puckey, and Elmer J. Fox.[52] The subject for the competition was finally published in February.[53] It was to be a "Memorial" on the axis of Roosevelt Road just east of the new Field Museum. The full title, "A Monument to a Great American Statesman," was published in the 1923 exhibition catalog. The competition was to be conducted in accordance with the rules of the Beaux-Arts Institute of Design, and nineteen men submitted an *ascus*.[54] The time allowed was relatively short, and by March a winner, Keith Cheetham, had been named. The jury submitted a written report and spent an entire evening at the club reviewing their

49. *ISA Monthly Bulletin* 6, no. 3 (September 1921): 11.

50. *ISA Monthly Bulletin* 6, no. 5 (November 1921): 9.

51. *ISA Monthly Bulletin* 6, no. 7 (January 1922): 9.

52. *ISA Monthly Bulletin* 6, no. 6 (December 1921): 7. It was also noted in the following month's bulletin that the committee was working, but no program for the competition was mentioned.

53. *ISA Monthly Bulletin* 6, no. 8 (February 1922): 7.

54. Ibid.

*Keith Cheetham, winner of the 1922 Traveling Scholarship Competition, came to Chicago from Australia (PP)*

findings.[55] Cheetham's design was listed, but not illustrated, in the 1923 exhibition catalog.

While the scholarship competition was under way, several club members also entered and took prizes in other competitions. The Le Brun Traveling Scholarship, sponsored by the New York Chapter of the AIA, was open to all. Club members H. W. Anderson and J. F. Booton both entered, and although neither won, they were mentioned in the resulting publicity. The Atelier Parsons's schedule was such that many of its participants simply could not participate in the Traveling Scholarship Competition. Atelier members did, however, regularly receive mentions or better in the jurying of their work. To motivate atelier members, the directors established the "Club Prize," to be awarded to "the Atelier student receiving the greatest number of 'values' for the current season." The prize was a year's active membership dues.[56] There were only so many hours in the day, and with five-and-a-half-day work-weeks, time was limited. It is remarkable that as much work was done as was reported in the professional press.

There is no record of just when the Thirty-fifth Annual Chicago Architectural Exhibition for 1922 was first scheduled. It must have been decided early in the fall, since both the ISA and the AIA exhibition committees were announced in the August issue of the *ISA Monthly Bulletin.* Chester H. Walcott was the AIA chairman and was asked to serve as the chairman of the joint committee for the exhibition. The Chicago Architectural Club committee members were not published until the 1922 catalog appeared. J. A. Kane, Paul Esser, C. W. Farrier, and W. M. McCaughey represented the club. Walcott's AIA group included H. H. Bentley and H. K. Franzheim. George Maher chaired the ISA committee, which consisted of Hubert Burnham, A. H. Hubbard, Clare C. Hosmer, and Charles L. Morgan. There were also a Committee on Hangings and Decoration and a Jury of Admission, all in keeping with traditions established in 1914. The first reference to the 1922 exhibition is in the minutes of the Illinois Society of Architects for November of 1921. There was considerable concern that the Joint Exhibition Committee had taken it upon itself to engage one John C. Baker to sell advertising for the catalog. There had been no catalog for the 1921 exhibition, and all concerned felt strongly that that had been a mistake. The ISA board in particular, and the AIA to some extent, felt that the committee had overstepped its authority in entering into an agreement with Mr. Baker. The debate went on for several weeks and it was not until early in 1922 that all agreed that John C. Baker would be acceptable as agent for the exhibition catalog.[57] He was told to proceed with selling advertisements for the catalog. It would be the first advertising to appear in an exhibition catalog since 1899.

The Thirty-fifth Annual Architectural Exhibition was scheduled for March 11 through April 9, 1922. The Woman's National Farm and Garden Association was again asked to participate. Mrs. Russell Tyson was named chairman of the group.[58] Numerous prizes, both cash and objects, were offered in various categories of exhibits. Casts of garden sculpture were awarded for the best exhibit, and the Garden Club of Hinsdale gave a second prize of fifty dollars for landscape gardening. Mrs. Charles A. Brown also offered fifty dollars for the best sundial. Jurors were Mrs. S. Helena Rosse of Highland Park, William Pilkin Jr. of Cleveland, and John W. Root Jr. of Chicago. In a preopening article it was announced that the previous year "this exhibit was of great interest . . . the present show . . . includes garden plans, back yard gardens, sun dials, and garden sculpture . . . The work of American sculptors will be represented by twenty-five pieces of garden sculpture chosen for this purpose by the National Sculpture Society of New York."[59] The Farm and Garden Association also sponsored a number of lectures during the exhibition, as it had done the year before.

55. *ISA Monthly Bulletin* 6, no. 9 (March 1922): 7.

56. *ISA Monthly Bulletin* 6, no. 7 (January 1922): 6.

57. This problem was discussed at several meetings of the ISA board of directors as well as the Executive Committee and recorded in the minutes between early December 1921 and January 1922. Those minutes are at the Chicago Historical Society in the records of the Illinois Society of Architects.

58. "Architects to Hold Exhibit," *Chicago Daily News,* February 11, 1922.

59. Marguerite B. Williams, "Art Notes," *Chicago Daily News,* March 8, 1922.

The Joint Exhibition Committee's plans for 1922 went beyond adding garden exhibits. The *Chicago Daily News* article reported that the exhibition also included a "group of room models made by the collaboration of New York mural painters, architects and interior decorators." The writer went on to say that all this would "serve to enliven the plans of skyscrapers and churches, which [are] from the exhibition proper of the architects." The exhibition went even further, as reported in the *Christian Science Monitor*, where a "Special Correspondence" noted that "mural painting, interior decoration, sculpture, and landscape gardening unite with the thirty-fifth annual Chicago Architectural exhibition, auspiciously installed, in the east galleries of the Art Institute."[60] Included were "an exhibit from the Architectural Association of London, . . . Sproatt & Rolph's Hart House, University of Toronto . . . [and] designs from the American Academy in Rome." The correspondent also commented on the murals, decorative elements, models of domestic interiors, and landscape architecture, as well as the usual architectural exhibits. Alfred Granger's design for a combination Cathedral and Office Building for the Protestant Episcopalian Diocese of Chicago and a similar, but larger, building by Bertram Goodhue of New York were singled out. Both were illustrated in the catalog as well

60. "Chicago Architectural Exhibit Proves Varied and Brilliant," *Christian Science Monitor*, March 15, 1922.

*Alfred Granger's Cathedral Building for the Protestant Episcopalian Diocese of Chicago, shown at the 1922 exhibition (CAC/22)*

*Bertram G. Goodhue's design for a larger cathedral, shown in the 1922 exhibition (CAC/22)*

*Malvina Hoffman's bronze figure for a fountain, submitted in 1922 (CAC/22)*

*George W. Maher & Son's design for the John B. Murphy Memorial Building, submitted to the 1922 exhibition (CAC//22)*

as in local newspapers. While the pre-exhibition comments had promised work from London, Paris, and elsewhere, there was no work by foreign architects included in the catalog, except for a single exhibit from Canada. Also promised were a number of works from related fields—murals, paintings, and sculpture. Most published reviews included this material in their comments but, for the most part, only sculpture was mentioned. Sculptors Malvina Hoffman, A. A. Weiman, Alois Land, and Edward McCartan were all well represented.

The 1922 catalog was in many ways an elegant departure from the past. It was hardbound with a printed paper cover over boards and a total of 270 pages. Fifty-one pages were devoted to advertising, as was the inside back cover. There were seventy-three advertisers, none of whom were architects. The catalog opened with a title page giving the basic information on the exhibition including its dates. It was followed by a listing of the various committee members, a page devoted to the Illinois Chapter of the AIA's medal of honor, and, after a frontispiece with a "View of Chicago" taken near Wolf Point, a foreword written by George W. Maher. Maher was somewhat restrained in his one-page essay. After years of arguing in the strongest terms for the development of an American architecture, he touched only peripherally on the subject. He did open by saying, "The spirit of progress is abroad. In every field of endeavor there are indications of the forward look, a desire for self expression, an examination of the problems that beset this country, a determination to establish America's place in the great world movement." He came close to continuing his argument for an American architecture, but ultimately did not do so. At the midpoint of his essay he wrote, "The architect has a noble tradition to guide him in his efforts. The historic past is available in all of its rich and myriad forms from which to draw upon for inspiration in the forming of a representative art." He was bowing to his colleagues who were looking to the past for inspiration. He concluded, "The judgment of the great public is the controlling factor in the end."

The frontispiece was the only page printed on the recto side. All the other pages, except the advertising, were printed on one side only, the verso. The catalog was divided into four sections: Residential, Public and Commercial, Ecclesiastical and Educational, and Sculpture and Carving. Each of the four sections listed the exhibitors represented therein. A list of the advertisers followed the illustrations. The title page, the medal of honor page, each section divider, and the final page of the

*Frank G. Fulton's "View of Chicago," used as the frontispiece for the 1922 catalog (CAC/22)*

list of advertisers all had a small sketch of a Chicago scene by Charles Morgan. Morgan's work eventually became legendary in Chicago. He prepared renderings for numerous Chicago architects, including the great and near great. It is not surprising that the club's annual editors chose to include his work in the pages of their catalog. The book was printed in dark sepia ink on beige paper. It did not include a complete listing of all the exhibitors. That was provided by a supplemental list prepared in a manner identical to that of the previous year. This small booklet was given gratis to each visitor.

Reviews of the 1922 exhibition were mixed. Eleanor Jewett of the *Chicago Tribune* was fairly noncommittal.[61] She mentioned the miniature rooms and the "mural paintings shown by the national Society of Mural Painters," which she thought gave the exhibition a "much needed touch of color." She also mentioned that the Woman's National Farm and Garden Association had opened its exhibit at the same time, and she was pleased that paintings brought a "change in the tone of the exhibit." She noted the names of several exhibiting architects but not what they exhibited, reserving such comments for a single sentence commending Frederick C. Hibbard for his "interesting sculptural . . . memorial to be erected in Shiloh National Park." In an article in the *Chicago Herald-Examiner,* Dan Fogle urged parents to "Take the Kids to Architects' Exhibit Today."[62] He too, found little to discuss in what was probably a tongue-in-cheek article. One of the longest, and strangest, reviews of the exhibition was the second article by Eleanor Jewett in the *Chicago Tribune.*[63] Once again, she really didn't write about the architecture, and she acknowledged that. She began, "Properly speaking, in an architectural exhibition the emphasis should be laid . . . upon architecture." She then proceeded to devote a full third of her article to the work of painter Grace Ravlin, whose work was in an adjacent gallery. (It may have been part of the exhibition, but is not referenced elsewhere.) She wrote briefly about the small models of interiors, which she found "most attractive." Eventually, she got to the architectural galleries, which had been arranged with "enlarged photographs of residences and business structures, each of which illustrates some excellency in architecture." The only specific building that to her mind merited mentioning was Bertram Goodhue's office building for "Protes-

61. Eleanor Jewett, "Architectural Exhibit Opens This Morning," *Chicago Tribune,* March 12, 1922.

62. Dan Fogle, "Take the Kids to Architects' Exhibit Today," *Chicago Herald-Examiner,* March 12, 1922.

63. Eleanor Jewett, "Art and Artists," *Chicago Tribune,* March 19, 1922.

*Frederick C. Hilbard's photograph of his design for the United Daughters of the Confederacy Memorial, Shiloh National Park (CAC/22)*

tant centralized religious activities." She admired much of the sculpture in the exhibition and found room to comment on the mural paintings. She also mentioned the names of several architects without listing their work. Most other local reviews were in the same vein. Only Lena M. McCauley of the *Chicago Evening Post* had a genuinely positive reaction.[64] She wrote, "How changed are the walls in the year since the earlier shows. Whereas plain drawings and plans and sketches calculated to interest the profession ruled in the long ago, today the scene has taken on popular color—sculpture and the allied arts of mural painting enliven the display . . . The interest is still concentrated on the parts of architecture, but it is the broader point of view . . . the mural painter and the sculptor, the maker of decorative iron grills, the designer of tapestries and the interior decorator, together with the landscape gardener, are vitally associated with noble buildings, from the picturesque studio home to the edifice for public use." She went on to discuss the specifics of the exhibition, generally in a favorable light. It seems the local press was simply not ready to review an architectural exhibition that was broad enough in scope to include material other than architecture.

The most comprehensive and intellectual review was published by the *Western Architect*.[65] The author, probably Robert Craik McLean, was disturbed by "the lack of local material." He stated that the "profession in Chicago was largely submerged in the showing of work from the East." He briefly discussed past exhibitions and then went on to say that it "has not been a year nor a series of years which produces exhibition of unusual merit." He felt that, at least in the current year, the "artists and sculptors have it over the architects . . . In Chicago, of all cities, one might expect to find a certain freedom of fancy, if tradition counts for aught. It was not to be found in this particular Exhibit." He added, "Chicago has a long ways to go to attain and retain the leadership which once was its heritage." He was clearly lamenting the lack of material from those architects who had, for so many years, been in the avant-garde, not just in Chicago but in the nation. He then noted that having "gotten rid of the worst which may be said of the Thirty-fifth Exhibit, there are several things wholly complimentary which, we presume, should have been expressed at the outset . . . there was, this year, a unity of purpose on the part of the hanging committee which deserves mention. The arrangement . . . and hanging . . . displayed a studied attempt to arrange with a view to material, sizes, color and subject matter that created comment of a most favorable character. Groupings of the work of a single architect gave some idea of his versatility and of his moods." The work of Adler & Work was singled out, as was that of Pond & Pond, Charles Morgan, Chester H. Walcott, and a few other Chicagoans. The bulk of his favorable remarks, however, were reserved for exhibits from out of town. He was concerned that the East Coast was disproportionately represented. Toward the end of his two-page review he wrote that "some day . . . the Chicago Architectural Exhibition should be a truly national one. It will not be until the Pacific coast and the country to the West is represented." He was impressed with the western work he knew of and concluded, "We should like to see more of it in the East."

When the Thirty-fifth Annual Exhibition was over, the Joint Exhibition Committee reported that they considered it a success and had cleared approximately eight hundred dollars.[66] They also recommended that the catalog be continued in the future.

✳

The annual meeting of the Chicago Architectural Club was held in the club rooms on May 1, 1922.[67] Newly elected officers included president C. W. Farrier, vice

64. Lena M. McCauley, "National Outlook at Architects' Show," *Chicago Evening Post*, March 14, 1922.

65. *Western Architect* 31, no. 5 (May 1922): 49–50.

66. Report of the Architectural Exhibits Committee of the Illinois Society of Architects, June 5, 1922, ISA Collection at the Chicago Historical Society.

67. *ISA Monthly Bulletin* 6, no. 11 (May 1922): 9. This same item included information on the summer plans, the atelier, and other information included hereinafter.

*David Adler and Robert Work's photograph of the house they designed for R. T. Crane on Jekyll Island, Georgia (CAC/22)*

president Gerald Barry, and Alwin Wiersha and Chas. H. Market as treasurer and secretary. Directors James A. Kane and C. H. Sierkes were carried over, and J. B. Lindquist, J. Schierhorn, and M. H. Goetz were elected to two-year terms. Retiring president Elmer J. Fox was asked to serve a one-year term as director, filling out the slate for 1922–23. Records indicate that the club had added thirty-six new members and had ten resignations as well two new allied members. The club was flourishing both in membership and in funds. The treasurer reported a healthy bank balance and, in a change to the bylaws, the club decided to pay the treasurer, although the amount was not recorded. Summer was upon the club and, as usual, its affairs were somewhat reduced. It did set up a summer outdoor sketch class, and during the month of May was host to the Third Traveling Exhibition of the Beaux-Arts Institute of Design Medal Designs. That show included a drawing by Jerry Loebl, a member of the club and a student at the Chicago School of Architecture. In July the club hosted a similar traveling exhibition, this time of Class A medal drawings.[68]

The club's 1921–22 Atelier Parsons was not quite finished in May. It had one last problem to complete by May 22, in addition to a summer problem that would be due on September 18. In a departure from past practice, it was decided that atelier leaders (the *massier,* who was in charge in the absence of the patron, and the *sous massier,* second in command) were to be elected at the annual meeting rather than by the atelier members themselves. At the last minute, all agreed that this would not take effect until the following year. By August, the 1922–23 atelier program had been received and published. It was expected to be the best attended to date. No count of (or names of) participants was ever published, but the club regularly noted the number of problems forwarded to New York for judgment. In November of 1923, the club published a chart showing a "compilation of the number and classification of the graded problems sent by the various independent ateliers to the Beaux-Arts Institute of Design during a representative period last year." Of the twenty-seven ateliers listed, excluding universities, only three had submitted

68. *ISA Monthly Bulletin* 7, no. 1 (July 1922): 11.

*Charles Morgan's rendering for Board of Education architect John C. Christiansen, one of several sketches he provided for the 1922 catalog; Morgan's work became widely admired over the next few years (PAB)*

more problems for grading than the Atelier Parsons. The atelier had become the major activity of the Chicago Architectural Club. Its influence on other activities was evident in the various club-sponsored competitions, most prominently the Annual Traveling Scholarship Competition, which was, by 1923, being conducted along the same lines as any other Beaux-Arts program. The atelier's crowded schedule did not, however, hinder the club's other activities.

In the fall of 1922, the club began to publish its programs in advance as it had done many years before. The Entertainment Committee announced in July that it would hold a club picnic in Palos Park in August, a golf tournament had been arranged, and a special meeting would be held in November to announce the programs for the rest of the year. That same evening, Archie Morphett and Pierre Blouke gave short talks about their trips abroad, courtesy of the funds won in Traveling Scholarship competitions.[69] Regular in-house competitions were held, including the "Tiny Trib," in response to the Tribune Tower Competition, which had captured the interest of architects throughout the world.[70] The Education Committee continued its policy of devoting one evening each month to educational efforts.

69. *ISA Monthly Bulletin* 7, no. 4 (October 1922): 7.

70. *ISA Monthly Bulletin* 7, nos. 6–7 (December–January 1923): 11.

*Sketch by Charles Morgan used in the 1922 catalog (CAC/22)*

*Zimmerman, Saxe & Zimmerman's house for Lowell S. Hoit in Chicago; it has many of the characteristics of the Prairie houses built fifteen years earlier (CAC/22)*

On January 29, 1923, Thomas Tallmadge gave a talk on Christopher Wren. The members, particularly those who had not had the advantage of education beyond high school, were always interested in the history of architecture. Almost every month there would be an announcement of the acquisition of books related to history in the club library, which was, of course, open to all. In addition to its ever-increasing list of books, the club continued to subscribe to all the major professional magazines.

Broes Van Dort once again provided fifty dollars in prize money for the annual Sketch Competition, this time for "A Bridge Plaza." Alfred Granger and William J. Smith of the Illinois Chapter of the AIA were the judges and spent the rest of the evening in conversation with the members, which is remarkable considering that Granger was simultaneously chairing the jury for the Tribune Tower Competition. The same evening it was announced that the club would sponsor at least one brief in-house competition each month with small cash prizes.

By early 1923, the Chicago Architectural Club was already well along in its plans for the Annual Traveling Scholarship Competition and the Thirty-sixth Annual Chicago Architectural Exhibition. Other events over which CAC members had no control would, however, dominate the architectural scene in Chicago in 1923 and beyond. By far the most momentous was the announcement in December of 1922 of the winner of the Tribune Tower Competition.

*Principal rendering of the Tribune Tower submitted by Howells & Hood (TT)*

# New Excitement
# in Architecture

CHAPTER NINETEEN

During the last weeks of 1922 and the early part of 1923, the public's interest in architecture was at a level not seen in Chicago since the World's Columbian Exposition thirty years earlier. A period of labor strife had been over for six months and architects were generally busy. Members of the Chicago Architectural Club were especially conscious of the new public awareness of architecture. The winner of the great Tribune Tower Competition, Howells & Hood of New York City, had been announced at a special ceremony on December 2, 1922. The public learned the winner's name when they opened their Sunday papers on December 3.[1] The competition had been announced on June 9, 1922, at a banquet at the national convention of the American Institute of Architects held in the central hall of the crumbling Fine Arts Building in Jackson Park, the last remaining structure from the World's Columbian Exposition. The timing of the announcement was clearly intended to ensure that the competition would, by association with the national AIA, have the approval of architects throughout the United States.

The banquet at the Fine Arts Building had been arranged as part of a campaign initiated several years earlier by a small group of Chicagoans, headed by George W. Maher, who wanted the building restored to its original grandeur. The announcement of the Tribune Tower Competition had not been part of the original plans—it was merely serendipitous. At the previous year's AIA convention in Washington, D.C., the Illinois chapter had been well represented with thirteen delegates, four alternates, and five ex officio delegates, including national directors Richard E. Schmidt and N. Max Dunning, as well as past national president Irving K. Pond. These twenty-two men were a formidable group. They had proposed to the AIA's board of directors that the 1922 convention be held in Chicago. Four months later, Illinois chapter president Albert Saxe had received a letter from national AIA president Henry H. Kendall accepting the invitation.[2] In the meantime, the Illinois chapter had been continuing its efforts to get support for its plan to restore the Fine Arts Building.

Although this project had been discussed for several years, it was only in September of 1919 that it had gained credibility. Lorado Taft, an honorary member of the Illinois Chapter of the AIA and the Chicago Architectural Club, had spoken at a meeting of the Illinois chapter and suggested that the Fine Arts Building, then usually referred to as the Columbian Field Museum, be restored and preserved as

*William Dean Howells (TT)*

*Raymond Hood (TT)*

1. The best discussion of the competition, and all that went on before and after, is in Katherine Solomonson, *The Chicago Tribune Tower Competition* (New York: Cambridge University Press, 2001). It is a remarkable work of scholarship and has been used as a basic source throughout unless specifically noted otherwise.

2. *ISA Monthly Bulletin* 6, no. 4 (October 1921): 7.

*Eliel Saarinen's design for the Tribune Tower (TT)*

an art museum.[3] He hadn't mentioned that the collection of material in the Fine Arts Building was to be transferred to the new Field Museum shortly thereafter.[4] At the annual meeting of the Illinois chapter on June 8, 1920, it had been reported that "considerable progress has been made toward a plan of perpetuation."[5] Two weeks later, at the annual meeting of the Illinois Society of Architects, a resolution had been put forth requesting the "South Park Commissioners to defer decision on removing this building until careful examination of its physical condition can have been made, and suggestions for its further use be submitted for their consideration." The resolution had been discussed at some length, and an eloquent plea for the building's restoration and preservation had been made by George W. Maher. His remarks had been printed verbatim in the *ISA Monthly Bulletin* along with the resolution.[6] While it had not been stated, there was clearly a cooperative spirit between the AIA and the Chicago Architectural Club in proceeding with what was to be a monumental task. The Illinois AIA assigned the project to its Committee on Municipal Art and Town Planning, chaired by George W. Maher.

The committee's principal focus in 1920 and early 1921 was enlisting the aid of other civic organizations. In a report on committee activities published in May

3. *ISA Monthly Bulletin* 4, no. 3 (September 1919): 5–6.

4. *ISA Monthly Bulletin* 4, no. 12 (June 1920): 6.

5. Ibid., 4.

6. *ISA Monthly Bulletin* 5, no. 1 (July 1920): 9–10.

*The Tribune Tower Competition was announced at the closing banquet of the national AIA convention at the deteriorating Fine Arts Building in Chicago in 1922 (WA)*

*The restored Fine Arts Building in Chicago's Jackson Park, rededicated as the Museum of Science and Industry*

of 1921, it was noted that "the leading clubs of Chicago and civic organizations by resolution have endorsed the . . . actions of the committee. The South Park Board . . . stated in a letter, that no action will be taken by the Board relative to the wrecking of this building at the present time."[7] The AIA and the ISA were then challenged to get something started. They had to show their resolve to restore the Fine Arts Building in some concrete way before the South Park commissioners changed their minds. Furthermore, with the national AIA convention in June, it was imperative that progress be demonstrated in order to be certain of the support of the national organization. Their plans were outlined in a lengthy article in the May 1922 issue of the *ISA Monthly Bulletin*. The two groups agreed to jointly fund "a careful estimate of the cost of restoring the Fine Arts Building located in Jackson Park, otherwise known as the Columbian Field Museum." They also sought permission "to restore a portion of the building," which was granted by the South Park commissioners. That permission was given subject to the costs all being borne by the AIA and the ISA and any other civic groups that might be involved. This was important, since the bulk of the estimated sum of $7,500 needed for the cost estimate and other preliminary work had already been pledged by the Second District of the Illinois Federation of Women's Clubs. The remaining funds were raised, and work was begun on the restoration of the northwest corner of the building. The Chicago Architectural Club was not in a position to support the project financially, but did support it philosophically and regularly updated its members on the progress. A report of the work under way was published after the convention in the July 1921 issue of the *Architectural Forum*.[8] That article estimated that the cost of the restoration would be $1.64 million, which ultimately proved to be far too conservative. While the preliminary work was not yet finished when the national AIA held its annual banquet in the rotunda of the building in 1922, enough had been done to interest architects throughout the United States, who began to enthusiastically sup-

7. *ISA Monthly Bulletin* 5, no. 12 (June 1921): 6.

8. George W. Maher, "The Restoration of the Fine Arts Building of the World's Columbian Exposition," *Architectural Forum* 35, no. 1 (July 1921): 35–36.

port the restoration. That support encouraged Chicago philanthropist Julius Rosenwald to contribute a total of $3 million to the restoration of the building as an industrial museum, later renamed the Museum of Science and Industry. Plans were prepared by Graham, Anderson, Probst & White in 1926. Funds were not yet in hand, and before they came available, Alfred Shaw, Sigurd Naess, and Charles F. Murphy split away from Graham, Anderson, Probst & White. The final drawings and supervision of the restoration were completed by Shaw, Naess & Murphy.

The credit for restoring the Fine Arts Building has to go to George W. Maher, who headed the committee that insisted that the building be saved and brought the AIA and the ISA together in a cooperative effort to start the project. It is interesting to note that he was doing this literally at the same time he was writing essays for the *ISA Monthly Bulletin* advocating "An Indigenous Architecture," which was, in many ways, the antithesis of what the Fine Arts Building symoblized Whatever conflicting thoughts he may have had, George W. Maher was dedicated to the preservation and restoration of the Fine Arts Building, and the work he did prior to the AIA convention in 1922 was key to its ultimate success. He continued to devote time and effort to the project after the convention, but he never gave up his devotion to the idea that the Chicago School was the future of architecture.

In October of 1922 Maher drafted an essay titled "The Chicago School of Design."[9] It began, "The 'Chicago School' or as often termed 'The Prairie Style' of design originated in Chicago and thereby established a certain prestige or distinction in the realm of art." He went on to describe what is today termed the Prairie School of architecture. There is no doubt of his intent. He stated that "Chicago and its suburbs are well represented. We shall, therefore, refer to a few examples" and named a number of buildings, four by Sullivan, two by Wright, and four of his own. None was residential, although he noted that there were "many residences and other types of buildings here and abroad." He named only one architect, Louis H. Sullivan. (The final version published in the *Christian Science Monitor* named Sullivan, as well as Frank Lloyd Wright and George W. Maher. It included two illustrations, one by Sullivan and the other by Maher.) Maher's essay, obviously well thought out, ended with the statement, "The 'Chicago School' of design has been inaugurated. The movement will never die since it is a product of a virile life, it is American since it originated in America. It is well and favorably known abroad and has brought distinction to this great city. It should be encouraged as an indigenous or creative product of the middle west." With one exception this essay appears to have been the last bit of writing Maher prepared for publication,[10] albeit one that never saw print in its original form.[11] He essentially gave up public activity in 1923,[12] and left much of the day-to-day work in his office to his son, Philip, who joined him as a partner in February of 1922 after becoming licensed in mid-1921.[13]

The work toward restoring the Fine Arts Building in Jackson Park, the annual banquet of the AIA held there, and the announcement of the Tribune Tower Competition during the banquet all served to draw Chicagoans' attention to the architectural activity in their city. Oddly enough, all these events came at a time when most construction was at a standstill because of labor problems. Fortunately, those problems were soon resolved.[14]

The Chicago Architectural Club never ceased its activities during this period, laboring long and hard to continue its programs and following the work of senior colleagues in the AIA and the ISA. The two groups often held special

9. A three-page typescript of this essay is in box 19 of the ISA archives at the Chicago Historical Society. It is bylined George W. Maher and dated October 14, 1922. A revised version appeared in the *Christian Science Monitor* on November 13, 1922. A least twice as long, the article nevertheless uses some of Maher's language verbatim. It is signed "P.O.W." The editor changed Maher's term "Prairie Style" to "Prairie School"; it is the earliest known use of that term in print.

10. The exception was George W. Maher, "Restoration of the Fine Arts Building of the World's Columbian Exposition," *Architectural Forum* 35, no. 1 (July 1921): 35–37.

11. Two other articles with George W. Maher's byline did appear in professional journals: "An Architect's Relation to Town Planning" in the *American Architect* of January 1923 and "The Hinsdale Community Development" in the same journal in March 1924 (attributed to "George W. Maher & Son").

12. Maher had suffered a nervous disorder from time to time throughout his life. In late 1922, possibly early 1923, he began a series of confinements to sanatoriums, to no avail. On September 12, 1926, he took his own life while at his summer home in Douglas, Michigan.

13. The firm was known thereafter as George W. Maher & Son, Architects.

14. The major resolution of labor problems in Chicago at this time was the so-called Landis Award, whereby judge Kennesaw Mountain Landis served as an arbiter to establish fair and equitable wage rates for most of the building trades in Chicago.

*The members' table at the Cliff Dwellers Club, where innumerable plans germinated (WRH)*

events in the club's quarters, largely because the facilities of the Adventurers Club on the floor below were available for large groups for sit-down dinners. During this time, one of the club's most distinguished honorary members was involved in two significant activities. Louis H. Sullivan had arranged to write *The Autobiography of an Idea* and to prepare a series of drawings for the Burnham Library of Architecture titled *A System of Architectural Ornament According with a Philosophy of Man's Powers*. Both were eventually published by the Press of the American Institute of Architects.[15]

The two books had their genesis at the members' table of the Cliff Dwellers Club, where the city's architects, including many members of the Chicago Architectural Club, often took lunch. Sullivan had been an honorary member of the Cliff Dwellers since 1912, and after 1916, when he was no longer able to afford membership in the exclusive Chicago Club, he became a regular at the Cliff Dwellers.[16] In late 1922, over lunch, some of Sullivan's architect friends suggested that he prepare a series of drawings illustrating his philosophy of ornament.[17] It can be surmised through various letters and other documents that those friends included Andrew Rebori, N. Max Dunning, Pierce Anderson, Howard Van Doren Shaw, Thomas Tallmadge, I. K. Pond, Henry Holsman, and George Nimmons. It is possible that George Elmslie was also involved, and Frank Lloyd Wright was in touch with Sullivan during this period as well, sometimes "loaning" him money. Later on, a contemporary review of *A System of Architectural Ornament* stated that the fund was subscribed to by ten Chicago architects, the Armour Institute of Technology, and the Burnham Library. Apparently, Sullivan's friends arranged for the Burnham Library to contribute five hundred dollars, later shared equally with the Armour Institute of Technology. They themselves provided another five hundred dollars to finance the project. It was a way of supplying funds to Sullivan at a time when he desperately needed money, and getting a valuable document in return.[18] Originally planned to be thirty plates, the book was eventually reduced to twenty.

Sullivan had finished several preliminary plates by June 1922, when the national AIA held its convention in Chicago. During the second day of formal convention affairs, Sullivan was recognized on the floor by national president Henry H.

15. The story of these two books has been told several times by various authors. The best are George E. Pettingill, "The Biography of a Book: Correspondence Between Sullivan and the Journal," *AIA Journal* 63 (June 1975): 42–45, and George E. Pettingill, "'A System of Architectural Ornament . . .': Further Sullivan-Journal Correspondence," *AIA Journal* 63 (September 1975): 28–30. The story of *The Autobiography of an Idea* is also recounted in Russell Lewis, "Sincerely, Louis H. Sullivan," *Chicago History* 15, no. 1 (Spring 1986): 36–63. None contains all the documentation of Sullivan's work, and further information is at both the AIA Library in Washington, D.C., and the Ryerson and Burnham Libraries of the Art Institute of Chicago. A few items are also in private hands.

16. Honorary members of the Cliff Dwellers were, and still are, excused from paying dues. They do, however, pay for their meals and drinks. Oral history has it that in the last years of

Sullivan's life, his many friends at the club saw to it that his monthly food bills were paid, although he was not served liquor.

17. No accurate list of these friends has survived.

18. There is some confusion about how much and how Sullivan was actually paid. A letter dated March 29, 1922, from Howard Shaw to Marian Comings, the Burnham librarian, states that the library's contribution was to be $250. It is the author's opinion that the Burnham Library paid $250, the Armour Institute paid another $250, and $500 was contributed in $50 units by ten architect friends. Those contributions apparently went directly to Sullivan, as is indicated in a letter dated February 2, 1922, from Sullivan to Thomas Tallmadge (in the author's collection), that acknowledges "receipt of your favor of Jan 28th '22, and of the Nimmons and Dunning cheques of $50.00 each to apply on act [*sic*] of the set of drawings.

Kendall. Kendall remarked that Sullivan had been "drawing a series of plates illustrating the philosophy of ornament as devised and perfected by him. Some twelve or more are now under glass on exhibition at the Art Institute." He went on to ask Sullivan if he "would like to say a word in regard to this matter." Sullivan responded that "along about January the Burnham Library . . . thought it would be well if I would put on record a number of drawings to illustrate the philosophy and lines of designs which I devised at the expense of some 40 years of experience . . . There are thirty plates in all, twelve of which have been completed . . . It will probably take four months to complete the remaining plates." Some of the plates on exhibit were preliminary drawings, but dates on the final sheets indicate that about eight plates had been finished by then. The remaining plates were completed over the next several months, during which time Sullivan had extensive correspondence with AIA editor Charles H. Whitaker regarding their eventual publication. Sullivan's autobiography was not, as some have suggested, part of the same project.

He started the autobiography a month or so after beginning the drawings for *A System of Architectural Ornament*. According to Sullivan, it grew out of a mid-January 1922 conversation "with Andy Rebori . . . a few evenings since . . . he said 'why don't you write your autobiography? That would be very interesting.'" That talk led to a series of letters between Sullivan and Whitaker. These letters and those concerning the drawings he was preparing were written over the same period of time, although the two projects were seldom discussed in the same correspondence. Notable exceptions were in two of Sullivan's letters to Whitaker. On March 21, 1922, Sullivan wrote that "during the past 40 calendar days I have turned out 3 chapters of the book and 3 plates for the Burnham Library." Then, on August 2, 1923, he wrote that the "literary work has covered a period of almost 18 months, the drawings 17, and I am very tired." They were approved for publication at about the same time, apparently in September of 1923.[19]

Both books were finished just days before Sullivan's death. In a memo to Sidney J. Adler, N. Max Dunning wrote that during a visit with Sullivan he realized how fast Sullivan was slipping away, and he "wired the officers of the Press of the Institute to rush out, if it was humanly possible, one volume of the 'Autobiography of an Idea' and one volume of the plates so I could show them to Mr. Sullivan before he passed away." It was done, and Sullivan had the pleasure of seeing his work in print a few days before his death on April 14, 1924.[20]

19. See C. H. Whitaker's letter of September 26, 1923, to Sullivan. The original is now in the AIA archive in Washington, D.C.

20. Numerous authors have used the Dunning memo dated April 28, 1924, as a reliable source of information concerning Sullivan's last days. The original is now in the Ryerson and Burnham Libraries in Chicago.

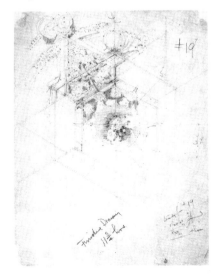

*Sullivan's preliminary sketch of plate no. 19 for* A System of Architectural Ornament *(AIC)*

*Final drawing for plate no. 19 (AIC)*

Between the time Sullivan finished his two books and their publication, he continued to write. His last published article was a lengthy review in the *Architectural Record* titled "Concerning the Imperial Hotel, Tokyo, Japan," on the building designed by his former colleague, Frank Lloyd Wright.[21] He spoke highly of it, ending his remarks with the statement that "the Imperial Hotel stands unique as the high water mark thus far attained by any modern architect. Superbly beautiful it stands—a noble prophecy." Earlier he had stated, "I have had occasion recently to comment upon the splendid interpretation of the spirit of the American people manifest in the design submitted in the competition for the Tribune Building in Chicago—by a Finlander—Eliel Saarinen . . . It is in this sense that we are now about to contemplate the new Imperial Hotel in Tokyo, Japan." Louis Sullivan could give no higher accolade to Wright than to compare his work to that of Saarinen.

His article on the Tribune Tower had appeared in the same journal two months earlier.[22] There he opened his critique with a philosophical discussion concerning those who were "Masters of Ideas, and those who are governed by ideas." He came down on the side of the "masters," declaring them "master of courage; the free will of adventure is in them. They stride where others creep." He then briefly reviewed the program of the Tribune Tower Competition, specifically the requirement to "secure the design for a structure distinctive and imposing—the most beautiful office building in the world." After further review, he commented that "in this light, the second and the first prize stand before us side by side. One glance of the trained eye, and instant judgment comes: that judgment which flashes from inner experience, in recognition of a masterpiece. The verdict of the Jury of Award is at once reversed, and the second prize is placed first, where it belongs by virtue of its beautifully controlled and virile power. The first prize is demoted to the level of those works evolved of dying ideas." The essence of his remarks was that the Tribune Tower Competition did produce "the most beautiful office building in the world," but that the jury did not recognize it.

Sullivan was not the only one critical of the jury's choice. I. K. Pond, Thomas Tallmadge, and others saw the results in a similar vein. So did much of the architectural community of Chicago, many of whom had followed the competition closely, and some of whom had entered their own designs. A review of the list of architects who submitted designs indicates that fifteen were men who were, or had

21. *Architectural Record* 53, no. 4 (April 1923): 333–52.

22. *Architectural Record* 53, no. 2 (February 1923): 151–57.

*Frank Lloyd Wright's design for the Imperial Hotel in Tokyo (Taliesen)*

been, members of the Chicago Architectural Club. Many other members were involved in the competition as employees of firms that had entered. Five of those companies were "invited competitors"—large, successful firms where numerous club members would have been employed. The competition was the subject of a number of lectures and many casual conversations during the nearly five-month period it was under way. (The Tiny Trib Competition sponsored by the club in December of 1922, after the winners of the big award had been announced, was won by club member Jack Howells, who was not related to John Mead Howells of Howells & Hood, the Tribune Tower designers. Neither his drawing nor any of the other competitors' work has survived.)[23]

The architecture that was designed after the Tribune Tower Competition was decidedly new and certainly different. While the tower did inspire some architects with its Gothic detailing, far more chose to emulate the work of Eliel Saarinen. The big firms in particular—Holabird & Roche, Graham, Anderson, Probst & White, James Gamble Rogers, Alfred Alschuler, and many others—drew inspiration from various Tribune Tower designs. It would be several years, however, before the results of this work would begin to be seen at the annual exhibitions.

23. Ibid.

*Rendering of Chicago's London Guarantee Building by Alfred Alschuler, shown in the 1923 architectural exhibition (CAEL/23)*

*Rudolph J. Nedved (PP)*

The 1923 exhibition was the last that was planned and promoted primarily by the Chicago Architectural Club, albeit with the help and cooperation of the Chicago Chapter of the AIA and the Illinois Society of Architects. It was a transitional year when many Chicago architects were preoccupied with other matters. As in the recent past, the three groups formed a Joint Exhibition Committee. A separate Jury of Admission made up of senior architects and a Reception Committee of younger members were formed to assist in the mounting of the exhibition. The dates, May 1 through May 31, had probably been settled in late 1922, but no reference to the exhibition appears until January, when it is mentioned as an aside with no details in the club's column in the *ISA Monthly Bulletin*.[24] The first detailed discussion of the exhibition is in a letter dated February 8, 1923, to F. E. Davidson, president of the ISA, from Elmer J. Fox, chairman of the Joint Exhibition Committee.[25] (Apparently an identical letter went to the presidents of the AIA and the CAC.) Fox noted that the committee proposed "to employ a manager." They had agreed on John C. Baker, the same man who performed the task in 1922. Fox's letter stated that the committee sought "the approval and thorough cooperation of the Boards of Directors of the A.I.A.-Illinois Chapter, Illinois Society of Architects and Chicago Architectural Club." He asked each group to sign a copy of the letter and return it to him. Fox was obviously making certain that the concerns of these groups in 1922 were not repeated in 1923. No record of agreement with the committee's plans has survived, but apparently all concerned did agree, since the committee proceeded as outlined in Fox's letter. The club's column in the February 1923 *ISA Monthly Bulletin* had an article about the exhibition, but again little detail was included.[26] It did say that the club had "again taken the initiative in the preliminary program for this year's exhibition." The rest of the article essentially said that it would be the club's last year as the prime mover of the exhibition. While the CAC encouraged its members to exhibit, it was also noted that the club "takes great pride in its record of Exhibitions thus far but feels it has a greater need of expanding further in the direction of education for younger men." It was the first statement of intent to form a new group to take over the annual exhibitions.

The first widely distributed notice of the Thirty-sixth Annual Chicago Architectural Exhibition was in the March 1923 issue of the *Western Architect*.[27] It named the principal committee members, but also noted that "Clare C. Hosmer, A.I.A., is acting as director, and to his office . . . all correspondence concerning the Exhibit should be sent."[28] Hosmer and the Joint Committee made certain decisions in the planning of the exhibition that made it different from those of the previous years. They had discovered that there was to be an exhibit of contemporary British architecture in the United States that would coincide with the Chicago show. It was to be held at the Philadelphia T-Square Club, where space was limited. Therefore, all concerned agreed that the British work should be divided equally between Chicago and Philadelphia. Eugene Clute, editor of *Pencil Points* magazine, made the selection of drawings for each venue, allocating about 150 to Chicago. The Art Institute of Chicago was also sponsoring its Twenty-first Annual Exhibition of Applied Arts at the museum during the same period. Since the Art Institute had assumed the rather onerous task of hanging both shows, it elected to combine them in the east galleries of the second floor of the museum. Thus, there were three different, but more or less compatible, exhibitions under way at the same time in the same spaces. In most cases, press reviews covered all three together. At the same time, a hundred designs for the Tribune Tower Competition, which had been in a traveling exhibition for three

24. *ISA Monthly Bulletin* 7, nos. 6–7 (December–January issue): 11.

25. This letter is in the files of the Illinois Society of Architects at the Chicago Historical Society, and is on the letterhead of the Chicago Architectural Club.

26. *ISA Bulletin* 7, no. 8 (February 1923): 7.27. *Western Architect* 32, no. 3 (March 1923): 34.

28. Architect Clare C. Hosmer served as director of both the 1923 and 1924 exhibitions, after which he left Chicago and moved to Florida.

*Rudolph Nedved's charcoal on board sketch of his design for "A Neighborhood Center for the Fine Arts," the winner of the 1923 Annual Traveling Scholarship Competition (CT)*

*Exhibition of the Tribune Tower Competition drawings at the Art Institute of Chicago (TT)*

*Trinity Methodist Episcopal Church in Chicago, designed by Tallmadge & Watson, shown in the 1923 architectural exhibition (CAEL/23)*

months, were exhibited in another section of the Art Institute. It was a feast for aficionados' eyes.

The Chicago Architectural Club elected to have its annual banquet on April 30, after which members and the press were invited to a preview of the exhibition hosted by the Reception Committee headed by Pierre Blouke. The club used the occasion to announce the winner of the 1923 Annual Traveling Scholarship, which had been juried the day before. The program, which had only been published at the club, was for "A Neighborhood Center for the Fine Arts." The winner was Rudolph J. Nedved, who was then with Tallmadge & Watson.[29] The club medal for second place went to George Nedved, who was Rudolph's uncle, although they were about the same age. R. E. Dando was also commended for his design. None of these appeared in the 1923 catalog since it was already completed, but the first two did appear in the "Index of Exhibits," which was distributed free with the catalog. Rudolph Nedved's winning design was published in the *Chicago Tribune* along with a notice of the exhibition.[30]

Most Chicago newspapers reviewed the combined exhibitions, usually in a positive manner. In the *Chicago Post*, Lena M. McCauley stated that "the combination of the thirty-sixth annual Chicago Architectural exhibition with the twenty-first annual Applied Arts show is interesting because of the intimate relationship between the two. On the other hand, each exhibition loses its individuality."[31] In an unsigned review in the *Highland Park Illinois Press*, however, one critic wrote, "Particularly pleasing is the very installation, made possible by combining the exhibits of the Chicago architectural show with the applied arts." Oddly enough, the applied arts exhibition and the British architects' work were often reviewed separately, usually in a positive vein, while the architectural exhibit was discussed only as part of the three exhibits as a whole. I. K. Pond wrote in the *Christian Science Monitor* that "another annual architectural exhibition is on at the Art Institute . . . held in conjunction with a display of examples of craftsmanship, products of the applied arts, so called, under the direct patronage of the Art Institute . . . In their haste certain committeemen of the architectural organizations expressed themselves as unsatisfied with the exhibition arrangement this year, objecting to the interspersion of objects of applied art among purely architectural exhibits. A calmer view will in all probability change their attitude, and perhaps . . . will come to feel

29. Rudolph J. Nedved (ca. 1898–ca. 1985) was one of the CAC members who served in France during WWI and stayed on to study at the École des Beaux-Arts. After four months at the École, he returned to Chicago and completed his degree at the Armour Institute.

30. "Neighborhood Center for Fine Arts—$1000 Prize Winner," *Chicago Sunday Tribune*, May 6, 1923.

31. Lena M. McCauley, "Beauty in Crafts at Art Institute," *Chicago Post*, May 8, 1923.

. . . they were not so far wrong . . . when, in the interest of harmony they signed away their right to participate in the pleasure of 'hanging' and left that delectable function completely in the hands of the Art Institute."[32]

The exhibition was also reviewed by the professional press. An unsigned review in the *American Architect* began, "To use a homely but forceful expression, 'sometimes the tail wags the dog.' We are reminded of this when we regard the present architectural exhibition in Chicago. In any joint exhibition of architecture and the arts and crafts to which architecture is related, architecture as the oldest and most enduring of all the arts, should dominate. In previous years, it has. This year it does not."[33] The reviewer's primary objection seems to have been that the exhibitions were combined. When he discussed the architecture, he was kinder. He stated, "The material shown this year is excellent, in some respects better than ever . . . the architects of Chicago and the middle West know their work." His colleague writing for the *Western Architect* had similar thoughts and lamented that "the Joint Architectural Committee . . . gave over to the Art Institute the hanging of the Exhibit. The result was a scattering of architectural material, disconcerting to the architects, at first glance, but not so bad for the public. At least it transferred . . . the burden of 'hanging' [to others]." He then went on to praise many of the exhibits, noting that the "prize winning drawings for the Chicago Tribune Competition, home from their travels, appeared in this Exhibit."[34] His primary intent was apparently to convey the value of architectural exhibitions in general.

Several reviewers made comments about the 1923 catalog. It was similar to that of 1922, although it did have more front matter, including material on the Traveling Scholarship, the Lake Shore Trust and Savings Bank's Annual Gold Medal Competition, and the Chicago Chapter of the AIA's medal of honor.[35] The remainder of the book followed the format of the previous year's catalog almost exactly. With it, as noted earlier, was an index of all the exhibitors, including the English contributors. Disconcertingly, the club page in the *ISA Monthly Bulletin* for June 1923 reported that there was "no representation of the Club whatsoever in the Exhibition this year."[36] This statement was not quite true, since both George and Rudolph Nedved had their entries in the Traveling Scholarship Competition exhibited. Furthermore, a number of the other exhibitors were either current members of the club or had been members in the past. Still, the annual exhibition had ceased to be the club function it had once been.

Following the closing of the exhibition, the Chicago Architectural Club met on May 7, 1923, to elect new officers. The election was reportedly the "smallest in the history of the Club."[37] The following slate was "steamrollered through": Pierre Blouke was named president, with Paul J. McGrath as vice president. George M. Nedved and Lawrence E. Allen were asked to serve as secretary and treasurer. Gerald Barry and James A. Kane were elected to two-year terms as directors and Robert E. Dando to a one-year term. Charles H. Sierkes took a two-year term as associate director. The treasurer's annual report indicated that the club was in good shape financially, with nearly two thousand dollars in the bank, but it also had over two thousand dollars in accounts receivable. The annual report concluded, "This year must and will be a big year for the Chicago Architectural Club." It was to be.

Three events that took place during the next two years had a major impact on the Chicago Architectural Club, the Chicago Chapter of the AIA, and the Illinois Society of Architects. First, it was decided that it was no longer feasible to mount the annual architectural exhibition as a joint effort between the three groups; a separate

32. Irving K. Pond, "Architecture: The Thirty-sixth Annual Chicago Architectural Show," *Christian Science Monitor*, May 10, 1923.

33. *American Architect* 113, no. 2421 (June 6, 1923).

34. *Western Architect* 23, no. 6 (June 1923): 69–70.

35. The Illinois Chapter of the AIA had been split in two a few months earlier when the Central Illinois Chapter was formed. In May of 1923, the former Illinois Chapter became the Chicago Chapter of the AIA.

36. *ISA Monthly Bulletin* 7, no. 12 (June 1923): 6.

37. *ISA Monthly Bulletin* 7, no. 11 (May 1923): 6.

Charles E. Fox (PC)

organization was needed. Second, John J. Glessner agreed to deed his famous H. H. Richardson house to the Chicago Chapter of the AIA upon his death, if the architectural community worked together to purchase the S. S. Beman-designed Kimball House across the street as a meeting place for Chicago's architectural societies. Third, a new organization, the Architects Club of Chicago, was formed to buy and hold title to the Kimball House.

The three sponsoring organizations of the annual exhibition had received essentially identical reports from their representatives on the Joint Exhibition Committee after the 1923 exhibition. The club had already expressed the desire to be released from responsibility for the exhibition in the February 1923 *ISA Monthly Bulletin.* The other two organizations had no difficulty approving the idea. In June of 1923, Chester Walcott, on behalf of the AIA, and Charles E. Fox, on behalf of the ISA, suggested that a new organization be formed to handle the annual exhibition. The basic plan was to create a "permanent and continuous organization" that would carry on the exhibition. Charles E. Fox suggested the following:

> That the Exhibition be a corporation not for profit, in which the three members societies [sic] hold stock in equal amounts.
>
> That each of the three members societies appoint one-third of the Directors, the first appointments being for one, two and three year terms, after which one vacancy would occur in each society each year for a three-year term; or some other method of permanent continuing [sic] organization permitting of the cooperation of the Societies and the continuance of the personnel of the management.[38]

Fox ended his report, "We believe that if some such continuing organization were set up, the Architectural Exhibition might within a very few years be raised to a point of municipal interest and national importance which would reflect honor on the participating societies, credit to the participants, and benefits to the entire profession."

On June 26, 1923, Frank E. Davidson, after three years as president of the Illinois Society of Architects, declined to serve another term. In his place, Charles E. Fox was elected.[39] Fox had, of course, been chairman of the Illinois Society of Architects' Exhibition Committee in 1923, and it was under his leadership that the new Architectural Exhibition League was organized.[40] Little was published concerning the organization of the league, although the ISA did approve the concept at its November 1923 meeting.[41] The AIA took longer. The plan was first suggested in June 1923, when Chester Walcott made his formal report,[42] and it was raised again at the December 1923 meeting of the chapter's Executive Committee.[43] It was finally approved at the January 28, 1924, meeting of the Executive Committee.[44] Just over two weeks later, on February 14, 1924, the first meeting of the board of directors of the Chicago Architectural Exhibition League took place at noon in the offices of Marshall & Fox. Charles E. Fox, Alfred Granger, and Pierre Blouke, representing the ISA, the AIA, and the CAC, were all present. Article III of the corporate documents required that they, as presidents of their respective groups, be on the board. It also required two more from each group be elected, so that two-thirds of the board would be holdovers each year. The board passed the typical bylaws and elected Leon Stanhope, John Armstrong, Hubert Burnham, C. W. Farrier, George M. Nedved, and Perry W. Swern to fill out the group. James A. Huffman was asked to serve as temporary secretary at that first meeting, but C. W. Farrier was later elected

38. This language was in the report Charles E. Fox presented to the ISA on June 9, 1923. He noted that it was the result of a joint meeting of committee members from the three sponsoring groups.

39. *ISA Monthly Bulletin* 8, no. 1 (July 1923): 1.

40. Charles E. Fox (1880–1920) was a major figure in Chicago's architectural scene. He was born in Pennsylvania and educated at MIT. He began his professional life in the office of Holabird & Roche around 1896, and left in 1905 to join Benjamin Marshall in forming Marshall & Fox, where he remained until his death. Highly regarded by his colleagues, he was a member of the AIA, the ISA, and the CAC.

41. *ISA Monthly Bulletin* 8, no. 5 (November 1924): 2.

42. *Chicago Chapter AIA Leaflet,* no. 7 (September 1923): 6.

43. *Chicago Chapter AIA Leaflet,* no. 11 (January 1924): 2.

44. *Chicago Chapter AIA Leaflet,* no. 12 (February 1924): 2–3.

permanent secretary. Pierre Blouke was elected president, and Charles E. Fox and Alfred Granger were elected vice presidents. Hubert Burnham was chosen as treasurer. A short time later, the league's board of directors performed its first official task, appointing the Jury of Admission for the 1924 exhibition, to be held from May 1 through 31. Chester H. Walcott from the AIA, Irving K. Pond from the ISA, Walter Frazier from the CAC, painter William P. Welsh, and sculptor Albin Polasek were asked to serve.[45] The Chicago Architectural Exhibition League would henceforth be responsible for the annual exhibitions.[46]

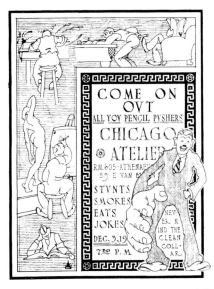

*The new Chicago Atelier attracted many of the aspiring young architects in Chicago (PP)*

While the Chicago Architectural Club was no longer primarily responsible for the exhibitions, the members did not lose interest in the show, nor did they curtail their other activities. Late in 1923, on November 13, the club held the first of a series of one-night sketch problems.[47] The program for the design of "A Reviewing Stand in a Stadium" was under the general direction of Fred Hodgdon. No first place was awarded that evening, but members were encouraged to continue to participate. The following month, the *ISA Monthly Bulletin* reported that the club was conducting a "construction class" and a "long awaited" life class was under way.[48] A brief report on the atelier activities was published, as was a lengthy excerpt of a letter from Rudolph Nedved, the 1923 Traveling Scholarship winner, with the admonition that every reader should "make up your mind that next year, you, as holder of the Traveling Scholarship will be seeing the things he describes." Fred Hodgdon was reported to be the chairman of the Scholarship Committee. The forthcoming annual exhibition was only briefly mentioned in a note that made it clear that it would be handled by the newly organized Architectural Exhibition League, "a long felt need in the architectural life of Chicago."

In December 1923, the club's Atelier Parsons found it had some competition. Under the leadership of the highly regarded Armour Institute professor Edmund S. Campbell as patron, a new atelier was organized. On December 3, 1923, nearly eighty men turned out in response to an invitation to participate. Andrew Rebori, formerly part of the Atelier Bennett, was on hand to give a talk and to critique the sketches produced by prospective members on that first evening. They met in the old quarters of the Chicago Architectural Club at the Athenaeum on Van Buren Street. Many club members chose to work with the new group, probably because the quarters at 40 South Clark Street were so crowded.

On February 12, 1924, the club dispensed with its sketch night and entertained Eliel Saarinen, who "gave a talk on his plan for the development of the Chicago lake front."[49] After taking second honors in the Tribune Tower Competition, Saarinen elected to leave Finland in 1923 and settled in Evanston, Illinois. Four days after Saarinen's lecture an "*esquisse* for the Foreign Traveling Scholarship was held . . . [and] drawings . . . [were to] be in 'charette' the last week in March." There was a good deal of interest in the scholarship in 1924, with fourteen men participating in the competition.[50] In the same issue of the *ISA Monthly Bulletin* it was announced that the 1924 architectural exhibition would again have Mr. Clare C. Hosmer as director. He was to be paid a small stipend, and his presence would relieve the volunteers of much of their day-to-day duties.

The Traveling Scholarship Competition closed on March 21, 1924.[51] Its program had "called for the design of a Memorial Reading Room in a State Capitol. The room was to be a memorial to those who lost their lives in the Great War." Of the fourteen men who had submitted an *esquisse*, nine finished the final drawings. The jury, made up of Messrs. Mundie, Adler, Holabird, Burnham, and Beersman,

*Eliel Saarinen (TT)*

45. This information is all from the *Minutes Book of the Chicago Architectural Exhibition League,* now on deposit at the Art Institute of Chicago. There are fifteen pages, plus three pages of resolutions appended. For reasons that are not clear, page 15 of the first board minutes of the league was typed by another machine, although the language makes it clear that the appointments referred to were made at that meeting. The minutes are signed by Pierre Blouke, president, and C. W. Farrier, secretary.

46. The Great Depression brought about the demise of the exhibitions, but the corporation lived on until it was liquidated in June of 1953. At that time, there was $1,671.87 in the treasury, which was donated to the Burnham Library to be used in microfilming and cataloging records of buildings of Chicago.

47. *ISA Monthly Bulletin* 8, no. 6 (December 1923): 5.

48. *ISA Monthly Bulletin* 8, no. 7 (January 1924): 7.

49. *ISA Monthly Bulletin* 8, no. 8 (February 1924): 7.

50. *ISA Monthly Bulletin* 8, no. 9 (March 1924): 7.

*Ferdinand Eiseman (PP)*

*Ferdinand Eiseman's winning design of 1924 (CAEL/24)*

awarded the prize to Ferdinand Eiseman. Edwin Ryan placed second, and George Conner was third. On April 18, Mundie gave a general criticism of the drawings at the monthly meeting of the local chapter of the AIA. All were shown in the 1924 exhibition and later at the June meeting of the Chicago Chapter of the AIA. The notice in the *ISA Monthly Bulletin* reported that "some of the competitors worked at the University of Pennsylvania, some at the Chicago Atelier, some at the Atelier Parsons, and some worked their problems up outside."

While the annual scholarship competition was under way, the Atelier Parsons continued to get recognition for its work. One member, Harry Bieg, submitted drawings for the second preliminary of the Paris Prize and was placed, thus making him eligible for the finals. Club member Ed Nelson received a first mention in the most recent Beaux-Arts problem, and all the men in the Parsons atelier who submitted drawings on the same problem received mentions. The note that some of the members had worked at "the Chicago Atelier" made it clear that there was no animosity between the two ateliers. The Chicago Atelier was, as noted earlier, not part of the Chicago Architectural Club, although a number of club members participated in its work.

Shortly after the announcement of the Traveling Scholarship Competition winner, the Chicago Architectural Club's board of directors met on April 7, 1924, to plan for the annual meeting on May 5.[52] No longer encumbered by the responsibility of sponsoring the annual exhibition, the club was in a much better position to plan its future. That future looked bright: there was over fourteen hundred dollars in the bank, less than three hundred dollars in payables, and sixteen hundred dollars in receivables. Furthermore, the club had received assurance from the Chicago Chapter of the AIA and the Illinois Society of Architects that they would participate equally in funding the traveling fellowship, which greatly reduced the club's financial burden, since the winner now received a thousand dollars. At the directors' meeting, the board appointed a Nominating Committee and asked for a report from the Traveling Scholarship Committee. They noted that the board planned to submit an amendment to the constitution at the annual meeting, creating a "senior membership for older members of the club who are not able to take an active part in club affairs but who wish to be members in spite of that fact."

The Nominating Committee assembled the following slate for 1924–25: George Nedved as president, Pierre Blouke as vice president, William Sponholtz as secretary, and Louis Pirola as treasurer. In the director slots, Paul McGrath was recommended for the two-year opening, and Clarence Farrier, Fred Hodgdon, and Fred Thomsen were selected for the one-year tours. The slate as presented was not passed without changes, some of which came promptly, others over the next few weeks. Pirola declined to serve, and L. E. Allen, the previous year's secretary, was elected in his stead. Thus, three of the previous year's four officers remained on the board, albeit in different positions. Blouke was also assigned to be the "Official Correspondent" in lieu of C. W. Farrier, who was now a director. The position, which was created in 1923, was essentially that of editor of the *ISA Monthly Bulletin*'s club news page. One of the sitting directors, Gerald Barry, resigned effective May 1, and Gerald Bradbury was appointed to fill out his term. By October, McGrath, Farrier, Hodgdon, and Thomsen were on the board and C. H. Sierkes was the only holdover from the previous year.

The board's suggestion for a change in the constitution to create a senior membership was presented at the annual meeting and passed.[53] It provided that "active members who have been in good standing for eight years or more shall be eligible for 'Senior Membership.' Senior Members shall have all the privileges granted to [an] Active Member." The most significant event of the annual meeting was a recommendation by the Scholarship Committee to clarify the rules and eligibility for participation in the annual Traveling Scholarship Competition. The Scholarship Committee, headed by Fred Hodgdon, with Messrs. Reed, Venning, Dunning, and Schaefer, felt that the competition should be held "on as high a plane of accomplishment in architectural design as possible" and suggested rules by which it should be conducted. The rules were not greatly different from those used in the past, but it was the first time they had been codified. They recommended that each "entrant must be 30 years of age or under and must have passed the two years previous to this competition as architect's assistant or student of architecture, wholly, or in combination within the territory represented by the Chicago Chapter of American Institute of Architects, and must be recommended by three members of the Chicago Chapter." This was a change, in that previously the competition had been open to all, nationwide. Members of the club in good standing who met the age requirement were also eligible. Any winner was granted a year's membership in the club without payment of dues but was also required to advise the club "as to time of departure, itinerary, work to be done abroad, duration of trip and plans for engaging in architectural education in Chicago after return." The last recommenda-

52. Ibid.

53. *ISA Monthly Bulletin* 8, no. 11 (May 1924): 7.

tion was that the name of the competition should remain "'The Chicago Architectural Club Traveling Scholarship,' in order that the fine traditions associated with it may survive." This provision was undoubtedly prompted by the fact that the scholarship was "now financed [in equal parts] by the Chicago Chapter AIA, the Illinois Society of Architects, and the Chicago Architectural Club," as reported in remarks by retiring president Pierre Blouke at the annual meeting. Blouke noted that the club atelier had made great progress in the previous year, and that club members had been invited to participate in AIA and ISA meetings. He spoke also of the formation of the Chicago Architectural Exhibition League. He made no mention that he had been elected the first president of the league.

✤

The club continued its various activities, using its space at 40 South Clark Street to great advantage. The Adventurers Club dining facilities remained an attraction, not only to club members, but to others as well. The Chicago Chapter of the AIA was now holding nearly all its meetings at the club. There may, however, have been another reason that the AIA was using the space.

In April 1924 it was announced that the Art Institute of Chicago had demanded that the chapter "immediately remove the portraits owned by the Chapter which have long adorned the walls of the club-room occupied by the Chapter and the Illinois Society of Architects," an action that, it was felt, could "be construed by architects in only one way, and that is that the presence of the Architectural bodies in the halls of the Art Institute is unwelcome; and that the Art Institute no longer desires the aid and co-operation of the Architectural Profession."[54]

The *ISA Monthly Bulletin* article went on to say, "Without doubt, after this month there will be no further meetings of either of the Architectural Societies held in the club-rooms of the Art Institute. It is also probable that future Architectural Exhibits conducted by the Architectural Exhibition League will be conducted elsewhere." This last statement was somewhat premature, because the 1924 exhibit had already been scheduled to be held at the Art Institute and would continue to be held there through 1928. But the architects were not just worried about the loss of the club room. The *ISA Monthly Bulletin* article continued, "A number of prominent architects are wondering if this attitude of the present management of the Art Institute means that in a short time the Burnham Library will also be forced to find more congenial headquarters." Fortunately, this did not come to pass. There was some competition in collecting architectural books over the next few years. The Chicago Architectural Club had, for many years, been building a library of its own. During the next fifteen years, after the Art Institute became difficult to work with, the club accumulated a library of nearly a thousand volumes. The exact disposition of these books has never been determined, but many eventually ended up in the Burnham Library collection.

The ISA article included a review of the problems the previous year's exhibition had experienced, none of which had been discussed earlier. It went on, "Most of our members are familiar with the circumstances attending the hanging of last year's Architectural Exhibits, when many of the exhibits which had been passed by the jury were later rejected by the officials of the Art Institute, who had demanded that all exhibits should be hung by its employees, the result being that this year many of the leading architectural firms who have for years sent their best work to the annual Architectural Exhibition have refused to submit anything, and have stated that they will continue to do so as long as the Architectural Exhibits are hung in the halls of the Art Institute." This paragraph explained, at least partially, why

54. "Architects and the Chicago Art Institute," *ISA Monthly Bulletin* 8, no. 10 (April 1924): 4.

the club was continually urging its members to prepare for and submit work to the annual show. Clearly a number of members, particularly those who worked for larger firms, were angry about the previous year.

The article continued, "The question is, who and what is the Art Institute of Chicago? No doubt, most of our readers are familiar with the fact that the ground occupied by the Art Institute was donated to the Art Institute by the City of Chicago with certain provisions in the deed that no admission fees should be charged on certain days of the week. It will also be recalled that the funds necessary to build the original buildings was [sic] donated by the World's Columbian Exposition Company. They will also recall that the Art Institute is maintained quite largely by donations from the South Park Board whose annual contribution is said to be eighty thousand dollars. These funds are, of course, contributed by the taxpayers of the South Park System, some of whom are architects. Many architects are curious to know, if considering the gifts and the donations which have made the Art Institute possible, as well as the donations which are necessary to provide for its continual upkeep which comes from the purse of the taxpayers, as to why the management of the Art Institute has assumed such an intolerant attitude." The article did not answer that question.

The problem was addressed, however, in an article prepared in 1982 by John Zukowsky, then associate curator of architecture at the Art Institute of Chicago.[55] In this succinct article, Zukowsky suggests that changes in the management and board of trustees of the Art Institute of Chicago were probably responsible for the change in attitude. He speculates about whether the director appointed in 1921, Robert B. Harshe, was responsible, or whether it was the result of changes in the board of trustees. Zukowsky refers to a second article in the *ISA Monthly Bulletin*, in the July–August 1929 issue, that supports his contention.[56] That article states, "The years bring many changes. Mr. Hutchinson who was really the father of the Art Institute and the patron and friend of Chicago architects and of every movement making for the beautification of Chicago has gone to his great rest. The Art Institute has grown by leaps and bounds and new kings have risen 'who knew not Joseph.'" Zukowsky wonders if the replacement of Hutchinson, after his long illness and death in late 1924, by Potter Palmer as board president in 1925 further exacerbated the problem or if it was the increasing demands of the architects that caused the rift in relations. He also points out that there had already been a problem in 1923, when the need for space for the exhibition in the Art Institute had been almost more than could be provided. In spite of the difficulties in 1924, the exhibition was mounted as scheduled in May. It would continue to be held at the Art Institute for the next four years, but relations would become increasingly strained.

The *ISA Monthly Bulletin* article concluded, "At any rate, the fact of the Architects being kicked out of the Art Institute means that they must redouble their efforts to secure for themselves adequate headquarters where the portraits of those who were the great builders of Chicago may be allowed to remain in peace." This final paragraph confirmed what had only been vaguely acknowledged for the past two years. The architects of Chicago needed a home of their own. They would address the problem in a creative manner while the 1924 exhibition was still in place.

The Thirty-seventh Annual Exhibition was also called the First Annual Exhibition of the Chicago Architectural Exhibition League. Under the direction of Clare C. Hosmer, the problems of the previous year were alleviated. The Exhibition of Applied

55. John Zukowsky, "The Chicago Architectural Club, 1895–1940," *Chicago Architectural Journal* 2 (1982): 170–74. Zukowsky later became the John H. Bryan Curator of Architecture at the Art Institute of Chicago. He left Chicago in 2004 to become the director of the Westcott Foundation in Springfield, Ohio.

56. *ISA Monthly Bulletin* 9, nos. 1–2 (July–August 1929): 6–7.

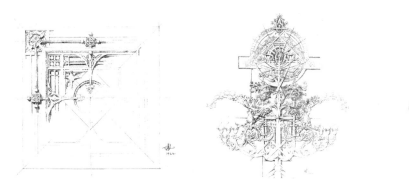

*Four of the twenty drawings Louis Sullivan prepared for* A System of Architectural Ornament *(AIC/SSO)*

Arts, which had been held in the same space the year before, was again scheduled to coincide with the architectural exhibition, but was held in a different gallery. Segregating the smaller decorative articles from the strictly architectural exhibits was far more satisfactory to the architects. Hosmer kept tight control on the mounting of the exhibits and, while the Art Institute staff did assist in the hanging, he saw to it that the drawings, renderings, and models were placed to best advantage.

The exhibition contained 374 separate exhibits. It was well received by the press, and reviews were published by most Chicago newspapers. The most notable exhibit was the display of the twenty plates of drawings completed a year earlier by Louis H. Sullivan. In the first published review, the *Chicago Herald-Examiner* commented that "architects will be attracted first to the original sketches by Louis Sullivan, sketches from his last book compiled. These works in pencil and pen show that the genius who designed the Chicago Auditorium, many World's Fair buildings and so many of the familiar things of beauty in the loop, such as Carson, Pirie & Scott's door, retained his vitality until his recent death."[57] In spite of the reporter's obvious errors, the essence of what he had to say was true. A more accurate and comprehensive review appeared in the *Chicago Illinois Post*.[58] After some

57. "Architects Open Annual Exhibit at Art Institute," *Chicago Herald-Examiner*, May 4, 1924.

58. "The Architects' Annual," *Chicago Illinois Post*, May 6, 1924.

*Drawings prepared by Hugh Ferriss to explain the New York zoning laws, shown in the annual architectural exhibition of 1924 (PP)*

favorable opening comments, the reviewer wrote that "of first importance artistically is the memorial group of twenty drawings constituting 'A System of Architectural Ornament,' executed for the Burnham Library of Architecture in 1922 and 1923, by Louis H. Sullivan, who died recently. These drawings arranged by themselves on a wall of a large gallery attract an unbroken succession of viewers, especially of young architects, who appreciate the masterly manner of presentation of an idea and its execution. Mr. Sullivan's spiritual interpretation of architecture is as inspiring in his drawings as it was in his teachings to young architects. To many, this group, 'A System of Architectural Ornament,' is the outstanding feature of the entire exhibition." The reviewer covered the exhibition exhaustively. He discussed the material from the American Academy in Rome, the Traveling Scholarship drawings, and a number of exhibits from out of town. He was also impressed with "Hugh Ferriss's Studies of the zoning law in New York." The reviewer found room for nearly every architect's name in his three-column article, although most were not credited with specific designs. The only bylined review was written by Eleanor Jewett for the *Chicago Tribune*.[59] She had clearly taken the time to look at the show and had chosen her words carefully. After two opening paragraphs concerning the exhibit on applied arts, she critiqued the architectural exhibition. She found it to be "a little stiff and formal . . . From its nature it could hardly be otherwise." She noted that there were "groups of photographs and of plans in black and white; there are multitudes of insides and outsides, odd corners, roofs, niches, glimpses of long living rooms and less long bedrooms; there are mysterious diagrams showing the effects of the zoning laws; there are renderings of office buildings, stern, simple, impressive, and of other structures, such as tombs, less simple but, perhaps because unavoidable, more impressive." She was especially impressed with Holabird & Roche's plans for the new Palmer House Hotel and some of the exhibits of gardens. She missed seeing the work of Charles Morgan, who did not exhibit in 1924, but she was pleased with the show as a whole.

The review in the *Chicago Post* was devoted to "two entries of 'A Study of the Zoning Law,' by Hugh Ferriss of New York. The architect has used the heart of a great city, New York, and buildings by Bertram Goodhue to illustrate his argument."[60] The remainder of the article illustrated the buildings Ferriss used in his demonstration.

The *Western Architect* did not review the exhibition. Instead, the editors, probably Robert Craik McLean, remarked only that it was now in the hands of the Chicago Architectural Exhibition League. It was, they said, "a marked and intelligent advance in presentation of architectural design for professional and public inspection."

Several reviewers commented on the catalog, all praising it. It was similar to those published in 1922 and 1923, but slightly larger. It opened with a title page explaining the new organization, the Chicago Architectural Exhibition League, followed by a page of the officers of the three groups that made up the league through appointments to its board of directors. This was followed by a listing of the board members, with officers and the names of the Jury of Admission. Charles C. Hosmer led this list as director. After a brief commendation page, the Chicago Architectural Club Traveling Scholarship got a full page listing all past winners plus the current winner, Ferdinand Eiseman. The rules guiding the awarding of the Chicago Chapter of the AIA's medal of honor merited their own page, followed by a page devoted to the Lake Shore Trust and Savings Bank's Annual Gold Medal Competition for "The Best Building Improvements in the North Central District." This competition, now in its second year, resulted in two gold medals and two honorable mentions, whereas the Chicago Chapter of the AIA once again failed to find any building wor-

THE GERM: THE SEAT OF POWER

*Sketch by Louis Sullivan (AIC/SSO)*

59. Eleanor Jewett, "Applied Arts and Architecture New Institute Exhibits," *Chicago Tribune*, May 11, 1924

60. "At Architects' Annual," *Chicago Post*, May 13, 1924.

*H. H. Richardson's John J. Glessner House (HABS)*

thy of its medal of honor. The next two pages were devoted to an appreciation of Louis H. Sullivan written by Thomas E. Tallmadge and illustrated with one of Sullivan's drawings.

A foreword by Charles E. Fox preceded the illustrations of exhibits. The catalog was divided into four sections: Residential, Public and Commercial with Sketches, Ecclesiastical and Educational, and Arts and Crafts. Ninety-five exhibits were illustrated. Some architects' work was shown in more than one category, since only eighty-three exhibitors' names were included in the supplementary index of exhibits that listed all the exhibitors and their contributions. The pages of the catalog were not numbered, and the illustration pages were printed on one side only. The paper was the same cream-colored stock used in 1922 and 1923, again printed in sepia ink. The catalog proper was 230 pages, with 72 pages of advertising following the illustrations. Many of the advertisements included illustrations of the entries. It was the largest catalog ever published for an annual exhibition.

Coincidentally, during the exhibition the national AIA held its annual convention in Washington, D.C. There had been a preconvention meeting of the Chicago Chapter of the AIA to plan the activities for the convention. Charles E. Fox was chairman of the meeting. He was then also serving as president of the Illinois Society of Architects. (During those days, it was customary for the national AIA to welcome nonvoting delegates from the Illinois Society of Architects to its conventions, and Fox was, obviously, serving a dual role at the preconvention meeting.) The meeting was held just prior to the May gathering of the Chicago chapter, which, despite the problems with the Art Institute, was being held at the club room of the institute. On the way to that meeting, Alfred Granger, president of the chapter, suggested to several of the members accompanying him that he had a bottle of scotch and should they join him at his table for dinner, the evening might pass more pleasantly.[61] (Apparently, neither Prohibition nor the Art Institute's ban on liquor bothered Fox and his colleagues.) At that dinner, it was suggested that the

61. This story has been told several times, most completely in *ISA Monthly Bulletin* 9, no. 4 (November–December 1924). It was repeated in the *Architects Club of Chicago Monthly Bulletin* 1, no. 1 (January 1925). All the information regarding the Glessner House, the Kimball House, and the circumstances resulting in the formation of the Architects Club of Chicago was taken from these sources.

Kimball House (GHM)

John J. Glessner House at Eighteenth and Prairie just south of Chicago's Loop "would be an ideal building to house the architectural profession in Chicago."

The subject of new quarters for the architectural profession was very much on the minds of all those present, in view of the position taken a month earlier by the Art Institute. The ISA had already had one meeting concerning a new space and had voted to move its executive offices to 160 North La Salle Street on May 1, 1924.[62] The Chicago Architectural Club rarely used the Art Institute space, although it was authorized to do so. As the story goes, it was Charles Fox who suggested that AIA chapter president Alfred Granger approach Mr. Glessner suggesting that he "provide in his will that the architects should have the first opportunity to purchase his house." Alfred Granger was the ideal person to approach Glessner. He had grown up in Zanesville, Ohio, Glessner's hometown, and their families had undoubtedly known each other. It is also likely that Alfred Granger had worked on the drawings of the Glessner House while employed in Richardson's office during his tenure at MIT. In any case, Granger agreed to the idea and spoke with Glessner a few days later.

John Glessner "was genuinely pleased that the AIA should want to preserve his house and told Mr. Granger that he would discuss it with his family, etc., with

62. *Chicago Herald-Examiner,* April 20, 1924.

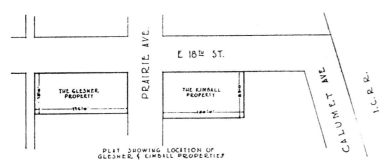

Site plan showing the Glessner and Kimball houses (ISA)

*John J. Glessner House was ideally suited to serve as the headquarters for Chicago's architectural community (GHM)*

the outcome that he shortly afterwards advised President Granger that he was prepared to give his home to the Chicago Chapter, AIA," subject to a life estate for himself and his wife in the house. He did, however, stipulate that "the architects must secure and occupy as their headquarters the Kimball house located directly across Prairie avenue from his home." Glessner was concerned about protecting the neighborhood, particularly since the Pullman House, which had been at the northeast corner of Eighteenth and Prairie, had been torn down just months before. An agreement in principle was reached almost immediately and all concerned began work on an appropriate "deed of gift" to transfer the house to the Chicago Chapter of the American Institute of Architects.[63] It was executed on December 1, 1924, by Mr. and Mrs. Glessner and by Alfred Granger for the AIA, and attested to by Howard L. Cheney, the chapter secretary.

The members of the Chicago Chapter of the AIA realized that the "securing and occupancy of the Kimball House which was made mandatory by the Glessner legacy appeared to be too great an undertaking for the Chicago Chapter, AIA to undertake alone." Therefore, they asked the Illinois Society of Architects and the Chicago Architectural Club to join them in the endeavor. A three-party agreement between the groups was prepared before the deed of gift was executed.[64] It was dated November 25, 1924, a week earlier. The contract between the three organizations stated that each would share "in all of the privileges and benefits to be derived from the Glessner gift of his home; the other societies sharing with the Chapter in the maintenance and operation of the building. The title of the Glessner home, however, will be vested in the Chicago Chapter, AIA, which was one of the conditions of the Glessner gift."

It was also necessary to devise a method of purchasing and holding title to the Kimball House. A plan was worked out whereby the house would be purchased by a trust, which would, in turn, lease it to a new organization, the Architects Club of Chicago. That club was incorporated on December 10, 1924. The new club was to

63. A copy of the entire deed of gift is included in the appendix.

have four classes of members: proprietary, regular, nonresident, and honorary. The proprietary members, at first limited to a hundred, were asked to subscribe to a sum of a thousand dollars each in order to raise funds for the purchase.[65] The purchase of the Kimball House by the trust was finalized on December 15, 1924.[66] By January 1, 1925, seventy-seven full shares, three half shares, fifteen quarter shares, and two sixteenth shares had been subscribed for a face value total of nearly $82,500, the price of the house. After January 1, the price of a share went up to twelve hundred dollars. Eventually a total of a hundred thousand dollars was raised. Proprietary shareholders were to be paid a return of 7 percent on their investment and were excused from initiation fees and dues. Regular members were to pay an initiation fee of a hundred dollars and yearly dues of fifty dollars. It was agreed that members in good standing of the three participating groups would be eligible for membership in the new club and would not be required to pay an initiation fee or dues beyond what they had paid to their primary organizations. The participating groups were required to share in the operating costs of the Kimball House. The new club elected to admit members who were not involved with any of the three groups, primarily contractors, material suppliers, bankers, and any others connected with the building industry.

With all the necessary legalities worked out, the Architects Club of Chicago began preparing the Kimball House for occupancy by the Chicago Chapter of the AIA, the Illinois Society of Architects, and the Chicago Architectural Club early in 1925. The plan was that each group would lease space for "the holding of their regular meetings and functions, and that the garage of the Kimball residence shall be remodeled and leased to the sketch club as the home of its atelier. Thus the three professional organizations will have their homes in the Kimball residence as tenants of the Architects' Club of Chicago until the Chapter shall secure by deed of gift the Glessner home, when it is planned that the three professional organizations shall move across the street with their headquarters and the Glessner House be maintained in perpetuity as the official home of the three professional organizations, the garage of the Glessner home being remodeled and occupied by the atelier of the sketch club, and the wonderful Glessner home be occupied as an art gallery by the architectural organizations and as an architectural public library . . . It is also planned . . . to equip a number of rooms in the club so that guests of any of its members from other cities may be put up and treated to real club hospitalities. Of course, a grill and other club equipment will be installed as early as possible." Thus, with the deed of gift, the three-party agreement, the Architects Realty Trust (which held title to the Kimball house), and the new Architects Club of Chicago all in place, the work to adapt the Kimball House to its new use was ready to begin.

The formal announcement that "the Architects Club of Chicago is now a reality" came in the *ISA Monthly Bulletin* of January 1925.[67] The officers were president C. E. Fox, first vice president Alfred Granger, second vice president Andrew Lanquist, secretary Pierre Blouke, treasurer F. E. Davidson, and a five-man group of directors, Clarence Farrier, George Nedved, J. C. Llewellyn, George C. Nimmons, and Richard E. Schmidt. All were then, or had been at one time, members of the Chicago Architectural Club. In that same issue of the *ISA Monthly Bulletin*, the Chicago Architectural Club announced that it was changing its name back to the Chicago Architectural Sketch Club, effective February 1, 1925, to "avoid the confusion which would arise from the similarity of names" with the Architects Club of Chicago.

The officers and members of the Executive Committee of the Chicago Architectural Club had participated in every step of the formation of the new Architects Club of Chicago and all the other legalities required to see it to fruition. They did

64. A copy of the agreement is included in the appendix.

65. Those who purchased their shares early were granted a hundred-dollar discount, so they paid only nine hundred dollars.

66. The Architects Realty Trust was directed by trustees Alfred Granger, Charles E. Fox, and Andrew Lanquist. The Kimball House, which had been a boardinghouse, was purchased from George J. and Caroline Williams. Initially, there was a forty-thousand-dollar mortgage due on October 13, 1928.67. *ISA Monthly Bulletin* 9, no. 7 (January 1925): 1.

*Harry Bieg won the Paris Prize with this design in 1924 (PP)*

not, however, neglect the other activities of the club. Without the demands of mounting the annual exhibition, the primary work of the club was the Parsons atelier. It had been remarkably successful the previous year, with virtually all its members taking at least a few awards. It had had some friendly competition from the Chicago Atelier organized in December of 1923 under Edmund S. Campbell, a popular professor at the Armour Institute of Technology. That atelier had also had a substantial number of winning entries in the various competitions conducted by the Beaux-Arts Institute of Design. Unfortunately for the Chicago Atelier, Campbell was chosen to be dean of the Beaux-Arts Institute of Design in New York City in the fall of 1924, and his atelier could not continue. Many of his students simply joined the Parsons atelier at 40 South Clark Street. It made for a crowded space but was one more reason for the club to be pleased about the possibility of moving to the Kimball House.

In October it was reported that the "chief activity of the Architectural club in the past few months has been the holding of farewell dinners to the winners of the local and national scholarship at which good times were had by all in the bidding 'Bon Voyage' to Eiseman, Pirola, Donald Nelson and a few other satellites of the Atelier."[68] The same article noted that the "result of the summer problems is now out and the Atelier batted 100% and better in the Class B Project receiving one First Mention Place (to be published later), one first Mention and one Second Mention. In the Class B Analytique problem the writer believes that all received mentions or better with one exception." Pirola and Nelson had both won scholarships to MIT as

68. *ISA Monthly Bulletin* 9, no. 3 (October 1924): 7.

69. *Pencil Points* 6, no. 2 (February 1925): 81–82.

Donald S. Nelson (PP)          Louis Pirola (PP)          Harry K. Bieg (PP)

a result of their work in the atelier.[69] The big honor, however, went to Harry K. Bieg, who won the Seventeenth Paris Prize of the Society of Beaux-Arts Architects.[70]

In November 1924 it was announced that "the Chicago Architectural Exhibition will be held this year in February, instead of in May, in Blackstone Hall, Art Institute of Chicago."[71] This earlier date resulted from a recommendation made by director Clare C. Hosmer the previous year in hopes that solicitation for advertising would be enhanced by starting in late 1924 rather than waiting until spring.[72] At the same time, Hosmer advised the board of the Chicago Architectural Exhibition League that he would be unable to continue in his position because he was relocating to Florida. This was a blow to the league since he had performed admirably, but it did prompt the board to "establish an office at 721 N. Michigan Avenue . . . and to engage a secretary at a salary of not to exceed thirty-five dollars ($35.00) per week."[73] Pierre Blouke, then president of the Chicago Architectural Exhibition League, was at that time employed by Marshall & Fox at the same address.

Thus Chicago's Thirty-eighth Annual Architectural Exhibition was scheduled at the Art Institute for a full month, February 2 through March 2, 1925. The expected rift between the architectural societies and the Art Institute of Chicago had not yet fully come to pass.

70. Notice of the award was first published in the Omaha, Nebraska, *Bee* on August 3, 1924. A longer article was published in *Pencil Points* 5, no. 9 (September 1924): 73.

71. *Western Architect* 33, no. 11 (November 1924): 120.

72. Chicago Architectural Exhibition League Minutes of June 26, 1924, now on deposit at the Art Institute of Chicago. A complete copy is in the author's collection.

73. That position was filled by Margaret S. Jones, who worked out of the downtown office of Marshall & Fox at 721 North Michigan Avenue. I was privileged to meet Ms. Jones's granddaughter while writing this book; it was she who brought to my attention the fact that Margaret S. Jones is listed in the 1925–28 catalogs as the corresponding secretary.

*Announcement of the opening of the new Kimball House club space (PP)*

# A New Home

CHAPTER TWENTY

A key concern of the Chicago Architectural Club members and their colleagues in early 1925 was the remodeling and furnishing of the Kimball House to make it habitable for the three societies, the Chicago Chapter of the AIA, the Illinois Society of Architects, and the club. The building had been used as a rooming house for several years and the first task was eliminating the temporary walls that had been installed. Much of the work was done by members of the club who may have had little money to contribute but did have time. They worked evenings and weekends. It was as much a social activity as it was work.

Early in 1925, before the house could be used by the new owners, it was discovered that it was "necessary to revamp the entire heating system and to entirely rewire the building. This added work, which was not contemplated."[1] It caused a delay in opening the house, but all concerned still expected it to be ready for regular use in the spring. The additional expense also prompted a more vigorous drive for members of the Architects Club of Chicago, particularly proprietary members, who, after 1924, paid twelve hundred dollars for their memberships. The trustees of the Architects Realty Trust—Messrs. Granger, Fox, and Lanquist—hosted a luncheon on January 9, 1925, at the Auditorium Hotel for proprietary members of the new club. All were urged to recruit at least five new regular members as soon as possible, and new proprietary members were particularly welcome.[2] Richard E. Schmidt was appointed chairman of the campaign. There were already, at the time of the luncheon, seventy-seven full proprietary members and thirty-three fractional proprietary members. The goal, later revised, was to have 150 proprietary members, 500 regular members, 200 nonresident members, and 25 honorary members. The goal for proprietary members and regular members was ultimately changed to a combined total of four hundred. Proprietary members were excused from any initiation fees or dues. Fractional proprietary members were excused from the same fraction of fees and dues as their fraction of ownership. It was not until October 15, 1925, that the Architects Club's acting president, Alfred Granger, announced that "388 regular members had been elected and urged those present to secure the twelve additional applications which must be had before the club is really fully organized."[3] This was after work on the Kimball House had essentially been completed and all the three tenant groups had moved in.

*Extraordinary newel post, still standing in the front hall of the Kimball House (WRH)*

1. *ISA Monthly Bulletin* 9, nos. 6–7 (February–March 1925): 1.

2. *Architects Club of Chicago Bulletin* 1, no. 1 (January 1925): 1.

3. *ISA Monthly Bulletin* 10, no. 2 (October 1925): 1. The total apparently included proprietary members who were treated like regular members, except for dues payments.

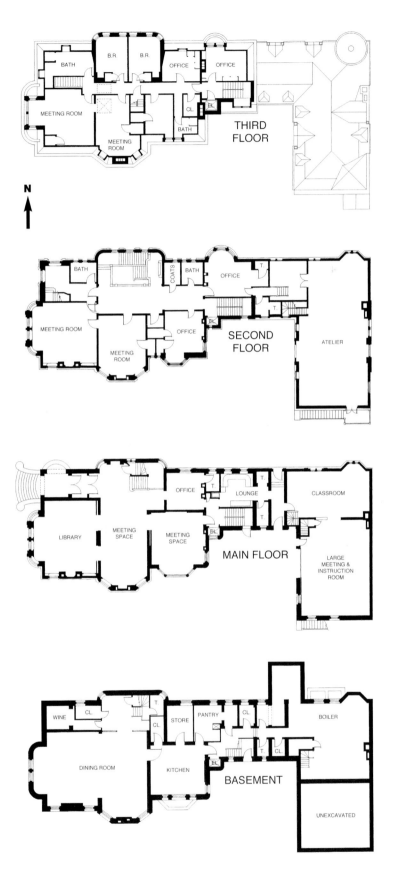

*Kimball House floor plans, drawn by Danielle Ever*

The plan was that the Architects Club of Chicago, which owned the building through the Architects Realty Trust, would "lease quarters in the Kimball house to the Chicago Chapter AIA, to the Illinois Society of Architects, and to the Architectural Club for the holding their regular meetings and functions, and that the garage of the Kimball residence shall be remodeled and leased to the Sketch club as the home of its Atelier."[4] Ultimately, the three groups expected to continue to occupy the Kimball House even after they took over the Glessner House and transferred some of their activities to that building, including the "development and operation of a free public library."

There were no furnishings in the house, and a call went out to the members of all three societies for help. Even before the purchase was finalized, the editors of the *ISA Monthly Bulletin* published a plea to all concerned.[5] They noted that "furniture and complete household equipment must be secured, pictures and other works of art proper for a professional club are desired, and particularly books relating to architecture and building." They were particularly concerned about building a library, and the article ended with a request that "every architect and member of the club . . . look through his own private library and make a list of books and pamphlets on Architecture and building subjects that they would be willing to donate as the nucleus of the club library." The members of all three groups responded generously, and furnishings and other accoutrements were quickly acquired. Perhaps more significant, the collection of historic portraits of architects was brought to the clubhouse and hung in the major rooms of the first floor. It had been removed from the Art Institute club room a year earlier and, in the interim, had been hung in a room at the University Club where the AIA had been offered space after its eviction from the Art Institute.[6]

It took nearly four months for the work at the Kimball House to be completed. During this time, a resident manager for the new facility, a Mr. Sayles, was hired to supervise activities at the clubhouse. This was necessary largely because it was expected that numerous meetings, large and small, plus atelier activities would need careful coordination, and someone had to be in charge of day-to-day activities. Furthermore, luncheon and dinner meetings were planned, and food service required that a chef and servers be hired on an "as needed" basis. The new manager was not responsible for supervising construction, but he did watch over the house while work was under way. Fortunately, not a great deal of construction was needed other than the electrical and heating renovation.

The first "meeting of any kind" at the Kimball House was held on Tuesday, April 28, 1925, when the Illinois Society of Architects reported that the "regular meeting of the Society" was held in its new quarters. Dinner was served prior to the business of the evening.[7] Shortly thereafter, it was reported that the next meeting of the Illinois Society of Architects would be held at the Kimball House on May 26 and that the "furnishings of the club building will be completed at that time."[8] The front room on the ground floor, really a raised basement, had been fitted up as a dining room with a kitchen immediately to the east and two adjacent food-storage rooms. A cloakroom and lavatory completed this area. The remainder of the ground floor was given over to service spaces such as the boiler room. The main floor had three large public rooms that members could use as club rooms where they could meet and talk. Fortunately, most of the exquisite cabinetry and bookcases designed for the Kimball family by S. S. Beman had survived. The largest room, facing Prairie Avenue, served as the library. There were two small meeting rooms on the north, one with access to a lavatory. A small elevator served all floors, and there was access to the garage-coach house, which had two floors adapted for use as an atelier and for large meetings. The second floor of the main building had several large rooms, originally bedrooms, which were now used as offices for the Architects Club

4. *ISA Monthly Bulletin* 9, nos. 4–5 (November–December 1924): 3.

5. Ibid, 7.

6. *Chicago Chapter AIA Leaflet*, no. 52 (April 1929): 8.

7. *ISA Minutes Book, 1925*, Chicago Historical Society Archives, 95.

8. *ISA Monthly Bulletin* 9, nos. 8–9 (April–May 1925): 1.

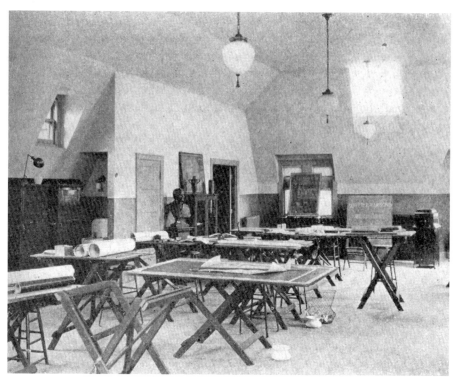

*The Kimball coach house provided an ideal space for the club's atelier (PP)*

of Chicago and the three leasing groups. There were two full bathrooms on this floor. For a time, the Architectural Exhibition League also maintained an office at the Kimball House, where corresponding secretary Margaret S. Jones held forth. Several of the eight rooms on the third floor were set aside for overnight guests. Each had its own in-room lavatory, and there was a full bath on that floor as well. The attic was one large room, probably originally a ballroom. The Kimball House was as near to an ideal space as could be imagined for the architectural professions of Chicago. It worked well for several years until it and the Glessner House had to be given up for reasons that had nothing to do with their suitability.

After the Illinois Society of Architects began holding its meetings at the new clubhouse, virtually all the regular meetings of the ISA, the Chicago Chapter of the AIA, and the Chicago Architectural Club, as well as many of their committee functions, were held at the Kimball House. At the April meeting of the ISA, members were treated to "a most minute inspection of the various rooms in the club building, those present were most enthusiastic over the new Atelier for the Chicago Architectural Sketch Club. The Sketch Club now has one of the most delightful Ateliers of any sketch club in the United States."[9] The atelier members also found their quarters in the former Kimball garage, which were accessible at any time, to be especially attractive.

While the arrangements were being made to acquire the Kimball House, the Chicago Architectural Club was still occupying its quarters at 40 South Clark Street. Its lease ran through the end of April 1925. The club's activities had been reported only sporadically during the last half of 1924, usually only in the *ISA Monthly Bulletin*. During this period, it was customary for most architectural clubs in the United States to regularly report their activities in *Pencil Points* magazine.[10] There were a number of brief items concerning the Chicago Architectural Sketch Club included in 1924, usually about atelier activities, but late in the year they tapered off. However, in February of 1925 there was a lengthy essay on the club's activities that

9. Ibid.

10. *Pencil Points, A Journal for the Drafting Room* was an offshoot of the *Architectural Review*. For eighteen months before the magazine was issued separately, it had been "shown throughout the country . . . in the leaflet issued under the same title," as reported in *Pencil Points* 1, no. 1 (June 1920): 5. A regular feature of *Pencil Points* was a section that reported the activities of the various clubs throughout the United States.

led off by observing that with "great gobs of enthusiasm and activity the Architectural Sketch Club of Chicago (formerly *The Chicago Architectural Club*) has entered upon what promises to be one of its most active years."[11] The club had already announced its name change in the January 1925 issue of the *ISA Monthly Bulletin*.[12] The *Pencil Points* article went on to discuss the successes of the Parsons atelier, pointing out that "two of its junior members, Donald Nelson and Louis Pirola were the successful competitors for the scholarship offered by the Massachusetts Institute of Technology, where they are now busily engaged in soaking up an architectural education as representatives of the Club." Also mentioned were several other atelier members who had won awards and the atelier's preparations for offering a "life class" in sketching under the tutelage of member Robert Dando. G. Broes Van Dort was commended for offering his now annual fifty-dollar prize for a ten-hour sketch problem. The competition, "A memorial tablet . . . to a great man," was juried by Andrew Rebori. Edward Herter took the prize.

The club's year had officially started in September 1924, but it hadn't really begun its social activity until December 5, when it had hosted a dinner party for seventy-five members at the Adventurers Club dining room on the floor below its space. On December 21, the entire club had been invited to tour the Northwestern Terra Cotta Company by Charles H. Sierkes, a senior member of the company and an associate director of the club. The *Pencil Points* article covered the formation of the Architects Club of Chicago in some detail and noted that a major effort in 1925 was to be the "accumulation of a technical library covering all phases of the building industry."

The Thirty-eighth Annual Architectural Exhibition, which opened on February 2, 1925, at Blackstone Hall in the Art Institute of Chicago, did not merit coverage in the *Pencil Points* article. It was, as usual now, under the sponsorship of the Chicago Architectural Exhibition League. No one was particularly happy with the new location of the exhibition in Blackstone Hall. It would remain there for two years. In an article published in the *Leaflet* of the Chicago Chapter of the AIA in 1929, Henry Holsman wrote bitterly that in 1925 "the Exhibition was hung in the basement among store room casts."[13] Blackstone Hall was in the rear of the first floor of the Art Institute and accessible from the main floor only by a pair of staircases—in other words, in the basement. It was also the exhibition area of casts that were used both as exhibits and for drawing classes by the students at the School of the Art Institute. Most of those pieces remained in place during the exhibition. It was, understandably, not a satisfactory solution and was one more problem that eventually resulted in the exhibition being moved out of the Art Institute, although it was moved back to the east galleries in 1927 and 1928.

The 1925 exhibition remained in place for a full month. It did not, however, receive the kind of attention it had in the past. While there were several brief mentions of the show in various newspapers, the only lengthy review was by Marguerite B. Williams in the *Chicago Daily News*.[14] She referred to the setting of the exhibition in the opening of her piece when she wrote, "The Gothic doorways and sculpture of Blackstone hall at the Art institute provide the setting for the plans of the latest American skyscrapers, factories and college buildings which go to make up the thirty-eighth annual Chicago architectural exhibition." She made the point that it was these kinds of buildings that dominated the exhibition. She singled out James Gamble Rogers's work for Northwestern University, as well as the Bunte Building by Schmidt, Garden & Martin as a contemporary factory building and the Chicago Methodist Temple Building by Holabird & Roche as a transitional work in the evolution of the skyscraper. She remarked that she was sorry that there was "nothing by Frank Lloyd Wright, who lately refused attractive offers to rebuild

*One of several Albert Kahn pencil sketches shown at the 1925 exhibition (PP)*

11. *Pencil Points* 6, no. 2 (February 1925): 81–82.

12. *ISA Monthly Bulletin* 9, no. 5 (January 1925): 5.

13. *Chicago Chapter AIA Leaflet*, no. 52 (April 1929): 8.

14. Marguerite B. Williams, "Art to Have Place in Coming Skyscrapers," *Chicago Daily News*, February 5, 1925.

*Bunte Building candy factory by Schmidt, Garden & Martin (PC)*

Japan and returned to Chicago to devote himself to planning industrial buildings." She noted that although "the eyes of the world are now turned to America as the possible creator of a new style in architecture which some believe will rejuvenate all art, the architectural exhibition gives little hint of it." Apparently she didn't understand that one of the buildings she had singled out, the Bunte Building, was actually a superb example of modern American architecture, and not, as she said, from "the modern German School." She discussed some of the minor pieces without naming names, except in the case of a "magnificent scale drawing of Castellans by Henry Sternfeld, a Beaux Arts prize student." She enjoyed "the delightful little pencil sketches of Italy signed 'A. K.,' a Detroit architect who designs industrial buildings." Obviously, she had no inkling of just how important the work of Albert Kahn would be in the near future. Finally, she did mention the "1924 prize-winning design of Harry K. Bieg in the Paris competition of the Beaux-Arts Institute of Design, and a group of airplane photographs of American gardens belonging to the Burnham library."

The photographs mentioned by Ms. Williams and others were the only part of the exhibition found worthy of mention by the *ISA Monthly Bulletin*.[15] Its article

15. *ISA Monthly Bulletin* 9, nos. 6–7 (February–March 1925): 1.

noted that "many noticed the photographs displayed by Burnham Library. Some of these were labeled 'purchased from funds subscribed by Chicago architects.'" More than three hundred photographs had been recently acquired as a result of a plan put forth by the late Pierce Anderson, who had been chairman of the Burnham Library Acquisitions Committee. Charles Hodgdon, an active member of the Chicago Architectural Sketch Club, had been appointed to select the purchases. Several individual architects had made contributions, and the Furst-Kerber Cut Stone Company had made a large contribution. The collection was made available for loan to architects and students of architecture, and is still a part of the permanent collection of the Burnham Library.

Just before the opening of the 1925 annual exhibition, the Illinois Society of Architects announced at its January meeting that a senior member, Julius Huber, had donated his library and a steel engraving of the Cologne Cathedral to the society. The collection was reputed to be valued at thirty thousand dollars. At the same time, F. E. Davidson, the editor of the *ISA Monthly Bulletin,* suggested that a competition be held for the design of a bookplate for the society, and offered fifty dollars for the winning design. ISA financial secretary Palmer offered to cover the expense of the printing plate for the bookplate. At first the competition was to be open only to members of the sketch club, but it was quickly revised to include members of the Chicago Chapter of the AIA and the ISA.[16] A detailed search of available records did not reveal any evidence that the competition ever took place. It is highly likely that the ISA elected to merge the Huber books with the library already assembled by the Architectural Sketch Club at the Kimball House. All the books eventually became part of the collection of the Architects Club of Chicago.

The new Architects Club seemed to be especially anxious to establish its own library. The Chicago Architectural Club had always been interested in building a library and had done so. For example, in the *ISA Monthly Bulletin* of December-January 1922–23, there was a report from club librarian George M. Nedved that a number of new volumes had been added to the CAC library.[17] Now, however, it seemed that the new Architects Club of Chicago and the Chicago Architectural Sketch Club were planning to merge all the books available, including the Huber collection, into a single collection. This appears to be confirmed by the fact that in 1935, the Architects Club of Chicago had a competition for the design of a new bookplate for its library.[18] The library eventually grew to substantial size. In 1926, architect Arthur Woltersdorf prepared an article for publication in the *Chicago Record-Herald* titled "The Architects Club of Chicago and Its Library."[19] He wrote, "In the salon and directors' room (the old dining room) are cases containing one of the finest architectural libraries in the country. This library was assembled by the Architects Club of Chicago. It includes many monumental works and is devoted largely to historical buildings in different European countries as well as America. There are . . . in all 187 titles comprising 550 volumes. Accretions to the library come mainly through gifts. An outstanding gift was the architectural library of the late Architect Charles Frost." He went on to discuss the types of books in the library and how they were used. At the Burnham Library, there is a typewritten list of books that shows the "Chicago Architectural Club Inventory as of March 5, 1939 at Architects Club of Chicago."[20] That list includes 740 volumes and is dated March 5, 1939, just prior to the time the Chicago Architectural Club moved to the Merchandise Mart. There is no record of what happened to those books.[21]

During the first few months of 1925, many members of the Chicago Architectural Sketch Club were helping with the renovation of the Kimball House, but they were also carrying on their regular affairs at the club rooms at 40 South Clark Street. Activities included a freehand sketching class with nude models and a

*Julius Huber (M of I)*

16. The story of this gift and the plan for a competition are told, in slightly different versions, in the minutes of the January 1925 ISA monthly meeting and in *ISA Monthly Bulletin* 9, nos. 6–7 (February–March 1925): 1.

17. *ISA Monthly Bulletin* 7, nos. 6–7 (December–January 1922–23): 11.

18. *ISA Monthly Bulletin* 19–20, nos. 12-1 (June–July 1935): 5. This article would seem to indicate that the earlier competition for an ISA bookplate was never completed.

19. A typewritten copy of this article is in the Woltersdorf file at the Burnham Library. It does not state the date of publication, but it is known that Woltersdorf regularly wrote for the *Chicago Record-Herald.*

20. This was first brought to my attention by Zukowsky, "The Chicago Architectural Club," 170–74. I am also grateful to Bart Rychbosch, archivist at the Art Institute of Chicago, for providing a copy of the same list.

21. Research for this book unearthed only two volumes that carried a stamp indicating they were from the Chicago Architectural Club library. Some books at the Burnham Library at the Art Institute of Chicago appear to have come from the same source but as gifts from individuals rather than as a collection.

*Frank E. Davidson (PC)*

*Theodore Hofmeister in the club atelier (PP)*

structural class for those expecting to take the licensing examination. William B. Parsons continued to serve as the patron of the atelier, but he had asked Paris Prize winner Arthur F. Adams, then with Rapp & Rapp, to join him as co-patron.[22] The atelier provided space and criticism for the participants who, for the most part, devoted their time to projets authored by the Beaux-Arts Institute of Design. The atelier space was also used by participants in the Annual Traveling Scholarship Competition, which was still a major program of the Chicago Architectural Sketch Club. In early February 1925, the club's Scholarship Committee, composed of chairman Fred Hodgdon, Earl Reed Jr., Rudolph Nedved, George Nedved, Frank Venning, and Pierre Blouke, wrote the program for the 1925 competition. It was to be the design for an "air line station [airport] projected into the future fifty years."[23] For the first time, the rules of the competition required that the finalists "finish the last week of the competition in the Sketch Club Atelier and the nine finalists did so."[24] Future scholarship competitions were all held under the jurisdiction of the atelier.

The 1925 jury, made up of E. H. Bennett, Raymond Hood, Alfred Shaw, and Gilbert Hall, awarded first place to Theodore Hofmeister. In its announcement of the award, the club noted that now "that the Atelier is part and parcel of the Architects Club it is hoped that the Architect Members of the Club will show a more intimate relationship with members of the Atelier." This did not mean that the atelier was no longer strictly a function of the Chicago Architectural Sketch Club, but only that it was part of the larger Architects Club of Chicago, as was the sketch club. Hofmeister's award came too late to be shown at the 1925 exhibition. It was shown the following year, but was not illustrated in the catalog.

The sketch club officially moved into the Kimball House on May 29, 1925. An announcement of the pending move sent to all members and many friends of the club was titled "The Grand Start." More than seventy-five members and guests turned out for the celebration. The last events held at the old quarters were the announcement of the 1925 Traveling Scholarship Competition on April 26 and the annual meeting on May 5. New officers elected in 1925 included president Robert E. Dando and vice president George M. Nedved, with E. J. Ryan and G. A. Bradbury chosen as secretary and treasurer. Pierre Blouke and Rudolph Nedved were asked to serve two-year terms as directors, with C. W. Farrier and Paul J. McGrath in one-year terms. W. F. Thomsen and C. H. Sierkes were elected to represent the associate members, each for a single year.

The first scheduled event in the fall of 1925 was a new adventure, a golf tournament on October 3. The Atelier Parsons officially opened shortly thereafter, although two club members, T. O. Menees and P. Schweiker, had each submitted solutions to a Class B summer project, "A Memorial Wall Fountain." On October 28, 1925, the Architects Club of Chicago invited the senior class in architecture from the University of Illinois to be its guest for the day.[25] Sketch club members served as hosts and the "day was spent in visiting the various architectural offices in the city and in the evening the guests repaired to the club rooms for dinner. After partaking of a very excellent dinner, the balance of the evening was devoted to a program arranged by the Architectural Sketch Club." Following dinner, a number of prominent architects, including Andrew Rebori and Charles Morgan, spoke with the students and took questions. The program was well attended, with more than 125 members and guests. It was the first of many similar events. The club invited the senior class of the Armour Institute of Technology "to take their sketch problem

22. Arthur F. Adams won the Paris Prize in 1910 for his design of a Municipal Interborough Trolley Station and Assembly Hall. He had taken second honors the year before.

23. *ISA Monthly Bulletin* 9, nos. 6–7 (February–March 1925): 3.

24. *ISA Monthly Bulletin* 9, nos. 8–9 (April–May 1925): 9.

25. *Pencil Points* 6, no. 12 (December 1925): 86.

Members of the club preparing for the Beaux-Arts ball (CACJ)

Invitation to a sketch club function (PP)

as guests of the club in the Atelier on Sunday, Nov. 1. Mr. Wm. Smith will officiate as their *patron*. Club members and Atelier men are urged to turn out."[26] It was the beginning of a long and fruitful relationship between the club and the Armour Institute.

In late November, the sketch club members were invited to tour the Decorators Supply Company in Chicago, and a few weeks later they had a tour of the ornamental ironworks of A. E. Coleman. While these events were generally educational, the club's Entertainment Committee regularly arranged for nights of recreation. For example, on December 18 they sponsored a Beaux-Arts ball. The description of the ball noted that "some sixty members and guests assembled in the Atelier of the Architectural Sketch Club where they posed to a very industrious photographer, who snapped them as a group of the club's representative members . . . [they then] adjourned to the club's dining room where they feasted quite royally . . . The Congress Hotel formed the final destination where . . . they very swiftly merged into a still larger, more colorful group of playfellows out for a good time . . . in the wee, small hours of dawn that John Smith, the pencil pusher and his fair companion decided to call it an evening and wended their weary but happy way homeward."[27]

The same issue of the *ISA Monthly Bulletin* reported on two other events. First, the club had sponsored the Dickey Architectural Competition "to try and effect a cure for the recent bad habit of erecting buildings, some of whose exposed walls were unsightly and irritating to the eye. After due consideration of the various means of accomplishing this cure, the idea of ridicule was accepted as providing the greatest opportunities." The competition apparently got great response despite its somewhat cynical proposition. It was juried by E. S. Hall, H. B. Wheelock, G. W. Rapp, and J. C. Bollenbacher, all respected practitioners. Robert E. Dando was awarded first prize of $250, Charles Morgan got second prize of $100, and three other prizes of $75, $50, and $25 went to the runners-up. The drawings were exhibited for two weeks at the Kimball House. A few weeks later, the club exhibited sketches made by two members, George Conner and Otto Cerny, during their travels abroad.

In February 1926, the club held a "Stag Party" with dinner at the clubhouse, followed the next day by a tour of the Northwestern Terra Cotta Company's

26. *ISA Monthly Bulletin* 10, no. 2 (October 1925): 3.

27. *ISA Monthly Bulletin* 10, no. 4 (January 1926): 3.

*Frederick Theodore Ahlson's winning design for the Twenty-sixth Annual Traveling Scholarship Competition (CDN)*

28. *ISA Monthly Bulletin* 10, no. 6 (March 1926): 5.

29. Ibid.

30. Ahlson's winning design was published only in the *Chicago Daily News*, on May 24, 1926, where his name was erroneously given as "Robert." It was reported, also erroneously, in *ISA Monthly Bulletin* 11, no. 7 (January 1927), that he was "at Harvard for this year." He was actually at Yale, as reported in *ISA Monthly Bulletin* 11, no. 11 (May 1927).

31. Ahlson eventually moved to Seattle, Washington, and became a partner in Miller & Ahlson.

32. *ISA Monthly Bulletin* 11, no. 8 (February 1927): 5.

33. This rule was reported in the *ISA Monthly Bulletin*, but in *Pencil Points* in March 1927 it was noted that nonmembers would require recommendations from three members of the Chicago Chapter of the AIA.

34. *ISA Monthly Bulletin* 11, no. 9 (March 1927): 5.

35. *ISA Monthly Bulletin* 11, no. 10 (April 1927): 3–4.

36. Ibid., 7.

Chicago plant, courtesy of associate member Charles H. Sierkes. At about the same time, the club once again began its structural class for members and others planning to take the architectural licensing examination.[28] The club was fulfilling one of its basic original goals, turning young men into architects. More than forty men were enrolled.

The Traveling Scholarship Competition for 1926 was announced and published in March of that year.[29] The problem was "A Public Administrative Center for the City of Chicago" that involved the "creation of a great axial highway and parkway from Grant Park on the east to the western city limits . . . along the present line of Congress Street." It was to be a "civic feature of architectural, sculptural, and landscape beauty, as well as a great traffic artery." It was also to create "a great civic plaza between the present La Salle Street and the river to locate the municipal and county departments, administrative offices and various courts." Obviously, it was inspired by the *Plan of Chicago* published seventeen years earlier. The program went on to describe the plaza buildings in some detail. It was probably the most complex problem the club had ever presented for the competition and was conducted along strict Beaux-Arts Institute of Design rules. A program for an *esquisse* was issued at the club on March 6, 1926, with the proviso that the final drawings were due at noon on April 25, probably in an effort to include them in the annual exhibition, which was scheduled to open on May 1.

The winner of the scholarship was Frederick Theodore Ahlson. Second and third places were awarded to George Nedved and Robert Switzer. Ahlson had been employed by David Adler as a draftsman during the 1925–26 year. After winning the 1926 Traveling Scholarship, Ahlson entered Yale in the fall of 1926.[30] He spent the 1926–27 year there, and took his European tour in the summer of 1927. He then spent a year at Georgia Institute of Technology before returning to Yale, where he received a bachelor of fine arts in 1930. He never returned to Chicago.[31]

The Chicago Architectural Sketch Club's Scholarship Committee began planning the next year's Traveling Scholarship Competition early in 1927. In February, the club announced that a "preliminary sketch is to be made in the Club Rooms on Saturday, March 5th, from 2 to 11 o'clock. The finished drawing is to be turned in on Sunday, May 1st, at noon."[32] Under the new rules, competitors did not need to be club members if they had been recommended by a member of the Chicago Chapter of the AIA.[33] Entrants were required to be U.S. citizens under thirty years of age. Club members in good standing for at least a year, within the age limit, did not require a sponsor. The new rules also stated that the winner was to use the thousand-dollar award money for a "European trip lasting not less than six months." This rule was probably established because the 1926 winner, Fred Ahlson, apparently spent only three months in Europe. In March, the 1927 program for the Traveling Scholarship was briefly mentioned in the *ISA Monthly Bulletin* after fifteen preliminary sketches had already been submitted.[34] The full program was published the following month.[35]

The competition was to design a three-part World War I memorial, "A War Memorial in a Small City," consisting of a monument, a memorial hall, and an auditorium, all of which could be connected or treated as separate entities on a single site 250 feet long by 200 feet wide. It was to be "a fitting memorial to the valor and sacrifices of those . . . who fought and died abroad." The site work was an important part of the design and was to include walks, terraces, colonnades, and plantings. The competitors worked in the sketch club atelier, even though it was not part of the atelier program.[36] The jurying of the competition was "held on the afternoon of May second, and the awards were announced at the Annual Meeting [of the Chicago Architectural Sketch Club] that evening." Richard Powers of Boston

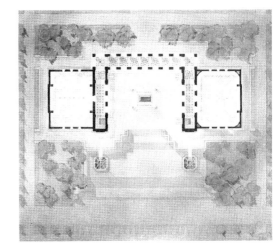

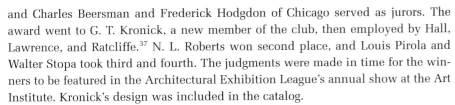

G. T. Kronick's winning design for the Twenty-seventh Annual Traveling Scholarship Competition (CAEL/27)

*Gerald T. Kronick (PP)*

and Charles Beersman and Frederick Hodgdon of Chicago served as jurors. The award went to G. T. Kronick, a new member of the club, then employed by Hall, Lawrence, and Ratcliffe.[37] N. L. Roberts won second place, and Louis Pirola and Walter Stopa took third and fourth. The judgments were made in time for the winners to be featured in the Architectural Exhibition League's annual show at the Art Institute. Kronick's design was included in the catalog.

The 1928 Traveling Scholarship Competition was conducted under the same rules used in 1927. In anticipation of the Chicago World's Fair scheduled for 1933, the Scholarship Committee elected to ask for a "Permanent Chicago Building" for the fair. The idea was to "retain the building after the fair . . . as a recreational headquarters" with "a grand entrance hall, restaurant and dining terraces, exhibition hall and combination observation tower and aviators' beacon light."[38] The opening work on the competition took place on March 10 in the club atelier, with twenty-four men submitting preliminary designs. Eleven submitted final designs on May 7 and were juried the same day by chairman Charles Beersman, E. H. Bennett, Gilbert Hall, Fred Hodgdon, and George Robard. The winners were announced that evening at the club's annual meeting. Louis Pirola, a longtime member of the club, took first honors, followed by Paul McCurry, Eugene Voita, and Helmer Anderson, in that order. Pirola had been active in a number of club competitions in the past and had won a two-year scholarship to MIT in 1924. That award, sponsored by the Atelier Parsons, was one of several Pirola received. Although he spent two years at MIT, he received most of his education through his activities at the Chicago Architectural Sketch Club and the club's atelier. He would remain active in the club until its demise many years later. Pirola's winning design and those of the three runners-up were exhibited in the Chicago Architectural Exhibition League's last show at the Art Institute of Chicago in 1928. While it was not illustrated in the catalog, Pirola's design was published in the July 1928 issue of *Pencil Points*.

The exhibitions at the Art Institute between 1926 and 1928 were fraught with problems that grew out of the relationship between the institute and the professional architectural societies that had used the club room there for many years. Relations between the Art Institute and the architectural societies of Chicago had been

37. Gerald T. Kronick was born in Chicago in 1904 and attended public school there. After he graduated from the University of Minnesota in 1926, he returned to Chicago.

38. *Western Architect* 37, no. 6 (June 1928): 124; *Pencil Points* 9, no. 7 (July 1928): 457. Both journals had essentially the same text and published the winning design in their plate sections.

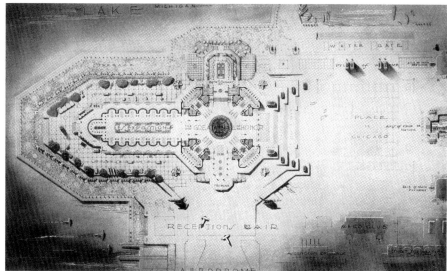

*Louis Pirola won the Twenty-eighth Annual Traveling Scholarship Competition with this design for a structure for the 1933 World's Fair (PP)*

steadily deteriorating since early in 1924, when the Chicago Chapter of the AIA had been asked to remove its portrait collection from the walls of the club room it had been using for over a decade. The AIA had pulled out of the Art Institute almost immediately and found quarters in the University Club. It had remained there until the Kimball House was acquired, and had then become a tenant of the Architects Club of Chicago. The ISA took longer to leave the Art Institute, but it too took up residence at the Kimball House in early 1925 when it was ready for occupancy. Because the Chicago Architectural Club had continued meeting in its rooms at 40 South Clark Street, the eviction from the Art Institute had meant little to the club members. They simply waited until their lease expired and moved into the Kimball House in May 1925. The greatest impact of the Art Institute's unfortunate policy was the diminution of the annual architectural exhibition that began in 1925, when it was relegated to Blackstone Hall, instead of a major exhibition area.

The format of the 1925 exhibition, and that of its catalog, was essentially duplicated during the next three exhibitions. The 1926 exhibition catalog went so far as to use the same frontispiece and cover photographs on the index of exhibits. The front matter followed the 1925 example almost exactly, with one exception. Pages 10 and 11 were facing pages illustrating the Glessner House and the Kimball House with text by Pierre Blouke representing the Architectural Exhibition League and Gerhardt F. Meyne writing for the Architects Club of Chicago. Blouke lauded John J. Glessner for his generosity in leaving his house to the Chicago Chapter of the AIA and inspiring the Chicago architectural societies to form the Architects Club of Chicago in the Kimball House across the street. Meyne devoted his brief essay to a description of what the Architects Club of Chicago was and what it hoped to accomplish. His words were followed by a description of one of the first events at the Kimball House, the Dickey Competition, which had been held in 1924.[39] Next came a rather strange introduction to the catalog by Thomas E. Tallmadge, who stated that "this exhibition should be of especial interest, for . . . in the past twenty-five years great changes have occurred to architecture." He cited various new types of buildings and then wrote, "The skyscraper, always considered a purely American problem, is today reaching a solution and redeeming the total failure that the architects of the last generation had made of it." Later critics would probably agree with his words, if not his choice of buildings. The skyscrapers illustrated in the 1926 catalog were hardly the best of the period. McNally & Quinn showed a drawing of the Verona, and Robert S. De Golyer exhibited his design for an apartment building on Lake Shore Drive. Tallmadge & Watson's odd design for a Collegiate Club that was never built was also exhibited, as was the unbuilt design of Rebori, Wentworth, Dewey & McCormick, Inc., for the Midland Club Competition. Probably the best design shown in this category was Holabird & Roche's Passavant Hospital. Another building of some merit was the Ward Dental Center on the Chicago campus of Northwestern University by James Gamble Rogers.

The 1926 exhibition had been announced to the profession in January[40] and to the public in April.[41] Local newspaper coverage was modest. Only a few articles appeared, most of which concentrated on two items in the exhibition: Frederick Ahlson's winning Traveling Scholarship design and a special display of the work of French architect Jacques Carlu. Carlu had won the French Prix de Rome in 1919, and in 1926 he became a professor of architecture at MIT. One of his students was D. S. Nelson, who had won a scholarship through a special competition held by the Atelier Parsons. Carlu was highly regarded both as an architect and as a teacher. An entire section of the 1926 exhibition and catalog was devoted to his work. *Chicago Daily News* critic Marguerite B. Williams wrote that "the question of architectural style seems to overshadow every other in the domain of art today. Frank Lloyd Wright tried to answer it by turning his back on the past, while the American Institute men have thought that they saw the solution by adhering strictly to tradition. Neither seems to be bringing us as rapidly as we could wish to that much-awaited and talked of American renaissance. But in the meantime we are glad to get the viewpoint of Jacques Carlu, the French architect, who is one of the most conspicuous figures in American architectural circles today. He comes to us straight from the hotbed of modern French architecture, and sees the situation with a fresh eye. The architectural exhibition at the Art Institute brought Jacques Carlu to Chicago last week. He came to arrange his plans and drawings and those of his students at the Massachusetts Institute of Technology—without which this year's architectural exhibition at the Art Institute would have been quite a tame affair."[42] She went on to discuss Carlu and his philosophy at great length, ignoring the rest of the exhibition. She quoted him extensively and near the end of her column wrote, "He feels that we are handicapped in our progress by fear, a failure to introduce into our art that willingness to venture which runs through so many of

39. *ISA Monthly Bulletin* 10, no. 4 (January 1926): 3. The results of the Dickey Competition (discussed later in this chapter) were also published in the catalog. The *ISA Monthly Bulletin* page with this article is erroneously headed "The Architects Club of Chicago—Monthly Bulletin."

40. Ibid., 1.

41. "Annual Exhibition of Architecture May 1 to June 1," *Chicago Tribune*, April 11, 1926. It was announced as the "third annual exhibition of architecture and allied arts, conducted under the auspices of the Chicago Architectural Exhibition League." The catalog stated that it was the "Thirty-ninth Annual Exhibition."

42. Marguerite B. Williams, "Jacques Carlu Discusses Our Chances for an American Style in Architecture," *Chicago Daily News*, May 5, 1926.

Nineteen twenty-six was the year of the skyscraper, as illustrated by drawings in the Chicago Architectural Exhibition League's catalog. Left to right: the Verona apartment building by McNally & Quinn; Robert S. De Golyer's apartment building at 1120 Lake Shore Drive; Rebori, Wentworth, Dewey & McCormick's competition entry for the Midland Club; James Gamble Rogers and Childs & Smith's perspective of the Ward Dental Center; and Tallmadge & Watson's "Tentative Design" for a Collegiate Club in Chicago.

Holabird & Roche's design for the Passavant Hospital, shown in the 1926 exhibition (CAEL/26)

our other accomplishments." A careful reading of the catalog would lead one to agree with Ms. Williams. The problem, however, was due more to the lack of exhibits from major offices. There was good work being done in Chicago in 1926. While the exhibition may not have been an aesthetic success, it was a financial success. Hubert Burnham, the treasurer for the exhibition, reported that a net profit of $1,855.86 had been realized.[43]

In 1927 the Chicago Architectural Exhibition League, now under the leadership of Rudolph J. Nedved as president, succeeded in convincing the powers at the Art Institute that holding the annual exhibition in Blackstone Hall was simply not acceptable. Nedved was also serving as president of the Chicago Architectural Sketch Club at the same time. He was tireless in both capacities. The exhibition was scheduled to take place in the east galleries of the Institute, an excellent space where it had been held a number of times in the past. There was still a problem, however, since the Art Institute insisted that the exhibition take place from

43. Chairman Robert C. Ostergren's report to his colleagues in the ISA, dated June 17, 1926, now in the archives at the Chicago Historical Society.

*An extraordinary design by Jacques Carlu, submitted to the 1926 exhibition (CAEL/26)*

44. *ISA Monthly Bulletin* 11, no. 9 (March 1927): 5.

45. Lena M. McCauley, "Architectural League Opens Annual Exhibit," *Chicago Evening Post*, June 21, 1927.

June 25 through August 1. The dead of summer was hardly an appealing time to hold such an exhibition, particularly since air-conditioning was still in its infancy and had not been installed in the space provided. The dates were announced in March of 1927.[44]

The catalog for the 1927 exhibition listed 452 exhibits, but there were actually more. In an interview before the opening, President Nedved commented, "The 1927 show is unusually large and interesting. A feature of the year is an exhibition of

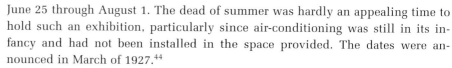

*Martin H. Braun won the Architectural Exhibition League's High School Competition with this drawing of a "Caprarola Window" (CAEL/27)*

*Monument to Pioneer Women, one of the twelve sculptures shown at the 1927 exhibition (PC)*

*"Town Hall" design, a student problem from the Atelier Parsons-Adams completed by Paul Grosse (CAEL/27)*

*Drawing by Arthur Deam, completed while he was at the American Academy in Rome in 1925 (CAEL/27)*

*Drawing of a Mayan temple exhibited at the 1925 annual exhibition by Sarkis Shirinian, a student at the Armour Institute (CAEL/27)*

*The University of Illinois was represented in the 1925 annual exhibition by this drawing of "A Spanish Colonial Church" by Phillmore Jacobson (CAEL/27)*

models for a 'Monument to the Pioneer Woman.'"[45] Twelve statues were to be shown, all by prominent American sculptors. They were part of a traveling show that would be seen in twelve cities, and by fortunate coincidence were being shown along with the 1927 architectural exhibition. Nedved also noted that a number of prominent eastern architects had been invited to show, as well as several large Chicago firms. He was most pleased, however, with the work done by the Chicago Architectural Sketch Club atelier, the Armour Institute of Technology, the University of Illinois, the American Academy in Rome, and the Beaux-Arts Institute of Design. The exhibition included a special showing of work from some of Chicago and Cook County's technical high schools. For the first time, the recently organized Women's Architectural Club showed some of its work.[46] The Tribune Company exhibited nineteen examples of designs from its Small Homes Competition. Clearly the sketch club was succeeding in returning to its roots by showing the work of aspiring young practitioners. A number of student sketches and drawings from past Traveling Scholarship winners were on the walls. Professional work was also shown, including that of Adler & Work, Alfred Alschuler, Paul Cret, Holabird & Roche, H. T. Lindberg, Ben Marshall, and Rebori, Wentworth, Dewey & McCormick. Work from the east included "America's Tower of History" by Bertram Goodhue, rendered by Hugh Ferriss.[47] The Chicago Chapter of the AIA, for the first time in five years, chose to award its medal of honor. It went to architects John Mead Howells and Raymond Hood for their design of the Tribune Tower. The buildings shown were almost universally derivative. The modern movement seen a few years earlier was still on the drawing boards of several Chicago firms and would appear in bricks and mortar only a few years before the Great Depression.

With Rudolph Nedved at the helm of both the sketch club and the Architectural Exhibition League, the members of the club made a valiant effort to remain true to their origins while looking toward the future. Nedved was enthusiastic about the showing of the club's work and other work by students, but he was almost apologetic about the relatively modest showing by senior architects' offices. He was quoted as saying, "Since drawing-rooms and ateliers are busy places in these days when our skyscrapers, manufacturing districts, and suburban residences

46. In 1921, Elizabeth Martini was the only woman in Illinois both licensed and in active practice. She placed an ad in a Chicago newspaper stating, "Only girl architect lonely. Wanted—to meet all the women architects in Chicago to form a club." Several respondents joined her to form the Chicago Women's Drafting Club, which survived only two years. In 1927, the first Women's World's Fair prompted another effort, the Women's Architectural Club, with nine members. It lasted about fifteen years and was eventually absorbed by the local AIA, after which it became known as the club of architects' wives—certainly *not* the intent of its founders. Following the Second World War, Chicago Women in Architecture was organized and is still an active group. An excellent history of Chicago's women architects can be found in Sabra Clark, *Chicago Women in Architecture, A Creative Constellation* (1984).

47. Marguerite B. Williams, "Here and There in the Art World," *Chicago Tribune*, June 29, 1927.

*Benjamin Marshall's design for the Bryn Mawr Beach Apartments, submitted in 1927 (CAEL/27)*

*The Tribune Tower (PC)*

*Bertram Goodhue's "Tower of History" design, rendered by Hugh Ferriss (CAEL/27)*

seem to come into existence in a night, not all the business men take time to make entries at the Art Institute. Their hearts are loyal to the cause, while they have no minutes to gather drawings or prints for exhibition. This explains why names were missing last year and may make it clear why others are absent today." They would soon make an appearance.

Nedved's concern about the lack of big firms in the exhibition did not seem to bother the press. The exhibition was covered extensively by Chicago's newspapers. Perhaps that was because of the higher quality of the work in 1927, but more likely it was because the show was more appropriately mounted than it had been in the previous two years. The *Chicago Tribune*'s critic, Eleanor Jewett, wrote that the exhibition "opens this afternoon in the east wing galleries of the Art Institute. The exhibit is one which formerly has been . . . installed in much less spacious quarters. In fact, it has usually had to scurry around and dissolve itself into its various component parts to fill the cold distances of Blackstone hall, that serene retreat of tombs and armored horsemen . . . today it has come into its own. Architecture has been placed where it deserves to stand in the formal halls of the exhibition wing."[48] In her mind, the 1927 exhibition was a success, no matter that the great Chicago

48. Eleanor Jewett, "Architecture Comes Into Its Own in Annual Exhibition at Institute," *Chicago Tribune*, June 25, 1927.

*Paul Cret's drawing for the Harding Memorial Competition, shown in 1927 (CAEL/27)*

*H. T. Lindeberg's photograph of the Lisbeth Ledyard Residence in Stockbridge, Massachusetts (CAEL/27)*

buildings of the 1920s were yet to be seen.

The 1928 exhibition, the last to be held at the Art Institute of Chicago, was the forty-first. It was announced in March and scheduled for May 19 to June 7.[49] Rudolph Nedved continued as president of both the Chicago Architectural Exhibition League and the Chicago Architectural Sketch Club. Eventually, it became codified that the "President of the Chicago Architectural Club automatically becomes the President of the Architectural Exhibition League" in the league's minutes of April 17, 1934.[50] Thus the Chicago Architectural Club would eventually take back much of the authority and responsibility for the annual exhibitions.

Before the 1928 exhibition opened, the Architectural League of New York held its annual show in February. Holabird & Root exhibited five recent designs, all rendered by Gilbert P. Hall.[51] The New York exhibition was something of a trial run, since Holabird & Root's work, among the firm's best, would be shown in the Chicago exhibition. Arthur T. North, the reviewer for the *Western Architect*, commented that it was "good to see Chicago represented by designs such as these which indicate that the modern school of architecture will find an adequate expression in that city. Chicago has been very disappointing architecturally for so long a time."[52] Chicagoans did not, of course, agree with Mr. North. The Architects Club of Chicago thought enough of the work being done in Chicago to hold its own First Annual Exhibition at the Kimball House in early April of 1928 before the Exhibition League's show was mounted at the Art Institute. It was actually a large exhibition. The *ISA Monthly Bulletin* for March of 1928 described it as a show that "coordinates in one exhibit all the phases of the buildings industry, and at the same time embodies and expresses the very ideals of this Club."[53] This was, of course, a reference to the Architects Club of Chicago. The exhibition included "everything illustrative of the process of construction from the sketch to the completed project." The show took over the entire second floor of the Kimball House, and much of it remained in place for several weeks. Architects, contractors, and suppliers all responded enthusiastically. In May a list of the participants in the Architects Club's First Annual Exhibition was published in the *ISA Monthly Bulletin*, after it had been reported that nothing "this Club has undertaken has met with such hearty and

49. *ISA Monthly Bulletin* 12, no. 9 (March 1928): 7.

50. Chicago Architectural Exhibition League Minutes of April 17, 1934, from the author's collection.

51. Gilbert P. Hall (1884–1971) was born in Brooklyn, New York, and received his basic education there. He earned a bachelor of architecture at Cornell University in 1909, after which he studied at the École des Beaux-Arts in Paris, where he received a certificate in 1914. He joined Holabird & Roche (later renamed Holabird & Root) in 1914 and remained there his entire career, primarily as a designer. His distinctive classic renderings, especially those of 1920s deco buildings, are superb examples of the perspectivist's art.

52. "The Passing Show," *Western Architect* 37, no. 3 (March 1928): 63–64.

53. *ISA Monthly Bulletin* 12, no. 9 (March 1928): 8.

54. *ISA Monthly Bulletin* 12, no. 11 (May 1928): 6.

*Gilbert Hall (T&R)*

general approval."[54] Like the New York show, it was a kind of trial run for the Chicago Architectural Exhibition League's Forty-first Annual Exhibition the following month. There appears to have been some overlap with the annual exhibition, since it was reported that it was "opening during the first week in April and continuing for a period of two months."[55] It is probable that at least some of the material shown at the Kimball House was also shown at the Art Institute.

Prior to the opening of the Forty-first Annual Exhibition, the Exhibition Committee prepared a lengthy press release that was sent to all Chicago newspapers and numerous other outlets, both locally and nationally. The emphasis was on the plan to exhibit models of important new structures and the work of students, some of which had been shown in New York at the Architects Club. Seven models of buildings that had been prizewinners at the recent Chicago Garden Show were now part of the annual architectural exhibition.[56] They included the Board of Trade Building, the Chicago Civic Opera, 333 North Michigan, the Chicago Motor Club, the Schroeder Hotel in Milwaukee, and the Chicago Daily News Building. The press release worked wonders; more than a dozen major pre-exhibition notices were published.

The exhibition itself got good, if somewhat abbreviated, reviews. Marguerite B. Williams gave it favorable comments, noting that "not since the World's Fair days has architecture taken on so fascinating an outlook in Chicago as at the present moment. The new buildings under way west of the loop, the coming World's Fair now being planned, and the discussions on the new style in the current architectural journals give new zest to this most conservative of the arts."[57] Her remarks predated the opening by three days, but she had probably been given access to the show while it was being mounted. (It was not, by the way, hung by the Exhibition Committee. That task had been assumed by Harold O. Warner, staff architect for the Art Institute.) Ms. Williams published a second review after the exhibition was in place.[58] This time she was more enamored of the drawings, but she still concentrated on the work of Holabird & Root, particularly the designs of John W. Root Jr.

55. *Western Architect* 37, no. 3 (March 1928): 66.

56. "Show Models of Buildings," *Chicago Journal*, May 7, 1928.

57. Marguerite B. Williams, "Here and There in the Art World: The Architectural Show," *Chicago Daily News*, May 16, 1928.

58. Marguerite B. Williams, "Here and There in the Art World: Skyscraper Series," *Chicago Daily News*, May 23, 1928.

*Perspective of the Civic Opera House by Graham, Anderson, Probst & White (CAEL/28)*

*Chicago Daily News Building (AIC)*

*George Elmslie's design for the Capitol Savings and Loan Building in Topeka, Kansas (WRH)*

*Board of Trade Building at the foot of La Salle Street by Holabird & Root (CAEL/28)*

and the renderings by Gilbert Hall. She was enthusiastic about the 333 North Michigan Avenue Building. She noted that it was the "first to be completed . . . [of a] whole series of drawings for buildings exhibited . . . by Holabird & Root." (Ms. Williams was the first to acknowledge that the firm was no longer Holabird & Roche, but had changed its name in 1928 and was now Holabird & Root.) She also understood that these "buildings exemplify the outcome of the Chicago zoning law which restricts a building to 167 feet in height but permits a tower of unlimited height provided it does not occupy over 25 per cent of the ground area." This was, of course, a major benefit that Chicago architects had over their colleagues in New York, where zoning laws required a series of setbacks that were difficult to deal with from a designer's point of view. Ms. Williams found little else worth comment in the exhibition, but toward the end of her column, she did find room to praise the work of Charles Morgan, whose renderings had become a regular feature at the annual exhibitions. She also found words for the skyscraper, which she felt was "about our only real claim to modernism, except those abortive efforts of Sullivan with his banks and Wright in his residences."

Eleanor Jewett's article in the *Chicago Tribune* was enthusiastic about the new architecture of Chicago.[59] She noted that "business is speaking. The great driving force which is impelling all kinds of enterprise onward and again onward is speaking. There is no activity today which is not yearning and pushing toward larger development, and larger quarters in which to house it." She was ecstatic about the office buildings in the 1928 exhibition. She wrote that they were "in sincerest truth temples to industry." She was particularly impressed with the Board of Trade Building by Holabird & Root, and she also liked the firm's 333 North Michigan Avenue Building, the Chicago Motor Club, and the Schroeder Hotel in Milwaukee, as well as others.[60] A number of these buildings, not yet built, were exhibited as mod-

59. Eleanor Jewett, "Architectural League Exhibit Wins Praise," *Chicago Tribune*, May 27, 1928.

60. The work of Holabird & Root is covered in great detail in Robert Bruegmann, *Holabird & Roche, Holabird & Root, An Illustrated Catalog of Works, 1880–1940* (New York: Garland, 1991). This three-volume compendium is far more than a mere catalog. Bruegmann has identified and described literally every building designed in the period noted in the title; his book is indispensable to anyone seeking information concerning the long tenure of this important firm.

els. Ms. Jewett also understood the trend toward city living and wrote that the "homes of yesterday, houses of modest height rooted to the ground are today giving way to apartment hotels stretching to staggering heights . . . Cities which cannot easily spread out may spread up, and have done so." Other items in various newspapers echoed these comments. The *Christian Science Monitor* noted that one of "the smaller galleries is largely devoted to work by Holabird and Root . . . and it is really the high spot in the show."[61] The remainder of the exhibition was barely mentioned. There was actually a good representation of work by smaller offices, including H. T. Lindeberg, Howard Cheney, Childs & Smith, and Robert De Golyer, and for the first time in many years, George G. Elmslie exhibited three of his distinctive buildings. The Chicago Architectural Sketch Club showed Louis Pirola's winning Traveling Scholarship drawings and those of the three runners-up. The Forty-first Annual Exhibition at the Art Institute of Chicago was decidedly a success, but it was to be the last at that venue.

One could argue that 1926 to 1928 were years when the Chicago Architectural Sketch Club was preoccupied with its annual Traveling Scholarship Competition and, to some degree, the annual exhibition at the Art Institute of Chicago. That was hardly the case. The club continued to be heavily involved in the affairs of its atelier, now permanently installed on the second floor of the Kimball coach house, and in other activities that entertained and educated its members. The Kimball House was open at virtually all hours, and the club members made good use of the most elegant quarters they had ever had.

The Chicago Architectural Sketch Club was by far the most active occupant of the Kimball House. The atelier, housed in the coach house, was in use literally every evening, and there was at least one other club event planned every week. Both the atelier and the clubhouse became gathering places for young architects, and it was not at all unusual for members and their friends to show up in the evenings just to relax. In June of 1926, the sketch club acquired a pool table that was set up on the first floor of the coach house, which had become the meeting place of choice for most club members. Not long after, the atelier members and the sketch club purchased a radio—a new form of entertainment—for the room. They also installed their own telephone.[62] The Chicago Chapter of the AIA did use the clubhouse for its board meetings and occasionally held other events there. AIA members were also more or less regulars at the Thursday luncheons, at which all were encouraged to participate. Many members of the AIA and the ISA enjoyed coming to the Kimball House just to mix with their younger colleagues.

The Illinois Society of Architects had been a key player in organizing the Architects Club and acquiring the Kimball House, and it was the first group to hold regular meetings there. In March 1926 however, the ISA's secretary wrote to the Architects Club to advise that the society had "decided that, at least for a time, it will hold its Board meeting in the Loop."[63] He apologized profusely for the decision, but said that the ISA felt the clubhouse location was simply too inconvenient for most of its members. It was not the first problem the ISA would have with the clubhouse and the sketch club.

In fact, the Illinois Society of Architects had never been a strong supporter of using the Kimball House as its headquarters. In April of 1926, several members of the ISA advocated the development of an "Architect's Office Building" to be built at some downtown site and occupied solely by architects (and, presumably, by the

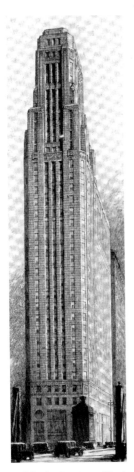

*Holabird & Root's 333 North Michigan Avenue Building (CAEL/28)*

61. *Christian Science Monitor*, June 7, 1928.

62. *ISA Monthly Bulletin* 11, no. 2 (August 1926): 3.

63. Ralph C. Harris to Architects Club of Chicago, March 9, 1926, ISA Archive, Chicago Historical Society.

64. *ISA Monthly Bulletin* 10, no. 6 (April–May 1926): 6.

ISA).[64] A committee consisting of chairman Leon E. Stanhope, H. B. Wheelock, and H. L. Palmer was appointed to look into the matter. This group reported back within a week that "the project was practical and feasible and they believed the time is right to enter into such a project." They also recommended that the Chicago Chapter of the AIA be brought into the planning process and that a committee be formed to find an appropriate location for such a building. Insofar as a designer was concerned, they took the unusual step of suggesting that the two organizations, in joint executive session, "select five architects by written ballot, who were to be the architects of the building." On April 21, 1926, that was done and H. B. Wheelock, D. H. Burnham Jr., A. H. Granger, M. C. Chatten, and N. Max Dunning were named. A site selection committee of R. C. Ostergren, H. L. Palmer, and Leon E. Stanhope was also chosen. It is highly likely that this entire scheme was the brainchild of H. L. Palmer, who, while not an architect, was the financial secretary of the Illinois Society of Architects and had never been enthusiastic about using the Kimball House as the headquarters for the society. In his defense, it should be pointed out that the Kimball House was eighteen blocks south of the center of downtown Chicago, and transportation was difficult, to say the least. Palmer never moved his office there, preferring to remain in his Loop headquarters. In any case, shortly after the initial planning for an architects' building was done, the project was abandoned. It did, however, demonstrate the reluctance of some to use the Kimball House as originally intended. Ultimately, that reluctance was a major factor in the loss of the Kimball House as an architectural headquarters.

*Rudolph J. Nedved (PP)*

❖

In May 1926, the sketch club held its annual meeting and election of officers at its new quarters.[65] The members treated the evening as a party, complete with dinner, dancing, and movies. It was on that evening that Rudolph J. Nedved was first elected president. Before the entertainment began, A. F. Adams was made an honorary member. The club then effectively took the summer off, although the members did continue to use the atelier space and the first-floor room below on a regular basis. There was a "Summer Problem" at the atelier, which had to be sent in by September 13, and the new atelier season was scheduled to begin on September 18, 1926.[66] Ferdinand Eiseman, the 1924 Traveling Scholarship winner, had returned from Europe and was appointed *massier* of the atelier, with Paul Grosse as his assistant, or *sous massier*. The atelier was now known as Parsons-Adams, in recognition of the participation of A. F. Adams, who had become the primary critic and patron of the atelier, although W. E. Parsons still made himself available from time to time.

*Elizabeth Kimball Nedved (PP)*

As the 1926–27 season began, the Chicago Architectural Sketch Club commenced its scheduled activities with an enthusiasm not seen in some time. Every firm in Chicago was busy and so were the club members. Not only was the atelier active, with more than forty participants, but other classes were offered as well. A watercolor class was organized with President Nedved's wife and fellow architect, Elizabeth Kimball Nedved, as instructor, and the classes for candidates for the licensing examination were scheduled to start midyear, as was a life-drawing class. There was also a Golf Committee, and the members regularly played on weekends at club-sponsored tournaments. The first formal social event of the year was a dance held in the atelier space on December 10.[67] It was reported that about "a hundred couples were present to enjoy the excellent music and refreshments and to admire the work of the Decorations Committee who had worked days transforming the Atelier to a scene from Fairyland." All who attended looked forward to joining

65. Ibid., 5.

66. *ISA Monthly Bulletin* 11, no. 3 (September 1926): 7.

67. *ISA Monthly Bulletin* 11, no. 6 (December 1926): 5.

their colleagues in future events of a similar nature. Unfortunately, the sketch club and the architectural community lost two old friends when both George W. Maher and Charles E. Fox passed away in the fall of 1926.

With the advent of the new year, the Chicago Architectural Sketch Club began a practice it would continue for the next several years. Since, for the time being at least, it was no longer responsible for the annual architectural exhibition, it elected instead to hold small exhibits of members' work at the Kimball House. The first of these opened in mid-January and remained in place for a month. More than 150 watercolors and pencil travel sketches by Joseph F. Booton, Eugene Fuhrer, and Ferdinand Eiseman were shown. All three had spent time in Europe during the previous two years. Booton had won the Stewardson Memorial Scholarship from the T-Square Club of Philadelphia in 1924, Fuhrer had won the 1923 Traveling Scholarship from the Armour Institute, and Eiseman had been the winner of the club's Traveling Scholarship in 1924.[68] The sketch club also reestablished the sketching evenings at the clubhouse on a more or less regular basis, with prizes for the winners chosen either by ballot or a jury of senior architects at the end of each evening.[69] In February 1927, there was an in-house competition for "A Wrought Iron Gate to a Private Estate" with prizes of twenty-five, fifty, and seventy-five dollars for the best three of the twenty-two entries. John Story took first prize, with Homer Huntoon and G. T. Kronick at second and third. Kronick, a new member, was later named the winner of the 1927 Traveling Scholarship. In early March, the club sponsored another competition, for "A Cast Iron Store Front." Only two prizes were awarded, Edmund Ryan taking first and Hal Pereira second. Another competition in April, which attracted a good deal of interest, was for the cover design for a new printing of the club's constitution. This was actually the annual competition for which longtime associate member G. Broes Van Dort provided prize money. First prize of twenty-five dollars went to Louis J. Blume, second of fifteen dollars went to Ralph H. Carlbury, and Edmond W. Enthof was given an honorable mention but no prize money. The designs were submitted anonymously and were judged by the board of directors. None of the drawings for any of these competitions was published. During this period, all members of the club were invited to monthly meetings of the Chicago Chapter of the AIA, which gave them an opportunity to interact with their older colleagues and hear excellent speakers. This plethora of activity brought about a substantial interest in the club, and new members were added almost every month. The Chicago Architectural Sketch Club was taking full advantage of the facilities provided by the Kimball House at 1801 South Prairie Avenue.

The sketch club's annual meeting on the first Monday in May 1927 began with dinner and refreshments, and filled both dining rooms of the Kimball House. Rudolph Nedved was reelected president and T. O. Menees was renamed treasurer. Jerome R. Cerny was elected secretary, and Robert E. Dando was chosen as vice president. After the evening's business was finished, the members were entertained by professional performers. They then adjourned to the atelier, where Joe Booton, the chairman of the Traveling Scholarship Committee, "gave a talk explaining the reasons for the Jury's decisions" with all entries available for review.[70]

On June 14, 1927, the sketch club held its final meeting of the season, and committee assignments for the year were announced. Only the club's atelier would continue formal activities over the summer, but the club secretary announced that

68. "Sketch Club Holds Exhibit at Chicago Architect's Club," *Chicago Sunday Tribune*, January 23, 1927.

69. *Pencil Points* 8, no. 1 (January 1927): 51.

70. *ISA Monthly Bulletin* 11, no. 11 (May 1927): 7.

at the "end of the summer's grind a lively party is planned which will coincide with the date of the judgment [of the summer problem] in New York. Several other events are planned that the Atelier may mix play and work more often."[71] Before the summer was over, the club learned that Donald S. Nelson, who had won the Special Student Scholarship to MIT while working in the Atelier Parsons in 1924, had been awarded the Twentieth Paris Prize in Architecture by the Society of Beaux-Arts Architects.[72] He was the only member of the Chicago Architectural Sketch Club ever to win that award. Nelson's prizewinning drawings were exhibited at the Architects Club of Chicago in October of 1927. When that exhibit closed, the sketch club sponsored an exhibition of more than "200 drawings, sketches and water colors by students of the Lake Forest Foundation for Architecture and Landscape" during the month of November.

The Illinois Society of Architects was becoming increasingly disenchanted with the Kimball House in early 1927. In May, it asked the Architects Club if it had the right "to discontinue its relationship with the Architect's Club of Chicago and as to the effect of this action if it should be taken." In a carefully phrased reply, the attorney for the Architects Club advised Alfred Granger, president of the club, that the three-party agreement between the Chicago Chapter of the AIA, the Chicago Architectural Club, and the Illinois Society of Architects was a binding agreement and that the society could not disregard its contractual obligation to the other parties. Furthermore, he stated that when the Architects Club of Chicago was organized, it was "very definitely understood that all three of such organizations would hold their meetings at the club house." This was an obvious allusion to the fact that the Illinois Society of Architects had ceased holding its regular meetings at Kimball House in March of 1926.[73] Records indicate that the ISA did continue to support the Architects Club of Chicago by paying a small monthly rent, but seldom used the clubhouse for regular meetings.

A similar problem occurred when the Architectural Exhibition League decided to move its corresponding secretary, Margaret S. Jones, to the office of its president, Rudolph Nedved, in Chicago's Loop. It is understandable that the two needed to be in more or less continuous contact, particularly during preparations for the annual exhibitions. It was, however, just one more loss of one of the six groups—the AIA, the ISA, the CASC, the CASC atelier, the Exhibition League, and the Architects Club—originally expected to maintain office space at the Kimball House. The clubhouse was not being used nearly as much as had been intended and expected when the Architects Club of Chicago was organized. This was not the case insofar as the Chicago Architectural Sketch Club was concerned. The CASC continued to use the space both for its atelier and for other club activities until the Depression curtailed many of its activities.

The sketch club atelier, with the addition of a third patron, Arthur F. Deam, now became the Atelier Parsons-Adams-Deam.[74] It was now one of the major, if not the most important, elements of the sketch club's activities. Its competitions were conducted strictly in accordance with the rules of the Beaux-Arts Institute of Design, which provided the projets used by the patrons. The first problem in the fall of 1927 was put before the members on September 17, with the second following on September 24. Senior architects and members of the club not actively working in the atelier were encouraged to stop by and observe the work in progress. The sketch club page in the *ISA Monthly Bulletin* for September 1927 noted that it was "always an inspiring sight to see a problem get started, especially the first one of

71. *ISA Monthly Bulletin* 11, no. 12 (June 1927): 5.

72. *Pencil Points* 8, no. 8 (August 1927): 501. Nelson won a number of prizes during his student days. In addition to those noted, he also won the Fontainebleau Scholarship, after completing both his junior and senior work in a single year at MIT, and another scholarship for a year of postgraduate design at MIT. While at Fontainebleau in 1925, he won the Jean Paul Alaux Prize, and after returning to MIT he won the Emerson Prize, as well as the Chandler and Despradelle prizes and several other prizes for Beaux-Arts work. After completing his education, he chose to remain in the east and never returned to Chicago.

73. There is an undated document in the ISA files at the Chicago Historical Society titled "Attendance Record," which notes that the average attendance in the 1922–23 year was sixty, but after the society started holding meetings at the Kimball House, it dropped to forty-five in both the 1923–24 and 1924–25 years, and then to thirty-one in the 1925–26 year. The following year, 1926–27, when the ISA met at a downtown location, attendance went up to an average of thirty-eight per meeting. This document may have been prepared to support the position that the Kimball House location did not benefit the society.

74. Arthur F. Deam (1895–1974) began his education at Ohio State University and later transferred to Columbia University, where he graduated with a bachelor of architecture. In 1923, he won the Prix de Rome. At the time of his appointment to the atelier, he was employed in the office of D. H. Burnham and Company.

the year, and even if you are not taking a problem yourself it will be worth your time to come to the club rooms on either of the above dates. The older members of the profession are always welcome at any of our affairs and we would be delighted to see more of them around and watch us at our work."

The appeal of the space at the Kimball House and the many activities of the sketch club helped in recruiting new members. Under the leadership of Rudolph Nedved, the membership increased dramatically. In October 1927, the sketch club column in the *ISA Monthly Bulletin* reported that "at the last Director's meeting sixty-two new men were taken in and added to our active list." In the same issue, it was noted, "We were told recently that [for] the first problem of the season" in the atelier "there were forty *esquisses* sent in. A later check shows that a more correct idea . . . was nearer to seventy-five." The writer went on to assert that "the Atelier is booming and overflowing with work, but also looking to the playtime side of life as well for they are planning on having a big party soon, but, of course, it will be at a later date than the club Halloween Party on October 31st."[75] The atelier was clearly a great attraction to both old and new members and would, for the next few years, dominate the activities of the sketch club. Two months later, it was reported that the sketch club had added several more new members to the club. The problem now was "where to put the new men. Our Massier, Louis Pirola, cannot find enough tables and stools for them all."[76]

In the same issue of the *ISA Monthly Bulletin,* the sketch club column noted that "the Competition for a cover for our magazine has not brought in any results. The closing date is now set for December 10th as we will have another publication then and we want to use it." This was the first mention of a new sketch club publication. It had had space in the *ISA Monthly Bulletin* since August of 1920 and it was also on the ISA's mailing list from that date forward. Over the years, the size of the space, which started as a full page, fluctuated, but it was nearly always at least a full column or a half page. During that period, the ISA and the club had an excellent relationship. As noted earlier, the relationship had deteriorated in 1926 and 1927, when the ISA found the new quarters at the Kimball House to be less than to its liking. Furthermore, with the sketch club expanding rapidly, it was felt that having a separate CASC journal would be more appropriate. Therefore, in the fall of 1927, the club elected to launch *Treads and Risers.*[77] Eventually, it became quite sophisticated, with long articles, items concerning club activities, and enough advertising to support it. Like many other similar ventures, however, it was a victim of the Great Depression, and it died in 1931 after a little more than four years of publication. By then, the sketch club no longer had an outlet for distributing information to its members, since its last column in the *ISA Monthly Bulletin* had been in April of 1928.

❋

By the end of 1927, the Chicago Architectural Sketch Club was thriving. It dominated the activities at the Kimball House and was by far the most active participant in the Architects Club of Chicago. Its atelier filled the coach house to overflowing, and both floors had to be used to accommodate all the young men who took advantage of the programs offered. In December there were 184 active members, and a total of 252 if one counted seniors, associates, nonresidents, and honorary members. In 1928, membership went up to 262 actives and 315 in all categories. Nineteen twenty-nine saw 315 actives and 322 total, and 1930 still had 248 actives and 310 total. But by 1931, membership began to shrink, with only 213 active members

75. *ISA Monthly Bulletin* 12, no. 4 (October 1927): 4.

76. *ISA Monthly Bulletin* 12, no. 5 (November 1927): 5.

77. A notice in the November 1927 issue of the *ISA Monthly Bulletin* was the first published evidence of the proposed journal. It began to appear in early 1928, apparently at first as a mimeographed newsletter and later as an excellent magazine devoted to the affairs of the Chicago Architectural Sketch Club. Only a few copies were found during the research for this book. There was a notice in *Pencil Points* 9, no. 9 (September 1928): 608, stating that the magazine was being published and that the sketch club was eager to exchange journals with other clubs.

and 255 total. The Depression was beginning to have an effect. There are no published records of numbers of members after 1931, although the club continued to be active and the atelier was still popular.

The sketch club began the new year of 1928 with a Twelfth Night ball at the clubhouse, which was a great success.[78] It was followed by an inspection trip to the Northwestern Terra Cotta Company's plant with a turnout of sixty members, reminiscent of events long past. The Northwestern Terra Cotta Company had always supported the club, and a few weeks later, Gustav Hottinger, the president of the company, made a generous donation to the Art Institute of Chicago to establish a class in architectural modeling as part of the Industrial Art School. That class, like others at the institute, was popular with members of the sketch club.

In the meantime, regular sketch club meetings, with speakers and competitions, continued to be held at the clubhouse. In 1928, a number of members were active in preparing for the annual architectural exhibition to be held at the Art Institute of Chicago from May 19 to June 7, even though it was now sponsored by the Chicago Architectural Exhibition League.

On May 7, 1928, the Chicago Architectural Sketch Club held its annual meeting. Director Gerald Bradbury was elected president, and former two-term president Rudolph J. Nedved was elected vice president. Director Joseph F. Booton was chosen as secretary, and T. O. Menees was reelected treasurer.[79] A complete new slate of directors was named, including Edwin F. Anderson, Francis Baldwin, Helmer N. Anderson, T. H. Hofmeister, Albert Eiseman Jr., and William Thomsen. At the same time, the Atelier Parsons-Adams-Deam named Albert Eiseman Jr. as *massier* and J. D. Kerchenfaut as *sous massier*. President Bradbury, his officers, and the club directors had a new phase of activity ahead of them. The 1928 annual exhibition was the last to be held at the Art Institute. Major changes were also ahead for the administration of the Traveling Scholarship Competition, and it would be the last year before the Great Depression would have a devastating effect on the members of the sketch club and architects in general.

78. *ISA Monthly Bulletin* 12, no. 8 (February 1928): 6.

79. *Western Architect* 37, no. 5 (May 1928): 110.

*The Brick House, designed by architect Andrew Rebori, was featured at the 1933–34 Century of Progress in Chicago. Rebori was an active member of the Chicago Architectural Club from 1911 forward and served as patron of the Club's atelier. (CP/HF)*

# Depression, Decline, and Demise

CHAPTER TWENTY-ONE

The annual meeting of the Chicago Architectural Sketch Club on May 7, 1928, was not only the time for the election of officers, it was also the occasion for announcing the winner of the 1928 Traveling Scholarship. Louis Pirola took the prize.[1] A month later the sketch club treasurer, T. O. Menees, wrote to his counterpart at the Illinois Society of Architects, Robert C. Ostergren, requesting that the ISA forward its third of the prize money, $333.33.[2] A penciled note at the bottom of that letter indicates that the check was to be sent. It was enclosed with a letter to the club from the ISA secretary, Walter A. McDougall. McDougall advised the sketch club that while they were "granting your request for this money, the Board of Directors does not sanction the present method of procedure, and insists that in the future when you propose to hold such a competition with the expectancy that certain of the money will be paid by the Illinois Society of Architects, they must first be advised of such proposed competition and your Club must have the authority of the Society, and be directed by them in all such competition." This seemingly antagonistic letter was hardly in keeping with the policy of some years' standing that the ISA and the AIA would jointly cover the expenses of the Traveling Scholarship. It was an indication of the growing estrangement between the Illinois Society of Architects and the Chicago Architectural Sketch Club.

The Chicago Architectural Sketch Club, the Chicago Chapter of the AIA, and the Illinois Society of Architects had begun a formal cooperation fourteen years earlier, in 1914, when the annual exhibition was first mounted under the direction of a Committee on Exhibition made up of members from all three groups. The prize for the Traveling Scholarship that year was six hundred dollars, and it had been provided entirely by the club. The following year, the club's name was no longer used exclusively and the exhibit was called the Chicago Architectural Exhibition. All three groups had been given equal billing in both the catalog and the publicity. The club, however, had continued to administer and fund the Traveling Scholarship.

The Traveling Scholarship was discontinued in 1916 due to the war in Europe, and no award was made that year. In 1917, the club instead sponsored an American Traveling Scholarship with $325 in prize money. No awards were made in 1918 or 1919. In 1920, when the Foreign Traveling Scholarship was again awarded, the prize was a thousand dollars donated by the Northwestern Terra Cotta Company.

1. Louis Pirola (ca. 1905–ca. 1969) was a diehard member of the Chicago Architectural Club. He was elected president in 1932 and became a director in 1941, a position he held for six years. He then served as treasurer for three years and secretary for fifteen years, until the final dissolution of the club corporation in 1967.

2. T. O. Menees's letter, dated June 6, 1928, is in the files of the Illinois Society of Architects, now at the Chicago Historical Society. While there is no similar letter on file addressed to the Chicago Chapter of the AIA, it can be assumed that one was sent to the AIA as well.

Late in 1920, anticipating problems with the club's ability to keep funding the Traveling Scholarship, the ISA and the AIA had enthusiastically endorsed a change in the club's constitution to provide for allied members. This allowed members of the AIA and the ISA to be club members at modest dues of five dollars a year. The money was to be used to fund the Annual Traveling Scholarship, which was now $750. For the next three years, this strategy was a great success, and about 125 allied members joined the club. Their dues were enough to cover most of the Traveling Scholarship expenses.[3]

By 1923 the Traveling Scholarship winner's prize money had been raised again, to a thousand dollars. It was also the year that the ISA and the AIA had agreed to share equally in funding the prize.[4] From that date forward, each of the three organizations would contribute one-third of the prize, and no objections to this arrangement have been found in the records of any of the three groups. In fact, there are letters on record from the ISA to the sketch club in 1925, 1926, and 1927, documenting the payment of its share of the prize money. The only hint of the ISA's misunderstanding of the situation, as well as any potential problems, was in 1927, when the ISA secretary wrote that the society had "already guaranteed one-third of the scholarship . . . this sum [$333.33] will be forthcoming after the competition is held and when the winner is ready to commence his travels."[5] Therefore it seems strange that in 1928 the ISA would send a letter demanding more control over the competition, a position it had never taken before.

During the following months there was a vigorous exchange of correspondence between the club and its two sister organizations regarding the future of the Traveling Scholarship. The two primary matters under discussion were the need to increase the stipend to twelve hundred dollars, and the possibility that the Chicago Architectural Sketch Club should no longer contribute funds to the award. Its place would be taken by the Architects Club of Chicago. The assumption was that there was a conflict of interest if the sketch club both administered and funded the scholarship.

The records concerning this controversy over how the Annual Traveling Scholarship would be administered and funded are somewhat confusing. For example, in July of 1928, the *ISA Monthly Bulletin* reported that the Architects Club of Chicago had "recently joined with the Chicago Chapter, AIA, and the Illinois Society of Architects in assuming the responsibility for the expense of the annual traveling scholarship of the Architectural Sketch Club. In the future, the jury judging the award will be appointed by the presidents of the three architectural societies."[6] This seems perfectly clear and straightforward, except that there are a number of letters postdating that notice wherein the relationship between the four groups, including the sketch club, is discussed—actually debated—at some length. Apparently, the three groups had agreed in principle about how the Traveling Scholarship would be handled, but it had not been codified.

There are three letters in the ISA files, now at the Chicago Historical Society, all written by Emery Stanford Hall, that discuss the matter in rather confusing detail.[7] Hall's position is difficult to understand. He was a member of the AIA, the ISA, the sketch club, and the Architects Club of Chicago. He was intensely interested in architectural education, and it was from this point of view that he objected to the sketch club funding the Traveling Scholarship. In a letter written in November 1929 to Bertram A. Weber, then treasurer of the Chicago AIA, he noted that he had suggested that the ISA "withdraw their support from the Sketch Club Traveling Scholarship, and that efforts be made to establish an Architects' Travelling Scholarship sponsored entirely by the regular architectural societies without any financial support from the Architectural Sketch Club." The plan was that sketch club members would participate in the competition for the scholarship but would have

3. In 1924, the constitution was again changed and all the allied members were transferred to the associate category. Few of them remained on the roster.

4. *ISA Monthly Bulletin* 8, no. 11 (May 1924). The decision by the AIA, the ISA, and the club to jointly finance the Traveling Scholarship award is first mentioned here; when that decision was made is not specified.

5. Ralph C. Harris (ISA) to the Architectural Sketch Club, February 9, 1927, ISA Archive, Chicago Historical Society.

6. *ISA Monthly Bulletin* 13, no. 1 (July 1928): 7.

7. Emery Stanford Hall (1869–1939) was a prominent architect in Chicago. He graduated from the University of Illinois in 1895 and was deeply involved in all aspects of architecture and the related professional societies until his death.

no control over it. He went on to state that "unfortunately, news of this arrangement got out before the negotiations were completed and was generally misunderstood." This is probably a reference to the notice published in the *ISA Monthly Bulletin* the previous July. He went on to say that "the amount of money now contributed by the sketch club towards the scholarship could be better expended in increasing the efficiency of its educational work." He closed by noting that it had been difficult to get all concerned together to finalize the situation. Two months later, in early February of 1929, Hall wrote to Gerald Bradbury, then president of the Chicago Architectural Sketch Club, to advise that "it seems to have been impossible up to the present time to have located a meeting of the Joint Committee on Travelling Scholarship and the Architectural Sketch Club at a time when all the members could attend." He did, however, advise Bradbury that plans now called for a total prize of twelve hundred dollars that would be funded equally by the ISA, the AIA, and the Architects Club. He also outlined some suggested rules for the conduct of the competition and named a proposed Donor Committee consisting of Harry L. Bentley for the AIA, Alfred C. Granger for the Architects Club, and himself for the ISA. He proposed that he would also act as temporary chairman of the committee. The next relevant letter is from Hall to H. B. Wheelock, wherein Hall expressed astonishment that Wheelock had misunderstood the proposed plans. He sent Wheelock the entire file on the subject and advised him that he and his colleagues had drafted an agreement between the AIA, the ISA, the Architects Club, and the sketch club that would settle the matter.

The agreement, which still survives, was pretty straightforward.[8] It not only provided for a Donor's Committee to be made up of the contributing societies, but also specified rules for jury selection and payment of the prize money in installments. Some provisions were left to be "worked out to the satisfaction of the Committee." After all this confusion, the only real changes were the amount of prize money and the addition of the Architects Club of Chicago as a donor in lieu of the Chicago Architectural Club.

During the long delay, preparations for the 1929 Annual Traveling Scholarship Competition had already begun. In a letter dated May 25, 1929, Emery S. Hall reported to the Illinois Society of Architects' board of directors that an agreement had been reached and that he recommended they execute it. He also reported that in the meantime, the program for 1929 had been approved by all concerned and "been conducted by the sketch club under rules and regulations approved by the Donor's Committee, and final drawings of competitors submitted for adjudication."

The 1929 Traveling Scholarship program was "A Housing Development for a city block 300 ft. by 600 ft., to include the buildings and gardens." It was an extremely ambitious program. The jury—three chosen from a list of nine—was made up of F. W. Puckey, E. H. Clark, and E. H. Klaber. They unanimously chose the submission by Albert Eiseman Jr.[9] Albert Bacci was given a first mention and Ralph Emerson a second mention. The award was announced at the annual meeting of the sketch club on the first Monday of May in 1929.[10] Emery Stanford Hall had been meticulous in seeing to it that the rules of the Donor's Committee were followed. In September, he wrote to his colleagues Granger and Bentley to advise that Eiseman had worked out a possible outline for his trip and suggested that the committee meet with him to "discuss and make recommendations for his best educational advantage." He also suggested a schedule of payments to Eiseman to be made on a monthly basis over the six-month tour. Surviving records indicate that his recommendations were followed.

The 1930 Traveling Scholarship seems to have been conducted along the same lines. There is, however, virtually no information concerning the competition until a

*Emery Stanford Hall (WRH)*

8. A copy is in the ISA files at the Chicago Historical Society. It was signed by J. C. Bollenbacher for the AIA on April 10, 1929; Howard White for the ISA on May 31, 1929; Alfred Granger for the Architects Club of Chicago on April 10, 1929; and Gerald Bradbury for the Chicago Architectural Sketch Club on April 28, 1929. There are a number of errors in the document, but its intent is clear.

9. Albert Eiseman Jr. was born and educated in Chicago. All his architectural training was at the atelier of the Architectural Sketch Club of Chicago. At the time he won his traveling scholarship, he was massier of the atelier and was employed in the office of David Adler.

10. The information concerning the award, including illustrations, was published in *Pencil Points* 10, no. 7 (July 1929): 496–97.

*Albert Eiseman Jr. (PP)*

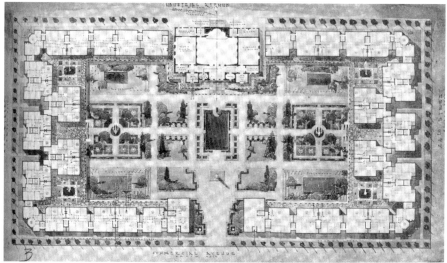

*Albert Eiseman Jr. won the Twenty-ninth Annual Traveling Scholarship Competition with this design for "A Housing Development" (PP)*

11. Alexander H. Bacci (1904–ca. 1975) was born in Chicago and received a BS in architecture from the Armour Institute of Chicago. He traveled extensively in the Far East after receiving his degree, before winning the traveling scholarship. At the time he won the scholarship he was employed in the Chicago office of Howells & Hood. Later he became a partner in the Chicago office of Schmidt, Garden & Erikson.

12. *Pencil Points* 11, no. 7 (July 1930): 593.

13. The competition was always referred to as if there had never been any hiatus in the years it was awarded. In fact, no scholarship was awarded from 1916 through 1919, due to the war in Europe.

letter dated May 7, 1930, from E. S. Hall transmitted to the three "Donor's Societies" wherein he advised that "a Competition has been held for this year's Travelling Scholarship. Judges were appointed and the Competition was judged on Monday, May 5." He went on to say that the judges, who were chosen by the sketch club, were Louis Ritter, Chester Wolcott, Philip Mayer, and Charles Bohassac. Thomas Tallmadge was asked to serve but arrived too late to help. Alexander Bacci was chosen as the winner of the competition.[11] S. T. Johnson and A. Crisevsky were named as first and second mentions. The subject of the competition was unusual, as it was not a building: it was a "bridge, suggested as one of a series of fixed bridges between Michigan Avenue and Wells Street, spanning the Chicago River."[12]

During 1931, there was even less information on the Thirty-first Annual Traveling Scholarship.[13] Without any explanation, the Donor's Committee did not fund the scholarship. The Great Depression had affected the architectural profession to such a degree that funds simply were not available. Instead, the prize of twelve

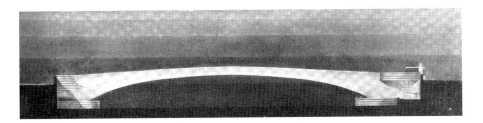

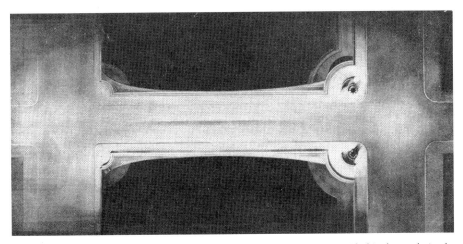

*Alexander Bacci won the Thirtieth Annual Traveling Scholarship Competition with this elegant design for "A Fixed Bridge over the Chicago River" (PP)*

hundred dollars was donated by William K. Fellows of Hamilton, Fellows & Nedved in Chicago.[14] Fellows was a longtime supporter and past president of the sketch club, who first became a member in 1895. The program for the competition was prepared by a committee composed of George M. Nedved as chairman, Louis Pirola, and Edmund J. Ryan. It called for "A *Curative-Bath Establishment,* similar to the Spas in Europe."[15] The drawings were due on May 31. The jury of five architects included Rudolph J. Nedved as chairman, Philip Maher, David W. Carlson, Ernest A. Grunsfeld Jr., and Carl A. Erickson. The results were published in *Pencil Points.*[16] The winner was Albert J. De Long, who would graduate from the Armour Institute of Technology shortly after winning the prize.[17] Thomas A. Carter took second place, and F. F. Polito, Wallace Miles, and Gosta Sjolin were named as honorable mentions.

14. *Pencil Points* 12, no. 5 (May 1931): 388.

15. *Pencil Points* 12, no. 8 (August 1931): 615.

16. Ibid., 614–15.

17. Albert Joseph De Long (1909–ca. 1985) was born in Chicago. He attended the Armour Institute, where he received his degree in 1931. After returning from his traveling scholarship trip to Europe, he worked in the office of Holabird & Root. He joined Skidmore, Owings & Merrill in 1955 and finished his career there.

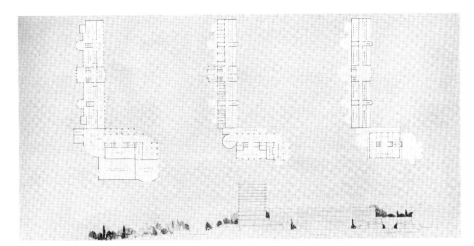

*Albert J. De Long won the 1931 Traveling Scholarship Competition with his "Curative-Bath Establishment" design. His master site plan is shown on page 570(PP)*

*Albert J. De Long's site plan for the
"Curative-Bath Establishment" (PP)*

The Thirty-second Annual Traveling Scholarship was awarded to Robert Benedict Brout in May of 1932.[18] Once again, information regarding the competition is sparse. The first published record of the 1932 competition was in the July issue of *Pencil Points*.[19] The elaborate program called for the design of "A Collaborative School of Fine Arts" in the United States that would eliminate the need for American students to do graduate work in Europe. The site was an island of two hundred thousand square feet north of an unspecified shoreline. A bridge was an optional part of the program. Fifty students were to be accommodated; twenty-five of them were to be architects and the others were to be sculptors, painters, and

18. Robert Benedict Brout (1907–ca. 1972) was born in Chicago and attended Crane Technical High School. He spent a year at Iowa State College and three years at the Armour Institute. At the time of the competition, he was employed by Alexander & Grandt, Architects, in Chicago.

19. *Pencil Points* 13, no. 7 (July 1932): 500–501.

*Robert Benedict Brout (PP)*

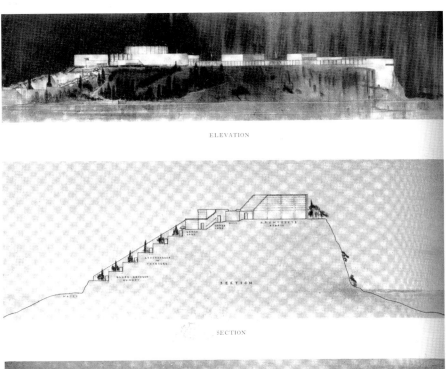

ELEVATION

SECTION

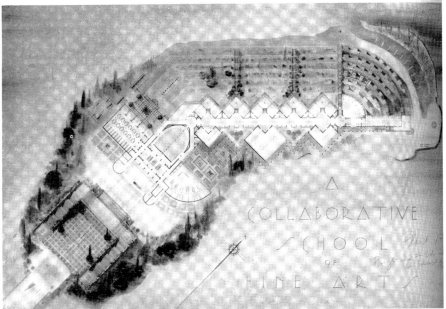

*Winning design for the competition for "A Collaborative School of Fine Arts," submitted by Robert Brout (PP)*

landscape architects. Provisions were to made for an auditorium, an exhibition hall, general studios for each discipline, and living quarters for students with dining facilities. Visiting professors would be accommodated in the student quarters, since no permanent faculty housing would be provided. The competition winner, Robert Benedict Brout, had been a member of the Chicago Architectural Sketch Club since 1929 and had participated in the Atelier Adams-Nelson, where he did his work on the competition drawings. When Brout received his twelve hundred dollars in prize money he used it, as required by the rules of the competition, to travel in Europe. What was originally intended to be a six-month tour became a five-year stay. When he left Chicago in the fall of 1932, opportunities for architects were approaching an all-time low due to the Depression. He elected to remain overseas, where his prize money was enough to sustain him for some time. Eventually, he found work and did not return to Chicago until mid-1937. The Chicago Architectural Club then sponsored an exhibition of his European drawings at the Kimball House. It filled all the public rooms on the first floor and a good portion of the second. Brout left Chicago shortly thereafter and ultimately ended up in California, where he practiced until his death around 1972.

The Traveling Scholarship that went to Brout in 1932 was the last to be awarded. There simply was not enough money in any of the professional societies' coffers to fund the award, and no individuals were willing to pick up the tab. Twice there are references to Beaux-Arts balls that were intended to raise money for the "scholarship fund," but there is no further reference to a scholarship during the Depression. There was a brief spurt of activity in 1940, when the club moved to new quarters and announced that the Traveling Scholarship would be resumed.[20] It was not. The Second World War and other events were too much to overcome.

The Traveling Scholarship was one of the club's major undertakings between 1928 and 1932, despite the problems associated with its administration by the Illinois Society of Architects and Emery Stanford Hall. The scholarship had always been highly sought after, and many members entered the competition, although at least half of them typically fell by the wayside before the final drawings were submitted for jurying. The work was usually done in the club atelier in the Kimball coach house, although that was not mandatory. One of the problems the competitors had to face was that the atelier did not give them time off to prepare their designs for the scholarship competition.

The club's atelier continued to be patronized by a steadily declining number of club members and a few outsiders. Some members chose to join private ateliers or attend organized classes elsewhere, such as Chicago Technical College.[21] Most members continued to use the club facilities at the Kimball House on a more or less daily basis. A number were active in the annual architectural exhibition although, technically, the club was not responsible for its presentation. The club's president continued to be automatically appointed president of the Chicago Architectural Exhibition League, which did have responsibility for the exhibition. With the Art Institute of Chicago out of the picture, the 1929 show was mounted at the Arts Club in the Wrigley Building annex at 410 North Michigan Avenue. The space, designed by architect Arthur Heun, was relatively small but delightful.

In a meeting of the board of directors of the Chicago Architectural Exhibition League on October 16, 1928, Gerald Bradbury, who was president of the sketch club, was officially appointed president of the league. For unknown reasons, he served only until January of 1929, when Pierre Blouke was elected "Director of the

20. *ISA Monthly Bulletin* 24, nos. 8–9 (February–March 1940): 5.

21. Several architects sponsored private ateliers between 1928 and 1940. Most used the programs provided by the Beaux-Arts Institute of Design. Occasionally a student from one of these ateliers would be listed as a winner of an award, but few ateliers were notable, except for Chicago Technical College, which regularly posted winners. The college was founded informally in 1903, when two men from the Chicago Bridge & Iron Works began giving evening classes on structural engineering. The institution was formalized in 1904, when it took a room on the fifth floor of the Athenaeum Building, where the Chicago Architectural Club had had space in the early 1890s and again in the early twentieth century. The college was organized to educate engineers and, as such, resembled the Chicago Architectural Club in many ways, except that it was a private, profit-making venture. In 1905, the school was fortunate to have structural engineer Frank A. Randall joins its faculty. (Randall is remembered primarily for *History of the Development of Building Construction in Chicago*, a key reference for anyone researching Chicago's architecture.) The college began using programs prepared by the Beaux-Arts Institute of Design around 1924, which attracted a great many students and soon formed the school's largest division. Students had the option of enrolling only in these design classes, which were conducted essentially as ateliers, instead of taking the full curriculum. Chicago Technical College thrived from around 1920 until 1955 for two important reasons: its classes were relatively inexpensive and could be taken during the day or evening, and after World War II the school took advantage of the G.I. Bill of Rights and trained thousands of young people. Unfortunately, it was not accredited either in engineering or architecture, and its graduates sometimes had a difficult time getting licensed. The school survived until 1977.

League," for which he was to receive the sum of a thousand dollars. All the other officers were to remain the same as the previous year, except for former president Bradbury, who assumed the office of secretary. It was Blouke who made the arrangements with the Arts Club after preliminary contact was made by Alfred Granger.[22] Blouke scheduled the exhibition for Friday, May 24, through June 13.[23] Blouke mailed a four-page brochure to the architects of Chicago outlining the rules for exhibiting. The brochure also named the officers of the league, the Jury of Admission, and the Reception Committee, whose responsibility was to open the exhibition at a tea sponsored by the Arts Club on the afternoon of May 24.

The league officers elected to forgo an illustrated catalog and advertising in 1929. Instead, they asked former advertisers as well as others to become patrons of the exhibition in order to cover costs. An "Index of Exhibits" was published, similar to the lists published in the past in conjunction with the illustrated catalogs. The league's officers and committees were listed at the end of the booklet, followed by two lists of patrons, one the architects, twenty-six in all, and the second the sixteen suppliers who supported the exhibition.

The 1929 exhibition was somewhat smaller than the previous year's, primarily because of the smaller space. There were fifty-three exhibitors who had 171 listings in the catalog. It got generally favorable reviews, although somewhat fewer than in the past. The *Art World*'s review by Charles Victor Knox opened, "A wide range of architectural activity . . . from an 'air restaurant' perilously poised, like a daisy, on a slender stalk to house plans for the Architects' Small House Service Bureau."[24] The "air restaurant" was a student project the reviewer felt could be favorably compared with Buckminster Fuller's Dymaxion House. He went on to describe a number of the entries in a positive light. Knox was impressed by B. K. Johnson's "municipal observatory," another student project. He was also impressed that "a group of grain elevators may be an asset rather than a detriment to the landscape," as designed by J. M. White. The Chicago War Memorial design by Howard Cheney

22. Minutes of the Meeting of the Chicago Architectural Exhibition League, January 14, 1929. The originals are at the Ryerson and Burnham Libraries at the Art Institute of Chicago. A copy of the complete set is in the author's collection.

23. Assistant Secretary of the Arts Club to Pierre Blouke, January 25, 1929, Archives of the Newberry Library, Chicago.

24. Charles Victor Knox, "Chicago Architects Exhibition," *Art World*, May 8, 1929.

*Eagle on the east facade of the Chicago Club, displayed in the 1929 exhibition (George Gabauer photo)*

*The Arts Club of Chicago, a superb space in which to view exhibitions (ArtsC)*

and Eliel Saarinen was noted as a "conception of considerable merit." Knox's focus, however, was on the skyscraper designs by Holabird & Root, most of which had not yet been built. Finally, he admired a "fine model for an eagle for the front of the Chicago Club" exhibited by sculptress Viola Norman.

Ernest L. Heitkamp's review in the *Chicago Herald-Examiner* was very different.[25] He began by asserting, "Chicago has an unprecedented opportunity at the present juncture in its history to create an architectural entity and beauty unexampled in this country. Chicago is being literally rebuilt, remade, in our time. Fortunately the Chicago Plan is coming to fruition before it [is] too late." He went on in this vein for several paragraphs, regretting only that he found "too little of response to this need of Chicago. It is natural, of course, that young architects should busy themselves much with the lesser demands which can be more readily and surely converted into revenue and income; but . . . young architects . . . should respond to this newer need and opportunity of Chicago." He was concerned that buildings of the "so called 'modern idea' which have attracted world-wide attention in the East" were not being built in sufficient numbers in Chicago. He was convinced that "if New York can build these, Chicago can do it better—better because of its spirit, because of its room, because of its courageous determination to rebuild and remake itself, because of its peculiar opportunity to create and carry through a united architectural effort." Heitkamp was using the exhibition at the Arts Club as a platform to encourage the architects of Chicago to show the world what they could do. In his entire article, he did not mention a single specific building. It was, nevertheless, a positive statement. The 1929 exhibition was a success.

One exhibit came in late and thus was not part of any review. It was Thomas Tallmadge's design for the memorial marker to be installed over the grave of Louis Sullivan at Graceland Cemetery. Tallmadge wrote to the Arts Club to advise that he was bringing in a model of the monument for display during the exhibition. The Arts Club wrote to Blouke to ask if this late entry should be allowed.[26] It was shown and was the subject of an article in the *Chicago Sunday Tribune*. Several items appeared in the professional press regarding the design of the monument, most of which are mentioned in a 1975 article in the *Prairie School Review*.[27] A committee of architects, including John Van Bergen, Walter Stockton, Howard White, Jens Jensen, William Gates, Martin Ryerson, and Henry Babson, with Thomas Tallmadge as chairman, had been established to prepare a suitable marker for Sullivan's grave. At first, all agreed that George Elmslie should design the marker. His design, for unstated reasons, was rejected. Tallmadge then prepared an alternate design that was executed in a slightly smaller version than originally envisioned. Elmslie was not pleased. He wrote to the members of the committee, proclaiming, "I particularly desire publication be given to the fact that I did not design the memorial as it is being built . . . I want it made clear that I did not, and could not with my intimate knowledge, based on years of association of Sullivan's philosophy and ideals, design the present structure."[28] An examination of the two designs, both of which survive, makes Elmslie's concerns evident.[29] The Tallmadge scheme is essentially an art deco design, with little reference to what Sullivan might have done. Nevertheless, the model of the monument was shown at the exhibition and the reporter for the *Chicago Tribune* wrote that it was "simple in design, the memorial to one of the few geniuses Chicago has produced will take the form of a pink granite boulder—seven feet high. On the front will be a bronze medallion, now being modeled by Kristian Snyder . . . one of Sullivan's friends . . . a reproduction of one of the plates made just before his death . . . for the Art Institute."[30] The center of the medallion had a bas-relief of Sullivan modeled by Emory Seidel.

25. Ernest L. Heitkamp, *Chicago Herald-Examiner*, Sunday, June 2, 1929.

26. A note to Blouke regarding this matter is in the Arts Club files. The model was illustrated in the *Chicago Sunday Tribune* of June 2, 1929, with an article about Sullivan and the proposed monument.

27. Lenore Pressman, "Graceland Cemetery: Memorial to Chicago Architects," *Prairie School Review* 12, no. 4 (Fourth Quarter 1975): 13–18.

28. George Elmslie to Thomas Tallmadge, July 10, 1929, Burnham Library Collection, Art Institute of Chicago.

29. Drawings for both designs are in the author's collection, a gift from Henry Tideman.

30. In Tallmadge's copy of *A System of Architectural Ornament*, in the author's collection, plate 19 is marked up to instruct Snyder on his work.

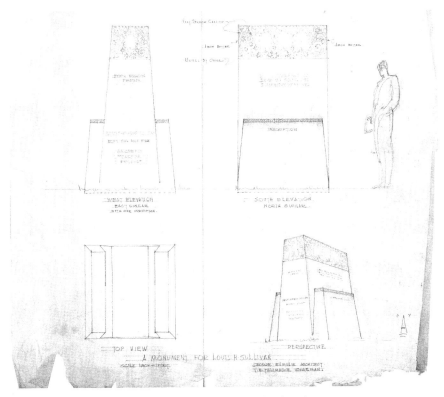

*George Elmslie's rejected design for Louis Sullivan's grave marker (WRH)*

*Thomas Tallmadge's design for Sullivan's memorial was installed, although at a smaller scale than originally proposed (WRH)*

*Sullivan's grave marker as it appears today (WRH)*

A year later the Chicago Architectural Exhibition League once again mounted its annual exhibition at the Arts Club of Chicago. It was essentially a rerun of the 1929 exhibition. The invitations and the instructions were all adaptations of the previous year's materials.[31] The exhibition was larger, however, with forty-eight individuals and firms showing 244 items. The index of exhibits was displayed in the same format it had been in 1929, with the officers and patrons at the end of the pamphlet. There were sixty-five patrons listed, but in 1930 architects and suppliers were not listed separately.

Again the *Art World* was the primary reviewer of the exhibition.[32] Lena M. Mc-Cauley was very positive in her comments, noting that "at the peak of its 43rd year the Chicago Architectural Exhibition League has staged a display of drawings and models in the galleries of the Arts club, witnessing the fact its members are alive to the changing time." She complimented the jury—Venning, Hofmeister, Iannelli,

31. Virtually all the documentation regarding the exhibition is now in the archive of the Arts Club at the Newberry Library in Chicago.

32. Lena M. McCauley, *Art World*, May 27, 1930.

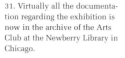

*The plaque on Sullivan's grave marker was modeled after plate 19 in* A System of Architectural Ornament; *the pencil markings were made by Tallmadge, who owned this copy of the book, now in the author's collection*

Ewell, and De Golyer—on its selections, observing, "A high order of interest is maintained." She was pleased with the work submitted by students from the Armour Institute and the University of Illinois, which she saw as "evidence of an awareness of the classics in relation to the creative work of the ambitious present." McCauley singled out Holabird & Root's "masterpiece," the Chicago Daily News Building, for special praise. It had just been awarded the Chicago Chapter of the AIA's medal of honor. She felt that it was "among the monumental buildings that do honor to Chicago." In an aside, she also commended several other Holabird & Root buildings in the exhibition. She praised the twelve designs proposed for the Century of Progress as well, one of the few projects in the exhibition featuring work by out-of-town architects. Ralph Walker, Paul Cret, and Raymond Hood were all included, along with local architects E. H. Bennett, Hubert Burnham, and John Holabird. McCauley made a point of naming several designers without identifying their buildings, all in a positive light. While there were a few other brief notices about the exhibition, none was comprehensive. The show, however, was generally deemed a success, despite the onset of the Depression.

In 1931 the Chicago Architectural Exhibition League again worked with the Arts Club to mount its annual show. The surviving documentation indicates that it too was modeled on previous years' exhibitions; even the dates, May 15 through June 6, were almost identical. Forty-eight firms and individuals presented 224 exhibits. Fifty-seven patrons were acknowledged in the back of the index of exhibits. Nineteen thirty-one is the only year for which a listing of the amounts contributed by the patrons has survived. The minutes of the Chicago Architectural Exhibition League for November of 1931 list forty-four contributors who gave a total of $865.

*By the time the completed Chicago Daily News Building was shown in the 1930 exhibition, it had already won the Chicago Chapter of the AIA's gold medal (AIC/HALIC)*

*The Adler Planetarium designed by Ernest Grunsfeld won the AIA gold medal in 1931 (AIC/HALIC)*

*Chicago Chapter of the AIA's gold medal (photo by WRH, courtesy of Anthony Grunsfeld)*

33. "Annual Exhibit of Architects Opens May 15th," *Chicago Tribune*, May 10, 1931.

34. C. J. Bulliett, *Chicago Evening Post Magazine of the Art World*, May 19, 1931.

35. Marguerite B. Williams, "Chicagoan Wins Medal on Design of Planetarium," *Chicago Daily News*, May 21, 1931.

The amounts vary from as much as seventy-five dollars to as little as five. The exhibition was announced in the *Chicago Tribune* a few days early and it was reviewed by most of the local press.[33] C. J. Bulliet wrote a review for the *Chicago Evening Post* that discussed the state of architecture in Chicago.[34] He noted that the exhibition included "buildings already accomplished, buildings about to be and dream buildings that may get no further than the enthusiastic sketch of builders of castles in Spain." He observed that the opening had drawn "200 architects and laymen . . . [and] there was a goodly stream of people intent upon seeing what has been done recently in Chicago and what is projected." He was most impressed by the Adler Planetarium, which had just received the Chicago Chapter of the AIA's gold medal. He felt it deserved "the honor, for the planetarium, quite apart from the majesty of its purpose, is the most impressive work, architecturally, in the show." The planetarium was also lauded by the *Chicago Daily News* in an article by Marguerite B. Williams.[35] Williams's review went further to discuss many of the items in the exhibition, including "Charles Morgan's imaginative conception of Frank Lloyd Wright's glass skyscraper, a series of water colors of Italian buildings by A. H. Bacci and Carol Lou Burnham's architectural sketches done in Europe." She was disappointed that the "allied arts seem rather meagerly represented except for Frank Sohn's vitrolite panels, Emil Lehman's bronze gate, Walter Williams' sculptural reliefs and a few other exhibits."

Williams ended her comments by noting that while "the Arts Club is turning from its French moderns . . . to act as patron to this small and somewhat specialized exhibition of our local architects and students, the public is viewing the popular display of models and plans of Jubilee week at Marshall Field's tearoom. That widespread interest in architecture which the American skyscrapers has given us should lead still others to see A. C. Webb's very romantic drawings of New York buildings which in their colored stone remind us of old Assyrian and Egyptian towers. The latter are at the Carson Pirie Scott & Co. galleries this month." Williams's column concluded, "Perhaps it is not as great a calamity as it appears that we have no longer the big architectural exhibitions at the Art Institute that we used to. What the public lacks now is the opportunity to see what Europeans and easterners are doing."

There were no more exhibitions at the Arts Club. The Chicago Architectural Exhibition League met on December 8, 1931, and "it was generally agreed to conserve the capital of the organization by not conducting such an exhibition [in 1932]."[36] In 1932 and 1933, however, there was considerable discussion about having an exhibition of some sort. At first it was suggested by the board of the Chicago Architectural Exhibition League that a small "air castle" show be held at the Architects Club. Shortly thereafter, the league was offered space at the site of the World's Fair, the 1933 Century of Progress. Three booths were to be available to the league free of charge. After considerable debate, it was concluded that the league could not bear the expense of mounting shows at both the Architects Club and the World's Fair. At the instigation of Louis Pirola, the recently elected president of the sketch club and the Chicago Architectural Exhibition League, the league ultimately decided to accept the offer of space at the fair. Pirola was able to rally a group of members of the sketch club, and a small exhibition was held in 1933. In December of 1933, the minutes of the Chicago Architectural Exhibition League recorded that an average of about seven hundred people per day saw the exhibition, a total of about seventy-five thousand. The Executive Committee of the league then authorized the reimbursement of seventy-five dollars to Pirola for his out-of-pocket expenses and acknowledged that he was "highly commended for the type and kind of show and the conduct of same."[37] A similar motion was put before the full board of the league a few days later, when plans were made for an exhibition at the fair in 1934. However, at a meeting of the league four months later, it was reported that few potential exhibitors were interested, and it was "moved and seconded that the idea be given up entirely."[38] The 1933 exhibition at the Century of Progress was the last ever mounted under the auspices of the Chicago Architectural Exhibition League.[39]

Meanwhile, many sketch club members had been looking forward to participating in the 1933–34 Century of Progress since the late 1920s. The first indication of a more than casual interest in the fair was the program for the 1928 Traveling Scholarship Competition. It called for a design for a "Chicago Building for the 1933 World's Fair and Exposition." The competition, won by Louis Pirola, was for a design that could be retained after the fair was long gone. It was not, of course, built, but the idea was one that excited the members of the Chicago Architectural Sketch Club. None of them had a major involvement as a designer for the fair, but many were employed by the various firms that designed the structures of the fair. A national commission had been organized in 1928 to plan the fair, headed by Harvey Wiley Corbett of New York. He was aided by committee members from San Francisco, Philadelphia, and New York, as well as Edward H. Bennett, John A. Holabird, and Hubert Burnham from Chicago.[40] The Chicago Architectural Sketch Club followed the planning of the fair with great interest. Late in 1928, the sketch club published an article in its journal, *Treads and Risers,* by Charles S. Peterson, vice president of the Chicago World's Fair trustees, that succinctly outlined the plans under way for the fair.[41] He described the process by which Bennett, Holabird, and Burnham were chosen to represent Chicago as commissioners and as designers of some of the structures at the fair. Nathaniel Owings, who would later organize Skidmore, Owings & Merrill, was tapped as the development supervisor for the fair. The *Treads and Risers* article had opened with the statement that the "younger architects of Chicago may see open before them in 1929 very much the same kind of an

36. Minutes of the Executive Committee of the Chicago Architectural Exhibition League, December 8, 1931, from the author's collection.

37. Minutes of the Chicago Architectural Exhibition League, December 5, 1933, from the author's collection.

38. Minutes of the Chicago Architectural Exhibition League, April 17, 1934, from the author's collection. At this meeting it was made official that in the future "the President of the Chicago Architectural Club automatically becomes the President of the Architectural Exhibition League"; what had been the practice for several years became codified.

39. The minutes of the league during the next several years indicate that the subject was brought up nearly every year, but no exhibition was ever held. The Chicago Chapter of the AIA did have a small exhibition at the Art Institute of Chicago in the fall of 1941.

40. "Architects Plan Chicago World's Fair," *East Chicago Indiana News,* December 14, 1928. The article also noted that "Island No. 1" (now called Meigs Field) was under construction at the time and would be an integral part of the fair.

41. The article was reprinted in *Pencil Points* 10, no. 2 (February 1929): 124.

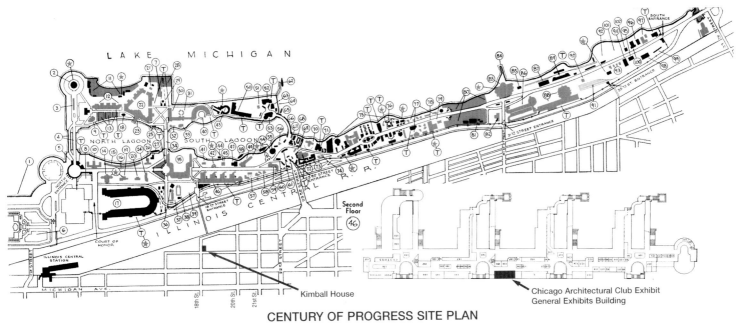

LAKE MICHIGAN

NORTH LAGOON

SOUTH LAGOON

ILLINOIS CENTRAL R.R.

Court of Honor

ILLINOIS CENTRAL STATION

MICHIGAN AVE.

18th St. 20th St. 21st St.

Second Floor

Kimball House

Chicago Architectural Club Exhibit
General Exhibits Building

**CENTURY OF PROGRESS SITE PLAN**

*The 1933 World's Fair site was easily accessible from the Kimball House*

opportunity as that which opened before their predecessors in 1891." Ultimately, a great many Chicago architects, both individuals and firms, participated in planning the fair. More than fifty members of the club were involved to some degree in designing the buildings. Those not involved kept a sharp eye on the proceedings and often visited the site immediately to the east of the Kimball House, which was accessible by a footbridge over the Illinois Central tracks.

As plans for the fair progressed, the sketch club kept up its usual schedule of activities. The atelier was submitting an average of forty problems to New York for judgment at the end of each Class B problem. It also sponsored an exhibit of student drawings from the École in Paris in late 1928 and continued to invite other architectural organizations to visit.[42] On Monday, May 6, 1929, the club held its annual meeting, with nearly a hundred members present.[43] After an excellent dinner and entertainment, Gerald Bradbury was reelected president. E. F. Anderson and F. M. Baldwin were elected vice president and secretary, and T. O. Menees was reelected treasurer. The list of directors for the year included Harold Spitznagel, William Thompson, Thomas Mulig, and Howard Bordewich for two-year terms. V. R. Rund and T. M. Hofmeister were chosen for one-year terms. Several past presidents, including J. C. Llewellyn, W. B. Mundie, Pierre Blouke, and C. Herrick Hammond, spoke of their own experiences with the club, and Hammond, who was then serving as president of the national AIA, was elected an honorary member. Following the annual meeting, formal meetings of the sketch club were suspended for the summer, although some members of the atelier continued to work on summer problems. There was a summer sketch competition for all members, with a prize of fifty dollars for the best group of sketches. (No winner was announced.) When the fall atelier schedule was posted, nearly fifty members of the club signed on. They, along with the regular club membership, began a series of monthly "get-together-Smokers" at the clubhouse, which brought out dozens of members, as did a regular schedule of speakers. Alfonso Iannelli, who remained in Chicago after working with Frank Lloyd Wright on the Midway Gardens, lectured from time to time, fascinating the members with his grasp of the relationship between sculpture and architecture.

42. *Pencil Points* 10, no. 2 (February 1929): 127.

43. *Pencil Points* 10, no. 6 (June 1929): 422.

44. *ISA Monthly Bulletin* 14, nos. 6–7 (December–January 1930–31): 9.

Early in 1930, the Architects Club of Chicago elected to mount a second exhibition of architects' and craftsmen's work at the clubhouse.[44] A similar exhibition had been a great success in 1928, and all concerned felt that it would not compete with the Architectural Exhibition League's show since they contained different material. The Architects Club decided that in 1930 "in addition to the architects' work and materials, student work will also be shown." All the local schools participated. It also announced that in "order to make the exhibition more representative nonmembers have been invited to exhibit as well as members of the club." The exhibition, while sponsored by the Architects Club, was largely handled by members of the sketch club. CASC member David A. Pareira served as chairman.[45] After it was hung there was an informal opening on February 11 and a formal opening a week later. The show got good coverage in the professional press but very little in the popular press. The sketch club's journal, *Treads and Risers*, gave it a favorable, illustrated review.[46] In the same issue, the 1930 annual exhibit of the Chicago Architectural Exhibition League was announced for May 15 through June 7, and the Evanston–North Shore Association of Architects announced its Third Annual Architectural Exhibition for March 17–29 at the public library in Evanston. Dates for all these exhibitions were chosen with care to avoid conflicts.

*Eric Gugler and Roger Bailey won the competition for a World War I memorial with this design (PP*

While all this was taking place, there was a major national competition for a World War I War memorial in Chicago. Numerous Chicago firms entered, including many that employed members of the sketch club, but first honors went to the team of Eric Gugler and Roger Bailey from Detroit. Second prize went to Chicago architect Benjamin H. Marshall, whose late partner, Charles E. Fox, had been instrumental in organizing the Chicago Architectural Exhibition League and the Architects Club of Chicago. Several members of the sketch club worked in his office. Marshall's published perspective was far more impressive than Gugler and Bailey's. Chicago architects Nimmons, Carr & Wright shared third place with New York architects Voorhees, Gmelin & Walker.

Just before the Forty-third Annual Architectural Exhibition opened at the Arts Club of Chicago, the sketch club held its annual meeting at the Kimball House. Francis Baldwin was elected president. No other elected officers' or directors' names were published.

As the annual meeting was being held, another important architectural event was happening at Princeton University. Frank Lloyd Wright delivered six lectures

45. *Pencil Points* 11, no. 3 (March 1930): 224.

46. *Treads and Risers* 3, no. 3 (March 1930): 16.

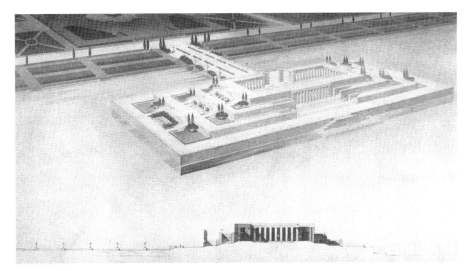

*Ben Marshall's design for a World War I memorial took second place in the competition (PP)*

*Frank Lloyd Wright's 1931 exhibition at the Art Institute of Chicago. (CHS)*

there in May of 1930, later published in *Modern Architecture, Being the Kahn Lectures for 1930.* A concurrent exhibit of Wright's work was touring the United States. It came to Chicago in September of 1930, just as the Chicago Architectural Sketch Club was preparing for its 1930–31 activities. The Wright exhibit opened on September 27, and Marguerite B. Williams reviewed it a few days later in the *Chicago Daily News.*[47] Ms. Williams noted that the exhibit "was drawing interested crowds," and that there was "an air of excitement there last Saturday afternoon as men gathered around the tables of plans and books and perused the epigrams taken from Mr. Wright's Princeton lectures, printed on the wall. Quite informally, as in his own studio at Taliesen, drawings and plans of unexecuted projects are all mixed in with photographs of executed ones, sculptural models and the gay mosaics designed by Mr. Wright in the special process of his associate, Charles Morgan. With the exception of a few of his latest projects, the exhibition is the same as that which attracted so much attention in New York last spring. And from the demands for tickets to Mr. Wright's lectures at the Art Institute, Oct. 1 and 2, it looks as though Chicago is now giving Mr. Wright its tardy homage."[48] The great majority of those tickets were used by members of the Chicago Architectural Sketch Club.

In November 1930, *Pencil Points* reported that "the Architectural Sketch Club is one of the oldest professional organizations in Chicago, but it caters primarily to the younger draftsmen and students and its aims are almost entirely education."[49] The same article noted that the club's "principal activity is the Atelier which . . . conducts several prize competitions yearly and in the Spring conducts the Annual Foreign Scholarship." The article went on to state that "minor activities of the club include lectures and talks by prominent men in the architectural and building field and social affairs for the club members and their friends twice a year." It also noted that the club conducted a structural design class and that "about three hundred and thirty active, senior, and non-resident members indicates that the club fills a definite need in Chicago's architectural life and that the club is striving to do its share in raising the standard of architectural design and practice in Chicago."

Despite this positive publicity, 1931 was a quiet year for the Chicago Architectural Sketch Club. The downturn brought about by the recession was taking a toll on architects in general, and particularly the younger men. After a relatively uneventful first half of the year, the annual meeting, held on the first Monday of May, brought the reelection of Francis Baldwin as president and George Nedved as vice president. V. R. Rund and T. O. Menees were chosen as secretary and treasurer. The six directors were Howard Bordewich, Albert Heino, T. M. Hofmeister, Thomas

47. Marguerite B. Williams, "Art Institute Draws Crowds with Exhibits," *Chicago Daily News,* October 4, 1930.

48. The two lectures Wright delivered were published by the Art Institute of Chicago in a paperbound issue of two thousand copies titled *Two Lectures on Architecture by Frank Lloyd Wright,* now extremely rare.

49. *Pencil Points* 11, no. 11 (November 1930): 906.

*Members of the Tech Architectural Club in 1931 (PP)*

Mulig, Paul Rauch, and associate William Thomsen. Except for the Annual Traveling Scholarship Competition, which was now sponsored by the club atelier, most activities at the clubhouse had become informal social events. The entire membership
was pleased to learn that sketch club member Benjamin Lane Smith had won the
Warren Prize in 1931. It was just one of his many awards from the Beaux-Arts Institute of Design for the previous year's work. George D. Recher had received a first
medal in the Emerson Prize and had been a contender for the Warren Prize. Thomas
J. Mulig took home a second medal for one of his designs for an interior project.

The atelier continued to participate actively in Beaux-Arts problems and
other special competitions. In June 1931, it was announced that R. F. Weber of the
club's Atelier Adams-Nelson had won first prize of five hundred dollars for the design of a steel bridge.[50] The competition was sponsored by the American Institute
of Steel Construction. At almost the same time it was announced that sketch club
member Eugene Voita had won first prize of two thousand dollars in a competition
to design an elevated steel water tank. That competition, first announced in September of 1930, was sponsored by Chicago Bridge & Iron Works. It drew entries
from throughout the United States, with 691 applications to participate and 152
designs submitted.[51]

The Chicago Architectural Sketch Club regularly participated in events of related groups and often provided speakers. In 1923, Chicago Technical College had
organized a student group called the Tech Architectural Club, modeled after what
was then called the Chicago Architectural Club. It became very popular at the col-

50. *Pencil Points* 12, no. 6 (June 1931): 460.

51. The designs were published in *Elevated Tank Designs Submitted in a Competition Sponsored by Chicago Bridge & Iron Works* (Chicago, 1931), now extremely rare.

lege, with virtually every student architect and some engineers participating. It held regular meetings with speakers, often from the sketch club. Each year, it published an annual of the work of architectural students at the college. As time went by, students from the architecture department began to participate in the Beaux-Arts Institute of Design projets and their work was often noted in the various professional journals where results of ateliers were published.[52]

Another group that had a peripheral relationship with the Chicago Architectural Sketch Club was the Women's Architectural Club of Chicago. First organized in 1927, it had exhibited drawings, photographs, and models at the Women's World's Fair held in Chicago that spring.[53] It had exhibited again at the second Women's World's Fair the following year, and after that had met on a regular basis in various architects' offices. It was the first organization of its kind, and its monthly dinner meetings were always "liberally and enthusiastically attended." The members chose not to be affiliated with the Chicago Architectural Sketch Club and went their own way. Key figures in the organization were Mary Ann Crawford, Bertha Yerex Whitman, Ruth Perkins, Vera Lund, Helen Brown, and Elizabeth Kimball Nedved, who was married to Rudolph Nedved, two-term president of the sketch club and the Architectural Exhibition League. (Both Nedveds had graduated from the Armour Institute of Technology, and they traveled extensively in Europe together after being married in London. Eventually Elizabeth and Rudolph had become partners in the firm organized by Dwight Perkins, which became Hamilton, Fellows & Nedved after his retirement. Elizabeth Nedved had become the first woman member of the Chicago Chapter of the AIA in 1926.) By 1932, the Women's Architectural Club was holding two meetings a month, often with competitions among members, not unlike the ones held in the early days of the Chicago Architectural Club. It also introduced "an associate membership designed for women interested in architecture who would not otherwise be qualified for membership in the Club."[54]

In the fall of 1930, there had begun to be hints that the Architects Club of Chicago was not thriving as all concerned had intended. The problem seemed to be that only the sketch club was regularly using the facilities of the Kimball House, and even its activities were generally confined to the coach house, where the atelier was held. In September, Carl Heimbrodt, the secretary of the Architects Club, had written to the Illinois Society of Architects and the Chicago Chapter of the AIA, inviting them to meet with the board of directors of the Architects Club at the Kimball House on September 24 to discuss matters of mutual interest.[55] While specifics were never published, it becomes clear from reading the minutes of the ISA and subsequent reports of the activities that took place at the clubhouse that the point of the meeting was to encourage increased use of the club facilities.

During the following year, the Architects Club began a serious effort to recruit more members and to involve all of them in club activities. Those activities were not confined to architecture. The Architects Club sponsored nine golf outings during the summer of 1931, culminating in a tournament on September 24, 1931.[56] One hundred and fourteen members and guests turned out and everyone got a prize. The club also sponsored a "trek to Browns Lake, Wisconsin, in mid-August with twenty members participating." In the fall of 1931, the group announced that future activities would include "speakers, smokers, and social events," as well as monthly meetings of the AIA, the ISA, and the sketch club. It also chose to initiate a "new and important feature . . . the development and planning of modern tenement buildings along a unified city plan." Eventually a document on the subject was

52. The most reliable listing of winners of Beaux-Arts Institute of Design projets was the *Bulletin of the Beaux-Arts Institute of Design*, which began publishing in 1924 and continued until 1952. Results were also published in other journals from time to time.

53. *Pencil Points* 9, no. 1 (November 1928): 734.

54. *Pencil Points* 13, no. 12 (December 1932): 846.

55. A copy of Heimbrodt's letter, dated September 18, 1930, to Walter A. McDougall, secretary of the Illinois Society of Architects, is in the ISA Archive at the Chicago Historical Society.

56. *Pencil Points* 12, no. 11 (November 1931): 849.

57. Henry K. Holsman, *Rehabilitating Blighted Areas, Report of the Committee on Blighted Area Housing* (Chicago: Architects Club of Chicago, 1932).

published by Henry K. Holsman.[57] In November 1931, the Chicago Chapter of the AIA held a joint meeting with the Architects Club at the Kimball House to present the gold medal to Ernest Grunsfeld for his Adler Planetarium design. More than 150 people attended, including Max Adler and Dr. Fox from the planetarium.

Ten days later, the Architects Club held its annual Thanksgiving dinner and a formal welcome-home party for the club's president, Alfred Granger, who had spent a year in Europe. At the end of the evening, a collection was taken to help the architects' contribution to the general relief fund. Times were becoming more and more difficult. The Architects Club continued to make every effort to encourage its members and member societies to make use of the Kimball House. Under the leadership of a new club manager, W. B. Thompson, members were regularly sent invitations to attend the "Thursday Luncheon Meetings" at the clubhouse. Lunch was fifty cents, and an interesting speaker was almost always scheduled. The Architects Club expanded this plethora of activity in 1932–33 by sponsoring "tournaments at the Club house in bridge, chess, backgammon, and ping-pong; as well as several quartets, orchestras, and a minstrel aggregation."[58] There was a monumental effort to give the Architects Club of Chicago a reason for being. For a time it seemed to be working.

By the 1930s, the sketch club's Atelier Adams-Nelson had long since taken on a life of its own. In November 1931, it held its "fortieth" annual smoker at the Kimball House.[59] It was customary to hold the annual smoker on November 23, the same date the patrons' dinner at the École des Beaux-Arts in Paris was held. Alfred H. Granger was the guest of honor, and he, William E. Parsons, Edward H. Bennett, Arthur F. Adams, Joseph F. Booton, Arthur F. Deam, Francis Puckey, and Andrew Rebori were elected "ancien patrons," which the atelier members felt they merited because of their past support. The senior patron was now Donald S. Nelson, who was himself a graduate of the club's atelier.

Early in 1932, perhaps taking a cue from its parent organization, the Architects Club of Chicago, the sketch club began sponsoring field trips and events at the Kimball House on a more regular basis. The Adler Planetarium was the focus on Friday evening, March 4, 1932.[60] The members were honored to have Ernest Grunsfeld lead the excursion, which was followed by a lecture by senior planetarium staff member professor Fox. A few weeks later, at the annual meeting on the first Monday in May, Louis Pirola was elected president for 1932–33, and Francis Baldwin, Thomas J. Mulig, and William Thomsen were chosen as vice president, secretary, and treasurer, respectively.[61] When fall came, most meetings were highlighted by lectures by Chicago architects, such as Eugene Klaber on "Faddism vs. Reality" and Irving K. Pond on "Is Modern Architecture Modern?" The most ambitious program was the Architects' Ball at the Drake Hotel, organized by member Ralph Gross. Most events, however, had to be done at very modest expense. Many of the members simply could not afford to do otherwise. The early months of 1933 brought more of the same. In May of 1933, Ralph F. Gross was elected president and Thomas Mulig was named secretary.[62]

The members of the Chicago Architectural Sketch Club continued to use the Kimball House as their headquarters in 1933 and beyond, but few events were scheduled. The atelier continued to operate, but its numbers began to shrink. One of the few events in which the members of the sketch club were able to participate was a three-day conference at the Kimball House in October, organized by the Architects Club, entitled "Preparation for Entrance to Architectural Practice."[63] (Since most members were out of work, what better time to hang out their own shingles?)

58. *Pencil Points* 13, no. 11 (November 1932): 769.

59. *Pencil Points* 13, no. 1 (January 1932): 59. This was probably a misnomer since it would have meant that the first atelier smoker was held in 1891. The Chicago Architectural Club did not have its own atelier until 1908, when the Atelier Bennett was organized.

60. *Pencil Points* 13, no. 4 (April 1932): 285.

61. *Pencil Points* 13, no. 12 (December 1932): 847. The results of the annual election were never published per se. These names are from a later article on other events at the club.

62. Ralph F. Gross (1874–1971) would continue as president (except during 1937 and 1938, when Thomas Mulig served as president and Gross was a director) until 1967, when the club's corporation was dissolved. From 1942 on, the club's address was 1119 North Harding, Ralph Gross's home address. The only source of other officers' names were the annual reports to the Illinois secretary of state.

63. *ISA Monthly Bulletin* 18, nos. 4–5 (October–November 1933): 6.

Those members who had been employed had spent most of their time preparing the drawings for the 1933 Century of Progress. After the fair opened, visiting the site became a popular pastime, since most offices no longer needed draftsmen's services, and those who had started their own practices had no work. Many members were involved in helping the Chicago Architectural Exhibition League mount "an exhibition of architects' drawings, also the work of painters and sculptors . . . shown in the . . . General Exhibits Building at a Century of Progress."[64] The exposition coincided with another show, the Exhibition of Early Modern Architecture (Chicago 1870–1910) mounted at Marshall Field & Company, which had been part of an exhibition at the Museum of Modern Art in New York City the previous year.[65] It was basically a collection of photographs illustrating the development of the skyscraper, and many of the buildings depicted had been designed in offices where members of the club had been employed. Club members took more than a little pride in showing visitors that work, as well as the contemporary work on the lakefront just east of their clubhouse.

The Art Institute of Chicago also took advantage of the World's Fair to mount an exhibit of the work of Louis Sullivan in the Burnham Library in 1933.[66] The medal awarded to Sullivan by the French Union Centrale des Arts Decoratifs for his design of the Transportation Building at the Columbian Exposition was exhibited along with a selection of photographs of his other designs. Sullivan's drawings for *A System of Architectural Ornament* were also shown, as were a number of his original manuscripts, deposited at the library by George Grant Elmslie.

By 1934, the Great Depression was having a devastating effect on the architects of Chicago and the Architects Club was in dire straits. Membership was falling and few of the meetings of the AIA and the ISA were being held at the Kimball House, further reducing income. Only the sketch club and its atelier were using the space on a regular basis, and the income that generated was insufficient to meet the obligations of the Architects Club. In May 1934, the Membership Committee penned a somewhat humorous but obviously desperate letter to the proprietary members of the club, urging them to bring in new members. If it worked, there is no record of it. At about the same time, the members of the Chicago Architectural Sketch Club held their annual meeting on May 7, 1934, and reelected Ralph Francis Gross as president and Thomas J. Mulig as secretary. On that same date, the club filed a

64. Ibid., 7.

65. *ISA Monthly Bulletin* 18, nos. 2–3 (August–September 1933): 7–8.

66. Ibid., 3.

*Sullivan's medal for the Transportation Building, exhibited by the Art Institute in 1933 (AIC)*

"change of name" with the secretary of state. It was noted that "Article 1, Section 1 be changed to read, The name of the Club shall be The Chicago Architectural Club." Section 2 was changed to read, "The Club shall be conducted for the purpose of advancing the Education, knowledge and ethics of the Architectural Profession. It shall sponsor an Atelier and other classes in the field of Architectural Education." It was the first time that ethics and the atelier were specifically called out in the club's bylaws. No reason for the change was recorded, but it probably came about as a way of formalizing the name by which the club was almost universally known to the members and the public.

One of the last formal competitions in which members of the Chicago Architectural Club participated was sponsored by the Architects Club of Chicago. Announced in May 1935, it called for the design of a club bookplate. The program required that "competitors must be architectural designers and draftsmen residing within a radius of forty miles of Cook County Courthouse, Illinois. Drawings must be 6 1/2 by 8 1/2 inches on white paper 10 1/2 by 14 inches. The design shall be in black and white for reduction to 3 1/4 by 4 1/4 inches and reproduction from zinc etching. The design must incorporate 'Ex Libris' and 'The Architects Club of Chicago.'" First prize was to be fifty dollars, second prize was twenty-five, and third prize was ten. Entries were due at 1801 South Prairie Avenue by noon on Monday, July 15, 1935. They were to be judged by August 1. The jury was made up of the members of the Library Committee: Walter M. Buchroeder, George F. Fairbrass, and chairman Arthur Woltersdorf. The competition got only a modest response, and the three winners, Ray Stuermer, Eugene F. Stoyke, and Mary Ann E. Crawford, had their designs published in the *ISA Monthly Bulletin* in August–September 1935. The jury was disappointed that more designers had not entered, but felt that the low number was offset by the "especial brilliance of the designs submitted." As a final thought, the jury stated that it hoped that "the few entries were a sign of increased activity among designers in more lucrative work and a sad reflection that the bookplate has perhaps been swept out of modern thought along with the overmantel of complicated shelves and mirrors holding the beloved gimcracks of the extinct Vic-

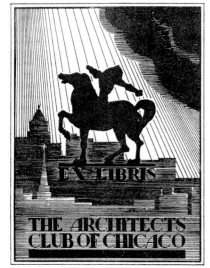

*The winning entries in the 1935 competition for an Architects Club of Chicago bookplate were designed by, from left, Ray Stuermer (first prize), Eugene F. Stoyke (second), and Mary Ann E. Crawford (third) (ISA)*

torian era, the last remains of which are slowly being trucked out of the neighborhood of this club."[67] This last statement was undoubtedly prompted by an event then taking place on Prairie Avenue, which was noted in the *ISA Monthly Bulletin* a few months later.[68] Under the headline "Sic Transit Gloria," it was reported that "it is not without regret that Chicago says goodby to one of the last of the old Prairie Avenue mansions. When the stately yellow brick house at the north end of the street, part of the estate of Mrs. H. J. Reynolds, goes under the auctioneer's hammer Monday, together with its period furniture and priceless objects of art, only two of its companions will remain—the Robert Gregory home and the Marshall Field home, the latter seldom used."[69]

✳

The Chicago Architectural Club, with a large contingent of members present, joined the Chicago Chapter of the AIA, the Illinois Society of Architects, the Chicago Architectural Exhibition League, and the Women's Architectural Club in November 1935 in sponsoring a dinner at the Kimball House in honor of a visit by Swiss-born French architect Le Corbusier. It was the final stop on his tour of America and his largest audience in Chicago. He had spoken at the Arts Club and the Renaissance Society at the University of Chicago two days earlier. French consul M. Rene Weiller introduced Le Corbusier, and the lecture was translated by Robert Jacobs, a young American who had worked in Le Corbusier's office for some time. The lecture was delivered in the coach house atelier space. Slides and a short film were also shown. The lecture was not published verbatim, but it was covered in some detail in the *ISA Monthly Bulletin* by Mr. Gilmer V. Black, whose article was quite benign.[70] In the following issue, however, Thomas E. Tallmadge was not so kind.[71] He was disappointed by what he had heard. He noted that he "understood better what Le Corbusier did not say and was more alive to the golden opportunity he lost than impressed by what seemed to me a very little message." He went on to say, "I will make, therefore, no comment on what he said. It seemed to me old stuff. But how we would have thrilled if he had told us something of the great movement of Puritanism in architecture, of which he is the chief reformer, which has stricken, as a sin, ornament from our buildings as Cotton Mather snatched the brooches from the pretty white throats of the New England girls; or the debt that the New Architecture owes to Louis Sullivan; or of the rich mine that the European Secessionists discovered in Frank Lloyd Wright's book of his works in 1912."[72]

✳

In early 1936, the architects of Chicago learned that their friend and benefactor John J. Glessner had died on January 20. Glessner, who had deeded his house to the Chicago Chapter of the American Institute of Architects in 1924, had retained a life estate in the house. Mrs. Glessner had died in 1932, and the house was now to pass to its new owners, the Chicago Chapter of the AIA. This gift came at a most difficult time. It was the height of the Great Depression, Chicago's architects were without work of significance, and the three professional societies that had agreed to share the Glessner House were broke.

On February 15, 1936, less than a month after Glessner's death, Emery Stanford Hall, the president of the Chicago Chapter of the AIA, invited Arthur Woltersdorf to visit the Glessner House with him. Tom Tallmadge joined them during their tour. The house was still occupied by a butler, a chauffeur, and several other servants. After an hour or so they were met by Mrs. Blewett Lee—Glessner's daughter,

67. ISA Monthly Bulletin 20 (August–September 1935): 2 plus illus. page.

68. *ISA Monthly Bulletin* 20, nos. 6–7 (December–January 1935–36): 2.

69. That article was taken from the *Chicago Herald-Examiner.* It was not correct. In addition to the Gregory and Marshall Field houses, the Kimball House (home to the Architects Club), the Coleman-Ames House, and the Marshall Field Jr. House still stood on the east side of Prairie Avenue between Sixteenth and Twentieth streets. On the west side were the Keith House at 1900 and two party-wall houses just south of the Glessner House at 1800. At the time, Moholy-Nagy was preparing to use the Marshall Field House as the headquarters for his Chicago Bauhaus.

70. *ISA Monthly Bulletin* 20, nos. 6–7 (December–January 1935–36): 1–2.

71. *ISA Monthly Bulletin* 20, nos. 8–9 (February–March 1936): 6.

72. This remark was a clear reference to Frank Lloyd Wright, *Ausgefuhrte Bauten und Entwurfe von Frank Lloyd Wright,* or its companion volume, *Ausgefuhrte Bauten.* Both arrived in the United States about 1912.

Frances—who gave the three visitors a wonderful account of the house and its history.[73] Thus, all concerned knew what they were getting. Three months later, the ISA called a meeting with the Chicago Chapter of the AIA and the Chicago Architectural Club for a special Glessner House conference.[74] The minutes of that meeting have survived intact.[75] The three professional societies that made up the Architects Club of Chicago were well represented. Twenty-seven men attended and nine more participated by proxy.

John Holabird and E. S. Hall had prepared sketches showing what needed to be done to the house to adapt it for use by the Architects Club of Chicago, which would continue to function as an umbrella group. Two cost estimates had been prepared, one for twenty-two thousand dollars, representing the ideal situation, and a second for ten thousand dollars, which would permit the various groups to "function adequately." Several other estimates comparing the cost of operating the Glessner House with that of continuing in the Kimball House were also presented. Probable income was also estimated. The costs and income appeared to be enough to justify accepting the Glessner House, and the group agreed that it would assume possession on June 1, 1936. In the meantime, plans for financing the various programs and other expenses would be made and, ideally, an endowment fund would be established. The cost of maintenance until the group took possession was estimated at five hundred dollars, which was to be divided among the three societies. (Later on, Mrs. Lee, representing the Glessner heirs, agreed to continue to maintain the house until September 1, except for paying the taxes.) Ralph Gross, president of the CAC, stated that "the Chicago Architectural Club recognizes its responsibility in connection with the three-fold contract existing between these architectural groups, and expressed the view that his group would assist financially in accordance with its financial capacity, but he did not feel that his organization should be expected to contribute to this fund on an equal basis with the Chicago Chapter and the Illinois Society." The assembled group agreed. Thus, a plan was established to make the Glessner House the headquarters of Chicago's architectural societies.

One of the stumbling blocks, however, was the value of the Kimball House, which had sunk to about seventeen thousand dollars. There were back taxes due as well. A number of meetings were held during the following year in an attempt to get all concerned to agree on a course of action. The Chicago Architectural Club continued to use the Kimball House and its coach house during this period; the other societies used it only sporadically.

The key to success would be the cooperation of the Architects Realty Trust, which owned the Kimball House and leased it to the Architects Club of Chicago, which, in turn, leased it to the three societies. The proprietary members of the Architects Club had purchased shares in the Architects Realty Trust totaling nearly a hundred thousand dollars to purchase and refurbish the Kimball House in 1924–25 and now the property was worth a fraction of that. The money invested in the Kimball House, and more, would be needed if the Glessner property were to be taken over. The proprietary members were simply not willing to sacrifice their investment for what amounted to less than twenty cents on the dollar.

Another, unstated, problem that had haunted the Architects Club from the beginning was that many members, particularly those from the Illinois Society of Architects, were not willing to make the rather arduous trip to Eighteenth and Prairie on a regular basis. They wanted a way to meet downtown in Chicago's Loop, and by subtly refusing to encourage their colleagues in the AIA to make a stronger effort to find the means to take over the Glessner House, they torpedoed the deal. The committee in charge managed to delay a final decision for several months, while the patient Glessner heirs continued to bear the cost of maintaining the house. Nev-

73. Arthur Woltersdorf made notes during his visit about Mrs. Lee's comments. He then prepared an essay that was published in *ISA Monthly Bulletin* 20, nos. 10–11 (April–May 1936): 7–8.

74. H. B. McEldowney to Elmer C. Jensen, May 20, 1936, ISA Archive, Chicago Historical Society.

75. That document, dated May 25, 1936, was five pages in total, and is now in the ISA Archive at the Chicago Historical Society.

ertheless, in April 1937 Emery Stanford Hall reported to his colleagues at the Chicago Chapter of the AIA that "it was necessary for the Chapter now to take over the property or release it, according to the Glessner Estate's attorney. Fact finding committees had determined that the Chapter, without an endowment fund, would be unable to handle the property. No assurance of an endowment was at hand and authority was asked of the Chapter for the Executive Committee to take definite action and, if necessary, surrender the deed to the estate. The Chapter voted the Executive Committee such authority."[76] Shortly thereafter, in mid-1937, the Chicago Chapter of the AIA gave up its claim to the Glessner House.[77] It was, in retrospect, a terrible decision. Had the AIA held on for only two or three years, all concerned would have seen the economic downturn reversed, and the long-term care and maintenance of the Glessner House would have been assured. It was not to be.

❊

The Architects Club of Chicago continued to operate from the Kimball House at 1801 South Prairie Avenue. It made a valiant effort to keep the clubhouse alive. The Chicago Architectural Club was still using it on a regular basis, as was the atelier, but its contribution of funds was simply not enough to maintain the house. Several moneymaking schemes were proposed. For example, in June 1937 a notice in the *ISA Monthly Bulletin* advised, "A few attractive rooms are available at the Architects Club of Chicago, 1801 South Prairie Avenue, for young men in the building industry. They are offered at inviting rentals and, coupled with the environment and advantages of the club, should make a most desirable home for young men, especially those interested in the building industry or in architecture."[78]

For reasons never explained, in spite of its earlier decision to meet in the Loop rather than at the Kimball House, the Illinois Society of Architects once again began holding its regular meetings at the Kimball House in the fall of 1937. Many of the ISA members were proprietary members of the Architects Club, and they were undoubtedly seeking to protect their investment until the house could be sold. On September 28, 1937, at an ISA meeting at the Kimball House, Thomas Mulig, president of the Chicago Architectural Club, "made an announcement relative to the Beaux Arts Mexican Ball to be held . . . at the Drake Hotel for the benefit of the Chicago Architectural Club Scholarship Fund, asking the endorsement of the Society."[79] That endorsement was granted. The minutes of the meeting also noted that the "work of Robert Benedict Brout," a former Traveling Scholarship winner, adorned the walls of the clubhouse.

The most important event of the evening, however, was a forty-minute speech by Ladislaus Moholy-Nagy, who had recently arrived from Germany to open what was to be the "New Bauhaus" on October 18 in the old Marshall Field Mansion, a block south of the Kimball House. It must have seemed like the salvation of the Architects Club. Architects and students were expected to flock to the area. Moholy-Nagy's group did, for a time, cooperate to some degree with the Architects Club, particularly in making use of the atelier space in the Kimball coach house. It was never, however, a close relationship. The New Bauhaus did not subscribe to the teaching methods advocated by the Beaux-Arts Institute of Design and the Chicago Architectural Club's atelier.

Moholy-Nagy and his colleagues at the New Bauhaus were not the only German nationals to come to Chicago in the late 1930s. On March 20, 1936, John A. Holabird, as head of a search committee for a new director of the Architecture School at the Armour Institute of Technology, had written to Ludwig Mies van der Rohe to if Mies would consider the position. Mies expressed interest.[80] After a good

76. *ISA Monthly Bulletin* 21–22, nos. 12-1 (June–July 1937): 5.

77. A concise explanation of the situation was published in *ISA Monthly Bulletin* 22, nos. 2–3 (August–September 1937): 7–8. It was a verbatim report of the Joint Ways and Means Committee on the Glessner House project.

78. *ISA Monthly Bulletin* 21–22, nos. 12–1 (June–July 1937): 6.

79. The minutes of this meeting are in the ISA Archive at the Chicago Historical Society.

80. The story of Mies van der Rohe's arrival in Chicago is told in detail in chapter 6 of Franz Schulze, *Mies van der Rohe, a Critical Biography* (Chicago: University of Chicago Press, 1985), a book that is indispensable to the study of Mies and his lifework.

deal of correspondence and several visits to Chicago, Mies accepted the position and moved to the United States in late 1937. He immediately began work on a curriculum that he expected to inaugurate at Armour. It was a great departure from the Beaux-Arts-influenced programs used by nearly every school of architecture in the United States and by literally all the ateliers, including the one run by the Armour Institute and the Art Institute of Chicago and that of the Chicago Architectural Club. Mies met with several senior members of the Armour Institute in February 1938 to discuss the transition to his new program and where the students would be taught. Would the Armour Institute's relationship with the Art Institute continue or would another location be more suitable? For a time, serious consideration was given to using the Glessner House, then owned by the Armour Institute, which had acquired it after the Chicago Chapter of the AIA had returned it to the Glessner estate. Ultimately, all concerned elected to continue working with the Art Institute for the time being. Mies then left Chicago for several months to wind up his affairs in Germany. He returned in August and began his work as director of the School of Architecture in the fall of 1938.

John Holabird, like many of the architects involved in bringing Mies van der Rohe to Chicago, was a former member of the Chicago Architectural Club. He and his colleagues all felt that the addition of Mies to their ranks would further enhance Chicago's already glowing reputation for producing innovative architecture. On October 18, 1938, a formal dinner was held at the Palmer House to welcome Mies to Chicago. There were more than 450 guests—the elite of Chicago's architects—most of whom were or had been members of the Chicago Architectural Club at some time in the past fifty years. It is said that Mies himself invited Frank Lloyd Wright to make an introduction.

Reports of what Wright said vary widely—there were several different versions published by Wright himself. There was, however, an article in the *ISA Monthly Bulletin* by Dorothy G. Wendt, which was probably as accurate as any. She described the event in great detail, recounting the statements of all who spoke. She reported on what Wright had to say under the subhead "Frank Lloyd Wright Rebukes His Confreres." In what appears to be at least a partial transcript, she wrote that "Frank Lloyd Wright thought the atmosphere of the evening was 'too learned, too highly educated,' to provide the time or place for the discussion of the ideals of an organic architecture. 'Since Europe has taken over American architecture,' said Mr. Wright, 'and it serves the country right, I am proud to *give* you Mies van der Rohe. I give him to you more perhaps than you realize—more, perhaps, than he realizes. When the ideals of an organic architecture do prevail, as they will, the entire structure of what we now call education will lie in the dust. It will not even be a picturesque ruin. This thing is going to begin at the beginning once more—where architecture always begins. It begins anew at least every generation. Why not every hour? The eclecticism of this country could get the ideals of an original architecture in no other way than from a foreign country. Let us be grateful.'"[81] Miss Wendt, a graduate of the Armour Institute, also reported on the dinner and included a lengthy summary of Mies's presentation. Mies concluded with a quotation from Thomas Aquinas: "Beauty is the radiance of the truth." Even Wright, who had left the room, would have agreed.

Shortly after the dinner for Mies, the Art Institute of Chicago mounted an exhibition of his work, from December 15, 1938, to January 15, 1939. The members of the Chicago Architectural Club took a long look at what this German was bringing with

*Ludwig Mies van der Rohe (WRH)*

81. *ISA Monthly Bulletin* 23, nos. 6–7 (December–January 1938): 1–2. Wright's remarks were also published in the *Weekly Bulletin of the Michigan Society of Architects*, which was used by Kevin Harrington, professor of architectural history at the Illinois Institute of Technology, in an essay recapitulating the various versions of the speech. "Table Talk: Ludwig Mies van der Rohe" was published in *Chicago Architectural Journal* 9 in 2000.

*Mies van der Rohe exhibition at the Art Institute of Chicago in 1938–39, the first of several showings of his work over the next half century (AIC)*

him to Chicago. It, and what Moholy-Nagy was doing in the Marshall Field Mansion just down the street from their clubhouse, was new and different from anything they had encountered in their education. That and the coming war would change architecture forever.

The Chicago Architectural Club had come into being at a unique time in the history of architecture. In 1884, Chicago—and the rest of the world—was ready for a new architecture. A new kind of architect was needed, and the club provided a forum for the development of those architects. For a half century, the club members had observed, and indeed influenced, a revolution in design and building. By 1939, another revolution was at hand. It was time to move on.

Carbide and Carbon Building, Burnham Brothers, 1929 (AIC)

Home Insurance Building by Jenney & Mundie, 1885 (PC)

Promontory Apartments, Mies van der Rohe, 1946–49 (courtesy of Tim Samuelson)

*A meeting of the newly reconsituted Chicago Architectural Club at the Graham Foundation in 1985. Myron Goldsmith is at the podium and to his left are Helmut John, Stanley Tigerman, and Bruce Graham (Graham Foundation Photo)*

# Epilogue: Significant Events Leading to the Revival of the Chicago Architectural Club

In the late 1930s and early 1940s, as the United States began girding itself for the Second World War, a general diminution of interest in architecture was the first and foremost reason it seemed unimportant to continue the Chicago Architecture Club. In comparison to the overwhelming need to arm a nation threatened by war, the traditions of aesthetic posturing common to the École des Beaux-Arts' educational methods that had been transplanted to American architectural schools seemed insignificant. Clearly, the need for an architectural club that had originally been organized for the apparently esoteric purposes of reading scholarly papers and conducting exhibitions of drawings, with occasionally published catalogs, was anything but significant in the face of genuinely awesome worldwide events.

The second reason for the demise of the Chicago Architectural Club was intrinsically architectural in nature. By the end of the 1930s, the case for modern architecture was pretty much universally accepted in the United States. (If anything, the Second World War enhanced its acceptance by dint of need reinforcing the functional imperative so central to modernist tenets.) Clearly, the purpose of an organization whose foundation was laid a full half century earlier could have precious little meaning by 1940. There seemed to be little value in presenting exhibitions of architectural drawings, which had been discredited by the modern movement's apologists who, more coolly, detached themselves from individual cultism through the vehicle of architectural model making. Pamphleteering also seemed pointless in an era whose preoccupations were anything but intellectual, as rationalism became a realistic way of architectural life. As Chicago specifically, and American architects generally, came to identify with the belief systems central to modernist thought, organizations such as the Chicago Architectural Club were seen as inconsequential. The club had served and outlived its purpose.

Third, and most important, was the powerful presence of Mies van der Rohe, who, in 1938, took control of the Chicago School of Architecture, jointly administered by the Art Institute of Chicago and the Armour Institute (later to become the Illinois Institute of Technology). It was Mies's presence more than anything else that inadvertently contributed to a general lack of interest in the Chicago Architectural Club. After all, one of the overriding reasons for establishing the club in the first place had been to facilitate communication. Pluralistic thought (and, I might add, its inevitable argumentative aspect) was central to the original purpose of this organization, and communication as such is often most legitimate when disparate attitudes require communicating. In the presence of an overriding collective agreement connected with the work and the teachings of Mies van der Rohe, this aspect was ostensibly unnecessary.

It is not as if these three reasons for discouraging interest in the Chicago Architectural Club were momentary—the three combined held sway for more than three decades in a city always in search of an answer. Not until well after Mies's death in 1969 were efforts made to reassess Chicago's ultimately pluralistic architectural traditions. Such eccentric figures as Bertrand Goldberg, Walter Netsch, and Harry Weese grew old bereft of sycophants primarily because of the new zeitgeist mentality connected with the absolute acceptance of both the syntax and symbolism of Mies's modernism. Little communication existed between the architects of the 1950s and 1960s who were faced with the Miesian dictum "Build, don't talk." Without any particular goal, architects began to talk again in the 1970s and 1980s.

In the spring of 1975, Harry Weese, then president of the Chicago Chapter of the American Institute of Architects, convened a seminal luncheon meeting. The purpose was to discuss possibilities for architects to exhibit their work in Chicago in conjunction with the American bicentennial celebration. A. James Speyer, curator of twentieth-century art at the Chicago Art Institute, Steven Prokopoff, director of the Museum of Contemporary Art, John Entenza and Carter Manny Jr., former and current directors of the Graham Foundation for Advanced Studies in the Fine Arts, and I attended that meeting. In response to an inquiry as to what the various institutions had in mind with respect to architecture for the forthcoming national celebration, it was noted that the Art Institute's calendar was "booked" and that the MCA had scheduled the exhibition "One Hundred Years of Chicago Architecture" (first presented in Germany some years earlier), jointly curated by Oswald Grube, Peter Pran, and Franz Schulze. Thus, yet another representation of the traditionally held view of Chicago architecture was to be regurgitated (the Sullivan-Mies linkage, etc., etc.).

A suggestion was made that perhaps a kind of *salon des refusés* might be constructed to represent a more diverse view of Chicago's several architectural traditions and that Larry Booth, Stuart Cohen, Ben Weese, and I might cocurate such an event. Harry Weese offered the lobby of Time-Life's Chicago headquarters as a likely site for such an event, the Graham Foundation (and later the National Endowment for the Arts) offered to financially back the exhibit, and thus the project got under way.

The first showing of that exhibition occurred in the spring of 1976 at the Cooper Union in New York City; it then returned to Chicago to stand in contradistinction to the canonical Chicago show mentioned earlier, with the two shows opening simultaneously in May 1976. The two exhibitions received a great deal of attention and publicity, and Ada Louise Huxtable wrote a major review in the *New York Times*. The show traveled to Harvard University, the University of California at Berkeley, and elsewhere.

Since the exhibition enjoyed such a great success, the four organizers decided to expand it to seven architects, adding Thomas Hall Beeby, James Ingo Freed (then dean of architecture at IIT), and James L. Nagle. Calling themselves the "Chicago Seven" (after the antiestablishment political group of a decade earlier), they produced an exhibition and catalog of their work in December 1976 at Chicago's Richard Gray Gallery. With the addition of Helmut Jahn, the Chicago Seven, together with the Graham Foundation, sponsored a major international conference on the state of architecture at the Graham Foundation in autumn 1977. Included were such architects and critics as Peter Eisenman, Michael Graves, Frank O. Gehry, John Hejduk, Craig Hodgetts, Charles Jencks, Anthony Lumsden, Richard Meier, Cesar

Pelli, Robert A. M. Stern, James Stirling, Thomas Vreeland, William Turnbull Jr., and the Seven (Eight). By December 1977, the Seven had organized their second public exhibition at Chicago's Walter Kelly Gallery, based on Andre Breton's parlor game *cadavre exquis* (exquisite corpse). By 1978, the Seven (Eight) were increased to eleven, with the addition of Gerald Horn, Kenneth Schroeder, and Cynthia Weese; monthly meetings were held and the decision was made to organize a competition based on the Exquisite Corpse show of 1977. By May 1978, the competition had been held; 169 entries were tabulated, with eight solutions honored together with twenty-one runners-up. An exhibition of the winning schemes, together with a symposium, was held at the Graham Foundation and the projects were displayed at the Walker Art Center in Minneapolis.

The last event organized by the Chicago Seven revisited the original Chicago Tribune Competition of 1922–23. This idea was conceived in 1979, realized in 1980, and curated by Stuart Cohen, Rhona Hoffman, and me. The exhibition, which opened at Chicago's Museum of Contemporary Art in May 1980, traveled to ten other locations before retiring in May 1982. Rizzoli International published *Chicago Tribune Tower Competition/Late Entries,* which included reprints of the original 1923 results as well as guest essays by George Baird, Juan Pablo Bonta, Charles Jencks, Vincent Scully, and Norris Kelley Smith.

By the close of 1979, the remaining ten members of the Chicago Seven (James Ingo Freed had returned to architectural practice in New York City with I. M. Pei) clearly saw that the pluralistic origins of the group were central to its ideology (or lack thereof). Thus, the idea of reinstating the Chicago Architectural Club came into being. From a list of sixty designers, historians, and critics, more than forty accepted an invitation to join the newly reestablished club, and by autumn 1979 its first meeting was held at the Graham Foundation. James W. Hammond was installed as its first president and the ten members of the Chicago Seven as its first Executive Committee. Monthly meetings (exclusive of the summer months) began, and continue to the date of this writing.

Ten meetings are now held each calendar year, featuring papers read by such varying visiting and resident architects and scholars (beginning in the 1980s) as Alfred Caldwell, Alan Chimacoff, Peter Eisenman, Wilbert R. Hasbrouck, James Kenneth Kettlewell, John McDermott, Steven Peterson, George Ranalli, Thomas Schumacher, Robert A. M. Stern, David van Zanten, Lauretta Vinciarelli, and Judith Wolin, as well as adult jurylike "show-and-tell" presentations of new and recent architectural projects by club members. The first annual exhibition of projects by the club membership was held at the Graham Foundation in the spring of 1981 and the first annual catalog was published by Rizzoli International with articles by Wilbert R. Hasbrouck, Judith Wolin, Fazlur R. Khan, Allan Greenberg, John McDermott, Anders Nereim, Stuart Cohen, and me.[1] The first annual catalog was edited by Anders Nereim and dedicated to George Fred Keck (1895–1980), who, shortly before his death, had been made an honorary member of the club. The catalog contained reproductions of projects represented in the first annual exhibition together with remarks by Robert A. M. Stern, Evans Woollen, Gene Summers, and Thomas Schumacher.[2]

In 1981, Carter Manny Jr. was elected president of the club by the Executive Committee in accordance with its bylaws.[3] In 1982, the Executive Committee voted to limit the membership to a maximum of eighty active resident members. The club's second annual journal contained projects by the membership with related comments by a jury of Peter Eisenman, Daniel Libeskind, James Stirling, Evans Woollen, and Faruk Yorgancioglu, who were appointed to select projects to be exhibited at the Chicago Art Institute's new department of architecture. The catalog highlighted Benjamin Marshall, whose work was discussed in an essay written by

1. This effort can be compared to the early involvement of John W. Root Sr., Daniel H. Burnham, Peter B. Wight, Louis Sullivan, Dankmar Adler, and other senior men who supported the original club.

2. The reconstituted club was, in many ways, acting the way the founders and members of the club had in the late nineteenth century.

3. Subsequent presidents of the club have included Stuart Cohen, Jeanne Gang, Kevin Harrington, James L. Nagle, Drew Ranieri, John Ronan, Ben Weese, Cynthia Weese, Dan Weese, Richard Whitaker, and Stephen Wierzbowski.

William Westfall. Sadly, the club lost its first regular resident member in March 1982, when the preeminent structural engineer Fazlur R. Khan passed away.

The *Chicago Architectural Journal* (initially published by Rizzoli International), edited by club members,[4] first reappeared in 1981. Competitions, the first for "Tops," began in 1983. The Burnham Prize, with a three-month residency at the American Academy in Rome, was initiated in 1984.[5]

Of the original Chicago Seven, only Stuart Cohen and Ben Weese are still members in 2005. While in 1979 the club was populated only by architects, by 2003 landscape architects, historians, interior designers, structural engineers, photographers, and even one real estate developer grace its 120-person membership. As of 2005, the *Chicago Architectural Journal* is published biennially, and the Chicago Prize Competition has joined the Burnham Prize as a biennial event.

The architectural dialogue that began before the turn of the twentieth century seems to be alive and well and at home in twenty-first-century Chicago.

Stanley Tigerman

*A somewhat different version of this essay was first published in an early issue of the Chicago Architectural Journal. Additional information was gleaned from an essay by Kevin Harrington, and in conversation with John Ronan and Wilbert Hasbrouck.*

4. Journal editors have included Deborah Doyle, Kevin Harrington, Michael Lustig, Anders Nereim, and David Woodhouse.

5. The Burnham Prize is essentially the equivalent of the Annual Traveling Scholarship that the original club organized.

# Appendix 1: Constitution of the Chicago Architectural Sketch Club

The constitution for the Chicago Architectural Sketch Club was written by a committee from the eighteen founders of the Club. It included Harry Lawrie, George Beaumont, William Zimmerman, J. H. Carpenter, and Irving K. Pond. They reviewed various other similar organization's constitution's and by-laws and within two weeks presented a constitution and by-laws for consideration.

On March 12, 1885, the founders met and after review (and apparently some revisions) formally adopted the work of the committee. The final constitution, with its by-laws, is shown below in its entirety as published in the *Inland Architect* in April of 1885. The only changes we have made are the correction of a few obvious typographical errors. It was presented to the membership as a whole on March 27, 1885 at the first regular meeting of the club.

## CONSTITUTION.

Article I.—Name.
The name of the Association shall be "The Chicago Architectural Sketch Club."

Article II.—Object.
The object of this Association shall be the advancement and improvement of its members in all matters pertaining to architecture.

Article III.—Methods.
The methods of this Association shall be:
  By regular meetings of its members.
  By increasing the facilities for study.
  By readings or lectures on professional subjects.
  By the friendly discussion of practical matters.
  By competition in design and drawing for exhibition.
  By visiting selected buildings.
  And by, any other means determined upon by the Association.

Article IV.—Membership.
This Association shall consist of Senior, Junior and Honorary members.

Article V.—Officers.
Section 1. The officers of this Association shall consist of a President, two Vice-Presidents, a Secretary, Treasurer, and Executive Committee, elected annually at the first regular meeting in November.
Sec. 2. The Executive committee shall consist of the officers of the Association and two Senior members.
Article VI.—Qualifications of Members.
Section 1. Any person having served three years in an architect's office or in kindred arts is eligible for Senior membership.
Sec. 2. Any person having served one year in an architect's office or in kindred arts is eligible for Junior membership.
Sec. 3. Any person may be an Honorary member who shall be elected as such because of interest manifested in the Association.
Sec. 4. Honorary and Junior members shall have all the privileges of the Association except that of voting, and shall not be eligible to office.

Article VII.—Amendments.
This Constitution may be amended by a two-thirds vote of the Senior members present at any regular meeting, provided, that the meeting shall be composed of a majority of the Senior members of the Association, a copy of the amendment having been posted 30 days at the regular place of meeting, and read at the two consecutive meetings previous.

## BYLAWS

Article I. Applications.
Section l. Any person desiring to become a member of this Association shall send his application to the Executive Committee. This application being indorsed by two Senior members of the Association, who are personally acquainted with the applicant.
Sec. 2. All applications for membership shall be accompanied by a drawing made by the applicant, which, upon his election to membership, shall become the property of the Association.

Article II. Election of Members
Section 1. The Executive Committee, upon receiving an application for membership, shall investigate the standing of the applicant, and act upon the same within the time of two consecutive meetings.
Sec. 2. Election of members shall be by ballot, and two negatives shall reject.
Sec. 3. All discussion of applicants shall be considered strictly confidential.
Sec. 4. Junior members of one year's standing, as such, may be advanced to Senior membership, as an award of merit for superior progress.
Sec. 5. Rights and Duties of Members.—The interest in and use of all property belonging to the Association shall be equally vested in all members, such property not to be removed from the rooms of the Association. It shall be the duty of every member to attend all regular meetings. It shall be the duty of each member to advance the interest of the Association to the best of his ability.
Sec. 6. No person shall take from the Association rooms any article belonging to the Association, or mutilate, deface, or destroy the same.
Sec. 7. All interest in the property of the Association of members reigning, or otherwise ceasing to be members, shall be vested in the Association.
Sec. 8. Each member shall be required to deliver a paper, or submit, at least, two drawings during the year, which shall remain the property of the club.
Note.—It is desired that, when possible, sketches shall conform to the uniform sizes, 8 x 12, or 14 x 17, and made with pen and ink, that they may be photo-engraved.
Sec. 9. Resignations.—All resignations shall be made, in writing, to the Executive Committee, but a resignation shall not discharge the member presenting it from any unpaid dues or penalties.

ARTICLE III.—Meetings.
Sec. l. Annual Meeting.—The annual meeting shall be the first regular meeting in November, and shall be held for the election of officers, and for the transaction of such other business as shall properly come before the Association.
Sec. 2. Order of business at annual meetings.
  1. Annual address.
  2. Calling the roll.
  3. Report of Secretary.
  4. Report of Treasurer.
  5. Report of Executive Committee.
  6. Appointment of Auditing Committee upon Treasurer's Report.
  7. Election of officers as per By-Laws.
  8. Reports of special committees.
  9. Consideration of reports of committees.
  10. Miscellaneous business.
  11. Reading of papers, debates, and addresses.
  12. Closing address.
  The order of exercises may be changed by a majority vote of the meeting.
Sec. 3. The annual address shall be delivered by the President, or an alternative appointed by him.

Regular Meetings.

Section 1. There shall be a regular meeting of the Association every alternate Monday evening.

Sec. 2. The place of meeting shall be determined by the Executive Committee.

Sec. 3. Order of Business at regular meeting.
1. Calling roll.
2. Reading minutes and reports.
3. Old business.
4. New business.
5. Collection of dues and penalties.
6. General discussion of work.
7. Report of Judges.
8. Adjournment.

Sec. 4. Fifteen senior members and a presiding officer shall constitute a quorum for business.

Sec. 5. Special meetings may be called at any time by the Executive Committee whenever the President shall have been requested to call a meeting by the written request of five members, setting forth the purpose of said meeting, and all members shall be notified by the Secretary. At any such special meeting, no business other than that specified in the call shall be transacted, except by unanimous consent of the members present.

Sec. 6. In any question of debate the Association shall be governed by Roberts' Rules of Order.

Sec. 7. All subjects and essays, before being presented before the Association, must be referred to the Executive Committee for approval.

Article IV.—President.

The President of the Association, or, in his absence, the senior Vice-President present, shall preside at all meeting of the Association and of the Executive Committee. In the absence of the President and Vice-Presidents a presiding officer shall be chosen, without ballot, by the Association. Vice-Presidents shall preside over regular committees.

Article V.—Secretary.

Sec. l. The Secretary of the Association shall keep a record of the proceedings of the Association and of the Executive Committee, and of all matters of which a record shall be deemed advisable by the Association, or the Executive Committee. The Secretary shall notify the members of their election, shall keep a roll of the members of the Association, shall issue notices of all special meeting, shall conduct the correspondence, and shall be keeper of the seals of the Association.

Sec. 2. The records and the correspondence, except in relation to the qualifications of candidates for membership, shall at all reasonable times be open to the inspection of any member of the Association.

Sec. 3. In consideration of the onerous duties of the Secretary, he shall be exempt from all dues or other duties during term of office.

Article VI.—Treasurer.

The Treasurer of the Association shall collect, and, under the direction of the Executive Committee, disburse the funds.

He shall keep the accounts of the Association in a book belonging to it, which shall at all time be open to inspection of the Executive Committee. He shall report at any annual meeting, and oftener if required, upon the state of the treasury. The accounts of the Treasurer shall be audited by a committee of two elected by the Association at the annual meeting; the committee to report before the close of the meeting. No member of the Executive Committee shall be a member of the Auditing Committee.

Article VII.—Finance.

Section 1. Fees and Dues.—The initiation fee shall be three dollars for active members. No initiation fee shall be required of Honorary members. The monthly dues of all members shall be twenty-five cents. The initiation fee shall be paid, upon the admission of the candidate, to the Treasurer of the Association. The monthly dues shall be paid at the first regular meeting in every month.

Sec. 2. No candidate shall be entitled to membership until his initiation fee is paid.

Sec. 3. If any member shall fail to pay his dues for three successive months, the Treasurer shall cause him to be notified, and unless the sum shall be paid by the next meeting thereafter, he shall be reported to the Executive Committee.

Sec. 4. Any member who has paid the regular dues, and is absent from the city for a continuous period of six months, shall be exempted from the payment of dues for the period of his absence, if he shall have given previous written notice to the Treasurer of his intention to be absent.

Article VIII.—Committees.

Section 1. Executive Committee.—The Executive Committee shall consist of the President, Secretary, Treasurer, two Vice-Presidents, and two other members. It shall meet for the transaction of business as often as necessary. Four members shall constitute a quorum. Vacancies in its own number shall be filled by the committee for the remainder of the term. The Executive Committee shall be subject in all respects, except as the expenditures, to such instructions and limitations as may from time to time be prescribed by the Association. It shall control and manage its property, and enforce the preservation of order and obedience to its rules. It shall make all necessary purchases and contracts, but shall have no power to make the Association liable for any debt or debts to an amount exceeding one-half that which, at the time of contracting the same, shall be in the Treasurer's hands in cash, and not subject to prior liabilities. It shall have the power to solicit subscriptions for furthering the purposes of the Association. At every annual meeting it shall report its proceeding, and may at any time recommend such ;measures as it may deem advisable. The Executive Committee has power to arbitrate between members consulting it in regard to disputes relative to the affairs of the Association. It shall have charge of the library with authority to expend such sums of money as may be voted therefor by the Association, or provided by voluntary subscription. It shall obtain judges for the competitions, and shall appoint the Committees on Current Work; govern all competitions, and perform the general work of the Association.

Sec. 2. The Executive Committee shall receive proposals for admission of candidates, and is to decide, by ballot, whether the general standing of the candidate qualifies him for membership in the Association. If the decision is favorable, the committee will report candidate's to the Association as members. If the decision is unfavorable, the committee will notify the proposers of the candidate, and a reconsideration is to be left to the discretion of the committee.

Sec. 3. Censure and Expulsion of Members.—If the conduct of any member shall appear to the Executive Committee to be injurious to the interests of the Association, or contrary to the Constitution and By-Laws, the Executive Committee shall inform him thereof, and if, in its opinion, the nature of the offense requires it, dismiss him.

Sec. 4. Special committees shall be appointed when required, and presided over by one of the Vice-Presidents, who shall report their proceedings to the Executive Committee, and act in harmony with its decisions.

Article IX.—Amendment.

At any regular meeting of the Association these By-Laws may be amended, in same manner as provided for in Constitution.

# Appendix 2: Glessner and Kimball House Agreements

When the agreement was reached in principle between the Chicago Chapter of the American Institute of Architects and John J. and Frances M. Glessner for the chapter to assume ownership of the Glessner House after the death of both Mr. and Mrs. Glessner, various other legalities had to be taken care of in order to ensure that the Glessners' wishes were carried out. Below are transcriptions of those agreements, all or in part, in chronological order as they were executed:

1. Agreement between the Chicago Chapter of the AIA, The Illinois Society of Architects, and The Chicago Architectural Club wherein they agree to cooperate future activities regarding the Glessner House and the Kimball House. (11/25/1924)

2. The Deed of Gift from the Glessners to the Chicago Chapter of the AIA. (12/1/1924)

3. Organization of The Architects Club of Chicago. (12/10/1924) A brief description.

4. Organization of The Architects Realty Trust. (12/15/1924) A brief description.

Taken from The Architects Club of Chicago *Monthly Bulletin*, Vol. I, No. 1, January, 1925.

## AIA, ISA, CAC AGREEMENT TO COOPERATE

THIS AGREEMENT entered into this 25th day of November, A. D. 1924, by and between the CHICAGO CHAPTER OF THE AMERICAN INSTITUTE OF ARCHITECTS, hereinafter called the first party, THE ILLINOIS SOCIETY OF ARCHITECTS, hereinafter called the second party, and THE CHICAGO ARCHITECTURAL CLUB, hereinafter called the third party, each of said parties being a corporation not for profit organized under the laws of the State of Illinois,

WITNESSETH: That

WHEREAS, the first party is or shortly is to become the donee under a deed of gift from John J. Glessner and wife of the property at 1800 Prairie Avenue, Chicago, Illinois, described as follows:

Lots 39 and 40 and the north 19 feet of lot 38 in block 9 in the Assessor's Division of the southwest fractional quarter of section 22, township 39 north, range 14 east of the third principal meridian now occupied by the said John J. Glessner and wife as a residence, said first party to obtain possession thereof upon the death of said John J. Glessner and wife, or prior to that time should the said John J. Glessner and wife, or the survivor of them, abandon their residence in said property; and

WHEREAS, said gift to said first party is conditioned upon the use of said property for various architectural and kindred purposed as set forth in said deed of gift; and

WHEREAS, said gift is further conditioned upon the occupancy and control by one or more of the parties hereto, of the premises known as the Kimball residence at 1801 Prairie Avenue, Chicago, Illinois, which it is considered by the parties hereto can best be accomplished by their combined efforts in the organization of a club which shall be representative of the architectural and building interests of the Chicago district;

NOW, THEREFORE, in consideration of the mutual covenants hereinafter set forth, of the sum of one dollar ($1.00) in hand paid by each of the parties hereto to the other, receipt of which is hereby acknowledged, and of other good and valuable considerations, said parties have agreed and by these presents do agree as follows:

FIRST: Each of said parties hereto shall use its best efforts and endeavors, jointly with the other parties hereto, to form a club which shall be representative of the architectural profession and the building industries of the Chicago district, which club shall purchase and occupy to aforesaid Kimball property as a club house during the lifetime of said John J. Glessner and wife, thereby complying with the condition imposed by the said John J. Glessner in the gift aforesaid.

SECOND: Immediately upon the first party obtaining ownership or control of the said Glessner house above described, the said second party and third party, respectively, shall have equal privileges with the first party in the use and occupancy of said Glessner house and shall pay the expenses for maintenance, up-keep, repairs, replacement, taxes, if any, insurance and any an all other expenses and carrying charges incident to the maintenance, operation and up-keep of said property for the purposes set forth in the deed of gift from said John J. Glessner and wife, and the purposes hereinafter set forth, in the following proportions: The third party shall pay such sum as shall be determined by mutual agreement of the first party and the second party, and said first party and second party shall each pay one half of the remainder of said expenses. In the event that either the second party or the third party shall fail or refuse to pay promptly its share of the expenses above referred to, its right to share in the privileges of said property shall immediately cease and shall not be re-acquired until its share of all such delinquent expenses is paid. Liability to contribute to current and future expenses shall not be affected by any such loss of privileges. In the event that said second party or third party shall fail to pay its share of said expenses for the period of one year or more, the first party shall have the right upon thirty days' notice in writing the terminate this agreement with respect to said delinquent party, and thereupon all of its rights and privileges under this agreement shall finally cease and determine.

THIRD: The said Glessner property shall at all times be devoted to the purposes of and architectural museum and gallery, an architectural library which shall be open to the public, an atelier or school for the use of the members of the third party, and as a place of assemblage for architectural meetings of the respective parties hereto.

FOURTH: Subject to the terms and conditions of the Glessner gift the management and control of said property shall be vested in a board of trustees, three in number, one appointed by the board of directors of each of the parties hereto.

FIFTH: The first party shall have the right by and with the consent of both of the other parties hereto to convey the title to said Glessner property unto trustees for the purpose of organizing a corporation to establish, maintain and manage a free public library on said property under and in compliance with the terms of the statutes of the State of Illinois.

IN WITNESS WHEREOF the parties hereto have caused this instrument to be duly signed by their respective presidents, thereunto duly authorized, and their respective corporate seals to be affixed, attested by their respective secretaries, all done in triplicate the day and year first above written.

### CHICAGO CHAPTER OF THE AMERICAN INSTITUTE OF ARCHITECTS

S E A L
Attest:
S/Howard L. Cheney      by    S/Alfred Granger

| Secretary | President |
| --- | --- |
| | S/G. C. Nimmons |
| | S/R. E. Schmidt |

### THE ILLINOIS SOCIETY OF ARCHITECTS

S E A L
Attest:
S/Ralph C. Harris      by    S/Chas. E. Fox

| Secretary | President |
| --- | --- |
| | S/F. E. Davidson |
| | S/J. C. Llewellyn |

### THE CHICAGO ARCHITECTURAL CLUB

S E A L
Attest:
S/Wm. C. Sponholz      by    Geo. M. Nedved

| Secretary | President |
| --- | --- |

1.            D E E D   O F   G I F T

THIS DEED OF GIFT entered into this 1st day of December, A.D. 1924, between JOHN J. GLESSNER and FRANCES M. GLESSNER, his wife, of the City of Chicago, State of Illinois and the City of Littleton and State of New Hampshire, Donors, and CHICAGO CHAPTER OF THE AMERICAN INSTITUTE OF ARCHITECTS, a corporation not for profit incorporated under the laws of the State of Illinois, donee, WITNESSETH:

THAT, WHEREAS, the Donee is a society organized for the promotion of art and science as it is given expression particularly in architecture, and is desirous of preserving some outstanding example of the work of noted architects as embodied in a building constructed by one of them as an architectural museum and gallery; as a place of assemblage of architectural organizations, and as an atelier for younger men; and,

WHEREAS, the Donors are the owners and occupants of a certain dwelling house in the City of Chicago designed and built for them by HENRY HOBSON RICHARDSON, Architect, and are desirous of seeing this preserved as a type of his work and as a contribution to the science and art of architecture, and used for the purposes above enumerated;

NOW, THEREFORE, in consideration of the premises, and of the conditions and covenants hereinafter prescribed and entered into, JOHN J. GLESSNER AND FRANCES M. L. GLESSNER, the Donors, do hereby give, grant and convey every right, title and interest to the CHICAGO CHAPTER OF THE AMERICAN INSTITUTE OF ARCHITECTS, the Donee, in the following described premises, to-wit:

Lots thirty-nine (39) and forty (40), and the North Nineteen (19) feet of Lot thirty-eight (38) in Block Nine (9), in the Assessor's Division of the Southwest fractional quarter of Section Twenty-two (22), Township thirty-nine (39) North, Range Fourteen (14) East of the Third Principal Meridian, situated in the City of Chicago, County of Cook and State of Illinois;

except a life estate in said premises hereby reserved to the Donors, JOHN J. GLESSNER and FRANCES M. GLESSNER, and the survivor of them.

The conditions of said gift and conveyance, and the covenants of the Donee which shall run with the land, are as follows:

The premises shall be used generally within the powers and purposes now appearing in the Articles of Association of the Donee.

The house is to be used solely for the purposes of architecture and the allied arts and sciences, such as an architectural museum and gallery, an architectural library, a place of assemblage for legitimate meetings of architectural organizations, and an atelier for the instruction of younger men in the principles of the architectural profession and offices of administration.

The house is to be known as GLESSNER HOUSE, and so styled, named and referred to in all public announcements and in any literature issued concerning and in connection therewith; the address for receiving and sending mail shall contain this name as a part thereof.

The premises, including the building thereon, is to be kept in good and substantial repair, said building to be preserved architecturally in the same condition as when received—likewise the finish of the building, both inside and out, shall be maintained as it is at the time of receiving possession thereof by the Donee. (Windows may be substituted for doors in the garage—the kitchen may be converted into a gallery, and the smaller rooms on the second floor may be consolidated.) The offices of administration shall be maintained upon the second floor—the atelier shall be maintained in the part now used as a garage, and the rooms on the main floor shall be the galleries and library of the museum.

The monogram of the architect, which is carved in the outer wall above the front entrance, shall be preserved intact and visible. The photographic copy of the architect's portrait now hanging in the main hallway, shall be maintained in the library and in good condition.

The Donee further agrees to fully respect the life estate reserved to the Donors, agreeing that the Donors shall have the right to use and occupy said premises during the lifetime of said Donors, and the survivor of the, without any condition or limitation whatsoever, the Donors having the right, during said term, to occupy said premises, either part, or all of the time, or to permit others to occupy the same; to make such repairs, alterations and changes, other than structural or architectural, as they, the said Donors, may deem necessary for their comfort and for the preservation of said premises.

The Donee further agrees to assume the payment of all taxes, general or special, and other municipal or Governmental charges, which may become due after the decease of the survivor of the Donors.

The Donee further agrees that neither it, nor any assignee, licensee, lessee, successor, or purchaser for value, shall use said premises in any other manner, nor for any purposes other than above described (other architectural organizations may be permitted to share in the privileges of the house within the limitations of this gift upon such terms as the Donee may from time to time prescribe), agreeing that if it shall abandon said premises, or said premises shall be used for any other purpose than above described, or any material change shall be made in the structure or finish of said building, or said Donee shall in any manner lose its title by operation of law, then all right, title and interest therein to said premises shall immediately revert to the heirs of the Donors, if any such event shall occur during the lifetime of any of the grandchildren of the Donors; provided that if, after a period ending with the decease of the last surviving grandchild of the Donors the neighborhood and surrounding use of property shall so completely change as to make it wholly undesirable and objectionable to continue said premises for the uses and purposes above prescribed, the Donee and the premises shall be freed from the restrictions and reservations above prescribed in the same manner as if the same had never existed, it being the express intention of both parties, however, that said restriction, reservations, covenants and agreements, until the happening of such event or events, shall be binding as covenants running with the land.

The Donee agrees to occupy the property at 1801 Prairie Avenue, Chicago, Illinois, know as the Kimball property, either as owner or tenant during the lifetime of the Donors, and the survivor of them, or to procure and maintain the use or said premises during said lifetime of the Donors as an Architect's club by some organization, the majority of whose members shall be architects, or persons engaged in some phase of the building industry.

IN WITNESS THEREOF the Donors have executed and delivered this Deed of Gift as of the day and year first above written, and the Donee has accepted said Gift and agrees to all of the covenants, conditions and limitations therein as of said date.


John J. Glessner      (SEAL)

Frances M. Glessner      (SEAL)

CHICAGO CHAPTER OF THE AMERICAN INSTITUTE OF ARCHITECTS

(SEAL)
By Alfred Granger, President

ATTEST:

Howard L. Cheney, Secretary
*Note: The signatures were notarized by M. B. Axford, 12/1/1924*

The following was appended to the above agreement.

## THE ESCROW AGREEMENT

J. J. GLESSNER, and the CHICAGO CHAPTER OF THE AMERICAN INSTITUTE OF ARCHITECTS agree that the deed to GLESSNER HOUSE, which has been duly executed by both parties, shall be delivered to Franklin Hess and held by him in escrow until the condition therein contained concerning the acquiring of 1801 Prairie Avenue has been consummated by acquiring title to said premises for the purpose of complying with said condition, and when so consummated, shall be delivered by Franklin Hess at once to the Chicago Chapter of the American Institute of Architects.

DATED this 1st day of December, A.D. 1924.

JOHN J. Glessner   (SEAL)

CHICAGO CHAPTER OF THE AMERICAN INSTITUTE OF ARCHITECTS

By Alfred Granger, President     Escrow accepted. Franklin Hess.

3.        THE ARCHITECT'S CLUB OF CHICAGO, INC.

On December 10, 1924, The Architects Club of Chicago, Inc. was organized to be the primary tenant and lease holder of the entire Kimball House. The Club was organized in such a manner that it would have individual members but members of the AIA, the ISA, and the CAC would be eligible for any class of membership through their individual organizations. This effectively provided for these three organizations to have their headquarters at the Kimball House which was the primary function of The Architects Club of Chicago. Each group had its own lease with The Architects Club of Chicago which permitted the use of Kimball House for meetings, etc. Each also had an office where their records were kept. The provision for individual members of the Architects Club permitted others to use the facilities even if they were not members of any of the primary lessee's organizations. Insofar as the Chicago Architectural Club was concerned, it provided them with a Clubhouse, an office, space for meetings, and an excellent atelier. Ultimately, the CAC was the primary user of the Kimball House.

4.        ARCHITECTS REALTY TRUST

Following the execution of the Agreement dated November 25, 1924, the receipt of the Deed of Gift from the Glessners' dated December 1, 1924, and the Incorporation of The Architects Club of Chicago on December 10, 1924, three architects, namely Alfred Granger, Charles E. Fox and Andrew Lanquist formed the Architects Realty Trust. The purpose of that Trust was to provide a vehicle for the purchase of the Kimball House as required by the terms of the Deed of Gift from the Glessners.'

The Architects Realty Trust was a lengthy document that laid out a plan for the purchase of the Kimball House by architect's who purchased shares therein, usually in units of $1,000, in order to raise the amount needed to buy the Kimball House. About $100,000 was raised initially, although more shares were sold later to cover additional costs. The Trust was dated December 15, 1924 and the purchase of the Kimball House was finalized on that date.

In addition to the Legalities outlined in the Trust, it included the rules and regulations under which the Trust would operate. It provided for election of future trustee, etc. but was primarily formed to hold title to the Kimball House. Upon its formation, the Trust immediately entered into the agreement to lease the Kimball House to The Architects Club of Chicago as provided in the agreement dated December 10, 1924.

# Appendix 3: List of Members

This list was compiled using a number of sources. The first names assembled were those of the eighteen founders, who were listed in the March 1885 issue of the *Inland Architect and Building News*. Almost every month for the next several years, that journal published the names of the members who attended meetings of the club. Names were also published in the *Sanitary News* and the *Building Budget*. Members' names are recorded here as they appeared in the month and year the first time they were listed.

The first formal publication of members' names was in *Sketches,* which was published in December of 1892. Both regular and associate members were listed. In 1894, exhibition catalogs began to be published, and they included members' lists, which were reviewed for additional names in the process of compiling this list. These exhibition catalogs were a primary source of members' names for the next few years. In 1905, the *Handbook for Architects and Builders* began publishing an annual list of the club's members, and from that year until the demise of the club, it and the annual exhibition catalogs were primary sources for this list.

From 1935 through 1940, when neither of the above references sources were regularly published, the annual reports to the Illinois secretary of state provided a list of officers' names, but members' names were not included. It was very difficult to be certain that all members were included during this period. Nevertheless, I have attempted to be as comprehensive as possible.

Names are spelled as found in the above references. (Some names have only initials, although full names were generally used in the text.) Only obvious misspellings have been corrected. Some members belonged to the club for only a year or so, while others remained active for decades. The various categories of membership—junior, associate, etc.—are listed as they were recorded in the first source in which they were encountered. Many members advanced to other categories.

| Abbott, Frank B. | 3/04 |
| Aberle, Wilbert J. | 1926 |
| Ablamowicz, S. V. | 1921 |
| Ackerman, Ed. | 1906 |
| Adams, A. F. | 1927 Hon. Mem. |
| Adelsperger, Roland | 3/97 |
| Adler, Dankmar | 2/92 Assoc. Mem. |
| Ahlson, Fred. | 1923 |
| Albert, Ernest | 12/90 |
| Alderman, W. N. | 1929 |
| Alexander, Isadore | 1925 |
| Alexander, L. | 1925 |
| Allen, John K. | 3/87 Hon. Mem. |
| Allen, Lawrence E. | 1921 |
| Alling, Van Wagenen | 3/00 |
| Allison, Al. | 1926 |
| Alschuler, Alfred S. | 4/96 |
| Alstrom, John | 1922 |
| Alyea, Thomas | 1915 |
| Ames, Millard E. | 1906 |
| Amory, W. Austin | 3/99 |
| Anderson, A. B. | 4/92 |
| Anderson, A. L. | 1930–31 |
| Anderson, A. W. | 1921 |
| Anderson, B. D. | 1929 |
| Anderson, Edwin F. | 1925 |
| Anderson, Helge A. | 1911 |
| Anderson, Helmer N. | 1927 |
| Anderson, Herbert F. | 1920 |
| Anderson, Herbert W. | 1929 |
| Anderson, S. D. | 1921 |
| Anderson, Sidney C. | 1930–31 |
| Anderson, W. E. | 1928 |
| Andrew, W. H. | 1913 |
| Andrews, Alfred B. | 1924 |
| Anderson, Carl A. | 1918 |
| Anderson, Edwin, F. | 1916 Hon. Mem. 1923 |
| Anderson, Pierce | 4/02 |
| Andrew, C. B. | 1922 |
| Andrews, Alfred B. | 4/02 |
| Andrews, A. G. | 3/03 |
| Andrews, Elliott R. | 1911 |
| Androvette, Geo. E. | 5/95 Assoc. Mem. |
| Angell, Austin | 1912 |
| Armstrong, J. A. | 1908 |
| Appel, Henry L. | 4/02 Assoc. Mem. |
| Applebach, Henry | 1920 |
| Archer, C. G. | 1926 |
| Archer, Charles S. | 1919 |
| Arneson, S. V. | 1928 |
| Arnold, Hugo | 5/95 |
| Arnold, Miss Jennie | 5/95 First woman |
| Arnvig, Sigurd | 1923 |
| Aroner, Jacob S. | 1910 |
| Ashton, R. J. | 1917 |
| Atchison, John D. | 3/00 |
| Atwood, Charles B. | 12/92 |
| Awsumb, George | 1908 |
| Baars, Jas. Den. | 12/92 |
| Bacci, Alex H. | 1927 |
| Bacon, Francis. T. | 3/03 |
| Bacon, Harry | 3/93 |
| Bagge, Christian U. | 1904 |
| Baily, Hugh | 1929 |
| Baird, Eldon G. | 1928 |
| Baird, Wm. N. | 1930–31 |
| Baker, Frank S. Baker | 3/99 |
| Baldwin, Francis. M. | 1922 |
| Baldwin, John E. | 1915 |
| Balfour, A. N. | 1928 |
| Balkin, Louis | 1910 |
| Bannister, George S. | 1921 |
| Bargman, E. F. | 3/01 |
| Barker, Frank | 4/98 |
| Barnes, H. H. | 1920 |
| Barnum, Geo. L. | 1914 |

| | | | | | | | |
|---|---|---|---|---|---|---|---|
| Barry, Gerald, Jr. | 1916 | Boothby, Donald | 1931–32 | Cenek, R. R. | 1913 |
| Barry, W. H. | 3/04 | Booton, J. F. | 1922 | Cerny, Jerome Robert | 1925 |
| Bartholomew, F. L. | 4/05 | Bordewich, Howard | 1927 | Cerny, Jerry J. | 1906 |
| Bartlett, Harry O. | 1928 | Bossert, H. F. | 1922 | Chaddock, De Clifford | 3/03 Assoc. Mem. |
| Bartolomae, Francis | 3/00 | Boston, Jos. F. | 1925 | Chaffee, D. C. | 7/94 |
| Barton, Francis M. | 3/01 | Boulwood, C. E. | 12/89 | Chance, J. H. | 1928 |
| Batchen, J. C. | 11/6 | Bourke, Robert E. | 3/00 | Charles, W. T. | 1910 |
| Batwell, Edward A. | 11/92 | Bownton, Herbert E. | 1925 | Charvat, Anthony | 1921 |
| Baum, M. G. | 1928 | Bowstead, Harry G. | 1910 | Chase, Frank | 1909 |
| Beach, G. S. | 1921 | Boyington, W. W. | 2/92 Assoc. Mem. | Chase, Robert | 1913 |
| Beaumont, George | 3/85 Charter Mem. | Brabant, Gifford | 1912 | Chatten, M. C. | 1900 |
| Beck, D. W. | 1921 | Bradbury, G. A. | 1922 | Chayes, Frank | 1928 |
| Beauley, William J. | 4/91 | Braeger, William | 5/94 | Cheatle, Augusta | 1930–31 |
| Beck, B. E. | 1929 | Brand, Gustave A. | 1905 | Cheatle, Edwin | 1930–31 |
| Beckerleg, E. L. | 3/04 | Brandt, Oscar E. | 3/97 | Cheetam, F. K. | 1921 |
| Beckwith, Harry C. | 1910 | Brandt, Robert | 1926 | Cheney, H. L. | 1912 |
| Beeckman, Julius | 4/89 | Braun, Alfred | 1914 | Childs, Frank A. | 3/03 |
| Beel, Jay Bassett | 3/98 | Braun, Henry H. | 12/88 | Christian, O. C. | 11/86 |
| Beers, Herbert F. | 4/05 | Braun, Isadore H. | 1920 | Christensen, C. W. | 1912 |
| Beers, M. L. | 12/92 | Breckenridge, P. C. | 1928 | Christensen, Howard | 1925 |
| Behel, Vernon W. | 3/04 | Brinkman, William. J. | 1891 | Christensen, John C. | 1921 |
| Behr, E. Theodore | 3/99 Assoc. Mem. | Brinsley, Herbert. G. | 1893 | Christiansen, Roy T. | 1920 |
| Behrens, Elmer | 1923 | Bristle, Joseph | 1910 | Church, Myron H. | 3/85 Charter Mem. |
| Behrends, Edward | 1920 | Brittingham, B. M. | 4/96 Assoc. Mem. | Ciarcoschi, S. | 4/05 |
| Behrends, John | 1910 | Brout, Robert | 1929 | Civkin, Victor | 1928 |
| Behrens, Elmer F. | 1917 | Brown, A. G. | 2/92 | Clark, Edwin H. | 1910 |
| Beidler, A. W. | 4/05 | Brown, Arthur H. | 1921 | Clark, Edward C. | 3/99 Assoc. Mem. |
| Beidler, Herbert B. | 1928 | Brown, Arthur T. | 1928 | Clark, L. C. | 1910 |
| Beil, Carl | 1909 | Brown, Clarence G. | 1910 | Clark, Robert | 2/92 Hon. Mem. |
| Beilin, Sidney J. | 1928 | Brown, O. G. | 3/91 | Clark, Wm. Jerome | 1921 |
| Belden, Edgar S. | 12/94 | Brown, Richard | 1920 | Clarke, Edwin B. | 4/05 |
| Bellas, Chas. | 1912 | Browning, Alex. | 3/04 Assoc. Mem. | Clay, W. W. | 2/92 Assoc. Mem. |
| Beman, D. W. | 1910 | Brush, Chas. E. | 3/04 | Cleary, Charles W. | 1910 |
| Beman, S. S. | 5/94 Assoc. Mem. | Brydges, E. Norman | 3/05 | Clifford, D. F. | 3/04 |
| Benedict, Jules B. | 3/00 | Buchroeder, W. M. | 1930–31 | Clow, Wm. E. | 1911 Hon. Mem. |
| Benisch, H. J. | 1920 | Buck, Lawrence | 7/94 | Cloyes, F. O. | 12/92 Assoc. Mem. |
| Benkert, Ernest A. | 1926 | Bucket, Arthur C. | 1910 | Cobb, Henry Ives | 5/94 Assoc. Mem. |
| Benn, William W. | 1929 | Buckley, Ralph J. | 1911 | Coffin, Arthur | 1921 |
| Bennett, Arthur J. T. | 3/04 | Buckmaster, W. A. | 1930-31 | Coffman, Geo. W. | 3/99 |
| Bennett, Edward H. | 1921 | Buell, Temple H. | 1920 Hon. Mem. 1923 | Cohen, Isidore | 3/04 |
| Bentley, Harry H. | 1911 | Buhmann, Chas. J. | 3/04 | Cohn, Irving | 1928 |
| Berglund, E. | 1929 | Bultman, Wm. C. | 1921 | Cohen, S. Bruce | 1929 |
| Bergstrom, Harold G. | 1928 | Budina, A. D. | 1921 | Colburn, Howard F. | 1930–31 |
| Berlin, Robert C. | 1921 | Burdett, Samuel | 1919 | Collins, Harry B. | 1921 |
| Berndt, Frank J. | 12/92 | Burger, Walter D. | 1928 | Colpoyes, F. H. | 12/89 |
| Bernhard, Adolph F. | 11/92 | Burghoffer, Leon | 1903 | Combs, Roger M. | 4/96 Assoc. Mem. |
| Berry, Addison C. | 3/86 | Burnham, D. H. | 2/92 Assoc. Mem. | Conley, Walter | 1928 |
| Best, Theo. D. | 1912 | Burnham, Hubert | 1910 | Conner, G. D. | 1921 |
| Bethel, Vernon W. | 1910 | Burnham, W. Stewart | 1922 | Connoly, J. | 1929 |
| Betts, Wm. B. | 1911 | Burrill, Loraine S. | 1929 | Conroy, John J. | 1912 |
| Bicknell, Alfred H. | 3/04 | Busch, Wm. | 1910 | Cook, Norman W. | 1908 |
| Bieg, Harry K. | 1922 | Buschbaum, Emanuel | 1928 | Cook, Wm. G. | 1906 |
| Biegalski, Cosmio | 1929 | Bushnell, Ed S. | 12/92 Assoc. Mem. | Cooke, Thomas E. | 1927 |
| Binford, W. H. | 1928 | Cahn, Edgar B. | 3/99 | Coolidge, Charles A. | 5/94 Assoc. Mem. |
| Birge, Chas. Eliot | 5/95 | Callahan, Carl | 1920 | Corbeky, L. J. | 1913 |
| Bjork, A. E. | 1905 | Cameron, Edgar | 3/00 | Cornell, Paul Jr. | 3/00 Assoc. Mem. |
| Blake, Charles F. | 3/04 | Camp, E. M. | 5/95 | Corse, R. P. | 1910 |
| Blake, Charles G. | 1927 | Campbell, Donald | 4/04 | Cortez, Louis A. | 1928 |
| Blake, Edgar O. | 1921 | Campbell, E. R. | 1910 | Corwin, Eugene C. | 1917 |
| Blake, Theodore L. | 1/86 Hon. Mem. | Campbell, Harry S. | 1916 | Coughlen, Gordner C. | 1913 |
| Blauner, Louis | 1917 | Capron, E. F. | 4/05 | Coverly, Charles O. | 1928 |
| Blomfield, James | 1910 | Capraro, Axel V. | 1921 | Coxhead, J. H. | 10/86 |
| Blomgren, Charles E. | 1929 | Carlburg, R. H. | 1921 | Cramer, Ambrose C. | 1916 |
| Bloom, Richard | 1929 | Carlson, Clifford | 1915 | Crane, K. E. | 1928 |
| Blouke, Pierre | 1915 | Carlson, Elmer C. | 1919 | Cranford, R. N. | 3/97 |
| Blum, R. F. | 1925 | Carlson, George C. | 1928 | Criz, A. | 1931–32 |
| Blume, Louis J. | 1926 | Carlson, Glen | 1928 | Crizevsky, A. | 1930–31 |
| Blummer, Oscar | 5/95 | Carlson, Richard J. | 1920 | Crockett, E. B. | 4/96 |
| Bochin, B. P. | 1927 | Carlsson, Axel | 1928 | Crofoot, Fred D. | 1906 |
| Bock, Richard W. | 3/97 | Carman, Chas. W. | 3/04 | Crombie, R. A. | 1921 |
| Bock, Theo. | 1912 | Carnegie, Wm. C. | 1921 | Crowther, Joseph C. | 1928 |
| Bodett, Roy C. | 1917 | Carpenter, J. H. | 3/85 Charter Mem. | Crowe, J. G. | 3/06 |
| Bodinus, Wm. S. | 1929 | Carr, Charles A. | 3/97 | Crowe, Robert | 1926 |
| Bodle, A. T. | 1912 | Carr, Harry W. | 1911 | Crofoot, Fred | 1925 |
| Boehm, R. P. | 1927 | Carrier, D. G. | 5/94 Assoc. Member. | Crowther, Fred | 1911 |
| Boggesen, Walter | 1928 | Carson, Robert | 1928 | Culbertson, H. W. | 11/86 |
| Bohm, Chas. H. | 1930–31 | Casse, E. Jackson | 1921 | Cummings, R. H. | 1922 |
| Bohre, Albert | 1928 | Cassel, Earl D. | 1923 | Cummings, Ralph W. | 1928 |
| Bollenbacher, J. C. | 1911 | Caukins, Eugene L. | 12/85 | Cunningham, P. J. | 4/96 |
| Bonner, Charles | 3/04 | Cauley, Frank M. | 1923 | Curtis, J. Arthur | 1927 |

Dady, Wm. E. 1920
Dalsey, Harry I. 1912
Dando, Robert E. 1921
Dauchy, Samuel 4/96 Assoc. Mem.
Davenport, Henry F. 1930–31
Davidson, F. E. 1921
Davis, Frank L. 3/89
Davis, Seymour 11/92
Dawson, Arthur 12/90
Dazey, Harry L. 1910
Dean, A. F. 1928 Hon. Mem.
Dean, Arthur R. 4/96
Dean, Charles F. 3/05
Dean, George R. 7/94
Deane, E. Eldon 9/91
De Arment, F. H. 1921
De Golyer, Robert S. 1921
De Money, F. O. 1921
Demuth, John 1923
Denell, R. A. 12/87
Dennen, Thomas 1928
Denslow, L. E. 3/04
de Sanno, Raymond F. 1917
Dewson, Edward 3/85 Charter Mem.
Dieball, Ed. H. 1930–31
Dillon, Henry R. 4/96 Assoc. Mem.
Dillon, John R. 7/94
Dinkelberg, E. P. 3/04
Dixon, L. B. 2/92 Assoc. Mem. W
Dobbert, R. H. 1922
Dodd, John M. 3/04
Dodge, Charles 12/87
Doll, Clarence 1924
Donderdale, G. 3/06
Doran, Wm. J. 1925
Dornbush, Chas. H. 1930–31
Dougherty, F. E. 1921
Downe, Edwin L. 3/06
Downey, Aloysius N. 3/03
Downs, E. L. 1906
Downton, Herbert E. 1912
Dreyer, Detlef J. 1921
Drielsma, J. A. 1925
Driver, H. G. 1927
Drummond, Wm. E. 3/01
Duncan, Jas. S. 1930–31
Dunderdale, Geo. 1911
Dungan, Thomas A. 5/95
Dunham, Geo. Foote 1901
Dunning, A. G. 3/03 Assoc. Mem.
Dunning, Hugh 1909
Dunning, N. Max 4/96 Hon. Mem. 1923
Dunning, W. H. 1911
Dukkee, A. R. 2/92
Dutton, L. B. 3/85 Charter Mem.
Dwen, R. G. 3/06
Eames, Arthur R. 3/87
Eberhart, Doyle S. 1923
Eberly, Walter K. 1917
Eberson, Drew 1928
Edbrooke, Harry W. J. 3/97
Edholm, W. L. 1929
Edquist, Carl B. 1928
Eggebrecht, William 4/96
Ehresman, D. D. 1924
Eich, George B. 4/02
Eichberg, S. Milton 1921
Eichenbaum, Edward E. 1928
Eiker, Charles F. 3/04
Eischen, R. M. 1921
Eiseman, Albert, Jr. 1927
Eiseman, Ferdinand 1921
Eisenberg, Maurice L. 1926
Ekberg, Arthur B. 1928
Elcock, E. G. 1910 Hon. Member
Eliel, Roy 3/97
Ellinger, F. L. 12/87
Ellingwood, F. L. 3/86
Ellis, C. M. 1916
Ellis, H. W. 3/06

Ellis, Edmund L. 12/92
Emerson, Ralph Waldo 1928
Emery, Jesse Lee 3/99 Assoc. Mem.
Enders, Frank 9/88 Hon. Mem.
Enders, Oscar R. 3/86
English, John W. 1913
Enthof, Edmond W. 1926
Eppinghausen, Chas. 5/94
Erickson, Allen E. 1920
Ernst, Henry F. 1916
Esser, Curt A. 1920
Esser, Paul F. 1916
Eugene, Alex K. 1929
Evans, Alfred F. 1/93
Evans, Floyd 1917
Ewen, John Meiggs 2/92 Assoc. Mem.
Falnbigl, Ferdinand 4/02 Assoc. Mem.
Falkner, Chas. D. 1921
Falkenau, Victor 3/04
Fanning, Chas. G. 3/06
Faro, R. Vale 1928
Farrell, James A. 1928
Farrier, C. W. 1917
Fasold, Frank 1930–31
Fehlow, Albert C. 1918
Fellheimer, Alfred 4/96
Fellows, William K. 1895
Ferguson, Louis A. 4/96 Assoc. Mem.
Ferris, John T. 1912
Ferris, William J. 1926
Fielder, August 4/96
Fierbaugh, J. F. 1929
Finch, Lloyd H. 1930–31
Fischer, Fred A. 1912
Fischer, Harry L. 1929
Fischer, John R. 1895
Fisher, Howard T. 1930–31
Fisher, John B. 5/95
Fisher, Percy E. 1910
Fisher, R. E. 1910
Fishman, Maurice 1912
Fisk, Louis A. 4/96
Fisher, Reynolds 2/92 Assoc. Mem.
Flaks, Francis A. 1921
Flanders, John J. 3/04
Fletcher, Robert C. 1921
Fleury, Albert 3/04
Floto, Julius 4/96
Fogel, Reuben W. 4/02
Foley, Michael 1928
Forte, Attilio 1927
Fortin, Joseph T. 1921
Fosso, William R. 1928
Foster, Arthur 1921
Fowler, Harry C. 1928
Fox, Charles E. 1921
Fox, Elmer J. 1916
Fox, John J. 1921
Fox, William Paul 1921
Fraenkel, T. O. 12/85
Franklin, Robert L. 1915
Franzen, Clarence E. 1924
Franzheim, H. Ken. 1921
Frary, I. E. 1910
Frederick, G. W. 1929
Freeman, Ernest 3/04
French, B. L. 2/92
Froelich, Robert S. 1931-32
Froh, J. T. 1913
Frost, Charles S. 2/92 Assoc. Mem.
Frybort, Chas. Fisher 1912
Fuhrer, Eugene 1924
Fuller, L. E. 3/99
Fyfe, James L. 2/92
Gage, Thomas G. 3/00
Gamoll, H. L. 1925
Garden, A. J. 12/91
*(probably an error)*
Garden, Edward G. 2/92
Garden, F. M. 2/92

Garden, H. M. G. 12/91
Garden, J. E. 12/91
*(probably an error)*
Gardner, Richard H. 4/96 Assoc. Mem.
Gates, Ellis D. 3/03 Assoc. Mem.
Gates, Wm. D. 5/95 Assoc. Mem.
Gaubert, Leon 3/04
Gay, Henry Lord 12/86 Hon. member
Gaydos, Frank J. 1928
Gerber, Arthur U. 3/04
Gerrity, J. F. 1929
Giannini, Orlando 3/00 Assoc. Mem.
Gibb, William R. 11/86
Gibian, E. H. 1921
Gibson, Charles H. 1930–31
Gilbert, Irving M. 1909
Gillette, Edwin F. 1908
Gilloffo, S. 1928
Gindele, Chas. W. 1911 Hon. Mem.
Glidden, Homer H. 3/01
Gliotto, Leonard J. 1920
Glube, Harry 1923
Goetz, M. H. 1917
Goetz, M. L. 1925
Golden, Howard 1930–31
Goldman, Jos. 1928
Gollnick, Louis R. 1928
Goo, Robert 1929
Goodwin, J. M. 5/94
Gorges, Franz 1917
Gorman, Edward D. 1929
Goudy, F. W. 3/97
Gould, O. C. 1925
Grace, William 4/04
Graham, Ernest R. 12/92 Assoc. Mem.
Granger, Alfred H. 3/99
Granger, Donald K. 1923
Gray, George C. 3/01 Assoc. Mem.
Greeley, M. L. 3/04
Green, Herbert H. 3/05
Green, W. M. 12/86
Greenfield, George H. 1912
Greengard, B. C. 1912
Greenwald, Leslie J. 1924
Griesbach, Henry F. 4/96
Griffin, Walter B. 3/00
Grimgaard, O. H. 1926
Grimmer, Vernon 1928
Grindel, John F. 1930–31
Griswold, R. E. 1913
Grosguth, Joseph, Jr. 1929
Gross, R. J. 1925
Grover, Oliver D. 4/96
Gruenfeld, Caspar 3/00
Grundy, James 12/87
Guarino, Joachim 1924
Guerini, Anibal 5/94
Guilbert Ernest F. 4/92
Gunn, C. A. 1908 Assoc. Mem.
Guenzel, Louis 1921
Gurd, G. A. 12/89
Gustafson, Arthur C. 1930–31
Gustafson, Virgil E. 1928
Gylleck, Elmer A. 1920
Gylleck, Waldo G. 1929
Haagen, Paul T. 3/03
Haganey, Jas. A. 4/05
Hahn, Stanley W. 1928
Haigh, Arthur 1925
Haight, Arthur H. 4/05
Hale, Alfred R. 1916
Hall, A. G. 1910
Hall, Emery Stanford 1921
Hall, Gilbert P. 1921
Hall, Irwin R. 4/02
Hall, John L. 5/94
Hall, Oliver A. 3/05
Hallin, E. L. 1920
Hals, Harold 3/03
Hamel, T. S. 3/06

| | | | | | |
|---|---|---|---|---|---|
| Hamilton, I. G. | 1930–31 | Hodgkins, Howard G. | 5/94 | Johnson, Gilbert V. | 1930–31 |
| Hamilton, J. L. | 3/03 | Hoeppner, E. A. | 8/89 Hon. Mem. | Johnson, Harold T. | 1928 |
| Hammett, Ralph W. | 1927 | Hofer, Victor G. | 1928 | Johnson, Ingwald L | 1921 |
| Hammond, C. Herrick | 4/05 Hon. Mem. | Hoffman, Emil J. | 3/06 | Johnson, Jens A. | 4/04 |
| Hanebuth, Edgar C. | 1928 | Hoffman, John F. | 3/97 | Johnson, John | 1/93 |
| Hanifin, Arthur C. | 1906 | Hofmeister, T. M. | 1926 | Johnson, Morris O. | 3/00 |
| Hanipin, Arthur | 1910 | Hohagen, Paul | 1907 | Johnson, N. E. | 1908 Assoc. Mem. |
| Hansen, A. T. | 1911 | Hokanson, P. L. | 3/04 | Johnson, Rueben H. | 1921 |
| Hansen, Herbert C. | 1927 | Holabird, John A. | 1921 | Johnston, Ernest D. | 1923 |
| Hansen, Leslie M. | 1931–32 | Holabird, Wm. | 5/94 Assoc. Mem. | Johnston, Percy T. | 1912 |
| Hansen, Roy E. | 1926 | Holana, J. | 1930–31 | Jones, L. C. | 1922 |
| Hanson, O. C. | 5/95 | Holcomb, H. F. | 1922 | Joy, S. Scott | 1921 |
| Hanson, Clarence | 5/95 | Holmes, Harold | 1912 | Junge, W. H. | 4/86 Hon. Mem. |
| Hanter, Herman | 1926 | Holmes, Morris G | 12/85 | Junkin, J. P. | 1911 |
| Hanzlik, Sidney | 1927 | Holmes, N. H. | 3/04 | Kable, Chas. Howard | 4/05 |
| Harbeck, Jervis R. | 4/02 | Holslag, Edward J | 1905 | Kable, J. Frank | 1906 |
| Harder, Julius | 9/91 | Holsman, Henry K. | 3/98 | Kalter, W. L. | 1909 |
| Harger, A. | 1928 | Holstead, Abram | 1909 | Kalthoff, F. Jr. | 1921 |
| Harper, W. W. | 4/05 | Holyoke, T. T. | 11/89 | Kamm, Robert F. | 1928 |
| Harris, Chester R. | 3/97 | Hompe, A. W. | 12/87 | Kane, J. A. | 1921 |
| Harris, Ralph C. | 1911 | Hooper, C. Lauron | 5/95 Assoc. Mem. | Kannenberger, Werner | 1929 |
| Harris, R. Keith | 1913 | Hooper, Wm. T. | 1911 Hon. Mem. | Karlin, Irving M. | 1928 |
| Hart, W. B. | 3/04 | Horn, Benj. A. | 1912 | Karlinsky, Irving | 1920 |
| Haselbooth, Ray | 1928 | Horrocks, P. A. | 1906 | Kartowicm, Frank | 1929 |
| Haselburn, Robert G. | 1929 | Hougaard, Perry V. | 1920 | Kastrup, Carl J. | 1927 |
| Hatsfeld, Edwin | 1929 | Houpert, Pierre | 1908 | Kattenbrun, James A. | 1928 |
| Hatzfeld, Clarence | 4/96 | Howland, John Roche | 1928 | Kay, Stanley W. | 1929 |
| Hawley, Elmer R. | 1925 | Hubbard, Archie H. | 1921 | Kehm, August | 3/06 |
| Hazelton, H. T. | 4/05 | Hubbard, Philip | 1925 | Keiller, David | 3/04 |
| Haupt, Oscar | 5/94 | Hudson, Harry F. | 4/05 | Keller, Norman E. | 1927 |
| Hauser, D. W. | 1921 | Huey, William B. | 1909 | Kelly, Joe | 1928 |
| Haviland, C. A. | 1912 | Hughes, T. C. | 1914 | Kelly, John H. | 3/99 |
| Hawkins, G. A. | 3/85 Charter Mem. | Hulbert, C. P. | 1907 | Kemmler, Junius A. | 1930–31 |
| Hayes, C. L. | 1911 | Hulfield, Jos. | 1921 | Kendall, R. C. | 1928 |
| Haynes, Kenneth | 1929 | Hulla, John | 3/97 | Kendall, R. R. | 5/94 |
| Hazelton, H. F. | 12/87 | Hunt, Frederick. S. | 2/92 Hon. Mem. | Kennedy, Everratt L. | 1921 |
| Hazelton, T. | 7/87 | Hunt, Leigh B. | 4/02 | Kennedy, John J., Jr. | 1928 |
| Heer, R. N. | 1913 | Hunt, Myron H. | 5/95 | Keppler, Frederick | 12/86 |
| Heim, L. H. | 12/87 | Hunter, David C. | 4/02 | Kershenfaut, J. Donald | 1926 |
| Heino, Albert | 1928 | Hunter, Herman | 1927 | Kessell, Chas. A. | 3/85 Charter Mem. |
| Heinz, C. P. | 1910 | Huntoon, Homer | 1927 | Keys, Fred | 12/92 Assoc. Mem. |
| Heinz, George P. | 3/00 | Huszagh, Ralph D. | 1922 | Kibby, Chas. H. | 5/95 |
| Heinz, L. H. | 12/88 | Hutton, Gordon J. | 3/04 | Kilby, C. H. | 5/94 Assoc. Mem. |
| Heinz, Lorenz | 1921 | Hyett, Robert T. | 1909 | Killen, E. Greble | 4/96 Assoc. Mem. |
| Heinz, S. H. | 12/89 | Hyde, Robert M. | 1921 | Kimball, C. D. | 4/96 |
| Helder, C. Will | 3/04 | Hyland, Paul V. | 3/00 | Kimbell, Arthur | 1915 |
| Helmkamp, H. L. | 12/89 | Ignalzi, Rinaldo L. | 1931–32 | Kimbell, E. C. | 3/04 |
| Hemmings, Edw. C. | 3/98 | Ingram, Horace C. | 1909 | Kimbell, M. N. | 3/04 |
| Henderson, A. W. | 1920 | Insley, E. E. | 3/00 | Kimbell, S. S. | 3/04 |
| Hendrickson, Arthur | 3/97 | Insensee, Frederic M. | 1924 | Kingsley, Donald | 1927 |
| Hengels, Heenry C. | 1911 | Ireland, F. W. | 1909 | Kinnavy, Michael | 1926 |
| Henschien, H. Peter | 1921 | Isenberger, Robert | 1926 | Kirkpatrick, F. W. | 4/96 |
| Hepner, R. H. | 1928 | Jackson, H. W. | 5/94 | Kirkpatrick, R. A. | 4/96 |
| Herbeck, J. R. | 1901 | Jacob, V. H. | 1927 | Klees, Fred | 5/9 Assoc. Mem. |
| Hercz, Arthur | 3/97 | Jacobson, Phillmore | 1926 | Kleinfell, A. C. | 3/89 |
| Herlin, George W. | 1911 | James, E. R. | 1910 | Kleinhaus, Geo. F. | 1930–31 |
| Herman, Milton | 1927 | Jameson, Wm. S. Jr. | 1929 | Kleinpell, W. E. | 2/89 |
| Herr, Thornton A. | 1909 | Janes, M. F. | 1930-31 | Klewer, W. L. | 12/87 |
| Herter, Edward | 1923 | Janik, Ladislav | 1928 | Klinger, E. A. | 1921 |
| Heselbroth, Ray | 1926 | Janson, Edw. F. | 1922 | Knezicek, Wm. K. | 1920 |
| Hess, Louis F. | 1917 | Jansson, E. F. | 1928 | Knickerbocker, E. B. | 1928 |
| Heth, Ralph | 1928 | Jenkins, A. M. | 1912 | Knisely, Harry C. | 5/95 Assoc. Mem. |
| Hetherington, J. T. | 3/85 Charter Mem. | Jenkins, Harry. D. | 4/96 | Knox, Arthur H. | 4/05 |
| Hetherington, T. D. | 3/85 Charter Mem. | Jenney, W. L. B. | 2/92 Hon. Mem. | Knudsen, Harold No. | 1928 |
| Heun, Arthur | 12/88 | Jenney, Max | 5/95 | Koch, W. W. | 1910 |
| Hewitt, Herbert E. | 2/92 | Jennings, George H. | 3/97 | Koenig, William | 1925 |
| Higgins, J. Smith | 1909 | Jensen, Elmer C. | 11/90 | Kohfeldt, Walter J. | 3/06 |
| Highwood, Donald H. | 1928 | Jensen, Jens | 3/04 | Koll, H. C. | 4/96 |
| Hill, Edgar A. | 1930-31 | Jillson, Byron H. | 1921 | Koenigsberg, Nathan | 1921 |
| Hill, Francis J. | 3/99 | Jobson, Frank C. | 5/86 | Kostrup, Carl J. | 1926 |
| Hiller, Eugene F. | 1908 | Joerger, G. | 1929 | Kovar, Frank | 1926 |
| Hinchcliff, George E. | 1915 | Jogerst, Joseph P. | 1909 | Krause, J. W. | 5/94 |
| Hine, Cicero | 3/85 Charter Mem. | Johns, B. D. | 1929 | Kroman, M. Louis | 1925 |
| Hinman, C. G. | 1928 | Johnson, B. Kenneth | 1925 | Kronich, David | 1928 |
| Hirsch, Fred R. | 5/86 | Johnson, Albin | 1926 | Kronick, Gerald T. | 1927 |
| Hobbs, Ray. M. | 1911 | Johnson, Carl W. | 1928 | Kruchton, C. K. | 1921 |
| Hodgdon, Charles | 1921 | Johnson, Charles G. | 1930–31 | Kucharik, John | 1927 |
| Hodgdon, Fred M. | 1913 | Johnson, E. M. | 1931–32 | Kuestner, Louis E. | 1928 |
| Hodgdon, J. M. | 1922 | Johnson, Ernest D. | 1922 | Kuezick, William | 1928 |
| Hodgkins, Harold C. | 1906 | Johnson, E. V. | 1906 | Kuklin, Abraham | 1930–31 |

| | | | | | |
|---|---|---|---|---|---|
| Kurtz, David P. | 1929 | Lyons, Harry | 1910 | Millikin, H. C. | 1920 |
| Kutsche, Arthur W. | 3/97 | Macardell, Cornelius | 1928 | Millikin, H. O. | 1921 |
| Lagergr4en, Gustav P. | 1921 | MacLeish, Norman H. | 1929 | Minchin, Sidney B. | 1913 |
| Lammers, Herman C. | 3/99 | MacLellan, Albert C. | 1928 | Mitchell, Robert B. | 1929 |
| Lampe, C. W. | 1914 | McCarthy, C. A. | 1920 | Mitton, Eugene | 1928 |
| Land, H. H. | 1920 | McCarthy, Joseph W. | 1921 | Mohr, Frederick J. | 4/05 |
| Lane, Harry L. | 1912 | McConville, L. E. | 1921 | Moonin, Harry | 1929 |
| Lang, Louis A. | 3/00 | McCoughey, W. F.,Jr. | 1921 | Moravec, Bohumil T. | 1928 |
| Langerstrom, Art O. | 1912 | McCullough, W. J. B. | 3/85 Charter Mem. | Morrison, Harry H. | 1928 |
| Lanquist, A. | 3/04 | McCurry, Paul D. | 1927 | Mortinson, H. W. | 1929 |
| Lantz, R. S. | 1930–31 | McDonald, James W. | 4/96 | Mitchell, John A. | 3/99 |
| Larson, Harry | 1928 | McEldowney | 1924 | Mittelbusher, Edwin | 1927 |
| Larson, Roy | 1916 | McFetridge, W. H. | 3/98 Assoc. Mem. | Moulding, Thomas | 1925 |
| Lau, Willy H. | 4/02 Assoc. Mem. | McGrath, Paul J. | 1920 | Monberg, H. Lawrence | 1919 |
| Lauer, Martin W. | 3/04 | McGrew, Chas. B. | 1913 | Monberg, Otto | 1921 |
| Lautrup, Paul C. | 2/92 Assoc. Mem. | McGrew, Kenneth A. | 1920 | Montgomery, John T. | 3/04 |
| Lawrence, A. J. | 1913 | McKeeby, M. Sanford | 1909 | Morden, W. W. | 1919 |
| Lawrie, Harry | 3/85 Charter Mem. & | McKey, Harry | 1925 | Morehouse, Merritt J. | 1921 |
| | Hon. Mem. | McLaughlin, Geo. W. | 1930–31 | Morgan, Chas. L. | 1914 |
| Layer, Robert | 1921 | McLaren, Robert J. | 1921 | Morgan, Elisha | 1911 |
| Leach, Joseph P., Jr. | 1928 | McLean, Robert C. | 3/85 Charter Mem. & | Morgan, Harry T. | 1921 |
| Le Duc, Albert | 1928 | | Hon. Mem. | Morgenstierne, Chris. | 3/04 |
| Leavell, John Calvin | 1910 | McMurry, Oscar L. | 3/04 | Morin, H. J. | 1917 |
| Ledebuhr, A. E. | 1921 | McQuire, John J., Jr. | 1930–31 | Mork, Raykmond | 1915 |
| Lee, Charles S. | 1925 | McWhirter, Robert | 5/94 | Morphett, Arch S. | 1925 |
| Lee Vee, Raymond | 1928 | Magnuson, Harry E. | 1925 | Morphette, Archie J. | 1912 |
| Lehle, Louis | 1921 | Maher, George W. | 12/86 | Morrison, James R. | 1915 |
| Lehman, L. E. | 1920 | Maher, Philip B. | 1921 | Morse, Burton E. | 3/99 |
| Lehmann, Ludwig E. | 1918 | Mahler, H. H. | 4/05 | Morse, W. A. | 12/90 |
| Lengel, C. M. | 1927 | Mahon, Robert B. | 1926 | Morton, ? | 12/89 |
| Lescher, Theo. A. | 1910 Hon. Mem. | Mair, Clark F. | 1926 | Moulding, Jos. W. | 3/04 |
| Le Vieque, E. J. | 1921 | Maixon, T. N. | 1913 | Moulding, Thomas | 1920 |
| Levi, Simeon C. | 1922 | Maiwurn, R. H. | 1926 | Mountjoy, F. E. | 4/95 |
| Levings, M. M. | 3/04 | Maldaner, Arthur | 1905 | Mudge, J. Wilbur | 1926 |
| Levine, Samuel | 1931-32 | Mallinger, John W. | 1921 | Mueller, Arthur | 1929 |
| Levinson, M. B. | 1922 | Malmquist, B. | 1921 | Mueller, Floyd C. | 1915 |
| Leviton, Morton | 1921 | Maly, Albert F. | 1924 | Mueller, H. E. | 1921 |
| Levy, Albert D. | 1928 | Manasse, Dewitt J. | 1913 | Mueller, Paul F. P. | 11/86 |
| Levy, Alex L. | 1921 | Mann, Paul F. | 1909 | Mulig, Thomas J. | 1927 |
| Levy, Samuel H. | 4/92 | Mansfield, John | 5/94 | Mullay, Thomas H. | 12/91 |
| Lewin, Edward P. | 1921 | Marchese, Frank | 1911 | Mullen, J. Bernard | 1906 |
| Lewis, Le Roy, Jr. | 1921 | Marienthal, Oscar B. | 3/00 | Muller, Louis Jr. | 3/91 Hon. Mem. |
| Lewis, W. C. | 2/92 | Markle, Charles H. | 1920 | Mundie, William B. | 4/86 Hon. Mem. |
| Leyden, Tho. F. H. | 5/95 | Markowich, Joseph | 1928 | Murison, Richard V. | 1923 |
| Liebert, Theodore E. | 1929 | Marling, Franklin, Jr. | 1915 | Muscarello, Victor | 1928 |
| Liedberg, Hugo J. | 3/97 | Marsh, Harry L. | 3/03 | Naess, Ivar | 4/96 |
| Lilleskau, John | 3/91 | Marshall, Benj. H. | 1921 | (1899 listing as Viehe-Naess) | |
| Lillig, M. A. | 1929 | Martin, E. D. | 3/04 | Nagle, Callard P. | 3/04 |
| Lindblad, Alfred | 1916 | Martin, Edgar O. | 4/05 | Naper, Herbert J. | 4/02 |
| Lindeberg, G. L. | 1921 | Marshall, B. H. | 3/03 | Naramore, Floyd A. | 1908 |
| Linden, Frank L. | 11/86 | Marshall, Sylvester | 3/04 | Nathan, Bernard | 1925 |
| Lindquist, Joseph B. | 1917 | Marvin, Chas. H. | 3/04 | Necheles, L. | 1924 |
| Lindstrom, R. S. | 5/94 | Marx, Sam A. | 1910 | Nedved, George M. | 1921 |
| Link, John G. | 1908 | Matteson, Victor A. | 4/96 | Nedved, Rudolph J. | 1922 |
| Linke, John E. | 4/05 | Matthes, Carl E. | 1916 | Neebe, John K. | 1921 |
| Linke, John G. | 1910 Hon. Mem. | Matz, Herman L. | 5/95 Assoc. Mem. | Nelson, Charles F. | 3/98 |
| Lippencott, Roy A. | 1911 | Mauch, Max | 4/96 Assoc. Mem. | Nelson, D. S. | 1923 |
| Liska, Emil | 4/05 | Mayer, Carl G. | 1929 | Nelson, De Witte | 1919 |
| Little, Edmund Cook | 3/00 | Mayer, C. H. | 1914 | Nelson, Edgar | 1925 |
| Lively, Frank L. | 1/86 | Mayger, A. Guy | 1914 | Nelson, Edward O. | 4/95 |
| Livingston, T. | 5/95 | Maynard, H. S., Jr. | 1911 | Nelson, E. S. | 1911 |
| Llewellyn, Joseph C. | 5/95 | Mayo, Vivian B. | 1923 | Nelson, Theo. W. | 1930–31 |
| Llewellyn, Ralph C. | 1909 | Mazzone, Samuel | 1928 | Nettenstrom, Elmer | 1906 |
| Loebl, Jerry | 1921 | Meadowcroft, Miner | 1916 | Neubauer, Adolph | 3/98 |
| Lohmuller, F. S. | 4/96 | Meder, Everett S. | 1924 | Nevara, Walter | 1923 |
| Long, Birch B. | 4/96 | Meiselbar, W. | 1928 | Newberry, Robert T. | 3/99 |
| Long, F. B. | 3/03 | Meldrum, John | 1923 | Newbold, Roy E. | 1921 |
| Longley, Dwight H. | 1910 | Mendes, Oscar | 4/88 | Nichols, Robert N. | 1925 |
| Lord, Charles Carroll | 1928 | Mendius, H. | 1918 | Nicolai, A. Erwin | 1926 |
| Lord, W. B. | 6/86 | Menees, T. O. | 1924 | Niedecken, George M. | 3/98 |
| Lorch, Emil | 4/02 | Merrill, Ed. | 1927 | Niedecken, Mary M. | 3/98 |
| Love, Robert J. | 1909 | Messer, John W. | 1912 | Nielsen, L. L. | 1930–31 |
| Lovedale, Geo. F. | 1910 | Mexelberger, Joseph | 8/89 | Niemz, Arthur R. | 12/87 |
| Lovedall, George C. | 1921 | Michaelsen, C. S. | 1909 | Nimmons, George C. | 3/00 |
| Lovell, Sidney | 4/96 | Middlescauf, John | 4/89 | Nitsche, Edward A. | 1913 |
| Lowe, Elmo C. | 1906 | Miers, Clayton | 1926 | Nocheles, L. | 1923 |
| Lucas, H. J. | 1918 | Millay, Thomas | 3/91 | Noelle, Joseph B. | 4/02 |
| Lucas, Um. Bates | 1907 | Miller, Joseph A. | 12/87 | Nordquist, Robert G. | 1928 |
| Lund, Charles E. | 12/91 | Miller, W. F. | 4/05 | Nordstrand | 1929 |
| Lundberg, D. R. | 1917 | Millet, Louis J. | 4/95 | Norrgard, Werner E. | 1927 |

| | | | | | |
|---|---|---|---|---|---|
| Norling, E. | 1921 | Poole, W. E. Jr. | 1930–31 | Rondel, Victor E. | 3/04 |
| Norske, Helmut F. | 1921 | Porter, Alex G. | 1929 | Roney, Henry B. | 1916 |
| Nyden, John A. | 1921 | Poschenreiter, F. J. | 1930-31 | Roos, Carl L. | 12/92 |
| Nye, H. E. | 3/06 | Posthuma, Folkert | 3/99 | Root, John W. Sr. | 1886 Hon. Mem. |
| Oak, Clarence | 1928 | Potthoff, M. A. | 1908 | Root, John W. Jr. | 1923 |
| Oborn, Charles Wm. | 1929 | Potts, J. Oliver | 3/04 | Root, L. P. | 1921 |
| O'Neill, John P. | 1928 | Poulsen, Edw. J. | 4/02 | Rose, Arthur | 1928 |
| Oberhammer, Hans | 1927 | Poulsen, Geo. F. | 1908 | Rose, W. L. | 1913 |
| Obermaier, Charles W. | 12/91 | Powers, Horace S. | 3/04 | Rosenthal, A. B. | 4/02 |
| O'Connell, Thomas F. | 3/04 | Prather, Fred V. | 1912 | Ross, H. J. | 11/90 |
| Ohlheiser, John | 5/88 | Pratt, H. D. | 1928 | Ross, Torey, Jr. | 1921 |
| Ohlheuser, Joseph R. | 12/92 | Preis, C. G. | 1912 | Ross. H. T. | 12/91 |
| Okeberg, E. N. | 1921 | Prendergast, R. W. | 1928 | Rothe, Walter | 1926 |
| Oldefest, E. G. | 1910 | Presto, William C. | 1913 | Rother, Eugene P. | 1921 |
| Oleson, O. S. C. | 5/94 Assoc. Mem. | Pringle, W. L. | 1913 | Rouleau, Arthur | 5/95 |
| Oliver, Ralph H. | 1922 | Prins, E. Paul | 3/06 | Rouleau, Harvey | 1914 |
| Olson, Bernard | 1923 | Pritz, Richard | 1930–31 | Roth, Emery | 11/90 |
| Olson, E. | 1921 | Probst, Albert John | 1928 | Roucoli, Louis | 1927 |
| Oman, S. S. | 1922 | Prosser, H. B. | 5/95 Assoc. Mem. | Rowe, C. B. | 1921 |
| Orth, A. Beatty | 2/92 | Pruyn, Wm. H. | 1922 | Rowe, L. P. | 1921 |
| Orth, Gustav | 1920 | Puckey, F. W. | 1914 | Royer, J. W. | 1921 |
| Ostergren, Robt. C. | 1909 | Purcell, William G. | 3/04 Assoc. Mem. | Rudd, Melvin | 1927 |
| Ostrom, Paul | 1913 | Purrington, D. V. | 5/95 Assoc. Mem. | Ruge, P. H. | 3/03 |
| Otis, W. A. | 3/85 Charter Mem. | Pyle, L. S. | 1929 | Rund, Vaclac R. | 1928 |
| Ott, Charles F. | 1918 | Quinn, P. Edwin | 1917 | Rundin, Rudolph | 1924 |
| Otten, Ralph H. | 1928 | Raab, J. D. | 2/92 | Rupinski, E. W. | 1924 |
| Ottenheimer, Henry A. | 12/91 | Rabig, Chas. E. K. | 1909 | Russ, Edward | 1925 |
| Paffrath, Kasper | 1913 | Rabito, Guy | 1924 | Russell, Fenton | 1925 |
| Page, Harvey L. | 3/00 | Rabun, Elmer R. | 1926 | Russell, William A. | 1915 |
| Palmer, H. L. | 1921 | Rader, B. H. | 1906 | Russeque, G. M. | 11/90 |
| Pareira, David A. | 1929 | Rae, W. R. | 3/87 | Russy, Anthony F. | 3/04 |
| Pareira, Hal | 1929 | Raeder, Henry | 1921 | Ryan, Edward | 1924 |
| Parker, John M. | 3/97 Assoc. Mem. | Raftery, John H. | 1930–31 | Sachtleben, Albert | 1929 |
| Parker, John W. | 12/92 Assoc. Mem. | Ramsey, George L. | 1924 | Salisbury, Robert H. | 1912 |
| Parker, Walter H. | 4/05 | Ramsey, Wm. E. | 4/05 | Sandbloom, Axel | 1/93 |
| Parmentier, Fernand | 6/88 | Rapp, George L. | 3/01 | Sandegren, Andrew | 4/04 |
| Parmelee, E. Dean | 1912 | Rauch, Paul V. | 1925 | Sandegren, Andrew | 1930–31 |
| Parmelee, F. | 12/89 | Rawson, Lorin A. | 3/98 | Sandquist, Oliver C. | 1927 |
| Parrock, H. P. | 1909 | Rebori, Andrew N. | 1911 | Sandstrom, L. E. | 1928 |
| Parsons, Wm. E. | 1921 Hon. Mem. | Recher George D. | 1930–31 | Sandstrom, R. S. | 1919 |
| Paschen, Jacob | 4/05 | Reed, Earl H., Jr. | 1909 | Sanford, Truit E. | 1924 |
| Pastel, Alfred H. | 1921 | Reese, Theodore F. | 5/95 Assoc. Mem. | Sargent, Norman D. | 1928 |
| Pattison, Edward B. | 3/04 | Rehder, J. G. H. | 1920 | Sargisson, Robert L. | 1910 |
| Pattison, James Wm. | 3/97 | Reichert, Will G. | 4/05 | Saunders, George L. | 1917 |
| Patton, Normand S. | 2/92 Assoc. Mem. | Reiner, Eugene B. | 1926 | Savage, C. E. | 1920 |
| Paulson, E. J. | 1909 | Reinhardt, G. A. | 3/01 | Save, Carl M. | 1911 |
| Peabody, Arthur | 12/92 Assoc. Mem. | Reinhold, O. | 1913 | Saxe, Albert M. | 1906 |
| Peerstone, E. D. | 1908 | Renholdt, Martin | 1925 | Schaefer, C. Bryant | 7/87 |
| Pentecost, Ashton | 11/86 | Renwick, Edward A. | 1921 | Schaefer, J. W. | 1911 |
| Peirera, Hal | 1925 | Repp, Geo. W. | 1911 | Schaefer, W. J. | 1913 |
| Perkins, Dwight H. | 12/88 | Rezny, Adrian | 1927 | Schardt, Otto | 1915 |
| Perkins, F. W. | 3/97 Assoc. Mem. | Rhinelander, John | 1922 | Scheaffer, Matthias | 1930–31 |
| Perr, Nelson J. | 1911 | Rice, J. L. | 4/02 | Schell, Geo. J. | 4/96 |
| Petersen, J. Edwin | 1928 | Rich, Charles, C. | 1908 | Schiewe, Ed. A. | 1920 |
| Petersen, Jens C. | 4/02 | Rich, William M. | 1930-31 | Schimck, A. F. | 1920 |
| Peterson, Alfred | 1928 | Richards, J. V. | 1912 | Schleslinger, A. R. | 2/92 |
| Peterson, Charles G. | 1912 | Riddle, Herbert H. | 1921 | Schlossman, N. J. | 1921 |
| Peterson, Karl E. | 1926 | Riddle, Louis W. | 1921 | Schlessinger, W. | 12/90 |
| Peterson, Martin | 4/05 | Ridley, T. Ralph | 1910 | Schmidt, Richard E. | 3/86 |
| Peterson, Stanley M. | 1917 | Rieger, Morris D. | 1928 | Schmidt, Rudolph. O. | 3/00 |
| Pfeiffer, George L. | 1921 | Riley, Ivan H. | 1927 | Schmidt, Hugo | 3/99 |
| Pfoff, John H. | 1926 | Rippel, Fred O. | 1917 | Schock, F. R. | 2/92 Assoc. Mem. |
| Phillips, John H. | 3/00 | Ritman, Howard B. | 1928 | Schoenberg, George | 12/87 |
| Phimister, D. G. | 8/89 Hon. Mem. | Roach, Wilbur L. | 1925 | Schoeing, J. A. | 1922 |
| Pierce, E. F. | 3/99 Assoc. Member | Roberts, E. E. | 1921 | Scholer, Fred | 1911 |
| Piit, Benita A. | 1930–31 | Roberts, N. L. | 1927 | Schonne, C. W. | 1928 |
| Pingrey, Roy E. | 1921 | Robertson, Alexander | 4/88 | Schott, Fred | 1908 |
| Pirola, Louis | 1922 | Robertson, David | 5/95 | Schrader, Ernest | 1912 |
| Pischel, Fred | 5/95 | Robinson, Albert E. | 1906 | Schroeder, Chas. W. | 1931–32 |
| Place, Richard | 12/92 | Robinson, Argyle E. | 1921 | Schroeder, Fred E. | 1913 |
| Pleins, Leo H. | 1921 | Robinson, F. B. L. | 3/04 | Schroeder, William | 1912 |
| Poetsch, W. C. | 1923 | Robinson, Michael | 1930-31 | Schuchkardt, Wm. H. | 4/96 |
| Poetsch, W. R. | 1923 | Roche, Martin | 5/94 Assoc. Mem. | Schumm, Walter | 3/97 |
| Polacek, C. | 1928 | Rodatz, Jacob | 3/04 | Schwartz, A. A. | 1911 |
| Polito, Frank F. | 1930–31 | Rodde, Herbert L. | 1929 | Schwartz, Ervin | 1928 |
| Polk, Willis | 3/01 | Roesch, Charles E. | 4/02 Assoc. Mem. | Schweiker, Paul | 1925 |
| Pomeroy, James T. | 1920 | Roeske, Clemons | 1922 | Schye, Ole A. | 4/89 |
| Pond, Allen B. | 12/90 | Rogers, John A. | 5/95 | Scoffeld, Hubert | 3/00 |
| Pond, Irving K. | 3/85 Charter Mem. & Hon. Mem. | Rognstad, Sigurd A. | 1919 | Scribbins, John A. | 1910 |
| | | Rolle, Walter C. | 1915 | Seablom, Harry R. | 1921 |

| Name | |
|---|---|
| Seamen, Emil H. | 12/88 |
| Seeler, Alfred J. | 1907 |
| Sehafer, W. A. L. | 3/98 |
| Seip, Carl R. | 1928 |
| Selby, George W. | 5/95 |
| Senescall, L. C. | 1927 |
| Seney, Edgar F. | 3/97 |
| Sevenhouse, H. | 1928 |
| Sevic, Wm. | 1921 |
| Seyfarth, Robert | 4/05 |
| Shank, Ed. | 1906 |
| Shankland, R. M. | 3/04 |
| Shattuck, Walter F. | 3/04 |
| Shaver, Thomas | 1927 |
| Shaw, H. Van Doren | 5/95 |
| Shaw, E. C. | 1920 |
| Shaw, Roger D. | 1928 |
| Sheblessy, John F. | 3/97 |
| Sheddy, Ray | 1927 |
| Sheffield, A. H. | 1917 |
| Sheldon, Geo. | 1930–31 |
| Sheldon, Karl H. | 1921 |
| Shellenberger, Jesse | 1925 |
| Sheppard, H. E. | 3/04 |
| Shirinian, Sarkis | 1929 |
| Shparago, Carl | 1928 |
| Shreves, Robert | 1929 |
| Shuma, William F. | 1925 |
| Sieja, E. W. | 1921 |
| Sierks, Chas. H. | 1918 |
| Silberschlag, Ernest E. | 1927 |
| Silbert, I. J. | 1918 |
| Silha, Otto A. | 3/04 |
| Siljander, A. J. | 1913 |
| Sillani, Muzio | 1919 |
| Simmons, H. H. | 1911 |
| Sincere, Edwin M. | 1912 |
| Sir, Arthur J. | 1925 |
| Sjolin, Gust. | 1926 |
| Skinner, Otis A. | 1920 |
| Skubic, Leroy F. | 1930–31 |
| Slovine, G. J. | 1911 |
| Small, John S. | 1910 |
| Smith, Ben L. | 1930–31 |
| Smith, George S. | 1924 |
| Smith, John R. | 1910 |
| Smith, Luther L. | 3/00 Assoc. Mem. |
| Smith, Oliver C. | 12/87 |
| Smith, R. E. | 2/92 |
| Smith, William J. | 3/98 |
| Smith, Wm. Sooy | 5/95 Assoc. Mem. |
| Snell, H. W. | 1909 |
| Snyder, D. W. | 1925 |
| Snyder, J. W. | 3/04 |
| Sobel, Herbert | 1927 |
| Sollet, R. F. | 12/87 |
| Sollit, Ralph T. | 3/03 Assoc. Mem. |
| Sohn, Frank | 1912 |
| Somers, Albert S. | 1910 |
| Somlyo, J. | 1920 |
| Sommer, A. L. | 1917 |
| Sommers, A. L. | 1925 |
| Sorensen, Albert H. | 1911 |
| Spaulding, Keith | 1906 |
| Spector, Charles S. | 1928 |
| Spencer, C. B. | 1921 |
| Spencer, Charles B. | 1921 |
| Spencer, N. S. | 1921 |
| Spencer, Robert C. | 10/93 |
| Spierling, Ernest J. | 5/94 Assoc. Mem. |
| Spindler, Oscar | 4/96 Assoc. Mem. |
| Spitzer, Maurice | 1921 |
| Spitznagel, Harold T. | 1928 |
| Sponholz, W. C. | 1922 |
| Springer, Chas. E. | 3/04 |
| Stander, Adolph | 3/00 |
| Stanhope, Leon E. | 3/04 |
| Stanton, F. C. H. | 1912 |
| Stark, Chester A. | 1928 |
| Starck, E. F. | 5/95 |
| Starmer, Chas. E. | 1931-32 |
| Starr, Harry C. | 5/95 |
| Stauder, Adolph | 3/01 |
| St. Clair, C. T. | 1928 |
| Steele, Harry Y. | 1928 |
| Stege, John D. | 1912 |
| Steigley, Arthur C. | 1912 |
| Stein, Paul | 1925 |
| Steinborn, Edward | 1917 |
| Stermer, Chas. E. | 1930–31 |
| Steward, Claude A. | 1915 |
| Stewart, P. C. | 11/90 |
| Stopa, Walter | 1927 |
| Storey, John | 1924 |
| Story, John | 1927 |
| Strahan, George H. | 11/92 |
| Strandberg, C. Ber | 1930–31 |
| Strelka, Leo | 1922 |
| Strong, B. P. | 1926 |
| Struble, Henry | 3/04 |
| Studor, Erwin | 1924 |
| Sturges, Howard P. | 1921 |
| Sturm, Meyer J. | 3/98 |
| Sturnfield, Charles H. | 1921 |
| Sugarman, L. B. | 1920 |
| Sullivan, Louis H. | 2/92 Hon. Mem. |
| Sullivan, Andrew W. | 1928 |
| Sumarkoff, Leonard P. | 1928 |
| Surmann, J. F.,Jr. | 1911 |
| Sutter, Barnard | 1917 |
| Sutter, J. H. | 1925 |
| Svoboda, A. F. | 1927 |
| Swanson, Arthur P. | 1931–32 |
| Swanson, H. F. | 11/90 |
| Sweet, John E. | 1928 |
| Swenson, Carl | 1910 |
| Swensson, Walter | 1917 |
| Switzer, Robert M. | 1926 |
| Taber, A. R. | 1928 |
| Taft, Lorado | 3/90 Hon. Mem. |
| Taggert, John A. | 1910 |
| Tallmadge, Thomas E. | 3/01 |
| Taylor, Edward P. | 3/99 |
| Taylor, Edward L. | 3/00 |
| Taylor, Howell | 1921 |
| Takylor, H. Walter | 1929 |
| Taylor, Victor F. | 3/04 |
| Teich, Frederick J. | 1921 |
| Teisen, Axel V. | 1921 |
| Thisslew, Charles | 1921 |
| Thomas, H. S. | 4/96 |
| Thomas, E. T. | 1913 |
| Thompkins, Albert S. | 1930–31 |
| Thompson, George D. | 1928 |
| Thompson, Harold | 1927 |
| Thompson, Magnus | 1928 |
| Thompson, Le Roy W. | 1926 |
| Thomson, H. C. | 1911 |
| Tomlinson, H. W. | 3/98 |
| Thomsen, F. T. | 1921 |
| Thomsen, Wm. F. | 1925 |
| Thorud, Bet M. | 1921 |
| Ticknor, James H. | 1921 |
| Timm, Paul | 1925 |
| Torgenson, Henry | 3/98 Assoc. Member |
| Torrance, James B. | 3/04 |
| Tourtelotte, Ralph N. | 1925 |
| Tracey, Chas. A. | 5/94 Assoc. Mem. |
| Traphagen, O. G. | 12/92 Assoc. Mem. |
| Traube, George F | 1928 |
| Trautretter, J. W. | 1928 |
| Traxler, Victor | 5/95 |
| Treat, Samuel A. | 5/95 |
| Troast, S. A. | 12/89 |
| Trost, H. C. | 12/88 |
| Trow, R. C. | 1925 |
| Trowbridge, C. V. | 12/92 |
| Trowbridge, C. W. | 12/85 |
| Tucker, C. S. | 1928 |
| Tumbleson, A. T. | 1923 |
| Turner, J. W. | 1921 |
| Turner, R. M. | 10/86 |
| Tuttle, A. B. | 1908 |
| Twose, Geo. M. R. | 3/99 |
| Twyman, Joseph | 3/00 Assoc. Mem. |
| Tyson, Arthur | 1928 |
| Ueberroth, Otto V. | 1917 |
| Uffendell, Wm. G. | 1908 |
| Uhrie, L. J. | 1931–32 |
| Ullman, Henry | 3/99 Assoc. Mem. |
| Unverzagt, Arthur G. | 4/02 |
| Upman, Frank | 4/96 |
| Van Balen, John C. | 1928 |
| Van Bergen, John S. | 1922 |
| Van Dort, G. Broes | 1925 |
| Vance, Lyle | 1911 |
| Van den Berghen, A. L. | 4/96 Assoc. Mem. |
| Van Dort, G. Broes | 3/98 Assoc. Mem. |
| Van Inwagen, Jas., Jr | 3/01 Assoc. Mem. |
| Van Kirk, Sidney | 1929 |
| Vennetti, Charles H. | 1928 |
| Venning, Frank | 1908 |
| Verity, Geo. W. | 1906 |
| Vesley, Wm. J. | 1920 |
| Vibelius, Fred N. | 1929 |
| Viehe-Naess, Ivar | 1921 |
| Viscarrielo, Vincent | 1929 |
| Vitzthum, Karl M. | 1921 |
| Voelker, William H. | 1916 |
| Vogel, L. C. | 1909 |
| Volens, N. | 1913 |
| Vollert, Harold | 1930–31 |
| von Gunten, O. | 1912 |
| von Holst, Herman. V. | 3/97 |
| von Rosen, Chas. | 3/06 |
| Vrooman, Geo. | 1911 |
| Wagner, Fritz, Sr. | 2/92 Hon. Mem. |
| Wagner, Fritz, Jr. | 1909 Hon. Mem. |
| Wagner, Ernest J. | 10/86 |
| Wagner, H. V. | 10/86 |
| Waid, D. E. | 4/96 |
| Wakeness, Leonard | 1921 |
| Walcott, Chester H. | 1906 |
| Walker, Frank C. | 4/04 |
| Walker, William E. | 3/04 |
| Wall, R. J. | 1921 |
| Wallace, M. R. | 1920 |
| Wallden, Elmer F. | 1923 |
| Wallsworth, Allan G. | 1927 |
| Walsh, Robert A. | 1928 |
| Wamness, Leonard | 1919 |
| Wandell, Ivar | 1915 |
| Warine, J. T. | 3/85 Charter Mem. |
| Warren, Clinton J. | 2/92 Assoc. Mem. |
| Warren, George E. | 1918 |
| Waterman, Harry H. | 3/04 |
| Watson, George E. | 5/94 Assoc. Mem. |
| Watson, J. Nelson | 3/00 |
| Watson, Robert Bruce | 3/00 |
| Watson, Vernon | 3/01 Assoc. Mem. |
| Waxelberger, J. | 1/86 |
| Weary, Edwin D. | 3/00 Assoc. Mem. |
| Weaver, Roy | 1924 |
| Weber, Alfred P. | 1921 |
| Weber, Arthur M. | 1928 |
| Weber, Peter J. | 12/91 |
| Weber, Robert F. | 1929 |
| Webber, A. M. | 1921 |
| Webster, Maurice | 1921 |
| Wechselberger, J. | 4/86 |
| Weich, Peter J. | 1923 |
| Weinper, B. V. | 1930–31 |
| Weirick, Ralph | 3/01 |
| Weiss, Edw. W. | 1922 |
| Weiss, John W. | 1906 |
| Welling, Frank P. | 1911 |
| Wells, Frederick | 1912 |
| Wells, William A. | 3/99 |
| Wendland, William R. | 3/99 |
| Wenisch, W. F. | 1917 |

| | |
|---|---|
| Wentworth, John | 1916 |
| Werenskjold, Ralph | 1911 |
| Wheelock, Harry B. | 3/85 Charter Mem. |
| White, Charles E. | 1911 |
| White, F. C. | 1910 |
| White, Howard J. | 1921 |
| White, J. A. | 3/97 Assoc. Mem. |
| White, James M. | 1921 |
| White, Melville P. | 3/00 |
| Whitehouse, Francis | 12/92 Assoc. Mem. |
| Whittlesey, Charles F. | 12/88 |
| Wiemz, A. C. | 3/89 |
| Wiener, Jerome L. | 1915 |
| Wieneke, Geo. F. | 1920 |
| Wiersba, Alwin | 1921 |
| Wilcox, A. L. | 3/99 |
| Wilder, Edward T. | 5/95 |
| Wilkins, S. W. | 1920 |
| Wilkinson, F. H. | 1925 |
| Wilkinson, L. E. | 1908 |
| Wilkinson, L. C. | 1909 |
| Willatzen, Andrew | 4/05 |
| Willatzen, C. P. | 1904 |
| Willett, James R. | 2/92 Assoc. Mem. |
| Williams, Paul G. | 1917 |
| Williams, Theo. S. | 1912 |
| Williamson, J. C. | 12/89 |
| Williamson, Robert B. | 7/86 |
| Williamson, Wm. G. | 1885 Charter Mem. |
| Willis, H. S. | 1910 |
| Wilmanns, August C. | 4/96 |
| Wilson, Horatio R. | 3/04 |
| Wilson, Joseph W. | 4/05 |
| Winiarski, M. F. | 1922 |
| Winslow, Benjamin E. | 3/04 |
| Winslow, Carleton M. | 3/99 |
| Wirt, Frederick B. | 3/04 |
| Wirts, Stephen M. | 2/92 |
| Wittekind, Henry W. | 3/97 |
| Walcott, Chester H. | 1908 |
| Wolfarth, William | 3/04 |
| Wolff, Rudolph | 1911 |
| Woltersdolf, Arthur | 5/94 |
| Wood, Frank Elmer | 1928 |
| Wood, Richard | 7/86 |
| Woods, John R. | 3/04 |
| Woodman, Andrew | 1908 |
| Woodyatt, Ernest | 3/04 |
| Woolson, Theron | 1920 |
| Work, R. G. | 3/97 |
| Work, Robert | 1921 |
| Wright, Clark C. | 3/03 |
| Wright, Wm. C. | 1920 |
| Wuehrmann, Wm. G. | 1910 |
| Wyles, Thomas R. | 3/99 |
| Wyman, A. D. | 1905 |
| Yardley, Ralph W. | 1921 |
| Yerkes, Waren F. | 1923 |
| Yetter, Paul L. | 1928 |
| York, John D. | 4/05 |
| Young, Hugo | 1909 |
| Young, Leo | 1926 |
| Youngburg, John E. | 1921 |
| Youngburg, J. E. | 11/90 |
| Zakharoff, Alexis A. | 1923 |
| Zelenka, Anthony J. | 1924 |
| Zettel, John | 4/94 |
| Ziegle, Adolph E. | 1925 |
| Zimmerman, Alfred | 4/96 |
| Zimmerman, Hugo H. | 3/00 |
| Zimmerman, Ralph | 1921 |
| Zimmerman, William | 3/85 Charter Mem. |
| Zumkeller, Rev. Emil | 1926 |

| Club Events | Concurrent Events | Officers |
|---|---|---|
| *1857* | American Institute of Architects established | |
| *1859* | Illinois Chapter of the American Institute of Architects chartered | |
| *1863* | École des Beaux-Arts established basic teaching method | |
| *1865* | Course work in architecture at MIT | |
| *1867* | Boston Society of Architects founded | |
| *1868* | Course work in architecture at the University of Illinois | |
| *1871* | The Chicago Fire destroys a major portion of the business district | |
| | Course work in architecture at Cornell University | |
| *1873* | University of Illinois establishes Department of Architecture | |
| | Nathan C. Ricker receives first architectural degree in the United States at Illinois and inaugurates the architecture program | |
| | *Architectural Sketchbook* founded by Osgood | |
| | Course work in architecture at Syracuse University | |
| *1876* | *American Architect and Building News* founded by Osgood | |
| *1880* | Architectural Sketch Club of New York founded | |
| *1881* | P. B. Wight starts "fireproof" company to produce fireproof tiles | |
| | Architectural League of New York founded | |
| | Course work in architectur at Columbia University | |
| | *Inland Architect and Builder* launched | |
| *1883* | Western Association of Architects (WWA) organized | |
| *1884* | | |
| | J.B. Carpenter proposes a sketch club in an aricle and letter to *Inland Architect* | |
| | Jenney's Home Insurance building started | |
| **Chapters One & Two** **1885** | Miluakee and Des Moines Sketch Clubs founded | *March 1885* P   Carpenter 1V  Pond, I K 2V  Lawrie S   Williamson T   McLean |
| Chicago Architectural Sketch Club (CASC) organized in March | Illinois State Association of Architects organized with Root as chairman | |
| Meetings held in Builder's Exchange | Illinois Chapter of AIA has first meeting in years | |
| Members Participate in second annual exhibition of the New York Architectural League | Richardson gets commissions for Marshall Field Warehouse, Glessner House, and McVeigh House | *November 1885* P   Lawrie 1V  Beaumont 2V  Carpenter S   Williamson T   Kessel |
| Presentations by Junge, Pond, McLean, Lawrie | S. S. Beman designs Pullman | |

| Club Events | Concurrent Events | Officers | |
|---|---|---|---|
| Bi-weekly meetings started; in-house competitions monthly | Death of H. H. Richardson | *November 1886*<br>P   *Lawrie (resigns)*<br>1V   *Beaumont (becomes President)*<br>2V   *Pond, I.K.*<br>S   *Williamson*<br>T   *Trowbridge* | *Chapter Two*<br>*1886* |
| CASC exhibits with WAA National Convention | CASC shows work at Minnesota Industrial Exposition | | |
| 1st Annual Banquet. (The 1st Annual Exhibition started the following year.) | | | |
| Active program of competitions, presentations, and exhibitions draws press coverage | Inland Architect and Builder becomes *Inland Architect and News Record* | *November 1887*<br>P   *Beaumont*<br>1V   *Kessel*<br>2V   *Mundie*<br>S   *Williamson*<br>T   *Wagner* | *Chapter Three*<br>*1887* |
| Root, Sullivan,and  Jenney agree to judge competitions on regular basis | National AIA convention in Chicago; exhibition features drawings by CASC members | | |
| Root is made an honorary member | Second annual exhibition of Architectural League of New York at Salmagundi Club | | |
| M Fundraising for larger quarters at the Art Institute of Chicago | | | |
| 1st Annual CASC Exhibition | | | |
| New quarters at Art Institute | Sketch clubs formed in Buffalo, Detroit, St. Paul, Rochester, and Atlanta | *November 1888*<br>P   *Williamson*<br>1VP *Mundie*<br>2VP *Christian*<br>S   *Kessell*<br>T   *Wagner* | *1888* |
| Begin assembling CASC Library | Buffalo proposes a national league of clubs | | |
| Start purely social evenings | | | |
| Sullivan suggests more structured "programmes" for competitions | | | |
| Second Annual CASC Exhibition | | | |
| Competitions for Robert Clark Medal and Phimister Medal announced | | | |
| CASC is incorporated | Merger of WAA and national AIA | *November 1889*<br>P  *Mundie\**<br>1VP *Kessell*<br>2VP *Christian*<br>S  *Gibb*<br>T  *Wagner*<br><br>*\*Elected after Williamson declined 2nd term* | *Chapters Four*<br>*1889* |
| Johannes Gelert designs Clark medal | Sketch clubs formed in Boston, Syracuse, Columbus, Minneapolis, St. Louis, New York, Newark, and Denver | | |
| First Clark and Phimister competitions gain national recognition for CASC | Art Institute announces evening architecture classes | | |
| Clark competition, An Apartment House won by Claude Bragdon | By-law change to admit non-residents and to permit members who had become architects to stay in the Club | | |
| Phimister competition, A Public Library, won by T. G. Holyoke | | | |
| Third Annual CASC Exhibition | | | |
| W. B. Mundie wins second Clark competition | Illinois Association of Architects merges with the Illinois Chapter of the AIA | *November 1890*<br>P  *Williamson*<br>1VP *Fraenkel*<br>2VP *Mundie*<br>S  *Gibb*<br>T  *Wagner* | *Chapters Five & Six*<br>*1890* |
| Fourth Annual CASC Exhibition | Congress enacts World's Columbian Exposition Act | | |
| | Jackson Park selected as WCE site | | |
| | University of Pennsylvania architecture program started | | |
| | Minneapolis and San Francisco clubs inaugurated | | |

| Club Events | Concurrent Events | Officers |
|---|---|---|
| **Chapters Five & Six continued**<br>**1891**<br><br>Half of club membership working on WCE under Burnham<br><br>Club moves to Athenaeum<br><br>Budget pressure on the Club<br><br>Adler appointed chairman of Clark competition jury<br><br>Third Clark competition, won by George G. Will<br><br>First proposal for an exhibition catalog<br><br>Fifth Annual CASC Exhibition | Death of John Wellborn Root<br><br>Burnham selects architects for WCE buildings<br><br>Art Institute announces a two-year curriculum, three terms each year for day classes only<br><br>City of Chicago Public Library competition announced as a national competition<br><br>Burnham's office, now directed by Perkins, designs Masonic Temple, Monadnock Block, and Washington Park Refectory | *November 1891*<br>P   Kessell<br>1VP   Kleinpell<br>2VP   Heun<br>S   Youngberg<br>T   Wagner |
| **Chapter Six**<br>**1892**<br><br>Club elects to publish *SKETCHES*, first official catalog, with ad designs required of members<br><br>Root Memorial competition for grave marker won by P. J. Weber<br><br>Fourth Clark competition won by Axel Sandbloom<br><br>Sixth Annual CASC Exhibition | Illinois AIA mounts first annual exhibition at Art Institute with catalog; many drawings by CASC members done for firms.<br><br>Chicago Society of Artists, fourth Annual Black & White exhibition; several CASC members participate | *November 1892*<br>P   Fraenkel<br>1VP   Gibb<br>2VP   Linden<br>S   Garden, Hugh<br>T   Wagner |
| **Chapters Six & Seven**<br>**1893**<br><br>Club begins year in January, not November, due to Fair<br><br>Move to Masonic Temple space in May<br><br>Begin several years of association with Chicago Society of Artists<br><br>Very little data published between March and December after Secretary Edward Garden resigns<br><br>Fifth Clark Competition won by W. Pell Pulis<br><br>No CASC 1893 Exhibition | WCE open from May through October<br><br>Burnham elected AIA National President while simultaneously chairman of the World Congress of Architects<br><br>New Art Institute building completed with space for Chicago School of Architecture (Art Institute & Armour Institute), now a four-year college<br><br>Massive layoffs after work at the Fair; Nationwide depression begins<br><br>Desire Despradelle, from École des Beaux Arts becomes head of MIT Architecture Department | *November 1893*<br>P   Garden, Hugh<br>1VP   Wirts<br>2VP   Schlesinger (resigned)<br>new 2VP   Heun S Garden, Edw. (resigned)<br>new S   Schlesinger (resigned)<br>new S   Dillon<br>T   Wagner |
| **Chapter Seven**<br>**1894**<br><br>Seventh Annual CASC Exhibition in new Art Institute galleries<br><br>First permanent Exhibition catalog published<br><br>Sixth Annual Clark competition won by Willard Hirsh | CASC moves to South Michigan Avenue to share space with Chicago Society of Artists<br><br>Gold Medal offered by Chicago AIA<br><br>Society of Beaux-Arts Architects organized in New York<br><br>Cleveland and Baltimore clubs organized<br><br>Illinois AIA receives large collections of books and photographs including library from France and the "Adams" photo collection<br><br>First Annual Chicago Building Trades & Material Exhibition<br><br>American Academy in Rome organized largely through the efforts of Burnham and McKim | *November 1894*<br>P   Dean<br>1VP   Jensen<br>2VP   Garden, F<br>S   Dillon<br>T   Belden |

| Club Events | Concurrent Events | Officers | |
|---|---|---|---|
| | | | *Chapter Eight* |
| | | | *1895* |
| CASC becomes Chicago Architectural Club (CAC) | Art Institute & Armour Institute merge activities | *October 1895*<br>P   Dean<br>1VP  Schmidt<br>2VP  Hunt<br>S   Garden, F<br>T   Wilder | |
| Eighth Annual Exhibition mixes architects and artists | *Brochure Series* begins publication | | |
| First series of Bohemian nights on alternate Mondays in lieu of formal presentations | Beaux-Arts Institute of Design inaugurated | | |
| | Patton, et al, form Municipal Improvement League | | |
| New Constitution written to admit practicing architects | P. B. Wight reconciles Lake Front plans using Patton's work as a basis | | |
| Elmer C. Jensen wins first Illinois AIA Gold Medal | Perkins designs Steinway Hall; Wright designs Winslow House; Sullivan designs Guarantee Building | | |
| Seventh Annual Clark competition won by A. B. Le Boutillier | | | |
| | Lakefront Park planning becomes a major interest of the business and architectural community of Chicago including CAC | | |
| | Detroit and San Francisco clubs organized a second time | | |
| | | | *Chapters Eight & Nine* |
| | | | *1896* |
| Ninth Annual Exhibition is reviewed by P. B. Wight as best ever; he is concerned with influence of French methods in schools and suggests omitting professional architects from CAC exhibitions | *American Architect & Building News* starts series of competitions for clubs | *October 1896*<br>P    Schmidt<br>1VP  Perkins<br>2VP  Bernhard<br>S   Brown<br>T   Waid | |
| | Chicago members of Illinois AIA press for licensing of architects; architect Nothnagel elected to the State Legislature as advocate | | |
| CAC challenged to address the plan for Lake Front Park | Chicago Architects' Business Association (CABA) formed and eventually becomes largest architectural group in Illinois | | |
| Eighth and final Annual Clark competition won by David G. Meyers | American Luxfer Prism Company formed | | |
| | Providence, RI, and Pittsburgh clubs organized | | |
| | | | *1897* |
| Tenth Annual Exhibition is largest ever held | Chicago Arts & Crafts Society is organized at Hull-House | *October 1897*<br>P   Garden, E<br>   resigned 2/98<br>1VP Kirkpatrick<br>   Became Pres.<br>   2/98<br>1VP Eggebrecht<br>S   Dunning<br>T   Llewellyn | |
| CAC moves from South Michigan to Art Institute club rooms | Licensing law passed in Illinois, first in US | | |
| Several architects offer to act as patrons of CAC following example of the Society of Beaux-Arts | Hunt, Spencer and Wright move into Steinway Hall to share space with Perkins | | |
| F. W. Kirkpatrick becomes CAC president | Wright hired by Luxfer Prism Co as consultant | | |
| | Business depression continues with new office buildings a drag on the market | | |
| | Washington, DC, club organized | | |
| | First exhibition of the American Academy in Rome shown in Chicago | | |

| Club Events | Concurrent Events | Officers |
|---|---|---|
| **Chapters Nine & Ten**<br>**1898**<br><br>Eleventh Annual Exhibition held jointly with Arts & Crafts Society<br><br>1st Projet (Group) Drawings exhibited<br><br>Kirkpatrick reorganizes CAC<br><br>First syllabus published in several years | The 18/Deipnosophists/Committee on the Universe regularly meeting<br><br>Luxfer Prism Company announces national competition with Wright as consultant<br><br>Notre Dame establishes School of Architecture<br><br>Springfield, MA, club organized<br><br>Illinois AIA moves to Art Institute | *October 1898*<br>*P    Llewellyn*<br>*1VP  Zimmermann*<br>*2VP  Holsman*<br>*S     Dunning*<br>*T     Wilmanns* |
| **Chapter Eleven**<br>**1899**<br><br>Twelfth Annual Exhibition—Dean's essay in catalog outlines plans for Architectural League of America<br><br>Sullivan speaks on Principles of Architectural Design<br><br>Lakefront Park design competition announced | W. B. Griffin graduates from U of Illinois and joins Perkins, et al, in Steinway Hall<br><br>Architectural League of America (ALA) organized in Cleveland<br><br>Sullivan's essay "The Modern Phase of Architecture" read at ALA convention<br><br>Ohio State establishes School of Architecture<br><br>Toronto club organized | *October 1899*<br>*P    Llewellyn*<br>*1VP  Spencer*<br>*2VP  Holsman*<br>*S     Long*<br>*T     Wilmanns* |
| **1900**<br><br>Thirteenth Annual Exhibition<br><br>CAC now directing activity toward civic affairs; offers design of shelters & playground to Park District<br><br>Exhibition includes NY "Tenement House Exhibit," objects by Arts & Crafts Society and Chicago Woman's Club | J. C. Llewellyn new president of ALA<br><br>Chicago building at worst point in 12 years but reverses dramatically at end of year<br><br>Perkins designs University of Chicago Settlement house; Wright and Perkins struggle over Abraham Lincoln Center building<br><br>Burnham starts Marshall Field's store on State Street<br><br>C. R. Ashbee visits Chicago | *October 1900*<br>*P    Holsman*<br>*1VP  Spencer*<br>*2VP  Weber*<br>*S     Long*<br>*T     Bernhard* |
| **Chapter Twelve**<br>**1901**<br><br>Fourteenth Annual Exhibition includes much avant-garde work<br><br>Wright's "Art & Craft of the Machine," first delivered at Hull House, featured in exhibition catalog<br><br>First Annual Traveling Scholarship won by N. Max Dunning<br><br>Constitution rewritten | Sullivan's "Kindergarten Chats" published in *Interstate Architect and Builder*<br><br>Wright's designs for "A Home in a Prairie Town" and "A Small House with Lots of Room in It" published in *Ladies Home Journal* and exhibited widely<br><br>University of Illinois, Kansas City, and San Francisco (3rd time) organize clubs<br><br>Third Annual ALA Convention held in Philadelphia<br><br>Chicago's "Lakefront Park" becomes "Grant Park" | *May 1901*<br>*P    Spencer*<br>*1VP  Lorch*<br>*2VP  Hemmings*<br>*S     Phillips*<br>*T     Bernhard* |

| Club Events | Concurrent Events | Officers |
|---|---|---|
| | | *1902* |
| Fifteenth Annual Exhibition dominated by emerging Prairie School architects | Fourth Annual Architectural League of America convention in Toronto; Chicago's influence is superseded by Eastern architects | *May 1902*<br>*P Brown*<br>*1VP Edbrooke*<br>*2VP Beauley* |
| Traditionalist members of CAC satirize by mounting a "Gallery of Grotesque" | Despradelle's enormous drawings dominate the annual exhibition, but this influence is short lived | *S Benedict (resigned)*<br>*S Jenkins*<br>*T Starr* |
| New slate of officers elected after Exhibition ensures traditional architects will be represented in next exhibit | | |
| John H. Philips wins second Annual Traveling Scholarship | | |
| | | *Chapter Thirteen* |
| Sixteenth Annual Exhibition returns to traditional designs | Marshall Field offers $10 million for museum on lakefront | *1903* |
| CAC invited to participate in Society of Beaux-Arts competitions | Burnham wants museum in Grant Park | *May 1903*<br>*P Fellows*<br>*1VP Hamilton* |
| Burch Burdett Long wins third Annual Traveling Scholarship | P. B. Wight is the prime proponent of free space on the lake front | *2VP Tallmadge*<br>*S Hyland*<br>*T Starr (resigned)* |
| | Olmsted Brothers receive basic data for lake front design from Burnham | *T Nelson* |
| | City Club of Chicago organized | |
| | Fifth Annual ALA convention in St. Louis | |
| | | *Chapters Thirteen & Fourteen* |
| Seventeeth Annual Exhibition; work on Grant Park by numerous CAC members dominates the show | McLean leaves editorship of *Inland Architect* in Chicago to be editor of *Western Architect* in Minneapolis | *1904* |
| "Salon des Refusées" mounted by moderns at Riverside | No ALA Convention | *May 1904*<br>*P Hamilton*<br>*1VP Wittekind* |
| Perkins prepares report to establish the Forest Preserve District; he and ten others prepare a plan to relieve the congestion of downtown Chicago. | Washington University (St Louis) and University of California establish architectural schools | *2VP Marsh*<br>*S Pattison*<br>*T Nelson* |
| Second eviction of CAC from the Art Institute | Twin City Architectural Club organized | |
| Club moves to Dexter Building | Burnham/Olmsted plans for museum in Grant Park continue to be controversial | |
| CAC officers establish stability for rest of decade Thomas E. Tallmadge wins the fourth Annual Traveling Scholarship | | |

| | Club Events | Concurrent Events | Officers |
|---|---|---|---|
| **Chapter Fourteen** | | | |
| **1905** | Eighteenth Annual Exhbition | Sixth Annual ALA convention in Pittsburgh | |
| | C. Herrick Hammond wins fifth Annual Traveling Scholarsip | Chicago officers elected at ALA; representatives recommend member clubs establish ateliers based on the Beaux-Arts system | *May 1905*<br>*P    Nelson*<br>*1VP Pattison*<br>*2VP Silha* |
| | CAC in good financial shape | Holden atelier (short lived) established in Chicago | *S    Kable*<br>*T    Denslow* |
| | Pen and ink and watercolor classes encouraged; concern that this skill has been lost in the last sixteen years | Carnegie Institute establishes an architectural school | |
| **1906** | Nineteenth Annual Exhibition with many Eastern jurors; half of entries from outside Chicago | Wright exhibits Japanese prints at the Art Institute in a room adjacent to the CAC Exhibition | *May 1906*<br>*P    Alschuler*<br>*1VP Mahler* |
| | Herbert Green wins the sixth Annual (three-stage) Traveling Scholarship | Architectural League Annual published; key element in spreading avant-garde beyond the Midwest | *2VP Hyland*<br>*S    Wilson*<br>*T    Brush* |
| | | Burnham agrees to prepare a Plan of Chicago; enlists Bennett as assistant | |
| | | University of Michigan establishes an architectural school | |
| | | Los Angeles Club organized | |
| | | Seventh Annual ALA convention in New York | |
| **1907** | Twentieth Annual Exhibition reduces work shown by non-Chicagoans | McLean concerned that Chicago concentrates on small matters, not beautification of the City | *May 1907*<br>*P    von Holt*<br>*1VP Hammond* |
| | Exhibition not widely reviewed except for Wright rooms by Harriet Monroe | Alabama Polytechnic establishes architectural progam | *2VP Green*<br>*S    Zimmermann*<br>*T    Silha* |
| | Will Reichert wins seventh Annual Traveling Scholarship | Portland, OR and North Carolina organize architectural clubs | |
| | | Twin City Club splits into separate clubs in St. Paul and Minneapolis | |
| **1908** | Twenty-first Annual Exhibition installed in setting designed by Wright for Japanese prints | CAC, Illinois Architects Business Association and Illinois AIA invite Ashbee to Chicago a second time | *May 1908*<br>*P    Hammonnd*<br>*1VP Naramore* |
| | Municipal Art League exhibit overlaps CAC exhibit | Tenth ALA convention in Detroit; ALA now exists essentially only on paper; last Annual, mostly work from East | *2VP Reichert*<br>*S    Lowe*<br>*T    Haagen* |
| | George Aswumb wins eighth Annual Traveling Scholarship | McLean pans CAC in *Western Architect* for criticizing Burnham's Lake Front plan | |
| | | Georgia Tech and Tulane establish architecture programs | |
| | | Columbus, OH, and Wilmington, DE, establish clubs | |

| Club Events | Concurrent Events | Officers | |
|---|---|---|---|
| | | | *1909* |
| Twenty-second Annual Exhibition; 40 percent of entries from outside Chicago; includes Atelier Bennett | Illinois AIA re-establishes Gold Medal for CAC exhibition | *May 1909*<br>P    Lowe<br>VP  Talmadge<br>S    Haagen<br>T    Nettenstrom | |
| CAC has "patron of the Atelier" as an officer | Marshall & Fox's Blackstone Hotel completed | | |
| Future atelier work in Chicago is loosely connected with CAC; atelier facilities in club open around the clock | *Plan of Chicago* unveiled<br><br>University of Texas establishes architectural program | | |
| Hugh Dunning wins ninth Annual Traveling Fellowship | Seattle organizes a club | | |
| | Milwaukee Club splits into Architectural Association and Draftsman's Club | | |
| | CAC participates in first Minneapolis exhibition | | |
| | | | *1910* |
| Twenty-third Annual Exhibition | Chicago Board of Education brings unfounded charges against Perkins; he founds successful school design firm | *May 1910*<br>P      Gillette<br>1VP  Marx<br>2VP  Ingram<br>S      Ridley<br>T      Levings | |
| CAC generally accepted as the most important architectural Association in Chicago | | | |
| Clarence J. Brown wins tenth Annual Traveling Scholarship | Art Institute lists 23 art oriented groups meeting in their "clubroom" | | |
| | Holabird & Roche complete Monroe Building | | |
| | Ashbee writes introduction of Wright's Wasmuth portfolio | | *Chapter Fifteen* |
| | South Bend, IN, organizes a club | | *1911* |
| Twenty-fourth Annual Exhibition—large number of skyscrapers and many examples of Prairie School; American Academy in Rome has large number of exhibits | Cass Gilbert proposal for Woolworth Building in New York | *May 1911*<br>P    Gillette<br>VP  Lippincott<br>S    Wuehrmann<br>T    Awsumb | |
| | Griffin designs and builds solid Rock House | | |
| Midpoint of CAC existence begins when virtually all major Chicago architects were then or had been members | Popular press recognizes early modern movement as a new architecture | | |
| Reunion of early CASC/CAC members | Catholic University establishes architectural program | | |
| Entries in competitions more & more parallel to École; influence of Wright's Studio waning | Blackstone Hotel wins Illinois AIA Gold Medal | | |
| W. B. Betts wins eleventh Annual Traveling Scholarship | | | |
| | | | *1912* |
| Twenty-fifth Annual Exhibition; smallest in years; CAC considers abandoning exhibitions | Death of Daniel H. Burnham | *May 1912*<br>P    Silha<br>VP  Surmann<br>S    Wuehrmann<br>T    Awsumb | |
| CAC leaves Dexter building for Art Institute space | Puckey assumes responsibility for the Chicago Atelier, now becoming key element in CAC education efforts | | |
| Arthur C. Hanifin wins 12th Annual Traveling Scholarship | Pond urges local AIA to cooperate more closely with CAC | | |
| | Griffin wins Canberra competition in Australia | | |
| | Architectural Draftsmen of North America organized in Chicago | | |
| | Illinois AIA opposes Greek architectural theme of Lincoln Memorial in Washington | | |

| | Club Events | Concurrent Events | Officers |
|---|---|---|---|

**1913**

*Club Events*

Twenty-sixth Annual Exhibition with catalog dedicated to Burnham; Sullivan has a retrospective room; many avant- garde entries

Armory Show in New York City overlaps both City Club of Chicago's Housing Exhibition and the CAC exhibition

Club suffers as Prairie School coalesces and members devote less time to club affairs

Club begins to lose position as Chicago's most influential architectural organization

R. G. Wolfe wins thirteenth Annual Traveling Scholarship

*Concurrent Events*

Illinois AIA appoints Perkins, et al., to define American architecture/modern design for AIA Journal (never published)

Eleven issues of *The Western Architect* devoted to early modern movement

Interaction with City Club of Chicago, using their facilities; cooperation on several citywide activities

Cliff Dwellers Club used for occasional meetings

City Club of Chicago organizes competition for Development of a Quarter Section of Land

Chicago Architects Business Association changes name to Illinois Society of Architects (ISA)

*Officers*

*May 1913*
P   Awsumb
VP  Wuehrmann
S   Bentley
T   Wagner

## Chapter Sixteen
**1914**

*Club Events*

Twenty-seventh Annual Exhibition sponsored with help of AIA & ISA

Wright is given an entire room at exhibition for his own material; charges of bribery dismissed by Illinois AIA

Harriet Monroe describes Wright as a Secessionist in her reivew

*Concurrent Events*

New Draftsman's organization competes for younger members

World War I begins in Europe; many members of CAC called to active duty

Madison WI organizes club

*Officers*

*May 1914*
P   Awsumb
VP  Llewellyn
S   Brabant
T   Wagner

**1915**

*Club Events*

W. J. Schaeffer wins fourteenth Annual Traveling Scholarship

Twenty-eighth Annual Exhibition, now held jointly with CAC, IL AIA, ISA, & Art Institute thus starting a relationship that would last more than twenty years

Fred M. Hodgdon wins the fifteenth Annual Traveling Scholarship

*Concurrent Events*

Ateliers use "programmes" issued by Beaux-Arts Institute of Design

End of dominance of CAC, now one of three groups of architect-oriented groups in Chicago

Two women win City Club Neighborhood Center competition

Burnham's portrait and others unveiled at Illinois AIA meeting at Cliff Dwellers

AIA and ISA begin regular meetings in the Club Room at the Art Institute

*Officers*

*May 1915*
P   Llewellyn, R
VP  Bentley
S   Brabant
T   Wagner

## Chapter Seventeen
**1916**

*Club Events*

Twenty-ninth Annual Exhibition, one of the few exhibitions photographed in situ; Atelier Puckey exhibits "representing CAC"

École des Beaux Arts becomes the principle source of inspiration for the CAC in its educational efforts through the American organization of École graduates called The Society of Beaux-Arts Institute of Design

Traveling Scholarship cancelled due to war in Europe

*Concurrent Events*

Illinois AIA appoints Perkins, Maher and Woltersdorf as a committee to prepare a "definition" of American architecture

Illinois AIA grows but ISA largest organization in the state; CAC is now the smallest

ISA Monthly Bulletin established

*Officers*

*May 1916*
P   Bentley
VP  Wagner
S   Leavell
T   Stanton

| Club Events | Concurrent Events | Officers | |
|---|---|---|---|
| | | | *1917* |
| Thirtieth Annual Exhibition; Atelier Puckey exhibits "representing CAC" | Wright mounts a major exhibition of Japanese Prints at the Arts Club of Chicago | *May 1917*<br>P   Wagner<br>VP   Leavell<br>S   Franklin<br>T   Stanton | |
| American Traveling Scholarship, sponsored in lieu of the Annual Traveling Scholarship, awarded to Roy Larson | United States enters World War I | | |
| | | | *1918* |
| Thirty-first Annual Exhibition is one of the largest due to the sub-exhibit of "Historic Architecture" by Tallmadge, which takes up an entire gallery | Illinois AIA calls for photographs to document Tallmadge's list of modern buildings | *May 1918*<br>P   Franklin<br>VP   Morphett<br>S   Ashton<br>T   Rognstad | |
| CAC returns to Athenaeum Building | Permanent collection is suggested; now part at the Art Institute, part at the Chicago Historical Society | | |
| Now 91 members, 31 in active service; many stay in France to study at the École after war is over | Rebori, et al, designs for North Michigan development | | |
| No Traveling Scholarship offered | | | |
| | | | *1919* |
| Thirty-second Annual Exhibition features work from the last five years; very little avant garde; many city plans | In a speech to the Illinois AIA, Lorado Taft suggests that the Fine Arts building from the WCE be restored as art museum | *May 1919*<br>P   Morphett<br>VP   Hodgdon<br>S   Fox<br>T   Rognstad | |
| Club Atelier now under Parsons as patron | City Planning becoming a major interest of Chicago Architects | | |
| Traveling Scholarship still on hold | Plans for bridging Chicago River at Michigan Ave are prepared by Rebori | | |
| | | | *1920* |
| Thirty-third Annual Exhibition highlights the Chicago School and Sullivan in particular | Maher writes three major articles each titled "An Indigenous Architecture" | *May 1920*<br>P   Fox<br>VP   Esser, P<br>S   Esser, C<br>T   Rippel | |
| CAC now has the only atelier in Chicago | ISA Monthly Bulletin dedicates page to CAC news | | |
| Club struggles to survive, looks back on seven years of decline; moves to Adventurers' Club | AIA extends blanket invitation to all CAC members to attend chapter meetings | | |
| Pierre Blouke wins twentieth Annual Traveling Scholarship | Architectural League of New York Exhibition material destroyed by fire | | |
| Allied member catagory added to fund Traveling Scholarship | National AIA relaxes rules so more practitioners can participate and become members | | |
| | | | *Chapter Eighteen*<br>*1921* |
| Thirty-fourth Annual Exhibition with painters, sculptors, other groups; no catalog | George Maher begins campaign to restore the WCE Fine Arts Building in Jackson Park | *May 1921*<br>P   Fox<br>VP   Esser, C<br>S   Lindquist Barry, G<br>T   Markle Kane | |
| Resurgence in membership, from 182 to 337 | The third Traveling Exhibition of the Beaux-Arts Institute of Design Medal Awards visits Chicago hosted by CAC | | |
| Atelier speaks "French;" CAC now completely in tune with Beaux-Arts teaching | | | |

| Club Events | Concurrent Events | Officers |
|---|---|---|

**1922**

| Club Events | Concurrent Events | Officers |
|---|---|---|
| Thirty-fifth Annual Exhibition; catalog resumed; East disproportionately represented | Howells & Hood announced as Tribune Tower Competition winner at National AIA convention in Chicago | *May 1922*<br>P  Farrier<br>VP  Barry<br>S  Maraket<br>T  Wiersha |
| Sullivan plates hung | At Cliff Dwellers, members suggest that Sullivan do *An Autobiography of an Idea* and that he prepare plates for *A System of Architectural Ornament*. Funds for the two projects are raised | |
| "Tiny Trib" competition held by CAC in response to Tribune Tower Competition | | |
| CAC resumes publishing programs in advance | | |
| Keith Cheetham wins 22nd Annual Travaeling Scholarship | | |

*Chapter Nineteen*

**1923**

| Club Events | Concurrent Events | Officers |
|---|---|---|
| Thirty-sixth Annual Exhibition; concurrent with Applied Arts exhibit, British architecture, and Tribune Tower competition; not primarily a club function; only modest CAC participation | CAC, AIA, ISA form separate organization, Architectural Exhibition League, to manage exhibitions | *May 1923*<br>P  Blouke<br>VP  McGrath<br>S  Nedved<br>T  Allen |
| Rudolph Nedved wins twenty-third Annual Traveling Scholarship | Sullivan lauds Saarinen's second-place design for Tribune Tower; it has great influence in Chicago | |
| | Rebori works with new "Chicago" atelier with Campbell from Armour | |
| | Chicago Technical College forms Tech Architectural Club | |

**1924**

| Club Events | Concurrent Events | Officers |
|---|---|---|
| Thirty-seventh Annual Exhibition; no longer under CAC control; Sullivan's plates given a prominent location; Hugh Ferris's work exhibited | Sullivan completes both of his books which are published just before his death | *May 1924*<br>P  Nedved, G.<br>VP  Blouke<br>S  Sponholtz<br>T  Allen |
| Ferdinand Eiseman wins 24th Annual Traveling Scholarship | AIA & ISA fund Traveling Scholarship, rules codified | |
| | Glessner agrees to deed his house to Chicago AIA upon his death subject to the architectural community buying and using the Kimball House | |
| | Art Institute demands that Ilinois AIA remove portraits from AIC clubroom, severs relationships with architectural organizations although exhibitions continue | |
| | Concern that the Burnham Library will be forced to move | |
| | Architects Club of Chicago organized | |

*Chapter Twenty*

**1925**

| Club Events | Concurrent Events | Officers |
|---|---|---|
| Thirty-eighth Annual Exhibition in Blackstone Hall at Art Institute | Kimball House renovated by CAC, AIA, ISA | *May 1925*<br>P  Dando<br>VP  Nedved<br>S  Ryan<br>T  Bradbury |
| CAC sponsors Beaux-Arts Ball at Kimball House to raise funds | CAC changes name to the Chicago Architectural Sketch Club (CASC) to avoid confusion with newly established Architects Club of Chicago | |
| Theodore Homeister wins twenty-fifth Annual Traveling Scholarship | | |

| Club Events | Concurrent Events | Officers | |
|---|---|---|---|
| | | | **1926** |
| Thirty-ninth Annual Exhibition; section of exhibition and catalog devoted to French Architect Carlu now at MIT; few exhibits from major offices | ISA decides to hold meetings in the Loop; Palmer appoints committee for site selection for new headquarters | *May 1926*<br>P   *Nedved*<br>VP *Dando*<br>S   *Cerny*<br>T   *Menees* | |
| Kimball Coach House becomes a center of activity for members | Death of George W. Maher | | |
| Frederick Ahlson wins twenty-sixth Annual Traveling Scholarship | Death of Charles E. Fox | | |
| | | | **1927** |
| Fortieth Annual Exhibition; Chicago Technical High Schools show work, Women's Architectural club shows work; Tribune Company exhibits Small Homes Competition; CASC again showing younger members' work; exhibition covered extensively in the press | Women's Architectural Club formed; exhibits with second Women's World's Fair | *May 1927*<br>P   *Nedved, R.*<br>VP *Dando*<br>S   *Cerny*<br>T   *Menees* | |
| | Nelson, Atelier Parsons 1924, wins Paris Prize from the Institute of Beaux-Arts | | |
| Small exhibits of members work held at Kimball House | Chicago AIA Gold Medal awarded to Howells & Hood for the Tribune Tower | | |
| Membership in the Atelier (now Atelier Parson-Adams-Deam) increases dramatically | CSAC begins its own journal, *Treads & Risers* | | |
| T. G. Kronick wins twenty-seventh Annual Traveling Scholarship | | | |
| | | *Chapters Twenty & Twenty-one* | |
| | | | **1928** |
| Forty-first Annual Exhibition; last to be held in the Art Institute; many architectural models shown of various commercial buildings | Codified that CASC president automatically becomes president to Architectural Exhibition League, thus regaining control | *May 1928*<br>P   *Bradbury*<br>VP *Nedved*<br>S   *Booton*<br>T   *Menees* | |
| First Annual Exhibition of the Architects Club of Chicago | Last Club column in ISA Bulletin | | |
| CASC sponsors Paris École Drawing Exhibit | Last year before the Depression has major effect on club | | |
| Louis Pirola wins twenty-eighth Annual Traveling Scholarship | ISA forwards money for Annual Traveling competition but says CASC must have authority from the Society | | |
| | | *Chapter Twenty-one* | |
| | | | **1929** |
| Forty-second Annual Exhibition; at Arts Club; no illustrated catalog | Women's Architectural Club now meeting regularly Tacoma building demolished; AISC does a "forensic" examination of the steel frame to confirm that it actually was a "skyscraper" | *May 1929*<br>P   *Bradbury*<br>VP *Anderson*<br>S   *Baldwin*<br>T   *Menees* | |
| Tallmadge model of monument for grave of Sullivan exhibited | | | |
| Albert Eiseman Jr wins twenty-ninth Annual Traveling Scholarship | Stock Market crashes | | |
| | Death of Birch Burdette Long | | |
| | | | **1930** |
| Forty-third Annual Exhibition held at Arts Club | Adler Planetarium built | *May 1930*<br>P   *Baldwin*<br>VP *Hofmeister*<br>S   *Nedved, R.* | |
| Second exhibition of architects' and craftsmen's work at Kimball House | Wright delivers six Princeton Kahn lectures, later published; his exhibit tours nationally | | |
| Alexander Bacci wins thirtieth Annual Traveling Scholarship | | | |

|  | Club Events | Concurrent Events | Officers |
|---|---|---|---|
| **1931** | Forty-fourth Annual Exhibition<br><br>CASC Atelier submitting an average of forty problems to New York for each problem issued by the Beaux Arts Institute of Design<br><br>Albert de Long wins thirty-first Annual Traveling Fellowship funded by W. K. Fellows | *Treads & Risers* ceases publication<br><br>More than fifty members work on the Century of Progress Fair<br><br>Architects Club of Chicago takes collection for General Relief Fund<br><br>Adler Planetarium wins AIA Gold Medal | *May 1931*<br>P   Baldwin<br>VP  Nedved, G<br>S   Rund<br>T   Menees |
| **1932** | No Annual Exhibition for first time<br><br>Sketch Club sponsoring more smaller events at the Clubhouse, largely social<br><br>Last Traveling Scholarship awarded to R. Benedict Brout | Women's Architectural Club holding 2 meetings per month including competitions<br><br>Chicago architects' work shown at the Museum of Modern Art<br><br>Death of Mrs. John Glessner<br><br>Architects Club of Chicago sponsors variety of events to attract members | *May 1932*<br>P   Pirola<br>VP  Baldwin<br>S   Mulig<br>T   Thomsen |
| **1933** | Exhibition space provided to Club at 1933 World's Fair; Chicago; Architectural Exhibition League is manned by CASC but no exhibit mounted<br><br>Few events sponsored, number of members shrinks, no work after Fair opens | Century of Progress (World's Fair) opens<br><br>Sullivan's work shown at Burnham Libary | *May 1933*<br>P   Gross<br>S   Mulig |
| **1934** | No interest at repeat Exhibition at 1933-34 World's Fair<br><br>Chicago Architectural Sketch Club changes name back to Chicago Architectural Club | Architects Club of Chicago in dire straights, because of a great shortfall in income and few meetings of ISA or AIA at Kimball House | *Officers from 1933 reelected* |
| **1935** | No Annual Exhibition<br><br>No Traveling Scholarship | CAC participates in last competition sponsored by Architects Club, a Club bookplate for the library<br><br>Kimball House essentially abandoned by all but CAC | *May 1935*<br>P   Gross<br>VP  Young<br>S   Mulig<br>T   McPherson |
| **1936** | No Annual Exhibition<br><br>No Traveling Scholarship<br><br>CAC essentially the only (occasional) user of Kimball House | Death of John Glessner dies<br><br>Glessner House a gift to Chicago AIA; 3 societies (AIA, ISA & CAC) are broke and unable to accept the House due to back taxes on Kimball House, maintenance & preference for the Loop as a meeting location; therefore offer rejected<br><br>Mies van der Rohe invited to Armour Institute by Search committee seeking new director of the Department of Architecture | *Officers continue in place* |

| Club Events | Concurrent Events | Officers | |
|---|---|---|---|
| | | | *1937* |
| No Annual Exhibition | New Bauhaus makes use of Kimball coach house but does not use teaching methods of Atelier. Soon moves to Marshall field House a few doors south of Kimball | *May 1937* | |
| No Traveling Scholarship | | *P   Mulig* | |
| | | *S   Berbiera* | |
| Rooms advertised for rent to architects at the Kimball | | *T   McPherson* | |
| | Chicago Chapter AIA formally gives up deed to Glessner House | | |
| Le Corbusier speaks at joint meeting of Chicago Architects at Kimball House | | | |
| | Mies accepts position at Armour, works on new curriculum | | |
| | | | *1938* |
| No Annual Exhibition | Mies meets with Armour Institute faculty and others regarding transition to his new program | *May 1938* | |
| | | *P   Mulig* | |
| No Traveling Scholarship | | *S   Rodde* | |
| | At formal dinner welcoming Mies, Wright rebukes architectural community for its lack of understanding the need for new education techniques. He closes by "giving" Mies to Chicago | *T   Anderson* | |
| | Art Institute mounts exhibition of Mies's work | | |
| | Armour Institute acquires Glessner House | | |
| | | | *1939* |
| No Annual Exhibition | Architects Club of Chicago moves to Fine Arts building on Michigan Avenue | *May 1939* | |
| | | *P   Gross* | |
| No Traveling Scholarship | | *S   Van Balen* | |
| | Chicago AIA portrait collection moved from Kimball House to storage | *T   Anderson* | |
| | M World War II under way in Europe | | |
| | | | *1940* |
| Chicago Architectural Club opens new quarters in the Merchandise Mart | Chicago Architectural Club moves to the Merchandise Mart but is unable to maintain itself as an active organization* | *May 1940* | |
| | | *P   Gross* | |
| | | *S   Van Balen* | |
| | | *T   Anderson* | |

*After 1940, the club carried on until 1964 but only in a superficial manner. About ten members, headed by Ralph Gross, Louis Pirola, and Albert Eiseman held the primary offices during this period. The Chicago Architectural Club formally dissolved on November 14, 1967 after failing to file any annual reports after 1965.

# Bibliographic Note and Acknowledgments

The sources used in compiling information for this study were extensive and essentially all are dealt with in the footnotes. A complete bibliography would be of little further value, since many references are to brief anonymous articles. During our research it became clear that few scholars have addressed architectural clubs in general, or the Chicago Architectural Club in particular, and the impact that these largely amateur groups wielded on the profession in the late nineteenth and early twentieth centuries.

While no previously published book covers the Chicago Architectural Club in detail, there are a few works to which I am especially indebted. Background data was first brought to my attention by Siegfried Giedeon in his *Space, Time and Architecture,* followed by *The Chicago School of Architecture* by my colleague Carl Condit. It was Condit who pointed me toward the work of younger architects in Chicago. His own interests were directed at a few of the great figures of the early Chicago school of architecture, particularly those of the late nineteenth century. Condit was quick to acknowledge that much of the work of these architects owed a good deal to their young colleagues who spent their days over drawing boards developing and refining the designs of their firms' principals. After Condit came H. Allen Brooks, whose *The Prairie School; Frank Lloyd Wright and His Midwest Contemporaries.* Brooks's book covers much of the same era as my own, but from a different point of view. Finally, there is one more recently issued study that deserves note; *From Craft to Profession: The Practice of Architecture in Nineteenth-Century America,* by Mary N. Woods, is an excellent prelude to this volume. None of these books has covered the ground addressed here before, but I am indebted to each of these authors for setting a standard of excellence in scholarship, interest and readability, which I hope has been equaled in my work.

My basic training in research and writing was acquired while my wife and I edited and published *The Prairie School Review.* The *Review* was devoted to the work of Louis Sullivan, Frank Lloyd Wright, and others of similar but less known accomplishments. During the fourteen years we published the *Review,* we collected an impressive amount of reference material and became adept at using it. Much of what we did was related in some manner to the work of members of the Chicago Architectural Club. The last issue of *The Prairie School Review* was issued in 1981, at about the time my interest in the Chicago Architectural Club began in earnest.

The initial work on this study began in 1979 when Stanley Tigerman asked me to present a brief lecture to the first meeting of the newly reconstituted Chicago Architectural Club. That presentation was taped and I later edited it into an article for the first issue of *The Chicago Architectural Journal* in 1981. The manuscript was laid aside and little additional work was done until I retired from fulltime architectural practice at the end of 1996. At the suggestion of my wife, Marilyn Hasbrouck, who certainly was the inspiration for, if not the coauthor of this book, the present work was started. Two grants from the Graham Foundation in Chicago, which covered the cost of travel and data assembly throughout the United States, were a great help.

My initial expectation was that the writing would be done in a year. I assumed that the majority of information would be found in the *Inland Architect*, an important journal of architecture published in Chicago between 1883 and 1908. It was critical, but certainly not the only source regarding the Chicago Architectural Club. In the early days, the *Inland Architect* published the minutes of every meeting of the club. When a report of the first year's activities was published in December of 1885, it was noted that the club was grateful for the publicity accorded them by the *Inland Architect,* but also by the *Building Budget*, and the *Sanitary Engineer.* This prompted a review of not only those, but every journal of architecture published in the United States during the late nineteenth and early twentieth centuries. There were many, and nearly all included information regarding the Chicago Architectural Club. This was primarily because the club distributed minutes to the press after every meeting, a practice that continued until the onset of World War II. Not only did the various journals publish the activities of the club, they also included illustrations of the work of its members. Line drawings in particular were often printed, sometimes the only record of extraordinary work. It remained only to be mined by patient search.

In addition to the journals of architecture published during the life of the Chicago Architectural Club, another source was simply indispensable. From its inception, the Chicago Architectural Club sponsored an annual exhibition of the work of its members and others with a catalog that named the exhibitors and usually included illustrations. The first six catalogs are often referred to, but none have surfaced after extensive research. (It is assumed that they were simply lists that were not intended to be saved.) There were no catalogs in 1892 or 1893, probably because of the World's Columbian Exposition. In 1893 the club did issue *Sketches,* which was actually a compilation of selected drawings done by members over a period of several years. In 1894 the club issued its *Catalogue of the Seventh Annual Exhibition,* the first catalog that survived and can be found in various libraries throughout the United States. After that a catalog of some sort, often elaborate but sometimes scant, was issued every year until 1931. I am fortunate to own a complete set of these publications and have drawn extensively from them in preparing this work.

Finally, there are two other sources of printed data that were essential to the completion of this book. The first was the *Handbook for Architects and Builders,* which was published by the Chicago Architects' Business Association, predecessor to the Illinois Society of Architects, between 1898 and 1938 missing only five years during the depths of the Great Depression. A complete list of club members was included every year from 1904 through 1932. The same organization published a monthly bulletin beginning in 1916, and after August of 1920 gave the Chicago Architectural Club a page in each issue, this proved to be an excellent record of club activities.

The sources named above were all essential to the assembly of the material needed for an understanding of the Chicago Architectural Club. They, and too many others to name, were located in widely dispersed libraries. The assistance of the staff of these institutions was invaluable. Most are identified in the footnotes and the source list that follows, but a few merit special note. It would have been impossible to mine the data we needed without the staff assistance and collections now in Chicago at the Harold Washington Library, the Newberry Library, and the University of Illinois campus libraries both in Chicago and Champaign, Illinois. The Center for Research Libraries and the John Crerar Library, both on the University of Chicago campus, were extremely important, as was the Northwestern University Library in Evanston, Illinois. The Chicago Historical Society's research center has collected material concerning Chicago's architecture for many years, and it was made available to me. Finally, no one could possibly do research of this kind without the collections and staff at the Ryerson and Burnham Libraries at the Art Institute of Chicago, where librarian Jack Brown is both knowledgeable and helpful; he was always willing to review my progress and suggest further areas of research. He continues to maintain an extraordinary scrapbook collection of clippings concerning activities at the Art Institute of Chicago, a practice that began in the nineteenth century. Much of the material, now on microfilm, pertains to the Chicago Architectural Club and related activities. Along with this is an unsurpassed collection of photographs relating to Chicago architects and architecture. All the staff at the library were courteous and helpful but I cannot forget Susan Perry, whose knowledge and pleasant assistance was always available.

We were fortunate in that other libraries throughout the United States were always ready to help. One of our earliest visits was to St. Louis, where the Public Library has one of the great collections of architectural material, including several key items we needed. The same can be said for the Missouri Historical Society, also in St. Louis. We had access to the architectural archives at the University of Minnesota, where Alan Lathrop helped us to find material not available elsewhere. The Milwaukee County Historical Society was also useful. A trip to the East Coast found incredible archives at the Boston Society of Architects and at the AIA Library in Washington, D. C. In New York we found important information in the Avery Library at Columbia University and material regarding Irving K. Pond at the American Academy of Art. More Pond material, much regarding the CAC, was found at the Bentley Library at the University of Michigan in Ann Arbor.

Finally, I am eternally indebted to several people who have read all or part of my manuscript and discussed it with me at length. Professor Emeritus Paul E. Sprague (University of Wisconsin) read the text at an early stage and his erudite comments have made it better at every step of the way. John Zukowsky, then the John Bryan Curator of Architecture at the Art Institute of Chicago, read substantial portions of the manuscript and made important suggestions. Professor Emeritus Franz Schultz (Lake Forest College) and Professor Emeritus Stuart Cohen, FAIA, (University of Illinois in Chicago) both reviewed the manuscript and offered useful suggestions, as did Professor David T. Van Zanten (Northwestern University). Stanley Tigerman read the manuscript and very kindly agreed to prepare the Epilogue.

An initial computer-generated layout of the entire book was prepared by my designer son, John W. Hasbrouck, whose skill in such matters never ceases to amaze me. This work provided a basic framework, which was a great help to all concerned. John also made the scans of all the illustrations and his comments have made the final appearance of the book far more satisfactory. My architect son,

Charles R. Hasbrouck, patiently listened to my discussion of progress and when I needed help, he loaned me a young man from his office to prepare drawings needed for the book. Charles and Susan Dinko Hasbrouck also gave us grandson Benjamin Wil Hasbrouck, who has been my loyal, unquestioning supporter in all things for what amounts to most of his life. Perhaps I can one day return the favor. There is, of course, no one who deserves more credit for this work than my wife, Marilyn J. Whittlesey Hasbrouck. With her fulltime day job as president of the Prairie Avenue Bookshop occupying most of her time during the week, she was always ready to work with me evenings and weekends. She was with me for thousands of hours of conversation, countless visits to libraries and sites of various kinds, and meetings with more potential sources than I can remember. It was she who worked side by side with me to do an initial layout of the book and then do it again when it proved to be, in our judgment, too long. She also prepared the initial draft of the Chronology, which we expect to be critical to the use and understanding of what became a complex book.

In closing, I must thank Gianfranco Monacelli for his confidence in me, which began long before the manuscript was finished. He is fortunate that he has an excellent staff at The Monacelli Press. Advice and assistance was always available from Andrea Monfried and Evan Schoninger, who took our original layout and made it even better. Most notable was my editor, Noel Millea, who made it her goal to make me a better author. To my everlasting gratitude, I think she succeeded. Should there be errors of any sort, they are mine alone. Finally, my sincere thanks go to Elizabeth White, who ultimately assembled all the pieces and put the book in final form. I hope that everyone is as pleased with the result as I am.

**—Wilbert R. Hasbrouck, FAIA**

| Abbreviations | Full name or title of source |
|---|---|
| AA | *American Architect* |
| AABN | *American Architect and Building News* |
| AC | *American Contractor* |
| AIA | American Institute of Architects Library |
| A&B | *Architecture and Building* |
| AIC | Art Institute of Chicago, Ryerson & Burnham Libraries (Inst. Coll.) |
| AIC/CDA | C. D. Arnold collection |
| AIC/DHB | Daniel H. Burnham collection |
| AIC/FR | World's Columbian Exposition "Final Report..." |
| AIC/HALIC | Historic Architectural & Landscape Collection |
| AIC/SC | Sullivania Collection |
| AIC/SSO | Sullivan's System of Ornament Collection |
| ALA | Architectural League of America |
| ARev | *Architectural Review* |
| BB | *Brickbuilder* |
| BHL | Bentley Historical Library |
| B&P | *Brush & Pencil* |
| BS | *Brochure Series* |
| BBU | *Building Budget* |
| BWCE | *Building of the Worlds Columbian Exposition* |
| CD | Cliff Dwellers Club |
| CHB | *Complete Home Builder* |
| CM | *Century Magazine* |
| CRL | Center for Research Libraries |
| CAC | *Chicago Architectural Club (Catalog)* |
| CAEL | *Chicago Architectural Exhibition League (Catalog)* |
| CASC | *Chicago Architectural Sketch Club (Catalog)* |
| CCB | *Chicago Central Business and Office Building Directory* |
| CDN | *Chicago Daily News* |
| CCAL | Chicago Commission on Architectural Landmarks |
| CH | *Chicago Herald* |
| CHS | Chicago Historical Society |
| CPL | Chicago Public Library |
| CSAC | *Chicago School of Architecture Catalog* |
| CT | Crombie Taylor collection |
| CTR | *Chicago Tribune* |
| CLRD | *City Residential Land Development* |
| CW | *Clay Worker* |
| DF | *Decorator and Furnisher* |
| EBR | *Engineering and Building Record* |
| EPL | Edwardsville Public Library |
| ER | *Engineering Record* |
| F. M. Weinstein | Chicago Field Museum |
| FF | *Forms & Fantasies* |
| HAU | Harvard Universitiy Archives |
| HW | *Harper's Weekly* |
| HU | Harvard University Library |
| IA | *Inland Architect [and Builder]* and/or *[and News Record]* |
| ISA | Illinois Society of Architects |
| LO | *Land Owner* |
| MCAA | *Missouri's Contribution to American Architecture* |
| MCHS | Milwaukee County Historical Society |
| MLMW | Collection of Michael Levitin and Meredith Wise/Mendes |
| MofI | *Men of Illinois* |
| MTB | Masonic Temple Promotional Brochure [1891] |
| WMH | Western Missouri Historic Manuscripts Collection-Kansas City |
| NEMMI | New England Manufacturer s and Mechanic s Institute |
| NL | Newberry Library |
| NWA | *Northwestern Architect* |
| NWAA | Northwest Architectural Archives, U of Minnesota |
| NWUA | Northwestern University Archives |
| NYAL | New York Architectural League |
| OHS | Olmsted Historic Site |
| PAB | Prairie Avenue Bookshop |
| PAC | *Pittsburg Architectural Club Catalog* |
| PC | Private Collection |
| PCA | Portland Cement Association |
| PofC | *Plan of Chicago* |
| PSR | *Prairie School Review* |
| RTPC | *Railway Terminal Problem of Chicago* |
| RL | Ricker Library |
| StLAC | *St. Louis Architectural Club Catalog* |
| SBRA | Shepley Bullfinch Richardson & Abbott |
| SN | *Sanitary News* |
| Taliesin | Taliesin Archives |
| TCR | Photograph Courtesy of TCR Corp. Archives |
| UI | University of Illinois Library, Champaign |
| VANR | *H. H. Richardson and His Work*, Van Renssalear |
| WA | *Western Architect* |
| WCEC | *World's Columbian Exposition Official Catalog* |
| WCPR | *World 's Congress/Parliment of Religions* |
| WRH | Collection of the author |
| YANUL | Tom Yanul, Big Shot Photo |

# Index

Note: The "Club" in entries stands for "Chicago Architectural Club." Italic page references indicate illustrations or photographs.

Abraham Lincoln Center, 259, *261*
Adams, Arthur F., 544, 559, 585
Adams, W. Henri, 172
Addams, Jane, 222, 367
Addison, John, 103
Adler, Dankmar, 7, 50, 61, 79, 85, *85*, 90, 106, 115, 116, 124, 126, 138, 143, 147, 156–57, 162, 173, 203, 216, 229, *436*, 438, 523
Adler, David, 465, *505*
Adler, Sidney J., 515
Adler Planetarium, 578, *578*, 585
Adler & Sullivan, 57, 85–86, 123, 131, 156, 185, 214, 478
    office floor plan, *123*
Adler & Work, 504, 553
Adventurers Club, 488, 514, 526
    dining room, *498*
Agriculture Building, *133*
Ahlschlager, Walter W., 465, *467*
Ahlson, Frederick Theodore, 546, 549
    competition design, *546*
Albert, Ernest, 125–26, 169
    drawing of building, *169*
Albricht, E. G., 420
Aldis, Arthur, 495
Alford, William H., 498
Allen, John K., 65, 66, 83
Allen, Lawrence E., 521, 525
Alschuler, Alfred S., 274, 327, 330, 345, 375, 425, 517, *517*, 553
Alvord, John W., 404
American Academy in Rome, 205–8, 432
*American Architect, The*, 197
*American Architect and Builder's Monthly, The*, 30
*American Architect and Building News, The*, 30, 132
*American Architect and News Record, The*, 31
American architecture, 428–29, 451–52, 462, 485–87
*American Builder and Journal of Art, The*, 30
American Express Building (Richardson), *25*
American Federation of Art, 445
American Institute of Architects (AIA), 9–10, 15, 20, 30, 63, 98, 100, 103, 106, 124, 177, 267, 364
    convention and exhibition (1916), 445
    convention banquet, *511*
    convention catalogue cover, *78*
    gold medal, *578*
    *See also* Chicago Chapter of the American Institute of Architects; Illinois Chapter of the American Institute of Architects
American Institute of Steel Construction, 583
American Luxfer Prism Company, 216–22, 242
American Merchants Union Express Company Building, 23

American Radiator Company, 374, 381, 382, 420
American Technical Association, 421
American Terra Cotta and Ceramic Company, 352, 475
American Terra Cotta Company, 349–51
American Traveling Scholarship, 484, 565
Anderson, Edwin F., 580
Anderson, Helmer N., 547
Anderson, Herbert F., 476, 491
Anderson, H. W., 492, 494, 500
Anderson, J. M., competition design, *341*
Anderson, Pierce, 303, 333, 514, 543
Anderson Pressed Brick Company, 41, 44
Anderson Silver Medal, 98, 100
Andrews, Elliot R., 394, 403
Annual Chicago Architectural Exhibition, 63–64, 75–77, 99–100, 167–68, 181–88, 196, 197, 203, 208–9, 223, 229–33, 244, 252, 259, 262, 278, 286, 290, 307–8, 314, 321, 352, 354, 358, 360, 368, 373, 380, 389–90, 392–93, 399, 402, 408, 421, 422–23, 431–32, 439, 444, 445–46, 454–56, 460–61, 467, 468, 474, 478, 483, 492, 494–95, 496–97, 500, 507, 518, 527–28, 535, 541, 548–49, 551–52, 555, 556, 572–73, 576, 577, 579, 581
    catalog, 77, 141, 181–83, 187, 201, 208, 230, 239, 241, 251, 259, 265, 278, 292, 306–7, 318, 352, 355, 360, 368–69, 373, 381, 390, 393, 399, 408, 424, 444–45, 458, 468, 476, 500, 502, 521, 529–30, 548–49, 573
    catalog, advertising in, 390, 500
    catalog covers, *141, 183, 200, 240, 418, 443*
    cessation of (1932), 579
    Club's loss of control of, 483–85
    first (1892), 141
    installation photos, *250, 449, 455, 496, 573*
    invitation, *347*
    new leadership of, 518, 521–22
Annual Traveling Scholarship Competition, 274–75, 283–84, 289–90, 301, 303–6, 317, 321, 330–36, 368, 374, 381–82, 385, 386, 408, 420, 426, 432, 434, 441, 443–44, 453, 459, 471, 475, 484, 490, 493–94, 506, 507, 520, 523–24, 525, 544, 546–47, 553, 560, 565–72
    cessation of, 572
    funding of, 565–66
    site plan for competitors, *330*
Applied Arts Exhibition, 518–19
architects
    first woman, 132*n5*
    importance of travel to education of, 111
    licencing of, 8–9, 204–5
    training of, 8–9, 49–51, 57, 90–91, 162, 241, 287, 344–45, 364,

376–77, 450–54, 483–85
*Architects' and Mechanics' Journal*, 30
Architects Club of Chicago, 9, 522, 532–33, 543, 549, 555–56, 561, 566, 584–85, 589, 590
    exhibition at Kimball House, 581
    library of, 543
Architects Realty Trust, 533, 537, 589
*Architectural Annual*, 248
Architectural Association of Minnesota, 21
*Architectural Association Sketchbook*, 30
architectural clubs, generally, 15, 103, 197, 448, 450
    architectural sketches from members, *102*
    catalogs put out by, 140–41, 183
    national league of, 71, 98
Architectural Decorating Company, 490
Architectural Draftsmen of North America, 420–21
Architectural Exhibition League, 540, 555, 561, 572–73
Architectural League of America, 8, 9, 244, 246–48, 261, 264, 271, 287–88, 300, 342–45, 351–52, 358, 403
    birthplace of, *247*
    convention attendees, *268, 269*
    conventions, 267, 277, 364
    demise of, 364
    emblem of, *248*
Architectural League of New York, 18–19, 28, 29, 56, 65, 77, 82, 87, 98–99, 100, 140, 247, 456, 476, 555–56
    meeting of, *20*
*Architectural Record*, 30
*Architectural Review and American Builder's Journal, The*, 30
*Architectural Sketchbook, The*, 30
*Architecture and Building*, 31, 107
architecture schools, 310, 446–47, 595
    in Chicago, 82, 90
*Architektonische Skizzenbuch*, 30
Armory Show of Modern Art, 412–13
Armour Institute of Technology, 162, 163–64, 301, 370, 452, 514, 544–45, 590, 591, 595
Armstrong, John, 522
Arnold, C. D., 156
Arnold, Hugo, 229
Aroner & Somers, 415
Art Institute of Chicago, 44–45, 91–92, 104, 124, 140, 158, 163–64, 167, 208–10, 301, 367, 369, 370, 374, 387–88, 416–17, 431, 444, 462, 475, 518, 535, 551–52, 555, 586, 591, 595
    architecture classes, 136
    exhibitions, 8
    relations with the architectural societies of Chicago, 526–27, 547–48
    School of the Art Institute, 377, 439
Art Institute of Chicago Building, 65, 137, 156, 162–64, *162*, 169, 253
    floor plans, *163, 209*
    interior, *164, 169*
Arts and Crafts Society, 230–33, 252,

255–56, 278
Arts Club of Chicago, 572–73, 576, 579
    interior, *573*
Ashbee, Charles Robert, 273–74, *273*, 286, 364, 365–67
Ashbee, T. S., 232
Ashland Block, 117, *119*
Ashton, R. J., 466
Atchison & Edbrooke, 306
    building design, *306*
Atelier Adams-Nelson, 585
Atelier Bennett, 364–65, 368, 403, 448
Atelier Bennett-Rebori, 365, 434, 448
Atelier Fitzwilliam, 288, 364
Atelier Holden, 364
Atelier Masqueray, 364
Atelier Parsons, 491, 499, 505–6, 524, 534, 544
Atelier Parsons-Adams, 559
Atelier Parsons-Adams-Deam, 561
Atelier Puckey, 365, 434
    exhibition design, *452*
Atelier Rebori, 365
atelier system, 136, 288, 309–10, 345, 364–65, 377, 385, 439–40, 447–48, 451–54, 499
Athenaeum (trade school), 52
Athenaeum Building, 125, *126*, 466
Atwood, Charles, 129, *130*, 131, 138, 147, 148, 150, 155, 210, 313
    building by, *135*
    building design, *195*
Auditorium Building (Adler & Sullivan, 1889), *68*, 69–70, 85–86, *86*, 153, 162
    interior, *272*
Awsumb, George, 332, 340, 371, 394, 403, 415, 438, 439, 453, 459
    building by, *464*
    building design, *334*
    competition design, *335, 340, 453*
Ayer's Building, 243

Babcock, Charles, 451
Babson, Henry, 574
Bacci, Albert, 567, *569*
    competition design, *569*
Bacci, Alexander H., 568, 578
Bacon, Harry, 150
Bacon, Henry, 147, 400, 426, 428
    monument design, *401*
Bagge, Christian U., 381
    competition design, *381*
Bagley, Frederick, House, *169*
Baha'i Temple, exhibition model, *497*
Bailey, Roger, 581
    competition design, *581*
Bailey, Vernon Howe, 472
Bajor, William R., 369
Baker, John C., 500, 518
Baldwin, Francis, 580, 581, 582, 585
Baldwin, Frank C., 137, 364
Bargelt, Louise James, 446, 456, 478
Barnum, George Lloyd, 454, 460, 485, 489, 490, 492, 494, 499
    building design, *447*
Barr, Charles H., 244
Barry, Gerald, Jr., 498, 499, 505, 521, 525
Barry, J. K., house, *28*
Bartlett, Frederic C., 367, 439
    window design, *367*
Bartolomae, Francis M., 253
baseball games, 71, 92

Bauer, August, 22
Bauman, G. A., 373
    *The Builders* (painting), *374*
Baumann, Frederick, 124, *437*, 438
Bay City High School, plan, *479*
Beach, Gordon, 491
Beacon of Progress, 290–91
Beauley, William Jean, 141, 299, 300, 301, 308, 400
    competition design, *300*
Beaumont, George, 26, 27, 33, 35, 37–38, 43, 46, 49, 59, *59*, 63, 73, 75, 79, 82, 89–90, 125, 193, 196, 204, 380
    illustrations by, *50*
Beaux-Arts Institute of Design, 344–45, 365, 385, 450, 484, 534, 561
    Medal Designs, 505
Beaux-Arts style, increasing use of, in early part of 20th century, 445
Beeckman, Julius, 114
Beers, Herbert P., 404
Beersman, Charles, 523, 547
Behel, Vernon W., 331
Behr, E. Theodore, 300
Beil & Hermant, 360
Belden, Edgar S., 158, 173, 252
Bell, Carl, 355
    *Labor* (sculpture), *355*
Beman, Solon Spencer, 130, 219, 254, 293, 333, 386, *436*, 437, 522, 539
    competition design, *220*, *255*
    interior design, *324*
Benedict, Jules B., 290, 299, 300
Bennett, Edward H., 190, 371, 372, 385, 403, 452, 458, 467, 491, 495, 544, 547, 577, 579, 585
    urban design, *470*
Bentley, Harry H., 416, 439, 454, 500
Bentley, Harry L., 567
Berg, Carl, 430
Berlin, 35
Bernard, Wilhelm, 404
Bernhard, Adolph F., 201, 272, 286, 300
Bernhard, Wilhelm, 431
    competition design, *405*, *430*
Berry, Addison C., 93, 148
    competition design, *95*
Betts, William B., 381, 390
    competition design, *381*
Bieg, Harry K., 524, 535, *535*, 542
    competition design, *534*
Birge, Charles E., 181, 186, 188, 189, 190
    competition design, *182*
Birren, Joseph, 489
Bischof, J. H., 452
    competition design, *388*
Bishop, Lucile, 395
Black, Gilmer V., 588
Blackall, Clarence H., 100, 111, 265, 310, 352
Blackstone Hotel, *375*
Blair, Lyman, House (274 South Michigan Avenue), 165, *166*
Blashfield, Edwin Howland, 99
    medal by, *99*
Bliss & Faville, 282
Blouke, Pierre, 494, 506, 520, 521, 522–23, 525, 533, 535, 544, 549, 572–73, 580
Blume, Louis J., 560

Board of Trade Building (Holabird & Root), 557, *557*
Boari, Adamo, 215, 219, *220*, 243, 254
    competition design, *220*, *242*, *256*
Bock, Richard W., 179, 185, 187, 190, 230, 280, 350, 360, 409
    sculpture, 230, *230*, *297*, *351*, *361*
Bognild, Enoch, 341
Bohassac, Charles, 568
Bollenbacher, J. C., 545
Booton, Joseph F., 500, 560, 585
Bordewich, Howard, 580, 582
Boston Architectural Club, 84, 140, 244, 247
Boston Portfolio Club, 30
Boston Society of Architects, 28, 29, 30
Boston Terra Cotta Company, 36
Bourke, Robert E., 286, 300
Boutwood, Charles E., 145
Bowen, Howard, 221
Boyd, David Knickerbacker, 259
Boyington, William W., 79, 131, 162
    building by, *132*
Brabant, Gifford, 438, 439
Bradbury, Gerald A., 525, 544, 567, 572, 573, 580
Bragdon, Claude Fayette, 93, 279, 398, 446
    competition design, *97*
Braun, Henry H., 87, 143
    competition design, *88*
Braun, Martin H., competition design, *552*
*Brickbuilder, The*, 339–40, 398, 404, 415
    competitions, 336–41
Brickbuilder Publishing Company (Boston), 189
Brick House (Rebori), *564*
Briggs, F. H., 137
*Brochure Series*, 189
Brogdon, Claude, multi-plate exhibit, *448*
Brooks, H. Allen, 216
Brout, Robert Benedict, 571–72, *571*, 590
    competition design, *571*
Brown, Arthur George, 151, 190, 201, 299, 301, 305, 380, 421
Brown, Mrs. Charles A., 500
Brown, Charles Francis, 438
Brown, Clarence G., 336, 374, 381, 394
Brown, C. M., 452
Brown, Glenn, 265
Brown, Helen, 584
Brown, O. G., 125
Browne, Charles Francis, 142
Browne's Bookstore, 362
Brunner, A. W., urban design, *316*
Buchroeder, Walter M., 587
Buck, Lawrence, 167, 169, 216, 280, 291, 343, 355, 361, 375, 392, 409, 473, 478
    building by, *475*
Buckingham, Clarence, 361
Bucklen Building (Oscar Cobb, 1884), 166
Buffalo Architectural Sketch Club, 71, 98, 109
    competition designs by members, *62*
Builders and Traders' Exchange, 33, 40, 44, 54, 67, 98, 194
    Silver Medal, 100
*Building Budget, The*, 31, *32*, 47, 93, 96,

104, 170
Building Trades and Material Exhibition, 170–72, *171*
Bulliet, C. J., 578
Bunte Building, *542*
Burgess, Ida, 244
Burghoffer, Leon, 403
Burling & Whitehouse, 131
Burnham, Carol Lou, 578
Burnham, Daniel Hudson, 7, 8, 20, 46, 61, 79, 92, *105*, 106, 120, 129, 131, 145, 147, 148, 155, 177–79, *178*, 190, 194, 207–8, 209–11, 222, 271, 272, 291, 313–14, 327–29, 348–49, 354, 355, 360, 400, 408, 424, 437, *437*, 438, 523
    cup awarded to, *178*
    park design, 195, *328*, *371*
    *Plan of Chicago* (1909), 190, 301, 314, *316*, 317, 328–29, 342, 349, 371–72, 419, 467, 468
Burnham, D. H., Jr., 559
Burnham, Hubert, 437, 500, 522, 551, 577, 579
Burnham Brothers, 465
Burnham Library of Architecture, 514–15, 526, 543, 586
Burnham & Root, 7, 45, 57, 71, 92, 105, 117, 120–24, 129–31, 214
    floor plan, *122*
    interior of offices, *122*
    library, *129*
Bush-Brown, H. K., 271
Bushnell, E. S., 142
Butts, William, 53
Byrne, Barry, 385, 416, 478
    building by, *477*

Cady, Jeremiah Kiersted, 203, *204*, 229, 235
Caleb H. Marshall Scholarship, 374, 380
*California Architect and Building Review*, 31
Calumet Building (Burnham & Root, 1884), 45
Cameron, Edward, 24
Campbell, Edmund S., 446, 523, 534
Cannon & Fetzer, 450
Carbide and Carbon Building (Burnham Brothers), *593*
Carlbury, Ralph H., 560
Carlson, David W., 569
Carlu, Jacques, 549
    exhibition design, *551*
Carnegie, Andrew, 286–87
Carpenter, James H., 9, 17–18, *19*, 21, 25, 27, 31, 35, 37–38, 43, 44, 46, 66, 197
    architectural sketches, *17*, *31*, *33*
Carpenter, N. H., 327, 438
Carr, Charles A., 238, 252, 253, 272
Carrere, John, *316*
Carter, Thomas A., 569
Case, John Watrous, 287
Caukin, Eugene L., 40
Cement Products Exhibition Company, 394
Cenek, Robert R., 434
Central Art Association, 233, 234
Central Music Hall, *154*
Century of Progress World's Fair (1933), 547, 577, 579–80, 586

site plan, *580*
Cerny, Jerome R., 560
Cerny, Otto, 545
Charity Organization Society of the City of New York, 252
Charnley House, *464*
Chatten, M. C., 559
Chatten & Hammond, 375
Cheetham, Keith, 499, *500*
Cheney, Edwin H., 423
Cheney, Howard L., 532, 558, 573
Chicago
    1909 plan, 190, 301, 314, 317, 328–29, 342, 349, 371–72, 419, 467, 468
    architectural clubs in, 379
    beautification of, 360
    building activities in, 19, 45, 210, 289
    competition for the World's Colombian Exposition, 105
    innovative architecture of, 7–8
    view of, *502*
Chicago Architects' Business Association (CABA) (later renamed the Illinois Society of Architects), 104, 204–5, 364, 365, 372–73, 377, 379, 388, 417, 419, 421
Chicago Architectural (Sketch) Club, 8, 9, 79, 106, 144–45, 247, 251, 318, 364
    announcement, *536*
    annual banquet, 54, 56, 63–64, 75–77, 99–100, 145–48, 158–59, 173, 193, 227, 342–43, 493, 520
    architectural sketches by members, *37*, *38*, *47*, *55*
    atelier of, 345, 354, 403, 448, 484, 488–89, 490–91, 499, *540*, 558, 559, 561–62, 572, 583, 585
    attention given to in architectural press, 329–30
    bimonthly competitions, 187–88
    Bohemian nights, 179, 190
    bookplate, *587*
    classes, 145, 173, 179, 188, 190, 224, 559
    club rooms and furnishings, *66*, 151, 166
    club seal, 139, *140*
    competition designs by members, *47*, *49*, *63*, *71*, *84*, *112*, *125*, *167*, *173*
    competition judges, 60–61
    competitions and prizes, 35–42, 46, 75, 87, 106
    constitution and by-laws, 28–29, 31, 84, 179, 236–37, 286, 329, 493, 525
    demise of, 595
    design for lakefront, *199*
    drawings by members, ownership of, 53
    elections, 59, 190, 223, 237–38, 309, 327, 363, 394, 403, 415, 438, 454, 460, 466, 474, 487, 497, 504, 521, 525, 544, 559, 560, 565, 580, 582, 585, 586
    Executive Committee, 46, 257
    exhibition drawings by members,

*64*
exhibitions as part of program, 53–56
female members, 65
founders reunion of, 380
founding of, 13, 17, 25–29
honorary membership, 56, 59
incorporation, 85
initiation sketch by member, *176*
invitations, *139, 354, 545*
"Ladies Night," 224
library, 69
logo, *278*
meetings, 35, 60
meeting spaces, 33, 40, 44–45
membership, 56, 180, 420, 443, 454, 498, 505, *545*, 562–63
membership card, *13, 15*
membership entry fees, 68
menu card, *75, 100, 117, 138*
minor exhibitions, 300, 560, 587
mug, *320*
musical comedy staged by, 372, *373*
name changes, 13, 180, 483, 533, 587
newsletter of, 562
presentations and talks, 48–51, 60, 70
quarters, 65–68, 124–25, 153, *154,* 177, 209, 221, 318–20, 388–89, 404, 416–17, 419, 441, 455, 466, 488–89, *489,* 492, 537, 544
revival of name in recent times and reconstitution of Club, 10, *594,* 595–98
sketch classes, 489, 543
sketching trips, 71–72, 77, 92, 166
sketch problems posed, 523
student drawing, *179*
success of, 43, 47
syllabi and year's programs, 48–49, 106, 138, 148, 150, 155, 165, 189, 196, 203, 229, 238, 274
training given by, 52–53
Chicago Architectural Exhibition League, 522, 529, 579, 586
Chicago Arts and Crafts Society, 222–23, 277
Chicago Atelier (Campbell's), 524, 534
poster, *523*
Chicago Automobile Club, 289
Chicago Board of Education, 373
Chicago Bridge & Iron Works, 583
Chicago Builders' Club, 237
Chicago Ceramic Club, 185
Chicago Chapter of the American Institute of Architects, 9, 224, 518, 522, 529, 532, 537, 548, 558, 566, 584, 588–90
Chicago Cultural Center, 137
Chicago Daily News Building, *556,* 577, *577*
Chicago Face Brick Association, 382, 444
Chicago Fire of 1871, 8, 19, *22–23,* 51
*Chicago Herald,* 64
Chicago Historical Society, 462
Chicago lakefront, 8, 313, 329
plan, *315*
Chicago Manual Training School, 52
Chicago Master Masons, 15

Chicago Opera House (Cobb & Frost, 1885), 45, *45*
Chicago Public Library, 136–37, 156, 224
Chicago Real Estate Board, 194
Chicago River, bridge plan, *456, 467*
Chicago School of Architecture (joint venture of the Art and Armour institutes), 162, 163–64, 188, 301, 370, 387, 595
Chicago school of architecture (stylistic approach), 7, 45–46, 229, 355, 391, 462–63, 465, 473, 475–76, 478, 484, 485–87, 513
philosophy of the major architects of, 51
Chicago Society of Artists, 160, 165, 168, 183, 190, 194, 195, 209
Chicago Technical College, 572, 583
Chicago Woman's Club, 90, 260
Childs, Frank A., 468
Childs & Smith, 478, *551,* 558
Christian, Oswin C., 69, 71, 72, 85, 93, 99, 107, 114, 150
competition design, *94*
Church, Frank W., 365
Church, Myron H., 26, 46, 49
drawing of building, *27*
Church, Walter S., 365
Cincinnati Architectural Club, 98, 100, 108
Cincinnati Chapter of the American Institute of Architects (AIA), 247
Cincinnati Sketch Club, 89
City Club of Chicago, 419–20, 429–31
competitions, 404–8
City Club of Chicago Building, *399*
Clark, Edwin H., 567
Clark, Edwin R., 175
Clark, Robert, 79, *79,* 82–83, 99, 116
donation by, 77
*See also* Robert Clark Testimonial Competition
Clark, T. M., 111
classical revival architecture, 450–54
Claus, Alfred, 48
Clay, William W., 229, 320, 438
Clay Products Exposition, 398
Cleveland, L. D., 22
Cleveland, Ohio, 316
Cleveland Architectural Club, 183, 197, 247
Cleveland Chapter of the American Institute of Architects (AIA), 247
Cliff Dwellers Club, 514, *514*
Clow, William E., 420
Cloyes, F. O., 132
Clubhouse for Architects Competition, 229
Clute, Eugene, 518
Cobb, Henry Ives, 85, *85,* 115, 126, 130, 143, 173
Cobb & Frost, 71
Codman, Henry, 105, *105*
Coffin, Arthur S., 420
Coleman, A. E., 545
Colonial Fireplace Company, 354
Columbia University, 51, 310
Columbus (Ohio) Architectural Sketch Club, 87, 89, 107

Combs, Roger M., 289, 394
Comes, John, 186
Comey, Arthur C., 404, 405
Committee on the Universe, 235
concrete, 395–96
Conner, George D., 524, 545
*Construction News,* 373, 400–401
Cook, Walter, 265
Cook County Courthouse, 351, 353
Coolidge, Charles A., 149, *150,* 155, 173, 203, *204,* 253, 310
Coolidge & Carlson, 320
Coonley, Avery, 235
Corbett, Harvey Wiley, 579
Cornell Architectural Sketch Club, 107
Cornell University, 49, 51, 451
Corse, Redmond P., 371, 452
Coxhead & Coxhead, 282
Cram, Ralph Adams, 221, 246, 291
Cram and Wentworth, 100
Crane, R. T., Jr., 456
Crawford, Mary Ann E., 584, 587
competition design, *587*
*Crayon, The,* 30
Cret, Paul, 553, 577
monument design, *554*
Crisevsky, A., 568
Crofoot, Fred, 466
*Croquis d'Architecture,* 30
Crunelle, Leonard, 360
Cudel & Hercz, 186

Dando, Robert E., 520, 521, 541, 544, 545, 560
Davidson, Frank E., 485, *485,* 518, 522, 533, 543, *543*
David Swing Settlement Building, 258
Davis, George R., 149
Davis, H. E., 452
Davis, Zachary, 472
Dawson, Arthur, 125
Deam, Arthur F., 561, 585
architectural sketch, *553*
Dean, George R., 158, 167, 173, 179, 189, 190, 201, 224, 229, 231, 232, 233, 234, 238, 239, *240,* 241, 257, 264–65, 274, 277–79, 285, 292, 293, 297
building design, *294, 295*
competition design, *239*
cover design, *240*
essay by, 240–41
Dean and Dean, 464, 468, 478
Deane, E. Eldon, 132–34, *133, 153*
Decorators Supply Company, 545
De Golyer, Robert S., 549, 558, 577
building by, *550*
De Long, Albert J., 569, *569*
competition design, *569, 570*
de Mari, Valere, 404
Dennell, R. A., 83, 87, 91
competition design, *94*
Denver Architectural Sketch Club, 158
Des Moines, Iowa, 48
Des Moines Sketch Club, 25, 28, 46
Despradelle, Desire, 290–91, *291,* 310
Detroit Architectural Club, 189, 197, 247
Dewhurst, Frederic E., 349
Dewson, Edward, 26, 27, 33, 38
design for award, *104*
drawing of an interior, *40*
illustration by, *39*
Dexter Building, *302, 327,* 404, 416

Club quarters at, 318, 327
interior, *319, 320*
loss of, 419
D. H. Burnham and Company, 183, 185, 210–11, 308, 355, 398, 495
railroad station design, *407, 457*
Dibelka, James B., *445*
Dickey Architectural Competition, 545, 549
Dillard, Frank G., 351
Dillon, Henry R., 223, 229
Dillon, John Robert, 13, 165, 173, 174, 180, 189, 190, 197
Dillon Competition, site plan for competitors, *224*
Dow, Arthur W., 287
Downs, E. L., 363
Downton, Herbert E., 439, 454, 460, 466, 474
draftsmen, 420–21
clubs for, 48
considered professionals, 26
training of, 8–9, 17–18, 52–53, 67
Drummond, William E., 7, 275, 283, 284, 385, 392, 396, 400, 406, 419, 478
building by, *395*
building design, *401, 478*
competition design, *283, 285*
Dukkee, A. R., 150
Dunning, Hugh B., 336, 365, 369, 381
competition design, *337*
Dunning, Nelson Max, 180, 223, 224, 228, 229, 231, 234, 237, 238, 246, 247, 248, 253, 271, 275, 278, 283, 288, 299, 307, 336, 340, 343, *343,* 346, 349, 351, 360, 364, 365, 400, 499, 509, 514, 515, 525, 559
architectural sketches, *308, 350*
competition design, *282*
Dunning, N. Max, 8, *236*
Dutton, L. B., 26

E. Bonnett & Son, 211
École des Beaux-Arts (Paris), 76, 187, 207, 237, 248, 288, 309–10, 385, 447, 450, 585
educational methods, 384, 447, 591, 595
Edbrooke, H. W. J, 299
Eggebrecht, William, 223, 238, 239
cover design, *240*
Eidlitz, Leopold, 221
Eighteen, the, 234–36, 257, 277–78
Eiseman, Albert, Jr., 534, 567, *568*
competition design, *568*
Eiseman, Ferdinand, *523,* 524, 529, 559, 560
competition design, *524*
Elcock, E. G., 331, 333, 420
Electricity Building (at WCE), *134*
Elicott Square Building (Buffalo), 185
Eliel, Roy, 318, 322
Elliott, J. Wilkenson, 320
Ellis, Harvey, 279
Elmslie, George Grant, 7, 514, 558, 574, *557*
Sullivan grave marker design, *575*
Emerson, Ralph, 567
Enders, Frank, 75
Enders, Oscar, 59, *59,* 69, 73–74, *74,* 75, 77, 81, 82, 83, 98, 100, 107,

108, 111, 271
   competition design, *81*, *87*, *109*, *112*
Enthof, Edmond W., 560
Eppinghausen, Charles F., 188
   architectural sketch, *203*
Erickson, Carl A., 569
Esser, Curt A., 487, 498
Esser, Paul F., 474, 487, 495, 500
Evans, Alfred P., 82, 140, 156
   competition design, *82*
Evanston-North Shore Association of Architects, 581
Ewell, James Cady, 577
Ewen, John Meigs, 92, 117, 145, 148, 216
Eyre, Wilson, 245, 291, 320, 474

Fairbank, N. K., 162
Fairbrass, George F., 587
Falkenau, Victor, 321, 330
Farmer's National Bank of Owatonna (Sullivan), *413*
Farrier, Clarence W., 487, 490, 500, 504, 522, 525, 533, 544
Faulkner, C. D., 387
   competition design, *388*
Fehleisen, Mr., 46
Fellheimer, Alfred, 221
Fellows, William K., 206, 241, 271, 274, 301, 309, 333, 374, 461, 569
Ferriss, Hugh, 529, 553, *554*
   architectural sketch, *528*
Ferry, George B., 343
Fiedler, August, 180
Field, Marshall, 310, 327
Field Columbian Museum, 194, 310, 327–28, 495, 509, 511
Field & Medary (Philadelphia), 219
Field Museum of Natural History, 8, 194, 313, 342, 372, 495
   model of, *402*
Fifth Avenue Art Galleries, 65
Fine Arts Building (WCE), 131, 310, 400, *494*, 495–96, *495*, *511*, *512*
   interior, *157*
   plans and views, *152*, *402*
   restoration of, 509–13
First Regiment Armory, 117, *118*
Fisher, J. E., 219
Fisher, John B., 368, 371
Fitzwilliam, F. J., 288, 345
Flagg, Ernest, 291, *325*
Flanders, J. J., *28*
Fletcher, Sir Bannister, *History of Architecture*, page from, *127*
Fleury, Albert, 352
Fogle, Dan, 503
Foreman, Henry G., 351
Forest Preserve District of Cook County, 317, 351
Forestry and Dairy Building (WCE), *135*
Fox, Charles E., 522, *522*, 530, 531, 533, 537, 560, 581
Fox, Elmer J., 8, 474, 487, 490, 493, 498, 499, 505, 518
Fraenkel, Theodore (Teddy) O., 56, 69, 71, 83, 85, 87, 92, 93, 99, 107, 108, 114, 134, 135, 145, 158, 180, 183, 186, 380
   competition designs, *68*, *70*, *88*, *91*, *140*
Fraenkel & Schmidt, 156

Francis J. Plym Fellowship in Architecture, 399
Franklin, Robert L., 454, 460, 466, 468–69
Franzheim, H. K., 500
Frazier, Walter, 523
French, William M. R., 136, 164, 197
French, W. R., 424
Friedlander, J., 186
Frost, Charles S., 149, *150*, 180, 543
   exhibition design, *434*
Frost & Granger, 245, 280, 323, 386
   interior design, *324*
Fuhrer, Eugene, 560
Fuller, Buckminster, 573
Fuller, George A., 216
Fuller, Henry, 235
Fulton, Frank G., photograph of Chicago, *502*
Furst-Kerber Cut Stone Company, 543

Gage Building (Louis Sullivan), *298*
Garbett, Edward Lacy, *Rudimentary Treatise on the Principles of Design in Architecture*, 113
Garden, Edward G., 7, 82, 141, 142, 158, 160, 165, 201, 223, 224, 227, 228, 275
   competition design, *142*, *159*
Garden, Frank M., 82, 148, 173, 190, 224, 227, 257, 274
   competition design, *150*
Garden, Hugh M. G., 7, 82, 137, 145, 149, 154, 158, 167, 171, 178, 181, 185, 190, 221, 229, 230, 231, 235, 241, 271, 278, 280, *281*, 287, 288, 293, 320, 373, 380, 395, 495
   competition designs, *139*, *182*
   designs for lakefront, *201*
   drawing of building, *184*
Garden brothers (Hugh, Frank, and Edward), 140
"Gas-Lite," 39
Gates, William D., 238, 318, 323, 350–51, 420, 574
   ceramic mug, *320*
Gates Potteries, 350
   poster invitation, *326*
Gay, Henry Lord, *34*, 35, *35*, 37, 38–40, 47, 63, 75, 77, 79, 80, 96, 103–4, 124, 170
   competition set by, *41*
Gelert, Johannes Sophus, 86, 155, 178, 438
   bust of Root, *178*
   Clark medal, plaster model, *86*
George A. Fuller Company, 118, 217
George W. Maher & Son, building design, *502*
Giannini, Orlando, 323
Gibb, William R., 71, 99, 111, 115, 142, 145, 147, 380
   competition design, *113*
Gibbs, A. D., 452
Gilbert, Cass, 390
Gillespie, Charles H., 175
   competition design, *174*
Gillette, Edwin F., 390, 394, 402, 431
Gindele, Charles W., 374, 381, 382, 420
Glessner, John J., 23, 522, 531–32, 549, 588
Glessner House (Richardson), 9–10, *27*,

*530*, 531–32, *532*, 539, 540, 549, 588–90, 591
   site plan, *531*
Goetz, M. H., 505
Goldberg, Bertrand, 596
Goodhue, Bertram Grosvenor, 343, 472, 501, *501*, 503, 553, *554*
Goodwin, J. M., 147
Goodyear, William Henry, 224
Gookin, Frederick W., 235, 352, 361
Gookins, James F., 260
Graham, Anderson, Probst & White, 465, 467, 513, 517, *556*
   railroad station design, *466*
Graham, Ernest R., 177, 210, 406
Graham Foundation for Advance-ment in the Fine Arts, 10
Granger, Alfred H., 24, 236, 238, 320, 346, 354, 454, 478, 501, 507, 522–23, 530, 531–32, 533, 537, 559, 561, 567, 573, 585
   building by, *501*
Grant Park, 8, 193, 301, 310–14, 327–28, 342, 371, 372, 458
   plan, *315*, *329*, *349*
Great Depression, 10, 562–63, 568, 572, 577, 586, 588
Green, Dwight E., 48
Green, Herbert H., 331, 342, 476
   competition design, *331*, *332*
Green, James C., competition design, *116*
Greengard, Bernard C., 8, 382, 387, 408, 476, 489
   competition design, *387*
Grey, Elmer, 186, 268–69, *268*, 278, 285, 293, 450
Griffin, Marion Lucy (Mahony), 7, 416
Griffin, Walter Burley, 7, 215, 271, 331, 365, 368, *369*, 375, 380, 384, 385, 395, 396, *397*, *398*, 398, 400, 402, 403, 406, 409, 411, *411*, *412*, 414, 416, *416*, 427, 450
Gross, Oskar, 392
Gross, Ralph Francis, 585, 586, 589
Grosse, Paul, 559
   building design, *552*
Grover, Oliver D., 186, 439
Grueby Faience Company, 244
Grunsfeld, Ernest A., Jr., 569, 585
   building by, *578*
Guaranty Building (Adler & Sullivan), *184*, 238
Guenzel & Drummond, 430, 450
   exhibition design, *434*
   railroad station design, *407*
Guerin, Jules, 215, 348, 371
Guerini, Annibal, 165
Gugler, Eric, 581
   competition design, *581*
Guilbert, Ernest F., 148, 175, 186, *186*
Gunther, Arthur, 341
   competition design, *341*
Gustafson, A. C., 453

Haagen, Paul Topping, 333, 363, 365, 371, 373
Hahn, Fred, 186
Haig, J. A., 446
Hale, C., 420
Hall, Emery Stanford, 423, 545, 566–67, *567*, 568, 588, 589, 590
Hall, Gilbert P., 544, 547, 555, *555*, 557

Hall, W. C., 310
Hallberg, L. G., 193, 204
Hall of Fame plan, 437–38
Halperin, C., 387
   competition design, *388*
Hamilton, Fellows & Nedved, 569
Hamilton, J. L., 309, 321, 327, 345
Hammond, C. Herrick, 330, 342, 345, 354, 363, 380, 494, 580
   competition design, *330*
Hampe, A. W., 50
*Handbook for Architects and Builders*, 443, 493
Handy, Frank, 233, 235, 238
Handy & Cady, 231
Hanifin, Arthur C., 381, 453
Hansen, Harold M., 51
Harbeck, Jarvis, 290
Harder, Julius F., 133, 142, 145, 155, 259, 287
   competition design, *96*
Harper, W. W., competition design, *311*, *341*
Harris, Arthur, competition design, *87*
Harrison, Benjamin, 104, 105
Harrison, Carter, 158
Harshe, Robert B., 527
Hartwell & Richardson, 156
Hastings, Thomas, 179
Hatzfeld, Clarence, 229, 238, 252, 253
Hawkins, G. A., 26
Hayden, Sophia G., 132, *133*
Hazelton, H. T., 64
Healy & Millet, 232
Heayden, P. C., 364
Heer, R. N., 426
Heimbrodt, Carl, 584
Heino, Albert, 582
Heitkamp, Ernest L., 574
Hekanson, Oscar M., 205
   competition design, *207*
Hemmings, E. Charles, 272, 286, 300
Henderson, W. H., 87
Henderson, William, 106
Henry R. Dillon Club House Competition, 234
Herinant, Leon, 355
Herlin, George B., 369
Herter, Albert, 363
Herter, Edward, 541
Hetherington, J. T., 26
Hetherington, T. D., 26
Heun, Arthur, 75, 83, 87, 93, 106, 107, 111, 115, 125, 134, 135, 142, 143, 165, 179, 189, 216, 231, 236, 293, *296*, 320, 572
   competition design, *95*, *116*
Hewitt & Emerson, building by, *434*
Hibbard, Frederick C., 503
Higginbotham, H. N., 314, 327
Highland Park, 458
Hilbard, Frederick C., monument by, *503*
Hill, Henry W., 90
Hine, Cicero, 26
   architectural sketch, *12*
Hinkle Gold Medal, 98, 100, *101*
Hirsh, F. R., 137
Hirsh, Willard, 175
Hodgdon, Charles, 543
Hodgdon, Frederick M., 8, 386, 434, 466, 474, 476, 494, 523, 525, 544, 547
   competition design, *386*

Hodgkins, H. G., 216
Hoeppner, E. A., 142, 143, 145, 149
Hoerman, Carl, 458
Hoffman, Curtis, 219
Hoffman, Malvina, 502
    sculpture, 502
Hoffmann, Donald, 112
Hofmeister, Theodore M., 543, 544, 576, 580, 582
Hoit, Henry F., 213, 213, 215
    drawing of building, 212
Holabird, John A., 7, 439, 446, 495, 523, 577, 579, 589, 590, 591
Holabird, William, 39
Holabird & Roche, 57, 185, 243, 307, 307, 351, 353, 390, 465, 478, 495, 517, 529, 541, 549, 550, 553, 557
    park design, 479
Holabird & Root, 137, 555, 556, 557–58, 574, 577
    building by (333 North Michigan Avenue), 558
Holden, B. E., 345, 364
Holmes, Kathryn, 444
Holmes, M. G., 49, 69
    competition design, 69
Holsman, Henry K., 238, 252, 271, 272, 274, 286–87, 364, 490, 514, 541, 585
Holyoke, T. G., 93
    competition design, 96
Home Insurance Building (Jenney and Mundie, 1885), 23, 24, 25, 45, 593
Home Traveling Scholarship, 387, 460
Hompe, A. W., 75
Hood, Raymond, 509, 544, 553, 577
Hooker, George E., 404
Hoover, J. W., 301
Hornbostel, H., 186
Hosmer, Charles C., 529
Hosmer, Clare C., 500, 518, 523, 527–28, 535
Howe-Davidson, Martha, 56
Howells, Jack, 517
Howells, John Mead, 517, 553
Howells, William Dean, 509
Howells & Hood, 509, 517
    Tribune Tower design, 508
Hubbard, A. H., 500
Huber, Julius, 543, 543
Hudnut, Joseph, 430
    competition design, 430
Huffman, James A., 522
Hull-House (Pond & Pond), 222–23, 222
    plan, 258
Hunt, Elmer, 201, 237, 392
Hunt, Jarvis, 406, 408, 411, 467
Hunt, Myron, 183, 186, 190, 210, 213, 214, 221, 223, 224, 236, 243, 243, 265, 278, 280, 293, 458, 472
Hunt, Richard Morris, 85, 100, 130, 147, 185
Hunt & Grey, building by, 393
Huntoon, Homer, 560
Husser, Joseph W., 263
    House, 263, 273, 361
Hutchinson, Charles, 527
Hutchinson, Charles B., 145, 148
Hutchinson, Charles L., 437
Hyde, Henry M., 412

Hyett, Robert Teal, 336, 381
    competition design, 337
Hyland, Paul V., 274, 309, 336

Iannelli, Alfonso, 446, 576, 580
    mural design, 442
Illinois, 18, 21–22, 103
    architecture of, 462–63
Illinois Association of Architects, 23, 33, 106, 170
Illinois Chapter of the American Institute of Architects, 19, 21–23, 103–4, 104, 106, 124, 140, 165, 170, 178, 193, 204–5, 208, 221, 247, 252, 363–64, 365, 371, 372, 374, 376–77, 379, 380, 399, 412, 416–17, 419, 421, 428–29, 431, 437, 439–40, 443, 451, 465, 475, 483, 484, 492–93, 513
    Gold Medal Competition, 180–81, 393–94
    new space, 388–89
Illinois Industrial University, 51
Illinois Institute of Technology, 595
Illinois Society of Architects (ISA), 9–10, 417, 431, 437, 439–40, 443, 475, 483, 488, 513, 518, 522, 530, 531, 532, 537, 539, 543, 548, 558–59, 561, 565, 566, 584, 589, 590
    membership certificate, 492
    Monthly Bulletin, 485, 488, 493, 521, 543, 562
Illinois State Association of Architects, 21, 39–40, 90, 103
Illsley, C. E., 41
Imperial Hotel, Tokyo (Wright), 516
Improved Housing Association, 251–52, 254
Industrial Chicago, The Building Trades, 25
Ingeman, A. S., 368, 452
Ingram, Horace C., 376, 389–90, 393
    competition design, 389
Inland Architect, 31, 32, 43, 65, 83, 179, 330
Inland Architect and Builder, 31
Inland Architect and Building News, The, 13–15
Institute of Building Arts, 103–4, 170–71, 194
Interstate Exposition Building, 162
Ittner, William B., 322, 323, 343, 361
Ives, Halsey, 235

Jackson, Emery B., 469, 495
Jackson, H. W., 160
Jackson, John F., 190, 205
    competition design, 192, 207
Jackson Park, 105, 105, 119, 129, 194, 303, 310, 400
    Pavilion, 119
    Refectory Building, 120, 121
Jacobs, Robert, 588
Jacobson, Phillmore, architectural sketch, 553
James, E. R., 336
    competition design, 338
Jamieson, James P., 96n50
Janin, Fernand, 371, 446
J. C. Llewellyn & Company, 468

Jenkins, Harry Dodge, 188, 201, 224, 300, 354, 368, 369
    competition design, 301
Jenney, William Le Baron, 7, 23, 42 n16, 46, 51, 56, 60–61, 60, 61, 66, 69, 75, 79, 83, 92, 100, 106, 112, 114, 115, 117, 136, 138, 155, 164, 173, 233, 265, 360, 437, 438
Jenney & Mundie, 130
Jensen, Elmer C., 111, 124, 147, 165, 172, 173, 179, 185, 189, 193, 224, 229, 254, 352, 354, 439
    competition design, 112, 181
Jensen, Jens, 317, 375, 404, 431, 574
Jewett, Eleanor, 496, 503, 529, 554, 557
Johnson, B. K., 573
Johnson, E. V., 346
Johnson, Jens A., 403, 416, 420
Johnson, John W., 134, 143, 172, 173, 179, 181, 189
    competition design, 172, 173, 182
Johnson, S. T., 568
Johnston, C. H., 19n5
Johnston, Percy T., 384, 452
    competition design, 384
Jones, George B., 472
Jones, Jenkin Lloyd, 259
Jones, Margaret S., 540, 561
Junge, W. H., 36

Kable, Charles H., 331
Kahn, Albert, 175, 542
    exhibition drawing, 541
Kalter, W. L., 368
Kane, James A., 498, 500, 505, 521
Kansas City Exposition, 73
Kartowicm, F. G., 452
Kees & Colburn, 343
Keith, Elbridge, House, 464
Kelsey, Albert, 248, 248, 264, 267, 287, 406
Kemeys, Edward, 169
Kendall, Henry H., 509, 514–15
Kennedy, J. C., 404
Kenyon, W. M., 134
    drawing of building, 134
Kervic, F. W., 395
Kessell, Charles A., 26, 27, 46, 63, 66, 72, 73, 74, 81, 85, 99, 131, 134, 135, 145, 380
    competition design, 94
    drawing of building, 34
Kimball House, 9–10, 522, 531, 532–33, 537–38, 544, 548, 549, 558–59, 560, 561–62, 572, 584–86, 589, 590
    coach house, interior, 540
    floor plans, 538
    interior, 537
    revamping and furnishing of, 537–39
    site plan, 531
Kimbell, Arthur, 454, 460
Kirkland, Alexander, 80
Kirkpatrick, Francis (Frank) W., 8, 213, 215, 223, 228, 228–29, 234–37, 243, 257
Klaber, Eugene H., 567, 585
Kleinpell, Walter H., 253, 272, 278, 300
Kleinpell, William E., 51, 83, 117, 134, 141–42, 144, 252
Knapp, George A., 455, 461, 468

Knox, A. J., 340, 342
    competition design, 333
Knox, Charles Victor, 573
Koch, W. W., 403
Kohinoor drafting pencils, 421–22
Krehbeil, Albert H., 461
Kronick, Gerald T., 547, 547, 560
    competition design, 547
Kurtz, Charles, 235

Lake Front Park, 193–201, 203
    site plan for a competition, 253, 254
Lake Michigan, 8
Lake Shore Trust and Savings Bank, 529
Lamb, Frederick S., 300
lampposts competition, 341–42
Land, Alois, 502
Lanquist, Andrew, 533, 537
Larson, Roy, 460
    competition design, 461
Lautrup, Paul C., 7, 20–21, 22, 24, 26, 139, 349
Lawrence, A. J., 455, 461, 474, 487
Lawrence, Edgar H., 406
Lawrie, Harry, 25, 27, 28, 31, 35, 46, 46, 48, 48, 49, 56, 59, 380
Leavell, John Calvin, 381, 390, 439, 454, 460
Lebenbaum & Marx, building by, 377
Le Boutillier, Addison B., 190
    competition design, 191
Le Brun Traveling Scholarship, 489, 500
Le Corbusier, visit to Chicago, 588
Lee, Mrs. Blewett, 588–89
Lehman, L. Emil, 578
Leiter, Levi Z., 216
Lescher, Theodore A., 345, 371
Le Vieque, E., 498–99
Levings, Mark M., 327, 331, 394, 403
Levy, Samuel H., 239
Leyden, Thomas F. H., 175
    competition design, 174
Liedberg, Hugo J., 219
Liesch, Pierre, 205
Lilienberg, Albert and Ingrid, 404, 405
Lilleskau, John, 201, 274, 341, 360
    competition design, 341
Lincoln Memorial (Washington, D.C.), 428
Lincoln Park Refectory (Perkins, Fellows & Hamilton), 395, 477
Lindeberg, H. T., 553, 555, 558
Linden, Frank L., 64, 67, 85, 99, 115, 125, 134, 135, 141, 145, 158
Linden Glass Company, 169
Lindquist, J. B., 494, 498, 505
Lion House at Lincoln Park, interior, 413
Lippincott, Roy A., 394, 403, 412
Lively, Frank L., 66, 71, 380
Livingston, Thomas, 205
Llewellyn, Joseph C., 8, 51, 223, 229, 231, 237, 238, 243, 247, 252, 267, 271, 274, 287, 288, 300, 301, 320, 364, 374, 399, 416, 421, 438, 439, 533, 580
    architectural sketch, 53
    urban design, 470
Loebl, Jerry, 505
London, 35
London Guarantee Building, 517
Long, Birch Burdette, 215, 224, 229, 230, 238, 241, 243, 252, 260, 265,

272, 274, 275, 278, 279, 283, 305–6, 308, 352, 354
  competition design, *239*, *282*, *304*
  cover design, *279*
  park design, *264*, *265*
Lorch, Emil G., 271, 286, 287, *287*, 288, 376–77
Lord, W. B., 66, 69
Lord & Hewlett, 320
Love, Robert J., 416, 420, 439
Lowe, Elmo C., 345, 363, 364, 370, 374, 429
Lund, Vera, 142, 584
Lundberg, D. R., 498
Luxfer Prism Company, 234
  Competition, 237

MacHarg, W. S., 136, 164
Machinery and Electricity Building (Trans-Mississippi Exposition), *231*
Madden, Martin B., 194–95, *195*
Madlener House, 10
Maher, George W., 50, 73, 280, *298*, 320, 321, 360, 375, 392, *392*, 400, *401*, 404, 409, 411, 414, 421, 424, 428, 429, 450, 451, 457, *457*, 465, 478, 484, 485–87, 495, 500, 502, 509–10, 513, 560
  Maher, Philip, 513, 569
Mahony, Marion L., 213, 215, 223, 230, 365, 384, 385, 406–7
  competition design, *366*
  fixture design, *410*
Mallers Building (John J. Flanders, 1884), *44*, 45
Mann, Frederick M., 186, 364, 399
Mann, Paul F., 368
Manny, Carter H., 10
*Manufacturer and Builder, The*, 30
Marble, Oliver W., 19*n7*
Market, Chas. H., 505
Markle, Charles H., 498
Marling, Franklin, Jr., 454
Marquand, H. S., 452
Marsh, Harry L., 327
Marshall, Benjamin H., 374, *375*, 553, *554*, 581
Marshall Field Annex Building, 211, *212*
Marshall Field & Company, 586
Marshall Field Mansion, 590
Marshall Field Warehouse (Richardson), 23, *26*, 211
Marshall & Fox, 465
Martin, Edgar D., 235
Marx, Samuel A., 345, 371, 376, 395, 446
Masonic Temple, 117, *118*, 151, 153–54, *153*, *154*
Massachusetts Institute of Technology (MIT), 49, 51, 117, 310, 451
Matteson, Victor A., 229
Matz, Hermann L., 289, 398
Mauch, Max, 252, 272
Mauran, John Lawrence, 343
Mayer, Philip, 568
Mayger, A. G., exhibition design, *433*
McArdle, M. P., 160
  competition design, *161*
McCartan, Edward, 502
McCarthy, J. G., 51, 100
McCaughey, W. M., 500

McCauley, Lena May, 427, 446, 457, 463, 504, 576–77
McCormick, Alexander, 235
McCormick, Cyrus H., 216
McCullough, W. J. B., 26
McCurry, Paul, 547
McDougall, Isabel, 355
McDougall, Walter A., 565
McGrath, Paul J., 494, 521, 525, 544
McKim, Charles Follen, 145, 148, 207, 373
McKim, Mead & White, 130
McKowell, Mary, 430
McLean, Robert Craik, 13–15, *14*, 17, 19, 21, 25, 26, 28, 31–33, 38, 43, 46, 48, 60, 61, 67, 71, 81, 82, 94–96, 99, 114, 115, 125, 126, 136, 145, 148, 154, 167–68, 193, 197, 209, 224–25, 247, 263, 292, 330, 331, 342, 349, 360, 370, 380, 403, 421–22, 436–37, 448–50, 458, 475, 504, 529
McLeod, James A., 65
McNally & Quinn, 549, *550*
McVeagh, Franklin, 23
McVeagh House (H. H. Richardson), *27*
Mead, George H., 430
Mead, Marcia, 430
  competition design, *430*
Mendelssohn, Fisher & Lawrie, 46*n24*
Menees, T. O., 544, 560, 565, 580, 582
Meseke, Frederick J., 395
Meyers, David G., 205
  competition design, *206*
Meyne, Gerhardt F., 549
Michigan, 18, 310
Michigan Avenue, 467, 472
Midland Terra Cotta Co., 475
Midway Gardens, model of, *426*
Mies van der Rohe, Ludwig, 7, 10, 590–92, *591*
  exhibition, *592*
  move to Chicago, 595
Miles, Wallace, 569
Miller, J. A., 112
Millet, Louis J., 92, *92*, 136, 164, 179, 181, 188, *188*, 190, 195, 203, *204*, 229, 233, 275, 301, 461
Milwaukee, 73–74
Milwaukee Architectural Club, 48
Milwaukee Exposition, 73
Milwaukee Exposition Building, *74*
Milwaukee Public Library, 169, 234
  Wright's design for, *170*
Minneapolis Architectural Club, 362, 370
Minneapolis Industrial Exposition, 54
Minneapolis Sketch Club, 107
Missouri, 21
Mobley Building (Detroit), 185
modern movement, 385–86, 595–96
Moholy-Nagy, Ladislaus, 590, 592
Molitor, John, 352
Monadnock Building, 117, *119*
Monroe, Harriet, 356–58, 400, 411, 426
Monroe Building (Holabird & Roche), *391*
Montauk Building (Burnham & Root, 1882), *44*, 45
Montgelas, Albrecht, 456
Montgomery Ward Building, 245
*Monument to Pioneer Women* (sculp-

ture), *552*
Moody, Walter, 406
Mora, Luis F., 363
Morgan, Charles L., 444, 489, 500, 503, 504, 529, 544, 545, 557, 578, 582
  architectural sketches, *482*, *506*
Morgan, L. Henry, 186
Morgan Park, Minnesota, plan, *464*
Morgenstern, Christian, 330
Morphett, Archibald S., 454, 460, 466, 468, 474, 487, 494, 506
Morris, William, 348
Morse, Burton E., 253, 272
Morse, F. W., 380, 453
Morse, W. A., 134, 147
Moulton, Robert H., 372, 390, 393
Moylan, Martin, 66, 70
Mueller, Paul F. P., 51, 70, 85, 106, 114
Mulig, Thomas J., 580, 582–83, 585, 586, 590
Mullay, Thomas H., 380
Mullen, J. Bernard, 416, 420, 439, 490
Mulligan, Charles J., 370, 399, 434, 439
  monument by, *400*
Mundie, William Bryce, 7, 23, *23*, 26, 51, 64, 65, 66, 69, 72, 75–77, 82, 85, 87, 89, 98, 99, 107, 108, 114, 115, 125, 165, 173, *173*, 179, 186, 224, 274, 322, 323, 523, 580
  competition design, *58*, *70*, *87*, *90*, *91*, *108*, *116*
Municipal Art League of Chicago, 341–42, 363, 364
Municipal Improvement League, 194–96, 313
mural paintings, 363
Murphy, Charles F., 513
Museum of Science and Industry, 513

Naess, Sigurd, 513
Naramore, Floyd A., 363, 365
Nash, Joseph, 446
*National Builder, The*, 30
National Life Insurance Building, *36*
National Trust of Great Britain, 273
Nedved, Elizabeth Kimball, 559, *559*, 584
Nedved, George M., 499, 520, 521, 522, 525, 533, 543, 544, 546, 569, 582
Nedved, Rudolph J., 8, *518*, 520, 521, 523, 544, 551, 553, 555, 559, *559*, 560, 561, 562, 569, 584
  competition design, *519*
Nelson, Donald S., 534, *535*, 541, 549, 561, 585
Nelson, Edward O., 309, 327, 345, 349, 394, 524
Nelson, E. S., 466, 474
Netsch, Walter, 596
Nettenstrom, Elmer T., 363, 371, 394, 403
Neu, Matthew, 370
New Bauhaus, 590
Newberry Library, 90–91
Newhall, Louis C., 344
Newton, Francis, 363
New York Chapter of the American Institute of Architects (AIA), 500
*New York Sketchbook, The*, 30

New York Sketch Club, 84, 107, 140
Niemz, Arthur, 216
  competition design, *95*
Nimmons, Carr & Wright, 581
Nimmons, George C., 374, 376, 403, 408, 409, 411, 414, 450, 499, 514, 533
Nimmons & Fellows, 280, 306–7, 346, *347*, 375
  competition design, *307*
"No. 12," 72
Norman, Viola, 574
North, Arthur T., 555
*Northwestern Architect, The*, 31, 54
Northwestern Terra Cotta Company, 238, 331, 375, 475, 541, 545, 565
Northwestern University, 82
  Settlement House, *259*
Norton, Francis L., 160
Norton, John, 432
  exhibition design, *433*
Nothnagel, Charles W., 205, *205*
Nourse, William Ziegler, 493

Oak Park Studio (Wright's), 217, 230, 384–85
Ohlheuser, Joseph, 147
Oldefest, Edward G., 372, 376, 390, 466
Olin, M. T., 211
Oliver, Maude I. G., 370, 390, 428
Olmsted, Frederick Law, 105, *105*, 177, 194, 313
Olmsted, Frederick Law, Jr., 313
Olmsted, John C., 313–14
Olmsted Brothers, 313–14, 320, 328, 371
  park design, *315*, *329*, *371*
Olsen, C. M., 137
Orpheus Theater (Aroner & Somers), *415*
Orth, A. Beatty, 93, 112
  competition design, *97*
Osgood, James Ripley, 30–31, *30*
Ostergren, Robert C., 365, 559, 565
  competition design, *366*
Ostertag, Blanche, 230, 361
Otis, William A., 25, 92, *92*, 136, 164, 185, 224, 320
Otis & Fuller, 92*n39*
Ottenheimer, Henry L., 231, 320
Ottenheimer, Stern & Reichert, 450
Owings, Nathaniel, 596
Own Your Own Home Exposition, 489–90

Palmer, Charles, 39
Palmer, H. L., 543, 559
Palmer, Potter, 527
Pareira, David A., 581
Paris, 35
Paris Salon, 494–95
Parker, Lawton, 438
Parker, Walter H., 331
  competition design, *333*
"Park Improvement" shelter, *265*
Parmelee, E. Dean, 381
Parmentier, Fernand, 93
  competition design, *95*
Parsons, William E., 452, 488, 490–91, 544, 559, 585
Partridge, W. O., 233
Pattison, Edward B., 327
Pattison, James W., 363
Patton, Florence, 423
Patton, Normand S., 90, 190, 193, 194,

*194*, 195, 196, 313
  designs for lakefront, *198–99*
Patton & Fisher, 123, 185
  floor plan and interior, *123*
Patton & Miller, 375
Peabody, Robert S., 310
Peabody & Beauley, 307, *307*
Peabody & Stearns, 130
Peck, F. W., 162
*Pencil Points*, 540
pencils, 421–22
Pennell, Joseph, 208
People's Bank of Cedar Rapids (Sullivan),
  *414*
People's College, 125
Pereira, Hal, 560
Perkins, Dwight Heald, 7, 24, 50, 117–20,
  *118*, *121*, 143, 185, 193, 201,
  *201*, 204, 210–11, 213, *214*,
  221, 223, 224, 229, 230, 231,
  233, 234, 235, 237, 238, 241,
  247, *256*, 257, 259, *260*, 271,
  272, 274, 278, 280, *292*, 300,
  303, 314, 316–17, 318, 320,
  333, 351, 360–61, *361*, 368,
  373, 374, 392, 398, 409, 429,
  431, 439, 451–52, 454, 457,
  465, 484, 584
Perkins, Eleanor, 210
Perkins, Fellows & Hamilton, 412, 414,
  458, 465, 478
  building by, *440*, *459*, *477*
Perkins, Frederick W., 171, 459
Perkins, Lucy Fitch, 143, *143*, 201, 243
  interior design, *243*
Perkins, Ruth, 584
Perkins & Selby, *210*, 214
Perkins & Hamilton, *395*
Permanent Exhibit and Exchange, 36, *39*,
  *40*, 103, 170
  convention, 63
  floor plan, *39*
Peters, R. H., 452
Peterson, Charles S., 579
Peyraud, Frank C., 368
Philadelphia Architectural Club, 247
Philadelphia T-Square Club, 100, 197,
  247, 362, 518
Philbrick, Allen E., 438, 439
Phillips, John H., 275, 283, 286, 290, 300,
  301, 339, 352, 354–55
  competition design, *282*, *284*
Phimister, D. G., 77, 81, 99
Phimister Competition, 85, 86, 87, 89,
  93–98
Pickel Marble and Granite Company of St.
  Louis, 41
Pierron, E., competition design, *341*
Pietsch, Eugene L., 233, 351
Pietsch, Theodore Wells, 134, 216, 227,
  245, 447
Pilkin, William, Jr., 500
Pinkham, Walter E., 137, 143
  competition design, *139*, *144*
Pinkham, W. L., 86n24
Pirola, Louis, 525, 534, *535*, 541, 547,
  558, 562, 565, 569, 579, 585
  competition design, *548*
Pischel, Fred, 181
Pittsburgh Architectural Club, 247, 410
Pittsburgh Chapter of the American
  Institute of Architects, 247
Place, Richard, 147

*Plan of Chicago* (Burnham, 1909), 190,
  301, 314, 317, 328–29, 342,
  349, 371–72, 419, 467, 468
Plumbers' Association, 15
Plympton and Trowbridge, 100
Polasek, Albin, 523
Polito, F. F., 569
Polk, Willis K., 279, 303, 307
  San Francisco project, *279*
Pond, Allen B., 27, 111, 134, 215–16, *216*,
  222, *222*, 223, 235, 236, 257
Pond, Irving K., 26, 31, 40–41, 42–43, 46,
  92, 109, 111, 136, 138, 147,
  148, 164, 173, *173*, 183, 188,
  *188*, 190, 215–16, *216*, 222,
  223, 234, 235, 236, 238, 257,
  265–66, 330, 354, 364, 373–74,
  380, 399, 402, 429, 430–31,
  439, 451, 476, 494, 509, 514,
  516, 520, 523, 585
  competition design, *42*
  drawing, *110*
Pond & Pond, 185, 216, 231, 243, 257,
  272, 280, 293, 318, 320, 343,
  374, 375, 399, 406, *440*, 459,
  478, 504
  design, *296*
  railroad station design, *407*
Pope, John Russell, 428
Porter, Washington, 194
Post, George B., 130
Postle & Mahler, 389
  competition design, *389*
Powers, Horace S., 309, 380, 422
Powers, Richard, 546
Prairie Avenue, 588
Prairie school of architecture, 7, 120, 215,
  229, 298, 355, 370, 385, 392,
  513
Preston, Jessie M., 294
Price, Chester Boyce, 343
  competition design, *343*
Price, Hugh A., competition design, *341*
Prindeville, Charles H., 439
Pringle, W. L., 488
Promentory Apartments (Mies), *593*
Providence Architectural Club, 197
Puckey, Francis W., 403, 420, 421, 424,
  441, 448, 452, 461, 468, 499,
  567, 585
Pulis, W. Pell, 160
  competition design, *159*
Pullman Building (Beman, 1884), *44*, 45
Purcell, Feick & Elmslie, 409, 411
Purcell, William Gray, 310, 336, 398
  competition design, *312*, *339*
Purcell & Elmslie, 450, 473, 478
  design, *473*
Purington, D. V., 100

Rabig, C. E. K., 452
Rae, William R., 72, 287
  competition design, *90*
railroads, 406–8, 419
*Railway Review*, 83, 87
Rapp, George W., 100, 545
Rauch, Paul, 583
Ravlin, Grace, 503
Reade, Christina M., 186
Rebori, Andrew N., 434, 448, 452, 465,
  467, *469*, 472, 473, 478, *481*,
  491, 514, 523, 541, 544, *564*,
  585

Rebori, Wentworth, Dewey & McCormick,
  549, 553
  competition design, *550*
Recher, George D., 583
Reed, Earl H., Jr., 368, 468, 489, 525, 544
Reichert, Will G., 331–32, 363, 368
Renwick, James, 56n43
Rice, Florence Chauncey, 175
  competition design, *175*
Richardson, Henry Hobson, 23–24, *23*,
  106, 117, 185, 211, 462, 522,
  *530*
  office staff photo, *118*
Richardson Romanesque, 25
Richmond, John, 143–44, 160
  competition design, *161*
Ricker, Nathan Clifford, 51–52, *51*, *52*, 85,
  *85*, 115, 126, 136, 143, 173,
  376, 399, 451
Ricker Library at the University of
  Illinois, 51n33
Ridley, T. Ralph, 375, 376
  building by, *376*
Riordan, Roger, 18
Ripley, H. G., 134, *135*
Rippel, Fred O., 474, 487, 498
Ritter, Louis, 568
Rixson, O. C., 156, 186
Robard, George, 547
Robert Clark Testimonial Competition, 77,
  79, 87–89, 93–98, 113, 115,
  137, 143, 155, 160, 173–75,
  188, 190–92, 203, 205, 223
  jury, 85, 126
  medal, 86, *86*
  subjects for competitors, *89*, *114*,
  *155*
Roberts, N. L., 547
Robertson, Alexander S., 93, 398
  advertisement drawn by, *146*
Robinson, Charles Mulford, 431
Robinson, Harry F., 395
  competition design, *396*
Roche, Martin, 7, 421, 424, 439, 446
Rogers, James Gamble, 235, 275, 320, 321,
  517, 541, 549
  drawing, *551*
Rogers & Manson, 336
Rognstad, Sigurd A., 466, 474, 487
Rookery Building (the Rookery), *131*, 217
Root, John Wellborn, Jr., 7, 21, 46, 50, 56,
  57, 59, 60–61, *60*, 61, 66, 67,
  92–93, 100, 105–6, *105*, 113,
  116, 117, 129, 145, 148, 155,
  178, 185, 221, 241, 438, *446*,
  465, 500, 556
  bust of, *178*
  essay by, 112–13
  monument, *148–149*
  "Style" (paper), 59
Root Memorial Competition, 148
Rosenwald, Julius, 513
Ross, Albert R., 100
Ross, Denman W., 287
Ross, Henry J., 112
Rosse, Mrs. S. Helena, 500
Roth, Emery, 124, 142
  competition design, *142*
Royal Insurance Building (William W.
  Boyington), 27, *45*
Rund, V. R., 580, 582
Russell, E. J., 300

Ryan, Edmund, 560, 569
Ryan, Edwin, 524
Ryan, E. J., 544
Ryerson, Martin, 456, 574

Saarinen, Eliel, 386, 516, 517, 523, *523*,
  574
  Tribune Tower design, *510*
Sailor, Homer S., 387
  competition design, *387*
St. Gall, Switzerland, monastery plan, 120
St. Louis Architectural Club, 197, 244,
  246, 267
St. Louis Hydraulic Pressed Brick
  Company, 41, 46
St. Louis Sketch Club, 89, 107
St. Paul Sketch Club, 107
Salmagundi Club, 56
Sandbloom, Axel, 143, 238
  competition design, *144*, *239*
*Sanitary News, The*, 31, *32*, 64
Saunders, George, 460
Saxe, Albert, 509
Sayles, Mr. (manager of Kimball House,
  539
Schaefer, C. Bryant, 75, 83, 107, 108, 112,
  142, 143, 145, 167, 380
  advertisement drawn by, *146*
  competition design, *94*, *108*
Schaeffer, W. J., 382, 386, 408, 426, 525
  competition design, *383*
Schenck, Anna Pendleton, 430
  competition design, *430*
Schierhorn, J., 505
Schlesinger, A. L., 150, 165
Schlesinger, Alfred R., 158, 167, 168
Schlessinger, W., 117
Schmid & Schieden, 186
Schmidt, Garden & Erikson, 465
  building by, *432*, *435*
  building design, *472*
Schmidt, Garden & Martin, 467, 472, 473,
  478, 541
Schmidt, Richard E., 7, 66, 70, 125, 186,
  190, 201, 231, 235, 243, 245,
  271, 287, 288, 293, 297, 308,
  320, 429, 432, 509, 533, 537
  building design, *299*
  competition design, *87*, *245*
Schock, F. R., 117
Scholer, Frederick, 404
School of the Art Institute, 377, 439
Schuyler, Montgomery, 414
Schwartz, A. A., 382, 408
Schweiker, Paul, 544
Schweinfurth, J. A., 111
Seidel, Emory, 574
Selby, George W., 211
Sewell, Frederick S., 219, 221
Shankland, E. C., 177, 210
Shattuck, Walter Francis, 136, *136*, 164,
  *300*, 301
Shattuck Competition, 254
Shaw, Alfred, 513, 544
Shaw, Howard Van Doren, 7, 190, 231,
  *233*, 238, 265, 307, 320, 330,
  343, 354, *393*, 411, 431, 459,
  465, 467, 468, *471*, 495, 499,
  514
Shaw, Naess & Murphy, 513
Sheblessy, John F., 205
Shepley, Rutan & Coolidge, 24, 100, 137,
  156, *162*, 163, 185, 214, 224,

231, 272, *427*
Sherman, John B., 328–29
Sherman Park, 328
Shipman, S. V., 124
Shirinian, Sarkis, architectural sketch, *553*
Shrigley, Arthur, 205
Sierkes, Charles H., 453, 466, 474, 488, 505, 521, 525, 541, 544
Silha, Otto A., 8, 327, 352, 394, 403, 424
Silsbee, Joseph Lyman, 7, 61, *61*, 73, 112, 320
Sjolin, Gosta, 569
Sketch Club of New York, 197
Sketch Club of San Francisco, 107
sketch clubs, generally, 18–19, 25, 89, 100–101, 107
Sketch Club Team, 92
Sketch Competition (of CAC), 507
*Sketches* (club portfolio), 147
    advertisements in, *146*
    cover design, *142*
Skigly, H. C., 369
Smith, Benjamin Lane, 583
Smith, F. Hopkinson, 245
Smith, Herbert A., 476
Smith, Oliver C., 69
Smith, Orson, 462
Smith, R. E., 141
Smith, William J., 494, 499, 507, 545
Snook, James, 56*n43*
Snyder, Kristian, 574
Society of Beaux-Arts Architects, 9, 224, 246, 247, 288, 309–10, 344–45, 365, 447–48, 450, 451, 452, 484
Sohn, Frank, 578
Soldier Field, 478
Sollitt, Oliver, 72–73
Sommers, E. S., 396
Sooy-Smith, William, 224
40 South Clark Street club quarters, 488–89, 492, 526, 540
South Park System of Chicago, 119, 512
Spencer, Robert Clossen, Jr., 7, 82, 137, 156–57, *157*, 169, 183, 186, 188, *188*, 190, 210, 213, *214*, 219, 221, 223, 224, 227, 229, 231, 233, 234, 235, 237, 238, 241, 242, 243, 245, 252, 257, 259, 260, 261, 265, 271, 272, 274, 275, 278, 280, 282, 285, 286, 287, 289, 290, 292, 297, 300, 301, 320, 343, 380, 398, 419, 422, 429, 430, 454, 480
    architectural sketch, *138*
    designs, *201, 232, 241, 291, 293*
    Club logo by, *278*
    competition design, *219, 261*
    cover design, *200*
    drawing of building, *169, 233*
Spencer & Powers, 368, 375, 398, 409, 450, 478
    buildings by, *369, 375, 477*
Spitznagel, Harold, 580
Sponholtz, William C., 525
Stanhope, Leon E., 522, 559
Stanton, Frederick C. H., 454, 460
Starbuck & Rose, 211
Starr, Harry C., 190, 229, 290, 299, 300, 309
State Board of Architectural Examiners, 205

State Historical Society, 462
State of Illinois Building (WCE), *132–133*
Steinway Hall, *202*, 210, 212–16, *212*, 228, 277
    floor plans, *215*
    Room 1107, 215, 228
Steinway Hall Group, 216, 231, 384, 422
Sternfeld, Henry, 542
Stevens Point, Wisconsin, Normal school, *210*, 211
Stewardson Memorial Scholarship, 560
Stewart, Peter C., 112, 124
Stine, Wiber M., 164
Stockton, Walter, 574
Stopa, Walter, 547
Story, John, 560
Stoyke, Eugene F., 587
    competition design, *587*
Stuermer, Ray, 587
    competition design, *587*
Sturgis, R. Clipston, 438
Sullivan, Louis Henry, 7, 21, 39, 46, 50, 56, 60–61, *60*, 66, 69, 75–76, 92–93, 98, 106, 120, 139, 162, 174–75, 185, 203, 217, 221, 238, 241, 248, 266, 269, 271, 275, 277–78, 280, 284–86, 288, 293, 297, 300, 306, 325, 343, 346, 351, 358, 367, 375, 376, 384, 385, 387, 408, 411, 414–15, 424, 426–27, 437, 438, 447, 450, 451, 454, 462, 463, 465, 473, 475–76, 478, 486, 487, 495, 513, 514–15, 528–29, 530, 586
    buildings, *280, 298, 413, 414*
    building designs, *293, 323, 409*
    cover design, *276*
    exhibition, *480*
    furnishing design, *299*
    grave marker, 574–76, *576*
    medal given to, *586*
    ornamental design, *185, 360, 378, 515, 528*
    page of essay, *226*
    "Style" essay, 69
    writings, 514–16
Surmann, John F., Jr., 403, 416, 421, 423
Swern, Perry W., 522
Switzer, Robert M., 546
Symons, Gardner, 374
Syracuse University, 51

Taft, Lorado, 85, *85*, 100, 106, 115, 126, 138, 139, 143, 145, 147, 148, 155, 173, 195, 235, 238, 244, 509
Tallmadge, Thomas Eddy, 275, 286, 299, 300, 309, 318, 321, 322, 343, 354, 368, 371, 374, 380, 403, 411, 421, 435, 458, 461–62, 465, 468, 472–73, 476, 484, 507, 514, 516, 530, 549, 568, 574, 588
    competition design, *283, 317*
    park design, *478*
    Sullivan grave marker design, *575*
Tallmadge & Watson, 375, 398, 409, 414, 450, 473, 478, 549
    buildings, *376, 475, 520*
    designs, *474, 551*
Taylor, Isaac, 59*n2*

Tech Architectural Club, 583–84, *583*
*Technologist, The*, 30
Temple, Seth J., 275
Tenement House Exhibition, 252, 253–54, *255, 257*
Terra Cotta Competition, 404
    sketch for competitors, *238*
Tharp, N., 134
Thomas Moulding Company, 274
Thompson, William B., 580, 585
Thomsen, Fred, 525
Thomsen, W. F., 544
Thomsen, William, 583, 585
Throop Institute (Hunt & Grey), *393*
Thule, Adolph, 137
Thumb Tack Club, 164, *164*, 301
Thurber Galleries, 362
Tilton, John N., 320
Tomlinson, Henry Webster, 215, 217, *217*, 236, 238, 247, 252, 277
Toronto Architectural Eighteen Club, 247
Toronto Architectural Sketch Club, 109
Trans-Mississippi International Exposition, 230
Transportation Building (Louis Sullivan), 120, 463, 487
Traxler, Hazel, 444
Traxler, Victor, 208, 307
    competition design, *208, 230*
*Treads and Risers*, 562
Treat, Samuel A., 22, 39, 85, *85*, 115, 124, 126, 143, 155, 171, 173, 194, 195, 204, 374
Tribune Company, 553
Tribune Tower (as built), *554*
Tribune Tower Competition, 507, 509, 516–17, 518, 553
    exhibition of designs for, *519*
Trost, Henry C., 87, 106, 124, 142
    competition design, *87*
Trowbridge, C. W., 49
Trunk, Ben W., 160
    competition design, *159*
"T. Square," 17, 21
T-Square Club. *See* Philadelphia
Turner, R. M., 56
    competition design, *90*
Tuttle, Arthur B., 368
Twose, George M. R., 197, 232, 255
Twyman, Joseph, 257, 347–49
    exhibition, *348*
Tyson, Mrs. Russell, 500

Union League Club (William Le Baron), *45*
Union Station, plans for, *407*
Universal Portland Cement Company, 365
University of Chicago, 292, *427*
University of Illinois, 49, 51–52, 399, 451, 544
    at Champaign, 165
Upman, Frank, 223, 224
U.S. Government Building (WCE), plan and elevation, *132*

Van Bergen, John S., 385, 450, 574
Van Brunt & Howe, 130
Vanderpoel, John H., 155, 195
Van Dort, G. Broes, 499, 507, 541, 560
Van Dort Sketch Competition, 499
Van Inwegen, James, Jr., 289

Van Osdel, J. M., 204
Van Pelt, John, 186
Venning, Frank L., 456, 460, 525, 544, 576
Vinson, L. C., 373
Viollet-le-Duc, *Discourses*, 113
Vogel, Louis C., 416, 439
Vognied, Enoch, competition design, *341*
Voita, Eugene, 547, 583
von Holst, Hermann V., 201, 229, 236, 238, 239, *240*, 345, 355, 358, *358*, 364, 368, *394*, 410, *410*, 421
Voorhees, Gmelin & Walker, 581
Vorse, Norman T., 343
Vrooman, George, 453

Wachter, Robert L., 444
Wacker, Charles H., 216, 406, 437, 468
Wagner, Ernest J., 63, 73, 75, 85, 99, 106, 115, 124, 134, 135, 145, 149, 158, 380
Wagner, Fritz, 66, 72, 73, 125, 138, 143, 147, 148, 238, 331
Wagner, Fritz, Jr., 403, 416, 421, 438, 439, 454, 455, 460
Waid, Dan Everett, 201
Waid & Cranford, 231
Walcott, Charles, architectural sketch, *465*
Walcott, Chester H., 344, 468, 500, 504, 522, 523
    park design, *458*
Walcott, Julie C., 468
Walker, C. Howard, 100, 287
Walker, Frank C., 331, 368, 381, 452
    competition design, *311*
Walker, Hobart A., 82, 140
    competition design, *83*
Walker, Ralph, 577
Wallebrecht, H., monument design, *445*
Waller, Edward C., 216–17
Ward, A. Montgomery, 7–8, 194, 313, 314, 328
Ware, William R., 117, 148, 451
Warine, J. T., 26
Warner, Harold O., 556
Warren, Clinton J., 185
Washington Architectural Club, 247
Washington Park, 119
    Refectory, 119
Washington University, 452
Waterman, H. H., 320
Watson, J. Nelson, 272, 274
Watson, Vernon S., 333
    competition design, *335, 336*
Wayne Hardware Company, 98
Weary, Allen B., 343, 469
Webb, A. C., 578
    exhibition design, *433*
Weber, Bertram A., 566
Weber, Peter J., 148, 272, 330, 361, 364, 380
    competition design, *149*
Weber, R. F., 583
Webster, H. Effa, 428
Webster, J. C., 361
Wees, J. L., 219, 221
Weese, Harry, 596
Wegmann, John, 149
Weiman, A. A., 502
Weirick, Ralph W., 305–6
    competition design, *305*

Wells, Newton A., 271, 289, 364
Wells, W. A. & A. E., 243
Welsh, William P., 523
Welton, William L., 190, 205
    competition design, *192, 341*
Wendt, Dorothy G., 591
*Western Architect, The,* 330, 415, 450
*Western Architect and Builder,* 31
Western Association of Architects (WAA),
        7, 15, 20–21, 41, 46, 54, 100,
        103, 170
    convention catalogue cover, *78*
    exhibitions, 56
    expansion of, 21
    program cover, *16*
    seal of, *21*
Western Society of Architects, 39, 98
Western Society of Engineers, 194
Wexelberger, Joseph, 92
Wheeler, Arthur, 235
Wheelock, Harry B., 26, 204, 229, 545,
        559, 567
Wheelock & Clay, 117
Wheelwright & Haven, 156
Whitaker, Charles H., 515
White, Catherine M., house, 243
White, Charles E., 375
    building design, *376*
White, Howard, 574
White, James M., 287, 573
White, Stanford, 148
Whitman, Bertha Yerex, 584
Whittlesey, Charles, 72
Widow Clark House, *464*
Wiersha, Alwin, 505
Wight, Peter B., 7, 13, 23, 168, 171,
        184–86, 193, 194, 195–96,
        197–200, 204, 221–22, 224,
        227, 229, 252, 313, 314, 328,
        380, 399, 402, *436, 438*
    interior by, *104*
    plan for lakefront, *198–199*
Wilder, Edward T., 190
Wilkinson, L. E., 336, 364
    competition design, *339*
Will, George G., 137
    competition design, *138*
Willett, James R., 22, 115
Willett & Pashley, 185
Williams, David S., 221
Williams, Marguerite B., 462–63, 541,
        549, 556–57, 578, 582
Williams, Walter, 578
Williams, William, 490
Williamson, R. B., 41, 147
    song by, 76
Williamson, W. G., 26, 27, 31, 38, 39, 41,
        43, 46, 67, 69, 70, 73, 75, 79,
        80, 85, 87, 99, 106, 114, 124,
        147, 155, 380
    competition design, *43, 88*
    drawing, *27*
    drawing of interior, *66, 67*
Wilmanns, August C., 223, 238, 252, 271,
        289, 300
Wilson, Horatio Reed, 7, 19, *21,* 320
Wilson, Joseph W., 331, 336
    competition design, *333, 340*
Wilson, Ruth, 444
Wilson & Marshall, 19n7
Windrim, Jas. H., 131
Winkel, B. J., 420
Winnebago Building (Chicago), 185

Winslow, Carleton M., 239, 252, 253
Winslow, Mr. and Mrs. Herman, 223
Winslow, William H., 212, 216–17
Winslow Brothers, 169
Winslow House (Wright, River Forest,
        Illinois), 212
Wirts, Stephen M., 142, 145, 158
Wolcott, Chester, 568
Wolfe & Lenzen, 450
Wolff, Rudolph G., 382, 386, 408, 452
    competition design, *382*
Woltersdorf, Arthur F., 173, 398, 402, 404,
        421, 428, 429, 438, 452, 457,
        465, 484, 587, 588
Woman's National Farm and Garden
        Association, 490, 495, 496,
        500, 503
Women's Architectural Club of Chicago,
        553, 584
Women's Temple, 117, *118*
Women's World's Fairs, 584
Wood, Richard, competition design, *90*
Woodlawn Presbyterian Church (Harry
        Lawrie), *28*
Woolley, Clarence M., 381, 420
Woolley, Taylor, 424
Woolworth Building, *393*
Work, Robert, *505*
World Congress of Architects, 156, 177
World's Columbian Exposition, 104,
        153–76, 177–78, 310, 385, 400,
        463, 487
    architectural exhibition at, 156
    designing of, 129–51
    events leading up to, 104–28
    plan of buildings, *130*
    plan of grounds, *128*
    Service Building, *130*
World War I, 380, 441, 443–44, 454,
        460–61, 484
World War II, 10, 444, 595
Wrenn, John H., 361
Wright, F. A., 77
Wright, Frank Lloyd, 7, 86, 106, 120, 169,
        173, *173,* 175, 186, 210, 212,
        213, 214, *214,* 217, 221, 223,
        224, 231, 233–34, 238, 241,
        247, 257, 259, 261, 262, 265,
        266, 267, 269–71, 273–74, 275,
        278, 279, 285, 292, 293–94,
        297, 308, 321, 343, 350,
        352–53, 355, 356–58, 361–63,
        365, 367, 370, 384–85, 386,
        392, 404, 405, 408–9, 411,
        414–15, 423–24, 426–27, 428,
        432, 446, 450, 460, 480, 495,
        513, 514, 516, *516,* 541, 549,
        578, 580, 581–82, 591
    building designs, *260, 409, 410*
    competition design, *170*
    drawings, *216, 218, 262, 263*
    exhibitions by, *353, 356–357, 362,*
        *425, 582*
    furniture design, *295*
    letter to Harriet Monroe, *359*
    office planned by, *217*
    park design, *266–67*
    pottery design, *350*
    puppet theater, *425*
    speech introducing Mies, 591
    urban design, *406*
Wuehrmann, William G., 8, 365, 382, 383,
        394, 403, 408, 416, 421, 423,

    424
    competition design, *384*

Yale & Towne Manufacturing Company,
        186, *187*
Yerkes Observatory, *186*
York, John Devereaux, 352, 390, 421
    monument design, *392*
Youngberg, J. C., 112
Youngburg, John E., 61, 124, 126, 131,
        134–35, 139, 142, 143, 145,
        149
    advertisement drawn by, *146*
Young Turks, 231, 368, 375

Zettel, John, 143
Zettler, Emil R., 408, 461
Zeublin, Charles, 236
Zimmerman, A. G., 27, 237–38
Zimmerman, Hugo H., 300, 309, 327, 368,
        485
    caption design, *485*
Zimmerman, Saxe & Zimmerman, build-
        ing by, *507*
Zimmerman, William Carbys, 26, 149,
        *150,* 216, 399
    drawing of building, *28*
    prison design, *400*
Zueblin, Charles, 257, *257,* 278
Zukowsky, John, 527